MUSIC
EDUCATION
RESEARCH

MUSIC
EDUCATION
RESEARCH

An

Anthology

from the

Journal *of* Research *in* Music Education

Edited by Harry E. Price

MENC
MENC
MENC
MENC
Music Educators National Conference

Contents

IV. CHILDREN'S PERCEPTION, DISCRIMINATION, AND PERFORMANCE ABILITIES

V. PERFORMANCE AND ADULT DISCRIMINATION

VI. TEACHER BEHAVIOR AND STUDENT RESPONSE

VII. OBSERVING AND EVALUATING MUSIC TEACHING

VIII. RESPONSES TO MUSIC

IX. REINFORCEMENT AND MUSIC

X. SPECIAL POPULATIONS AND MUSIC

XI. MULTICULTURAL ISSUES AND MUSIC

XII. OTHER ISSUES IN MUSIC EDUCATION

XIII. THE PAST AND THE FUTURE

JRME INDEX

Introduction

The *Journal of Research in Music Education* (*JRME*) was first published in the spring of 1953. In its forty-five-year history, more than 950 research articles have been published. It contains, by far, the most comprehensive accumulation of music education research in any single source. The fact that the *JRME* has taken its rightful place as the flagship journal in the field is a tribute to those with the foresight to establish it, especially Allen Britton. The unquestionable impact of the *JRME* is owed to its founders; the editors who have guided it—Allen P. Britton (1953–72), Robert G. Petzold (1972–78), James C. Carlsen (1978–81), George Duerksen (interim 1981–82), Jack Taylor (1982–88), and Rudolf E. Radocy (1988–94); the numerous editorial board members who contributed their valuable time and invaluable expertise in advising authors and selecting manuscripts; and, most of all, the hundreds of authors whose distinquished research it contains. The purpose of this anthology is to present exemplars of research. The articles were selected from *JRME* on the basis of their distinction, representation of various topics and methodologies, and focus on issues central to music education and the Music Educators National Conference (MENC) research agenda.[1]

SELECTION PROCESS

The task of selecting from this impressive corpus was daunting and humbling. On what basis were these decisions to be made? Given that *JRME* is a research journal, it made sense that research should be used to inform the decision. The first sources that were consulted to select the articles were studies entitled "Influential *Journal of Research in Music Education* Articles as Indicated by Authors of Two or More Studies" by Harry E. Price and Evelyn K. Orman[2] and "Cited Quantitative Research Articles in Music Education Research Journals, 1975–1990: A Content Analysis of Selected Studies" by Charles P. Schmidt and Stephen F. Zdzinski's.[3] In Price and Orman, authors who had published two or more articles in *JRME* were surveyed and asked to chose studies in *JRME* that they felt "have had the greatest impact on the field, have withstood the test of time in importance to the profession, and/or have added significantly to the body of knowledge about the effects of music and music teaching."[4] Responses to the survey resulted in a list of thirty-seven articles, all of which have been included in this anthology.

Schmidt and Zdzinski identified studies that were cited most often by articles published in *JRME, Bulletin of the Council for Research in Music Education, Psychology of Music, Journal of Music Therapy, Contributions to Music Education,* and *Missouri Journal of Research in Music Education.* Their study was limited to quantitative research, and it examined the citations of 922 descriptive and experimental studies. Eleven articles from *JRME* were among the fifteen most cited articles, and these are included in this anthology.

Subsequent to compiling articles for inclusion based upon research studies, some works were added for the purposes of balance among topics and modes of inquiry. A few other articles, published subsequent to the two research studies that served as the foundation for initial selection, have been included because they were deemed consequential or exemplars of approaches to research.

It must be remembered that prior to selection for this anthology, these articles underwent a stringent review process before acceptance for publication. The current *JRME* process is one of blind peer review, in which a manuscript is submitted to the editor. If deemed appropriate for review, all cues that identify the author(s) are removed, and the manuscript is sent to three members of the Editorial Committee. Committee members have been selected based on evaluations of their credentials, first by the current Editorial Committee and then by the Executive Board of the Music Education Research Council. The Council forwards two names for each opening to the National Executive Board of the Music Educators National Conference, which makes the final appointments. Individuals who review a manuscript are unaware of the identities of the other reviewers and do not confer. They assess the manuscript on a set of criteria and provide written feedback. This process between the author and reviewers continues until an article is deemed acceptable or unacceptable for publication. Once a manuscript is accepted, the publication staff at MENC puts the final polish on manuscript text and presentation before the work goes to the printer. Consequently, it is not inaccurate to say all the articles that appear in the *JRME,* whether or not included in this anthology, have undergone arduous screening and editing.

USEFUL FOR MANY PURPOSES

Given the stringent selection process, the studies included in the *Anthology* become useful for many purposes. First, the studies provide a historical perspective and serve as models for those who are actively pursuing research, whether they are novices or experienced scholars. The *Anthology* can also serve as a set of readings for graduate music education students enrolled in courses involving research. Beyond these utilitarian functions, there is benefit from understanding the implications of the research.

The format and printing styles of the articles included in the *Anthology* vary widely; this is because they are reprints of the original journal, which has gone through several style changes over the course of its forty-five-year history. The language in some of the older articles may seem archaic or the methodology simplistic, but they must be read in the context of their time and how they have contributed to music education research.

ORGANIZATION OF STUDIES

In a broad sense, musical scholarship can be said to encompass "any scholarly activity directed toward the investigation and understanding of the facts, the processes, the developments, and the effects of the musical art."[5] There has been an effort to group the studies in a logical way while recognizing that other taxonomies might have worked as well. Regardless of organizational structure, the studies presented here may be said to represent the highest form of music education scholarship.

Reflections on Music Education Research

The *Anthology* begins as each issue of *JRME* does, with a "Forum." It was introduced in the Summer 1984 issue and has been used to makeannouncements, highlight articles contained in an issue, and muse about many aspects of music scholarship and education. The particular Forum chosen for the *Anthology* presents the idea that there are many ways of accessing truth, and the ignorance of any approach diminishes its pursuit.

The Forum is followed by an adaptation of the Senior Researcher Award Acceptance Address given by the first award recipient, Clifford K. Madsen, in 1988. This award is given by the Society for Research in Music Education (at special sessions at MENC's national biennial in-service conferences) to "a researcher who has a record of scholarly publication sustained for a minimum of fifteen years beyond the date of his or her initial published research; demonstrates in his or her publications creativity, originality, and the sustained productivity in research that has clear implications for music teaching or for greater understanding of the processes of music learning or of the human response to music; and has a continuing influence on contemporary research in music education."[6] In his address, Madsen suggests music education research priorities and reminds us that teaching does not inhibit research and that research and teaching should be complementary.

Philosophical Conceptualizations

The opening section of the *Anthology* is followed by a section entitled "Philosophical Conceptualizations." Philosophies of music and music education have ancient roots. In contemporary music education, there have been a few seminal books and the occasional journal article to provoke either new conceptualizations or reflections on previous ones. This area of music education is a critical one. Educators are constantly making choices for themselves and their students concerning the purposes of music education, how to teach, what to teach, and what repertoire to use. They ask themselves: "On what basis do we make these choices and others?"

Philosophy, whether it be professional or personal, should define the bases for our choices of actions; conversely, one could argue that what we do defines our philosophy. Philosophical inquiry helps us to illuminate our thinking and generate clarity of purpose and perspectives. It can generate many hypotheses worthy of other systematic inquiry. As we work our way methodically through ideas, we may find that we revise or even reject those ideas that we held dear. How do we make decisions regarding what we will do, what we will teach, and how we will teach, if we have not brought lucidity to what we believe?

Historical Conceptualizations

The articles included in the section entitled "Historical Conceptualizations" are examples of documentation, discovery, and analysis of events, persons, and artifacts of the past. History is the discipline that underlies all scholarly pursuits, be they qualitative or quantitative. It puts all future research in a context. A researcher must be conversant with historical developments before attempting to forge ahead. Whatever the direction of research, including philosophical, historical, ethnographical, descriptive, behavioral, and experimental, it must begin with a careful examination of relevant history. What has happened previously in other settings? What work has been done in the past? What was its meaning? Who did it and why was it done? What was its impact? How does it relate to what I am doing? How can the relevant history inform me?

Children's Perception, Discrimination, and Performance Abilities

Examination of children's abilities has merited considerable attention in music teaching and research. The next section contains a wide range of studies under the title "Children's Perception, Discrimination and Performance Abilities." It is fascinating to learn how capable children really are. In some instances, researchers have found that successful music instruction rests not so much on the question of the child's maturity or ability but on the quality of communication among children and adults.

Teachers need (and children merit) all the insights that research can provide. How soon should we be teaching what? What can be perceived by children of different ages and levels of sophistication? When can children make different musical discriminations? What can we expect students to do at what age and developmental level? What are the relationships among perception, discrimination, and performance? Even with all the research that has been done in these areas, many fundamental questions remain to be answered about children's musical abilities.

Performance and Adult Discrimination

Music performance is the wellspring from which a great deal of music education has risen, and one would think that with the long presence of music performance among humans, there would be a commensurate body of research in performance; this is not the case. "Music is basically an applied art, and if the making of music is to progress (outside of professional ensembles), we need a good deal of research that is much more comprehensive and sophisticated than that attempted at present."[7]

The articles in the section entitled "Performance and Adult Discrimination" provide models of systematic inquiries into the acts involved in performing music and the abilities to make musical discriminations. The pairing of performance with discrimination seems logical because, intuitively, they would seem to be highly related; however, the evidence does not appear to support this supposition.

While a musician must be able to discriminate to perform, higher abilities to make discriminations do not lead to better quality performances. What are factors that affect performance? What processes need to be developed to be a fluent musician? Exactly how does discrimination relate to performance and to what degree? Does performance enhance discrimination, and are they interactive? The relationships among the abilities to make musical discriminations and to perform are unclear, and until there is more systematic study of performance along with discrimination, these relationships will remain obscure, and the ability to teach these skills will not reach its potential.

Teacher Behavior and Student Response

The section entitled "Teacher Behavior and Student Response" is a compelling one for music educators because the studies included in it examine what teachers do and the impact of their behaviors on students. Teaching is an interaction among teachers, students, and the classroom environment. Any research that provides insights into these issues and their relationships helps to further the understanding of the educational process. There are many ways to examine the teaching process, and frequency and magnitude are two methods that have received considerable attention.

The studies presented in this section examine fundamental issues about classroom and ensemble teaching environments. There are many questions, both basic and complex, that deserve careful study. How can teachers best structure music learning for positive affect, attentiveness, and achievement? What impact do different patterns of music instruction have? What kinds of responses do different types of activities elicit? What can we do to best keep our students engaged and help them achieve? Clearly, research to gain a better understanding of the music teaching process merits attention.

Observing and Evaluating Music Teaching

The next group of studies is entitled "Observing and Evaluating Music Teaching." There is so much to learn about teaching that it would be naive to believe that there is a single seminal issue in this area. In spite of the daunting challenge, it is paramount that practitioners, teacher educators, and researchers understand better the music teaching process. We need to identify good teaching practices; we need to carefully define them, utilize them, attempt to teach people to use them, and then assess the situation to see if indeed they are occurring and how effective they are. When is it appropriate to apply concepts developed in other subjects to music instruction? What are the salient issues in teaching music? Once identified, how can educators best learn to implement best practices? As links between teaching practice and learning are made, what are the appropriate applications and evaluations that should take place?

Responses to Music

When we examine music teaching, we also must take a considered look at music's effects, as do the studies in the section entitled "Responses to Music." How people respond to music must be a central issue to music education. One principal area of examination has been that of affective responses to music. There is no question that music is a potent force and its emotional value may be a source of that power. Among other factors, it appears that the function of music within a culture is another source of its sway.

Given the power of music, we need to consider the influences that shape our reactions. What are the qualities in music to which we respond? How do their alterations affect that response? Are there culturally shared feelings or experiences that occur when listening to music? What is it about music that is so compelling? Are there things that music teachers do that can have an influence on the way students respond to music and that can assist them? A better understanding of these and other questions about music may help educators to share the musical experience.

Reinforcement and Music

The study of music education would not be complete without an examination of the power of music and the teacher. The studies in the section entitled "Reinforcement and Music" span three decades and represent what is one of the most investigated areas in music education. Much of this research has provided basic knowledge that we now take for granted. Some of these studies may seem simplistic or the language archaic, but the reader must remember that the basic knowledge we now take for granted had a genesis. It is the power of the ideas within these studies that makes them transcend time.

Special Populations and Music

The next section (as well as the following one) in the *Anthology* deal with diversity—diverse students and diverse musics. The research in these areas is fairly recent and thus limited in providing a breadth of insight that is needed today. Increased diversity in the classroom involves all types of students with differing abilities, and the studies in the section entitled "Special Populations and Music" deal with issues of working with these students. Music classrooms have some history of being homogeneous and exclusive, but this is decreasingly the case. New laws and enlightened teachers are working to provide opportunities for all students to be involved with music.

Indeed, some teachers are finding that a varied student population provides a richness of which they were previously unaware.

Research in special populations has become increasingly important as music teachers seek to find better ways to make accommodations. Teacher and peer attitudes may be bigger impediments than any other issue. Continuing research is needed to help teachers and students succeed. What can students with different disabilities contribute to the music class? What can teachers in general music and performance settings do to help students of differing abilities? What accommodations can we make to enhance musical experiences and contributions? Can a diverse classroom enrich all who participate? More objective evidence is needed in this area.

Multicultural Issues and Music

In the section entitled "Multicultural Issues and Music," the authors deal with culturally diverse students and musics. In the United States, populations of diverse ethnicities and nationalities are growing rapidly. This country may be the most multicultural in the world. Music education in the United States has historically been Eurocentric with some folk traditions, but the content is broadening just as society is. What is the impact of the increased intermingling of cultures and their musics?

The studies presented here are a testament to that change. There is a desire to examine musics of many cultures and ways to teach them. There is an interest in considering whether persons of other cultures should be introduced to musical and pedagogical concepts in the same ways that students have been introduced to music in the Western tradition. What impact does the teaching of multicultural music have? Can it be understood? Do the affect and meanings translate? How authentic do experiences need to be to function as multicultural? There are many questions to be addressed in a world of increased communication and interaction among peoples and music.

Other Issues in Music Education

The section entitled "Other Issues in Music Education" is composed of studies that do not fit into the previous sections of the *Anthology*. The importance of these studies is that they have been identified as areas that are influential or critical to music education and research. Among other questions, the five studies in this section ask: How might we best approach and understand composition and other creative processes? What impact does studying music, or time away from other academics, have on achievement? What are the gender issues that come into play in music, and how can we work against stereotyping? What are the motivation issues for students in music, and how can we best use and shape them for the students' benefit? What are the workplace health issues for the music educator, and how do we create safe environments? The extent to which questions such as these are asked and examined is only limited by a researcher's knowledge and imagination The need for more work in these and other areas exists, and the studies in this *Anthology* may provide models and impetus.

The Past and the Future

The last section contains the text of the 1996 Senior Researcher Award Acceptance Address given by Cornelia Yarbrough. This address, entitled "The Future of Scholarly Inquiry in Music Education," includes analyses of the past and current research published in *JRME*, discusses trends, and provides some thoughtful comments about where she believes the future lies. Yarbrough makes recommendations for directions of research and discusses interdisciplinary efforts, philosophical inquiry, empirical methodology, and research in applied music.

This *Anthology* concludes with a comprehensive title index of *JRME* (1953–1997). The articles chosen for the *Anthology* examine many, but far from all, important questions in music education, and this index provides an extensive view into past research. Reflecting this, one could try to predict what the future holds with educational reforms, a changing society, and enhanced knowledge due to systematic inquiry, but I dare not speculate. As the researchers in the *Anthology* have done,[8] we move ahead and strive for enlightenment in the areas of import and interest to music educators.

—Harry E. Price, editor of JRME *(1994–2000)*

NOTES

1. Music Educators National Conference, "A Research Agenda for Music Education: Thinking Ahead," *Teaching Music* 5, no. 4, (1998): special insert.

2. Harry E. Price and Evelyn K. Orman, "Influential Journal of Research in Music Education Articles as Indicated by Authors of Two or More Studies," *Research Studies in Music Education* (A journal fostering music education research in Australia, New Zealand, and East and Southeast Asia) 6 (1996): 59–69.

3. Charles P. Schmidt and Stephen F. Zozinski, "Cited Quantitative Research Articles in Music Education Research Journals, 1975–1990: A Content Analysis of Selected Studies," *Journal of Research in Music Education* 41 (1993): 5–18.

4. Price and Orman, 62.

5. Otto Kinkeldey, "Musical Scholarship and the University," *Journal of Renaissance and Baroque Music* 1 (1946): 11.

6. No author, *Journal of Research in Music Education* 45 (1997): 328.

7. Clifford K. Madsen," Senior Researcher Award Acceptance Address," *Journal of Research in Music Education* 36 (1988): 134

8. The authors of the studies included in the *Anthology* are from the following institutions: Arizona State University; Central Michigan University; Columbia University; Florida International University; Florida State University; Georgia State University; Indiana University; Kansas State University; Kent State University; Louisiana State University; Loyola University; McGill University in Montreal, Canada; Michigan State University; Northwestern University; Ohio State University; State University of New York (SUNY) at Buffalo; Syracuse University; Towson State University; University of Alabama; University of Arizona; University of Georgia; University of Illinois; University of Kansas; University of Maryland; University of Michigan; University of Minnesota; University of Missouri–Columbia; University of Texas at Austin; University of Utah; and University of Washington.

I.

Reflections

on

Music Education

Research

Forum

Harry E. Price, Editor
Journal of Research in Music Education

JRME 1997, VOLUME 45, NUMBER 1, PAGES 4–5

Caves are curious places. Historically, they provided shelter from the outside world. They are secure and generally stable, and they provide consistent environments. They change only as the Earth changes, and the deeper you penetrate them, the less light there is. In caverns, one of the favorite demonstrations is to turn out the lights to demonstrate that, in such intense blackness, you can't even see your hand in front of your face.

Philosophers have understood all too well the dangers of caves. Plato's cave allegory illustrates one of these. Even when near light, people who keep their backs to it see only shadows of themselves and of objects that pass nearby. Unless they turn toward the light, all they see and hear are reflections. The "unenlightened" prisoners in the allegory may be said to be prisoners of knowledge that is distorted and incomplete.

We in music education are fortunate to have an ever-increasing number of sources for enlightenment. In the past two decades, there has been a blossoming and rejuvenation of English-language research journals at international, national, regional, and state levels. We now have new and relevant journals, which include *The Australian Journal of Music Therapy* (founded in 1989), the *British Journal of Music Theory* (1987), the *Bulletin of Historical Research in Music Education* (1980), *Music Therapy Perspectives* (1982), *PMEA* [Pennsylvania] *Bulletin of Research in Music Education* (resumed publication in 1992), the *Philosophy of Music Education Review* (1993), *The Quarterly Journal of Music Teaching and Learning* (1990), *Research Studies in Music Education* (1993), the *Southeastern Journal of Music Education* (1989), and *Update: Applications of Research in Music Education* (1982). Additionally, special research interest groups (SRIGs), which were formed by the Society for Research in Music Education (SRME), publish newsletters that often carry information about research.

The number of journals is a sign of robust research activity and an increased depth of research in our field. As with any mature discipline, there are flagship, second-tier, and third-tier national and international journals, as well as those with more focus on specific regions or states. What most of these journals have in common is breadth of coverage and a referee process. A refereed journal speaks to quality control, and breadth speaks to enlightenment across content areas and research methodologies. However, if journals become too narrow in their content, it is possible that we might become like the prisoners in Plato's cave, with narrow and distorted views, uninformed by other perspectives of knowledge. Although there is a need among researchers to have interchange about their respective modes of inquiry, the content of their work needs to be disseminated to all. The purpose of research is knowledge and enlightenment, not research techniques or bias.

How unfortunate it would be to try to work toward the future without a firm ground in what has transpired. Without historiography and ethnography, we remain ignorant about how we became what we are. One cannot imagine any quest for knowledge without the love of wisdom, which is at the heart of philosophy. Empirical research without a strong historical foundation and a grounding in philosophy is diminished by their absence; conversely, historiography, ethnography, and philosophy are weakened in the absence of enlightenment provided by empirical evidence.

As we draw from narrower and narrower sources of knowledge, we fall prey to ignorance born of being in a cave of limited edification. Harkening back to both Plato and Aristotle, Francis Bacon speaks, in his doctrine of Idola, of *sources for profound errors and superstitions in the nature of the mind.* The idol of the cave is one of his four idols. Those who are susceptible to the idols of the cave or den interpret everything according to a personal viewpoint and tend to lack objective observations. As we are drawn further into this cave, our perceptions become narrower, and we are increasingly predisposed to error.

A proliferation of journals that promote all sources of knowledge elevates music education and all forms of research. However, trends and discussions of vehicles that focus on type of methodology rather than content take us further into a cave. These ill-conceived divisions could be qualitative and quantitative. Within the qualitative category, we could further isolate knowledge by historiography, ethnography, philosophy, and what is now termed qualitative research. In the quantitative division, we could have behavioral, experimental, descriptive, and statistical research methodology journals. We could even further divide some of these into elementary general, secondary general, elementary instrumental, elementary choral, and secondary choral categories. It is possible to suggest that nothing informs anything else.

Having taken this argument to the absurd, I would suggest that all pursuits of knowledge inform all others. To ignore any is to be ignorant. Philosophical and historical inquiry uninformed by empirical evidence is very deep in a cave; conversely, empirical evidence without solid philosophical and historical foundation is a pursuit operating without illumination.

If journals are established based upon methodologies, then what is the place of the content? The purpose of research is a quest for enlightenment, and the greater the variety of modes of inquiry for sources of knowledge, the closer we come to a complete truth.

Clifford K. Madsen is the first recipient of MENC's Senior Researcher Award. This article is an adaptation of a speech he presented to the Society for Research in Music Education at the MENC national biennial in-service conference, Indianapolis, April 22, 1988.

Clifford K. Madsen, *Florida State University, Tallahassee*

JRME 1988, VOLUME 36, NUMBER 3, PAGES 133–139

Senior Researcher Award Acceptance Address

I wish to thank very much those people who have made this award possible. First, the Music Education Research Council and the National Executive Board of MENC. Second, my colleagues at Florida State University (FSU)—I think that those people with whom one works most closely know one best. I would also like to thank all those involved in the Center for Music Research at FSU who help make my research possible. Third, I would especially like to thank the students whom I have had the privilege of teaching over the years and with whom I have interacted and addressed research issues.

It has been said that there is no better job than to be a tenured professor at a major university. This is especially true if the subject matter one deals with is music. Although music teachers at all levels have the privilege of interacting with people and music, there are only a few who have been given the time, within the requirements of their job, to add a little to the sum total of knowledge. It seems obvious to me as I interact with K-12 teachers that it is they who not only make the most difference with students but who also work the hardest. For those of us who may have forgotten how difficult it sometimes is even to schedule a rest room break, the relative luxury of university teaching should carry an added responsibility.

The responsibility for me is to be a researcher, to work carefully in both basic and applied models and to find and test those aspects that contribute either to greater understanding or to a better application of the information found. I find the research process to be exciting and

---

For copies of this speech, contact Clifford K. Madsen, Center for Music Research, School of Music, Florida State University, Tallahassee 32306.

personally rewarding. Indeed, I am one of those individuals who gets to do what I love best: research combined with teaching.

I am somewhat distressed, however, with aspects that seem to inhibit research in music education within institutions of higher learning. It is often said that a heavy teaching assignment reduces research productivity. This is often the case, but it seems to me that the primary enemy is not teaching but unnecessary meetings. Disregard for faculty time has no parallel when it comes to scheduling meetings. While faculty participation in the running of a university is both important and necessary, it seems that quality time is far more important than total time, and every attempt should be made to limit meetings. As one might suspect, I have collected data on this aspect as well as other issues dealing with use of time, and I would suggest that a great deal of research could be accomplished during the time devoted to committee meetings. This might seem obvious, but it needs to be stated.

Some time ago I was asked to help the National Association of Schools of Music develop a research agenda for music. I spent considerable time thinking through many issues relating to research that seemed to be perennial and finally decided that several basic aspects were especially important because of their potential influence within our profession. Much of the following is taken from that original work (Madsen, 1985a).

It seems that there are three basic areas that need to be analyzed and developed in much greater detail before we can expect research to have the influence it deserves. These are (1) investigating attitudes toward all issues relating to applied music study; (2) examining those aspects that pertain to transfer of knowledge, including research dissemination; and (3) developing and supporting researchers within schools of music.

The first aspect concerns applied music study. It seems that issues relating to applied study are both extremely important and complex. Music is basically an applied art, and if the making of music is to progress (outside of professional performing ensembles), we need a good deal of research that is much more comprehensive and sophisticated than that attempted at present. It would be wise to consider current practices of musicians in this regard, for it seems that the way musicians pass on their applied art has not substantially changed in hundreds of years. Young Wolfgang Amadeus Mozart was instructed by his father Leopold in much the same manner as applied music is taught today—one-on-one—in an apprenticeship model. The essence of this model seems to rely on individual musicianship (craftsmanship) and the ability of the student to learn from the master. Furthermore, it is tremendously expensive, especially in institutions of higher education. The tremendous facility required for professional performance demands optimal efficiency, but much time is wasted when conflicting opinions, which could be tested experimentally, are argued and debated. This does not imply that Leopold Mozart was not a good instructor for young Wolfgang; he obviously was. It does seem unfortunate, however, that some applied musicians still do not recognize anything outside of "apprenticeship" in the study of applied music or that most aspiring musicians are not Mozarts (Madsen & Madsen, 1978).

Until we start to unravel the philosophical complexities of why people pursue this difficult task, the sociological issues concerning status, and the psychological issues relating to self-concept and personal motivation, we will probably not change the attitudes surrounding applied study. Also, the entire area of systematic inquiry and subsequent technological advances needs to be investigated in relationship to its perceived value by performing musicians. Research needs to be conducted in the psychological, sociological, and philosophical areas to determine what constitutes the structures that contribute to present attitudes. For example, if an aspiring performer "needs" to study with a distinguished teacher or has a propensity to eulogize his present teacher regardless of competence or even reputation, as some of my data suggest, then it seems useless to try to prove that a great deal of time could be better spent working with a computer to develop pitch discrimination or that group lessons with rotating graduate assistants provide better progress for freshmen. Any research investigating a "better method" or a particularly effective technique will not be valued unless we can understand and subsequently predict the variables of wanting to perform and wanting to study with a particular individual as well as how other complex issues relating to applied music might interact.

The second basic area relates to research dissemination and therefore to transfer. Years ago people talked about "disciplining the mind" to produce an informed citizen or effective person or whatever it was that they deemed important. Yet, psychological experimentation seemed to indicate that the mind could not be "trained" except for specific constructs or tasks and that there was no transfer unless one specifically taught for transfer, both vertical and lateral (Gagne, 1974). Vertical transfer or the arrangement of hierarchical constructs seems to receive much greater attention (e.g., the Kodály concept, music theory sequencing) than does lateral transfer or the ability to bring knowledge relating to one situation into another situation that seems to be disparate. Even the transferable value of formal music theory and history instruction to performance or vice versa has yet to be empirically documented, let alone the transfer of subtle musical concepts from one performance situation to another. Issues relating to effective curricular sequencing, as well as specific relationships among the various performance styles, need special attention. It seems to me that the most important education issues relate to a person's ability to make transfers.

Transfer also seems to be the key to gaining greater meaning from research reports as well as all other reading, and I have suggested (Madsen, 1985b) that until each of us as a professional is capable of answering the important question of how this information can relate to us, it is probably fruitless to seek any easy solutions to our many problems. I suggest that many of the reasons given for not reading research may not be the "real" reasons. It seems that one important detriment to research dissemination relates to an inability to transfer information from the research report to one's own teaching situation. I have proposed some things that could be done to teach for transfer, and I have also reported a procedure whereby research reports can be analyzed and understood: I designed, tested, and redesigned a special one-page form that summarized each research study and asked participants to make several differentiations (Madsen, Greer, & Madsen, 1975; Madsen & Prickett, 1987). Even if musicians could not understand the entire article, they were asked to read the abstract and the discussion. Then they were asked to provide answers to several important questions such as "What did the research attempt to do?" and "What constituted the measurement?" Attempts were made to understand the statistical or graphic data analyses. More important, each musician was asked to write a short paragraph stating what he or she considered to be the basic importance of the study as well as a paragraph concerning how results could be generalized or transferred to other subjects or situations. The last two paragraphs proved the most useful in helping readers relate the study to their own teaching or performing situations. Musicians became progressively better in analyzing and making transfers from published research studies. They also became more sophisticated in their critical analysis and more discriminating in their reading. Another series of studies (Hanser & Madsen, 1972; Madsen, 1982; Madsen & Furman, 1984) indicates that most music students, undergraduate and graduate, can do quite sophisticated research on their own after having read and studied published research.

The third aspect important to the research process is to develop competent researchers. This is a long-term process—Opus 1 doth not a composer make and Opus 1 doth not a researcher make. As long as the dissertation remains the paramount if not the only research product attempted, it is inconceivable that systematic literature will be developed that will help shape music practices. There seem to be several problems and issues that relate to developing researchers, not the least of which involves the question of why some people desire such strong identification with the research community without doing any research.

One problem is with the traditional curricular structure of graduate education regarding the discrepancy between subject matter specialties (e.g., elementary, vocal, band), methodological specialties (e.g., philosophical, historical, descriptive, experimental), and specific subspecialties (e.g., aesthetic learning, computer applications). I suggest that differentiations concerning selection of a major professor for university music students be made along methodological and special interest lines rather than traditional subject matter classifications. For example, I find it difficult to see how a choral director could be sophisticated enough to direct all dissertations that involve historical, philosophical, descriptive, or experimental aspects relating to choruses, let alone be knowledgeable in all the subspecialties necessary for guidance. Therefore, I suggest that the major professor should direct work that is within his or her methodological expertise rather than tied to subject matter expertise, and the professor whose expertise lies in the appropriate subject matter should serve as an additional consultant. Certainly, it would be better to have one person with both abilities, but this is often not possible.

An ideal environment in which to develop a competent researcher would be one that starts early in developing general musical sensitivity combined with research prowess. I suggest that we begin by teaching research to undergraduates. We might start with those young people who are sophisticated musicians and are truly curious, especially about the nature of teaching and learning and about perceptual or creative processes in music. It is unlikely that insensitive musicians or insensitive people will develop sensitive research projects. The undergraduate might begin early to integrate theory and practice so that learning methods of research is continuously interwoven with solving actual music problems. If long-term practices are not submitted to empirical investigation, the methods of teaching and research that have always been taught in certain ways go unchallenged and curricula become rigid and unresponsive to current needs. Alternatively, continuous investigation without actual practice tends to become esoteric and removed from the real world of making music. After the undergraduate has attempted several short projects and has read some research literature, the student needs to get out into the practicing profession to appreciate better the mammoth demands of "doing it" (e.g., teaching, professional touring, or working as a music therapist). After several years of doing this, the student might return for a beginning graduate degree or might intersperse graduate work with his or her employment. Prospective researchers might help senior graduates or professors with projects while taking statistics, design, and measurement courses. It is especially important that they do a thesis that is publishable.

Perhaps the most important objective for prospective researchers is to begin early to write and, if possible, to publish (even if they coauthor their studies with more experienced scholars). It is at the master's level that a few students decide to attempt an advanced degree and thereby commit themselves to advanced research. Writing initiates the student into a community of scholars who are committed to research.

I suggest this process in contrast to current practice, which consists of adding a scholarly product (i.e., a dissertation or treatise) to many other burdensome requirements toward the pursuit of a doctorate. During doctoral study, identification with a major professor should be strong. It seems axiomatic that the major professor should present a model for important research behavior, but there is also a need for research critics and research administrators. These people are very important to the research process, and without them, research products would be nonexistent or hopelessly naive. The doctoral student should do many research projects during residency study so that one or two projects of publishable quality can be completed for the preliminary (comprehensive) examination. The dissertation should be an almost entirely independent endeavor so that little if any help is necessary from the supervising committee. In this manner the doctoral graduate emerges fully capable of doing research as well as directing other research without "farming out" the statistical or measurement problems to others.

Nevertheless, the nurturing process is still not complete unless the researcher has a network of concerned, highly critical, but supportive people with whom to interact. In this regard, groups are formed with persons of similar interests who possess these qualities. To work toward this end, I instituted in 1974 a National Conference on Research in Music Behavior, which has met every two years and continues to bring together researchers of similar interests who are academically critical yet socially supportive. All persons affiliated with this group are currently highly productive and continue to provide leadership in music research. Additionally, in 1980 the Center for Music Research was formally established at the Florida State University under the capable leadership of Jack Taylor. As Bennett Reimer (1985) has suggested, other schools should provide opportunities for various focal research interests so that literature can be developed that includes specific thrusts.

I hope that these three issues, if appropriately addressed, will help in the development of sophisticated research that is important for advancing knowledge, promoting greater efficiency, and enhancing the quality of music experiences. Traditionally, rewards in higher education go to people who do whatever can be done within their chosen specialty: If one is a violinist, one plays; if one is a composer, one composes; if one teaches theory, one theorizes (in refereed journals, of course), and so on. Yet, additional knowledge concerning those aspects that could help us with our important work remains elusive, and research does not begin to enjoy the respect it should have. Perhaps some day research will be so valued in the music community that researchers will state proudly one of Cornelia Yarbrough's phrases, "*Research* is my performing instrument."

In summary, it seems that findings from research and subsequent technology would be especially beneficial in applied music study, but as long as those whose major responsibility is to teach applied music do not really value these procedures, the procedures will not be encouraged or used. Additionally, musicians and music teachers get ideas to try out in whatever manner they can. Transferring from reading the research reported in professional journals is one good source of these ideas, and working toward objective evaluation of any idea is certainly useful. Most important, researchers are ordinary people and therefore subject to the encouragements and punishments of their environments. It has always been difficult for me to understand how research can flourish when only punishing consequences prevail. Unfortunately, we have a few people in our research community whose primary goal seems to be criticism, and they produce little, if any, research. We not only need to be highly critical; we need to be supportive and nurturing as well. It seems to me that the often-perceived gap between the rigorous requirements of scientific inquiry and the art of music begins to narrow with attempts that include both pursuits. Therefore, in developing long-term aesthetic goals, we must strive to provide effective support for research efforts as well. I am pleased that MENC originated the Senior Researcher Award because I believe it is an important step in that direction. I am most grateful to have received this honor.

REFERENCES

Gagne, R. M. (1974). *Essentials of learning for instruction.* Hinsdale, IL: Dryden.
Hanser, S. B., & Madsen, C. K. (1972). Comparisons of graduate and under-graduate research in music therapy. *Journal of Music Therapy, 9*(2), 88–93.

Madsen, C. K. (1982). Graduate versus undergraduate scholarship: What should be our expectations? *College Music Symposium, 22*(1), 73–77.

Madsen, C. K. (1985a). Developing a research agenda: Issues concerning implementation. In National Association of Schools of Music, *Proceedings: The 60th Annual Meeting.* Reston, VA. Author. Used by permission.

Madsen, C. K. (1985b). Making research apply to your classroom. *Music Educators Journal, 71*(8), 18–19.

Madsen, C. K., & Furman, C. E. (1984). Graduate versus undergraduate scholarship: Research acquisition and dissemination. *Journal of Music Therapy, 21*, 170–176.

Madsen, C. K., Greer, R. D., & Madsen, C. H., Jr. (Eds.). (1975). *Research in music behavior: Modifying music behavior in the classroom.* New York: Teachers College Press.

Madsen, C. K., & Prickett, C. A. (Eds.). (1987). *Applications of research in music behavior.* Tuscaloosa: University of Alabama Press.

Madsen, C. K., & Madsen, C. H., Jr. (1978). *Experimental research in music.* Raleigh, NC: Contemporary Publishing.

Reimer, B. (1985, Summer). Toward a more scientific approach to music education research. *Bulletin of the Council for Research in Music Education, 83*, 17–21.

II.

Philosophical

Conceptualizations

Leonard Meyer's Theory of Value and Greatness in Music

BENNETT REIMER

JRME 1962, VOLUME 10, NUMBER 2, PAGES 87–99

Introduction

IN HIS BOOK *Emotion and Meaning in Music*, published in 1956,[1] Leonard B. Meyer set forth an explanation of musical experience which drew upon the resources of modern psychological knowledge and his own background as a practicing musician and aesthetician. It was Meyer's purpose to present an account of meaning and communication in music based upon a systematic application of certain psychological theories to the phenomenon of musical responsiveness. These theories have to do with pattern perception, and the myriad ways in which the manipulation of patterns gives rise to affect and meaning.

A few years later Meyer made "Some Remarks on Value and Greatness in Music" in the *Journal of Aesthetics and Art Criticism*.[2] This essay was an attempt to carry some of the insights of his book (and others seemingly gained subsequent to the book's publication) to conclusions of a nature which seem to me far more fruitful than any he was able to draw previously. This essay will be dealt with in some detail, for it is felt that the conceptions contained in it are of great assistance in formulating a clear and valid understanding of the function of musical experience, and, by extension, of aesthetic experience in general. In so doing, the main premises of his book will be touched upon, but in a context which is felt to be more meaningful than would be possible if one treated the book alone. The purpose for explaining Meyer's conceptions is, of course, that they are felt to have great bearing on the field of music education. Some specific applications of the ideas dealt with here to music education will be attempted in the conclusion.

Synopsis of Meyer's Argument

The question "What makes music great?" is one that must be met in some manner by everyone who is deeply concerned with this art. Meyer's attempts at understanding the nature of value in music have led him to questions as to the nature of value in general, and finally to the realm of metaphysics. He recognizes that attempts to systematize one's views as to greatness in music are frought with hazards and uncertainties. But one cannot escape making them. It is impossible to avoid making value judgments, both for oneself and for others, when dealing with music as a practicing musician and teacher. And in order to explain how and what music "communicates," some system of ordering of values is necessary.

As first glance the problem seems capable of a relatively easy solution.

---

[1] Leonard B. Meyer, *Emotion and Meaning in Music* (Chicago: University of Chicago Press, 1956).

[2] Leonard B. Meyer, "Some Remarks on Value and Greatness in Music," *Journal of Aesthetics and Art Criticism*, XVII (June, 1959), p. 486.

Everyone recognizes certain technical criteria for excellence in a piece of music. It must have consistency of style (a unified system of expectations and probabilities), clarity of basic intent, variety, unity, and so on. But these things, while they may enable us to distinguish a good piece from a downright bad one, will hardly tell us the difference between a fairly good piece and a very good one, let alone distinguish for us the characteristics of greatness. For example, the tune "Twinkle, twinkle little star" possesses style, unity, and variety. If we ask why Bach's *B Minor Mass* is better than "Twinkle, twinkle little star"— using *only* these technical categories in our answer—we would have to admit that both are equally good. This, of course, is patently untrue.

Nor can the criteria of length, size, or complexity, *as such,* provide the answer to our question. All of us know small pieces which are obviously better works than some large pieces.

At this point Meyer suggests that we turn to particular musical examples to see what we can learn from them. Restrictions of space lead him to choose two fugue subjects, and to confine his analysis to them, with the understanding that they will serve to raise some of the basic considerations relating to value and to greatness, and that these

considerations apply with equal force to complete works, even of the greatest magnitude. The two themes he chooses are one by Geminiani (Fig. 1), and one by Bach (Fig. 2).

No attempt will be made here to present in full Meyer's treatment of these two fragments, for this would entail a lengthy and detailed excursion into his analytical techniques. For an understanding of his method one must consult *Emotion and Meaning in Music,* which is mainly concerned with such analyses. The purpose here is to point out the kinds of things he looks for in music, and the conclusions he draws from the degree of their presence or absence.

Thus, he points out that the themes are similar in basic melodic structure. Both begin on the 5th degree of the scale and move to the tonic—in Bach's case through the 3rd of the scale—and then skip an octave. The resulting gap gives a sense of incompleteness, which, complemented by the rhythmic instability of the first musical shape, calls for a filling in. We expect a descending melodic line to follow, and to come to rest ultimately on the tonic tone. This in fact does happen, but with crucial differences. The Bach theme moves down slowly, with delays and diversions, through related harmonic areas. It establishes as it goes various levels

Fig. 1

Fig. 2

of melodic activity and intent, with various potentials to be realized. These delays are rhythmic as well as melodic. The Geminiani theme, on the other hand, moves almost directly to its goal. Although the second measure, being chromatic, contains the potential for different modes of continuation, it moves to the very likely B, and then directly to the inevitable E. When the theme falls to this obvious consequent with neither delay nor diversion it seems like a platitude—a musical cliché. Even the rhythm moves with no disturbance from the initial upbeat to the final obvious downbeat.

From these observations Meyer draws a fundamental premise. "Value," he says, "has something to do with the activation of a musical impulse having tendencies toward a more or less definite goal, *and with the temporary resistance or inhibition of these tendencies.*" To point up the importance of the element of resistance he suggests we rewrite the Bach theme in such a way that this element is eliminated (Fig. 3).

consistent stylistic context, the musical event will have little value. Third, if the goal is never reached, or if the tendencies which have been activated dissolve in the press of irrelevant and over-complex diversions, then value will tend to be limited.

The notion which relates value to the inhibition of goal-oriented tendencies has been touched upon by several writers. Robert Penn Warren, in an article titled "Pure and Impure Poetry,"[3] stated, ". . . a poem, to be good, must earn itself. It is a motion toward a point of rest, but if it is not a resisted motion, it is a motion of no consequence. For example, a poem which depends upon stock materials and stock responses is simply a toboggan slide, or a fall through space."

John Dewey states it in a more general way in *Art as Experience.*[4] "Impulsion forever boosted on its forward way would run its course thoughtless, and dead to emotion. . . .The only way it can become aware of its nature and its goal is by obstacles surmounted and means employed. . ."

Fig. 3

The theme is now as banal as the Geminiani.

Three further premises are drawn. First, that a melody or work which establishes no tendencies, if this can be imagined, would be of no value. Of course these tendencies need not be powerful at the outset, but may be developed during the course of the work. Second, that if the most probable goal is reached in the most immediate and direct manner, assuming a

In recent years certain concepts have been developed in the field of information theory in which the relationship between value and resistance seems implicit. In order to apply these concepts to our problem, it is necessary to examine in more detail the nature of goal-tendency processes.

[3] Robert Penn Warren, "Pure and Impure Poetry," *Kenyon Review*, V (1943), p. 251.
[4] John Dewey, *Art as Experience* (New York: Minton, Balch and Co., (1934), p. 54.

Musical events take place in a context of stylistic probability. Any tone taken singly could be followed with equal probability by a great number of different tones. If a sequence of two tones is stated the number of probable consequent tones is somewhat smaller, and hence the probability of the remaining alternatives is somewhat increased. As more tones are added, and consequently more relationships between tones are built up, the probabilities of a particular goal become increased. In Bach's theme the probability of any particular tone following the first D is very small, since the number of possibilities is very large. As the line moves downward through Bb and A, however, the probabilities of the G become very strong. When it is reached this first little musical pattern seems ended. Then the pattern, after the octave skip, becomes the unit of motion, and is set up as the basis for estimating probability on a higher architectonic level. The *variety of events* in the theme, as well as the *delays* noted previously, make the particular sequence of events seem *much less probable* than the sequence of events in the Geminiani theme.

Here information theory applies. It states that if a situation is highly organized so that the possible consequents have a high degree of probability, and the probable occurs, the information given by the message (or musical event) is minimal. On the other hand, if the musical situation is less predictable—if there is *not* a high degree of probability that a certain consequent will follow a given antecedent—then the information contained in the musical message will be high. Thus, the more probable the message, the less its information.

Since resistances, or deviations, are by definition disturbances in the goal-oriented tendencies of a musical impulse, these deviations lower the probability of both the particular consequent and the piece as a whole. Thus they create or increase information. And one may reasonably conclude that what creates or increases the information in a piece of music increases its value.

This is not to say that a completely random series of stimuli, since it contains a low degree of probability, will contain a high degree of information. Actually, a random series will in all likelihood communicate nothing. Music depends upon the existence of an ordered system of probabilities which makes the several stimuli or events mutually relevant. Randomness of choice is always limited by the fact of musical style.

Information theory suggests that the notion of resistance, or deviation, relates to the notion of uncertainty. The lower the probability that any one particular sequence of events will take place—that is, the lower the probability that the total message will be any particular one—the greater the uncertainty as to what the events and the message will actually turn out to be. And also the greater the information the total event will contain. Thus the greater the uncertainty, the greater the information. The relationship between resistance and uncertainty is quite clear. Whenever a tendency is inhibited, as by a deviation, slight uncertainty is experienced. What seemed so probable that alternatives were not considered now seems less so. For the mind, in attempting to account for the deviation, is made aware of the possibility of less probable, alternative conclusions.

A distinction must be made between the type of uncertainty which is desirable and that which is undesirable.

Desirable uncertainty arises as a result of the structured probabilities of a musical style. Information is a function of this type of uncertainty. Undesirable uncertainty arises when the probabilities are simply not known because the listener's responses are not relevant to the style. Further, uncertainty must be distinguished from vagueness. Uncertainty presumes a basic norm of clear-cut probability patterns, so that even the ambiguous is felt to be goal oriented. Vagueness, on the other hand, involves a weakening of the syntactical relationships among the musical elements. As a result the sense of musical tendency is enfeebled.

After a further analysis of Geminiani's theme in relation to a parallel example from language, Meyer summarizes what has been learned from the excursion into the relationship of information theory to music and to value. First, we find that resistance, or more broadly, deviation, is a correlative of information. Since information is valuable the hypothesis as to the importance of deviation has received confirmation. Second, the inquiry points to a relationship between information and deviation on the one hand, and uncertainty on the other. This implies that uncertainty is somehow related to value.

Testing the Hypotheses

As a test of the plausibility of his hypotheses, Meyer suggests that we apply them to the question of the difference between primitive music and art music. Doing so might well reveal another aspect of the relationship between tendency inhibition and value. The fundamental difference between sophisticated art music and primitive music (and "primitive music" does not include the highly sophisticated music

which some so-called "primitives" play) lies in speed of tendency gratification. The primitive seeks almost immediate gratification for his tendencies, whether these be biological or musical. He cannot tolerate uncertainty. The tonal repertory of the primitive is limited not because he can't think of other tones, but because distant departures from the certainty of the tonic and lengthy delays in gratification are insufferable to him. It is not his mentality which is limited, but his maturity. Popular music may be distinguished from jazz under this notion. While "pop" music, whether of the tin-pan alley or the Ethelbert Nevin type, makes use of a fairly large variety of tones, it operates with such conventional clichés that gratification is almost immediate and uncertainty is kept to a minimum.

An important aspect of maturity, both of the individual and of the culture within which a style arises, is the willingness to forego immediate and probably lesser gratification for the sake of future ultimate gratification. Understood generally, self-imposed tendency inhibition and a willingness to bear uncertainty are indications of maturity. "And this, I take it," says Meyer, "is not without relevance to considerations of value."

The Ordering of Values in Music

The above argument hints at a rather puritanical view of value in music. What of some of the other values to be gained from music, such as the sensuous pleasure of beautiful sound, and the enjoyment of the associations music evokes? Are these without value?

The problems raised by these questions, says Meyer, are problems of the relation of pleasure to value and of the ordering of values. At first it seems that we do distinguish between what is pleasurable and what is good. But both immediate gratification and delayed gratification are pleasurable, and both are valuable. This value relates to a quality of musical experience. It arises out of the transaction between the listener and the musical work. It is not inherent in the musical object as such, or in the listener as such. Thus, the value of a particular musical experience is a function of the listener's ability to respond according to the style of the work, and the mode of his response.

There are three large areas of musical response and enjoyment. These are the sensuous, the associative-characterizing, and the syntactical. Though all music involves all three to some extent, some works emphasize one aspect and minimize the others. At one end of the continuum is the immediate gratification of the sensuous and the excited outburst of uncontrolled, pent-up energy. At the other end is the delayed gratification arising out of perception of and response to the syntactical relationships, intellectual and/or emotional, which shape and mold musical experience. The associative aspect functions with either. It can color the sensuous pleasure with the satisfactions of wish-fulfillment. Or it can shape one's expectations as to the probabilities of musical motion by characterizing musical events. Our estimate of the character of a theme shapes our expectation as to how it will behave. And the way it behaves influences our opinion as to its character. So the syntactical and the characterizing facets of musical responsiveness are inextricably linked.

But the question of the ordering of values remains. Are the different aspects of musical enjoyment equally valuable? Is a piece of music which

appeals to sensuous-associative pleasure as good as one which appeals to syntactical-associative pleasure? To say that "each is good of its kind" is to evade the problem.

An idea from the discussion of primitive music and art music can be applied here. It was observed that the willingness to inhibit tendencies and tolerate uncertainties is a sign of maturity. Now the converse of this is also true. Maturation and individualization are themselves products of the resistances, uncertainties, and problems with which life confronts us. It is only by coming to grips with resistances in our environment that self-awareness develops, that we achieve self-realization. And from this it follows that since evaluation of alternative probabilities and understanding of relationships among musical events leads to self-awareness and individualization, the syntactical response is more valuable than those in which the ego is dissolved and loses itself in sensuality or reverie. For this reason, works involving deviation and uncertainty are better than those which offer more immediate satisfaction.

The difficulty with this appears to be the fact that aside from the most primitive musico-emotional outbursts and the most blatant appeals to the sensuous element found in some popular music, there are no musical works in which syntactical elements do not play an important role. But it must be recognized that while we might evaluate the response of *listeners* on the basis of weighing sensuous-associative and syntactical elements present in the response, we can only evaluate musical *works* syntactically. For the degree of presence or absence of sensuous and associative aspects in a piece of music is a completely subjective matter. Who is to say which piece has greater sensuous appeal or evokes the more poignant associations? The question of which is greater or which is lesser music must be answered in terms of the syntactical organization of the music.

From the syntactical viewpoint then, what things determine value in music? We have already noted that complexity, size and length are not in themselves virtues, as we have learned from many a bombastic and empty work of large proportions. Still, in so far as a complex work must contain, as it runs its course, a good deal of resistance and uncertainty—and presumably information—value is thereby created. This seems more plausible when we consider that as we get to know a complex work better our enjoyment of it is increased, for our comprehension of the permutations and interrelations among the musical events increases the information we receive.

Of course there are limits to the efficacy of complexity. The human mind can handle only so much complexity of pattern. It is also true, however, that first experiences with a piece might be unrewarding because of a seeming overcomplexity, while familiarity may later make the same work understandable and meaningful. At any rate, it seems clear that complexity, while not a sufficient cause of value, is somehow closely related to value.

But what of relatively simple works such as Schubert's song "Das Wandern," or a Mozart minuet? Are they not valuable precisely because of their simplicity? It seems probable that much of the value of such "simple" music is associative, since its appeal is to childhood, remembered as secure and untroubled. Yet we still cannot say that there is a one-to-one correspondence between complexity and value. For again, we are all aware that some relatively simple pieces are far more rewarding than some larger, more complex works.

This problem may be resolved by the realization that information is judged not in absolute, but in relative terms. We evaluate a work not only by the output of information, but by the relationship of information gained to musical means invested. Those works are judged good which yield a high return of information for the musical effort made. Musical information is thus evaluated both quantitatively and qualitatively. Two pieces might yield the same amount of information yet not be equally good because one is less economical and elegant than the other. On the other hand, a piece which is somewhat overstated may be better than a more economical piece because it contains substantially more information and hence provides a richer musical experience.

Greatness in Music

Musical communication, says Meyer, is qualitative in another sense than the syntactical. The *content* of musical experience is also an important aspect of its quality. And with this statement he leaves the concepts of information theory, which are only concerned with music's syntactical nature, and he also parts company from those aestheticians who contend that musical experience is devoid of content. And his argument moves from the consideration of value as such to the consideration of greatness. It also moves directly into the realm of metaphysics.

When we talk of greatness, Meyer says, we are dealing with a quality of experience which transcends the syntactical. Greatness is another order of value, in which self-awareness and individualization arise out of the cosmic uncertainties that pervade man's existence. The sense of the inadequacy of reason in a capricious and inscrutable universe, the feeling of isolation and loneliness in a hostile environment, the awareness of insignificance and finitude, all lead man to ultimate and inescapable questions and concerns. These ultimate uncertainties—which are at the same time ultimate realities—are made conscious in great music. We are made aware of them not as a result of syntactical relationships alone, but from the interaction of these with the associative facet of music. This interaction, which both shapes and characterizes musical experience, gives rise to a profound wonderment and to a deeper insight into the mystery of existence. In the very act of sensing this mystery we are driven to a higher level of consciousness, of individualization. And the nature of uncertainty too has changed. It has become a means to an end, rather than an end to be suffered.

The greatest works, then, are those which combine value of the highest order with the most profound (or what some philosophers would call "sublime") content. "Excellence" in a piece of music depends on syntactical elements, while "greatness" includes considerations of content. This is why it makes sense to speak of a "great work" that doesn't quite "come off." We mean that it seeks to make us aware of ultimate uncertainties, but fails in execution. We can also distinguish between a "masterpiece" and a "great work" under this notion. Some of Bach's Inventions, for example, are masterpieces of musical excellence, but are not great works.

Great music, in causing the listener to become aware of the ultimate concerns of life—to experience them existentially, as it were—has a profound-

ly disturbing, even shattering effect. As a general rule "suffering" is evil, because it brings about a regression towards immaturity, toward primitivism. But when the individual is able to master it through understanding, suffering may ultimately be good. It is painful, as is medical treatment, but it leads to a higher level of consciousness and to a more sensitive, insighted conception of the very nature and meaning of existence. All maturation, all self-discovery, is in a very real sense somewhat painful. It is the wonder of great art that through it we can approach this highest level of consciousness without paying the painful price exacted in real life, and without the risk of that self-dissolution which real suffering often brings. The ultimate value of art is its ability to individualize the self, by making the self aware of those things which concern it ultimately.

It becomes clear, then, that the hypothesis as to the relation of resistance and uncertainty to value transcends the realm of aesthetics. In the final analysis the question which must be asked is metaphysical. "What is the meaning and purpose of man's existence?" "Though one's answer," says Meyer, "can be rationalized and explained—though one can *assert* that it is through self-realization that man becomes differentiated from the beasts —it cannot be proved. Like an axiom, it must be self-evident."

Subjective Nature of
Meyer's Procedure

Leonard Meyer's conception of value and greatness in music, as sketched above, presents the reader with some useful insights and with some thorny problems. The basic idea of separating considerations of value from those of greatness seems to be extremely helpful. It states quite clearly what the listener realizes intuitively—that "something" differentiates the skillful and complex from the great. Before commenting on Meyer's conception of what that "something" is, a difficulty in his procedure for determining value through analyses of the syntactical elements of music will be considered.

When following an analysis by Meyer, we are struck with the great skill and deep musical and psychological understanding he exhibits as he works through a musical fragment. So struck are we, that occasionally it occurs to us that it would be almost impossible for anyone else to match exactly his analytical skill. In fact, one must confess that aside from the more obvious points he makes, the procedure seems to border upon the subjective. We recognize his intent, and the fact that music can logically lend itself to an analysis of this type. But in actual practice it often seems that the very nature of the symbols requires that many of the judgments made about them be based upon a subjective evaluation of their function and purpose.

A parallel example of this is found in the dream analyses of Carl Jung and Sigmund Freud. The dream symbols these men deal with are similar to musical statements in that they are both capable of myriad interpretations at various levels. A musical theme may even be compared to a central symbol in a dream sequence. Both seem to serve as unifying elements, and their behavior has much to do with the "meaning" of the total symbol. Jung and Freud maintain that dream symbols can be analyzed according to systematic application of certain principles and procedures, as does Meyer with music. Yet anyone who has studied the dream interpretations of these two eminent psychiatrists realizes that if one were to reach the same conclusions in every case that they reach, one would have to, in some sense, *be them*, bringing to the task not only their knowledge and intelligence, but their background, preferences, attitudes, and even ambitions. Their conclusions seem logical and straightforward, yet we wonder if anyone else could have arrived at exactly those conclusions if working separately. In fact, we do know that agreement among psychiatrists in such matters, aside from the most elementary and obvious cases, is practically nonexistent.

Such seems to be the case with music. Some analytical techniques, notably in the several systems of harmonic analysis, provide consistent and highly workable tools for extracting certain items of information about particular pieces of music. The information gained through Meyer's system is, of course, of a different order, and seems to depend on judgments which are of necessity subjective. This is not to say that the information gained is thus invalid and unimportant, either in the case of dreams or of music. The point is that Meyer's analytical technique does not provide a completely accurate measure of syntactical complexity in music, but indicates the directions one must take in order to evaluate for oneself the degree of such complexity.

From this it follows that there is no absolute scale of value or excellence in music based upon the degree of syntactical complexity it contains. Aside from the impossibility of accurately measuring one piece against another in this regard, there is also the problem of differentiating between the mediocre, the good and the excellent. At what point does music become "good" rather than "mediocre," or "excellent" rather than "good"? We can only say that a piece may meaningfully be called "better" or "worse" than another piece of equal magnitude on the basis of the syntactical complexity and skill of handling it seems to exhibit as compared to the other piece. But of course this is no small accomplishment. For it means we have a realistic and useful method to help us in formulating value judgments which are based upon more than sheer intuition.

Application to Music Education

The entire conception of excellence in music as a function of syntactical organization can be applied with great benefit to the field of music education. If it is the purpose of music education to provide means by which the student may apprehend and evaluate musical excellence, it would seem necessary that the major portion of musical instruction be concerned with explication of music's syntactical nature.

This is a notion of far-reaching significance. It can be applied to all levels of musical instruction and to all types of musical instruction. It is a notion which can permeate all aspects of teaching and learning in music, giving them both direction and sustenance. In short, we seem to be confronted with a central principle capable of ordering and directing a major portion of activities in the field of music education. While much activity in this field is, in fact, directed toward fostering just this awarenecss of music's syntactical nature, there is seldom present the kind of clear justification for so doing which Meyer's theory provides. And in a field in which activities and objectives are so infrequently grounded upon justifiable principles, the fact that at least one

such principle does exist must be noted with more than passing interest.

But as one ponders the manifold applications of this idea to actual practices in the teaching of music, it becomes clear that involvement with musical syntax alone would hardly be sufficient to develop the kind of sensitivity and understanding which this art seems capable of giving. One feels that concern with the values of "excellence" and "information" alone is somehow sterile and clinical. Certain very common practices in the teaching of music theory immediately come to mind as examples of the sterility of total involvement in musical syntax to the exclusion of natural musical responsiveness.

We seem to be presented with a paradox. On the one hand we draw from Meyer's analysis of value the principle that musical excellence is a function of the skill of manipulation of syntactical elements. If we are to become sensitive to musical excellence we must concern ourselves with these elements. At the same time we find that common practices in music education, notably in the teaching of theory, lead to a certain clinical emptiness as a direct result of concern with musical syntax. It seems clear that what the musician calls "musicality," or the "musical" values, must enter in. The practicing musician and the sensitive listener intuit the presence in music of certain values which are larger than the total of musical devices employed. These values are related to what Meyer calls "greatness" —a quality which he feels is in some measure dependent on the "content" of the music.

When speaking of "content" in music, one steps into a field which has traditionally been marked by bitter controversy. The classical statement of opposition to the view which holds that it is possible to speak of musical content as something apart from musical syntax is Eduard Hanslick's *The Beautiful in Music*.[5] The cogency of Hanslick's argument, aided by personal factors which made it more pointed and impassioned than a scholarly dissertation usually turns out to be, had the effect of clearing the air of many of the misconceptions of Romantic thought. From this first statement of opposition to the Referentialist point of view, the literature dealing with musical "meaning" or musical "content" has until recent years favored the "Absolutist" point of view. The Absolutists insist that musical meaning lies exclusively within the context of the work itself, in the relationships set forth among the musical elements. The Referentialists contend that in addition to syntactical, abstract meanings, music also communicates meanings which refer to the extramusical world of concepts, emotional states, etc.

It is not necessary to enter this debate here, but it must be pointed out that the thinking on this matter has mellowed somewhat from the extreme attitudes both sides held at the outset. It seems evident that both views contain a good deal of validity, and that it is possible, without alienating any but the staunchest supporters of each side, to somewhat reconcile the two. For it has come to be realized by many writers that absolute meanings and referential meanings are not mutually exclusive. This is not to say that anyone who has given serious consideration to this problem condones the practice of relating particular musical events to particular extramusical

---

[5] Eduard Hanslick, *The Beautiful in Music* (London: Novello, Ewer and Co., 1891).

reactions on the part of the listener. This type of musical response is not considered valid or important by either Absolutists or Referentialists. The argument is at the level of what Meyer calls syntactical responsiveness, and hinges on whether "meaning" at this level remains purely musical or whether it can relate to values which are part of life in general. Meyer is one of the growing number of thinkers who conclude that music and the arts, when they operate at the level of greatness, do indeed carry us into the realm of human values, and at a point at which these values can only be discussed in metaphysical terms.

This turn of thought is not an isolated phenomenon. It is interesting to note that in the field of depth psychiatry, particularly as practiced by the Existentialists and by Carl Jung and his school, metaphysical considerations are beginning to play a larger and more important part. And even from the realm of the applied sciences come indications that at certain levels and under certain conditions metaphysical problems become highly pertinent and highly applicable to advances in understanding.

At any rate it is Meyer's contention that it is only when music illuminates and makes conscious to the listener the ultimate uncertainties that it can be called great. If we accept this view, we find that the terms which must be used to explain greatness in music are terms which are somewhat foreign to the vocabulary of musicians and aestheticians. Meyer talks of "self-realization," of "the nature and meaning of existence," of "suffering" and "ultimate uncertainties" and "ultimate realities." These terms are the common coin of another realm—that of religion. Indeed it is the very purpose of religion to make these concepts clear and understandable.

When the term "religion" is used in this connection, it should be made plain that it is used in its widest and most abstract sense. The term "religion" is not used to mean any of the organized systems of worship and morality which go by the names of Christianity or Judaism or Buddhism. Rather the word is employed in the sense of John Dewey's conception— that any experiences or concepts which illuminate or order those aspects of existence which concern man ultimately are religious experiences, religious concepts. This is both a definition of religion and an attitude towards it. It involves the idea that religious considerations can pervade all of experience, without relating in any way to organized systems which have for their purpose the structuring of these experiences in preset ways. Susanne Langer states this view in slightly different terms than Dewey, but with the same intent. For Langer, "religion is a gradual envisagement of the essential pattern of human life, and to this insight almost any object, act, or event may contribute."[6] The point both make, a point which is essential to an understanding of music's highest function, is that any experience which touches upon values which are called, in philosophical and theological terms, ultimate values, is religious experience.

According to Meyer's description of greatness in music, it becomes quite clear that at this level music's function is essentially a religious one. "The ultimate value of art lies in its ability to individualize the self," says Meyer. Self-individualization has been recognized for ages, of course, to be one of

the most vital and significant functions of religion. It receives its classical statement in the ancient admonition "know thyself," which implies that in so knowing, one shall "know God." This notion, that one must "look inward" to find truths which seem basic, has been expressed in philosophy and literature throughout history, and is receiving verification in modern times in psychology and depth psychiatry. It is this notion which is being applied by Meyer to music, and according to it the function of music and the arts can be described, in a very real sense, as being a religious function.

Accepting this line of reasoning, we can make a further statement. If music education has for its purpose the development of the student's comprehension of and sensitivity to musical greatness, then its purpose is essentially a religious one. Music education, when operating with music at the level of greatness, is essentially religious education. This statement can only be made, one must hasten to point out, in the light of the definition of religion suggested above. It is in this light, of course, that it *is* made. The point is that the statement *can* be made, and can be well defended by pointing to arguments from the field of aesthetics and arguments from the field of religion.

The implications of this notion seem to me to be immense. For here we approach a conception of the function of music and of music education which makes it possible to explain both the feelings of reverence with which great music has always been regarded, and the impelling desire of those who have experienced the greatness of music to make such experience available to everyone through musical education. Stated simply, our notion is that the function of great music is

---

[6] Susanne K. Langer, *Philosophy in a New Key* (New York: New American Library, 1953), p. 126.

to provide insights which may be called religious, and that the function of music education, when operating at its highest level, is to make these insights generally available. Hence, music education is, when fulfilling its function, religious education.

But how does one teach to promote the kind of response to music which takes advantage of its highest potential? How does one insure that the insights gained from musical activity are insights which are deep and valuable? What methods does one use to help the student gain the kind of illumination from music which can be called religious?

Methods and devices for developing an awareness of musical structure are widely known and used. These include all the ways in which knowledge of music's syntactical nature is fostered. Some of these methods are efficient, some inefficient, but there is general agreement as to the goal of instruction at this level. It is to develop "knowledge of" music, which usually means an understanding of the syntactical functions of the musical elements and some ability in manipulating one or more of these elements through writing, playing, singing, etc. The problem is, how can we make certain that musical instruction will have as its outcome something more than knowledge of the musical elements and their use? We feel that deeper insights than those dealing only with musical excellence do in fact come about as a result of instruction, but they often seem to come about in spite of, or aside from our efforts, rather than as a direct result of these efforts.

The problem raised here is not, of course, capable of an easy solution.

Such writers as James Mursell in *Education for Musical Growth*[7] and elsewhere, and Charles Leonhard and Robert House in *Foundations and Principles of Music Education*,[8] are very much concerned with ways and means of insuring that the "immediate musical experience" will be the core of all musical instruction. It seems clear that musical instruction which is limited to dealing with musical knowledge and musical skill to the exclusion of opportunities for natural musical responsiveness is both misguided and beside the point for all but the professional musician and musician-in-training. But even if we assume that certain methods of teaching will tend to lead to affective experiences of musical form, the problems of the quality of these experiences, the possibility of developing their quality, and the upward limit to which this quality might be developed, remain unsolved. At this point we enter the relatively unexplored region of the relationship between aesthetic experience and religious experience, how either or both might be developed, and the effect of the development of one upon the development of the other. It is suggested here that Leonard Meyer's theory of value and greatness in music makes the solution of issues such as these of vital importance to the formulation of a philosophy of music education broad enough to take into account music's potential as an agent of self-realization.

University of Illinois

---

[7] James L. Mursell, *Education for Musical Growth* (Boston: Ginn and Co., 1948).
[8] Charles Leonhard and Robert W. House, *Foundations and Principles of Music Education* (New York: McGraw-Hill Book Co. Inc., 1959).

Throughout Western history, various philosophies of music education have been articulated by intellectual, political, and religious leaders. A common factor in the various philosophies is the relationship between music education and society. Since the middle of the 20th century, writers on music education philosophy have been mostly music educators, rather than societal leaders. They have, for the most part, abandoned the many historical justifications of the profession in favor of aesthetic philosophy. The utilitarian values of music education that have formed its historical philosophical basis have been rejected during the last 30 years because they have little to do with music. Music is now taught for the sake of music, and the link that has historically connected aesthetics with societal needs has been broken.

Michael L. Mark *Towson State University, Towson, Maryland*

JRME 1982, VOLUME 30, NUMBER 1, PAGES 15–21

The Evolution of Music Education Philosophy from Utilitarian to Aesthetic

Philosophies of music education have been articulated by many societal leaders throughout history. A review of those with whom music educators are generally familiar reveals that the writers understood the aesthetic value of music, but did not think of it, in itself, as justification for music education. Justification was based on the fact that the aesthetic development of the individual influenced behavior in such a way that a better citizen (in terms of cultural, civic, religious, or other values) was expected to be developed.

The literature of ancient Greece contains many statements describing the role of music education in the development of the individual. Plato strongly emphasized the necessity for music (meaning all of the arts) in education to maintain traditional cultural values and to develop the ideal citizen. Discussion of the topic is found in his *Protagoras*(Hamilton & Cairns, Eds., 1961, p. 322), *Laws* (1961, pp. 1,251–1,257, 1,264–1,267, 1,294, 1,343, 1,370–1,374, 1,300–1,303, 1,386–1,387, 1,394–1,396, 1,400), and *Republic*(1961, pp. 623, 643–647, 654–656, 753–754). Aristotle cited historical precedents for music education, saying that music is

Requests for reprints should be sent to Michael L. Mark, Dean of the Graduate School, Towson State University, Towson, Maryland 21204.

valued for "intellectual enjoyment in leisure" and that it "...is a sort of education in which parents should train their sons, not as being useful or necessary, but because it is liberal or noble." (Ross, Ed., 1921, 1,383:30). The Greek scholar Athenaeus, discussing Damon, said, "...Damon of Athens and his school say that songs and dances are the result of the soul's being in a kind of motion; those songs which are noble and beautiful produce noble and beautiful souls, whereas the contrary kind produce the contrary" (Gulick, trans., 1937, p. 389). Roman authors also discussed music education in reference to the development of the citizen. The orator Quintilian stated that music was a necessasy part of the ideal training program for orators, who were among the most respected members of the Roman intelligentsia (Smail, 1936, pp. 47–55). The Roman statesman and scholar Boethius, in summarizing the musical practices of the ancient world, reviewed many of the viewpoints held by Greek and Roman schools of thought about the influence of music on the development of the individual and the relationship of the influence to society (Bower, 1967, pp. 31–44).

The Middle Ages also produced many leaders concerned about music education. During a period of retreat from the greater world by the Holy Roman Empire and of church dominance over civic and governmental affairs, the basis of music education was the need for individuals to be religiously influenced by music. Again, music education was seen as a tool for the formation of the adult who would best fulfill those functions expected of him or her by the society of which he was a part. Charlemagne established a basic curriculum that included music throughout the Carolingian Empire in his decree "that there should be schools for boys who can read. The Psalms, the notation, the chant, and arithmetic and grammar [ought to be taught] in all monasteries and episcopacies..." In the same decree, he specified that all clerics were to learn the Roman chant thoroughly (Ellard, 1956, pp. 54–55). Seven centuries later the Protestant Reformation continued to confirm the value of music in the development of the citizen, beginning with the writings of Martin Luther.

Many well known European educators who influenced American education advocated music education. Comenius (who was also a minister) was specific about how and why music and art were to be taught. (Monroe, 1908, pp. 48–49; Comenius, 1923, pp. 194–202, 259, 261, 268, 274). Pestalozzi recognized the need for music education for the development of, among other things, a peaceful and serene family life, and of nationalistic feelings in children (Green, 1916, pp. 228–229). Froebel advocated music education (and other arts) as a means of developing an understanding of the universe and man's place in it (1908, pp. 225–229). This goal was not unlike that of the classical quadrivium, in which music, as a mathematical subject, was expected to reveal the nature of the universe and the relationship of man to it. Spencer presented an argument for the power of music to further emotional development. He stated, "...music must take rank as the highest of the fine arts—as the one which, more than any other, ministers to human welfare." (1951, p. 76; 1980, pp. 28–33, 70–81).

MUSIC EDUCATION IN AMERICA

Music was not a part of the normal educational program in colonial America, but was considered an important aspect of life in the theocratic New England colonies. The New England ministers spoke and wrote of it frequently, often in impassioned tones. One of the most influential ministers, Cotton Mather, wrote that music was a natural part of worship and religion (Swan, Ed., 1977, pp. 10–11). Over a century later, Lowell Mason justified music education on the same basis and wrote about the benefits of music instruction for moral character development. He added other justifications—improved health and development of intellectual discipline (1834). It was on the basis of those same factors that the special committee of the Boston School Committee considered music as a school subject. The committee's report stated:

> Judged then by this triple standard, intellectually, morally, and physically, vocal music seems to have a natural place in every system of instruction which aspires, as should every system, to develop man's whole nature.... Now the defect of our present system, admirable as that system is, is this, that it aims to develop the intellectual part of man's nature solely, when for all the true purposes of life, it is of more importance, a hundred fold, to feel rightly, than to think profoundly (*Boston Music Gazette*, 1838).

The Boston School Committee adopted music as a curricular subject on the basis of the recommendations contained in the report. This was a turning point in music education history because the way was now prepared for music to become a regular component of the public school curriculum, which it did in most American school systems during the course of the next century. Music was usually adopted by local boards of education on essentially the same justifications as those accepted in Boston in 1838. Horace Mann, the first secretary of the Massachusetts Board of Education, reported in 1844 that music instruction was successful in Massachusetts; his judgment was based on the threefold standard of morality, intellect, and health (1891, pp. 445–463). Although his judgment may have been subjective, he spoke for the state's board of education and the citizens of Massachusetts, and he influenced educational policy-making bodies in many other states.

Early in his career, John Dewey wrote about aesthetic feeling, saying that "the end of art is to produce a perfect harmonized self" (1887, p. 274), thus restating Plato's justification for education in the arts. Dewey said in 1897, "We need to return more to the Greek conception, which defined education as the attaching of pleasure and pain to the right objects and ideals in the right way" (pp. 329–330). Dewey was concerned about the development of the individual as a social being. The introduction of the *Progressive Music Series*, derived from Dewey's philosophy, stated:

> The general aim of education is to train the child to become a capable, useful, and contented member of society. The development of a fine character and of the desire to be of service to humanity are results that lie

uppermost in the minds of the leaders of educational thought. Every school subject is valued in proportion to its contribution to these desirable ends. Music, because of its powerful influence upon the very innermost recesses of our subjective life, because of its wonderfully stimulating effect upon our physical, mental, and spiritual nature, and because of its well-nigh universality of appeal, contributes directly to both of the fundamental purposes of education. By many of the advanced educators of the present day, therefore, music, next to the "three R's," is considered the most important subject in the public school curriculum (1916, p. 9).

In 1954, Benjamin Willis, superintendent of schools in Chicago, stated:

At the risk of underemphasizing many of the other important functions of music in the curriculum at all levels of education today, I believe I would put *education for citizenship* as its most important function. This concept is a very logical and necessary base from which many of the other values to be derived from music as a part of education, can follow. This is music's most important stake in education" (Morgan, 1955, p. 3).

The societal and educational changes brought about by the decline of progressive education, World War II, the Cold War, the repercussions of Sputnik, the dawn of the age of technology, and other events resulted in the need for music educators to redefine their profession in order to identify their place in the emerging technological society. Music Educators National Conference addressed itself to the need by appointing the Commission on Basic Concepts in 1954. The purpose of the commission was to articulate the philosophical and theoretical foundations of music education. The commission's work was published in *Basic Concepts in Music Education* (Henry, Ed., 1958). Although meant to serve as a basis for future development, it is ironic that, with the exception of one author, *Basic Concepts* was the philosophical culmination, in the United States at least, of thousands of years of utilitarian philosophy. Several authors discussed music education philosophy in utilitarian terms. They include Madison (p. 21), Mueller (pp. 120–122), McKay (pp. 138–139), Burmeister (pp. 218–219, 234), House (p. 238), and Gaston (pp. 272–274). *Basic Concepts* also contained an article by Allen Britton, who articulated a different philosophy, which later came to be called "aesthetic education." It was characterized by total emphasis on the aesthetic development of the child and rejection of extramusical values as part of the philosophical justification of music education. Few authors have addressed themselves to music education philosophy since the publication of *Basic Concepts*. The very small body of literature suggests that educational philosophy, the historical basis of music education philosophy, was replaced by aesthetic philosophy. Aesthetics had been, until that time, the philosophical basis of the art of music, rather than of music education. Where earlier writers had sought to link the two philosophies in order to indicate how aesthetic development led to societal fulfillment, the philosophy of aesthetic education concentrated only on aesthetics, breaking the link with societal needs. Bennett Reimer stated in *A Philosophy of Music Education*:

If music education in the present era could be characterized by a single, overriding purpose, one would have to say this field is trying to become "aesthetic education." What is needed in order to fulfill this purpose is a philosophy which shows how and why music education is aesthetic in its nature and value (1970, p. 2).

Britton wrote in *Basic Concepts in Music Education*:

Music, as one of the seven liberal arts, has formed an integral part of the educational system of western civilization from Hellenic times to the present. Thus, the position of music in education historically speaking, is one of great strength. Unfortunately, this fact seems to be one of which most educators, including music educators, remain unaware. As a result, the defense of music in the curriculum is often approached as if something new were being dealt with. Lacking the assurance which a knowledge of history could provide, many who seek to justify the present place of music in American schools tend to place too heavy a reliance upon ancillary values which music may certainly serve but which cannot, in the end, constitute its justification. Plato, of course, is the original offender in this regard, and his general view that the essential value of music lies in its social usefulness seems to be as alive today as ever (1958, p. 195).

Charles Leonhard agreed with Britton. He wrote:

While reliance on statements of the instrumental value of music may well have convinced some reluctant adminstrator more fully to support the music program, those values cannot stand close scrutiny, because they are not directly related to music and are not unique to music. In fact, many other areas of the curriculum are in a position to make a more powerful contribution to these values than is music (1965, p. 43).

The Tanglewood Symposium in 1967 appeared to be an attempt to counter the new philosophy. Its purpose was to explore the present and future relationship between music education and society. The resulting document, the *Documentary Report of the Tanglewood Symposium*, presented many viewpoints of the relationship. However, the summarizing statement, "The Tanglewood Declaration," dealt for the most part with the place of music in the curriculum, rather than with societal needs that can be met by music education. Only one of the eight articles of the declaration referred to individual student needs. The inference might be drawn that the concern for the development of a citizen who is in some way different because of music education was not of the highest priority to the symposium participants.

Little has been written on music education philosophy since the publication of Reimer's work in 1970. One concludes from the lack of current literature, from the impact of Reimer's work, and from the emphasis on the subject at local, state, and national conferences, that aesthetic education is recognized to be the prevailing philosophy.

SUMMARY

Music education philosophy developed over 2,000 years. The developmental process was not evolutionary because the philosophy remained essentially the same from Plato's time to mid 20th century. Developmental factors, indicated in the large body of literature of music education philosophy, resulted from differences between societies in various cultures over an extended period of time. In every case, the philosophical justification for music education was its effect on the development of the citizen and its ability to influence people to be more effective citizens. Around the middle of the 20th century, music education philosophers no longer expressed the need to relate aesthetic development to societal needs and goals. From that time on, the prevailing philosophy of aesthetic education has supported the teaching of music for aesthetic development without expressing the value to society of the aesthetically developed individual.

REFERENCES

Aristotle. *Politica, Book 7.* In W. D. Ross (Ed.), *The Works of Aristotle,* vol. 10. London: Oxford University Press, 1921.

Athenaeus. *The Deipnosophists.* (C. B. Gulick, trans.). Cambridge, Massachusetts: Harvard University Press, 1937.

Boston Musical Gazette, 18, Nov. 28, Dec. 12, 26, 1938.

Bower, C. M. Boethius' "The principles of music," an introduction, translation and commentary. (Doctoral dissertation, George Peabody College for Teachers, 1967). *Dissertation Abstracts International,* 1967, *28,* 2279A. (University Microfilms, no. 67–15,005).

Charlemagne. *Monumenta Germania historica,* Leges II, Capitulari regum Francorum I. In G. Ellard. Master Alcuin, liturgist. Chicago: Loyola University Press, 1956.

Comenius, J. A. *The great didactic.* (M. W. Keatinge, trans. and Ed.). London: A. & G. Black, Ltd., 1923).

Dewey, J. The aesthetic element in education. In *Addresses and proceedings of the National Education Association.* Washington, D. C.: National Education Association, 1897.

Dewey, J. *Psychology,* 1887. In *The early works of John Dewey: Psychology.* Carbondale: Southern Illinois University Press, 1967.

Froebel, F. *The education of man.* New York: D. Appleton and Company, 1908.

Green, J. A., Ed. *Pestalozzi's educational writings.* New York: Longmans, Green & Co., 1916.

Henry, N. B., Ed. *Basic concepts in music education.* Chicago: National Society for the Study of Education, 1958.

Leonhard, C. The philosophy of music education—present and future. In *Comprehensive musicianship: The foundation for college education in music.* Washington, D. C.: Music Educators National Conference, 1965.

Mann, H. *Life and works of Horace Mann: Annual reports of the secretary of the board of education of Massachusetts for the years 1839–1844.* Boston: Lee and Shepherd Publishers, 1891.

Mason, L. *Manual of the Boston Academy of Music for instruction in the elements of vocal music on the system of Pestalozzi.* Boston: Boston Academy of Music, 1834.

Mather, C. *The accomplished singer.* Boston, 1721. In Swan, J. C. (Ed.), *Music in*

Boston. Boston: Trustees of the Public Library of the City of Boston, 1977.

Monroe, W. S. *Comenius' school of infancy.* Boston: D. C. Heath & Co., Publishers, 1908.

Parker, H.; McConathy, O.; Birge, E. B.; and Miessner, O. *The progressive music series,* teacher's manual, vol. 2. Boston: Silver, Burdett and Company, 1916.

Plato. *Protagoras, Laws, Republic.* (E. Hamilton and H. Cairns, Eds.). Princeton, New Jersey: Princeton University Press, 1961.

Reimer, B. *A philosophy of music education.* Englewood Cliffs, New Jersey: Prentice-Hall, 1970.

Smail, W. M., trans. *Quintilian on education,* book 1. Oxford, England: Clarendon Press, 1938.

Spencer, H. *Education: Intellectual, moral, and physical.* New York: D. Appelton and Company, 1890.

Spencer, H. *Literary style and music.* New York: Philosophical Library, 1951.

June 1, 1981

The literature of music, religion, and philosophy, especially aesthetics, forms the basis from which a definition for imagination is offered: Imagination is a power of the whole of human consciousness that employs intuition, perception, thinking, and feeling. A definition for each of the four facets is suggested and explored. These facets are then combined in various ways leading to the tentative formulation of three types of imagination with the third type comprised of two subtypes. A developmental sequence is implied based on research in aesthetic and cognitive developmental theory. Suggestions for the cultivation of imagination through music are offered along with implications for further research.

Mary J. Reichling, *Indiana University, Bloomington*

JRME 1990, VOLUME 38, NUMBER 4, PAGES 282–293

Images of Imagination

The purpose of this article is to suggest various types of imagination and to explore the possibility of stages or levels of imaginative development. The views of selected writers concerning the nature of imagination will be examined. Components of these views will be brought together to see what images of imagination might emerge.

In general, recent literature of a theoretical nature in music has focused on creativity rather than imagination. For example, Vaughan (1973) presents creativity as "the life of the mind at its highest order of functioning" (p. 35). Howard, in his 1982 book *Artistry: The Work of Artists*, has viewed artistry epistemologically and drawn from his experiences as a singer. There seems, however, to be a paucity of philosophical research concerning imagination in music. Often creativity and imagination are used synonymously, particularly in the psychological literature. For purposes of this article, imagination is understood in some way to precede the creative act. Hence, creativity and imagination are viewed as distinct but related. In music, creativity, or a creative work, becomes the outward expression of imagination.

Imagination: The Musician's Image

Most musicians agree that the imagination is in some way central to the experience of music. Copland (1952/1970), for example, writes of the imaginative mind in relation to the listener, the interpreter, and the creator of music. He states that the imagination must take fire to provide a wholeness to the musical experience by balancing and combining music's elements. Imagination's ability to function through time in the presentation of the musical event is, to Copland, one of the rarer manifestations of consciousness. Similarly, Sessions (1950/1974) writes that the music listener takes music into consciousness and remakes it through imagination. He holds that the composer's imagination gives form to the musical impulse, and that the performer then recreates that impulse. In

This research was conducted at the Indiana State University School of Music under the direction of Estelle Jorgensen. I am indebted to her for her assistance throughout the project. For copies of this article, contact Mary J. Reichling, 800 North Smith Road, Apartment 33X, Bloomington, IN 47408.

doing so, the performer is not only faithful to the text, but applies personal insights discovered through his or her imagination.

A different view of imagination is offered by Ives and Busoni. For Ives (1920/ 1962), imagination is expressed referentially through metaphor, poetry, or some extramusical association. From Busoni's aesthetic, one concludes that music imitates nature, and its purpose is to interpret feelings (1911/1962). Elsewhere he writes that imagination, form, and feeling shape his compositions, giving his music a personal style (1967/1979). These three entities are essential to the artist. Yet another position is presented by Boulez (1971), who writes about the paralysis that can result from restricting a work to the composer's creative imagination. He holds that a composer cannot foresee the current or future consequences of a composition or its potential apart from its historical time.

Still other views of the role of imagination in the musical experience are offered by teachers and performers. Pablo Casals states that it is imagination that allows the performer to grasp the composer's original musical idea. The performer, then, is able to give full meaning to the music as it is brought from score to reality (Corredor, 1956). Nadia Boulanger suggests that while each person is unique, it can be commonly agreed that two plus two equals four; if the imaginative mind finds a different answer, however, then something else has occurred, the results of which are unknown (Monsaingeon, 1985/1988). Boulanger concludes that "the imaginative person has an option on the unknown" (p. 110).

Imagination: Images from Other Fields

Further information about imagination is provided by writers outside the field of music. Among them are religious thinkers and philosophers, particularly aestheticians. Religious thinkers affirm the importance of imagination in a different way. Imagination is assigned the function of mediating between appearances and truth, since it tolerates images that oppose the laws of nature. Kroner (1941) suggests that imagination can both conceive and generate miracles and myths. He goes so far as to state that one can come to belief only with the assistance of imagination.

Eliade writes of a mythical imagination (Calinescu, 1977). Myths are reenacted in rituals through which the imaginary transcends time and space and is made "real" and temporally embodied (Eliade 1959/1961; Girardot & Ricketts, 1982). Ritual has a special connection with the arts, as is evident in the use of dance, gesture, music, poetry, visual art, and metaphor to help convey the meaning of the ritual (Calinescu, 1977; Lynch, 1960). Thus religion, through its rituals, has had a profound influence on the artistic imagination as well. For example, oratorios, passions, and Masses are among the musical works that have resulted from the Christian tradition.

Philosophers, especially aestheticians, also offer various definitions and functions for imagination. For example, Hume views imagination as a distinctive type of thinking and holds that the data of imagination are ideas (Wilbanks, 1968). Kant (1781/1965) writes about "productive" imagination that brings sensation and understanding together creating a "second nature out of the material supplied to it by actual nature" (p. 165). To illustrate, imagination finds ways of representing the arts to members of an audience who in turn use their imaginative power to surpass what is observed or heard (Warnock, 1976). Furthermore, Husserl (1920/1958) holds that while imagination may rely on experiential and perceptual data, it can go beyond these data to nonempirical intuitions that do not stem from sensory existence. This might be demonstrated by imagining a faun such as that suggested in Debussy's *Prélude à l'après-midi d'un faune.*

The function of intuition in imagination is also central in the aesthetic of Croce (1922/1965), who considers intuitive knowledge obtained through imagination to be one of the primary forms of knowledge. Intuition includes both unifying perceptions of the real and images of the possible; thus Croce can say that imagination is the "intellectual intuition of art" (p. 295).

Coleridge (1965/1975) distinguishes between a primary and secondary imagination. Primary imagination is the usual instrument of perception common to all persons. Secondary imagination, however, differs in both degree and mode of operation. "It dissolves, diffuses, dissipates, in order to re-create; or where this process is rendered impossible, . . . it struggles to idealize and unify" (p. 167). Thus, for Coleridge, secondary imagination is creative or artistic and involves intuition, whereas primary imagination is reproductive and grounded in perception.

Another view of imagination is presented by Langer (1953), who holds imagination to be humankind's utmost conceptual power. It is the source of insight and belief, the oldest faculty that is uniquely human, and the power that generates the arts and is directly affected by them (Langer, 1957). Langer also holds that epistemologists who define the image as a replica of sense impressions miss the mark. The important trait is that they are symbolic. Symbols may be visual or auditory; they may be vague, fleeting, or even sensuously different from what they represent. Thus the work of art is the image of a feeling that Langer calls the "Art Symbol" (Langer, 1957). "Art [including music] is the creation of forms symbolic of human feeling" (Langer, 1953, p. 40). The emotive content, art's form, is presented directly to the imagination, and the meaning (vital import) is apprehended intuitively (Langer 1957).

In summary, four facets of imagination seem to emerge from an analysis of the various conceptions of imagination just reviewed. First, intuition is given prominence by Kant, who suggests an intuitive or transcendental nature for imagination. Husserl writes specifically of the intuitive nature of imagination. Kroner and Eliade both set the intuitive nature of imagination in opposition to perception. Croce states that intuitive knowledge is obtained through imagination. Ives also suggests the intuitive or transcendent nature of imagination. Similarly, Copland describes imagination as having an intuitive function.

Second, perception is also an aspect of imagination, especially in the reproductive imagination presented by Kant. Warnock likewise discusses perception's role in imagination. Coleridge views perception dominant in primary imagination; intuition prevails in secondary imagination. Howard includes perception in his imagination continuum. Busoni suggests that imagination imitates nature, thus giving perception importance.

A third facet of imagination that emerges form the writings cited here is thinking, sometimes termed reasoning or cognition. Hume considers imagination the faculty of mind that produces ideas, prerequisite to thinking. Warnock assigns imagination a cognitive function. Langer suggests that art presents forms of feeling for contemplation. Contemplation establishes the link to thinking. Ives appears to assign a cognitive dimension to "substance" in his conception of imagination. Although Copland gives particular prominence to intuition, he also assigns thinking a place in his conception of imagination.

A fourth facet of imagination that can be found in the writings presented thus far is feeling. Langer in particular stresses the importance of feeling and assigns it a cognitive dimension. Ives associates feeling with "manner" in his substance-manner duality. Copland assigns feeling a primary role in imagination and considers music's ability to move listener, performer, and composer a unique artistic phenomenon. Like Langer, Copland gives emotion a cognitive function as he suggests that those involved in a musical event are able to contemplate the event at the same time they are engulfed in it.

Thus intuition, perception, thinking, and feeling recur throughout the various conceptions of imagination. Generally, they do not appear in isolation but occur in some combination. At times, one may be given prominence over another. At this point, imagination might be viewed as a power of the whole of human consciousness that employs intuition, perception, thinking, and feeling. A close inspection of the meaning of each of these four facets of imagination is fundamental to the ensuing discussion.

FOUR FACETS OF IMAGINATION

Intuition

Intuition might be defined as an immediate rather than a mediated mode of knowing. In this usage, intuition does not necessarily have to rely on the senses or reasoning, that is, mediated knowledge, for its content. Instead, knowledge is gained directly, without intervening agents or causes, as a kind of gestalt, a grasp of the whole, an insight. The insight may occur as a leap from the known to the unknown in the manner described by Dewey (1934/1958): "When old and new jump together, like sparks when the poles are adjusted, there is intuition" (p. 266).

Insight may also proceed from the unknown to the known. Here the unknown is that which has not yet been conceived in thought while the known is that which comes to mind in an other-than-rational process. For example, Mozart described how compositions came to him in a flash while he was riding or walking (Holmes, 1868). He did not know how they came, nor could he force them into existence. This suggests the intuitive leap from the unknown to the fully known. Here, intuition may be defined as a quality aligned with thinking but distinct from reasoning. Mozart did not come to know his works through a deductive reasoning process; they were sudden gestalten. He was, however, certainly able to think about and reflect upon his intuitively gained knowledge. This is not to say that reason is never applied to such knowledge, but only that reasoning is not a part of the initial insight. Images formed through intuition need not rely on the senses, although such images may be informed by experience.

Perception

The next facet of imagination to be explored is perception. The focus here is on philosophical or theoretical conceptions of perception, explored in depth by Fleming (1962), rather than on the psychological processes of perception. Perception, unlike intuition, is a mediated mode of knowing. Thus knowledge is gained through the mediation of the five senses, that is, hearing, sight, touch, smell, and taste. This definition also suggests that the basis for forming images is grounded in the sense world. Of particular interest for musicians are aural images of the type Copland (1952/1970) calls the "sonorous image." It seems that the literature about music gives greater import to visual images, which are merely contiguously related to a musical work, than to sonorous images that bear a causal connection to the musical composition and its performance (Laske, 1977).

In addition, the images formed either through intuition or perception seem real. In this view, just because an image is founded in the sense world does not make it more real than one that has no physical existence, such as Husserl's flute-playing centaur. The concepts of reality denoted here have a long and distinguished history that can be traced to Plato and Aristotle. Plato's allegory of the cave, found in his *Dialogues* (Rouse, 1956), points to the reality of that which exists in the mind, while Aristotle, in his *Metaphysics* (Hope, 1952), designates that which exists in the sense world as the real. The notion of the image proposed here does not limit images to the sense world or the world of the mind. Neither is supreme; rather, both are implied.

Knowledge obtained through perception, as with intuition, is distinct from reason. Perceptions and intuited knowledge, however, may be subjected eventually to a reasoning process. Furthermore, I suggest that knowledge gained by either of these two modes is made recognizable through experience. In this usage, experience is more than knowledge or skill gained through repetition (as might be suggested by the phrase "an experienced piano tuner"). In this case, experience is phenomenologically and existentially construed to include what is actually experienced as well as the undergoing of an experience (Allen, 1982). The experience might be axiological, perceptual, or mystical; as such, experience is personal and subjectively informs knowledge or truth, thereby making reality recognizable. Perception, then, is another facet of imagination.

Thinking

This facet might have been termed reasoning or cognition, but thinking seems to offer a broader view and avoids possible ambiguities among cognition, perception, cognitive perception, and sense perception. Thinking, as presented here, offers three modes of knowing. The first is deductive thinking, reasoning from the general to the specific. The second is inductive thinking, reasoning from the specific to the general. An approach to joining these two modes might be illustrated in the forming of images. Many specific details may unite to form a general, overall image that then can be broken up into several component images. For example, viewing a score of a Chopin prelude generates an aural image. The observation of details such as melody, rhythm, harmony, and form may yield an image that is a gestalt, several discrete images, or both. Similarly, the performance of a composition may occur within the context of a total sonorous image of the work, the context of its component images, or some combination of these. Casals suggests that no image is isolated, though each note is important in itself, but rather that images are like links in a chain that connect what has been with what will be (Corredor, 1956).

The third mode of thinking suggested here is analogical or reasoning through association, that is, through the drawing of comparisons by attribution, metaphor, and symbol. Some aspects of resemblance are perceived between things otherwise unlike. Here musical images might be illustrated with comparisons such as "the music is like a rushing stream" or "the music is heroic." The first example represents analogy by attribution. Qualities intrinsic to a rushing stream are ascribed to the music so that in some way the listener has an image of the sound of that music. The second example demonstrates analogy by metaphor or direct comparison. Langer writes, as stated above, that art [including music] is the image of a feeling—the "Art Symbol." Thus, to speak of music as a feeling in Langerian terms is to know music through analogy.

Analogical thinking is rooted in ambiguity and connotation, the poetic or symbolic. On the other hand, induction and deduction, the universal and the denotative or literal, are the foundation of the reasoning process (Leone, 1980). As with intuition and perception, thinking presents another facet of imagination.

Feeling

The fourth facet of imagination offered for consideration is feeling, which may also be viewed as another mode of knowing. Whereas perception included touch, feeling as used here is not identified with the five senses. Feeling is usually associated with the interpretation of some bodily state, but that is not the definition offered here either (Alston, 1967/1972). Rather, feeling is assigned a cognitive dimension. Ricoeur (1978), for example, suggests that feelings are not merely inner states but are really "interiorized thoughts" (p. 156). Thus feeling, in Riceour's view, is not contrary to thought; "it is thought made ours" (p. 156). Scheffler (1986) extends this notion and writes about the cognitive emotions. He suggests that emotion without cognition is blind, while cognition without emotion is vacuous. For example, the emotions serve cognition as a stimulus to the scientific imagination—"the joy of verification and the feeling of surprise" (p. 353). Furthermore, the emotions are a source of imaginative patterns and perform a selective function among these patterns. It seems then that Scheffler is assigning an epistemological status to the cognitive emotions.

Goodman (1985) also dispels the dichotomy of knowing and feeling by suggesting a cognitive function for the emotions, particularly in the aesthetic experience. He writes: "Emotion in aesthetic experience is a means of discerning what properties a work has and expresses" (p. 148). Similarly, Langer (1957) writes that feelings are not involuntarily vented in the artistic process, nor is the work of art intended as a catharsis. Rather, the work of art presents forms of feeling for contemplation. These feelings are conceived as the symbolic form is created. In addition, works of art "are images of feeling, that formulate it (feeling) for our cognition" (p. 25). Clearly, Langer is also assigning a cognitive dimension to feeling. Thus, feeling is another mode of knowing.

In summary, this discussion of the four facets of imagination—intuition, perception, thinking, and feeling—has provided a vantage point for further exploration of imagination. What image or images of imagination emerge as a result of combining in various ways some or all of these facets? Might such combinations yield types or levels of imagination? Furthermore, if types do appear, is any developmental sequence implied?

TYPES/LEVELS OF IMAGINATION

The First Image: Fantasy or Magical Imagination

One-year-old children have been observed engaged in pretend play (Flavell, 1977). For the very young child, a pencil becomes a rocket ship as fantasy overcomes reality and the properties of the pretended object fuse with the actual object (Gardner & Winner, 1978). By age 4 or 5, children are able to distinguish the real from the pretended object but, since the boundaries of appearance and reality are not yet fully established, the distinction assumes little importance. It seems that perception dominates in this imaginative play. Objects used are concrete and perceived through touch, sight, and so forth. An object is transformed in imagination to another object that is one with the perceived object. The imagined object may also be "seen" or "touched" because, for the very young child, the real object *is* the imagined object; the pencil is the rocket ship; and no distinction is made between appearance and reality. The object becomes known and assumes meaning for the child through imagination.

Studies concerning the aesthetic development of preschool children show similar results (D'Onofrio & Nodine, 1980; Parsons, 1975). For example, children were viewing a reproduction of the Currier and Ives painting *Preparing for Market*. One child responded that he liked the work very much. When asked why, he said that it was because the painting reminded him of his cowboy hat. Yet, there were not cowboys or cowboy hats in the painting. Thus, for the young child, imagining the hat and seeing the painting were one (Parsons, 1975), in a manner similar to which the rocket ship and the pencil had become one.

It seems that this initial level of imaginative development relies primarily on perception. Among the other three facets of imagination, feeling is probably present because the imaginative play is pleasurable. The child, however, is not yet able to identify feelings and reflect on them (Flavell 1977); feelings are not functioning as a mode of knowing or recognizing imagination. Neither intuition nor reasoning seems to be present; there is no grasp of the whole and no distinction between appearance and reality. The reasoning process has been shown to appear later in children's development (Flavell, 1977). Thus, though objects are magically transformed in imagination, they remain in the concrete world of the senses. This first type of imagination might then be called fantasy or magical imagination.

If this first type of imagination is assumed to be present as described, several implications may be offered for the cultivation of imagination through music among preschoolers. Music becomes fantasy, magic, fun, and pretend play. It is "browsing and the encouragement of vivid freshness" (Whitehead, 1929/1961, p. 33). Though Whitehead places this stage of romance a little later in the child's development, he leaves room for flexibility in its application. He holds that experiences at this point influence how the child's future will be shaped by ideals and colored by imagination (pp. 26, 28).

Children, then, may be given the utmost freedom and encouragement to image the music as cowboy hats, rocket ships, brooms carrying buckets of water, dancing flowers, and anything else they wish (D'Onofrio & Nodine, 1980; Flavell 1977; Gardner & Winner 1978; Parsons 1975). Preschoolers might use props and act out the fantasy in the real-sense world. When appearance and reality join, anything can happen with magical imagination.

The Second Image: Reproductive or Literal Imagination

Next, if reason is added to perception, another type of imagination seems to emerge. Reason enables the child to distinguish fantasy from reality. Research indicates that children in middle childhood (approximately ages 6–12) are primarily concerned with the literal and real rather than fantasy and pretending. Children over age 6 or so engage in forms of play such as sports, games, and hobbies (Flavell, 1977). An example of this attraction to literalness may be seen in Gardner and Winner's 1978 study of metaphorical development in children. They found that during middle childhood, children were unable to imagine the connection between the terms of a metaphor (pp. 130–131). Instead, they sought a literal meaning. This desire for literalness was also evident in D'Onofrio and Nodine's 1980 study of aesthetic development in children: the children that they studied were consistently upset when a painting did not conform to reality and satisfy the nominative rules for form and content.

The research just cited supports the type of imagination proposed here that combines perception and reason. Objects are imagined as they exist in concrete, observable reality, not as magically transformed. Symbol and referent are the same. Thus reason is functioning in some way; but analogical thinking is not evident, since children at this level are not able to comprehend the metaphor. Speculative or deductive thinking also seems to be absent, as demonstrated by the child's inability to transcend the terms of the metaphor. Children do, however, seem to be able to reason inductively or empirically, as illustrated by their ability to view a painting and determine that it conforms to the rules or conventions of form and content. The distinction drawn here between deductive and inductive reasoning abilities is congruent with Piaget's theory of cognitive development (Flavell, 1977).

At this stage of development, it seems that intuition is largely absent. These children do not grasp the whole either in metaphor or in abstract works of art that lack conformity with the real world of the senses. On the other hand, feeling does seem to be present and functioning in a limited way as a mode of knowing. The dissonance or incongruity that the child feels when a work of art lacks conformity with reality suggest that there may be apposing feelings of pleasure and satisfaction when the work does represent the real world. Thus, in some way, emotion or feeling helps the child to discover certain qualities that are present or absent from the work of art and so functions as a mode of knowing. This second type of imagination might be described as reproductive imagination in the Kantian sense (Kant, 1781/1965), or literal imagination after Crossan (1981).

The second type of imagination, if it occurs as suggested in the research cited, presents several implications for cultivation through the musical education of children between ages of 6 and 12 (Crossan, 1981; D'Onofrio & Nodine, 1980; Flavell, 1977; Gardner & Winner 1978; Parsons, 1975). These ages probably are the best time to begin study of an instrument. Children will be concerned about holding their instruments correctly and playing them properly, according to the "rules." Similarly, a study of the rudiments of music such as pitch, rhythm, form, and notation are in order. With these tools, children might cultivate imagination through composing for their instruments. In addition, music listening might encourage imagination by including a study of the lives of composers and events that may have occasioned particular works. Following musical forms may also be enjoyable for the child, particularly in a simple set of variations such as Mozart's "Ah! vous dirais-je, Maman." Finally, listening to works such as the *1812 Overture* that relate to historical events might also encourage development of literal imagination.

The Third Image: Metaphorical and Paradoxical Imagination

The addition of intuition brings the last facet of imagination together with perception, thinking, and feeling at the level of adolescence and adulthood. This combination, it is suggested, yields the full and complete development of imagination as a power of the whole of human consciousness. Within this final stage of development, two subtypes of imagination may emerge, depending on the ways in which the facets—perception, feeling, thinking, and intuition—interact. Specifically, metaphorical and paradoxical imagination are posited here as two subtypes. This theory is congruent with that of Crossan (1981), who also suggests metaphorical and paradoxical imagination, except that he views these as separate stages rather than subtypes. The terms metaphorical and paradoxical imagination will provide the focus for analysis according to the facets of imagination already presented.

Let us explore the metaphor, "Music changes its clothes" (adapted from Read, 1967), to see what is occurring in imagination. First of all, there is an element of surprise and playfulness. Then there is the recognition of literal untruth but not deliberate falsehood (Goodman, 1985). This apparent contradiction propels imagination to search for the underlying truth (Swanson, 1978). To do so, the imagination must suspend, in the Husserlian sense, the ordinary reference and seemingly abolish it in search of an underlying "primordial" reference (Husserl, 1920/1958; Ricoeur 1978). Discovery yields understanding and pleasure.

It seems that all facets of imagination are involved as an image of the metaphor is formed. Perception provides the concrete literal meanings for the terms. It is necessary to understand these before intuition can make the leap or the connection to the referent. Thinking, or reasoning, then finds the many dimensions of underlying truth in the metaphor. Feeling as cognitive emotion is present in surprise and the joy of discovery (Scheffler, 1986). In this example, one might think of music wearing a classic line, or a more modern style. Another application might be to several versions of the same work, such as the Brahms F-minor *String Quintet* (1862), later arranged as the F-minor *Sonata*, op. 34b, for two pianos, and finally set as the F-minor *Piano Quintet*, op. 34a (1864). When the concept of metaphor is applied to music, the writings of Susanne Langer particularly come to mind. As cited earlier, art, and by extension, music, is the image of a feeling—the Art Symbol. Thus, to speak of music as a form or image of human feeling is to consider music a metaphor. Also, Ives (1920/1962) presents a program for the "Thoreau" movement of his *Second Piano Sonata* that suggests another way in which music may be viewed as a metaphor. Here, music represents a place and all the qualities of nature and life found there. If one accepts that music is a metaphor in some way, then several implications for the development of metaphorical imagination result. Students at this level would likely need assistance in identifying the music as a metaphor. They might be guided in discovering and experiencing the music's expressive meaning through giving imaginary form to the sensory content. Lastly, aesthetic value may or may not be ascribed to the underlying truth.

The foregoing exploration of metaphorical imagination and its relationship to music leads to the next consideration: Might a paradoxical imagination also emerge as a subtype from a blending of the four facets of imagination? Paradox in this usage denotes a dialectical contradiction, that is, a self-contradictory statement (Colie, 1966). The liar paradox illustrates this: A musician may make this statement that "All musicians are liars." The paradox arrests thought and dazzles the imagination as one tries to grapple with a statement that disobeys the laws of logic (Colie, 1966). Religious literature, apart from that of the Renaissance, seems to provide timeless paradoxes through which imagination empowers belief. In a way, religious imagination becomes paradoxical or contradictory in the religious experience as it tolerates images that oppose the laws of nature. The earlier citation applies here: Imagination can both conceive and generate miracles and myths. As stated previously, Kroner (1941) goes so far as to state that one can come to belief only with the assistance of imagination; he is identifying a paradoxical imagination.

In an essay published in 1981, Crossan writes that paradoxical imagination is not merely another type of imagination but is "the highest stage and final level of imaginative development" (p. 56). As one explores the interaction of the four facets and their relationship to imagination as just described, two facets seem to dominate: thinking and intuition. Reason is continually challenged to find an image that resolves the contradictions with which it is presented. Intuition leaps for an unknown that cannot be found. Herein lies a key difference between metaphorical and paradoxical imagination. Metaphorical imagination seeks and finds the underlying truth; paradoxical imagination searches, challenged to its limits, turned back on itself, but never finds resolution (Colie, 1966). The initial feeling of surprise when the paradox is first heard impels the imagination toward finding an explanation. If Scheffler's view concerning the significance of surprise is applied here, it might be suggested that "epistemic distress" results from the "painful disorientation" of paradoxical imagination's hopeless search for resolution (Scheffler, 1986).

In this regard, Crossan suggests that some people refuse to contend with paradox and seem incapable of responding to its challenge. Perhaps the arts provide some means of addressing paradoxical imagination. In Shakespeare's *King Lear*, for example, Lear finds vision in blindness. Some of Escher's lithographs and engravings seem to defy perspective. Both of these art forms cultivate and challenge paradoxical imagination. In music, the application is more difficult to find and tentative at best. John Cage's *Imaginary Landscape no. 4* for 12 radios reflects his philosophy that sounds should not be vehicles for communication of feeling. Music is no longer a symbol but exists as pure sound in a Zen-like approach. Here music seems to lose its inner form as symbol because meaninglessness becomes music's meaning (Hofstadter, 1979). Cage's (1961) answer to the purpose of writing music is paradoxical: "a purposeful purposelessness or a purposeless play" (p. 12). In a different way, the paradoxical imagination may also be cultivated through music by works such as Wagner's *Parsifal* and *Der Ring des Nibelungen*, Mozart's *Die Zauberflöte*, and Strauss's *Don Quixote*. The myths or stories that these works express through texts, programs, thematic transformation, and leitmotifs cultivate and challenge paradoxical imagination.

DISCUSSION

While a theoretical basis concerning the nature of imagination has been suggested, it is tentative and needs further development and analysis, particularly with respect to the third type or level of imagination. Is the third type comprised of two subtypes or might each, if viewed differently, constitute a third and fourth? Do the types occur in levels or are they sequential with one a prerequisite to the next? Additional theoretical work in these areas is warranted.

A link between imagination and creativity was suggested at the beginning of this paper. If creativity is imagination expressed in perceptual form, are creative forms a result of imagination? If this were the case, it would seem to imply that imagination precedes creation. The relationship between imagination and creativity needs exploration and clarification at a conceptual level.

Research is needed at both the empirical and the practical level. Studies of an empirical nature, perhaps similar to the one done by D'Onofrio and Nodine (1980) with children and visual artworks but with application to music, might verify or suggest changes in the types and levels of imagination offered here. At a practical level, some of the implications of these ideas for music education might be explored. For example, if the four facets of imagination function somewhat as suggested, how might each of these be encouraged? Perhaps teachers might develop a program of music education for the cultivation of imagination drawing upon and expanding on some of the suggestions offered in this article and then testing the program in the classroom. Many teachers, perhaps, are already intuitively teaching in a manner that reflects the four facets and various types or levels of imagination presented here. If so, the case-study method may provide a useful approach to determining what is occurring in such learning situations. On the other hand, it may prove necessary to rethink school music programs. It may be that metaphorical and paradoxical imagination at the adolescent and adult levels will provide a rationale for an integrated arts curriculum in high schools and colleges. Certainly, these issues merit further attention from the music education community.

REFERENCES

Allen, D. (1982). Phenomenological method and the dialectic of the sacred. In N. Girardot and M. L. Ricketts (Eds)., *Imagination and meaning: The scholarly and literary worlds of Mircea Eliade* (70–81). New York: Seabury Press.

Alston, W. P. (1972). The nature of feeling. In P. Edwards (Ed.), *The encyclopedia of philosophy* (pp. 483–484). New York: Collier/Macmillan. (Original work published 1967)

Boulez, P. (1971). *Boulez on music today* (Susan Bradshaw & Richard Bennett, Trans.). London: Faber.

Broudy, H. (1972). *Enlightened cherishing: An essay on aesthetic education.* Urbana: University of Illinois Press.

Busoni, F. (1962). Sketch of a new esthetic of music. In (Th. Baker, Trans.)., *Three classics in the aesthetics of music* (pp. 73–102). New York: Dover. (Original work circa 1911)

Busoni, F. (1979). *The essence of music.* (R. Ley, Trans.). Westport, CT: Hyperion, 48. (Original work published 1957)

Cage, J. (1961). *Silence*. Middletown, CT: Wesleyan University Press.

Calinescu, M. (1977). "Imagination and Meaning: Aesthetic Attitudes and Ideas in Mircea Eliade's Thought." *The Journal of Religion* 57(1), 1–15.

Coleridge, S. T. (1975). *Biographia literaria* (rev. ed.). New York: Dutton. (Original work published 1967)

Colie, R. (1966). *Paradoxia epidemica: The Renaissance tradition of paradox*. Princeton. NJ: Princeton University Press.

Copland, A. (1970). *Music and imagination*. Cambridge, MA: Harvard University Press. (Original work published 1952)

Corredor, J. M. (1956). *Conversations with Casals* (André Mangeot, Trans.). New York: Dutton.

Croce, B. (1965). *Aesthetic* (rev. ed.). (D. Ainslie, Trans.). N.p.: Noonday Press (Division of Farrer, Straus, & Giroux, USA). (Original work published 1922)

Crossan, J. D. (1981). Stages in imagination. In C. Winquist (Ed.), *The archeology of the imagination*. Thematic studies of *The Journal of the American Academy of Religion, 58*(2), 49–62.

Dewey, J. (1958). *Art as experience*. New York: Capricorn-Putnam. (Original work published 1934)

D'Onofrio, A., & Nodine, C. (1980). Parson's model painted realistically. *Journal of Educational Research, 14*(4), 103–106.

Eliade, M. (1961). *The sacred and the profane* (W. Trask, Trans.). New York: Harper and Row Torchbook. (Original work published 1959)

Flavell, J. (1977). *Cognitive development* (2nd ed.). Englewood Cliffs, NJ: Prentice-Hall.

Fleming, B. N. (1962). The nature of perception. *Review of Metaphysics, 16*(2), 259–295.

Gardner, H., & Winner, E. (1978). The development of metaphoric competence: Implications for humanistic disciplines. *Critical Inquiry, 5* (Autumn), 123–141.

Girardot, N., & M. L. Ricketts (Eds.). (1982). *Imagination and meaning: The scholarly and literary worlds of Mircea Eliade*. New York: Seabury Press.

Goodman, N. (1985). *Languages of art* (2nd ed.). Indianapolis, IN: Hackett.

Hofstadter, D. (1979). *Gödel, Escher, Bach: An eternal golden braid*. New York: Basic Books.

Holmes, E. (1868). *The life of Mozart, including his correspondence*. New York: Harper and Brothers.

Hope, R. (Trans.). (1952). [Aristotle's] *Metaphysics*. New York: Columbia University Press.

Howard, V. A. (1982). *Artistry: The work of artists*. Indianapolis, IN: Hackett.

Husserl, E. (1958). *Ideas*. (W. R. B. Gibson., Trans.). New York: MacMillan. (Original work published 1920)

Ives, C. (1962). Essays before a sonata. In *Three classics in the aesthetic of music*. New York: Dover. (Original work published 1920)

Kant, I. (1965). *Critique of pure reason* (N. K. Smith, Trans.). New York: St. Martin's Press. (Original work published 1781)

Kroner, R. (1941). *The religious function of imagination*. New Haven, CT: Yale University Press.

Langer, S. (1953). *Feeling and form*. New York: Charles Scribner.

Langer, S. (1957). *Problems of art*. New York: Charles Scribner.

Laske, O. (1977). *Music, memory, and thought* (Monograph). University Microfilms International.

Leone, S. (1980). Metaphoricity, language, and the mind. *Dissertation Abstracts International, 42*, 4436A.

Lynch, W. (1960). *Christ and Apollo: The dimensions of the literary imagination*. New York: Sheed and Ward.

Monsaingeon, B. (1988). *Mademoiselle: Conversations with Nadia Boulanger* (R. Marsack, Trans.). Boston: Northeastern University Press. (Original work published 1985)

Parsons, M. (1975). A suggestion concerning the development of aesthetic experience in children. *Journal of Aesthetics and Art Criticism, 34*(3), 305–314.

Rouse, W. H. D. (Trans). (1956). *Great dialogues of Plato*. New York: Mentor.

Read, H. (1967). *The philosophy of modern art*. New York: World-Meridian Books.

Ricoeur, P. (1978). The metaphorical process as cognition, imagination, and feeling. *Critical Inquiry, 5* (Autumn), 143–159.

Scheffler, I. (1986). "In praise of the cognitive emotions." In *Inquiries: Philosophical studies of language, science and learning* (347–352). Indianapolis, IN: Hackett.

Sessions, R. (1974). *The musical experience of composer, performer, listener.* Princeton, NJ: Princeton University Press. (Original work published 1950)

Swanson, D. R. (1978). "Toward a Psychology of Metaphor." *Critical Inquiry* 5 (Autumn), 163–166.

Vaughan, M. (1973). "Cultivating Creative Behavior." *Music Educators Journal, 59*(8), 35–37.

Warnock, M. (1976). *Imagination.* Berkeley and Los Angeles: University of California Press.

Whitehead, A. N. (1961). *The aims of education.* New York: NY: Mentor Books. (Original work published 1929)

Wilbanks, J. (1968). *Hume's theory of imagination.* The Hague, Netherlands: Martinus Nijhoff.

April 17, 1989

George N. Heller, *The University of Kansas*

JRME 1985, VOLUME 33, NUMBER 1, PAGES 4–6

On the Meaning and Value of Historical Research in Music Education

The story and study of the past, both recent and distant, will not reveal the future, but it flashes beacon lights along the way and it is a useful nostrum against despair.[1]

—Barbara W. Tuchman

Historical research in music education has been in and out of favor since the first publication of Edward Bailey Birge's monumental *History of Public School Music in the United States* in 1928. Reasons for this are difficult to discern, though changing perceptions of meaning and value must surely play some part. The present climate of increasing interest may well be part of a larger story that future historians will be able to write, but for the moment it seems appropriate to try to give the enterprise some definition and defense. Life is too short to spend much of it in activities that have little import and serve no appreciable ends.

It is perhaps tautological to say that historical research is what historians do, but the current emphases on behaviorism within the field and on existentialism and phenomenology in society at large make this a reasonable starting point. Briefly stated (and somewhat oversimplified), historians do three things: They gather, organize, and report evidence of the recent and remote past in order to explain the present and prepare for the future.

Barbara Tuchman's description of history as "the story and study of the past" recognizes the importance of two activities that might be called historiography and historical research. Historiography here is taken to include the various problems of narrative, while historical research is concerned with gathering and organizing evidence.

Technical considerations of the historian's work have been well, if somewhat pedantically, described in manuals, and will not therefore be taken as central to the present discussion.[2] Rather, the activities of historians in gathering, organizing, and reporting evidence and the consequences of these are the focus here. Underlying this discussion is the question of whether or not history may be considered a science or an art or some kind of hybrid of the two. Given the current popularity of (and reaction to) science and technology, this question looms so large in the background it cannot be ignored. The tendency to presume that

---

1. Tuchman, *Practicing History* (New York: Alfred A. Knopf, 1981), p. 55. Originally part of an address, "The Historian's Opportunity," American Historical Association, Dec. 1966; subsequently published in *Saturday Review*, No. 50, 25 Feb. 1967, p. 29.

2. For a summary of these with reference to music education, see George N. Heller and Bruce D. Wilson, "Historical Research in Music Education: A Prolegomenon," *Bulletin of the Council for Research in Music Education*, No. 69, Winter 1982, pp. 1–20.

research is and must be scientific is so strong that it must be taken into account.

Historians in the late nineteenth century and for much of the twentieth borrowed heavily from the methods and practices of scientists. Leopold von Ranke's call to uncover history *wie es eigentlich gewesen ist* (as it actually happened) suggested a single, knowable true past discoverable only by pursuing rigorous investigations with scientific precision and attention to detail. Historians did not merely gather evidence, they proposed hypotheses and tested them in post hoc designs borrowed from the natural sciences in what might be called retroactive longitudinal studies. The present culmination of the scientific trend is seen in two sub-disciplines: quantohistory and psychohistory. While quantohistory has considerable merit, particularly where economics or demography are important considerations, it is problematic in areas where extant information is not easily quantifiable or where quantification fails to answer the important questions under study. The current interest in psychohistory—application of principles and ideas borrowed from psychoanalysis to historical problems—may be fruitful in some biographical studies; it also may be a too zealous attempt to align history with science.

While there is much in science for historians to admire, the search for laws and causes by proposal and testing hypotheses cannot be adopted as a method for historical investigation. Evidence gathered by such a process will too often confuse and lead astray. Human affairs do not always proceed lawfully, and causes are almost always manifold and related in extremely complex ways. Proposing hypotheses in advance insidiously leads to selection of evidence in undesirable ways; if one knows what the object of search is, he or she is almost sure to find it. Too often the salient questions cannot be known in advance and must be permitted to emerge as the evidence accumulates. Laws and causes may be derived from history by sociologists and other behavioral scientists, but the search for them is not the central task of historians. History may lead to the formulation of hypotheses and their subsequent acceptance or rejection, but they cannot be allowed to control the search for evidence.

Organizing evidence in a historical investigation is primarily concerned with the passage of time, that is, with chronology. Simultaneous events pose severe problems for historians that are seldom solved but are only handled with varying degrees of success. Music education history must be concerned with the developments of musical styles and forms, with trends in education generally, and with events and conditions in the culture. While other disciplines are obligated to explain how simultaneous developments in these three areas relate to one another at any given moment in time, historians must primarily explain them as they unfold. Sequence is fundamental to history. That human affairs proceed from multiple, often disparate, antecedents is a complication that can only be handled on a case by case basis. Sorting out the complexities is not the kind of problem that yields to predetermined formulas or methods, and it is not often done without controversy, criticism, and dissent. Thus even the very best of history is subject to revision in light of more persuasive arguments, differing points of view, or new evidence.

History as it actually happened is one thing, historical narrative is quite another. What Barbara Tuchman called "the story of history" is the description of the past written at a later, sometimes much later, date by an individual who may or may not have been present. Writing history, sometimes erroneously called making history, is a problem for all who take the field seriously. Explaining what happened means bridging the gap between present readers and past events. Science offers little help and many unfortunate examples. Historians, like all story tellers, whether of fact or of fiction, take on the responsibility of explaining their findings in comprehensible and interesting language. Historians cannot invent words willy-nilly to describe what happened but must with very few exceptions limit their tale to the available language. Rather than turn to science for help in this task, historians must look to literature. History may sometimes be scientific in pursuit of the truth, but it must also be artistic in telling the truth. History unread is of dubious value to anyone. It is the special task of the historian to inspire, even to impel, the reader to turn the page.

All research is in a sense historical. Even the most avant garde experiments cannot be reported until after they have taken place. The future cannot be reported, recounted, or re-anythinged. Research is by definition a second going over, another search. Because history conveys a sense of linear progression, or pendular swings, or cyclic trends, it is possible to imagine—occasionally with striking clarity—that the future is knowable, even predictable. Because predictions turn out often to be on or near the mark, it seems reasonable to conclude inevitability. Statistical estimates of probability are too often confused with knowledge of things not yet experienced.

Barbara Tuchman's phrase "beacon lights along the way" alludes to the potential contributions history may make. Beacon lights, however, are not the brilliant sun of high noon. History no more than science can foretell events with unerring certainty. What history can provide is an understanding of possibilities that results from knowledge of past achievements and "a useful nostrum against despair." History can inform its readers on the events and ideas of the past, it can show the results of persistence through time. This characteristic of the discipline is useful to music educators, particularly in the current atmosphere. That music has been taught and learned throughout history and in every known culture is a historical fact. Vast evidence exists to give nourishment to impoverished spirits. Belief in the future does not require knowledge to an absolute certainty, it only requires the demonstration of potential, of possibility for success. Knowledge of possible consequences—whether quantified or not—helps the human spirit to venture into the unknown, to persist when times are tough.

History that best serves the profession informs and inspires its readers. Authenticity in history may be the product of science and knowledge; credibility transcends both of these and may well be a matter of faith or belief. Gathering all the available evidence, organizing it logically, and reporting it in clear and interesting prose are the tasks of historical research. Illuminating the passage of time and comforting the souls of its readers are history's finest results.

III.

Historical Conceptualizations

Ernest F. Livingstone

JRME 1967, VOLUME 15, NUMBER 4, PAGES 243–277

The Place of Music in German Education
From the Beginnings Through the 16th Century

A T PRESENT Germany's eastern border is the Oder-Neisse line approximately 80 miles east of Berlin.[1] This line was established by the Potsdam Conference of 1945, which marked the end of the German Empire. It is of no small interest that at the beginning of the Empire in 800, this eastern border was almost identical with the one established in 1945. After the Frankish King Charlemagne had bitterly fought the Saxons for over 30 years, he succeeded in annexing their territory (what is now the land between Hanover and Bremen and part of Westphalia) and extended control over the Slavs as far east as the Peene River, only a few miles west of the Oder. At the same time, Charlemagne helped Pope Leo III against the (Germanic) Lombards who threatened from northern Italy. He defeated them, thus also becoming King of the Lombards. Charlemagne entered Rome where, on Christmas Day of 800, the Pope put an imperial crown on his head during the church service. The old Roman Empire seemed to have been resurrected under a militant Christian leader who had converted many pagans, mostly by force, and whose grandfather had successfully defended Christianity against the onrushing Moors. King Charlemagne had become Emperor, and the fact that his empire included all the major territories which had accepted Christianity, and that it was almost as large as the European part of the ancient Roman possessions, in time created the name of "Holy Roman Empire."[2]

Though Charlemagne was the king of a Germanic tribe, he cannot be called a German ruler in the proper sense of the word because the back-

---

[1] The most important materials used for this article are: Friedrich Paulsen, *Das deutsche Bildungswesen in seiner geschichtlichen Entwicklung* (Leipzig, 1960), and Friedrich Paulsen, *Geschichte des gelehrten Unterrichts an den deutschen Schulen und Universitäten I* (Leipzig, 1896), if quoted, referred to as Paulsen 1 and 2 respectively.

[2] Spain, which had become Moorish in 711, was not part of it; attempts to penetrate into Spain failed (cf. *Chanson de Roland*). The distinction between "Emperor" and "King" is not clear. Originally, only a king crowned by the Pope could call himself emperor. But with the house of Habsburg the title became hereditary (from 1273 on); coronation by an archbishop became a formality.

bone of his empire was present-day France. This is where the Franks had lived for 300 years before him and where they had become assimilated into the Gallo-Roman civilization. At his death in 840, Charlemagne's son left the empire to his three sons. Lothar, the eldest, inherited the imperial crown and with it the oldest Roman lands, i.e., the *Rhein*, *Meuse (Maas)*, *Mosel*, and *Rhône* countries, the Alps, and Italy as far as the boundary of the Papal states. *(Patrimonium Petri* was guaranteed to the Pope by Charlemagne's father, Pippin, in exchange for the anointment as King to replace the Merovingians.) Of the two other sons, Ludwig (Louis) received the east and Karl (Charles) the west. The first agreement between them, the Oaths of Strasbourg, was written in Old French and Old German, an indication of how heterogeneous the empire really was. When Lothar's son died, his share was divided between Ludwig and Karl, not without serious misgivings and quarrels; Ludwig, then the stronger, received the lion's share and thus the German nation was born.[3]

The first *praeceptor Germaniae* (teacher of Germany) was Rhabanus Maurus (780?-856), a student of Alcuin. He was the originator of the Carolingian Renaissance of learning, and later became abbot of the monastery at Fulda, the first famous center of culture in Germany. He was at the end of a long development as well as the beginning of a new one for the young German nation which had just become one independent part of the European empire of Charlemagne.

The idea of the necessity of education had never died completely, not even during the Dark Ages (ca. 500-800). While the Roman Empire crumbled away, Cassiodorus (ca. 485-580), chancellor of Theodoric, King of the Ostrogoths, who had occupied Italy and ruled it *de facto*, forsook this high position. In his later years he turned from worldly fame to religious fervor and founded a monastery in his native province of Calabria. In his principal work, *Institutiones divinarum et humanarum rerum*, he exhorted his monks to exercise painstaking scholarship so as to understand the Holy Scriptures as profoundly as possible.[4] It was of the greatest significance that the Benedictines, originally interested in performing practical good works, took over this idea and introduced it in Germany through its Christianization by St. Boniface (d. 754). Very early, the Benedictine monks also showed an interest in liturgical music and therefore gave music a prominent place in their activities.

Bishop Chrodegang of Metz (in office 742-766) made his cathedral school, established for the promotion of the Roman liturgy, a center of learning not only for the clergy but also for children who showed promise.[5] Many of these, though not all, entered the clergy at the end of their

---

[3] Treaty of Mersen (870). The central, and strategically as well as economically important, part of Lothar's domain was Lorraine, in German Lothringen, i.e., Lothar's land; no fewer than 33 Franco-German wars were, in part, caused by the desire for its possession between 845 and 1945.

[4] Blume, *Die Musik in Geschichte und Gegenwart*, II, 804f.

[5] A. Walter, "Der Musikunterricht in Deutschland von den ältesten Zeiten bis zum ersten Jahrtausend," *Kirchenmusikalisches Jahrbuch II* (1887), 40.

training. For the singing school at Metz and at his palace school, Charlemagne (ruled 768-814) ordered that the ideas of St. Benedict and Bishop Chrodegang be followed. He imported singers from the *Schola Cantorum* in Rome and sent promising native youths to Rome for more thorough training. These men came back after the completion of their studies to establish important schools at bishops' sees and monasteries. In the Carolingian Empire school boys learned to sing at a very early age so they could assist the churchmen or monks in singing their choral prayers; in fact, some antiphons and responses were sung only by the boys.[6] The ability to sing Psalms, sacred songs, and hymns from memory was the basic goal of the boys' general education. Memorization was of extreme importance since notation in the form of neumes did not allow a correct "reading" of the music and was only an aid to memory. Consequently the teaching of songs and hymns took so much time that except for (Latin) grammar, no other subject was so time-consuming as music.[7] Even at that time the aim of musical education was not only to raise *cantores* (singers) but to make *musicos* of them as well, i.e., people with a knowledge of "theory," meaning philosophy of music and aesthetics.[8]

The method applied to reach these aims consisted mainly of explanation in dialogue or question-and-answer form (erotematic form), in which most early textbooks (except the *scholiae,* commentaries to other works) were written, and of demonstration and imitation or repetition. This type of method did not change significantly for almost a thousand years. An especially helpful device for musical instruction was the monochord, in use long before the Guidonian Reform.[9]

The career of a serious music student at the time of Charlemagne and his successors can best be illustrated by a short biography of the music theorist[10] Walahfrid Strabo. He was born in 806 in Suebia (southern Germany) and attended the monastery school at Richenau where he received what was then a thorough general education by studying the seven liberal arts.[11] At age 17 or 18 he began the advanced study of music from the writings of Boëthius and The Venerable Bede. (At that stage a student had already learned to play the organum, harp, flute, trumpet, or zither and had mastered the art of singing from memory.) Now the study of music proper followed mathematical principles: numerical relationship of tones and modes, rules of composition, character of instruments, place, value, and function of music in life and learning. As a matter of course, Strabo went on to study theology and as a clergyman with great musical knowledge and experience, rose high and was widely honored. He became dean at the monastery of St. Gall, then abbot of Reichenau, and was entrusted with several imperial missions as the

---

[6] Walter, p. 43.
[7] Walter, p. 43f.
[8] Walter, p. 41.
[9] George Schünemann, *Geschichte der deutschen Schulmusik* (Leipzig, 1928), pp. 14ff.
[10] Eitner, *Quellenlexikon* IX, 304.
[11] See below, next paragraphs.

authorized representative of the emperor. He died in Reichenau in 849.[12] How important a place music occupied in education at that time can be seen from the statement of Rhabanus Maurus that he who is not familiar with music cannot adequately discharge the duties of an ecclesiastical office.

While music was of great importance, it was, of course, not the only subject taught. Charlemagne announced an ambitious education program for his realm in his *Epistola de litteris colendis* (Letter on the necessity of studies) of 787, upon which the synods of Aachen in 789 and 803 acted by decreeing the establishment of schools in all monasteries and cathedrals. In these all boys who, or whose parents so desired, should learn reading, singing, the computation of holidays in the calendar, and Latin. In addition, it was declared that the knowledge of the liturgy and its music was necessary for consecration to any ecclesiastical office. Though universal education could not yet be enforced,[13] all boys were encouraged to attend one of the three types of schools—monastery, cathedral, or parish schools. In the latter the rudiments of reading, writing, and the singing of Psalms and simple songs were taught. No tuition was charged in any school but voluntary gifts were accepted.

Even the girls took some part in the slowly expanding education and culture. Convents sprang up beside the monasteries. In these some girls (though by far fewer than the boys who had the choice of three types of schools) could acquire a good education with the result that learned nuns were by no means unusual. In the 10th century Hrotswitha von Gandersheim wrote the drama *Paphnutius*, which contained a didactic dialogue on music, while in the 12th century St. Hildegard von Bingen was the authoress of widely read works on theology, natural science, and medicine, and many sacred musical compositions including a play with music called *Ordo virtutum*.[14]

By the time of Rhabanus (or Hrabanus) Maurus (780?-856), the greater schools, i.e., the monastery and cathedral schools, taught the seven *artes liberales*.[15] (Latin) grammar, rhetoric, and dialectic were the *artes sermocinales* (verbal arts), better known by Boëthius' term *trivium*, while arithmetic, geometry, music, and astronomy were the *artes reales*, better known as the *quadrivium*. The principal textbooks used were those of Alcuin, who was born in England and became *Rector* of the monastery school at York. Later he was the organizer of Charlemagne's educational program and lived in Tours. Alcuin wrote on many subjects of the *trivium* and *quadrivium;* most of the works on the latter are lost except for the treatise *De Musica,* which is a treatment of the eight modes

---

[12] Walter, p. 44f.

[13] The first law in Germany containing provisions to enforce general school attendance was the *Weimarische Schulordnung* (School Statutes of the Land of Weimar) of 1619. See below, p. 270f.

[14] Schünemann, p. 14; Blume, *MGG* VI, 389ff, Carpenter, *Music in the Medieval and Renaissance Universities* (Norman, Okla., 1958), p. 25.

[15] The seven *artes liberales* came down to the Middle Ages in the form established during the Roman Empire described by Martianus Capella (5th century A.D.).

(with definitions taken from Cassiodorus), their names, significance, and relation to the letters.[16]

From the 9th century on, many theorists like Hucbald, Hermannus Contractus, and Cotto experimented with various types of notation as they were aware of the unreliability of the neumes then in use. They complained that there were as many differences in singing a melody as there were teachers. The schools of St. Gall and Metz, under the influence of the singer Romanus, introduced letters added to the neumes, resulting in the manner of writing known mainly through the Codex Montpellier of the 11th century. Hucbald wrote text syllables between different lines according to their intervallic distance, which others tried to indicate by observing a fixed place above or below a center. This center was soon marked by a line analogous to that used for the writing of letters.[17] Drawing from all these suggestions, Guido d'Arezzo (d. ca. 1050) introduced an exact notation on four lines. This was revolutionary because emphasis had to be shifted from rote learning to the re-creation of a piece of music from the written page without first hearing it and then slavishly imitating the heard melody until it was securely memorized. It also made possible the fixation of new music and thus the development of greater creativity. Finally, it greatly contributed to the unification of the liturgy and thus indirectly to the strengthening of the authority of the Church. From Guido's time on, the goal of practical music education was sight-singing by means of solmization rather than memorization by rote, and it remained so through the 16th century. Yet it must not be forgotten that in spite of his concern with sightsinging and his delight in, and even boasting about, his pupils' phenomenal successes, Guido esteemed the theoretical knowledge of music to be of greater value than its performance, and in this respect he was a typically medieval man: "There is a great difference between musicians and singers. The latter perform, [while] the former know that which music consists of. For he who executes what he does not know, is termed a beast."[18] Thus it happened that in spite of Guido's joy over the practical application of his method, notation gradually became an end in itself, not only a means to an end; it became more complicated and more "learned" or even "secret," especially with the expansion of polyphony. It embodied in itself a complete course of music and became the chief subject in the cathedral and court schools of the later Middle Ages.[19]

After learning notation for several years, the students studied polyphony and composition, athough the latter were reserved for the most exceptional pupils; the majority learned only notation and sightsinging of melodies. There is no evidence concerning the average duration of the study of notation as it probably depended on individual aptitude. Con-

---

[16] Blume, *MGG* I, 325 f; Schünemann, pp. 5ff.
[17] Schünemann, p. 17f.
[18] Carpenter, p. 25.
[19] Guillaume de Van, "La Pédagogie musicale à la fin du moyen âge," *Musica Disciplina* II, 81f.

temporary pictures and elementary treatises show that young children (*pas encore mués,* i.e., before the change of voice) sang *super librum,* i.e., without reading, guided by adults and supplementing their insufficient knowledge of notation with their memories. When a student had finally mastered the rudiments of notation and sightsinging, he had *artem.* This was not "art" in our sense of the word but "skill." Music in its totality, however, was considered *scientia,* comprising the intricacies of notation and all its mathematical components such as interval relationships, scale structures, modes rhythmic and ecclesiastical, and the like. As all advanced subjects at the height of the Middle Ages, music was imbued with complicated, secret, and exclusive devices so as to be reserved for an intellectual elite.[20]

Principal aids in teaching and learning music as well as other subjects were various types of treatises: the *eisagogé* (introduction), usually in erotematic form; the *scholia,* a commentary on an original work by marginal annotation or in dialogue form; and the *speculum* (mirror), the most speculative and comprehensive kind fashioned after theological works. There already existed a *vocabularium musicae* in alphabetical order, probably compiled in the 11th century by an Italian.[21]

While the commanding influence of the Guidonian Reform on the further development of music and music education was readily recognized, the awareness of its over-all significance was not so apparent. While in the other subjects of the *trivium* and *quadrivium,* as taught in the first half of the Middle Ages, memorization was paramount, the encouragement to re-create and to create in the field of music contributed to the preparation of the minds for the acceptance of the great intellectual changes leading to the Renaissance of the 12th cetury. This began with the flourishing of the cathedral schools and closed with the rise of the earlier universities; it started with the bare outlines of the seven liberal arts and ended with the possession of Roman and canon law, many "newly" discovered works of Aristotle translated into Latin by the Arabs, "new" works of Euclid and Ptolemy, and works of Greek and Arabic physicians. It saw a revival of the Latin classics in prose and verse, the great feudal epics of France, and the lyric poetry of Provence; it saw the earliest works in Middle High German and the height and passing of Romanesque art and the growth of the Gothic style of architecture.[22]

This great revival centered in the cathedral schools, especially those of Chartres and Orléans. The curriculum of these and soon of other cathedral schools added the complete works of Euclid, the logic of Aristotle as laid down in his *Organa,* and the Latin classics in prose and poetry (though still under the discipline of grammar). As the Guidonian Reform had loosened up the process of mechanistic learning, so the intro-

---

[20] de Van, pp. 75, 81.
[21] Carpenter, p. 30.
[22] This passage, from line 29 on this page, is a condensation of Haskins, *The Renaissance of the Twelfth Century* (Cambridge, Mass., 1928), pp. 6-8.

duction of classical Latin literature equally led to re-creative and creative endeavor. Unfortunately this was not of long duration; in the 13th century law and dialectics acquired a greater importance and consequently, rhetoric, logic, and systematic thought triumphed over literary enjoyment and free expression.[23] The result was again a preponderance of formalistic and artificially complicated learning, except perhaps in practical music. But the teaching of advanced music was more and more isolated in France—then leading in music as well as the other intellectual pursuits—by being relegated to special *écoles des maîtrises* attached to the cathedral schools and the court schools that were established by the French kings and dukes during the 13th century.[24]

The study books from the 12th century on were the works of the transmitters of ancient learning: Martianus Capella (5th century A.D.), who wrote on the seven liberal arts and gave an outline of each; Priscianus (ca. 500) on Latin grammar and literature; Boëthius (ca. 500) on theology, philosophy, and music; Isidore of Seville (ca. 600), whose *Etymologies* was the medieval encyclopedia; and The Venerable Bede. Priscianus' *Institutiones,* the standard textbook for Latin grammar and literature, was rather extensive; therefore many schools preferred the simpler *Ars Major* or the even briefer *Ars Minor* of Donatus (late 4th century). The latter work, often memorized, discussed in erotematic form the eight parts of speech within the equivalent of ten printed pages. Priscianus also wrote a shorter work in which he dissected the first twelve lines of the *Aeneid*. In this work three pages were devoted to the first word, *arma,* explaining its grammatical classification and function and all its derivatives. In some instances parts of the *Aeneid* itself were read (mostly for its grammatical rather than its literary value) and also Cicero's *De inventione* (for its rhetorical significance). The *Disticha,* attributed to Cato (later Roman Empire), the *Fabulae* of Avianus (ca. 400), and the *Eclogue* of Theodolus (9th century)—often bound together—served for the teaching of both Latin and morals. But soon the invasion and victory of logic and dialectic influenced the choice of textbooks. In the poem "The Battle of the Seven Arts" by Henri d'Andeli (ca. 1250), Donatus and Priscianus fight a losing skirmish against Logic; soon the *Doctrinale* of Alexander de Villa Dei (Villedieu), a dry systematic grammar in 2,645 hexameters, triumphs over them.[25] In its first part, the *Doctrinale* deals with Inflections, in its second with Syntax, in its third with Quantity (of syllables), Accent, and *Figurae* (fixed ways of speech). It had been intended for advanced students, who were supposed to learn from memory all the exceptions, and was very instrumental in evolving the medieval Latin, which had become quite different from the classical Latin in structure as well as in vocabulary. Terms such as *substantia, essentia, existentia, quantitas, qualitas, identitas, causalitas,*

---

[23] Haskins, p. 39f.
[24] de Van, pp. 75, 78. See also below, p. 266.
[25] Haskins, pp. 81, 130ff.

finalitas, quidditas(!), and *haecceitas*(!) were either newly created or given new meanings adapted to the terms used in Aristotelian philosophy. The *Doctrinale* was immensely popular until the 16th-century humanists did away with it. Going back to the classical Latin, the humanists were utterly horrified by the "monstrosities" of the new language and had nothing but contempt for this medieval Latin. This was an unfair judgment as this language was the vehicle for such beautiful poetry as the *Dies Irae, Stabat Mater, Salve Regina,* and the like, and for such elegant prose as the *Imitatio Christi.*[26]

With the *Doctrinale* appeared the signs of the practical trend in rhetoric: Evrard de Bethune's *Grecismus,* a work on the etymological derivation of words (not on the Greek language), Alberic's *Breviarium de Dictamine* or the art of letter writing, and the Bolognese Professor Boncompagno's *Antiqua Rhetorica.*[27] Imaginary letters where written by masters and students, especially at the cathedral school of Orléans, concerning correspondence between Paris and Helen, Ulysses and Penelope, Winter and Spring, Soul and Body, Life and Death, Man and Devil. At the same time the practical side of life received its due attention as can be seen from this sample:[28]

> To his father H., C. sends due affection. *This is the salutation.* I am much obliged to you for the money you sent me. *This is the captatio benivolentie.* But I would have you know that I am still poor, having spent in the school what I had, and that which recently arrived is of little help since I used it to pay some of my debts and my greater obligations still remain. *This is the narration.* Whence I beg you to send me something more. *This is the petition.* If you do not, I shall lose the books which I have pledged to the Jews and shall be compelled to return home with my work incomplete. *This is the conclusion.*

From another letter one can glimpse student life at a cathedral school in the 12th century:[29]

> To their very dear and respected Parents M. Martre, knight, and M. his wife, their sons send greetings and filial obedience. This is to inform you that, by divine mercy, we are living in good health in the city of Orléans and are devoting ourselves wholly to study, mindful of the words of Cato, "To know anything is praiseworthy," etc. We occupy a good and comely dwelling, next door but one to the schools and market place so that we can go to school every day without wetting our feet. We have also good companions in the house with us, well advanced in their studies and of excellent habits—an advantage which we well appreciate, for as the Psalmist says, "With an upright man thou wilt show thyself upright," etc. Wherefore lest production cease from lack of material, we beg your paternity to send us by the bearer money for buying parchment, ink, a desk, and the other things which we need, in sufficient amount that we may suffer no want on your account (God forbid!) but finish our studies and return home with honor. The bearer will also take charge of the shoes and stockings which you have to send us, and any news as well.

---

[26] Paulsen 2, p. 43f.
[27] Haskins, pp. 81, 130ff.
[28] Haskins, p. 144.
[29] *Loc. cit.*

A more detailed description of student life at these times is furnished by the autobiography of John of Salisbury. "As a lad" he went into Gaul (in 1136) to study and acquired "at the feet of the famous Abaelard the first rudiments of the dialectic art . . . with entire greediness of mind." After Abaelard left the church school of Mont Ste. Geneviève, John continued the study of dialectic with Master Alberic and Robert of Melun, spending a total of two years. Then Alberic went to Bologna (to the recently founded university concentrating mainly on law) and there he "unlearned that which he had taught, yea, and returned and untaught the same; whether for the better or no, let them judge who heard him before and since." (This seems indicative of the gradual penetration of the new learning with greater emphasis on law and science, demonstrated by a new flare-up of the controversy between nominalists and realists which ended in the conflict between Aristotelianism and Platonism.) Then John studied grammar with William of Conches at Chartres for three years and with Richard l'Evêque, who impressed him with his personal integrity and virtue, and from whom he received a review of the *trivium* and certain things of the *quadrivium* which he had not learned from a previous teacher, the German Hardwin. He also took up rhetoric again "which Master Theodoric had treated only meagerly" and which Peter Helias now "supplied more plentifully." He (John) supported himself as the tutor of children of noble persons while reviewing and studying informally under the great Adam du Petit-Pont who introduced him to Aristotle, a rare privilege since he, Adam, "was wont to do this to none or few but his own scholars." (Teachers generally depended on their fees for earning an adequate livelihood.) Poverty forced John to become a teacher but, while teaching, he continued his studies, now in logic and theology. "Thus engaged in diverse studies near twelve years passed by" him, and he revisited his old companions on Mont Ste. Geneviève. He found them "as before"; they had stagnated and had progressed only in one point: "they had unlearned moderation and knew modesty no longer." And thus experience taught him that "whereas dialectic furthers other studies, so if it remain by itself it lies bloodless and barren."[30] In spite of this criticism, he was so subject to the thinking of his period that he approved of its general temper with the words *"littera sordescit, logica sola placet"* (the letter [meaning language and literature] dulls [the mental faculties], logic alone is pleasing [has value]).[31]

Several characteristic features of medieval education can be gleaned from the preceding passage:

1. There was leisureliness of studies and great lengths of time were spent on their pursuit.

2. There was a personal, almost private bond between master and student though the school was "public" in the sense that it was estab-

---

[30] Haskins, p. 373f.
[31] Paulsen I, p. 22.

lished and, in part, maintained by the Church or later also by a ruler's court.

3. As a consequence of the above, there was frequent traveling and moving around of students who either followed their favorite teachers when they moved, or who wanted to sample the teachings of as many famous men as their situation permitted. A result of this was the rise of the Goliardi, a group of young, satirical, and ribald poets. (Until the 20th century it was the custom of German students who could afford it to attend two, if not more, universities and to take it easy at least during the first two semesters.)

4. There was a lack of rigidity in the plan of studies. The above autobiographer (John of Salisbury) first studied dialectic, and only later studied grammar which would logically have come first; he intermingled the study of the *trivium* and *quadrivium*. There seemed to be no strict age limits for the beginning nor division between master and student; while studying he taught, while teaching he studied, the emphasis shifting according to the situation and the teachers or students available.

The title of such a student-teacher was *Locatus,* from *locus* (place, of a group or class in the originally common single school room). He was the lowest in rank and helped the *Magister* by taking care of a lower group in one corner while the latter worked with a higher group in another. The head of a cathedral school was the *Magister scholarum* or *Scholasticus.* Originally he taught all children in all subjects, but with the expansion of knowledge and the growth in the number of pupils in the schools, he hired one or more assistants called *Socii, Provisores* or, if well trained, *Magistri.* In addition, he chose a *Locatus* from among the older proficient students. Since the 12th century, the office of the teacher who gave instruction in music (among other subjects) was definitely separated from that of the *Scholasticus.* His title was from then on *Cantor,* and for a considerable time his rank was second in the faculty.[32]

The teaching method was essentially the same as it had been in the early Middle Ages: (a) *praecepa* (rules), (b) *exempla,* and (c) *imitatio.* The last was not only imitation but also usually memorization, though the introduction of logic and dialectic and the increasing complexity of musical notation sharpened the students' minds for more original thinking.[33] Carpenter[34] concurs by saying that after Guido, and especially with the development of polyphony, the problems of rhythm and notation became the principal subject matter, displacing the memorization of music.

In order to secure the desired results, the masters maintained a very harsh discipline. The rod was in constant use not only to punish misbehavior but also to speed up slow comprehension and to correct or, as

---

[32] Schünemann, p. 5.

[33] de Van, p. 89: "The objective (of late medieval notation) surpasses by far that of simple cerebral gymnastics because it keeps the mind alert and saves it from automatic reactions leading to mechanistic processes."

[34] Carpenter, p. 28.

it was hoped, to prevent errors. Without the slightest hesitation St. Adelheid gave a nun who sang wrong a box on the ear with the effect that the nun thenceforth was endowed with the clearest and most beautiful voice. Konrad von Fuezbrunn (12th century) tells in his *Childhood of Jesus* that upon learning the letter *Aleph*, the Child wanted to give its significance right away and received a beating for His rashness and precocity. To add insult to injury, a child was to kiss the rod and say, "Dear rod, if it were not for you, I would never do well."[35] Some primary textbooks were even called *sparadorsum* (spare the back). He who spoke in his native tongue instead of Latin had to hang the *asinus* (donkey) around his neck, and he who had it last in the day received a beating. There was also the *lupus* (wolf) chosen from among the pupils, who had to spy out and write down all cases of infraction so that the guilty could be duly punished in class.[36]

However, not all aspects of school life were harsh. There was room for celebrations: December 28, the Day of the Innocents, was a great children's festival, the preparations for which were begun around St. Nicholas Day (December 6). The best student was selected "prefect" and was assisted by two "court chaplains." On the day itself the "prefect" assumed the honor and dignity of the bishop (or abbot), and even sang the high clergyman's part in the Holy Office and blessed the procession. The singing of the boys, adorned by special tropes, made this service a very special occasion. The pupils "ruled" over church and school; they could even "arrest" any adult and hold him until he bought his freedom. In spring and summer pupils went to the woods to pick green branches, and even the cutting and home-taking of the dreaded rods was itself a joyous occasion accompanied by songs and ending with a procession through the town. Another important day was March 12, the feast of St. Gregory, on which day the school year began. The children elected a "bishop" for the day; they played games and received gifts, especially fruit and baked goods as on many other holidays.[37] These things are mentioned to dispel the conception of the Middle Ages as a dreary period constantly directed toward the life hereafter.

What happened to the boys when they had outgrown the rod and the children's games? When they were 12 to 15 years old (for an exact age for entering or leaving school did not exist), many would leave school altogether without seeking any further education. The more gifted, and those who could afford it or who had the stamina and spirit of adventure to fend for themselves, somehow would stay on if their school or some of their teachers had something more to offer, or they would look for another more advanced school. But eventully the cathedral and monastery schools could not accommodate the rising tide of students and, above

---

[35] Schünemann, p. 52: "Liebe ruot, trute ruot,/werestu nit, ich thet niemer guot." (Middle High German)

[36] Schünemann, pp. 54, 144.

[37] Schünemann, pp. 55, 134.

all, could no longer offer them the advanced education they desired. There were many reasons for this which can be touched upon here only in a very cursory manner. When, before the year 1000, many devout Christians anticipated the "millennium" and thought that judgment day was close at hand, a new spirit flowed through the monasteries. Since their foundation in the 7th and 8th centuries, the monks had labored in and for the world, especially in agriculture and teaching, though the ideal of their members was flight from the world. This dualistic attitude was clearly shown by the fact that they had run two kinds of schools, the *schola interna* for those who actually intended, or whose parents intended for them, to take their vows at maturity, and the *schola externa* for those who wanted an education but did not want to become monks or perhaps not even clergymen at all. In the first two and three hundred years of their existence the monks had become rich enough through grants, bequests, and special privileges that they were in danger of acquiring a rather worldly attitude. Sensing this and fearing the approach of the millenium, they reformed under the leadership of the monastery of Cluny and turned away from the world, thus losing interest in their *schola externa*. By the 12th century their influence on education, except that of novices, had declined.

From this development a great flowering of the cathedral schools should be expected. This did in fact occur, but was of a shorter duration and lesser impact than one might surmise. The cathedral school of Notre Dame and several church schools in Paris gradually consolidated themselves into a new institution of learning, the university, which soon eclipsed the great cathedral schools in other French cities such as Orléans, Chartres, and Rheims. These, not being in the capital of the monarchy, had not so many churches and learned men to develop a similar institution, nor had they at that time a teacher of the stature of Abaelard in Paris. The cathedral school by itself, however great it might have been, could not cope with the tremendous influx of new knowledge and new fields of learning.[38] Here again the poem "The Battle of the Seven Arts," already mentioned, illuminates the situation. It deals with the allegorical battle between Paris and Orléans (famous for its course in literature) and awards the palm of victory to Paris. Her fame, especially in theology and philosophy, spread far and wide and ever faster so that by 1200 it was generally said that Italy had the Papacy, Germany had the Empire, Paris had Learning.[39] While Paris did not have the first university in Europe, it had the first north of the Alps and the first to grow out of cathedral and church schools. Oxford followed in the late 12th century and Cambridge soon after. In Germany, the University of Cologne (1388) had the same origin as the University of Paris; Prague (1348) and Vienna (1365) were founded by imperial initiative; and

---

[38] Haskins, *The Rise of the Universities* (New York, 1923), pp. 19ff.
[39] Haskins, p. 28.

Erfurt (1379), Heidelberg (1385), and most of the others were founded by order of the territorial princes. All were confirmed by Papal Bull and all followed the model of Paris.

The cathedral schools could still have held their own by continuing to concentrate on the seven liberal arts in spite of the fact that the universities taught the same in their arts faculties, as such overlapping of instruction was not uncommon in the later Middle Ages. "Mobility within the educational system, lack of strict demarcation of age, class, or type of school were typical for the Middle Ages as for all young cultures; only in the 19th century there emerge such strict divisions."[40] After some time, however, the cathedral schools had to cope not only with the competition of the universities, but also with the rise of the city schools, especially in Germany. With the increase of trade caused by the crusades and the consolidation of political authority of kings and territorial princes, the cities grew in wealth and power and soon understood that it was to their advantage to have schools within their walls. Even where cathedral schools existed, the cities wanted schools of their own to train their children to become good and productive burghers rather than clergymen. However, so profoundly was learning identified with the clergy that the city left the actual teaching to the churchmen. Though it never attacked the authority of the Church as such, it often quarreled with local churchmen over administrative control; since it held the purse strings, the city invariably won out. It can be safely assumed that the choristers at the non-cathedral church schools formed the nucleus of the city schools. With the Reformation, the monastery and cathedral schools in northern and central Germany and in Württemberg also became city schools. Thus, the entire foundation of St. Thomas at Leipzig—monastery, church, and school—passed into the hands of the city council.[41]

The schools in the cities varied in number, size, and quality depending on the size and wealth of the city. The city council appointed the *Ludimagister* or *Rector* (head of the school), who then hired the other teacher or teachers according to the size of the school. These were called *Socius, Provisor, Baccalaureus* (from the 14th century on, if he held such a degree), and *Locatus* (if he was taken from among the older students). Later, they were often called simply according to their rank: *primus, secundus, tertius,* and so on. Only the *Cantor* was at first appointed not by the *Rector* but by the church authorities in consultation with the city council because of his importance for the church service.

Since instruction in the city schools, also given by churchmen, did not essentially vary from that in the church school (it was rather a question of emphasis), the victorious city school soon found a competitor of its own in the private schools. These schools concentrated on practical education in the vernacular for both boys and girls, and required no Latin.

---

[40] Paulsen 2, p. 319.
[41] Carpenter, p. 256.

The city and church authorities repeatedly tried to curb the activities of these *Winkelschulen* (corner schools), as they were derisively called, but they survived and eventually became the roots of the elementary schools. Thanks to the private schools and the (learned) city schools, almost every city dweller at the end of the Middle Ages knew how to read.

Despite the waning of their importance, the cathedral schools in France, together with the court schools, fulfilled one great mission. The great musicians of the Franco-Flemish period were trained in their *écoles des maîtrises* (singing schools attached to the cathedral schools), not at the universities which followed the tradition of favoring theoretical or speculative music at the expense of practical music. In the universities music remained a science, while in the *écoles des maîtrises* it was truly an art. The coveted title of *musicus* which previous centuries had bestowed only on theorists was snatched away from the university and given to the composers of the 15th and 16th centuries purely on the strength of their genius.[42] It is no wonder that music declined at the universities and was finally removed from their programs of study around the middle of the 16th century.[43] In 1545/46, Adrian Petit Coclico's drive for the establishment of a professorship in music, though supported by his students and the University of Wittenberg, failed because of the refusal of the Elector Johann Friedrich. A similar move on behalf of Sixt Dietrich, also at the University of Wittenberg, had also failed; Salamanca remained the only European university with a special chair for music.[44] This did not mean, however, that the universities turned their backs on music altogether. Great theorists and music teachers maintained some connection with the universities. They were, however, no longer full members of the faculty but rather academic music directors without the prestige and salary of professors.[45] Often they were under contract with the university to teach privately those students who so desired. Among those taught in the universities were Luscinius, Glareanus, Listenius, Figulus, Coclico, Heinrich Faber, and Hermann Finck.[46]

This peculiar position of the music teacher around 1500 who was under contract with the university to give private lessons, to give a few lectures on music (as part of the mathematics course), and to help with the musical aspects of academic festivals, but who derived his main income as a secondary school teacher of music and academic subjects, throws light on the typical overlapping not only of subject-matter but

---

[42] de Van, p. 78.

[43] G. Pietsch, "Zur Pflege der Musik an den deutchen Universitäten . . .," *Archiv für Musikforschung* III (1938), 302.

[44] Carpenter, p. 268.

[45] P. *Wagner*, "Zur Musikgeschichte der Universität," *Archiv für Musikwissenschaft* III (1921), p. 8f.

[46] Carpenter, pp. 264ff.; Pietzsch, p. 304.

also of personnel in secondary schools and universities. So, for instance, many men were *Cantors* at St. Thomas, students, and lecturers at Leipzig University at the same time. The *Cantors* at St. Stephen in Vienna studied and taught law or theology at the university there.[47] As will be shown later (see page 272), some larger secondary schools taught almost the whole program of the arts faculty, and may well have done as good and thorough a job in that as did many universities. Even the life of the older secondary school students in the late Middle Ages did not differ much from that of the university students. There were so many traveling and roving students away from the control of their parents that manuals had to be issued setting down rules for behavior, as for instance: remember God, obey your masters, behave in church, lift up your voice in the church choir, keep your books clean, pay your bills promptly, wash your face and hands in the morning but visit the baths only with permission, do not run on ice nor throw snowballs, on Sunday play only in the churchyard, never use dice, and always speak Latin. The manuals also contained courtesy phrases in Latin including prefabricated excuses, and there were manuals on etiquette which would seem rather crude by our standards.[48]

The autobiography of Burckhardt Zengg gives a good picture of this kind of life. He was born in 1396 at Memmingen in southern Germany, and attended the school of his town for four years. Then, at age 11, he was sent to an uncle, a clergyman at Krain, who sent him to school in Reisnitz where he stayed for seven years. Since his uncle died and his father, having remarried, withheld his mother's estate from him, Burckhardt was then on his own. He returned to Memmingen and took up his schooling again. He was the tutor of two brothers in exchange for lodging in their home. After one year he fell in love, whereupon he quit school and became apprentice to a furrier. He endured his work at the furrier's for only fourteen days, and left Memmingen again. He went to Biberbach where he obtained lodging without board from an old shoemaker. As he disliked begging for food in the streets, he went to Ehingen on the advice of another student. There he saw others singing and begging, lost his shyness, and joined them. After half a year, an older student convinced him to come with him to Balingen by promising to help him there, a promise which he did not keep. So Burckhardt first stayed at a smith's as a tutor, then at an innkeeper's who provided him with room and board. After one year he went to Ulm where he stayed at the town piper's as tutor, but now he had to beg for his food again. The next year found him at Augsburg where he had gone with the aim of being ordained for the lower clergy, but he found employment with a merchant instead and gave up school. After serving several masters in Augsburg and Nürnberg for some years, he married and immediately lost his job. However, from his wife's spinning and his work as copyist

---

[47] Carpenter, pp. 256, 226.
[48] Haskins, pp. 95 ff.

they earned enough for a decent living. Through this last occupation he came to the attention of the town council and was sent to deliver a message to King Sigismund. This enhanced his prestige in the town so that he ended his checkered career as a successful merchant.[49]

If the secondary school and university students in part shared the same life and much of the same study program, what made the essential difference between the secondary schools, or "learned" schools as they were then called, and the universities? There were three principal factors that set the university apart as a unique institution:

1. The university was a corporation as its name *universitas* implies. This term originally did not refer to the universality of learning but to the totality of a group. The *universitas societas magistrorum discipulorumque* (all-including society of masters and students) was a corporation organized along the lines of a guild. It may have started as an association of students who wanted to protect their interest against the townspeople charging high rents or high prices in general, or against the professors charging high fees or being frequently absent, as was the case in Bologna. Or a university may have developed from an association of professors of various learned schools, as was the case in Paris and the other universities north of the Alps.[50] Their corporative character was strengthened by Papal Bulls and by privileges given by a king, territorial prince, or city government such as the exemption from taxes and especially the jurisdiction over their own members. When an ambitious ruler threatened to infringe on these privileges, the university simply prepared to move to another place since it usually owned very few buildings and often none; such preparation was usually sufficient to make the ruler change his mind.

The student body was originally constituted by "nations" according to the origin or home of the students. At its beginning the University of Paris had four such nations: the French, including the Latin peoples; the Norman; the Picard, to which also belonged students from the Low Countries; and the English, comprising also the Germans and the peoples from northern and eastern Europe. These groupings varied, of course, with the political changes during the centuries. This whole situation seems not to have been a very happy one as each "nation" had and voiced a long list of prejudices against the others, which led to frequent friction and violent fights.[51] This eventually led to their abolition, but in their prime it was they who chose the *Rector*, the head of the university, whose office was at first merely ceremonial so that often even a distinguished student was elected. The real executive power was vested in the chancellor, a powerful churchman and member of the faculty.

There were actually four faculties, each headed by a *Decanus* (dean): arts, canon law, medicine, and theology. Of these, the arts faculty was the

---

[49] Paulsen 2, pp. 23-35.
[50] Haskins, pp. 13ff, 24.
[51] Haskins, pp. 24ff.

lowest and had the most students (about two-thirds). It was here that there was much overlapping with the learned schools. After many centuries the arts faculty developed into the Philosophical Faculty and, much earlier, the faculty of canon law became the general Law Faculty dealing with all aspects of the law.

2. This organization of faculties distinguished the university from the learned school in that the latter pursued only some, very rarely all, of the program of the *facultas artium*. Canon law, medicine, and theology were reserved to the university; in fact, the addition of these to the "arts" was the very reason and justification for the existence of the universities as has been shown above.

3. The faculty acted as a body and a unit when conferring degrees, and it was there that its great prestige lay. The establishment of degrees was an entirely new idea in education; while the Greeks and Romans certainly had higher education, they knew nothing of certificates, diplomas, or degrees. But with the increase of knowledge and a greater organization and division of education on various levels, the student could no longer be sure whether a master was competent or not, nor could the Church risk having people as teachers whose ignorance or heretical ideas would have had a bad influence on the younger generation. Therefore examinations were instituted and licenses to teach were issued to candidates who had proved their competence to the satisfaction of the Church and university authorities as represented by the chancellor of the university. Out of these licenses developed the *magister artium* (master's degree) for full teachers and the *baccalaureus artium* (bachelor's degree) for assistant teachers. The later was necessary because the demand for teachers always seemed to exceed the supply. The degree of *doctor* (learned scholar) was reserved to the higher faculties of medicine, law, and theology.

As for the program leading to these degrees, a statute of the University of Leipzig from 1410 lists the following required courses for the B.A. and M.A. with their textbooks and approximate time of study:[52]

(a) *Baccalaureus artium:*
    I. Grammar.
        1. Last two books of Priscianus (2 months)
    II. Logic
        1. Tractatus *(Summulae)* of Petrus Hispanus (2½ to 3 months)
        2. The "Old" Logic (3 to 4 months) [According to the Paris Statute of 1254 this consists of (1) the *Introduction to the Categories* by Porphyry; (2) the *Categories* and *On Interpretation* by Aristotle; (3) the *Divisions* and *Topics*, except Book IV, by Boëthius.]
        3. The "New" Logic, except *Topics* (6½ to 7 months) [According to the same statute this comprises *Prior and Posterior Analytics* and the *Sophistical Refutations* by Aristotle.]

---

[52] E. P. Cubberlyy, *Readings in the History of Education* (Cambridge, Mass., 1920), pp. 169ff.

III. Natural Philosophy [Aristotle].
 1. *Physics* (6 to 9 months) [This subject eventually took over the time originally allotted to music in most universities.]
 2. *On the Soul* (2 months)

IV. Mathematics.
 1. *On the Material Sphere* by Sacrobosco (5 to 6 weeks)

(b) *Magister artium:*

 I. Logic.
 1. *Logic of Heytisbury* [No time is given; this may have been an introductory or review course for those who needed it.]
 2. *Topics* by Aristotle (3 to 4 months)

 II. Moral and Practical Philosophy [all by Aristotle].
 1. *Ethics* (6 to 9 months)
 2. *Politics* (4 to 9 months)
 3. *Economics* (3 weeks)

 III. Natural Philosophy [all by Aristotle].
 1. *On the Heavens and the Earth* (3½ to 4 months)
 2. *On Generation and Destruction* (7 weeks to 2 months)
 3. *Meteorics* (3½ to 4 months)
 4. *Parva Naturalia* (2½ to 3 months) [The *libri*, here meaning chapters, on:]
 a. "Sense and Sensible Things"
 b. "Sleep and Waking"
 c. "Memory and Recollection"
 d. "Longevity and Shortlivedness"

 IV. *Metaphysics* (5 to 9 months) [Aristotle].

 V. Mathematics.
 1. Astronomy: *Theory of the Planets* by Gerard of Cremona (5 to 6 weeks)
 2. Geometry: Euclid (5 to 9 months)
 3. Arithmetic: *Common Arithmetic* by Sacrobosco (3 weeks to 1 month)
 4. Music: Music [*Tractatus de Musica*] by Johannes de Muris (3 weeks to 1 month)
 5. Optics: *Common Perspective* by Johannes de Pisa (3 to 3½ months)

If all these courses were taken successively, one arrived at about 2 to 2½ years of study for the B.A. and an additional 3½ to 5½ years for the M.A. This time may have been shortened by taking some courses concurrently or lengthened because of poor preparation upon entering or of poor work and study habits after matriculation. Since a student could begin his university studies as early as age 15, it was possible under the most favorable conditions to earn the M.A. at age 20-21. In most cases the successful master's candidate had to promise to lecture at his university for up to two years in the arts faculty. These two years were often used for working toward the doctor's degree in one of the three higher faculties.[53]

---

[53] Wagner, p. 68f.

For the degree of *doctor*, the content of the courses was also firmly established. The studies centered on Hippocrates and Galenus for medicine, on the *Decretum* of Gratianus for canonic law and the *Corpus Iuris Civilis* of Justinian for civil law, and on the Holy Scriptures with various commentaries and the *Summa Theologica* by Thomas Aquinas for theology. Both master's and doctor's candidates had to defend a thesis in a grand public *disputatio*. No safe indication of the time spent on obtaining the doctor's degree can be given because this depended on too many factors in each individual case.

The method in all faculties was lecture, commentary, summation of a given text, and disputation. It must be noted, however, that in the arts faculty, especially at the beginning, the methods and strict discipline, except beating, of the secondary schools were used. This is not surprising because many students were much younger than the entering college students of today. Older students, if not living by themselves in rented rooms, stayed in "colleges" established and operated as residence halls by the university or in *bursae* run by individual masters. The younger boys often lived in special *paedagogia* under strict supervision with "built-in tutors" or they were sent back to the nearest learned school for remedial work in their weak points, this work being done under the ultimate control of the *paedagogium*. This institution, together with the other better learned schools, evolved into the *Gymnasium* in Germany or the *lycée* in France. In some cases, such as St. Stephen in Vienna, the whole cathedral school was directly supervised by the university.[54]

A characteristic document illustrating this overlapping of method and content in secondary schools and universities until the 16th century is the music notebook of the Wittenberg student Georg Donatus. Its content did not exceed the material learned in the city school but its lack of organization and emphasis on problematic points showed that a certain amount of basic knowledge was assumed and this part was reviewed very briefly if at all. Thus not the whole material was retaught, but the interest was extended to those chapters not carefully done or not well understood in the secondary school. These items were quite numerous because the schools often had little time for more difficult theoretical problems because of the many singing performances in church and community.[55]

This leads to a brief investigation of what the universities required in music before this subject was eliminated from the curriculum around the middle of the 16th century. As has been shown above, Leipzig (and other universities following its example) required very little—only 3 weeks to 1 month of Johannes de Muris—and that almost at the end of the M.A. program, a stage that relatively few students ever reached. Many did not even go as far as the B.A. In the Oxford statutes, how-

---

[54] Carpenter, p. 102.

[55] A. Aber, "Das musikalische Studienheft des Wittenberger Studenten Georg Donat (um 1543)," *Sammelbände der Internationalen Musikgesellschaft* (SIMG) XV (1913), 68-98.

ever, music figured from 1431 until the 19th century. In 1431, one year of music, mainly Boëthius, was required for the M.A.; in Cambridge, a statute from the late 15th century prescribed that the first year of the B.A. program be divided between arithmetic and music. In 1507, the study of music was made optional at Leipzig. But Cracow and Salamanca, the only university with a special chair for music, maintained vigorous programs of practical and theoretical music for many years.[56]

To summarize the findings on education through the Middle Ages, it seems best to outline the hypothetical career of a medieval scholar from its beginning to its end. However, it must be kept in mind that such an outline gives a norm from which there were many deviations due to location, period, and individual differences. Three major levels of education (or stages) can be roughly distinguished:

1. Elementary level—church or parish schools and first years of learned schools, later also private schools: The study of the alphabet by means of little wax tablets (therefore the term *tabulistae* for pupils at this stage), reading and memorization of Psalms, daily practice of singing, later also writing on parchment; in some but not all of these schools the beginnings of Latin grammar and memorization of Latin phrases for the more gifted pupils.

2. Intermediate level—cathedral and monastery schools, later also city and court schools, to be subdivided into three stages:

a. *Tabulistae:* the beginners (see above).

b. *Donatistae:* students able and ready to learn Latin grammar out of Donatus; they learn also some simple arithmetic and *musica plana.*

c. *Alexandristae:* students far enough advanced to study the very comprehensive grammar of Alexander de Villa Dei, mentioned above (p. 249). At this stage the schools vary widely; the better schools may cover the whole range or part of the seven liberal arts (e.g., Priscianus, Virgil, and Cicero) and teach a great deal of *musica figuralis* with all the complicated problems of notation, rhythm, and proportions; other schools may teach only some more grammar and arithmetic and the rudiments of music, such as *scala, voces, mutatio, cantus,* and perhaps *ligaturae.*

3. Higher level—universities, better cathedral, monastery, court, and city schools covering part of the arts program only, to be again subdivided into three stages:

a. The *baccalaureus artium* program, a thorough study of the liberal arts.

b. The *magister artium* program, a deepening of the study of philosophy and mathematics and some study of natural science.

c. The *doctor* program, specializing in medicine, canon or civil law, or theology.[57]

In the second or third decade of the 15th century the Dominican professor at Vienna, Johannes Vider, listed the following hierarchy of sub-

---

[56] For abortive attempts at establishing a professorship in music at Wittenberg, see above, p. 256.

[57] For details see above, pp. 259ff.

jects in the university curriculum (in ascending order) : grammar, rhetoric, logic, geometry, arithmetic, music, astronomy, metaphysics, ethics, imperial law, canon law, theology.

Throughout the Middle Ages and still in the 16th century, *sacra theologia* was the queen of all disciplines of learning and had the greatest prestige. In spite of the expansion of learning since the 12th century, the maxims of Anselm still held: Faith precedes science, fixes its boundaries, and prescribes its conditions; and the better known *credo ut intelligam, non intelligo ut credam* (I believe in order that I may know, I do not know in order to believe).[58] Next to faith, in the late Middle Ages, the authority of Aristotle was almost as great as that of the Scriptures. Ever since Thomas Aquinas, it was felt that God had to be reached through *ratio* (reason) and *revelatio*. This *fides quaerens intellectum*, the drive for the union of faith and reason, was most characteristic of this period.

When the great hope of transforming faith into knowledge proved to be false, the Renaissance, with disgust and contempt, turned away from scholastic mental acrobatics and toward a creative revival of classical antiquity in art and literature. To the Renaissance man the latter had nature, truth, beauty, perfection, and freedom, while the Middle Ages were filled with Gothic barbarism. Making such a harsh judgment, the men of the Renaissance and Humanism overlooked, or did not want to see, the fact that medieval life was also made up of war and conquest, hunts and tournaments, love and joy of life, humor, hero epics and love of poetry, and architectural works of exquisite strength and beauty. The new ideal of the Italian Renaissance was definitely aristocratic and aesthetic with a certain contempt of anything common, even common man and common morals. The contrast of distinguished and common, beautiful and ugly, fine and coarse, soon overshadowed that of good and evil. Luther's Reformation was an ethical-religious and German-popular reaction against this aristocratic-aesthetic ideal from Italy. The clash was so great that it generated in Luther a violent hatred both of the late-medieval ideal of learning with its pagan Aristotle at the head, and of the humanists. Luther might have reduced education to the minimum standard of the "common man" if it had not been for his friend and collaborator, Philip Melanchthon. This man combined (Protestant) faith and the desire for knowledge in a way far superior to and far more practical than the scholastic philosophers so that he became the founder of a whole nation's school system, elementary as well as secondary, and rightfully earned the title held by his spiritual ancestor Rhabanus Maurus more than six hundred years before: *praeceptor Germaniae*. How much he was liked and respected for what he did for the cause of German education is shown by the little word "our" that the people soon added to this distinguished title. Thus he is known to posterity as *praeceptor noster Germaniae*.

---

[58] Haskins, p. 70.

To implement this fusion of faith and knowledge with the best possible result, Melanchthon turned to the schools and universities. Like all great reformers, he preferred to build upon what he found rather than to destroy and rebuild; he preserved the educational structure in the German lands and let it grow organically to fulfill the new tasks that Reformation and Humanism imposed. Thus it is not surprising that in the 16th century one finds a very similar organization of education as in the late Middle Ages. But gradually new and more carefully differentiated types of schools came into existence. A well arranged list of these types is given by Steinhäuser. Comment will be made on individual items as is deemed necessary:[59]

[a] University character
- *Academica*
- *Lyceum*
- *Gymnasium* — formerly *studium generale* or *universitas*
- [Upper division of Jesuit college]

[b] Schools of advanced character where Latin is taught
- [1] *Gymnasium, Academicum illustre* [intermediate stage between school and university]
- [2] Schools of Princes, of States, and Monastery schools [*Fürstenschulen, Landesschulen, Klosterschulen*]
- [3] Learned schools, Pedagogic Institutes [*Gelehrtenschulen, Pädagogien*]
- [4] [Lower division of Jesuit college]

[c] Schools of less advanced character where Latin is taught
- [1] Secondary schools [*Partikularschulen*] (under city administration)
- [2] Secondary school [*Trivialschulen*]
- [3] Latin schools
- [4] Large city schools — sometimes only called city schools or [city] council's schools [*Ratsschulen*]

[d] Evangelical schools without Latin elementary school character
- [1] German schools [*deutsche Schulen*]
- [2] Corner schools [*Winkelschulen*]
- [3] Writing schools [*Schreibschulen*]
- [4] [Sometimes just] City schools [*Stadtschulen*]
- [5] [Evangelical parish schools in villages]
- [6] [Catholic parish schools in villages]

[for boys and girls]

---

[59] Steinhäuser, *Die Musik an den Hessen-Darmstaedtischen Lateinschulen im 16. und 17. Jahrhundert und ihre Beziehungen zum kirchlichen und bürgerlichen Leben.* (Giessen, Doctoral dissertation, 1936), p. 6. The same or a very similar organization of schools exists in the rest of Germany. Additions and original German are enclosed in brackets.

Comments:

[a] More and more of the functions of the university arts faculty passed to this group of the best of the learned schools, continuing the trend that began with the overlapping of the two in the late Middle Ages (see above, pp. 259, 261f.). All three types were preparing for, as well as performing, some of the studies at the universities so that a student with this kind of schooling would obtain his baccalaureate degree much faster than students coming from lesser schools. In fact, the term *Gymnasium* was often used by the humanists as a synonym for 'university; it also denoted the upper classes of schools established by princes.[60]

[b] For the terms *Gymnasium* and *Academicum illustre* see [a] above. They are listed also in this group because some were not quite so demanding as the arts faculties of the universities. The names in [2] are regional variants of the same type, learned schools established by a prince. The term *Landesschule* is more generic, *Fürstenschule* applies chiefly to Saxony, *Klosterschule* (from the ancient monastery school, i.e., church property confiscated by the prince and used for school purposes) applies to Württemberg. In [3], *Gelehrtenschulen* and *Pädagogien* were specifically university-preparatory schools for future scholars, while the chief aim of the schools in [2] was the training of competent higher administrative officers in the service of the prince, though students of these schools were also encouraged to attend a university later. Remarkably, the admission to these schools depended more on ability and character than on social rank, and applicants were examined in their knowledge of grammar, etymology, syntax, zeal, and fear of God. This was possible because most of these schools dispensed with the lowest classes and accepted students at a slightly more advanced age. Pupils were enrolled for 5 to 6 years between the ages of 12 and 20. The schools in [2] and [3] were usually boarding schools (*Internate*) while those in [1] were mostly day schools.

Most schools in classifications [a] and [b] had 5 classes, though the division into (year-long) classes was not very strict. The first class learned the reading and writing of very simple Latin, it was the direct continuation of the lowest group (*primus locus*) of the Middle Ages. Classes 2 and 3 studied mainly the Latin language; they resulted from the division of the old intermediate group (*secundus locus*). In classes 4 and 5, Latin literature, Greek language, and philosophy were taught; these classes originated from a division of the old advanced group (*tertius locus*). A few of these schools had less than 5 classes, others had more as, for instance, Sturm's *Gymnasium* at Strasbourg had 10 (year-long) classes (see below, pp. 272ff.).

The Jesuit college was the Catholic counterpart of the Protestant learned school but its upper division, for training future members of the

---

[60] Thomas Woody, *Fürstenschulen in Germany after the Reformation* (Menasha, Wis., 1920), p. 6.

order, ranged far beyond the scope of the learned school in subject matter and duration. These *studia superiora* comprised 3 years of philosophy and 4 years of theology centered on Thomas Aquinas whose pronouncements had almost the force of law. The *studia inferiora*, however, were modeled after the Protestant schools with the same division into classes, the same general goal of mastery of the Latin language shown through eloquence, re-creation of classical poetry, and rather frequent performances of classical dramas. Their performances were more frequent, in fact, than those in the Protestant schools, for the Jesuits were especially fond of devices that attracted wide attention. This factor also determined their attitude toward music; while they at first disliked it as a school subject, they soon admitted it half-heartedly but went all out in hiring professional musicians for their school dramas and school and church festivals. In their reports they would always mention the "stupendous" effect that the massed "military instruments" had had on the audience. This was in part also to impress the rich donors who supported the Jesuit schools without being allowed any influence on them.

[c] This class of schools was under the control of the city council and an ecclesiastical advisor. The educational activities proper were run by the *Ludimagister* or *Rector,* nearly always a clergyman or at least a man with theological training, and very often also the city scribe. Some of these schools were at the same level as the learned schools, especially in the larger cities. The variety of names does not necessarily suggest a difference in programs or standards. The multiplicity of names is primarily of historical origin. A *Trivialschule* was a school teaching the *trivium* as was a *Partikularschule*. The *studium particulare* meant the same as the *trivium,* while the *studium generale* comprised all the seven liberal arts. Most of these schools also prepared for entrance into a university but did not carry their students as far as the first two types.[61]

[d] This group was the stepchild among educational institutions, frowned upon by secular and ecclesiastical authorities alike. Therefore all these schools were private establishments which survived and even flourished despite harassments by the authorities because they fulfilled the vital need of giving a minimum education to those who had not much ability, or little time or money to spend on schooling. They also had the moral backing of Luther's educational writings demanding that boys with no desire for learning should at least attend an elementary-type school and that girls should have the opportunity to hear the Gospel one hour per day, in German or Latin.[62] These schools taught boys and

---

[61] Robbins, *Teachers in Germany in the 16th Century* (New York, 1912), p. 21, and Sternfeld, "Music in the Schools of the Reformation," *Musica Disciplina* II (1948), 109.

[62] ". . . dass man die Knaben, die nicht studieren sollen, eine Stunde oder zwei lasse zu solcher Schule gehen," in *Letter to the Christian Nobility of the German Nation (Schrift an den christlichen Adel deutscher Nation),* 1520 (St. Louis Ed. X, 266ff.), ". . . darinnen des Tags die Maidle eine Stunde das Evangelium hörten, es wäre zu deutsch oder lateinish," in *Letter to the Mayors and Aldermen . . . in behalf of Christian Schools (An die Bürgermeister und Ratsherren . . . I),* 1524 (St. Louis Ed. X, 453ff.)

girls reading and writing in German. After all of the school statutes in the first thirty years of the era of the Reformation had considered only Latin schools and many had expressly outlawed German schools, the school statutes of Württemberg (1559) and Kursachsen (1580) permitted them in small villages, but only where Latin schools did not exist. Instruction was given by the sexton who then could not be a policeman and/or game warden at the same time that he was a teacher.[63] Filling a real need, these schools were eventually recognized also in the cities because they trained boys for the lower civil service and gave a minimum education to girls.[64]

Most school statutes of the 16th century, however, mentioned only the Latin school for which they prescribed the following curriculum: the first level began with the reading and writing of simple Latin phrases and even the learning of a little of Donatus and Cato; on the second level (in one or two classes) the pupils learned Latin grammar and the reading of Latin prose works; the third level (in one or two classes) received the true humanistic instruction in Latin poetry and eloquence, and in philosophy. Greek was reserved for the gifted and offered only in the cities (with the exception of some princes' schools). At that time the Latin school was the "public school" proper.

This "public school" was still dominated by the church in its outlook as well as its organization. The prince (or the city) appointed an administrative body, the *Konsistorium,* composed of lawyers and clergymen, to discharge the state's (or the city's) new responsibility for the protection and maintenance of churches and schools. The highest authority in church and school matters was the General Synod made up of the *Konsistorium* and the district superintendents. Next in authority came the Particular Synod comprised of the superintendent and all the clergy of the district. General regulations and their enforcement by means of "visitations" (inspections) arose from several needs: that the schools should teach the "pure" Lutheran doctrine, that they should be efficiently run and have an adequate number of talented boys and qualified teachers, and that they should at least provide a minimum education to enable all people to participate in the church service and to know the rudiments of their religion. Though Luther at first favored a free development of the schools, he soon had to consent to regulations because of the rapid establishment of new schools and the annexation of Catholic church schools which obviously had had different objectives. Eventually, ever more detailed regulations resulted from the dual control of church and state.[65] Thus many important church statutes (*Kirchenordnungen*) containing regulations of the schools, and independently published school statutes (*Schulordnungen*) were written in the first 50 years

[63] Paulsen 1, p. 47.
[64] Robbins, p. 21.
[65] Woody, p. 9.

of the era of the Reformation, mainly by Melanchthon and Bugenhagen or by men under their influence.[66]

As early as 1528 *visitatores* (inspectors) went to every parish to investigate the care of the souls (*Seelsorge*), the instruction of youth (*Kindererziehung*), and the care of the poor (*Armenfürsorge*). In the records of these inspections, called *Registraturen* or *Protokolle*, one finds remarks such as the following: in 1555 a *Cantor* at Liebenwerda in Saxony had to be admonished because he preferred hunting to organ playing; in 1557 a *Cantor* at Trettin was dismissed because of indolence, drunkenness, and brawling. Some *Cantors* (and, of course, also other teachers) were placed on probation for as long as three years. But on the whole, there was more praise than blame; e.g., all the teachers at St. Thomas and St. Nicolai in Leipzig were highly commended in 1580.[67] The inspectors were appointed by the secular authorities from the nobility and intelligentsia; most of them were so thorough that they questioned each boy in the school and also checked the schools' facilities, such as the kitchens, for cleanliness.[68]

The main object of their investigations was, however, the teachers. In small schools there were at least two, *Rector* and *Cantor,* for the latter was very instrumental in the church service. In schools with three teachers the order usually was *Rector, Cantor,* Sexton.[69] The rank of the *Cantor* began to decline after the division into three groups or levels was abandoned in favor of the separation into more classes, and this trend continued and increased in the 17th century as the *Cantor* was removed more and more from academic teaching. In the larger Latin schools where there was a *Conrector,* the *Cantor,* if he was not the *Conrector* himself (which happened not too frequently), dropped to fourth place: (1) *(Ludi)rector, Magister,* or *Meister (Schulmeister)* ; (2) *Conrector, Subrector, Supremus,* or (sometimes) *Cantor;* (3) *Baccalaureus* or *Pädagoge;* and (4) *Cantor, Infimus, Baccalaureus,* or *Pädagoge.* With five teachers the order was the same, with the *Medius* occupying third place between the *Conrector* and *Baccalaureus.* An assistant teacher was called *Praeceptor, Collaborator, Socius,* or *Gesell.* In Hamburg the order was *Rector, Subrector, Cantor,* and four *Pädagogen*; in Annaberg (Saxony) it was *Schulmeister, Supremus, Medius, Cantor,* and *Infimus;* in Pomerania it was *Ludirector, Conrector, Cantor,* and at least two *Collaboratores.* The *Locatus,* student-teacher of the Middle Ages, gradually disappeared from the scene.[70] With the decreasing prestige of the *Cantor* went a lowering of his qualifications; while *Rector* of a better school had to be a *magister artium,* this was no longer required of the *Cantor.*

---

[66] Robbins, pp. 9ff. He gives a list of *Schulordnungen* on pp. 15ff, their text is given by R. Vormbaum, *Die evangelischen Schulordnungen des 16. Jahrhunderts* (Gütersloh, 1860). For an example from such a *Schulordnung,* see below, pp. 272ff.

[67] Robbins, pp. 31ff.

[68] Woody, p. 39.

[69] Sternfeld, p. 110.

[70] Robbins, p. 22f.

In some places the prospective teachers were examined, especially in grammar and catechism, before they were appointed by the *Rector*; the *Rector*, in turn, was named by the *Konsistorium*. The teachers in the princes' schools received a fixed salary plus room and board while those in the city schools had several sources of income, such as some remuneration from the city council, students' fees paid quarterly, and many kinds of *Akzidentien*, i.e., revenue from students' performances, public singing, participation in funerals, weddings, and the like. As will be shown from an autobiographical account of the period, the prestige of a teacher, unless he was a *Rector*, was not very high and many a teacher considered his position as a stepping-stone to the more honorable pastorate. The social position of the teachers was all the lower since even the new clergy itself came from the peasant and artisan classes; in the 16th century, school service was church service on a lower level.

Sternfeld[71] provides some figures on the teacher-student ratio at the princes' schools in Saxony: at Meissen 4 (*Rector*, two *Baccalaurei*, *Cantor*) to 60; at Merseburg 4 to 70; at Pforta 5 (*Rector*, three *Baccalaurei*, *Cantor*) to 100. Since these schools were totally maintained by the princes, this ratio must be considered more favorable than average. Pupils were admitted to different schools at different ages. Some ambitious educators like Sturm, Trotzendorf, and Meander made students start serious Latin studies at the age of 8 and kept them until age 18; before that they had already had two years of reading and writing elementary Latin, music, and calligraphy.[72] The princes' schools admitted boys at age 14 or 15 and kept them three years before sending them to a university.[73] This shows that entrance to a university now was usually at age 18 as compared with 15-16 in the late Middle Ages because the learned schools had expanded their curriculum and taken over much subject matter formerly taught by the arts faculty; the schools with more than five classes, especially, went very far in this respect. The school year still lasted about ten months, and the school day consisted of six hours in general, with Wednesday (or Thursday) and Saturday afternoons free from regular classes but not from remedial work or preparation for Sunday's church services.[74] As in earlier times any form of advanced education was reserved for boys; girls had to attend the parish school in the village and the private elementary school in the cities, mostly without Latin, where they learned reading, writing, the catechism, and singing, though they never performed in public or in church.[75]

Neither method nor discipline changed much from that of the late Middle Ages. The students' attendance at all church services, not only Sundays, was compulsory. Often the sermon topic was discussed at length

---

[71] Sternfeld, p. 111.
[72] Sternfeld, p. 110.
[73] Woody, p. 11.
[74] Paul Monroe, *A Textbook in the History of Education* (New York, 1928), p. 435.
[75] Schünemann, p. 57.

in class the following day.[76] The method of instruction was still *praecepta* (rules), *exempla, imitatio* (on lower levels this was memorization). Practical imitation, especially in respect to classic Latin authors, and *usus* (practical application) in these and especially in music became important since the 16th century already believed in "learning by doing." However, most of the factual information was gained merely as the by-product of language and literature studies and there was little science or mathematics, except some arithmetic, in the normal curriculum of the average Latin school. Even after the invention of printing the students themselves had few textbooks; most of them studied from notes taken during lectures.[77] Latin grammar and eloquence formed the principal part of the program while the teaching of religion expanded from the memorization of Bible passages, prayers, and Psalms to a preparatory course in theology with the exposition of a Gospel or other parts of the New Testament. In some more advanced schools this was even from the Greek text. In spite of a more practical bent, the studies were still extremely formal; little was left to the choice of the individual teacher, nothing to the student as to method or material studied except, perhaps, in music which was probably the freest of all subjects.[78]

In most schools, discipline remained as harsh as it had been in the Middle Ages. The rod was still the constant companion of the teacher, but a new spirit emerged in the princes' and the Jesuit schools. In the former, the teacher was generally forbidden to strike the pupil or to pull his hair or ears; the rod was to be used only as a last resort, with restraint and without tyranny or harshness.[79] The explanation for this may partly be that the students were already somewhat older when they entered this type of school. But in the Jesuit schools the attitude toward beating was the same regardless of the boy's age. There the classroom teacher was never to use force and if corporal punishment was deemed necessary, it was administered in moderation by the *Corrector* only. The Jesuits had other means of enforcing discipline, such as developing in the students an extreme ambition coupled with a fierce spirit of competition, mutual spying among students, and instilling fear in a boy's conscience.

The most interesting disciplinary novelty was the compulsory school attendance for all children, first demanded by Charlemagne, then by Luther in his three famous writings on education.[80] Like Charlemagne, he did not live to see this idea enacted into law. But finally, in 1619, the Weimar school statue threatened parents with punishment for failing to send their children to school and also devised a method of enforcement

---

[76] Sternfeld, p. 105.

[77] See above, p. 261 about the notebook of Georg Donatus.

[78] Woody, p. 33f.

[79] Woody, pp. 22, 25.

[80] See above, note 62; cf. also Luther's *Sermon on the Duty of Sending Children to School (Sermon, dass man die Kinder zur Schule halten solle)* (St. Louis Edition X, 416ff.).

by ordering all ministers and school principals to keep up-to-date registers of all children of 6 to 12 years in their respective districts. With this statute, soon followed by others with the same provisions, the public elementary school was born.

To summarize the findings one may again follow from his auto-biography, the career of a man representative of this period. Georg Naubitzer was born in 1560 at Mittweida in central Germany. His father was a *diaconus* (deacon who assisted the pastor, especially in tak-ing care of the poor and the sick), his mother had a girls' school (one of the private *Winkelschulen*) until her death in 1599. In 1572 he received his first communion and in 1574 he assisted his schoolmaster (principal) in staging a play. In the same year he left his home town to go to Torgau (which had a large school of splendid reputation thanks to Johann Walther who had taught there). He attended this school for six years, of which three were spent in *Sekunda* and *Prima*, i.e., on the higher level. During these six years he was a *paedagogus* (tutor and caretaker of children) in four different households; he had much housework to do, had to do the marketing, had to work in a tannery and in a brewery, which was heavy work, and received his fair share of beatings. When he worked for a doctor, he did not have too much housework, but had to do more tutoring and hosting at parties, had to write prescriptions and often fetch his master from the tavern. While in Torgau, he matriculated (registered) at the University of Wittenberg in July 1578, but in 1580 he went to the University of Leipzig instead because it had offered him a place in its *convict* (a house where students received free room and board for rendering minor services to the university). When he arrived in Leipzig, he presented a letter of recommendation from his *Rector* in Torgau, was examined by the *Magister* of the *convict*, and was accepted on August 1, 1580. A week later, he made a valedictory speech at Torgau entitled *De gratitudine*, after which he returned to Leipzig to begin his studies on August 19. He had table No. 5 in the mess hall under senior Johannes Hipp and lived on the upper floor of the *Paulinerkolleg* with a learned and peaceable young roommate. On July 14, 1582 he delivered his first sermon at the *Paulinerkirche* (St. Paul's Church). In 1585 he was *Korrector* (not *Conrector*), i.e., proofreader, in a Leipzig publish-ing house. On September 16, 1586 he was appointed schoolmaster and town scribe at Sonnenwalde, a small town in Thuringia, whereupon he was dismissed from the Elector's stipend (for his studies at Leipzig) *bona pace et honesto testimonio*. He now accepted private pupils and ate with their families. On October 24, 1587 he married *Kunigunde,* daugh-ter of the previous town scribe's widow. On December 27 he preached his first sermon at Sonnenwalde. For over a year his wife served in the local count's household so that he was separated from her to his great sorrow. In 1593, after an examination in Leipzig, he was ordained as a deacon in Sonnenwalde. On June 5 of that year he administered his first confession and on June 6 he conducted an entire church service for the first time. He was harassed by the *Amtsschösser* (a town tax official) because of his punitive sermon on the Seventh Commandment against this man. On October 13, 1595 he accompanied his first criminal to the place of execution. In 1600 he finally became pastor at Weisstropp, where he died after 1634.[81]

Georg Naubitzer's schooling closely conforms to the contents of the school statute of Württemberg of 1559, the first such statute elaborated in detail. It was designed after Melanchthon's ideas, and established six classes instead of five as the norm. An outline of its content would look like this:[82]

1.   Teutsch (German) Schools

Beginning school. Boys and girls (but) separate. Instruction in reading and writing German, religion, and music. Such schools to be set up in every village and hamlet. Teachers in such schools to be relieved from beadle and mass services in the churches. These schools free, and for the masses.

2.   Latin Schools

A fully equipped school to have six classes, but many had less. These known as private schools.[83] They were divided into six classes, as follows:

First or Lower Class. (9 to 11 years of age.) Pupils in this class learned to pronounce and read Latin and began building up a vocabulary. Readings from Cato.

Second Class. (10 to 12 years of age.) Cato continued, Declensions and conjugations. Grammar studied. Vocabulary enlarged. Translation from the Latin catechism. Much drill on phrases. Music taught.

Third Class. (11 to 13 years of age.) Much drill on phrases. Reading of fables and dialogues. Letters of Cicero begun. Readings from Terence for elegance and purity. Syntax begun. Music continued.

At close of this year might be transferred to the Cloister Schools (3).

Fourth Class. (12 to 14 years of age.) Cicero's "Letters to his Friends"; his treatises on "Friendship" *(De amicitia)* and "Old Age" *(De senectute); and* Terence to be read. Syntax finished; prosody begun. Music continued. Greek grammar begun, with readings from the smaller Greek catechism of Brentius.

Fifth Class. (13 to 15 years of age.) All previous work to be perfected. In this class read Cicero's "Familiar Letters" *(Ad familiares)* and his "Offices" *(De officiis).*[84] Also Ovid's *de Tristibus,* and the Gospels in Greek and Latin. Much attention to prosody and to exercises in style. Music continued.

Sixth Class. (14 to 16 years of age.) Cicero's "Speeches," Sallust, and the *Aeneid* of Vergil to be read. Much attention to the elegancies of the Latin tongue, and to pure poetical diction. Successful imitation of the idiom and phraseology of Cicero the aim. In Greek to complete the grammar, and to read Xenophon's *Cyropaedia* and the larger catechism of Brentius. Music, especially

---

[81] Paulsen 2, p. 332f.

[82] Literally taken from Cubberley, *Readings in the History of Education* (Cambridge, Mass., 1920), p. 250f.

[83] This interpretation is misleading. Though the students paid a quarterly fee to their teachers, these schools were maintained by the state or by the city.

[84] These are poor translations: *Ad familiares* means (Letters) to relatives or intimate friends; *De officiis* means On Duties (or Obligations).

sacred, to be practiced, and the recitations of the day to be begun by singing either the *Veni sancte Spiritus* or the *Veni Creator Spiritus.*
Conversation, both in and out of school, to be in Latin.
Logic and Rhetoric to be read in this class.

3. The Lower Cloister or Grammar Schools

Could be entered after completing the Third Class, at 12 to 14 years of age. Designed for selected boys, who were to be trained for the service of the Church.
Course of study paralleled the three upper classes of the Latin Schools, but with much more emphasis on theological doctrine.

4. The Higher Cloister Schools

Entered at 15 to 16 years of age to prepare for the university, which was usually entered at about 16 or 17.[85]
Read Cicero and Vergil. Continued emphasis on style and purity and elegance of diction. Phrase book constructed.
Continue Greek grammar, and read Demosthenes.
Continue music, and study musical theory.
Continue Logic and Rhetoric.
Begin Arithmetic and Astronomy.
Disputations fortnightly on questions of grammar, logic, rhetoric, or the sphere.
Strict discipline, and emphasis on theology.

5. The State University at Tübingen

Studies: Greek, Hebrew, Latin, Logic, Rhetoric, Mathematics, and Theology.

The ideas put into practice by this school statute were first laid down by Melanchthon in the Saxony Plan of 1528, and were actually instructions for school inspectors.[86] He advocated the teaching of Latin as the only language and wanted to eliminate German, Hebrew, and even Greek from the secondary schools, which seemed strange for a humanist. However, he was not concerned with the fame of the schools or of their teachers—in fact he criticized them for their vanity—but with ascertaining that amount and quality of instruction which would best suit the pupils and avoid their being overburdened. At that time he still followed the old division into three groups (*Haufen*). The first group consisted of children learning to read (in Latin) beginning with the familar creed, the Lord's Prayer, and other prayers. They then took up Donatus and Cato in very small segments. In addition they were made to sing together. The second group consisted of pupils who knew how to read and were beginning the study of grammar. But first he stated that this group, like the other two, was to have music during the first hour of every afternoon. The studies of this group were comprised of the fables of Aesop and the *Paedology* of Mosellanus, followed by selections from the *Colloquies* of Erasmus. The pupils memorized moralizing sentences

---

[85] Entrance into university at this time was closer to 18. It is hard to see how this program could have been finished in only one year.
[86] The following is condensed from Cubberley, pp. 247-249.

from the ancient classical writers. After Aesop, Terence was read and then the "harmless" comedies of Plautus. The hour before noon was always reserved for grammatical studies in the second and third groups: etymology, syntax, and prosody (metric). Grammar was repeated and drilled over and over again. The third group was composed of selected, very proficient students only. Grammar studies and prosody were deepened and supplemented by the reading of Vergil, Ovid's *Metamorphoses*, and Cicero's *De officiis* (On Duties) or *Ad Familiares* (Letters to Friends). Idiomatic constructions and prominent figures of speech were discussed and memorized. The learning and making of verse was deemed very important for building a good vocabulary. When he had sufficiently mastered grammar, the student went on to logic and rhetoric. Compositions in letter or verse form were assigned every week for the second and third groups, and teachers and students were always to speak only Latin.

The most characteristic sentence in the Saxony Plan was the following: "For no greater injury can befall learning and the arts than for youth to grow up in ignorance of grammar." Grammar was considered the principal means of attaining *pietas, eloquentia* (as a reaction against scholasticism and its dialectic), and *sapientia* (wisdom, or better: knowledge). The linguistic approach to and form of literature were more important than its content. However, the frequent use of language in writing and speech-making did not necessarily yield the expected character-building result as can be seen from a speech made by the *Professor Eloquentiae* Erasmus Schmidt about the topic *De America* upon the occasion of his promotion to *magister artium* at the University of Wittenberg in 1602. It was utterly insipid, a vehicle for showing off the speaker's vast accumulation of knowledge. He quoted Homer, Virgil, Plato, Aristotle, Strabo, Pliny, Ophir (a navigator from the Old Testament), and concluded his oration with the following words: ". . . may He (God) awaken in us not so much a burning desire to explore this earth as rather the longing to enter that celestial home where we all have the right of citizenship."[87] This statement is illustrative of the lack of interest in science and of the favoring of theology and linguistic proficiency even at the university level.

This can be shown even more clearly by excerpts from the program of the Philosophical Faculty (formerly Arts Faculty) of this university from the year 1561:[88]

h.6: M.[89] A. Lemeiger, Rhetoric, 4 hrs. weekly: Mon. Tues. *praecepta rhetorices,* Thurs. Fri. explanation of Cicero's letters and orations.
h.7: M. Sebastianus, Geometry and Astronomy after Euclid and Ptolemy, 4 hrs.
h.8: Dr. Vitus Winshernius, Greek Authors, 4 hrs.
h.9: M. P. Vincentius, Dialectic, Mon. Tues.; Dr. V. W., Greek Grammar, Wed.; Dr. C. Pencer, History, Sat.

---

[87] Paulsen 2, p. 346f. note 1.
[88] Paulsen 2, p. 225.
[89] M. before instructor's name means *Magister (artium).*

h.12: M. B. Schönborn, *de dimensione terrae,* 4 hrs.; later Pliny, *Meteora Pontani.*

h.1: M. M. Plochinger, *Elementa sphaerica et arithmetica,* 4 hrs. (for younger students).

h.2: M. Esromus, Physics, 4 hrs.; M. E. Menius, Latin grammar with Terence, Plautus, Vergil, Ovid, 4 hrs.; M. P. Vincentius, Ethics, Wed.

h.3: Dr. J. Maior, Poetics, with explanation of Latin poets, especially Vergil, 4 hrs.

h.4: M. P. Vincentius, Cicero, *de oratore,* then Livy alternating with Homer, Thurs. Fri.

How versatile a true humanist could be is best understood by a listing of all the subjects which Melanchthon taught in the upper courses at Wittenberg: rhetoric, dialectic, physics, ethics, history (which after 1588 expanded as it replaced Latin grammar, by then effectively taught in the secondary Latin schools), Greek grammar, explanation of Latin authors (Christian and pagan) and Greek authors (Homer, Demosthenes, Sophocles, Euripides, Thucydides), Hebrew, and Old Testament. Respect for this man should grow still further when it is considered that he wrote textbooks for many of his teaching subjects and also several for the secondary-school level. After his retirement, six instructors were needed to replace him![90]

The regular program leading to the B.A. degree contained dialectic, rhetoric, poetics, and elements of mathematics and physics; the M.A. course offered Greek language and literature, Aristotle's physics and ethics (from the original), mathematics after Euclid, and astronomy after Ptolemy. The programs were the result of a university reform carried out by the humanists around 1520. Orators and poets could and did now become professors, the medieval Latin was replaced by the classical, new translations of Aristotle were substituted for older ones, and he was more frequently read in the original. Poetry and eloquence (public speaking), with the reading and imitation of classical writers, now became examination subjects. New professorships for the Greek language and literature were established, and the old extensive grammar of Alexander de Villa Dei was discarded. New textbooks were introduced, written by humanists such as Melanchthon, Camerarius, and Reuchlin, or older textbooks were reinstated if they were short and practical as, for instance, Donatus. Everything possible was done to enable the student to master Latin and oratory techniques as well as the great Cicero himself had done!

This same goal was also pursued by the Jesuit schools, and with more energy, as the whole order dedicated itself to teaching and influencing people to remain good Catholics or to return to the Catholic religion. Their ultimate aim of reestablishing the dominion of the Roman Catholic Church was promoted by a strict organization along military lines not only outwardly but also inwardly through the absolute obedience to their superiors. They won great influence over the ruling

---

[90] Paulsen 2, p. 224.

classes in the southern and western parts of Germany because many noble families and quite a few ruling houses sent their sons as boarding students to the Jesuit schools. Besides boarding students, the Jesuits also accepted day students from the city in which their school was located. These two groups followed only the *studia inferiora* while a third group, the novices (*nostri*), also residents of the school, went on to the *studia superiora* to become members of the order themselves. While the *studia inferiora* closely resembled the course of the better Protestant Latin schools with the obvious differences in religious instruction, the *studia superiora* were a specifically Jesuit creation. They replaced a full university course for future members of the order, comprising a three-year course in philosophy followed by a four-year course in theology. Thomas Aquinas formed the center of all higher studies from which one was allowed to deviate only in an extreme necessity and then only *summa reverentia*.

This attitude explains both the phenomenal success of the order in the 16th and 17th centuries[91] and its fairly rapid decline in the 18th. The rigid organization and educational program (the *ratio studiorum* of the fourth general Aquaviva remained in force from 1599 to 1836) insured great continuity and universally high standards as long as the Jesuit schools taught approximately the same material as the other learned schools. They were superior to their Protestant counterparts because of the better and much longer training of their teachers, the better discipline of teachers and students, and a stronger devotion to the cause since the Jesuits had no families and were able to dedicate all their energy to their task. They also succeeded in recruiting rich donors willing to support their schools without claiming any control whatsoever over their administration. Lastly, they got their results by sophisticated and even spectacular means (as shown above pp. 265f.) and by sometimes making the ends justify their means. On the other hand, their extreme conservatism and reluctance to adopt new ideas coupled with their basic aim of absolutely subduing the individual to church and society doomed them to eventual failure, especially in a period of intellectual revival and curiosity as was the 18th century.

However, the true source from which a broad middle-class musical culture developed was the Protestant school. In the larger of these, several choirs of different abilities prepared music for the church services on Sunday and for many religious occasions outside of the services, while the Jesuits concentrated on far fewer but all the more spectular performances, mostly with hired soloists and instrumentalists who reinforced the school choir. Another support for a broad musical culture can

---

[91] The Jesuit *Gymnasium* in Cologne, founded in 1556, already had 80 pupils by 1560, including many non-Germans, and 12 teachers; at the end of the 16th century it had 1,010 students. Arnold Schmitz-Bonn, "Archiv-Studien über die musikalischen Bestrebungen der Kölner Jesuiten im 17. Jahrhundert," *Archiv für Musikwissenschaft* III (1921), 423.

be found in the fact that many musical students, after they left their Protestant school, entered the adult religious singing society of their town called *Kantorei*. These *Kantoreien* were also under the direction of the *Cantor* who therefore knew the adult singers very well and was respected by them. The final conclusion is that music was an integral part of life in school, church, and community in Protestant Germany at the turn of the 16th and 17th centuries. Adults as well as students, overwhelmingly from the middle-class, took an active part in all kinds of musical performances. This gave the musical culture of that period a far broader base than elsewhere and was to a large extent responsible for creating the cultural climate in which flowered great composers like Schütz and Bach.

Rensselaer Polytechnic Institute
Eastman School of Music

Period writings about singing activity from early eighteenth-century Boston and current data on singing in the United States provide material for a comparison of sex-related differences in public singing involvement. This material shows that, in America, there has been a marked shift from male to female predominance in public singing interest. Males arrogated singing leadership to themselves in early Boston and urged women to sing. Today, adolescent and adult American males are much less publicly involved with singing than are females. A cursory analysis of this phenomenon suggests that an inversion of leadership interest in public singing by sex has taken place in America. This interpretation, however, does not explain the facts, and music educators have some cause for concern that choral singing involvement of both sexes will continue to wane.

J. Terry Gates, *State University of New York at Buffalo*

JRME 1989, VOLUME 37, NUMBER 1, PAGES 32–47

A Historical Comparison of Public Singing by American Men and Women

One matter often overlooked in accounts of vocal music in colonial America (circa 1600–1780) is the apparent lack of involvement of women in public singing. The tune book compilers were men, singing in taverns and fraternal societies was presumably a male amusement, writers calling for music literacy among congregations were male, and singing masters and music teachers advertising in colonial newspapers were male. In the preface to the 1723 edition of John Tufts's *An Introduction to the Art of Singing Psalm-Tunes*, the author called attention to this problem:

> What a vast Addition would it be to the Pleasure of Singing, if we had more *Female* voices assisting in that Holy Exercise, and the sweet and sprightly Voices of our *Children*. *Women* have certainly greater Advantages to attain the Skill of Singing than *Men*. They have generally good Voices, and more Leisure than Men have; and the Obligations to Praise GOD are as full, and

My thanks to Mai Hogan Kelton, a researcher living in Northport, Alabama, for bringing to my attention some of the material on early hymnody. Also, thanks to Thomas M. Dicken, a minister from Eau Claire, Wisconsin, for information on the issues surrounding St. Paul's authorship of portions of biblical letters to the Corinthians and Timothy. For copies of this article, contact J. Terry Gates, State University of New York at Buffalo, Buffalo 14260.

binding. And as to our *Children*, how affecting the Sight, how vast and charming the Pleasure to have them sweetly joining with us in our *Family-Worship*, as well as in the *Publick Assemblies*, in singing forth the praises of the Great CREATOR! and this even by some almost as soon as they can speak plain, and begin to read. O that this time for the *singing of Birds were come!* [italics in original][1]

In America, there has been a marked shift from male to female involvement with public singing from colonial times to the present. Males took leadership roles in public singing and music literacy in early Boston and urged women to sing; today, adolescent and adult males are much less involved with public singing than are females. This shift in involvement might suggest that American women have replaced men as leaders in public singing. This suggestion does not explain the facts. A more adequate analysis suggests that the movement away from public singing among males merely has been delayed in females and that American music educators are going to experience serious difficulty in maintaining the current level of female interest in public singing in the future.

BOSTON IN THE 1720s

In the early 1720s, Boston's twelve thousand inhabitants were experiencing periodic general fires, a smallpox epidemic (Bonner 1722), and several lively controversies. The godliness of smallpox vaccinations was heatedly debated in newspaper editorials and open letters. At least one printer, James Franklin (in whose shop his younger brother, Benjamin, was then an apprentice), went to jail defending the right of the press to print material that criticized the government's laxity in protecting shipments and sailors from being taken by pirates (Franklin 1980). The uncertain occupational fortunes of church pastors provided fuel for public exchanges of views of their competence—a situation that might remind Americans today of the employment adventures of head coaches in university and professional athletics.

These were not times in which matters of trivial interest would take much attention from writers and pamphlet readers. Thus, both the Boston music literacy movement (also called "regular singing," or "singing by rule" or "by note") and printed observations about the singing of women and children add to the importance of the era for American music education historians. During the decade of the 1720s, Thomas Symmes (1720, 1723), Thomas Walter (1721, 1722, and 1723), Cotton Mather (1721), Peter Thacher, John Danforth, and Samuel Danforth (1723), John Tufts (1721, 1723, 1726, and 1728), and others, aided by their dual importance as leading clergymen and intellectuals (and supported by the publisher Samuel Gerrish [Gates 1988a]), had spread the message that the incompetent and contentious congregational singing of the time was undermining godliness. The message was also intended for children. Isaac Watts (1715) wrote a highly regarded version of the Psalms especially for children. Children and adolescents were encouraged to sing by Increase and Cotton Mather (1721);

Symmes (1720); Thacher, Danforth, and Danforth (1723); and Tufts (1723).

For the most part, these men were members of the intellectual elite of the time. They were not only in positions to have informed opinions about singing and music literacy; they also had the power to enact remedial programs. Their extensive writings ranged widely in subject matter—from natural disasters to medicine, from alcoholism to theology—and they did not always agree. Except for Tufts, their musical writings comprised relatively small but highly effective proportions of their outputs. The extent of their agreement that singing as it was then practiced was a major deterrent to godliness was remarkable. They also agreed that music literacy for all congregation members was the preferred solution to this problem rather than advocating silence, forming select choruses of the musically skilled, or using musical instruments. Their criticisms of the status quo were uniformly sharp.

Most of the invective, however, was directed toward men. Men were roundly chastised for singing too loudly, too high, too low, holding pitches too long, using melismas, using more than one tune at the same time, not encouraging women's singing, and being led (by Satan) into contentiousness because they were too ignorant and too stubborn to learn to read music (Mather 1721; Rowe 1722; Symmes 1720, 1723; Thacher, Danforth, and Danforth 1723; Walter 1722). Those who resisted learning to read music were dubbed "anti-regular singers," and this term's acronym ("A.R.S.'s") was used in some references to these people (Symmes 1723). Many of the writings designed to meet this problem were revised and reissued several times between 1720 and 1730, providing evidence of their popularity in and around Boston (see Gates 1988a).[2]

These writers combined advice about singing with their calls for music literacy, but treated these two matters quite differently. Issues in singing had to do with tone quality, intonation, rhythm, and the variation in commitment to public singing among men, women, and young people. Calls for music literacy dealt mainly with the amount and variety of repertoire and the reasons for learning to read music. In addition, the writers argued for singing schools and for using one or another of the music-reading systems available at the time (Gates 1988b). Little appears in print about secular singing in early eighteenth-century America, but song sheets and other musical broadsides do survive (Lowens 1964). They were used in fraternal societies and taverns that were populated almost exclusively by men. (For this article, I drew inferences about sex-related public [religious] singing activity represented by the Boston material and, for the moment, must leave unanalyzed matters of tone quality, intonation, repertoire, singing schools, and notation systems.)

Most advocates of regular singing found it necessary to deal directly with the problem of convincing women to sing in church. Symmes (1720), in the first of the decade's important publications on regular singing, outlined the major arguments for women's singing that Cotton Mather (1721) and Walter (1722) dealt with in more detail:

Q[uestion]. 8. *Do not the Handmaidens of the Lord, need to be put forward in this Duty?* . . . Were there not *Women-Singers*, as well as *Men-Singers* of old?

Would it not be very proper for them to have suitable Instructions and *Schools* on convenient Seasons? Are not they to be employed in *Singing GOD's Praises* in the Heavenly World, and why should they not in the Churches and Families on Earth? Have they not the pleasantest Voices (generally Speaking), and how will they answer it to GOD who gave them such Voices, if they don't improve them in *Singing His Praises?* [italics in original] (p. 19)

There was ample encouragement for women to sing in public worship, not only suggested in the material quoted above but also in the opinionated Cotton Mather's (1741) advice for women:

The *Sabbath* she calls *her Delight*; nor will she waste the sacred Hours of it in the *naughty Superfluities* of Diet and Rayment; but be as often as well as she can in the Congregation of the People of God; and there, as her *Voice* makes a sound that shall be not *Base*, for the Musick of the Publick *Psalms*, thus her *Heart* is an *Altar* from whence, during the whole Solemnity, there ascend unto God, *the Sacrifices which he Desires.* [italics in original] (pp. 28–29)

Women were to make themselves obedient to God through psalm-singing and public worship rather than to occupy themselves with preparing special foods and worrying over their sabbath-day appearance.

Thacher, Danforth, and Danforth (1723) permitted, urged, and nearly required women to sing. They cautioned, however, that women should not become singing teachers. They cited 1 Corinthians 14:34 as their biblical authority and added: "Undoubtedly they *may* and *ought* [to sing in the church]. . . .They are restrained from being *Authoritative Teachers*, as the next verse [verse 35] shows; but not from being *Melodious Singers* there. . ." (pp. 15–16). Children, nonmembers, and unconverted persons were encouraged to sing if they would ". . .behave themselves orderly and inoffensively" (p. 16).[3]

Boston's singing problem was neither new nor unique.[4] The notion of whole-congregation singing was part of the Protestant Reformation in Germany, and the pressure for general literacy in Protestant congregations grew to statutory significance in mid-seventeenth-century England. This movement resulted in mechanisms for learning to read music that included "patent" notation systems, tune book introductions, and singing schools. These mechanisms were placed in service around Boston in the early 1700s. Thacher, Danforth, and Danforth (1723) urged New England congregations to follow the lead in learning to sing by rule of ". . .Boston, Roxbury, Dorchester, Cambridge, Taunton, Bridgewater, Charlstown [*sic*], Ipswich, Newbury, Andover, Bradford, and other Places. . ." (p. 7).

Most American writers advocated the singing-school approach to regular singing. Presumably, singing teachers were to receive a stipend for their services, although little is known about the commercial aspects of early eighteenth-century regular singing beyond the sale of publications. A British clergyman, J. Rowe (1722) warned New Englanders that singing teachers had nothing but commercial motives: Their purpose as a group was to sell knowledge that should have been easily available to everyone. He went on to say that the study of his numeric music reading system materials (available for purchase in the colonies) made paid singing teachers unnecessary.

Thacher, Danforth, and Danforth (1723) revealed that young people not only attended singing schools, but they also pressured older men to do the same. They flaunted their music-reading skill in congregational singing and complained about their elders' defective singing in meetings. This, of course, irritated the older men. Since the older men held the power to decide on congregational programs, this hindered the establishment of singing schools in some congregations and increased the need for assistance through the kind of pamphlets studied by the author while researching this article. Furthermore, the motives of the young people who advocated singing schools were considered suspect. Their real desires were thought by their elders to center more on the increased social opportunities singing schools provided than on musical learning. Symmes (1723) discounted parental objections to regular singing (that singing schools gave young people an excuse to ". . . tarry out a[t] nights disorderly") by pointing out that singing psalms was preferable to ". . . learning *Idle, Foolish,* yea *pernicious Songs* and *Ballads,* and [singing schools will] banish such *Trash* from their Minds. . ." [italics in original] (p. 17).

The older men used age as an excuse for staying away from singing schools. They claimed that they were too old to learn a new way of singing, but Thacher, Danforth, and Danforth (1723) quoted Symmes (1720, 14) as an authority (without citing him) to counter this claim: ". . . many have learnt to Sing by Note, some upwards of Forty Years of Age, who never could (tho' they be desirous of it) ever learn one Tune in the usual way."

Despite the dangers that young people would use singing schools for social purposes or would treat psalm-singing lightly (Symmes 1720, 17) and that singing teachers had commercial motives, the leading clergymen and intellectuals advocated that whole congregations—men, women, and children—learn to read music in two or three evenings per week, instructed by a skilled person. In country parishes, the schoolmasters were advised to teach singing,[5] and all ministers were to encourage their congregations to learn to sing by rule (Symmes 1720, 20, 21).

Several inferences can be made from these writings: Women (and children) were being urged to join congregational singing, primarily for religious reasons; public singing was largely associated with adult males (in and probably out of churches); and the advantages of adding a social dimension to evening singing schools by urging women and children to attend were not lost on those who advocated this method of reform.[6] The picture that emerges from these writings is simply that women did not engage in public singing. The decade of the 1720s in Boston is remarkable in music education history because of the scholarly attention that Boston's intellectual and religious elite gave to music literacy and the persistence with which they argued for regular singing and singing schools as the preferred means for its implementation. It is also remarkable for its contrast with the current state of affairs in America.

AMERICA IN THE 1980s

Public singing in America is still alive if not well. The ubiquity of choral programs in schools, places of worship, and communities provides both men and women ample opportunities to engage in public singing, and singing at public events is still widely practiced. Current American choral directors find that a primary challenge of that work is the recruitment of male singers. Although enrolling large numbers of female singers in choruses is far from automatic, the statement that characterizes our national condition in this regard is that public singing is a female pursuit. Despite some pockets of strong male involvement (in folk singing, in entertainment and commercial music, in barbershop choruses, in shape-note singing [Kelton 1984], and in college male choruses), singing among American males has probably never been held in lower regard. Outside of choruses, male singing has all but disappeared from taverns; singing in gatherings of fraternal organizations and service clubs is perfunctorily engaged in for largely forgotten purposes; and male singing in church congregations and sporting events arguably lacks not only skill but spirited commitment to singing or the social benefits of this activity.

Recent data add substance to these impressions. Table 1 shows that the gap between sexes in singing outside of school widened sharply with age, especially during the junior high school years of those who are now young adults.

Instrumental and vocal music participation in American secondary schools shows sharp sex-related differences (see Table 2). Although the sexes are equally divided in instrumental music involvement, the female percentage of the secondary school population involved in choral activities surpasses the male percentage by greater than a 5:2 margin.

These ratios seem to reflect a relatively new phenomenon. As recently as fifty years ago, a more balanced ratio was apparent. In 1932–33, 28.3 percent of high school boys and 29.9 percent of high school girls were in choruses (Reavis and Van Dyke 1933, Fig. 12, p. 95). Sex separation was promoted within chorus programs and in many other aspects of school life, and sex ranked third (after interest and ability) as a qualification for extracurricular activity membership (p. 98). Despite the relatively high percentage of high school students in choruses, only 10.4 percent of high school choral members continued vocal music activities in adult life (pp. 154, 155), and music groups ranked eighth on a list of twelve extracurricular activities that alumni recommended to freshmen (p. 162).

More recently, during the second National Assessment of Educational Progress (NAEP) in music (1978–79), 83.0 percent of nine-year-old boys and 85.8 percent of nine-year-old girls reported being taught music in school in that school year (NAEP 1981, Table 12, p. 33). Almost half of the nine-year-old children (47.2 percent of the boys and 47.5 percent of the girls) said they sang "just for fun" in their music classes (NAEP 1981, Table 16, p. 36). Despite this widespread involvement of both sexes in

Table 1
Responses on Singing from the Second National Assessment of Educational Progress in Music

	Percentage of "yes" responses	
Age-group	Males	Females
Sing just for fun?		
Age 9	38.3[a]	52.5[a]
Age 13	47.1	72.8
Age 17	58.0	83.7
Sing with friends for fun?		
Age 9	30.4	49.7
Age 13	24.6	57.5
Age 17	34.4	62.7
Sing in a church or community music group?		
Age 9	42.4	44.9
Age 13	22.6	30.9
Age 17	15.1	25.4
At least one of the above?		
Age 9	69.0	81.0
Age 13	59.6	84.2
Age 17	63.8	88.3

[a]All data statistically significant at the .05 level.
Data from the National Assessment of Educational Progress (NAEP), 1981, Table 10, pp. 30–31.

elementary school general music, only 3.3 percent of nine-year-old boys and 5.8 percent of nine-year-old girls said they would sing in a music group if they had one free period a day in school (NAEP 1981, Table 5, p. 12).

Responses of nine-, thirteen-, and seventeen-year olds were nearly equal between the sexes to the question, "Can music change the way you feel?" The three age-groups responded affirmatively at 73.6, 93.6, and

Table 2
Secondary School Student Participation in Vocal and Instrumental Music Groups

	Percentage		
Group	All	Males	Females
Band/orchestra	20.7	20.9	20.4
Choir/choral groups	17.6	9.1	24.9

Data from the National Association of Secondary School Principals (NASSP), 1984, p. 17.

96.3 percent, respectively. At no age level were the sexes separated in respect to this question by more than 2.4 percentage points (NAEP 1981, Table 6, p. 13; these results are statistically nonsignificant at the .05 level). Despite this nearly unanimous agreement about the emotional powers of music, both male and female secondary students' ratings of music class placed it sixteenth in importance in a list of eighteen school subjects, but both sexes rated music second to sports and fitness and ahead of automobiles in importance in everyday life among a list of eight activities. In a 1987 Roper Poll (Greer and Gude 1987) 95 percent of a national sample of American young people ($N = 1,000$) reported feeling good about being Americans. But, as a group, the young people polled ranked singing "The Star-Spangled Banner" last in a list of ways to express their patriotism. Also, in high schools, 52.6 percent of female students and 33.6 percent of male students listed music as a hobby or special interest, but 3.5 percent of female students and 1.3 of male students (another ratio greater than 5:2) listed music as a career they were interested in pursuing, according to the National Association of Secondary School Principals (NASSP 1984, pp. 10, 27, 28, 62). Although large percentages of students of both sexes find music attractive and important in out-of-school life, very small percentages are willing to commit their time and effort to involvement in a choral group or to exploring music as a career.

Sex differences in most performance tasks on the first NAEP in music were not wide. There was, however, an important sex difference in singing ability:

> Females of all ages generally attained higher percentages of acceptable scores on the performance items than did their male counterparts. . . . The exercises that involved singing familiar songs like "America" and the round ["Are you Sleeping"] were the exercises upon which the greatest discrepancy between male and female scores appeared. On these exercises, as many as 20 or 30 points separated the male from the female percentages. (Rivas 1974, p. 25)

In addition to differences in singing behavior between sexes, social values (e.g., sex steteotyping) have historically produced other differences in behavior between sexes (as in type of clothing, hair styles, and occupational choices). Sex-related differences in some of these general behaviors, however, are beginning to disappear. Reported motivations for getting college degrees, for instance, show that males and females differ in expressing these values far less today than they did as recently as 1975 (see Figure 1). Not only are male and female college students' motivational profiles becoming adrogynously "bunched," but the direction and amount of change within the individual values represented in Figure 1 are similar between sexes over the last two decades.

CONCLUSION

The picture that emerges from these data is clear: We can reasonably infer that 2½ centuries ago in Boston, males dominated public singing. Data from the 1930s indicate that membership in high school choruses

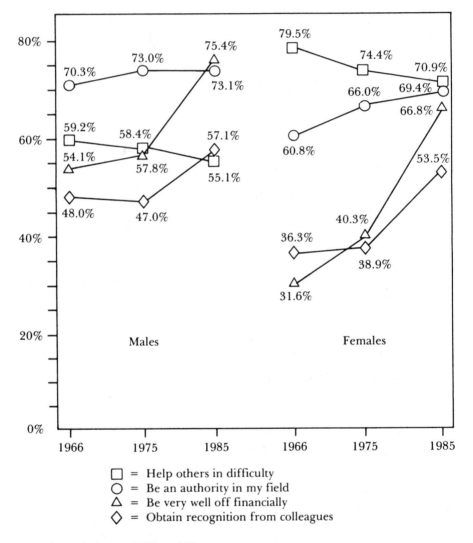

= Help others in difficulty
= Be an authority in my field
= Be very well off financially
= Obtain recognition from colleagues

Data from Ottinger, 1987, p. 135.

Figure 1. Objectives considered to be very important in getting a college degree (other than to raise a family).

was equally divided between sexes. Today, males who are now young adults in our society were far less willing to be identified publicly with singing as secondary school students than were females, and the data do not bode well for a turnaround. Music educators have cause to be alarmed at what these data confirm about the public singing attitudes of American males.[7]

There can be no doubt that a gradual but profound shift has occurred. Women of early eighteenth-century Boston had to be coaxed to sing in public by men, inferring that women did not. Parity was apparently reached in American high schools as recently as the 1930s. Today, the American men whose musical activities of a decade ago reflected little involvement in choral singing are hard to recruit for choruses. This apparent inversion of the sexes' commitment to public singing was gradual enough over 265 years to escape correction by many generations of music educators. Changes this gradual are not explained easily.

Research on music participation has revealed weak explanations of the dropout–retention phenomenon, at least in instrumental music (Gates 1988c). Results suggest that music participation, including public singing, is based on grounds much broader than the questions asked in such research. In this article, I make the assumption that public singing is the expression of social values—probably those based on sex steretyping and status attainment—rather than being motivated by educational pedagogical, or aesthetic interests. Although a further analysis of the relationship of social values and singing behavior is certainly warranted, it is safe to begin to assume that the social behavior of both sexes, possibly including public singing, is expressive of increasingly androgynous social values (see Figure 1). Sex steretyping, at least, may be disappearing as the basis for certain traditional differences in behavior between sexes. If it is true that public singing is an expression of social values, and if females are adopting previously male social values (as Figure 1 may indicate), then the percentage of girls and women involved in public singing should gradually drop to that of boys and men.

An alternative interpretation based on a cursory examination of these data might seem to be that women have replaced men in singing leadership in our society. Missing from this explanation, however, is the kind of reasoned advocacy for singing directed toward the opposite sex that influential men displayed in early eighteenth-century Boston. The analytical attention that Walter, Mather, Symmes, and other intellectual leaders lavished on musical literacy and singing in the earlier era gave music literacy advocates an advantage that is not present today. Like these earlier male intellectuals, twentieth-century female leaders have directed their influence toward a wide range of social issues. Unlike those of eighteenth-century Boston men, however, modern women's wide-ranging interests do not include arguing for music literacy or expressing concern for the low percentage of boys and men in public singing. The feminization of the music teaching profession during the last century in the United States has not been sufficient to fill this leadership gap.

Clearly, the explanation that there has been some sort of singing leadership inversion between the sexes is not plausible. There is little evidence that leading women who do not have a vested interest in recruiting male singers for specific choruses consider increased male singing (or music literacy) to be much of an issue.

This historical trend deserves analysis, however, because of what it portends for the future of choral participation among the general population. (Select choruses probably will not be affected.) The slow rate of the change in public singing noted in this article suggests that hypotheses that relate broad social values to public singing will illuminate the phenomenon best. It is clear from the eighteenth-century writings that men sang heartily, if not well, and sang out of an expressed conviction that they were duty-bound to do so, a conviction that was reinforced because it was based on ascendent social and religious values.

The variety of rationales used by early nineteenth-century music educators and others to support public singing by girls and women (see Birge [1939] for a good account) probably helped music educators tap some important social values in support of women's involvement in singing. Men led this effort too; public singing was already socially reinforcing to adolescent and adult men, and it apparently continued to be so until sometime after the 1930s. The drastic reduction in the percentage of boys in high school choruses from the 1930s to the present is further evidence that the basis for reinforcement of American boys' singing has eroded. The involvement of high school girls in choruses is little changed in percentage now from the level it was in the 1930s (see Table 2). The similarity in percentages suggests that public singing is at least as reinforcing for girls now as it was in the decade prior to World War II. The current trend toward the androgyny of expressions of some social values (see Figure 1), however, unfortunately seems to presage an erosion of this reinforcement.

The explanation that seems to account for the facts (and deserves deeper analysis) is that the social and cultural values that drive public singing behavior (probably those based on sex sterotyping) are not as highly regarded today as they were in Boston of the 1720s or American high schools of the 1930s. It is reasonable to expect that public singing will become less and less reinforcing to women as we approach the turn of the century. Singing seems to have been reinforcing to early eighteenth-century men and early twentieth-century boys. We cannot draw this same conclusion about the American male's current interest in public singing.

Writings urging early eighteenth-century Boston women to feel duty-bound to sing in public worship would have been received as shallow and legalistic if they were not based on strong cultural and social values. These writings were serious urgings written by knowledgeable and influential men. It would be difficult to expect the same sort of seriousness from similar leaders today. The confluence of cultural, social, and political factors that supported calls for public singing and music literacy in Boston in the 1720s or in American high schools in the

1930s is not in evidence today, and a serious advocacy for public singing from America's intellectual elite (of either sex) is nonexistent.

IMPLICATIONS

For these basic reasons, music educators must expect that the percentage of women in choruses will decline. Members of the profession now must resolve to base choral programs on a clearer view of currently ascendant social and cultural values than some of our current practices display. These values go deeper than musical or educational (or communications-industry) fashions, which are merely expressions of these values. Fashions, including popular music styles, can be thought of as behavior expressive of a social value that reinforces a controlled change. The value foundations of behavior (such as fashion) are difficult to isolate and name, but there are choral leaders currently solving the problem of recruiting and retaining students of both sexes. Information about successful practice not only deserves the wide dissemination it currently gets, but it also needs much deeper analysis. Such analysis can provide the solid foundations for lasting remedies to choral recruiting problems. More important, it can contribute to an adequate theory of music participation and a higher quality of professional criticism.

The job ahead is to integrate an intelligent, professionally defensible theory of music participation with theories of aesthetic values. Because of our traditionally artistic orientations, reconciling what will seem like excesses on the side of social values with our musical values will require considerable skill. This discussion will be neither comforting nor easy, but it must begin soon in the choral and general music fields. Professionally, we will not only need to take immediate and massive steps to slow the movement of American males away from public singing, but we will also need to increase our attention to recruiting and retaining female singers as well. Regrettably, the indications are clear that women's interest in public singing will decline to the level of men's. We will need to read the signs of similar trends better in the future.

NOTES

1. The entire preface is quoted in Finney (1966, 165–6). The authorship of this "Publisher's Preface" is somewhat unclear. Samuel Gerrish published the 1723 Tufts, as he did practically all the extant material having to do with the Boston regular singing movement of the 1720s (Gates 1988a). There is evidence that Gerrish felt strongly about this matter, but there is nothing to suggest that he would have (or could have) written so eloquently about it. Lowens (1964) ascribed Gerrish's interest in the movement to commercial motives (pp. 39ff.). This allegation, in my opinion, deserves review, although few clues to the truth of this matter remain. It would seem that, if the regular singing movement provided an unusually good market, other publishers would have been selling in it. Gerrish seems to have left nothing in print more creative than advertising copy and handbills for his book auction business, and my efforts to locate his personal and business papers have proved unsuccessful. Until evidence to the contrary emerges, we must assume that Tufts was the author of this passage, although few samples of his writing are extant. I believe that the writer could have just as easily been Thomas Symmes or, perhaps more

likely, Thomas Walter. The resolution of this question is important to music education historians since the purview of its author adds to or subtracts from its plausibility. For the present, I will accept Tufts (of Newbury-Port, a day's journey from Boston) as author, with Gerrish's assent as evidence that the passage fairly represented the actual state of affairs in the region. (See also Britton and Lowens 1953; Crawford and Krummel 1983; Gates 1988b; and Lowens 1954.)

2. For a collection of reprinted primary sources about this controversy, see Hood (1846). For contemporary scholarship about the regular singing movement, see Britton (1950) or Lowens (1964) and Temperley (1981). Britton (1950, 23–60) provided a brief analysis of the politico-religious context of regular singing in the early 1700s and discussed the movement's most important printed matter extant in 1950 in a dissertation that Metcalf (1968, viii) called the ". . . most essential single source for accurate and reasonably complete bibliographical information on American tune books through 1800."

3. In 1 Corinthians 13 and 14, the writer discussed spiritual gifts and charged those who display them with the dual requirement that they be motivated by love and that they benefit others in the gathering. Verses 34 and 35 of Chapter 14 come near the close of this passage: "As in all the churches of the saints, women are to remain quiet at meetings since they have no permission to speak; they must keep in the background as the Law itself lays it down. If they have questions to ask, they should ask their husbands at home: it does not seem right for a woman to raise her voice at meetings" (Jones 1966, 306–7). In 1 Timothy 2:11–12, this view was reinforced: "During instruction, a woman should be quiet and respectful. I am not giving permission for a woman to teach or to tell a man what to do" (Jones, 1966, 359). Biblical scholars assert that Paul's letters to Timothy were written by a trusted associate (see Jones 1966, 264), and there is some controversy about the authorship of his letters to the Church at Corinth. Other parts of the second chapter of 1 Timothy support Mather's (1741) admonishments about women's sabbath-day concerns for their appearance. Denying women the right to teach singing on these biblical grounds while burdening them with the responsibility to sing in church services may seem to split hairs; but ample other foundations exist in the Bible in support of public singing by women, especially in the Old Testament. In addition, most New Testament scholars now agree that Paul's associate did not write either the passage in Corinthians, nor did he write the similar passage found in 1 Timothy 2:11–12; both sections were added later by editors and probably represent inaccurate interpretations of Paul's message, since many women played an active role in the early Hellenic Christian Church.

4. Lucas Osiander, who died in 1604, was motivated by the poor state of psalm-singing in Nurenberg to move the melody to the top staff in printed congregational music so that psalm tunes were ". . . set in such a way that the whole congregation [including women] can join in them" (quoted in Liemohn 1953, 48). Early seventeenth-century British sources, however, mentioned boys but not women in the endeavor to improve congregational singing (see Dearnley 1970, 148ff). Attempts to have trained singers (i.e., a choir) support congregational singing, a consistent panacea since the Reformation, met with the same result as it does today. The assignment to the choir of the responsibility for the singing ". . . either made the congregation mute or left them to their own unharmonious devices" (Dearnley 1970, 149).

Church music in the British Isles during the turbulent mid-seventeenth century was affected by political matters: the contentious reign of Charles I, the Civil War and Protectorate, and the restoration of the monarchy under Charles II. (For a much-disputed account, see Burney 1789; see also Scholes 1934.) The duty of singing and of obtaining psalmbooks and learning to read them was extended beyond the choir by a 1644 House of Lords ordinance, which reads: "It is the duty of Christians to praise God publickly by singing of psalms together, in the congregation, and also privately in the family. In singing of psalms the voice is to be audibly and gravely ordered; but the chief care must be to sing with understanding and with grace in the heart, making melody unto the Lord. That the whole congregation may join herein, every one that can read is to have a psalm-book, and all others, not disabled by age or otherwise, are to be exhorted to learn to read. But for the present, where many in the congregation cannot read, it is convenient that the minister, or some fit person appointed by him and the other ruling officers, do read the psalm, line by line, before the singing thereof" (Ordinance passed in the British House of Lords, 4 January, 1644, quoted in Burney 1789, Vol. 2, p. 341).

It was during and after the period of this edict that printed psalmbooks, containing not only the metricized Psalms but some music also, began to appear in large numbers in England. Musical writings by John Playford and Thomas Ravenscroft were among the most admired and used. Following continental reformationists, seventeenth-century British Puritans severely restricted music in churches to the singing of the Psalms and made literacy a high priority. Both the restriction to Psalms and the religious duty to sing them persisted in the assumptions underlying eighteenth-century treatises about psalm singing in New England: All were to sing Psalms. The demand for music literacy, however, had not been reflected in early Boston practice, and this demand resurfaced in Boston during the 1720s.

5. The admonition that schoolmasters should teach singing when no singing teacher was available was apparently an American idea. Its persistence in the present will not be lost on most readers. The assumption that elementary education majors should learn to teach music as part of their preparations comes from an idea that predates the American Revolution. Because most elementary education majors are women, the future of this professional practice may be in doubt.

6. Hood's (1846) lively account of the controversy and what was known of attempts to resolve it through music education included long quotations from sources of the period. Although much has been learned about this era since Birge (1939) summarized the establishment of eighteenth-century singing schools, recent music education historians have drawn from this research few insights more instructive than those of Birge.

7. Some of these data are reprinted in Steinel 1984.

REFERENCES

Birge, Edward Bailey. 1939. *History of public school music in the United States—new and augmented edition*. Boston: Oliver Ditson Co.

Bonner, John. 1722. *[Map of] The town of Boston in New England*. Boston: Captain John Bonner and William Price.

Britton, Allen P. 1950. *Theoretical introductions in American tune books to 1800*. Ann Arbor, MI: University Microfilms, No. 1505.

Britton, Allen P., and Irving Lowens. 1953. Unlocated titles in early American sacred music. *Music Library Association Notes* 11 (December):33–48.

Burney, Charles. 1789. *A general history of music*. (Reprinted in 1957 by Dover Publications, New York.)

Crawford, Richard, and D. W. Krummel. 1983. Early American music printing and publishing. In *Printing and society in early America*, ed. William Leonard Joyce et al., 186–227. Worcester, MA: American Antiquarian Society.

Dearnley, Christopher. 1970. *English church music 1650–1750*. New York and London: Oxford University Press.

Finney, Theodore M. 1966. The third edition of Tufts' *Introduction to the art of singing psalm-tunes*. *Journal of Research in Music Education* 14 (Fall):163–70.

Franklin, Benjamin, V, ed. 1980. *Boston printers, publishers, and booksellers, 1640–1800*. Boston: G. K. Hall.

Gates, J. Terry. 1988a. Samual Gerrish, publisher to the 'regular singing movement' in 1720s New England. *Music Library Association Notes* 45 (September):15–22.

Gates, J. Terry. 1988b. A comparison of the tune books of Tufts and Walter. *Journal of Research in Music Education* 36 (Fall):169–93.

Gates, J. Terry. 1988c. Recruiting and retention studies: Rethinking the assumptions. Research paper presented at the New York State School Music Association Annual Convention, November 29, 1988, Kiamesha Lake, New York. (Manuscript available from the author: c/o Music Department, SUNY at Buffalo, Buffalo, NY 14260.)

Greer, Cynthia, and Karl Gude. 1987. Parents doing OK, national survey says. Associated Press. *Naperville [Illinois] Sun*, 26 November, 6C. (Nationally syndicated report of poll by The Roper Organization.)

Hood, George. [1846] 1970. *A history of music in New England*. Reprint. New York: Johnson Reprint Corporation.

Kelton, Mai Hogan. 1984. Analysis of the music curriculum of *The Sacred Harp* (American tune book, 1971 edition) and its continuing traditions. Ed.D. diss., University of Alabama, Tuscaloosa.

Liemohn, Edwin. 1953. *The chorale*. Philadelphia: Muhlenberg Press.

Lowens, Irving. 1954. John Tufts' *Introduction to the singing of psalm-tunes* (1721–1744): The first American music textbook. *Journal of Research in Music Education* 2 (Winter):89–102.

Lowens, Irving. 1964. *Music and musicians in early America*. New York: Norton.

Mather, Cotton. 1721. *The accomplished singer*. Boston: Samuel Gerrish.

Mather, Cotton. 1741. *Ornaments for the daughters of Zion*. 3d ed. Boston: S. Kneeland and T. Green.

Metcalf, Frank J. 1968. *American psalmody*. New York: Da Capo. (Originally issued in 1917 by Heartman, New York.)

National Assessment of Educational Progress (NAEP). 1981. *Music 1971–79: Results from the second national music assessment* (Report No. 10-MU-01, November). Denver: Education Commission of the States.

National Association of Secondary School Principals (NASSP). 1984. *The mood of American youth*. Washington, DC: National Association of Secondary School Principals.

Ottinger, Cecilia A. (comp.). 1987. *1986–87 fact book on higher education*. New York: American Council on Education and Macmillan.

Reavis, William, and George E. Van Dyke. 1933. *Nonathletic extracurriculum activities* (Bulletin 1932. No. 17: National Survey of Secondary Education; Monograph No. 26). Washington, DC: U.S. Office of Education.

Rivas, Frank W. 1974. *The first national assessment of musical performance* (Report 03-MU-01). Denver: Education Commission of the States.

Rowe, J. 1722. *Singing of psalms by seven constituted sounds, opened and explained*. Boston: N.p.

Scholes, Percy A. 1934. *The puritan and music: In England and New England*. London: Oxford University Press.

Steinel, Daniel V., ed. 1984. *Music and music education: Data and information*. Reston, VA: Music Educators National Conference.

Symmes, Thomas. 1720. *The reasonableness of regular singing*. Boston: Samuel Gerrish.

Symmes, Thomas. 1723. *Utile dulci*. Boston: Samuel Gerrish.

Temperley, Nicholas. 1981. The old way of singing: Its origins and development. *American Musicological Society Journal* 34:511–44.

Thacher, Peter, John Danforth, and Samuel Danforth. 1723. *Cases of conscience about singing psalms*. Boston: Samuel Gerrish.

Tufts, John. 1721. *An introduction to the art of singing psalm-tunes*. Boston: Samuel Gerrish (unlocated, but see Britton and Lowens 1953).

Tufts, John. 1723. *An introduction to the art of singing psalm-tunes*. 3d ed. Boston: Samuel Gerrish.

Tufts, John. 1726. *An introduction to the singing of psalm-tunes*. 5th ed. Boston: Samuel Gerrish.

Tufts, John. 1728. *An introduction to the singing of psalm-tunes*. 7th ed. Boston: Samuel Gerrish.

Walter, Thomas. 1721. *The grounds and rules of musicke explained*. Boston: Samuel Gerrish.

Walter, Thomas. 1722. *Sweet psalmist of Israel*. Boston: Samuel Gerrish.

Walter, Thomas. 1723. *The grounds and rules of musicke explained*. 2d ed. Boston: Samuel Gerrish.

Watts, Isaac. 1715. *Honey out of the rock*. Boston: Samuel Gerrish.

September 9, 1987

FRAY PEDRO DE GANTE PIONEER AMERICAN MUSIC EDUCATOR

George Heller

JRME 1979, VOLUME 27, NUMBER 1, PAGES 20–28

Fray Pedro de Gante was an important figure in the history of American music education. His life and work in Mexico City predate similar activities in the United States by at least a century. He worked in a radically changing ethnic and sociocultural environment and was a principal agent in the acculturation process. In teaching music he also became involved in the arts in general education, multicultural education, and student teaching. He was the first European to teach music in the Western hemisphere and taught thousands of students during his 45-year tenure. His school served as a model for later Franciscan schools in the southwestern United States. The documents show that he was not only successful by European standards, but that he was also highly respected and admired by the Indians he taught.

Key Words: cultural background, geographical environment, historical period, historical research, music teacher, socioeconomic status, teaching ability.

In *Foundations and Principles of Music Education,* Charles Leonhard and Robert House (1959, p. 39) note the need for music teachers to know the history of music education. They point out the need to understand continuity, growth and development, antecedents and consequences, and the context in which music has developed in American schools. Their argument is contained in the statement, "Without doubt, the issues in music education today have been met in other forms by our predecessors."

Four centuries ago, Fray Pedro de Gante faced challenges that still confront today's serious-minded music educators. That he handled them successfully makes it worthwhile to know more about him; that he did things in music education for the first time in the Western hemisphere makes the study of his life and work even more important. Many of the current ideas in music education—career education,

Fray Pedro de Gante is portrayed here by the artist Aubin.

the arts in general education, and multicultural education—are not new. These ideas and others are part of the introduction of European music in the schools of the Western hemisphere. The story may not be well known not only because the time of its occurence is remote and the place somewhat distant, but also because the primary sources are not yet readily available in English.

The introduction of European music, and with it European language, religion, politics, economics, and culture, is a pivotal point in the history of American music and music education. Though it is difficult to ascertain in the literature, music education held a vital role in pre-Columbian America. What occurred in Mexico City during the sixteenth century was not so much an initiation as it was a transformation. As with many other signal events in the history of music education, a single personality was the dynamic force behind the event. Fray Pedro de Gante's work in Mexico City from 1523 to 1572 succeeded in transplanting the achievements of Renaissance Europe in the New World. It demonstrates an interesting contrast with the failure of similar efforts by missionaries to merge the European and indigenous cultures in the United States a century later.

De Gante's success was probably the result of his background of education and experience, his energetic attitude toward his mission, and his skill in human relations. Though he faced many problems, he was also blessed with some fortuitous circumstances. He worked in an area that was formerly an imperial capital, and the people with whom he worked had a heritage that included music education in a context not unlike that which de Gante sought to develop.

The primary sources for de Gante are his five extant letters, reports from his contemporaries, and a short biography written by a colleague in the Convent of San Francisco in Mexico City. The first letter was written on July 27, 1529, from Mexico City and was addressed to his brothers and sisters in Flanders. The second, third, and fourth letters were written in Mexico City and were all to the Spanish King (and Holy Roman Emperor) Charles V; they were dated October 31, 1532; July 20, 1548; and February 15, 1552. The fifth letter was to Philip II and was written shortly after the death of his father, Charles V. It was sent from Mexico City and dated June 23, 1558 (Heller, 1973, pp. 155–185). The short biography by Mendieta was part of a four-volume study on the work of the Franciscans among the Indians of Mexico, first published in 1596 (Mendieta, 1945, pp. 53–57).

Pedro de Gante lived the first 40 years of his life in Flanders, in what is now Belgium. Both his letters and Mendieta's biography state that he was born in Ygüen, a town that is probably the equivalent of the modern Ayghem-St. Pierre on the outskirts of Ghent. The date of his birth is not known, but a report to the inspector-general of the Council of the Indies, written in late 1569 or early 1570, gives his age as 90 years (García Icazbalceta, 1941, p. 7). This would make his birth date either 1479 or 1480.

His early years saw the twilight of an era of opulence for Flanders and its Burgundian rulers. Situated in the delicate balance between France,

Germany, and England, Flanders reached a cultural zenith in the fifteenth century. Life in the great cities of Bruges, Ghent, Liége, Louvain, Brussels, and Dijon was the most cosmopolitan in Europe from 1420 to 1460. It was even rated as superior to life in Florence, then under the spell of the great Cosimo de' Medici (Durante, 1957, p. 127).

Following this grand climax, the road downhill began with the merger of Burgundy and Austria. Flanders became part of the dowry of the daughter of a Burgundian prince, thus being attached to the Hapsburg Empire. Ultimately, the area became a part of the Holy Roman Empire when Charles V began his reign in 1515.

This homeland of de Gante was in the midst of another turmoil that was greater than the political machinations of kings and emperors—the Reformation. Martin Luther was but four years younger than de Gante and was also a cleric with a pioneering mission. Savonarola in Florence, Erasmus in Flanders and England, and Henry VIII in England were beginning to influence events. The printing presses of Venice, Germany, and Paris were initiating popular, vernacular, and secular currents that would continue through modern times. In music, de Gante could hardly have avoided the achievements of Franco-Flemish polyphony. His youth and early adulthood were the years in which Ockeghem, Tinctoris, Obrecht, Isaac, Josquin, Glareanus, Pierre de la Rue, and many others were reaching maturity.

De Gante's music education was probably taken at the University of Louvain in Flanders (González Vera, 1868, p. 383). According to Carpenter, Louvain was modeled after the University of Cologne (Carpenter, 1959, p. 240) where music held a traditional place in the mathematical quadrivium along with arithmetic, geometry, and astronomy. Texts were by such classic authors as Aristotle, Isidorus, and Boethius. The *Musica* of Jean de Muris was required reading. Rudolf Agricola probably was on the Louvain faculty at the time of de Gante's study. Louvain also followed the English practice of providing scholarships for boys who provided the music for the cathedral, an example de Gante followed later in Mexico City.

In the midst of this atmosphere of music achievement, political change, social and religious turmoil, and incipient decline from greatness, Charles V came to Ghent in 1522 bringing news of Cortés's discovery and conquest of Mexico. That year de Gante was living in the Franciscan convent of Ghent under the command of Fray Juan de Tecto. He and another Franciscan priest, Fray Juan de Ayora, petitioned the King to be allowed to go to the New World to evangelize the Indians. Permission was granted.

The three Franciscans departed Ghent on April 27, 1522, and went in the retinue of the King of England to visit Charles V's sister, Catherine of Aragon. The royal entourage arrived in Spain at the port of Santander on July 22, 1522. Thus, de Gante and his two companions became part of the great Flemish emigration that saw Josquin, Isaac, and many others achieve fame in other lands. According to de Gante's first letter, they departed Seville on May 1, 1523, and arrived in Mexico at the port of Villa Rica on August 13, then traveled inland to Mexico City (Heller, 1973, pp. 155–159).

The conquest of Mexico City by Cortés in 1519 left most of the former Aztec capital in ruins, and the rebuilding was not completed when the three Franciscans arrived in Autumn of 1523. They therefore went to the city of Texcoco, the capital city of a tribe that had been allied with Cortés, which was across the lake from Mexico City. The missionaries were cordially welcomed by Cortés and the Texcocoan chieftain, Ixtlilxochitl, whose grandson of the same wrote an account of the occasion. In that account, he noted that the three friars were given rooms for a school in the palaces of a former chieftain, Nezahualcoyotzin (Ixtlilxochitl, 1952, p. 398).

The friars had to learn the language before evangelizing the Indians. De Gante described the task as being so difficult that it was accomplished not by him, but by God. He complained of the lack of letters and writing that might have served him as aides to learning the idiom. Whatever the difficulties may have been, sources agree that he not only learned the language better than either of his two companions, but was also more proficient than any of the later arrivals. Bishop Zumárraga testified to de Gante's excellence in the language of the Aztecs, as well as his diligence in caring for 600 youths or more, in a letter to Franciscans in France, dated June 12, 1532 (Oroz, Mendieta, and Suárez, 1947, p. 55). De Gante was not always easily understood by his Spanish-speaking colleagues, but Mendieta wrote that the Indians had no difficulty in understanding him when he spoke Nahuatl (Mendieta, 1945, pp. 53–54).

De Gante's first school for the sons of leaders of the Indian tribes was opened in Texcoco sometime prior to the arrival of Fray Martín de Valencia and his group of 12 Franciscans in 1524. During the day at Texcoco he taught his students to read, write, and sing; at night he preached and taught Christian doctrine. In the Spring of 1527 he moved the school to Mexico City. By 1529, eighteen months after moving the school, he wrote that he was teaching reading, writing, singing, and religion to 500 sons of the leading Indian families. Since he had so many students and only two assistants, he developed a system of training the most able students to become his assistants.

De Gante ran more than a school for the Indian boys. His building served as chapel, school, and community gathering place for the entire Indian community in Mexico City. He supervised the work of educating the young and spreading the Spanish and Catholic heritage throughout the area. He spread his influence to the surrounding countryside, erecting churches and schools, and staffing them with his graduates. According to one source, he built as many as 100 churches in the Valley of Mexico during his years there (Mendieta, 1945, pp. 54–55).

Comprehensive arts education or "the arts in general education" were not familiar terms in de Gante's time, but he was an outstanding practitioner of these "new" ideas. He had studios built adjacent to his school for his children to learn painting. He taught arts and crafts, stone masonry, carpentry, sewing, and embroidery, as well as music and the academic subjects. He organized groups (cofraídas) of singers and instrumentalists to provide music for the churches, and he organized groups of craftsmen and artists to decorate them. These groups were probably modeled after the guilds that abounded in Flanders in his youth and were similar to those known to have been in existence at the University of Louvain and other schools that followed the English system of allowing boys to work their way through school.

The number of students who attended his school attest to de Gante's popularity and success. His letters follow the growth of the school until it reached 1,000 students in 1589. Judging from the sorrow that swept the country when he died, he remained popular and his school continued to flourish.

De Gante's sensitivity in working with the Indians was best demonstrated in an event reported to Philip II in the letter of 1558. In that letter, he tells of how he discovered the importance of music in religious celebrations in pre-conquest times. Noting the importance of dance and vocal and instrumental music to the Aztecs, he provided the students with dance costumes on which religious motifs had been painted. Then he set verses written in Nahuatl to Indian tunes. The verses were from the Catechism that he translated and adapted so the Indians could sing them to familiar tunes.

The fifth letter also describes in some detail the daily routine of the students under de Gante's supervision. The report reveals that the character of the school was similar to that of a monastery. The students observed canonical hours, reciting and singing the divine offices. This regimen was probably a case of de Gante teaching as he had been taught rather than an attempt to prepare the Indian boys to take ecclesiastical orders.

In his later letters, de Gante's concern seems to be more with the social problems of his students than with the academic. He writes less about how well they are doing in learning music and other subjects and more about how they are being mistreated by the Spaniards. He exposed at great length the injustices and abuses the Indians were forced to endure, and he was not afraid to invoke the king's favor to help win support for his proposals for reform. The problems for the Indians seemed to increase with the rise of Spanish immigration and the decline of Spain's wealth and political power in Europe.

De Gante also suffered some difficulties in his relations with his contemporaries as a result of his outspoken defense of the Indians. Rumors were a nagging problem for him to contend with. One of these concerned a widely circulated notion that he was the illegitimate son of Charles V. This idea is clearly refuted by the fact that he was twenty years old when Charles V was born. Other writers have speculated that he was the son of Philip the Handsome (Duke of Burgundy), but this is hardly likely since the two were about the same age. A close personal relationship did exist between the friar and Charles V, but probably because they were both from Flanders rather than from any blood relationship.

Regardless of his relations with his peers, there can be no question about the feelings of the hundreds of thousands of Indians he served. Mendieta (1945, pp. 54–55) quoted the Archbishop of Mexico, Alonso de Montúfar, who commented on the strength of de Gante's following among the Indians, "I am not the Archbishop of Mexico, but rather, Fray Pedro de Gante, a lay brother of San Francisco." Montúfar was not only describing the high regard the Indians held for their teacher, but he was also aware that de Gante was the first choice of Charles V to be archbishop. De Gante refused this position and he also turned down opportunities for ordination as a priest. The first such offer was made by Pope Paul II, the second was by the provincial-general of the Franciscan order, and the third was by the papal nuncio to the Spanish court in connection with the king's offer to make de Gante the archbishop of New Spain. He apparently felt he could better accomplish his goals in a teaching position that kept him in direct contact with the Indian community.

Among the many incidents reported by his contemporaries is one that underlines the affection of the Indians for de Gante. At one time he was exiled for a short period to a nearby town on the order of the provincial-general. The exile was the result of false testimony that led to a reprimand (Torquemada, 1969, p. 431). Mendieta (1945, p. 55) describes his return to Mexico City:

> The natives also loved this servant of God very much, especially the natives of Mexico City, as they showed on his return from Tlaxcalla, where he had been exiled for a short time. They received him with a beautiful flotilla of canoes, and made a solemn ceremony in the style of a naval combat on the great lake of Texcoco, and they carried him to his quarters with much rejoicing.

Fray Pedro de Gante died in mid-April, 1572. The exact date is not known, but a portrait by a contemporary artist, Aubin, notes that he was buried on Sunday, April 21, 1572. All sources agree on the year, though some speculate that he died on June 29, the day of his patron saint (García Icazbalceta, 1896, pp. 35–56). His death caused great outbreaks of sympathy and mourning among the Indians (Mendieta, 1945, p. 56):

> The natives felt much sadness and pain, and they showed it in public. At his burial many of them shed copious tears, and many of them wore signs of mourning which are normally worn when one's father dies.

Following the official burial rites, each of the cofraídas he founded held separate ceremonies in the various towns and villages in the Valley of Mexico. The offerings given at these various services were much larger than normal, even in the poorest parishes. For many years following his death, services were held and offerings were given in his name for the benefit of the needy. The convent of San Francisco in Mexico City received provisions for the entire year from the memorial services held for de Gante.

The Indians asked and received permission for de Gante to be buried in the chapel of San José where he had spent most of his life teaching. His remains were lost in 1862 when the convent and its chapel were razed to make room for a street that still bears his name, Calle de Gante (García Icazbalceta, 1896, pp. 35–56).

In 1572, the provincial of the Franciscans in New Spain wrote to Philip II to report de Gante's death (González Vera, 1868, p. 386):

> We have lost one of our greatest workers in Fray Pedro de Gante. God took him to his reward as He takes all who serve Him well. It would be a great burden to Your Majesty if I told of all the work he accomplished here, because the country is full of his fame. He was a tireless shepherd, working fifty years and dying among the sheep. . . . The Indians owe him a great debt of gratitude, and we friars are also in his debt for the many favors the very Christian father of Your Majesty granted us because of the close relationship between him and Fray Pedro.

Fray Pedro de Gante's impact on music education in the Western hemisphere was enormous. Almost single-handedly he taught 1,000 students each year. Fully 100 years before any sizeable colonization efforts were noticeable in North America, his students in Mexico City were singing European music, copying Franco-Flemish polyphony, playing and building violins and organs, and composing and teaching music in the European style. His teaching and his school served as models for other Franciscans and their missions throughout Central America and as far north as San Francisco, Arizona, New Mexico, Texas, and Colorado. He may have had a direct influence on Fray Juan de Padilla, also a Franciscan, who was probably the first teacher of European music in what is now the United States.

The problem of cultural change is a pervasive one in music education. It occurs in communities that are experiencing changing socioeconomic characteristics; it happens when new graduates of music schools take their first jobs in small, rural communities, and it happens when adult teachers work with members of the youth culture. The process of cultural change is affected by the degree of change, the intensity of the contact, and the contact agents. The results may be merger, incorporation, or extinction. Pedro de Gante faced a cultural change of immense degree and intense contact. His actions as a contact agent helped control the circumstances of the contact in such a way as to result in merger of the indigenous Indian culture with the immigrant Spanish culture. His success is unparalleled in the history of music education.

References

Carpenter, Nan Cooke. *Music in the medieval and renaissance universities*. Norman, Oklahoma: University of Oklahoma Press, 1959.

Durant, Will. *The reformation. The story of civilization*, (Vol. 6). New York: Simon and Schuster, Inc., 1957.

García Icazbalceta, Joaquín. *Obras* (Vol. 3). Mexico· City: V. Agüeros, 1896.

García Icazbalceta, Joaquín (Ed.). *Códice franciscano*. Mexico City: Salvador Chávez Hayhoe, 1941.

González Vera, Francisco de. *Revista de España* (Vol. 3). 1868.

Heller, G. N. *Music education in the valley of Mexico during the sixteenth century.* Unpublished doctoral dissertation, University of Michigan, 1973.

Ixtlilxochitl, Fernando de Alva. *Obras históricas* (Vol. 1) (Alfredo Chavero, Ed.). Mexico City: Editoria Nacional, 1952.

Leonhard, C., & House, R. *Foundations and principles of music education.* New York: McGraw-Hill Book Company, Inc., 1959.

Mendieta, Fray Gerónimo de. *Historia eclesiástica indiana* (Vol. 4). (Joaquín García Icazbalceta, Ed.). Mexico City: Editorial Chávez Hayhoe, 1945.

Oroz, Pedro; Mendieta, Gerónimo de; & Suárez, Francisco. *Relación de la descripción de la provincia del Santo Evangelio que es en las Indias occidentales que llaman la Nueva España.* (Fidel de J. Chavet, Ed.). Mexico City: Aguilar Reyes, 1947.

Torquemada, Fray Juan de. *Monarquía indiana* (Vol. 3). Mexico City: Editorial Porrua, 1969.

University of Kansas
Lawrence

*The distinguished music scholar Charles L. Seeger (1886–1979) viewed music edu-
cation as playing a critical role in the development of American musical life. During
his long career, he made an important contribution to the history, philosophy, and
sociology of music education. The purpose of this study was to identify a primary
aspect of Seeger's contribution by exploring one of his ongoing professional concerns—
American music for American children. The study progresses from a profile of Seeger
the music educator to his approach to music in American culture, his plan for revi-
talizing music in American education, and, finally, an appraisal of his criticisms
and recommendations. Music in American education, he believed, would better serve
American society if some vital connections with school music were activated
or renewed. The writer identifies these as the child's own music, American vernacular music in general, other music professionals (and particularly musicologists), and
the cultural-political context in which music and education function. Seeger played a
significant role in introducing vernacular music into the schools, in extending the
definition of American music in the curriculum, in presenting music as a cultural
subject, and in assisting music educators in dealing with musical diversity in the
classroom.*

Marie McCarthy, *University of Maryland*

JRME 1995, VOLUME 43, NUMBER 4, PAGES 270–287

On "American Music for American Children": The Contribution of Charles L. Seeger

Charles Seeger is universally acclaimed as one of the foremost
music scholars of the twentieth century. His preeminence was gained
"not because he was famous for any one thing, but for the collec-
tivity of all his contributions to the American music scene and to
American society."[1] Since many of his writings are conceptually complex and semantically dense, scholars have been reluctant to explore
his works and apply his ideas to issues in contemporary music scholarship.[2] Furthermore, Seeger has been viewed narrowly as a musicologist with tenuous connections to music education. An overview of
the major histories of music education in the United States indicates

Marie McCarthy is an assistant professor in the Department of Music, University of
Maryland, College Park, MD 20742.

clearly that Seeger's legacy to and leadership in the profession is minimally acknowledged and totally unexplored.[3] The primary purpose of this article is to present Charles Seeger the music educator—to induct him, as it were, into the annals of music education history—and to begin to explore the wealth of his contribution and legacy to the profession. In a sense, this is a response to Seeger's biographer when she stated: "My hope—and I think his would be, too—is that this book will initiate more in-depth and definitive research into each facet of Seeger's work."[4]

A comprehensive study of Seeger's contributions to music education is not possible within the scope of the present study. This initial exploration focuses on one of the dominant themes of his career—the relationship of music and culture as applied to American society. Within this theme, Seeger frequently addressed "the missionary role of educators in 'making America musical'"[5] and their responsibility in expanding the definition of American music for American children. The motivation for choosing this topic over a host of others from his immense corpus of literature is twofold. First, Seeger was a primary innovator and activist in introducing vernacular music into American public schools in the 1940s. In that capacity, he had a fundamental impact on professional practice and paved the way for subsequent efforts to broaden school music repertoire. Second, an examination of his role in promoting music as a cultural subject in the curriculum provides insights into the multiple dilemmas and paradoxes music educators face today in accommodating diversity and in linking school music with vernacular music culture.

"American Music for American Children," a Seeger article cited in the title of this study, was published in the Novem-ber–December 1942 issue of *Music Educators Journal*.[6] It described the project on "American Songs for American Children," which was presented earlier that year by Seeger, among others, at the national biennial conference of the Music Educators National Conference (MENC) in Milwaukee, Wisconsin. Viewed in the context of his entire career, the title served as a symbol for one of his ongoing professional concerns, and the article may be explored and interpreted at a number of different levels. First, the article communicated to music teachers a new definition of school music and promoted folk music as worthy of inclusion in the curriculum. Second, Seeger's arrival at this perspective was the result of years of forethought and scholarship on the role of music in culture, society, and education. Third, it provided clear testimony of an intellectual and musical journey that Seeger had made from an elite, nineteenth-century view of music for music's sake to a democratic, twentieth-century view of music rooted in its sociocultural functions. Fourth, it demonstrated his quest for a definition of American music beyond the hegemonic European one of previous decades. Finally, his efforts to define American music for American children offered a stimulus for a lively debate in contemporary music education as to the usefulness of such a definition. His ideas can provide that same stimulus today as we try to answer such questions as: Is it futile to attempt to define American music in the curriculum? Have we surpassed a discussion of such an issue? Is it a topic that is related to the contemporary debates in the multicultural education movement?

Charles Seeger the Music Educator

Seeger was raised in a bicultural environment because his father's business ventures took the family back and forth between the United States and Mexico City. In 1904, he entered Harvard University where, against the wishes of his parents, he pursued studies in music. He later wrote:

> My youthful ambitions and ideals by the time I got to Harvard were to avoid going into business. ... When I told my father that I was going to be a composer, he was horrified. He said: "But gentlemen are not musicians." ... He pointed out the impracticality of it and the argument closed.[7]

After graduating from Harvard *magna cum laude* in music in 1908, Seeger spent two and a half years in Europe. In 1912, he was hired as chairman of the Music Department at the University of California at Berkeley, and remained there until 1919. One of his appointments while at Berkeley was to a committee on music education, and "his committee service meant that he spent a few weeks each spring visiting public high schools in the California foothills."[8] In these years at Berkeley, during subsequent periods back in New York at the Institute of Musical Art (1921–33) and the New School for Social Research (1931–35), and later in Washington, D.C., as music adviser for various federal projects (1935–41), Seeger's intellectual ideas were formed. The period during which he was most involved in music education extended from 1940 to 1953, coinciding with his tenure as chief of the Music Division of the Pan American Union (PAU, now called the Organization of American States). His intense engagement with the music education profession during this period is reflected in the fact that all but one of his writings on education appeared between 1940 and 1953.[9]

Seeger conducted his scholarly inquiry from multiple vantage points. This is consonant with Gilbert Chase's view of Seeger's ideas as transcending all categorical boundaries.[10] Unlike other scholars who focused their life's work on questions that lay within the increasingly narrow confines of disciplinary terrain, Seeger, driven by an "intellectual curiosity of such enormous proportions, touched every aspect of the music world."[11] Music education thus occupied a central position in his grand scheme of intellectual inquiry. In 1947, he was publicly identified with the music education profession in his article in the *Music Educators Journal,* "Music Education and Musicology: A Musicologist Who Is Also a Music Educator Examines the Ivory Tower from the Grassroots Point of View."[12]

He served in many leadership roles. The pivotal figure in his relationship with national and international music education was Vanett

Lawler who, as Executive Secretary of MENC, also served as education consultant to PAU and worked closely with him.[13] Seeger made presentations at several music teachers' national conventions, including presentations at the Music Teachers National Association (MTNA) conventions in 1940 and 1946, and MENC's national conferences in 1942 and 1944. He was a member of the MENC Music Education Research Council (1944–48) and organized a committee on music education and musicology.[14] His aim was to nurture positive relationships between the two professional groups (music educators and musicologists). In general, he advanced thinking on the role of music in education not only in the United States but also in the various Latin American countries; he also supported music education through the key role he played in the founding of the International Society for Music Education in 1953.[15]

Of central importance to his contribution to music education were his efforts to promote American vernacular music in the public schools. In collaboration with his wife Ruth Crawford Seeger and Vanett Lawler, among others, he organized the publication of folksong materials for use in schools, directed the collection of recordings of folk music from various Latin American countries, served as consultant to several publishing houses on American folk music for children, and made presentations to teachers on the value and use of folk music in the classroom.

After 1953, the year Ruth died, his direct connections with the music education profession weakened. He moved from Washington, D.C., to California, and a new phase of his life began. Although he published little in the music education field after that, his seminal ideas on the relationship between music in society and in education continue to be relevant, insightful, and applicable to contemporary dilemmas and challenges in music education.

Music in American Culture: A Grassroots Approach

An exploration of Seeger's theory of music in culture, and in American society in particular, is a prerequisite to understanding the nature and significance of his contribution to the history, philosophy, and sociology of American music education. Perhaps the most important factor in the formation of his approach was his intense observation of and reflection on the musical values and practices of American people in communal contexts, especially during the years 1920–1940. Having a classical music education himself at Harvard University followed by an extended period of time as opera director at the Cologne Municipal Opera, Seeger had internalized the values of Western art music culture.

His intellectual curiosity led him to question the nature of value in connection with music. With his first wife Constance and their three children, Charles, John, and Peter, he set out from New York in November 1920 and traveled to North Carolina, intending to perform "good" classical music for people who were deprived of that musical experience. However, he and Constance soon realized that their definition of "good" music "did not impress their audiences, for they had their own music that they valued."[16] Seeger observed and interacted with banjo and fiddle players and gained some insights into the relationship among music, the individual, and society. He learned, as Dunaway put it, that "music transplants poorly ... especially in the name of civilization."[17] No doubt this journey into the musical life of the South impacted his future thinking about and advocacy for folk music in culture and in education.

Seeger was further directed toward the study of folk music by his student, Ruth Crawford, who later became his wife. (Charles and Constanse's marriage deteriorated during the 1920s and the couple separated. Ruth became a student of Seeger's in 1929, and they married in 1932.) She worked with Carl Sandberg on *The American Songbag* (1927) and became increasingly involved in the collection and arrangement of folk songs for publication. Although Seeger himself did little with folk music until after 1935,[18] his strong beliefs about acknowledging the music of the people were established in the 1920s. As Kerman put it, "Seeger always worked to promote music that comes from 'below,' rather than music imposed from 'above.'"[19] A striking example of this approach is evident in his work within the Composers Collective in New York (1931–35). In an interview with David Dunaway, he described his guidelines for the field workers:

> I had a whole list of things they [field workers] were to do. First, they would probably find that they could work with music in the school, but for God's sake, don't give them a songbook, don't teach [the children] songs you like, but find out what songs they like to sing, and get them to sing them. Find out what their singing games are and encourage them to sing and play them, instead of looking down on the games and forbidding them, as some of their parents had been doing.[20]

Similarly, as music adviser to Roosevelt's Resettlement Administration in Washington, D.C. (1935–41), he advocated that social workers ought "to encourage the singing and playing of songs the children knew and loved."[21] His experiences had taught him that "music must serve. That you must use the music that the people have in them already."[22] Seeger's involvement with projects that nurtured music in various social contexts during the 1920s and 1930s laid the foundation for his philosophy of vernacular music in education. He witnessed the vitality of the vernacular, and "his deep and wide social consciousness"[23] recognized and responded to the human values involved in music-making. As he put it later, "For cross-traditionally, music is above all a value system."[24]

As Seeger became more involved in various American musical genres beyond art music, he realized that the traditional concept of "folk" music was narrow and unsatisfactory. In its place, he used the term "vernacular music, which he viewed much more broadly."[25] The traditional concept of folk music, in Seeger's view, created problems in that attention has tended to be directed mainly to material artifacts—structures, particular "pieces" of speech, and music—their collection, their classification, in repertorial canons, their sequestration in bodies of collectanea often as not regarded as private property by collectors and sometimes even copyrighted in the collectors' names.[26]

This approach to folk music lacked the vitality he had witnessed in the folk music practices of American people. Instead of attempting to keep folk music alive "as something quaint, antique, and precious," he wrote, "let us say 'the folk is changing—and its songs with it.'"[27] He argued that folk music was not merely composed of pieces that "stay still" while one contemplates them.[28] Rather, it was "a summary of the way of life of a culture community … a veritable code of individual and social behavior."[29] In essence, his definitions embraced the neglected area of the social functions of music:

In the Western world, music is talked about to a greater extent in terms of structure—concrete structures, at that—with immutable beginnings, endings, and inner construction.[30]

The desire to promote the study of music in terms of its social functions motivated Seeger to develop a theory of music in total culture. He delivered two papers on the topic at MTNA national conventions in the 1940s: "Music and Culture" (1940), and "Music and Musicology in the New World" (1946). What did he consider important to impart in a music teachers' forum? The goal of his 1940 paper was to draw teachers' attention to the fact that no longer could they focus narrowly on the structural aspects of music. As he told his listeners, "The concept of total culture is before us and constitutes a challenge which … we must accept, apparently, whether we like it or not."[31]

He then identified basic assumptions about music that permeated Western intellectual circles, assumptions that teachers carried as products of a Western educational system. First, he discussed the assumption that music progressed from lower to higher stages, from folk to art music. "Traced by the 'advanced' culture," he said, "a fixed, one-directional evolutionary pattern led somewhat naively to itself as representing the highest stage."[32] Second, he warned teachers to "be careful to avoid the fallacy that music is a 'universal language.'"[33] He explained this by pointing out that "what music we know, we know only in the frame of our own culture, in which a certain place and function is allowed to it by custom."[34] He urged teachers to learn more about various idioms of American music culture, while acknowledging the difficulty of moving beyond their own.

For any one of these idioms is some way like a language—one has to learn it in order to understand it and estimate its value—and sometimes even to discover it. It is not easy for a person brought up in the tradition of one music idiom to acquire understanding (and still less, ability to express himself) in the tradition of another idiom.[35]

Seeger's dialogue with music teachers on assumptions about music continued in an article published in 1941 in the *Music Educators Journal*. He brought before them assumptions that originated in Europe and that dominated American music during the previous century. These assumptions included the notions that music was a universal language, that the best music was written music, and that the basis for music education was in written techniques and in the performance of written masterpieces.[36]   Again, he addressed the functional approach to music: "While it is true that musical 'good' is inherent in music itself, it is equally true that it is to be found also in the function the music serves."[37]   Returning to the MTNA forum in 1946, he presented teachers with a comprehensive approach to studying music within the context of the culture as a whole. It embraced musical traditions, methods of transmission, quantitative distribution of traditions, idioms, criteria of evaluation, development of services, and integration of traditions, idioms, and services into the culture.[38]

As Seeger's vista for viewing music in culture broadened and deepened, he began to consider the complexity of the American music scene—the multiplicity of traditions serving different functions and their interrelationships. He identified four types of music idioms— folk, primitive or tribal, art, and popular music—and was careful to point out from the beginning that the relationships among them were highly complex, unexplored, and controversial. Later in his career, he reported that

> modern scholarship sees the relationship between the four music idioms less as a one-way street between exclusive classes and more as a reciprocal two-, three-, or even four-way activity of give-and-take within the social body as a whole.[39]

In numerous writings, and particularly those written expressly for music teachers, Seeger focused on transmission of the various idioms to demonstrate their interrelationships. He described three varieties: "exclusively oral, mixed oral and written, and predominantly written."[40]   In reality, the transmission of music in the Western hemisphere was viewed in simplistic, dualistic, and dichotomous terms: oral or written modes to correspond with folk or cultivated music, respectively. This "pitted oral and written traditions against each other"[41] and created regrettable chasms among the idioms. On the surface, oral and written traditions refer innocently to the manner in which music is inherited, disseminated, and left to one's descendants. "Undoubtedly, this 'manner-in-which' molds the traditional *forms which music takes*. But the social function of the music groups ... in a culture molds the kind and range of *content* or meaning of those forms, and through this, the forms as well."[42]   In other words, a focus on the manner of transmission was necessary but not sufficient for acquiring an understanding of music's social function.

Seeger proceeded to illustrate his argument by examining music in the United States. His analysis shed light on the history of music in American culture and education. He defined American music "first, as designating the music and music activity actually existing in the United States; second, as referring to the part of this music that expresses or characterizes the American people as distinguished from other peoples."[43] He identified four elements that shaped the development of music in the United States—the Native American, the European, the African, and the music brought back by wealthy Americans and professional music students who went to Europe during the nineteenth century "and acquired, with the psychology of the colonist returning to the mother country, a musical attitude and taste of distinct and peculiar character." It was in terms of this fourth element, he claimed, that American music education had grown.[44]

Because of this belief, he was critical of the course taken by music education in the public schools during the nineteenth century. Lowell Mason, in his opinion, spearheaded the group who "sought to substitute, throughout the areas it can influence, not only the products but even the process of the written tradition for those of the oral."[45] He also associated Mason with "a small vanguard of private citizens" who "set themselves with almost religious zeal to 'make America musical' in the exact image of contemporary Europe as they saw it."[46] This goal underpinned music in the schools where "until after 1900 the music education movement bogged down in the boredom and difficulty of solfège (note-reading) and of dull, genteel textbooks.[47] Meanwhile, as the American music industry grew, a "sell-America-music" group emerged that was concerned with "the taste preferences of the people—that is, the quality judgements of buyers." One of their largest markets was the public school. However, the materials demanded there were not necessarily what the children wanted but, rather, what the teachers wanted. Seeger believed that after the establishment of the Music Supervisors National Conference in 1907, change took place. The music education profession

abandoned authoritarian leadership of the make-America-musical group for the more democratic opportunism of the sell-America-music group. Instead of offering school administrators an upper-class, intellectual, divine, quasi-European art, the Conference tried to find out what the administrators would buy and pay for in the way of music. This turned out to be the somewhat old-fashioned, middle-class popular music of the day. By giving them this in quantity and at the same time allowing the 'good music boys' to work within such a frame as best they could, a revitalization of music education in the schools took place, the magnitude and quality of whose effect upon the use of music in the United States can scarcely yet be estimated.[48]

In the context of folk music, Seeger saw a close relationship between its rejection by the schools and by urban music intellectuals and the musical immaturity of the nation. He observed, "It may be said that one mark of a mature and vigorous people is its *ability to be at home with itself,* to accept itself and to value itself for what it is."[49] A major integrative force was necessary to unite the various traditions of music that expressed or characterized the American people. To achieve this goal, he turned to music education "as an integral part

of American music as a whole—as possibly the most effective agency
we have for the integration of American music within itself and within the culture of which it is a part."[50] He recognized the launching
of the project "American Songs for American Children" at the 1942
MENC biennial convention, as

> the most momentous single step to be taken toward the time when the United
> States will *be at home with its own music.* This step is the adherence of the music
> educators of the United States to the principle that one essential basis of music
> education in a country is the folk music of that country.[51]

Furthermore, for Seeger, to be at home with one's own music was
a necessary but not sufficient end for music education. A complementary goal was that the individual be "*at home in the world at large*—
to give and take in the free intercourse of peoples without too much
regrettable loss on any side."[52] Seeger's contribution to the understanding and development of American music in culture and education did not stop at the philosophical level. He worked arduously to
organize and disseminate folk-music materials for educational use.
From his presentations and writings, there is evident a plan for the
implementation of his theory in education.

Music in American Education: Some Vital Connections

Seeger considered music education to be a critical and influential
partner in the development of American musical life as a whole. His
writings throughout his career reflect this belief, especially those
published or delivered during 1940–53, the period in which he was
most intensively involved with music education. As critic, philosopher, and sociologist, his contributions provide insights into music
education that transcend the time period in which they were made.
His recommendations to the music education profession were based
on observations of its strengths and shortcomings. These were articulated in a statement read before the National Institute on Music
Education in Wartime, held in Chicago, November 12–14, 1942. On
one hand, he identified the many strengths of the profession's
endeavors and achievements—devoted teachers, improving teach-
er-training programs, an incredible number of ensembles in the
schools, the widening scope of music education from nursery to
graduate levels, increased integration with other subjects of instruction, and good working relations with many groups in public life. At
the same time, he observed a general lack of vitality and dynamism
in the structures, networks, and processes of music education—lack
of development of creative techniques in the schools, lack of utilization of oral tradition in the classroom, lack of contact with contemporary fine-art composers, "lack of use of music as a vehicle of living
thought, feeling, or whatever it is that music embodies or conveys
from one person to another, or from one group to another," and
rather poor public relations with fields such as musicology.[53]
Some vital connections[54] were missing, in Seeger's opinion—con-

nections that he sought to activate, nurture, and strengthen in his leadership roles in music education. The inertness he witnessed in school music could be reversed by changing the nature of the relationship between the child's and the school's music cultures, by broadening the repertoire of school music, by increased communication among all music professionals, and by considering music in its cultural-political context, both in society and in education.

Of primary importance for Seeger was making a vital connection between school music and the child's own music. Already in his work in New York in the 1930s, he advocated listening to and accepting the children's music as a base for formal music instruction. Seeger was attuned to the educational thought of his day and the child-centered, experiential approach to schooling, "for, as we all know, it is an inescapable principle of modern education that the child should first be grounded in a knowledge of his own native environment and traditions."[55]   More than thirty years later, in another article published in the *Music Educators Journal,* Seeger reiterated this principle: "From a musical point of view, the prime concern in education would seem to be acquisition of competence in one's own music, the tradition inherited, cultivated, and transmitted by the members of the sociocultural continuum into which one has been born."[56]   His definition of competence was focused on the practice of music: he believed that "*music is primarily in the making of it;* only secondarily in the listening to it."[57]   Although Seeger believed that, in many ways, children were musically sophisticated when they entered school, he observed that few American children "possess the ability to improvise even a single line of sound that constitutes a simple melody such as they have to improvise the not entirely different single line of sound that constitutes a simple sentence."[58]

A second vital connection needed to be in place to improve the child's ability to use music as naturally as language—that is, the use of vernacular music in the classroom, presented as a living, functional means of personal and collective expression. The goal of public school music education in its first century was that of presenting music as "a good in itself." Addressing music educators in 1942, Seeger reported a change toward the presentation of music as "good for something."[59] Inherently, this change in perspective and approach created a set of challenges for music educators who were schooled in the narrow Western definition of music literacy as synonymous with reading notation and re-creating musical works.

To help teachers encounter the challenges, Seeger provided philosophical and pedagogical direction in addition to the provision of appropriate materials in the larger context of his work with Ruth Seeger, Vanett Lawler, and the Pan American Union. His first major statement to music teachers on the topic of folk music occurred on March 30, 1942, at the MENC biennial conference in Milwaukee. As part of the general session on "American Songs for American Children,"[60] Seeger addressed the future of the American folk song. A subsequent report in the *Music Educators Journal* conveyed the significance of this event:

Music educators left the folk song session with a new insight into the importance of American folk song in education and the responsibilities of their profession in the utilization of this material.[61]

In the Foreword to *American Songs for American Children,* Seeger stressed that in order for the United States to be at home with its own music, music educators needed to adhere to the principle that "one essential basis of music education in a country is the folk music of that country."[62] To adhere to the principle, teachers needed careful guidance, since the use of folk music in the schools was, in his opinion, "nothing short of a revolution." In fact, to have folk music handled properly would take generations of teacher training.[63]

He proceeded in subsequent writings to point out some of the unique features of folk music and effective pedagogical strategies for its transmission. As distinct from art music, a folk song or tune transmitted orally depended on the variation principle. No one, absolute, authentic version existed, a fact that needed to be reflected in pedagogy where the guiding principle should be that of variation as opposed to "repetition of the single, authentic text."[64] Seeger believed that using this principle to guide music teaching and learning would help remedy the lack of creative activity he was critical of in music education.

A further concern was the translation of folk music from unwritten to written forms. He warned that "abstraction of the notes from the style of singing and playing is one of the worst sins against proper folklore study."[65] An alternative means of transmitting folk music was the recording. He offered this comparison: "What print is to the art of speech in a literate world, the record would seem to be in the musically illiterate world."[66] Seeger continued to confirm the role of mass media as a means of "bypassing the bottleneck of notation" of the folk song and of learning to sing "from hearing the voices of authentic singers."[67] The question of authenticity was as alive in the 1940s as it is today. Seeger empathized with music educators who encountered difficulty in knowing whether they have "in hand a genuine folk song or a false one," based on the variation in quality of materials being printed. He anticipated that the emerging field of comparative musicology would provide leadership in this respect.[68] First, music educators needed to reach out and draw on the resources of related fields such as musicology. This constituted a third artery in the network of connections basic to vitalizing music in education.

In his vision for music in American culture and education, Seeger stressed the need for a close relationship between musicologists and music educators. Many of his writings refer to the tensions and diffident relations existing between these groups. His 1947 article, "Music Education and Musicology," provided some historical background to this situation. In his opinion, American musicology was steeped in nineteenth-century values and practices and failed to provide music educators with a vital, contemporary view of music. He wrote:

> In the fight for a twentieth-century educational approach to the problem of music in the schools, music educators had to fight nineteenth-century educational practice as it existed in the conservatories of music. Not having at hand a twentieth-century musicology with which to strengthen their hand, there was evolved, as the next best weapon, a strong trend toward anti-intellectualism in music. This gave music educators freedom from bondage to outworn tradition and enabled them to forge the unique instrument they now possess.[69]

Seeger's conviction about the interdependence of these music professions did not stop at the level of criticism. He brought together members of both groups at the 1944 MENC biennial convention in St. Louis. A committee on music education and musicology was established, chaired by Seeger. It started out "as a kind of sub-committee of the Research Council."[70] Similar forums were authorized in the American Musicological Society and the MTNA.

He continued to promote increased communication between the groups, emphasizing that "the time has come when few of us can afford to tend our home garden as if it were a thing in itself, independent of the rest of the world."[71] It seems that his pleas and efforts had limited influence on building a vital connection between music educators and musicologists. Almost two decades later, Johannes Riedel, writing on the sociology of music and music education, referred to the conflict that existed between the same two groups and revisited Seeger's plea toward unity and cooperation in promoting the use of music in the life of human beings.[72] The sociological and cultural context of music, as Riedel pointed out, was the common ground for musicologists and music educators.

Another context of which Seeger was acutely aware and in which he was actively involved was the political context of music in culture and in education. During his career, he witnessed developments in American music that resulted from the two World Wars, and, later, the multicultural music movement of the 1960s and 1970s. Music served political agendas in music education programs such as American Unity through Music during World War II. These agendas did not necessarily end in the post-war years. In fact, Seeger observed increased political influence on music's development. Writing in the *Music Educators Journal* in 1972, he concluded that the task of music education "has become cultural-political on a large scale."[73]

American Music for American Children: An Epilogue

Charles Seeger's contribution to American music education is unique in several ways. Rarely do we find a major scholar from outside the profession playing as significant and active a role within the profession as Seeger chose. Each scholarly discipline, in his opinion, incorporates "a world view of its own."[74] Seeger penetrated the "world view" of music education and disturbed the equilibrium with his radical views, his sometimes harsh criticisms, his arresting ideas, and his progressive thinking. However, it is the very disturbance of the profession's "world view" that makes his contribution dynamic and worthy of exploration and continued study.

What sets him apart as a musicologist–music educator is the central role he granted music education in the development of American musical life. His appraisal of and recommendations for the profession were made in that broad sociocultural and political context. From this vantage point, he was able to identify points of tension or potential conflict in music education. Thus, he was in a position to make recommendations for empowering music students and teachers, for making music programs relevant to American sociocultural life, and for strengthening the fiber of American musical life.

Not only did Seeger observe and criticize from the outside, but he entered the forum and communicated meaningfully with music teachers and those in leadership positions. His dialogue with them embraced a broad spectrum—from the history, philosophy, and sociology of music education to repertoire and pedagogical issues. It is noteworthy that he emphasized, albeit indirectly, the importance of music education history for teachers. Seeger expressed regret that music educators were, in his opinion, ignorant of the historical forces that informed their philosophy and shaped their practices:

> So American educators have had to get along with second- and third-hand echoes of European philosophies of music. Besides being considerably distorted, these echoes are out of date. The foundations of music education in the United States are, then, strictly twentieth century upon their educational side but garbled nineteenth century on the musicological side. And worst of all, the music educators do not know it.[75]

Although some may not agree with much of his revisionist thought on the history of American music education, Seeger does provide an alternative perspective for viewing music education in the context of total American culture. He is quite critical of the course taken by Lowell Mason and his colleagues in establishing music in American education. More than one century later, armed with a different "world view," Seeger doubtless found it tempting to graft the values and paradigms of his own view onto the actions and practices of predecessors.

In an almost contradictory vein, he identified Mason and his followers with the "make-America-musical" group. The goal of their mission corresponded, in essence, with the one Seeger envisioned for American music education in his era. The difference lay in the definition of a musically educated American. In keeping with the general MENC theme of the 1940s, "Widening Horizons for Music Education," Seeger sought to expand the musical horizons and broaden the musical perspectives of teachers and students by motivating change not only in the content of music curricula but also in the processes of music transmission in school culture.

Seeger was by no means a pioneer in addressing the use of folk music in education. There is abundant historical evidence that folk music, in various forms and definitions, had been used in music education for decades previously. He, however, sought to abandon former definitions that treated folk repertoire as museum pieces that could be decorated with the ornaments of Western harmony and preserved in written form. Folk music, for Seeger, was the vernacular of the people—what the people value, transmit, and change—a pulse of life in their communities. A folk song was not an esoteric piece from a distant land; rather, it was a living tradition from a local community. Thus, Seeger highlighted for teachers the importance of interfacing school music with music traditions in the surrounding communities.

Related to this concept was his innovative thinking on music as a cultural subject, with emphasis placed on its social function. Considering the fact that it is only in recent years that music educators have begun to approach music from the sociocultural perspective, Seeger's 1940 MTNA presentation "Music and Culture" was revolutionary in its paradigmatic base and its conceptual canvas, and laden with ideas whose time had not yet come. More tangible, though perhaps no less radical, to music educators' experience and world view was his definition of American music for children. No doubt the impact of World War II shaped this definition. For example, the promotion of Latin American music reached a climax during the 1940s, the intensity of which has not been equalled since that period. Although Seeger advocated all American musics for children, the focus of his promotional efforts was on Anglo-American and Latin American folk music, with minimal attention devoted to Native American or African American music. Theoretically, I believe that his thinking was catholic and inclusive; the focus of his efforts reflected the political assumptions and expectations of his time and, in a sense, the limitations of his world view.

In addition to expanding the context of school music repertoire, Seeger also sought to change the process of music transmission in the classroom. He elevated the status of oral processes and attempted to diffuse the dichotomous view of orality and literacy as being synonymous with folk and art music, respectively. The heart of the music education process, in Seeger's opinion, was "doing" music. In contemporary terms, he might be considered a proponent of the praxial philosophy of music education, advocating practice-focused, value-centered, people-oriented music teaching and learning that was socially and culturally contextualized. Music, for him, was "above all a value system," a belief that grew out of his own observations of the role of music in people's lives.

All of his recommendations were aimed at creating or renewing connections that he considered vital to American music education—connections with the child's own music; with American vernacular music in general; with other music professionals, particularly musicologists; and with the cultural-political context in which American music and education are situated. Seeger's prediction and hope that "comparative musicology" would provide music educators with a twentieth-century philosophy of music have been realized to a certain extent, reflected in the increased communications between music educators and ethnomusicologists in the last two to three decades. Each scholarly discipline, as Seeger pointed out, has its own world view. In the context of American musical life, it is necessary to be aware of, communicate with, and learn from other disciplines whose mission is also to "make America musical."

On the theme of "American Music for American Children," Seeger's legacy is rich and provocative, with many of his ideas applicable to the dilemmas and challenges of American music education today. He expanded the definition of American school music, promoted the use of vernacular music in the schools, heightened awareness of the function of music in American culture, and paved the way for dealing with musical diversity in American schools. In a sense, his attempts to define "American music for American children" illustrate that it is a dynamic concept, constantly in transition. American musical life was as diverse in the 1940s as it is today. What Seeger provided were some principles and avenues of approach to deal with diversity, regardless of the particular music cultures in question. His ideas addressed perennial questions regarding music in American culture and education. His voice lives on in the multivocal and complex dialogue of contemporary music education.

Notes

1. Ann M. Pescatello, *Charles Seeger: A Life in American Music* (Pittsburgh and London: University of Pittsburgh Press, 1992), vii.
2. Seeger's biographer, Ann Pescatello, writes that "Seeger had frequently rued the fact that people did not read his scholarly articles—or, if they did, they had no comments or criticisms to make about them." *Charles Seeger: A Life in American Music*, 274. In "Reminiscent of Charles Seeger," Mantle Hood referred to Seeger's "long list of publications too seldom read, too little comprehended." *Yearbook of the International Folk Music Council* 11 (1979), 99.
3. In Michael L. Mark and Charles L. Gary, *A History of American Music Education* (New York: Schirmer Books, 1992), the authors refer to the influence Seeger had on Vanett Lawler during her time as education consultant to the Pan American Union, stating that "her close association with Charles Seeger was fortuitous," 249.
4. Pescatello, xii.
5. Archie Green, "Charles Louis Seeger (1886–1979)," *Journal of American Folklore* 92 (October–December 1979): 397.
6. Seeger, "American Music for American Children," *Music Educators Journal* 29 (November–December 1942): 11–12.
7. Charles Seeger, dictated to Peggy Seeger Cohen, April 22, 1977, in Pescatello, 37.
8. Pescatello, 64.
9. *Ibid.*, 303.
10. Gilbert Chase, An Exagmination Round His Factification for Incami-

nation of Work in Progress. (Review Essay and Reminiscence)." *Yearbook of the International Folk Music Council* 11 (1979), 143.
11. Pescatello, 285.
12. *Music Educators Journal* 33 (January 1947): 10–11. The latter part of the article title is perhaps an editor's addition. Either Seeger identified himself with the profession or the editor wished him to be presented as a music educator to the professional community.
13. For a detailed study of Vanett Lawler's work with the PAU, see Christy Izdebski and Michael L. Mark, *The Bulletin of Historical Research in Music Education* 8 (January 1987): 1–32.
14. Seeger was a member of numerous MENC committees in the 1940s and early 1950s, including the American Folk Song Committee, the Committee on Creative Music Projects, the National Committee on Song Writing Project, and the editorial board of the *Music Educators Journal*.
15. For a detailed description of Seeger's contribution to international music education, see Marie McCarthy, "'Canticle to Hope': Widening Horizons in International Music Education, 1939–1953." Paper delivered at the Twenty-first Biennial World Conference of the International Society for Music Education, Tampa, FL, July 18–23, 1994 and subsequently published in the *International Journal of Music Education* 25 (1995), 38–49.
16. Pescatello, 82–83.
17. David Dunaway, *How Can I Keep from Singing: Pete Seeger,* rev. ed. (New York: Da Capo Press, 1990), 34.
18. Pescatello, 111.
19. Joseph Kerman, *Contemplating Music: Challenges from Musicology* (Cambridge, MA: Harvard University Press, 1985), 156.
20. Seeger to Dunaway, in David K. Dunaway, "Charles Seeger and Carl Sands: The Composers' Collective Years," *Ethnomusicology,* 24 (May 1980), 168.
21. Pescatello, 140.
22. Seeger to Dunaway, "Charles Seeger and Carl Sands," 168.
23. Chase, 142.
24. Seeger, "The Music Compositional Process as a Function in a Nest of Functions and in Itself a Nest of Functions," *Studies in Musicology 1935–1975* (Berkeley: University of California Press, 1977), 153. Based on a 1966 article, "The Music Process as a Function in the Context of Functions," *Yearbook, Inter-American Institute for Musical Research* (New Orleans, LA: Tulane University, 1966).
25. Bruno Nettl, "The Dual Nature of Ethnomusicology in North America," in *Comparative Musicology and Anthropology of Music,* ed. Bruno Nettl and Philip V. Bohlman (Chicago: University of Chicago Press, 1991): 268.
26. Seeger, "The Folkness of Nonfolk and the Nonfolkness of the Folk," in *Studies in Musicology,* 335. Based on a 1966 article, "The Folkness of the Nonfolk vs. the Nonfolkness of the Folk," in *Folklore and Society* (Hatboro, PA: Folklore Associates, 1966).
27. Seeger, "Folk Music in the Schools of a Highly Industrialized Society," *Journal of the International Folk Music Council* 5 (1953): 44; reprinted in *Studies in Musicology,* 330–34.
28. Seeger, "The Compositional Process," 140–41.
29. Seeger, "Folk Music in the Schools," 40.
30. "The Music Compositional Process," 140.
31. Seeger, "Music and Culture," *Proceedings of the Music Teachers National*

   Association, 35th Series (1941).
32. *Ibid.,* 112.
33. *Ibid.,* 122.
34. *Ibid.,* 115.
35. *Ibid.,* 118.
36. Seeger, "Inter-American Relations in the Field of Music: Some Basic Considerations," *Music Educators Journal* 27 (March–April 1941): 18.
37. *Ibid.*
38. Seeger, "Music and Musicology in the New World," *Proceedings of the Music Teachers National Association, 40th Series* (1946): 38–39.
39. Seeger, "Folk Music," *Collier's Encyclopedia,* vol. 10 (New York: P. F. Collier, Inc., 1965), 132.
40. Seeger, "Music and Musicology," 40.
41. Seeger, "American Music for American Children," 11.
42. Seeger, "Music and Culture," 118.
43. Seeger, "American Music for American Children," 11.
44. *Ibid.,* 12.
45. Seeger, "Folk Music in the Schools," 41.
46. Seeger, "Music and Class Structure in the United States," in *Studies in Musicology,* 225. First published in *American Quarterly,* 9 (Fall 1957): 281–94.
47. *Ibid.,* 226.
48. *Ibid.,* 230. In "American Music for American Children," Seeger identifies the "somewhat old-fashioned" popular music as that of Foster, Work, Root, Emmet, Band—on the whole, a nineteenth-century, cosmopolitan style, 12.
49. Seeger, "American Music for American Children," 11.
50. *Ibid.*
51. Seeger, Foreword to *American Songs for American Children* (Chicago: MENC, ca. 1942), 3.
52. Seeger, "American Music for American Children," 11.
53. Seeger, in "Proceedings of the National Institute on Music Education in Wartime," Chicago, November 12–14, 1942. Unpublished paper, MENC Historical Center, University of Maryland at College Park, 163–64; published subsequently in the *Music Educators Journal* 29 (January 1943): 12–14.
54. The identification of "some vital connections" results from the author's interpretation of Seeger's writings.
55. Seeger, "Inter-American Relations in the Field of Music," 65.
56. Seeger, "World Musics in American Schools: A Challenge to Be Met," *Music Educators Journal* 59 (October 1972): 107.
57. *Ibid.,* 111. Seeger had voiced this opinion throughout his career. For example, in "The Musician: Man Serves Art/The Educator: Art Serves Man," *UNESCO Courier* 6 (February 1953): 12. Reprinted in *The Australian Journal of Music Education* 30 (April 1977): 15–16.
58. Seeger, "World Musics in American Schools," 107.
59. "Proceedings of the National Institute on Music Education in Wartime," 162.
60. The project was undertaken in cooperation with the MENC American Unity Through Music Committee, with assistance from the Rockefeller Foundation. Charles and Ruth Seeger edited the music and text, and Alan Lomax wrote the explanatory notes.
61. "American Songs for American Children," *Music Educators Journal* 38 (May–June 1942): 29.

62. Seeger, Foreword to *American Songs for American Children,* 3.
63. Seeger, "Notes on Music in the Americas," *Bulletin of the Pan American Union* 79 (June 1945): 344.
64. Seeger, "Folk Music in the Schools," 334.
65. "Folk Music," in *Collier's Encyclopedia,* vol. 10 (1965), 132.
66. Seeger, "Notes on Music in the Americas," *Bulletin of the Pan American Union* 79 (June 1945): 344.
67. "Folk Music in the Schools," 334.
68. Seeger, "Music Education and Musicology," in *Music Education Source Handbook,* ed. Hazel Nohavec Morgan (Chicago: MENC, 1947), 196.
69. *Ibid.,* 197.
70. Conference Digest of the Music Educators National Conference, "Widening Horizons for Music Education," 9th Biennial Meeting, St. Louis MO, March 2–8, 1944; MENC Historical Center, College Park, MD.
71. Seeger, "Music and Musicology in the New World," 47.
72. Johannes Ridel, "The Function of Sociability in the Sociology of Music and Music Education," *Journal of Research in Music Education* 12 (Summer 1964), 158.
73. Seeger, "World Musics in American Schools," 111.
74. Seeger, "Toward a Unitary Field Theory for Musicology," in *Studies in Musicology,* 107. Originally in *Selected Reports,* vol. 1, no. 3, Institute of Ethnomusicology (Los Angeles: University of California, 1970).
75. Charles L. Seeger, "Music Education and Musicology: A Musicologist Who Is Also a Music Educator Examines the Ivory Tower from a Grassroots Point of View," *Music Educators Journal* 33 (January 1947), 11.

Submitted November 15, 1994; accepted January 23, 1995.

The Easy Instructor (1798-1831)

A History and Bibliography of the First Shape Note Tune Book

IRVING LOWENS and ALLEN P. BRITTON

JRME 1953, VOLUME 1, NUMBER 1, PAGES 30–55

A CRUCIAL problem faced by our earliest music educators — and one whose difficulties puzzle us still— was how to teach successfully the core skill of reading music at sight. The approach through notational reform, now considered hopelessly quixotic, came in for a good deal of attention in eighteenth and early nineteenth century America. Indeed, the first music textbook published on this side of the Atlantic, John Tufts' *An Introduction to the Singing of Psalm Tunes* (Boston, 1721, perhaps earlier), presented an innovation which was no doubt of some value in a situation where the art of reading orthodox notation had virtually disappeared. The nub of the problem was to devise a system in which pitch, time, and solmization were combined into a single, easily assimilated notation. The Tufts solution, apparently not wholly original,[1] was to abandon ordinary notes entirely and to substitute upon the staff the initial letters of the four solmization syllables (fa, sol, la, mi) then in universal use in Great Britain. Time values were indicated with punctuation marks. This was quite adequate for the traditional psalm tunes Tufts included in his clearly written and unpretentious little pamphlet, but the system was unwieldy and ill-adapted to music of greater

complexity. It failed to win adherents, although the *Introduction* itself proved to be something of a best-seller, going through eleven editions.

Among the ingenious notations which followed in the wake of the Tufts experiment, none was more remarkable than the "shape note" system which made its first public appearance in the pages of a quite extraordinary tune book, *The Easy Instructor*, "by" William Little and William Smith. The shape note idea was the kind of inspired solution to a knotty problem which seems perfectly obvious once it has been suggested. It consisted merely of using a differently shaped note head to represent each of the four syllables. Thus, a triangular note head represented fa, a round note head sol, a square note head la, and a diamond note head mi. In all other respects, the notation was completely orthodox. (See illustration on opposite page.)

The clear advantages of the shape note system are almost immediately apparent. Providing an individual shape for each syllable enables anyone, after a modicum of attention to the matter, to name the proper syllables of any piece of music instantaneously. One of the genuine difficulties in ordinary solmization lies in the fact that keys change and hence do (or fa in the fasula system) does not remain in the same place. The student must make continual mental computations.

---

[1] See Sirvart Poladian, "Rev. John Tufts and Three-Part Psalmody in America," *Jour. of the Amer. Musicol. Soc.*, IV (Fall 1951), 276-277.

Illustration 1. A page from *The Easy Instructor*. Courtesy of the Clements Library, University of Michigan. (See "Edition F" in check list, page 45, also Illustration 4, page 44.)

With shape notes, this is completely avoided. A somewhat subtler advantage is that the shapes are continually before the singer whether he happens to be singing words or syllables. Thus, the true function of any solmization system—that of aiding in the automatic identification of scale degrees— is emphasized and capitalized upon through shape notes in a fashion impossible in any system which permits abandonment of the process of syllabification when words are sung. Comparison of the shape note system with that of Tonic Sol-Fa, so successful in the British Isles, highlights the superiority of the *Easy Instructor* idea. The symbols of Tonic Sol-Fa are not posited upon a staff, and hence the pictorial suggestion of tonal direction provided by staff notation is lost. Failure to use the staff demands a complicated method of octave identification, and failure to use regular notes demands a similarly complicated method of representing time values. Furthermore, Tonic Sol-Fa is quite independent of orthodox notation, whereas the shape notes utilize the standard notation and add to it a graphic, quickly comprehended key to relative scale degrees.

No one who has witnessed the astonishing sight-singing virtuosity exhibited by the shape note singers of the rural South today, trained with what is basically the *Easy Instructor* method, can possibly doubt the effectiveness of the device. Had this pedagogical tool been accepted by "the father of singing among the children," Lowell Mason, and others who shaped the patterns of American music education, we might have been more successful in developing skilled music readers and enthusiastic amateur choral singers in the public schools. The reasons for the rejection of shape notes — Thomas Hastings, one of their most vociferous early detractors, called them "dunce

notes"[2]—had nothing to do with the system's merits or demerits. The shape notes from their very inception were closely associated with a remarkable indigenous music which began its development in Connecticut in the 1780's and shortly afterward blanketed New England and the Middle Atlantic states.[3] The "reformers" who quickly arose in earnest protest against this first flowering of American musical expression, all too conscious of the European musical tradition and possessed of an inferiority complex regarding peculiarly American cultural manifestations, eventually saw to the elimination of this music from American life, at least in the North. In the meantime, the shape note system and the music itself became completely identified. Shape notes came to be regarded in urban centers as the musical notation of the country people, the naive, simple people who sang for their own enjoyment songs in a strange, almost primitive native idiom. Leaders of fine city choirs, busy with Pucitta and Neukomm as well as Handel and Haydn, would have nothing to do with such music nor with such notation. Inevitably, the city choir leaders became first music teachers in the public schools. Shape notes were never admitted to the classroom. As a result, the child who learns music in our schools today must do so without the aid that they might give.[4]

The earliest reference to *The Easy Instructor* and to the shape note system is to be found in a "title-page"

---

[2] *Musical Magazine*, I (July 1835), 87.

[3] For a brief analysis of this music, see Allen P. Britton, "The Musical Idiom in Early American Tune Books," *Jour. of the Amer. Musicol. Soc.*, III (Fall 1950), 186.

[4] This entire subject is dealt with in the unpubl. diss. (University of Michigan, 1949) by Allen P. Britton, "Theoretical Introductions in American Tune Books to 1800" (University Microfilms, No. 1505), pp. 313-332.

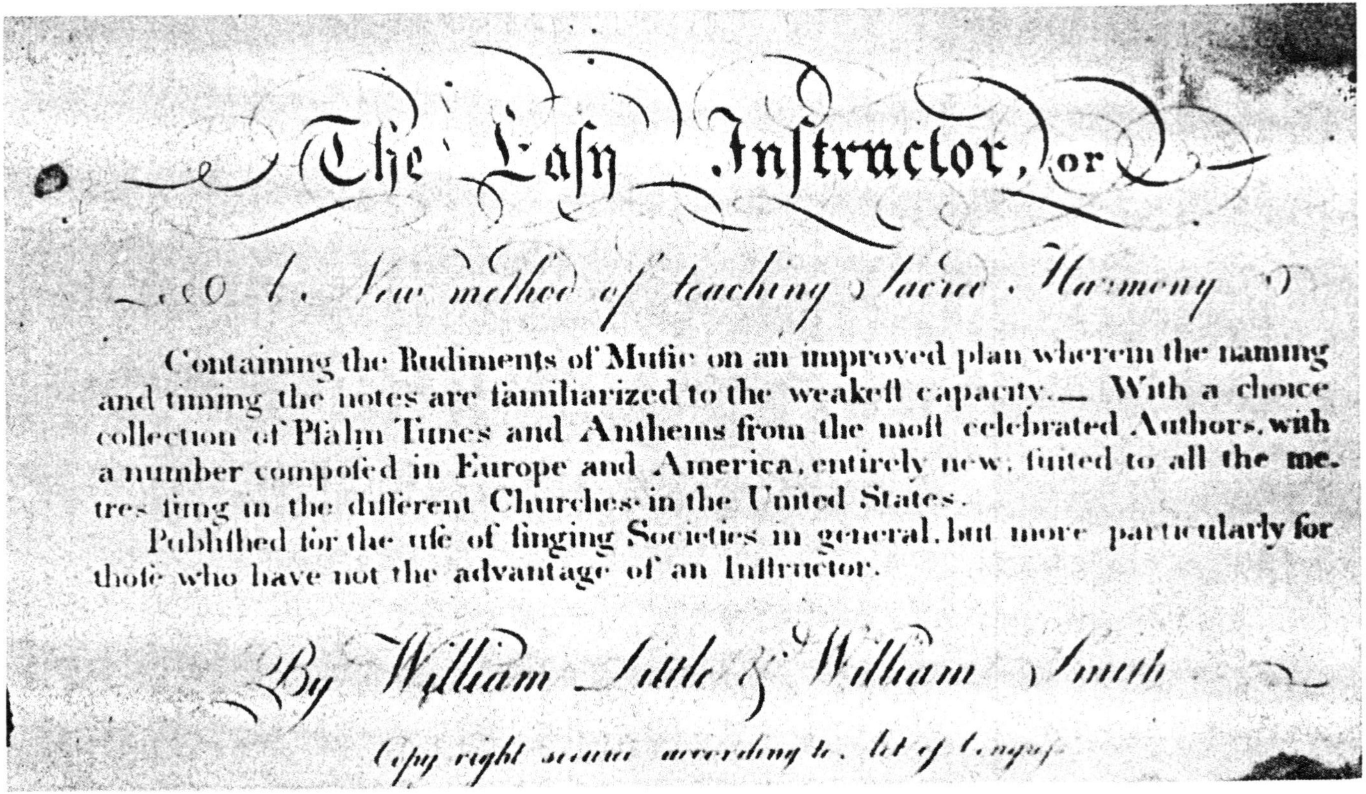

Illustration 2. Edition Aa. Title page of the 1802 edition of *The Easy Instructor.* Reproduced from a photograph of the original by courtesy of the Case Memorial Library, Hartford Seminary Foundation. (See check list, page 47.)

which was deposited for copyright in the Southern District of Pennsylvania on August 15, 1798:

THE *Easy Instructor,* or a New Method of teaching *Sacred Harmony,* containing the Rudiments of *Music* on an improved Plan, wherein the Naming and Timing the notes, are familiarized to the weakest capacity.

Likewise, an Essay on Composition, with directions to enable any person with a tolerable voice, to take the air of any piece of Music at sight, and perform it by word, without singing it by note. Also, the Transposition of Mi, rendering all the keys in music as easy as the natural key, whereby the errors in Composition and the press may be known. Together with a choice collection of Psalm Tunes, and Anthems, from the most celebrated Authors in Europe, with a number composed in Europe and America, entirely new; suited to all the metres sung in the different Churches in the United States.

Published for the use of Singing Societies in general, but more particularly for those who have not the advantage of an Instructor.

By EDWARD STAMMERS,
WILLIAM LITTLE.
*Copy right secured according to
Act of Congress.*[5]

Surprisingly, the name of Edward Stammers appears where one might expect to find that of William Smith. Who was Stammers? His name appears in every known edition of *The Easy Instructor,* together with that of Richard T. Leech, in connection with a report of a committee of the Uranian Society of Philadelphia printed therein.

The report reads as follows:

PHILADELPHIA, August 15, 1798.
The Committee appointed by the URANIAN SOCIETY of PHILADELPHIA, to examine a Singing Book, entitled, "THE EASY INSTRUCTOR," BY WILLIAM LITTLE,

REPORT......That having carefully examined the same, they find it contains a well digested system of principles and rules, and a judicious collection of tunes: And from the improvement of having only four significant characters, indicating, at sight, the names of the notes, and a sliding rule for timing the same, this book is considered easier to be learned than any we have seen.

Were it possible to acquire the sound of the eight notes but by imitation, they verily believe they might be obtained by the help of this book, even without an instructor.

The Committee are of opinion the Author merits the patronage and encouragement of all friends to Church Music:

Which is submitted to,

EDWARD STAMMERS,
RICHARD T. LEECH.[6]

Three aspects of this report present special difficulties when considered together: (1) the date coincides with that of the Pennsylvania copyright entry; (2) Little is given as sole author in the body of the report; (3) the names of Stammers and Leech are preceded by the phrase "which is submitted to."[7] A number of questions

---

[5]From the original at the Library of Congress (M2116 L77). The authors here wish to express their thanks to the staff members of the Music Division, the Descriptive Cataloging Division, and the Rare Book Room for unstinted assistance and cooperation. Grateful acknowledgment is also made to the staffs of the New York Public Library, the Newberry Library, the Case Memorial Library of the Hartford Seminary Foundation, the Brown University Library, the Clements Library of the University of Michigan, and many others for their cooperation over a period of years without which this study would have been impossible.

[6]Ed. A, pp. [3]-4. What the "sliding rule" might have been remains a matter of conjecture. No further reference to it occurs in the introductory musical instructions. The title of Benjamin Dearborn's *The Vocal Instructor,* copyrighted in Massachusetts in 1797 but apparently never published, mentions "a sliding music scale, never before publish'd in which a moveable index points out the names and distances of the notes in all their variations." See Evans' *American Bibliography,* No. 32021.

[7]The complete phrase appears before the names of Stammers and Leech only in Eds. A-Da. In Eds. Db-I, the phrase reads, "which is submitted," thus making it appear that the two men *submitted* to the report. In Eds. J-BB, the whole phrase is omitted, and Stammers and Leech seem to be the *signers* of the recommendation.

arise. Since report and copyright entry were submitted on the same day, why is not Stammers credited as co-author in both? Did Stammers actually assist Little in compiling the book, or was he engaging in some way to sponsor its publication in return for credit as co-author? What is the meaning of the strange closing phrase, i.e., did Stammers and Leech *submit* or *receive* the report? Since Little is given as sole author in the report, how is it that the name of William Smith is given as co-author on the title-page of all known printed editions? (A further difficulty arises in connection with the 1802 New York copyright to be discussed below, which, like the report, gives Little as sole author.) None of these questions can now be answered with certainty although some general conclusions regarding the Stammers-Little-Smith relationship will presently be deduced.

The "choice collection of Psalm Tunes, and Anthems, from the most celebrated Authors *in Europe* [italics supplied], with a number composed in Europe and America, entirely new" of the 1798 copyright entry clearly does not pertain to any of the known early editions of the tune book, all of which contain almost exclusively American music in the distinctive native idiom. This description of an *Easy Instructor* unknown in print presupposes a compiler familiar with the European tradition, which Stammers certainly must have been. As a member of a prominent singing society and the compiler

of a posthumously published tune book, the *Philadelphia Chorister* (Philadelphia: J. McCulloch, 1803),[8] Stammers was obviously quite capable of having edited *The Easy Instructor* and devised the shape note system. Whether he actually did so must remain an unanswered question; what little evidence is now available points to the probability that he was responsible only for instructions and music in the 1798 manuscript, which, so far as is known, never achieved publication under the title *Easy Instructor*. The invention of the shape note system itself, however, is even more difficult to establish, although here probability favors Little as its originator.

William Little's very obscurity as a practicing musician lends some credence to this theory. The phrase in the 1798 copyright deposit, "whereby errors in . . . the press may be known," and the typographical nature of the shape note concept give rise to the suspicion that someone engaged in the printing trades was in some way associated with the venture. If this supposition is correct, the William Little who was an obscure printer in Philadelphia during 1802 and 1803[9] may well have been Stammers' associate. The assumption that Little was a printer interested in music (he was interested

---

[8]Stammers is listed as a baker in the Philadelphia directories of 1798 through 1802. In 1803 appears, "Stammers, widow of Edward, baker." As the directories were invariably published in the October preceding the dated year, Stammers apparently died prior to October, 1802. It is possible that his *Philadelphia Chorister* is actually the original manuscript of *The Easy Instructor* in print, since it corresponds fairly well with the description of content in the 1798 copyright of the latter work. The only *Philadelphia*

Chorister located to date is at the New-York Historical Society. The authors would like here to express their indebtedness to Miss Geraldine Beard of the Society's staff for considerable help in establishing the chronology of the early Albany printing firms sketched in this study.

[9]H. Glenn Brown and Maude O. Brown, *A Directory of the Book-Arts and Book Trade in Philadelphia to 1820* (New York, 1950), p. 76. A William Little—perhaps the same individual—was also active in New York as a printer during 1808 and 1809; see George L. McKay, *A Register of Artists, Engravers, Booksellers, Bookbinders, Printers & Publishers in New York City, 1633-1820* (New York, 1942), p. 44.

enough to do a little composing, for four of his tunes appear in the earliest known edition, see Ed. A below) rather than a professional musician helps to explain why another collaborator, William Smith, became necessary when Stammers died before *The Easy Instructor* appeared in print, and also the peculiarly distant relationship between Little and the tune book of which he was supposedly one of the compilers.

Although it is clear from the Uranian Society committee report that a manuscript utilizing shape notes must have been in existence in 1798 before William Smith entered the picture, it is extremely doubtful that the work was published in that year or that it was ever published at all in the form in which it received the recommendation. The existence of a copyright entry is by no means proof that a title actually achieved publication. As it was only necessary at that time to file the *name* of a book to receive copyright protection, not an actual copy of the book itself, early copyright records are filled with ghost titles of books which were never printed. This appears to have been the case with the original manuscript of *The Easy Instructor* seen by the committee of the Uranian Society. The unique 1798 "title-page" preserved at the Library of Congress was apparently imprinted for the specific purpose of entering the title in the copyright records, and examination proves that it bears no possible physical relationship to any printed copy of the book known today.

The only record of a 1798 edition of *The Easy Instructor* appears in a thoroughly self-contradictory entry in Evans' *American Bibliography*, No. 34004:

LITTLE, WILLIAM. The Easy Instructor; or, a new method of teaching sacred harmony. Containing, I. The rudiments of music on an improved plan, wherein the naming and timing of the notes are familiarized to the weakest capacity. II. A choice collection of psalm tunes and anthems, from the most celebrated authors, with a number composed in Europe and America, entirely new; suited to all the metres sung in the different churches in the United States. Published for the use of singing societies in general, but more particularly for those who have not the advantage of an instructor. By William Little and William Smith. [Philadelphia. 1798. Pp. 74. Obl. 12mo.]

Evans evidently transcribed the title page from one of the undated Albany editions published between 1808 and 1816 (Eds. F-0*b*; see Illustration 4). The imprint appears to have been supplied on the basis of the known 1798 Pennsylvania copyright and the dated report of the Uranian Society committee—which Evans erroneously associates with the advertisement signed by Little and Smith to be found in all known editions (see fn. 12). The 74-page collation seems inexplicable, but the nature of the entry strongly suggests that it is an attempted reconstruction of a book not actually examined.[10] This supposition is strengthened by the fact that Evans locates no copy of this purported edition. Why he failed to use the title as given in the 1798 Pennsylvania copyright, with which he was familiar, remains a mystery. Thus, it must be assumed that no 1798 edition was actually published until more convincing evidence of its existence is uncovered.

Because very little factual information is available, any account of *The*

[10]The Massachusetts Historical Society copy of Ed. R. may perhaps be the source of the Evans entry. The following, written in a nineteenth century hand, appears on the fly-leaf: "This Book is probably the 4ᵈ Ed. of the Easy Instructor has 127 pages & index makes 128 pages—& issued abt 1818. The First Ed. had 74 pages, 2ᵈ Ed. 104 pages & 3ᵈ Ed. has 112 pages. The Preface by Little & Smith dated 'Phil. Aug. 15, 1798' is the Same in Each Ed. But the Music & Tunes are quite different in Each Ed. W. Latham."

Easy Instructor between 1798 and 1802, when the genuine first edition (see Ed. A below) seems to have appeared, must be largely speculative. The gap of four years between manuscript and book may be accounted for by the typographical novelty of the project and the not inconsiderable difficulty of preparing suitable plates. During this period Stammers died, and Little entered into collaboration with one of the most tantalizingly mysterious figures in the history of American music, William Smith. Certainly, he is not to be confused with the comparatively prominent Rev. William Smith who published *The Churchman's Choral Companion* (New York, 1809). While the authors have not as yet managed to destroy Smith's anonymity, they have been able to uncover one very faint and perhaps fruitless clue to his identity. In the manuscript letter books of Daniel Read, one of the most distinguished practitioners of the American idiom, are five letters written between 1794 and 1802 addressed to an otherwise unknown New York singing master called William H. Smith.[11] The content of the letters does not preclude the possibility that this was Little's associate. Unfortunately, New York directories and other contemporary sources such as newspapers disclose no William Smith or William H. Smith engaged in musical activities during this period. In 1803 and 1806 our Smith was evidently a resident of Hopewell, New Jersey, as this is the place given in the dated prefaces of a tune book published unilaterally by him, *The Easy Instructor, Part II* (discussed in detail below).

Whoever Smith might have been, he apparently differed sharply from Stam-

mers in musical taste. The 1798 copyright describes a tune book with a European orientation, whereas the music in the earliest known edition, presumably compiled by Smith, is almost entirely American. Since both Smith and Little were composers in the American idiom (Smith is represented by one number in Ed. A and Little by four), the change in orientation seems understandable enough. Both men must have originally worked well together, for by 1802 they had gathered "upwards" of 3000 subscriptions for *The Easy Instructor,* a number presaging its future success.[12]

Perhaps because of Stammers' death and Smith's *locus vivendi,* the scene of *Easy Instructor* activity shifted from Philadelphia to New York some time between 1798 and 1802. There, at last, the firm of G. & R. Waite (which was apparently more interested in selling patent medicines and lottery tickets than book publishing, to judge from their advertisements) announced on November 25, 1802, in the New York *Chronicle Express,* "This day is published . . . THE EASY INSTRUCTOR; or A New Method of Teaching Sacred Harmony by William Little & William Smith. . . ."[13] A few weeks *after* publication, on December 10, 1802, Little deposited the title of the book in the District of New York for copyright. Apparently for the specific purpose of befuddling later generations of scholars, Little signed himself sole author.[14] The peculiarity of the copy-

[11]See Irving Lowens, "Daniel Read's World: the Letters of an Early American Composer," *Music Library Association Notes,* IX (March 1952), 233-248.

[12]Ed. A, "Advertisement," p. [3]. In later editions the August 15, 1798, date is typographically set so that it appears to pertain to the advertisement rather than to the recommendation printed immediately below it. That the date pertains to the recommendation is clear in Ed. A.

[13]The complete advertisement is quoted in Frank J. Metcalf, "The Easy Instructor; a Bibliographical Study," *Mus. Quar.* XXIII (January 1937), 91.

[14]The 1802 copyright entry is also quoted in its entirety in Metcalf, p. 90.

right situation makes it evident that Smith was a junior partner in the venture, and that Little's was the controlling interest. The 1802 copyright also makes it amply clear that Little wished to retain undivided control of *The Easy Instructor* and that he had perhaps become somewhat suspicious of Smith's intentions.

No copy bearing an 1802 date or a G. & R. Waite imprint has been located, but Edition A (see the check list below) conforms to all the particulars of the 1802 advertisement and copyright entry and is presumed, on circumstantial evidence, to be the genuine first edition. Edition A, four copies of which have now been located, is the *only* known edition which could possibly be that advertised. Furthermore, one bit of evidence turns the possibility into probability. The preface to Smith's *Easy Instructor, Part II* (see below), dated 1803, begins as follows: "The Publisher of this work meeting with great encouragement in the first edition of the '*Easy Instructor*,' is induced to publish a second edition, and having added the flats and sharps, so that the singer may take his choice, either to sing by characters or by line and space, he hopes to meet the approbation and patronage of the friends to Vocal Music." The music in Edition A is *without* "flats and sharps" (i.e. key signatures) excepting for three numbers only. Unless Smith had published an earlier edition of *Part II*, an extremely unlikely event, it must be presumed that Edition A is the "first edition" he refers to.

The sole identifiable remnant of the 1798 manuscript appearing in Edition A would appear to be the preface, which consists basically of the first six paragraphs and a portion of the seventh of the preface to Ralph Harrison's *Sacred Harmony* (London, 1784). This same preface had been utilized at least twice before by American tune book compilers, by John Poor in his *Collection of Psalms and Hymns* (Philadelphia: J. McCulloch, 1794), and, more significantly, by Andrew Adgate in his *Select Psalms and Hymns* (Philadelphia: Young and McCulloch, 1787). As Adgate was one of the founders of the Uranian Academy of Philadelphia, of which the Uranian Society was a direct outgrowth,[16] the possible connection between the preface and Stammers, an official of the Uranian Society, is obvious.

Of the 105 compositions included in Edition A, only five are of European origin; even these were old American favorites which had appeared in almost every New England tune book from the time that Daniel Bayley of Newburyport commenced to reprint the works of the English singing masters William Tans'ur and Aaron Williams in the 1760's. The American compositions, among them forty-one claimed as "never before published," are excellent examples of the characteristic native idiom of the time. Thus, between 1798 and 1802, the European musical bias of Stammers had been transformed into the thoroughly American one of Smith, with Little serving as a bridge between the two musicians. From a strictly musical point of view, the interest of *The Easy Instructor* is considerably enhanced because of this change in orientation; from the point of view of the future acceptance of the shape note idea by the eventual arbiters of musical progress in America, the change was disastrous. In this manner, the individual tastes of a single obscure musician, William Smith, may have changed the whole future course of American music history.

In the year after *The Easy Instruc-*

---

[16]See O. G. Sonneck, *Early Concert-Life in America, 1731-1800* (Leipzig, 1907), pp. 103-120.

tor appeared in print, Smith, apparently without help from Little, brought out another tune book making use of the shape note system:

THE Easy Instructor OR A New method of teaching Sacred Harmony. PART II. Containing the Rudiments of Music on an improved plan.—With a choice collection of Psalm Tunes, a number of which are entirely new. By William Smith & Co.

The omission of any reference to "European music" on the title-page and the absence of any in the collection itself bear out the idea that Smith's preference was for American music in the native idiom. Where the book was published is not known, but a physical resemblance between the title pages of *Part II* and Edition A arouses the suspicion that the Waite firm was also responsible for this imprint. No copyright record has been located, and the strong probability is that no application was made, as *Part II* does not appear to have been authorized by Little. Little was the sole owner of the 1802 copyright, and Smith may have overstepped the bounds of propriety, if not of legality, with the curious author ascription on the title-page of *Part II* where the senior partner is reduced to the unenviable status of an "& Co." There seems to be little doubt that the appearance of *Part II*, with its nonchalant disregard of Little, did not help build amicable relations between the two. Indeed, indications are that it caused a complete break, for when a second edition of *Part II* was published in 1806, "& Co." was no longer on the title-page, and Smith appears as sole author.

A disagreement about *Part II* may well have precipitated the next phase in the history of *The Easy Instructor*. If Little was in fact a printer by trade, the book must have been at best a peripheral interest, and the rupture of

his partnership with Smith deprived him of a collaborator. Perhaps annoyance decided him to sell out on the best possible terms. Perhaps he considered the copyright, already violated by Smith, no longer of any particular value. At any rate, some time between 1803 and 1805—no record of the transaction has been found—he apparently sold or reassigned the copyright to a trio of Albany, New York, printers, possibly suggested to him by G. & R. Waite, who maintained a branch of their firm in that city. Thereafter, neither of the co-authors of Edition A seems to have been in any way connected with the book, and another person assumed the responsibility for its ever-changing musical content. All the introductory material remained unaltered throughout all editions.

In Albany *The Easy Instructor* really hit its stride, thanks to the astuteness of an editor who successfully followed the musical fashions of the moment. A veritable flood of editions, the first in 1805 and the last in 1831, poured from the presses. Tens of thousands of copies were sold, and the tune book became celebrated throughout the country, extending its influence far beyond its Albany base. If Little was then still alive, he must have regretted his decision to dispose of the copyright, which suddenly had become an extremely lucrative property.

One of the most intriguing of the many historical riddles in connection with *The Easy Instructor* is the identity of its Albany editor, who certainly deserves a small niche in the musical hall of fame. Who chose the music and decided what changes should be made from edition to edition? The little evidence available points to Daniel Steele (1772-1828), one of the three figures who obtained the 1802 copyright from Little. There is no reason to believe that either of the other two, Charles

R. Webster (1762-1832) or his twin brother George Webster (1762-1821), was sufficiently interested or skilled in music to undertake the difficult editorial task. Both were prominent printers in the community, and there is no indication in their well documented life histories that they participated in any musical activities; their only connection with music seems to have been their publishing activities, which are known to have commenced as early as 1800. On the other hand, Steele, although a lesser figure in Albany local history and consequently a more obscure one, may have been the singing master who advertised as follows in the Albany *Argus* of December 16, 1817:

SINGING SCHOOL

Mr. Steele will commence school this evening for the purpose of instructing youth in the Rudiments of vocal Music, at the Session Room of the Presbyterian Church in Beaver Street. Those who are desirous of attending, can become members by applying at the room.

Although no definite evidence that Steele functioned as a practicing musician earlier than 1817 has been found, there are indications that this may have been a part-time career engaged in over a long period of time, simultaneously with his book-selling and printing activities. The tune books he advertised for sale as early as 1801 strengthen the impression that he was more than casually interested in music. The fact that creative revision of *The Easy Instructor* virtually ceased at the close of his life is suggestive; until more information comes to light, it should probably be assumed that the Albany editions published prior to 1828 are the product of Steele's imagination and labor.

Apparently, the transaction between Little and the Albany group did not include the transfer of the original plates, as a new set engraved by Henry W. Snyder, an Albany craftsman, was used for the earliest group of Albany editions (Eds. B, C. D*a*, D*b*, and E), the first of which was issued in 1805 and the last in 1808. Snyder's work was more skillful than that of the anonymous original engraver, who may perhaps have been Little himself, but it is still quite crude compared to the productions of other engravers active during the same period. Although the music editor radically revised the contents, omitting twenty-five tunes from the first edition and adding twenty-two others, he did not change its emphasis upon music in the native idiom.

Beginning with the first undated Albany *Easy Instructor* (Ed. F), the engraved music plates characteristic of prior editions were abandoned. This and subsequent editions were printed from a type-font designed specifically for the shape note system.[16] The origi-

---

[16]One might naturally assume that this was the first such type-font in existence, but the facts are otherwise. About a year after the appearance of Ed. A, Andrew Law, one of the most prominent singing masters of the day, brought out the fourth edition of his *Art of Singing* (Cambridge: W. Hilliard, 1803) "printed upon a new plan." This particular edition and later publications of Law's were printed typographically with shape notes identical to those in *The Easy Instructor*. However, Law interchanged the characters for fa and la and entirely abandoned the use of staff lines. Significantly, he made no claim that the shapes were his own invention but stressed the fact that the staff was eliminated, strongly implying that this was the essence of his "new plan." Yet, in a book published six years later, *The Art of Playing the Organ and Piano Forte* (Philadelphia: Jane Aitken, c. 1809), he did insist that he had a shape note system ready for publication as early as 1786, but could not print it because it was then impossible to obtain type. But if Law's system was ready in 1786, why could not the shapes have been engraved? At that time almost all tune books, including Law's own, were printed from engraved plates. Law cannot be credited with the invention of the shape note system, but he no doubt was first to make typographical use of the characters.

nator of this font was undoubtedly either William Wood or Obadiah R. Van Benthuysen, whose names are found in the colophon of Edition F. The probability is that Van Benthuysen deserves the major share of the credit, as Wood disappears from the history of *The Easy Instructor* after the appearance of this single edition, while Van Benthuysen continued his association with the book throughout its existence, first as its typographer and later as its printer. In 1809 Van Benthuysen formed a brief partnership with George Newton (see Eds. G and H). Thereafter he continued in business independently (see Eds. I and J) until 1812, when he joined forces with Robert Packard (see Eds. K and all following Albany editions). The firm of Packard and Van Benthuysen was to become illustrious in the annals of the Albany printing trade, continuing in existence throughout the nineteenth century and well into the twentieth, finally closing its books in 1922.[17]

Typographical editions of *The Easy Instructor* were brought out at the rate of one or two each year from 1808 to 1822. Thereafter, as the demand for the book tapered off, they were issued at bi-yearly intervals with one exception. The printing record of *The Easy Instructor* demonstrates that it probably reached the peak of its popularity between 1814 and 1817. Editorial changes, presumably made by Steele to keep the collection up to the moment, followed a clear-cut pattern. In each new edition, a greater or lesser number of old American favorites was deleted and new and fashionable European

tunes were added (see Table VIII). At irregular intervals, extra eight-page signatures containing almost exclusively European music were also added, thus progressively enlarging the number of pages from 104 in the first typographical edition to 136 in the last. At the same time, the uniquely native flavor of the early editions was gradually watered down to the point where the character of its music was practically indistinguishable from that of the "reform" collections. Indeed, except for title, instructions, and notation, there is but little resemblance between the early and late editions of *The Easy Instructor*.

Before the last of the engraved editions came out in 1808, other publishers, particularly in Pennsylvania, had become aware of the phenomenal success of *The Easy Instructor* and imitations began to appear in print. Ironically, one of the first of these brings the story back to Philadelphia, where the history of *The Easy Instructor* had its inception in 1798. The John Jenkins Husband[18] edition of Andrew Adgate's *Philadelphia Harmony* (Philadelphia: M. Carey, 1807; also 1811)[19] appeared in a shape note guise derived in conception from *The Easy Instructor*, although its editor used considerably different shapes. During the same year the Philadelphia musician-bookseller Charles Woodward brought out his *Ecclesia Harmonia* (Philadelphia, 1807; another ed. publ. by W. W.

---

[17]See John Clyde Oswald, *Printing in the Americas* (New York, 1937), p. 226, and Clarence T. Brigham, *History and Bibliography of American Newspapers, 1690-1820* (Worcester, 1947), I, 587. The authors are deeply indebted to Dr. Brigham and the American Antiquarian Society for supplying them with much helpful information.

[18]An English musician who apparently arrived in the United States in 1806 or 1807. He has a stronger claim to immortality if the tune "Revive Us Again" (better known in secular circles as "Hallelujah, I'm a Bum"), attributed to him in Lester Hostetler, *Handbook to the Mennonite Hymnary* (Newton, Kansas, 1949), pp. 253-254, is actually his composition.

[19]Although Adgate died in the yellow fever epidemic of 1793, the publication of this popular collection was continued, the last edition appearing in 1811.

Woodward, 1809), in which the shape note idea was borrowed intact, although he also used differently shaped note heads, while a year later Nathan Chapin and Joseph L. Dickerson's *The Musical Instructor* (Philadelphia: W. McCulloch, 1808; also 1810) appeared in a seven shape system of which the Little and Smith shape notes formed the basis.

With the publication of the first of the typographical editions, a more important series of imitations, also printed typographically, was brought out by John Wyeth, a Harrisburg publisher. The first to be issued, Joseph Doll's *Leichter Unterricht* (Harrisburg, 1810; also 1814, 1821; Vol. II, 1815) was not only a direct plagiarism in translation of the Little and Smith title, but a direct appropriation of the distinctive shapes as well. As the *Leichter Unterricht* was designed to appeal to the German-speaking Pennsylvania population which would not ordinarily be reached by such a book as *The Easy Instructor*, its compiler chose primarily music from the continental European tradition, although he did include some of the favorite native American tunes set to German texts. Wyeth's comprehensive *Repository of Sacred Music* (Harrisburg, 1810; also 1811, 1812, 1814, 1816, 1818, 1823, 1826, 1834), on the other hand, duplicated the character of *The Easy Instructor* almost exactly, but masqueraded its indebtedness to the earlier tune book under a totally different title. There appears to be strong evidence that nearly half its 156 tunes were taken directly from various editions of *The Easy Instructor*, as in many cases Wyeth reprinted without change distinctive typographical errors and mistakes in composer ascription found only in the Little and Smith work. One of the most significant music publications of the early nineteenth century was Wyeth's *Repository*

of Sacred Music, Part Second (Harrisburg, 1813; also 1820). This proved to be the first really influential anthology of what George Pullen Jackson has termed spiritual folk song, and *Part Second* was a major source drawn upon for materials by later compilers such as Ananias Davisson, James M. Boyd, Joseph Funk, Allen D. Carden, William Walker, and many others.[20] It undoubtedly set the pattern for the distinctive combination of Yankee psalm and fuging tunes and secular folk melodies which constitutes the Southern folk hymnody tradition out of which such magnificent tune books as Walker's *Southern Harmony* and White and King's *Sacred Harp* grew. *Part Second* was perhaps more important than *The Easy Instructor* itself in the eventual dissemination of the shape note idea to the South. Still another of Wyeth's shape note publications was Johannes Rothbaust's bilingual *Die Franklin Harmonie, und leichter Unterricht* (Harrisburg, 1821; Vol. II, 1821), reprinted by a different publisher as a second, revised edition under the English title *The Franklin Harmony and Easy Instructor* (Chambersburg: H. Ruby, c. 1830). This curious tune book, with its frank indebtedness to *The Easy Instructor* flaunted on its title-page, exhibits a most interesting crossblend of German and Anglo-Saxon music traditions in its contents.

The firm name Websters & Skinner, found in the second engraved Albany edition of *The Easy Instructor* (Ed. C), came into existence on May 19, 1806, when Elisha W. Skinner, the brothers Webster's nephew, joined them in their

---

[20]For a study of the important role played by this tune book in the development of the Southern tradition, see Irving Lowens, "John Wyeth's *Repository of Sacred Music, Part Second;* a Northern Precursor of Southern Folk Hymnody," *Jour. of the Amer. Musicol. Soc.,* V (Summer 1952), 114-131.

THE EASY INSTRUCTOR,

OR, A NEW METHOD OF TEACHING

SACRED HARMONY.

CONTAINING,

The Rudiments of Music on an improved Plan, wherein the Naming and Timing of the Notes are familiarized to the weakest Capacity.

With a choice Collection of Psalm Tunes and Anthems from the most celebrated Authors, with a Number composed in Europe and America, entirely new; suited to all the Metres sung in the different Churches in the United States.

Published for the use of Singing Societies in general, but more particularly for those who have not the advantage of an Instructor.

By WILLIAM LITTLE AND WILLIAM SMITH.

ALBANY:

Printed by CHARLES R. and GEORGE WEBSTER, and DANIEL STEELE, Proprietors of the Copy-right ; and sold at WEBSTER's Bookstore, corner of State and Pearl Streets, and at STEELE's Bookstore, near the Court House, in Court Street.

1805.

Illustration 3. Edition B. Courtesy of the New York Public Library. (See check list, page 47.)

business. In the fall of 1811, Elisha's two brothers, Hezekiah and Daniel, were taken into partnership and the firm then became known as Websters & Skinners. Despite mutations in the firm's name, the *Easy Instructor* copyright seems to have remained the sole property of the two Websters and Daniel Steele. Understandably enough, the three men were not anxious to surrender their lucrative property to the public domain when the copyright on the work was due to expire on December 10, 1816. One of the three, apparently George Webster, hit upon a clever idea to prolong their control of the shape note idea regardless of the expiration of the copyright, which could only be renewed, according to the law, by the original owner. On February 28, 1816, a patent covering the casting and use of the shape note types was granted to George Webster, obviously as agent for the Albany trio. Most unfortunately, the original patent application, which ordinarily would have been preserved, was destroyed in one of the many fires which ravaged the United States Patent Office early in its career, and only a bare notice of the patent grant is extant. Were the details of the application itself available, considerable information about the early history of *The Easy Instructor* might have been gathered from it. Notice of the patent grant is found on the title-page of the 120-page Edition P, published shortly after the expiration of the copyright, where the familiar phrase "Proprietors of the Copy-Right" is omitted and in its place appears the legend: "The Music Types used in printing this Book are secured to the Proprietors by Patent Right." This notice is unquestionably the genesis of the term "patent notes," frequently used in later years as a synonym for shape notes.

With the expiration of the copyright,

the proprietors apparently decided to license other publishers to cast and use their patented shape notes and to reprint *The Easy Instructor* itself. The first to obtain a license seems to have been William Williams of Utica, New York, whose name is found in the list of authorized agents printed on the title-page of Edition P. Williams, who was also the publisher of Thomas Hastings and Solomon Warriner's influential *Musica Sacra* (Utica, 1816; many later editions),[21] brought out editions of *The Easy Instructor* in 1818 and 1820 (Eds. S and W), using the 120-page Edition P as prototype. His only editorial change was to delete a single long American tune and to substitute for it three shorter European ones, thus giving his editions, both of which are identical in content, a total of 127 compositions as compared with the 125 of his model. Working with the unfamiliar shape notes apparently proved somewhat troublesome to him, as his editions are poorly executed and are replete with typographical errors in both music and text. Only one other printer, J. Pace of Cincinnati, is known to have brought out an authorized *Easy Instructor*. The Pace imprint, published in 1819 (Ed. U), used the first of the Williams editions as the source of its music rather than the 120-page Albany edition, in some instances duplicating textual errors found there only. The Cincinnati edition omits the last thirteen tunes in the Utica edition.

That the Albany group failed to sell additional licenses is not surprising. Part of their plan, possibly conceived at the same time application for a patent was made, may well have been to cut the ground out from under the feet of their self-manufactured competitors by issuing revised editions

[21]See John C. Williams, *An Oneida County Printer, William Williams, Printer, Publisher, Editor* (New York, 1906).

THE EASY INSTRUCTOR;

OR,

A NEW METHOD OF TEACHING

Sacred Harmony.

CONTAINING

I. THE RUDIMENTS OF MUSIC on an improved Plan, wherein the Naming and Timing of the Notes are familiarized to the weakest Capacity.

II. A choice Collection of PSALM TUNES and ANTHEMS, from the most celebrated Authors, with a number composed in in Europe and America, entirely new ; suited to all the Metres sung in the different Churches in the United States.

Published for the Use of SINGING SOCIETIES in general, but more particularly for those who have not the Advantage of an INSTRUCTOR.

BY WILLIAM LITTLE AND WILLIAM SMITH.

PRINTED, *Typographically*, at ALBANY,

BY WEBSTERS & SKINNER AND DANIEL STEELE, (Proprietors of the Copy-Right,)

And sold at their respective Bookstores, at the corner of State and Pearl-Streets, and a few doors south of the Old City-Hall, in Court-Street ; by T. & J. SWORDS, EVERT DUYCKINCK and WILLIAM FALCONER, *New-York* ; MATHEW CAREY, JOHNSON & WARNER, WILLIAM W. WOODWARD and HOPKINS & EARL, *Philadelphia* ; and INCREASE COOK, *New-Haven.*

Illustration 4. Edition F. Courtesy of the Clements Library, University of Michigan.
(See check list, page 47.)

while selling licenses to reprint the old. Thus, on the one hand, they hoped to reap a profit from the sale of permissions, while on the other, they maintained command of the market by continuing to adjust the content of their own editions to conform to the changing musical tastes of the moment. On the latter account, all Albany editions published after Edition P are designated "revised and enlarged." These, the last of which appeared in 1831, bring to a close the history of *The Easy Instructor*.

The check list which follows is an attempted solution to one of the most complex bibliographical problems in the entire range of American printing history. The authors cannot presume to have untangled all the snarls and to have evaded all the booby-traps hidden in the jungle of *Easy Instructor* editions and issues, but they believe they have been successful in establishing the chronology of those editions they have examined, and have ascertained exact dates of publication within one year. The solution of this problem is of more than bibliographical interest. With each printing accurately dated and placed in proper chronological order, *The Easy Instructor* becomes an extremely accurate barometer of American musical tastes over a period of nearly three decades. The tale told by the addition of one tune and the deletion of another is invaluable, highly detailed documentation of a significant, though much neglected aspect of our cultural development. Two bibliographical studies of *The Easy Instructor* have previously appeared in print, one by Frank J. Metcalf[22] and another by Lester Condit.[23] The Metcalf study, although fragmentary and based on incomplete

data, is quite valuable; those interested in comparing his results with those of the authors should consult Table VIII, where the numbers assigned to the editions seen by Metcalf are listed in conjunction with letters assigned in this study.

A Check List of Editions and Issues

In the following list, each edition is assigned a letter in accordance with the chronology of its publication. Separate printings which embody no changes of title, imprint, or content have been defined as issues of a given edition and are indicated by combining a lower case italic letter with that assigned the edition (e.g. A*a*, A*b*). Unless otherwise indicated, omitted titles and imprints or various sections thereof may be presumed similar to those of the edition or issue next above. Location symbols are those used by the *Union List of Serials*. Except for capitalization of initial letters, which has been followed exactly, no attempt has been made to indicate original typography; however, reference is made to the method of printing (i.e. whether from engraved plates or from type). Titlepages of key editions have been reproduced photographically. Although dozens of points of distinction among editions and issues were ascertained and tabulated in preparing the chronology given below, only those unique points are given which may serve easily to identify a particular edition or issue. Special attention is called to the eight tables, which are designed to give comparative data succinctly. Table I distinguishes all undated typographically printed editions, and Table VIII is a conspectus of all editions and issues. Since William Smith's *The Easy Instructor, Part II* is a completely separate work, its two editions are not included in this list.

---

[22]See fn. 13 for reference.

[23]"Editions of Little & Smith's *Easy Instructor*," *Papers of the Bibl. Soc. of Amer.*, XL (Third Quarter 1946), 233-236.

TABLE I. A CONDENSED IDENTIFICATION CHART FOR UNDATED ALBANY EDITIONS

104-page editions

Edition	Title-page points	
	Typographer	*Last dealer's name*
F [1808]	none	Increase Cook
G [1809]	Van Benthuysen & Newton	Increase Cook
H [1809]	Van Benthuysen & Newton	M. Cary [sic]
I [1810]	O. R. Van Benthuysen	D. Allenson & Co.

112-page editions

Edition	Title-page points		Other points	
	Typographer	*Last dealer's name*	*Page 61**	*Page 81*
J [1811]	O. R. Van Benthuysen	E. Lewis	Salisbury	Judgment Anthem
K [1812]	Packard & Van Benthuysen	E. Lewis	Salisbury	Judgment Anthem
L [1813]	Packard & Van Benthuysen	William Norman	under "n"*	Judgment Anthem
Ma [1814]	Packard & Van Benthuysen	E. Lewis	under "m"	Judgment Anthem
Mb [1814]	Packard & Van Benthuysen	E. Lewis	under "e"	Judgment Anthem
Mc [1815]	Packard & Van Benthuysen	E. Lewis	before "D"	Judgment Anthem
N [1815]	Packard & Van Benthuysen	E. Lewis	between "n" and "m"	Judgment Anthem
Oa [1815]	Packard & Van Benthuysen	E. Lewis	between "n" and "m"	New York
Ob [1816]	Packard & Van Benthuysen	E. Lewis	under "D"	New York

120-page edition

Edition		
P [1817]	There is only one edition of 120 pages	

127, [1]-page editions: "Revised and Enlarged"

Edition	Title-page points		Other points	
	Steele's firm name	*Steele's address*	*Page [3]†*	*Miscellaneous*
Q [1817]	Daniel Steele	472 S. Market St.	roman	Anthm [sic], p. 89
R [1818]	Daniel Steele	472 S. Market St.	roman	Endfield [sic], p. 23
T [1819]	Daniel Steele	472 S. Market St.	roman	Armeley [sic], p. 41
V [1820]	Daniel Steele	472 S. Market St.	italic	Armley, p. 41
X [1822]	Daniel Steele	435 S. Market St.	italic	Armley, p. 41
Ya [1824]	D. Steele & Son	437 S. Market St.	italic	Armley, p. 41
Yb [1826]	D. Steele & Son	437 S. Market St.	roman	Armley, p. 41
AA [1830]	Oliver Steele	437 S. Market St.	roman	Armley, p. 41

EDITION A*a*: [see illustration] The Easy Instructor, or A New method of teaching Sacred Harmony. Containing the Rudiments of Music on an improved plan, wherein the naming and timing the notes are familiarized to the weakest capacity.—With a choice collection of Psalm Tunes and Anthems from the most celebrated Authors, with a number composed in Europe and America, entirely new; suited to all the metres sung in the different Churches in the United States. Published for the use of singing Societies in general, but more particularly for those who have not the advantage of an Instructor. By William Little & William Smith Copy right secured according to Act of Congress. [New York: G. & R. Waite, 1802]

[2], 105 (i.e. 106) pp. No. 12 is repeated in the paging. T.-p. and pp. 12*b*-105 engraved; pp. [1]-12*a* typeset. 14 x 23.5 cm. CtHC.

This issue may readily be distinguished by the presence of a printed key signature of A major on p. 87, at the beginning of Daniel Read's tune "Stafford." It was advertised as just published on November 25, 1802, in the New York *Chronicle Express*, by the firm of G. & R. Waite.

EDITION A*b*: [same]
CtHWatk, DLC, MWA.

This issue, otherwise identical to A*a*, lacks the key signature on p. 87 referred to above. Apparently, the signature was originally engraved as an oversight and later expunged from the plate. It shows through faintly in the DLC copy. Other key signatures appear in both issues only with Morgan's "Judgment Anthem," pp. 99-105, and Babcock's "Admonition," pp. 63-64. A facsimile of the DLC title-page appears in Metcalf (see note 13 above), opposite p. 92.

EDITION B: [see illustration] . . . By William Little and William Smith. Albany: Printed by Charles R. and George Webster, and Daniel Steele,

Proprietors of the Copy-right; and sold at Webster's Bookstore, corner of State and Pearl-Streets, and at Steele's Bookstore, near the Court-House, in Court-Street. 1805.

108 pp. T.-p. and pp. [2]-12 typeset; pp. 13-108 engraved. 13.5 x 23 cm. NN.

The engraver's signature, "Snyder Sculp," appears at the foot of p. 108.

EDITION C: . . . Smith. Albany: Printed by Websters & Skinner, and Daniel Steele, Proprietors of the Copy-Right; and sold at their respective Bookstores at the corner of State and Pearl-Streets, and near the Court-House, in Court-Street. 1806.

108 pp. T.-p and pp. [2]-12 typeset; pp. 13-108 engraved. MWA.

EDITION D*a*: . . . Albany: . . . Pearl-Streets, and a few Doors South of the Court-House, in Court-Street. 1807.

108 (i.e. 104) pp. Nos. 9-12 are omitted in the paging because smaller type was used to print the introductory matter. T.-p. and pp. 13-108 engraved; pp. [2]-8 typeset. NjR.

This is the last edition in which the full phrase, "which is submitted to," appears immediately preceding the names of Edward Stammers and Richard T. Leech at the foot of p. [3].

EDITION D*b*: [same]
ICN, MWA, NjR, NN.

This issue, otherwise identical with D*a*, has a new type set-up for the introductory matter which may quickly be identified by the absence of the word "to" from the phrase on p. [3] referred to above and by the presence of a misprint "INSTUCTOR" in the caption on p. 7.

EDITION E: . . . Albany: . . . 1808.

108 (i.e. 104) pp., as D*a-b*. CtHWatk, IU, MWA, NNUT.

EDITION F: [see illustration] . . . Containing I. The Rudiments of Music . . . . II. A choice Collection of Psalm

Tunes . . . . Printed, Typographically, at Albany, By Websters & Skinner and Daniel Steele, (Proprietors of the Copy-Right,) And sold at their respective Bookstores, at the corner of State and Pearl-Streets, and a few doors south of the Old City-Hall, in Court-Street; by T. & J. Swords, Evert Duyckinck and William Falconer, New-York; Mathew Carey, Johnson & Warner, William W. Woodward and Hopkins & Earl, Philadelphia; and Increase Cook, New-Haven. [1808]

104 pp.; typeset. 13.5 x 23 cm. See Tables I and II. DLC, MiU-C, NN.

At foot of p. 104: "Van Benthuysen & Wood, Typographers." In this and all succeeding editions the music is printed from type. Obadiah R. Van Benthuysen and William Wood apparently established their typographical firm in November 1807. It was in existence through November 1808, only. This edition, which clearly must have appeared some time after the last dated edition and some time before the dissolution of the partnership, thus was unquestionably published in 1808, probably during the latter part of the year.

EDITION G: . . . Albany, . . . by T. & J. Swords, Everet [sic] Duyckinck and William Falconer, New-York; Wm. J. M'Cartee, Schenectady; A. Seward, Utica; Tracy & Bliss, Lansingburgh; Parker & Bliss, Troy; and Increase

Cook, New-Haven. Van Benthuysen & Newton, Typographers. [1809]

104 pp.; typeset. See Tables I and II. CtHC, DLC, ICN, MWA, N, NjR (2), NNUT, RPB.

A facsimile of this title-page is in Metcalf (see note 13 above), opposite p. 93.

EDITION H: . . . Albany, . . . Troy; Increase Cook, New-Haven; and M. Cary [sic], Philadelphia. Van Benthuysen & Newton, Typographers. [1809]

104 pp.; typeset. See Tables I and II. ICN(2), MiU-C.

Obadiah R. Van Benthuysen and George Newton apparently established their firm in November, 1808. It was in existence only through December, 1809. Eds. G and H were thus in all probability both published in 1809, and could not have appeared after that date. Because Eds. E and F both appeared in 1808, it is extremely doubtful that Ed. G was actually printed before 1809, although this is theoretically possible.

EDITION I: . . . Albany, . . . New-Haven,; [sic] M. Cary [sic], Philadelphia; J. Bogert, Geneva; J. D. Bemis, Canandaigua; P. Potter, Poughkeepsie; E. Lewis, Newburgh, [sic, comma] and D. Allenson & Co. [sic, no comma] Burlington, N.J. O. R. Van Benthuysen, Typographer. [1810]

104 pp.; typeset. See Tables I and II. ICN, N.

This edition was advertised as "just published" in the [Albany] *Balance & New-York*

TABLE II. CONTENT CHANGES IN 104-PAGE EDITIONS

Page	F	G and H	I
34	Southwell	Mount Sion	....
35	Sherburne	Williamstown	....
38	Caldwell, Williamstown	Sherburne	....
70	Babel, Plymouth	....	Concord
93	23rd Psalm, 29th Psalm	....	Arnheim, *Arlington
100	Crucifixion	....	*Newark
101	(cont.), *Newmark	*................	*Columbia *................

*Of European origin.

TABLE III. CONTENT CHANGES IN 112-PAGE EDITIONS

Page	J	K	L	Mabc	N	Oab
16	Whitestown	....	....	....	*Dalston *Martyrs	*................ *................
24	Calvary, *Mear	.... *................	*Mear, *Evening Hymn	*................ *................	*................ *................	*................ *................
34	Mt. Sion	....	*Tunbridge	*................	*................	*................
35	(cont.), Williamstown	....	Williamstown, *Pleyel's	*................	*................	*................
39	Sharon	....	*St. Asaph's	*................	*................	*................
42	Grafton	*Bethesda	*................	*................	*................	*................
43	(cont.), Coronation	Coronation Sutton				
53	Stratfield	....	....	....	*Portugal, *Hymn	*................ *................
57	Ballstown	....	....	....	*Pelham	*................
61	Salisbury	....	*Denmark	*................	*................	*................
62	Lena	....	*(cont.)	*................	*................	*................
64	Rome	....	....	....	*Sunday, *Bedford	*................ *................
65	Judgment	....	....	*Pleyel's 2d	*................	*................
68	Berne	....	Lena			
69	Providence	....	Salisbury	....	New. Jordan	
71	Brentwood, *Bangor	.... *................	.... *................	*Bangor, *Salem	*................ *................	*................ *................
77	Heavenly Vision (cont.)	....	*Portugal	*................	*Irish	*................
81–	Judgment					
84	Anthem					*New York
85	(cont.)	....	....	....	....	*(cont.), *Munich
86	(cont.)	....	....	....	....	*Musick
87	(cont.)	....	....	....	....	*German
88	(cont.)	....	....	....	....	*Green's 100, *Dunchurch
92	*Piermont	*................	*................	*Portsmouth	*................	*................
95	Westminster	....	*Rutland	*................	*................	*................
96	Exhortation	....	....	*Portuguese Hymn	*................	*................
97	Milton	....	....	*Plympton	*................	*................
98	Christian Song	....	*Ashley	*................	*................	*................
99	(cont.), China	....	China, *Bethel	*................	*................	*................
101	Columbia, *Newmark	.... *................	.... *................	*Newmark, *St. Thomas	*................ *................	*................ *................
105	*Pleyel's, *Silver St.	*................ *................	*Silver St.	*................	*................	*................
110	Winter, Funeral Thought	....	....	*St. Michael's	*................	*................

*Of European origin.

THE EASY INSTRUCTOR;

OR,

A NEW METHOD OF TEACHING

Sacred Harmony.

CONTAINING,

I. The RUDIMENTS OF MUSIC on an improved Plan, wherein the Naming and Timing of the Notes are familiarized to the weakest Capacity.

II. A choice Collection of PSALM TUNES and ANTHEMS, from the most celebrated Authors, with a number composed in Europe and America, entirely new; suited to all the Metres sung in the different Churches in the United States.

Published for the Use of SINGING SOCIETIES in general, but more particularly ft.. those who have not the advantage of an INSTRUCTOR.

By WILLIAM LITTLE AND WILLIAM SMITH.

The Music Types used in printing this Book are secured to the Proprietors by Patent Right.

ALBANY:

PRINTED FOR WEBSTERS & SKINNERS AND DANIEL STEELE, (PROPRIETORS,)

And sold at their respective Book-Stores, at the corner of State and Pearl-streets, and at No. 472 South Market-street; by T. & J. SWORDS, E. DUYCKINCK, COLLINS & Co. and D. SMITH, New-York; M. CAREY, B. WARNER, W. W. WOODWARD and A. SMALL, Philadelphia; J. CUSHING, Baltimore; H. HOYT, New-Haven; WILLS & LILL', Boston; G. GOODWIN & SONS, Hartford; P. POTTER, Poughkeepsie; B. F. LEWIS, Newburgh; E. NORMAN, Hudson; PARKER & BLISS, Troy; TRACY & BLISS, Lansingburgh; DODD & STEVENS, Salem; H. STEVENS, Schenectady; W. WILLIAMS, Utica; J. BOGERT, Geneva; J.D. BEMIS, Canandaigua; SKIN .ER & CROSBY, Auburn; S. H. & H. A. SALISBURY, Buffalo.

PACKARD & VAN BENTHUYSEN, PRINTERS.

Illustration 5. Edition P. Courtesy of the General Library, University of Michigan. (See check list, page 53.)

State Journal on February 6, 1810. Condit (see note 23 above) reports an edition identical with Ed. I except that the name of M. Carey [Cary] is missing from the list of booksellers. The authors have been unable to locate such an edition. As the title-page is incorrectly transcribed in other respects, the omission of the bookseller's name may perhaps have been an oversight or a typographical error.

EDITION J: . . . Albany, By Websters & Skinners and Daniel Steele, . . . Duyckinck [sic, no comma] New-York; Wm. J. M'Cartee, . . . E. Lewis, Newburgh. O. R. Van Benthuysen, Typographer. [1811]

112 pp.; typeset. See Tables I and III. RPB.

Van Benthuysen was in business alone between December, 1809, and the fall of 1812; therefore, Eds. I and J, which bear his name as sole typographer, must have been published between these dates. Ed. J. however, must have appeared between the fall of 1811 and that of 1812, as its title-page gives the printers as Websters & Skinners, a change in title which took place in the fall of the former year.

EDITION K: . . . Albany, . . . Evert Duyckinck, New-York; . . . Packard & Van Benthuysen, Typographers. [1812]

112 pp.; typeset. See Tables I and III. DLC, ICN, OCHP.

EDITION L: . . . Albany, . . . New-York; A. Seward, Utica; Tracy & Bliss, Lansingburgh; Parker & Bliss and Solomon Wilber, Jun. [sic, no comma] Troy;

Increase Cook, New-Haven; Matthew Cary [sic], Philadelphia; J. Bogert, Geneva; J. D. Bemis, Canandaigua; P. Potter, Poughkeepsie; William E. Norman, Hudson. Packard & Van Benthuysen, Typographers. [1813]

112 pp.; typeset. See Tables I and III. MWA, MiU-C, NN.

EDITION M*a*: . . . Albany, . . . New-York; Riggs & Stevens, Schenectady; A. Seward, Utica; Tracy & Bliss, Lansingburgh; Parker & Bliss, Troy; M. Carey, Philadelphia; . . . Poughkeepsie; E. Lewis, Newburgh. Packard & Van Benthuysen, Typographers. [1814]

112 pp.; typeset. See Tables I, III, and IV. CBB (2), ICN (2), MWA (2), NN, NNUT.

EDITION M*b*: [same, except comma omitted after "T. & J. Swords"] [1814]

See Tables I, III, and IV. CtHWatk. MBC, N.

EDITION M*c*: [same] [1815]

See Tables I, III, and IV. CtHC, MWA.

EDITION N: [same] [1815]

112 pp.; typeset. See Tables I, III, and IV. N, NN, NNS, RPB.

EDITION O*a*: [same] [1816]

112 pp.; typeset. See Tables I, III, and V. MB, N, NNUT.

EDITION O*b*: [same] [1816]

See Tables I, III, and V. MWA (2).

TABLE IV. COMPARISON OF ISSUES, EDITION M

Page	Points	M*a*	M*b*	M*c*
17	Last two words, upper line of text, "Sutton"	Surprize, And	Surprize, And	Suprise [sic], and
61	First letter of word "soft" in relation to letters in "Denmark"	under "m"	under "e"	before "D"

REVISED AND ENLARGED EDITION.

THE EASY INSTRUCTOR;

OR,

A NEW METHOD OF TEACHING

Sacred Harmony.

CONTAINING,

I. The Rudiments of Music on an improved Plan, wherein the Naming and Timing of the Notes are familiarized to the weakest Capacity.
II. A choice Collection of PSALM TUNES and ANTHEMS, from the most celebrated Authors, with a number composed in Europe and America, entirely new ; suited to all the Metres sung in the different Churches in the United States.

Published for the Use of SINGING SOCIETIES in general, but more particularly for those who have not the advantage of an INSTRUCTOR.

By WILLIAM LITTLE AND WILLIAM SMITH.

The Music Types of this Book,, as to casting and using, are secured by Patent Right to GEORGE WEBSTER, of the city of Albany. Rights to make or use them may be obtained of him.

ALBANY :

PRINTED FOR WEBSTERS & SKINNERS AND DANIEL STEELE, And sold at their respective Book-Stores, at the corner of State and Pearl-streets, and at No. 472 South Market-street.

PACKARD & VAN BENTHUYSEN, PRINTERS.

Illustration 6. Edition Q. Courtesy of the Library of Congress. (See check list, page 53.)

EDITION P: [see illustration] . . . The Music Types used in printing this Book are secured to the Proprietors by Patent Right. Albany: Printed for Websters & Skinners and Daniel Steele, (Proprietors,) And sold at their respective Book-Stores, at the corner of State and Pearl-streets, and at No. 472 South Market-street; by T. & J. Swords, E. Duyckinck, Collins & Co. and D. Smith, New-York; M. Carey, B. Warner, W. W. Woodward and A. Small, Philadelphia; J. Cushing, Baltimore; H. Howe, New-Haven; Wells & Lilly, Boston; G. Goodwin & Sons, Hartford; P. Potter, Poughkeepsie; B. F. Lewis, Newburgh; E. Norman, Hudson; Parker & Bliss, Troy; Tracy & Bliss, Lansingburgh; Dodd & Stevens, Salem; H. Stevens, Schenectady; W. Williams, Utica; J. Bogert, Geneva; J. D. Bemis, Canandaigua; Skinner & Crosby, Auburn; S. H. & H. A. Salisbury, Buffalo. Packard & Van Benthuysen, Printers. [1817]

120 pp.; typeset. CtHWatk, DLC (2), MWA, MiU, PPeSchw, RPB, SCU.

This is evidently the earliest edition printed after the lapse, on December 10, 1816, of the original New York copyright, which ran for fourteen years; a patent notice is substituted for the copyright notice appearing on the title-pages of previous editions. A patent on the casting and use of the shape note types was issued to George Webster, of the firm of Websters & Skinners, on February 28, 1816. The original notice of the patent was apparently destroyed in one of the fires which ravaged the U.S. Patent Office early in its history, and so no details as to the exact nature of the patent are available. See also Eds. S, U, and W, which are derivatives of this edition, apparently printed by license of the holders of the patent.

EDITION Q: [see illustration] Revised and Enlarged Edition. The Easy Instructor; . . . The Music Types of this Book, as to casting and using, are secured by Patent Right to George Webster, of the city of Albany. Rights to make or use them may be obtained of him. Albany: Printed for Websters & Skinners and Daniel Steele, And sold at their respective Book-Stores, at the corner of State and Pearl-streets, and at No. 472 South Market-street. Packard & Van Benthuysen, Printers. [1817]

127, [1] pp.; typeset. See Table VI. CLU, DLC, MdBJ.

This edition was advertised as "just published" in the Albany *Gazette & Daily Advertiser* on November 6, 1817.

EDITION R: [same] [1818]

127, [1] pp.; typeset. See Table VI. CSU, MHi, N, NHi, NN.

EDITION S: [text of title-page same as Ed. P through "Patent Right," then:] Utica: Printed by William Williams, No. 60, Genesee Street. 1818.

126, [1] pp.; typeset. CtY, DLC, ICN (2), MH, MWA, OClWHi.

EDITION T: [same as Ed. Q] [1819]

127, [1] pp.; typeset. See Table VI. ICN.

TABLE V. COMPARISON OF ISSUES, EDITION O

Page	Points	Oa	Ob
[3]	In line beginning, "The Committee . . ."	URANIAN SOCIETY	URANIAN SNCIETY [sic]
[4]	First word, second line	ample	the
5	Last word on page	of	ensue
61	First letter of word "soft" in relation to letters in "Denmark"	between "n" and "m"	under "D"

TABLE VI. CONTENT CHANGES IN 127, [1]-PAGE EDITIONS

Page	Q	R	T, V, X-AA
20	New Durham,	*Gilboa	*...............
	Invitation		
21	Mortality,	*Wells,	*...............
	*Wells	*Brighthelmstone	*...............
22	Ocean	*Blendon,	*...............
		*Messiah	*...............
38	Sherburne	*Christmas,	*Dundee,
		*Chelmsford	*...............
45	Delight	*Pensance	*...............
102	Exhortation	*Arundel,	*...............
		*St. Ann's	*...............

*Of European origin.

EDITION U: [text of title-page same as Ed. P through "the advantage of an instructor," then:] By Little and Smith. Cincinnati: Printed by J. Pace, No. 106, Main-Street. 1819.

112 pp.; typeset. OC.

EDITION V: [same as Eds. Q and T, except that "Sacred Harmony" is printed in shadowed rather than plain black letter] [1820]

127, [1] pp.; typeset. See Table VI. ICU, MiU-C.

EDITION W: [same as Ed. S, except that the date has been changed to:] 1820.

126, [1] pp.; typeset. CtY, MWA, NN.

EDITION X: [same as Ed. V, except that Daniel Steele's address is given as 435 South Market-street] [1822]

127, [1] pp.; typeset. See Table VI. ICN, MWA.

Daniel Steele was at the street address given in this edition only between April and September, 1822.

EDITION Ya: [same as Ed. X, except that the imprint reads:] . . . and D. Steele & Son, . . . and at No. 437 South Market-street. . . . [1824]

127, [1] pp.; typeset. See Tables VI and VII. MnU, MWA.

EDITION Yb: [same] [1826]

See Tables VI and VII. CtHWatk, OClWHi.

EDITION Z: [same, except that the imprint reads:] . . . and Oliver Steele . . . 1828.

127, [1].; typeset. See Table VI. DLC, MWA, N, NNUT.

EDITION AA: [same, except that the imprint is without date] [1830]

127, [1] pp.; typeset. See Table VI. DLC.

EDITION BB: [same, except that the imprint is dated:] 1831.

135, [1] pp.; typeset. MWA, N.

An extra signature of music has been added to this, the last edition of *The Easy Instructor*.

TABLE VII. COMPARISON OF ISSUES, EDITION Y

Page	Points	Ya	Yb
4	First word, second line	ample	example
5	Last word on page	of	persons
61	First letter of word		
	"soft" in relation to	under "D"	before "D"
	letters in "Denmark"		

TABLE VIII. CONSPECTUS OF EDITIONS AND ISSUES

Edition	Place if other than Albany	Metcalf number	Pages	Number of musical compositions			
				Indexed	Actually printed	Of Amer. origin	Of Eur. origin
Aa [1802]	[New York]		[2], 105 (i.e. 106)	105	105	100	5
Ab [1802]	[New York]	A	[2], 105 (i.e. 106)	105	105	100	5
B 1805			108	102	102	88	14
C 1806		3	108	102	102	88	14
Da 1807			108 (i.e. 104)	102	102	88	14
Db 1807		4	108 (i.e. 104)	102	102	88	14
E 1808		5	108 (i.e. 104)	102	102	88	14
F [1808]		6	104	95	95	76	19
G [1810]		7	104	94	94	75	19
H [1809]			104	94	94	75	19
I [1809]		8	104	95	95	73	22
J [1811]		10	112	106	105	75	30
K [1812]		11	112	107	106	75	31
L [1813]		12	112	107	106	68	38
Ma [1814]		13	112	104	105	61	44
Mb [1814]			112	104	105	61	44
Mc [1815]			112	104	105	61	44
N [1815]		15	112	107	108	57	51
Oa [1816]			112	111	113	56	57
Ob [1816]		14	112	111	113	56	57
P [1817]		16	120	124	125	50	75
Q [1817]		17	127, [1]	139	139	34	105
R [1818]			127, [1]	141	141	27	114
S 1818	Utica	22	126, [1]	127	127	49	78
T [1819]			127, [1]	141	141	27	114
U 1819	Cincinnati		112	111	112	49	63
V [1820]			127, [1]	141	141	27	114
W 1820	Utica	23	126, [1]	127	127	49	78
X [1822]		18	127, [1]	141	141	27	114
Ya [1824]		19	127, [1]	141	141	27	114
Yb [1826]			127, [1]	141	141	27	114
Z 1828		20	127, [1]	142	141	27	114
AA [1830]			127, [1]	142	141	27	114
BB 1831		21	135, [1]	142	153	27	126

Hyattsville, Maryland
School of Music, University of Michigan

Carl E. Seashore's tests of musical aptitude, originally published in 1919, were a logical outgrowth of first, centuries of research and thinking on sensory discrimination and specification, and second, applications to psychological research of Charles Darwin's theory of evolution. These two fields came together when English anthropologist Francis Galton (1822–1911) devised tests of sensory perception to test individual mental capacity in the 1870s and 1880s. Galton, who modeled his tests on those devised previously by physicists, included measures of musical perception in his test batteries. He believed that individual differences are quantifiable and that discrete measures of sensory acuity, including musical discrimination, would provide at least an indirect measure of intelligence. Galton influenced American psychologist James Cattell (1860–1944), who in turn influenced Seashore. Because Seashore, like all experimental psychologists of his day, was a sensory psychologist, he produced tests that were criticized from the beginning for being sensory and atomistic. Nevertheless, Seashore's work fired the imaginations and profoundly influenced the work of the first generation of American music education researchers.

Jere T. Humphreys

JRME 1993, VOLUME 41, NUMBER 4, PAGES 315–327

Precursors of Musical Aptitude Testing: From the Greeks through the Work of Francis Galton

The name usually associated with early musical aptitude testing is Carl Emil Seashore (1866–1949), whose research beginning just before the turn of the twentieth century resulted in the world's first standardized tests of musical aptitude, published in 1919.[1] The most influential music psychologist of his era, Seashore inspired an intense interest in music education research and musical aptitude testing among music education researchers beginning in the 1920s. These facts are recognized by modern music educators, but heretofore, the antecedents of Seashore's prolific, influential research efforts have not been documented.

Seashore's pioneering efforts did not occur in isolation; on the contrary, he built upon the work of a long line of philosophers, physicists, and psychologists with similar goals, beliefs, and methods. This article describes the most important of those antecedents, beginning with early speculation about sensory perception, continuing through the influence of sensory physiology, atomistic chemistry, and

For copies of this article, contact Jere T. Humphreys, School of Music, Arizona State University, Tempe, AZ 85287-0405.

evolutionary theory, and ending with Francis Galton's use in the late nineteenth century of musical discrimination tests to measure individual mental capacity. Seashore's tests have been criticized for being sensory and atomistic; this article demonstrates that, given the heritage on which Seashore built, they hardly could have been otherwise.

Sensation

The first person known to have been interested in sensation was the Greek philosopher Heraclitus (ca. 540 – ca. 475 B.C.), who postulated that thought is derived from the senses. He was followed by Alcmaeon of Croton (ca. 500 B.C. – ?), who developed theories of vision, hearing, smell, and taste, and speculated about the relationship of these senses to the brain. Next came the first person known to have dealt with perception as distinguished from sensation, Empedocies of Akragas (ca. 490 – ca. 430 B.C.), who speculated that sense organs are affected by emanations given off by the perceived objects. Building on Empedocies's work, Democritus (ca. 470 – ca. 370 B.C.) wrote that atoms of the body come into contact with atoms outside the body, resulting in both sensation and perception. Democritus was also probably the first to speculate about the important phenomenon of sensory thresholds.[2]

The next person of note to study sensation and perception was the Greek philosopher Aristotle (384–323 B.C.). Once a devotee of Plato's (428 or 427/348 or 347 B.C.) mode of introspective thinking, Aristotle gradually came to recognize the importance of empirical observation to scientific inquiry. He then proceeded to give direction to his empiricism by identifying the five human senses: vision, audition, smell, taste, and touch. Unlike Plato, who distrusted sensory perception as a means for discovering higher truths, Aristotle believed that knowledge is acquired through the senses, after which it is received by the brain through a part of the human psyche—the faculty of intelligence. Furthermore, he believed that "art is an intellectual activity [that] constitutes one stage in the evolution of thought from sensory perception to wisdom."[3] Aristotle's views about empiricism and sensory perception—including relationships between sensation, perception, and thought—have constituted the mainstream of the field of psychology ever since his time.[4]

From the Greek period through the end of the nineteenth century, much of the history of psychology can be traced through the search for increasingly specific information about the psychological senses. Boethius (ca. 480 – 524 A.D.), in his enormously influential *De Institutione Musica* (The Principles of Music), questioned "the exact nature of [the] senses," as well as "the actual property of ... objects sensed." He concluded that "the answers to these questions are not so obvious." He went on to state that

> sight is present in all mortals. But whether we see by images coming to the eye or by rays sent out from the eye to the object seen, this problem is in doubt to the learned, although the common man is not conscious of doubt. ... The same thing can be said of the other senses, especially concerning aural perception.[5]

Boethius may have been the first to advocate scientific study of musical perception:

> The power of the mind ought to be directed toward fully understanding by knowledge what is inherent in us through nature. Thus just as erudite scholars are not satisfied by merely seeing colors and forms without also investigating their properties, so

musicians should not be satisfied by merely finding pleasure in music without knowing by what musical proportions these sounds are put together.[6]

After the Middle Ages, during which little progress was made in this field, came the Renaissance and its great enthusiasm for studying natural and human phenomena. John Locke (1632–1704) led the way in sensory research by differentiating between primary and secondary qualities of sensation.[7] He was followed by Isaac Newton (1642–1727), who divided the spectrum into colors,[8] and Charles Bell (1774–1842), François Magendie (1783–1855), and Johannes Peter Müller (1801–1858), all of whom studied relationships between nerves and sensation.[9] Other important research was done on touch by Ernst Heinrich Weber (1795–1878) and Maximillan Ruppert Franz von Frey (1852–1932), and on vision and audition by Hermann Ludwig Ferdinand von Helmholtz (1821–1894).[10] In addition to these and other sensory specification studies came attempts to measure sensation and perception. Among the most important early measurement studies were by Pierre Bouguer (1698–1758), who studied perception of lights of different intensities.[11]

Studies designed to measure musical perception occurred relatively early. One of the most important early musical studies was by Charles Eduard Joseph Delezenne (1776–1866), who in 1827 measured the least discernable differences in musical pitch by musically trained and untrained subjects.[12] Other studies of musical perception were conducted by physicists on musical consonance as early as 1799, on timbre by 1830, and on upper and lower thresholds of the hearing of tones as early as 1831.[13]

Sensory measurement took a giant leap forward in 1834, when Ernst Weber identified what appeared to be a scientific, naturally occurring law on which such measurements could be based. He proposed that the "just noticeable difference" between stimuli that vary—weights, sights, sounds, and the like—occurs in constant ratio to the magnitude of the stimuli being compared, and that the size of the smallest perceivable difference between stimuli is determined in part by the original intensities of the stimuli, not just by the absolute difference between them. Weber's theory drew little attention until Gustav Theodor Fechner (1801–1887) elaborated on it in 1860, developing a complicated formula for determining relationships between stimuli and sensations. Fechner dubbed the principle "Weber's law."[14]

Although Weber's law was the source of considerable controversy in psychology and was later found not always applicable, it provided a strong impetus for the fusion of philosophical speculation and physiological research on sensation in the middle of the nineteenth century. The result was the emergence and growth of the related fields of experimental psychology and psychophysics.[15] For the remainder of the century, experimental research on sensory perception, including musical perception, constituted the mainstream of psychology.

The Theory of Evolution

At about the time Weber's law gave physicists a theoretical basis for measuring sensory perception, another theory changed the course of psychology even more radically: In 1859, Charles Robert Darwin (1809–1882) published a theory of evolution in his work *On the Origin of Species by Means of Natural Selection, or the Preservation of Favoured Races in the Struggle for Life.*[16] Darwin suggested that variations between individual members of a given species function within the evolutionary process to isolate certain "optimal configurations" by which a given species can be perpetuated. In short, the theories of natural selection, survival of the fittest, and evolution are based in part upon the premise that individuals differ from each other.[17]

Before Darwin's theory was published, scientists had searched not for individual differences, but for natural laws that govern all living things. Physicists like Delezenne, Weber, Fechner, and Helmholtz, and other scientists like Wilhelm Wundt (1832–1920), the most influential psychologist of the nineteenth century, did not think in terms of variations in human attributes and capabilities. Rather, they sought to identify and quantify aspects of the body and behavior common to people in general.

After Darwin, a new type of investigator appeared, scientists who based their research on the theory of evolution. They, too, sought to quantify body part sizes and certain aspects of human behavior, but, unlike the traditionalists, those influenced by evolutionary theory attempted to identify differences between people rather than commonalities among them. They reasoned that the concept of variation within a given species implies quantity for everything governed by the natural selection process. They reasoned further that anything with quantity is susceptible to measurement. Accordingly, they, like their colleagues who continued to search for natural laws governing commonalities, began to measure height, weight, arm length, head size, and other parts of the human anatomy.

Francis Galton's Mental Testing Research

After physical measurement came attempts to measure simple behavioral and psychical differences, and it was at this stage that musical perception testing took the turn that eventually led to musical aptitude testing. The first person to apply Darwin's principles to the study of human characteristics other than relatively straightforward physical dimensions was Darwin's half cousin, English anthropologist Francis Galton (1822–1911).[18] It was he who first experimented with testing mental ability.[19]

Galton was an innovator, but he did hold certain conventional beliefs, one of which was in the veracity of faculty psychology, the leading nineteenth-century psychological theory. Faculty psychologists believed that the mind is composed of separate compartments, or faculties, each of which operates more or less independently.[20] The sensory faculties were thought to correspond roughly to specific faculties of the brain.

Another influence on Galton came from the field of atomistic chemistry, a field then enjoying considerable success and prestige due to the recent discovery of chemical elements. With Wilhelm Wundt leading the way, "elementalism" became the watchword of psychology, as he, Galton, and others began to search for and measure specific elements of consciousness. Given the centrality of sensation in the history of psychological thinking up to that time, as well as the dominance of faculty psychology, it is not surprising that Wundt and Galton turned first to the psychological senses, which to them constituted the elements of the mind.[21]

Still another view of Galton's, this one dating back to Aristotle, was that all knowledge is obtained through the five senses. Galton began to deviate from conventionalism, however, when he hypothesized that a measure of sensory acuity would provide a crude measure of a person's level of intelligence. This erroneous belief, which for a time was held widely, was one of the fundamental premises that helped launch the mental testing movement.

Finally, Galton made an even larger leap when he hypothesized that mental ability is normally, or randomly, distributed within a given population. Galton's inspiration for this hypothesis came from the work of Belgian astronomer, mathematician, and statistician Adolphe Quetelét (1796–1874), who had calculated earlier in the century that the measurements of certain body parts and other phenomena form normal distribution curves.[22] Because the theory of evolution assumes random, or chance, selection, and because it was becoming clear by then that at least some physical characteristics are normally distributed, Galton assumed that mental phenomena are distributed normally as well:

> There is no bodily or mental attribute ... which cannot be ... consolidated into an ogive [distribution curve] with a smooth outline, and thenceforward be treated in discussion as a single object.[23]

Later, he wrote that he had

> applied this same law [normal distribution curve representing height] to mental faculties, working it backwards in order to obtain a scale of ability.[24]

For all these reasons, when Galton set out to study mental ability by measuring individual differences in psychological functions, he devised a series of tests designed to measure sensory discrimination ability, which he believed would prove to be distributed normally. Others were already studying sensory discrimination, principally German physicists led by Helmholtz and German psychologists led by Wundt, but Galton's tests differed from those of the German investigators in that they were designed to identify differences between individuals rather than traits common to all people. Furthermore, Galton's tests, unlike the German tests, were designed to be administered quickly and easily to large numbers of people. The main difference between the Galton and German tests, however, was the purpose for which they were to be used: Galton contended that tests of sensory discrimination would be "indicative of judgment and thus of intelligence,"[25] two traits that he believed varied considerably among individuals.

Galton's concept of variation in mental ability differed radically from the prevailing view of human mental ability. Wundt, for example, believed that deviations from the average result from error—not measurement error but human error, representing deficiencies in the deviating individuals. Wundt and others therefore tended to dismiss variations between individuals. Conversely, Galton sought to identify and measure individual differences, which he considered to be naturally occurring phenomena.

To determine differences in mental ability, Galton sought to " 'sample' a man with reasonable completeness," to "measure *absolutely* where ... possible, otherwise *relatively* ..., the quality of each selected faculty" [emphasis in original]. The next step was to

> estimate the combined effect of these separately measured faculties in any given proportion, and ultimately to ascertain the degree with which the measurement of sample faculties in youth justifies a prophecy of future success in life....[26]

Galton, who previously had studied instances of genius within families, was convinced as early as 1865 of the pressing necessity of obtaining a multitude of exact measurements relating to every measurable faculty of body or mind, for two generations at least, on which to theorize.[27]

After 1869, when he outlined his basic tenets on human genius and its tendency to run in families in his first book, *Hereditary Genius: An Inquiry into Its Laws and Consequences*, Galton began to conduct experiments on human variability. He was beginning to conclude by then that his anthropometric research was superficial and provided little information about the mind, his real interest. For that reason, he turned increasingly to psychometrics, or mental measurement.[28]

One of his first attempts at psychometrics came in the 1870s, when he asked a number of elementary and secondary schools to make certain measurements of their students.[29] When this effort failed, he began to conduct some crude experiments on his own.

Galton's Musical Discrimination Research

Studies of musical discrimination were among Galton's first psychometric experiments. As early as 1876, he worked on a brass whistle (the "Galton whistle") capable of producing variable pitches, which he used to test the perception of upper limits of pitches by different people and animals.[30] Among his findings were that there is "a remarkable falling off in the power of hearing high notes as age advanced," and that cats are superior to most other animals in high-frequency pitch perception. His attempts to measure the hearing of insects failed.[31] Galton was not the first to make those kinds of measurements relating to music, but he seems to have been the first to use them specifically to identify differences in ability between individuals.

In 1882, Galton wrote an article in which he recommended the establishment of anthropometric laboratories, partly to conduct intelligence testing. In this famous article, the first publication ever to suggest intelligence testing in anything like its modern form, Galton advocated the testing of sensory discrimination ability, among other things. He acknowledged the vast body of extant research on sensory discrimination, but said that "the work remaining to be done is to select out of extant instruments those that are sufficiently inexpensive and quick in manipulation to be appropriately placed in an anthropometric laboratory....[32] Within the realm of sensory discrimination, Galton specified in this article only "the more important measurements": those of sight, sound, touch, and muscular sense. For sound, he suggested measuring "keenness" of hearing, "the appreciation of different grades of loudness," and the perception of "different notes."[33]

One year after the publication of this article, Galton published his landmark book, *Inquiries into Human Faculty and Development*, now regarded by some historians of psychology as the beginning of both the scientific study of individual psychology and of mental testing.[34] In this book, Galton described his experiments on human variability conducted during the previous fourteen years, since the publication of his *Heredity Genius* in 1869. Among the experiments described were those on musical discrimination.

Galton believed he was measuring intellectual ability, at least indirectly, with his pitch perception and other sensory tests:

> The only information that reaches us concerning outward events appears to pass through the avenue of our senses, and the more perceptive the senses are of difference, the larger is the field upon which judgment and intelligence can act.[35]

He also noted that "the discriminative faculty of idiots is curiously low," and that

the trials I have as yet made on the sensitivity of different persons confirms the reasonable expectation that it would on the whole be highest among the intellectually ablest....[36]

As for music, he speculated, after mentioning the principle of just noticeable differences, that although people might possess equal ability to hear very loud and very soft sounds, "they may differ as to the number of intermediate grades of sensation." He suggested that musicians do not necessarily have more ability than others to hear loud and soft sounds, but he implied that they should be able to discriminate more finely within their ranges.[37]

The year after Galton's *Inquiries* was published, he established an anthropometric laboratory as part of the International Health Exhibition that opened in London in 1884. At this laboratory Galton and his associates measured exhibition attendees, charging them a "threepenny fee" for the privilege. When the health exhibition closed in 1885, he moved his laboratory into the Science Galleries at the South Kensington Museum in London.[38] Altogether, Galton made seventeen measurements on each of 9,337 people, who ranged in age from five to eighty years.[39]

Probably the most important result of Galton's anthropometric laboratory was his development of the rudiments of statistical correlation, which he devised to determine the "relation between two variables partly dependent on a common set of influences."[40] In addition to that significant accomplishment, Galton published some of the data collected at his anthropometric laboratory, including results of his tests of strength of pull, standing and sitting height, arm span, weight, breathing capacity, strength of squeeze, swiftness of blow, and keenness of sight.[41] He was able to make only one generalization about human variability from the data, and that was an incorrect one: that women are inferior to men in sensory ability (except for the sense of touch), as well as in the nonsensory abilities measured. He attributed these discrepancies to differences in inherited abilities.[42]

Galton's musical discrimination measurements included those of keenness of hearing and highest audible pitch. The only published information on the results of these measurements concerns the perception of highest audible tones. The tones were produced by a set of five whistles ranging in pitch from 10,000 to 50,000 cycles per second (Hz). Galton's table of results includes data from males age twenty-three to twenty-six years ($n = 206$) and forty to fifty years ($n = 317$), and females age twenty-three to twenty-six years ($n = 176$) and forty to fifty years ($n = 284$). Males surpassed females in the ability to hear high notes in both age categories. (Virtually all subjects could hear the 10,000-Hz tone.) Galton barely refrained from declaring his data normally distributed:

The results fall into a very fair curve; however, it would be hardly justifiable to give percentiles, because the values on which the curve is based are wide apart [20, 30, 40, and 50 thousand Hz]. I therefore limit myself to giving a table of percentages for the convenience of comparison.[43]

It is clear that Galton thought of his musical discrimination tests in relation to mental aptitude and not musical aptitude per se. He may have been the first, however, to propose the need for musical aptitude tests:

It is perfectly conceivable that the Artistic Faculty in any person might be somehow measured, and its amount determined, just as we may measure Strength, the power of Discrimination of Tints, or the tenacity of Memory.... It is reasonable to expect that the Scheme [distribution] of the Artistic Faculty would be approximately Normal in its proportions, ... [and] that the same law of inheritance might hold good in the Artistic Faculty that was found to hold good both in Stature and in Eye colour.[44]

Although Galton did not experiment with sensory perception in music in relation to musical aptitude, he attempted to deal with aptitude indirectly.[45] In the early 1880s, he offered prizes to families for providing him with family records, which he compiled into a collection titled "Records of Family Faculties." To compile data on the artistic faculty, one of the many faculties he studied, he simply asked adult subjects from some 150 families whether they considered themselves artistic. He defined artistic persons as those "especially fond of music and drawing," but he conceded that his list of artistic persons "no doubt includes many who are artistic in a very moderate degree."[46]

Galton found, among 894 subjects, that 28 percent were artistic males and 33 percent were artistic females, a difference he attributed not to heredity, as he did with sex differences in sensory discrimination, but to the inclusion of more music and drawing in girls' education. He did admit that although men and women probably "differ little in their artistic capacity, ... such difference as there is in adult life is somewhat in favour of women."[47]

Conclusions

The most important discoveries and insights leading to Carl Seashore's early attempts to measure musical aptitude were the centuries of speculation and research on sensory perception and Darwin's theory of evolution, both of which led to Francis Galton's pioneering work in mental testing. Galton's work was especially influential on later music testing. His concept of individual differences, his strong belief in inherited abilities, and his discovery of statistical regression and correlation all became cornerstones of the mental testing movement from which Seashore drew his inspiration and methods. Galton built on centuries of speculation and research on sensory perception, applied Weber's law, used the new techniques of experimental psychology, adapted new discoveries in chemistry, and, most important, fused all these things with the theory of evolution to identify individual differences and develop tests to examine these differences. In music, he speculated about and gathered data on aptitude, measured individual sensory perception, and suggested the feasibility of measuring musical aptitude directly. Galton's methods of measuring both mental and artistic ability were crude, and he was mistaken about many things, but, for better or worse, one segment of the mental testing movement followed his course for many years.

In the 1890s, when Galton turned his attention to other matters, the United States became dominant in the mental testing movement. The movement was led by James McKeen Cattell (1860–1944), who had studied with Galton in the 1880s. Cattell continued Galton's work, including experiments on musical discrimination, coined the term "mental test," and for a generation led the American mental testing movement of which Seashore and other important American psychologists were part. Under Cattell's leadership, the mental testing movement soon came to have powerful political, social, and educational implications, especially in the United States.

Fewer than ten years after Galton closed his anthropometric laboratory in

London, Seashore began laboratory experiments that led to the publication of his tests of musical aptitude. It is no wonder that Seashore's work strongly reflects the centuries of psychological research on sensation, one of the "three great topics" that led to modern scientific psychology.[48] Because the two other "great topics" were learning and motivation, neither of which became popular until after the turn of the century, Seashore, like all experimental psychologists trained in the nineteenth century, was a sensory psychologist. It is also not surprising that Seashore was influenced strongly by Francis Galton, the scientific genius who founded mental testing only a short time before Seashore began work on his tests of musical aptitude, tests that fired the imaginations of the first full generation of American music education researchers.[49]

NOTES

1. Carl E. Seashore, Don Lewis, and Joseph G. Saetveit, *Seashore Measures of Musical Talents* (New York: The Psychological Corporation, 1919).

2. Zusne, *Names in the History of Psychology: A Biographical Sourcebook* (Washington, DC: Hemisphere Publishing Co., 1975), 1–4.

3. Michael L. Mark, *Source Readings in Music Education History* (New York: Schirmer Books, 1982), 35.

4. Zusne, *Names*, 7–8; and Renford Bambrough, *The Philosophy of Aristotle* (New York: The New American Library, 1963), 230.

5. Boethius (Anicius Manilus Torquatus Severinus), *De Institutione Musica*, Book I; excerpts quoted in Mark, *Source Readings*, 64.

6. *Ibid.*, 68.

7. John Locke, *An Essay Concerning Humane Understanding: In Four Book* (London, 1690), Book II, Chapter 8; excerpts quoted in Richard J. Herrnstein and Edwin G. Boring, eds. *A Source Book in the History of Psychology* (Cambridge, MA: Harvard University Press, 1965), 14–17. For more information on the history of sensory specification and measurement see *ibid.*, 1–88.

8. Isaac Newton, two-part paper delivered to the Royal Society of London on December 9 and 16, 1675; published in Thomas Birch, *History of the Royal Society of London* (London, 1757), III, 262–63; excerpts quoted in Herrnstein and Boring, *Source Book*, 7–8.

9. Charles Bell, *Idea of a New Anatomy of the Brain: Submitted for the Observation of His Friends* (London: Privately printed, 1811), 21–24, 28–29, 34–37; François Magendie, "Expériences sur les fonctions des racines des nerfs rachidiens," *Journal de Physiologie Expérimentale et Pathologique* 2 (1822): 276–79, and "Expériences sur les fonctions des racines des nerfs qui naissent de la moelle épinière," *ibid.*, 366–71; and Johannes Müller, *Handbuch der Physiologie des Menschen*, Book V (Coblenz, 1838), Introduction; excerpts quoted in Herrnstein and Boring, *Source Book*, 17–33.

10. E. H. Weber, "Der Tastsinn und das Gemeingefühl," in Rudolph Wagner, ed. *Handwürterbuch der Physiologie* (Brunswick, 1846), vol. III, part 2, 481–588; Max von Frey, *Vorlesungen über Physiologie* (Berlin: Springer, 1904), 308-26; H. L. F. von Helmholtz, *Die Lehre von den Tonempfindungen* (Brunswick, 1863); and H. L. F. von Helmholtz, *Handbuch der Physiologischen Optik*, vol. II (Leipzig, 1860); excerpts quoted in Herrnstein and Boring, *Source Book*, 34–58.

11. Pierre Bouguer, *Traité d'Optique sur la Gradation de la Lumière*, Book I (Paris, 1760); excerpts quoted in Herrnstein and Boring, *Source Book*, 60–62.

12. C. E. J. Delezenne, "Sur les valeurs numériques des notes de la gamme," *Recueil des Travaux de la Société des Sciences, de l'Agriculture et des Arts de Lille (1827): 4–6;* excerpts quoted in Herrnstein and Boring, 61–64. Perhaps the first study on pitch perception thresholds was conducted in 1700: Joseph Sauveur, "Des intervales des sons, et son appli-

cation à tous les systèmes et à tous les instruments de musique," *Hist. Acad. Sci. Paris* (1701): 299–366; cited in Edwin G. Boring, *Sensation and Perception in the History of Experimental Psychology* (New York: Appleton-Century-Crofts, Inc., 1942), 339.

13. Ernst Florens Friedrich Chladni, "Ueber die wahre Ursache des Consonirens und Dissonirens," *Allgemeine musikalische Zeitung* (1800/1801): 337, 353; and R. Willis, "On the Vowel Sounds, and on Reed Organ-Pipes," *Cambridge Philosophical Society 3* (1830): 231–68; cited in David Medford Butler, "An Historical Investigation and Bibliography of Nineteenth Century Music Psychology Literature," vol. I (Ph.D. diss., Ohio State University, 1973), 62, 65. F. Savart, "Sur la perception des sons graves," *Annales de Chimie et de Physique* 47 (1831): 69–74; cited in Boring, *Sensation and Perception*, 333.

14. Herrnstein and Boring, *Source Book*, 64–75.

15. *Ibid.*, 60; and Edwin G. Boring, *A History of Experimental Psychology*. 2nd ed. (New York: Appleton Century-Crofts, 1950), 158.

16. Charles Darwin, *On the Origin of Species by Means of Natural Selection, or the Preservation of Favoured Races in the Struggle for Life* (London: Dent, 1859).

17. Herbert Spencer, not Darwin, coined the term "survival of the fittest," although it is compatible with the latter's theory; likewise, Darwin's was by no means the first theory of evolution, only the first reasonably coherent and documented one.

18. German biologist August Welsmann (1834–1914) and Austrian monk Gregor Mendel (1822–1884) were Galton's Darwinian counterparts in the worlds of animal and plant research, respectively.

19. Achievement testing of various types has an extremely long history, and attempts had been made before Galton's day to identify "mental defectives." Nevertheless, the mental testing (psychometrics) movement in psychology was set in motion by Galton's efforts to test mental aptitude.

20. Jere T. Humphreys, "The Child-Study Movement and Public School Music Education," *Journal of Research in Music Education* 33 (Summer 1985): 80.

21. The influence of the discovery of chemical elements on the emerging field of psychology is represented vividly in a book published in 1896 by the well-known psychologist Edward Titchener (1867–1927), in which he listed the "known" sensory elements, along with blank spaces for those yet undiscovered; Edward Bradford Titchener, *An Outline of Psychology* (New York: Macmillan 1897; reprint of the first edition, 1896), 66–67. Titchener was probably influenced by a table drawn up in 1869 by the Russian chemist Dmitri Mendelyeev (1834–1907), which included a list of all known chemical elements, along with gaps from which the existence of other elements was eventually inferred.

22. For more information about Quetelét, see Frank H. Hankins, *Adolphe Quetelét as Statistician* (New York: AMS Press, 1968; reprint of the first edition, New York: Columbia University Press, 1908).

23. Francis Galton, *Inquiries into Human Faculty and Development* (London: Macmillan, 1883), 52.

24. Francis Galton, *Hereditary Genius: An Inquiry into Its Laws and Consequences* (London: Julian Friedmann Publishers, 1978; reprint of the 1869 first edition and preface to the 1892 second edition), xi–xii.

25. Boring, *A History*, 487.

26. Franics Galton, *Memories of My Life*, 2nd ed. (London: Methuen & Co., 1908), 267.

27. *Ibid.*, 244.

28. Karl Pearson, *The Life, Letters and Labours of Francis Galton*, vol. II. (Cambridge, England: Cambridge University Press, 1924), 211. Anthropometrics ("man measurements"), the measurement of human physiological features, was one of the immediate forerunners of psychometrics, the measurement of mental abilities and achievement.

29. Galton, *Memories*, 244.

30. Pearson, *The Life*, vol. II, 212.
31. Galton, *Inquiries*, 26, 39–40.
32. Francis Galton, "The Anthropometric Laboratory," *The Fortnightly Review* 31 (March 1882): 336.
33. *Ibid.*
34. Kathryn W. Linden and James D. Linden, *Guidance Monograph Series*, Series III, "Testing." Shelley C. Stone and Bruce Shertzer, eds. (Boston: Houghton Mifflin Co., 1968), 7.
35. Galton, *Inquiries*, 27.
36. *Ibid.*, 28–29.
37. *Ibid.*, 27–28.
38. Galton, *Memories*, 245–47.
39. Francis Galton, "On the Anthropometric Laboratory at the late International Health Exhibition," *The Journal of the Royal Anthropological Institute of Great Britain and Ireland* 14 (1885): 206, 213, 216.
40. Galton, *Inquiries*, 27. Galton's discovery of the fundamental principles of statistical regression also contributed heavily to the mental testing movement.
41. Francis Galton, "Tables of Observations," *The Journal of the Royal Anthropological Institute of Great Britain and Ireland* 18 (October 1889): 420–30. These tables include statistics for twenty-three- to twenty-six-year-old male subjects only. For more information about Galton's anthropometric laboratory findings, see Francis Galton, "Retrospect of Work Done at My Anthropometric Laboratory at South Kensington," *The Journal of the Royal Anthropological Institute of Great Britain and Ireland* 22 (1892): 33.
42. Francis Galton, *Natural Inheritance* (London: Macmillan, 1889), 199–201. Darwin, too, believed in the superiority of male sensory and locomotive abilities; see Charles Darwin, *The Descent of Man and Selection in Relation to Sex*, 2nd ed. (New York: American Publishers Corporation, 1874), 225.
43. Francis Galton, "Some Results of the Anthropometric Laboratory," *The Journal of the Anthropological Institute of Great Britain and Ireland* 14 (1885): 286. Although Galton claimed superiority for males over females on this particular "faculty," chi-square comparisons computed from Galton's data by the present author indicate no statistically significant percentage differences between sexes on any frequency (20, 30, 40, or 50 thousand Hz) for subjects ranging in age from 23–26 or those 40–50 years of age. (The eight χ values with 1 degree of freedom each range from 0.00 to 1.8, all $p \geq .05$).
44. Galton considered musical ability part of the "artistic faculty"; *Inquiries*, 158–59.
45. Typically, nineteenth-century research on musical aptitude, conducted primarily in Germany, dealt not with musical aptitude in the general population, but with abilities of major composers and with relationships between musical ability and various abnormalities; Butler, "An Historical Investigation," 79.
46. Galton, *Natural Inheritance*, 154.
47. *Ibid.*, 156.
48. Herrnstein and Boring, *Source Book*, 1.
49. Jere T. Humphreys, "Applications of Science: The Age of Standardization and Efficiency in Music Education," *The Bulletin of Historical Research in Music Education* 9 (January 1988): 19–21.

REFERENCES

Bambrough, Renford. *The Philosophy of Aristotle*. New York: The New American Library, 1963.
Bell, Charles. *Idea of a New Anatomy of the Brain: Submitted for the Observation of His Friends*. London: Privately printed, 1811. In Herrnstein, Richard J., and Edwin G. Boring. *A Source Book in the History of Psychology*. Cambridge, MA: Harvard University Press, 1965,

pp. 17–19, 23–26.
Birch, Thomas. *History of the Royal Society of London* (London, 1757). In Herrnstein, Richard J., and Edwin G. Boring. *A Source Book in the History of Psychology*. Cambridge, MA: Harvard University Press, 1965, pp. 7–9.
Boethius (Anicius Manlius Torquatus Severines). *De Institutione Musica*, Book I. In Mark, Michael L. *Source Readings in Music Education History*. New York: Schirmer Books, 1982, pp. 64–68.
Boring, Edwin G. *A History of Experimental Psychology*, 2d ed. New York: Appleton Century-Crofts, 1950.
———. *Sensation and Perception in the History of Experimental Psychology*. New York: Appleton-Century-Crofts, Inc., 1942.
Bouguer, Pierre. *Traité d'Optique sur la Gradation de la Lumière*. Book I. Paris, 1760. In Herrnstein, Richard J., and Edwin G. Boring. *A Source Book in the History of Psychology*. Cambridge, MA: Harvard University Press, 1965, pp. 60–62.
Butler, David Medford. "An Historical Investigation and Bibliography of Nineteenth Century Music Psychology Literature." Vol. I. Ph.D. diss., Ohio State University, 1973.
Chladni, Ernst Florens Friedrich. "Ueber die wahre Ursache des Consonirens und Dissonirens." *Allgemeine musikalische Zeitung* (1800/1801): 337, 353. In Butler, David Medford. "An Historical Investigation and Bibliography of Nineteenth Century Music Psychology Literature." Vol. I. Ph.D. diss., Ohio State University, 1973, p. 65.
Darwin, Charles. *The Descent of Man and Selection in Relation to Sex*, 2d ed. New York: American Publishers Corporation, 1874.
———. *On the Origin of Species by Means of Natural Selection, or the Preservation of Favoured Races in the Struggle for Life*. London: Dent, 1859.
Delezenne, C. E. J. "Sur les valeurs numériques des notes de la gamme." *Recueil des Travaux de la Société des Sciences*, de l'Agriculture et des Arts de Lille (1827): 4–6. In Herrnstein, Richard J., and Edwin G. Boring. *A Source Book in the History of Psychology*. Cambridge, MA: Harvard University Press, 1965, pp. 62–64.
Galton, Francis. "The Anthropometric Laboratory." *The Fortnightly Review* 31 (March 1882): 332–38.
———. *Hereditary Genius: An Inquiry into its Laws and Consequences*, reprint of the 1869 first edition and preface to the 1892 second edition. London: Julian Friedmann Publishers, 1978.
———. *Inquiries into Human Faculty and Development*. London: Macmillan, 1883.
———. *Memories of My Life*, 2d ed. London: Methuen & Co., 1908.
———. *Natural Inheritance*. London: Macmillan, 1889.
———. "On the Anthropometric Laboratory at the late International Health Exhibition." *The Journal of the Royal Anthropological Institute of Great Britain and Ireland* 14 (1885): 205–21.
———. "Retrospect of Work done at my Anthropometric Laboratory at South Kensington." *The Journal of the Royal Anthropological Institute of Great Britain and Ireland* 22 (1892): 32–35.
———. "Some Results of the Anthropometric Laboratory." *The Journal of the Royal Anthropological Institute of Great Britain and Ireland* 14 (1885): 275–87.
———. "Tables of Observations." *The Journal of the Royal Anthropological Institute of Great Britain and Ireland* 18 (1889): 420–30.
Hankins, Frank H. *Adolphe Quetelét as Statistician*. New York: AMS Press, 1968 [reprint of the first edition, New York: Columbia University Press, 1908].
Herrnstein, Richard J., and Edwin G. Boring, eds. *A Source Book in the History of Psychology*. Cambridge, MA: Harvard University, 1965.
Humphreys, Jere T. "Applications of Science: The Age of Standardization and Efficiency in Music Education." *The Bulletin of Historical Research in Music Education* 9 (January 1988): 1–21.
———. "The Child-Study Movement and Public School Music Education." *Journal of Research in Music Education* 33 (Summer 1985): 79–86.
Linden, Kathryn W., and James D. Linden. *Modern Mental Measurement: A Historical Perspective*. Guidance Monograph Series, Series III, "Testing." Shelley C. Stone and Bruce Shertzer, eds. Boston: Houghton Mifflin Co., 1968.
Locke, John. *An Essay Concerning Humane Understanding: In Four Books*. London, 1690. In Herrnstein, Richard J., and Edwin G. Boring. *A Source Book in the History of Psychology*. Cambridge, MA: Harvard University Press, 1965, pp. 14–17.

Magendie, François. "Expériences sur les fonctions des racines des nerfs qui naissent de la moëlle épinière." *Journal de Physiologie Expérimentale et Pathologique* 2 (1822): 366–71. In Herrnstein, Richard J., and Edwin G. Boring. *A Source Book in the History of Psychology.* Cambridge, MA: Harvard University Press, 1965, pp. 19–22.

———. "Expériences sur les fonctions des racines des nerfs rachidiens." *Journal de Physiologie Expérimentale et Pathologique* 2 (1822): 276–79. In Herrnstein, Richard J., and Edwin G. Boring. *A Source Book in the History of Psychology.* Cambridge, MA: Harvard University Press, 1965, pp. 19–22.

Mark, Michael L. *Source Readings in Music Education History.* New York: Schirmer Books, 1982.

Müller, Johannes. *Handbuch der Physiologie des Menschen.* Book V. Coblenz, 1838. In Herrnstein, Richard J., and Edwin G. Boring. *A Source Book in the History of Psychology.* Cambridge, MA: Harvard University Press, 1965, pp. 26–33.

Pearson, Karl. *The Life, Letters and Labours of Francis Galton,* Vol. II. Cambridge, England: Cambridge University Press, 1924.

Sauveur, Joseph. "Des intervales des sons, et son application à tous les systèmes et à tous les instruments de musique." *Hist. Acad. Sci. Paris* (1701): 299–366. In Boring, Edwin G. *Sensation and Perception in the History of Experimental Psychology.* New York: Appleton-Century-Crofts, Inc., 1942), p. 339.

Savart, F. "Sur la perception des sons graves." *Annales de Chimie et de Physique* 47 (1831): 69–74. In Boring, Edwin G. *Sensation and Perception in the History of Experimental Psychology.* New York: Appleton-Century-Crofts, Inc., 1942, p. 333.

Seashore, Carl E., Don Lewis, and Joseph G. Saetveit. *Seashore Measures of Musical Talents.* New York: The Psychological Corporation, 1919.

Titchener, Edward Bradford. *An Outline of Psychology.* New York: Macmillan, 1897 [reprint of the 1896 first edition].

von Frey, Max. *Vorlesungen über Physiologie.* Berlin: Springer, 1904. In Herrnstein, Richard J., and Edwin G. Boring. *A Source Book in the History of Psychology.* Cambridge, MA: Harvard University Press, 1965, pp. 49–58.

von Helmholtz, H. L. F. *Die Lehre von den Tonempfindungen.* Brunswick, 1863. In Herrnstein, Richard J., and Edwin G. Boring. *A Source Book in the History of Psychology.* Cambridge, MA: Harvard University Press, 1965, pp. 44–49.

———. *Handbuch der Physiologischen Optik.* Vol. II. Leipzig, 1860. In Herrnstein, Richard J., and Edwin G. Boring. *A Source Book in the History of Psychology.* Cambridge, MA: Harvard University Press, 1965, pp. 40–44.

Weber, E. H. "Der Tastsinn und das Gemeingefühl," in Rudolph Wagner, ed. *Handwörterbuch der Physiologie.* Vol. III, Part 2, 481–588. Brunswick, 1846. In Herrnstein, Richard J., and Edwin G. Boring. *A Source Book in the History of Psychology.* Cambridge, MA: Harvard University Press, 1965, pp. 34–39.

Willis, R. "On the Vowel Sounds, and on Reed Organ-Pipes." *Cambridge Philosophical Society* 3 (1830): 231–68. In Butler, David Medford. "An Historical Investigation and Bibliography of Nineteenth Century Music Psychology Literature." Vol. I. Ph.D. diss., Ohio State University, 1973, p. 62.

Zusne, Leonard. *Names in the History of Psychology: A Biographical Sourcebook.* Washington, DC: Hemisphere Publishing Co., 1975.

July 2, 1992

IV.

CHILDREN'S

PERCEPTION,

DISCRIMINATION,

AND

PERFORMANCE

ABILITIES

The Development of Auditory Perception of Musical Sounds By Children in the First Six Grades

ROBERT G. PETZOLD

JRME 1963, VOLUME 11, NUMBER 1, PAGES 21–43

MUSIC EDUCATORS are agreed as to the significance of music reading skills in the musical development of the individual. Skill in music reading is considered an essential element of both musical understanding and appreciation, and of independent musical performance. Although there is little agreement regarding the degree of music reading skill which children in the elementary school should be expected to develop, the basic music program of the schools does give considerable emphasis to a variety of activities designed to facilitate the development of a minimal level of such skill. There is also general agreement among music educators that a carefully planned "music reading readiness" program designed to provide opportunities for the child to develop an aural understanding of the melodic, rhythmic, and interpretative elements of music should precede any sequence of music reading activities. It is expected that the child will, as a result of growing competence in the aural perception of musical sounds, be able to proceed effectively to the visual perception of music symbols in music reading because they are already familiar with the "sound vocabulary" of music represented by these symbols. Recommendations regarding the general nature of such "readiness" programs have been based upon collective practical experience rather than upon systematic research.

Since the future musical growth of the child depends upon developing this aural understanding, it is necessary to be able to identify accurately the stages through which such development moves. It is particularly important that we understand fully the nature of this auditory perception when programs of instruction in music reading are planned.

Purpose of the Study

The primary need for an investigation of this kind arises from the lack of information available concerning the development of auditory perception by children in the elementary grades.[1] The writer became involved with this problem of auditory perception as he carried forward certain research relating to music reading by children in the upper elementary grades.[2] The results of this exploratory investigation revealed a relatively low level of music reading accomplishment and suggested that part of the difficulty might be attributed to lack of an aural understanding of the musical symbols. A survey of professional

---

[1] The research reported herein was performed pursuant to a contract with the U. S. Office of Education, Department of Health, Education, and Welfare.

[2] Robert G. Petzold, "The Perception of Music Symbols in Music Reading by Normal Children and by Children Gifted Musically," *Journal of Experimental Education*, XXVIII (June 1960), 271-319.

literature failed to provide much information regarding either the various levels of accomplishment associated with the auditory perception of musical sounds, or with the developmental aspects of such perception.

The basic purpose of the study was to determine the differences between children at each of the first six grade levels in the ways in which they perceive and respond to the auditory presentation of musical sounds. The identification of such differences would permit a more precise definition of the nature of the development of the child's ear response to the elements of music.

The study dealt primarily with the melodic element of music, that element which is later visually perceived in terms of pitch symbols as the child begins to read music. Approximately 600 children, randomly selected from grades one through six of the total elementary school population in the public schools in Madison, Wisconsin, were used in the study. The testing carried forward in the project was all individual; the data was gathered by tape-recording the pupil responses in the testing situation and later transforming these responses to syllabic (sol-fa) notation. Tape-recording the responses eliminated the need for immediate scoring at the time the test was given, thus insuring accuracy of data since questionable responses could readily be repeated for verification. The several tests used in the study were also tape-recorded to insure uniformity of testing procedures.

Experimental Studies

An extensive analysis of the professional literature relating to the musical development of children showed this literature to be grouped into two general categories: (a) professional literature which includes courses of study, books in the field of music education which deal primarily with methods of teaching music, and articles in professional journals; and (b) research literature in the fields of psychology, child development, music education, and music.

The information available in the first category, despite its significance, contains the opinions, personal experiences, and recommendations based upon personal experiences which frequently serve as guides in planning programs of instruction in music education. Such information is readily available to the reader and need not be reviewed at this time. The authorities are in general agreement that one aspect of the musical development of the individual begins with developing, through those kinds of activities which involve the auditory perception of musical sounds, an awareness and understanding of the several elements of music. Once the individual has achieved a reasonable degree of competence in terms of the aural recognition of such elements, it is believed that this then establishes a satisfactory basis for involving the individual in those types of activities which give experience in becoming familiar with the abstract symbolic representation of the several musical elements. This completely logical sequence of events has gained widespread acceptance despite the fact that such a sequence has not been verified by careful and systematic investigation.

The research literature dealing with the dual problems of auditory perception and the musical development of children is not extensive and only those studies considered relevant to the present investigation will be mentioned. Comparatively little information exists regarding the musical growth of children of elementary school age. Several major studies dealing with the music development of younger children, ages two and one-half to six, point up the need for similar work with older children.[3] These studies are relevant to the present investigation because they emphasize the need for giving careful consideration to the pitch level and pitch range to be used in tests which require a singing response. They further indicate that vocal control is directly related to the concept of pitch, for if good vocal control is present, as evidenced by accurate reproduction of aural stimuli, the concept of pitch has been differentiated from other musical concepts present in the total musical experience. Since the writer planned to measure auditory perception in terms of a singing response to an aural stimulus it was necessary to establish the soundness of such a procedure.

Auditory perception is frequently defined as melodic or tonal memory and a limited, but significant body of research literature is available on this

[3] Edith N. Drexler, "A Study of the Ability to Carry a Melody at the Pre-School Level," *Child Development*, IX (September 1938), 319-332; Melvin S. Hattwick, "The Role of Pitch Level and Pitch Range in the Singing of Pre-School, First Grade, and Second Grade Children," *Child Development*, IV (1933), 281-291; Arthur T. Jersild and Sylvia Bienstock, "The Influence of Training on the Vocal Ability of 3-Year Old Children," *Child Development*, II (1931), 272-291; Arthur T. Jersild and Sylvia Bienstock, "A Study of the Development of Children's Ability to Sing," *Journal of Educational Psychology*, XXV (October 1934), 481-503; Arthur T. Jersild and Associates, *Training and Growth in the Development of Children* (Child Development Monographs, No. 10, 1932), Chapter 8; Ruth Updegraff, Louise Heiliger, and Janet Learned, "The Effect of Training upon the Singing Ability and Musical Interest of 3-, 4-, and 5-year Old Children," *University of Iowa Studies in Child Welfare*, XIV (1938), 83-131; Harold Williams, C. H. Sievers, and Melvin Hattwick, "The Measurement of Musical Development," *University of Iowa Studies in Child Welfare*, VII (1933), No. 1.

subject. The studies of Drake, Karlin, Lundin, Kwalwasser, Dykema, Mainwaring, Seashore, Semenoff, and Wing have been concerned with developing tests capable of measuring musical talent, with musical memory as one significant factor in such talent. Other researchers have been more directly concerned with defining the nature and function of tonal memory, particularly in terms of aural perception.[4] Ortmann defines the types of common tonal patterns and identifies the relative difficulty of each type. Heinlein was concerned with the factors which operate in the aural perception of tonal configurations, especially the nature and difficulty of such configurations. Bugg and Herpel differentiated between "tonal memory" and "musical memory," concluding that "tonal memory," defined as the ability to remember isolated tones, is an essential factor of superior pitch, timbre, and rhythmic judgments.

The limited amount of research literature emphasizes the need for studies which deal with the musical development of children. Existing sources fail to provide an objective and an adequate basis for recommending the kinds of instructional procedures which will result in developing an aural understanding of the melodic element of music. The data from the writer's previous study showed a relatively consistent level of accurate response to aural stimuli by fourth, fifth, and sixth grade children, but there was little parallel success in responding to the

[4] Eugene G. Bugg and Lloyd Herpel, "The Significance of Tonal Memory for Musicality," *Journal of General Psychology*, XXXV (July 1946), 3-15; Otto Ortmann, *On the Melodic Relativity of Tones*, (Psychological Monographs, XXXV, No. 1, 1926); Otto Ortmann, "Some Tonal Determinants of Melodic Memory," *Journal of Educational Psychology*, XXIV (September 1933), 454-467.

symbols representing the visual presentation of these same stimuli.[5] This inability to relate the visual symbols to the appropriate sounds appears to indicate that an aural understanding of musical elements is a necessary beginning as we consider the musical growth of children.

Procedures

The study was structured to examine perception of musical sounds as the aural identification of the similarities and differences between tonal configurations. Two types of tests were needed: (1) a test which would yield data regarding the aural perception of short tonal configurations, varied as to length and complexity; and (2) a test which would provide data regarding the auditory perception of larger and more complete musical ideas such as those found in the musical phrase, this data to be interpreted in terms of the rate at which children learned such phrases as well as in terms of the amount of recognition taking place.

Analysis of Song Materials

Since the subjects for the study were to be selected from the first six grades it was necessary to have test items with which they would be reasonably familiar as well as items which were capable of discriminating between the various levels of accomplishment. For these reasons it was decided to construct test items on the basis of the frequency with which certain tonal configurations appeared in the song materials used by children in these grades. One of the first steps taken in the study was a detailed analysis of materials in the basic song-texts to identify such common configurations. In the writer's previous study, an extensive analysis had been made of 326 songs written in major keys, resulting in identifying common tonal configurations.[6] The present study was to be concerned with the aural perception of minor as well as major tonal configurations and so the analysis was continued. The present analysis utilized 145 songs in minor keys which were selected from seventeen of the basic song-texts used by children in grades two, four, and six. The data from the two analyses were combined, giving a total of 64 common major and minor tonal configurations. It is significant to note that these 64 configurations, although they represented only 8 percent of the total number of configurations which had been identified, accounted for 57 percent of the total frequency count! These were used as a basis for constructing the melodic items for the tests.

Although the study was to be primarily concerned with the melodic element of music, the writer felt it would be of considerable interest to explore the possible effect upon auditory perception when the rhythmic element was combined with the melodic element. This decision made it necessary to analyze song materials in order to identify common rhythmic patterns. It is difficult for the musically untrained individual to differentiate aurally between certain basic rhythmic patterns because such differences are frequently notational in character. For example, the ♩♩♩ pattern in rapid ⁴⁄₄ may sound much like the ♩♪♪ pattern in slow ²⁄₄. Similarly, the ♩♩ pattern in ¾ sounds very much like the ♩♪ pattern in ⁶⁄₈. Because of this apparent lack of difference in terms of sound, the writer limited the analysis to songs written in ¾ and ⁴⁄₄ to avoid

---

[5] Petzold, pp. 298-300.

[6] Petzold, pp. 274-279.

unnecessary duplication of effort. A total of 1047 songs selected from fifteen basic song-texts were examined.

The major problem of establishing objective criteria for accurately identifying rhythmic patterns in music still remains to be solved. There is little research available to serve as a guide despite the fact that developing the ability to read rhythmic notation accurately represents a significant problem area for the music teacher, particularly in instrumental music. One factor which makes difficult the consistent application of any criterion for identifying rhythmic patterns in songs is the interrelationship existing between the syllables of the text and the notation of the melodic line. It is also evident that a pattern must contain at least three tones, preferably of unequal duration, in order to convey a feeling of movement. With this in mind, the writer arbitrarily established the musical measure as the basis for identifying the length of a rhythmic pattern. In certain situations the half-measure became the more logical basis of identification. Where neither of these seemed to apply the text was carefully examined and the identification made in terms of both the text and the musical measure. A total of 45 common rhythmic patterns were identified in this fashion and, since these 45 patterns accounted for 91 percent of the total frequency count, they were used in constructing rhythmic test items.

The Sample

The design of the study called for a stratified sample randomly drawn from the normal population of children in grades one through six, this population being undifferentiated in terms of musical ability. It had been determined that approximately 660 pupils could be tested during the time available for collecting the data. This stratified sample, with the pupils selected at random within each grade level, maintained the appropriate proportions of the total population in terms of school size, enrollments in a given grade, and number of boys and girls.

Test Construction

The time element was an important factor in developing the final form of each test since it had been discovered in an earlier study that children of this age are unable to work efficiently and effectively on tasks requiring considerable concentration for periods of time much in excess of twelve minutes. A second reason for using tests which could be completed within a ten-to-fifteen-minute testing session was the practical necessity of considering the length of the music period in the school. Arrangements to use children in the project had been approved with the understanding that all testing was to be done during the child's regular music period. Careful planning of the length of each test would permit effective use of this time, as well as insure maximum cooperation and effort from each child. After considerable exploratory work, four tests were developed for use in the study.

1. 45-Item Test

This basic test was designed to provide data regarding the auditory perception of short tonal configurations. Such data would make it possible to identify various levels of accomplishment as well as to confirm the presence of possible growth patterns in the development of auditory perception. It was necessary for the test to contain a reasonably large number of items which varied as to length and complexity. Items were selected on the basis of an item analysis of responses to an exploratory test given to 125 children. This test of 60 items was reduced to a total of 45, items eliminated being those which ranked "poor" in discriminating power and either "very easy" or "very difficult" in terms of difficulty. The final form of the test could be completed within a twelve-minute testing session and contained approximately equal numbers of 3-, 4-, 5-, 6-, and 7-tone patterns. These items represented the following kinds of musical contours: (a) scale patterns, ascending and descending; (b) chord patterns, ascending and descending; (c) disjunct patterns; and (d) conjunct and disjunct combinations of scale and chord patterns. The 45 test items were arranged in order of difficulty from "easy" to "difficult."

2. 20-Item Test

This test was designed to give data regarding the consistency of pupil responses to short tonal configurations. For this purpose it was decided to use three presentations of a stimulus and, observing the time limitation for a given testing session, this would permit the use of 20 to 25 items. Reference to the item analysis of the exploratory test resulted in identifying 30 items with high discriminating power which ranked in the middle of the difficulty range. Twenty items were selected and the total list was randomized for each of three successive presentations. Had three successive presentations of each item been made before moving to the next item it is doubtful that the data could have been interpreted in terms of the consistency of response since rote learning would then have influenced the pupil's performance.

3. Rhythm Test

The tests described thus far were used to measure auditory perception of only the melodic element of music, each test utilizing tones of equal duration. The music we hear and perform represents a combination of all the basic elements of music, particularly melodic and rhythmic. The rhythmic structure of a melodic line frequently serves to give the melody an identity which is unique, a factor of considerable assistance in learning and retaining that melody. The writer is interested in exploring this area and identifying the relationships which may exist between these two basic elements in terms of their effect upon the auditory perception of musical sounds. The scope of the present study would not permit more than a preliminary investigation which might suggest research techniques and procedures for later use. It was decided, therefore, to administer the basic 45-Item Test to one group of children with these items re-written so that each represented a common rhythmic, as well as tonal, configuration.

4. Phrase Test

The three tests thus far described measure auditory perception of short tonal or tonal-rhythmic configurations. Music, although it may be reduced to small melodic segments for purpose of analysis, usually involves larger, more complete musical ideas. Much of the music learned by children in the elementary grades is the result of extensive rote teaching, a procedure which appears to be retained in the teaching of vocal music at even higher levels of our educational system. In order for children to learn songs rapidly and effectively by rote procedures, or procedures which combine rote learning with music reading, it is essential that they develop a sense of tonal memory which enables them to perceive readily and retain the essential elements of larger musical ideas. It is particularly important for the child to retain a mental image of the sound of the phrase long enough to be able to judge the accuracy of his own performance as compared with the stimulus.

The writer has long felt that the auditory perception of larger musical units represents a highly significant problem area in the musical growth and development of the individual. For this reason the present study included a test designed to gather such information. In constructing the Phrase Test, the following criteria were utilized:

1. This larger musical unit, preferably a four-measure phrase, should be reasonably musical without duplicating any familiar song.

2. Each phrase should utilize only the more common tonal configurations in order to insure some measure of success for most individuals.

3. The melodic line should include a simple, repetitive rhythmic pattern to permit easier recognition, more consistent organization, and greater retention since there were to be no accompanying texts which could be associated with the melody.

4. The phrase should encompass a reasonable singing range to permit the children to sing easily and without tension.

Two phrases, one in major and one in minor, were finally selected by an informal jury of composition students, theory teachers, and elementary school music teachers. Each phrase was presented a total of ten times and the child was to sing as much of the phrase as possible after each presentation. The starting pitch of the phrase was given immediately prior to each singing trial. In order to minimize pupil frustration arising from lack of success, the child was given the opportunity to hear the phrase twice before attempting to sing it.

Testing Procedures and Test Scoring

Throughout the study, each child was tested individually in a separate testing room. The 45-Item Test was given to all children participating in the study. Since it was not possible to administer all four of the tests to each child, the children in the total sample were, at each grade level, randomly assigned to one of three sub-groups. Following this assignment, one of the three remaining tests was randomly assigned to each sub-group. Each sub-group contained approximately equal numbers of children at each of the first six grade levels.

To insure uniformity of testing procedures, all of the tests were tape-recorded. The aural presentation of the test item was played by a piano, with this aural presentation followed by an interval of silence which was varied in accordance with the length of the test item. For all of the tests the child was expected to make a singing response which duplicated the stimulus during this interval of silence. A second tape-recorder in the testing room was used to record the entire testing session for each child. There seemed to be no way of effectively measuring accuracy of aural perception except in terms of some type of musical performance. A vocal response was considered to be most appropriate because all of the children had had experience in singing as part of the regular music program in the schools.

The writer was aware that the decision to use a singing response as a measure of accurate aural perception created a problem in that an incorrect response might result from inadequate vocal control rather than from inability to accurately perceive the stimulus. To minimize this problem, the writer developed a comprehensive scoring system which attempted to reflect the degree to which the child was aware of the nature of the stimulus, as well as the degree to which he was able to control the singing voice. Data from the earlier exploratory study was used to identify the several common types of responses made by children in responding to the aural presentation of short tonal configurations. These responses, together with the scoring procedures, are as follows:

Type A. The response is an exact imitation of the stimulus—2 points for each tone of the item. A correct 7-tone item would be scored 14 points.

Type B. Part of the response is correct, the remainder either changed or omitted—2 points for each correct tone provided these tones are reproduced in the correct sequence. For example, an item "do re mi fa sol" might result in a response of "do re mi sol la." Only the first three tones are correct as to pitch and sequence and the item would be scored 6 points. In some instances there was no way of determining whether the child forgot the beginning of the item but retained the final tones, whether he retained the beginning but started on the wrong pitch and then omitted the final tones, or whether he thought the item contained fewer tones than was the case. For example, "mi fa sol" might have been the response made to "do re mi fa sol." To eliminate the need for guessing as to the exact nature of the response, such a response was scored as Type F, giving it 1.25 points or 12.5 percent of the value of a 5-tone item.

Type C. The interval relationships between the tones of the response duplicate those of the stimulus but the response is transposed—50 percent of the total possible item value. For example, the child hearing "do re mi" might lose the starting pitch and sing "re mi fi." This response would be scored 3 points, 50 percent of the total possible item value of 6 points.

Type D. The response follows the general direction or contour of the stimulus and contains the correct number of tones but the pitches are not duplicated—25 percent of the total possible item value. For example, the item "do mi do" might result in a response of "mi sol mi." Since the response contains the correct number of tones and has a shape similar to that of the stimulus it would be scored 1.5 points, 25 percent of the total value of 6 points.

Type E. The response contains the correct number of tones but the pitches and/or direction are different—12.5 percent of the total possible item value. A response of "mi re do" to the item "do re mi" would be scored .75 points, 12.5 percent of the total possible item value of 6 points.

Type F. The response follows the general direction of the stimulus but contains neither the correct pitches or the correct number of tones—12.5 percent of the total possible item value. A response of "do mi sol *mi*" to the item "la ti do *la sol*" appears to show directional recognition of the item and is scored 1.25, or 12.5 percent of the total possible item value of 10 points.

The 45-Item, Rhythm, and 20-Item tests were all scored in terms of these six types of responses. The Rhythm Test was designed to ascertain the possible effect that the addition of the rhythmic element might have upon the auditory perception of tonal configurations, as such. It was assumed that the melodic character of the tonal pattern was not significantly altered when the pattern was stated rhythmically. Since the Rhythm Test was given to a group of children who had earlier taken the 45-Item Test, performance on the two tests could more easily be compared if similar scoring methods were used. Therefore, rhythmic accuracy was not a factor in scoring the Rhythm Test, only melodic accuracy.

The nature of the Phrase Test precluded application of the scoring system developed for the other tests. The writer felt that interpretation of each trial in terms of one or more of these six general types of responses would necessitate making certain subjective judgments which would, in turn, be subject to error. It was decided to use the number of tones correctly reproduced in each measure as the basis for scoring each trial. Since there were 15 tones in the phrase, two points for each correct tone gave a total of 30 points as the perfect score for any trial. Two kinds of scores were then calculated for the Phrase Test:

a. The "mean correct score" for the entire test represented the child's achievement in terms of the number of tones correctly reproduced. This score, with a possible score range of zero to 30, was obtained as follows:

$$\text{"mean correct score"} = \frac{\text{sum of the scores for each trial}}{\text{number of trials}}$$

b. A "rate-of-learning" score (RL) represented a single score which would describe the test gains made by the subject from the first trial to the last, as well as a score which would take into account the number of trials needed to make those gains.

$$\text{RL Score} = \frac{\text{Score on final trial minus score on 1st trial}}{\text{Perfect score (30) minus score on 1st trial}} \times \frac{100}{\text{N of trials}}$$

The RL scores ranged from 0 to 100 but did not include negative scores which might result had the final trial been poorer than the first trial. Other clarification of the scoring procedure for the Phrase Test is as follows:

a. The subject whose final trial either represented no gain over the score on the initial trial, or whose final trial was lower than the score on the initial trial, was given an RL score of zero.

b. The criterion of success consisted of two consecutively perfect trials and, since the child was given the opportunity to hear the phrase twice before attempting to sing, it would be entirely possible for the first and second trials to be perfect. Application of the scoring formula would result in an RL score of zero since no improvement between initial and final trials was noted, or even possible. This seemed illogical in view of the superiority of such children as compared to the children in "a" above and, to differentiate between such cases, children with perfect scores on both the initial and second trials were given an RL score of 100.

The RL score, since it was a gain score rather than an achievement score, worked to the disadvantage of subjects who may have had high "mean correct scores" on the initial trial but then either failed to improve their performance or else required several trials to attain a perfect performance. Therefore, in discussing the results of the Phrase Test, both kinds of scores will be utilized.

These scoring methods have been discussed in some detail because scoring constitutes a major problem in carrying forward research in the area of music testing. It is of greatest importance that the scores obtained for a given test reflect both the nature of the task involved and the kind of skill or competence the test is designed to measure. Music educators have frequently defended the use of subjective scoring systems for the many aspects of musical accomplishment and performance on the assumption that the things being measured could not be scored objectively because of the unique characteristics of music. The writer feels that continued research activity will eventually result in a much greater degree of objectivity than has been considered possible. Such objectivity will, in turn, have far-reaching effects upon the music instruction taking place at all levels of our educational system.

Results of the Study

In summarizing the results of the study, the significant data for each of the several tests will be discussed separately to facilitate the presentation.

The 45-Item Test.—Although a total of 660 children had been scheduled to receive this basic test, usable data was obtained for 606 children.

One of the first steps taken with regard to the test was to ascertain the reliability of the test itself. A detailed item analysis for each grade of the total sample was carried forward and the procedures need not be detailed because they are generally known. The Kuder-Richardson Formula No. 20 was used to compute the reliability coefficient of the test:

$$r_{tt} = \frac{n}{n-1} [\frac{\sigma^2_t - \Sigma pq}{\sigma^2_t}]$$

To complete the standard error of measure, the usual formula was used:

$$\sigma_e = \sigma_t \sqrt{1 - r_{tt}}$$

The reliability coefficients and standard errors given below indicate that the test possessed a high degree of stability and internal consistency at all grade levels. (See Table 1)

TABLE 1

RELIABILITY COEFFICIENTS AND STANDARD ERRORS OF THE BASIC 45-ITEM TEST

Grade	r_{tt}	σ_e	Grade	r_{tt}	σ_e
1	.95	2.29	5	.97	2.31
2	.96	2.34	6	.97	2.34
3	.96	2.39	1-6	.97	2.36
4	.97	2.37			

One purpose of the test was to determine whether any significant differences were found between grade levels. The data in Table 2 shows that for the total group, boys and girls combined, there is a higher mean score at each successive grade level, with a marked increase for sixth grade. To ascertain the significance of these observed differences, "t" tests were made between grades at one-, two- and three-year intervals with the results given in Table 3.

TABLE 3

COMPARISONS BETWEEN GRADE LEVELS FOR THE 45-ITEM TEST, SHOWING THE SIGNIFICANCE OF THE DIFFERENCES IN TERMS OF "T" VALUES

1-Year Interval		2-Year Interval		3-Year Interval	
Grades	"t"	Grades	"t"	Grades	"t"
1 & 2	1.583	1 & 3	2.065*	1 & 4	2.861**
2 & 3	0.601	2 & 4	1.318	2 & 5	1.971*
3 & 4	0.634	3 & 5	1.237	3 & 6	5.281**
4 & 5	0.634	4 & 6	4.811**		
5 & 6	4.114**				

*Significant at the 5% level.
**Significant at the 1% level.

When we consider the grades at one-year intervals the differences between the means are significant only for grades five and six. When a two-year interval is taken we find the differences to be significant for grades one and three and grades four and six. A

TABLE 2

MEAN SCORES AND STANDARD DEVIATIONS, CLASSIFIED BY
GRADE AND VARIABLE, FOR THE 45-ITEM TEST

Grade	Total Group			Boys			Girls			Experience Group I			Experience Group II		
	N	$\bar{X}$	SD	N	$\bar{X}$	SD	N	$\bar{X}$	SD	N	$\bar{X}$	SD	N	$\bar{X}$	SD
1	120	193	108	62	186	107	58	200	108	27	158	99	22	253	102
2	103	216	106	43	196	98	60	229	109	27	173	81	23	242	110
3	93	225	122	51	212	124	42	242	118	29	188	122	23	296	107
4	102	236	118	47	233	122	55	239	115	32	203	95	28	289	118
5	102	247	121	42	240	116	60	252	124	22	192	114	38	303	111
6	86	316	105	52	316	104	34	316	108	14	272	93	24	358	113
1-6	606	236	120	297	230	120	309	241	118	151	191	106	158	292	116

TABLE 4

DISTRIBUTION, BY GRADE, OF SCORES WITHIN EACH OF THE
COMPETENCE LEVELS ESTABLISHED FOR THE 45-ITEM TEST

Grade	Level 1 (0-140.5)		Level 2 (141-226)		Level 3 (226.5-332.0)		Level 4 (332.5-460)	
	N	%	N	%	N	%	N	%
1	43	36	34	28	28	23	15	12
2	30	29	28	27	29	28	16	16
3	23	25	26	28	24	26	20	22
4	26	26	24	24	24	24	28	28
5	23	23	26	26	24	24	29	28
6	6	7	15	16	24	28	41	48

	Q_1 (141)	Q_2 (226.5)	Q_3 (332.5)

TABLE 5

MEAN SCORES AND STANDARD DEVIATIONS, CLASSIFIED BY
GRADE AND VARIABLE, FOR THE RHYTHM TEST

Grade	Total Group			Boys			Girls			Experience Group I			Experience Group II		
	N	$\bar{X}$	SD	N	$\bar{X}$	SD	N	$\bar{X}$	SD	N	$\bar{X}$	SD	N	$\bar{X}$	SD
1	36	189	106	12	157	84	24	199	115	7	126	60	3	214	64
2	30	238	125	12	213	135	18	254	114	6	237	88	6	243	121
3	24	228	120	12	192	123	12	265	106	5	162	31	6	288	114
4	22	259	105	8	265	93	14	256	111	10	230	83	8	293	132
5	26	276	136	12	244	142	14	303	126	7	190	149	9	368	90
6	27	349	105	17	329	122	10	384	53	5	320	129	10	370	112
1-6	165	253	128	73	238	134	92	263	122	40	209	114	42	314	124

three-year interval shows the differences between the means to be significant for all comparisons. This suggests that although children in the middle grades, three, four and five, perform similarly, there are marked differences in accomplishment between the lower and upper grades.

The relatively large standard deviations, which are very similar from grade to grade, indicate that the individual scores are distributed over a fairly wide range. Inspection of the data showed the following score ranges for each grade: grade one, 12-401; grade two, 31-458; grade three, 9-460; grade four, 26-450; grade five, 20-460; and grade six, 82-460.

Another basis for comparing the performances of children in each of the grade levels utilizes the frequency distribution of the scores. The six grades were first combined into a single distribution for this purpose and the 25th, 50th, and 75th percentiles were found for the total sample. This gave $Q_1 = 141$, $Q_2 = 226.5$, and $Q_3 = 332.5$. When these score values had been located for the total sample it became possible to identify four competence levels for the test and to use these as a basis for comparing the performances at each grade level. Table 4 summarizes this information, showing the percentage of children in each grade earning scores located within each of the four competence levels identified: Level 1, below Q_1; Level 2, Q_1 to Q_2; Level 3, Q_2 to Q_3; Level 4, above Q_3. The percentage of scores which lie within the inter-quartile range, Q_1 to Q_3, tends to remain relatively constant from grade level to grade level while there is a noticeable increase in the percentage of children earning scores above Q_3 as we examine each successively higher grade level. This analysis further tends to support the position

that age, as identified by grade level, implies a musical growth and maturity that is directly related to competence in the auditory perception of the melodic elements of music.

One of the instructional problems which faces the teacher of music results from the markedly different attitudes which boys and girls have toward music. There is no sound basis for assuming that these differences can be attributed to differing abilities. In a previous study the writer found no significant differences between boys and girls as they engaged in certain music reading activities. To determine whether such differences might exist with the auditory perception of musical sounds, the performances of boys and girls were compared at each grade level. The data in Table 2 shows the girls to have higher mean scores than the boys at each grade level, except grade six. To ascertain fully the significance of these differences, "t" tests were made and the results showed that none of the "t" values approached the 5 percent level of significance. The hypothesis that the means of the boys differed significantly from the means of the girls may be rejected, results which confirmed the writer's previous findings.

Programs of musical activities are frequently influenced by an assumption that additional musical training and out-of-school contact with music is significantly related to the musical growth and development of the individual. Since the tests used in this study required a response in terms of musical performance it was reasonable to expect that these varying kinds and amounts of musical experiences might be reflected in the children's test scores. A *Musical Experience Information Sheet* was developed to collect data regarding the musical training of the child, as well as information regarding the nature and extent of musical activity in the home. The information was furnished by the parents and *Information Sheets* were returned by 506 children of the total sample. An "experience score" was calculated for each child, a frequency distribution of the scores was constructed, and the upper and lower quartiles then identified. Children with scores below the 25th percentile were identified as Experience Group I (low "experience scores"); those whose scores were above the 75th percentile were identified as Experience Group II (high "experience scores"), and those with scores falling within the inter-quartile range were not assigned to either group. The data presented in Table 2 clearly shows that children in Experience Group II earned scores on the 45-Item Test that were considerably higher, an average of 92 points, than those earned by children in Experience Group I. The "t" tests made between the two groups at each grade level showed that the differences between the means were significant at the 1 percent level for all grades except grades two and six, these being significant at the 5 percent level. It would appear that the hypothesis of "no difference" could be rejected and that musical experience is a significant factor in performance on tests of this kind. However, other hypotheses regarding the nature of this relationship between experience and achievement, particularly in terms of auditory perception, should be formulated and tested.

Rhythm Test.—This test was, it may be recalled, similar to the 45-Item Test in that it used the same test items presented rhythmically as well as melodically. Approximately 200 children had been scheduled to receive the Rhythm Test in addition to the basic 45-Item Test. However, since many children were not available for testing, usable data for the Rhythm Test was obtained for 165 children. This data is summarized in Table 5. As was the case with the 45-Item Test, the means of the total group are higher at each successive grade level, except grades 2 and 3. The "t" tests made between the grades at one-, two-, and three-year intervals are given in Table 6. These show that the differences between the means are significant in only four of the twelve comparisons, and that three of these involve the sixth grade. In view of this, it appears that the hypothesis of "no difference" is tenable for one- and two-year intervals but must be rejected for the three-year interval. This similarity with the "t" tests made for the 45-Item Test is to be anticipated since these two tests had the same melodic content. In addition, the scoring system was the same for both tests, with items scored in terms of melodic accuracy rather than taking into account rhythmic accuracy as well.

TABLE 6

COMPARISONS BETWEEN GRADE LEVELS FOR THE RHYTHM TEST, SHOWING THE SIGNIFICANCE OF THE DIFFERENCES IN TERMS OF "T" VALUES

1-Year Interval		2-Year Interval		3-Year Interval	
Grades	"t"	Grades	"t"	Grades	"t"
1 & 2	1.821	1 & 3	1.445	1 & 4	2.532**
2 & 3	0.267	2 & 4	0.642	2 & 5	1.084
3 & 4	0.895	3 & 5	1.280	3 & 6	3.754***
4 & 5	0.469	4 & 6	2.927**		
5 & 6	2.153*				

*Significant at the 5% level.
**Significant at the 2% level.
***Significant at the 1% level.

The secondary purpose for scoring the Rhythm Test in this manner was to permit comparisons between performance on the two tests in an attempt to ascertain whether the introduction of the rhythmic element significantly affected the auditory perception of the *melodic* element. Table 7 gives the data for both the Rhythm Test and the 45-Item Test for this group of children. Correlations between the two test scores were calculated for each grade, the resultant "r's" are as follows:

Grade	"r"
1	.92
2	.94
3	.96
4	.94
5	.96
6	.94

This indicates that the two tasks are very closely related, as might be expected, and that children could be expected to perform at much the same level of competence on either test.

TABLE 7

MEAN SCORES AND STANDARD DEVIATIONS, CLASSIFIED BY GRADE, FOR CHILDREN TAKING BOTH THE RHYTHM AND 45-ITEM TESTS

Grade	N	Rhythm test X	Rhythm test SD	45-item test X	45-item test SD
1	36	189	106	174	103
2	30	238	125	217	118
3	24	228	120	205	111
4	22	259	105	239	110
5	26	276	136	262	125
6	27	349	105	339	100
1-6	165	253	128	236	123

The data in Table 6 also shows that the means for the 45-Item Test are lower than those for the Rhythm Test at every grade level and for all grades combined. Since the Rhythm Test was given at least two months later than the 45-Item Test it is not reasonable to assume that children were able to remember the test items. The higher means for the Rhythm Test might reflect the influence of previous practice and familiarity with the task, or they might suggest that the rhythmic organization of the melodic items makes them easier to perceive and retain. However, the "t" tests for the significance of the differences between the means of the two tests failed to yield any "t" values which approached the 5 percent level of significance. This would indicate that the addition of the rhythmic element to melodic items had no appreciable influence upon the auditory perception of such items, that the presence of rhythm proved to be neither a help or a handicap. Therefore, it appears reasonable to assume that the higher means on the Rhythm Test reflect the influence of previous practice on a related task but, lacking a control group who had taken only the Rhythm Test, the assumption cannot be verified at this time. The fact that the differences between the means of the two tests were not significant is of considerable interest because it has been generally assumed that auditory perception is influenced in some fashion when more than one musical element is present in the stimulus.

Analysis of the data for the 45-Item Test showed that the differences between the means of the boys and the girls were not significant at any grade level. Although the data presented in Table 5 again show that the girls have higher means than the boys, the "t" tests failed to yield any "t" values which met the 5 percent level of significance. It becomes apparent that factors other than musical competence may be present in a situation which so consistently results in girls earning higher scores than boys. Such factors might include attitudes toward the task, attitudes toward music activities in general, level of aspiration and motivation, and general singing competence. The study did not concern itself with an examination of these other factors, particularly since the performances of boys and girls did not differ significantly.

Comparisons between experience groups did not produce results similar to those obtained for the 45-Item Test. Part of this might be attributed to the fact that only 50 percent of the children taking the Rhythm Test provided us with data regarding their musical background. Table 5 shows that children in Experience Group II earned mean scores that were an average of 85 points above the mean scores of Experience Group I. The "t" tests made between the two groups at each grade level showed that the only significant difference between the means was found for fifth grade, significant at the 2 percent level. When the six grades were combined the difference between the means of the two groups gave a "t" value which was significant at the 1 percent level. It is highly probable that had data regarding this musical experience been available for all children taking the Rhythm Test, the results of the "t" tests would have been very similar to those made for the 45-Item Test. There is no sound basis for assuming that such musical experience could be related to one task and not to a second, very similar task.

20-Item Test.—The primary function of this test was to ascertain the degree to which children were able to give consistent responses to given auditory stimuli. The twenty items, selected on the basis of an item analysis of items used in the exploratory test, were randomized for each of three suc-cessive trials. It was not the intent of this test to determine the number of trials needed to obtain a consistently accurate response, and successive presentations of the same item were avoided. Approximately 200 children had been scheduled to receive this test in addition to the 45-Item Test. Usable data on the 20-Item Test were obtained for 164 children. The test items were scored exactly as items on the 45-Item Test had been scored, with the total test score derived by summing the scores on each trial and dividing by the number of trials. Table 8 summarizes, by grade and variable, the scores for this test.

No marked differences were observed between the means for the several grades. The "t" tests made between grades at one-, two-, and three-year intervals gave "t" values which met the criterion of a 5 percent level in only one of the twelve comparisons, that for grades five and six, which was a one-year interval. The "t" values for grades one and four and grades three and six, three-year intervals, very closely approached the 5 percent level of significance, and the hypothesis of "no difference" between means taken at this larger interval may not be retained with complete confidence.

The information given in Table 8 shows that the girls again earned higher mean scores than the boys, except at the sixth grade level. The "t" tests made to ascertain the significance of these differences resulted in a "t" value for grade two which was significant at the 5 percent level. This is the first test for which an obtained "t," when comparing the performance of boys and girls, has met the criterion of significance. However, in view of the evidence thus far presented, the writer feels that this is quite probably the result of chance and would continue to accept the hypothesis that no difference exists.

Data regarding musical experience was secured from only 69 of the 164 children taking the 20-Item Test. Consequently the small number in each group at each grade level creates certain problems of interpretation. The mean scores for each Experience Group are presented in Table 8. The limited number of cases, especially at the sixth grade level, tends to make the "t" tests of little value. However, the observed difference between the means of the two groups were significant at the 2 percent level for all but grades two and five. It would appear that experience is a factor in achievement on tests of this type.

The 20-Item Test was, of course, very closely related to the 45-Item Test since the content was identical though not as extensive. The correlations between scores for the two tests ranged from .82 to .96. All were significant far beyond the 1 percent level, results to be expected since performances on two almost identical tests were compared.

The primary function of this test was to ascertain the consistency with which children responded to the same stimulus. The data for each of the three trials, not presented here for reasons of space, showed that the mean scores and standard deviations remained relatively unchanged from one trial to the next. This suggests that at all grade levels children were able to give consistent responses to each presentation of the item. Had the responses been markedly different from trial to trial this lack of consistency would have been reflected in the test scores. Further, the similarity of means from trial to trial suggests that the practice effect of one or two trials had little effect upon the score achieved.

The "t" tests made between each pair of trials at each grade level (Trials I and II, Trials I and III, and Trials II and III) yielded values which were between 85 and 90 percent levels of significance with many of them approaching the 99 percent level. The hypothesis that children do make consistent responses as reflected by consistent scores from trial to trial obviously may not be rejected for this sample.

To study further the consistency of pupil response, an extensive and detailed analysis was carried forward of the responses made by each child to each test item on each trial of the test. It was assumed that many children might perform consistently, but incorrectly as well as correctly, singing the *same* response each time a given stimulus was presented. The analysis of item responses identified, for each child, those items which received identical responses for either two of the three trials or for all three trials. A separate tabulation was made for correct and incorrect item responses, responses which were, however, identical from trial to trial. The tabulated results are too extensive to be presented in this report but showed that the total sample performed at a 60 percent level of consistency. At each grade level more than half of the items received identical responses for either two or three of the three trials, with a range of 54 percent for grade one to 73 percent for grade six. This percentage of identical responses included both correct and incorrect responses to the items. It is interesting to note that while the percentage of correct responses to items for two or three of the trials increased from 35 percent in grade one to 61 percent in grade six, the percentage of identical but incorrect responses for two or three of the

Table 8

Mean Scores and Standard Deviations, Classified by
Grade and Variable, for the 20-Item Test

Grade	Total Group			Boys			Girls			Experience Group I			Experience Group II		
	N	X̄	SD	N	X̄	SD	N	X̄	SD	N	X̄	SD	N	X̄	SD
1	34	105	53	21	103	57	13	108	46	8	84	31	5	164	9
2	29	114	48	7	77	25	22	126	47	8	87	53	7	119	35
3	28	114	53	13	111	46	15	116	58	9	61	34	8	156	43
4	31	131	54	16	122	57	15	140	48	10	101	50	4	168	37
5	24	110	48	11	108	49	13	112	47	7	93	45	9	119	51
6	18	144	47	9	150	36	9	137	56	2	160	2	2	200	0
1-6	164	118	52	77	112	53	87	123	52	44	88	47	35	144	46

Table 9

Mean Scores and Standard Deviations, Classified by Grade and
Variable, for the Phrase Test, Using "RL" Scores

Grade	Total Group			Boys			Girls			Experience Group I			Experience Group II		
	N	X̄	SD	N	X̄	SD	N	X̄	SD	N	X̄	SD	N	X̄	SD
1	38	2.28	2.30	24	1.88	1.92	14	2.98	2.70	9	3.00	2.27	9	1.96	1.43
2	32	3.46	3.75	15	3.15	2.77	17	3.74	4.42	9	1.79	2.12	9	6.01	5.26
3	33	7.49	17.02	19	4.78	5.78	14	11.17	24.79	13	4.17	3.15	9	14.60	30.30
4	41	7.10	17.00	19	11.45	23.75	22	3.35	4.57	11	3.56	2.93	15	13.41	26.38
5	34	8.42	10.52	13	7.11	13.16	21	9.23	8.38	5	3.40	4.68	14	11.24	12.25
6	34	14.74	19.77	21	16.60	22.80	13	11.73	12.94	5	13.90	19.00	11	21.69	26.23
1-6	212	7.19	14.15	111	7.58	15.87	101	6.75	11.97	52	4.29	7.31	67	11.94	21.51

Table 10

Mean Scores and Standard Deviations, Classified by Grade and
Variable, for the Phrase Test, Using "Mean Correct" Scores

Grade	Total Group			Boys			Girls			Experience Group I			Experience Group II		
	N	X̄	SD	N	X̄	SD	N	X̄	SD	N	X̄	SD	N	X̄	SD
1	38	9.37	5.64	24	8.48	4.97	14	10.88	6.87	9	8.90	5.23	9	11.86	4.25
2	32	9.48	5.39	15	8.91	5.25	17	9.98	5.46	9	6.13	2.61	9	13.77	6.72
3	33	13.84	6.12	19	13.26	5.82	14	14.63	6.43	13	11.85	5.93	9	16.57	6.46
4	41	11.06	6.44	19	12.46	7.53	22	9.85	5.01	11	10.95	4.74	15	12.63	7.57
5	34	14.36	7.48	13	13.05	6.91	21	15.17	7.70	5	10.74	7.13	14	17.18	6.08
6	34	16.75	7.14	21	16.78	7.39	13	16.70	6.71	5	14.98	8.93	11	17.55	7.75
1-6	212	12.39	6.95	111	12.14	7.01	101	12.66	6.87	52	10.35	6.18	67	14.97	7.05

trials remained at a relatively constant 13 percent beyond grade two. This analysis indicated that several presentations of a given auditory stimulus will result in identical responses approximately 60 percent of the time. Had more trials been available it is anticipated that the level of consistency would have been even higher.

Phrase Test.—This test was designed to provide data regarding the auditory perception of longer, more complete melodic entities such as encountered in the phrase. The task of perceiving and responding to short tonal patterns which are presented only once is considerably different from a task involving a phrase of four measures that is presented several times in succession. There were a total of ten presentations of the phrase, with a response to be given after the second and each succeeding presentation. It was considered unwise to expect children to be capable of making a successful response after a single presentation since the resulting frustration might seriously affect their attitude toward the task. These several learning trials made it possible to identify, by means of the scoring system presented earlier, the rate at which children were able to learn the phrase as well as the overall achievement represented by the number of tones correctly reproduced.

The basis for scoring the Phrase Test differed from that for the other tests in that only tones correctly performed were scored. The perfect score for any response trial was 30 points, two points for each of the 15 tones. The "mean correct" score was obtained by summing the scores for each trial and dividing by the number of trials. No individual could have a score higher than 30. The RL (rate-of-learning) score described the gains made by the individual from the initial to the final trial, and although the range of possible scores was 0 to 100, a score of 11.1 or higher was possible only if the subject's final trial was perfect. Consequently, the means and standard deviations are relatively small values, reflecting the scoring system used as well as the difficulty of the task.

Usable data was obtained for 212 children taking the Phrase Test and is summarized in Tables 9 and 10. Once again there is improvement from grade level to grade level and, in terms of the RL scores, the sixth grade mean reflects the large number of children who had perfect final trials. When the RL scores are considered, a pronounced gap is observed between grades two and three and grades five and six. A similar gap is observed between grades two and three for "mean correct" scores. The "t" tests between grades did not give results which were similar to those obtained for the other tests. The "t" values, summarized in Table 11, show that with the RL scores the differences between the obtained means are significant only for the three-year interval between grades three and five. For the "mean correct" score, the differences between the means are significant in six of the twelve comparisons, most of these involving comparisons between grades at one- and two-year intervals. In other words, if the rate at which children are able to learn materials is the basis for comparison, there is almost no significant change in performance from grade level to grade level. However, when achievement is considered, the results indicate significant changes in performance from grade level to grade level. The "mean correct" score on the Phrase Test reflects the same kind of competency involved in performance on the other tests but

TABLE 11

COMPARISONS BETWEEN GRADE LEVELS FOR THE PHRASE TEST, SHOWING
THE SIGNIFICANCE OF THE DIFFERENCES IN TERMS OF "T" VALUES

1-Year Interval			2-Year Interval			3-Year Interval		
Grades	"t_1"	"t_2"	Grades	"t_1"	"t_2"	Grades	"t_1"	"t_2"
1 & 2	1.590	0.081	1 & 3	1.841	3.159***	1 & 4	1.712	1.223
2 & 3	1.289	3.001***	2 & 4	1.173	1.104	2 & 5	2.480**	2.983***
3 & 4	0.096	1.862	3 & 5	0.264	0.306	3 & 6	1.580	1.762
4 & 5	0.387	2.026*	4 & 6	1.773	3.579***			
5 & 6	1.621	1.329						

Note: "t_1" for "RL" scores, "t_2" for "mean correct" scores.
*Significant at the 5% level.
**Significant at the 2% level.
***Significant at the 1% level.

produces considerably different results when grades are compared. The RL scores measure an additional factor and the writer considers it significant that the ability to learn a short musical phrase from aural presentation alone does not appear to be significantly affected by the experience and maturity one associates with each higher grade level. Although this hypothesis is tenable, in terms of the results which have been presented, it needs careful examination because it does not agree with the widely accepted viewpoints of professional music educators. Other types of tests and other hypotheses need to be developed in order to completely explore this kind of musical learning.

Tabulation of the individual test scores showed a noticeable increase in the percentage of children in grades five and six whose scores indicated an ability to learn the phrase within the ten-trial testing session. The percentage of children at each grade level who learned the phrase is as follows: grade one, none; grade two, 6 percent; grade three, 12 percent; grade four, 15 percent; grade five, 38 percent; grade six, 50 percent, and grades one to six combined, 20 percent. The Phrase Test included a second phrase in the minor

mode which has not yet been discussed. Only 25 of the 212 children taking the Phrase Test were able to proceed to this second phrase within the time limits of the single testing session. These were children who had required no more than six trials to learn the first phrase and consequently had additional time available for testing. Of the 25 children attempting this second phrase, 16 were able to achieve a perfect learning trial, and all were in grades five and six.

The "mean correct" score describes the achievement of the individual in terms of the average number of tones correctly reproduced. It was found that many children had relatively high 'mean correct" scores, but because little or no improvement was noted between the initial and final trials, the RL score was quite low. One way to identify the degree to which this kind of situation prevailed was to calculate the correlations between the two kinds of test scores, the RL score and the "mean correct" score. These correlations were as follows: grade one, .28; grade two, .78; grade three, .59; grade four, .72; grade five, .74; grade six, .64. All correlations are positive and show, especially for first grade children, that the ability to reproduce part of the phrase correctly does not necessarily result in improvement from trial to trial. This suggests that the learning process involves considerably more than just having the child listen to the material without giving him any suggestions regarding his progress. It is quite probable that the correlations would have been considerably higher, thus reflecting the fact that children had achieved some degree of effective learning which was related to their initial achievement, had the testing procedures employed one or more of the following devices:

1. The examiner describes and demonstrates the nature of the errors made, calling them to the attention of the pupil.

2. The pupil is given an opportunity to hear the recording of his response so he can compare his performance with the stimulus.

3. The pupil is given an opportunity for drill on troublesome intervals before proceeding with the next learning trial.

4. Some children, for various reasons, could have been given the opportunity to learn only a section of the phrase before proceeding to the rest of the phrase.

5. Provision for additional learning trials, particularly in those cases where the child appeared to be uncertain as to the nature of the task.

The writer was not, however, interested in using such devices since the purpose of the test was to ascertain the amount of learning which resulted solely from the individual's aural perception of the stimulus. The degree to which the child is able to perceive, retain, organize a response, and then compare this response to the stimulus in order to effect appropriate changes in succeeding attempts depends upon

the level at which auditory perception functions. To introduce external teaching devices creates the situation in which the child is not independent, but dependent upon the teacher for all learning which takes place.

Further evidence that learning musical material involves factors other than accurate auditory perception is provided by the correlations which were calculated between the scores earned by this group of children on the 45-Item Test and the two kinds of scores on the Phrase Test. These correlations, given below, are keyed as follows: $1=$ 45-Item Test score; $2 =$ RL score on Phrase Test, and $3 =$ "mean correct" score on Phrase Test. It will be noted that the "r_{13}" is higher than the "r_{12}" in every instance. All of the correlations except the "r_{12}" for grades 1 and 3 are significant at the 1% level.

Grade	"r_{12}"	"r_{13}"
1	.28	.79
2	.42	.57
3	.38	.79
4	.44	.58
5	.66	.86
6	.54	.70
1-6	.47	.74

The data for the tests thus far discussed showed that the differences between the means of the boys and girls were not significant at any grade level. These same findings are to be noted for the Phrase Test and this information is presented in Tables 9 and 10. None of the "t" tests yielded "t" values which met, or even approached, the criterion of significance at the 5 percent level, and the hypothesis of "no difference" continues to be tenable.

Tables 9 and 10 also summarize the scores on the Phrase Test for the two experience groups. Unfortunately, data regarding this experience was available from only 119 of the 212 children taking the test. The data shows consistently higher means for Group II and it is interesting to note that for the RL scores, the standard deviations of Group II are considerably larger than those of Group I. The "t" tests gave results which would appear to indicate that this type of musical experience is not reflected in a task which involves the learning of musical material from auditory stimuli alone. These tests showed that for both kinds of scores the hypothesis of "no difference" between the two experience groups is tenable in all instances except when the six grades are combined and when the second grade is considered. The "t" values for both scores when the six grades were combined were at the 2 percent level of significance and the "t" value for grade two met the 5 percent level of significance. This is quite different from the results of similar "t" tests for the other tests where the hypothesis could be rejected at almost every grade level considered. It is quite evident that other hypotheses regarding the relationship of musical background and experience and degree and rate of musical learning will need to be tested.

Summary and Conclusions

Some of the more significant findings of the study may be summarized as follows:

1. No significant differences were found between boys and girls in terms of their performance on tasks concerned with the auditory perception of musical sounds. For only one of the 35 comparisons involving this variable did the mean score of the boys differ significantly from that of the girls.

2. The hypothesis that age, defined in terms of grade level, is a significant factor in the development of auditory perception, may be accepted with certain reservations. The data showed that when the two grades being compared were taken at one-year intervals the differences between the means were significant in only six of 25 comparisons, with four of these at the fifth and sixth grade levels. When a two-year interval was used, the differences between the means were significant in five of twenty comparisons, three of these for grades four and six. Finally, when a three-year interval was used, the differences between the means were significant in seven of the fifteen comparisons, with four additional comparisons closely approaching the 5 percent level.

3. The hypothesis that musical training and out-of-school musical experience is a significant factor in the development of auditory perception may not be rejected with confidence since significant differences between the means of these two groups were obtained in 17 of 35 comparisons. Three additional comparisons closely approached the 5 percent level of significance and nine of the remaining fifteen comparisons were near the 25 percent level. The 45-Item Test, because data regarding this variable had been obtained for a substantial number of children, gave results which clearly supported this hypothesis with the "t" values significant at every grade level.

4. The competence levels which had been established for the 45-Item Test indicated that the proportion of children earning high scores tended to increase at each successively higher grade level, accompanied by a decrease in the proportion of children earning low scores. The proportion of children with scores falling within the inter-quartile range remained relatively stable from grade level to grade level. These results

tend to support the conclusion that grade level and competence in responding to aural stimuli are directly related provided such comparisons are limited to above-average competence groups. The data cannot indicate the nature of this relationship at other competence levels since it is unable to reflect the possible changes which might occur in the individual child as he advances from grade level to grade level.

5. The hypothesis that the addition of the rhythmic element to a melodic pattern has a significant influence upon the auditory perception of such melodic material may be rejected since none of the "t" values between the means of the two tests approached the 5 percent level of significance. The data support the conclusion that the presence of rhythm has no appreciable influence upon the auditory perception of melodic items.

6. The data for the 20-Item Test showed that at all grade levels, children were capable of making consistent responses to a given auditory stimulus. From 52 to 73 percent of the items received the same response in two or three of the three trials. The mean scores for each of the several trials at each grade level also reflected this consistency since none of the "t" values obtained for each pair of trials met the criterion of the 5 percent level of significance.

7. Analysis of the data for the Phrase Test showed that the scores which identified the rate at which children were able to learn musical material did not reflect the variables of age and musical experience nearly as much as did scores which identified overall achievement. However, inspection of the raw data showed that more children in the upper grades demonstrated the ability to learn such musi-

cal material than was observed for children in lower grades.

8. The correlations between the several tests and the 45-Item Test are, except for the Phrase Test, uniformly high. This suggests that the auditory perception of short tonal configurations precedes the auditory perception of larger musical units. It is expected that the data secured for the same children over a period of several years would provide a better basis for identifying the nature of this relationship.

9. Throughout the study it is evident that the sixth grade sample may well have been the result of randomly selecting a large number of musically superior children. It is also possible, in view of the performance of the fifth grade group, that random selection resulted in the inclusion of a relatively large number of children with below-average musical ability. For both groups the probability that this sample contains a normally distributed population in terms of musical ability is somewhat suspect.

The more important implications of the study may be summarized as follows:

1. There is considerable evidence that age and auditory perception are related if lower and upper grades are compared, but the relationship is not as evident when grades are compared at one- and two-year intervals. It is reasonable to assume that these observed differences result from factors other than age, particularly the cumulative influence the music program of the school has upon the child.

2. The existence, within each grade level, of children with marked differences in terms of musical competence and ability, vocal control, and aural understanding further emphasizes the need for developing teaching proce-

dures and activities which will take account of these differences and result in more effective learning on the part of all children. One is forced to question the continued acceptance of the practice of scheduling music classes and categorizing music activities in terms of grade level, *per se*.

3. The research procedures employed in the study are reliable but very inefficient. There is widespread need for efficient and objective measures of the several aspects of musical competence and understanding. Instruments need to be developed which will permit testing in group situations.

4. The results of the study suggest that the music program of the school must include a variety of activities designed to stimulate and challenge the child if children are to develop an aural understanding of musical sounds.

Rote learning of songs, particularly if the process is carried on in a routine way, fails to provide the child with opportunities to become independent; to develop the ability to evaluate critically the accuracy of responses as compared with the stimulus; or to become aware of the subtle differences between similar but not identical musical material. Aural understanding, which is the reflection of accurate auditory perception, results from intelligent thought and not from mechanical imitation, from judgments made independently by the child in terms of his understanding of basic musical concepts and not from judgments made for the child by the teacher. Music educators need continually to evaluate the music program in terms of the attitudes and skills the program is seeking to develop.

School of Music, University of Wisconsin

Robert G. Petzold

JRME 1969, VOLUME 17, NUMBER 1, PAGES 82-87

Auditory Perception by Children

THE WRITER HAS, through a series of research projects supported by the University of Wisconsin and the United States Office of Education, been concerned with identifying the ways in which children in elementary school (ages 6 to 12) perceive and respond to the auditory presentation of musical sounds. The need for investigations of this kind arises from the lack of available information concerning the development of skills associated with auditory perception. Literature relating to the musical development of children repeatedly emphasizes the desirability of beginning with those activities which focus attention upon aural perception and recognition of the several basic musical elements. The resultant aural understandings are considered essential to the subsequent, or even parallel, development of skills associated with intelligent and sensitive musical listening and performance. Traditional music education in the elementary schools usually begins with a relatively simple "readiness" program. It is expected that once the individual has achieved minimal competence in terms of the aural recognition and understanding of basic elements of music, he can then successfully undertake music reading activities. It has been further assumed that activities which require visual perception and some overt response to musical symbols are meaningful only when the individual is already familiar with the musical ideas being symbolized. However, few of the assumptions and practices have been verified by systematic investigation.

The writer became involved with the problem of auditory perception in connection with exploratory research concerned with music reading competencies possessed by children in the upper elementary grades (ages 10, 11, and 12). The several tasks utilized in this study required singing responses to the visual presentation of: (a) a set of short tonal configurations, each given individually in a set of learning trials, the items randomized for each successive trial; and (b) a short song, eight measures in length, which utilized these same tonal configurations. The major findings of the study showed:

1. There were no significant differences between grade levels (4, 5, and 6) in terms of competence in learning to read tonal configurations.

2. The level of achievement in reading simple tonal configurations without external assistance was relatively low for all grades, with considerable guessing taking place.

3. Older children were able to learn to read the song at a faster rate (fewer learning trials with greater accuracy) even though this appears to be a more complex task than reading tonal configurations.

4. Musically superior children, so identified on the basis of a number of criteria measures, learned all material at a rate three to four times faster than average subjects, with a correspondingly higher level of accuracy.

5. For all reading tasks utilized in the study, the results showed that little improvement in music reading competence took place during the two-year period between fourth and sixth grades, despite the fact that these children all received regular classroom music instruction with music specialists.

6. Analysis of the responses to visual and aural stimuli indicated that the major source of music reading difficulty might be traced to an inadequate aural understanding of the musical sounds represented by the symbols.

In view of the results of this study, the writer decided to postpone further investigation of the music reading process in order to pursue a more limited, but essential, inquiry dealing with auditory perception. A series of studies extending over a six-year period has recently been completed.

PROCEDURES

The overall project contained two major aspects: (a) a longitudinal study of three groups of children covering a total period of four, five, and six years respectively; and (b) a series of one-year pilot studies dealing with melody, rhythm, timbre, and harmony. The children for the longitudinal study were drawn at random from the first three grades; the children participating in the annual pilot studies were selected at random from the first six grades so that each such sample was stratified with respect to grade, sex, and socioeconomic location of the school. All samples were drawn from the total public elementary school population of Madison, Wisconsin.

The several tests used during the project had been constructed by the writer on the basis of information obtained from extensive analyses of the rhythmic, harmonic, and melodic characteristics present in the song materials children use. All of the tests required that the child make some kind of overt musical response to an *aural presentation* of the test item. In view of the children's experience with singing as part of the regular music program of the schools, most of these were singing responses. All of the testing was individual, the tests were tape recorded to insure maximum uniformity of testing procedures, and all pupil responses were recorded during the testing session of subsequent processing. More than 6000 tests were administered during the total project.

MAJOR FINDINGS

There can be no detailed discussion of each of the one-year pilot studies or the longitudinal study. The salient findings, drawn from all of the studies, are sufficient to indicate the general nature of the research.

1. The differences between boys and girls, in terms of the auditory perception of musical sounds, appear to be related to the nature of the task. Two of the three groups that had been given the 45-item test of tonal configurations showed boy-girl differences that were significant at the .01 level and this was also observed for the timbre study which utilized the same test content. There were no significant differences between boys and girls for the harmony or rhythm studies or for the phrase test of the longitudinal study. In general, boys and girls in the first two grades showed greater similarity of performance, regardless of the task, than was observed for the upper grades.

2. All of the tasks showed that the differences between grades 1 and 3 were always significant at the .01 level; that the children in grades 3 through 6 usually performed at approximately the same level of accuracy indicating that a plateau had been reached; and that the greatest gains were usually noted between grades 1 and 2 even if they were not always significant. Older children tended to perform with greater accuracy than did young children although the longitudinal study showed that the effects of practice can usually counteract the initial advantage of age.

3. The longitudinal study showed that children with low or high scores for the initial year did not usually change their position with respect to their peers during subsequent years, continuing to earn low or high scores.

4. With respect to responses made to melodic items, there was a definite pattern which indicated that the large number of nonmelodic responses made by first grade children were usually eliminated by second grade when greater vocal control had been attained. The next stage, usually reached by grade 4 or 5, was to eliminate those responses which indicated only awareness of the contour and number of tones, thus increasing the number of partially correct responses. The final stage was to transform partially correct responses to correct responses. The difficulty of the item had a direct bearing upon the rate at which this change took place since the total process was completed much earlier in the grades for easy items.

5. The data for the phrase test used in the longitudinal study shows that learning a short musical phrase without external assistance was an extremely difficult task. Children in grades 5 and 6 were more competent than younger children, but only one-third of the sixth grade group managed to learn the phrase in 10 trials. Only eight out of 90 children were capable of learning the phrase by grade 4, retaining this skill for subsequent years. Furthermore, a second phrase given when these children reached sixth grade showed that they performed at only the third grade level of competence. This suggests that the learning process itself had not changed significantly during four years despite experience with a task of this kind.

6. The ability to learn a musical phrase was not strongly influenced by the accuracy with which children were able to respond to short

melodic items. High scores on the 45-item test did not insure that the phrase, using these same items, would be learned.

7. When melodic items were presented by media other than the piano, children responded with significantly less accuracy to flute and piano than to violin and soprano voice (timbre study).

8. The timbre study showed that item difficulty was a function of melodic content and not of timbre.

9. The harmony study showed that the accuracy with which children responded to melodic items was not significantly influenced when harmonic versus nonharmonic treatments were compared. However, when the complexity of the harmonic treatment given to *both* the stimulus and response was considered, children responded with greatest accuracy when the response was accompanied by a simple three-chord progression. The multichord progression accompanying the response was found to seriously inhibit melodic accuracy.

10. The harmony study also showed that when harmonic accompaniment was present for both stimulus and responses, three distinct levels of accuracy appeared: grades 1 and 2, grades 3 and 4, and grades 5 and 6.

11. The rhythm study showed that although children responded with greater accuracy to the rhythmic rather than the melodic content of a melodic-rhythmic test item, comparisons between responses to melodic-rhythmic items versus pure rhythmic items did not produce significant differences in terms of the accuracy of those responses.

12. In general, the ability to respond accurately to the aural presentation of rhythmic patterns of medium difficulty and to maintain a steady beat did not change significantly once the child had completed second grade.

13. All children experienced significantly more difficulty in maintaining a steady beat at the slower tempos of 92 and 60 beats per minute and that children in grades 1 and 2 found the tempo of 60 especially difficult, responding with larger deviations than those noted for the other two grades.

14. Throughout the project it was evident that most children, approximately 85 percent, had learned how to control the singing voice by grade 2 but that approximately 8 percent of the "problem singers" in grade 1 remained so throughout their total elementary school experience.

CONCLUSIONS AND IMPLICATIONS

The major hypothesis that age (grade level) is a significant factor in the development of auditory perception is sustained with limitations. For most tasks it is obvious that this reaches a plateau no later than grade 3 but there are indications that the most significant changes occur between grades 1 and 2. This agrees, in part, with those who advocate a readiness program but it also suggests that unless greater attention is paid to the development of aural understandings when the child is in first grade, this will seriously inhibit his subsequent musical development. It is also evident that most first grade children can develop sufficient aural understandings so they are able to participate successfully in music reading activities, provided such activities utilize simple melodic and rhythmic figures. The study identified, in terms of item difficulty, many such patterns which first grade children responded to with considerable accuracy. The results clearly indicate that complex melodic, rhythmic, and harmonic items are too difficult for young children and that even older children continue to experience difficulty with such items.

The fact that a plateau is generally reached by grade 3 does not indicate that full development has been attained with respect to these kinds of tasks. This suggests that the music program must continually provide the child with more challenging musical tasks so that obvious changes can take place in the upper grades. Almost every task utilized in the study showed that there was, even after grade 3, opportunity for continued improvement on the part of a substantial number of children. The fact that relatively few sixth grade children have attained sufficient musical understanding so as to enable them to learn a simple musical phrase without any external assistance is but one example.

The findings of the overall project indicate that there is a tendency for girls to perform with greater accuracy than boys. It would appear, however, that these differences, particularly for children in the upper grades, can be attributed more to attitude, motivation, and level of aspiration than to basic differences in terms of musical competence. The girls generally continued to improve their performance at each successive grade level, four through six, while the boys showed either slight improvement or did poorer in grade 6 than in grade 5. The writer believes that part of this is related to the attitude of the boys toward using the singing voice —they lack both confidence and competence in being able to view singing as a natural musical response. The fact that no significant differences between boys and girls appeared for the harmony or rhythm studies is not to be ignored. Certainly much more attention needs to be given to the nonmusical differences between boys and girls as musical experiences are planned, materials selected, and teaching procedures reviewed and revised.

The results of the study also emphasize that the ability to imitate the aural presentation of certain kinds of musical ideas is not a measure of the understanding children have of such ideas. The tenuous relationships which exist between duplicating short melodic items and learning a phrase containing those items indicates a mechanical approach to the first task and a lack of understanding and musical thought for the second task. The same relationship was noted between the ability to imitate rhythmic patterns and to maintain a steady beat. Children need to learn how to think musically, how to analyze and evaluate the factors that are present in a musical situation. The fact that performance accuracy is not inhibited when certain of the basic elements of music are presented in combination (i.e. melody-rhythm, melody-harmony, timbre-melody) indicates that children are capable of responding to the more complete musical situations. Children will respond to that which they are asked to respond to, even in complex auditory situations, and it may not be necessary to treat each of these elements as separate entities to be combined into musical wholes at some later time.

Throughout the project the writer was impressed by the interest in the tasks that was verbally expressed by the children. Their eagerness to concentrate and to do their best indicated that they are, at all grade levels, intrigued by such musical tasks. This suggests that the music programs should provide children with frequent opportunities for overt individual performance so that systematic evaluation by both student and teacher can take place. Such opportunities require time and the average music teacher, faced with large classes, full teaching schedules, and the usually limited amounts of time provided by the school, can hardly be expected to carry forward such activities. It is also evident, because of the plateau already referred to, that children cannot continue toward developing a minimal level of musical growth and understanding unless the school is able to provide both time and opportunities for such growth, as well as qualified teachers.

The research techniques and procedures employed in the study were adequate. The study identified several interesting and highly significant problems which warrant further investigation, particularly problems which would involve a series of learning sessions. There is a considerable amount of data from the present project which the writer wishes to examine more carefully and systematically before planning the next steps in the anticipated series of projects relating to the. musical development of children.

Two studies were completed to investigate young children's ability to identify single and combined musical elements in response to listening, movement, and singing activities. Study 1 was an examination of the effects of short-term instruction on preschool children's ability to apply decentration to musical tasks. Subjects (N = 30) were divided into (a) an experimental group, which participated in four small-group instruction sessions designed to teach the discriminations fast/slow and smooth/choppy as well as these elements' four possible combinations and (b) a posttest-only control group. Results indicated that instruction was significantly related to subjects' ability to identify and label musical characteristics, and that subjects were significantly more accurate with single versus double discrimination responses. Study 2 was designed to replicate aspects of the previous study, with the addition of singing as a response mode and age as a variable. All the preschool-age subjects (N = 42) received the instruction component of Study 1. Results of the listening test again indicated that subjects were significantly more successful with the single discrimination task and that older children scored significantly higher than younger children. The subjects were better able to label simultaneous musical characteristics in their own singing than in recorded listening examples. Conclusions drawn, based on both studies, include: (1) preschool-age children can easily learn to make and label single discriminations; (2) most young children may not be ready for music listening tasks requiring attention to more than one element at a time; (3) children's ability to make discriminations based on their own performance may develop earlier than their ability to make discriminations in listening situations; and (4) initial indications of discrimination may be demonstrated through singing in simultaneous imitation with a model.

Wendy L. Sims, *University of Missouri—Columbia*

JRME 1991, VOLUME 39, NUMBER 4, PAGES 298–310

Effects of Instruction and Task Format on Preschool Children's Music Concept Discrimination

Researchers have completed a variety of studies to identify and evaluate young children's musical skills, knowledge, and preferences, which have provided useful and enlightening insights into early-childhood musical development. As Scott (1987) pointed out, however, the profession still has some critical needs, including a "solid body of literature determining either short- or long-term effects of music instruction with the young," as well as "theories of musical development which could serve to provide a framework for our thinking and a focus for our research" (p. 11).

This study was supported by a research grant from the University of Missouri-Columbia College of Education. The author would also like to acknowledge the assistance of Jennifer Ashley Young. For copies of this article, contact Wendy L. Sims, 138 Fine Arts Center, University of Missouri, Columbia, MO 65211.

One aspect of musical development that has been of particular interest to researchers is young children's ability to discriminate between contrasting musical elements such as loud/soft or fast/slow. According to Zimmerman (1984), "a developmental sequence pervades research findings in music concept formation, with concepts developing in the following order: volume, timbre, tempo, duration, pitch, and harmony" (p. 72). McDonald and Simons's (1989) review of the research literature resulted in the identification of a similar sequence. Most of the numerous studies on which these conclusions were based were examinations of young children's ability to discriminate an isolated musical element in the context of songs, musical excerpts, single pitches, or patterns. Since music is characterized by the simultaneous interaction of a number of elements, however, determining how young children respond to more than one element at a time seems important to developing a more complete understanding of children's responses to music.

Little is known yet about how young children respond to simultaneous musical elements, although music educators have suggested, and some research seems to indicate, that young children tend to "center" their attention on one characteristic of a musical stimulus to the exclusion of others (Hargreaves, 1986; Petzold, 1981; Shuter-Dyson & Gabriel, 1981; Sims, 1988, Young, 1982; Zimmerman, 1986). Although this conclusion is based primarily on examination and application of the child development theories of Jean Piaget, the extent to which his ideas pertain to musical development has yet to be determined empirically.

The most substantial work in this area is the body of research in which authors sought to relate Piaget's theories of conservation to the development of musical thought (see Serafine, 1980, and Hargreaves, 1986, for reviews of this literature). The results of these studies are inconclusive, however, and there is some question as to whether musical tasks can approximate or be analogous to Piagetian conservation tasks (Bartholomew, 1987; Hargreaves, 1986; Serafine, 1980). One question as to the appropriateness of the music tasks arises due to the mixed results of studies in which experimenters attempted to determine whether performance on musical conservation tasks can be improved with instruction (Hargreaves, 1986; Shuter-Dyson & Gabriel, 1981; Zimmerman, 1986). According to the theory, children progress through stages of development characterized by distinctive patterns of thinking and approaches to problem solving, the acquisition of which are developmental in nature and *not* amenable to direct training.

The Piagetian stage of development into which most preschool-age children would fall is the preoperational stage. One characteristic of this period is the child's tendency to "center his attention exclusively on some single feature or limited portion of the stimulus array that is particularly salient and interesting to him, thereby neglecting other task-relevant features" (Flavell, 1977, p. 81). The ability to decenter, or to consider several characteristics of a stimulus simultaneously, is a basic perceptual skill. As it represents only one component of the conservation response, it is a less complex and more easily isolated construct than conservation, and may be more appropriate for musical application. While the complete process of conservation has received much attention in the literature, there is little research available that addresses children's ability to make musical judgments and discriminations requiring decentration, or how and when this ability develops. As the ability to perceive and discriminate is considered critical to concept development (Gagne, 1977; Greenberg, 1976), information about the development of decentration not only will provide knowledge relevant to developmental theory, but also might have an impact on techniques and materials selected to provide musical experiences and instruction for young children.

One study has directly addressed developmental aspects of the ability to apply decentration to a music listening task. Sims (1988) examined subjects' ability to demonstrate decentration during a nonverbal movement-to-music activity that required the untrained subjects to respond to two musical characteristics simultaneously. Results indicated that there were qualitative differences among the responses of four groups: preschoolers, first and second graders, third graders, and nonmusician college students. It was concluded that "there may be identifiable stages in the development of the ability to demonstrate decentration in response to a musical stimulus" (Sims, 1988, p. 125). Sims also noted that the relationship between these results and child development theory would be clarified by determining whether the discrimination required would be amenable to instruction. The first study reported in the present article examined the effects of short-term instruction on the ability of preschool children to decenter, or make responses requiring two simultaneous musical discriminations. The study was designed to explore further the possible relationship between children's musical behavior and developmental theory, as well as to provide basic information about characteristics of young children's music concept discrimination skills.

STUDY 1

METHOD

The subjects for this study were children ranging in age from 4 years 0 months to 5 years 1 month, enrolled in three preschools with similar programs. Music was included in the daily activities at all three schools, with greatest emphasis placed on rote singing of children's songs and playing singing games with fingerplay or motions. The children represented middle-class families with a variety of ethnic backgrounds. All children who were in attendance for each session served as subjects, resulting in a final $N = 30$ (3 children were eliminated due to absences). Subjects were randomly divided into an experimental group ($n = 15$) and a posttest only control group ($n = 15$). The average age of the children in each group was 4 years 6 months.

The experimental variable consisted of short-term instruction designed to teach the children to respond to two musical characteristics at the same time. Two pairs of contrasting characteristics related to tempo (fast/slow) and style of articulation (smooth/choppy) were selected since these discriminations were relevant to the musical task used by Sims (1988), which was being replicated. These characteristics also seem to work well because the two sets of terminology are different enough so as not to be inherently confusing to young children, as seems to be the case with language related to other concepts, such as high/low and loud/soft (McDonald & Simons, 1989). Although children's ability to make discriminations based on tempo has received much attention in the research literature, there has been little research addressing children's ability to discriminate between styles of articulation, and results have been inconclusive (Taebel, 1974, Young, 1982).

For this research, "fast" was operationally defined as examples where beats per minute equaled or exceeded 110, with "slow" examples defined as pieces with beats per minute of 80 or fewer. "Smooth" excerpts consisted of flowing, connected melodies or chords (e.g., the main theme from Smetana's "Moldau" or the cello theme from Camille Saint-Saëns's *Carnival of the Animals* "Swan" section), whereas "choppy" was defined as short and detached notes or chords, including but not limited to staccato and pizzicato passages (e.g., phrases performed by the xylophone in the *Carnival of the Animals* "Fossils" section or the sections featuring piano from the "Javanaise" movement of Claude Bolling's *Suite for Flute and Jazz Piano*). Graduate students in music education were used to establish that the examples clearly exemplified the desired characteristics.

Subjects in the experimental group were divided into small groups of three or four, and participated in four 20-minute small-group instructional sessions. Instruction was designed to provide a variety of experiences with each characteristic, and included many opportunities for the characteristics to be labeled verbally, as labeling and language are important in discrimination and concept learning (McMahon, 1986; Zimmerman, 1984). Instruction was sequenced as follows: Day 1—fast/slow; Day 2—review fast/slow, begin smooth/choppy; Day 3—review smooth/choppy, begin combinations fast and smooth, slow and smooth, fast and choppy, slow and choppy; Day 4—review combinations. All characteristics and their combinations were presented through speech, singing, movement, and listening activities, and experience with each element always preceded labeling.

A posttest was designed to elicit information related to several areas of investigation. One component was a listening test, consisting of short excerpts and procedures similar to those used during the instructional activities. The musical selections were different from those used during the lessons, to test for transfer of the concepts, rather than for the association of labels with specific pieces. For two items, subjects were asked to label the example as either "fast or slow," for two "smooth or choppy," and for two they were asked to listen for both pairs of characteristics, "smooth or choppy AND fast or slow." Subjects were told which set(s) of elements to listen for prior to listening, and were presented with the choices again after the excerpt was played. During the administration of this section of the posttest, no assistance with the terms or their usage was provided to children in either the experimental or control groups.

The second component of the posttest was the movement-to-music activity developed and tested by Sims (1988), based on the piece "Kangaroo" from *Carnival of the Animals*. Subjects were instructed that they would be hearing music that had been composed to describe a kangaroo, and to listen for the parts of the music that sounded like the kangaroo was hopping (short, detached tone clusters) and the parts that sounded like the kangaroo had stopped (sustained cadential chords). During the "hopping" sections, they were to hop like a kangaroo, but "stop to rest and look around" when the music sounded like the kangaroo had stopped hopping. Correct responses to these sections would demonstrate the smooth/choppy discrimination. The discrimination of primary interest, however, occurs during the last phrase of the short piece, during which the choppy "hopping" figures are played, but with a change in tempo. In the previous study, the young children stopped hopping at this point, apparently confused about the change and not seeming to recognize that the music was still characterized by the hopping figures, while many of the older children and all of the college students continued hopping. Of interest to the present study is whether the experimental subjects, after receiving instruction in which they experienced and verbalized that music could display two characteristics at once, would demonstrate this double discrimination by continuing to hop when the hopping sounds were slower. Prior to performance of the movement activity, practice was provided through the use of an experimenter-constructed recording, consisting of examples of "hopping" and "stopping" sounds similar to those in the stimulus piece, but with no change of tempo.

Upon completion of the movement activity, the children were asked to listen to the last phrase of the "Kangaroo" and to indicate whether it was "smooth or choppy." This final test component provided for a comparison of the movement response and verbal response to this phrase.

All posttests were administered in individual sessions lasting approximately 8 minutes and occurring three days after instruction for the experimental group. Verbal answers were recorded on answer sheets, and movement responses were recorded on videotape. A continuous observation procedure was used to transcribe the movement data for analysis (Sims, 1988). For each second of the "hopping" segments, the transcribers recorded on specially constructed observation forms whether or not the subject was hopping. Interobserver reliability, calculated for 57% of the responses, and was equal to .976.

RESULTS

There were four questions on the posttest (excluding the final question about the "Kangaroo") that required the subjects to discriminate and label a single characteristic of a musical excerpt, and two double discrimination items that required two answers each, resulting in a total of four responses in this category, as well. A two-factor, repeated-measures analysis of variance (ANOVA) was used to compare the responses of the experimental and control groups on the single and double discrimination items. Results indicated significant main effects for treatment condition $[F(1, 28) = 8.12, p < .05]$ and for type of discrimination $[F(1, 28) = 48.61, p < .05]$, with no significant interaction (see Table 1). The experimental group scored significantly higher than the control group, and both groups scored significantly higher on single as compared to double discrimination items (see Table 2).

Table 1
Summary Table: Repeated-Measures ANOVA Comparing Experimental and Control Groups on Single and Double Discrimination

Source of variance	SS	df	MS	F
Between subjects	*29.73*	*29*		
Groups	6.66	1	6.66	8.12*
Residual	23.07	28	0.82	
Within subjects	*39.00*	*30*		
Discrimination	24.06	1	24.06	48.61*
Group × Discrimination	1.08	1	1.08	2.18
Residual	13.86	28	0.495	
Total	*68.73*	*59*		

*$p < .05$.

All subjects were able to demonstrate the choppy/smooth (hopping/stopping) discrimination related to the movement activity by the end of the short practice example. Responses to the double discrimination section of the activity were considered to be correct if the subject hopped during or after the fifth second of the last phrase, the place at which the tempo change occurred. Seven experimental and five control subjects made correct responses, whereas the remaining 18 children, 60% of the subjects, stopped at the change in the music and did not resume hopping.

Table 2
Results of Listening and Singing Discrimination Tasks

STUDY 1

| | Listening discrimination | |
	Single (4 items)	Double (4 items)
Experimental group		
M	3.87	2.33
SD	0.35	0.82
% correct	96.67	58.33
Control group		
M	2.93	1.93
SD	1.16	0.70
% correct	73.33	48.33

STUDY 2

| | Listening discrimination | | Double discrimination |
	Single (4 items)	Double (4 items)	After singing (8 items)
Younger children			
M	3.28	1.81	4.90
SD	0.90	0.68	1.14
% correct	82.14	45.24	61.30
Older children			
M	3.76	2.57	5.76
SD	0.62	0.87	1.51
% correct	94.04	64.28	72.02

Thirteen children in the experimental group and 9 in the control group answered the final listening question, after the movement activity, with the correct response of "choppy." Of these 22 children, only 8 were correct in performance of their movement response, while 3 of the 8 children who answered "smooth," which was incorrect, did perform with correct movements.

DISCUSSION

The results of this study clearly demonstrate that preschool children are capable of learning to identify and label musical characteristics with very few errors after a brief program of instruction. In examining the cell data (see Table 2), it is clear that the experimental group did very well on the single discrimination items (only 2 errors in 60 responses), making 23% more correct responses than the control group. Neither group was particularly successful with the double discrimination items, however, with both responding near the chance level, and only a 10% advantage for the experimental group. The dramatic difference in the experimental group's single versus double discrimination scores should particularly be noted. These data appear to be consistent with Piaget's theory—that young children tend to center on only one aspect of a stimulus at a time, and that the ability to decenter is acquired through development and experience rather than through instruction.

Only a few children in this study were successful in demonstrating double discrimination in the movement activity, and these responses did not seem to be dependent on participation in instruction or the ability to provide the correct verbal label. These results are similar to those reported by Sims (1988), and they reinforce the conclusion that most young children are not ready for, nor receptive to, music listening tasks requiring decentration responses.

The results of the control group are consistent with the body of research that has revealed that children do not express musical ideas well verbally (Flowers, 1984; McMahon, 1986; Petzold, 1981; Sims, 1986; Young, 1982). The success with which the experimental group *did* learn to do this, however, indicates that young children are receptive to learning and using language to describe music. The experimental group children were able to retain the terminology during the three days between instruction and testing. It would be informative for future research to determine the length of retention for this type of learning. Although the experimental group children had successfully performed songs and movements that used the combination of characteristics during instruction, they were not able to provide the correct labels during the posttest. While these results seem consistent with child development theory, the possibility that children could successfully demonstrate, rather than label, two musical characteristics simultaneously warrants further investigation, and will be examined in Study 2, which follows.

STUDY 2

The purpose of Study 2 was to replicate and extend the first study, in part to investigate the speculation that children might be able to demonstrate combined musical elements through a nonverbal response mode, in this case, singing. Another purpose of Study 2 was to determine whether results similar to those of Study 1 would be obtained in a more usual large-group instructional setting, as opposed to the small groups used in the first study. Of particular interest was the previous study's finding that the children learned to label concepts in a single discrimination task very easily. Although children's difficulty in providing verbal labels for musical concepts has been well documented in the research literature, most of the studies in this area did not incorporate instruction into the research design. Replication of the results in a more typical preschool classroom situation would strengthen the implications for early childhood music instruction.

One new aspect considered was whether the children could make use of two elements at a time while singing a familiar song in a purely imitative rote manner. Elicited imitation has been cited as a valuable research tool in the field of language development (Dale, 1972; Slobin & Welsh, 1971). According to Slobin and Welsh (1971), "in repeating a sentence, one must filter it through one's own productive system" (p. 176). An intriguing transfer to the music task may be that if children are able to imitate the desired characteristics, they are demonstrating through production an initial stage of discrimination or comprehension. A second, more sophisticated production behavior of interest was whether the children could sing a familiar song "on command" incorporating two characteristics specified by the teacher.

The singing response mode was of interest in the context of this replication for an additional reason. In the first study, the simultaneous discrimination task at which the children were not successful required them to answer questions in response to recordings of orchestral or piano music. One possibility, investigated in the current study, is that it may be easier for children to identify simultaneous musical characteristics in a version of a song they have just sung that exemplified those characteristics. It is possible that direct experience and interaction with the musical material might facilitate analysis and discrimination on a task that seems to be difficult for preschool children.

METHOD

The subjects for this study were children enrolled in three classrooms at two preschools that are comparable to the preschools that provided subjects for Study 1. Although 56 children participated in one or more of the four instructional sessions, only the children in attendance for all of the sessions were considered subjects for the study, resulting in a total N of 42. The children ranged in age from 2 years 9 months to 5 years 11 months, with an average age of 4 years 3 months. Given the wide range of ages represented in this study, the effect of age on the activities tested here was of interest. In order to investigate possible age differences, two age-groups, younger ($n = 21$, M age = 3 years 6 months), and older ($n = 21$, M age = 5 years 0 months), were designated.

In the previous study, the effects of instruction were investigated using an experimental group/no-contact control group design, and results indicated that students receiving instruction were significantly and substantially better at performing the discrimination tasks than were control group students. Since instruction was not to be a variable in the present study, all subjects in this study participated in the instructional procedures so that they would be familiar with the terminology and types of activities.

Unlike the first project, in which instruction took place in small groups, subjects in the current study received instruction in their regular classes. During this study's four 20-minute instructional sessions, 14 to 22 children were present in each class, with class size varying due to absences. This was considered to represent a more typical setting for preschool music activities than was the small-group setting. The lesson plans used were the same as those taught in the earlier study.

All subjects were posttested individually by the experimenter within 3 to 5 days after the completion of instruction. As in the first study, the experimenter administered the test and was generally positive and encouraging but provided no specific feedback or reaction to the students' responses.

The first component of the test was the same listening task used in the previous study, consisting of short recorded musical excerpts, two of which the children were asked to label as "fast or slow," two as "smooth or choppy," and two as both "smooth or choppy AND fast or slow." The second and third components of the test were singing tasks and were designed specifically for the current project. All sung responses were tape recorded for subsequent analysis. Sung responses were of interest only as they related to the concepts being examined, and were not analyzed for pitch or rhythmic accuracy. The song "Rain, Rain, Go Away" was used for both singing tasks because it was short, familiar, and easy to sing. Throughout the lesson sequence, it had been sung by the children using the contrasting elements and their combinations. The song was reviewed with each subject prior to its use as a test activity.

One singing activity was designed to assess the children's ability to incorporate the elements studied into a song. Subjects were asked to sing the song four times, using each combination of fast/slow with smooth/choppy (e.g., "Please sing 'Rain

Rain' for me fast and choppy"). Four orders of the paired elements were constructed and assigned to subjects at random to control for possible order effects. The method of analyzing these responses is described in the Results section.

For the second singing task, the children were asked to sing the song with the experimenter. They were instructed to "sing 'Rain Rain' with me, just the way that I sing it." The only cues available to the children were from the musical rendition itself, as the descriptive terminology was *not* used verbally to identify how the song would be performed. Since the children were expected to join in and match the model, their responses were imitative in nature. This process will be operationally defined as "simultaneous imitation," as opposed to echo-style imitation. A simultaneous format was selected so that the effects of memory inherent in an echo format would be minimized. Again as a control, four different orders of the combined characteristics were used, and assigned to subjects at random. After completing each version, the child was asked whether the song had been fast or slow, and smooth or choppy. There were two purposes of this activity: (1) to determine whether the children would be able to demonstrate the discrimination and vocal control necessary to match the combination of characteristics used by the model, and (2) to determine whether the children could provide labels to describe characteristics of their own singing.

RESULTS

A two-factor, repeated measures analysis of variance (ANOVA) was used to compare the mean scores on the single and double discrimination listening task for the older and younger age-groups. Results indicated that older children scored significantly higher than the younger children [$F(1, 40) = 13.43, p < .05$], and other scores were significantly higher for single versus double discrimination items [$F(1, 40) = 61.21., p < .05$], with no significant interaction (see Table 3). These results, particularly those of the older children, are quite comparable to those obtained in Study 1 with respect to means and percentages correct (see Table 2).

There were four items on the posttest that required the children to sing with the experimenter and then identify both the fast/slow and smooth/choppy characteristics of the version sung. This resulted in eight "double discrimination after

Table 3
Summary Table: Repeated-Measures ANOVA Comparing Younger and Older Children on Single and Double Discrimination.

Source of variance	SS	df	MS	F
Between subjects	32.29	41		
Age	8.06	1	8.06	13.43*
Residual	24.23	40	0.60	
Within subjects	62.00	42		
Discrimination	37.34	1	37.34	61.21*
Age × Discrimination	0.41	1	0.41	0.67
Residual	24.25	40	0.61	
Total	94.29	83		

*$p < .05$.

singing" items. No significant difference was found between age-groups for these items, $t = 1.16$, $p > .05$ (see Table 2). All children approximated the tempo and style of articulation of the model when singing with her.

The fourth component of the posttest was the "sing on demand" section. Subjects were asked to sing "Rain Rain" four times, each with a different combination of the two sets of musical elements being studied. Some children would not sing the song alone or stated that they could not sing it in the manner requested and refused to try. Therefore, data will be reported for only the 27 children who completed all four versions. These subjects included 63% of the younger children, $n = 12$, and 65% of the older children, $n = 15$.

Upon listening to the tape-recorded sung responses, it immediately becomes apparent that the children were not successful at incorporating the characteristics requested into their singing. The most informative way to analyze these responses was to examine the four responses made by each child, to determine what, if any, relationship existed among each set of responses. No child's performance reflected the correct relationships for all four versions. About half (14) of the subjects sang the song almost exactly the same way all four times. Of the remaining 13 subjects, only 4 correctly incorporated the contrast between smooth and choppy, and another 2 approximated a correct relationship between tempos. The responses of the remaining 7 children reflected changes among versions, but these were incorrect changes, all related to dynamic level. Three children sang louder in response to the "fast" instruction, two sang louder when the request to sing "choppy" was included in the instructions, and two remaining children sang louder for one or two examples, but without a pattern evident. To explore the tempo responses further, each response was timed to the nearest second. The number of beats per minute was calculated based on the 8 beats constituting the song (8 beats times 60 seconds divided by number of seconds of singing). These results should be considered to be estimates only, however, because many performances did not maintain a steady beat. The average beats per minute for each of the four versions were approximately: fast/smooth, 127; fast/choppy, 104; slow/smooth, 105; slow/choppy, 102. Inspection of these data reveal little systematic variation among tempos, other than for the fast/smooth version, which was performed about 25% faster than the other versions.

DISCUSSION

One purpose of Study 2 was to replicate the teaching and testing procedures used with the experimental group in Study 1. As presented in Table 2, the single discrimination listening responses of the "older" group in Study 2 (M age = 5 years 0 months) were quite comparable to the responses of the slightly younger experimental group in the previous study (M age = 4 years 6 months). Study 2's "younger" group (M age = 3 years 6 months), while scoring a bit lower than the experimental group in Study 1, scored higher than the Study 1 no-instruction control group, even though the average age of the control group was one year older (M age = 4 years 6 months). These data, while further reflecting age differences in discrimination ability, also seem to suggest that single discrimination instruction can be very effective for 4- and 5-year-olds, and moderately effective even with 3-year-old-children. It is also conceivable that the large-group setting proved less effective for the youngest children.

The subjects were almost equally unsuccessful in responding to the double discrimination listening task in both studies, although the group of children with the highest average age (Study 2 "older" group) performed a bit better than the other three groups. It may be concluded that Study 2 generally did replicate the results of Study 1. The children in both studies performed single discriminations quite successfully after instruction, but most responded at near the change level on double discrimination items.

This replication strengthens the prior conclusion that most young children are not ready for music listening tasks requiring attention to more than one element at a time, and supports the speculation that the ability to do this may be acquired through development and experience rather than through direct instruction. The age differences described in this study and the substantially higher scores of the older children versus younger on the double discrimination listening task provide additional support for this conclusion. Teachers should be aware that preschool-age children tend to focus on one element during music listening tasks, perhaps to the exclusion of others. Activities during listening experiences, such as movements directly related to a specific musical characteristic (Sims, 1986), might be planned to ensure that the students are attending to the *desired* element or contrasts. Based on the replication of the success with which the children learned to apply terminology to single discriminations, and the fact that this occurred in the context of both large- and small-group classroom settings, it may be concluded that the early years, which are a time of rapid language acquisition, would seem to be an ideal time to begin building children's music vocabulary and discrimination skills.

The effectiveness of singing to facilitate children's ability to demonstrate decentration may be examined by comparing the scores on the listening and singing double-discrimination labeling tasks. On the listening task, the younger children made correct responses 45% of the time, and the older, 64%. After singing a version of the song that incorporated two of the elements, however, younger children were able to label what they had just sung with 61% accuracy, and older children were correct 72% of the time. While the "after singing" scores might be considered only moderately successful, they are substantially more successful than the listening-only format, particularly for the younger children. One reasonable conclusion based on this comparison may be that children's ability to make discriminations based on their own performance is developmental in nature, and is evidenced earlier than their ability to make discriminations in more abstract listening situations. It also may be true that even if they hadn't been singing themselves, the a cappella melody would have elicited a higher number of correct responses than the stimuli consisting of more complex orchestral and piano pieces. Familiarity with the musical stimulus also may have been a factor affecting this task. Further research on the effects of stimulus complexity and familiarity on young children's discrimination responses might provide teachers with valuable methodological and sequencing information.

The children were all able to approximate the characteristics combined by the model in the singing of a familiar song even though they were not as successful in labeling these characteristics. Their ability to do this reflects their ability to make the appropriate discriminations, albeit at an initial level. This finding reinforces the validity of child-centered teaching methodologies that advocate an "experience first" approach to learning, and corroborates a number of studies that have suggested that children may perceive more than they can label (McDonald & Simons, 1989). It seems that although it might not be an effective use of a teacher's time to try to teach double discriminations directly to preschool children, a valuable foundation for future discrimination learning might be laid by incorporating double-discrimination experiences into singing activities. Research to explore children's ability to combine characteristics in movement would help determine if movement could also provide a productive methodology for early interaction with combined characteristics.

The preschool-age children in this study were not successful with the task that required them to sing a familiar song using two specified characteristics. There was some indication that "fast" in combination with "smooth" was the easiest characteristic for the children to understand and/or produce, possibly because that is the most "normal" way of singing from among the four combinations presented. Since the children could incorporate two characteristics into the simultaneous imitation activity, it seems that their difficulty with the "sing on demand task" was not the result of a vocal control problem, but rather was another reflection of the difficulty young children have in responding to verbal descriptors of music concepts. Because these data were obtained from the relatively small number of students who attempted all four versions ($n = 27$), these results should be viewed with some caution, although the number of the remaining children who indicated that they "did not know how" to sing in the manner requested actually seems to lend support to these conclusions. The possibility that preschool-age children might be successful in demonstrating one specified characteristic at a time in singing was not examined in this study, but would be a valuable area for further research.

The subjects in this study demonstrated discrimination through simultaneous imitation in singing with more success than through their independent production of singing responses. As mentioned previously, researchers in language acquisition have found that elicited imitation can be a valuable research tool. This may be true for research in music education, as well, as a child's imitation ability may provide an initial nonverbal indication of the child's perception or production ability. Further research to explore the relationship between imitation and production abilities, as well as the usefulness of both simultaneous and echo-style imitation as assessment tools in music, seems warranted.

Based on the results of these two studies, as well as research and theory cited above, a tentative sequence of development for the acquisition of music concept discrimination in listening and singing might be identified. It is speculated that the ability to produce sung responses imitating a specific musical characteristic is demonstrated first, followed by the ability to label the characteristic in the child's own performance and then in listening examples, with the ability to apply the specified concept to the production of a song developing last. In each case, the ability to make specific single discrimination responses would most likely precede the ability to make discriminations requiring the combination of these concepts or musical elements. This hypothesized sequence has the potential to contribute to the formulation of a developmental framework for the acquisition of music discriminations or concepts, and warrants further investigation. The exploration of the validity of these ideas certainly provides a wealth of possibilities for future research.

Given the attention currently being focused on musical experiences during the early childhood years as important to future musical development, there is still relatively little known about how children actually develop music skills and concepts. Determining sequences of development, as well as the types of activities and instruction that might be the most appropriate or effective for promoting musical growth and understanding in young children, should be an important goal for researchers in music education.

REFERENCES

Bartholomew, D. (1987). Problems with Piagetian conservation and musical objects. *Bulletin of the Council for Research in Music Education*, no. 93, 27–40.

Dale, P. S. (1972). *Language development.* Hinsdale, IL: Dryden Press.

Flavell, J. H. (1977). *Cognitive development.* Englewood Cliffs, NJ: Prentice-Hall.

Flowers, P. J. (1984). Attention to elements of music and effect of instruction in vocabulary on written descriptions of music by children and undergraduates. *Psychology of Music, 12,* 17–24.

Gagne, R. M. (1977). *The conditions of learning.* New York: Holt, Rinehart, & Winston.

Greenberg, M. (1976). Research in music in early childhood education: A survey with recommendations. *Bulletin of the Council for Research in Music Education*, no. 45, 1–20.

Hargreaves, D. J. (1986). *The developmental psychology of music.* Cambridge, England: Cambridge University Press.

McDonald, D. T., & Simons, G. M. (1989). *Musical growth and development: Birth through six.* New York: Schirmer.

McMahon, O. (1986). Implications of recent research into aspects of music in early childhood. *International Society for Music Education Yearbook, 13,* 161–164.

Petzold, R. G. (1981). Child development. In *Documentary report of the Ann Arbor Symposium* (pp. 42-48). Reston, VA: Music Educators National Conference.

Scott, C. R. (1987). Reaching the young child through music. *International Music Education, 14,* 11–20.

Serafine, M. L. (1980). Piagetian research in music. *Bulletin of the Council for Research in Music Education*, no. 62, 1–21.

Shuter-Dyson, R., & Gabriel, C. (1981). *The psychology of musical ability.* London: Metheun.

Sims, W. L. (1986). The effect of high versus low teacher affect and passive versus active student activity during music listening on preschool children's attention, piece preference, time spent listening, and piece recognition. *Journal of Research in Music Education, 34,* 173–191.

Sims, W. L. (1988). Movement responses of pre-school children, primary grade children, and pre-service teachers to characteristics of musical phrases. *Psychology of Music, 16,* 110–127.

Slobin, D. I., & Welsh, C. A. (1971). Elicited imitation as a research tool in developmental psycholinguistics. In C. S. Lavatelli (Ed.), *Language training in early childhood education* (pp. 170–185). Urbana: University of Illinois Press.

Taebel, D. K. (1974). The effect of various instructional modes on children's performance of musical concept tasks. *Journal of Research in Music Education, 22,* 170–83.

Young, L. P. (1982). An investigation of young children's music concept development using nonverbal and manipulative techniques. *Dissertation Abstracts International, 43,* 1345A. (University Microfilms No. DA8222205)

Zimmerman, M. P. (1984). The relevance of Piagetian theory for music education. *International Journal of Music Education, 3,* 31–34.

Zimmerman, M. P. (1986). Music development in middle childhood: a summary of selected research studies. *Bulletin of the Council for Research in Music Education*, no. 86, 18–35.

December 11, 1989

The purpose of this study was to determine (1) what terminology from their own vocabulary subjects would use to label music concepts and (2) if consistent terminology would be selected by children in grades two, three, and four, and by college students majoring in elementary or music education. A group-listening test was administered to the subjects. One music concept was varied in each of the 10 presentations of a well-known melody. Subjects were asked to write a word that described the characteristic change in each playing. When correctly describing music concepts, subjects of all ages used consistent and traditional terminology. However, when incorrect terms were chosen, there was little similarity in vocabulary between children and adults.

Harriet I. Hair *University of Georgia, Athens*

JRME 1981, VOLUME 29, NUMBER 1, PAGES 11–21

Verbal Identification of Music Concepts

Most of the current elementary methods classes and music textbook series base their curricula on a conceptual approach to music. Emphasis is placed on providing students with a variety of music activities that will give them an experiential basis on which to form and label concepts according to traditional music terminology. Yet, the use of traditional terminology for concepts in studies with young children continues to present research problems (Hitchcock, 1942; Zwissler, 1971; Taebel, 1974; Hair, 1977).

Children do perceive differences and changes in music stimuli long before they are able to label these changes appropriately (Andrews & Deihl, 1967). Numerous approaches have been used in investigating the identification and development of music concepts in children. Recent studies have given children appropriate descriptors (McDonald, 1974; Rost, 1976; Zwissler, 1971), avoided or discouraged verbalization (Schevill, 1971; Scott, 1978), asked children to make judgments and then explain their rationale (Botvin, 1974; Bettinson, 1976), used aural-visual tasks (Zaporozhets & Elkonin, 1971; Olson, 1978), examined the reinforcement value of music for cognitive learning tasks (Greer, 1978; Greer, Dorow, & Wolpert, 1978), and used nonverbal performance tasks (Van Zee, 1976; Hair, 1977). Taebel (1974) found that the test scores of children who were told exactly what attribute to listen for did not vary

Requests for reprints should be sent to Harriet I. Hair, Department of Music, University of Georgia, Athens 30602.

significantly from those who were asked to provide their own explanation of the change in the music.

In addition, labeling of music concepts by older students and adults has been investigated. Farnsworth (1969, p. 80) stated:

> Research by Schoen, Gatewood, Mull, and others has demonstrated beyond the possibility of doubt that synonymous words will be employed with some consistency to describe the character of much of our Western music whenever the listeners are drawn from roughly the same subculture. The degree of agreement is little affected by differences in listener intelligence, tested musical aptitude, musical training, or age level (if above the sixth grade).

These statements are supported by the research of Utley (1973) who found substantial agreement among the nontechnical vocabulary that junior-high students chose to describe music, and by Zimmerman (1971) who concluded that no specific music instruction experience bears a high relationship to verbal-descriptive skill development in high-school students. Jetter (1978) developed an instructional model for naming music phenomena to be used by preschool children. She claimed that achievement was not related to socioeconomic background, sex, or age.

Few of the previous studies have investigated the descriptive vocabulary of elementary school children. Thus, the question arose, would research with this age child provide data similar to that found with older children or adults?

The purpose of the present study was to determine (1) what terminology from their own vocabulary subjects would use to label music concepts and (2) if consistent terminology would be selected by children in grades two, three, and four, and by college students majoring in elementary or music education.

In addition, the following hypotheses were tested: Are there significant differences ($p < .05$) among mean correct scores of children grouped according to grade, ability, or sex? Are there score differences between children and adults? Are there score differences among adults—music and education majors, male and female music majors, female adults and major, or education majors at the beginning and end of music courses? Are there score differences among each group on individual test items?

PROCEDURE

A group-listening test was administered to the subjects. One music concept was varied in each of the 10 presentations of a well-known melody. Subjects were asked to write a word that described the characteristic change in each playing.

Subjects

The 299 subjects participating in this study included 226 children and 73 adults. All children attended the one elementary school that serves the Oconee County, Georgia, area. Nine classes of children were randomly selected from grades two, three, and four. Classes in each grade were divided into high, middle, and low ability groups based on scores from the Metropolitan Achievement Tests and on recommendations from the teachers. Only children with hearing impairments were excluded from the study. A music specialist taught the children one 30-minute lesson each week.

Of the total number of children, the subgroups numbered as follows: second grade, $n = 69$ (29 boys, 40 girls); third grade, $n = 71$ (38 boys, 33 girls); fourth grade, $n = 86$ (40 boys, 46 girls). The ability groupings numbered high = 78, middle = 91, and low = 57.

Of the 73 college students in this study, 56 were female elementary education majors who were tested at the beginning and end of their introductory music courses. Seventeen (six males and 11 females) were senior music education majors taking the elementary music-methods class.

The subjects were given a group-listening test, which lasted approximately 12 minutes, in their regular classroom during the normally scheduled music class. The test was administered by either the music teacher or the investigator. In order to control the teacher variable, all testing instructions and music examples played on a Steinway grand piano were recorded on tape by the investigator. Procedures of distributing answer sheets, handling the tape recorder, and answering questions were rehearsed jointly by both administrators. In addition, initial administrations of the test were rotated between and observed by both teachers.

A piano was used in the regular class and its timbre was considered familiar to the students. Two well-known tunes, "Happy Birthday" and "Twinkle, Twinkle, Little Star," were used in the testing. The music teacher verified that the children had played and sung these two songs many times during the school year. The college students had sung these songs previously in their methods class. The following taped instructions were given.

We can play or sing a song many different ways. We can use words to tell how the sound of the music changes. I would like to know what word you will choose to tell how the music sounds each time it is played. Here is an example. This is the way we usually play "Happy Birthday" (song played). Now, I will play it again. Listen and think of a word that tells how the music sounds (song played loudly). Do not tell anyone your answer. Write your word on your answer sheet by the word: example. (If the students did not understand the procedure, the tape was stopped at this time and the instructions clarified.) This is the way we play the song "Twinkle, Twinkle, Little Star" on the piano (song played). Now you will hear this song played 10 times. Each time you hear a number, you will hear the song played in a different way. Write a word beside the number that tells how the music sounds. If you cannot think of a word, put a question mark by the number. Are you ready to begin? Listen carefully. Here is number one. . . .

Initially the subjects heard the melody "Twinkle, Twinkle, Little Star" played as they would expect to hear it, with "normal" tempo, dynamics, and mode. The complete melody was then played 10 times. One element was changed in each subsequent example. The sequence of changing the elements was structured to make the contrast among the elements as obvious as possible. The difficulty of the items increased as the test progressed. The presentations of the melody were as follows: "normal" practice example, (1) loud, (2) soft, (3) fast, (4) slow, (5) high (one octave higher than the original), (6) low (one octave lower than the original), (7) sung (a cappella by the investigator), (8) harmonized, (9) parallel minor, and (10) with rhythmic change (dotted rhythm pattern throughout).

All examples were played in the key of C. These were within the singing range of the children, middle C to A above, except for items five and six. Examples were analyzed and tested to ensure that only one element was changed each time it was played. To determine the content validity of the test, five music faculty members listened to the test and agreed that the items clearly represented each concept. In addition, they verified the correctness of items given by the subjects.

RESULTS

Statistical analysis of the data involved t tests, two and three-way analysis of variance tests, and Duncan's multiple range tests. The total correct score of the test was 20 points. Each of the 10 items was weighted: correct = two points, partially correct = one point, incorrect = zero. Correct answers consisted of traditional music terms and their synonyms. Partially correct answers were those words that basically described the concept, but were not used in associative labeling in most music textbook series on methods classes. See Table 1. Analysis of total test scores (t tests) showed that there were significant differences ($p < .001$) between (1) children and adults, (2) music and education

Table 1—Vocabulary of Subjects Classified as Correct or Partially Correct

Item	Correct	Partially Correct
1	Loud, Forte, Noisy, Banging	Hammered, Hard, High, Pounding
2	Soft, Quiet, Pianissimo	Low, Gentle, Light, Faint, Weak, Timid, Whisper
3	Fast, Presto, Rapid, Rushed, Speedy, Accelerated, Hurry, Quick, Racey	Excited
4	Slow, Dragging, Drawn-out, Ritard, Large, Augmentation	Delayed, Labored, Tired, Hesitant, Lethargic, Languid
5	High, Treble, Shrill, 8va	Bright, Light, Screeching
6	Low, Deep, Bass, 8va	Heavy, Dark
7	Singing, A Cappella, Unaccompanied, Song, Human, Vocalized, Solo	Lyrical, Words, Talk, High-opera
8	Harmony, Chordal, Triadic, Accompany	Mixed, Low, Fuller, Together, Group, Two Hands, Double, Two Notes, Two Tunes, High and Low
9	Minor	Off-Key, Out of Tune, Not Tune, Different Key, Disharmony, Different Notes, Mysterious, Spooky, Scary, Gloomy, Sad, Ominous
10	Rhythmic Change, Uneven, Skipping, Syncopated, Dotted Rhythm, Off-beat	Chopt Up, Jumpy, In Pieces, Broken, Stopping, Split, Short, Hopping, Two at a Time, Stop Then Go, Halting, Part by Part, Hesitant, Slow Then Fast, Bouncy, Jazz, Bebop, Two Beats, In Sets, Sectioned, Doubled, Beat Change, Accented, Strong Beat

majors, (3) female adults and major, and (4) education majors at the beginning and end of music courses. There were no significant differences on total test scores between male and female music majors. See Table 2.

It was not possible to obtain total test scores for the low ability group in the second grade due to disruptive, inattentive behavior. Additional t tests showed that there were significant differences on total test scores among all combinations of children (grade and ability groupings) and adults (music and education majors).

A three-way analysis of variance test of the total test scores of children showed there were statistically significant differences among ability groupings, $F(15, 210) = 24.46$, $p < .001$. The Duncan test showed that the high ability group was significantly higher than the medium and low groups. But the two lower groups were not significantly different from each other.

An analysis of the differences in mean correct scores (t tests) between children and adults, and among adults on individual test items (Table 3), showed that the low ability second grade group completed only items 1 through 7. Because the scores for all of these items were significantly different from those of the adults, the remaining discussion will not include this group.

The items analyses on items 1 through 4 showed that significant differences varied according to groups and items. Nearly half of these significant differences were due to the children's scoring higher than the adults. On items 5 through 10 there were significant differences among children of all ability groups and all groups of adults (with the exception of education majors and children in the second-grade high group on item 7). Among adult groups significant differences were found more often on items 6 through 10.

Analysis of variance and Duncan's tests of children showed that girls scored significantly higher than boys on items 1, 2, and 3. There were significant differences ($p < .05$) among test-item scores by grades as follows: item 2, grade 4 > 2; item 3, grades 3, 4 > 2; item 4, grade 3 > 2; item 9, grade 4 > 2, 3. There were significant differences ($p < .05$) among test scores by ability groupings as follows: item 1, H > L; item 2, H > M, L; items 3 and 4, H, M > L; items 5 and 6, all groups were significantly different; items 7 through 10, H > M, L. The high ability groups were significantly higher than the low groups on all examples. But there were no differences between high and middle groups on three items, or between middle and low groups on six items.

The vocabulary given for each test item was analyzed according to each group of subjects. The words chosen most often are given in Table 4.

A large percentage of children and adults chose traditional vocabulary on the first four items. The use of traditional terminology dropped considerably on more difficult items as children chose a larger number of words per item and showed a wider distribution of responses to these words. Although children and adults chose a relatively large number of different words per item, only a few terms were common to both groups. See Table 5.

On item 1 (*loud*), the traditional term "loud" was used by 75% of the children and 68% of adults. The second most used term was "high," but this occurred only in the third grade. Low ability groups chose the term "soft," while high and middle ability groups used the term "low."

Seventy-two percent of the children and 59% of adults used the traditional term "soft" for item 2 (*soft*). The children's second choice was "low." A small

Table 2—*t* Tests of Means of Total Test Scores of Children and Adults

Group	Mean	SD	Minimum	Maximum	df	t
Children	9.68	3.42	0	19	282	13.74*
Adults	16.18	3.66	4	20		
Education Major	15.46	3.76	4	20	71	4.35*
Music Major	18.53	2.03	13	20		
Female Adults						
Education Major	15.46	3.76	4	20	66	5.543*
Music Major	19.08	1.44	16	20		
Education Major						
Beginning	14.64	3.73	4	20	54	4.998*
End	18.50	1.83	15	20		
Music Major						
Male	17.20	2.77	13	20	15	1.869
Female	19.08	1.44	16	20		

*$p < .001$

Table 3—Significantly Different Test Items between Groups

					Item					
Group	1	2	3	4	5	6	7	8	9	10
Children — Adults		X*		X	X	X	X	X	X	X
Music										
2nd High					X	X	X	X	X	X
2nd Middle					X	X	X	X	X	X
2nd Low	X	X	X	X	X	X	X	—	—	—
3rd High					X	X	X	X	X	X
3rd Middle		X			X	X	X	X	X	X
3rd Low					X	X	X	X	X	X
4th High					X	X	X	X	X	X
4th Middle					X	X	X	X	X	X
4th Low		X		X	X	X	X	X	X	X
Education										
2nd High					X	X		X	X	X
2nd Middle					X	X	X	X	X	X
2nd Low	X	X	X	X	X	X	X	—	—	—
3rd High			X[a]		X	X	X	X	X	X
3rd Middle		X			X	X	X	X	X	X
3rd Low		X[a]	X[a]	X	X	X	X	X	X	X
4th High		X[a]	X[a]	X	X	X	X	X	X	X
4th Middle					X	X	X	X	X	X
4th Low		X		X	X	X	X	X	X	X
Music								X	X	X	X
Female — Ed. vs. Music		X		X		X		X	X	X
Education — Beg. vs. End		X							X	X
Music — Male vs. Female										

[a]Perfect scores of children

*$p < .05$

number of children responded with the words "quiet," "slow," and "high." For item 3 (*fast*) 87% of the children and 74% of adults used the term "fast." Only four or five children chose the words "high" and "loud," respectively. All children in the third grade high and low groups used the term "fast."

The term "slow" was given for item 4 (*slow*) by 85% of the children and 74% of adults. All children in the third-grade high and low groups and in the fourth-grade high group chose the term "slow." A small number of children used the words "soft" and "low." The traditional term "slow" was the only word chosen by both children and adults.

For item 5 (*octave higher*), the term "high" was given by 29% of the children and 81% of adults. While only one child in the low groups used the word "high," this term was found in all other groups. The children's second choice of terms was "medium." Their third choice was "soft." This word was found in all groups of children. The only additional pitch-related terms chosen by the children were "low," "light," and "shrill."

The term "low" was given for item 6 (*octave lower*) by 33% of the children and 79% of adults. The low groups in the fourth and second grades did not use this term. The low second-grade group picked only the terms "loud" and "soft." The words found across all ability groupings and grades of children were "loud," "hard," and "slow." The term "high" was chosen by the high and middle groups.

Table 4—Words Chosen Most Frequently

Item	Children n = 226	Adults n = 73
1	Loud 169, High 12, Low 6	Loud 50, Hard 5, Harsh 4
2	Soft 156, Low 31, Quiet 6	Soft 52, Quiet 3, Pianissimo 3
3	Fast 197, Loud 5, High 4	Fast 54, Hurried 3
4	Slow 193, Soft 9, Low 6	Slow 54, Dragging 3, Largo 3
5	High 65, Medium 37, Soft 20, Regular (Normal) 11, Low 9, Loud 6	High 59
6	Low 84, Loud 27, Hard 15, Slow 12, High 14, Deep 6, Soft 6	Low 58, Deep 4
7	Singing (Song) 33, Voice 23, Soft 18, High 18, Slow 14, Low 10, Solo 7, Pretty 7, Medium 6	Singing (Song) 28, Voice 24
8	Loud 42, High 17, Good 14, Low 12, Slow 8, Medium 8, Harmony 6, Fast 6	Harmony 17, Chords 27, Accompanied 5
9	Slow 25, Low 21, Soft 12, Off-tune 12, Loud and Soft 10, Medium 8, High 7, Sad 7, Wrong (Goofed) 7	Minor 34, Off-key 8, Flat 6, Mistakes 6
10	Skipping 21, Slow 17, Loud 11, Happy 9, High 9, Fast 8	Syncopated 14, Rhythm (Time) Change 9, Choppy 6, Jumpy 4, Skipping 8, Dotted Rhythm 6

For item 7 (*sung*), the terms "singing," "vocalized," "voice," or "a person" were used by 23% of the children and 71% of adults. Two children in the low second-grade group, who had responded to all previous items by the word "piano," responded to this item with the word "talk."

Table 5—Descriptive Vocabulary of Children and Adults

Different Words	Common Words	Children	Adults
Item 1; C = 20; A = 17	Loud	169	50
	Hard	3	5
	Noise	3	1
	Banging	1	2
Item 2; C = 13; A = 12	Soft	156	52
	Quiet	6	3
	Light	1	1
Item 3; C = 12; A = 15	Fast	197	54
	Quickly	3	1
	Jumpy	1	1
Item 4; C = 10; A = 14	Slow	193	54
Item 5; C = 27; A = 14	High	65	59
	Light	3	1
	Shrill	1	1
Item 6; C = 31; A = 10	Low	84	58
	Hard	15	1
	Deep	6	4
	Bass	2	2
Item 7; C = 33; A = 18	Singing	33	28
	Voice	23	24
	Solo	7	1
	Regular	4	1
Item 8; C = 43; A = 19	Harmony	6	17
	Two Hands	1	5
	Treble and Bass Clef	1	2
	Together	1	1
Item 9; C = 36; A = 20	Minor	0	34
	Out-of-tune	1	8
	Wrong (Goofed)	7	6
Item 10; C = 54; A = 23	Skipping	21	8
	Fast	8	1
	Choppy	2	6
	Jumpy	2	2
	Jazzy	1	2

On item 8 (*harmonized*), children chose the term "harmony" in only 19% of the high fourth-grade group. The word "harmony" was given by 3% of the children and 23% of adults. The term "loud" was used by 20% of all groups of children. Their next most frequently chosen terms were "high," "good," and "low." Terms that related to the concept but occurred only one time were "up and down," "treble and bass clef," "two notes," "two tunes," or "two hands." The terms "high and low" were used by 6% of the children in the middle second- and fourth-grade groups and the third-grade high group.

On item 9 (*parallel minor*), the traditional term "minor" was used by 47% of the adult groups only. Music majors and education majors, at the end of their course, had only one person in each group who did not use the term "minor." The choice of terms used by the children was quite varied. The terms "slow" and "soft" were found among all groups of children except the high third-grade group. The word "low" was found in all groups except the low fourth grade. Only one occurrence of the term "sad" was found in each of the second-grade middle and high groups, while 16% of the fourth-grade high group used this term. One child in each grade used the word "scary."

For item 10 (*rhythmic change*), the word "skipping" was chosen by 10% of the children and 11% of adults. The low fourth-grade group did not use this term. The second term used most by the children was "slow." Repetition of other terms was relatively slight. Children selected a few other words that related to the concept: "2-beats," "in pieces," "stop then go," "two at a time," "split," and "in sets."

DISCUSSION

When correctly describing music concepts, subjects of all ages used consistent and traditional terminology. However, when incorrect terms were chosen, there was little similarity in vocabulary between children and adults. The number of different words chosen per item ranged from 23 to 72. Yet, only one to five words per item were common to both children and adults.

Children chose a larger number of words than adults for all concepts except "fast" and "slow." The children tended to repeat many of the same terms for the different concepts. It appeared that if they did not know the correct answer, they chose one of the terms that they associated with "music," without regard to its specific meaning. These were the traditional terms found in music textbook series and in methods classes, such as "loud," "soft," "fast," or "slow." The half-hour weekly music class that the children had was not sufficient to establish the correct meaning for these traditional labels.

Education majors at the beginning of the course chose more descriptive words than the other adults. Music majors and education majors at the end of their course used the least and most traditional terminology of all groups.

There were significant differences on test scores of children among ability groupings. However, ability groupings did not differ consistently in vocabulary choice. The number of times a word was used by a group varied more than the number of different words chosen. High groups simply chose the correct terms more often.

Item analyses showed that children generally did as well, and sometimes better, than adults on items 1 through 4. It appeared that children of these ages had already developed the concepts of tempo and dynamics and the traditional vocabulary to label them. Scores of subjects with additional age and training showed no significant improvement on these items.

The effects of music training seemed evident on the last four items. Children had some difficulty in labeling the concepts of pitch, rhythmic change, and timbre. They clearly did not have the vocabulary to describe the concepts of minor mode or harmony. The greatest differences between adults and children were on these items.

In addition, education majors at the beginning of the course showed a great drop in scores for the last four items. Music and education majors, at the end of their course, had consistently high scores on all items, with the exception of the scores of the education students for rhythmic change.

In comparing scores of children and adults, one should note that the groups of children consisted of a random sample of ability levels. One might assume that the adult collegiate subjects had a higher ability level than the normal population. The college students' larger vocabulary may have made their choice of words more confusing. The fact that the adult groups scored higher only on the items related to more abstract or technical terminology suggests new means must be found to bridge this gap in terminology that is meaningful to children. As Hitchcock (1942) suggested, perhaps sound-descriptive terms would be more appropriate for children than the traditional terminology.

Most educators assume that it is important for children to verbally label music concepts. Further investigations need to determine how linguistic skills develop and function in relation to music perception. Researchers should continue exploring how much and when associative training is needed before conceptual labels for aural stimuli become meaningful.

REFERENCES

Andrews, F. M., & Deihl, N. *Development of a technique for identifying elementary school children's musical concepts.* Final Report BR-5-0233 (September 1967), Pennsylvania State University, ERIC: ED 016 517.

Bettinson, G. *The relationship between the conservation of certain melodic materials and standard Piagetian tasks.* Paper presented at the Music Educators National Conference, Atlantic City, New Jersey, 1976.

Botvin, G. J. Acquiring conservation of melody and cross-modal transfer through successive approximation. *Journal of Research in Music Education,* 1974, *22,* 226-233.

Farnsworth, P. R. *The social psychology of music.* Ames: The Iowa State University Press, 1969, 80.

Greer, R. D. *An operant approach to motivation and affect: Ten years of research in music learning.* Paper presented at the National Symposium on the Applications of Psychology to the Teaching and Learning of Music, Ann Arbor, Michigan, 1978.

Greer, R. D. Dorow, L., & Wolpert, R. *The effect of taught musical affect on the learning ability of young children at cognitive musical tasks.* Paper presented at the Music Educators National Conference, Chicago, 1978.

Hair, H. I. Discrimination of tonal direction on verbal and non-verbal tasks by first grade children. *Journal of Research in Music Education,* 1977, *25,* 197-210.

Hitchcock, A. *The value of terminology in children's descriptions of changes in pitch direction.* Unpublished masters thesis, University of Minnesota, 1942.

Jetter, J. T. An instructional model for teaching identification and naming of music phenomena to preschool children. *Journal of Research in Music Education,* 1978, *26,* 97-110.

McDonald, D. Environment — a factor in conceptual listening skills of elementary school children. *Journal of Research in Music Education,* 1974, *22,* 205-214.

Olson, G. Intersensory and intrasensory transfer of melodic contour perception by children. *Journal of Research in Music Education,* 1978, *26,* 41-47.

Rost, W. J. The identification of elementary school children's musical concepts as a function of two types of musical literature and environment. *Bulletin of the Council for Research in Music Education,* 1976, *48,* 36-42.

Schevill, H. S. *Perceived order of auditory and visual stimuli in children.* Final report BR-1-1-043 (October 1971), Institute of Medical Sciences, San Francisco, ERIC: ED 057 923.

Scott, C. R. *Pitch concept formation in preschoolers: Its measurement.* Paper presented at the Music Educators National Conference, Chicago, 1978.

Taebel, D. *The effect of various instructional modes on children's performance of music concept tasks.* Paper presented at the Music Educators National Conference, Anaheim, California, 1974.

Utley, E. The development of a musical perception test free of technical vocabulary for use in grades six through twelve. *Bulletin of the Council of Research in Music Education,* 1973, *35,* 44-52.

Van Zee, N. Responses of kindergarten children to musical stimuli and terminology. *Journal of Research in Music Education,* 1976, *24,* 14-21.

Zaporozhets, A. V., & Elkonin, D. B., Eds. *The psychology of preschool children.* Translated by J. Shybut and S. Simon. Cambridge, Massachusetts: The MIT Press, 1971.

Zimmerman, W. W. Verbal description of aural music stimuli. *Journal of Research in Music Education,* 1971, *19,* 422-432.

Zwissler, R. N. *An investigation of the pitch discrimination skills of first-grade children identified as accurate singers and those identified as inaccurate singers.* Unpublished doctoral dissertation, University of California, Los Angeles, 1971.

November 26, 1979

The Responses of Children to Musical Tasks Embodying Piaget's Principle of Conservation

MARILYN PFLEDERER

JRME 1964, VOLUME 12, NUMBER 4, PAGES 251–268

ONE OF THE OBJECTIVES of the elementary music program is to foster the musical understanding of each individual child by helping him to organize the musical experiences comprising the music curriculum which he undergoes. In view of this objective the writer has long questioned the paradoxical dearth of research studies designed to determine how a child organizes his musical experiences. Some research studies concerning the musical abilities of children have been conducted by psychologists, but these are rarely cited in the elementary music literature as a basis for existing practices in elementary music education.

About two years ago the writer became involved with the research of Jean Piaget, a Swiss psychologist, in the areas of concept formation and the development of thought processes in children. If a child's musical learning is inseparable from other learnings and follows the same general patterns of development, it seemed obvious that music education might benefit from an application of Piaget's theory to musical development. From a consideration of several approaches to the problem evolved plans for a pilot study to investigate the relevance of Piaget's principle of conservation to musical learning.

Purpose of the Study

The purpose of the study was to devise musical tasks embodying the Piagetian principle of conservation of meter, tone, and rhythm and to determine the responses of eight five-year-old and eight eight-year-old children to these tasks. The musical tasks represented an attempt to embody the principle of conservation of tone and rhythm. In actuality each task represented an hypothesis to be empirically tested: developmental trends in the conservation of the specific musical concept could be discerned through the administration of the task to children of two different ages.

Development of Thought Processes

In developing his theory of intellectual growth and development, Piaget emphasizes not only the experiences of the child, but also the child's ability to utilize these experiences. His stages of intellectual growth represent a constant progression from a less to a more complete equilibrium manifested by the organism's steady tendency toward a dynamic integration—first of action patterns and perceptions and later of operations.

Piaget designates the first period in an infant's life as the sensori-motor period. Beginning with the organization of congenital reflexes and action patterns of the neonate, this period lasts until eighteen months to two years of age. For the newly-born the world consists of a blurred succession of aural and visual patterns and other sensations. The progressive use of experience enables the infant to find and build relationships between his sensori-motor functions and the external environment. According to Piaget the infant uses his own body and action patterns as reference points to build up the concept of an object as well as concepts of space and time in which both he as subject and external objects are located.[1]

Concept formation depends upon two primary factors—the acquisition of the symbol function and the elaboration of the mental operations by which concepts are formed. Since a concept involves the sign or symbol by means of which it is conveyed, language development plays an important role in the formation of concepts. Also of primary importance in the formation of concepts is the process by which the concept is formed. It is this process which Piaget sees as an elaboration of mental operations originating in the child's own activity. He traces this elaboration of the thought process from its substructure of sensori-motor intelligence through the preconceptual and intuitive phases of preoperational thought to operational or reflective thought.

The second period in the child's mental growth and development begins when the child is about eighteen months or two years of age and is identified by Piaget as the preoperational representation stage. This stage, beginning with organized forms of symbolic behavior, allows the child to represent the external world through the medium of symbols established by simple generalizations. Two phases are included in the second period: the preconceptual phase from eighteen months or two years to age four, and the intuitive phase from age four to

age seven or eight. Preconceptual and/ or intuitive thought is not a new power suddenly attained by the child or superposed all of a sudden on completely prepared mechanisms; it is an extension and expression of the intercoordinated schemata of sensori-motor behavior patterns beyond present and immediate perceptions and responses to the formation of concepts of a reality more remote in time and space. A gradual coordination of representative relations results in growing conceptualizations that in turn will take the child to the threshold of operational thought. Thought at this stage remains prelogical; judgments, inconsistent and in terms of single relationships, are intuitive and ego-centered. Perceptual domination causes the child to focus on only one aspect of a situation to the exclusion of other aspects; hence, he can deal with only one problem at a time and is unable to coordinate relationships.

It is at about age seven that operational thought structures are formed. Operational thought emerges when the basic stock of concepts formed at the preoperational level is organized or grouped into coherent systems. An operation begins its existence as an internalized action—as an imagined action carried out in thought. Not only are concrete operations internalized actions, they are actions which have been integrated with other actions to form reversible systems. But the operational systems at the concrete level are still fragmentary; they have not yet completely achieved an equilibrium, nor are they combined into a single structured whole. Although concrete thought remains essentially attached to empirical reality, it is an advance over intuitive thought of the preoperational stage in that it begins to extend "the

---

[1] Jean Piaget. *The Construction of Reality in the Child.* Translated by Margaret Cook. (New York: Basic Books, 1954).

actual in terms of the potential."[2] The child begins by acting, during the course of which he seeks to coordinate the sequence of results that he has obtained. But as he does so, he structures only the immediate reality upon which he acts.

The stage of formal operations, ages twelve to fifteen, marks the development of the child's ability to use the hypothetico-deductive procedures of science and logic. The individual at the stage of formal thought begins by reasoning about theoretical possibilities. From these hypotheses he proceeds to the empirical data. By beginning with theory he is able to establish or verify actual relationships between things encountered in the empirical situation. The process is the reverse of that found at the level of concrete operations where the child derived an elementary theory from his prior structuring of immediate reality. At the stage of formal operations he begins with that which is hypothetically possible and tests it empirically.[3]

Conservation

Central to Piaget's theory of concept development and essential for the appearance of the operational system of thought is the principle of conservation, or the invariance of a given empirical factor throughout observed changes of stage. Only as a given material element remains permanent and independent of changes in its form can the mind use it in building a conceptual framework of the physical world.

"Conservation principles are fundamental to disciplined thought."[4] Conservation is the resultant of operational reversibility and implies what Piaget calls the "coordination of differences."

Piaget views concept development in terms of conservation, marked by an increasing stability of a particular concept in the face of changes (often irrelevant) in the stimulus field. For Piaget conservation can be traced through a successive growth from the child's perceptually-dominated view of the reality of his experiential world to concepts representing that world. A utilization of the principle of conservation allows the child to think away visual qualities and concentrate on the logical relationships involved. When the child sees that the total amount of a quantity remains the same even when divided into smaller units, he is utilizing the principle of conservation. Conservation is justified by the properties of reversibility and compensation. Only when the child is able to return to the initial state of a given material by an inverse operation, does he arrive at conservation of that material.

By means of ingenious experiments embodying the principle of conservation and skillful questioning, Piaget determined to find out if a child acts in accord with the principle of conservation from the beginning of his mental activity, or if conservation is gradually constructed through pertinent experience. His experiments dealing with the manipulation of physical objects showed developmental trends in children's ability to conserve quantity, weight, and volume in the construction of these concepts. A variety of ex-

[2] Bärbel Inhelder and Jean Piaget. *The Growth of Logical Thinking from Childhood to Adolescence.* Translated by A. Parsons and S. Milgram. (New York: Basic Books, 1958), p. 248.

[3] Jean Piaget. *The Psychology of Intelligence.* Translated by M. Piercy and D. E. Berlyne. (London: Routledge and Kegan Paul Ltd., 1950).

[4] Lee J. Cronbach. *Educational Psychology.* Second Edition. (New York: Harcourt, Brace, and World Inc., 1963), p. 355.

periments enabled Piaget to trace the development of conservation from a stage of non-conservation at the beginning of the intuitive phase of thought through a transitional stage to conservation at the concrete operations level.

Three stages can be discerned in the development of conservation of specific properties. In the initial stage the child focuses on only one biasing aspect of the stimulus field. This is followed by an oscillatory stage where he shifts back and forth between the major biasing aspect and a competing one. The compensatory role of these two aspects begins to be suspected and, finally, the child arrives with certitude at the realization of absolute, exact conservation of the property concerned despite perceptual changes in the stimulus field.

Usually the child's reasoning from age four to six is marked by an absence of conservation with the intermediary stage occurring at about age six or seven. After age seven he reasons with necessary conservation and so is able to conserve quantities and numbers, to classify, to serialize, and to construct concepts of space and time which are typical of adults.

Musical Intelligence in the Light of Piaget's Theory

Any discussion of the musical experience "is based upon certain psychological assumptions and implies a certain view of the nature and functioning of the musical mind."[5] The musical experience can be emotional, perceptual, aesthetic, or to some degree intellectual, that is to say, conceptually mediated. Hence, musical development has many aspects. A rudimentary musical response is the sheerly emotional wherein the listener is aware only of a pleasant auditory impression. He is unable to grasp and respond to tonal-rhythmic movement because he cannot separate tonal and rhythmic patterns from the total complex of sound. Perceptual development refers to growth in the ability to differentiate between pitches, rhythm patterns, meter, timbre, and intensities. An individual grows aesthetically as he is able to respond to the expressive form of the music. "Having an aesthetic experience is a direct relation between perceiving sounds and a perceiver self, needing no intermediary of knowing and thinking."[6] Yet another aspect by which the musical development of an individual is judged is executant ability in a performance medium.

This study was concerned with the rational aspects of musical development. These rational aspects consist of the intellectual controls of operational thought pointed to by Piaget in his researches into children's development of concepts of quantity, weight, volume, and class inclusion.

As we have already seen, a key concept underlying the Piagetian theory of intellectual growth and understanding is that of conservation. For Piaget conservation is a "necessary condition of all experience and all reasoning."[7] If conservation is a necessary condition for all rational activity, musical thought should be no exception to the

---

[5] James Mursell. *The Psychology of Music.* (New York: W. W. Norton, 1937), pp. 287-288.

[6] Foster McMurray. "Pragmatism in Music Education," *Basic Concepts in Music Education.* Chapter II. The Fifty-Seventh Yearbook of the National Society for the Study of Education. (Chicago: University of Chicago Press, 1958), p. 54.

[7] Jean Piaget. *The Child's Conception of Number.* Translated by C. Gattegno and F. M. Hodgson. (London: Routledge and Kegan Paul Ltd., 1961), p. 3.

rule. Although the perceived contact between subject and object was visual or tactual-kinesthetic in the tasks described by Piaget, the perceptual contact might just as well be aural. This raises a most provocative question, "How might the principle of conservation apply to the development of musical thought?"

The essence of musical intelligence is the building of a stable framework of rhythmic, melodic, harmonic, and formal concepts through a progressive organization of musical experiences. It is this conceptual musical framework that permits an individual to reason about music. As long as the child is limited to the use of his spontaneous perceptions, the structural framework which he builds to represent his sound world is also limited. As he moves beyond the limits of his perceptual field, the mental schemata both structure and are structured by the refinement and improvement of perceptual stimuli. The child learns "to break up what is immediately perceived, to analyze it into its constituent parts and use these independently of the whole pattern of sight or sound in which they are presented."[8]

When listening to music one follows the unfolding of tonal patterns in temporal sequence. Even though changes occur in the spatial melodic movement, the listener conserves the metered rhythm so that he is cognizant of regular recurrent patterns of accentuation and duration within the musical measure. His ability to conserve this movement provides him with a forward-moving scheme of expectation that enhances both his musical responsiveness and his intellectual understanding of

the music. Or again, melodic patterns are varied both rhythmically and melodically as the composer manipulates and toys with his thematic material. In order to follow thematic manipulation intellectually and musically, the listener must be able to conserve pitch relationships and tonal patterns within the total musical configuration. Within this context the writer assumes that musical intelligence is a superior form of musical organization, represented by an equilibrium of cognitive structurings of musical elements that is built up through a utilization of the principle of conservation.

The orientation of the investigation was that stages from non-conservation (the result of perceptual centration) to an intermediate stage of conservation (reflected by a conflict between biasing perceptual centrations and intuitive regulations) to absolute conservation could be observed in the responses of five- and eight-year-old children to tonal and rhythmic patterns.

Procedure

Nine musical tasks were devised to study rational aspects of musical development as evidenced by the ability to conserve meter, tone, and rhythm. Preliminary experimentation with three eight-year-old boys in December, 1962, led to the development of the tasks concerning temporal conservation and conservation of rhythm patterns. All nine tasks are considered essential to the study although not all were investigated.

The six musical tasks to be described were selected for experimental use in a pilot study. These were as follows: Task IA and B, Conservation of Meter; Task IIIA and B, Conservation of Rhythm Pattern under Deformation of Tone; Task IV, Conser-

[8] M. D. Vernon. "The Development of Perception in Children," *Educational Research*, Vol. III, No. 1 (November 1960) 2-11, p. 10.

vation of Melody under Deformation of Durational Values; Task VI, Conservation of Tonal Pattern under Deformation of Pitch; Task VII, Conservation of Tonal Pattern under Deformation of Rhythm; and Task VIII, Conservation of Melody under Deformation of Accompaniment.

The six tasks were administered to eight kindergarten children and eight third grade children from two elementary schools in Champaign, Illinois, in a pilot study conducted during the Spring of 1963. The children were selected by their classroom teachers. The only criterion for selection was that they had no private music instruction.

Each child met individually with the investigator for four fifteen-minute sessions. A story told to the child by the investigator introduced each task. Task IA was preceded by a practice session with material comparable to that used in the task. Practice sessions for the remaining tasks are described in the stories. Then each tonal and/or rhythmic example (previously recorded on magnetic tape) was presented to the child. His responses to the task and to the questioning about the task were recorded by a second tape recorder.

The questioning procedure was varied according to the child's responses. If the child made a wrong response or did not appear to understand the task, the example was played for him a second and even a third or fourth time and additional questions asked. Sometimes the stimulus pattern and the rules of the game were also reviewed. Each task was designed not so much to determine the child's immediate aural perception as it was to try to discover how a child thinks about what he is hearing. This is believed to be analogous to the Piagetian method of testing.

Reinforcement in terms of a friendly smile and remarks such as, "You are doing fine," were provided by the investigator. The child was not told when he had made a mistake; rather he was encouraged to do his best at all times. Frequently the child was asked, "Can you tell me more about it?" in order to give the investigator additional clues as to his thinking.

Because of the relatively short attention span of the five-year-old not all of the items under each major task were presented to these eight children. Only the first two of the four items of Task IIIA and B and the first three of the four items of Task VI were presented to the kindergarten children. Tasks IA and B, IV, VII, and VIII were presented in their entirety to all children.

The protocols of the children were typed from the sound tape and scored from the typed copy. The number of correct first responses for Tasks IA and B, IIIA and B, VI, VII, and VIII was tabulated. Since all children did not make second responses to all of the tasks, subsequent responses were discussed in the interpretation of the protocols. For Task IV the number of correct responses after as many as four hearings was tabulated.

The Musical Tasks

Our musical tasks represent an attempt to trace stages of conservation in musical thought in five- and eight-year-old children. The tasks designed to study conservation of meter, tone, and rhythm are as follows: Task IA and B, Conservation of Meter; Task IIA and B, Conservation of Meter with One-to-One Correspondence; Task IIIA and B, Conservation of

Rhythm Pattern under Deformation of Tone; Task IV, Conservation of Melody under Deformation of Durational Values; Task VA and B, Seriation of Tones by Pitch; Task VI, Conservation of Tonal Pattern under Deformation of Pitch; Task VII, Conservation of Tonal Pattern under Deformation of Rhythm; Task VIII, Conservation of Melody under Deformation of Accompaniment; and Task IX, Conservation of Tonality.

Each of our conservation tasks requires a foil as did the tasks of Piaget. Conservation of a given empirical property results when that property remains invariant in the child's mind even though changes occur in its form or in the total stimulus field of which the property is a part. The foil represents the change made in the shape or presentation of a specific property to test the child's ability to conserve it. Table 1 summarizes the musical tasks, the property to be conserved, and the foil.

TABLE 1
THE MUSICAL TASKS

Task	Property Conserved	Foil
IA and B; IIA and B	Meter	Durational Values
IIIA and B	Rhythm Pattern	Tonal Pattern in IIIB
IV	Melody	Durational Values
VA and B	Tonal Series	Varying Pitches
VI	Tonal Pattern	Pitch Level
VII	Tonal Pattern	Rhythm Pattern
VIII	Melody	Rhythmic and Harmonic Accompaniment
IX	Tonality	Key of Accompaniment

Conservation of Meter

A major aspect of musical intelligence is the ability to conserve the meter. Once the temporal unit has become invariant in the child's thinking, other rhythmic concepts can be assimilated to it. From the basic structural concept of meter stem the schemata for relational reasoning in musical thought. Conservation of meter enables an individual to reason about the regular recurrent patterns of accentuation and duration within the measure and at the same time provides him with anticipatory schemata for interpreting the rhythmic flow of the music.

Task IA.—Task IA was designed to assess the ability of children to conserve meter as shown by their ability to discriminate between duple and triple meter. Six examples had been played at a tempo of MM $J = 84$ on a ten-inch drum and tape recorded. Three examples were in duple meter; three were in triple meter. The child was directed by the tape to "listen to number one," followed by the pattern, and so forth. The child answered verbally as to whether each stimulus pattern was in two or three. He was encouraged to clap, tap, or swing his arm on the accented first beat. In this and subsequent tasks the procedure was varied according to the child's response. Sometimes examples were repeated; at other times we went on to the next example.

Task IB.—Task IB was designed to determine the child's ability to conserve meter when he listens to music. The task was introduced in story form. Then a tape recording of two elementary songs performed on the piano at a tempo of MM $J = 112$ was played. The first song, *Halka Had a Rooster Red*, was in duple meter; the second, *Lavender's Blue*, was in triple meter. The child told the investigator whether each piece was in two or three. He was encouraged to clap or tap with the accent as he listened.

Conservation of Rhythm Pattern Under Deformation of Tone

An aspect of musical intelligence which logically follows conservation of meter is the ability to conserve the distribution of rhythmic elements within the measure when the tonal patterns vary. The ability to follow rhythmic patterns through tonal variations provides an individual with anticipatory schemata for organizing the rhythmic structure of the music. A musically intelligent individual conserves rhythm patterns as they unfold within the temporal flow of the music. He uses these patterns to interpret the rhythmic structure of the total composition.

Task IIIA and B.—Task IIIA consisted of four rhythm patterns played on a single tone bell. The task was presented within a story context. Four make-believe children, John, Mary, Bill, and Sue, were learning a dance pattern taught to them by the teacher. The task required the subject to select the child who played the pattern wrong. Task IIIB consisted of the same rhythm patterns played on different tone bells. The purpose was to determine the child's ability to conserve the rhythm patterns when presented in varying tonal contexts. The rhythm patterns had been played on Perfection Universal Song Bells and recorded. Each pattern was preceded by a direction, "John plays the pattern like this;" "Mary plays the pattern like this;" and so forth. Seven-inch cardboard dolls mounted on plastic stands represented the make-believe children.

A change of procedure in the administration of Tasks IIIA and B was made after the Tasks had been given

to three third grade children. To these three children all examples of IIIA were given and then those of IIIB. This procedure did not allow for a study of the immediate conservation of the rhythmic pattern when varying tonal patterns were added. Hence, it was decided to follow each rhythm pattern of IIIA with an immediate presentation of that pattern under deformation of tone. This resulted in an interweaving of Tasks IIIA and B in the presentations to the remaining thirteen children.

Conservation of Melody Under Deformation of Durational Values

Task IV.—The ability to follow a melody through variation in its rhythmic structure is another aspect of musical intelligence. Task IV was designed to assess a child's ability to conserve a melodic line when the durational values were altered. It was patterned after the Piagetian tasks designed to study the psychological development of concepts of time and speed in children. A four-measure phrase by Bartók[9] was immediately followed by the phrase in augmentation. A story about the dancing of a little girl and her jolly grandfather introduced the task. The children were asked two questions: Which dance tune was for the little girl and which was for the grandfather? Was the grandfather's dance tune the same as the little girl's or was it different? The children were allowed to hear the tune as many as four times. At each hearing their listening was focused on a different aspect of the two questions. Operational mastery of the task was

---

[9] Béla Bartók. *For Children*, Vol. 1, No. 5, "Play." (New York: Boosey and Hawkes, 1946), p. 5.

evidenced by the child's ability to answer both questions correctly.

Conservation of Tonal Pattern Under Deformation of Pitch

Task VI.—Task VI was designed to investigate the possibility that there are discernible stages in the child's ability to conserve a tonal pattern when it is transposed to different pitches. Piaget found that children under age six or seven do not grasp relationships between parts of complex figures. They perceive a global picture of the total shape of the parts but fail to note the manner in which the parts are fitted together. The ability to grasp relationships depends not so much upon an immediate perception of shape as it does upon the child's understanding of relationships. Ability to perform this task is dependent upon the child's perception of the relationship between the tones of a three-note figure. The setting for the task was a classroom situation in which the four make-believe children were being taught tonal patterns on the xylophone. The stimulus patterns had been performed on a Sonor Xylophone, one of the Orff instruments, and recorded. Each stimulus pattern was played twice for each subject. Then the investigator and the subject sang the pattern and used the hand to indicate pitch levels. Each of the make-believe children then performed the pattern which was preceded by a direction, "John plays the pattern like this;" "Mary plays the pattern like this;" and so forth. Our subjects had to determine who played the pattern incorrectly.

Conservation of Tonal Pattern Under Deformation of Rhythm

An aspect of musical intelligence logically following conservation of tonal pattern under deformation of pitch is the ability to follow tonal patterns through rhythmic variations. This component of musical intelligence can be described in terms of conservation of tonal pattern under deformation of rhythm. It is the reverse of conservation of rhythm pattern under deformation of tone (Tasks IIIA and B). A musically intelligent individual conserves tonal patterns as they unfold within the spatial flow of the music. These patterns allow him to interpret the over-all tonal structure of the total composition.

Task VII.—Task VII was designed to assess children's ability to conserve a tonal pattern when the rhythms are changed. Again the story depicting a classroom situation was used. The subjects listened twice to each recorded stimulus pattern played on the xylophone, and then sang it with the investigator. They listened to each make-believe child's performance of the three patterns on the xylophone in order to select the wrong pattern. Each pattern was preceded by a direction, "John plays the pattern like this," and so forth.

Conservation of Melody Under Deformation of Accompaniment

An important aspect of musical intelligence is the ability to conserve a melody when rhythmic and harmonic variations are introduced in the accompaniment. Task VIII was designed to ascertain how much interference of extraneous accompanying material children could bear and still conserve the melody.

Task VIII.—The melody of an Italian folksong[10] and four settings of

---

[10] M. Krone, I. Wolfe, B. Krone, and M. Fullerton. *Music Round the Town.* (Chicago: Follett Publishing Company, 1955), p. 118.

the melody had been performed on the piano at a tempo of MM $\rfloor$ = 92 and recorded. Both harmonic and rhythmic variation were introduced in the various accompaniments. One of the melodies was incorrect. The recorded piano performance of the melody was played for each child. The investigator sang the melody, inviting the child to try to hum along with her. Finally, the recorded performance was played again. Then each of the make-believe children in the hypothetical classroom played the melody with an accompaniment. Each melody was preceded by a direction, "John plays the melody like this," and so forth. The subjects were asked to select the incorrect melody. The correct melody was reviewed during the administration of the task.

Results of the Study

The protocols of the children's responses were analyzed according to Piaget's principle of conservation. Chapter V of the study was devoted to an interpretation of the protocols. In the following discussion of the results occasional reference will be made to the protocols.

To avoid confusion with the names of the make-believe children described in the tasks, the subjects have been given letter names followed by age. Hence, the kindergarten children are designated as follows: A5, B5, C5, D5, E5, F5, G5, and H5; the third grade children are designated A8, B8, C8, D8, E8, F8, G8, and H8.

In order to clarify the presentation of data the investigator arbitrarily assigned a value of one point for each correct first response to the items of Tasks IA and B, IIIA and B, VI, VII, and VIII. A value of two points was arbitrarily assigned to Task IV—one point for each of the two questions asked about Task IV—if the correct answers were given after as many as four hearings.

Task IA.—At the first hearing of Task IA, fourteen, or twenty-nine percent, of the total responses given by the five-year-old children were correct as shown in Table 2. Verbal explanations were marked by an absence of conservation. Their perception centered upon the number of impulses heard; there was no attempt to coordinate the differences in durational values. Hence, their responses about meter represented intuitive thought of the preoperational stage. When a question, "Do the little short notes take as much time as the longer notes?" was asked, the child would simply answer, "No."

TABLE 2
NUMBER OF CORRECT FIRST RESPONSES TO THE SIX EXAMPLES OF TASK IA

Kindergarten Children	Score
A5	1
B5	2
C5	1
D5	3
E5	1
F5	3
G5	1
H5	2
	14 or 29%*

Third Grade Children	Score
A8	2
B8	3
C8	2
D8	4
E8	4
F8	2
G8	6
H8	3
	26 or 54%*

* Out of a total N of 48 responses.

At the first hearing, twenty-six, or fifty-four percent, of the total responses given by the eight-year-old children were correct. The verbal explanations given by the third grade children to support their answers showed a growing conceptualization of meter. That these children were at the threshold of operational thought was evidenced by their beginning ability to utilize the logical principle of reversibility in discussing the examples. Their explanations indicated that five of the children were at the intermediate stage of conservation. Three were approaching absolute conservation, as evidenced by their ability to conserve meter. Ten initial answers tinged by perceptual illusion characterizing intuitive thought were changed to the correct answer when the children began to reason operationally.

Task IB.—The five-year-old children gave seven correct answers out of a total number of sixteen responses to Task IB, or approximately forty-four percent, after one hearing (Table 3).

TABLE 3
NUMBER OF CORRECT FIRST RE-
SPONSES TO THE TWO EXAMPLES
OF TASK IB

Kindergarten Children	Score
A5	0
B5	2
C5	2
D5	0
E5	0
F5	0
G5	1
H5	2
	7 or 44%*

Third Grade Children	Score
A8	1
B8	2
C8	1
D8	1
E8	2
F8	2
G8	1
H8	2
	12 or 75%*

* Out of a total N of 16 responses.

It is difficult to identify any conservation of meter from the answers given. One child (B5) justified duple meter by "two booms" and triple meter by "three booms." Three children (A5, D5, H5) arrived at the correct answers through their own activity of counting and clapping with the music. Two children (F5, E5) showed a definite absence of conservation; they tried to count out all of the tones heard and gave answers of "eleven and six," and "seven and nine" for the first and second examples, respectively. One child (G5) attempted to answer in terms of the accent: "It was a little louder and a little softer." Another child (F5) answered correctly at the initial hearing but could not support his answers with any kind of explanation.

The eight-year-old children had twelve out of a total number of sixteen responses correct, or seventy-five percent, after one hearing. Their answers showed evidence of conservation of the function of accent within the musical measure. Two of the children (A8, C8) commented that they found it easier to determine meter when the patterns were played on the drum. The fact that all eight-year-old children answered the second example, *Lavender's Blue*, correctly at the first hearing may indicate that the tune was familiar to these children.

Task IIIA and B.—Only two of the four patterns of Task IIIA and B were presented to the kindergarten children because of the limited attention span of the five-year-old child. The five-year-old children had difficulty conserving the rhythm patterns under deformation of tone. Perceptual centration upon the tone caused them to perceive correct rhythm patterns as incorrect. The investigator found that the children's own action of clapping out the rhythm pattern helped them to conserve it. A restatement of the task and definite questions about the rhythm patterns were further aids in the conservation of the rhythm patterns upon subsequent hearings.

TABLE 4
NUMBER OF CORRECT FIRST RESPONSES TO THE FIRST TWO RHYTHM PATTERNS OF TASKS IIIA AND B

Kindergarten Children	IIIA Score	IIIB Score
A5	6	6
B5	5	4
C5	3	2
D5	5	4
E5	7	6
F5	6	3
G5	5	2
H5	6	6
	43 or 67%*	33 or 52%*

Third Grade Children	IIIA Score	IIIB Score
A8	8	2
B8	8	7
C8	6	6
D8	8	5
E8	8	6
F8	6	8
G8	7	8
H8	6	4
	57 or 89%*	46 or 72%*

* Out of a total N of 64 responses.

Table 4 shows the first responses to Task IIIA and B. The examples were not presented a second time to the five-year-old child for further questioning if he showed signs of restlessness or inattentiveness. Of those that heard Task IIIA a second time, twelve out of sixteen wrong responses were changed to the correct response. One correct response was changed to a wrong response, but after a third hearing the correct answer was again given. Twenty-five items of Task IIIB that were incorrectly answered were heard a second time, of which

seventeen were changed to the correct response.

Four rhythm patterns, making a total of sixteen items, were presented to each eight-year-old child. The pattern of responses given by the eight-year-old children was similar to that of the five-year-olds. These children also found that it was more difficult to conserve the rhythm pattern under deformation of tone than to identify it when played on a single tone bell. Three of the eight-year-old children (B8, E8, G8) were able to pinpoint the errors made in the rhythm patterns. Only one five-year-old (F5) was able to do this and for only one item.

TABLE 5
NUMBER OF CORRECT FIRST RESPONSES OF THIRD GRADE CHILDREN TO TASK IIIA AND B

Third Grade Children	IIIA Score	IIIB Score
A8	14	7
B8	16	15
C8	13	12
D8	16	11
E8	16	14
F8	14	14
G8	15	16
H8	14	10
	118 or 92%*	99 or 77%*

* Out of a total N of 128 responses.

Table 5 shows that the eight-year-old children had 118 correct responses out of a total of 128 responses, or ninety-two percent, at the initial hearing of Task IIIA. Of those items that were heard a second time, eight out of ten wrong responses were changed to the correct response. A ninth wrong response was changed to the correct response with a third hearing. Twenty-five items of Task IIIB that were incorrectly answered were heard a second time, of which twenty were changed to the correct response. One correct response was changed to a wrong response with a second hearing.

A comparison of the five- and eight-year-olds' responses to the eight items of the first two rhythm patterns shows that the eight-year-old children had fifty-seven out of sixty-four, or eighty-nine percent, correct first responses to Task IIIA as compared with forty-three out of sixty-four, or sixty-seven percent for the five-year olds; forty-six out of sixty-four, or seventy-two percent correct first responses to Task IIIB as compared with thirty-three out of sixty-four, or fifty-two percent for the five-year-olds.

Task IV.—Four five-year-old children (A5, B5, C5, E5) were able to conserve the melody when the durational values were changed, while four children said that the tune changed. Three of the five-year-old children (C5, D5, G5) said that the end was faster than the beginning; one (A5) answered that it was the "same fast" all the way through. Their answers were dependent upon their perception.

Seven of the eight-year-old children were able to conserve the melody under deformation of durational values. Two eight-year-old boys (C8, H8) said that the beginning was twice as fast as the ending. This kind of answer indicated that they were trying to solve the task operationally by comparing tempi. The five-year-old children did not exhibit this kind of controlled judgment.

Table 6 shows that, in response to the two questions about Task IV, the eight-year-old children had fifteen out of sixteen, or ninety-four percent, correct responses as compared with eight out of sixteen, or fifty percent correct responses for the five-year-olds.

Task VI.—Only three of the four tonal patterns of Task VI were pre-sented to the five-year-old children because of their limited attention spans. The responses of the five-year-old children represent an intuitive phase of conservation. These children perceived the direction and contour of patterns, but failed to examine the intervallic relationships within the patterns. Four of the eight children (C5, D5, E5, G5) failed to notice the change of direction in the third example.

At the initial hearing sixty out of a total of ninety-six responses, or sixty-three percent of the five-year-olds' responses were correct. Twenty-six patterns that were incorrectly answered were heard a second time, of which fourteen were changed to the correct response. Two correct responses were changed to wrong responses.

TABLE 6
NUMBER OF CORRECT RESPONSES TO
TASK IV AFTER AS MANY AS FOUR
HEARINGS

Kindergarten Children	Score	Number of Hearings
A5	1	2
B5	2	2
C5	1	4
D5	0	2
E5	2	3
F5	1	3
G5	0	3
H5	1	3
	8 or 50%*	

Third Grade Children	Score	Number of Hearings
A8	2	3
B8	2	2
C8	2	2
D8	2	4
E8	2	1
F8	2	2
G8	1	3
H8	2	4
	15 or 94%*	

* Out of a total N of 16 responses.

Four tonal patterns were presented to the eight-year-old children. Their ability to conserve tonal patterns when transposed to different pitch levels did not differ appreciably from that of the five-year-olds. As with the five-year-old children, their perception centered upon the directional contour of the total pattern. Two of the eight-year-olds (C8, F8) failed to perceive the change of direction in the third example.

Table 7 provides a comparison of the five- and eight-year-olds' responses to the twelve items of the first three tonal patterns.

Table 8 indicates that at the first hearing ninety-eight out of a total of 128 of the eight-year-olds' responses, or seventy-seven percent, were correct. Twelve items that were incorrectly answered were heard a second time. Six of these were changed to the correct response.

TABLE 8
NUMBER OF CORRECT FIRST RESPONSES OF THIRD GRADE CHILDREN TO TASK VI

Third Grade Children	Score
A8	12
B8	13
C8	12
D8	12
E8	12
F8	11
G8	13
H8	13
	98 or 77%*

* Out of a total N of 128.

Task VII.—The five-year-old children had difficulty conserving tonal patterns when the rhythm patterns were changed. Their perception centered upon the rhythm; they found it difficult to abstract the tonal pattern from the tonal-rhythmic unit. Table 9 shows first responses for Task VII. Twenty items that were incorrectly answered were heard a second time. Eleven of these were changed to the correct response.

TABLE 7
NUMBER OF CORRECT FIRST RESPONSES TO THE FIRST THREE TONAL PATTERNS OF TASK VI

Kindergarten Children	Score
A5	8
B5	9
C5	5
D5	6
E5	9
F5	9
G5	9
H5	5
	60 or 63%*

Third Grade Children	Score
A8	8
B8	10
C8	9
D8	9
E8	9
F8	8
G8	10
H8	10
	73 or 76%*

* Out of a total N of 96.

TABLE 9
NUMBER OF CORRECT FIRST RESPONSES TO TASK VII

Kindergarten Children	Score
A5	9
B5	8
C5	9
D5	5
E5	9
F5	9
G5	8
H5	8
	65 or 68%*

Third Grade Children	Score
A8	11
B8	10
C8	8
D8	11
E8	8
F8	8
G8	11
H8	10
	77 or 80%*

* Out of a total N of 96 responses.

Three of the eight-year-olds (C8, E8, F8) found it difficult to conserve the tonal pattern. One child (G8) was able to describe the errors. Sixteen items that were incorrectly answered were heard a second time, of which eleven were changed to the correct response.

Task VIII.—In Task VIII, two of the five-year-old children (G5, H5) were able to select the third performance as being incorrect at the first hearing. A third child (C5) identified the wrong performance after a second hearing. Only A5 and B5 said, correctly, that Mary's elaborate setting was right. The record of first responses is given in Table 10. Twelve items that were incorrectly answered were heard a second time. Six of these were changed to the correct response.

TABLE 10
NUMBER OF CORRECT FIRST RESPONSES TO TASK VIII

Kindergarten Children	Score
A5	2
B5	3
C5	1
D5	2
E5	1
F5	2
G5	2
H5	3
	16 or 50%*

Third Grade Children	Score
A8	2
B8	3
C8	3
D8	2
E8	2
F8	2
G8	2
H8	2
	18 or 56%*

* Out of a total N of 32 responses.

The eight-year-old children responded to Task VIII as did the five-year-olds. No stages in growth of ability to conserve a melody with different accompaniments were evident. Only one child (E8) perceived the incorrect melody after one hearing. A second child (B8) was able to do so with a third hearing. Six of the eight children called the melody used in Mary's elaborate setting wrong. Twelve items that were incorrectly answered were heard a second time, of which only three were changed to the correct response.

Subtle melodic changes used with the same simple harmonic and rhythmic accompaniment as for the first setting of the melody created similar general effects of the two settings. An elaborate rhythmic and harmonic setting of the correct melody caused it to be perceived as incorrect. Perceptual concentrations upon the general effect of the total setting did not allow for a consideration of the melody *per se.* Because they lacked reversibility of musical thought, the children were unable to dissociate the melody from the musical unit in the performances of Mary and Bill.

Summary

The eight-year-old children were better able to conserve meter in Task IA and B and the tonal and rhythmic patterns of Tasks IIIA and B, IV, VI, and VII than were the five-year-olds. Only Task VIII failed to show a differentiation between the two groups. Task IA, Conservation of Meter, and Task IV, Conservation of Melody under Deformation of Durational Values, indicated differences in the kind of explanations given by the five- and eight-year-old children. The intuitive answers of the kindergarten children showed a lack of conservation and were indicative of preoperational thought. The answers of the eight-year-old children reflected the intermediate stage of conservation. Adumbrations of operational thought were indicated by answers of two children, A8 and C8 to Task IA, and by C8 and H8 to Task IV. Tasks IA and B and IV, dealing with durational values, seemed to present a better opportunity for operational thinking than did the tasks involving the conservation of tonal patterns.

Implications for Music Education

From the findings of the study the following implications can be drawn for elementary music education:

1. Stages of conservation were apparent in the children's various solutions to the rhythmic tasks involving conservation of meter. In many instances correct solutions were arrived at only with the intervention of the child's activity of clapping, swinging, tapping, or counting. The child seemed to reason with a form of sensori-motor intelligence wherein his own actions served as a guide for thought by providing a model to guide his judgment in solving the task. Overt interaction of the child with the musical problem would seem to be of primary importance. Opportunities for this interaction need to be provided.

2. A second implication points toward the necessity of models for the children to imitate. In working out the tasks involving conservation of rhythm patterns, the children's clapping of the pattern formed the model to which they matched the rhythm patterns heard in the task. These models served as feed-back mechanisms for the child. If the stimulus matched the model of the child's clapping, he could make a confident positive judgment, and conversely. Models supplied by the teacher should be properly matched to the child's existing mental schemata so that maximum development can be insured.

3. Because children's musical growth develops in stages, the musical experiences provided by the curriculum should stimulate a maximum amount of growth at each stage. A third implication points toward the necessity for supplying a variety of musical experiences. Musical problems to be solved must be commensurate with the child's musical understanding. Musical experiences designed to clarify incipient concepts must precede intellectualization of the specific concept in question. Too often the music program does not permit the child a wide enough range of musical experiences before he is asked to intellectualize these experiences.

4. A fourth implication for elementary music education is inherent in the very nature of the tasks. If musical intelligence can indeed be discussed in terms of conservation of tonal and rhythm patterns or themes, then experience with a large repertoire of these patterns in many and varied guises is necessary to sharpen the child's ability to discriminate between patterns and to follow thematic development of the patterns.

5. A fifth implication lies in the adaptation of the story settings for the tasks to live classroom situations. Here the children themselves would become the participants in the story. Conservation of a particular pattern would be determined by the child's ability to perform that pattern within varying tonal and/or rhythmic contexts. In a somewhat similar vein,

learning situations based on the child's use of his original rhythm patterns in varied tonal contexts and original tonal patterns in varied meters and rhythmic contexts would aid in the clarification of tonal and rhythmic relationships and would also provide the child with the kind of experience needed to build a conceptual musical framework.

Current practices in elementary music education are not entirely inconsistent with the implications drawn from the present study. Piaget's theory of intelligence with its essential principle of conservation can provide both a framework and a focus for the development of musical concepts which in turn will lead to musical literacy and independence.

Suggestions for Further Research

The pilot study conducted by the writer has shown that it is possible to apply the Piagetian principle of conservation to the development of musical thought. Much research needs to be done in this area before the three stages of conservation in conceptual growth identified by Piaget can be corroborated in the conservation of tonal and rhythmic patterns. The writer would like to suggest that further exploration is needed in the following areas:

1. An interpretation of the children's protocols has revealed that stages of conservation are more easily identified in the area of rhythm than in tone. Rhythm pertains to the temporal quality of the musical sound and includes basic schemes of time values within musical measures. Rhythm in this concrete sense can be clearly intellectualized by an individual who possesses reversibility of thought. The tasks in the areas of conservation of

meter and conservation of melody under deformation of durational values need to be refined and administered to large numbers of children.

2. Although the eight-year-olds were better able to conserve the tonal patterns than were the five-year-olds, their reasoning was based upon their perceptions and operational thought was not in evidence. When a child begins to decenter his attention from a musical unit in order to consider a specific musical element comprising that unit, his thought processes exhibit reversibility. How to get at this phenomenon is still a moot question. A sequence of tasks needs to be developed in the areas of conservation of tonal patterns under deformation of pitch and rhythm and conservation of melody under deformation of accompaniment.

3. Sets of carefully structured quesions need to be devised for each task in order to assure uniformity of administration. The way to develop these questions is through actual research. Only by using the questions in test situations can one determine their validity and relevancy, both for the task and for the child. Each task should be presented to each child the same number of times. The child should be allowed to hear the stimulus pattern a second time in order to have a frame of reference for the questioning.

4. Longitudinal studies concerned with conservation of tonal and rhythmic patterns need to be conducted with children through the ages of four to eight. This type of research would allow for the study of the development of conservation within individual children and would make possible a more accurate determination of the succession of stages of conservation.

5. Tests of pitch and rhythmic discrimination need to be given in addition to the musical tasks involving conservation of tone and rhythm. By comparing the results of the two kinds of tests it might be possible to determine to what extent the solution of the tasks embodying conservation is dependent upon perception and to what extent upon conservation leading to operational thought.[11]

Northwestern University

---

[11] This article is based upon the author's doctoral dissertation of the same title (University of Illinois, 1963).

This study examined the relationship between pitch-discrimination and vocal pitch-matching abilities of preschool and fourth-grade children. One hundred forty-four students were selected randomly and tested individually on both ability measures. Scores on the pitch-discrimination test served as the basis for three ability-level groups within each age group. Analysis of pitch-matching scores indicated a significant difference between the age groups, but not for the pitch-discrimination based ability groups; nor was there a significant age-by-ability group interaction. Rank-order correlations between the two measures were generally low, with the exception of the high-ability group of fourth-graders, where r = 61.

John M. Geringer, *University of Texas*

JRME 1983, VOLUME 31, NUMBER 2, PAGES 93–99

The Relationship of Pitch-Matching and Pitch-Discrimination Abilities of Preschool and Fourth-Grade Students

Descriptive and experimental research in music has investigated both perceptual and performance aspects of the elements of music. The ability to discriminate, as well as a basic understanding of the processes of perception concerning the components of music, is regarded by most music educators as fundamental not only to learning listening skills, but also as an implicit part of successful performance.

An area of continuing investigation concerns the perception of intonation and intonational performance. The actual relationship between pitch discrimination and satisfactory performance of intonation has remained primarily conjectural, although it would seem that a degree of pitch-discrimination ability is a prerequisite to skill in pitch matching (Hedden, 1980; Madsen & Geringer, 1976). It is conceivable that some studies have assumed that perception and performance are

---

For reprints of this article, contact John M. Geringer, Associate Professor of Music, Department of Music, University of Texas, Austin 78712.

synonymous. It is also possible that a rationale of some standardized music tests has been a tacit assumption of a correlation between pitch-discrimination skill and pitch-matching performance.

The few extant empirical studies directly comparing pitch discrimination and vocal pitch matching have yielded inconsistent results. An early investigation (Knock, 1922) of non-musically-trained adult subjects revealed a low and nonsignificant correlation. Analysis of data indicated that subjects in Knock's study were not matching pitches accurately enough to be hampered by the limitation of discrimination ability. A more recent study of sixth graders (Pedersen & Pedersen, 1970), using a rating system of pitch accuracy, indicated low-to-moderate relationships between pitch discrimination and vocal pitch production, the strength of which was somewhat different for two groups of subjects. Buckton (1977) found little correlation (.11) among 6- to 8-year-olds, but Zwissler (1971) found significant differences in pitch-discrimination skills between 6-year-olds selected as accurate singers and those selected as inaccurate singers. There have been other indications that in some situations performance and perception of intonation are significantly different. In a study involving both vocal and instrumental pitch matching, Geringer (1978) reported that the intonation perception of subjects' own performances was significantly less accurate and sharper in pitch than the actual performance of unaccompanied ascending scalar patterns.

There are many studies reporting the positive effects of training in improving pitch discrimination (Madsen, Edmonson, & Madsen, 1969; Sergeant, 1973) and pitch performance (Madsen, 1966; Madsen, 1974; Madsen, Wolfe, & Madsen, 1969) across a variety of ages. Investigations of early childhood populations also have reported success in training vocal ability (Jersild & Bienstock, 1934; Smith, 1963) and pitch discrimination (Petzold, 1969; Simons, 1964). However, there are few studies reporting that training in one ability results in improvement of the other. Buckton (1977) found a vocal program no more effective than an instrumental program in improving pitch discrimination, although both groups improved. In two instances of pitch discrimination training with elementary school subjects, there was no improvement in vocal pitch matching (Fullard, 1975; Porter, 1977). Porter found no evidence demonstrating that faulty singing is the result of inaccurate pitch perception.

The purpose of the present study was to examine the relationship between pitch-discrimination and vocal pitch-matching abilities of young children. Specifically, would preschool and fourth-grade subjects grouped according to ability on a pitch-discrimination task show significant differences performing a vocal pitch-matching task?

PROCEDURE

Subjects were 4- and 5-year-old children ($n = 72$), randomly selected from a large, ethnically mixed preschool (total enrollment of 450), and fourth graders ($n = 72$) randomly selected from five public schools. The experimenter spent 3 days prior to testing sessions interacting with the children and establishing rapport.

All experimental procedures had been pilot tested with other samples of 4-year-old children ($n = 18$) and fourth graders ($n = 12$). All subjects were tested individually for both the discrimination and pitch-matching tasks. The order of task testing was counterbalanced to prevent possible test-order bias.

The prerecorded pitch-discrimination test (PD) consisted of 12 trials of tonal pairs. The intervallic structures of test items were a descending tritone, an ascending minor third, a descending quarter tone (50 cents), one ascending and one descending eighth tone (25 cents), and four unison pairs. All tones were produced on a Johnson Intonation Trainer (timbre setting number 2) and were within the vocal ranges of the subjects (Welch, 1979). Three tapes were recorded with different test-item orders. All tapes were monitored with a Conn Chromatic Strobo-scope to insure pitch accuracy. Each tone had a duration of 1 second with a .1 second silence between tones of a pair. The intertrial duration was 10 seconds to allow subjects adequate time to respond. Subjects verbally stated whether the second tone of a pair was the same or not the same as the first tone, or whether they were uncertain. Flash cards with colored geometric figures were used to teach subjects and verify their ability to use the terminology appropriately. Criterion for aural testing was three consecutive correct discriminations and verbalizations regarding the visual stimuli.

The recording used for the vocal pitch-matching test (VPM) consisted of a simple, unaccompanied three-measure song with simple words, sung on scale degrees *do* (hear the), *re* (whistle), *mi* (of), *re* (the), and *do* (train, toot, toot). The master recording was made in three keys (C, E, and F♯ major) by a female vocalist viewing a strobotuner. A panel of graduate students in music education selected the most accurate version in each of the three keys, while viewing the strobe, so that all pitches were within ± 5 cents relative to equal temperament. The song was presented to individual subjects in each of the three keys, in counterbalanced orders. The experimenter instructed the subjects to sing back the sustained, final notes (*do*) of the examples, exactly as on the tape recorder. Thus, the pitches to be matched were well within the suggested singing ranges for both age groups (Welch, 1979). Subject responses were tape recorded for subsequent analysis.

RESULTS

Two scores were obtained for each subject. Individual PD scores were based on a summed ranking of correct/incorrect/uncertain across the 12 test trials, weighted according to the overall item difficulty. Item difficulty was based on percentages of correct responses. Correlations across subjects of item difficulty with decreasing size of intervals were very high: $r = 1.0, N = 6, p < .01$, for preschoolers and $r = .99, N = 6, p < .01$, for fourth graders. Internal consistency reliability for the PD test was .88 (Horst, 1953). The recorded pitches of subjects on the VPM test were analyzed by a panel using a strobotuner to determine the nearest semitone (reliability = .99, agreements/agreements plus disagreements). VPM scores of individuals were based on each subject's average semitone deviation across the three examples.

Subjects were assigned to ability level groups (high, middle, and low) for each of the age groups on the basis of relative standing on the PD scores. The Kruskal-Wallis Test indicated that these ability groups were indeed significantly different from each other on PD scores, $H(2)$ = 50.3, $p < .001$ for preschoolers; $H(2) = 59.4$, $p < .001$ for fourth graders. There was also a significant difference between the age groups, $Z = 2.86, p < .01$. Table 1 presents the weighted mean PD scores for age and ability groups.

Table 1 — Age and Ability Group Weighted Means of Pitch-Discrimination Scores

Ability Groups	Preschool	Fourth Grade
High	1.22	.43
Middle	3.06	.80
Low	7.63	2.19

Raw scores on the VPM test were analyzed with a 2 (age) by 3 (ability group) analysis of variance. As can be seen in Table 2, there was a significant difference between the VPM scores of the fourth graders (mean deviation = .93 semitones) and the preschoolers, $M = 2.60$, $F(1, 138) = 41.46$, $p < .001$. More than half of the fourth graders' average pitch-matching scores were within .5 semitone, while the median deviation of the preschool subjects was approximately 2.5 semitones.

There was, however, neither a significant difference in the VPM scores of the PD-based ability groups ($F < 1$) nor a significant age-by-ability group interaction [$F(2, 138) = 1.95$, $p > .10$]. Examination of cell means and cell standard deviations (see Table 3) indicates little consistent pattern of difference among the preschool subjects. Means for the fourth grade pitch-matching scores appear to correspond with the ability groups. Cell deviations of the middle- and low-group fourth graders are almost three times as large as the high-ability group deviation.

In the attempt to further describe the nature of the relationship

Table 2 — Analysis of Variance: Age by Ability Group

Source	SS	df	MS	F	p
Age	99.92	1	99.92	41.46	.001
Ability Group	4.31	2	2.16	.89	ns
Interaction	9.42	2	4.71	1.95	.10
Within	332.99	138	2.41	—	—
Total	446.64	143	—	—	—

between vocal pitch matching and pitch discrimination, Spearman Rank Correlations were computed between these two variables. Overall correlations between the PD and VPM tests were low and not significant. The Spearman correlation was $-.13$ for preschoolers and .16 for fourth graders. Table 4 shows correlations within the ability groups between the two measures. It can be seen that the correlations were generally low and not significant, with the exception of the high-ability group of fourth graders, where $r = .61, p < .01$. For this group of subjects, there appears to be a moderate relationship between the two measures; that is, subjects scoring high on the PD test also tended to match pitches relatively accurately.

Table 3 — Age and Ability Group Means and Deviations of Vocal Pitch-Matching Scores

Ability Group	Preschool		Fourth Grade	
	M	SD	M	SD
High	2.92	2.19	.57	.58
Middle	2.33	1.40	.80	1.49
Low	2.55	1.70	1.43	1.51

DISCUSSION

This study represents an attempt to investigate the interrelationship between pitch-discrimination and vocal pitch-matching ability. An analysis of variance indicated significant differences in pitch-matching abilities between age groups of subjects, but showed no differences among the discrimination-based ability groups on pitch-matching scores. A Spearman coefficient revealed a moderate correlation between the two measures within the high-ability fourth graders. These results appear consistent with some previous investigations (Pedersen & Pedersen, 1970; Zwissler, 1971), although the empirical literature is not unambiguous (cf. review of literature).

A degree of caution is warranted in the interpretation of the results. Although extreme care was taken to verify the ability of the preschool children to respond in accordance with their best judgment, it is possible that response biases may have been operating. The relatively large

Table 4 — Spearman Rank Correlations of Vocal Pitch-Matching and Pitch-Discrimination Scores

Ability Group	Preschool	Fourth Grade
High	$-.10$	.61*
Middle	.33	$-.22$
Low	$-.03$	.01

*$t = 3.61, df = 22, p < .01$.

standard deviations for this age group suggest such a possibility. Different dependent variables—verbal estimation, production, or reproduction methods—possibly account for much of the inconsistency in the research literature. Because young children lack verbal sophistication, it is especially critical to develop reliable and valid methods of measurement for this population.

The relative lack of correlation between pitch-discrimination and vocal pitch-matching ability raises some interesting questions of relevance to music educators. It may be that the limitations of pitch-discrimination ability do not operate until the vocal pitch-matching deviations are small enough to be affected by the limit. It is possible that pitch discrimination and pitch matching are simply two independent abilities, or that maturation and training are necessary to develop an interrelationship. There is some indication of the latter in the present study, because the high-ability group of fourth graders showed a moderate correlation. It may be further conjectured that pitch matching is at least partly a function of physical development, whereas pitch discrimination can be viewed as a function of discrimination learning. It is also possible that specific pitch-discrimination skills are later developed as separate abilities concomitant with specialized training in different aspects of performance, (i.e., keyboard as opposed to vocal performance). Similar questions have been encountered in the development of standardized tests in music in an attempt to predict even broader aspects, such as musical success, achievement, or subsequent performance ability. Although the efficacy of early childhood pitch-discrimination training has been described in the literature, implicit in suggesting such training has been the assumption that its development has a positive influence on other aspects of musical learning. Much continued investigation seems advisable to further describe the nature of the relationship between pitch-discrimination and pitch-matching abilities, as well as possible relationships with broader aspects of learning to perform and listen to music.

REFERENCES

Buckton, R. A comparison of the effects of vocal and instrumental instruction on the development of melodic and vocal abilities in young children. *Psychology of Music*, 1977, *5*, 36–47.

Fullard, W. G. Pitch discrimination in elementary-school children as a function of training procedure and age. In C. K. Madsen, R. D. Greer, & C. H. Madsen (Eds.), *Research in music behavior*. New York: Teachers College Press, 1975.

Geringer, J. M. Intonational performance and perception of ascending scales. *Journal of Research in Music Education*, 1978, *29*, 32–40.

Hedden, S. K. Psychoacoustical parameters of music. In D. A. Hodges (Ed.), *Handbook of music psychology*. Lawrence, Kans.: National Association for Music Therapy, 1980.

Horst, P. Correcting the Kuder-Richardson reliability for dispersion of item difficulties. *Psychological Bulletin*, 1953, *50*, 371–374.

Jersild, A., & Bienstock, S. A study of the development of children's ability to sing. *Journal of Educational Psychology*, 1934, *25*, 481–503.

Knock, C. J. Visual training of the pitch of the voice. *Psychological Monographs,* 1922, *31,* 102–127.

Madsen, C. K. The effect of scale direction on pitch acuity in solo vocal performance. *Journal of Research in Music Education,* 1966, *14,* 266–275.

Madsen, C. K. Sharpness and flatness in scalar vocal performances. *Sciences de l'Art-Scientific Aesthetics,* 1974, *9,* 91–97.

Madsen, C. K., Edmonson, F. A., & Madsen, C. H. Modulated frequency discrimination in relationship to age and musical training. *Journal of the Acoustical Society of America,* 1969, *46,* 1468–1472.

Madsen, C. K., & Geringer, J. M. Preferences for trumpet tone quality versus intonation. *Bulletin of the Council for Research in Music Education,* 1976, *46,* 13–22.

Madsen, C. K., Wolfe, D. E., & Madsen, C. H. The effect of reinforcement and directional scalar methodology on intonational improvement. *Bulletin of the Council for Research in Music Education,* 1969, *18,* 22–33.

Pedersen, D. M., & Pedersen, N. O. The relationship between pitch recognition and vocal pitch production in sixth-grade students. *Journal of Research in Music Education,* 1970, *18,* 265–272.

Petzold, R. Auditory perception by children. *Journal of Research in Music Education,* 1969, *17,* 82–87.

Porter, S. Y. The effect of multiple discrimination training on pitch-matching behaviors of uncertain singers. *Journal of Research in Music Education,* 1977, *25,* 68–82.

Sergeant, D. Measurement of pitch discrimination. *Journal of Research in Music Education,* 1973, *21,* 3–19.

Simons, G. V. Comparisons of incipient music responses among very young twins and singletons. *Journal of Research in Music Education,* 1964, *12,* 212–226.

Smith, R. B. The effect of group vocal training on the singing ability of nursery school children. *Journal of Research in Music Education,* 1963, *11,* 137–141.

Welch, G. F. Vocal range and poor pitch singing. *Psychology of Music,* 1979, *7,* 13–31.

Zwissler, R. N. An investigation of the pitch discrimination skills of first grade children identified as accurate singers and those identified as inaccurate singers (Doctoral dissertation, University of California at Los Angeles, 1971). *Dissertation Abstracts International,* 1972, *32,* 4056A.

November 8, 1982

V.

Performance

and

Adult

Discrimination

Pitch and tempo discriminations within a musical context were investigated. Two hundred musicians and two hundred nonmusicians heard ten excerpts of relatively familiar orchestral music. Excerpts were presented in pairs in order to test the ability of subjects to discriminate how an altered excerpt differed in pitch and/or tempo from its unaltered presentation. Pitch levels and tempi of the excerpts independently or in combination increased, decreased, or remained constant compared to unaltered versions. Consistent with previous research, subjects identified correctly the examples of decreased pitch levels significantly more than pitch increase examples. It is surprising, however, that tempo increase examples, rather than tempo decreases, were identified more accurately. Additional study regarding listener discrimination of the elements of music and related preferences appears advisable, since these conceivably influence music instruction as well as the performance of music.

John M. Geringer, *University of Texas, Austin*
Clifford K. Madsen, *Florida State University*

JRME 1984, VOLUME 32, NUMBER 3, PAGES 195–204

Pitch and Tempo Discrimination in Recorded Orchestral Music among Musicians and Nonmusicians

In order to perform in ensembles, musicians must rely upon generally accepted frames of reference concerning the elements of music. Perhaps two of the most consequential aspects of musical and artistic performance are the deviation standards for pitch and tempo. While pitch is usually standardized so that the A above middle C is set to 440 Hz, there are accepted ranges, more or less, for the various tempo indications. Regardless, variations within and between performers in both pitch and tempo appear to result from artistic deviation, acoustical inconsistencies,

---

For reprints of this article, contact John M. Geringer, Department of Music, University of Texas at Austin, Austin 78712, or Clifford Madsen, Center for Music Research, Florida State University, Tallahassee 32306.

vibrato effects, and other environmental, physiological, and psychological factors.

There has been a considerable amount of recent research concerning the performance and perception of intonation or pitch. Many studies have documented a tendency for performance deviation in the direction of sharpness (Geringer, 1978; Geringer & Witt, 1984; Madsen, 1974; Papich & Rainbow, 1974; Salzberg, 1980). The perception of sharpness has been shown to be less accurate that flatness discrimination, particularly for older, more musically trained subjects (Geringer, 1978; Madsen, Edmonson, & Madsen, 1969; Madsen & Geringer, 1976; Madsen & Geringer, 1981). Studies assessing the preferences of subjects have also demonstrated proclivities to prefer the direction of sharpness to flatness deviations (Geringer, 1976; Geringer & Madsen, 1981).

Similarly, investigations have indicated a marked tendency for tempo performance deviations in the direction of fastness rather than slowness (Drake, 1968; Killian, 1982; Kuhn, 1977; Kuhn & Gates, 1975). Musicians and nonmusicians tend to discriminate tempo that decreases sooner and more accurately than tempo that increases (Kuhn, 1974; Madsen, 1979). Tempo preferences have also been for faster rather than slower tempi (LeBlanc, 1981; Wapnick, 1980a).

Several studies have attempted to incorporate pitch or tempo stimuli within a musical context as opposed to isolated tones or tempo beats. Wang (1983), in a study of modulated tempo with music majors, suggested that in addition to the direction of tempo change, musical style and rhythm may influence tempo discrimination. Wapnick's (1980b) subjects estimated magnitude of tempo changes of recorded piano music and metronomic beats to a standard tempo. Deviation scores were greater for fast tempo examples than for same and slower examples. Geringer (1976) found that subjects listening to recorded orchestral music preferred faster tape speeds relative to the unaltered recordings. These preferences could have resulted from higher pitch levels, faster tempi, brighter timbres, or any combination of the above variables. Wapnick's (1980a) study of recorded piano music attempted to isolate pitch, tempo, and timbre effects. Subjects indicated preferences for increased tape speed and for fast tempo and bright timbre when these variables were examined independently of the other factors.

The present study was an attempt to further investigate pitch and tempo discrimination of musicians and nonmusicians within a musical context. Using relatively familiar orchestral music as stimuli, excerpts were presented in pairs to the four hundred subjects. Pitch levels and tempi of the excerpts independently or in combination increased, decreased, or remained constant compared to unaltered versions. The study was designed to test the ability of subjects to discriminate how an altered excerpt differed in pitch and/or tempo from its original, unaltered presentation.

METHOD

Four hundred randomly selected subjects participated in the study; 200 were musicians and 200 were nonmusicians. The musicians were students enrolled in graduate and undergraduate music degree programs at the University of Texas at Austin and The Florida State University. Nonmusicians were defined as students not enrolled in music degree programs, not participating in music organizations, and having less than 2 years of private or group music study during their public school experience.

The orchestral music excerpts selected for the stimuli were those used in a previous study (Geringer, 1976). A representative list of 10 relatively familiar orchestral works from the Baroque through Romantic periods had been compiled by music history faculty, subject to the restriction that each excerpt have a different tonic. A pilot investigation ($N = 24$) indicated approximately 30 sec to be the optimal duration for these excerpts. A 30-sec excerpt from each of the 10 works was chosen (a) by the preponderance of tonic chordal structures, (b) by the lack of abrupt tempi changes, and (c) from the introduction or exposition section of the movement. (See Table 1 for a list of the 10 musical excerpts.)

A master tape was recorded with the 10 30-sec selections at a constant input voltage. A Lexicon Model 1200 Audio Time Compressor/Expander was used in conjunction with a Revox B77 variable speed tape recorder to prepare tapes for the experimental conditions. The Lexicon Model 1200 is a studio quality machine containing a microcomputer. This instrument is generally used in broadcast applications to compress or expand television material to fit a fixed period. The compressor/expander allows the pitch level of recorded material to be raised or lowered without altering the musical tempo during playback on a variable speed recorder. Alternatively, it can change tempo without changing recorded pitch level, or it will allow simultaneous tempo and pitch change. Unlike previous equipment, high-speed digital processing allows computer-generated electronic splicing virtually free from artifactual noise and distortion.

The experimental tape was prepared so that subjects heard each of the ten excerpts twice, presented in pairs for comparison. One member of each pair was an unaltered, approximately 30-sec version of each musical excerpt. Another member of each pair was altered by the compressor/expander in one of the following ways: pitch increased, decreased, or remained constant, while tempo increased, decreased, or remained constant. The three possibilities for pitch combined with the three tempo possibilities resulted in nine conditions of pitch/tempo alteration. A second condition of no change of either pitch or tempo was added to provide additional control. Pitch/tempo conditions were randomly assigned to each of the 10 excerpts. The pilot investigation showed little probability of differential excerpt bias ($F < 1.0$). Table 1 presents the 10 excerpts and the respective alterations in pitch and tempo.

The amount of change in either direction for both pitch and tempo was either +12% or -12%. A change in pitch level of 12% corresponds to a raising or lowering of pitch level by approximately one whole step. For example, subjects listening to an excerpt altered by a pitch increase alone heard the entire excerpt one whole tone higher than the original recording, while the original tempo was maintained (i.e., Beethoven's

Table 1
Orchestral Excerpts and Pitch/Tempo Alterations

Composer	Work	Movement	Measures	Key	Alteration Pitch	Alteration Tempo
Johann Sebastian Bach	*Brandenburg Concerto No. 5*	I	1–12	D	–	0
Ludwig van Beethoven	*Symphony No. 3*	I	1–26	E♭	+	+
Ludwig van Beethoven	*Symphony No. 8*	I	1–28	F	–	–
Johannes Brahms	*Symphony No. 1*	IV	61–76	C	0	–
Johannes Brahms	*Symphony No. 4*	I	1–15	e	0	+
George Frideric Handel	*Concerto Grosso, Op. 3, No. 2*	I	1–21	B♭	+	–
Franz Joseph Haydn	*Symphony No. 100*	III	1–22	G	+	0
Wolfgang Amadeus Mozart	*Symphony No. 40*	IV	1–39	g	–	+
Franz Schubert	*Symphony No. 8*	II	1–15	E	0	0
Peter Ilyitch Tchaikovsky	*Symphony No. 4*	II	41–56	A⁷	0	0

Note: + = increase; – = decrease; 0 = no alteration.

Symphony No. 8 excerpt was presented in G rather than F). Similarly, if an excerpt was altered by tempo increase alone, subjects heard an original tempo of 100 beats per minute at an altered tempo of 112 MM, while the original pitch level was maintained.

An additional measure of control was added to the experimental tapes to prevent subjects from rehearsing pitch levels and/or tempi after hearing the original presentation of the excerpts. Between members of each pair, subjects heard 12 sec of keyboard music in an unrelated key and tempo (excerpts from Vivaldi's *Seasons* concertos performed on synthesizer).

Subjects were tested in small groups of 10 to 15 in acoustically designed music studios. Excerpts were presented in counterbalanced orders. After listening to a given pair of excerpts, subjects were asked to determine how the second version of the excerpt differed, if at all, from the first. Subjects indicated on answer sheets whether the second version changed in pitch (by checking increase, decrease, or same) and/or tempo (by checking increase, decrease, or same) compared to the first version.

It should be noted that changes in pitch level and, to a lesser extent, changes in tempo will invariably result in differences in timbre as well. It would have been desirable from the viewpoint of experimental control to accomplish these pitch/tempo alterations without concomitant changes in timbre. This, however, is musically and practically impossible. The effect of pitch and tempo alteration on timbre was minimized by the use of a studio quality compressor/expander. In order to allow for these timbre and any other changes subjects conceivably might "hear" in the altered versions, space was provided on the answer sheet corresponding to each excerpt for subjects to indicate other perceived changes.

RESULTS

Initial analyses indicated that there were no significant differences with regard to geographical settings ($p > .05$), which was not surprising. Results also indicated that there were no significant differences between the number of correct responses of musicians versus nonmusicians ($p > .05$), which was somewhat surprising although consistent with some previous research.

Subjects did discriminate across the 10 musical excerpts [χ^2 (19, $N = 400$) = 373, $p < .001$] with regard to correct responses. Subjects also differentiated among the classifications (increase, decrease, and same) across trials [χ^2 (38, $N = 400$) = 2878, $p < .001$]. Table 2 presents total responses of subjects across excerpts. It can be observed that subjects did discriminate among the examples. In addition, the two trials intended to serve as control for the pitch and tempo alterations (Schubert &

Table 2
Total Response of Subjects across Excerpts (Correct Responses in Parentheses)

Excerpt	Pitch responses		Tempo responses	
Brahms (#4)	+	52	+	(215)
	0	(295)	0	152
	–	53	–	33
Handel	+	(118)	+	39
	0	99	0	92
	–	183	–	(269)
Schubert	+	67	+	78
	0	(239)	0	(240)
	–	94	–	82
Brahms (#1)	+	53	+	93
	0	(179)	0	119
	–	168	–	(188)
Mozart	+	154	+	(360)
	0	121	0	35
	–	(125)	–	5
Bach	+	37	+	94
	0	89	0	(148)
	–	(274)	–	158
Tchaikovsky	+	49	+	61
	0	(262)	0	(221)
	–	89	–	118
Beethoven (#3)	+	(251)	+	(294)
	0	90	0	72
	–	59	–	34
Beethoven (#8)	+	67	+	87
	0	106	0	135
	–	(227)	–	(178)
Haydn	+	(108)	+	56
	0	207	0	(195)
	–	85	–	148

Note: + = increase; – = decrease; 0 = no alteration.

Tchaikovsky) were perceived correctly by most students as having no changes.

The primary concern of this study was to investigate the ability of subjects to discriminate pitch and tempo alterations of relatively familiar orchestral excerpts. While it is possible that some of the subjects may possess a "fixed standard," enabling them to compare the initial presentation with an ideational standard, the second example compared to its original, unaltered version (or vice versa) was the principal consideration chosen for analysis. For example, in the first trial, initially presented as originally recorded and subsequently presented with a 12% increase in tempo, it can be seen that while 215 subjects perceived the tempo increase correctly, 185 subjects did not. Consequently, if all responses concerning tempo are analyzed in relationship to pitch (and vice versa), comparisons can be made regarding effects of these changes across the trials (see Table 3). Thus, it can be observed that when correct tempo responses were compared on the unaltered pitch trials, the perception of differences in tempo was not significant ($p > .05$). That is, when the pitch was not altered, subjects did not differentially discriminate among the tempo changes of faster, slower, or constant. When the pitch was increased, subjects did discriminate [χ^2 (2, $N = 400$) = 21, $p < .001$] across the categories, with the influence being greatest for the tempo increase classification. Also, when the pitch was decreased, there was a significant difference with increases in tempo still being discriminated most correctly [χ^2 (2, $N = 400$) = 115, $p < .001$].

Table 4 indicates that, across the trials, when tempo was maintained as originally recorded, there was a significant difference in pitch responses [χ^2 (3, $N = 400$) = 79, $p < .001$]. Pitch increases were correctly identified less frequently. When those tempo trials that increased were compared on the three pitch classifications, again there was a significant difference, with the unaltered classification indentified correctly most often [χ^2 (2, $N = 400$) = 70, $p < .001$]. Across the tempo decrease trials, subjects responded most correctly to the pitch decrease trials, relative to increased and unaltered pitch trials [χ^2 (2, $N = 400$) = 34, $p < .001$].

Table 3
Correct Responses for Tempo Changes with Pitch Constant

Tempo Change				Pitch Condition
+	0	0	–	
215	240	221	188	0
+	0		–	
294	195		269	+
+	0		–	
360	148		178	–

Table 4
Correct Responses for Pitch Changes with Tempo Constant

Pitch Change				Tempo Condition
+	0	0	–	
108	239	262	274	0
+	0	–		
251	295	125		+
+	0	–		
118	179	227		–

When subject responses are ranked according to number of correct answers across the alterations (Table 5), it can be observed that tempo increases exerted the greatest influence on correct identification. Apparently, subjects were better able to identify tempo increases compared to unaltered and decreased tempi, and compared to the three categories of pitch alteration [χ^2 (9, N = 400) = 471, p < .001]. The total number of correct responses for tempo changes was 1,506; total correct regarding pitch alterations was 1,103. There were 869 correct identifications of tempo increases, compared to 637 for tempo decreases. Correct responses to pitch increases totaled 477, correct pitch decrease responses totaled 626.

DISCUSSION

Many of the alterations in the music excerpts were perceived somewhat differentially, and it would appear useful to view each trial independently. Trials 3 & 7 were intended as control trials, in that

Table 5
Rank Order of Correct Responses by Pitch/Tempo Changes

Number Correct	Pitch	Tempo
545	+	+
510	0	+
485	–	+
483	0	0
479	0	0
422	–	0
405	–	–
387	+	–
367	0	–
303	+	0

nothing was altered. Yet, on Trial 3 (Schubert), 40% of subjects perceived some changes in pitch and tempo. Trial 7 (Tchaikovsky) apparently functioned quite similarly, with the exception that slightly more subjects perceived tempo and pitch decreases.

Responses on Trials 2 (Handel) & 4 (Brahms *Symphony No. 1*) also were somewhat similar. In Trial 2, over 65% of subjects incorrectly perceived the pitch to have decreased (when it actually was increased), while 67% indicated correctly a tempo decrease. For Trial 4, the decreased tempo on the second hearing could have influenced the perceived pitch decrease by 40% of the respondents. Trial 5 (Mozart) evidenced the greatest number of correct responses, 90% for the tempo increase. Again, the tempo perception conceivably "pulled up" the perception of pitch, where over 38% of the subjects responded incorrectly that the pitch had been increased. This example was also the fastest example initially of all the trials, which may account for the high accuracy in tempo change identification. One subject characterized this tempo as "musically outrageous."

On the Brahms *Symphony No. 4* excerpt (Trial 1), approximately 75% of the subjects perceived correctly that the initial pitch level was not altered, while somewhat fewer subjects (54%) identified correctly the tempo increase. The pitch decrease of Trial 6 (Bach) was perceived correctly by over 67% of subjects, yet only 37% indicated that the tempo remained constant while 40% perceived the tempo as slower in the second example. Trial 10 (Haydn) was misidentified by slightly over half the subjects as being unchanged in pitch, although approximately half perceived correctly no change in tempo. Trial 8 (Beethoven *Symphony No. 1*) was perceived correctly by a majority of the subjects as being both increased in pitch (63%) and tempo (74%). On Trial 9 (Beethoven *Symphony No. 8*), 57% of subjects perceived correctly the pitch decrease, yet only 45% identified the concomitant decrease in tempo.

It is interesting to note some of the comments written by subjects in the space provided for other perceived changes. As anticipated, many comments appeared related to perceived changes in timbre, i.e., texture changes, darker timbre, and bass changes. On 9 of the 10 trials, there were comments indicating that instrumentation had changed. This occurred even on the control trials, where subjects heard identical excerpts. Five of the trials received comments stating that the second example had been recorded by a different performing group. Several subjects stated that the dynamics had been altered, different music had been excerpted, or that the rhythm had been changed.

It should be remembered that excerpts from Vivaldi's *Seasons* concertos performed on synthesizer were presented to subjects between the first and second hearing of all 10 excerpts. Therefore, the Vivaldi interlude (intended to destroy musical memory) conceivably influenced perception of both the first and second hearing of each musical excerpt. Further, since subjects checked answers after hearing both versions plus the interlude, it is possible that the last heard example affected retroactively the perception of the first version as well. Additionally, if one views each trial as a whole, rather than as a strict discrimination task, it is conceivable that subjects may have responded in accordance with individual preferences for the variations in pitch and tempo. That is, given the relatively high quality of the pitch and tempo alterations, excerpts may have been heard as musically acceptable in both versions, and subjects may simply have preferred the musical context of, for example, the faster tempo version. This seems reasonable in view of several informal comments by subjects, stating that after a few measures of the second example, it was extremely difficult to remember pitch and tempo levels of the first heard example. The data reveal further support for this view by the apparent difficulty of the subjects to specify accurately the nature of the changes and corroborate the experimental decision not to investigate the perceived magnitude of changes between the versions.

As would be predicted by considerable previous research (c.f., review of literature), subjects identified correctly the examples of decreased pitch levels significantly more than pitch increase examples. However, it is surprising that tempo increase examples, rather than tempo decreases, were identified more accurately by subjects. This result is not consistent with most previous studies regarding tempo discrimination. Perhaps a general preference of subjects for faster tempi (LeBlanc, 1981; Wapnick, 1980a) may partially account for this finding. Comments written by subjects indicating that the faster version seemed "livelier" might corroborate this possibility. It is apparent that changes in tempo exerted the largest influence on correct identification compared to the pitch categories. This is consistent with the study of Wapnick (1980a) that used recorded piano music as stimuli. Regardless, continued investigation appears advisable. The additional study of listener discrimination of the elements of music and related preferences seems important, since these conceivably influence music instruction as well as the performance of music. The application of an audio compressor/expander to music research appears useful, in that it allows manipulation of musical elements independently and in combination within a musical context.

REFERENCES

Drake, A. H. (1968). An experimental study of selected variables in the performance of musical durational notation. *Journal of Research in Music Education, 16,* 329-338.

Geringer, J. M. (1976). Tuning preferences in recorded orchestral music. *Journal of Research in Music Education, 24,* 169-176.

Geringer, J. M. (1978). Intonational performance of ascending scales. *Journal of Research in Music Education, 26,* 32-40.

Geringer, J. M., & Madsen, C. K. (1981). Verbal and operant discrimination/preference for tone quality and intonation. *Psychology of Music, 9,* 26-30.

Geringer, J. M., and Witt, A. C. (1984). *An investigation of tuning perception and performance of string instruments.* Paper presented at the 10th International Seminar on Research in Music Education, Victoria, British Columbia.

Killian, J. N. (1982, February). *Tempo accuracy performance and perception.* Paper presented at the national convention of the Music Educators National Conference, San Antonio, TX.

Kuhn, T. L. (1974). Discrimination of modulated neat tempo by professional musicians. *Journal of Research in Music Education, 22,* 270-277.

Kuhn, T. L. (1977). Effects of dynamics, halves of exercise, and trial sequences on tempo accuracy. *Journal of Research in Music Education, 25,* 222-227.

Kuhn, T. L., & Gates, E. E. (1975). Effects of notational values, age, and example length on tempo performance accuracy. *Journal of Research in Music Education, 23,* 203-210.

LeBlanc, A. (1981). Effects of style, tempo, and performing medium on children's music preference. *Journal of Research in Music Education, 29,* 143-156.

Madsen, C. K. (1974). Sharpness and flatness in vocal performance. *Science de l'Art Scientific Aesthetics, 9,* 91-97.

Madsen, C. K. (1979). Modulated beat discrimination among musicians and nonmusicians. *Journal of Research in Music Education, 27,* 57-67.

Madsen, C. K., Edmonson, F. A., & Madsen, C. H., Jr. (1969). Modulated frequency discrimination in relationship to age and musical training. *Journal of the Acoustical Society of America, 46,* 1468-1472.

Madsen, C. K., & Geringer, J. M. (1976). Preferences for trumpet tone quality versus intonation. *Council of Research in Music Education Bulletin, 46,* 13-22.

Madsen, C. K., & Geringer, J. M. (1981). Discrimination between tone quality and intonation in unaccompanied flute/oboe duets. *Journal of Research in Music Education, 29,* 305-313.

Papich, G., & Rainbow, E. (1974). A pilot study of the performance practices of twentieth century musicians. *Journal of Research in Music Education, 22,* 24-34.

Salzberg, R. S. (1980). The effects of visual stimulus and instruction on intonation accuracy of string instrumentalists. *Psychology of Music, 8,* 42-49.

Wang, C. C. (1983). Discrimination of modulated music tempo by music majors. *Journal of Research in Music Education, 31,* 49-55.

Wapnick, J. (1980a). Pitch, tempo, and timbral preferences in recorded piano music. *Journal of Research in Music Education, 28,* 43-58.

Wapnick, J. (1980b). The perception of music and metronomic tempo change in musicians. *Psychology of Music, 8,* 3-12.

March 9, 1984

Clifford K. Madsen

JRME 1966, VOLUME 14, NUMBER 4, PAGES 266–275

The Effect of Scale Direction on Pitch Acuity in Solo Vocal Performance

The first indispensable requirement of music is a series of notes which stand in some recognizable relation to one another in respect to pitch.[1]

Without scales as a means of organizing the tonal material of music with respect to pitch, music as an art would be inconceivable.[2]

SCALES, which are inferred from music performed for centuries, have merited the arduous study of musicologists who have concerned themselves with the history of the development of our present diatonic scale. However, only casual mention is made in the literature regarding the performed direction of these scales. Although many attempts have been made to show that descending scale patterns were first used in primitive music, it appears that no author or investigator has conducted a study of the relationship between performed direction and specifically assigned pitches, i.e., intonation. Since the tonal element of music has been largely organized upon various scales, and because performers need to execute these scales with accurate intonation, it seems that an investigation should be made to determine the possibility of greater pitch acuity with respect to ascending or descending scale performance.

In reviewing the literature, it is found that while many historians believe descending scale patterns were first used in primitive music,[3]

---

[1] Glen Haydon, *Introduction to Musicology* (New York: Prentice-Hall, Inc., 1941), p. 159.

[2] Hubert H. Parry, *The Evolution of the Art of Music* (New York: D. Appleton and Co., 1930), p. 23.

[3] Parry, pp. 23-26. See also: Waldo Selden Pratt, *The History of Music* (New York: G. Schirmer, Inc., 1935), p. 27; and Robert W. Lundin, *An Objective Psychology of Music* (New York: The Ronald Press Co., 1953), p. 65.

these observations are mostly historical speculation. Authors of method books traditionally introduce scales in ascending patterns,[4] and the psychology of music texts[5] contain no information concerning the possibility of intonational differences between ascending and descending scale patterns. It is further noted that the studies directly concerned with intonation were conducted without considering the possibility that intonation and scale direction may have an important relationship.[6]

The writer conducted a pilot study to determine if the area warranted investigation.[7] Twelve members of seventh grade music classes served as subjects: four vocalists, four violinists, and four trombonists. Subjects were equated on the basis of IQ, musical aptitude, and musical achievement. Each of these groups was then divided into experimental and control groups. The subjects performed the C, D, and E harmonic minor scales, the control group performing the ascending form and the experimental group the descending form of the same scales. The performances were recorded and analyzed on a stroboscope which evaluated pitch according to the equi-tempered intonational system.[8] Since the total cent deviation for the group who performed the ascending scales was approximately four times as great as the total cent deviation for the group who

---

[4] See: C. H. Hohmann, *Practical Method for the Violin,* ed. L. L. Bostelmann, rev. ed. (New York: G. Schirmer, Inc., 1925), p. 5; Nicolas Laoureux, *A Practical Method for Violin,* trans. by Theodore Baker, third French ed. (New York: G. Schirmer, Inc., 1907), p. 10; C. Paul Herfurth, *A Tune A Day* (Boston: Boston Music Co., 1953), p. 17; Niccolo Vaccai, *Practical Italian Vocal Method,* trans. by Theodore Marzials, rev. ed. (New York: G. Schirmer, Inc., 1894), p. 3; D. A. Clippinger, *Class Method of Voice Culture* (Bryn Mawr, Pennsylvania: Oliver Ditson Co., 1932); Gerald R. Prescott and June C. Phillips, *Prep* (Minneapolis: Paul A. Schmitt Music Co., 1952), p. 9; Wayne Douglas, *Belwin Band Builder,* ed. Fred Weber (New York: Belwin Inc., 1953), p. 18; C. Paul Herfurth and Hugh M. Stuart, *Our Band Class Book* (New York: Carl Fischer, Inc., 1957), p. 19.

[5] See: James L. Mursell, *The Psychology of Music* (New York: W. W. Norton Co., 1937); Carl E. Seashore, *The Psychology of Music* (New York: McGraw-Hill, 1938); Max Schoen, *The Psychology of Music* (New York: Ronald Press, 1940); G. Revesz, *Introduction to the Psychology of Music* (New York: Ronald Press, 1953); Paul R. Farnsworth, *The Social Psychology of Music* (New York: The Dryden Press, 1958).

[6] See: Paul C. Greene, "Violin Intonation," *Journal of the Acoustical Society of America,* IX (1937), 43-44; James F. Nickerson, "Intonation of Solo and Ensemble Performance," *Journal of the Acoustical Society of America,* XXI (1949), 593; Herman L. Helmholtz, *Sensations of Tone,* trans. by A. J. Ellis (London: Longman, Green and Co., 1912); Charles Williamson, "Intonation in Musical Performance," *American Journal of Physics,* X (August 1942), 172; James A. Mason, "Comparison of Solo Ensemble Performances with Reference to Pythagorean, Just, and Equi-tempered Intonations," *Journal of Research in Music Education,* VIII (Spring 1960), 31; Wesley Pearse, *Intonation and Factors Influencing Its Attainment with Special Reference to the School Band* (Salt Lake City: Pearse Music Co., 1945).

[7] Clifford K. Madsen, "A Study of Directional Harmonic Minor Scale Solo Performance," *Utah Music Educator,* VII, No. 1 (January 1962), 13.

[8] Chromatic Stroboscope (Stroboconn), C. G. Conn Ltd., Elkhart, Indiana. An electronic device for rapid and accurate visual measurement of sound frequencies to within one hundredth part of one equi-tempered semitone.

performed the descending scales, the entire area seemed to warrant more thorough investigation.[9]

The purpose of this study was to determine: (a) if there are significant differences in the intonation of unaccompanied solo vocal performances with reference to scale direction; and (b) if there are any consistent patterns of intonational differences among the individual performers or groups of performers being investigated.

Six hypotheses were tested. It was hypothesized that: (a) all subjects perform with greater pitch acuity when descending the scale: (b) there is not a consistent pattern of differences between individual subjects or groups; (c) subjects with greater formal training perform with greater pitch acuity than untrained subjects and do not exhibit as much difference between ascending and descending patterns; (d) piano majors and violin majors sing with as much pitch acuity as do vocal music majors; (e) practice sessions improve intonation; (f) the relative difference between ascending and descending patterns remains constant regardless of practice.

PROCEDURES

Forty subjects participated in the study. Eight subjects were randomly chosen from five populations, representing five educational groups. The groups consisted of: (a) elementary school students; (b) high school students; (c) vocal undergraduate music majors; (d) piano undergraduate majors; (e) violin undergraduate music majors. Subjects were then randomly assigned to test conditions to eliminate any possibility of the results being explained on the basis of an order effect. The conditions were as follows: (a) *C* up-down; *D* up-down; (b) *C* down-up, *D* down-up; (c) *C* up-down, *D* down-up; (d) *C* down-up; *D* up-down; (e) *D* up-down, *C* up-down; (f) *D* down-up, *C* down-up; (g) *D* up-down, *C* down-up; (h) *D* down-up, *C* up-down.

Before the test began, all subjects were given the following recorded instructions:

This is an experiment which is concerned with scales. You are to sing the C and D major scales in both upward and downward patterns. You will be told which direction to sing first. After the first pattern there will be a brief pause and you will listen to music; then you will sing the other pattern. The first pitch of each scale will be played on the piano to help you get started. Please sing each pitch with the syllable "moo." The tempo or speed of the scales will be one second for each note; please listen to the metronome for this.

Each subject was then tested in accordance with the test condition to which he was randomly assigned. Prior to each performance, all subjects were given the first pitch of every scale from a piano tuned to the stroboscope. Between the directional patterns there was a two-minute

---

[9] A cent is the interval between two tones having as a basic frequency ratio the twelve-hundredth root of two (one hundredth of an equi-tempered semitone).

listening break which was intended to destroy tonal memory and to prohibit greater pitch acuity conceivably influenced from the preceding pattern.

Subjects from each of the five educational groups were divided, two subjects from each group, into four treatments. All subjects received tape-recorded instructions prior to the test to inform them of procedures. In the first treatment, subjects listened to five minutes of music in keys other than C and D to inhibit their mentally rehearsing the scales. Subjects in the second treatment were given a five-minute rehearsal session which was tape recorded and which was intended to improve pitch acuity on the ascending scales. Sixteen ascending C and D scales which were previously recorded with the piano were randomly presented. The first pitch of each scale was played for four seconds after which the entire scale was presented. Tape recorded instructions given to the second treatment were as follows: "You will not have a five-minute practice session on the scales. The first pitch of each scale will be played on the piano. Please sing along with the piano." Subjects in the third treatment were given a five-minute rehearsal session which was intended to improve their pitch acuity of descending scales. Sixteen descending C and D scales which were previously recorded with the piano were randomly presented. The first pitch of each scale was played for four seconds after which the entire scale was presented. Tape recorded instructions given to the third treatment were as follows: "You will now have a five-minute practice session on the scales. The first pitch of each scale will be played on the piano. Please sing along with the piano."

Subjects in the fourth treatment were given instructions explaining the purpose of the experiment and were instructed to perform accurately with no intonational difference between the ascending and descending patterns. Tape recorded instructions given to the fourth treatment were as follows:

> The group of subjects to which you belong has been chosen as an experimental group to test one of the major hypotheses of this study. It is assumed that all subjects will sing better in tune when they descend the scale as opposed to ascending the same scale, that is, you will sing better in tune when you go down than when you go up.
>
> Since this is the major basis for this study, please try as hard as possible to sing both directions *exactly the same*. Please try extremely hard to sing each direction with exactly the same intonation. Sing as accurately as possible on all pitches both up and down, but do not make any difference between the patterns.

Subjects then performed a second time. Previously subjects had been randomly reassigned to the original eight test conditions. The interims between the up-down, down-up patterns were again filled with two minutes of recorded music intended to destroy tonal memory and prohibit greater accuracy influenced by the first pattern. This recorded music was also used to eliminate the possibility of practice effects other than those intended, and it added a greater degree of control to the study.

After the completion of all recordings, tape loops were prepared from the master tapes. Each of the 2,560 loops contained one pitch which was analyzed on a stroboscope until a reading of cent variation from equitemperament could be determined. Comparative deviations were recorded in plus (sharp) and minus (flat) cents. All loops were analyzed four times to ensure rigid evaluation. An A440 tape loop prepared from the United States Bureau of Standards signal was used to periodically check the accuracy of the analyzing apparatus.

RESULTS

The main problem concerning the hypothesis that all subjects perform with greater pitch acuity when descending the scale was substantiated at a level of significance above .01 percent. The obtained results regarding pitch acuity during unaccompanied solo vocal performance of the descending scale were significant enough that, on the basis of chance

TABLE 1

ANALYSIS OF VARIANCE

Source of Variation	Sum of Squares	d.f.	Mean Square	F
Between Treatments	36,334	3	12,111	1
Between Groups	166,436	4	41,609	2.02
III vs. IV and V	29,365	1	29,365	1.43
I and II vs. III, IV, and V	93,479	1	93,479	4.54[a]
I vs. II	42,304	1	42,304	2.06
IV vs. V	1,288	1	1,288	1
II vs. I, III, IV, and V				
Treatments vs. Groups	419,161	12	34,930	1.70
Error$_1$	411,650	20	20,583	
Between Individuals	1,033,581	39	26,502	13.90[c]
Between Control and Experimental	1,697	1	1,697	1
Between Directions (Up and Down)	997,146	1	997,146	85.46[d]
(Control and Experimental) vs. Direction	3,413	1	3,413	1
(Control and Experimental and Direction) vs. Individuals	1,365,179	117	11,668	6.12[c]
Treatments vs. (Control and Experimental)	18,283	3	6,094	3.20[a]
Treatments vs. Direction	39,108	3	13,036	6.84[b]
Treatments vs. (Control and Experimental) vs. Direction	30,546	3	10,182	5.34[b]
Groups vs. Direction	85,821	4	21,455	11.25[b]
Treatments vs. (Control and Experimental and Direction) vs. Individuals	1,191,421	104	11,456	6.01[b]
Error$_2$	305,189	160	1,907	
Total	3,706,205	319		

[a] Significant at the 5% level.
[b] Significant at the 1% level.
[c] Significant at the .05% level.
[d] Significant at the .01% level.

alone, they could occur less than one time in 10,000. Table 1 (Analysis of Variance) indicates that when comparing direction (up and down) an F ratio of 85.46 was obtained. Table 2 shows the total cent deviation of the forty individual performances on two ascending scales and two descending scales for a total of 320 observations, each of which is a total cent deviation value summed across the eight tones of each scale. In only one instance was the cent deviation greater for the descending than for the ascending rendition of the same scale. The ascending total cent deviation (23,921) was approximately four times as great as the total cent deviation for the descending patterns (6,058). This difference was the most important result of the study, and it held over all treatments and between comparisons of experimental and control conditions. The first hypothesis is clearly substantiated at a level of significance high enough to indicate that there should be no question as to the validity of the proposition.

TABLE 2

COMPARISON OF TOTAL CENT DEVIATION FOR DIRECTIONAL
PERFORMANCES WITH INDIVIDUAL GROUPS

	Group 1	Group 2	Group 3	Group 4	Group 5	Total
Ascending	4,302	6,948	5,112	2,764	3,795	23,921
Descending	1,870	1,551	1,110	576	951	6,085

It was hypothesized that the relative difference between ascending and descending patterns would remain constant regardless of practice. The experiment has shown this hypothesis to be correct (Table 3). The relative difference between the up and down patterns was approximately the same, although there was a slight trend for the intonation of the ascending scales to improve and that of the descending scales to become worse.

The hypothesis that practice would improve intonation was not substantiated. The Analysis of Variance Table shows that the difference

TABLE 3

TOTAL CENT DEVIATION FOR CONTROL AND EXPERIMENTAL GROUPS
COMPARED WITH DIRECTIONAL PERFORMANCES

	Control	Experimental
Ascending	12,406	11,515
Descending	2,952	3,106

between the control and experimental mean square F ratio was less than one, and, therefore, insignificant. There was a significant difference between the various results of the experimental treatments. The F ratio between the control and experimental treatments was significant at the 5 percent level. The overall effect of the treatments did alter performance, but in the opposite direction from that predicted.

The pitch acuity of the two treatment groups (1 and 4) without intervening practice improved slightly, if not significantly, as far as cent deviation was concerned, while that of the other two groups (2 and 3), who were given practice designed to induce improvement, became slightly worse. The practice sessions were extremely short and were not intended to test the effect of extensive practice on intonation, but rather to add an extra control to the study. It was felt that if the directional variable held across treatments which were designed to influence performance in ways opposite to those being tested, there could be no doubt as to the validity of the directional variable.

A finding of importance concerned the differences between individuals. Results indicated that the mean cent deviation for the individual subjects when averaged across treatments, groups, and directions was highly significant and showed a great deal of variation. This also indicated that individual scores could not be precisely predicted by knowing the group or treatment to which a subject belonged. Some of the best and worst performers were found throughout groups and treatments, and this indicated that individuals were not from a homogeneous group. These findings substantiated the hypotheses that there would be no consistent patterns of differences between individuals.

It was predicted that subjects with greater formal training would perform with greater pitch acuity than untrained subjects, and the difference between ascending and descending patterns would be less. The between groups F ratio was insignificant, which showed that there was no overall difference when all groups were considered simultaneously. That is, when averaged over the levels of treatments and direction, and including control and experimental renditions, the means were not significantly different. However, there was a significant difference between the pre-college groups (elementary and high school) when compared to the college groups with musical training (vocal, piano, violin). The F ratio was 4.54 which was significant at the 5 percent level. The other comparisons were insignificant. Elementary subjects did not differ significantly from violinists and neither did vocalists differ significantly from pianists and violinists when the latter two were combined. The preceding results sustained the hypothesis that piano majors and violin majors sing with as much pitch acuity as vocal majors.

DISCUSSION

The scope of this study did not include the succeeding material, for generalizations which are projected are not valid unless specific controls are utilized to test certain variables. However, the writer believes that the performing musician and the music educator might be interested in some additional information which moves beyond the limited range of the study and suggests further research.

Group Patterns

Piano majors performed with more pitch acuity than any other group on both ascending and descending scales. This carried over to all other combinations of circumstances: control as opposed to experimental, or up as compared to down. The difference was not statistically significant, but theoretically it may be very important. The second-best group (as far as pitch acuity is concerned) was consistently the violin majors. However, it must be emphasized that neither pianists nor violinists differed significantly from vocal majors, and there was tremendous variation among individuals. The question as to why these groups consistently performed with greater pitch acuity than did the vocal majors should be investigated. A study should be designed to find if this pattern is consistent and attempt to isolate the variables contributing to the results if they should hold with cross-validation.

Another unusual circumstance concerns the superiority of the elementary group over the college vocal majors on ascending scale performance, whereas the younger students were inferior in performing descending scales. Why should the high school students perform worst on the ascending scales among all groups but better than the elementary when descending? The factor of individual difference is important but does not provide complete information. It might be that present methods of teaching music in elementary and high school tend to make students progressively worse on ascending scales. This receives slight additional confirmation when it is recalled that the treatment group which was given practice to improve pitch acuity on the ascending scales actually decreased in average pitch acuity after such practice. This information suggests another unanswered question which should be investigated.

Larger samples should also be gathered to try to design experiments which would hold training constant and attempt to explain the better performance of instrumentalists over vocally trained students. This difference was not statistically significant, but a replication of this or a similar type experiment could ascertain the exact degree of this difference and investigate significant variables. Teaching methods should be studied and both younger and older subjects should be compared while being matched on amount and type of early or additional training.

Individual Patterns

One grade school subject had been classified as a non-singer, and, after being randomly chosen, was reluctant to participate in the study because of this previous classification. It was noted that this subject had far less total cent deviation than most subjects. The descending pattern of the first C scale was unique in that it was almost a perfect reproduction of an equi-tempered scale with the exception of the seventh degree, which was sung B ♭ instead of B ♮. It might have been such unique activity which stimulated the non-singer classification, but it could be observed that this subject was sensitive to pitch, had a range of at least more than an octave, and had the ability to sing. These findings suggest research in this area. It might be found that such students could be helped with methodology primarily containing descending scalar material.

Another interesting observation concerns those subjects who were purported to have "perfect pitch." There were five in this category: one vocalist, two pianists, and two violinists. The most striking thing observed is the wide difference in these subjects' performances when compared to each other. It should be noted that these subjects exhibited the most difference regarding scale direction and intonation. Also, these subjects did not conform to the equi-tempered standard, which would seem likely, especially for the pianists. This suggests research concerning scale direction and intonation using only subjects who have "perfect pitch."

Generalization of Findings to Other Scales

It will be noted that the relative cent deviation difference between ascending and descending patterns was almost exactly the same for the pilot study as it was for the present experiment. This fact adds to the reliability of the present study. It should be observed also that the pilot study used the C, D, and E harmonic minor scales. In addition to vocal performances, the pilot study employed instrumentalists who performed on the trombone and violin. Therefore, it would appear that findings derived from the present study could be generalized to other scale constructions and also to other performing media.

Explanation of the Phenomenon

It was not the purpose of this study to ascertain why there is an intonational difference with respect to scale direction, but only to find if this difference exists and to what degree it is significant. However, theories are presented for the purpose of clarifying areas for future research.

It would seem that at least two explanations are pertinent in attempting to answer why this directional difference exists: (a) there might be a difference in the aural perception of melodic lines with reference to direction; and (b) the neuro-muscular reproduction of the conceptualized pitch might be dependent upon physical factors related to melodic direction. The evidence seems to support both of these tenets. The violinists (who performed with their instruments in the pilot study) exhibited the directional difference to almost the same degree as did those subjects who vocalized. String players considered ascending from an open string technically more advantageous, which would suggest that the difference is one of perception and not reproduction. However, the subjects who had "perfect pitch" demonstrated the greatest intonational difference with respect to direction, which might suggest that the difference exists only because of physical limitations when ascending the scale. It seems possible that both perception and neuro-muscular response might be responsible for this directional difference. Further research should be conducted in these areas to determine a basis for explaining this phenomenon.

CONCLUSIONS

On the basis of this study, it was concluded that:

1. There is a highly significant difference between the intonation of unaccompanied solo vocal performance with reference to scale direction. Vocal pitch acuity is highly superior when subjects descend rather than ascend the same C or D scale.

2. There are no consistent patterns of differences between individual subjects or groups.

3. Subjects with greater formal training perform with greater pitch acuity than untrained subjects. There is also more variability among untrained subjects and the relative difference between ascending and descending performances is markedly different from trained subjects.

4. Piano majors and violin majors sing with as much pitch acuity as do vocal majors.

5. Short, five-minute practice sessions do not significantly improve intonation. The manipulation of treatments in the study led to results which tended to be in the opposite direction of that predicted, but which were not statistically significant. The fact that treatment effects were not significantly different invalidates the contention that practice sessions improve intonation.

6. The relative difference between ascending and descending patterns remains constant regardless of practice.

Florida State University

DISCRIMINATION OF MODULATED BEAT TEMPO BY PROFESSIONAL MUSICIANS

Terry Lee Kuhn

JRME 1974, VOLUME 22, NUMBER 4, PAGES 270–277

Thirty professional musicians were presented with 12 stimulus examples consisting of beats produced on a metronome. Initial beat tempo rate (60, 90, 120, and 150 beats per minute) and tempo modulation direction (Decrease, Increase, and Same) comprised the independent variables. Two dependent variables, number of correct responses on modulation directions and time required to discriminate a tempo change, measured the effect of tempo rate and modulation. Subjects correctly identified significantly more Decrease and Increase examples than Same examples ($F = 8.92$; df = 2,58; $p < .01$). More Decrease examples were correctly identified than Increase examples; however, that difference was not significant. Decrease examples were identified in significantly less time than Increase examples ($F = 24.09$; df = 1,29; $p < .01$). Time differences attributable to tempo rates and interactions were not significant. A replication of this experiment by Randall S. Moore using high school music students as subjects yielded markedly similar results.

Key Words: aural discrimination, fundamentals, musician, statistical analysis, testing.

Beat is a term used to define the perception of a steady, recurring pulse. Single beats consist of a point in time/space and a duration to the next point (Pankaskie, 1965). In fast tempo a short time duration occurs between points; in slow tempo a longer time duration occurs between points. Beat tempo is commonly referred to as the rate of speed of a composition. A beat tempo can modulate, or change, by speeding up or slowing down.

Beat tempo and beat tempo modulation are essential elements of Western music, yet have been the subjects of relatively little research. Musicologists attest to the importance of tempo and tempo variation (Kolisch, 1943; Sachs, 1952; Turner, 1938). Farnsworth concludes that "of the variables which give meaning to music, tempo plays the largest role. . . . The listener is most likely to change the affective terms with which he describes a piece of music whenever its tempo is appreciably slowed or hastened. Other alternations of the musical matrix change less strikingly how he will describe the music he is hearing."[1]

In an attempt to establish criterion validity for the *Seashore Measures of Musical Talent*, Smith (1957) found positive correlations of .66 and .44 between total errors on rhythm performance of a motor task and discrimination scores on the rhythm subtest and on the auditory time subtest, respectively. This finding indicates that subjects producing beats evidenced more variance than subjects reproducing rhythms. Drake found "a marked tendency for subjects to shorten beats or play faster than a given, or required, beat while performing musical durational notation."[2] In contrast to Drake's findings, Greer (1966) reported data indicating that most subjects performed beats longer than the given beat tempo in an experiment testing the effect of different types of notation on temporal deviation.

The present experiment[3] investigated the discrimination accuracy and time required by professional musicians to identify a modulation in beat tempo. Specifically, it was hypothesized that there would be no significant differences in the (1) number of correct responses earned by subjects on Decrease, Increase, and Same examples; (2) time required by subjects to identify a modulation in beat tempo at 60, 90, 120, and 150 beats per minute; and (3) time required by subjects to identify beat modulation Decrease and Increase.

Subjects

Thirty professional musicians participated in this experiment. These musicians were performers or teachers whose primary income was earned through performing, conducting, or teaching applied music at the university level. Available subjects were selected from the University of Maryland, American University, the United States Air Force Band, and a professional musical theater orchestra.

Independent Variables

Two independent variables investigated in this experiment were initial tempo rate and tempo modulation direction. The auditory

---

[1] P. R. Farnsworth, *The Social Psychology of Music* (Ames, Iowa: Iowa State University Press, 1969), p. 83.

[2] A. H. Drake, "An Experimental Study of Selected Variables in the Performance of Musical Durational Notation," *Journal of Research in Music Education*, Vol. 16 (1968).

[3] This experiment was supported by a Faculty Research Award from the University of Maryland.

stimulus consisted of beats produced by a metronome and recorded on one channel of a stereo tape recording.[4] Four initial beat tempos were chosen to represent slow through fast tempos: 60, 90, 120, and 150 beats per minute. The initial rate for each of the four tempos continued for the first 6 seconds of each example after which the rate either modulated (increased or decreased) or stayed the same. Madsen, Edmonson, and Madsen, studying discrimination of pitch modulation, reported that "more same responses were missed than any other category" and suggested that studies with similar designs should also control for guessing by including a "same" category because musicians have a "propensity to 'hear' differences that do not exist."[5] A similar conclusion was drawn by Sergeant (1973).

Pilot studies and related materials (Madsen and Graham, 1970) suggested the use of a modulation rate of one beat per minute change every second. This modulation was accomplished by setting a metronome at the initial beat tempo for 6 seconds after which 10 seconds of continuous modulation was produced.

Sergeant (1973) suggests the use of a randomized order for items on psychological tests concerned with perception to insure that judgments are ". . . made solely on the evidence of stimuli contained within that item. No judgment made in response to one item should be influenced by a relationship to or comparison with other items. For this reason, it is generally desirable to avoid any kind of progressive structure or order of difficulty of items in a test."[6] All subjects were acquainted with the procedures and the type of stimulus examples. Half of the subjects then heard a randomized presentation of the 12 examples and the other half of the subjects were presented with the reverse order.

Dependent Variables

Reaction time, to the nearest .01 second, required by subjects to perceive a tempo modulation was measured using an electric stop clock. The stop clock was activated by a noise-operated relay triggered from a 1000-Hz sine wave tone recorded on the alternate channel of the stereo tape recording. A switch mounted in a chassis box was connected to both the stop clock and the subject's headphones. Pressing the switch terminated the sound to the headphones and stopped the clock simul-

---

[4] The following equipment was used in this experiment: Franz electric metronome, Model LM-FB-5; Sony TC-630 stereo tape recorder; Scotch 206 recording tape; Hunter noise operated relay, Model 320S; Lafayette stop clock, Model 54014; toggle switch; Koss stereo headphones, Model PRO 4AA; Sennheiser stereo headphones, Model HD 414.

[5] C. K. Madsen, F. A. Edmonson III, and C. H. Madsen, Jr., "Modulated Frequency Discrimination in Relationship to Age and Musical Training," *The Journal of the Acoustical Society of America*, Vol. 46 (1969), pp. 1468-1472.

[6] D. Sergeant, "Measurement of Pitch Discrimination," *Journal of Research in Music Education*, Vol. 21 (1973), pp. 3–19.

taneously. Thereby, subjects did not receive confirmation concerning the correctness of responses. Subjects heard only the beat modulation examples that were recorded on one channel of the recording. After pressing the switch, subjects circled a response on an answer sheet to indicate whether the tempo was perceived as increasing, decreasing, or staying the same. The experimenter recorded the elapsed time from the stop clock and reset the subject's switch. Time responses could vary between 0 and 16 seconds. Correct time responses for examples which increased and decreased could be from 6+ through 16. As the stimulus beats did not begin to modulate until 6 seconds had elapsed, any time response occurring between 0 and 6 was classified as an incorrect response. A correct time response for a Same example was 16, as subjects were not to press the switch stopping the clock unless a tempo change was perceived.

Individually tested subjects responded to 12 examples including four Increase, four Decrease, and four Same items each presented at initial tempos of 60, 90, 120, and 150 beats per minute. The number of correct responses scored on the Increase, Decrease, and Same categories was compared. However, because Same examples were included as a control for guessing and because the time expectation for correct Same responses differed from correct Increase and Decrease responses, Same examples were not included in the time data analyses presented in Tables 3 and 4.

Results

Results presented in Table 1 indicate that correct responses made by subjects on the modulation directions contained at least one significant difference among the three means ($F = 8.92$; df $= 2,58$; p $< .01$).

A Newman-Keuls Sequential Range Test of the three modulation direction means presented in Table 2 indicates that Decrease and Increase examples were correctly identified a significantly greater number of times than were Same examples. More Decrease examples were iden-

Table 1

ANOVA Summary Table Comparing Number of Correct Responses by Subjects on Tempo Modulation Direction Examples

Source	SS	df	MS	F
Between Subjects	18.90	29		
Within Subjects	46.00	60		
Modulation Direction	10.87	2	5.44	8.92*
Residual	35.13	58	.61	
Total	64.90	89		

* p < .01.

Table 2
Mean Number of Correct Responses Per Subject on Three Tempo Modulation Directions: Newman-Keuls Sequential Range Test*

	Decrease	Increase	Same
	3.73	3.47	2.90

*No significant differences exist between groups underscored by the line. All other comparisons between pairs of means are significant at the .05 level.

tified correctly than were Increase examples; however, that difference was not significant.

Results comparing the time required by subjects to respond to tempo modulations presented in Table 3 indicate that no significant differences existed among the means of the four initial rates $(F = .73;$ df $= 3,87;$ NSD). A significant difference did exist between the response means of modulation increases and decreases $(F = 24.09;$ df $= 1,29;$ p $< .01)$. The rate by modulation interaction was not significant $(F = 1.81;$ df $= 3,87;$ NSD).

Table 4 presents the mean number of seconds required by subjects to respond to stimulus examples at four initial tempo rates and two tempo modulation directions. Results from Table 3 indicate that the only significant difference was between modulation Decrease (11.64 seconds and Increase (13.14 seconds) means.

Table 3
ANOVA Summary Table Comparing Subject Response Times on Examples Presented at Four Initial Tempo Rates and Two Tempo Modulation Directions

Source	SS	df	MS	F
Between Subjects (S)	430.59	29		
Within Subjects	1070.74	210		
Rate (R)	9.38	3	3.13	.73
S x R	374.66	87	4.31	
Modulation (M)	134.63	1	134.63	24.09*
S x M	162.08	29	5.59	
R x M	22.88	3	7.63	1.81
S x R x M	367.11	87	4.22	
Total	1501.33	239		

*p < .01.

Table 4
Mean Number of Seconds Required by Subjects to Respond at Two Tempo Modulation Directions and Four Initial Tempo Rates

Modulation Direction	Rate				
	60	90	120	150	Mean
Decrease	12.06	10.83	11.84	11.84	11.64
Increase	12.80	13.29	13.30	13.18	13.14
Mean	12.46	12.06	12.57	12.51	12.39

Discussion

Analysis of the number of correct responses made by subjects on the modulated beat discrimination task concerning Increase, Decrease, and Same examples indicated that Decrease examples were correctly identified most frequently, followed by Increase and then Same examples. Mean Decrease-Same and Increase-Same differences were significant, but the mean Decrease-Increase difference was not significant (Table 2). Therefore, the first hypothesis of no significant differences among the mean number of correct responses earned by subjects on Decrease, Increase, and Same examples was rejected.

Statistical analysis of data failed to reject the second hypothesis of no significant differences among the mean number of seconds required by subjects to respond at four initial tempo rates.

Beat tempos that decreased were identified significantly sooner than beat tempos that increased. Therefore, the third hypothesis, which stated that there would be no significant differences in the time required by subjects to identify beat modulation Decreases and Increases, was rejected.

An alternative hypothesis explaining the results of this study suggests that a regular recurring pulse, such as beats per minute, changes at a different proportional rate when increasing and decreasing; that is, the tempo modulation from 90 to 91 represents less change than the movement from 90 to 89. Under this alternative hypothesis subjects would have been expected to identify changes at slower tempos sooner than changes at faster tempos, and differences among the four initial rates would have been expected. Results concerning initial tempo rates do not support this alternative hypothesis.

If subjects can discriminate tempo decreases more accurately and sooner than tempo increases, then performance errors would be expected to include primarily tempo increases. Tempo performance results consistent with this theory were reported by Drake (1968). Results of the present study parallel pitch discrimination findings reported by Madsen,

Edmonson, and Madsen in that "more same responses were missed than any other category."[7]

It is suggested that future studies using younger or less experienced subjects extend the stimulus examples to a length of 20 seconds, because subjects with less training and less consistent attention to beat tempos would probably require more time to respond than the professional musicians selected for this study.[8] Implications for at least three lines of related research are suggested by this experiment: (1) replication of the design of this study using actual music as the stimulus examples, (2) use of the methodology of this study at the initial tempo rate of 90 beats per minute to determine the tempo modulation discrimination time required by subjects representing different ages and amounts of musical training, and (3) transfer of this idea from a discrimination study to a music performance study.

References

Drake, A. H., "An Experimental Study of Selected Variables in the Performance of Musical Durational Notation," *Journal of Research in Music Education,* Vol. 16 (Winter 1968), pp. 329–338.

Farnsworth, P. R., *The Social Psychology of Music* (Ames, Iowa: Iowa State University Press, 1969).

Greer, R. D., "The Effect of Selected Notation on Temporal Deviation," (master's thesis, Florida State University, Tallahassee, Florida, 1966).

Kolisch, R., "Tempo and Character in Beethoven's Music," *The Musical Quarterly,* Vol. 29 (1943), pp. 169–187, 291–312.

Madsen, C. K., and R. Graham, "The Effect of Integrated Schools on Performance of Selected Music Tasks of Black and White Students," (unpublished

---

[7] Madsen, Edmonson, and Madsen, pp. 1468–1472.

[8] This experiment was replicated by Randall S. Moore at Florida State University using high school students attending a summer music camp as subjects. These students made many more errors than did the professional musicians; however, results were markedly similar to those reported in this study. The greater number of errors may be partially attributable to the length of the examples, which were identical to those used in the present study. Specifically, Table 1 analysis of the high school subject's data produced at least one significant difference among the three means ($F = 32.07$; df $= 2,48$; p $< .01$). The mean number of correct responses to Decrease, Increase, and Same examples were 3.73, 2.83, and 2.17, respectively. It will be noted that the mean number of correct responses for Decrease examples was the same as the mean earned by professional musicians (see Table 2). The means earned by high school subjects for Increase and Same examples were much smaller than those earned by professional musicians. Each of these three means was significantly different from the other two. Table 3 analysis of time response data from the high school subjects produced a significant difference only on Modulation Direction ($F = 8.82$; df $= 1,29$; p $< .01$). This result parallels the present findings. It would appear that either the additional training/experience and/or age results in increased ability to discriminate tempo modulations.

paper, Florida State University), presented at Music Educator's National Conference National Convention, Chicago, Illinois, 1970).

Madsen, C. K., F. A. Edmonson, III, and C. H. Madsen, Jr., "Modulated Frequency Discrimination in Relationship to Age and Musical Training," *The Journal of the Acoustical Society of America*, Vol. 46 (1969), pp. 1468–1472.

Pankaskie, L., "Rudiments of Rhythm," (unpublished paper, Florida State University, Tallahassee, Florida, 1965).

Sachs, C., "Rhythm and Tempo: An Introduction," *The Musical Quarterly*, Vol. 38 (1952), pp. 384–398.

Sergeant, D., "Measurement of Pitch Discrimination," *Journal of Research in Music Education*, Vol. 21 (Spring 1973), pp. 3–19.

Smith, O. W., "Relationship of Rhythm Discrimination to Meter Rhythm Performance," *Journal of Applied Psychology*, Vol. 41 (1957), pp. 365–369.

Turner, E. O., "Tempo Variation; with Examples from Elgar," *Music and Letters*, Vol. 19 (1938), pp. 308–323.

■ University of Maryland
College Park, Maryland

Alan H. Drake

JRME 1968, VOLUME 16, NUMBER 4, PAGES 329–338

An Experimental Study of Selected Variables in the Performance of Musical Durational Notation

THE ACHIEVEMENT OF high-quality standards of performance in rhythm is a goal of all conscientious music teachers and conductors of performing organizations. Substantial research in the areas of reading and performance of musical durational notation can be a significant aid toward the achievement of this goal.

Most of the studies in the field of rhythm during the first half of this century were performed by psychologists, and practically none of them attempted to measure response to actual notation. Those studies that did use notation did not attempt to measure the rhythmic response with a high degree of temporal accuracy. Even today, many excellent studies involving response to notated rhythm have relied upon subjective evaluation of the response to the notation.

This study was basically exploratory in nature and its general purpose was two-fold.[1] First, it was an exploration of the way trained players actually respond to rhythmic notation; and second, it was an attempt to develop a highly accurate instrumentation which would measure precisely the increments of time involved. Thus the scoring of error went beyond the usual "right or wrong" and attempted to measure exactly "how right" or "how wrong." The study was highly limited in the amount of information it attempted to uncover, but the results have pointed out some new directions in which future research in rhythmic response can be implemented.

PURPOSE OF THE STUDY

This study was designed to measure and compare three variables in performances of musical durational notation by musically trained subjects and to assess the influence of a specific experimental treatment upon the variables. The variables, as defined, were:

1. *Beat reproduction;* the ability of a subject to reproduce a given beat.

2. *Beat steadiness;* the ability of a subject to maintain a regularly recurring beat.

---

[1] This article is based upon the writer's doctoral dissertation of the same title (Florida State University, 1965).

SAMPLE ITEMS AND TEST ITEMS

Sample
Sample
Item No. 1
Item No. 2
Item No. 3
Item No. 4
Item No. 5
Item No. 6
Item No. 7
Item No. 8

Figure 1

3. *Beat subdivision accuracy;* the ability of a subject to place the beginning of each note within an observed beat into temporal positions so as to coincide with the mathematical divisions implied by the notation.

The experimental treatment was inducement to use imaged subdivisions of the beat, or to mentally divide a beat into two or more equal parts.

THE EXPERIMENT

The Sample

Thirty-two subjects were selected at random from the 218 freshman students enrolled in the Purdue University Bands in the fall of 1964. The sample consisted of students that graduated in 1964 from 31 different secondary schools in ten states. Since Purdue University does not have a music school, all of the subjects were enrolled in nonmusical curriculums. All of the subjects had been members of high school bands and had played their instruments for an average of 7.25 years. Before the beginning of the testing, the subjects were randomly assigned to either the control group or the experimental group, each of which numbered 16.

Test Items

Eight test items and two sample items consisting of durational notation were composed (Figure 1). These items contained combinations of sixteenth, eights, and quarter notes in 2/4, 3/4, 4/4, and 5/4 meters. The eight items were placed in randomized order and numbered from one to eight.

Apparatus

The subject responses and a one-second continuing time line were recorded on a multi-channel FM instrumentation tape recorder. The one-second time line also served as a metronome by producing clicks with the turn of a switch. Each subject responded to the written notation by tapping a key which produced the electrical impulses for the tape and which also produced an audible 1000 cps pure tone. (See Figure 2 for diagram of experimental apparatus.) The data contained on the magnetic tape were transfered into visual form through the use of a Dynograph chart recorder.

Experimental Procedure

Both the pretest and the posttest were given during a 30-minute appointment with each subject. The subject was first given an opportunity to acquaint himself with the apparatus and to practice tapping the key. A prepared set of general instructions was then read to the subject. Each test item was then presented individually on a card. After the subject tapped out the two sample test items, he was required to tap out the eight test items. Order and practice effects were controlled by changing the order of presentation in accordance with a Latin Square arrangement. After each test item was presented to the subject he was allowed 15 seconds to examine it. At the conclusion of the 15-second period the

DIAGRAM OF EXPERIMENTAL APPARATUS

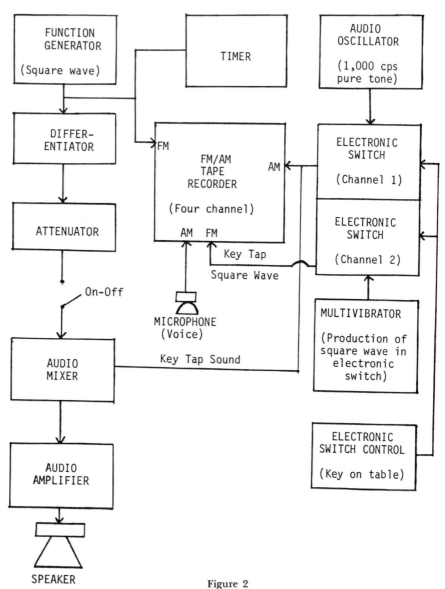

Figure 2

tape recorder was started, the metronomic clicks of one second interval were sounded, and the subject started when ready. The instructions had previously asked him to play the notation in the tempo indicated by the clicks. The clicking of the beat was sounded through the beginning of the second beat of the performance of the item and then silenced. This procedure was followed until all eight test items were tapped and recorded. This completed the pretest.

Then followed a period of instruction. Control group subjects were motivated to improve in performance by being told that practice would have a positive effect on their ability to play the items. Experimental subjects were given an explanation of imaged subdivisions of the beat and were asked to use them in the posttest. They were motivated to improve in performance by being told that the use of imaged subdivisions of the beat would have a positive effect upon their ability to play the items. The experimental treatment was that of inducement to use imaged subdivisions of the beat. After a five-minute practice period in which the subjects were given a sheet of eight items similar to the actual items, the posttest was presented. Except for the elimination of the two sample items, the posttest was identical to the pretest.

METHODS OF DATA ANALYSIS

Processing of Raw Data

The raw data consisted of 7,680 beats, 5,184 of which were subdivided into one, two, three, or four parts. Each beat length and note length was measured to the nearest half millimeter and recorded in the corresponding milliseconds. The lengths were measured from the beginning of one note or beat to the beginning of the next note or beat. The observed beat lengths for each beat, the required beat length (the one-second time line) for each item, and the beat subdivision deviation for each beat as computed by hand were transferred to IBM data processing cards in order that the desired statistical analyses could be run.

Error Measurements Used in Data Analysis

For each variable, variances based upon error deviations were computed following carefully defined specifications. The variances as obtained for each test item performed were the figures used in the statistical analyses. The definitions of the deviation and variance for each variable follow:

1. *Beat reproduction.* The beat reproduction deviation is the difference between a required beat length and the arithmetical mean of the observed beat lengths in a particular test item. The beat reproduction variance is the square of the beat reproduction deviation.

2. *Beat steadiness.* The beat steadiness deviation is the difference between an observed beat length and the mean of the observed beat lengths in a particular test item. The beat steadiness variance is the mean of the squared beat steadiness deviations for each item.

3. *Beat subdivision accuracy.* The beat subdivision deviation is the sum of the differences between the observed lengths of the notes within a particular beat as performed and the lengths of those notes as determined by the commonly accepted mathematical divisions for durational notation. The beat subdivision variance is the mean of the squared beat subdivision deviations in each item.

Statistical Analyses

The following data were computed:

1. The variances based upon error deviations for beat reproduction, beat steadiness, and beat subdivision accuracy for each test item as performed by each subject in the pretest and the posttest.

2. Analyses of variance to determine the significance of differences between subjects attributable to groups, tests, and items.

3. Correlations between all combinations of the variables by groups and tests.

4. Rankings of subjects by pretest scores and their relation to high school class ranks, instruments played, years of private instruction, and general musical performing ability.

SUMMARY OF RESULTS

Variances of the Experimental Variables

An examination of the variances for each experimental variable revealed a high degree of variation between subjects, between pretest and posttest, and between test items. The experimental group showed improvement at the posttest in all three variables. The control group showed improvement at the posttest in beat reproduction and beat steadiness but not in beat subdivision accuracy. The proportionate gains in the experimental group were greater than the gains in the control group from pretest to postest for all three variables (Table 1).

Ranks of Subjects and Comparison to Other Factors

An examination of the subjects as ranked in the performance of the three variables failed to show any noticeably marked relationship between the ranks and high school ranks, instruments played, and years of private lessons. A relationship was shown, however, between the ranks and musical performing ability as determined by audition (Table 2).

TABLE 1
GROUP MEANS OF VARIANCES FOR BEAT REPRODUCTION, BEAT STEADINESS, AND BEAT SUBDIVISION ACCURACY

Group	Test	Beat Reproduction Variance	Beat Steadiness Variance	Beat Subdivision Variance
Experimental	Pretest	4,786	12,575	9,373
Experimental	Posttest	1,781	6,019	6,824
Experimental	Both	3,284	9,297	8,098
Control	Pretest	13,335	14,029	12,101
Control	Posttest	9,325	9,807	14,170
Control	Both	11,330	11,918	13,136
Both	Pretest	9,061	13,302	10,737
Both	Posttest	5,553	7,913	10,497
Both	Both	7,307	10,607	10,617

Tests of Significance

1. *Analysis of variance for beat reproduction.* The overall difference in beat reproduction variances between the control group and the experimental group was highly significant. The interaction of groups by tests, which tested the influence of the experimental treatment, was very low

Table 2

Subjects as Ranked by Pretest Means of Variances with
Selected Information on Each Subject

Subject	Overall Rank	Beat Reproduction Rank	Beat Steadiness Rank	Beat Subdivision Accuracy Rank	High School Class Rank by Percentile	Instrument Played	Years of Private Instruction	Band Level in Purdue Bands
E 11	1	1	5	3	99	WW [a]	6	A
C 12	2	5	1	8	76	Brass	0	B
E 3	3	4	2	9	91	Brass	5	B
C 1	4	14	4	2	94	Perc. [b]	2	C
C 4	5	19	3	1	71	Perc.	8	A
E 14	6	2	11	11	76	WW	½	B
E 12	7	6	6	14	87	Brass	0	A
C 2	8.5	15	8	4	90	Brass	8	D
E 10	8.5	9	12	6	93	Brass	6	A
E 1	10	10	14	10	94	WW	½	A
E 15	11	3	10	23	95	Brass	3	B
C 10	12	13	9	16	98	WW	2	B
E 2	13	19	15	5	67	Brass	7	A
C 14	14	31	7	7	88	Perc.	8	B
E 6	15	11	20	15	95	WW	10	A
C 8	16.5	27	13	13	96	Perc.	0	C
E 5	16.5	7	21	25	88	String	½	A
E 13	18	25	18	12	69	Brass	3	C
E 4	19	8	23	29	83	WW	4	B
C 16	20	22	22	19	90	WW	1	A
C 13	21	16	30	18	78	Perc.	0	D
E 7	22.5	22	26	17	95	Brass	7	C
E 8	22.5	12	25	28	55	Brass	1	C
C 7	24	26	16	24	84	Brass	5	D
C 11	25	24	24	20	97	Brass	3	D
C 5	26	20	19	32	73	WW	3	C
C 3	27	32	19	26	70	WW	3	D
C 15	28	28	28	22	54	Brass	7	B
E 9	30	23	27	30	[c]	Brass	6	D
C 6	30	17	32	31	96	Brass	0	D
C 9	30	30	29	21	79	Brass	5	D
E 16	32	32	29	31	94	Brass	1	D

[a] Woodwind.
[b] Percussion.
[c] Not available.

TABLE 3
SUMMARY OF ANALYSES OF VARIANCE FOR VARIABLES USING LOGARITHMS
OF VARIANCE FOR EACH TEST ITEM, ALL SUBJECTS, PRETEST AND POSTTEST

Source of Variation	F Value	.05 F	.01 F
Beat reproduction:			
Groups, experimental vs. control	22.99**	4.17	7.56
Tests, pretest vs. posttest	3.50	4.17	7.56
Groups by tests (interaction)	.19	4.17	7.56
Items, both tests	1.30	2.05	2.73
Beat steadiness:			
Groups, experimental vs. control	1.90	4.17	7.56
Tests, pretest vs. posttest	21.49**	4.17	7.56
Groups by tests (interaction)	2.12	4.17	7.56
Items, both tests	5.04**	2.05	2.73
Beat subdivision accuracy:			
Groups, experimental vs. control	.57	4.17	7.56
Tests, pretest vs. posttest	4.59*	4.17	7.56
Groups by tests (interaction)	2.11	4.17	7.56
Items, both tests	6.35**	2.05	2.73

* Significant at .05 level of probability.
** Significant at .01 level of probability.

and not statistically significant (Table 3). An analysis of the statistics for beat reproduction in the total sample revealed a marked tendency to shorten beats, or play faster than the required beat (Table 4).

2. *Analysis of variance for beat steadiness.* There was a highly significant variation in beat steadiness variances in the total sample between the pretest and the posttest and between test items. However, the interaction of groups by tests although approaching low significance was not statistically significant. None of the other interactions were statistically significant.

3. *Analysis of variance for beat subdivision accuracy.* There was a significant variation in beat subdivision variances in the total sample between the pretest and the posttest and between test items. However, the

TABLE 4
DISTRIBUTION OF PLUS, MINUS, AND ZERO BEAT REPRODUCTION
DEVIATIONS BY GROUPS AND TESTS

Group	Test	Plus	Minus	Zero
Experimental	Pretest	45	82	1
Experimental	Posttest	55	71	2
Control	Pretest	24	104	0
Control	Posttest	46	82	0
		170	339	3

interaction of groups by tests although approaching low significance was not statistically significant. None of the other interactions were statistically significant.

Correlations

Significant correlations were found to exist between beat steadiness and beat reproduction and between beat steadiness and beat subdivision accuracy. The correlation between beat reproduction and beat subdivision accuracy was not statistically significant (Table 5). Rank correlations based upon the ranks of subjects for the variables tended to verify these results.

TABLE 5

CORRELATIONS BETWEEN EXPERIMENTAL VARIABLES BY GROUPS AND TESTS BASED UPON COMPARISON OF VARIANCES OF ALL TEST ITEMS

Group	Test	N	A vs. B	B vs. C	A vs. C
Experimental	Pretest	128	.37**	.34**	.01
Experimental	Posttest	128	.31**	.36**	.35**
Control	Pretest	128	.20*	.18*	−.07
Control	Posttest	128	.19*	.25**	.09
Both	Pretest	256	.24**	.24**	−.03
Both	Posttest	256	.22**	.28**	.15
Experimental	Both	256	.37**	.35**	.08
Control	Both	256	.21**	.21**	.00
Total Data		512	.25**	.25**	.04

A = Beat reproduction variances.
B = Beat steadiness variances.
C = Beat subdivision variances.
** Significant at .01 level.
 * Significant at .05 level.

CONCLUSIONS

Applicable to the study, the following conclusions were made:

1. Objective and precise measurements of beat reproduction, beat steadiness, and beat subdivision accuracy can be made of performances of musical durational notation.

2. There are large individual differences in the ability to perform musical durational notation.

3. There is a marked tendency for subjects to shorten beats or play faster than a given, or required, beat while performing musical durational notation.

4. Inducement to use imaged subdivisions of the beat while performing durational notation may cause an overall numerical improvement in beat steadiness and beat subdivision accuracy, but the amount of the improvement attributable to this treatment is not statistically significant.

5. Subject performance in beat reproduction under the limitations of this study is not significantly improved by inducement to use imaged subdivisions of the beat.

6. No noticeably marked relationship exists between the overall ranks of subjects in the variables measured and high school class ranks, instruments played, or years of private instruction.

7. A positive relationship exists between overall skill in the variables and general musical performing ability as determined by audition.

8. In comparing test item variances and subject ranks, significant correlations exist between beat steadiness and beat subdivision accuracy and between beat steadiness and beat reproduction, but not between beat reproduction and beat subdivision accuracy.

Following are recommendations for further research:

1. Analyses to compare error characteristics in each type of notational pattern, beat, and time signature.

2. Similar studies using different population samples with different treatments, test items, and instruction.

3. Studies to compare skill in the variables while performing at different tempos while playing instruments.

University of Southern Mississippi

EFFECT OF NOTATIONAL VALUES, AGE, AND EXAMPLE LENGTH ON TEMPO PERFORMANCE ACCURACY

Terry Lee Kuhn
Edith E. Gates

JRME 1975, VOLUME 23, NUMBER 3, PAGES 203–210

Seventy-two subjects drawn from six age groups clapped a notated rhythmic example while attempting to maintain a tempo given by metronome calibrated to 90 beats per minute. The example contained three sections that were counterbalanced to control for order. Section A of the example contained twelve beats of half notes, section B contained twelve beats of quarter notes, and section C contained twelve beats of eighth notes. Three forms of the example (ABC, BCA, and CAB) were randomly assigned to subjects. Dependent variable data consisted of the number of seconds required to perform each section of the rhythmic example. Seconds, measured to the nearest .01 second, were converted into beats per minute and expressed as deviation scores. No significant differences were produced among the three sections containing different notational values or among age groups of subjects. Significant differences were produced on order of presentation, indicating that performance tempo increased throughout the example. It was concluded that subjects evidenced a tendency to increase tempo during a clapped performance of a rhythmic example.

Key Words: age, aural discrimination, fundamentals, performance ability.

In order for studies in perception to have practical implications, relationships between perception and applied performance should be demonstrable. One purpose of this study was to determine if the results of a perception study could predict tempo changes in a rhythm performance task. In a recent tempo modulation experiment, professional musicians identified metronomic tempo decreases more accurately and significantly sooner than they identified metronomic tempo increases.[1] If one were to transfer that information from a perception discrimination task to a rhythm performance,

---

[1] Terry Lee Kuhn, "Discrimination of Modulated Beat Tempo By Professional Musicians," *Journal of Research in Music Education,* Vol 22 (Winter 1974), pp. 270–277.

one might argue that beat tempo changes would occur in the direction that is perceived least acutely. That is, it would be predicted on the basis of the perception study results that performance tempos would tend to increase because tempo decreases were perceived more accurately and quicker than tempo increases.

Smith conducted a study in an attempt to validate the auditory time and rhythm discrimination subtests from the *Seashore Measures of Musical Talent* by correlating those subtest scores with scores earned on a time performance and a rhythm performance test.[2] In a sense, experimental procedures in Smith's study are pertinent to this study in that results from aural discrimination measures were compared with a criterion performance measure. Smith found positive and significant correlations between discrimination and performance scores on the rhythmic subtest and performance of rhythms. However, Marciniak found no significant relationships between music perception and music performance. In interpreting these results, Marciniak intimated that lack of precision of the measurement may have obfuscated such relationships because "the levels of performance reflected the performance levels of bands, not individuals. The individuals' performance levels were measured only insofar as the band's performance is dependent on the collective performance of individuals."[3]

In a study investigating the performance of musical durational notation, Drake noted "a marked tendency for subjects to shorten beats or play faster than a given, or required, beat."[4] Although concerned with a different independent variable, Drake's findings support the hypothesized tendency for tempo to increase during performance.

Meyer reasoned that musical notation, in and of itself, cannot indicate what the tempo of a piece of music should be.[5] However, the results of an experiment led Linger to a slightly modified position on this matter. He maintained that "the visual appearance of a rhythmic pattern appears to be one of the primary influences in the process of establishing a tempo for performing the pattern."[6] Linger's subjects were asked to choose a beat tempo and perform rhythms notated with several different beat-note values. For example, the following three notations of the same rhythm pattern might have been presented to subjects, who would then choose a tempo and perform the pattern by tapping a telegraph key (see

[2] O. W. Smith, "Relationship of Rhythm Discrimination to Motor Rhythm Performance," *Journal of Applied Psychology*, Vol. 41 (1957), pp. 365–369.

[3] F. M. Marciniak, "Investigation of the Relationships Between Music Perception and Music Performance," *Journal of Research in Music Education*, Vol. 22 (Spring 1974), p. 43.

[4] A. H. Drake, "An Experimental Study of Selected Variables in the Performance of Musical Durational Notation," *Journal of Research in Music Education*, Vol. 16 (Winter 1968), p. 337.

[5] R. E. Meyer, *John Playford's "An Introduction to the Skill of Musick"* (doctoral dissertation, Florida State University, 1961).

[6] B. L. Linger, *An Experimental Study of Durational Notation* (doctoral dissertation, Florida State University, 1966), p. 36.

Figure 1). Linger's examples were longer than those given in Figure 1. Linger's analysis of the experimental data prompted the following explanation: "There appears to be a direct relationship between the *beginning* notes of a pattern and the choice of tempo for performing the entire pattern. If, for example, the beginning notes are half-notes, the tempo is slower; if the beginning notes are quarter-notes the tempo is faster, regardless of the notes in the remainder of the pattern.[7]

Figure 1. Three Notations of a Rhythm

A strong parallel to this study also exists in studies concerned with vocal intonation in which subjects have demonstrated increased discrimination on descending modulated frequencies combined with a tendency to perform more accurately on descending patterns as well as evidencing a tendency toward sharpness rather than flatness.[8] Greer found significant effects on external intonation ability when subjects attempted to match pitches produced in different timbres.[9]

Based on findings from previous research studies and pilot studies, the following research questions were posed: (1) Do different notational values cause differences in performance tempos? (2) Do different age groups of subjects perform a rhythm example at the same tempo? (3) Does performance tempo increase, decrease, or stay the same throughout a rhythmic example?

Method

Twelve subjects were randomly selected from each of six age groups. Age groups were established as grades one and two, three and four, five and six, seven through nine, ten through twelve, and college under-

[7] Linger, p. 37.

[8] C. K. Madsen, "The Effect of Scale Direction on Pitch Acuity in Solo Vocal Performance," Journal of Research in Music Education, Vol. 14 (Winter 1966), pp. 266–275; C. K. Madsen, "Sharpness and Flatness in Scalar Vocal Performance," *Sciences de l'Art-Scientific Aesthetics*, Tome 9, No. 1–2 (1974); C. K. Madsen, F. A. Edmonson III, and C. H. Madsen, Jr., "Modulated Frequency Discrimination in Relationship to Age and Musical Training," *Journal of the Acoustical Society of America*, Vol. 46 (1969), pp. 1468–1472; C. K. Madsen, D. E. Wolfe, C. H. Madsen, Jr., "The Effect of Reinforcement and Directional Scalar Methodology on Intonational Improvement," Council for Research in Music Education *Bulletin*, No. 18 (1969), pp. 22–33.

[9] R. D. Greer, "The Effect of Timbre on Brass Wind Intonation," in E. Gordon, ed., *Experimental Research in Music: Studies in the Psychology of Music*, Vol. 6 (Iowa City: University of Iowa Press, 1970).

graduates. All of the subjects had received adequate instruction in on-going school music programs to perform the notated rhythms. Subjects from fifth grade and higher were enrolled in a school music ensemble. Subjects were randomly assigned to perform the three sections of the example in one of the following sequences: ABC, BCA, or CAB. The three sections containing different rhythmic notational values were counterbalanced across subjects to control the influence of order of notational values on tempo. Figure 2 shows order ABC for the three sections of the example.

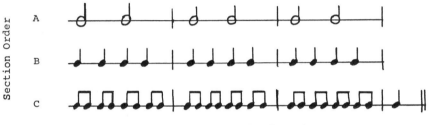

Figure 2. Rhythmic Notation Example

One additional note was included after the last section of the example to give a precise indication of the duration of the last beat of the example. Subjects were tested individually in a room isolated from extraneous sounds after listening to the following instructions: "You will hear a tempo of 90 beats per minute produced on a metronome. Listen carefully as long as you like, then clap the rhythm of the example while maintaining that tempo. The metronome will be turned off as you begin clapping. For the purposes of this study it is very important that you maintain a steady beat. Please avoid all rubato, accelerando, and ritardano. Do not slow down or speed up. Any questions? Ready. . . ."

All performances were recorded on channel A of a stereo reel-to-reel tape at 19 cm per second. A 1000-Hz sine wave tone was prerecorded on channel B to serve as a cue for time analysis. After data from all groups were recorded, individual performances were edited by preceding the initial attack of the first tone of each section of each example with leader tape. Timing of each of the three sections of each subject's performance of the example was accomplished by playing back the edited individual performances using the 1000-Hz cue tone to trigger a sound-activated relay, which in turn shunted a stop clock. In this way, a precise measurement of performance time was made for the three sections of each subject's performance of the example.[10]

---

[10] Equipment used in this experiment included a Franz Electric Metronome, Model LM-FB-5; Sony TC-630 Stereo Tape Recorder; Scotch 206 Recording Tape; Scotch Leader-Timing Tape; Hunter Noise Operated Relay, Model 320S; Lafayette Stop Clock, Model 54014; Editall Splicing Block, S-3; and Editall Splicing Tabs, CX-1.

Results

Differences among the three notational values nested within each subject's performance of the rhythmic example proved to be nonsignificant (F = 2.26; df = 2,132). Average tempo deviations from 90 beats per minute for the three notational values are given in Table 1. Of the three notational values, the quarter note was performed at a faster tempo than the half and eighth notes; however, the difference was not significant.

Table 1
Mean Tempo Deviation of Three Notational Values

Notational Values	Mean Tempo Deviation
A = ♩	+1.75
B = ♪	+3.08
C = ♪	+1.93

Average tempo deviations for each grade level group and for the order of performance of the three sections of the example are given in Table 2. Data in Table 2 indicate that all groups except undergraduates increased tempo during performance of the example. It will be recalled that the three rhythmic values were equally represented within the three sections performed; therefore, this increase is not explainable on the basis of different rhythmic values. Data presented in Table 2 were statistically

Table 2
Mean Tempo Deviation by Grade Level and Order of Performance

Grade Level	First Section	Second Section	Third Section
1–2	−1.08	2.42	4.67
3–4	1.42	6.17	7.17
5–6	.33	4.00	5.67
7–9	−1.08	1.00	1.00
10–12	1.08	3.83	5.33
Undergraduate	− .08	− .50	− .75
Combined Average	.10	2.82	3.85

analyzed using a two-factor analysis of variance test with repeated measures on the order of performance factor. A summary of this analysis is presented in Table 3.

Tempo differences among the six groups were not significant. The most accurate group performances were by the junior high (7-9) and undergraduate subjects; however, subject variability within groups was

Table 3
Analysis of Variance Summary Table Comparing Grade Level Groups and Order of Performance

Source of Variation	SS	df	MS	F
Between Subjects (S)	5276.34	71		
Grade Level Groups (G)	746.97	5	149.39	2.18
S within G	4529.37	66	68.63	
Within Subjects (S)	2960.66	144		
Order of Performance (O)	540.71	2	270.36	16.19*
G x O	214.90	10	21.49	1.29
O x S within G	2205.05	132	16.70	
Total	8237.00	215		

* $p < .01$

high enough to mitigate against significant differences among groups. The undergraduate group performed the rhythmic example most accurately and was the only group to decrease tempo over the three sections of the example. The average tempo decrease of the undergraduate group was very slight, ending only .75 of a beat slower than the given tempo.

Results of a Duncan Multiple Range Test comparing mean deviations of first, second, and third sections performed are presented in Table 4. The first section of the example was performed at a tempo slightly faster than 90 beats per minute and was performed significantly slower than the second and third sections of the example. The solid line in Table 4 indicates that the numerical difference between the second and third sections performed was not significant. The average deviation tempo of the first section (+ .10) was very close to the expected 90 beats per minute. However, the tempo deviation of the second section (+2.82) was significantly faster than the first section indicating that the greatest amount of tempo increase occurred relatively early in the example. The third section was performed faster than the second section (+3.85),

Table 4
Duncan Multiple Range Comparison of Tempo Deviation Means of First, Second, and Third Sections of Example

First Section	Second Section	Third Section
.10	2.82	3.85

suggesting a tendency toward a continuing tempo increase; however, the difference between the second and third sections was not significant.

Summarizing the results of this study, it was found that (1) different notational values did not influence tempo, (2) different age groups did not perform at significantly different tempos, and (3) tempo increased a significant amount throughout the performance of the musical example.

Discussion

If the entire example were to be performed at the expected tempo of 90 beats per minute then it would last for precisely 24 seconds, and each of the three sections of the example would have an expected duration of eight seconds. In terms of musical performance, this means that the average subject from the 10-12 grade level group began the example at a tempo of 91.08 beats per minute and increased the tempo to 95.33 beats per minute before the ninth measure. This amount of tempo fluctuation would appear to be unacceptable in applied performance; however, other factors must be brought into consideration in a musical performance. For instance, in this experiment subjects were requested to maintain a given tempo during a clapping performance. In an ensemble performance, however, the musical interaction among performers, the technical and idiomatic difficulties of the music, and the presence of a conductor may all exert influence on the performance tempo. Perhaps it is not objectionable to increase tempo in performance—both because it is difficult to perceive and because tempo increases can add an element of excitement to music.

Different notational values did not influence tempo. Results of this study appear to be in conflict with those presented by Linger inasmuch as subjects' tempos were influenced by notation in Linger's study but not in this study. This disparity is probably due to the difference in the structured testing situations: Linger's subjects were expected to choose their own tempo after viewing the notation and without any tempo reference point, whereas the subjects in this study were given a standard tempo to reproduce. The combination of these two findings suggests that Meyer's assertion that music notation cannot indicate the tempo of a piece may be incorrect in practice. That is, notation does suggest tempo to a performer unless a beat-note tempo is given.

Different age groups of subjects did not perform at significantly different tempos. This finding is not surprising because relatively few subjects represented each group and there was a fairly wide range of responses within each group.

One purpose of this study was to test the theory that subjects tend to increase tempo in performance because tempo decreases are discriminated more accurately and sooner than tempo increases. Experimental results indicated that tempo increases occurred throughout a musical example when subjects were attempting to maintain a given tempo. The explanation for this occurrence centers on the idea that more acute discrimination ability for tempo modulation decreases results in more tempo modulation increases in actual performance. Average tempo deviation on the first section performed was minimal; however, even though subjects attempted to maintain the given tempo throughout the remaining two sections of the example, the tempo increased by a significant amount, thus supporting the proposed theory.

■ University of Maryland
College Park, Maryland

VI.

Teacher Behavior

and

Student Response

COMPARISONS OF BEGINNING VERSUS EXPERIENCED ELEMENTARY MUSIC EDUCATORS IN THE USE OF TEACHING TIME

Michael J. Wagner
Eileen P. Strul

JRME 1979, VOLUME 27, NUMBER 2, PAGES 113–125

This study quantified and compared the amount of time three groups of nine teachers spent during elementary music classes pursuing various music classroom activities. Experienced teachers, teaching interns, and undergraduate teaching methodology students were each observed twice during fifteen minute segments of two elementary music classes in nine elementary schools. The amount of time spent in each of fourteen classroom activities, and the number and kind of reinforcements given were quantified. Interobserver reliability averaged .91. An attitude assessment was administered to all children following each class. Results indicate that experienced teachers spend significantly less time giving directions than do either of the other teacher groups. No other significant differences were found. Although there were no significant differences in student attitudes among teacher groups, the attitude assessments indicate that students are happy to be in music class, happy to participate, and spend time out of school pursuing music-related activities.

Key Words: aesthetic attitudes, assessment, elementary education, learning theory, music activities.

Methodology courses in music education are intended to guide prospective music teachers in the development of instructional skills, techniques, and teaching strategies. To this end, teacher training institutions often require field-based materials and internships, which include a wide variety of activities designed to prepare future teachers for constructive and successful careers in teaching. Courses in methodology are often structured by assuming that students enter with prior competence in areas of music specialization. Therefore, management techniques and school music issues, rather than music history, theory, and applied instrumental skills, are generally the major instructional concern during final teacher preparation leading toward the music teaching internship.

Many models of teacher education have been advanced, yet most have certain elements in common. It is generally assumed that knowledge of the subject matter (music) is a prerequisite to teaching at any level. Further, modeling an experienced teachers' presentation of subject matter seems necessary, along with mastery of rehearsal skills and cognitive strategies that make presentation of subject matter understandable and possible.

Recent studies involving reinforcement in educational classroom settings and music classrooms have been concerned with manipulating the classroom environment so that learning is the natural consequence of educational strategies and reinforcements (O'Leary & O'Leary, 1972; Becker, 1971). Methods of subject matter presentation (Hargiss, 1965; Porter, 1969), selection of subject matter (Greer, Dorow, Wacchaus, & White, 1973; Greer et al., 1974), kinds of reinforcements (Madsen & Madsen, 1972; Madsen, Moore, Wagner, & Yarbrough, 1975) and use of class time (Madsen, 1976; Forsythe, 1977), have all been studied carefully to ascertain their effectiveness. Efforts to quantify the behavior of teachers and students in the classroom have used interval recording techniques (Hall, 1974). Such observation forms employ constant intervals of time, codes for various operationally defined classroom activities, and behaviors that can be notated in a temporal way for post hoc analysis, and interobserver reliability checks (Flanders, 1970; Madsen & Madsen, 1974; Yarbrough & Madsen, 1976).

Results of behavioral techniques applied to classroom teaching in music education have been encouraging. According to Madsen, Greer, & Madsen (1975):

> Studies related to music in the schools offer the music education profession a new measure, a measure that might be termed a "power of music" measure; that is, measures of the effects of methodologies, teacher behaviors, and developmental variables that may be assessed in terms of whether they decrease or increase the effect of music in the lives of both children and adults. (p. 23)

Kuhn (1975) studied the effect of teacher approval and disapproval on student attentiveness, music achievements, and attitudes of fifth and sixth grade students in music classes. He reported that in classes where teachers contingently approved 80% of the time, students followed classroom rules better than did students who received high teacher disapproval. Murray (1975) studied the effects of teacher approval and disapproval on high school choruses and found that students who received 80% contingent approval rated their attitudes toward their music rehearsals significantly higher than those who rehearsed in a disapproval environment. Forsythe (1975) found that approval rates above 75% produced more attentiveness in elementary students than did a 75% disapproval rate. While a direct relationship between student music achievement and ratio of approval/disapproval has not been verified, it has been conjectured that students' attentiveness is indeed requisite to academic achievement.

Forsythe (1977) investigated elementary students' attending behavior in the music classroom as a function of the specific activity the students were engaged in. Findings indicated that students' attention is, in part, a function of the activity in which the student participates. Specifically, Forsythe concluded: (1) Elementary music teachers tend to allot differing amounts of class time to a variety of classroom activities. The emphasis is on verbal interaction (teaching), singing, and listening. (2) Off-task student behavior is related to the nature of the classroom activity engaged in, with those activities involving more "active" participation being more likely to promote on-task behavior. (3) The mean off-task behavior level of students is generally highest during periods of "getting ready" for other activities. Verbal interaction between students and teacher also produced higher levels of off-task behavior than singing, playing instruments, and so forth. (4) Off-task behavior levels of various activities do not correlate significantly with the amount of class time dedicated to those activities. (5) Off-task behavior levels are a function of the type of classroom activity, the teacher, and the curriculum emphasis of the music program. In general, there is no significant interaction among these three variables, suggesting that the effects of each are independent of the others.

In 1976, Moore introduced a form that attempted to quantify the activities used by teachers in the teaching of elementary general music. The *Music Teaching Reinforcement-Activities Form* (MTRA) was used to compare how experienced music teachers use time, compared to music teaching interns. Since time is a valued commodity for teachers, attempts to isolate how time is spent by model teachers might offer suggestions for improving uses of time for prospective teachers.

The present investigation attempts to compare (1) the use of music class time among experienced elementary music teachers, music teaching interns, and pre-interns; (2) the number and kind of reinforcements that these teachers use; and (3) students' attitudes toward music.

Procedure

Two music classes from grades four through six were randomly selected for study from each of nine elementary schools serving as preinternship and internship sites for music education students. Each of the elementary music specialists at these schools met accepted standards for supervising music education interns. Pre-interns were assigned to elementary schools using criteria of proximity to home, experience at particular socio-economic levels, and probable compatibility with supervising teachers. Placement of students in a field experience school was done using traditional teacher education criteria. The school in which the pre-interns did the field-based assignments of observation, lesson planning, and teaching, became the internship assignment for each music education student during the subsequent academic quarter. The music education students comprised the pre-intern ($N = 9$) and intern ($N = 9$) populations of the experiment, and were compared with experienced teachers ($N = 9$). For purposes of analysis, these populations were considered as three "experimental" groups.

Data were first gathered on pre-interns, then on experienced teachers, and finally, on interns. This schedule allowed observers over a 20-week period to plan observations with minimal schedule interruptions in classes at each elementary school.

Teacher observations in the present investigation were made using Moore's observation form (MTRA), which quantifies the number and kind of reinforcers used by elementary music teachers and categorizes how classroom teaching time is used. The MTRA is designed to record continuous events during a 15-minute segment of a general music class. The form includes: (1) the number and kinds of activities occurring chronologically in the music class, (2) the number of seconds spent in each activity, (3) the frequency of approvals and disapprovals given by the teacher, and (4) demographic information on grade level and class size.

During classroom instruction by teachers in each experimental category, three observations were made. Interobserver reliability between the two trained observers was .91. Data were not gathered during the first observation period. Each teacher was observed and data recorded for a period of fifteen minutes, four times (two in each class) over the five-week experimental period. All teachers were aware that they were being observed, but not informed as to the exact nature of the observations; only that "observations are a necessity in the training of interns." Observations made using the MTRA form categorized teaching time as follows:

Teaching Activities:
Academic instruction—Clarifying subject matter; teacher questions requiring short answers; lecturing. This activity is often described as teaching.

Discussion—An on-task conversation period in which students and teachers participate and interact.

Written assignments—Seat work requiring writing during the class period. The teacher acts as supervisor.

Directions—Teacher explaining rules or assignments and giving directions to students.

Music activities:
Singing—Vocal music performance activities in which students participate, with or without the teacher.

Playing instruments—Performance on musical instruments in which students participate, with or without the teacher. For example, playing xylophone, pianicas, ukeleles, recorders, and so on.

Rhythm—Students participating in activities related to rhythm, with or without the teacher. For example, echo clapping, playing drums, tapping, and so on.

Movement—Movements related to music performed by students with or without the teacher. For example, gross motor movement to music.

Listening—Attending to music that is played.

Nonteaching Activities:

Preparation—Teacher-directed activity where the teacher is getting ready to do something, such as passing out materials, waiting for student attention, arranging equipment or students before activity commences.

Talk—Teacher-directed conversation that is irrelevant or off-task to the classroom subject matter.

Interruption—Unavoidable distraction caused by external environment. For example, another teacher asks personal question, P.A. announcement, fire drill, and so on.

Lost control—Chaos. Normal student/teacher interactions no longer function contingently.

Other:

Combinations—Certain combinations of music teaching activities, such as singing and moving. Teacher divides class so that more than one activity takes place; also talk and seat work combinations.

Teacher reinforcements are categorized and recorded according to definitions outlined by Madsen and Madsen (1974). Definitions of reinforcement categories are:

Approvals:

Approval Academic—Approval for academic behavior. For example, the teacher indicates that the academic work is correct by using praise.

Approval Social—Approval for social behavior. The teacher gives any approving response paired specifically with appropriate social behavior.

Approval Academic Mistake—An approval mistake of reinforcement following academic behavior. Teacher indicates the academic response is correct when, in fact, the answer is incorrect.

Approval Social Mistake—An approval mistake of reinforcement follows social behavior that involves giving approval to inappropriate behavior.

Disapprovals:

Disapproval Academic—Disapproval for academic behavior. Any disapproval indicating that a student's response to academic work was incorrect.

Disapproval Social—Disapproval for social behavior given by the teacher following any disruption of the learning environment that interferes with learning.

Disapproval Academic Mistake—A disapproval mistake of reinforcement following academic behavior. The teacher indicates the student's academic answer is incorrect, when the answer is, in fact, correct.

Disapproval Social Mistake—A disapproval mistake of reinforcement following social behavior. The teacher gives disapproval when the social behavior was indeed appropriate to the classroom situation.

Portions of the "Affective Assessment" of the *Florida Catalog of Music*

Objectives were also used in the present study to assess elementary general music classes' attitude toward: (1) use of leisure time, (2) learning in music class, (3) singing, playing instruments, and listening activities in music class, and (4) the music class just completed. It seemed important to use an assessment technique that was not contingent upon the reading of directions. Therefore, this assessment was chosen because students received all directions orally and student choices were pictures or symbols instead of words.[1] Upon completion of each class, the nonverbal (picture/symbol) attitude assessment was administered to all students after the teacher had left the classroom. These procedures resulted in four observations and four sets of attitude surveys for each teacher in each group ($N = 27$).

Results

The number of seconds each teacher spent, for a total of 900 seconds (15 minutes) in each music class activity, served as the raw data for analysis. Time spent in each activity among experimental groups was compared using a One-Way Analysis of Variance (see Table 1).

Of all music class activities, only the time spent giving directions differed significantly between teacher groups. Results of a Newman-Keuls Multiple Comparison Procedure are indicated in Table 2. It can be seen that experienced teachers spent significantly less time giving directions to their music classes than did the other groups.

A comparison of the number of reinforcements in each category given to students among groups found no significant differences. Thus, there were no differences among groups in the number or kind of reinforcement given to children during elementary music classes (see Table 3).

It may be seen that approximately one-third of all reinforcement given by teachers was approval for correct academic responses. Slightly more than one-third of all reinforcement was disapproval for social behavior. The third most used category of teacher reinforcement was the approval of social behavior mistake, that is, the teacher approved of social behavior when it should not have been approved.

An attitude assessment was given at the conclusion of each music class taught by all teachers in each group. Table 4 shows results of the attitude assessment. Data were analyzed using χ^2 tests for independent samples to check for differences between teacher groups on each question, and no significant differences were revealed. Results of χ^2 tests for independent samples did reveal significant differences between choices for each of the first six questions (see Table 5). Question number seven was analyzed using a one-way analysis of variance, since selection of more than one choice was possible on this question (see Table 6). Significant differences were

---

[1] This technique was originally developed by J. L. Forsythe for project 106-3-70-029, Columbus, Georgia, E. S. E. A. Title III Elementary Music Project; George Coradino, project director.

found between means ($F = 153.13$; $df = 130, 4$; $p < .01$). Results of a Newman-Keuls Multiple Comparison Procedure revealed results about students' music activities at home, which are shown in Table 7.

Table 1
Percent of Time Spent in Music Class Activities

	Pre-Intern	Intern	Experienced Teacher	One-Way ANOVA F =	p
Teacher Activities					
Academic Instruction	25.31	26.36	32.84	1.01	N.S.
Discussion	5.39	.31	1.42	1.64	N.S.
Written Assignments	.82	.20	.86	.36	N.S.
Directions	15.00	13.00	7.50	3.98	<.05
Total Teaching Activities	46.52	39.87	42.62		
Music Activities					
Singing	5.01	6.08	11.91	1.19	N.S.
Playing Instruments	10.52	6.26	12.78	1.53	N.S.
Rhythm	4.62	2.69	1.73	1.26	N.S.
Movement	.02	.00	3.20	2.55	N.S.
Listening	2.99	7.53	.87	1.34	N.S.
Total Music Activities	23.16	22.56	30.49		
Nonteaching Activities					
Preparation	19.88	25.62	20.03	.72	N.S.
Talk	1.36	.68	3.58	2.95	N.S.
Interruption	2.47	.56	1.54	1.28	N.S.
Lost Control	5.62	9.04	.09	3.04	N.S.
Total Nonteaching Activities	29.33	35.90	25.24		
Other	.99	1.67	1.65	.39	N.S.
Total Time	100.00%	100.00%	100.00%		

Table 2
Neuman-Keuls Multiple Comparison of Means of
Time Spent Giving Directions between Three Teacher Groups

Pre-Interns	Interns	Experienced Teachers
132.8 (15%)	117.2 (13%)	67.2 (7.5%)
N.S.		

Underline indicates no significant differences. All other comparisons are significant at .05 level.

Discussion

Perhaps the most interesting finding of this investigation is the lack of significant differences among the three experimental groups of teachers. Significant differences were found in only one teaching activity. Experienced teachers gave directions in approximately one-half the time used by pre-interns and interns. Rate and kind of academic and social reinforcement did not significantly differ with respect to teacher group, and students' responses to the attitude survey were very similar for all three teacher populations. Apparently, student teachers model experienced teachers.

There should be some caution in the interpretation of these data because of the high variability among the teachers observed. Perhaps with a larger sample of teachers some of the apparent "differences" found in Table 2 would be significant as well. However, even with high variability, some striking aspects can be noted.

Although these data include an attitude assessment not included in Moore's pilot study, teacher/intern comparisons concerning the use of teaching time and reinforcement rate are remarkably similar. It should

Table 3
Comparisons of Percent of Total Reinforcement between Pre-Interns, Interns, and Experienced Teachers

	Percent of Total Reinforcement				
	Pre-Intern	Intern	Experienced Teacher	One-Way ANOVA F =	p
Approval Academic	32.42	28.69	36.88	.43	N.S.
Approval Social	2.34	2.74	2.71	.90	N.S.
Approval Academic Mistake	.40	.84	.23	.68	N.S.
Approval Social Mistake	17.89	15.82	9.95	.05	N.S.
Disapproval Academic	7.17	6.75	12.22	.99	N.S.
Disapproval Social	36.59	43.04	33.71	.77	N.S.
Disapproval Academic Mistake	.00	.64	.68	1.50	N.S.
Disapproval Social Mistake	3.19	1.48	3.62	.88	N.S.
Total Percent of Reinforcement	100.00	100.00	100.00		
Total Percent Approval	53.05	48.09	49.77		
Total Percent Disapproval	46.95	51.91	50.23		
$\bar{X}$ Number of Reinforcements per 15-minute Observation	27.94	26.33	24.55		
Total Number of Reinforcements	503	474	442		

be noted that Moore's pilot data were gathered in Eugene, Oregon, and the data for the present investigation were gathered in Miami, Florida.

Table 4
X̄ Number of Responses to Student Attitude Assessment; Pre-Interns Versus Interns Versus Experienced Teachers

	Pre-Intern	Intern	Experienced Teacher	Possible Response
1. Choose the picture that	6.2	6.4	6.9	Art
shows what you would	3.8	2.8	3.4	Reading
most like to do during	5.5	5.7	5.2	Music
free time at school.	12.3	12.1	11.2	Phys. Ed.
Choose one.	.3	.2	.2	No Answer
2. Choose the picture that	18.4	16.3	16.9	Happy Face
shows how you feel	7.9	7.8	8.3	Neutral Face
about LEARNING in	.8	2.1	1.1	Sad Face
music class.	.9	.8	.4	Question Mark
Choose one.	.1	.1	.1	No Answer
3. Choose the picture that	18.9	18.5	17.2	Happy Face
shows how you feel	5.9	6.1	6.6	Neutral Face
about SINGING in	2.4	2.1	2.7	Sad Face
music class.	.8	.4	.3	Question Mark
Choose one.	.1	.1	.0	No Answer
4. Choose the picture that	19.8	17.6	19.4	Happy Face
shows how you feel about	5.3	4.3	4.7	Neutral Face
PLAYING INSTRUMENTS	2.0	4.1	2.0	Sad Face
in music class.	.9	1.0	.7	Question Mark
Choose one.	.1	.2	.0	No Answer
5. Choose the picture that	19.3	18.3	18.3	Happy Face
shows how you feel about	5.7	6.0	6.1	Neutral Face
LISTENING TO MUSIC	2.2	2.0	1.7	Sad Face
in music class.	1.0	.6	.8	Question Mark
Choose one.	.1	.2	.0	No Answer
6. Choose the picture that	20.9	18.1	17.8	Happy Face
shows how you felt about	5.2	5.7	6.9	Neutral Face
music class *today.*	1.4	2.3	1.6	Sad Face
Choose one.	.5	.9	.7	Question Mark
	.1	.1	.1	No Answer
7. Choose the picture that	10.9	10.7	10.8	Singing
shows which of these	22.9	22.8	22.1	Records
activities you do at	20.3	19.8	20.3	Radio
home. Choose as many as	9.5	10.1	7.4	Play Instrument
you do at home.	.6	.8	.5	None

Table 5
Combined X̄ Number of Student Responses
to Teachers on
Attitude Assessment Items

	Music	Read-ing	Art	Phys. Ed.	No Answer	p
1. Choose the picture that shows what you would *most* like to do during free time at school.	6.8	3.3	5.5	11.9	.2	<.001

	Happy Face	Neutral Face	Sad Face	Question Mark	No Answer	
2. Choose the picture that shows how you feel about LEARNING in music class.	17.2	8.0	1.3	.7	.1	<.001
3. Choose the picture that shows how you feel about SINGING in music class.	18.2	6.2	2.4	.5	.06	<.001
4. Choose the picture that shows how you feel about PLAYING INSTRUMENTS in music class.	18.9	4.8	2.7	.9	.1	<.001
5. Choose the picture that shows how you feel about LISTENING TO MUSIC in music class.	18.6	5.9	2.0	.8	.1	<.001
6. Choose the picture that shows how you felt about music class *today*.	18.9	5.9	1.8	.7	.1	<.001

	Singing	Playing Re-cords	Radio	Play Instru-ments	No Answer	
7. Choose the picture that shows which of these activities you do at home. Choose as many as you do at home.	10.8	22.6	20.1	9.0	.6	<.01

Table 6
One-Way Analysis of Variance
of Choices for Attitude Assessment
Question Number 7

Source	SS	df	MS	F
Between	34,110.92	4	8,527.73	153.13*
Within	7,239.85	130	55.69	
Total	41,350.77			

*$p < .01$

Table 7
Neuman-Keuls Multiple Comparison of Students' Responses
to Musical Activities Engaged in at Home

Records	Radio	Singing	Playing Instruments	None
22.6	20.1	10.8	9.0	.6
		N.S.		

Underline indicates no significant differences. All other comparisons are significant at the .01 level.

Forsythe (1977) found that although different teachers tended to allot varying amounts of time for different activities, the emphasis was on teaching, singing, and listening. The present investigation found the emphasis on teaching (academic instruction), preparation (getting ready to do an activity), and playing instruments (although singing was also emphasized). Curricular emphasis can explain the rankings of singing, listening, and playing instruments. Teaching, however, seems to be the primary activity found by Forsythe, Moore, and the present study. It is interesting to note that preparation takes considerable time in elementary general music classes. It would seem important for teacher training programs to place emphasis on reducing the amount of time necessary for changing activities.

The effects of approval reinforcement (greater than 75% contingent approval) have been shown to significantly increase attending behavior (Forsythe, 1975), increase the following of classroom rules (Kuhn, 1975), and increase positive attitude toward choral rehearsal (Murray, 1975). In this investigation, teachers' reinforcement rate showed approximately a 50% approval rate. Although pre-intern and intern teachers in this study had observed and quantified teachers' approval/disapproval ratios as a portion of their teacher training and had studied previous research in this area, they did not increase their own approval/disapproval ratio beyond those of their supervising teachers. It would seem important that pre-interns, interns, and experienced teachers increase the number of approvals (particularly social approvals) given contingently in their classes. A corresponding decrease in approval social mistakes of reinforcement would also be appropriate.

Although a majority of students report that they would rather engage in physical education activities, they reported that they were happy to be in music class and happy to participate in learning, singing, and playing instruments. Students' attitudes did not vary significantly from each other, regardless of teacher category. Data further indicated that students spent time out of school pursuing music-related activities.

Conclusions

With regard to use of teaching time, rate of reinforcement, and student attitudes, the pre-intern, intern, and experienced teacher did not seem to differ in the classroom. Speculation may occur as to what changes take place as a prospective music teacher prepares for a career in music education. It seems important for future research to give pre- and posttests to students in each experimental teacher group. Consequently, student academic achievement may be determined as a function of the use of teaching time. It is possible that the effective use of teaching strategies may be the area most important to music teacher preparation.

By the very nature of teacher education programs, studies in this area use population sizes that are often small, thus the possibilities for generalizing to other populations are limited. Yet, due to the consistency of the findings, further investigation seems important so that curriculums for the training of teachers of music can be based upon empirical data.

References

Becker, W. (Ed.) *An empirical basis for change in education.* Chicago: Science Research Associates, Inc., 1971.

Flanders, N. A. *Analyzing teaching behavior.* Reading, Mass.: Addison-Wesley Publishing Co., Inc., 1970.

Florida catalogue of music objectives. (Rev. ed.) Tallahassee: Florida Department of Education, 1974.

Forsythe, J. L. The effect of teacher approval, disapproval, and errors on student attentiveness: Music versus classroom teachers. In C. K. Madsen, R. D. Greer,

& C. H. Madsen (Eds.), *Research in music behavior*. New York: Teachers College Press, Columbia University, 1975.

Forsythe, J. L. Elementary student attending behavior as a function of classroom activities. *Journal of Research in Music Education*, 1977, *25*, 228-239.

Greer, R. D., Dorow, L. G., Wachhaus, G., & White, E. R. Adult approval and student's musical selection behavior. *Journal of Research in Music Education*, 1973, *21*, 345-354.

Greer, R. D., Dorow, L. G., & Randall, A. Music listening preferences of elementary school children. *Journal of Research in Music Education*, 1974, *22*, 284-291.

Hall, R. V. Behavior modification: The measurement of behavior. In *Managing behavior* (Rev. ed.). Kansas City, Kans.: H. & H Enterprises, Inc., 1974.

Hargiss, G. The development of an evaluation of self-instructional materials in basic music theory for elementary teachers. *Council for Research in Music Education Bulletin*, No. 4, 1965, 1-6.

Kuhn, T. L. The effect of teacher approval and disapproval on attentiveness, music achievement, and attitude of fifth-grade students. In C. K. Madsen, R. D. Greer, & C. H. Madsen (Eds.), *Research in music behavior*, New York: Teachers College Press, Columbia University, 1975.

Madsen, C. K. *Modifying life's time*. Unpublished manuscript, Tallahassee: Florida State University, 1976.

Madsen, C. K., Greer, R. D., & Madsen, C. H. (Eds.). *Research in music behavior*. New York: Teachers College Press, Columbia University, 1975.

Madsen, C. K., & Madsen, C. H. Selection of music listening or candy as a function of contingent versus noncontingent reinforcement and scale singing. *Journal of Music Therapy*, 1972, *9*, 190-198.

Madsen, C. H., & Madsen, C. K. *Teaching/discipline: A positive approach for educational development, expanded second edition for professionals*. Boston: Allyn & Bacon, 1974.

Madsen, C. K., Moore, R. S., Wagner, M. J., & Yarbrough, C. A comparison of music as reinforcement for correct mathematical responses versus music as reinforcement for attentiveness. *Journal of Music Therapy*, 1975, *12*, 84-95.

Moore, R. S. Videotaped comparisons of beginning versus experienced elementary music specialists in the use of teaching time, and development and piloting of the 'music teaching interactions-activity form'. Paper presented at Second National Symposium on Research in Music Behavior, Milwaukee, Wis., 1976.

Murray, K. C. The effect of teacher approval/disapproval on the performance level, attentiveness, and attitude of high school choruses. In C. K. Madsen, R. D. Greer, & C. H. Madsen (Eds.), *Research in music behavior*. New York: Teachers College Press, Columbia University, 1975.

O'Leary, K. D., & O'Leary, S. G. *Classroom management: The successful use of behavior modification*. New York: Pergamon Press, Inc., 1972.

Porter, H. B. An integrated course in music literature, theory, and ensemble performance for talented high school students. *Council for Research in Music Education Bulletin*, No. 16, 1969, 47-48.

Yarbrough, C., & Madsen, C. K. *Competency based approach to music education: Observation and field manual*. Syracuse, N.Y.: S.C.A.M.E., Center for Instructional Development, Syracuse University, 1976.

Florida International University
Miami

ELEMENTARY STUDENT ATTENDING BEHAVIOR AS A FUNCTION OF CLASSROOM ACTIVITIES

Jere L. Forsythe

JRME 1977, VOLUME 25, NUMBER 2, PAGES 228–239

This study investigated the extent to which attending behavior (on-task parti-cipation) of students in elementary music classes is a function of the activities in which students engage. On-task behavior also was examined for possible relationships with teachers and curriculum. A total of 262 in-class observations of 10 to 20 minutes each were conducted at all grade levels (K-6) taught by 11 elementary music teachers during one academic year. An interval recording technique was used to record the number of students judged to be off-task during a series of 15-second intervals. Symbols representing 11 different activities were placed on the form. Factor analysis produced significantly different levels of off-task behavior relating to activity, teacher, and cur-riculum. Such activities as playing instruments and singing yielded low levels of off-task behavior; students showed higher off-task levels during periods of "getting ready" for activities and during periods in which teachers and stu-dents were interacting verbally. A significant interaction occurred between teacher and activity only when the "getting ready" activity was included in the analysis. Off-task levels did not correlate significantly with the amount of time spent on the various activities. These results suggest that attending behavior is, in part, a function of the nature of the activity in which students participate.

Key Words: activities, curriculum, elementary schools, elementary teacher, students

The value of classroom observation as a data-gathering procedure has been recognized for many years (Wright, 1960), despite dif-ficulties in quantifying student and teacher behavior (Medley and Mitzel, 1963; Rosenshine and Furst, 1973). A wide array of observa-tion forms and procedures is in current use (Dunkin and Biddle, 1974; Erbes, 1972), but the emphasis in classroom research has been upon the observation of social behavior (Becker, 1971). The theoretical assumption underlying this emphasis is that appropriate social behavior is necessary for successful academic learning. For example, attending behavior (concentration on or participation in surrounding activity) is a type of social behavior often regarded as prerequisite to academic learning. The student who does not attend to an academic learning task, many believe, is not likely to learn from it. Another notion is that attending behavior may parallel affective behavior, especially when attending is shown to be a function of the phenomenon attended to and not a result of other contingencies such as fear, desire for teacher approval, and so on. This relationship is supported by Krathwohl, Bloom, and Masia (1964) insofar as they list "attending behavior" as the basic level of affective responsiveness in the taxonomy hierarchy. Participating in and attending to learning experiences and activities appears to be closely related to a higher order of involvement. If attending behavior in music classrooms can be shown to be a function of the nature of the activity pursued, elementary music teachers may need to consider such information in lesson planning. Concern for this possibility led to the present study.

Purpose and Procedure

The purpose of this study was to examine the extent to which the attending behavior of students in elementary music classrooms is a function of the activities in which students engage. The differential effects of teachers and several curriculum emphases also were examined.

The observation form and procedure used for data collection were developed by Madsen and Madsen (1974). The observation procedure involves an interval recording technique (Hall, 1974), that allows observers to record student behavior within discrete time periods. It requires operational definitions of the behaviors observed, interobserver agreement checks, and accurate interval regulation.

Attending behavior, or on-task behavior, was operationally defined as appropriate attending to and/or participating in classroom activities and events. Students judged not to be responding appropriately during each interval were recorded as being off-task.

The observation form contained 25 interval boxes, each representing 15 seconds of observation time. Observers were instructed to scan the class from left to right during the 15-second interval and count the number of students who were off-task. Five-second record intervals allowed the observers to record the frequency data onto the form. A prerecorded cassette tape was used to regulate accurate "observe" and "record" intervals by cueing the observers as they listened to the tape through an earplug. Most music classes lasted 20 or 30 minutes, but observers were instructed to allow a brief period for students to adjust to their presence before beginning observation. Typically, one observation form was completed over approximately 10 minutes of class time. When possible, however, two forms were used for a given class period, thus providing data that represented almost the entire period.

Three trained observers spent three units of five consecutive school days—at the beginning, middle, and end of the year—during one academic year. They gathered a total of 262 separate observations (one complete form) across nine project teachers and two "control" (traditional) teachers. Sample observations from all elementary grade levels were included. Interobserver agreement checks were found to average .72. This figure was based upon a conservative criterion of agreement. To be considered an agreement, observers were required to agree within 10 percent of the total number of students present during a 15-second interval. For example, in a class of 20 students, agreement within two students was required. If one observer recorded five students off-task while the other recorded only two, a disagreement would be counted for that interval. The formula for computing agreement level was standard: agreements ÷ (agreements + disagreements).

To examine off-task levels in relation to the class activity occurring during each interval, an activity coding system was used (see Table 1). The observer placed symbols in the interval box with the off-task behavior figure for each interval. Off-task percentages thus could be determined for each activity.

Although it was not the original purpose of the data collection procedure to determine what proportion of class time teachers were dedicating to the different activities, this information proved to be a useful byproduct of the resulting data. It served two purposes. First, it was used to help maintain some degree of experimental control in a curriculum evaluation project within which these data were gathered (project 106-3-70-029, Columbus, Georgia, E.S.E.A. Title III Elementary Music Project). That project

Table 1
Activity Code Key

Symbol	Activity Description
T	Predominance of teacher talking (includes instruction, asking questions, verbal interaction with students)
S	Students singing (group or individual)
L	Students listening to music (live or recorded)—considered passive since other symbols refer to active listening (for example, M for moving to music)
P	Students playing instruments (includes echo clapping, tapping on desk, that is, nonvocal "performance")
M	Students moving to music (dancing, expressive movement, and so on)
S & M	Students singing and moving to music simultaneously
S & P	Students singing and playing instruments simultaneously
VR	Verbal rhythm (chanting words of a song in rhythm or chanting rhythm syllables)
C	Composing, creating sounds, and so on (not an imitative response)
G	Getting ready (teachers and students) for learning activities (getting instruments, passing out books, and so on)
O	Other (for example, interruptions at the door)

compared four unique curricula emphases with the "traditional" elementary school program (control). Each group was distinguished by an emphasis upon certain types of experiences: singing, playing instruments, creating, and listening. While an emphasis was not to be at the total exclusion of other activities, adequate stress on unique experiences was essential. However, observational data obtained during the first observation (see Tables 2-4) revealed that teachers were not adequately providing for unique approaches. Although ideal laboratory control was never considered a practical goal, it was obvious that teachers could improve their allotment of class time for experimental purposes. Feedback from the data resulted in greater clarity of curriculum emphases.

The second purpose served by the class time proportion data was to allow for an analysis of the relationship between off-task behavior levels and percent of class time. It seemed plausible that such a relationship might exist, since a common notion concerning elementary students is that activities should be varied frequently to avoid boredom and off-task behavior.

Raw data obtained from the observation forms first were reduced for each observation period (one complete form) by calculating the percent of

Table 2
Behavioral Observation I
Mean Percent of Class Time Activity and Off-Task Behavior

Activity Symbol		Vocal Experience	Listening Experience	Creative Experience	Instrumental Experience	Control Experience
T	Percent class time	61.0	41.4	58.3	47.2	38.5
	Percent off-task	10.1	7.8	10.4	11.0	11.1
S	Percent class time	20.3	17.4	14.7	13.9	40.1
	Percent off-task	4.2	4.6	5.7	4.7	5.9
L	Percent class time	1.1	18.1	2.5	6.7	11.2
	Percent off-task	4.0	7.1	4.8	8.6	12.6
P	Percent class time	11.9	2.1	12.3	19.4	3.9
	Percent off-task	5.8	3.0	7.8	14.4	4.1
M	Percent class time	.5		5.7		1.3
	Percent off-task	5.0		8.0		7.0
S&M	Percent class time	1.1				
	Percent off-task	14.0				
S&P	Percent class time	1.5	5.9	.4	2.5	2.1
	Percent off-task	1.0	2.0	3.0	5.3	5.7
VR	Percent class time					
	Percent off-task					
C	Percent class time			2.3		
	Percent off-task			11.5		
G	Percent class time		9.8	8.0	9.9	
	Percent off-task		14.6	32.0	19.7	
O	Percent class time	.9	.7	2.8	.3	2.4
	Percent off-task	0	3.0	9.7	3.0	14.5

class time in which each activity occurred and the mean percentage of off-task behavior recorded for each activity. Percentage of class time was calculated by dividing the number of intervals in which the symbol was recorded by the total number of intervals of the observation (for example, five "S" symbols ÷ 25 intervals = 20 percent of class time spent singing). Off-task behavior percentages for each activity were calculated by dividing the number of students off-task in each interval by the number of students in the class during that interval. The percentage figures then were averaged for the observation period. These basic data could be combined further into means for teachers, groups, and so forth. Both descriptive and inferential statistics were employed to provide a comprehensive analysis.

Results

Initially, data were reduced to means by group for each activity code symbol. The results for each of the three observations are presented in Tables 2-4.

Table 3
Behaviorial Observation II
Mean Percent of Class Time Activity and Off-Task Behavior

Activity Symbol		Vocal Experience	Listening Experience	Creative Experience	Instrumental Experience	Control Experience
T	Percent class time	56.6	32.1	45.2	40.0	37.9
	Percent off-task	5.7	6.0	6.3	9.0	10.9
S	Percent class time	15.8	10.0	8.1	11.1	35.4
	Percent off-task	2.8	5.3	5.7	6.6	8.9
L	Percent class time	3.2	40.0	5.8	3.5	5.2
	Percent off-task	3.0	5.6	3.7	9.9	9.4
P	Percent class time	2.0	9.9	4.9	28.1	.8
	Percent off-task	5.3	1.0	5.0	4.8	0
M	Percent class time	8.5	3.3	.4	.1	7.2
	Percent off-task	1.3	6.0	0	9.0	12.0
S&M	Percent class time		.9		.6	6.3
	Percent off-task		4.0		5.5	9.4
S&P	Percent class time	.7			1.1	
	Percent off-task	0			11.0	
VR	Percent class time	3.0	.4	.9	1.6	
	Percent off-task	9.0	15.5	7.0	.5	
C	Percent class time			25.3		
	Percent off-task			5.4		
G	Percent class time	9.6	3.3	9.2	12.6	6.2
	Percent off-task	3.9	4.8	10.5	9.5	15.7
O	Percent class time			.1		.2
	Percent off-task			12.0		12.0

Different amounts of class time and different levels of off-task behavior resulted in relation to classroom activites. Table 5 provides a ranking of the mean amounts of class time devoted to each activity. It is interesting to note that "teaching" consumed the major portion of class time, followed by "singing" and "listening." Although these data reflect a rather large sampling of classrooms, eleven teachers, and five "approaches," the composite picture reveals a basically traditional allotment of class time. Teachers spent, on the average, nearly the same amount of class time "getting ready" as they did "playing instruments" in class. This finding seems especially consequential, considering that the average amount of contact time with students was 24 hours for the year.

Off-task levels are ranked by symbol in Table 6. Students apparently exhibited most off-task behavior during "getting ready" periods. This finding may not be surprising, but it should be noted that students were coded as off-task if they behaved inappropriately at any time. Behavioral definitions of appropriate behavior are possible even for periods during which the relevant activity is not entirely clear.

Table 4
Behavioral Observation III
Mean Percent of Class Time Activity and Off-Task Behavior

Activity Symbol		Vocal Experience	Listening Experience	Creative Experience	Instrumental Experience	Control Experience
T	Percent class time	43.4	43.1	26.6	24.3	27.7
	Percent off-task	4.3	11.3	4.1	7.0	12.7
S	Percent class time	32.7	5.4	11.7	16.5	35.1
	Percent off-task	3.6	7.4	4.7	4.6	10.7
L	Percent class time	2.6	33.3	6.1	10.1	17.7
	Percent off-task	2.4	10.0	4.7	4.1	10.7
P	Percent class time	2.9	1.6	3.4	31.0	.9
	Percent off-task	1.8	0	.5	3.0	4.3
M	Percent class time	3.8	8.2			5.7
	Percent off-task	0	8.5			12.5
S&M	Percent class time				.3	.3
	Percent off-task				0	8.0
S&P	Percent class time	.5			2.1	
	Percent off-task	5.0			1.0	
VR	Percent class time	3.1		1.8	.8	.6
	Percent off-task	2.9		1.5	1.0	12.3
C	Percent class time	1.1		33.4		
	Percent off-task	0		4.1		
G	Percent class time	9.7	9.8	14.8	14.9	9.5
	Percent off-task	4.4	18.2	6.2	6.3	13.1
O	Percent class time	.3		1.0	.5	.1
	Percent off-task	3.0		6.3	0	8.0

An inference that might be drawn from the ranked data in Table 6 is that students seem to be more on-task as the nature of the activity demands or promotes involvement. Thus, participating in verbal interactions (T) lends itself to higher levels of off-task behavior than playing instruments, singing, and so on. This finding reinforces the notion that student involvement relates to the attention-consumption level of educative activity. A hypothesis remaining to be tested, however, is whether "action" activities also lead to the greatest learning. The present data suggest that on-task behavior is related to the nature of the activity in which students participate. At the same time, off-task levels were generally quite low, regardless of activity. Previous studies have reported that collective means of off-task student behavior in music classes are significantly less than those in regular classes (Forsythe, 1975).

Table 5
Class Time Ranking by Symbol

Activity Symbol		Average Percent of Class Time
O	(other)	.6
VR	(verbal rhythms)	.6
S&M	(singing and moving)	.9
S&P	(singing & playing)	1.6
M	(moving to music)	2.9
C	(creating)	4.1
G	(getting ready)	8.5
P	(playing instruments)	8.9
L	(listening)	11.1
S	(singing)	19.2
T	(teaching)	41.6

Table 6
Off-Task Ranking by Symbol

Activity Symbol		Average Percent Off-Task
S&P	(singing and playing)	3.8
P	(playing instruments)	4.1
C	(creating)	5.3
S	(singing)	5.7
VR	(verbal rhythms)	6.2
M	(moving to music)	6.3
O	(other)	6.5
L	(listening.)	6.7
S&M	(singing and moving)	6.8
T	(teaching)	8.5
G	(getting ready)	12.2

To investigate whether a relationship existed between percent of class time given to each activity and the level of accompanying on-task behavior, Pearson product-moment correlations were computed between these two variables across all teachers (separately) and observations (combined). No significant correlation resulted. The necessity for equal sample sizes in each factor cell precluded the use of all activity symbols, groups, and teachers in factor analysis. Following the recommendations of Glass and Stanley (1970), proportional cell sizes were obtained, for as many factors as practical, by randomly eliminating a few excess data points to achieve optimum sample sizes in which confidence could be placed. Adequate data were available for a comparison of all four project groups, and control, in relation to at least three classroom activities (teaching, singing, and listening). The third variable under consideration was "teacher." Since each group was staffed by two teachers, comparisons between teacher pairs within groups were made possible. The analysis of variance results for the first set of factors are shown in Table 7.

Significant differences were found for each of the main effect variables. No significant interactions occurred, however. The data reveal that off-task behavior levels were indeed a function, in part, of the activities in which

Table 7
Analysis of Variance: Activity* X Group X Teacher

Source	df	MS	F	p	
Activity	2	255.83	10.42	.001	
Group	4	395.94	16.12	.001	
Teacher	1	1090.01	44.38	.001	
A × G	8	26.21	1.87	.39	N.S.
A × T	2	19.23	.78	.46	N.S.
G × T	4	11.36	.46	.76	N.S.
A × G × T	8	41.62	1.69	.10	N.S.
Within	360	24.56			

* Includes teaching, singing, and listening

Table 8
Mean Off-Task Behavior: Five Groups X Three Activities

Activity	Control	Vocal	Creative	Instru-mental	Listening	Total Means
Teaching	11.73	5.89	8.35	9.08	8.62	7.01
Singing	7.54	3.00	6.04	6.46	6.96	6.00
Listing	10.35	2.54	5.08	6.96	9.12	6.81
Total Means	9.87	3.81	6.49	7.50	8.23	

the students engaged, at least with respect to the three activities involved in this analysis. Table 8 shows that the average off-task behavior level was highest during "teaching" activities and lowest during "singing" activities. Though these results may not appear surprising, they are made perhaps more meaningful by the fact that no interaction between teacher and activity occurred. That is, it would appear that off-task behavior was, in part, a function of the activity, irrespective of the teacher involved.

Four of the five groups involved yielded a sampling of activities sufficient to permit the analysis of the activities in Table 8 plus "getting ready." From Table 9 it can be seen that significant differences again resulted for each of the main variables. However, a significant interaction between teacher and activity did result in this analysis. Apparently, the effect of the teacher was not independent of the classroom activity when "getting ready" was included as an activity.

An analysis of the mean off-task percentages in Table 10 shows that "getting ready" activities produced a higher level of off-task behavior than other activities. "Singing" was again the activity with the lowest off-task mean.

Table 9
Analysis of Variance: Activity* X Group X Teacher

Source	df	MS	F	p	
Activity	3	466.02	11.01	.001	
Group	3	274.73	6.49	.001	
Teacher	1	2183.19	51.60	.001	
Int A × G	9	57.06	1.35	.21	N.S.
A × T	3	142.20	3.36	.02	
G × T	3	30.52	.72	.54	N.S.
A × G × T	9	41.41	.98	.46	N.S.
Within	384	42.31			

* Includes teaching, singing, listening, and getting ready

Table 10
Mean Off-Task Behavior: Four Groups X Four Groups

Activity	Control	Creative	Instru-mental	Listening	Total Means
Teaching	11.73	8.35	9.08	8.62	9.45
Singing	7.54	6.04	6.46	6.96	6.73
Listening	10.35	5.08	6.96	9.12	7.88
Getting Ready	13.00	9.89	8.54	15.12	11.64
Total Means	10.65	7.34	7.76	9.95	

Table 11 shows the results of a factor computation involving three groups and four activities (includes "playing instruments"). Once again, all main effect variables were significant and no interactions were significant.

Mean off-task levels in Table 12 indicate that "listening" activities yielded the lowest level of off-task behavior while "teaching" again produced the highest level.

Conclusions and Discussion

From the analysis of these data, the following conclusions about the sample can be drawn:

(1) Elementary music teachers tend to allot differing amounts of class time to a variety of classroom activities. The emphasis is on verbal interaction (teaching), singing, and listening.

(2) Off-task student behavior is related to the nature of the classroom activity engaged in, with those activities involving more "active" participation being more likely to promote on-task behavior.

Table 11
Analysis of Variance: Activity* X Group X Teacher

Source	df	MS	F	p	
Activity	3	137.24	5.90	.001	
Group	2	285.06	12.26	.001	
Teacher	1	397.13	17.08	.001	
A × G	6	18.32	.79	.58	N.S.
A × T	3	54.73	2.35	.07	N.S.
G × T	2	14.16	.61	.55	N.S.
A × G × T	6	44.18	1.90	.08	N.S.
Within	288	23.25			

* Includes teaching, singing, listening, and playing instruments

Table 12
Mean Off-Task Behavior: Three Groups X Four Activities

Activity	Vocal	Creative	Instru-mental	Total Means
Teaching	5.89	8.35	9.08	7.77
Singing	3.0	6.04	6.46	5.18
Listening	2.54	5.08	6.96	4.86
Playing Instruments	4.23	6.89	5.27	5.46
Total Means	3.91	6.59	6.94	

(3) The mean off-task behavior level of students is generally highest during periods of "getting ready" for other activities. Verbal interaction between students and teacher also produces higher levels of off-task behavior than singing, listening to music, playing instruments, and so forth.

(4) Off-task behavior levels of various activities do not correlate significantly with the amount of class time dedicated to those activities.

(5) Off-task behavior levels are a function of the type of classroom activity, the teacher, and the curriculum emphasis of the music program. In general, there is no significant interaction among these three variables, suggesting that the effects of each are independent of the others.

One of the major findings of this study was the lack of significant relationships between off-task behavior levels produced by various classroom activities and the amount of class time given to those activities. The data did not support the common notion that elementary school children must be provided with highly varied activities to maintain their attention. Moreover, this notion was invalid for this sample regardless of grade level, since correlation analyses were computed for each teacher's observations separately (per classroom) as well as collectively (all teachers, all observations), producing no significant results.

While it may not be surprising to find that off-task behavior levels were a function of the nature of the classroom activity, the absence of significant interactions with other variables places this finding in a more consequential light. Previous research presented in the *Journal of Applied Behavioral Analysis* has thoroughly demonstrated that teacher attention is a powerful variable affecting the on-task behavior of children. Therefore, it was puzzling that only one significant interaction between teacher and classroom activity occurred in this sample. In the present study teachers acted as their own control, insofar as classroom activities varied within a given classroom under the same teacher. Thus, fluctuations in off-task levels accompanying changing activities would seem to have been a function of those activities and not of the teacher. Significantly different off-task levels were evident between teachers within each group, but the pattern of off-task with respect to activities was similar. The only exception was the analysis that included the "getting ready" activity. Interaction did occur in this analysis, suggesting that the teacher variable is not independent of activity when preparatory activity is a factor. To the extent that this activity accounts for the interaction, the results are understandable, especially considering the potential for teacher differences in managing "getting ready" periods.

On-task behavior, of course, represents only one of many dependent behaviors in the music classroom. The hypothesis that such "social" behavior is related to either cognitive learning or affective responsiveness remains to be explored and tested. The operational definitions upon which any investigation relies are subject to prescribed limitations—at least until future findings suggest a broader implication. In the present study, the opposite of off-task behavior (not attending) was considered, by definition, on-task behavior (attending). But this distinction remains only a logical assumption until additional research demonstrates the extent to which appearing on-task is shown to be related to learning and enjoying music. Several implications for music teaching may be drawn from this study's findings. If attending behavior is indeed primarily a function of the nature of the activity in which students engage, as these data suggest, teachers may need to consider using more contrived contingencies for maintaining participation when students are pursuing an activity that may have high educative value but low probability of involvement. For activities that are not inherently consuming or reinforcing, students may need, for example, powerful teacher approval in order to sustain effort and attention through less desirable experiences. Another possibility might be to employ a version of the Premack principle, by which higher involvement activities are made contingent upon participation in lower ones. Elementary music teachers may be able to make use of the power of certain music activities in establishing contingent relationships for learning and enjoyment.

References

Becker, W. C., ed. *An Empirical Basis for Change in Education.* Chicago: Science Research Associates, Inc., 1971.

Dunkin, M. J., and B. J. Biddle. *The Study of Teaching.* New York: Holt, Reinhart and Winston, Inc., 1974.

Erbes, R. L. "The Development of an Observational System for the Analysis of Interaction in the Rehearsal of Musical Organizations." Unpublished doctoral dissertation (Urbana: University of Illinois, 1972).

Forsythe, J. L. "The Effect of Teacher Approval, Disapproval, and Errors on Student Attentiveness: Music Versus Classroom Teachers." In C. K. Madsen, R. D. Greer, and C. H. Madsen, eds., *Research in Music Behavior.* New York: Teachers College Press, Columbia University, 1975, pp. 49-55.

Glass, Gene V., and J. C. Stanley. *Statistical Methods in Education and Psychology.* Englewood Cliffs, New Jersey: Prentice-Hall, Inc., 1970.

Hall, R. V. *Behavior Modification: The Measurement of Behavior.* In "Managing Behavior." Revised edition. Kansas City, Kansas: H & H Enterprises, Inc., 1974.

Krathwohl, D. R., B. S. Bloom, and B. B. Masia. *Taxonomy of Educational Objectives Handbook II: Affective Domain.* New York: David McKay Company, Inc., 1964, p. 95.

Madsen, C. H., and C. K. Madsen. *Teaching/Discipline: A Positive Apprach for Educational Development.* Expanded second edition for professionals. Boston: Allyn and Bacon, 1974.

Medley, D. M., and H. E. Mitzel. "Measuring Classroom Behavior by Systematic Observation." In N. L. Gage, ed., *Handbook of Research on Teaching.* Chicago: Rand McNally, 1963, pp. 247-328.

Rosenshine, B., and N. Furst. "The Use of Direct Observation to Study Teaching." In R. M. W. Travers, ed., *Second Handbook of Research on Teaching.* Chicago: Rand McNally, 1973, pp. 122-183.

Wright, H. F. "Observational Child Study." In P. H. Mussen, ed., *Handbook of Research Methods in Child Development.* New York: John Wiley and Sons, Inc., 1960, pp. 71-139.

■ Ohio State University
Columbus, Ohio

EFFECT OF MAGNITUDE OF CONDUCTOR BEHAVIOR ON STUDENTS IN SELECTED MIXED CHORUSES

Cornelia Yarbrough

JRME 1975, VOLUME 23, NUMBER 3, PAGES 134–146

The purpose of this experiment was to investigate the effect of magnitude of conductor behavior on performance, attentiveness, and attitude of students in mixed choruses. Four mixed choruses (one university and three high schools) were rehearsed under three conditions: (1) with regular conductor, (2) with high magnitude conductor, and (3) with low magnitude conductor.

Magnitude was defined a priori by the experimenter and subsequently observed using the Music Conductor Observation Form developed for this study. In addition the effect of magnitude was measured by (1) judges' ratings of audiotaped musical performances, (2) behavioral observation of student attentiveness, and (3) self-report of student attitude.

Although results indicated no significant differences in musical performance, attentiveness, or attitude ratings among baseline and the two experimental conditions, high and low magnitude, three of the groups received their lowest ratings under the low magnitude condition, off-task percentage was lower during the high magnitude condition, and data demonstrated student preference for the high magnitude conductor.

Key Words: attitudes, choral organization, conducting, expressive devices, rehearsal, vocal instruction.

Historically, conductors have been responsible for directing performing groups—orchestra, chorus, band, opera—in order to bring about complete coordination of all players and singers. The use of hands to indicate melodic motion was a technique of not only early Egyptian and Sumerian conductors but also early conductors of Gregorian chant. In addition to melody, conductors have historically been responsible for the beat or pulse of music. This was sometimes indicated by an audible downward motion of the foot (early Greeks), an upward and downward hand motion (fifteenth and sixteenth centuries), or the use of the hand, a rolled-up sheet of paper, or wooden stick to produce slightly audible strong and weak beats (seventeenth century).

In the nineteenth century, conductors, rather than sitting at the harpsichord or singing within the choral ensemble, became more independent and authoritative. These conductors stood in front of the group and used a baton. Some present-day choral conductors have discarded the baton and augment strict conducting patterns with highly expressive motions.[1] While there is much debate concerning the behaviors that constitute good conducting, it would appear that no decisive conclusions acceptable to everyone have been reached. Most conducting texts deal with technical skills concerning beat patterns, baton technique, interpretation of the musical score, and the like. However, the variable of magnitude, i.e., what a conductor can do to make a rehearsal more exciting, has not previously been explored. Although it is assumed that most performers would prefer playing or singing under an exciting conductor, few attempts have been made to precisely define what exciting conducting is, and isolate those skills and behaviors that directly contribute to an effective rehearsal. This study is an attempt to investigate this illusive aspect of conducting—magnitude of conductor behavior.

Review of Literature

Behavioral studies in music that have manipulated the behavior of the conductor or music teacher in order to modify the behavior of the student can be classified into three general areas: social behavior, academic behavior, and music preference/attitude. These studies indicate that in the case of performance groups, the teacher is not the *source* of reinforcement that maintains appropriate behavior. Instead it is suggested that music itself functions as the reinforcement which maintains attending behavior. That is, regardless of the nature of teacher reinforcement, approval or disapproval, students appear to be on-task in music performance groups.[2]

---

[1] Willi Apel, *Harvard Dictionary of Music*, (Cambridge, Massachusetts: Belknap Press of Harvard University Press, 1967), pp. 196-198.

[2] J. Forsythe, "The Effect of Teacher Approval, Disapproval, and Errors on Student Attentiveness Comparing Music Versus Classroom Teachers," in C. K. Madsen, R. D. Greer, and C. H. Madsen, Jr., eds., *Research in Music Behavior* (New York: Columbia University, Teachers College Press, in press). C. K. Madsen, and C. H. Madsen, Jr., "Selection of Music Listening or Candy as a Function of Contingent Versus Noncontingent Reinforcement and Scale Singing," in C. K. Madsen, et al., eds., *Research in Music Behavior*, (New York: Columbia University, Teachers College Press, in press). K. Murray, "The Effect of Teacher Approval/Disapproval on Musical Performance, Attentiveness, and Attitude of High School Choruses," in C. K. Madsen, et al., eds., *Research in Music Behavior* (New York: Columbia University, Teachers College Press, in press).

Furthermore, it appears that musical performance, whether it be scale singing or the performance of a choral work, improves regardless of the ratio of teacher approvals/disapprovals or other kinds of rewards (pennies, listening to rock music, and so forth).[3] Finally, tentative results of research on the effect of teacher behavior in music classes on preference and attitude suggest that while approval/disapproval ratios do not seem to affect musical performance, high approval does influence attitude and preference. High school students appear to like both the music and the rehearsal of conductors who use high approval. Additionally, younger students receiving music listening lessons under conditions of adult high approval selected more of that music than subjects under low approval conditions.[4] It should be noted, however, that these studies failed to manipulate a variable within teacher behavior—that of magnitude, or intensity of reinforcement.

Behavioral literature outside the field of music has recognized the importance of speed, consistency, and potency of reinforcement. Although no studies were found that specifically manipulated intensity of teacher behavior, several emphasized the necessity of (1) dramatic change of pace, (2) dynamic presentation of materials, and (3) direct, personal delivery of reinforcement in order to affect student performance.[5] In a study concerning the effectiveness of direct verbal instruction on IQ performance and achievement in reading, and arithmetic, Englemann emphasized the importance of the teacher's being interested, excited, and creating drama and suspense by varying pacing, rhythm, loudness, and pauses.[6]

Since it appeared that no attempt had been made in previous experimental studies in music to isolate and define magnitude of teacher response operationally, this study was designed as an initial effort to vary magnitude of teacher behavior in order to study the effect of these varia-

---

[3] C. K. Madsen, D. C. Wolfe, and C. H. Madsen, Jr., "The Effect of Reinforcement and Directional Scalar Methodology on Intonational Improvement," *Council for Research in Music Education*, No. 18 (Fall 1969), pp. 22-23. R. D. Greer, A. Randall, and D. Timberlake, "The Discriminative Use of Music Listening as a Contingency for Improvement in Vocal Pitch Acuity and Attending Behavior," *Council for Research in Music Education Bulletin*, No. 26 (Fall 1971), pp. 10–18. K. Murray, "The Effect of Teacher Approval/Disapproval on Musical Performance, Attentiveness, and Attitude of High School Choruses," in C. K. Madsen, et al., eds., *Research in Music Behavior* (New York: Columbia University, Teachers College Press, in press).

[4] Murray. See also, R. D. Greer, L. G. Dorow, G. Wachhaus, and E. R. White, "Adult Approval and Students' Music Selection Behavior", *Journal of Research in Music Education*, Vol. 21 (Winter 1973), pp. 345–354.

[5] K. D. O'Leary and W. C. Becker, "The Effects of the Intensity of a Teacher's Reprimands on Children's Behavior," *Journal of School Psychology*, No. 7 (1968-1969), pp. 8-11. K. D. O'Leary, K. F. Kaufman, R. E. Kass, and D. S. Drabman, "The Effects of Loud and Soft Reprimands on the Behavior of Disruptive Students," *Exceptional Children*, No. 38 (1970), pp. 145-155.

[6] S. Engelmann, "The Effectiveness of Direct Verbal Instruction on I.Q. Performance and Achievement in Reading and Arithmetic," in W. C. Becker, ed., *An Empirical Basis for Change in Education* (Chicago: Science Research Associates, 1971), pp. 461-483.

tions on student responses. Specifically its purpose was to investigate the effect of magnitude of conductor behavior on performance, attentiveness, and attitude of students in selected mixed choruses. Thus, student performance, attentiveness, and attitude were observed in two experimental conditions: under conductor behavior operationally defined as *high magnitude;* and under conductor behavior operationally defined as *low magnitude.*

Procedures

Subjects used in this study were members of randomly selected student mixed choruses in Tallahassee, Florida (N = 207).[7]

The experiment was conducted during the regular rehearsal time and in the normal rehearsal room for each chorus. One experimental teacher, one observer, three media technicians, and audiovisual equipment surrounded the group during the experiment. One and one-half rehearsal periods were used for acclimation purposes. During this time regular rehearsals were continued within the experimental environment. The regular teacher was present only for the acclimation period and baseline rehearsal.

One SATB choral composition, "Alleluia" by Randall Thompson,[8] was selected after consultation with the conductors of the choruses on the following bases: (1) It was unfamiliar to the chorus members. (2) It was short and simple enough for high school choral groups to achieve an adequate performance level within a 16-minute time period as well as difficult enough to be discriminative. (3) It could be divided into sections similar in text, rhythm, harmony, and melody. The first section (11 pages) was then divided into two parts, one of which was used for baseline and the other for both experimental conditions. Baseline music consisted of pages 3-6, measures 1-25. Experimental music consisted of pages 7-11, measures 26-55.

Baseline data was recorded during the last half of the second regular rehearsal period. During baseline the regular director rehearsed the first section of Thompson's "Alleluia." Each director was told to use the rehearsal time as he wished and that at the end of the 16-minute rehearsal period the chorus would be asked to sing as much of the section as possible without accompaniment.

On the third day the experimenter taught the second section of Thompson's "Alleluia" under two conditions during two experimental rehearsal sessions each lasting 16 minutes. The rehearsal plan for each session was identical. Verbal instructions to be given to each choral group were written in the experimental conductor's score to control for instructional content, i.e., to insure that all groups received identical

---

[7] Leon High School, Godby High School, University High School, and Florida State University Choral Union.

[8] Randall Thompson, "Alleluia" (Boston: E. C. Schirmer Music Co., 1940).

instructions under each experimental condition. Rehearsal sessions were counterbalanced across choral groups and rehearsal periods.

The experimental conditions, high and low magnitude of teacher behavior, were operationally defined *a priori* by the experimenter (See Figure 1). At the beginning and end of each experimental rehearsal, each chorus sang an uninterrupted *a cappella* performance of the section that was recorded for subsequent rating by judges. Following posttest performances for both baseline and experimental sessions, an attitude scale was administered.

Figure 1
Operational Definition of High and Low Magnitude

Teacher Behavior	High Magnitude	Low Magnitude
Eye Contact	Maintains with group and/or individuals throughout rehearsal.	Never looks at individuals or group. Looks at music, ceiling, or occasionally in direction of piano.
Closeness	Frequently walks or leans toward chorus or particular section.	Stands behind music stand at all times. Music stand is always a minimum of four feet from chorus.
Volume and Modulation of Voice	Volume constantly varies. Wide range of volume as well as speaking pitch. Voice reflects "enthusiasm and vitality."	Volume remains clearly audible but the same approximate volume and pitch throughout rehearsal. Voice reflects little "enthusiasm and vitality."
Gestures	Uses arms and hands to aid in musical phrasing. Great variety of movement. Varies size of conducting patterns to indicate phrases, dynamics, and the like.	Strict conducting pattern, never varying. Uses arms and hands for attacks and releases. Exact movements.
Facial Expressions	Face reflects sharp contrasts between approval/disapproval. Approval is expressed by grinning, laughing aloud, raising eyebrows, widening eyes. Disapproval is expressed by frowning, knitting brow, pursing lips, narrowing eyes.	Neutral mask. No frowns. No smiles.
Rehearsal Pace	"Rapid and exciting." Quick instructions. Minimal talking. Less than one second between activity. Frequently gives instructions to group while they are singing.	"Slow and methodical." Meticulous care and detail in instructions. Always stops group to give instructions.

During the experimental sessions a ratio of 50 percent approval/50 percent disapproval teacher responses contingent on appropriate academic and social behavior was maintained. Control of the experimental conductor's approval/disapproval verbal responses was achieved by providing a feedback chart indicating the frequency of each type of response. Following each approval or disapproval given by the experimenter during an observation interval, an observer recorded the response and flipped the corresponding card. In order to achieve a more natural response, the experimental conductor was free to give contingent approval and disapproval responses at any time during the rehearsals.

Equipment

Videotape recordings of teachers and students, using two cameras to provide a split-screen effect, were made to provide *ex post facto* analyses. Therefore, both magnitude and frequency of teacher responses as well as frequency of student responses could be ascertained. Audiotape recordings were also made for subsequent judgment of musical performances. Prerecorded observe/record cassette tape was used to synchronize observations of video tapes. The following equipment was used: one Sony AV 3600 Videocorder, one Sony AV 3650 Videocorder, two Sony AVF 3200 Video Cameras, two Canon Zoom Lenses V5 × 20, one Sony 8″ Monitor—Model CVM 920U, one Sony Special Effects Generator—SEG-1, one Sony TC 355 Stereophonic Audio Tape Recorder, one Craig Cassette Audio Tape Recorder—Model 2621, one Sony 3-Channel Microphone Mixer—MX 600M, two Shure Unisphere B Microphones—Model 588SA, one Sony F-98 Cardiod Microphone and Lavalier, two Atlas Sound Microphone Stands, three Thoro Test Dynamic Earphones—15 Ohm/EP-4, and Thoro Test Stereo Headphones—SHP-2.

Behavioral Observation Procedures

After the experiment, two trained observers recorded overt student off-task behavior by viewing videotapes. Observation was time sampled and consisted of ten-second observe intervals and five-second record intervals. A prerecorded cassette tape providing verbal cues, "observe" and "record," was mixed into the sound recorded on videotape. The video camera was focused on a maximum of five students during each "observe" interval and was rotated on the "record" cue throughout each rehearsal so that all chorus members were observed. Student on/off-task was defined as follows:

On-Task: Active—When student is supposed to be singing, he must be singing and looking at either the music or teacher. Passive—When student is not supposed to be singing, he must be quiet and looking at

either music, teacher, or chorus members who are singing. Other—Student must follow instructions given by teacher.
Off-Task: Observably not on-task.

Observers viewed videotapes of experimental sessions and recorded frequency of verbal approval and disapproval responses. Verbal approval/disapproval teacher responses were defined as follows:

A = Approval. Any observable (aural) endorsement of an appropriate rehearsal behavior: verbal approvals.

(A) = Approval Error. Any verbal approval of an inappropriate rehearsal behavior.

D = Disapproval. Any observable (aural) reprimand of an inappropriate rehearsal behavior: verbal disapprovals.

(D) = Disapproval Error. Any verbal disapproval of an appropriate rehearsal behavior.[9]

Other observational data provided by subsequent analyses of videotape recordings concerned how rehearsal time was actually spent by both students and teacher. Time used for performance, nonperformance, and section rehearsals was recorded by observers *ex post facto* using the following categories of behavior:

I = Instruction. Teacher giving verbal directions concerning the music, performing an example, asking and answering questions concerning the music or its performance. Also, the accompanist may be performing an example.

S = Singing. Teacher singing or speaking in ensemble with students.

O = Other. Other teacher responses not fitting above categories, e.g., long pauses, jokes, or verbalizations not concerning the music or its performance.

N = Nonperformance. Chorus or any part of chorus is not singing during the majority of the observation interval.

P = Performance. Entire chorus is singing or speaking in ensemble during the majority of the interval. Mutually exclusive from "N."

S-A-T-B. Section(s) is (are) singing or speaking during the majority of the observation interval. These categories are mutually exclusive from "P" and "N" but not from each other.

Frequency of off-task student behavior, frequency of teacher approval/disapproval responses, and rehearsal time were recorded by observers using a Choral Rehearsal Observation Form developed by Murray.[10]

The main aspect of experimental interest in the present study concerned teacher magnitude. To observe magnitude of teacher behavior, a new observation form was developed based on the *a priori* operational

---

[9] C. H. Madsen, Jr., and C. K. Madsen, *Teaching/Discipline: A Positive Approach for Educational Development,* (Boston: Allyn and Bacon, expanded second edition for professionals, 1974).

[10] Murray.

definitions of high and low magnitude (Figure 1). Using this form observers recorded frequency of conductor behaviors in eight categories: activity, body movement, conducting gestures, eye contact, facial expressions, speech speed, voice pitch, and voice volume. Space was also provided for listing mannerisms such as foot tapping, bouncing, overuse of certain words, finger snapping, touching face, hair, glasses with hands, and so forth.

Observers viewed videotapes three times for each observation form. For the Choral Rehearsal Observation Form observers recorded (1) total number of students observed and number of students off-task during the first viewing, (2) teacher approvals/disapprovals during the second viewing, and (3) teacher/student activity during the third viewing. For the Music Conductor Observation Form, observers recorded (1) activity, body movement, and conducting gestures during the first viewing; (2) eye contact and facial expression during the second viewing; and (3) speech speed, voice pitch, and voice volume during the third viewing. If annoying mannerisms were noticed, observers viewed videotapes a fourth time to count frequency of occurrence.

Observer Reliability

Observation reliability was computed using the following ratio:

$$\frac{\text{Agreements}}{\text{Agreements plus Disagreements}}$$

Three observers were used for the Choral Rehearsal Observation Form. Reliability on 25 percent of the cases was computed for all possible pairs of observers. Average reliability was .84. Four observers recorded observations in the eight categories of the Music Conductor Observation Form. Average reliability between all possible pairs of observers was .83.

Results

A panel of expert judges heard 20 audiotaped pre- and postperformances in random order. Intonation, blend, balance, tempo, dynamics, tone quality, rhythm, phrasing, ensemble, diction, style, and overall artistic effect (musicality) were rated from 1 (poor) to 4 (excellent). Interjudge reliability (agreement) was tested using a Spearman rank correlation coefficient.[11] Results show high reliability ($r_s = .97$, p $<.05$) indicating little disparity between sets of rankings.

A Friedman two-way analysis of variance by ranks[12] reveals no significant difference in the posttest performance ratings among the two ex-

---

[11] Sidney Siegel, *Nonparametric Statistics for the Behavioral Sciences* (New York: McGraw-Hill, 1956), pp. 202–213.

[12] Siegel, pp. 166-172.

perimental conditions and baseline ($x_r^2 = 4.50$, p >.05). However, it is noted in Table 1 that three of the four groups received their lowest ratings under the low magnitude condition and two groups received their highest ratings under the regular director (baseline), respectively.

Concerning pre- to posttest performance gain scores, it appears that regardless of experimental condition (high or low magnitude), the most gain for all groups occurred during the initial 16-minute rehearsal period (see Table 2). A Wilcoxin Matched Pairs Signed Ranks test[13] on pre- and posttest gain (difference) scores for the high and low magnitude conditions indicates no significant difference in performance gain between the two experimental conditions (T = 5, N = 2, p >.05). Therefore, it seems possible that an order effect cancelled any effect that magnitude may have had on performance.

Although data presented in Table 3 demonstrates that students were less off-task under the high magnitude condition than under either the low magnitude or baseline (regular conductor), a Friedman two-way analysis of variance shows no significant differences in the percentage of off-task behavior among the two experimental conditions and baseline ($x_r^2 = 6$, p >.06). Regardless of conditions, students were more off-task during section rehearsals or during nonperformance or instruction parts of the rehearsal. As might be expected, students were most on-task while the entire group was singing (see Table 4). It is interesting to note that no order effect is apparent here. Regardless of order of condition, more students were attentive during the high magnitude than during either baseline or low magnitude.

A Friedman two-way analysis of variance was used to test differences in rank order of mean attitude ratings among baseline and the two experimental conditions for each question on the attitude scale. No significant differences are indicated on any of the comparisons. Table 5 indicates mean attitude ratings for each question on the attitude scale.

The Wilcoxin Matched Pairs Signed Ranks test reveals a significant difference in mean attitude ratings toward the experimental conductor between the high magnitude and low magnitude conditions (p <.05). Students did prefer the high magnitude conductor (mean attitude rating = 7.39) over the low magnitude conductor (mean attitude rating = 6.76) as demonstrated by mean attitude scale ratings (10 = high; 1 = low). However, it should be considered that perhaps the attitude ratings did not sufficiently discriminate in that all conductors were rated high.

Discussion

Results from this study indicate that magnitude of conductor behavior had no significant effect on the performance, attentiveness, and attitude

---

[13] Siegel, pp. 75-83.

Table 1
Postperformance Ratings

Group	Baseline	High Magnitude	Low Magnitude
1	1	3	2
2	2	1	3
3	2	1	3
4	1	2	3
Means	1.5	1.75	2.75

Table 2
Pre- and Posttest Difference Scores

Group	Rehearsal Order	High Magnitude	Low Magnitude
1	Low–High	−2	20
2	High–Low	29	9
3	Low–High	16	19
4	High–Low	11	−4

Table 3
Percentage Off-Task Behavior

Group	Baseline	High Magnitude	Low Magnitude
1	17.88	7.22	12.50
2	17.59	7.44	22.38
3	12.98	4.54	13.56
4	45.07	35.15	42.22
Means	23.38	13.58	22.66

Table 4
Mean Percentage Off-Task Behavior

Activity	Baseline	High Magnitude	Low Magnitude
Nonperformance	29.91	10.63	22.00
Performance	7.41	3.78	6.74
Section Rehearsal	31.44	23.67	33.39

Table 5
Mean Attitude Ratings

	Baseline	High Magnitude	Low Magnitude
Question: I Like This Music.			
	8.87	7.87	8.14
	7.86	7.96	8.09
	6.00	6.76	6.04
	7.13	6.80	6.54
Means	7.47	7.35	7.20
Question: I Enjoyed Rehearsing This Music.			
	8.40	7.26	6.97
	7.55	7.59	7.92
	5.80	6.43	5.84
	6.70	6.63	6.23
Means	7.11	6.98	6.74
Question: During This Rehearsal I Was: (Degree of Participation).			
	7.72	6.82	6.21
	6.98	7.46	7.51
	6.37	7.28	6.45
	6.70	7.01	7.05
Means	6.94	7.14	6.81

of students in mixed choruses. However there was a significant difference in mean attitude ratings toward the experimental conductor between the high magnitude condition and the low magnitude condition, although it must be considered that regardless of the magnitude condition over 55 percent of all students rated the conductor from 6 to 10 (high) on the scale.

The first possible explanation for the above results concerns the variable of primary interest, magnitude. What is magnitude? Is it *more* behavior, i.e., more expressive than strict conducting gestures, more loud voice volume than soft, more approach body movement than stationary? Perhaps magnitude does not concern *more* of a behavior but rather novelty or difference in behavior. Indeed, the reinforcing effect of a conductor may be based solely on the ability to change behavior dramatically in all categories (body movement, voice volume, pitch, speed, activity, eye contact, conducting gestures, facial expressions) at precisely the right time during the rehearsal.

Results from observations using the Music Conductor Observation Form suggest that although in most cases there was a dramatic change of behavior from the low magnitude condition to the high magnitude condition, there was little dramatic change of behavior *within* the high magnitude condition. For example, conductors spent most of their time behind the music stand rather than moving toward the chorus or walking among the students during rehearsal. However, it is noted that the experimental conductor under the high magnitude condition had significantly more approach movement than either the regular conductor or the low magnitude conductor. Still there is little difference in body movement within the high magnitude condition. The mean frequencies of the subcategories of body movement under the high magnitude condition are: Approach—17.00; Departure—5.75; Stationary—43.25. This demonstrates that there was *more* of one behavior than a variety resulting from dramatic change of behavior. In addition, all conductors conducted primarily in strict patterns rather than with expressive gestures; all conductors showed a propensity for speaking with variable pitch, normal volume, and steady speed; and all conductors appeared to instruct more, i.e., stop the group to give instructions rather than teach or sing during student performance. Perhaps this similarity contributed to the lack of difference in performance. It would appear that reinforcement history of the chorus' interaction with conductors sets up patterns of behavior that can only be modified by extreme variation in conductor behavior. In this particular instance the variation in conducting gestures from baseline to high magnitude as well as from high to low magnitude may not have been extreme enough.

In the categories "eye contact," "facial expression," and "voice volume," the high magnitude conductor again appears to be significantly different from the low magnitude conductor but very similar to the regular conductor. However, an examination of the frequencies of the subcategories of eye contact, facial expressions, and voice volume within the high magnitude condition again reveals little variety of behavior. For example, eye contact with the group as well as facial approval dominated the high magnitude rehearsal, thus providing little variation or extreme contrasts in behavior. In addition, voice volume for the high magnitude conductor ranged from loud with very little volume change to the other extreme, whispering.

Future research might focus on increasing the variety of conductor behavior within each category or the isolation of specific categories of behavior. Varying conducting behavior by going from one extreme to another, i.e., shouting to whispering, intense individual eye contact to no individual eye contact, much body movement to no body movement, exaggerated approval to exaggerated disapproval to neutral facial expressions, might yield interesting results.

Another plausible explanation for the results of this study is that perhaps the amount of time spent on the same music affected the lack of significant performance score differences between experimental conditions. For example, the same 29 measures of music were used for both experimental conditions. These conditions were rotated so that for two groups a high magnitude rehearsal was first and for the other two, a low magnitude rehearsal was first. Results indicated that in every group the most performance gain occurred during the first 16-minute rehearsal regardless of condition (Table 2). Perhaps the amount of time spent on the music (massed versus spaced practice) during one rehearsal is an important variable. Indeed, it would appear that as the time spent on the music at one sitting increased, the gain in the performance of that music decreased—the law of diminishing returns. Future research might attempt to control for order effect by counterbalancing different music as well as the different conditions.

As noted in Tables 3 and 4, off-task percentages were greater under the regular conductor and the low magnitude conductor than under the high magnitude conductor. The relatively low percentage of off-task under the high magnitude conductor might be attributed to (1) a greater amount of group and individual eye contact, (2) a greater amount of approval body movement, and (3) a much higher percentage of contingent reinforcement under the high magnitude condition (Table 6).

Table 6
Mean Frequencies of Involvement Techniques

	Baseline	High Magnitude	Low Magnitude
Eye Contact	25.75	60.75	3.50
Approach	5.75	17.00	0.00
Contingent Reinforcement	23.04	51.56	24.00

In this study the ratio of reinforcement was maintained at 50 percent approvals/50 percent disapprovals for both experimental conditions, although the frequency of approvals/disapprovals was greater under the high magnitude condition. No significant differences in attitude about music, rehearsal, or participation were indicated between the two conditions. However, a significant difference in attitude toward the conductor was indicated in that students preferred the high magnitude conductor (mean attitude = 7.38) over the low magnitude conductor (mean attitude rating = 6.76).

Perhaps the most interesting results of the attitude survey indicated that regardless of condition, over 50 percent of the students rated music, rehearsal, conductor, and participation in the 6 to 10 (high) ranks. It would appear that either the attitude scale is nondiscriminative or that students like music regardless of other intervening variables, i.e., conductor, environment, and so forth. Future research might administer similar attitude scales in other subject areas to determine similarities or differences in responses.

■ Syracuse University
Syracuse, New York

The purpose of this study was to examine videotaped teacher and performer behavior during several high school ensemble rehearsals to determine the predictability of a dependent variable, frequency of off-task behavior, by the following carrier variables: performance time; nonperformance time; frequency of social and academic approvals and disapprovals, stops, complete and incomplete teaching units, errors, and teacher eye contact. Subjects were six high school ensemble teachers and randomly selected students from two mixed choruses, three bands, and one orchestra. Videotapes, using two cameras and a special effects generator for a split-screen effect, were made for ex post facto analysis. The predictability of off-task behavior carrier variables was examined, using a multiple regression analysis. The variability of off-task behavior caused by individual teacher differences was accounted for in a repeated measures design. Results indicated a strong relationship between off-task behavior and individual teachers, nonperformance activity, and teacher eye contact. The carrier variables in this model accounted for 81.38% of the off-task variability.

Cornelia Yarbrough *Syracuse University, Syracuse, New York*
Harry E. Price *Syracuse University*

JRME 1981, VOLUME 29, NUMBER 3, PAGES 209–217

Prediction of Performer Attentiveness Based on Rehearsal Activity and Teacher Behavior

Effective teaching may be defined to the degree that an evaluation of the effect of observed teacher behavior on student behavior is possible. Previous studies have focused on teacher/conductor behavior (Forsythe, 1977; Moore, 1976; Murray, 1975; Thurman, 1976; Wagner & Strul, 1979; Yarbrough, 1975), student/performer response (Forsythe, 1977; Froehlich, 1979; Murray, 1975; Yarbrough, 1975), and student/teacher interaction in classes and rehearsals (Erbes, 1972; Forsythe, 1975; Froehlich, 1979; Kuhn, 1975; Madsen & Alley, 1979; Madsen, Wolfe, & Madsen, 1975; Murray, 1975; Nolin, 1971). These studies clarify specific teacher characteristics and class activities that

Requests for reprints should be sent to Cornelia Yarbrough, School of Music, 200 Crouse College, Syracuse University, Syracuse, New York 13210.

may affect attentiveness. Attentiveness in music classes and rehearsals may be related, in part, to teacher reinforcement. For example, on-task student behavior was greater under highly approving teachers than under highly disapproving ones (Forsythe, 1975; Kuhn, 1975). Approval reinforcement significantly increased attentiveness (Forsythe, 1975), following classroom rules (Kuhn, 1975), and positive attitudes toward choral rehearsals (Murray, 1975). Furthermore, relationships may exist between off-task behavior and social disapproval, approval, and teacher errors (Forsythe, 1975).

Results of these studies demonstrate that attentiveness in music classes and rehearsals may also be related to the class or rehearsal activity. For example, children seemed less off-task in music classes than in other classes, regardless of the approval, disapproval, or error ratios of the teachers (Forsythe, 1975). In a study that examined attentiveness in various classroom activities, students were more on-task during activities that required active participation than during passive activities, such as instruction and verbal student/teacher interaction (Forsythe, 1977). Other studies indicated that verbal instruction produced the least on-task behavior and that singing activity produced the most (Madsen, Wolfe, & Madsen, 1975). Students are more on-task in choral and instrumental music rehearsals than in general music and other classes, despite low approval ratios of conductors (Madsen & Alley, 1979). These results suggest that music performance or active, rather than passive, tasks may be intrinsically reinforcing.

Data from a study on magnitude of conductor behavior (Yarbrough, 1975) indicated that, when a conductor's behavior is dynamic and dramatic, it may affect student performance, attentiveness, and attitude. Three of the four choral groups studied received their lowest performance ratings under the low magnitude condition; on-task percentage was higher during the high magnitude condition, and student attitude ratings were higher following the high magnitude condition.

The purpose of the present study was to define and analyze a complete teaching/learning model and its relationship to specific dependent variables, such as performance, attentiveness, or attitude. Specifically, the study examined videotaped teacher and performer behavior of several high shcool ensemble rehearsals to determine the predictability of frequency of off-task behavior by the following carrier variables: performance time; nonperformance time; frequency of social and academic approvals and dispprovals, stops, complete and incomplete teaching units, errors (including reinforcement and teaching sequence mistakes), and teacher eye contact (Mosteller & Tukey, 1977).

PROCEDURE

Subjects were six high school ensemble teachers and randomly selected students from two mixed choruses, three bands, and one orchestra. Rehearsals, conducted by the regular teachers, were videotaped in the regular rehearsal rooms at the normal rehearsal times. Two media technicians and audiovisual equipment surrounded the group during the recorded rehearsals, which took place approximately two weeks prior to a performance.

Videotape equipment included one Sony AV 3600 videorecorder, two Sony AVC 3200 video cameras, two Sony f = 16 − 64 mm zoom lenses, one Sony CVM

112 8″ television monitor, one Sony SEG-1 special effects generator, one Realistic 33-1056 condenser microphone, one Realistic 33-1057 stereo microphone mixer, and one Craig 2261 cassette audio tape recorder. A prerecorded cassette tape providing the verbal cues "observe" and "record" was mixed into the sound recorded on videotape. One video camera was focused on a maximum of six students during each "observe" interval and was rotated on the "record" cue throughout each rehearsal so that all ensemble members were randomly observed several times. The other video camera was focused on the teacher for the entire rehearsal.

After videotaping was completed, two trained observers viewed the videotapes and recorded overt student off-task behavior and teacher eye contact.[1] Observation was time sampled and consisted of 10-second observe intervals and five-second record intervals.

Student behavior was defined as follows: (1) on-task active—when students are supposed to be performing, they must look at either the music or teacher; (2) on-task passive—when students are not supposed to be performing, they must be quiet and look at the music, teacher, or ensemble members who are performing; (3) on-task other—students must follow instructions given by the teacher; (4) off-task—students are observably not on-task (Madsen & Yarbrough, 1980, p. 56).

Observers counted the number of performers in view and those observably off-task for each 15-second interval. A percentage of off-task behavior was then computed for each eight-minute rehearsal segment by dividing the number of students off-task by the total number observed for that segment. Four measures of off-task behavior were obtained for each of the six rehearsals observed.

Teacher eye contact was counted and recorded according to the following definitions: (1) groups—conductor looking at entire group or section for at least three continuous seconds, (2) individual—conductor looking at individual in group or accompanist for at least three continuous seconds, (3) music—conductor looking at music for at least three continuous seconds, (4) other—conductor looking at something other than group, individuals, or music for the entire interval (Madsen & Yarbrough, 1980, p. 63). Total teacher eye contact was considered the sum of the frequency of group and individual eye contact.

A verbatim typescript of each rehearsal, prepared as a basis for further behavioral analysis, was used in conjunction with the videotape to measure seconds spent in performance and nonperformance. Continuous time in minutes and seconds was recorded in the left-hand margin of the script, using a stopwatch accurate to one-tenth second. A notation was made in the script each time the teacher stopped the music. A change of activity was noted if it lasted three or more seconds. Performance was defined as playing or singing by the entire ensemble or by its smaller sections. Nonperformance was defined as teacher instruction, teacher reinforcement, or anything not involving students' music performance.

---

[1]Observation procedures were based on techniques developed in previous behavioral and descriptive research (Madsen & Madsen, 1974; Madsen & Yarbrough, 1980; Thurman, 1976), with the exception of the procedure for complete and incomplete teaching units, which was developed for this study and is based on the teaching/learning model presented by Becker, Englemann, and Thomas (1971). Observer agreement was computed by dividing total agreements by agreements plus disagreements. Average agreement was .91.

The typescript was also used in conjunction with the videotape to analyze and count complete and incomplete teaching units. A complete teaching unit consisted of sequential parts: (1) teacher presentation of a task, (2) student response, and (3) teacher reinforcement.

Each part was delineated into categories and was coded. The codes were entered in the left-hand margin of the typescript. Teacher presentation was coded "1" and was divided into four categories, which were coded and defined as follows: 1a, academic task presentation (telling students how to play a passage or where to begin playing); 1s, social task presentation (telling students how to behave or making announcements about future activities); 1c, conducting task presentation (a nonverbal modeling of the music or a nonverbal conducting signal for dynamic changes, beginning to play, stopping, style, phrasing, and tempo); and 1o, off-task statements (those not related to social or academic tasks).

Student response was coded "2" and was divided into four categories, which were coded and defined as follows: 2p, performance by the entire ensemble; 2s, sectional performance; 2v, appropriate verbal response; and 2nv, nonverbal response.

Teacher reinforcement was coded "3" and was divided into six categories, which were coded and defined as follows: 3va, verbal academic or social approval (positive statement about student behavior); 3vd, verbal academic or social disapproval (negative statement about student behavior); 3fa, facial approval (a positive facial gesture); and 3fd, facial disapproval (a negative facial gesture). Errors were coded and defined as: 3va or 3fa (encircled), approving of an inappropriate behavior; 3vd or 3fd (encircled), disapproving of an appropriate behavior; 3vd/fa or 3va/fd (encircled), conflicting feedback (verbal expression is different from facial expression). Sequence errors included reinforcement not related to the task presented and presentation of a new task, followed by reinforcement of a previous task.

Teaching units were then analyzed for completion and content. Videotapes were again observed with coded typescripts to carefully note and accurately describe facial expressions, subtle approvals and disapprovals, and sequence errors. All units that followed a 1-2-3 sequence without error were considered complete. A 1-2 sequence, in which student response was performance by the entire ensemble or by sections, was considered complete because music performance may serve not only as student response but also as reinforcement.

Incomplete units consisted of a teacher presentation of a task followed by: (1) not allowing student response, (2) a nonmusical student response with no teacher reinforcement, or (3) teacher reinforcement with no intervening student response.

Using the coded transcript, academic and social approvals, disapprovals, and errors were identified and counted. A verbal or facial reinforcement was counted as one approval or disapproval. A verbal reinforcement paired with a facial reinforcement was counted as one approval or disapproval if the reinforcements agreed, and as one error if the reinforcements conflicted.

Each teacher and ensemble was videotaped for one complete rehearsal. Each rehearsal was analyzed in four eight-minute segments, excluding warm-ups and announcements. The complete data set consisted of percentage of off-task behavior; number of seconds during which performance (entire group plus sectional) and nonperformance occurred; frequency of stops, academic and social approvals and disapprovals, errors, teacher eye contact, and complete and incomplete teaching units.

The predictability of off-task behavior by the frequency or percentage of carrier variables was examined, using a multiple regression analysis (Mosteller & Tukey, 1977; Neter & Wasserman, 1974). Carrier variables for the regression analysis were the percentage of nonperformance and disapproval; and frequency of errors, stops, teacher eye contact, and complete and incomplete teaching units. The variability of off-task behavior caused by individual teacher differences was accounted for by using a repeated measures design.

Data were analyzed, using a multiple regression technique (Statistical Analysis System, General Linear Models Computer Program, release 79.3 A, Syracuse University) (Table 1). Carrier variables were selected and entered in hierarchical order of perceived importance based on results of previous research literature.

By studying the sums of squares values for each carrier variable, one can compare the relative contribution of each variable to the prediction of off-task behavior. Table 1b portions out the sums of squares for Model 1050.70. The F values for each carrier variable represent partial F values; therefore, they are affected by the order in which the carrier variables are entered. This explains, in part, the importance of entering carrier variables in a priori hierarchical order.

Table 1—Multiple Regression Analysis

	Source	df	SS	MS	F	p	R²
(a)	Model	12	1,050.70	87.56	4.01	.01	.8138
	Error	11	240.42	21.86			
	Corrected Total	23	1,291.12				
(b)	Teachers	5	823.75		7.54	< .003	
	Nonperformance Time	1	101.40		4.64	< .05	
	Disapprovals	1	.08		0.00	< .95	
	Errors	1	.91		.04	< .84	
	Stops	1	12.20		.56	< .47	
	Teacher Eye Contact	1	87.15		3.99	< .07	
	Complete Teaching Units	1	3.06		.14	< .72	
	Incomplete Teaching Units	1	22.15		1.01	< .34	

RESULTS

Results indicate a strong relationship between off-task behavior and the individual teachers ($p <$ .003), nonperformance activity ($p <$ .05), and teacher eye contact ($p <$ .07). Data show minimal relationships between off-task behavior and disapprovals ($p <$ .95), errors ($p <$ .84), stops ($p <$ .47), complete teaching units ($p <$ .72), and incomplete teaching units ($p <$ .34). The carrier variables in this model accounted for 81.38% (R^2 = .8138) of the off-task variability. A strong relationship exists between the predicted values (represented by the carrier variables data) and the observed values (represented by the percentage of off-task [dependent] variable).

A more detailed examination of percentages of off-task time, approvals, disapprovals, comparing performance versus nonperformance rehearsal time revealed more off-task behavior during nonperformance activity for all six teachers, more performance than nonperformance time for five of the six teachers, more approval during performance for four of the six teachers, and more disapproval during nonperformance for four of the six teachers (Table 2).

Table 3 shows frequencies of academic and social approvals and disapprovals and total approvals and disapprovals. Data show a low frequency of social reinforcement and a high frequency of academic reinforcement. Two of the six teachers were more approving than disapproving.

Table 2—Percentage of Off-Task, Time, Approvals, and Disapprovals during Performance and Nonperformance

| | Performance | | | |
Teacher	Off-Task	Time	Approvals	Disapprovals
A	25.90	38.26	54.16	45.84
B	13.82	57.68	80.89	19.11
C	9.52	68.67	45.00	55.00
D	8.06	55.35	23.84	76.16
E	6.32	53.63	72.62	27.38
F	12.30	59.09	24.58	75.42
Mean	12.65	55.45	50.18	49.82
	Nonperformance			
Teacher	Off-Task	Time	Approvals	Disapprovals
A	34.66	61.74	37.60	62.40
B	26.19	42.32	53.87	46.13
C	37.11	31.33	48.26	51.74
D	24.11	44.64	40.67	59.33
E	23.38	46.37	35.38	64.62
F	31.94	40.91	21.72	78.28
Mean	29.56	44.55	39.58	60.42

Table 3—Frequency of Academic Versus Social Reinforcement; Total Approvals and Disapprovals

| | Academic | | Social | | Total | |
Teacher	Approvals	Disapprovals	Approvals	Disapprovals	Approvals	Disapprovals
A	36	52	3	1	39	53
B	86	32	2	8	88	40
C	25	30	1	1	26	31
D	27	57	3	0	30	57
E	67	50	1	3	68	53
F	22	66	2	5	24	71
Total	263	287	12	18	275	305
Mean	43.83	47.83	2.00	3.00	45.83	50.83

Data showed that students are most on-task under teachers with most eye contact and most off-task under teachers with least eye contact. There was no discernible pattern in the data concerning frequency of stops. (See Table 4.) Teaching units were analyzed for completion (Table 5). A unit that contained a student performance response was considered complete. Because the quantity of units varies with the amount of time spent in each activity and because activity is a strong carrier variable, it may not be possible to analyze teaching units as contributors to off-task behavior.

Table 4—Percentage of Off-Task, Frequency of Eye Contact, and Stops

Teacher	Off-Task	Eye Contact	Stops
A	30.75	42	52
B	18.71	108	58
C	17.69	55	38
D	13.42	117	39
E	13.24	95	53
F	20.33	69	47

Table 5—Frequency of Complete Units, Incomplete Units, Errors, and Percentage Off-Task

Teacher	Units Complete	Incomplete	Errors	Off-Task %
A	74 *48%*	80	13	30.75
B	111 *63%*	64	23	18.70
C	48 *46%*	56	12	17.68
D	76 *76%*	24	3	13.42
E	110 *60%*	72	9	13.24
F	71 *57%*	54	21	20.33

DISCUSSION

Because of few rehearsals and great variability among teachers, caution should be used in generalizing the results of this study to other rehearsal situations. However, some strong relationships justify further discussion.

More on-task behavior occurred during performance time than during nonperformance time, which supports previous research, indicating that music or activity may be intrinsically reinforcing. During nonperformance there were more disapprovals than approvals. However, because of the low frequency of social reinforcement as compared to academic reinforcement, it may be unwise to conclude that disapprovals increased off-task behavior. Few social tasks were presented or reinforced during these rehearsals. Perhaps future research will focus on teacher effectiveness in social task presentation/reinforcement versus academic task presentation/reinforcement. The dependent variable for social task reinforcement might be attentiveness, and the dependent variable for academic task reinforcement might be performance.

Many incomplete teaching units, those in which the teaching sequence did not include an opportunity for student response, were observed. Many reinforcement errors involving sequence mistakes (reinforcement that had nothing to do with the task presented) were also observed. Regardless of the number of incomplete units and the number of errors, these variables contributed minimally to off-task behavior. To further isolate possible effects of instruction, future research should focus on the relationship of the teaching unit sequence to academic and musical achievement, attitude, and attentiveness. The quality and completeness of teaching units may affect academic and musical learning. Furthermore, academic reinforcement may affect academic learning, social reinforcement may affect attitude and attentiveness, and activity (performance versus nonperformance) may affect attentiveness and musical achievement. Because there may be little transfer from teaching/learning of academic tasks to teaching/learning of social tasks, these effects should be isolated.

Data suggest variables that may contribute to students' attentiveness during nonperformance rehearsal time. For example, eye contact had a strong relationship to on-task behavior because the least teacher eye contact produced the most off-task behavior. Data also showed the absence of teaching and reinforcing of social on-task behavior. Previous research (Madsen & Madsen, 1974) indicated that, with more than 20% off-task behavior in the classroom, academic learning suffers. Therefore, teaching and learning may be more efficient if the social task is taught. The teacher who spent the most time in nonperformance had the most off-task student behavior. The most effective balance of time spent in performance and in instruction should be explored and carefully maintained.

This study may serve as a model for future descriptive research in natural settings. Data may be added to the established computer bank of teaching data. As observations increase, generalizations can be drawn from the results. Because the teaching/learning environments were videotaped, other variables may be added and observed in the future. Recommendations for further analysis include other dependent measures, such as performance quality and student attitude; a comparison of age groups (elementary, junior high, adult) and abilities (professional and amateur); and promising independent carrier variables that are controlled in carefully designed experiments. Promising independent carrier variables from this study are activity (performance and nonperformance) and eye contact.

REFERENCES

Becker, W. C., Englemann, S., & Thomas, D. R. *Teaching: A course in applied psychology.* Chicago: Science Research Associates, 1971.

Erbes, R. L. *The development of an observational system for the analysis of interaction in the rehearsal of musical organizations.* Unpublished doctoral dissertation, University of Illinois, 1972.

Forsythe, J. L. The effect of teacher approval, disapproval, and errors on student attentiveness: Music versus classroom teachers. In C. K. Madsen, R. D. Greer, & C. H. Madsen, Jr. (Eds.), *Research in music behavior.* New York: Teachers College Press, Columbia University, 1975.

Forsythe, J. L. Elementary student attending behavior as a function of classroom activities. *Journal of Research in Music Education,* 1977, *25,* 228-239.

Froehlich, H. Replication of a study on teaching singing in the elementary general music classroom. *Journal of Research in Music Education*, 1979, *27*, 35-45.

Kuhn, T. L. The effect of teacher approval and disapproval on attentiveness, music achievement, and attitude of fifth-grade students. In C. K. Madsen, R. D. Greer, & C. H. Madsen, Jr. (Eds.), *Research in music behavior*. New York: Teachers College Press, Columbia University, 1975.

Madsen, C. H., Jr., & Madsen, C. K. *Teaching/discipline: A positive approach for educational development, expanded second edition for professionals*. Boston: Allyn & Bacon, 1974.

Madsen, C. K., & Alley, J. M. Effect of reinforcement on attentiveness: A comparison of behaviorally trained music therapists and other professionals with implications for competency-based academic preparation. *Journal of Music Therapy*, 1979, *XVI*, 70-82.

Madsen, C. K., Wolfe, D. E., & Madsen, C. H., Jr. The effect of reinforcement and directional scalar methodology on intonational improvement. In C. K. Madsen, R. D. Greer, & C. H. Madsen, Jr. (Eds.), *Research in music behavior*. New York: Teachers College Press, Columbia University, 1975.

Madsen, C. K., & Yarbrough, C. *Competency-based music education*. Englewood Cliffs, N. J.: Prentice-Hall, 1980.

Moore, R. S. Videotaped comparisons of beginning versus experienced elementary music specialists in the use of teaching time, and development and piloting of the 'music teaching interactions-activity form.' Paper presented at Second National Symposium on Research in Music Behavior, Milwaukee, Wisconsin, 1976.

Mosteller, F., & Tukey, J. W. *Data analysis and regression*. Reading, Mass.: Addison-Wesley Publishing Co., 1977.

Murray, K. C. The effect of teacher approval/disapproval on the performance level, attentiveness, and attitude of high school choruses. In C. K. Madsen, R. D. Greer, & C. H. Madsen, Jr. (Eds.), *Research in music behavior*. New York: Teachers College Press, Columbia University, 1975.

Neter, J., & Wasserman, W. *Applied linear statistical models: Regression, analysis of variance, and experimental design*. Homeward, Ill.: R. D. Irwin, Inc., 1974.

Nolin, W. H. Patterns of teacher-student interaction in selected junior high school general music classes. *Journal of Research in Music Education*, 1971, *19*, 314-325.

Thurman, V. L. A frequency and time description of selected rehearsal behaviors used by five choral conductors. Paper presented at the Music Educators National Conference National Convention, Atlantic City, N.J., March, 1976.

Wagner, M. J., & Strul, E. P. Comparisons of beginning versus experienced elementary music educators in the use of teaching time. *Journal of Research in Music Education*, 1979, *27*, 113-125.

Yarbrough, C. Effect of magnitude of conductor behavior on students in selected mixed choruses. *Journal of Research in Music Education*, 1975, *23*, 134-146.

October 15, 1980

This study examined the effect of conductor academic task presentation, reinforcement, and student performance on attentiveness, achievement, and attitude of members of a university symphonic band. The band rehearsed five times under three treatment conditions: A—directions followed by ensemble performance; B—academic task presentations followed by directions and ensemble performance; and C—academic task presentations, directions, and ensemble performance, followed by conductor reinforcement. Results indicated attentiveness was a function of both performance time and treatment. All treatments resulted in gains for music achievement, with Treatment B resulting in the smallest and Treatment C resulting in the largest gains. Student attitudes were related significantly to music, conductors, and their interaction. Student ratings of rehearsal enjoyment and conductor as a good teacher were significantly related to treatments, with Treatment C consistently rated the highest.

Harry E. Price, *Virginia Polytechnic Institute and State University, Blacksburg, Virginia*

JRME 1983, VOLUME 31, NUMBER 4, PAGES 245–257

The Effect of Conductor Academic Task Presentation, Conductor Reinforcement, and Ensemble Practice on Performers' Musical Achievement, Attentiveness, and Attitude

Previous studies in music have focused on teacher/conductor behaviors including reinforcement (Forsythe, 1977; Moore, 1976; Murray,

For reprints of this article, contact Harry E. Price, 303 Performing Arts Building, Department of Music, Virginia Polytechnic Institute and State University, Blacksburg 24061.

This article is a revision of the author's doctoral dissertation, The Effect of Conductor Academic Task Presentation, Conductor Reinforcement, and Ensemble Practice on Performers' Musical Achievement, Attentiveness, and Attitude, Syracuse University, New York, 1981.

1975; Thurman, 1976; Wagner & Strul, 1979; Yarbrough, 1975; Yarbrough and Price, 1981), student/performer responses (Forsythe, 1977; Murray 1975; Yarbrough, 1975; Yarbrough & Price, 1981), and student/teacher interactions in classroom and rehearsal situations (Erbes, 1972; Forsythe, 1975; Kuhn, 1975; Madsen & Alley, 1979; Madsen, Wolfe, & Madsen, 1975; Murray, 1975; Yarbrough & Price, 1981). These studies indicated that attitudes and attentiveness may be related in part to teacher reinforcement (Forsythe, 1975; Kuhn, 1975; Murray, 1975), and magnitude (Yarbrough, 1975). Other studies demonstrated that students who were active participants in the classroom were more on task (Forsythe, 1977; Madsen & Alley, 1979; Madsen & Madsen, 1972; Madsen, Wolfe, & Madsen, 1969; Spradling, 1980; Yarbrough & Price, 1981), and had a more positive attitude (Spradling, 1980).

One effective teaching model that may be applicable to an ensemble setting is direct instruction, which is the implementation of a sequence that comprises the teaching model presented by Becker, Engelmann, and Thomas (1971). The model involves a three-step process: (1) the teacher presents a preceding stimulus, (2) the student(s) respond, and (3) the teacher presents a following stimulus by either giving the student(s) feedback or going on to another preceding stimulus.

While this model has been shown to be effective in teaching basic skills in mathematics and English (Becker & Engelmann, 1976; Berliner & Rosenshine, 1976; Brophy & Evertson, 1974; Rosenshine, 1979), the effect of direct instruction in an ensemble rehearsal has not been examined in a controlled study. However, one observational study has examined the applicability of the direct instruction model to the ensemble setting (Yarbrough & Price, 1981). This study examined videotaped teacher and performer behavior during several high school ensemble rehearsals to investigate the relationship of performance time, frequency of approvals and disapprovals, stops, teacher eye contact, complete and incomplete teaching units, and errors to the frequency of student off-task behavior. The term "teaching unit" refers to the three-step sequence as defined by Becker, Engelmann, and Thomas (1971). While Yarbrough and Price (1981) did not find a strong relationship between teaching units and attentiveness, they did show that the concept could be transferred to an ensemble setting and documented via the instrument developed. It appeared that an analysis of a rehearsal made in this manner gave a clear description of those activities and sequences that are germane to ensemble rehearsals. The purposes of this study were to (a) control the teaching presentation of a music performance task, student response, and teacher reinforcement/feedback, and (b) measure the effect of these variables on student attentiveness, attitude, and performance.

METHOD

Subjects were the members of the Syracuse University Symphonic Band at Syracuse University in New York. The band was a 48-member nonauditioned group composed primarily of nonmusic majors. The experiment was conducted during the regular rehearsal time and in the normal rehearsal room over 4 weeks. Two experimental conductors, three media technicians, and audio-visual equipment surrounded the group during the experiment. Two rehearsal periods (2.5 hours each) were used for acclimation purposes. Compositions at an appropriate level of difficulty were selected by the experimental conductors for this study. Six compositions that were chosen for six experimental conditions were: (1) *Third Suite*—Robert Jager (first movement, no repeats; and third movement, measure 23 to the end); (2) *Pageant*—Vincent Persichetti (third beat of measure 66 to the end), (3) *Divergents*—Frances McBeth (number 2, measure 12 to the end; and number 4), (4) *William Byrd Suite*—Gordon Jacob (number 1, measure 25 to the end; and number 3), (5) *William Bryd Suite*—Gordon Jacob (number 4), and (6) *William Bryd Suite*— Gordon Jacob (number 5, no repeats; and number 6).

The experiment included a pretest session, five treatment sessions, and a posttest session. Sight-reading of each of the compositions served as the pretest for musical performance. Each of the five treatment sessions included six musical compositions distributed across three treatments, administered by two conductors, in a pre-posttest design to test the effect of conductor behavior. The three treatments were: A—directions concerning where to begin playing followed by ensemble performance; B—academic task presentations followed by directions and ensemble performance; and C—academic task presentations, directions, ensemble performance, followed by conductor reinforcement. Each of the six musical compositions was paired with one of the three treatments throughout, such that two compositions received the same treatment with a different musical composition being used for each of the two conductors. Two experimental conductors administered each of the three treatments, and thus each rehearsed three compositions every session. The conductors alternated the three compositions that they rehearsed and the six compositions were presented in a different random order each session, to control for experimenter and order effect. Each treatment was 12 minutes long. Conductors were given the following instructions for each treatment to ensure that the treatments were implemented according to the *a priori* definitions.

Treatment A

(a) Verbalizations are only to consist of directions that tell the ensemble at what point to begin in the music. These are not to consist of any feedback or academic task presentations;
(b) Allow the ensemble to perform as much as possible; and
(c) The face should be a neutral mask at all times.

Treatment B

(a) In addition to directions, verbalizations are to include academic task presentations. The verbalizations are not to consist of any feedback or reinforcement, and must comprise 50% of the treatment time;

(b) The ensemble must perform for 50% of the treatment time; and
(c) The face should be a neutral mask at all times.

Treatment C

(a) In addition to directions and academic task presentations, verbalizations are to include appropriate reinforcement to the ensemble for the performance immediately preceding. The reinforcement should consist of 80% academic approvals and 20% academic disapprovals (Murray, 1975). Reinforcement should be directly related not only to student performance, but also to the task presented. Academic task presentations and reinforcement should each comprise 25% of the time;
(b) The ensemble must perform for 50% of the treatment time; and
(c) The face should appropriately reflect the verbal reinforcement with sharp contrasts between approval and disapproval. Facial approval is to be expressed by nodding the head vertically, grinning, laughing, smiling, raising eyebrows, and widening eyes. Facial disapproval is expressed by shaking the head horizontally, frowning, knitting the eyebrows, pursing the lips, and narrowing the eyes (Yarbrough, 1975).

The conductors' rehearsal time was monitored by a trained observer listening to a prerecorded signal tape. The observer cued the conductors by pressing a switch connected to signal lights mounted on the conductors' music stand, out of the view of the members of the ensemble (Spradling, 1980). A blue light cued the conductors to give academic task presentations and/or directions, a white light cued the conductors to have the ensemble play, and a green light cued the conductors to give reinforcement.

Control of the conductors' approval/disapproval ratio of verbal responses was achieved by providing a feedback chart indicating the frequency of each type of response (Murray, 1975; Yarbrough, 1975). Two flip charts were mounted on a music stand in view of the conductors, but outside the view of the ensemble members. One chart had green numbers representing approvals; the other had red numbers representing disapprovals. Following each approval or disapproval given by the experimenter, an observer flipped the corresponding green or red card.

Following each treatment, the musical composition was played in its entirety to assess any change across treatment sessions in musical performance. After the last treatment session, one additional session was scheduled to play all the musical compositions without preceding treatments. This was used as a posttest assessment for musical performance ratings.

Measurement procedures

Videotape recordings were used for assessment of attentiveness and documentation of treatments. A prerecorded cassette tape providing the alternating verbal cues "observe" (10-second cue) and "record" (5-second cue) was mixed into the sound recorded on videotape to synchronize observations of videotapes. One video camera was focused on a maximum of six students during each "observe" interval and was rotated on the "record" cue throughout each treatment condition so that all ensemble members were randomly observed several times. The other video camera was focused on the experimental conductor for each treatment.

After the experiment, two trained observers recorded overt student off-task behavior and teacher eye contact by viewing the videotapes independently. Student attentiveness was assessed according to the definitions by Madsen and Yarbrough (1980, p. 56). Observers counted the total number of students in view, and the number observedly off task for each 10-second interval. A percentage of off task was then computed for each 12-minute condition by dividing the number of students observed off task by the total number observed in that condition. Thus, one measure of off task was obtained for each condition observed each day.

Conductor eye contact was counted and recorded according to the definitions provided by Madsen and Yarbrough (1980, p. 63). Total conductor eye contact was considered the sum of the frequency of group and individual eye contact.

Time spent in performance and nonperformance was measured in seconds using a stopwatch accurate to 0.1 second. Performance was defined as playing by the entire ensemble or by its smaller sections. Nonperformance was defined as teacher instruction, teacher reinforcement, or anything not involving students' music performance (Yarbrough & Price, 1981).

Videotape recordings were also used to analyze and count complete teaching units. A completed teaching unit consisted of two or three sequential parts: (1) teacher presentation of a task; (2) student responses; and possibly (3) teacher reinforcement for student responses (Yarbrough & Price, 1981). Each part was delineated into categories and was coded.

Teacher presentation was coded 1 and was divided into five categories, which were coded and defined as follows: 1a—academic task presentation (telling students how to play a passage), 1d—directions (telling students where to begin playing), 1s—social task presentation (telling students how to behave or making announcements about future activities), 1c—conducting task presentation (a nonverbal modeling of the music or a nonverbal conducting signal for dynamic changes, beginning to play, stopping, style, phrasing, and tempo), and 1o—off-task statements (those not related to social or academic tasks).

Student response was coded 2 and was divided into four categories: 2p—performance by the entire ensemble, 2s—sectional performance, 2v—appropriate verbal response, and 2nv—appropriate nonverbal response.

Teacher reinforcement was coded 3 and was divided into six categories: 3va—verbal academic or social approval (positive statement about student behavior), 3vd—verbal academic or social disapproval (negative statement about student behavior), 3fa—facial approval (a positive facial gesture), 3fd—facial disapproval (a negative facial gesture), reinforcement errors, and sequence errors. Reinforcement errors were coded and defined as: 3va or 3fa (encircled)—approving of an inappropriate behavior, 3vd or 3fd (encircled)—disapproving of an appropriate behavior, and 3vd/fa or 3va/fd (encircled)—conflicting feedback (verbal expression is different from facial expression). Sequence errors included (1) reinforcement not related to task presented and (2) presentation of a new task, followed by reinforcement of a previous task.

Teaching units were then analyzed for completion and content. All units that followed a 1-2-3 sequence without error were considered complete units. Also, a 1-2 sequence in which the student response was entire ensemble or sectional performance (2p or 2s) was considered complete, recognizing the possibility that music performance may serve not only as student response but also as reinforcement.

Finally, academic and social approvals, disapprovals, and errors were identified and counted. A facial or verbal reinforcement was counted as one approval or disapproval. If a verbal reinforcement was paired with an appropriate (not conflicting) facial reinforcement, it was scored as two approvals or two disapprovals in an attempt to assess the magnitude of the reinforcement. This yielded an approval/disapproval ratio and the reinforcement frequency for each condition. The frequency and duration of teacher presentations as well as student responses were also extracted for further documentation and analyses.

Audiotape recordings of the pretest, posttreatment, and posttest music performances were used for subsequent judgment of musical achievement. Three expert judges, all experienced in conducting clinics, public school and university ensembles, and adjudicating, independently heard seven audiotaped pre-posttest performances of each composition in a different random order. Intonation, blend, balance, tempo, dynamics, tone quality, rhythm, phrasing, ensemble, articulation, style, and overall artistic effect (musicality) were rated from 1 (poor) to 4 (excellent).

Attitude was assessed by means of an attitude scale that had been adapted from the *Attitude Survey for Performance Group* (Madsen & Yarbrough, 1980, p. 143). This survey consisted of five questions in which the students rated how much they liked the music, enjoyed the rehearsal, liked the conductor, and were "turned on" during the rehearsal, as well as whether they thought the conductor was a good teacher. These items were scaled 1 (strongly disagree) to 10 (strongly agree). The survey was administered to the members of the musical ensemble following each condition on the first, third, fourth, and fifth sessions, in an effort to assess trends in attitudes, as well as daily attitudes.

Reliability

Observer agreement was computed for the videotape analyses by dividing total agreements by agreements plus disagreements. Average agreement for off task was .96, eye contact was .91, and teaching units was .95. Interjudge reliability on music performance scores was tested using a Kendall Coefficient of Concordance (Siegel, 1956, pp. 229–238). Results demonstrated a significant (alpha level = .05) concordance [W (Treatment A) = .783; W (Treatment B) = .585; W (Treatment C) = .757] among judges' ratings.

RESULTS

Before analyzing the effects of treatments on attentiveness, attitude, and achievement, it was necessary to determine whether the treatments were implemented as planned. Data gathered through the use of the Teaching Unit Observation System (Yarbrough & Price, 1981) were analyzed to indicate the relationship of the experimental conductors' actual implementation of the treatments to the *a priori* operational definition of those treatments. Data indicated that the three treatments were implemented according to the *a priori* operational definitions.

Data in Table 1 demonstrate that the students (ensemble members) were least off task during Treatment A. There also appears to be a trend toward less off task for Treatment C than for Treatment B. The lower

Table 1 — Mean Percentage of Students Off Task: Treatment by Day

Treatment	Day				
	1	2	3	4	5
A	6.73	7.31	5.78	9.15	5.26
B	15.38	18.04	16.36	14.05	11.22
C	10.80	17.86	13.64	11.79	11.38

off task for Treatment A was to be expected, in that it contained a considerably larger amount of student performance time than either Treatment B or C (561 versus 336 or 326 seconds respectively). This explanation is not viable for the trend of Treatment C towards less off task than Treatment B. The lower off task for Treatment C may have been a function of the treatment rather than performance time.

Mean musical performance scores for the treatments are summarized in Table 2. The mean performance gain for Treatment C was highest although that for Treatment A was close. Treatment B resulted in the smallest gain, which is almost one-half of that for Treatment C. While

Table 2 — Pre-Posttest Gain Scores for Musical Achievement, Treatment Summary

Treatment	Pretest	Posttest	Gain
A	12.50	21.58	9.08
B	13.32	18.17	4.85
C	14.17	23.70	9.53
Range	1.67	5.53	4.68

mean performance scores on the pretest had a narrow range, the range on the posttest was more than three times larger, indicating a differential treatment effect.

The data for each of the five questions on the attitude survey were analyzed by use of a multiple regression technique (Statistical Analysis System, General Linear Models Procedure, release 79.3A of SAS at Syracuse University, New York), with student responses to each question as the dependent measures. Carrier variables (Mosteller & Tukey, 1977; Neter & Wasserman, 1974) for these regression analyses were treatments, compositions nested within treatments, conductors, interaction of treatments with conductors, and interaction of compositions with conductors. These variables were coded and entered respectively using a hierarchical model in which the responses to each of the five items were used as the dependent measure. Variability due to individual subject differences was accounted for by using a repeated measures design. The questions were also analyzed by the use of graphical displays for treatment responses.

The effects of compositions, conductors, and their interactions were signifcant (alpha level = .05) for all five survey items, thus the music used and the conductor had an effect on the manner in which the students responded to all the survey items. In addition, a significant treatment effect was found for the students' ratings of rehearsal enjoyment, affective state ("turned on"), and the conductor as a good teacher; however, no treatment was indicated in rating the liking of the music or conductor (see Tables 3, 4, and 5).

The treatment effect indicated in these analyses is evident when the means are plotted on a graphical display such as that in Figure 1, which is typical of the results for the three survey items' responses that showed a treatment effect. Figure 1 is a display of the mean response by treatment session of the survey item in which students indicated how "turned on" they were.

Treatment C was consistently rated highest for all three of these items; however, in only one instance was Treatment B rated above Treatment

Table 3 — Dependent Variable: Rehearsal Enjoyment Rating, Multiple Regression Analysis Summary

Source	df	SS	MS	F
Model	58	1391.82	24.00	9.45**
Error	752	1908.60	2.54	—
Corrected total	810	3300.42	—	—
Subject	47	995.04	21.17	8.34**
Treatment	2	30.43	15.21	5.99**
Composition (treatment)	3	270.11	90.04	35.48**
Conductor	1	22.76	22.76	8.97**
Treatment* Conductor	2	.02	.01	.00
Composition* Conductor	3	73.46	24.49	9.65**

$*p < .01$
$**p < .0001$

Table 4 — Dependent Variable: "Turned On" Rating, Multiple Regression Analysis Summary

Source	df	SS	MS	F
Model	58	1040.96	17.95	9.39*
Error	752	1436.96	1.91	—
Corrected total	810	2477.93	—	—
Subject	47	773.08	16.45	8.61*
Treatment	2	34.61	17.30	9.06*
Composition (treatment)	3	147.19	49.06	25.68*
Conductor	1	42.69	42.69	22.34*
Treatment* Conductor	2	.14	.07	.04
Composition* Conductor	3	43.27	14.42	7.55*

*$p < .0001$

A. When the students were asked to rate the conductor as a "good teacher," Treatment C was again rated the highest, but Treatment A was rated the lowest only for this item (see Figure 2).

DISCUSSION

The results of this study indicate that of the three treatments investigated, the one that included academic task presentations, directions, student performance, and feedback was the most efficient. This treatment resulted in the largest musical performance gains and highest student attitude ratings. The results also indicate a clear superiority of feedback over no feedback as measured by attentiveness, attitude, and performance when performance time is comparable. This suggests that an ensemble director should not only concentrate on instruction and/or

Table 5 — Dependent Variable: Teacher Rating, Multiple Regression Analysis Summary

Source	df	SS	MS	F
Model	58	1362.83	23.50	22.86**
Error	737	757.44	1.03	—
Corrected total	795	2120.26	—	—
Subject	47	917.94	19.53	19.00**
Treatment	2	14.42	7.21	7.01*
Composition (treatment)	3	27.18	9.06	8.82**
Conductor	1	382.71	382.71	372.38**
Treatment* Conductor	2	1.93	.96	.94
Composition* Conductor	3	18.65	6.22	6.05*

*$p < .01$
**$p < .0001$

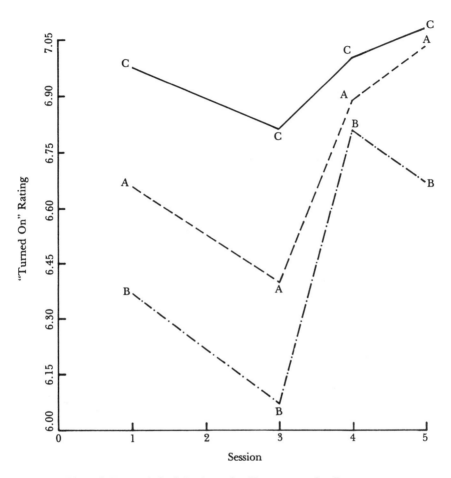

Figure 1. Plot of "Turned On" Ratings for Treatments by Day

student performance, but should also give appropriate feedback. These results support previous research in nonmusic settings (Becker & Englemann, 1976; Berliner & Rosenshine, 1976; Brophy & Evertson, 1974; Rosenshine, 1979).

A large gain in musical performance was noted for the treatment that only included direction and student performance. However, this might not have occurred had the study been carried out with an ensemble consisting of younger and less mature musicians who might have been more dependent on instruction.

As in previous research (Forsythe, 1977; Madsen & Alley, 1979; Madsen & Madsen, 1972; Madsen, Wolfe, & Madsen, 1969; Spradling, 1980; Yarbrough & Price, 1981) active student participation resulted in less off task. In this case, students were more attentive while performing. These data imply the need for varied techniques and approaches to instruction in a performance setting to ensure maximum effectiveness.

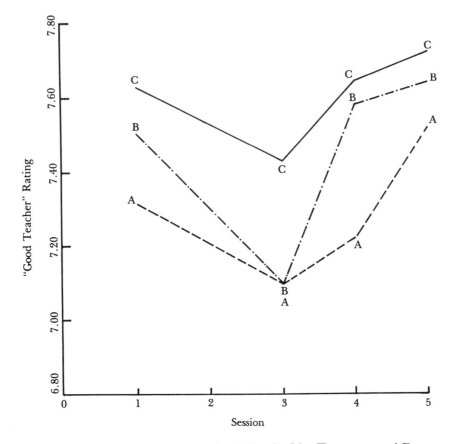

Figure 2. Plot of Conductor as a "Good Teacher" by Treatment and Day

There are many variables involved in ensemble rehearsals that bear examination. This study involved only one ensemble and two experimental conductors. While this clearly limits its generalizability, it does appear that techniques used in this study are viable for future ensemble research. The body of research that has attempted to experimentally manipulate variables in an ensemble setting is indeed limited, but with designs such as this it is possible that the implementation of this type of research will be more accessible. Also, as the body of literature increases, one may have a better understanding of those variables that contribute to a more effective rehearsal.

REFERENCES

Becker, W. C., & Engelmann, S. (1976). *Analysis of achievement data on six cohorts of low-income children from 20 school districts in the University of Oregon direct instruction follow through model.* Eugene: University of Oregon. (ERIC Document Reproduction Service No. ED 145 922)

Becker, W. C., Engelmann, S., & Thomas, D. R. (1971). *Teaching: A course in applied psychology.* Chicago: Science Research Associates.

Berliner, D. C., & Rosenshine, B. (1976). *The acquisition of knowledge in the classroom. Beginning Teacher Evaluation Study.* Technical report IV-1. San Francisco: Far West Laboratory for Educational Research and Development. (ERIC Document Reproduction Service No. ED 146 158)

Brophy, J. E., & Evertson, C. M. (1974). *Process-product correlations in the Texas teacher effectiveness study: Final report.* Austin, TX: Research and Development Center for Teacher Education. (ERIC Document Reproduction Service No. ED 091 394)

Erbes, R. L. (1972). *The development of an observational system for the analysis of interaction in the rehearsal of musical organizations.* Unpublished doctoral dissertation, University of Illinois.

Forsythe, J. L. (1975). The effect of teacher approval, disapproval, and errors on student attentiveness: Music versus classroom teachers. In C. K. Madsen, R. D. Greer, & C. H. Madsen (Eds.), *Research in Music Behavior.* New York: Teachers College Press.

Forsythe, J. L. (1977). Elementary student attending behavior as a function of classroom activities. *Journal of Research in Music Education, 25,* 228–239.

Kuhn, T. L. (1975). The effect of teacher approval and disapproval on attentiveness, musical achievement, and attitude of fifth grade students. In C. K. Madsen, R. D. Greer, & C. H. Madsen (Eds.), *Research in Music Behavior.* New York: Teachers College Press.

Madsen, C. K., & Alley, J. M. (1979). The effect of reinforcement on attentiveness: A comparison of behaviorally trained therapists and other professionals with implications for competency-based academic preparation. *Journal of Music Therapy, 16,* 70–82.

Madsen, C. K., & Madsen, C. H. (1972). Selection of music listening or candy as a function of contingent versus noncontingent reinforcement and scale singing. *Journal of Music Therapy, 9,* 190–198.

Madsen, C. K., Wolfe, D. E., & Madsen, C. H. (1969). The effect of reinforcement and directional scalar methodology on intonational improvement. *Council for Research in Music Education, 18,* 22–34.

Madsen, C. K., & Yarbrough, C. (1980). *Competency-based approach to music education.* Englewood Cliffs, NJ: Prentice-Hall.

Moore, R. S. (1976). Effect of differential teaching techniques on achievement, attitude and teaching skills. *Journal of Research in Music Education, 24,* 129–141.

Murray, K. (1975). The effect of teacher approval/disapproval on the performance level, attentiveness, and attitude of high school choruses. In C. K. Madsen, R. D. Greer, & C. H. Madsen (Eds.), *Research in Music Behavior.* New York: Teachers College Press.

Mosteller, F., & Tukey, J. W. (1977). *Data analysis and regression.* Reading, MA: Addison-Wesley Publishing Co.

Neter, J., & Wasserman, W. (1974). *Applied linear statistical models: regression, analysis of variance, and experimental designs.* Homeward, IL: Richard D. Irwin.

Rosenshine, B. V. (1979). Content, time and direct instruction. In P. L. Peterson, & H. J. Walberg (Eds.), *Research on Teaching* (pp. 28–56). California: McCutchan Publishing.

Spradling, R. L. (1980). *The effect of timeout from performance on attentiveness and attitude of university band students.* Unpublished doctoral dissertation, Florida State University.

Thurman, V. L. (1976). *A frequency and time description of selected rehearsal behaviors used by five choral conductors.* Paper presented at the Music Educators National Conference National Convention, Atlantic City, March.

Wagner, M. J., & Strul, E. P. (1979). Comparisons of beginning versus experienced elementary music educators in the use of teaching time. *Journal of Research in Music Education, 27,* 113–125.

Yarbrough, C. (1975). Effect of magnitude of conductor behavior on students in selected mixed choruses. *Journal of Research in Music Education, 23,* 134–146.

Yarbrough, C., & Price, H. E. (1981). Prediction of performer attentiveness based upon rehearsal activity and teacher behavior. *Journal of Research in Music Education, 29,* 209–217.

March 9, 1983

The purpose of this study was to examine extant research in effective teaching and to determine the extent to which results were being applied in music teaching. Rehearsals (N = 79) were analyzed to determine time spent in and correct sequencing of presentation of task, student responses, and reinforcement. Results demonstrated that (a) time spent in presenting musical information and appropriate reinforcement was about one-fourth of total rehearsal time, (b) an almost equal amount of time was spent giving directions as compared to musical information, (c) almost half the rehearsal time was devoted to performance, and (d) experienced teachers were highly disapproving of student responses, whereas preparatory teachers were highly approving.

Cornelia Yarbrough, *Louisiana State University*
Harry E. Price, *University of Alabama*

JRME 1989, VOLUME 37, NUMBER 3, PAGES 179–187

Sequential Patterns of Instruction in Music

Results of recent research support the notion that effective teaching involves the ability to sequence teaching and learning events in an optimal pattern of instruction. This optimal pattern, labeled *direct instruction* by Rosenshine (1976), was observed and first experimentally tested in reading and mathematics instructional situations at the primary level and later at the secondary level.

The teaching of a task can be broken into three components: (1) before the task is presented, the teacher gets the child's attention; (2) the task is presented in a routine designed to teach the task and to require the children to respond to a "do it" signal; and (3) the children are reinforced for right responses and corrected on wrong responses (Becker, Englemann, & Thomas, 1971, 306–315).

Comparisons of the direct instruction approach to other teaching approaches (e.g., open classroom model, cognitively oriented curriculum model, response education model, parent education model, behavior analysis model) clearly demonstrated its superiority in terms of producing student achievement of basic skills, cognitive understandings, and positive attitudes toward learning. Furthermore, teachers who were

---

For copies of this article, contact Cornelia Yarbrough, School of Music, Louisiana State University, Baton Rouge, LA 70803–2504

viewed as effective in helping students learn were those who were engaged in direct instruction (Berliner & Rosenshine, 1976; Brophy, 1979; Good & Brophy, 1974; Medley, 1977; Powell, 1978; Rosenshine, 1976, 1979). Direct instruction requires that a great deal of time be spent on academic activities and that teachers provide immediate and relative feedback using praise. The earliest model for direct instruction defined interactive units of teaching in which the sequential order of events, or pattern of instruction, was of paramount importance. Specifically, the pattern began with the teacher's presentation of the task to be learned, followed by student interaction with the task and the teacher, and solidified by immediate praise or corrective feedback related to the task presented (Becker, Englemann, & Thomas, 1971).

Results of recent studies in music have substantiated the presence of the direct instruction model in elementary music teaching (Moore, 1981; Rosenthal, 1982) and ensemble rehearsals (Yarbrough & Price, 1981). Early research revealed a significantly greater amount of intonational improvement when children were given instruction and contingent reinforcement, versus no instruction and noncontingent reinforcement (Madsen & Madsen, 1972). Later, researchers found that ensemble conductors who used a sequential pattern of instruction with musical task presentation followed by student performance of the task and immediate, related reinforcement were more effective in producing good performances, a high rate of student attentiveness, and positive student attitudes (Price, 1983). Results of other research showed that students clearly favored a teaching style in which the teacher structured a music concept and presented it verbally, allowed an opportunity for students to respond, and reinforced student responses (Jellison & Wolfe, 1987; Price, 1983). Jellison and Kostka (1987) studied elementary students' written recall of teaching content in music teaching cycles. Results indicated that the information recalled was specific musical information (as compared to nonspecific social information).

Music research isolating the effect of the complete and correct teaching cycle on student behavior is scant because, to date, the observation and control of the cycle have been difficult and cumbersome. The complexities involved in studying teaching effectiveness are recognized, and various researchers continue to grapple with these problems toward the goal of enabling those who train teachers to use complete, correct cycles so that effects may be studied. Although efforts toward this end have been unsuccessful up to now, progress has been made in the observation and isolation of the effects of each of the three components of the complete teaching cycle—teacher presentation of musical information (verbalization), student response (participation), and reinforcement (approvals versus disapprovals).

Verbalizations used in presenting musical information have been analyzed in recent research. Verbal-technical directions, demonstration/modeling, questioning, and instruction concerning musical elements (e.g., rhythm, dynamics, pitch) have been counted and timed (Carpenter, 1987; Moore, 1987; Thurman, 1978). Several researchers have examined the use of teaching time in music classes and rehearsals.

Thurman (1978) analyzed five choral rehearsals and found that the conductors devoted approximately 40% of their rehearsal time to verbal communications. In other research, observers found that experienced teachers gave fewer directions than inexperienced teachers (Wagner & Strul, 1979). In general, research results suggest that verbal behavior should be kept to a minimum, since it seems to be associated with increased student off-task behavior (Forsythe, 1977; Yarbrough & Price, 1981).

Furthermore, research in music has shown the effectiveness of active participation by students in increasing attentiveness and creating better attitudes toward instruction (Yarbrough & Price, 1981). Students were more on-task while involved in music activities compared to involvement in other academic work regardless of the teaching style used (Forsythe, 1977; Madsen & Alley, 1979; Sims, 1986; Spradling, 1985).

The effectiveness of the praise component of the model is well documented in music research, which demonstrates that student attentiveness is better under highly approving teachers than under highly disapproving ones (Forsythe, 1975; Kuhn, 1975) and that approval reinforcement significantly increased positive attitudes toward choral rehearsals (Murray, 1975). Still other researchers have supported using specific or descriptive praise as reinforcement following student responses (Madsen & Madsen, 1983; Madsen & Yarbrough, 1985). In spite of the overwhelming evidence of the efficacy of praise, recent descriptive research data showed that teacher-conductors were more disapproving than approving and that these disapprovals were more likely to be directed at musical behaviors than at social behaviors (Carpenter, 1987).

Although active participation and reinforcement have produced greater attentiveness and more positive attitudes, the presence of each component in the teaching cycle (presentation of task, student response, and reinforcement) in the correct sequence may be important in producing musical achievement (Jellison & Kostka, 1987; Jellison & Wolfe, 1987; Price, 1983). A large volume of research in education and a relatively few studies in music education substantiate a theory of effective teaching that proposes that effective teaching involves the application of interactive units of teaching in which the sequential order of events, or pattern of instruction, is of utmost importance. Specifically, the pattern begins with the teacher's presentation of the task to be learned, followed by student interaction with the task and the teachers. Student learning was then solidified by immediate praise or corrective feedback.

Therefore, the purpose of this study was to determine whether music teachers were applying in their own classrooms what has been demonstrated through research to be effective teaching. Specifically, rehearsals of experienced and preparatory instrumental and choral teachers were analyzed to determine how much time was being spent in various activities and whether teachers were using the correct sequence of teacher presentation of task, student response, and reinforcement. Comparisons of these observations to the research-established theoretical model of effective teaching were made to determine the potential for student achievement, attitude, and attentiveness.

PROCEDURE

Subjects were freshman music education majors (n = 30), sophomore music education majors (n = 19), experienced instrumental music teachers (n = 15), and experienced choral music teachers (n = 15). Freshman music education majors were videotaped teaching a song to preschool children; sophomores were trained to use direct instruction techniques (teacher presentation of musical task followed by student response and teacher reinforcement) and videotaped rehearsing their peers; and experienced instrumental and vocal teachers were videotaped in the regular rehearsal rooms at the normal rehearsal times. Experienced teachers were from New York, Georgia, Florida, Alabama, and Louisiana. Students were enrolled in music education degree programs at the University of Alabama, Tuscaloosa; Louisiana State University, Baton Rouge; and Florida State University, Tallahassee.

Verbatim typescripts (N = 79) of each of the above teaching situations were prepared. The typescripts were used to analyze, count, and time units of teaching and student performance. Units of teaching were categorized as teacher presentation of a task, student response, or teacher reinforcement.

Teacher presentation was coded "1" and was divided into subcategories as follows: 1a = academic musical task presentation (explaining musical aspects of the score, describing how the music is to be performed); 1s = social task presentation (telling students how to behave, presenting rules, planning social activities); 1d = giving directions (telling students who will play/sing, where to begin playing/singing); 1dc = counting beats, usually ending in "ready, play/sing," commonly known in other subject areas as "do it" signals; 1q = questioning (asking students questions about musical, social, or directional tasks); and 1o = interruptions in rehearsal such as teacher off-task statements and intercom announcements.

Student response was coded "2" and was divided into three subcategories, which were coded and defined as follows: 2p = performance by the entire ensemble or by sections; 2v = verbal response; and 2nv = nonverbal response.

Teacher reinforcement was coded "3" and was divided into two subcategories: 3va = verbal academic or social approval (positive statement about student behavior); and 3vd = verbal academic or social disapproval (negative statement about student behavior). Errors of reinforcement (such as approving of inappropriate behavior and disapproving of appropriate behavior) and specificity of reinforcement were also noted.

Teaching cycles were then analyzed for correct sequencing and content. All cycles that followed a 1–2–3 sequence without error were considered correct. Cycle mistakes occurred (a) when cycles contained only directions with no musical task content; (b) when directions interrupted the flow between musical task presentation and student performance; (c) when reinforcement was not related to the task presented; and/or (d) when a reinforcement mistake occurred.

An independent observer completed reliability observation for 25% of the videotaped teachers. Reliability was computed using the formula of agreements divided by agreements plus disagreements. Average reliability across all categories and teachers was .94 with a range of reliability from .74 to .99.

RESULTS

Using the direct instruction theoretical model for effective teaching as a guide, the authors calculated (in seconds) the time spent in correct and incorrect teaching cycles, presentation of musical tasks, directions, presentation of social information, questioning, classroom interruptions, student performance, student verbalization, student nonverbal responses, teacher approvals/disapprovals, and specific/nonspecific reinforcement for experienced band and choral directors, trained sophomore music education majors, and freshman music education majors. Percentage of time spent during each rehearsal was computed for each category (see Table 1).

Table 1 shows a greater percentage of time spent in incorrect than in correct cycles of teaching for all but the freshmen music education majors. More time was spent in presentation of tasks and student responses than in reinforcement across all groups.

Within the category of presentation of tasks, an almost equal amount of time was spent giving directions as compared to presenting musical tasks except in the trained sophomore group. The sophomores spent approximately 10% more time presenting musical tasks than giving directions. There was little attention to the presentation of social information and little questioning. Interruptions seemed to be numerous during rehearsals conducted by experienced teachers and by freshmen but were negligible during rehearsals conducted by sophomores.

Student responses for all groups were mostly performance-oriented, with few verbalizations and nonverbal responses. Almost half of the rehearsal time for all groups was spent in student performance. Interestingly, the percentage of time spent in giving directions plus the time spent in student performance equals well over half of the total rehearsal time (band = 66.14; chorus = 65.53; sophomores = 59.01; freshmen = 57.72).

Very little time, comparatively, was spent on reinforcement. If one considers the presentation of musical information and reinforcement for the correct performance of the musical task presented to be the primary components of teaching in the rehearsal situation, then it would seem that more structured practice than actual teaching occurred in the rehearsals observed. The percentage of time spent in presenting musical information plus the time spent in appropriate reinforcement was little more than one-fourth of the total rehearsal time except in the case of the sophomores (band = 26.66; chorus = 23.18; sophomores = 34.12; freshmen = 24.91).

Experienced teachers were highly disapproving while preparatory teachers were highly approving. All groups were more specific when using disapprovals as reinforcement.

DISCUSSION

The purpose of this study was to observe and analyze regular rehearsal situatibns and to determine whether music teachers were applying the results of research that demonstrates that there is a pattern of teaching (i.e., direct instruction) that results in high levels of student achievement, attitude, and attentiveness. Thus, occurrences of those variables of teaching effectiveness, as defined by the direct instruction model, were timed. Percentages of time spent for each component of the three-part sequential pattern of instruction (task presentation, student response, and reinforcement) were computed (see Table 1).

The presentation of musical information in rehearsals is occurring at a very low rate (less than 20% for all groups except the trained sophomores). The ability to speak appropriately about the musical score to students and to describe creatively what the music should sound like to young students is an art that may not have been developed in teacher training programs or through experience. Experienced teachers were very conscientious about catching the mistakes of students.

It was particularly disturbing to observe this high rate of disapproval among the experienced teachers. Numerous research studies have demonstrated that disapproval is not an effective feedback technique and, indeed, may even be counterproductive. The alternative, according

Table 1
Percentage of Time Spent in Teaching-Pattern Components

| | Teachers | | | |
Components of patterns	Band	Chorus	Sophomores (trained)	Freshmen (untrained)
Cycles of teaching				
Correct	18.39	34.52	36.51	70.25
Incorrect	81.61	65.48	63.91	29.75
Presentation of tasks	43.54	40.98	46.74	52.96
Musical information	18.11	17.22	26.47	18.75
Directions	20.19	16.30	16.75	20.36
Social information	0.56	1.23	0.91	2.08
Questioning	1.33	1.99	1.80	0.99
Interruptions	3.35	4.24	0.81	10.78
Student responses	47.91	53.06	45.60	40.88
Performing	45.95	49.23	42.26	37.36
Verbalizing	1.44	2.65	2.79	3.45
Nonverbal responses	0.52	1.18	0.55	0.07
Reinforcement	8.55	5.96	7.65	6.16
Approvals	1.62	2.44	5.60	5.47
Disapprovals	6.93	3.52	2.05	0.69
Approval/disapproval ratio	19/81	41/59	73/27	89/11
Specific/nonspecific ratio	70/30	59/41	57/43	47/53

to the theoretical model of direct instruction, may be to present corrective feedback. For example, instead of verbally punishing students for wrong notes, one might point out the correct notes and provide another opportunity for the student to get the wrong ones right. Also, a correct model might be presented to students to help them learn the musical task. Regardless, the authors recommend that those responsible for music teacher training programs examine the results of research in direct instruction and consider the importance of *initiating* student responses rather than simply *reacting* to them.

In addition, there seems to be too much extraneous verbalization, primarily in giving directions. Over half of the rehearsal time in the settings examined in this study was devoted to structured practice, i.e., the teacher gave directions regarding where to begin and who should play, then set tempo by counting one or more measures aloud (usually ending in "Ready, play/sing"). Subsequently, students would play until stopped by the teacher. This pattern of giving directions without musical information and cueing the response of students was the most common pattern observed among all groups of teachers.

The ability of sophomores and freshmen to maintain a highly positive reinforcement ratio is encouraging. However, specifying approvals is a skill that needs attention by these students as well as by experienced teachers. In addition, when an increase in the amount of musical information presented is achieved, a concomitant decrease in directions and increase in the amount of positive reinforcement must be sought.

Mistakes in correct sequencing (i.e., cycle mistakes) occurred most often in two ways: (a) when directions were given (that is, students' attention was focused on a particular place in the musical score), then musical information was presented followed by a "ready play/sing" signal, students played/sang, and the teacher stopped them with a disapproval for incorrect performance of something not presented to them before they responded; and (b) when musical information was given and then followed by a long list of directions concerning where students were to begin and who was to play. In the first instance, it would seem appropriate to recycle the musical information presented by praising those who achieved the objective and to give corrective feedback to those who had not. In the second instance, the lengthy list of directions disrupted the students' concentration on the musical information given. It might have been difficult for them to remember the musical task. Often, we select music that is so logistically difficult that we may be forced to spend too much time in "gathering the forces" and consequently have little time left to address musical issues.

Given the amount of research data supporting the use of complete and correct teaching cycles, the authors believe it is of paramount importance to develop techniques for teaching prospective teachers to present musical information, allow student response time, and appropriately reinforce the acquisition of that information. Future research will examine more closely the content and frequency of occurrence of musical information presented by experienced teachers toward the goal of developing training models for student teachers. In addition, it may be necessary to examine differences among teachers' reinforcement patterns in relation to ages of children being taught. Finally, the authors of this study must express appreciation and admiration for the experienced teachers who so graciously submitted themselves to such close scrutiny. These teachers also share the belief that, through research, we may be able to improve the quality of teaching in music education settings to enhance students' achievement, attentiveness, and attitudes.

REFERENCES

Becker, W. C., Englemann, S., & Thomas, D. R. (1971). *Teaching: A course in applied psychology.* Chicago: Science Research Associates.

Berliner, D. C., & Rosenshine, B. (1976). *The acquisition of knowledge in the classroom. Beginning Teacher Evaluation Study: Technical Report IV-1.* San Francisco, CA: Far West Laboratory for Educational Research and Development. (ERIC Document Reproduction Service No. ED 146 158)

Brophy, J. E. (1979). Teacher behavior and its effects. *Journal of Educational Psychology, 71,* 733–750.

Carpenter, R. A. (1987, March). A descriptive analysis of relationships between verbal behaviors of teacher conductors and ratings of selected junior high and senior high school band rehearsals. Paper presented at the Research in Music Behavior Symposium, Logan, Utah.

Forsythe, J. L. (1975). The effect of teacher approval, disapproval, and errors on student attentiveness: music versus classroom teachers. In C. K. Madsen, R. D. Greer, & C. H. Madsen, Jr. (Eds.), *Research in music behavior.* New York: Teachers College Press, 49–55.

Forsythe, J. L. (1977). Elementary student attending behavior as a function of classroom activities. *Journal of Research in Music Education, 25,* 228–239.

Good, T. L., & Brophy, J. E. (1974). Changing teacher and student behavior: An empirical investigation. *Journal of Educational Psychology, 66,* 390–405.

Jellison, J. A., & Kostka, M. J. (1987, March). Student or teacher as focus of attention and elementary students' written recall of teaching content within music teaching units. Paper presented at the Research in Music Behavior Symposium, Logan, Utah.

Jellison, J. A., & Wolfe, D. E. (1987). Verbal training effects on teaching units: An exploratory study of music teaching antecedents and consequents. In C. K. Madsen & C. A. Prickett (Eds.), *Applications of research in music behavior.* Tuscaloosa, AL: University of Alabama Press.

Kuhn, T. L. (1975). The effect of teacher approval and disapproval on attentiveness, musical achievement, and attitude of fifth grade students. In C. K. Madsen, R. D. Greer, & C. H. Madsen, Jr. (Eds.), *Research in music behavior.* New York: Teachers College Press, 40–48.

Madsen, C. H., Jr., & Madsen, C. K. (1983). *Teaching/Discipline: Behavioral principles toward a positive approach.* Raleigh, NC: Contemporary Publishing.

Madsen, C. K., & Alley, J. M. (1979). The effect of reinforcement on attentiveness: A comparison of behaviorally trained music therapists and other professionals with implications for competency-based academic preparation. *Journal of Music Therapy, 16,* 70–82.

Madsen, C. K., & Madsen, C. H., Jr. (1972). Selection of music listening or candy as a function of contingent versus noncontingent reinforcement and scale singing. *Journal of Music Therapy, 9,* 190–198.

Madsen, C. K. and Yarbrough, C. (1985). *Competency-based music education.* Raleigh, NC: Contemporary Publishing.

Medley, D. M. (1977). Teacher competence and teacher effectiveness. A review of process–product research. Washington, DC: American Association of

Colleges for Teacher Education. (ERIC Document Reproduction Service No. ED 143 629)

Moore, R. S. (1981). Comparative use of teaching time by American and British elementary music specialists. *Bulletin of the Council for Research in Music Education, 66–67*, 62–68.

Moore, R. S. (1987, March). The use of rehearsal time by a model conductor and children's choir. Paper presented at the Research in Music Behavior Symposium, Logan, Utah.

Murray, K. C. (1975). The effect of teacher approval/disapproval on musical performance, attentiveness, and attitude of high school choruses. In C. K. Madsen, R. D. Greer, & C. H. Madsen, Jr. (Eds.), *Research in music behavior.* New York: Teachers College Press, 165–180.

Powell, M. (1978). Research on teaching. *The Educational Forum, 43*, 27–37.

Price, H. E. (1983). The effect of conductor academic task presentation, conductor reinforcement, and ensemble practice on performers' musical achievement, attentiveness, and attitude. *Journal of Research in Music Education, 31*, 245–257.

Rosenshine, B. V. (1976). Recent research on teaching behaviors and student achievement. *Journal of Teacher Education, 27*, 61–64.

Rosenshine, B. V. (1979). Content, time, and direct instruction. In P. L. Peterson & H. J. Walberg (Eds.), *Research on teaching.* Berkeley, CA: McCutchan Publishing, 28–56.

Rosenthal, R. K. (1982). *A data-based approach to elementary general music teacher preparation.* Unpublished doctoral dissertation, Syracuse University.

Sims, W. L. (1986). The effect of high versus low teacher affect and passive versus active student activity during music listening on preschool children's attention, piece preference, time spent listening, and piece recognition. *Journal of Research in Music Education, 34*, 173–191.

Spradling, R. L. (1985). The effect of timeout from performance on attentiveness and attitude of university band students. *Journal of Research in Music Education, 33*, 123–127.

Thurman, V. L. (1978, April). *A frequency and time description of selected rehearsal behaviors used by five choral conductors.* Paper presented at the MENC National Biennial In-Service Conference, Chicago.

Wagner, M. J. & Strul, E. (1979). Comparisons of beginning versus experienced elementary music educators in the use of teaching time. *Journal of Research in Music Education, 27*, 113–125.

Yarbrough, C., & Price, H. E. (1981). Prediction of performer attentiveness based on rehearsal activity and teacher behavior. *Journal of Research in Music Education, 29*, 209–217.

May 2, 1988

VII.

Observing

and

Evaluating

Music Teaching

Information from a statewide norming study of all teachers was used to compare the performance of music teachers and other teachers on 10 competencies and a variety of classroom behaviors. Music teachers' competency scores were below the mean for all teachers on 7 of the 10 competencies; however, music teachers' scores on specific classroom behaviors showed virtually no difference from those of other teachers on 94 of the 117 behaviors included on the Classroom Observation Instrument (COR). Music teachers outperformed other teachers in using materials and eliciting student performance; however, they had lower frequencies in their use of various types of questions. On an opinion questionnaire, music teachers tended to support the evaluation program; however, a number expressed concerns about the validity of the competencies for music teachers and the evaluators' expertise.

Donald K. Taebel, *Georgia State University, Atlanta*

JRME 1990, VOLUME 38, NUMBER 1, PAGES 5–23

An Assessment of the Classroom Performance of Music Teachers

In the spring of 1987, the state of Alabama initiated the performance-based Career Incentive Program (CIP) for its more than 30,000 teachers. All teachers were observed in their classrooms and interviewed by their principals in an effort to establish norms or standards for evaluating teacher performance during the fall semester of 1987. More than 500 music teachers from across the state were involved in the norming study. The purposes of this study were (a) to describe the classroom performance of music teachers in comparison with other teachers and (b) to present information on the music teachers' perceptions concerning various aspects of the evaluation program.

STATEWIDE TEACHER EVALUATION

Since the time of Socrates, teachers have been evaluated by administrators, students, themselves, and others; however, only within the past 10 years have teachers been evaluated under programs promoted by

For copies of this article, contact Donald K. Taebel, School of Music, Georgia State University, Atlanta 30303.

state governments. Influenced by the accountability movement of the 1970s and, more recently, by calls for excellence in teaching, states have enacted various programs requiring the evaluation of school district personnel. Starting in states of the Southeast and expanding across the United States, programs for improving education have now been developed in 25 states (Borich & Fenton, 1977; Shulman, 1988; Southern Regional Education Board, 1988).

Although state programs differ in many ways, including their names, they share two common elements: They list criteria by which teachers are to be evaluated, and they specify methods of evaluation (Borich & Fenton, 1977). Much effort has gone into defining teaching as the demonstration of certain competencies that are believed to relate to student outcomes (Travers, 1981). The set of competencies often reflects a particular model or concept of teaching (Stallings, 1987; Wise, Darling-Hammond, McLaughlin, & Bernstein, 1984). Linked to the competencies are various methods for determining a teacher's level of competence, chiefly systematic observation in the classroom (Popham, 1986).

States have given considerable attention to the competencies used in assessment (particularly their definitions), reliability of measurement, and validity. Developers of statewide evaluation systems have tried to give explicit descriptions of each competency in terms of observable teacher actions to ensure high observer agreement. The validity of the competencies initially was determined by studies of educators' opinions; more recently, claims for the validity of the competencies have relied on the "teacher effectiveness" research base. From this vantage, states have proclaimed that the competencies used in their statewide assessment programs broadly apply to all grade levels and to all subject areas. In other words, these competencies are generic (Alabama State Department of Education, 1986; Borich & Fenton, 1977; Buttram & Wilson, 1987; Georgia State Department of Education, 1988; Johnson, Okey, Cappie, Ellett, & Adams, 1978).

Both researchers and teachers have challenged the putative "generic" competencies. Teachers argue that evaluation tools using the prevailing checklist approach, especially those grounded in the process-product model of instruction, are inappropriate (McLaughlin & Pfeifer, 1988). Popham (1986) contends that a defensible technology for appraising teachers has not yet been developed. Travers (1981) questioned the view of teaching as a set of competencies that are evaluated by a simplistic method. Stallings (1987) suggested that mandated examinations and instructional models restrict teachers' professional judgment. Wise and his associates (1984) noted that different techniques for evaluating teachers imply one of four conceptions of teaching, that is, as labor, craft, profession, and art. Each of these concepts of teaching will lead to very distinct evaluation systems ranging from a mechanical and highly systematized approach to one that is creative and open-ended.

Others who have reviewed the process-product research point out that these studies have been confined to elementary and mid-elementary grades and primarily to reading and mathematics instruction (Borich, 1979; Coladarci, 1988). They also note that effective teaching behaviors vary for students of different socioeconomic and intellectual characteristics, and for different grade levels, classes, and subject areas (Gage, 1978; Medley, 1977; Taebel & Medley, 1979; Wise et al., 1984).

Teaching behaviors that are effective when used in moderation (such as praise) can produce significant negative effects when overused or when applied in the wrong circumstances (Coker, Medley, & Soar, 1980; Soar & Soar, 1983). Effective practice is also dependent on the objectives and the content of lessons. Even Rosenshine (1987), a strong advocate of explicit instruction, recognized that these techniques may be ineffective when used with topics requiring complex learning. Stallings (1987) deplored statewide evaluation programs that claim to be based on effective teaching research but that select only research that is related to achievement test scores rather than to measures of problem-solving, creating, and valuing. In their analysis of teaching effectiveness research, Wise et al. (1984) observe:

> We consider this finding related to goals problematic because, if markedly different teaching behaviors lead to divergent results that can be deemed equally desirable, one cannot identify a single, unidimensional construct called effective teaching, much less delimit its component parts. One can, at best, pursue alternative models of effective teaching, making explicit the goals underlying each. (p. 27)

Andrews (1988) summarizes the state of teacher evaluation as follows:

> Almost everyone agrees that some way should be found to ensure the competence of teachers in public schools. Yet little agreement exists on how to define a good teacher, how to carry out an assessment to ascertain the quality of a teacher, or how to use assessment to nurture a teacher's growth throughout a career. (p. 2)

RELATED RESEARCH

In the 1986 assessment of beginning teachers in Georgia, the percentage of music teachers who passed the performance-based evaluation was lower than the mean on 7 of the 8 competencies (Taebel, 1987). In Humble, Texas, a large school system outside Houston, music teachers had mean lower scores on 8 of 10 competencies. In Florida, where the total score (rather than separate competency scores) is used, the average total score for all music teachers was lower than the average total score for all other teachers (Peterson, 1986).

Using a data source other than the classroom, Smith (1985) sought consensus validity of the competencies identified by the Florida Music Educators Association through a survey of FMEA members. Stafford (1987) produced a list of competencies needed to teach singing in elementary music classes.

Although not directly related to teacher evaluation, there are a substantial number of studies related to teaching behaviors that effective music teachers use in the classroom. Since such behaviors may be included in an assessment system, they are summarized here. Brand

(1985), in reviewing the research on effective music teaching, states that effective teachers demonstrate musicianship in accurate diagnosis and correction of errors and relate their lessons to student interests and needs. He adds that they also stay on-task, demonstrate enthusiasm and energy, use frequent eye contact, gestures, variation in facial expression, and modulation of speaking intensity. Curtis's (1986) work with successful junior high school general music teachers, and the work of Grechesky (1985) and Watkins (1986) with choral teachers, confirms the importance of nonverbal teaching behavior in instruction and management. Cox (1987) found that successful choral directors used familiar, enjoyable pieces at both the beginning and end of their rehearsals.

Price (1985) and Rosenthal (1985) in their reviews cite studies showing the importance of sequencing using a three-phase model of presenting, student activity, and reinforcement. Price also reviews the evidence for different types of feedback on student behavior and learning. Carpenter (1986) found that band directors tended to use disapproval more often than approval when giving feedback. In her review, McCoy (1985) notes that positive feedback in the form of praise is somewhat varied in its effect depending on its sincerity, relationship to the task, and the SES and achievement level of the students. She also reports that music teachers use different proportions of direct and indirect methods of teaching and that the effectiveness of one method over the other may depend on the experience of the students. Shehan (1984) reports that on measures of concept development, a heuristic approach was no different than a didactic approach, but that on measures of behavioral preference, the heuristic approach was better. Yarbrough's review (1985) supports the contribution of active involvement with music to both academic learning and on-task behavior.

One may conclude that adequate evaluation of music teaching should be sensitive to both direct and indirect models of teaching, capture nonverbal behaviors by the teacher and students (including affect), account for sequencing, and measure teacher musicianship as well as the typical verbal behaviors of presenting, questioning, and responding.

THE ALABAMA CAREER INCENTIVE PROGRAM

The enabling legislation for the Alabama Career Incentive Program (CIP) was passed in May 1985. The law provided for an incentive-based, merit-pay plan for teachers, based on their classroom performance and other professional activities. The assessment purportedly was based on both professional judgment of best practice and the research on teacher effectiveness (Wiersma, 1988).

The legislation established a working committee of teachers, school administrators, and community leaders to develop the evaluation program. This committee formulated 15 competencies representing the most important teaching activities, based on the committee's interpretation of research results and practice. The competencies then were defined in terms of behaviors and activities observable in classroom performance and overall professional work. Five competencies were associated with professional activities outside the classroom; the remaining 10 were the basis for classroom observation (Wiersma, 1988). The 10 classroom competencies, which are the focus of this study, are:

1. Presents organized instruction
2. Uses materials and equipment
3. Provides for practice and application
4. Monitors student achievement
5. Uses monitoring data
6. Manages classroom time
7. Maintains student behavior
8. Knows subject matter
9. Maintains a positive atmosphere
10. Communicates clearly and effectively

The Observation Instrument

Four instruments were developed for measuring teacher performance: (1) the Classroom Observation Record (COR), (2) the Pre-Observation Data form, (3) the Post-Observation Data form, and (4) the Evaluator Questionnaire. This study addressed only the Classroom Observation Record, or COR.

The COR is a low-inference inventory for recording classroom interactions and events. The 69 items of Section A were intended to measure a teacher's performance in the categories of instructing, questioning, responding, and managing. Section B contained 48 items to record general teaching methods and classroom organization (Alabama State Department of Education, 1986). The COR is a sign instrument rather than a category system instrument. A sign instrument contains many different items, whereas a category instrument, such as that of Flanders contains only a few items designed to capture a small range of classroom behaviors. Because sign instruments contain so many items, an item is coded only once during the coding period even if the behavior represented by the item recurs; however, category system items are coded every few seconds (Medley & Mitzel, 1963).

Scoring

During the spring semester of 1987, each Alabama teacher was observed twice, for at least 45 minutes each time. A Classroom Observation Record was completed for each 5 minutes of observation; thus, a minimum of 9 records were completed for each visit, or at least 18 records for the semester.

A competency score was derived by first developing a scoring key, an approach described by Medley, Coker, and Soar (1984). A cluster of items from the COR was used to form the scoring key for each of the 10 classroom competencies. The number of items in a key varied with each competency. Since the scores of different items varied greatly in frequency and also displayed non-normal distributions, the item scores had to be normalized and standardized before they could be aggregated to form a competency score.

The raw item scores were transformed using the "Probit" and "Standard" subroutines described in the *SAS User's Guide: Version 5 Edition* (SAS Institute, 1985). These transformed item scores, now T scores, were added together to yield a score for each competency. Finally, individual competency scores were standardized with the mean of all scores set at 50 and a standard deviation of 10 units. Standardizing the scores made it possible for a teacher to compare his or her scores with the group mean on the same competency; it also made it easier to compare one's relative position on one competency with the other competency scores.

Observer Agreement and Reliability

Observational data are vulnerable to error from a variety of sources, all of which may affect reliability (Evertson & Green, 1986). In the Alabama program, considerable attention was given to observer agreement coefficients (percentage of agreement) and the reliability of the scores. Of these two components of reliability, score reliability accounts for the greatest source of measurement error, namely, variability of a teacher's behavior on different occasions. Consequently, this measure invites greater confidence because it accounts for both consistency and stability of measurement (Frick & Semmel, 1978).

All observers were either building principals or, in a few districts, central office administrators. Teachers were not permitted to be observers. Observers were trained in 35 hours over a 2-week period that culminated in field-based observations of at least two different teachers. To be certified, each observer was required to reach an agreement level of 70% or above on at least four different records; the mean coefficient of agreement for all observers over all observations was 80%.

During the collection of real data, observers were monitored by district coordinators and records were checked for consistency of coding by the scanning program. A follow-up study was conducted six months after training to measure observer drift. After discovering that the mean percentage of agreement was 83%, researchers concluded that practice in collecting data together with the close monitoring had improved observation skills (Taebel, Schafer, & Coker, 1987).

Score reliability was determined for each of the 10 competencies, rather than for the total test score, using coefficient alpha. One competency (Competency 10) had a reliability of .42; all others had reliabilities ranging from .60 to .85. This range compares favorably with the reliabilities of measures reported for classroom performance measures by others (Froehlich, 1979; Medley, Rosenblum, & Vance, 1989). All human reports are inherently subjective to a degree; this fact must be accepted if observation is a source of data (Radocy, 1986).

METHOD

Data Sources

Several data sources were used in this study. Raw COR data for all teachers were available from the Teacher Evaluation Project at Georgia

State University. Standardized competency scores for a sample of music teachers came from several school districts in Alabama; questionnaire data came from cooperating teachers and their principals in these same districts.

Instruments

Two questionnaires were created for this study, one for music teachers and a similar one for principals. Music teachers first were asked to rate each competency regarding its appropriateness for teaching music on a four-point scale. They also were requested to comment on the adequacy of the evaluation system. These inquiries were made to determine the validity of the Alabama competencies from the perspective of music teachers in a manner similar to that used with other teachers in Georgia (Johnson et al., 1978; Taebel, 1980).

Music teachers also rated themselves on a 10-point scale (with 5 being average) on each of the 10 classroom competencies. Although the values of self-ratings in summative appraisals may be questioned (Popham, 1986), they are, nevertheless, used in professional development (Hoover & Carroll, 1987).

Principals also rated the competencies of their music teachers with a 10-point scale and offered suggestions for improving the evaluation system. Rating of a teacher's competency by a principal is commonplace, although this method also has been debated (Medley et al., 1984; Popham, 1986).

Samples

To compare performance on the 10 competencies, the standard scores of a sample of 130 music teachers were contrasted with the population mean of 50. The sample teachers represented 64% of the music teachers in several school districts of varying sizes throughout the state (Birmingham, Mobile, Montgomery, Huntsville, Dothan, Tuscaloosa, and Mountain Brook). Scores on the COR items were obtained from a random sample of 10% of all teachers in Alabama ($n = 3,191$) and a sample of 510 music teachers representing more than 90% of the music teachers in the state.

Questionnaire data were received from 152 music teachers and their principals. These data came from the same school districts listed above and represented about 75% of the population of those districts' music teachers.

Procedures

Data from the Classroom Observation Records were available for all teachers in the tape library at Georgia State University. The data for the music teachers and 10% of the other teachers were extracted and transferred to two separate tapes for analysis.

Questionnaires were distributed to music teachers and principals in January 1987 by district coordinators who had been associated with the state evaluation program. Questionnaires were returned to the district coordinators who, in turn, forwarded them to the researcher. By this time, music teachers and principals had had more than a year to review the competencies and evaluation procedures and had been through the complete evaluation process at least twice.

RESULTS

The results are organized around (a) the comparative competency scores and COR item scores and (b) the opinions of music teachers and principals derived from the questionnaires.

The first objective was to compare the music teachers' competency scores with those of all other teachers. Table 1 gives the mean score for each competency, the standard deviation, and the standard error of measurement. As an aid to interpretation, the percentile rank of the mean score of the music teachers is given. Of course, the percentile rank of the mean score for the population is 50. Since the mean of the population is known, a test statistic can be calculated by dividing the difference between the sample mean and the population mean by the standard error of measurement. The means were significantly ($p <.05$) lower on seven competencies and significantly higher on two. The lowest mean was on Competency 3, "Provides for practice and application," while the highest was on Competency 2, "Uses materials and equipment." The standard deviations were not as great as those of the population on the majority of competencies; however, music teachers showed greater variability on Competencies 2 and 6, "Manages classroom time."

Table 2 addresses the question of whether music teachers at different grade levels performed differently on these competencies. One-way analyses of variance indicated that, except for Competencies 2, "Uses

Table 1
Descriptive Statistics of Music Teachers' Competencies

Competency	Percentile	Mean	SD	SEM[a]	p
1 Presents . . . instruction	29	44.5	9.3	0.8	*
2 Uses materials/equipment	82	59.1	11.3	1.0	*
3 Provides for practice	29	44.4	9.2	0.8	*
4 Monitors student achievement	29	44.6	8.6	0.8	*
5 Uses monitoring data	51	50.1	10.2	0.9	NS
6 Manages class time	59	52.2	12.7	1.1	*
7 Maintains student behavior	40	47.5	9.7	0.8	*
8 Knowledge of subject matter	39	47.1	8.3	0.7	*
9 Maintains positive atmosphere	40	47.5	9.8	0.9	*
10 Communicates clearly	42	48.1	10.3	0.9	*

[a] Standard error of measurement.
* Significant at the .05 level.
NS = not significant.

Table 2
Mean Competency Scores at Elementary, Middle, and High School Levels

Competency	Elementary n = 52	Middle n = 38	High n = 40	p
1 Presents . . . instruction	46.6	42.5	43.6	NS
2 Uses materials/equipment	62.6	56.2	57.4	*
3 Provides for practice	43.3	44.2	46.2	NS
4 Monitors student achievement	44.3	44.7	44.7	NS
5 Uses monitoring data	49.2	50.2	51.1	NS
6 Manages class time	55.6	45.5	54.0	*
7 Maintains student behavior	46.3	46.8	49.7	NS
8 Knowledge of subject matter	46.0	46.3	49.4	NS
9 Maintains positive atmosphere	48.7	46.3	46.9	NS
10 Communicates clearly	47.4	48.3	48.8	NS

*Significant at the .05 level.
NS = not significant.

materials and equipment," and 6, "Manages classroom time," the differences among grade levels are not significant.

Elementary music teachers had significantly higher scores on Competency 2, "Uses materials and equipment," while middle school teachers had significantly lower scores on Competency 6, "Manages classroom time." Elementary music teachers had the lowest score of all music teachers on Competency 3, "Provides for practice and application." They also had lower scores than the others on 5 additional competencies.

Competency scores indicated a teacher's performance in a general way; however, these scores were derived from individual item scores from the observation instrument. These item scores of music teachers were compared with those of other teachers. The 42 items coded on more than 5% of the total number of records (for either group of teachers) are reported in Table 3. Seventy-five items were omitted because they were coded so rarely. The first two columns show scores as percentages to indicate the difference between music and other teachers. The next three columns report mean raw scores to show how music teachers differed by grade level. Since the COR is a sign instrument, an item was coded only once per record during a 5-minute time block even if the behavior recurred within the period. In Table 3, a mean raw score of 1 indicates that 1 of 18 records (time blocks) was coded on the average. In percentage terms, this represents about 5% of the total observation time.

Music teachers differed from others on the COR items by less than 5% on 20 of the 42 items. However, they had higher frequencies, by at least 5%, on 12 items and lower frequencies, by at least 5%, on 11 other items. Most differences were in the questioning category. This category included not only various types of questions (e.g., recall or application) but also indicated whether the teacher gave all students the opportunity to

Table 3
Frequency of Observations on COR Items in Percentages and Raw Scores Across All Records

COR Items	Percent of occurrence		Mean raw score		
	Nonmusic teachers $n = 3,191$	Music teachers $n = 510$	Elem $n = 137$	Middle $n = 148$	High $n = 225$
Instructing items					
Orienting					
1 Gets attention	9	12	2.3	1.7	2.2
2 States objective	8	7	1.9	0.9	1.1
Gives directions					
3 For immediate tasks	49	59	9.5	10.1	10.6
4 Clarifies assignment	11	15	3.0	2.3	2.7
Presents information					
5 Tells	54	56	9.5	9.0	10.5
6 Restates/emphasizes	18	24	3.7	4.2	4.3
Shows relationships					
7 To previous learning	5	5	1.2	0.8	0.8
Reviews material					
8 At beginning of class	6	5	1.2	0.9	0.7
9 Checks pupil progress	12	12	1.1	2.0	2.7
Questioning items					
10 Elicits performance—Volunteer	9	63	10.7	10.6	11.2
—Directed to individual	6	14	2.8	2.6	2.0
11 Divergent question—Volunteer	8	4	1.2	1.0	1.0
12 Application question—Volunteer	23	16	4.2	2.5	2.1
—Directed to individual	23	10	3.2	1.5	0.9
13 Recall question—Volunteer	33	24	5.5	4.2	3.4
—Directed to individual	33	12	3.1	2.3	1.2
14 Status question—Volunteer	20	18	3.0	3.4	2.8
—Directed to individual	9	5	0.8	0.9	0.8
Responding items					
15 Gives negative response	5	6	0.9	1.2	1.0
16 Corrects student work	16	22	3.0	4.0	4.1
17 Positive feedback	56	51	11.0	8.7	7.4
18 Neutral acceptance	16	17	2.9	2.0	2.2
19 Gives information	31	30	5.2	5.2	4.9
20 Gives cue or hint	15	12	3.2	1.8	1.8
Managing items					
21 Gentle—verbal	22	23	5.8	3.9	3.9
22 Direct—verbal	20	20	4.0	3.8	3.7
23 Gentle—nonverbal	4	6	1.3	0.8	1.0

(Continued on next page)

Table 3 *(continued)*

Class organization					
24 Whole class	81	93	15.8	15.1	16.9
25 Small group	13	6	0.8	1.3	0.8
Predominant teaching method					
26 Presentation	30	21	4.9	3.1	3.4
27 Guides practice	28	43	6.2	7.5	7.8
28 Review or recitation	21	13	2.9	2.2	1.7
29 Discussion	14	5	1.5	0.6	0.7
30 Assessment activity	10	10	1.1	1.7	2.0
31 Uses drill	6	27	2.7	5.0	5.5
Affective					
32 Expresses enthusiasm	13	20	4.2	3.0	3.7
33 Sets high expectations	9	21	2.5	3.2	3.7
Use of materials/equipment					
34 Print	69	62	8.1	10.7	12.2
35 Visual/no movement	40	19	4.6	3.2	2.4
36 Kinesthetic	12	37	4.9	6.8	6.5
37 Realia or models	7	9	1.5	1.5	1.7
38 Auditory—recordings	3	35	8.9	4.8	5.7

respond or if he or she directed the question to only one student. If the former, the item was identified as "Volunteer"; if the latter, the item was identified as "Directed." An extreme difference was found in teacher questioning identified as "Elicits performance," which was coded when the teacher asked a student to demonstrate a motor skill. This was, by far, the predominant type of question used by music teachers. With respect to questions calling for verbal responses, music teachers had lower scores, by more than 5%, on recall and application questions in both the volunteer and directed mode. These contrasts are displayed graphically in Figure 1.

Music teachers differed from others in demonstrating various teaching methods. Items in this category were coded only when the teaching behavior persisted for at least 1.5 minutes. As might be expected, music teachers used more drill and guided practice; however, they used less review, discussion, and presentation.

Discussion of Competency Scores and COR Item Scores

The competency scores and the COR item scores reflect two levels of measurement. An item score is a measure of the occurrence of a discrete, observed behavior within a certain time frame, whereas a competency score is derived by combining selected items that presumably define the competency. Therefore, item scores may be combined in different ways to produce different competency scores. If the definition of a competency, or the competency itself, were to change, the competency score also would change because different items would be combined to operationally define the competency.

The profile of the music teachers' classroom performance provided by the COR items was consistent with expectations. It showed high and low frequencies of behaviors that seemed to accurately depict typical music teaching.

On the other hand, the prevalence of low competency scores for music teachers was disquieting and perplexing. How can one account for so low an average on Competency 3, "Provides for practice and application," when one would anticipate that music teachers especially would be strong in this area? To fully interpret the competency scores requires a full exposition of the competency definitions and a list of the COR items that contributed to the score. To stay within reasonable bounds, only four competency scores are discussed here.

Music teachers had very high scores on Competency 2, "Uses materials and equipment." The definition gave the greatest weight to the use of a

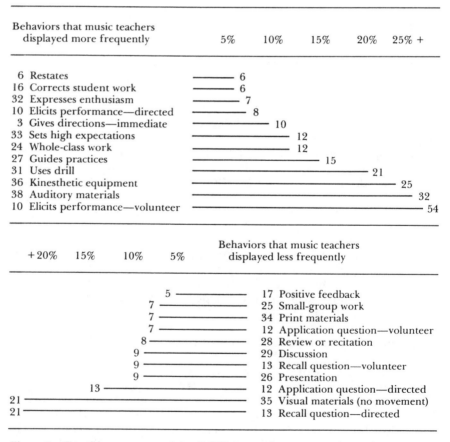

Figure 1. Graphic representation of differences between music teachers and other teachers on COR items showing percentage of difference.

variety of equipment and materials. Although not as strong as other teachers in their use of visual aids, music teachers used kinesthetic equipment (instruments) and auditory materials (recordings) with a much higher frequency. Of course, extensive use of varied materials in teaching music may be dictated by music's nature as an auditory art form as much as by any exceptional competency on the part of the music teacher.

A competency where music teachers, as a group, were at the 29th percentile was Competency 1, "Presents organized instruction." The items that contributed to this competency were from the instructing and questioning categories. While the music teachers' scores did not vary greatly from other teachers on items in the instructing category, they were not comparable on items in the questioning category. Their lower scores in the use of recall and application questions were not outweighed by their frequent use of questions calling for motor skill performance. Even though the item "Elicits performance" was included on the COR instrument, it was not used in this scoring key because the committee that drafted the definition of the competency failed to specify the development of motor skills as a form of instruction (Alabama State Department of Education, 1986). A similar problem existed with Competency 4, "Monitors student achievement." Scores on this competency were determined, in part, by the teacher's use of directed questions. From Table 3, we observe that the use of directed questions by music teachers was low in comparison to others. This same competency required the teacher to circulate through the group to check student work, a behavior rarely seen in a music class.

The lowest competency score was on Competency 3, "Provides for practice and application." Although music teachers scored well on the item "Guides practice," the competency was defined behaviorally by the teacher (a) circulating through the class and giving assistance as required and (b) assigning independent class work or homework. Again, these activities are infrequent in a music class.

These examples suggest that the competencies, even though only partially defined here, reflect an explicit teaching model as advocated by Madeline Hunter (Slavin, 1987) and others (Rosenshine, 1987). The results may indicate that this model, especially as defined by these competencies, is not serviceable for evaluating the performance of music teachers. This is not to say that some of the model's aspects may not be helpful to attain certain objectives in teaching music.

An alternate, if unwelcome, interpretation is that music teachers as a group are less competent that other teachers. Indeed, music teachers' competency scores generally were lower; but the item scores from the COR, a more objective description of performance, revealed that on rarely coded items (e.g., criticism), music teachers did not differ from other teachers (75 of 117 items). Furthermore, there was less than a 5% difference on 20 more frequently coded items. Finally, they had higher frequencies on 12 items and lower frequencies on 11 items (see Figure 1). These data may suggest that music teachers generally are comparable to others and that negative differences in performance may be offset by positive differences. If the capacity to exhibit "generic" competencies is randomly distributed among teachers, group differences in performance likely may be due to context variables, especially the subject area. Of course, some music teachers may be incompetent because they do things that nearly all observers agree are undesirable. However, until there is greater consensus on the behaviors associated with excellence in teaching, one may well question the competencies' construct validity rather than assume that the fault lies primarily with the music teachers (Coladarci, 1988; Ornstein, 1987; Peterson, 1987; Wise, et al., 1984).

Results from the Teacher and Principal Questionnaires

What did music teachers think about the competencies and the evaluation system? Data from the teacher questionnaires (see Table 4) revealed that, in general, music teachers agreed that these competencies are important for music teachers to demonstrate. On 7 of the 10 competencies, the majority of teachers marked "strongly agree," and only on Competency 5, "Uses monitoring data," were there sizable responses of disagreement. Yet, even here, the overall attitude was positive.

Fifty-five teachers (36%) commented regarding the evaluation system. One area of concern was the competency of the evaluators. One teacher said: "Only professionals in the field of music have the expertise to evaluate music teachers."

A second concern was over the administrative procedures, especially the limited time frame: "While the competencies are applicable, not all are used in one class period."

A third concern, expressed by 26 of those who wrote comments, was that the competencies were either not appropriate or not comprehensive enough to evaluate music teachers validly. Some believed that the model of teaching was ill-suited to music, especially to performance classes:

Table 4
Mean Ratings by Music Teachers and Their Principals on Each Competency

Competency	Music teacher rating on 4-pt. scale	Self-rating on 10-pt. scale	Principal rating on 10-pt. scale
1 Presents . . . instruction	3.6	8.8	7.9
2 Uses materials/equipment	3.4	8.8	7.9
3 Provides for practice	3.6	8.9	8.4
4 Monitors student achievement	3.4	8.6	8.0
5 Uses monitoring data	3.1	7.9	7.4
6 Manages class time	3.6	8.7	7.8
7 Maintains students behavior	3.7	8.7	7.8
8 Knowledge of subject matter	3.8	8.8	8.9
9 Maintains positive atmosphere	3.7	8.9	8.1
10 Communicates clearly	3.8	9.1	8.3

A high school band director is there to teach students to play instruments, not to make it into a theory or history class. Of course, some history, theory, and appreciation should be taught, but the bottom line is performance.

Teachers also suggested additional measures of their effectiveness. Thirteen music teachers suggested that evaluation of their competence also should include performance by their students at festivals, school events, or community activities.

Music teachers also were asked to rate themselves on the 10 classroom competencies, and principals were asked to rate their music teachers. A summary of these ratings appears in Table 4. Although the music teachers were told that a rating of "5" was an average rating, the majority of music teachers gave themselves ratings of 9 or 10 on all but one competency, which had a mean rating of 7.9.

The ratings by principals of their music teachers also were quite high, albeit somewhat lower than those of the teachers. The principals agreed with the teachers that the lowest performance was on Competency 5, "Uses monitoring data."

Correlations between the teacher and principal ratings were examined as were the correlations between the ratings and the competency scores. Each teacher self-rating on each competency was added together to produce a composite score. Principal ratings were also summed for each teacher as were the competency scores. These composite scores for each teacher were then correlated. The correlation of the teacher self-ratings with the principal ratings was .05. The correlation of teacher self-ratings with the competency scores was .02; while the correlation of the principal ratings with the competency scores was .18.

Discussion of Questionnaire Results

When rating the competencies, music teachers tended to support them as appropriate to teaching music. The questionnaire's timing may have contributed to the high ratings. Teachers had seen the COR forms; however, they had not seen the profile of their own competency scores and had only a naive awareness of the scoring procedure and no firsthand knowledge of the items that contributed to a competency score. Since the COR results may have been close to their expectations, teachers may have assumed that their competency scores would be satisfactory. A follow-up study would be necessary to determine whether teachers' perceptions changed after receiving their competency scores.

More than one-third of the teachers qualified their support by expressing concern over the validity of the competencies, the qualifications of the evaluators, and the failure to include student performance as an indicator of teaching effectiveness.

These data provide a degree of face validity for the competencies. However, some researchers question the validity of teachers' assumptions that certain competencies are contributors to student learning. Such competencies may be negatively related to student outcomes as often as they are positively related due to the interaction of competencies and grade level or subject area (Coker et al., 1980). Some music teachers felt that student achievement in performance classes might be compromised when giving more time to other dimensions of musicianship. Yet, as a group, music teachers were coded as "telling" (Item 5) slightly more often than other teachers, with high school music teachers coded higher than other music teachers. From this study, we cannot identify the specific content of instruction; however, other studies have suggested that instruction in theory and/or history in performance classes does not reduce performance skill (McCoy, 1985; Whitlock, 1981).

With respect to the concerns over the principal's ability to evaluate music teachers, Wise and his colleagues (1984) found in their survey of 32 school districts that "almost all respondents agreed that the principal lacked sufficient resolve and competence to evaluate accurately" (p. 22). They add that the respondents reported difficulty in having a generalist evaluator such as the building principal assess the competence of a specialist teacher. To overcome this problem, these researchers recommended that a master teacher serve as the evaluator, although they believed that, with specialized training, a building principal may become competent in this task.

Music teachers also proposed that student outcomes be included in the evaluation process. Even though this would pose major problems of measurement and weighting in music, a number of states are already moving toward the use of student outcome measures in evaluating their teachers (Southern Regional Education Board, 1988).

The self-ratings and the principal ratings were extremely high. This was expected since it is consistent with other results reported in the norming study where 98% of the teachers received near-perfect ratings by their principals (Taebel et al., 1987). It is also in accordance with Popham's view that "most of us are markedly partisan when we judge ourselves" (1986, p. 58). The low correlations of these ratings with the competency scores was likely due to the skewed distributions that restricted the ranges.

CONCLUSIONS AND RECOMMENDATIONS

Music teachers in Alabama received significantly lower scores than other teachers on 9 of 10 competencies, a result similar to comparisons made in Texas, Florida, and Georgia. However, inspection of the items that contributed to the competency scores showed that music teachers, on the majority of items, were similar except in the questioning area where dramatic differences were found, especially when a question called for a performance response. An evaluation system that relies excessively on verbal exchanges and cognitive learning may be inappropriate for music teachers. If systems use generic competencies, they should be defined so that verbal as well as nonverbal behaviors by the teacher and/or student are included.

Teacher evaluation provides many problems for research. One of the most important is to determine the contribution that "generic" competencies make to student learning. Also needed are studies that examine the relationship of generic competencies to curriculum-specific teaching behaviors (Gage, 1979). Such studies would need to use instruments that reliably measure a broad array of teacher and student behaviors, including nonverbal behaviors.

Research is also needed on the methods, procedures, and content of music teacher evaluation as practiced in various systems by principals or music supervisors. Although we have many recommendations from general education (McLaughin & Pfeifer, 1988; Medley et al., 1984; Wise et al., 1984), there is no known research on the evaluation of music teachers.

Music educators also may need to take a more active role in defining evaluation policies and procedures at the school district or state levels. In the words of Stallings (1987):

> It is time for teachers and teacher educators to become proactive, not just reactive, to each new legislative surprise. Excellence can be nurtured. It cannot be legislated. (p. 4)

REFERENCES

Alabama State Department of Education (1986). *Evaluator's manual: Career Incentive Program.* Montgomery, AL: Author. (ERIC Document Reproduction Service: ED 298 127)

Andrews, T. E. (1988). *Teacher assessment.* Reston, VA: Association of Teacher Educators.

Borich, G. D. (1979). Implications for developing teacher competencies from process-product research. *Journal of Teacher Education, 3*(1), 77–86.

Borich, G. D., & Fenton, K. S. (1977). *The appraisal of teaching: Concepts and process.* Reading, MA: Addison-Wesley.

Brand, M. (1985). Research in music teacher effectiveness. *Update: The Applications of Research in Music Education, 3*(1), 13–16.

Buttram, J. L., & Wilson, B. L. (1987). Promising trends in teacher evaluation. *Educational Leadership, 44*(7), 4–6.

Carpenter, R. A. (1986). *A descriptive analysis of relationships between verbal behaviors of teacher-conductors and ratings of selected junior high and senior high school band rehearsals.* Unpublished doctoral dissertation, The Ohio State University, Columbus.

Coker, H., Medley, D. M., & Soar, R. S. (1980). How valid are expert opinions about effective teaching? *Phi Delta Kappan, 62*(2), 131–134, 149.

Coladarci, T. (1988). The relevance of education research for identifying master teachers. *NASSP Bulletin, 72*(504), 90–98.

Cox, J. W. (1987). Rehearsal organizational structures used by successful high school choral directors. *Journal of Research in Music Education, 37*, 201–218.

Curtis, S. C. (1986). *An observational analysis of successful junior high/middle school general music teachers.* Unpublished doctoral dissertation, University of Oklahoma, Norman.

Evertson, C. M., & Green, J. L. (1986). Observation as inquiry and method. In M. Wittrock (Ed.), *Third handbook of research on teaching* (pp. 162–213). New York: Macmillan.

Frick, T., & Semmel, M. I. (1978). Observer agreement and reliabilities of classroom observation measures. *Review of Educational Research, 48*(1), 157–184.

Froehlich, H. (1979). Replication of a study of teaching singing in the elementary classroom. *Journal of Research in Music Education, 27*, 35–45.

Gage, N. L. (1978). *The scientific basis of the art of teaching.* New York: Teachers College Press.

Gage, N. L. (1979). The generality of dimensions of teaching. In P. L. Peterson & H. Walberg (Eds.), *Research on teaching: concepts, findings, and implications* (pp. 264–288). Berkeley, CA: McCutchan.

Georgia State Department of Education (1988). *Evaluation manual* (Field-test edition). Atlanta, GA: Author.

Grechesky, R. N. (1985). *An analysis of nonverbal and verbal conducting behaviors and their relationship to expressive musical performance.* Unpublished doctoral dissertation, University of Wisconsin—Madison.

Hoover, N. L., & Carroll, R. G. (1987). Self-assessment of classroom instruction: An effective approach to in-service education. *Teaching and Teacher Education, 3*(3), 179–192.

Johnson, C., Okey, J., Cappie, W., Ellett, C., & Adams, P. (1978). *Identifying and verifying generic teacher competencies.* Athens, GA: College of Education, University of Georgia.

McCoy, C. W. (1985). The ensemble director as effective teacher: A review of selected research. *Update: The Applications of Research in Music Education, 3*(3), 9–12.

McLaughlin, M. W., & Pfeifer, R. S. (1988). *Teacher evaluation.* New York: Teachers College, Columbia University.

Medley, D. M. (1977). *Teacher competence and teacher effectiveness: A review of process-product research.* Washington, DC: American Association of Colleges for Teacher Education.

Medley, D. M., Coker, H., & Soar, R. S. (1984). *Measurement-based evaluation of teacher performance.* New York: Longman.

Medley, D. M., & Mitzel, H. E. (1963). Measuring classroom behavior by systematic observation. In N. L. Gage (Ed.), *First handbook of research on teaching.* Chicago: Rand McNally.

Medley, D. M., Rosenblum, E. P., Vance, N. C. (1989). Assessing functional knowledge of the participants in the Virginia Beginning Teacher Assistance Program. *The Elementary School Journal, 89*(4), 495–510.

Ornstein, A. C. (1987). Teacher behavior research: Theory, practice, and recommendations. *NASSP Bulletin, 71*(503), 44–46.

Peterson, D. (1986). *Report for 1984–1985* [of the Teacher Evaluation and Assessment Center, University of South Florida]. Tampa, FL: University of South Florida.

Peterson, K. D. (1987). Teacher evaluation with multiple and variable lines of evidence. *American Educational Research Journal, 24*(2), 311–317.

Popham, W. J. (1986). Teacher evaluations: Mission impossible. *Principal, 65*(4), 56–58.

Price, H. E. (1985). Teaching in rehearsal: It's as easy as 1–2–3. *Update: The Applications of Research in Music Education, 4*(1), 11–13.

Radocy, R. E. (1986). On quantifying the uncountable in musical behavior. *Bulletin of the Council for Research in Music Education,* no. 88, 22–31.

Rosenshine, B. (1987). Explicit teaching and teacher training. *Journal of Teacher Education, 38*(3), 34–36.

Rosenthal, R. K. (1985). Improving teacher effectiveness through self-assessment: A case study. *Update: The Applications of Research in Music Education, 3*(2), 17–21.

SAS Institute (1985). *SAS user's guide: Version 5 edition.* Cary, NC: Author.

Shehan, P. K. (1984). The effect of instruction on the preference, achievement, and attentiveness for Indonesian gamelan music. *Psychology of Music, 12*(1), 34–42.

Shulman, L. S. (1988). A union of insufficiencies: Strategies for teacher assessment in a period of educational reform. *Educational Leadership, 46*(3), 36–41.

Slavin, R. (1987). The Hunterization of America's schools. *Instructor, 96*(8), 56–61.

Smith, A. B. (1985). *An evaluation of music teacher competencies identified by the Florida Music Educators Association.* Unpublished doctoral dissertation, Florida State University, Tallahassee.

Soar, R. S., & Soar, R. (1983). Context effects in the teaching-learning process. In D. C. Smith (Ed.), *Essential knowledge for beginning educators* (pp. 65–75). Washington, DC: American Association of Colleges for Teacher Education.

Southern Regional Education Board (1988). *Is "paying for performance" changing schools? The SREB Career Ladder Clearinghouse Report 1988.* Atlanta, GA: Author.

Stafford, D. W. (1987). *Perceptions of competencies and preparation needed for guiding young singers in elementary school music classes.* Unpublished doctoral dissertation, Florida State University, Tallahassee.

Stallings, J. A. (1987). Are we evaluating what we value? *The Journal of the Association of Teacher Educators, 9*(3), 1–4.

Taebel, D. K. (1980). Public school teachers' perceptions of the effect of certain competencies on pupil learning. *Journal of Research in Music Education, 28,* 185–197.

Taebel, D. K. (1987). The three r's: Reform, ratings, and research. In J. A. Braswell (Ed.), *The Proceedings of the 1987 Southeastern Music Education Symposium* (pp. 13–18). Athens, GA: University of Georgia.

Taebel, D. K., & Medley, D. M. (1979, April). *Generalizability of low inference measures of music teachers across observers, items, and classes.* Paper presented at the annual meeting of the American Educational Research Association, San Francisco, CA.

Taebel, D. K., Schafer, G., & Coker, H. (1987). *Alabama Performance-based Career Incentive Program: A report on the norming study of the spring semester, 1987.* Atlanta: Georgia State University Teacher Evaluation Project. (ERIC Document Reproduction Service: ED 302 578)

Travers, R. M. W. (1981). Criteria for good teaching. In J. Millman (Ed.), *Handbook of teacher evaluation.* Beverly Hills, CA: Sage Publications.

Watkins, R. E. (1986). *A descriptive study of high school choral directors' use of modeling, metaphorical language, and musical/technical language related to student attentiveness.* Unpublished doctoral dissertation, University of Texas at Austin.

Whitlock, R. H. (1981). *The design and evaluation of study materials for integrating musical information into the choral rehearsal.* Unpublished doctoral dissertation, North Texas State University, Denton.

Wiersma, W. (1988). *The Alabama Career Incentive Program: A statewide effort in teacher evaluation.* Atlanta, GA: Career Incentive Program—Teacher Evaluation Project, Georgia State University. (ERIC Document Reproduction Service: ED 298 128)

Wise, A. E., Darling-Hammond, L., McLaughlin, M. W., & Bernstein, H. T. (1984). *Teacher evaluation: A study of effective practices.* Santa Monica, CA: The Rand Corporation. (ERIC Document Reproduction Service No. ED 246 559)

Yarbrough, C. (1985). Indicators of affect for school music teachers. *Update, The Applications of Research in Music Education, 4*(1), 3–5.

September 3, 1989

One hundred fifty music teachers and students were asked to simultaneously observe, analyze, and write extemporaneously about 20 videotaped excerpts of live music situations. Subjects were divided on the basis of their expertise and experience into five groups of 30 people each: freshmen, juniors, novices, experienced teachers, and experts.

Responses were analyzed with differential points being given for accurate factual and inferential statements. Individual scores ranged from 17 to 205 points. Group means were widely differentiated and increased systematically as experience and expertise increased, and all differences between groups were significant except between the freshmen and juniors. A two-way ANOVA revealed that the difference in scores between experienced and expert teachers was not due solely to years of experience.

Jayne M. Standley and **Clifford K. Madsen,** *The Florida State University, Tallahassee*

JRME 1991, VOLUME 39, NUMBER 1, PAGES 5-11

An Observation Procedure to Differentiate Teaching Experience and Expertise in Music Education

Definitive conclusions about the process of evaluating teaching expertise are difficult to attain. Despite a plethora of research, the multitude of variables investigated seem to be inconsistently delineated and almost hopelessly confounded. Accepted criteria for defining teaching expertise are yet to be established and may vary across student age ranges (Brophy & Good, 1986), socioeconomic backgrounds (Berliner, 1985), and academic areas (Sanford & Evertson, 1983). For instance, some studies cite teacher reputation as a primary criterion of expertise (Berliner, 1976). Others observe the individual in the classroom and subsequently rate the performance according to a priori standards or, in some cases, according to poorly or vaguely defined parameters (Borich, 1986; Ornstein, 1986). Student performance on standardized tests is yet another frequently cited dependent measure often used without regard to differences in incoming student potential or school resources (McDonald, 1976). In some cases, teachers are even evaluated on the basis of their social and moral attitudes or philosophy, such as "liking children," church or volunteer participation, or ability to articulate a philosophy of education (Berliner, 1986).

Perhaps the reliance on these diverse and seemingly unrelated bases for evaluating teaching expertise stems from the lack of an accepted hierarchy of educa-

For copies of this article, contact Jayne M. Standley, Center for Music Research, The Florida State University, Tallahassee, FL 32306-2098.

tional outcomes to serve as a basis for judging. The debate over the most appropriate dependent measure of effective teaching continues and includes issues such as the students' acquisition of subject matter, the acquisition of values that help them to adapt and live adequately in contemporary society (Brophy & Good, 1986), and the efficiency of the environment in which learning occurs (Brophy, 1986; Good, 1979; Medley, 1977).

This lack of consensus on criteria for teacher comparison results in many researchers' equating expertise with years of teaching experience. The interaction of these two variables seems to further confound the global issue of teacher evaluation, either intentionally or unintentionally, since other research shows that the act of teaching requires hours of practice, thus generally improving over time (Berliner, 1976). However, the extent to which experience (versus other variables) actually accounts for the quality of the end result of teaching expertise is, as yet, undetermined.

A further complication in interpreting this research is the diverse array of qualifications of the judges or raters involved. Berliner (1986) points out that, in other professions, the act of judging is a rigorously acquired skill that requires prior personal success in the ability in question, training and testing in the skill of judging, and subsequent hours of practice in the activity of judging. Qualifications for judges are highly prized and stringently awarded. In the field of education, parents, media personnel, politicians, member of religious sects, students, and law enforcement officials commonly formulate evaluative opinions about "good teaching"; any and all judge primarily on the basis of their personal beliefs and opinions. The research in teacher expertise reflects this diversity; it is impossible to confirm reliability or validity across the various studies.

Some researchers have attempted to resolve these issues by identifying expert teachers (as determined by trained and qualified judges) and studying their classroom techniques in order to delineate unique skills and attributes (Berliner, 1986; Berliner & Tikunoff, 1976; Brandt, 1986). The results of these studies have shown that expert teachers process information and act differently than do novice teachers in several ways. Experts tend to view classroom situations and make inferences about the interaction rather than simply describe the literal aspects observed (Berliner, 1986). They use higher-order systems of categorization that reveal implicit inference combined with hierarchy and pattern recognition as an efficient and immediate analytical technique (Berliner, 1986; Brophy & Evertson, 1976; Haigh & Katterns, 1984).

Expert teachers also tend to be opportunistic planners, whereas novices reveal more "functional fixedness" in their proposed teaching strategies. For example, classroom experts plan by anticipating situations and generating contingencies for each of the several possible responses (Housner & Griffey, 1985). They then combine and creatively juxtapose contingencies with established teaching routines to simultaneously assess such issues as absenteeism, preparedness, knowledge, and attitude (Leinhardt, 1986). They continuously use this input to modify subsequent teaching procedures as they progress through the teaching session (Leinhardt & Greeno, 1986).

In one study, Berliner (1986) showed slides of classroom interactions to expert teachers, novices, and postulants (subject-matter experts from industry without teaching background) and interviewed all groups about what they saw. He found that expert teachers, but very few novices and postulants, had the ability to perceive clues in the slide and make correct inferences about the task, presence or absence of the teacher, and capabilities of the learners.

In the field of music education, research in teacher training has concentrated on teacher presentation attributes (Madsen & Geringer, 1989; Madsen, Standley, & Cassidy, 1989; Sims, 1986; Yarbrough, 1975); on use of reinforcement (Forsythe, 1975; Kuhn, 1974; Madsen & Alley, 1979); on efficiency in implementation of instruction (Madsen & Geringer, 1983; Moore, 1987); and on the effect of music versus nonmusic activities on student attentiveness (Kostka, 1984; Price, 1983; Yarbrough & Price, 1981). As yet, the global concept of teacher expertise in music education has not been subjected to systematic analysis.

The purpose of this study was to develop a task that would differentiate levels of expertise of music educators and therapists and to ascertain whether such expertise is independent of years of teaching experience.

PROCEDURE

One hundred fifty people involved at various levels in the study or professions of music education were asked to simultaneously observe, analyze, and extemporaneously write about 20 videotaped excerpts of a variety of music situations and interactions. Subjects were grouped on the basis of their recognized expertise and years of teaching experience into five groups of 30 persons each: (1) freshmen, first-time-in-college students who stated an intent to major in music education; (2) juniors, who had completed 2 years of college-level courses and who stated an intent to major in music education; (3) novice music educators, who had completed courses but were awaiting internship; (4) experienced music educators, with the required degree and 1 to 10 years of professional experience ($\overline{M}$ = 6.3); and (5) expert music educators, with the required degree and more than 10 years of professional experience ($\overline{M}$ = 15.6 years) who had also received recognition (e.g., formal commendations, awards) from their colleagues as having outstanding expertise.

The observation tape contained 20 one-minute excerpts separated from each other by 2 seconds of blank tape. The 20 examples consisted of music in special education interactions (n = 9) with mainstreamed groups and people who were mentally retarded, had cerebral palsy, were hearing-impaired, learning disabled, geriatric, abandoned, or were juvenile delinquents; music education interactions (n = 9) with general, instrumental, or choral groups at the elementary, middle school, and high school levels; and professional, formal music performances (n = 2) that included a piano concerto with both full orchestra and soloist shown and a violin solo accompanied by piano with only the violinist shown.

Subjects were told to observe each example and simultaneously write as much as they could about what they saw. No other directions were given concerning what to look for or write about. The tape was stopped after Example 10 for 1 minute to allow each subject to rest his or her hand, but no discussion was allowed about the task. Otherwise, the tape ran continuously.

Responses were analyzed on the basis of factual versus inferential content. Each accurate descriptor or factual statement about the audio/visual content was given 1 point (for example, "high school girls' chorus" = 3 points). Each inaccurate statement caused 1 point to be deducted (e.g., "high school band" = 0 points when the example clearly showed a high school orchestra with full string section). Each accurate, inferential statement was given 5 points (e.g., "These children are watching so intently the leader must be giving hand signals" = 5 points in response to an example where the leader was not shown and was, in fact, giving hand signals). An inaccurate inferential statement caused 5 points to be deducted (e.g.,

"This is a show choir in rehearsal [that] obviously has not been trained well" = – 5 points when the example was of a hearing-impaired, costumed dance group that did not sing, but performed a choreographed routine to a popular record in a television studio with cameras shown and signed beats being given by a leader, also shown).

Raters were faculty in music education, each with more than 10 years' experience in the preparation of teachers and in research concerning teacher effectiveness, who had been recognized by colleagues for their teaching expertise. Reliability was established through independent analysis of over 50% of the 150 samples and resulted in 98% agreement.

RESULTS

Scores were grouped according to the subject's experience or expertise. Table 1 shows means, score ranges, and standard deviations by group. Scores systematically increased as experience/expertise increased, and score ranges, though overlapping, were clearly differentiated across groups. The standard deviations were similar in all groups with the smallest deviation in the freshmen group.

Table 1
Observation Scores by Group

Value	Freshmen	Juniors	Novices (pre-interns)	Experienced teachers	Expert teachers
Mean score	58.6	70.5	94.7	110.6	147.5
Score range	22-103	29-120	46-147	67-166	107-205
Standard deviation	19.37	25.55	23.89	28.80	28.20
N	30	30	30	30	30

Total N = 150

Data were analyzed using a one-way analysis of variance (ANOVA) to compare mean scores across groups. ANOVA results are presented in Table 2 and indicate a significant difference in mean scores among groups ($p < .001$). Further analysis using the Newman-Keuls multiple comparison test showed all groups were significantly different from all others, except in one case. There was no significant difference between the freshmen and junior groups (see Table 3). All other groups showed increasingly higher scores on this task as group experience or expertise increased.

Table 2
ANOVA on Mean Observation Scores across Groups

Source	Sum of squares	df	Mean sum of squares	F
Between groups	146,262.49	4	36,565.62	57.45*
Error	92,296.07	145	636.53	

$*p < .001$

Table 3
Newman-Keuls Multiple-Comparison Procedure on Mean Scores by Group

Freshmen	Juniors	Novices (pre-interns)	Experienced teachers	Expert teachers
58.60	70.57	94.73	112.83	146.47

Note. Underlining indicates no significant difference ($p > .05$).

For the two groups that had prior teaching experience (i.e., those meeting the criteria for experienced teachers and those meeting the criteria for expert teachers), observation scores and years of teaching experience were subjected to a two-way ANOVA. This analysis showed the scores on only the observation task to be significantly different between the groups. The number of years of teaching experience was not a significant variable, nor was there a significant interaction between the two variables (see Table 4). Despite the fact that the expert teachers had an average of 15.6 years of teaching experience versus only 6.3 years for the experienced teachers, this variable did not account for the difference in scores on this task. Therefore, it was concluded that some variable other than longevity differentiated the expert teachers in completion of this task.

Table 4
Two-Way ANOVA: Years of Experience and Observation Score for Expert and Experienced Teacher Groups

Source	Sum of squares	df	Mean sum of squares	F
Years of experience	4747.63	5	949.53	1.18
Score	9487.03	1	9487.03	11.78*
Years of experience × Score	103.57	2	51.79	.06
Error	41,074.43	51	805.38	
Total	62,893.65	59	1065.99	

*$p < .001$

DISCUSSION

The observation task developed for this study resulted in clear differentiation of music teaching expertise and level of preparation in a music education degree program. Such a measure of pedagogical expertise can be valuable in a variety of ways. In the development of effective teacher training curricula, it can facilitate the delineation of requisite skills and help teacher educators teach hierarchical categorization of classroom interaction. As an observation tool, such a videotape also provides an opportunity for discussion of teacher/therapist effectiveness across a variety of situations. The score on this task was indicative of sensitivity to pedagogical expertise and values and therefore can be used as one component in a battery of assessment measures for screening and selection at various levels of the degree program, from the undergraduate major to the Ph.D. candidate. Additionally, it can separate those with music knowledge from those who are expert in the teaching of music knowledge.

Teacher evaluation is a primary component, albeit often a controversial one, in official policy decisions of state certifying agencies and systems providing educational services. As Berliner (1986) concluded in his search for the expert pedagogue, "in the ill-structured domains where surety about right action does not exist, the choice of a sensible solution strategy for a problem is an even more complex problem." A valid measure of expertise can be used not only to affect systemwide policies, but also to recognize those within the system who excel in both subject-matter knowledge and pedagogy. Furthermore, an established measure of teacher expertise based on documented criteria might reduce reliance on external and arbitrary evaluation by less-than-qualified judges.

Many professionals in teacher training believe that the internship period and the supervising teacher have the greatest impact on the preparation of the novice. An accurate measure of expertise could be valuable in selecting the best role models for this crucial phase of development.

"Domain-specific knowledge" is a characteristic of every kind of expert and is well worth pursuing in the scientific study of expert teaching (Berliner, 1986). The identification of masterful teachers in music can further research efforts by providing a source for the study of effective routines, teaching patterns, and classroom management techniques. The task developed for this study seems to clearly differentiate teacher expertise in music from other music knowledge and skills, and it provides a framework for future investigation in these areas.

REFERENCES

Berliner, D. C. (1976). Impediments to the study of teacher effectiveness. *Journal of Teacher Education, 27*(1), 5–13.

Berliner, D. C. (1985). Laboratory settings and the study of teacher education. *Journal of Teacher Education, 36*(6), 2–8.

Berliner, D. C. (1986). In pursuit of the expert pedagogue. *Educational Researcher, 15*(7), 5–13.

Berliner, D. C., & Tikunoff, W. J. (1976). The California beginning teacher evaluation study: Overview of the ethnographic study. *Journal of Teacher Education, 27*(1), 24–30.

Borich, G. D. (1986). Paradigms of teacher effectiveness research. *Education and Urban Society, 18*(2), 143–167.

Brandt, R. S. (1986). On the expert teacher: A conversation with David Berliner. *Educational Leadership, 44*(2), 4–9.

Brophy, J. (1986). Classroom organization and management, *Education and Urban Society, 18,* 182–194.

Brophy, J. E., & Evertson, C. M. (1976). *Learning from teaching: A development perspective.* Boston: Allyn and Bacon.

Brophy, J., & Good, T. L. (1986). Teacher behavior and student achievement. In M. C. Wittrock (Ed.), *Handbook of research on teaching* (pp. 328–375). New York: Macmillan.

Forsythe, J. L. (1975). The effect of teacher approval, disapproval, and errors on student attentiveness: Music versus classroom teachers. In C. K. Madsen, R. D. Greer, & C. H. Madsen, Jr. (Eds.), *Research in music behavior* (pp. 49–55). New York: Teachers College Press.

Good, T. L. (1979). Teacher effectiveness in the elementary school. *Journal of Teacher Education, 18*(3), 49–54.

Haigh, N., & Katterns, B. (1984). Teacher effectiveness: Problem or goal for teacher education. *Journal of Teacher Education, 35*(5), 23–27.

Housner, L. D., & Griffey, D. C. (1985). Teacher cognition: Differences in planning and interactive decision-making between experienced and inexperienced teachers. *Research Quarterly for Exercise and Sport, 56,* 45–53.

Kostka, M. J. (1984). An investigation of reinforcements, time use, and student attentiveness in piano lessons. *Journal of Research in Music Education, 32,* 113–122.

Kuhn, T. L. (1974). The effect of teacher approval and disapproval on attentiveness, musical achievement, and attitudes of fifth grade students. In C. K. Madsen, R. D. Greer, & C. H. Madsen, Jr. (Eds.), *Research in music behavior* (pp. 40–48). New York: Teachers College Press.

Leinhardt, G. (1986). Expertise in mathematics teaching. *Educational Leadership, 43*(7), 28–33.

Leinhardt, G., & Greeno, J. G. (1986). The cognitive skill of teaching. *Journal of Educational Psychology, 78,* 75–95.

Madsen, C. K., & Alley, J. M. (1979). The effect of reinforcement on attentiveness: A comparison of behaviorally trained music therapists and other professionals with implications for competency-based academic preparation. *Journal of Music Therapy, 16,* 70–82.

Madsen, C. K., & Geringer, J. M. (1983). Attending behavior as a function of in-class activity in university music classes. *Journal of Music Therapy, 20,* 30–38.

Madsen, C. K., & Geringer, J. M. (1989). The relationship of teacher "on-task" to intensity and effective teaching. *Canadian Music Educator, 30*(2), 87–94.

Madsen, C. K., Standley, J. M., & Cassidy, J. W. (1989). Demonstration and recognition of high and low contrasts in teacher intensity. *Journal of Research in Music Education, 37*(2), 85–92.

McDonald, F. J. (1976). Report on phase II of the beginning teacher evaluation study. *Journal of Teacher Education, 27*(1), 39–42.

Medley, D. M. (1977). *Teacher competence and teacher effectiveness.* Washington, DC: American Association of Colleges for Teacher Education.

Moore, R. S. (1987). Effects of age, sex, and activity on children's attentiveness in elementary school music classes. In C. K. Madsen & C. A. Prickett (Eds.), *Applications of research in music behavior* (pp. 26–31). Tuscaloosa: The University of Alabama Press.

Ornstein, A. C. (1986). Research on teaching: Measurements and methods. *Education and Urban Society, 18*(2), 176–181.

Price, H. E. (1983). The effect of conductor academic task presentation, conductor reinforcement, and ensemble practice on performers' musical achievement, attentiveness, and attitude. *Journal of Research in Music Education, 31,* 245–257.

Sanford, J. P., & Evertson, C. M. (1983). Time use and activities in junior high classes. *Journal of Educational Research, 76,* 140–147.

Sims, W. L. (1986). The effect of high versus low teacher affect and passive versus active student activity during music listening on preschool children's attention, piece preference, time spent listening, and piece recognition. *Journal of Research in Music Education, 34,* 173–191.

Yarbrough, C. (1975). The effect of magnitude of conductor behavior on performance, attentiveness, and attitude of students in selected mixed choruses. *Journal of Research in Music Education, 23,* 134–146.

Yarbrough, C., & Price, H.E. (1981). Prediction of performer attentiveness based on rehearsal activity and teacher behavior. *Journal of Research in Music Education, 29,* 209–217.

June 19, 1989

This study was designed to assess subjects' perceptions of teacher approval/disapproval given to elementary students compared to the actual responses of the teacher. Subjects were 109 graduate and undergraduate music therapy (n = 50) and music education (n = 59) majors enrolled in classes in behavioral techniques that constituted parts of teacher/ therapist training programs. Subjects viewed a 23-min videotape of an ongoing kindergarten music class involving listening, movement, and rhythm instrument performance activities. Subjects were instructed to write as many succinct statements as possible while observing the tape concerning the setting, teacher behavior, teacher/student interactions, lesson organization, and students' musical and social behaviors. Following the viewing, subjects evaluated various aspects of the approval and disapproval, using seven-point semantic differential scales, and also estimated the percentages of teacher time spent giving approval, disapproval, and instruction. All subjects inaccurately estimated the amount of teacher time devoted to approval and disapproval. There were significant differences between the two groups regarding the perceived use of teacher time, with music education students estimating a significantly greater amount of time devoted to approval (p < .01). Both groups indicated that there was "too little" approval given by the teacher; however, the music therapy subjects expressed this more strongly (p < .02). There were no significant differences between the two groups across other semantic differential scales. All subjects considered approval and disapproval to be generally "good," "meaningful," "beneficial," "valuable," and "effective." A significant difference between music therapy and music education majors was found in the number and content of written statements.

Clifford K. Madsen, *Florida State University, Tallahassee*
Robert A. Duke, *University of Texas at Austin*

JRME 1985, VOLUME 33, NUMBER 3, PAGES 205–214

Observation of Approval/Disapproval in Music: Perception Versus Actual Classroom Events

Sartre suggested that the only way we know ourselves is through the feedback we receive from others. If this notion is extended to include the general environment, then it might be possible to investigate systematically several issues concerning music. How are various "feed-

For reprints of this article, contact Clifford K. Madsen, Center for Music Research, School of Music, Florida State University, Tallahassee 32306.

back" modes interpreted by students? Feedback received from making music? Feedback from the sound of the music? Feedback from the teacher? Feedback from an accompanist or the group?

Prior to ascertaining the effects of feedback, one should decide specifically what it is that the feedback is intended to provide or produce. Some common aspects concerning feedback seem quite obvious. When considering the effect of gravity's feedback in teaching small children to keep their balance while walking, running, or perhaps later while riding a bicycle, the power of the "laws" is assumed. However, when considering the effects of approval/disapproval given to students, other issues are generally considered: What are our goals? Are our goals to produce more sensitive performances? Develop positive attitudes? Both?

If Sartre is correct in assuming that we must have feedback for knowledge, then perhaps we should start by considering the "feedback" received from listening to music. What constitutes appropriate feedback while listening to music? What knowledge is appropriate? If a musician is to intervene purposefully in this listening process (i.e., to teach), then where should instruction or teaching begin? Should it begin by choosing certain music for listening? Should it begin by teaching (i.e., giving feedback) about the music? In teaching for finer musical discriminations? It seems apparent that music, much like other pleasant sensations, including eating, can be enjoyed without a great deal of instruction. In this case the music-listening experience constitutes its own reward. Obviously, there are many, many people who listen to music without desiring much additional feedback. If one chooses to provide any feedback or to expand the music-listening experience, it would seem advisable that one do so carefully. Perhaps the goal would be to provide feedback in shaping musical performances (e.g., teaching someone to sing in tune). Regardless, it seems imperative that teachers know what outcome they intend such that feedback is both purposeful and effective.

A major problem arises at this point concerning desire versus effect. The effect of a teacher's feedback is not necessarily linked with the teacher's desire. The improvement, or lack thereof, of a musical organization in achieving greater musical sensitivity often is not tied in a cause-and-effect or contingent relationship to the feedback from the teacher. In empirical research, the dependent variable or effect is measured in relationship to the independent variable (intention), but it is the *effect*, not the intent, that takes precedence. Intentions, as it were, are eventually discarded if there is not a change in the dependent variable. Yet teachers may interact in an ineffective manner if their intentions are different from practice. It is the specific problem of intention that this research addresses: What constitutes the perceptions of music teachers concerning potential effectiveness of approval/disapproval given to students within a musical environment?

There seem to be many sources of feedback for students within a musical organization. Many would suggest that the performance of excellent music with both technical proficiency and musical sensitivity constitutes the best possible feedback for continuing participation, as well as for personal enjoyment. Others might allude to "winning" performances, physical movement, cognitive development, or peer social interchange. Some would suggest that the "approval" of the teacher is an important source of feedback, yet there appear to be many "perceptions" of teacher approval that inhibit teachers from its effective use.

In a general review of literature, Brophy (1981) suggested:

> Classroom-process data indicate that teachers' verbal praise cannot be equated with reinforcement. Typically, such praise is used infrequently, without contingency, specificity, or credibility. Often it is not even intended as reinforcement, and even when it is, it frequently has some other function (p. 5).

It would seem that if praise or verbal approval is to function appropriately then many issues must be taken into consideration. These issues concern differential effects based upon contingent versus noncontingent delivery (Madsen, 1982; Madsen & Madsen, 1983; Marlowe, Madsen, Bowen, Reardon, & Rouge, 1978), age (Thomas, Presland, Grant, & Glynn, 1978; White, 1975), relevant academic skills (Allyon & Roberts, 1974; Hundert, Bucher, & Henderson, 1976; Libb, Sachs, & Boyd, 1973), attribution (Dweck, 1975), and activity or music organization (Madsen & Alley, 1979).

In a study directly related to the present research (Madsen & Duke, 1985), subjects viewed a film designed to contrast high rates of teacher approval with equally high rates of teacher disapproval (Madsen & Madsen, 1975). Subjects then evaluated various aspects of the film using seven-point semantic differential scales and were also requested to list any specific teacher behaviors recalled. Results indicated that subjects trained in behavioral techniques considered approval to be significantly more "meaningful," "good," "valuable," and "effective" compared to those students without behavioral training. Perceptions of disapproval reflected similar, though less often significant, differences between the groups, and both trained and untrained subjects considered disapproval responses generally less effective.

Approval given to older students was viewed less favorably compared to that given to younger students. Untrained subjects perceived the teacher as being less sincere across all variables compared to the trained subjects. Trained subjects' assessment and recall of specific teacher behaviors observed were significantly more accurate than those of untrained subjects (Madsen & Duke, 1985).

The present research builds upon this previous work and attempts to more clearly ascertain what specific variables operate within a behaviorally trained group of individuals that would influence their perceptions of what and how specific feedback from a teacher functions within a music class.

METHOD

Subjects for the present investigation were 109 undergraduate and graduate music education and music therapy majors participating in a course concerning behavioral techniques in music. In light of previous research using videotape viewing (Gilbert & Stuart, 1977) and an earlier investigation that specifically addressed subjects' perceptions of approval and disapproval teacher responses in a film designed to contrast sequences of 100% teacher approval with 100% teacher disapproval (Madsen & Duke, 1985), it was decided to test the perceptions of subjects, trained in behavioral techniques and observation, viewing a film of an actual music classroom setting. Subjects enrolled in the music education curriculum ($n = 59$) were compared to those enrolled in music therapy ($n = 50$).

A videotape of a kindergarten general music class session was presented during the final week of a one-semester class in behavior modification in music. A classroom designed specifically for the use of audio-visual equipment was used for the presentation. Subjects were given the following verbal instructions:

> You will see a 23-minute videotape of a kindergarten music class. As you observe the lesson, notice as much as you can about what is going on in the classroom and write *brief* statements about what you see. Consider the following: setting, teacher behavior, teacher/student interactions, lesson organization, student musical behavior, student social behavior. Once again, make as many clear and succinct written observations as you can, and write them down as you watch the tape. If you have any questions, ask now.

The class activities shown in the videotape included a brief introductory discussion, a rhythm instrument demonstration and listening/performing activity, a movement activity, and roll-taking. Of the total class time, approximately 22% was devoted to teacher approval/disapproval. By actual count, the teacher's verbal responses included 18 approvals, 13 disapprovals, and 69 instructions/questions. Student on-task behavior was 92%. Reliability for the above was .98 (Agreements/Agreements plus Disagreements).

At the conclusion of the presentation, subjects were asked to evaluate various aspects of the observed approvals and disapprovals using seven-point semantic differential scales (Figure 1). In addition, subjects were asked to estimate the percentages of teacher time devoted to approval, disapproval, and instruction.

RESULTS

Results of t-test comparisons of group mean responses indicated that there were no significant differences between the music therapy and music education majors concerning the evaluation of the quality and effects of the teacher approval and disapproval observed in the videotape presentation. (See Table 1 for group means and corresponding t values.) In general, subjects in both groups rated the approval and disapproval favorably; that is, all of the group mean scores were on the positive side of each pair of bipolar adjectives. All subjects considered the teacher's responses as generally "good," "meaningful," "beneficial," "sincere," "valuable," and "effective." It is interesting to note that the one

Major _____ Year in school _____

Please evaluate the tape you have just seen. Answer each aspect carefully. It is important that you give your *honest* opinion concerning the teacher/student interaction.

Approval given by the teacher in the tape was:

		1	2	3	4	5	6	7	
1.	good	___	___	___	___	___	___	___	bad
2.	meaningful	___	___	___	___	___	___	___	meaningless
3.	beneficial	___	___	___	___	___	___	___	harmful
4.	insincere	___	___	___	___	___	___	___	sincere
5.	worthless	___	___	___	___	___	___	___	valuable
6.	effective	___	___	___	___	___	___	___	ineffective
7.	too much	___	___	___	___	___	___	___	too little

Disapproval given by the teacher in the tape was:

		1	2	3	4	5	6	7	
1.	good	___	___	___	___	___	___	___	bad
2.	meaningful	___	___	___	___	___	___	___	meaningless
3.	beneficial	___	___	___	___	___	___	___	harmful
4.	insincere	___	___	___	___	___	___	___	sincere
5.	worthless	___	___	___	___	___	___	___	valuable
6.	effective	___	___	___	___	___	___	___	ineffective
7.	too much	___	___	___	___	___	___	___	too little

How much of the teacher's time was devoted to approval/disapproval and instruction? Please indicate the percentages below.

Approval _____ %
Disapproval _____ %
Instruction _____ %
Total =   100%

Briefly describe any previous teaching, counseling, and/or leadership experience you have had (including length of time).

Figure 1.
Individual data sheet

aspect that received the most positive score for approval and disapproval from both the music therapy and education groups was that of teacher "sincerity."

There were significant differences observed between the two groups in the evaluation of the amount of approval and disapproval given by the teacher, and this appears to be the most consequential aspect of the study. One significant difference between music therapy and music education majors did occur in the evaluation of teacher responses in the "too much–too little" approval variable ($p < .02$), with the music therapy group expressing more strongly than music education students a perceived need for increased teacher approval. No significant difference was found on this variable concerning disapproval, with both groups

Table 1
Adjusted[a] Group Mean Scores for Music Therapy and Music Education Subjects

| | Group means | | | |
	Therapy	Education		
Approval				
Good	3.46	3.17	Bad	1.00
Meaningful	3.60	3.34	Meaningless	0.85
Beneficial	3.04	3.05	Harmful	0.04
Sincere	2.88	2.95	Insincere	0.22
Valuable	3.32	3.03	Worthless	0.96
Effective	3.68	3.46	Ineffective	0.74
Too much	5.80	5.22	Too little	2.53*
Disapproval				
Good	3.57	3.46	Bad	0.39
Meaningful	3.10	3.48	Meaningless	1.26
Beneficial	3.34	3.39	Harmful	0.18
Sincere	2.51	2.71	Insincere	0.79
Valuable	3.35	3.59	Worthless	0.90
Effective	3.48	3.75	Ineffective	0.83
Too much	3.59	3.85	Too little	1.06

*$p < .02$. All other comparisons $p > .05$.
[a]The items Sincere/Insincere and Valuable/Worthless were reversed on the subject response sheet.

perceiving the amount of disapproval as appropriate for the classroom setting.

Similar differences in the perception of teacher approval were observed in the estimation of time spent by the teacher. Table 2 presents the number of music therapy and music education students who indicated that a greater percentage of the teacher's time was devoted to approval, disapproval, or who indicated equal time was spent on each. Again, there was a significant difference between the responses of the two groups ($\chi^2 [2, N = 109] = 12.6, p < .002$), with the majority of music education majors indicating that more time was spent giving disapproval. In addition, a significant difference was found between the groups' mean estimations of approval time ($p < .0001$). In fact, the music education group mean of 24.1 is nearly twice that of the music therapy

Table 2
Number of Subjects Indicating Greater Percentages of Approval, Disapproval, or Equal Amounts of Each

	Approval	Disapproval	Equal
Therapy ($n = 50$)	12	30	8
Education ($n = 59$)	34	19	6

$p < .002$

Table 3
Mean Estimated Percentages of Teacher Time

	Therapy ($n = 50$)		Education ($n = 59$)		
	M	sd	M	sd	t
Approval	13.70	9.18	24.07	16.17	4.19*
Disapproval	17.98	12.83	18.29	12.49	0.12

*$p < .0001$

mean of 13.7 (see Table 3). There was no significant difference in the mean estimated percentages of disapproval time between the groups.

Subjects' written statements concerning observations made during the course of the film were categorized as to topic: activity, teacher, student, other. The activity category included statements that addressed in a general way the nature of the task or the quality of the lesson organization; for example, "demonstration of tambourine" or "class rules explained." Statements assigned to the teacher category described a specific teacher behavior or expressed an evaluation of the teacher; for example, "teacher used nonverbal cues" or "teacher very authoritarian; in control." Statements describing specific student behaviors or evaluating students' performance were included in the student category, for example, "Lester has hand raised" or "most students are with the beat." Statements concerning such things as the contents of the classroom, the placement of the chairs, the students' clothing, and similar miscellany were included in the other category.

Two independent judges completed the classification of subjects' written observations. Interjudge reliability was calculated for each subjects' responses by dividing the number of agreements by the total number of observations. The mean reliability across the subjects was .91.

It appears from the analysis of subjects' written responses that music therapy and music education majors attended to different aspects of the classroom situation depicted in the tape. There was a significant difference between the two groups across the four categories of observations (χ^2 [3, $N = 3,800$] = 44.53, $p < .0001$).

Table 4 presents the total number of statements recorded by group and category. Music therapy majors made more statements concerning the nature of the class activities than did the music education majors,

Table 4
Number of Total Subject Observations by Group and Observation Category

	Activity	Teacher	Student	Other	Total
Music therapy ($n = 50$)	423 (24%)	587 (34%)	614 (36%)	105 (6%)	1,729 (100%)
Music education ($n = 59$)	332 (16%)	821 (40%)	799 (39%)	119 (6%)	2,071 (100%)

$p < .0001$

while the number of statements categorized as teacher-related was greater for the music education group than the music therapy group. Music education students also recorded more observations in the student category than music therapy students.

It appears that students do perceive some aspects of behavior differently in relationship to specific training. Music therapy and music education subjects evidenced different perceptions of teacher time devoted to approval, and recorded different variables of classroom interactions.

DISCUSSION

The major issue concerning the preceding data is the discrepancy between what actually goes on in a classroom and how training or personal bias influences what people perceive of those classroom activities. Value judgments concerning "good," "bad," "meaningful," and so on seem to be very useful, yet the discrepancy between the perception of *both* groups of subjects compared to the actual classroom events suggests a need for continued research.

It should be remembered that all the subjects in the present study were enrolled in an observation class; had completed at least four independent observations, one with a reliability observer; and had been previously judged to be proficient observers. That is, subjects had demonstrated the ability to accurately count during ten-second intervals teacher approval/disapproval on selected student and teacher observation forms (Madsen & Madsen, 1983). Untrained subjects in an earlier study (Madsen & Duke, 1985) were not nearly as accurate in estimating teacher responses as were trained subjects. Yet in the present investigation, even trained subjects were not accurate in their post hoc estimation of approval/disapproval teacher responses.

Another issue of concern focuses on the age of the students involved. Piaget (1952) suggests that, for students at the preoperational level, most children attribute very concrete aspects to what the teacher says, while older students are much more reflective and do not internalize as readily. Thus, it might be difficult for a small youngster (as in the videotape demonstration) to separate doing a good job from being a good person or good musician. Older people who have not previously worked with this age group might therefore perceive these situations differently. There is some evidence to suggest that older people do view students differently depending upon how much praise students receive. Meyer, et al. (1979) found that high school students and adults viewed those students who receive praise after success and neutral feedback after failure as having low ability compared to students who receive neutral feedback after success and criticism after failure.

It is precisely the differentiated aspects of perception that make the study of effects extremely difficult. What one would like to receive in feedback for oneself, or specifically, what one perceives one would like to receive, makes it difficult to plan and implement instructional feedback systems because those systems might need to be different or even antithetical to one's own perceptions. In regard to these data, why is it that the therapy majors inaccurately estimated the approval time of the teacher and overestimated the disapproval time? Why did the music education majors overestimate the time spent giving approval and disapproval? And why did the therapy majors perceive a greater need for increased teacher approval in light of the high on-task level of the students?

These results may reflect the difference between those persons who view the subject matter as the paramount goal (i.e., music educators) compared to those who view the child's social activity as the major goal (music therapists). Of course, there may be any number of variables operating within each of these groups that could contribute to a differentiation. Yet in the present study, both the perceived rate and magnitude of approval seem to indicate that the goals one has for oneself or another influence the very perception of what specific feedback is actually taking place, let alone what feedback is most appropriate. Thus, the rate and balance of approval/disapproval seem to be inextricably interwoven with the perceived goals of the observer. If Sartre is correct in assuming that we only know ourselves from the feedback we receive from others, it would seem that we need a good deal more research concerning ourselves as well as those "others."

REFERENCES

Allyon, T. & Roberts, M.D. (1974). Eliminating discipline problems by strengthening academic performance. *Journal of Applied Behavioral Analysis, 7*, 71–76.

Brophy, J. (1981). Teacher praise: A functional analysis. *Review of Educational Research, 51*(1), 5–32.

Dweck, C. (1975). The role of expectations and attributions in the alleviation of learned helplessness. *Journal of Personality and Social Psychology, 31*, 674–685.

Gilbert J. P., & Stuart, M. (1977). A videotape procedure for assessing attitude toward disabled clientele: Procedural development and initial results. *Journal of Music Therapy, 14*(3), 116–125.

Hundert, J., Bucher, B., & Henderson, M. (1976). Increasing inappropriate classroom behavior and academic performance by reinforcing correct work alone. *Psychology in the Schools, 13*, 195–200.

Libb, J., Sachs, C., & Boyd W. (1973). Reinforcement strategies for token economies in a special classroom setting. *Psychological Reports, 32*, 831–834.

Madsen, C. K. (1982). The effect of contingent teacher approval and withholding music performance on improving attentiveness. In Proceedings of the Ninth International Seminar on Research in Music Education [Special issue]. *Psychology of Music*, 76–81.

Madsen, C. K., & Alley, J. M. (1979). The effect of reinforcement on attentiveness: A comparison of behaviorally trained music therapists and other professionals with implications for competency-based academic preparation. *Journal of Music Therapy, 16*(2), 70–82.

Madsen, C. K., & Duke, R. A. (1985). Behavioral training in music education: Perception of approval/disapproval in music education. *Bulletin of the Council for Research in Music Education, 85*, 119–130.

Madsen, C. K., & Madsen, C. H., Jr. (1975) *Approval vs. disapproval.* (16 mm color film; 30 min). Iowa City, IA: Amdecker, Films by Spectrum.

Madsen, C. H., Jr., & Madsen, C. K. (1983). *Teaching/discipline: A positive approach for educational development.* (3rd ed.). Raleigh: Contemporary Publishing.

Marlowe, R. H., Madsen, C. H., Jr., Bowen, C. E., Reardon, R. C., & Rouge, P. E. (1978). Severe classroom problems: Teachers as counselors. *Journal of Applied Behavioral Analysis, 11,* 53–66.

Meyer, W. W., Bachmann, M., Biermann, U., Hempelmann, M., Ploger, F. O., & Spiller, H. (1979). The informational value of evaluative behavior: Influences of praise and blame on perceptions of ability. *Journal of Educational Psychology, 71,* 259–268.

Piaget, J. (1952). *The origins of intelligence in children.* New York: International Universities Press.

Thomas, J., Presland, I., Grant, M., & Glynn, T. (1978). Natural rates of teacher approval and disapproval in Grade-7 classrooms. *Journal of Applied Behavioral Analysis, 11,* 91–94.

White, M. A. (1975). Natural rates of teacher approval and disapproval in the classroom. *Journal of Applied Behavioral Analysis, 8,* 367–372.

December 12, 1984

The purpose of this study was to investigate teacher intensity, *the global attributes of enthusiasm combined with an astute sense of timing in relation to classroom management and effective subject presentation and delivery. The authors also tried to ascertain whether high and low contrasts in teacher intensity could be taught to and then demonstrated by prospective music education student teachers (n = 20) and whether other music education majors untrained in the concept of intensity could recognize these contrasts (freshmen, n = 23; seniors, n = 22; and graduate students, n = 29). Results of the study indicated that intensity as a concept could be operationally defined, easily taught to prospective student teachers, ably demonstrated, and recognized with an extremely high degree of reliability across levels of sophistication within the music education major.*

Clifford K. Madsen, Jayne M. Standley, Jane W. Cassidy, *Florida State University*

JRME 1989, VOLUME 37, NUMBER 2, PAGES 85–92

Demonstration and Recognition of High and Low Contrasts in Teacher Intensity

The ability of a teacher to initiate and maintain a high level of student attention has been of major concern to researchers and teacher educators for years. To prepare future teachers for productive and effective teaching, it is necessary to identify those observable, quantifiable characteristics that separate expert teachers from novices (Brandt, 1986). Berliner (1986) has suggested a number of attributes needed for high teacher effectiveness and, therefore, high teacher intensity.

When used to refer to teacher presentation of subject matter, the terms *enthusiasm, magnitude,* and *affect* are used somewhat interchangeably, suggesting that teacher behavior can be executed and observed in varying degrees. Collins (1978) developed a measurement device that operationally defined eight teacher behaviors under low, medium, and high levels of enthusiasm. Behavioral descriptors were used in a training

---

For copies of this article, contact Clifford K. Madsen, Center for Music Research, Florida State University, Tallahassee, Florida 32306.

session designed to increase enthusiasm level of preservice elementary teachers. Collins's data, in the form of observer enthusiasm ratings, showed that experimental subjects increased their display of enthusiasm after training and that control subjects changed little from pretest to posttest, indicating that it is possible to train preservice teachers to increase teacher enthusiasm. McKinney et al. (1983) used the Collins model in an experimental training session. After treatment, teachers were asked to display high, medium, or low enthusiasm in the classroom on demand. Observers of these performances correctly assigned ratings to virtually all teachers across the three categories of enthusiasm, but the level of enthusiasm had *no* effect on posttest student achievement on a social studies task.

Music teacher behaviors of eye contact, closeness to students, volume and modulation of voice, gestures, facial expressions, and pacing were first operationally defined and differentiated as high and low levels of magnitude by Yarbrough (1975). In a choral rehearsal setting, the effects of high and low magnitude on student behavior were reliably observed. Students seemed to prefer and were more attentive during high magnitude conditions, although magnitude had *no* significant effect on performance level. Sims (1986) varied teacher affect (high versus low) and student activity (active versus passive hand movements) during music listening activities with preschool children. Changes in student off-task behavior were more obvious when high affect was followed by low affect than under the opposite condition.

Preliminary investigations specifically relating to the current project included three separate experiments. Experiment 1 (Standley & Madsen, 1987) compared videotaped performances of 42 freshman music education majors under two conditions: (a) each student speaking 30 seconds before the entire group of subjects about the individual's personal goals for a music career and (b) each subject leading a familiar song with a group of six preschoolers ranging in age from 4 to 5 years. Intensity, defined as sustained control of the student/teacher interaction with efficient, accurate presentation and correction of the subject matter combined with enthusiastic affect and pacing, was evaluated on a 10-point Likert scale. Correlation analysis indicated that intensity in speaking about oneself was *not* highly related to intensity in a music teaching situation (Spearman Rank Correlation Coefficient $r_s = .43$).

Experiment 2 (Standley & Madsen, 1987) assessed teacher intensity of three groups of music education/therapy majors engaged in a music task similar to Experiment 1: teaching a new song to a group of preschoolers ages 4 to 5 years. Subjects were 15 freshmen in their first semester of study, 15 senior music education majors in their final week of campus study prior to internship in the schools, and 15 senior music therapy majors in their final week of campus study prior to internship in clinical agencies. We rated subjects on intensity using a 10-point Likert scale. Mean scores for each group were compared with a Kruskall-Wallis one-way analysis of variance (ANOVA) and revealed significant differences ($H = 18.73$, $df = 2$, $\alpha < .001$). A Dunn's Multiple Comparison procedure determined the freshmen to be significantly lower in intensity ratings ($\bar{R} = 34.1$) than either the music education ($\bar{R} = 21.4$) or the music therapy seniors ($\bar{R}$ = 13.6). There was no statistical significance between the two senior groups. Results of these two studies suggested that intensity is a teaching skill that can be measured and that performance of a musical task may enhance the intensity of the teaching interaction.

Researchers in the third experiment (Madsen & Geringer, in press) focused on the relationship between demonstrated effective teaching and teacher intensity or teacher "on-task." Senior music education majors (n = 22) in their last week of student teaching made a videotape of their best teaching, which included both teacher and student responses. A panel of four expert teacher educators independently judged the videotapes using a 5-point Likert scale. Student teachers were evaluated on the basis of demonstrated effective teaching in relationship to student responses. Reliability among judges was W = .86. These same videotapes were then independently judged by two different experts trained in judging teacher "on-task" or intensity using an evaluative instrument specifically designed to assess behaviors relating to teacher intensity. These judges viewed videotaped examples of 15-second intervals and marked specific teacher behaviors. They also used a subjective rating scale to evaluate teacher intensity by assigning a rating of *low* (0) to *high* (10) at the end of each minute. Reliability for the judges was r_s = .85 on the more subjective rating. We then assessed the correlation between effective teaching and intensity. The Spearman Rank Correlation Coefficient was r_s = .92. Thus, results of the study suggested that intensity may be an important attribute of effective music teaching and warrants additional investigation.

METHOD

Our intent in this study was to ascertain whether high and low contrasts in teacher intensity could be quickly taught to and then demonstrated by prospective music education student teachers and whether subjects untrained in the concept of intensity could recognize these contrasts. Subjects were music education majors (N = 94) who were divided into one experimental and three control groups. The experimental group (student teachers) consisted of music education majors (n = 20) in their final week of on-campus preparation prior to beginning a public school internship with emphasis in general, choral, or instrumental areas. The three control groups were differentiated according to level of preparation in the music education or therapy major: freshmen (n = 23), seniors (n = 22), and graduate students (n = 29).

Prospective student teachers received one afternoon of training in a teaching session of 1.5 hours. Extreme contrasts in teacher intensity were modeled by the instructor across several specific musical activities (e.g., conducting the speaking of accurate rhythmic patterns or the singing of simple chord progressions or several folk songs). Student teachers then emulated these contrasts in teaching the same activities before their peers for short periods beginning with 10–15 seconds and extending to a few minutes.

The next day, we asked each subject to demonstrate high and low teacher intensity *contrasts* across 1 minute while teaching a self-selected music activity. The minute was divided into four 15-second intervals by the ringing of a bell. Differing combinations of high and low intensity had been randomly preassigned for the intervals of each minute and were known only to that subject. The presentation order of high and low intervals was counterbalanced by the experimenters and all possible orders of combinations were assigned.

At the conclusion of the first 20 demonstrations, we asked the subjects to repeat the task with each assigned high or low interval changed to the opposite concept (e.g., high-low-high-low to low-high-low-high). Again, a bell differentiated the four 15-second intervals within each minute. Both 20-minute demonstrations were videotaped, and the videotape included the sound of the bell that separated each 15-second interval. The numbers 1–4 were superimposed on the tape so that they appeared simultaneously with the auditory stimulus, providing an additional means of identifying the intervals. Equipment for this aspect of the study consisted of a VHS portable videocassette recorder (Panasonic, Model AG-2400), a color camera (Panasonic, Model WV3040K), and a character generator for superimposing numbers (Panasonic, Model WV-KB10). Videotapes were shown on two color monitors (Zenith, Model C 1382W and Panasonic, Model CTG-1911), arranged to maximize visibility for each participant.

Following the two demonstrations, the student teacher group was asked to view each 20-minute videotape and, for each 15-second interval, to mark an "H" indicating high intensity or an "L" indicating low intensity. Four intervals a minute for 20 minutes yielded a total of 80 intervals to be marked and a possible correct score of 80. At the end of the observation task, each subject was asked to give a self-rating of his or her own overall ability to achieve high intensity on a Likert-type scale from 1 to 10 (1 indicating *low intensity* and 10 indicating *high*). In addition, the prospective student teachers were asked to vote for the five people in the group they thought would be the best teachers. They were also asked to define "teacher intensity" and to state what they had learned about the particular task of contrasting high and low intensity.

Comparison of the responses ($n = 20$) on Tape 1 and Tape 2 yielded mean correct scores of 73.22 and 72.0, respectively. We computed agreement between the two observations using a Kendall Coefficient of Concordance that resulted in $W = .81$, which was statistically significant ($\chi^2 = 27.68$, $df = 17$, critical value = 27.59, $\alpha < .05$). We determined that the student teachers had adequately demonstrated high and low intensity such that it could be differentiated with accuracy across multiple observations.

Tape 1 was then shown to subjects within the three control groups who marked "H" or "L" at the end of each designated interval. Prior to the control observations, intensity was not taught, demonstrated, or defined. At the end of each four-segment minute, the videocassette recorder was placed in the pause mode for 5 seconds and control subjects gave each student teacher an overall ability to achieve high intensity rating from 1 (low) to 10 (high). At the end of the observation task, we asked the control subjects to define intensity by writing on the back of the observation form.

RESULTS

We compared observation scores and overall intensity ratings across groups and analyzed observation errors by interval and by subject. The single most important result was that intensity as a concept was operationally defined, easily taught to prospective student teachers, ably demonstrated, and easily recognized with an extremely high degree of reliability by almost all subjects in the study. The total rate of correct responses across the 15-second intervals was 82.7%. Additionally, the 20 overall intensity ratings (on a scale of 1–10) given by each subject within the control groups were compared for agreement with the Kendall Coefficient of Concordance, resulting in an extremely high reliability (W = .99) that was, of course, statistically significant (χ^2 = 55.87, df = 19, critical value = 43.82, α < .001). This result was considered extraordinary because the task involved rating a concept that was neither taught nor explained, yet agreement was almost 100% across subjects ranging from freshman level to graduate status.

The self-rating given by the student teachers who actually did the teaching task was then compared with the mean rating given by subjects within the untrained groups who had such high agreement among themselves. The Kendall Coefficient of Concordance then dropped to W = .74, which was not statistically significant (χ^2 = 28.12, df = 19, critical value = 30.14, α < .05), indicating low overall agreement. A t test comparing the student teachers versus the combined other groups yielded statistically significant results (t = 3.88, df = 38, α < .001) (see Table 1). These results show that the student teachers rated themselves an average of more than 2 points higher on a 10-point scale ($\bar{M}$ = 7.25) compared to the more objective observers ($\bar{M}$ = 4.41), who demonstrated highly consistent agreement among themselves. These findings substantiate prior research showing that self-ratings of students are both higher and less reliable when compared with those of other professionals (Greenfield, 1978).

Table 1
Analysis of High Versus Low Errors by Interval

	Beginning intervals		Changing intervals				Overall		
	Begin high	Begin low	Low to high	High to low	High to high	Low to low	Total high	Total low	Total
Intervals									
n	10	10	15	15	15	15	40	40	80
(Percentage)	(.125)	(.125)	(.187)	(.187)	(1.87)	(.187)	(.50)	(.50)	(1.00)
Errors									
n	298	80	371	147	174	232	843	459	1,302
(Percentage)	(.23)	(.06)	(.29)	(.11)	(.13)	(.18)	(.65)	(.35)	(1.00)

Total observers = 94; total intervals = 7,520; total errors = 1,302.
Error rate = .173.

We analyzed high versus low observation errors in Tape 1 by interval across all subjects (N = 94). Table 1 shows that almost twice as many errors occurred in recognizing high intensity (843) as in recognizing low intensity (459), with the bulk of the high errors occurring when student teachers were assigned a *change* from low to high (371) or were assigned to *begin* their demonstration with high intensity (298). This finding indicates that either acquisition or perception of high intensity is more difficult when compared to that of low intensity.

The observation errors of the student teachers were analyzed by subject, then rank ordered and compared with the rank of "best teacher votes" as awarded by the student teachers. A Spearman Rank Correlation Coefficient resulted in r_s = .64, which was statistically significant (t = 3.83, df = 19, critical value = 2.861, α < .01). The vote for "best teacher" correlated fairly highly with the subject's ability to demonstrate high and low contrasts in intensity.

We asked all subjects to define "intensity." Rates of responses varied. The fewest number of ideas was expressed by the student teachers (n = 20, comments = 37, $\bar{M}$ = 1.9) followed by freshmen (n = 23, comments = 62, $\bar{M}$ = 2.7) and seniors (n = 22, comments = 99, $\bar{M}$ = 4.5), with the greatest number of ideas expressed by the graduate students (n = 29, comments = 144, $\bar{M}$ = 4.97). Student teachers who were trained to demonstrate intensity were most concise about its definition. Number of expressions increased and varied with the length of time in the curriculum.

Table 2 shows degree of agreement among groups in the major ideas expressed and includes 14 items that accounted for 260 of the 342 total responses. Responses included by fewer than six persons were omitted, including 39 single ideas expressed solely by 39 different persons. Eye contact and proximity (the second and third most frequent responses) were not mentioned by any of the freshman subjects, who also omitted such specific instructional techniques as pacing; short, simple instructions; good posture; and the need for making music as opposed to talking. More advanced students are evidently taught these concepts in the curriculum, and they used such concepts to describe the teaching interactions observed. These items are very similar to the list compiled by Yarbrough (1975) to define high magnitude. Although the words used to define intensity varied greatly, agreement was very high in identifying intensity as either high or low, and it was also high on the overall rating of intensity.

Although they were not of major importance to this study, results were assessed to determine differentiation across groups. Table 3 shows the means and standard deviations of correct observation scores by group. With a possible maximum score of 80, means ranged from 73.22 (student teachers) to 63.04 (freshmen). The student teachers who were trained in demonstrating intensity scored higher than those groups who were untrained. A One-Way Analysis of Variance on these scores yielded significant results between groups (F = 5.05, df = 93, p < .001).

We believe that effective education in any field or area has to do with (a) student selection and (b) the demonstrated effects of teaching. Obviously, if the selection issue is the most important ("teachers are born not made"), the profession must find the important variables that constitute recruitment for effective teaching (as in Experiment 1). If skills can be taught, learned, and measured, the profession still has the same problem: What are the variables necessary for effective teaching?

Table 2
Definitions of Intensity by Group

Comment	Interns	Graduates	Freshmen	Seniors	Total
Enthusiastic, excited expression	5	22	11	11	49
Eye contact	7	15	0	9	31
Proximity; movement toward group	2	15	0	8	25
Concentration; attention to students or teaching; involvement	2	6	8	7	23
Strict, precise body movement or conducting gestures	1	8	3	10	22
Voice volume, pitch, inflection; change in voice	0	9	2	10	21
Energy; effervescence; vigor; pizzazz	3	10	3	3	19
No hesitation in voice; no filler words (uh, ah)	0	8	4	2	14
Planning; knowledge; competence	2	4	3	4	13
Pacing	1	7	0	4	12
Short, simple instructions	2	5	0	3	10
Good posture; change in posture	0	4	0	4	8
Confidence	1	3	2	1	7
Little talk, lots of singing; vary techniques to increase attention; as much time in learning activities as possible	4	1	0	1	6
Totals	30	117	36	77	260

Table 3
Group Means and Standard Deviations of Observation Scores

	Interns	Seniors	Graduates	Freshmen
n	20	22	29	23
Mean score	73.22	66.27	63.56	63.04
Standard deviations	1.93	1.8	2.27	2.24

$N = 94$

Other than knowledge of subject matter, two recurring variables concern (a) demonstrated teacher *enthusiasm* (high teacher affect) in live, positive student/teacher interactions and (b) a sense of *timing* in relationship to classroom management and effective subject matter presentation and monitoring. Both of these variables require the ability to "see oneself as others do" or to "know how one is coming across." Therefore, one's social awareness seems paramount. Teacher intensity in some ways seems to blend the attributes of enthusiasm and timing in that people who are perceived as having high intensity are enthusiastic as well as effective in managing the class. It is difficult to imagine an intense teacher who does not possess both these qualities.

Because previous researchers found a strong relationship between teacher intensity and teacher effectiveness, it seems that all issues relating to teacher intensity need to be investigated. These issues include student attentiveness, subject matter acquisition, the degree of intensity associated with the subject matter itself (i.e., the activity of making music), various levels of social and peer interaction that contribute to intensity, and the general level of teacher "on-task."

Issues concerning intensity are important in both selection and training of prospective teachers, especially in relation to student achievement. The experiments described in this article indicate that teacher intensity is an attribute that can be learned and demonstrated by preservice music teachers and that almost anyone can recognize it with very high reliability. Obviously, much more research is warranted.

REFERENCES

Berliner, D. C. (1986). In pursuit of the expert pedagogue. *Educational Researcher, 15*(7), 5–13.

Brandt, R. S. (1986, October). On the expert teacher: A conversation with David Berliner. *Educational Leadership,* pp. 4–9.

Collins, M. (1978). Effect of enthusiasm training on preservice elementary teachers. *Journal of Teacher Education, 29*(1), 53–57.

Greenfield, D. G. (1978). Evaluation of music therapy practicum competencies: Comparisons of self and instructor ratings of videotapes. *Journal of Music Therapy, 15*(1), 15–20.

Madsen, C. K., & Geringer, J. M. (in press). The relationship of teacher "on-task" to intensity and effective music teaching. *Canadian Music Educator.*

McKinney, C. W., Larkins, A. G., Kazelskis, R., Ford, M. J., Allen, J. A., & Davis, J. C. (1983). Some effects of teacher enthusiasm on student achievement in fourth grade social studies. *Journal of Educational Research, 76*(4), 249–253.

Sims, W. L. (1986). The effect of high versus low teacher affect and passive versus active student activity during music listening on preschool children's attention, piece preference, time spent listening, and piece recognition. *Journal of Research in Music Education, 34,* 173–191.

Standley, J. M., & Madsen, C. K. (1987). Intensity as an attribute of effective therapist/client interaction. *Quodlibet,* Summer, 1987, 15–21.

Yarbrough, C. (1975). The effect of magnitude of conductor behavior on performance, attentiveness, and attitude of students in selected mixed choruses. *Journal of Research in Music Education, 23,* 134–146.

September 9, 1987

The purpose of this study was to determine whether high and low contrasts of gestural intensity could be demonstrated by undergraduate beginning conductors and, furthermore, whether independent observers could recognize these contrasts. An investigator-developed stimulus videotape, illustrating beginning conductors in 1-minute demonstrations of intensity contrasts, was viewed by graduate and undergraduate music majors, undergraduate nonmusic majors, and high school music students. These subjects (N = 320) labeled each 15-second interval according to perceived contrast of intensity and indicated an overall intensity rating for each conductor. Results indicated a 77% correct response rate. Analysis yielded a significant difference in mean correct response between the graduate group and all other subjects, no significant difference in mean intensity ratings among subjects, and a high degree of reliability among the four experimental groups on overall intensity ratings.

James L. Byo, *School of Music, Louisiana State University*

JRME 1990, VOLUME 38, NUMBER 3, PAGES 157–163

Recognition of Intensity Contrasts in the Gestures of Beginning Conductors

The extensive amount of extant literature relating to conducting gesture is indicative of the topic's perceived importance in the fields of music and music education. Distinguished professional conductors and longtime students of conducting have written textbooks in which they attempt to teach conducting through isolation and description of specific elements of gestural technique (Green, 1987; Hunsberger & Ernst, 1983; Rudolf, 1950). Authors of empirical studies have examined gestures of the conductor through study of nonverbal conducting behavior (Berz, 1983; Roshong, 1978), through identification of conducting competencies in survey format (Parr, 1976; Spicer, 1977), and as an outcome of systematic observation of behavior (Madsen & Yarbrough, 1985; Price, 1985). Furthermore, precise definitions of conducting skills, opportunities to practice in conducting practica, immediate reinforcement through videotape feedback, and self-analysis are elements of conductor training that appear to enhance conducting skill development (Yarbrough, 1987).

If the nonverbal skills (gestures) of a conductor are to make a difference in attentiveness, attitude, and performance of musicians, it seems necessary that musicians (observers) be able to recognize qualitative differences in conducting gestures and, furthermore, be able to interpret the conductor's gestural intent

This article is based on the author's doctoral dissertation by the same title, awarded by Florida State University, Tallahassee, August 1988. For copies of this article, contact James L. Byo, School of Music, Louisiana State University, Baton Rouge, LA 70803.

accurately. If musicians can see these differences, both subtle and pronounced, one might expect a conductor whose gestures are technically correct *and* appropriately intense to elicit different musical responses than would one whose gestures are simply correct. If musicians cannot discriminate among various degrees of gestural intensity, one might question the need for gestural development beyond that which communicates only the most basic aspects of tempo, style, and dynamics.

Although previous research in conducting implies that the ability to demonstrate technically correct gestures may be a critical variable in conductor effectiveness, issues involving *intensity* of gesture have received far less data-based attention. If, in fact, "how the conductor 'acts' does make a difference" (Leinsdorf, 1981), it seems that intensity of nonverbal presentation might occupy a place of extreme importance in the conveyance of intention. Researchers in this area have investigated the effect of magnitude of conductor behavior on choir students' performance, attentiveness, and attitude (Yarbrough, 1975). Conductor behavior was differentiated into contrasts of high and low magnitude. Results indicated that students preferred the high-magnitude condition.

Several researchers have examined the concept of intensity as an attribute of effective teaching and as a stimulus for attentiveness in the music teacher/student interaction. Intensity, described as a leadership quality, is defined as "sustained control of the interaction as evidenced by efficient, accurate presentation and correction of the subject matter with enthusiastic affect and fast pacing" (Standley & Madsen, 1987, p. 16). Findings indicate that activity involving music seems to carry an intensity level of its own (Standley & Madsen, 1987); a relationship seems to exist between teacher intensity and effectiveness in the music classroom (Madsen & Geringer, 1989); and intensity training may improve efficiency of instruction (Cassidy, 1990). Continuing this line of research, the ability of preservice music education majors to demonstrate intensity contrasts was examined (Madsen, Standley, & Cassidy, 1989). Following a 1.5-hour training session and using a self-selected, nonconducted music activity as subject matter, students were asked to teach in preassigned, prescribed patterns of high and low intensity for 1 minute. Three independent groups of music majors observed these videotaped segments and labeled them according to perceived contrast of intensity. A high rate of correct responses indicated that intensity contrasts were recognized by those presumed to have little or no training in the concept of teacher intensity.

It is apparent from research in modeling that learning can be enhanced by the teacher's ability to present contrasting (correct and incorrect, positive and negative) models of performance (Sang, 1987). In effect, students are induced to see differences more clearly when presented with positive *and* negative examples as opposed to a positives-only approach. The contrast between dichotomous models may serve to limit the dimensions of learning tasks involving music concept instruction and acquisition (Haack, 1972; Jetter & Wolff, 1985).

In conducting, the concept of contrasted examples has not been formally investigated with regard to instruction in, or acquisition and recognition of, nonverbal skills. Given the nonverbal nature of the act of conducting, the varying degrees of intensity (intended or not) present in the deliveries of conductors, and research findings that indicate a link between intensity and effective teaching, there seems to be need for examination of the concept of intensity in conducting. Therefore, in this study, the researcher attempted to determine whether high and low contrasts in conductor intensity could be demonstrated by beginning conductors and whether observers untrained in the concept of intensity could see these contrasts. Specifically, independent observers' abilities to recognize nonverbal contrasts and rate overall degree of intensity were examined.

METHOD

The procedure for this study consisted of five phases: the development of an instructor videotape model containing high and low contrasts of conducting intensity; the development of competencies necessary for students to demonstrate high and low intensity contrasts; the development and subsequent analysis of a pilot videotape illustrating students in demonstrations of intended high and low intensity contrasts; the development of a final student-made videotape that served as the stimulus for this study; and independent observation of the stimulus videotape by various selected groups. The first four phases were nested within the course syllabus of a beginning instrumental conducting class. Students enrolled in this semester-long course were undergraduate music education majors ($N = 25$). The conducting class, which met for five 50-minute sessions per week, functioned as a conducting practicum or lab session 2 days per week.

The instructor-designed intensity-contrast videotape was a compilation of paired simulations of conductor behaviors as defined by descriptive and experimental research in this area. Each pair consisted of one positive and one negative example of gestural behavior. The purpose of the videotape was to illuminate the concept of conductor intensity by contrasting high-intensity models with low-intensity models. Student conductors viewed this 25-minute videotape during the first regular class session (Phase 1).

Instruction, specific to the development of competencies necessary for students to demonstrate intensity contrasts (Phase 2), included live instructor modeling of high and low contrasts through the teaching and conducting of three different music tasks for the instrumental lab ensemble. The music tasks ultimately would serve as vehicles through which student conductors would attempt to demonstrate contrasts. During this second phase, students practiced gestural contrasts with instructor guidance, which was based on contrasts of high and low intensity.

Phase 3 was a pilot to the study presented in this article. Each student attempted to demonstrate contrasts of high and low intensity across 1 minute while conducting the lab ensemble in a preassigned music task. The 1-minute segment was divided into four 15-second intervals during which each student was to demonstrate a preassigned pattern of high and low intensity (e.g., high, low, high, low). The sound of a bell indicated the beginning of a new 15-second interval and immediate progression to the next interval of the high and low pattern. Order of student presentation was random, and all possible high and low combinations were used.

The class subsequently observed a videotape of these 25 one-minute conducting segments and labeled each 15-second interval according to perceived contrast of intensity ("H" indicated high intensity; "L" indicated low intensity). Additionally, using a Likert scale that ranged from 1 to 10 (1 representing lowest intensity; 10, highest intensity), students indicated an overall intensity rating at the conclusion of each 1-minute segment. Student responses were analyzed for accuracy, with results indicating that demonstrations of contrasts generally functioned as intended (92% correct response rate).

With the exception of intensity-pattern assignments and order of student presentation, identical procedures were followed for development of a second videotape (Phase 4). Analysis of student responses yielded a 95% correct response rate. This videotape served as the stimulus for the final phase of this study (Phase 5). The first four procedural phases thus encompassed nine class sessions over a 5-week period.

Phase 5 consisted of independent observation of the stimulus videotape by 320 subjects divided into four groups according to age and musical experience. Music majors (graduate, $n = 80$; undergraduate, $n = 80$) and nonmusic majors

(n = 80) were students at two large, comprehensive universities and one moderate-sized, urban university. High school band and choir students (n = 80) were randomly selected from two intact performing ensembles. Three 19-inch television screens were used for the viewing procedure, which was administered to groups ranging in size from 2 to 40 subjects. The videotape ran continuously through 20 one-minute conducting segments (5 segments were eliminated randomly to limit tape length to 25 minutes). Subjects determined high intensity and low intensity across 15-second intervals and, using a 10-point Likert scale, gave an overall intensity rating for each completed conducting segment.

RESULTS

In the statistical analyses, only data from the final procedural phase were used. Observation scores (subjects' correct responses) were compared across groups, and observation errors were analyzed by interval across experimental subjects. An observation error was any subject response that deviated from a correct response. Correct responses were defined by actual intensity assignments that were validated by the 95% correct response rate of Phase 4.

Of 25,600 responses, 19,690 intervals were correctly identified, revealing a total rate of correct responses across all groups and intervals of 77%. Table 1 shows that more than twice as many errors occurred in recognition of high intensity (4,099) as in recognition of low intensity (1,866), despite equal distribution of high and low intervals on the stimulus videotape. High-intensity errors were analyzed in three categories: high intervals that occurred at the beginning of a conducting segment, high intervals preceded by a high interval, and high intervals preceded by a low interval. When all 1-minute segments that began with high intensity are considered, 33% of subject responses were in error. Response error rate for intervals that remained high was 33%, and for those that changed from low to high, it was 30%.

Similarly, low-intensity errors were analyzed in three categories: low intervals that occurred at the beginning of a conducting segment, low intervals preceded by a low interval, and low intervals preceded by a high interval. When all 1-minute segments that began with low intensity are considered, 14% of subject responses were in error. Response error rate for intervals that remained low was 12%, and for those that changed from high to low, it was 17%.

Table 1
Analysis of High Versus Low Errors by Interval

	Beginning intervals		Changing intervals				Overall		
	Begin high	Begin low	L-H	H-L	H-H	L-L	High	Low	Total
	Intervals								
N	13	7	13	18	14	15	40	40	80
%[a]	16	19	16	22	18	19	50	50	100
	Errors								
N	1,392	315	1,248	984	1,459	567	4,099	1,866	5,965
%[b]	33	14	30	17	33	12	32	15	23

[a] Percentages = number of intervals in category divided by total intervals.
[b] Percentages = number of errors in category divided by total responses within same category (number of intervals times 320).

To determine differences in response accuracy among experimental groups, data were analyzed using a one-way analysis of variance (ANOVA); mean correct responses across the four groups were compared. Results indicated a significant difference in mean correct responses among groups ($F = 10.22$; $df = 3, 316$; $p < .05$). Further analysis, using the Newman-Keuls multiple comparison test, yielded a significant difference ($p < .05$) in mean correct responses between the graduate group and all other groups. Graduate music majors were more accurate than were the other subject groups in identifying intensity contrasts as demonstrated by beginning conductors (see Table 2).

Table 2
Means for Correct Responses Across Groups

High school	Nonmusic majors	Undergraduate musicians	Graduate musicians
$M = 59.16$	58.27	61.51	65.87

Note. Underline indicates no significant difference ($p < .05$).

A second aspect of the experimental subjects' observation task was to assign an overall degree of intensity for each 1-minute conducting segment (on a scale of 1 to 10—lowest to highest intensity). A one-way ANOVA was used to compare mean intensity ratings among experimental groups (high school: $M = 4.69$, $SD = .91$; nonmusic majors: $M = 5.05$, $SD = 1.12$; undergraduate musicians: $M = 4.25$, $SD = .96$; graduate musicians: $M = 4.67$, $SD = 1.02$). Results indicated no significant difference in mean intensity rating among the four experimental groups ($F = .11$; $df = 3, 76$; $p > .05$). Additionally, the Kendall Coefficient of Concordance was computed to determine extent of agreement in intensity ratings. Results indicated a high degree of reliability ($W = .88$) among the four subject groups in this respect [$\chi^2(4, 20) = 66.88$, $p < .001$].

Relationships between the beginning conductor group and the four independent observer groups concerning perception of overall intensity rating were examined by calculating a mean rating from the beginning conductors' self and peer ratings ($M = 6.61$) and considering it in combination with that of the experimental subjects. Analysis, using the Kendall Coefficient of Concordance, revealed that there was significant agreement among those five groups [$\chi^2(5, 20) = 56.05$, $p < .001$, with reliability calculated at $W = .59$].

Results of a t test illustrated a significant difference in mean intensity ratings between experimental subjects and the beginning conductor group, $t(98) = 9.9$, $p < .001$. Beginning conductors' self and peer intensity ratings averaged nearly 2 points higher on a 10-point scale ($M = 6.61$) than did those of the independent observer groups ($M = 4.63$).

DISCUSSION

Results of the study presented here indicate that intensity, as a component of conductor affect, is recognizable across multiple illustrations and diverse levels of musical experience. Total rate of correct responses was 77%, a percentage that compares favorably to the 82.7% figure across 96 subjects attained from research on teaching (Madsen, Standley, & Cassidy, 1989). This result is considered extraordinary for two reasons. First, contrasts were modeled by undergraduate beginning conductors with little or no practical experience in conducting. One might expect intensity, as demonstrated by polished conductors, to be easy to recognize; however, the fact that it was a salient feature of beginning conductors, struggling to assimilate complex musical issues and gestural technique, is remarkable. It may be that the "contrasts" approach clearly delineated the nature of the task for students, in addition to making demonstrated variations in intensity more noticeable. This seems to support the modeling research of Haack (1972), Jetter and Wolff (1985), and Sang (1987).

Second, musical experience of the subject groups or independent observers varied greatly, ranging from that of highly sophisticated graduate music majors to that of undergraduate education majors with no formal music background. A correct response rate of 70% for nonmusic majors was the lowest of the four groups; yet it seems quite high for those with little knowledge of the subject matter. Perhaps exposure to the concept of intensity in arenas other than music, and the ability to transfer such knowledge to the field of conducting, may have reduced the complexity of the identification process, enabling nonmusicians to recognize intensity with a relatively high degree of accuracy.

Comparison of mean correct scores across the four experimental groups revealed that, of all subject groups, graduate music majors were the most accurate in identifying intensity contrasts. This suggests that musical experience may be a determinant of musicians' ability to detect intensity in conducting. Given the participants' diverse backgrounds as performers in conducted ensembles and as conductors in various media at different levels of sophistication, one might expect graduate music majors to be more cognizant of subtleties and nuances in conductor presentation. This exposes the possibility, however, that familiarity with the subject matter may have biased judgments in either a positive or negative direction.

In reference to the focus of this observation task—identification of intensity contrasts—it is conjectured that, although subjects were asked to make judgments concerning intensity, the *contrasts* in presentation may have been the more prominent variable.

It may be that subjects based identification on *differences* in presentation rather than actual intensity. This might explain a high-intensity response that, from an objective standpoint, was not highly intense but simply more intense than the previous interval. In this way, high scores could have been attained with little regard to demonstrated intensity.

Concerning overall intensity ratings, the high degree of reliability ($W = .88$) evidenced among the four subject groups was not only consistent with research findings concerning teacher intensity ($W = .99$) (Madsen, Standley, and Cassidy, 1989), but was remarkable considering the large sample size and the differences among groups. Essentially, subjects untrained in the concept of intensity and without benefit of common definition were in agreement concerning hierarchical placement of the 20 conductors with respect to overall rating. It seems that, regardless of musical experience, subjects were able to make reliable decisions related to intensity in conducting.

It was not surprising that self and peer intensity ratings by beginning conductors were significantly higher than those of the four experimental groups. These findings substantiate previous research that indicates that self-ratings of students are higher and less reliable than ratings assigned by independent observers (Greenfield, 1978; Madsen & Yarbrough, 1985; Price, 1985; Yarbrough, 1987).

The employment and documentation of a systematic procedure for intensity training were crucial aspects of the investigation described here, and this procedure distinguishes it from previous studies. Casual observations indicate that training in gestural contrasts seemed to be an effective means of improving nonverbal conducting skills. Given the episodic, ever-changing quality of much conducted music, the essence of skillful, musical conducting may be purposeful contrasts if, in fact, musicians are reliable in interpreting degree of gestural intensity.

The study described in this article seems to substantiate and extend previous research. Further examination of conductor intensity might focus on effect of intensity in conducting on performer achievement, attentiveness, and attitude; maintenance of high intensity by student conductors across successively longer periods of time; the application of the intensity training model used here to other university conducting settings to investigate its feasibility and usefulness across environments; and use of intensity training as an adjunct to current methods of conductor education.

REFERENCES

Berz, W. L. (1983). The development of an observation instrument designed to classify specific nonverbal communication techniques employed by conductors of musical ensembles (Doctoral dissertation, Michigan State University). *Dissertation Abstracts International, 44,* 270A.

Cassidy, J. W. (1990). Effect of intensity training on preservice teachers' instruction accuracy and delivery effectiveness. *Journal of Research in Music Education, 38,* 164–174.

Green, E. H. (1987). *The modern conductor.* Englewood Cliffs: Prentice Hall.

Greenfield, D. G. (1978). Evaluation of music therapy practicum competencies: Comparisons of self and instructor ratings of videotapes. *Journal of Music Therapy, 15*(1), 15–20.

Haack, P. A. (1972). Use of positive and negative examples in teaching the concept of musical style. *Journal of Research in Music Education, 20,* 456–461.

Hunsberger, D., & Ernst, R. (1983). *The art of conducting.* New York: Knopf.

Jetter, J. T., & Wolff, J. L. (1985). Effect of ratio of positive to negative instances on efficiency of musical concept learning. *Journal of Research in Music Education, 32,* 31–43.

Leinsdorf, E. (1981). *The composer's advocate.* New Haven: Yale University Press.

Madsen, C. K., & Geringer, J. M. (1989). The relationship of teacher "on task" to intensity and effective teaching. *Canadian Journal of Research in Music Education, 30,* 87–94.

Madsen, C. K., Standley, J. M., & Cassidy, J. W. (1989). Demonstration and recognition of high and low contrasts in teacher intensity. *Journal of Research in Music Education, 37,* 85–92.

Madsen, C. K., & Yarbrough, C. (1985). *Competency-based music education.* Englewood Cliffs: Prentice-Hall.

Parr, J. D. (1976). Essential and desirable music and music teaching competencies for first-year band instructors in the public schools (Doctoral dissertation, The University of Iowa). *Dissertation Abstracts International, 37,* 7601A.

Price, H. E. (1985). A competency based course in basic conducting techniques: A replication. *Journal of Band Research, 21*(1), 61–69.

Roshong, J. L. (1978). An exploratory study of nonverbal behaviors of instrumental music conductors (Doctoral dissertation, The Ohio State University). *Dissertation Abstracts International, 39,* 4587A.

Rudolf, M. (1950). *The grammar of conducting.* New York: G. Schirmer.

Sang, R. C. (1987). A study of the relationship between instrumental music teachers' modeling skills and pupil performance behaviors. *Bulletin of the Council for Research in Music Education, 91,* 155–159.

Spicer, R. (1977). The education of the band director, second report—"Competencies." *Journal of Band Research, 13*(1), 10–19.

Standley, J. M., & Madsen, C. K. (1987). Intensity as an attribute of effective therapist/client interaction. *Quodlibet,* Summer, 15–20.

Yarbrough, C. (1975). Effect of magnitude of conductor behavior on students in selected mixed choruses. *Journal of Research in Music Education, 23,* 134–146.

Yarbrough, C. (1987). The relationship of behavioral self assessment to the achievement of basic conducting skills. *Journal of Research in Music Education, 35,* 183–189.

February 13, 1989

Three experiments examined the effects of instruction, teaching practica, feedback from the course instructor, and videotaped self-observation on undergraduates' use of complete sequential patterns and sequential-pattern components. The complete sequential pattern is a teacher/student interaction sequence that follows the cyclical pattern of a teacher presentation of a task to be learned, followed by student interaction with the task and teacher, and then specific praise and corrective feedback related to the task. This model has undergone continuous refinement, has been found to be present in music settings, and is preferred by music teachers. There were significant increases (p < .01) in subjects' use of complete sequential patterns as defined in each experiment, feedback, and in approvals and their specificity.

Harry E. Price, *University of Alabama*

JRME 1992, VOLUME 40, NUMBER 1, PAGES 14–29

Sequential Patterns of Music Instruction and Learning to Use Them

Use of direct instruction, also termed explicit instruction, has been the object of recent research in music education in the form of sequential patterns (Benson, 1989; Duke & Blackman, 1989; Jellison & Kostka, 1987; Jellison & Wolfe, 1987; Moore, 1981; Price, 1983; Price & Yarbrough, 1991; Rosenthal, 1981, 1989; Wolfe, 1989; Yarbrough & Price, 1981, 1989; Yarbrough, Price, & Bowers, 1991). This research is an outgrowth of work by Becker, Englemann, and Thomas (1971), who described a teacher/student interaction model that follows the cyclical pattern of (1) teacher presentation of task to be learned, (2) student interaction with the task and teacher, and (3) reinforcement by immediate praise and corrective feedback related to the task.

Numerous studies have demonstrated the effectiveness of the direct instruction, or proactive, model in English and mathematics (Becker & Englemann, 1976; Berliner & Rosenshine, 1976; Brophy, 1979; Carnine, 1979; Good & Brophy, 1974; McDonald, 1976; Medley, 1977; Powell, 1978; Rosenshine, 1976, 1979, 1987). In addition, teachers have been trained to use the model's components in studies involving videotape self-observation (Carnine & Fink, 1978, Good & Brophy, 1974).

Duke and Blackman (1989) suggested that "'proactive' teachers are able to structure sequences of tasks in music that not only elicit a self-perception of success

For copies of this article, contact Harry E. Price, School of Music, Box 870366, The University of Alabama, Tuscaloosa, AL 35487-0366.

within students but also shape frequent successful (i.e., correct) student responses that may be reinforced contingently and specifically by the teacher" (p. 4).

Use of the direct instruction model, and specifically the three-step sequence of a sequential pattern, has been investigated in music teaching settings. Moore (1981) reported that this pattern occurred in elementary music settings of the United States and England. Investigators have found sequential patterns to exist and be a viable means of describing the teaching process also in applied music (Benson, 1989) and secondary school choral and instrumental ensemble settings (Yarbrough & Price, 1981, 1989).

Results of research on the effectiveness of direct instruction in nonmusic settings have been replicated by a study involving students in a music setting. Price (1983) investigated the effectiveness of using various sequential patterns in a university instrumental ensemble and demonstrated complete sequential patterns to be effective in enhancing performance, attentiveness, and positive attitudes. Jellison and Kostka (1987) examined the effect of elementary students' focus of attention within the context of complete sequential patterns and suggested the importance of continued study of sequential patterns.

> Given the amount of research data supporting the use of complete and correct teaching cycles [sequential patterns], the authors believe it is of paramount importance to develop techniques of teaching prospective teachers to present musical information, allow students response time, and appropriately reinforce the acquisition of that information. (Yarbrough & Price, 1989, p. 185)

Successful efforts to train elementary education and music education majors in the use of the complete sequential pattern model have been reported. In a study involving verbal training that focused on the first and third steps of the sequential pattern, antecedents (questions and directives) and consequents (approvals), subjects were trained to increase their use of these antecedents and consequents as well as their use of complete sequential patterns (Jellison & Wolfe, 1987). Use of specific approvals (consequents) and complete teaching units has also been increased through the use of visual prompts (Wolfe, 1989).

Self-observation of videotaped lessons has been used successfully to help music therapists and teachers improve their teaching (Alley, 1980; Greenfield, 1980; Hanser & Furman, 1980; Killian, 1981; Moore, 1976; Prickett, 1987; Rosenthal, 1981, 1989; Yarbrough, Price, & Bowers, 1991) and conducting skills (Madsen & Yarbrough, 1985; Price, 1985; Yarbrough, 1976, 1980, 1987; Yarbrough, Wapnick, & Kelly, 1979). Rosenthal (1981) employed a combination of course instructor and videotape feedback, and increased elementary music education majors' use of complete sequential patterns, with an increase in sequences containing academic content and decrease in sequences with none. A later study by Rosenthal (1989), involving course instructor and videotape feedback, increased music education majors' use of complete sequential patterns and specific feedback. Using videotaped models and videotape feedback, Benson (1989) increased the amount of time spent in musical tasks and giving specific feedback presented in an applied music setting.

In the three experiments presented here, I examined effects of various combinations of instruction, observation training, and practica, followed by competency-based videotape self-observation on subjects' use of sequential patterns. All three experiments included preliminary instruction and observation training in reinforcement principles, and videotaped practica while teaching/rehearsing peers, followed by subject self-observation with a peer reliability observer. A minimum of 75% interobserver agreement for the events was required for each observation using the formula [number of agreements/(number of agreements + disagreements)] × 100 (Madsen & Yarbrough, 1985). The first experiment had two practica; the second had a pretest, two practica, and a posttest; and the third experiment had three practica and a posttest (see Figure 1). Only in the first experiment did the subjects receive feedback from the course instructor regarding their teaching.

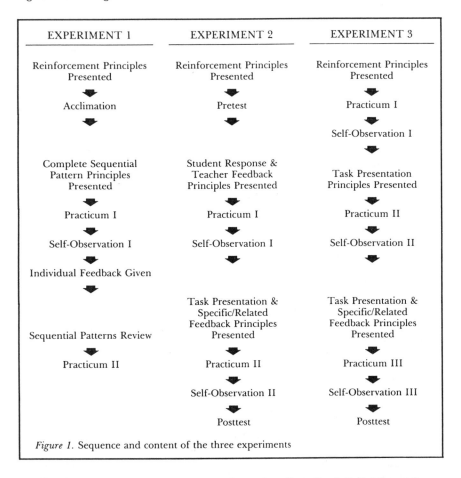

EXPERIMENT 1	EXPERIMENT 2	EXPERIMENT 3
Reinforcement Principles Presented	Reinforcement Principles Presented	Reinforcement Principles Presented
Acclimation	Pretest	Practicum I
		Self-Observation I
Complete Sequential Pattern Principles Presented	Student Response & Teacher Feedback Principles Presented	Task Presentation Principles Presented
Practicum I	Practicum I	Practicum II
Self-Observation I	Self-Observation I	Self-Observation II
Individual Feedback Given		
	Task Presentation & Specific/Related Feedback Principles Presented	Task Presentation & Specific/Related Feedback Principles Presented
Sequential Patterns Review		
Practicum II	Practicum II	Practicum III
	Self-Observation II	Self-Observation III
	Posttest	Posttest

Figure 1. Sequence and content of the three experiments

The three experiments encompassed continually refined definitions of complete sequential patterns. All experiments examined effects of instruction and self-observation on students' ability to successively approximate teaching using complete sequential patterns of instruction as defined in each experiment. In the first experiment, the complete sequence was defined as any 1-2-3 pattern where "1" was a task presentation that included directions, academic or social task, and "3" was any approval or disapproval feedback (Price, 1983; Yarbrough & Price, 1981). This definition was refined in the second and third experiments where a complete sequence was a 1-2-3 pattern that included a teacher presentation of an academic task and specific related teacher feedback (Price & Yarbrough, 1991;

Yarbrough & Price, 1989; Yarbrough, Price, & Bowers, 1991). The pattern definition used in Experiment 3 has been demonstrated to be preferred by experienced music educators and graduate music students (Price & Yarbrough, 1991; Yarbrough, Price, & Bowers, 1991).

EXPERIMENT 1

Procedures

Subjects were 18 undergraduate instrumental and vocal music education majors enrolled in a sophomore-level introductory music education clinical experiences course. This was the students' first music education course dealing with classroom techniques and included an initial teaching session, two practica, and two 4-week field experiences (see Figure 1). Students completed observation training and study of reinforcement principles presented in *Teaching/Discipline: A Positive Approach for Educational Development* (Madsen & Madsen, 1983) and *Competency-Based Music Education* (Madsen & Yarbrough, 1985) prior to an initial teaching experience. Students taught and were videotaped three times; they taught their peers for this and subsequent experiments. The first taping was a 5-minute teaching acclimation session for which they were instructed to teach anything pertaining to music. The students then observed their tapes and wrote a brief evaluation; for many students, this was their first time teaching a group.

Following completion of this initial teaching session, the students went into secondary schools for a minimum of three class periods a week for 4 weeks to observe and assist the music teacher; this field experience consisted primarily of observation. The students then returned to the university classroom and completed additional observation training in the application of reinforcement principles to ensemble settings in *Competency-Based Music Education* (Madsen & Yarbrough, 1985); received a 50-minute training session on the analysis and use of sequential patterns; and were instructed to use complete sequential patterns—defined as any sequence that followed a 1-2-3 pattern that included a direction, academic or social task, and feedback—to teach/rehearse for 10 minutes, using assigned choral music.

Each student/teacher was videotaped in Practicum I, observed the videotape with another class member, created a transcript of the practicum, and used the script in conjunction with the videotape to analyze the teaching for the components of sequential patterns. The students/teachers coded their practica according to categories similar to those used by Yarbrough and Price (1981, 1989) and Yarbrough, Price, and Bowers (1991). Teacher presentations were coded "1" and included four types of presentations defined as follows: "1a"—academic musical task presentation (talking about musical or performance aspects); "1d"—directions (giving directions regarding who will, or where to, sing); "1s"—social task presentation (presenting rules of behavior); and "1o"—off-task statement (unnecessary and irrelevant comments such as speaking to oneself). Responses were coded "2" in three categories: "2p"—performance (entire ensemble or sections performing); "2v"—verbal (ensemble members asking or answering questions, or making statements); and "2nv"—nonverbal (ensemble members nodding heads or moving in response to teacher instruction). The third part of the sequential pattern—feedback—was coded "3" in two categories: "3va"—verbal approval (positive statement about student performance or social behavior); and "3vd"—verbal disapproval (negative statement about student performance or social behavior).

Students went into secondary schools for another 4-week field experience, at the end of which they returned to the university classroom and met individually with the course instructor for 50-minute sessions. Each individual's Practicum I videotape was viewed using the student's transcript and analysis, as well as the instructor's analysis, and feedback was given regarding correct sequencing—any 1-2-3 sequence—and use of sequence components. Students also received a 50-minute sequential patterns review session in class. Within 1 week of the feedback and review sessions, students taught Practicum II, attempting to improve their use of sequential patterns while rehearsing the same music as in Practicum I. Each student again completed a script and analysis of Practicum II.

The course instructor and a reliability observer analyzed students' practica for frequency, duration, and sequencing of sequential pattern component behaviors. Analyses were based on the cycle and component definitions presented to the students, with any sequence following a 1-2-3 pattern considered correct. The reliability observer analyzed 25% of the practica, with a mean interobserver agreement of 96%.

Results

The purpose of Experiment 1 was to examine effects of instruction and teaching videotaped practica, followed by videotape self-observation and course instructor feedback, on the development of undergraduates' use of a 1-2-3 sequence of teaching, and the components of each part of the sequence. Data, from student self-observations and course instructor observations, were extracted for summary and analysis. Students were required to observe their videotapes with a class member and achieve a minimum of 75% agreement on the analyses of their teaching. Mean student/student agreement was 96% and 97% for Practica I and II respectively. Students' coded transcripts for Practica I and II were compared to the course instructor's for agreement, and mean instructor/student agreement increased from 61% to 71%. All reported data are from the teacher's observations for this and subsequent experiments.

Times spent in Practica I and II on all 1-2-3 sequences and all component behaviors—presentation of academic information, directions, social information, and off-task comments (teacher presentations); performance, verbal and nonverbal responses (student responses); and approvals and disapprovals (feedback)—were extracted. Table 1 summarizes the mean percentages of Practica I and II times spent in 1-2-3 sequences, as well as each of the component behaviors; teacher task presentation times for social task presentations, questions, and off-task comments have been combined. This table and those that follow report relative percentages of each session, rather than actual time, due to differing durations of the teaching sessions the data describe.

Data from Practica I and II were compared by means of one-way repeated measures analyses of variance. Significant increases for Practicum I to II were found for time spent in 1-2-3 sequences [$F(1, 17) = 12.49$, $p < .01$] and the third component of the sequence—teacher feedback—[$F(1, 17) = 5.61$, $p < .05$], and a significant decrease was found in the first component—teacher presentations—[$F(1, 17) = 5.27$, $p < .05$]. Mean time spent in 1-2-3 sequences increased by more than 51%, from 191 to 296 seconds—32% to 49%—of a 600-second (10-minute) practicum. Teacher feedback increased by more than 35%, from 34 to 46 seconds—6% to 8%. Time spent in teacher presentations decreased by 40 seconds, from 313 to 272 seconds—52% to 45%.

Table 1

Experiment 1: Mean Percentage of Time of Sequential Patterns, Sequence Components, and Component Behaviors

Sequence components	Practicum I	Practicum II
All 1-2-3 sequences	**31.9**	**49.3****
• 1-2-3 incomplete sequences	28.1	42.2**
• 1-2-3 complete sequences	3.8	7.1
Teacher task presentations	**52.1**	**45.4***
• Musical information	29.1	26.0
• Directions	19.3	16.8
• Other (social, questions, off-task)	3.7	2.6
Student responses	**42.2**	**46.9**
• Performing	37.5	43.9
• Verbal responses	3.7	2.6
• Nonverbal responses	1.0	0.4
Feedback	**5.7**	**7.7***
• Approvals	4.4	5.8*
Specific	2.0	2.6*
Unspecific	2.4	3.3
• Disapprovals	1.3	1.9
Specific	1.2	1.6
Unspecific	0.1	0.3
• Specific/unspecific ratio	55/45	54/46
Approval	45/55	44/56
Disapproval	89/11	83/17

* $p < .05$ ** $p < .01$

Since time spent on sequential pattern components was significantly different for Practicum I versus II, data for behaviors that comprise the components, teacher presentations (academic information, directions, social information, off-task comments), and feedback (approvals, disapprovals) were compared by means of one-way repeated measures analyses of variance. The only significant difference between behavior in Practica I and II was for approvals [$F(1, 17) = 6.50$, $p < .05$]. These increased by 35%, from 26 to 35 seconds, in Practicum II; however, the approval/disapproval ratio remained at approximately 75/25 for both practica.

EXPERIMENT 2

Procedures

Subjects ($n = 9$) were similar to those in Experiment 1 in the same introductory music education clinical experiences course. Course content was similar, and each student was videotaped teaching a 5-minute pretest, two 10-minute practica, and a 5-minute posttest.

The definition of a complete teaching sequence was refined, and a pretest-posttest design with two practica was used. Additionally, unlike Experiment 1, there was no course instructor feedback (see Figure 1). Students completed observation training and the study of reinforcement principles before teaching a 5-minute pretest for which music was assigned and no instructions were given.

Following the pretest, students went into secondary schools for 4 weeks to observe and assist the music teacher. They then returned to the university classroom and completed additional observation training in the application of reinforcement principles to ensemble settings, and attended a 50-minute instruction session on use and analysis of the second and third part of the teaching sequence, student response and teacher feedback. For Practicum I, music that was different from the pretest was used, and students were instructed to concentrate on student responses and teacher feedback. Following this 10-minute practicum, each student observed his or her videotape with another class member, created a transcript, and analyzed the transcript according to specific component behaviors—student performance, verbal and nonverbal responses, and teacher verbal approval/disapproval feedback.

Students then went into different secondary schools for another 4 weeks. They returned to the university classroom and received a 50-minute training session on analysis and use of the teacher task presentation component of sequential patterns and use of complete sequential patterns, with the added concept that in the 1-2-3 sequence the feedback needed to be *specific and related* to the task presented. For Practicum II, students were told to use teaching sequences consisting of musical task presentations, student interaction with the task, and specific related feedback and to rehearse the same music as in Practicum I.

Students analyzed this practicum using the same categories used in Practicum I plus five types of teacher presentations: four used in Experiment 1—academic musical task presentation, direction, social task presentation, and off-task statement—plus 1q, a question (asking questions about performing the music or if students know where to begin). In addition to all the component behaviors, teaching was analyzed for complete sequential patterns that required feedback to be specific and related to the task presented.

The last teaching assignment was a 5-minute posttest, modeled after the practica and pretest situations, and it used the pretest music to examine the ability to transfer the use of the concept of sequential patterns from music used in practica to different music. There were no performance criteria established for the pretest or practica; however, students were told that their posttest would be graded on the basis of a minimum competency of 80% of the feedback events being approving and 75% of the sequences being complete. Students' pretests, practica, and posttests were analyzed for duration of sequential pattern component behaviors, correct sequencing of components, and whether feedback was related and specific. Sequences that followed a 1-2-3 pattern were considered complete only when an academic task and specific related feedback were present. The course instructor and an independent observer analyzed all practica, resulting in a mean interjudge agreement of 94%.

Results

The purpose of this experiment was to examine the development of undergraduates' use of complete sequential patterns—academic task presentation, students' interaction with task, specific related feedback—through teaching practica in a laboratory situation that was videotaped, followed by videotape self-observation without any course instructor feedback. Data from student self-observations and course instructor observations were extracted for summary and analysis.

Reported mean student/student agreement figures were 99% and 95% for Practica I and II respectively; for Practicum I, students observed only student responses and teacher feedback, whereas they observed all component behaviors for Practicum II. Students' transcript analyses were compared to the course instructor's for agreement. Mean instructor/student agreement increased from 83% to 95% for student response and teacher feedback from Practicum I to II, with a mean agreement of 74% for all component behaviors in Practicum II. All reported data are from the teacher's observations.

Times spent on complete sequences—a 1-2-3 sequence with an academic task and specific related feedback—as well as other sequences that followed a 1-2-3 pattern, were extracted. As in Experiment 1, time spent in each sequential pattern component behavior was also extracted, as was information about whether approvals and disapprovals were specific or unspecific. Table 2 summarizes the data for mean percentages of pretest, practica, and posttest times; teacher task presentations of questions, social task presentations, and off-task comments have been combined, as have times of student verbal and nonverbal responses.

Table 2
Experiment 2: Mean Percentage of Time of Sequential Patterns, Sequence Components, and Component Behaviors

Sequence components	Pretest	Practicum I	Practicum II	Posttest
Complete sequences	**5.0**	**1.6**	**25.2**	**51.7****
Incomplete 1-2-3 sequences	13.5	14.1	13.5	7.4
Teacher task presentations	**54.5**	**48.4**	**45.5**	**48.4**
• Musical information	22.8	27.8	24.4	28.3
• Directions	27.3	18.8	19.2	18.8*
• Other (social, questions, off-task)	4.4	2.8	1.9	1.3
Student responses	**41.6**	**48.2**	**48.6**	**43.6**
• Performing	40.7	46.7	47.6	42.9
• Verbal/nonverbal responses	0.9	1.4	1.0	0.7
Feedback	**3.8**	**3.5**	**5.9**	**8.0****
• Approvals	3.0	3.2	5.4	7.7**
Specific	1.0	1.5	4.0	7.2**
Unspecific	2.1	1.7	1.4	0.5*
• Disapprovals	0.8	0.3	0.5	0.2*
Specific	0.8	0.3	0.5	0.2
Unspecific	0.0	0.0	0.0	0.0
• Specific/unspecific ratio	33/67	46/54	77/23	94/6**
Approval	25/75	41/59	74/26	94/6**
Disapproval	94/6	100/1	100/1	100/1

* $p < .01$ ** $p < .001$

Note: In instances where there is significant difference among pretest, practica and posttest, underscore indicates no significant differences, based on Scheffé F test, between specific observations at the .05 level.

Data from pretests, practica, and posttests were compared by means of one-way repeated measures analyses of variance. Significant differences were found among times spent in complete sequential patterns [$F(3, 24) = 19.86$, $p < .001$], with greater than a tenfold increase from 5% on the pretest to almost 52% on the posttest. A subsequent comparison of times spent in complete sequences determined that they increased significantly from Practicum I to II to the posttest; from 2% to 25% to 52% of the rehearsal time. The concept of complete sequences was taught after Practicum I and reviewed prior to the posttest, and students were informed that they would receive a grade for the posttest contingent on their ability to use complete sequences.

A comparison of mean times spent in the feedback component of the sequence indicated that component times were significantly different [$F(3, 24) = 13.94$, $p < .001$]. Students received substantial instruction in reinforcement concepts prior to the pretest and again prior to Practicum I, and had an opportunity to implement these concepts in their teaching; but it seems that it was necessary to present concepts of feedback specificity and relationship prior to Practicum II to help students incorporate more feedback in subsequent teaching. Within behaviors that constitute feedback, there was a significant difference in approvals [$F(3, 24) = 24.22$, $p < .001$], with a significant increase in Practicum II and posttest.

There was also a significant difference in the proportion of specific feedback [$F(3, 24) = 14.70$, $p < .001$], with an increase from 33% on the pretest to 94% on the posttest. This is a reflection of a significant increase in specific approvals [$F(3, 24) = 38.93$, $p < .001$], and significant decrease in unspecific approvals [$F(3, 24) = 6.14$, $p < .01$] from pretest to posttest. Specific approval time increased sevenfold, and unspecific disapprovals were almost nonexistent throughout. Although feedback remained predominantly approving, it changed in quality from unspecific to specific.

Teaching in Experiment 1 was reanalyzed in light of the evolving constructs used in Experiment 2. Complete sequences—a 1-2-3 sequence with an academic task and specific related feedback—and all other 1-2-3 sequences were extracted separately, as were specific and unspecific feedback. In Experiment 1 a significant increase was reported in use of 1-2-3 sequences ($p < .01$). These sequences could include any components as long as there was a task presentation, student response, and feedback; however, this post hoc analysis yielded a significant increase only for sequences that would be defined as incomplete in Experiment 2 [$F(1, 17) = 11.19$, $p < .01$], because they lacked an academic (musical) task presentation or specific related feedback. In Experiment 2, there was an overall decrease in incomplete sequences, while more stringent complete sequences increased significantly and dramatically.

There was also a significant increase for Experiment 1 in specific approvals [$F(1, 17) = 5.68$, $p < .05$]. Additionally there was a larger, although not significant, increase in unspecific approvals.

In general, all aspects of feedback increased in Experiment 1, while in Experiment 2 specific approvals significantly increased, and disapprovals and unspecific approvals significantly decreased. Proportion of specific to unspecific approvals in Experiment 2 increased significantly [$F(3, 24) = 18.84$, $p < .001$] and dramatically from 25% to 94%; in Experiment 1, proportions of specific to unspecific feedback remained fairly constant, with approvals at 45% and 44%.

EXPERIMENT 3

Procedures

Following the apparent success of the course structure—research design—and refined operational definitions of Experiment 2, the course structure was replicated with a different sample and an additional practicum replacing the pretest. This structure provided students with more opportunities (teaching sessions) to develop use of the complete sequential pattern model. This experiment was conducted with similar students ($n = 14$) in the same course, taught with similar content and structure. This time the students taught three 8-minute practica and an 8-minute posttest; as in Experiment 2, there was no course instructor feedback.

Students completed observation training and study of reinforcement principles prior to Practicum I. They were assigned music to rehearse for all practica, and for Practicum I they were instructed to concentrate on use of the reinforcement principles studied. Following this practicum, each person observed his or her videotape recording with another class member, created a transcript of the practicum, and analyzed it for reinforcement.

Students then went into secondary schools for 4 weeks to observe and assist the music teacher, returned to the university classroom, and received a 50-minute training session on analysis and uses of the teacher task presentation portion—academic musical task presentation, direction, question, social task presentation, off-task statement—of sequential patterns. For Practicum II, students were told to use 1-2-3 teaching sequences consisting of musical task presentation, student interaction with the task, and feedback.

Students created transcripts of their videotaped practica and analyzed them for teacher presentations, student responses, feedback, and sequences consisting of musical task presentation, student interaction with the task, and feedback. They did not analyze sequences for specific or related feedback, as they had not yet received instruction regarding the importance of these characteristics. Following Practicum II, students went into different secondary schools for another 4 weeks.

At the end of this 4-week period, the course instructor reviewed sequential patterns with the added concepts that in 1-2-3 sequences, feedback needed to be specific and related to the academic task presented. Each student then taught Practicum III and analyzed it for the presence of complete sequential patterns and all component behaviors, including whether feedback was specific and related. The last teaching assignment was an 8-minute posttest modeled after practica situations. Students were assigned a new piece of music to test their ability to transfer the use of complete sequential patterns of instruction to teaching different music and were told that their posttests would be graded on the basis of a minimum competency of 80% approval feedback and 75% complete sequences.

All practica and posttests were analyzed by the course instructor and an independent observer for duration of sequential pattern component behaviors, correct sequencing of the components, and whether feedback was related and specific. Mean interjudge agreement was 95%.

Results

Reported mean student/student agreement was 90%, 94%, and 96% for Practica I, II, and III respectively; students observed only their feedback for Practicum I, but all components for Practica II and III. Students' transcript analyses were compared to the course instructor's for agreement. Mean instructor/student agreement increased from 69% (feedback only), to 75% (all components), to 81% (all components plus specific and related feedback) for Practica I through III respectively. Reported data are those from course instructor observations.

Times spent on complete sequences were extracted, as well as time spent in each sequential pattern component behavior. Table 3 summarizes data for mean percentage of practica and posttest times; it combines teacher questions, social task presentations, and off-task comments, as well as student verbal and nonverbal responses.

Table 3
Experiment 3: Mean Percentage of Time of Sequential Patterns, Sequence Components, and Component Behaviors

Sequence components	Practicum I	Practicum II	Practicum III	Posttest
Complete sequences	**0.6**	**5.8**	**23.4**	**42.6****
Teacher task presentations	**47.4**	**41.6**	**43.1**	**45.0**
• Musical information	27.5	19.8	26.1	28.3
• Directions	17.1	19.7	15.7	15.7
• Other (social, questions, off-task)	2.8	2.2	1.3	1.0
Student responses	**48.7**	**53.2**	**48.6**	**47.0**
• Performing	48.3	50.4	48.3	46.9
• Verbal/nonverbal responses	0.5	2.8	0.3	0.2
Feedback	**3.9**	**5.2**	**8.3**	**7.9****
• Approvals	2.5	3.2	5.3	5.7**
Specific	1.0	1.2	3.6	5.1**
Unspecific	1.5	2.0	1.7	0.6*
• Disapprovals	1.4	2.0	3.0	2.3
Specific	1.3	1.8	2.6	2.1
Unspecific	0.1	0.2	0.4	0.2
• Specific/unspecific ratio	50/50	54/46	67/33	89/11**
Approval	36/64	31/69	62/38	87/17**
Disapproval	83/17	85/15	93/7	96/4

$*p < .01$ $**p < .001$

Note: In instances where there is significant difference among pretest, practica and posttest, underscore indicates no significant differences, based on Scheffé F test, between specific observations at the .05 level.

Data from practica and posttest were compared by means of one-way repeated measures analyses of variance. Significant differences were found among times spent in complete sequential patterns [$F(3, 39) = 26.29, p < .001$], with an increase from 1% of Practicum I to 43% of the posttest. A subsequent comparison of mean times spent in complete sequences determined that their use increased significantly from Practicum II to III to the posttest, increasing from 6% to 23% to 43% of the rehearsal time. The concept of complete sequences—academic task presentation, student response, specific related feedback—was taught after Practicum II, and reviewed prior to the posttest, and students were informed that the grade for the posttest was contingent on employment of complete sequences.

A comparison of mean times spent in the feedback portion of the sequence indicated a significant difference [$F(3, 39) = 6.91, p < .001$]; there was a significant increase from Practicum I to III. Prior to Practica I and II, students received substantial instruction in reinforcement concepts and had opportunities to implement feedback in their teaching; however, as in Experiment 2, it seems that instruction, prior to Practicum III, in concepts of specificity of feedback and its relationship to the task presented helped students incorporate more feedback.

Within behaviors that constitute feedback, there was a significant difference among overall approval and specific approval times [$F(3, 39) = 10.08$ and 16.45 respectively, $p = .001$], with both increasing significantly in Practicum III. Time spent in feedback more than doubled from Practicum I to posttest, and specific approval time increased fivefold. There was also a significant difference among unspecific approval times [$F(3, 39) = 4.92$, $p < .01$], with a significant decrease on the posttest. Times spent in disapprovals and their relative amount of specificity remained fairly constant. As in Experiment 3, feedback was predominantly approving and changed dramatically from unspecific to specific.

DISCUSSION

The implementation of these experiments in a music education class exemplifies the concept of an "experimenting teacher" or course instructor explicated in the fifth chapter of *Competency-Based Music Education* (Madsen & Yarbrough, 1985). These three experiments functioned on two levels: (1) examination of the effects of systematic instructional structures on acquisition of skills in use of complete sequential patterns through different combinations of instruction, course instructor feedback, practica, and videotape self-observation; and (2) refinement of constructs involved in sequential patterns of music instruction. Only in Experiment 1 was the complete sequential pattern defined as including any task presentation (direction, question, social or academic task), followed by a student response, and any teacher feedback. With subsequent examination of sequential patterns in school settings (Yarbrough & Price, 1989) and further development of the constructs and behaviors that comprise a sequential pattern (Price & Yarbrough, 1991; Yarbrough, Price, & Bowers, 1991), aspects of a complete sequential pattern were refined in Experiments 2 and 3 to require that the task presentation component include musical (academic) information, and that teacher feedback be specific and related to the task presentation. Development and refinement of these constructs influenced students' subsequent teaching.

As with any experiment that transpires over an extended period of time and has no control group, there can be alternative explanations for changes in subjects' behaviors; these might include influences of maturation, observations, vicarious learning, and other outside influences. However, given the specificity of the class focus, structure of in-class experiences around the sequential model of instruction, and consistency of results across three different groups in the three experiments, such alternative explanations are unlikely for changes that transpire within a one-semester music education class. All the experiments attempted to increase undergraduates' use of complete sequential patterns, as defined in each, by having students teach in a laboratory situation followed by videotape self-observation; the first experiment included course instructor feedback, while the next two did not. The experiments used a variety of combinations of pretests, practica paired with self-observation, and posttests (see Figure 1).

In all three experiments, undergraduates significantly increased their use of complete sequential patterns, as defined for each experiment. Students in Experiment 1 increased use of complete 1-2-3 sequences, as defined in this experiment; however, this increase was only for what was subsequently defined as incomplete sequences in the later two experiments, because they lacked an academic task or specific related feedback. In Experiments 2 and 3, students dramatically increased their use of complete sequences, and in Experiment 2, while all 1-2-3 sequences increased, incomplete sequences decreased (although not significantly) from the pretest to the posttest.

Amount of time spent on teacher feedback increased significantly in all three experiments, more than doubling in Experiments 2 and 3. These changes represent a relatively small proportion of the total practicum time; however, this proportion was comparable to that found in music classrooms/rehearsals (Yarbrough & Price, 1981, 1989). In all instances, overall approvals and specific approval feedback significantly increased; in Experiments 2 and 3, overall approvals more than doubled, and specific approvals increased more than fivefold. Also, in the final two experiments, unspecific approvals significantly decreased, resulting in a significant increase in the ratio of specific to unspecific approval feedback. As found in previous music classroom research (Carpenter, 1988; Yarbrough & Price, 1989), students initially tended to give unspecific approval feedback (> 75%), and disapprovals tended to be specific (> 80%). In both Experiments 2 and 3, level of specificity of approvals increased significantly, to greater than 85%, and consequently so did the overall ratio of specific to unspecific feedback; Experiment 1 did not exhibit this change. Amount of time spent in the other two sequential pattern components—teacher task presentation and student responses—did not change significantly across all three experiments.

For all experiments, the feedback component was covered at length in the classes and texts. Class lectures and textbooks emphasized the use of positive reinforcement, and this may have been reflected in the students' maintaining positive ratios, with final percentages of approximately 75%, 98%, and 72% approval levels for the three experiments. A positive ratio is not typical of those found in many classroom and ensemble settings (Carpenter, 1988; Madsen & Madsen, 1983; Yarbrough & Price, 1981, 1989).

There were significant changes in time spent in sequential patterns and some components for all three experiments. The final course instructor/student agreement, based on frequency data, increased from 71% to 74% to 81% for Experiments 1, 2, and 3 respectively; these were with, and then without, course instructor feedback. This increase in course instructor/student agreement replicates previous work involving student self-analysis of videotapes in basic conducting classes (Price, 1985; Yarbrough, 1976, 1980, 1987; Yarbrough, Wapnick, & Kelly, 1979). Improved operational definition of the teaching sequence and its component behaviors, and more self-observation opportunities, may have increased course instructor/student agreement across the three experiments, as well as serving to enhance aspects of students' teaching. Experiment 1 had an initial instructor/student agreement of 61% that increased to 71% after instructor feedback and teaching a second time. In Experiment 3, with refinement of operational definitions of the teaching sequence and its components and additional self-observation opportunities, Practicum I had 75% agreement that increased to 81% for Practicum III, with no intervening course instructor feedback.

These experiments demonstrate successful use of operational definitions and videotape self-observation for training students to use complete sequential patterns and better feedback in an ensemble setting. This structure is especially noteworthy given that the students did not require feedback from the course instructor to improve target behaviors. In Experiments 2 and 3, where there was no course instructor feedback and, after teaching only 25 and 24 minutes respectively, students dramatically improved time spent in correct sequences from 5% to 52% and from 1% to 43%. Students taught themselves, with the final use of complete sequential patterns being superior to the 18% and 34% respectively found in experienced band and choral directors who were not trained in the use of sequential patterns (Yarbrough & Price, 1989). This successful use of clear operational definitions and videotape self-observation suggests that the students in these experiments became more independent in assessing and improving teaching by relying less on external feedback.

Although these experiments demonstrated an effective method for improving the quantity and quality of sequential patterns used by prospective music teachers, work is still needed to improve these students' implementation of complete sequential patterns. Setting a priori performance criterion rates has enhanced teachers' use of feedback (Saudargas, 1972), and none were established for students in these experiments, with the exception of posttests in Experiments 2 and 3, on which students exhibited greater use of complete sequential patterns than in preceding practica. Setting criterion rates for complete sequential patterns and component behaviors, in addition to self-observation feedback, might lead to enhanced use of complete sequential patterns.

Subjects in these studies, when asked to teach new musical works, demonstrated the ability to transfer use of complete sequential patterns from one composition to another within the same setting. It remains to be seen if they are able to transfer implementation of complete sequential patterns to other settings, such as private lessons, elementary music classrooms, or ensemble rehearsals. We often assume that pedagogical techniques that are related in methods courses are then implemented in students' teaching. The present studies investigated students' abilities to demonstrate the techniques taught, but they did not examine whether use of sequential patterns then was transferred to other instructional settings.

Further work is also needed to examine the use and effectiveness of sequential patterns in music classroom, ensemble, and therapy settings. Current research is encouraging; however, there is a paucity of data on the effectiveness of use of complete sequential patterns on student achievement, attitude, and attentiveness.

The promises of the concept of the complete sequential pattern and its uses are evident. This concept of a teacher presenting a task, allowing for student interaction with the task, and giving specific related feedback is a viable pedagogical tool for training prospective music teachers and therapists. Sequential patterns can be used as a means of describing classroom or clinical settings for research or enhancing teaching quality. The specificity of the model also allows for careful investigation into uses of sequential patterns of instruction and their effects, and possibly even the establishment of optimal proportions of music classes and rehearsals that should be composed of complete sequences. Clearly, further descriptive and experimental research into what may be an operationally defined effective teaching model, the complete sequential pattern, is warranted.

REFERENCES

Alley, J. M. (1980). The effect of self-analysis of videotapes on selected competencies of music therapy majors. *Journal of Music Therapy, 17,* 113–132.

Becker, W. C., & Englemann, S. (1976). *Analysis of achievement data on six cohorts of low-income children from 20 school districts in the University of Oregon direct instruction follow through model.* Eugene, OR: Oregon University, College of Education. (ERIC Document Reproduction Service No. ED 145 922)

Becker, W. C., Englemann, S., & Thomas, D. R. (1971). *Teaching: A course in applied psycholo-*

gy. Chicago: Science Research Associates.

Benson, W. L. (1989). The effect of models, self-observation, and evaluation on the modification of specified teaching behaviors of an applied music teacher. *Update: The Applications of Research in Music Education, 7*(2), 28–31.

Berliner, D. C., & Rosenshine, B. (1976). *The acquisition of knowledge in the classroom. Beginning Teacher Evaluation Study* (Technical Report IV-1). N.p., CA: Far West Laboratory for Educational Research and Development. (ERIC Document Reproduction Service No. ED 146 158)

Brophy, J. E. (1979). Teacher behavior and its effects. *Journal of Educational Psychology, 71,* 733–750.

Carnine, D. W. (1979). Direct instruction: A successful system for educationally high-risk children. *Journal of Curriculum Studies, 11,* 29–45.

Carnine, D. W., & Fink, W. T. (1978). Increasing the rate of presentation and use of signals in elementary classroom teachers. *Journal of Applied Behavior Analysis, 11,* 35–46.

Carpenter, R. A. (1988). A descriptive analysis of relationships between verbal behaviors of teacher-conductors and ratings of selected junior and senior high school band rehearsals. *Update: The Applications of Research in Music Education, 7* (1), 37–40.

Duke, R. A., & Blackman, M. D. (1989, March). *Proactive teaching: The effect of sequential task hierarchy on teaching behavior, student performance, and student attitude.* Paper presented at the Research in Music Behavior Eighth National Symposium, Baton Rouge, LA.

Good, T. L., & Brophy, J. E. (1974). Changing teacher and student behavior: An empirical investigation. *Journal of Educational Psychology, 66,* 390–405.

Greenfield, D. G. (1980). The use of visual feedback in training music therapy competencies. *Journal of Music Therapy, 17,* 94–102.

Hanser, S. B., & Furman, C. E. (1980). The effect of videotape-based feedback versus field-based feedback on the development of clinical skills. *Journal of Music Therapy, 17,* 103–112.

Jellison, J. A., & Kostka, M. J. (1987, March). *Student or teacher as focus of attention and elementary students' written recall of teaching content within music teaching units.* Paper presented at the Research in Music Behavior Seventh National Symposium, Logan, UT.

Jellison, J. A., & Wolfe, D. E. (1987). Verbal training effects on teaching units: An exploratory study of music teaching antecedents and consequents. In C. K. Madsen & C. A. Prickett (Eds.), *Applications of research in music behavior* (pp. 135–148). Tuscaloosa: University of Alabama Press.

Killian, J. N. (1981). Effect of instructions and feedback on music teaching skills. *Journal of Music Therapy, 18,* 166–180.

Madsen, C. H., & Madsen, C. K. (1983). *Teaching/discipline: A positive approach for educational development* (3rd ed.). Raleigh, NC: Contemporary Publishing.

Madsen, C. H., & Yarbrough, C. (1985). *Competency-based music education.* Raleigh, NC: Contemporary Publishing.

McDonald, F. J. (1976). Report on phase II of the Beginning Teacher Evaluation Study. *Journal of Teacher Education, 27,* 39–42.

Medley, D. M. (1977). *Teacher competence and teacher effectiveness: A review of process-product research.* Washington, DC: American Association of Colleges for Teacher Education. (ERIC Document Reproduction Service No. ED 143 629)

Moore, R. S. (1976). The effects of videotape feedback and self-evaluation forms on teaching skills, musicianship, and creativity of prospective elementary teachers. *Bulletin of the Council for Research in Music Education,* no. 47, 1–7.

Moore, R. S. (1981). Comparative use of teaching time by American and British elementary music specialists. *Bulletin of the Council for Research in Music Education,* nos. 66–67, 62–68.

Powell, M. (1978). Research on teaching. *The Educational Forum, 43,* 27–37.

Price, H. E. (1983). The effect of conductor academic task presentation, conductor reinforcement, and ensemble practice on performers' musical achievement, attentiveness, and attitude. *Journal of Research in Music Education, 31,* 245–257.

Price, H. E. (1985). A competency-based course in basic conducting techniques: A replication. *The Journal of Band Research, 21,* 61–69.

Price, H. E., & Yarbrough, C. (1991). Validation of sequential patterns of instruction in music. *Canadian Music Educator: Research Edition, 33,* 165–173.

Prickett, C. A. (1987). The effect of self-monitoring on the rate of a verbal mannerism of song leaders. In C. K. Madsen & C. A. Prickett (Eds.), *Applications of research in music behavior* (pp. 125–134). Tuscaloosa: University of Alabama Press.

Rosenshine, B. V. (1976). Recent research on teaching behaviors and students achievement. *Journal of Teacher Education, 27,* 61–64.

Rosenshine, B. V. (1979). Content, time, and direct instruction. In P. L. Peterson & H. J. Walberg (Eds.), *Research on teaching* (pp. 28–56). Berkeley, CA: McCutchan Publishing.

Rosenshine, B. V. (1987). Explicit teaching. In D. C. Berliner & B. V. Rosenshine (Eds.), *Talk to teachers* (pp. 75–92). New York: Random House.

Rosenthal, R. K. (1981). *A data-based approach to elementary general music teacher preparation.* Unpublished doctoral dissertation, Syracuse University.

Rosenthal, R. K. (1989, March). *Effect of behavioral self-analysis on prospective teachers' use of teaching cycles.* Paper presented at the Research in Music Behavior Eighth National Symposium, Baton Rouge, LA.

Saudargas, R. A. (1972). Setting criterion rates of teacher praise: The effects of video tape feedback in a behavior analysis follow through classroom. In G. Semb, D. R. Green, R. P. Hawkins, J. Michael, E. L. Phillips, J. A. Sherman, H. Sloane, & D. R. Thomas (Eds.), *Behavior analysis and education* (pp. 253–261). Lawrence, KS: The University of Kansas Support and Development Center for Follow Through. (ERIC Document Reproduction Service No. ED 080 416)

Wolfe, D. E. (1989, March). *The effect of a visual prompt on changes in antecedents and consequents of teaching behavior.* Paper presented at the Research in Music Behavior Eighth National Symposium, Baton Rouge, LA.

Yarbrough, C. (1976, March). *The effect of videotaped observation and self-evaluation on rehearsal behavior of student conductors.* Paper presented at the National Biennial In-Service Conference of the Music Educators National Conference, Atlantic City, NJ.

Yarbrough, C. (1980). Competency-based conducting: An exploratory study. *1979 Proceedings: McGill Symposium in School Music Administration & Supervision* (62–73). Montreal, Québec, Canada: Faculty of Music, McGill University.

Yarbrough, C. (1987). The relationship of behavioral self-assessment to the achievement of basic conducting skills. *Journal of Research in Music Education, 35,* 183–189.

Yarbrough, C., & Price, H. E. (1981). Prediction of performer attentiveness based on rehearsal activity and teacher behavior. *Journal of Research in Music Education, 29,* 209–217.

Yarbrough, C., & Price, H. E. (1989). Sequential patterns of instruction in music. *Journal of Research in Music Education, 37,* 179–187.

Yarbrough, C., Price, H. E., & Bowers, J. (1991). The effect of knowledge of research on rehearsal skills and teaching values of experienced teachers. *Update: Applications of Research in Music Education, 9* (2), 17–20.

Yarbrough, C., Wapnick, J., & Kelly, R. (1979). Effect of videotape feedback techniques on performance, verbalizations, and attitude of beginning conductors. *Journal of Research in Music Education, 27,* 103–112.

June 9, 1989

VIII.

RESPONSES

TO

MUSIC

Harry E. Price, *The University of Alabama*

JRME 1986, VOLUME 34, NUMBER 3, PAGES 151–159

A Proposed Glossary for Use in Affective Response Literature in Music

INTRODUCTION

In 1982 members of the Affective Response Special Research Interest Group (SRIG), under the national chairmanship of Patrick McMullen, began an attempt "to define, clarify or place in perspective the terminology associated with this [affective response] area" (McMullen, 1982). These efforts were presented at a special session titled "The Affective Experience: A Dialogue," and were summarized by Asmus (1982).

During the Music Educators National Conference (MENC) National Convention in March 1984, members of the Affective Response SRIG discussed the continuing problems with the use of terminology in the field. It was felt that the terminology was used inconsistently or carelessly, thus contributing to difficulty in communication among members of the profession. It was decided that a survey of the literature in the field of affective responsiveness be undertaken by the SRIG in order to extract a listing of commonly used words and recommended definitions based upon common usage.

A proposed strategy was developed. It was presented for feedback at the Southern Division Convention of MENC (Price, 1985) and to the members of the Affective Response SRIG through the April 1985 issue of the *Affective Response SRIG Newsletter*. This strategy included the methodology to be used, with a listing of specific texts and journals to be surveyed. After feedback, the techniques and listing literature to be surveyed were revised and the survey was begun.

An interim glossary, along with the listing of books and journals surveyed to date, was distributed through the September 1985 *Affective Response SRIG Newsletter*. Included was a request for feedback on additional sources or terminology and modification of definitions. A second interim report was distributed through the January 1986 *Affective Response SRIG Newsletter*, which included this feedback and additional literature. A final report was distributed to active researchers in the

---

For reprints of this article, contact Harry E. Price, School of Music, The University of Alabama, Tuscaloosa, 35487–2876.

affective response field, glossary contributors, and all Affective Response SRIG members prior to a special session scheduled for the 1986 MENC National Convention. The proposed glossary was presented and reviewed, and recommendations were made for some revisions at the convention. This proposed glossary and its supporting documentation were approved, and it was recommended that it be disseminated to the music education research community to promote a more common usage of the language in affective response literature.

PROCEDURE

A representative sample of pertinent books (see Appendix A) and journals (see Appendix B) was surveyed. The content of this sample of literature was analyzed for both the quantitative and qualitative use of terminology. Through quantitative analysis of the literature, a listing of the most commonly used terms was developed. Following the development of this listing, an attempt was made to rationalize their qualitative content for the proposed glossary.

It was found that some terms were clearly explained, such as "generic style" or "behavioral preference"; however, many were ill-defined, at best. In many of these latter instances, it was necessary to deduce the meaning of terms from their contextual use. On other occasions, authors used different terms synonymously, such as "opinion" and "attitude," or "perception" and "discrimination." It was also found that in a number of articles, the same term was used with quite different meanings. The word "preference" was sometimes used in the manner in which "attitude" is defined in the proposed glossary.

Some of the terms and definitions listed are direct extractions from a single source, while other terms are a compilation from several. All of the terminology is related to music, however, to avoid constant repetition, the word "music" is not included in every definition.

GLOSSARY

aesthetic experience—Intense subjective and personal experience. Feelingful reaction. Requires perception, experience of feelings and reactions, and psychological involvement. (Abeles, 1980; Radocy & Boyle, 1979; Standifer, 1970)

affective response—Reaction involving feelings and emotions. Learned behavior resulting from a life history of interactions with musical stimuli; encompassing mood-emotional, preference, and taste responses. (Abeles, cited in Asmus, 1979, 1982; Haack, 1980)

appreciation—Awareness of salient characteristics. May imply a deeper involvement, understanding, and/or familiarity. Sometimes used to express a liking for or deeming worthy as expressed by seeking more. (Colwell, 1970; Hargreaves, 1984)

attitude—A learned predisposition reflecting the way one feels about a subject while not in the presence of that subject, which is not directly observable. Positive and negative evaluations, beliefs, and feelings regarding a phenomenon that may produce error in perception and recall. Generally used synonymously with opinion; however, opinion is a verbal reaction to a stimulus, and is directly observable (see *opinion*). Defined by the use of an attitude scale. (Colwell, 1970; Drinkwater, 1965; Edwards & Edwards, 1971; Jensen, 1970; Kuhn, Sims, & Shehan, 1981; Sanderlands & Larson, 1985; Wolman, 1973)

behavioral intention—Opinion or simulated preference expressed in the absence of a stimulus object, but with contextual referents given (e.g., What recording would a subject purchase if given $10.00?). Although a verbal response is solicited, a situational context is specified. (Kuhn, cited in Asmus, 1982, 1983; Kuhn, Sims, & Shehan, 1981; Yarbrough & Price, 1982)

behavioral preference—Differential response for one stimulus as opposed to another. Demonstrated choice through non-verbal actions, such as concert attendance, recording purchase, choosing to listen to specific music. Also called operant preference. (Geringer, 1982; Greer, 1981; Greer, Dorow, & Hanser, 1973; Greer, Dorow, & Randall, 1974; Kuhn, Shehan, & Sims, 1980; Kuhn, Sims, & Shehan, 1981; Morgan & Lindsley, 1966; Yarbrough & Price, 1982)

complexity—Low uncertainty with incongruity, establishing expectancies that are not followed. Information content, ranging from little information, and therefore boring, to so informative as to be difficult to comprehend and appreciate. (Crandall, 1967; Frith & Nias, 1974; Steck & Machotka, 1975)

discrimination—Perception of quantitative or qualitative differences. Detection of similarities and differences. (Bartlett & Dowling, 1980; Berlyne, & Madsen, 1973; Branning, 1971; Fullard, 1967, 1975; Mursell, 1964; Wolman, 1973; Zatorre, 1983)

emotion—A general affective reaction encompassing the feeling states. Affective experience. (Asmus, 1979; R. E. Radocy, personal communication, September 13, 1985: Schoen, 1968)

evaluation—To judge the relative worth, meaning, or significance. (English & English, 1958; Krathwohl, Bloom, & Masia, 1956; Wolman, 1973)

familiarity—Assumption of having heard it somewhere before. Predictability, as a result of repeated exposure to same or similar music. (Davies, 1978; Schoen, 1968; Schukert & McDonald, 1968)

generic style—Broad stylistic categories used to specify identifiable types of music within the concert and popular music traditions. (LeBlanc, 1979)

hedonic value—Reward value as judged by the capacity of a stimulus to reinforce a response, and degree of preference or pleasure reflected in verbal evaluations. A consequence of arousal-raising and arousal-reducing stimulus properties; includes pleasantness-unpleasantness, reward-punishment, positive-negative feedback, attractiveness-repulsiveness, and positive-negative incentive value. (Berlyne, 1970; McMullen, 1980)

information—Originality. Highly redundant events have low information content. (Davies, 1978)

interest—Perception of certain novelties that arise out of variations on the familiar. A term used to measure in the affective domain (see also *interesting*). (Bartlett, 1973; Colwell, 1970)

interesting—Holds the attention of the listener. An attitude that a stimulus object is significant, accompanied by selective attention toward that object. (English & English, 1958; Schoen, 1968; Wolman, 1973)

judgment—A critical evaluation or decision made after perception and discrimination. (Cuddy, Cohen, & Mewhart, 1981; Davies, 1978; Wolman, 1973; Zatorre, 1983)

opinion—Verbal reaction to an idea or a stimulus while in its presence. An evaluation is generally associated with the liking or disliking of a single phenomenon. (Kuhn, cited in Asmus 1982, 1983; Kuhn, Sims, & Shehan, 1981; Yarbrough & Price, 1982)

perceive—To be aware of, primarily through the senses (see also *perception*). (English & English, 1958; Wolman, 1973)

perception—The process through which sensory data are received by means of the senses and the individual becomes aware of features. The way an individual hears and interprets music. (Anderson, 1979; Davies, 1978; Harré & Lambe, 1983; Knieter, 1971)

preference—An act of choosing, esteeming, or giving advantage to one thing over another. Propensity toward something (see also *behavioral preference* and *verbal preference*). (Geringer, 1976; Kuhn, cited in Asmus 1982)

subjective complexity—Perceived complexity level or information content, which is mutable and a function of the listener and past musical experience. (Asmus, 1979; Davies, 1978; Heyduk, 1975)

taste—A person's overall attitude toward collective musical phenomena. Long-term commitment to musical preferences. A social matter that tends to vary with varying groups of people, places, and times, and that gives the impression that preference for one kind of music is better than preference for another. (Farnsworth, 1950; Haack, 1980; Krathwohl, Bloom, & Masia, 1956; LeBlanc, 1982)

values—What individuals consider good or beneficial to their well-being. Values are not innate, but are acquired through experience. (Harré & Lamb, 1983)

valuing—Believing (knowing) that a thing, phenomenon, or behavior has worth. (Krathwohl, Bloom, & Masia, 1956)

verbal preference—A choice; liking of something over something else. Demonstrated choice through verbal actions (spoken or written), based upon many musical and sociological factors, including musical contour, degree of symmetry, order, closeness to optimal level of complexity, societal pressures, and degree of enjoyment. Developed through training and familiarity. (Bauman, 1969; Davies, 1978; Eisenman, 1967; Eysenck, 1968; Frith & Nias, 1974; Looft & Baranowski, 1971; Radocy & Boyle, 1979)

DISCUSSION

This glossary was developed from the common use of terminology in the literature. The terms and their definitions were first included on the basis of the most common usage. After this, an attempt was made to rationalize commonalities and differences among words.

It came about as a result of concern, on the part of the music education community, about the lack of clarity with which the terminology in the field of affective response is used. The purpose is to promote a more common use of affective response language, and thus better communication and understanding in the field.

This glossary is not intended to be the terminal point for the development of the language in the field regarding affective responses to music. It is hoped that this presentation will stimulate thought regarding this field, and also possibly promote attempts toward communicational clarity in other fields.

The field of research regarding affective response to music is achieving a level of maturity and sophistication that requires care in the use of terminology. As the body of literature grows it is necessary to clarify use of the language. While the proposed definitions may not exactly conform to those with which some members of the music education community are accustomed, it would benefit the profession to work with common definitions, and thus ease both the comprehension and composition of the literature.

CONTRIBUTORS

Edward Asmus	Charlotte McKee
Ray Braswell	Wayne Nelson
Lori Gibson	Anne Osterle
Terry Kuhn	Rudolf Radocy

REFERENCES

Abeles, H. F. (1980). Responses to music. In D. A. Hodges (Ed.), *Handbook of Music Psychology* (pp. 105–140). Lawrence, KS: National Association of Music Therapy.

Anderson, P. (1979). Musical time and music as an art of time. *Journal of Aesthetics and Art Criticism, 38* 407–418.

Asmus, E. P. (1979). The operational characteristics of adjectives as descriptors of musical affect. *Dissertation Abstracts International, 40* 4289A. (University Microfilms No. 80–02, 797)

Asmus, E. P. (1982, Summer). "The affective experience: A dialogue" summary. *Affective Response SRIG Newsletter*, pp. 3–5.

Bartlett, J. C., & Dowling, W. J. (1980). Recognition of transposed melodies: A key-distance effect in developmental perspective. *Journal of Experimental Psychology: Human Perception and Performance, 6*, 501–515.

Bartlett, D. L. (1973). Effect of repeated listenings on structural discrimination and affective response. *Journal of Research in Music Education, 21*, 302–317.

Bauman, V. (1969). Teenage music preferences. *Bulletin of the Council for Research in Music Education, 15*, 46–51.

Berlyne, D. E. (1970). Novelty, complexity and hedonic value. *Perception and Psychophysics, 8*, 77–79.

Berlyne, D. E., & Madsen, K. B. (1973). *Pleasure, reward, and preference*. New York: Academic Press.

Branning, H. (1971). Audition preferences of trained and untrained ears on hearing melodic and harmonic intervals when tuned in just intonation of pythagorean ratios. *Bulletin of the Council for Research in Music Education, 23*, 29–32.

Colwell, R. (1970). *The evaluation of music teaching and learning*. Englewood Cliffs, NJ: Prentice-Hall.

Crandall, J. E. (1967). Familiarity, preference, and expectancy arousal. *Journal of Experimental Psychology, 73*, 374–381.

Cuddy, L. L., Cohen, A. J., & Mewhart, D. J. K. (1981). Perception of structure in short melodic sequences. *Journal of Experimental Psychology: Human Perception and Performance, 7*, 869–883.

Davies, J. B. (1978). *The psychology of music*. London, England: Hutchinson & Co.

Drinkwater, B. (1965). A comparison of the Direction-of-Perception technique with the Likert method in the measurement of attitudes. *Journal of Social Psychology, 67*, 189–196.

Edwards, J. S. and Edwards, M. C. (1971). A scale to measure attitudes toward music. *Journal of Research in Music Education, 19*, 228–233.

Eisenman, R. (1967). Birth-order and sex differences in aesthetic preferences for complexity-simplicity. *Journal of General Psychology, 77*, 121–126.

English, H. B., & English, A. C. (1958). *A comprehensive dictionary of psychological and psychoanalytical terms: A guide to usage*. New York: David McKay.

Eysenck, H. J. (1968). An experimental study of aesthetic preference for polygonal figures. *Journal of General Psychology, 79*, 3–17.

Farnsworth, P. R. (1950). *Musical taste: Its measurement and cultural nature*. Stanford, CA: Stanford University Press.

Frith, C. D., & Nias, D. K. B. (1974). What determines aesthetic preference? *Journal of General Psychology, 91*, 173.

Fullard, W. G. (1967). Operant training of aural musical discriminations with preschool children. *Journal of Research in Music Education, 15*, 201–209.

Fullard, W. G. (1975). Pitch discrimination in elementary-school children as a function of training procedure and age. In C. K. Madsen, R. D. Greer, & C. H.

Madsen (Eds.), *Research in Music Behavior* (151–164). New York: Teachers College Press.

Geringer, J. M. (1976). Tuning preferences in recorded orchestral music. *Journal of Research in Music Education, 24,* 169–176.

Geringer, J. M. (1982, July). Verbal and operant music listening preferences in relationship to age and musical training. Paper presented at the International Society of Music Educators 9th International Seminar on Research in Music Education, London, England.

Greer, R. D. (1981). An operant approach to motivation and affects: Ten years of research in music learning. In Music Educators National Conference, *Documentary Report of the Ann Arbor Symposium: National Symposium on the Applications of Psychology to the Teaching and Learning of Music* (pp. 101–121). Reston, VA: Music Educators National Conference.

Greer, R. D., Dorow, L. G., & Hanser, S. (1973). Music discrimination training and the music selection behavior of nursery and primary level children. *Bulletin of the Council for Research in Music Education, 34,* 30–43.

Greer, R. D., Dorow, L. G., & Randall, A. (1974). Music listening preferences of elementary school children. *Journal of Research in Music Education, 22,* 284–291.

Haack, P. (1980). The behavior of music listeners. In D. A. Hodges (Ed.), *Handbook of Music Psychology* (pp. 141–182). Lawrence, KS: National Association for Music Therapy.

Hargreaves, D. J. (1984). The effects of repetition on liking for music. *Journal of Research in Music Education, 32,* 35–47.

Harrace, R. & Lamb, R. (1983). *The encyclopedic dictionary of psychology.* Oxford, England: Basil Blackwell.

Heyduk, R. G. (1975). Rated preference for musical compositions as it relates to complexity and exposure frequency. *Perception and Psychophysics, 17,*84–89.

Jensen, J. P. (1970). Scandinavian research on "music and attitude." *Bulletin of the Council for Research in Music Education, 22,* 33–36.

Knieter, G. L. (1971). The nature of aesthetic education. In Music Educators National Conference, *Toward an aesthetic education.* Washington, D. C.: Music Educators National Conference.

Krathwohl, D. R., Bloom, B. S., & Masia, B. B. (1956). *Taxonomy of educational objectives, the classification of educational goals, handbook II: Affective domain.* New York: David McKay Company.

Kuhn, T. L. (1983, February). *Comparing the relative merits of rating scales and behavioral measures in the assessment of music preference.* Paper presented at the Southeastern Division Convention of the Music Educators National Conference.

Kuhn, T. L., Shehan, P. K., & Sims, W. L. (1980, November). *Relationships among bipolar verbal music preference descriptors and time spent listening to three simultaneously available music selections.* Paper presented at the National Symposium for Research in Music Behavior, New York.

Kuhn, T. L., Sims W. L., and Shehan, P. K. (1981). Relationship between listening time and like-dislike ratings on three musical selections. *Journal of Music Therapy, 18,* 181–192.

LeBlanc, A. (1979). Generic style music preferences of fifth grade students. *Journal of Research in Music Education, 17,* 225–270.

LeBlanc, A. (1982). An interactive theory of music preference. *Journal of Music Therapy, 19,* 28–45.

Looft W. R., & Baranowski, M. D. (1971). An analysis of five measures of sensation seeking and preference for complexity. *Journal of General Psychology, 85,* 307–313.

McMullen, P. T. (1980). Music as perceived stimulus object and affective responses: An alternative theoretical framework. In D. A. Hodges (Ed.), *Handbook of Music Psychology* (pp. 183–193). Lawrence, KS: National Association for Music Therapy.

McMullen, P. T. (1982, Summer). *Affective Response SRIG Newsletter*, p. 1.

Morgan, B. J., & Lindsley, O. R. (1966). Operant preference for stereophonic over monophonic music. *Journal of Music Therapy, 3*, 135–143.

Mursell, J. L. (1964). *The psychology of music.* Westport, CT: Greenwood Press Publishers.

Price, H. E. (1985, March). *A proposed strategy for the development of a glossary for use in affective response research.* Paper presented at the Southeastern Division Convention of the Music Educators National Conference.

Radocy, R. E. and Boyle, J. D. (1979). *Psychological Foundations of Musical Behavior.* Springfield, IL: Charles C. Thomas Books.

Sanderlands, L. E. and Larson, J. R. (1985). When measurement causes task attitudes: A note from the laboratory. *Journal of Applied Psychology, 70,* 116–121.

Schoen, M. (1968). *The effects of music: A series of essays.* Freeport, NY: Books for Libraries Press.

Schukert R. F., & McDonald, R. L. (1968). An attempt to modify the musical preferences of preschool children. *Journal of Research in Music Education, 16,* 39–44.

Standifer, J. A. (1970). Effects of aesthetic sensitivity of developing perception of musical expressiveness. *Journal of Research in Music Education, 18,*112–125.

Steck, L. & Machotka, P. (1975). Preference for musical complexity: Effects of context. *Journal of Experimental Psychology: Human Perception and Performance, 104,* 170–174.

Yarbrough, C., & Price, H. E. (1982, November). *The effect of instruction and repeated listening on behavioral preference, behavioral intent, verbal opinion, and ratings of familiarity and complexity.* Paper presented at the National Symposium for Research in Music Behavior, Tallahassee, FL.

Wolman, B. B. (1973). *Dictionary of behavioral sciences.* New York: Van Nostrand Reinhold.

Zatorre, R. J. (1983). Category-boundary effects and speeded sorting with a harmonic-interval continuum: Evidence of dual processing. *Journal of Experimental Psychology: Human Perception and Performance, 9,* 739–752.

APPENDIX A: BOOKS SURVEYED

Berlyne, D. E. (1974). *Studies in the new experimental aesthetics: Steps toward an objective psychology of aesthetic appreciation.* New York: Halsted Press.

Berlyne, D. E. & Madsen, K. B. (1973). *Pleasure, reward, and preference.* New York: Academic Press.

Colwell, R. (1970). *The Evaluation of Music Teaching and Learning.* Englewood Cliffs, NJ: Prentice-Hall.

Davies, J. B. (1978). *The psychology of music.* London, England: Hutchinson & Co.

Documentary Report of the Ann Arbor Symposium: National Symposium on the Applications of Psychology to the Teaching and Learning of Music. (1981). Reston, VA: Music Educators National Conference.

English, H. B. & English, A. C. (1958). *A comprehensive dictionary of psychological and psychoanalytical terms: A guide to usage.* New York: David McKay.

Farnsworth, P. R. (1950). *Musical taste: Its measurement and cultural nature.* Stanford, CA: Stanford University Press.

Farnsworth, P. R. (1969). *The social psychology of music.* Ames, IA: The Iowa State University Press.

Harré, R., & Lamb, R. (1983). *The encyclopedic dictionary of psychology*. Oxford, England: Basil Blackwell.

Hodges, D. A. (Ed.). (1980). *Handbook of Music Psychology*. Lawrence, KS: National Association for Music Therapy.

Hoffer, C. R. (1984). *The Understanding of Music* (5th ed.). Belmont, CA: Wadsworth Publishing.

Krathwohl, D. R., Bloom, B. S., & Masia, B. B. (1956). *Taxonomy of educational objectives, the classification of educational goals, handbook II: Affective domain*. New York: David McKay Company.

Madsen, C. K., Greer, R. D., & Madsen, C. H., Jr. (Eds.). (1975). *Research in music behavior: Modifying music behavior in the classroom*. New York: Teachers College Press.

Meyer, L. B. (1968). *Emotion and Meaning in Music*. Chicago: University of Chicago Press.

Mursell, J. L. (1964). *The psychology of music*. Westport, CT: Greenwood Press Publishers.

Ogden, R. M. (1968). *Hearing*. New York: AMS Press.

Radocy, R. E., & Boyle, J. D. (1979). *Psychological Foundations of Musical Behavior*. Springfield, IL: Charles C. Thomas Books.

Schoen, M. (1968). *The effects of music: A series of essays*. Freeport, NY: Books for Libraries Press.

Spears, E. M. (1947). *Music in Industry: Studies in Personnel Policy* (No. 78). New York: National Industrial Conference Board.

Toward an aesthetic education. (1971). Washington, D.C.: Music Educators National Conference.

Wolman, B. B. (1973). *Dictionary of behavioral sciences*. New York: Van Nostrand Reinhold.

APPENDIX B: PERIODICALS SURVEYED

Affective Response SRIG Newsletter (1981–85)
American Journal of Psychology (1965–85)
Bulletin of the Council for Research in Music Education (1965–85)
Journal of the Acoustical Society of America (1970–85)
Journal of Abnormal Psychology (1965–85)
Journal of Aesthetics and Art Criticism (1975–85)
Journal of Applied Psychology (1975–85)
Journal of Cognitive Psychology (1970–83)
Journal of Comparative Psychology (1975–85)
Journal of Educational Psychology (1975–85)
Journal of Educational Research (1965–85)
Journal of Experimental Psychology (1965–74)
Journal of Experimental Psychology: Human Perception and Performance (1975–85)
Journal of General Psychology (1965–85)
Journal of Music Therapy (1965–85)
Journal of Perception and Psychophysics (1965–85)
Journal of Research in Music Education (1965–85)
Journal of Social Psychology (1965–85)
Perception and Psychophysics (1965–85)
Psychological Bulletin (1965–85)
Psychological Review (1965–84)
Psychology of Music Journal (1981–84)
Scandinavian Journal of Psychology (1965–83)

May 5, 1986

MUSIC LISTENING PREFERENCES OF ELEMENTARY SCHOOL CHILDREN

R. Douglas Greer
Laura G. Dorow
Andrew Randall

JRME 1974, VOLUME 22, NUMBER 4, PAGES 284–291

Nonverbal tests using an episodic reinforcement device were conducted to ascertain the music preferences of children in elementary grade levels. The tests also provided data on listening attention span in these grades. Results indicated a growing preference for rock music over nonrock music with advancing grade level, with a critical change observable between third and fourth grade levels.

Key Words: activities (melodic, rhythmic), aesthetic preference, elementary education student, fundamentals

Background for the Study

Developmental research in music education has dealt primarily with aural discrimination of the components of music as affected by age, training, and grade level. Much of the developmental evidence to date may be obtained only through data derived from test construction (Colwell, 1968; Gordon, 1965) and pretest data from experimental studies. A few direct developmental studies have been accomplished, however, specifically including those of Petzold (1963), concerned with auditory discrimination, and Madsen, Edmonson, and Madsen (1969), concerned with detection and direction of pitch change. Other evidence regarding age and training effects may be obtained from pretest data of experiments concerned with harmonic discrimination (Hair, 1973), conservation (Pflederer, 1964), pitch matching (Greer, 1970; Hermanson, 1971), and vocalization and music reading (Dittemore, 1970).

No studies concerning the music preferences of children in elementary grade levels using nonverbal instrumentation were found.

Verbal instrumentation has been used to study music preference in numerous studies and some developmental data regarding the effect of age level and training are available (Rogers, 1957). Study of the actual listening choices of students has been made possible through the development of an instrument capable of allowing students to choose to listen to one type of music from alternative types, as well as change their choice at will, while simultaneously recording the student's listening time to each category of music. The instrument, an episodic reinforcement device, has been used in previous research (Greer, Dorow, Wachhaus, and White, 1973; Dorow, 1973; Greer, Dorrow, and Hanser, 1973).

The data discussed in this study were obtained with the episodic reinforcement instrumentation described, and were gathered to answer the following questions about children's preferences for rock and nonrock music, as well as their music listening attention span: (1) What are the within grade level preferences? (2) Do preferences change with grade level? (3) Does listening attention span change with grade level? (4) Are there differences between preferences for rock music when different nonrock music styles are offered as alternative choices?

Data Collection Procedures

One hundred thirty-four subjects were randomly selected from nursery school and grades one through six. Three metropolitan middle-low income schools were represented in the study. The nursery school population was from a school in one district; population of grades one through five was from one school, and population of grade six was from another school in a second district.

The subjects were tested individually for ten minutes on an episodic reinforcement device modeled after those used by Cotter and Spradlin (1971) and Lovitt (1965). Data consisted of the number of seconds each subject listened to two music categories, rock and nonrock, and a sound contingency control, white noise.

Two tape recorders (Revox model A77, and Wollensak model 6250) were used to reproduce prerecorded tapes of the rock and nonrock music and white noise. The two-track tape recorders allowed two music stimuli to be presented with one tape recorder, while the second tape recorder presented the white noise.

The rock music consisted of eight 75-second selections chosen from a rock radio station's "top twenty." The nonrock music category was comprised of three types of music: symphonic, classical piano, and Broadway show tunes. The eight 75-second nonrock selections for the nursery school, second, and third grade subjects were symphonic. For grades one, four, and five, the eight selections were classical piano, and for the sixth grade Broadway show tunes were used.

The rock, nonrock music, and white noise were channeled through earphones contingent on the subject's depression of keys. Continuous de-

Table 1
Listening Time in Seconds for Type of Music by Grade Levels

Grade Level	N	Nonrock Total	Nonrock Median	Nonrock Mean	Rock Total	Rock Median	Rock Mean	Total Listening Time	Total Listening Median	Total Listening Mean
Nursery	16	1219	94.5	76.19	1554	68.0	97.13	2773	92.0	173.31
First	20	3290	191.0	164.50	4692	248.0	234.60	7982	443.5	399.10
Second	19	3176	165.0	167.16	5375	289.0	282.89	8551	439.0	450.05
Third	19	3338	180.0	175.68	6120	298.0	322.11	9458	495.0	497.79
Fourth	20	2327	121.0	116.35	7964	393.5	389.20	10291	512.5	514.55
Fifth	20	2130	92.0	106.50	8464	422.5	423.20	10594	530.0	529.70
Sixth	20	1553	35.0	77.65	9999	540.5	499.95	11552	582.5	577.60

pression of any one key for one minute resulted in a relocation of the rock, nonrock, and white noise. In order to continue the same selection, the subject had to find its new key location. The number of seconds that each key was depressed was recorded on an Esterline Angus Chart recorder.

Subjects were taken individually by the experimenter into a room and were seated at a table on which earphones and a "press to hold" keyboard were located. A screen separated the subject from other equipment and experiment personnel. Each subject was instructed by the experimenter on the use of the "press to hold" keyboard. To familiarize the subject with the equipment, music categories, and the white noise, the experimenter pressed the subject's hand on each key for 20 seconds. The order of key depression during the instructional period was rotated to eliminate any association of experimenter approval with a particular key. The following verbal instructions were given: "This is part of a music workshop. I will return for you in a little while. While I'm gone you may press these keys." (Experimenter helps place earphones on subject. Experimenter takes subject's hand and presses each key for 20 seconds.) "You may begin." (Experimenter leaves room.)

Results

Table 1 shows the mean, median, and total number of seconds subjects in each grade level selected rock or nonrock music. The total selection time possible for any one subject was 600 seconds. The platykurtic distribution of the data warranted the use of nonparametric statistics (Glass, Peckham and Sanders, 1972; Siegel, 1956).

Overall differences between grade levels for the rock and nonrock music categories and total listening time were tested with the Kruskal-Wallis one-way analysis of variance. Significant differences were found for the rock ($H = 109.08$, $df = 6$, $p < .001$) and nonrock categories

Table 2
Summary Mann Whitney U Tests Between Grade Levels for Nonrock Music

Grade Level Comparison	Mann Whitney U	Direction
Nursery vs First	60.0*	First > Nursery
First vs Second	179.5	
Second vs Third	170.0	
Third vs Fourth	95.0**	Third > Fourth
Fourth vs Fifth	165.0	
Fifth vs Sixth	141.0	

* Significant at the .001 level, one-tailed test.
** Significant at the .01 level, one-tailed test.

(H = 57.55, df = 6, p < .001), and for total listening time (H = 129.87, df = 6, p < .001).

Subsequently, adjacent grade level comparisons were made using the Mann-Whitney U test. As shown in Table 2, the first graders listened to more nonrock music than the nursery school children. In addition, third graders listened to more nonrock than fourth graders, clearly indicating that after third grade the amount of time that children choose to listen to nonrock music decreases.

Grade level comparisons of the rock music category (Table 3) demonstrated an increase in rock listening time with the rise in grade levels. First graders listened to more rock than nusery school children, fourth graders more than third graders, and sixth graders listened more than fifth graders.

Comparisons of the total amount of listening time across grade levels (Table 4) revealed that first graders spent more total time listening than nursery school children. The sharp increase is perhaps attributable to a

Table 3
Summary Mann Whitney U Tests Between Grade Levels for Rock Music

Grade Level Comparison	Mann Whitney U	Direction
Nursery vs First	67.0*	First > Nursery
First vs Second	131.0	
Second vs Third	143.0	
Third vs Fourth	99.0*	Fourth > Third
Fourth vs Fifth	157.5	
Fifth vs Sixth	99.5	Sixth > Fifth

* Significant at the .01 level, one-tailed test.

Table 4
Summary Mann Whitney U Tests Between Grade Levels for Total Listening Time

Grade Level Comparison	Mann Whitney U	Direction
Nursery vs First	34.5*	First > Nursery
First vs Second	158.5	
Second vs Third	113.5**	Third > Second
Third vs Fourth	161	
Fourth vs Fifth	164	
Fifth vs Sixth	31.5*	Sixth > Fifth

* Significant at the .001 level, one-tailed test.
** Significant at the .01 level, one-tailed test.

Table 5
Order of Rock and Nonrock Preference by Grade Level

Grade Level	First Preference	Second Preference	Wilcoxen T
Nursery	Rock, Nonrock	—	47
First	Rock, Nonrock	—	47
Second	Rock	Nonrock	27.5*
Third	Rock	Nonrock	14*
Fourth	Rock	Nonrock	1*
Fifth	Rock	Nonrock	3*
Sixth	Rock	Nonrock	0*

* Significant at the .005 level.

greater listening attention span in first graders as compared to three-year-old children. Also, third graders had a greater total listening time than second graders, and sixth graders greater than fifth graders, an indication that listening attention span may increase with age and/or training.

The rank order of preference for rock and nonrock music was determined within each grade level using the Wilcoxon matched-pairs signed-ranks test (Table 5). Nursery and first graders showed an equal preference for both the rock and nonrock music whereas from second to sixth grade rock music was preferred.

Conclusions

General music students in the elementary grades, who are similar to those in the samples studied, will increasingly choose to listen to more rock music and less nonrock music with advancing age and/or grade level. There is no difference in preferences between the two categories of music for the nursery school children and the first graders, but by the upper grades the overwhelming preference of the children is rock music. Interestingly, the time between third and fourth grade appears to be a pivotal time in terms of musical taste. This time period has also been reported as a turning point for the acquisition of other music behaviors (Petzold, 1963; Gordon, 1965).

The children's preference for rock music will not surprise most music educators, but the degree to which nonrock music was increasingly avoided with advancing age and/or grade level may be unexpected. It must be stressed that the school populations studied were limited and that the sample sizes of the populations were small. However, the preference differences are large, consistent in direction, and compatible with general sociological theories concerning cultural conditioning. It is also conjectured that with increasing age and/or grade level, general music students become increasingly less amenable to nonrock music influences. This conjecture is not totally speculative but is based in part on pretest and posttest data for nursery school subjects; second and third graders (Greer, Dorow, and Hanser, 1973); first, fourth, and fifth graders (Dorow, 1973); and sixth graders (Greer, Dorow, Wachhaus, and White, 1973.

The music listening attention span (total listening time) increases uniformly and in a directionally predictable manner with advancement in grade level. It is clear that the older children listened to more music when given the choice of listening to noise, not listening, or listening to music, than the younger children. The increase in attention span is accompanied with a corresponding increase in choice of rock over nonrock. This preference trend may in part be attributed to the influence of mass media, a conclusion supported by the Surgeon General's report on the influence of television on children's behavior (Comstock, Rubinstein, and Murray, 1972).

The use of different categories of nonrock music with different grade levels may represent control limitations for the data. However, the use of Broadway show music as the nonrock selection for the sixth graders would have been expected to offset differences in rock and nonrock listening times. In fact, the converse was true, as sixth graders listened even less to the nonrock selections than the other grade levels. This finding suggests that the type of nonrock music used was not an important variable to be controlled. However, one previous study using a similar sample showed differences between nonrock music categories of jazz, music classics, and electronic music (Greer, Dorow, Wachhaus, and White, 1973). Although these differences were significant, they were slight in magnitude and were totally overwhelmed by the large magnitude of difference between the most preferred nonrock category and the rock category, with rock being most preferred. This latter finding was similar to the result of a similar preference study using sixth graders drawn from an entirely different population (Greer, Dorow, and Harrison, in press). If school music programs for general music students are to be influential in terms of the expansion of students' musical tastes, it seems clear that more must be known about what school-related variables influence taste. Future research should experimentally isolate specific instructional content and teacher behavior that influences the expansion of students' musical tastes.

References

Colwell, R., *Music Achievement Tests* (Chicago: Follett Educational Corporation, 1968).

Comstock, G. A., E. A. Rubinstein, and J. P. Murray, eds., U.S. Surgeon General's Scientific Advisory Committee on Television and Social Behavior; Reports and Papers (Rockville, Md.: National Institute of Mental Health, 1972).

Cotter, V. W., and J. E. Spradlin, "A Non-Verbal Technique for Studying Music Preference," *Journal of Experimental Child Psychology*, Vol. 11, No. 3 (1971), pp. 357–365.

Dittemore, E. E., "An Investigation of Some Musical Capabilities of Elementary School Students," *Studies in the Psychology of Music*, Vol. 6 (Iowa City: University of Iowa Press, 1970).

Dorow, L. G., *The Effect of Teacher Approval/Disapproval Ratios on Student Music Selection Behavior and Concert Attentiveness* (doctoral dissertation, Columbia University, 1973).

Glass, G. V., P. D. Peckham, and J. R. Sanders, "Consequences of Failure to Meet Assumptions Underlying the Analysis of Variance and Co-variance," *Review of Educational Research*, Vol. 42, No. 3 (1972), pp. 237–288.

Gordon, E., *Musical Aptitude Profile* (Boston: Houghton Mifflin, 1965).

Greer, R. D., "The Effect of Timbre on Brass-Wind Intonation," *Studies in the Psychology of Music*, Vol. 6 (Iowa City: University of Iowa Press, 1970).

Greer, R. D., L. Dorow, and S. Hanser, "Music Discrimination Training and the Music Selection Behavior of Nursery and Primary Level Children," *Council for Research in Music Education*, Vol. 35, No. 4 (Winter 1973), pp. 30–43.

Greer, R. D., L. Dorow, and L. N. Harrison, "Aural Discrimination Instruction and the Preferences of Sixth Graders for Music Listening, Story Listening, and Candy," In C. K. Madsen, R. D. Greer, and C. H. Madsen, Jr., *Research in Music Behavior* (New York: Teachers College Press, in press).

Greer, R. D., L. G. Dorow, G. Wachhaus, and E. R. White, "Adult Approval and Students' Music Selection Behavior," *Journal of Research in Music Education*, Vol. 21, No. 4 (Winter 1973), pp. 345–354.

Hair, H., "The Effect of Training on the Harmonic Discrimination of Children in the First Grade," *Journal of Research in Music Education*, Vol. 21, No. 1 (Spring 1973), pp. 85–91.

Hermanson, L., *An Investigation of the Effects of Timbre on Simultaneous Vocal Pitch Acuity of Young Children* (doctoral dissertation, Columbia University, 1971).

Lovitt, T. C., *Narrative Rate Preferences of Normal and Retarded Males as Assessed by Conjugate Reinforcement* (doctoral dissertation, University of Kansas, 1965).

Madsen, C. K., F. A. Edmonson, and C. H. Madsen, Jr., "Modulated Frequency Discrimination in Relationship to Age and Musical Training," *The Journal of the Acoustical Society of America*, Vol. 46, No. 2, Pt. 2 (1969), pp. 1468–1472.

Petzold, R., "The Development of Auditory Perception of Musical Sounds by Children in the First Six Grades," *Journal of Research in Music Education*, Vol. 11 (Spring 1963), pp. 21–43.

Pflederer, M., "The Responses of Children to Musical Tasks Embodying Piaget's Principle of Conservation," *Journal of Research in Music Education*, Vol. 12 (Winter 1964), pp. 251–268.

Rogers, V. R., "Children's Musical Preferences," *Elementary School Journal*, Vol. 57 (1957), pp. 433–435.

Siegel, S., *Nonparametric Statistics for the Behavioral Sciences* (New York: McGraw-Hill, 1956).

■ Teachers College, Columbia University
New York, New York

GENERIC STYLE MUSIC PREFERENCES OF FIFTH-GRADE STUDENTS

Albert LeBlanc

JRME 1979, VOLUME 27, NUMBER 4, PAGES 255-270

The primary intent of this study was to find fifth-graders' most preferred generic music style and identify the critical competitors of that style, if any existed. A short listening test was developed to measure preference for different generic styles of music. Ambient sound was employed as a reference point to anchor the response scale. The test was administered to 278 students of varying socioeconomic status and ethnic background in 11 fifth-grade classrooms in the greater St. Louis area. Test reliability was evaluated in terms of stability of preference responses over time. Naturalistic behavioral observation was employed during test administration to secure a rough confirmation or denial of the truthfulness of student preference responses. Easy-listening pop music was the most preferred generic style and five other generic styles earned preference ratings that would qualify them as critical competitors. An exploratory factor analysis was conducted on preference responses and four factors were obtained and interpreted in an oblique solution.

Key Words: activities (melodic, rhythmic), aesthetic experience, aesthetics, attitudes, aural discrimination, psychological processes, tests, theory.

In his review of attitude and preference research in music, Wapnick (1976) traces a continuing interest in music taste.[1] A highlight of the early research in this area was the sequential and interrelated work of Hevner, who experimented with the affective character of major and minor modes (1935), melody, harmony, and rhythm (1936), pitch and tempo (1937), and developed the adjective circle and a

---

[1] Data for this study was collected as part of the evaluation of an aesthetic education curriculum package conducted by the author. The package was developed by the Aesthetic Education Program of CEMREL, Inc., a national educational laboratory funded in part by the National Institute of Education. No endorsement of these findings by the National Institute of Education should be inferred.

series of discrimination tests to facilitate her work. Much of the early research into taste in music is summarized in Farnsworth's 1950 monograph.

Comparatively few studies published after 1950 deal exclusively with taste and preference as the central research problem. Cattell and Saunders (1954) explored music preference as a possible tool for personality diagnosis, while Keston and Pinto (1955) studied it in relation to intelligence and personality variables, and Hedden (1973) examined autochthonous and experimental characteristics as possible determinants of the listener's reaction to music. Bartlett (1973) studied the effect of repeated listenings on music preference, Duerksen (1972) and Radocy (1976) have shown the effect of experimentally created bias upon listener judgments, and Inglefield (1972) demonstrated the impressive power of the adolescent peer group to redirect music preferences. McMullen (1974, 1976; McMullen & Arnold, 1976) has examined music preference in the context of information theory and Berlyne's approach to experimental aesthetics, and Greer, Dorow, Wachhaus, and White (1973), and Dorow (1977) have dealt with music preference in the context of behavior modification techniques. A study by Greer, Dorow, and Randall (1974) is a rare example of published contemporary research in which music taste is the central concern. Citing a need for sequential and interrelated studies of the taste phenomenon, LeBlanc (Note 1) has advanced a theoretical model of sources of variation in music taste that may be useful in the design of future studies.

The objectives of this study were:

1. To develop a prototype, group-administered listening test to measure expressed preference for different generic styles of music.
2. To assess the reliability of the test in terms of stability of responses across time.
3. To explore various procedural options within the framework of the pencil-and-paper listening test, and the possibility of using behavioral observation to gain a rough confirmation or denial of the truthfulness of student responses.
4. To measure comparative preference for different generic styles of music.
5. To conduct an exploratory factor analysis of preference responses to identify some of the stimulus characteristics accounting for the preference response.

For the purposes of this study, music taste was considered to be synonymous with expressed music preference, and generic style was defined as broad stylistic categories used to specify identifiable types of music within the concert and popular music traditions. It was assumed that the response to a stimulus representing a particular generic style would be indicative of the response toward that style in general.

Procedure

Test Development

Music excerpts thought to be clear-cut examples of different generic styles were selected. Working with classical piano music and Broadway tunes as competitors to rock music, Greer (1974) found a statistically significant preference for rock music in grades four through six. The present study used other generic styles to compete with rock music for preference ratings and used recordings of ambient sound to anchor the rating scales in the same way that Greer et al. used white noise in their 1974 study.

An effort was made to vary the tempo and performing medium as well as the generic style of the examples. Ambient sound stimuli were given less time than were the music examples because there was no phrase structure to maintain. Examples were arranged in a random sequence and recorded on reel-to-reel tape at a professional recording studio with a 15-second response interval between each example.

Forsythe (Note 2) and Kuhn (Note 3) have successfully used bipolar response continuums anchored with smiling and frowning faces in preference studies with young children. In evaluation studies conducted for the Aesthetic Education Program of CEMREL, Inc., LeBlanc used the semantic differential with seven-point response continuums with fifth-grade students. The only problems experienced with the semantic differential involved vocabulary, and this was not a concern in the present study because a simple preference response was the only information desired. The response sheet consisted of 16 seven-point response continuums anchored by the words "like" and "dislike." To counteract possible response set biasing, the polarity of every second scale was reversed and two forms of the response sheet were prepared, with each form reversing different scales. The recorded tape and its response sheet were called the Sound Organization Preference Index (SOPI).

Three groups of graduate students in music education critiqued the test before it was used with fifth-grade students.[2] The first group was asked to supply, as a constructed response, the name of the generic style they thought each example represented, and the results were compared with the researcher's list of targeted generic styles. There were no disagreements at this point except for different terminology used to indicate essentially the same meaning. In some cases descriptors were revised or combined to give a clearer indication of the generic style they were intended to describe.

---

[2] The researcher gratefully acknowledges the help of students in his psychology of music seminar at the University of Texas at Austin, and of students in the seminars of Lewis B. Hilton of Washington University and Robert G. Sidnell of Michigan State University.

For the next step of review, the second and third groups of graduate students listened to each example with a sheet listing the targeted generic style and a seven-point scale for rating each music selection representing that style. They were also asked to rate each excerpt for durational adequacy since each stimulus had been taped up to the first cadence point or musically logical phrase ending rather than the standard 30-second duration used in some previous studies. The criterion used to evaluate durational adequacy was whether or not the recorded stimulus was of sufficient length to present a clear example of generic style. No outstanding deficiencies were identified at this point in the review process, although several items were flagged for reevaluation after the pilot trial.

The draft version of SOPI and a standard set of verbal directions were pilot tested with two classes of fifth-grade students, who were invited to comment about the test as soon as they finished it. Two of the 16 items were revised as a result of student and reviewer comments. Contents of the final version of SOPI are given in Table 1. The stimulus tape required 12 minutes playing time, and a complete administration was accomplished in 20 minutes.

SOPI was administered to 278 fifth-grade students from 11 classrooms in the greater St. Louis area. Students in the selected classrooms provided a wide variation of socioeconomic and racial background, and both inner-city and suburban sites were included in the study. Racial composition of the classes varied from entirely black to entirely white, while the integrated classes varied in terms of proportion and identity of a majority race. To comply with protection of human subjects regulations and to remove any danger of response biasing by authority figures, students responded to SOPI anonymously. In the classrooms where reliability was being measured in a test-retest design, students were given an ID card with a number that was used to match their test and retest response sheets. ID cards were kept by the school principal, but they were distributed to students at the time of retest to remind them of their number, and then the cards were destroyed.

Reliability Analysis

A test-retest design was employed to measure reliability in terms of the stability of student responses over time. Eight out of the 11 participating classes took the test twice, although retest data were discarded for Class 3 because the teacher's class control had deteriorated to a state of ineffectiveness by the time of the retest. In the test-retest study 10 days was the shortest period of elapsed time and 91 days was the longest.

The mean preference ratings that had been accorded to each stimulus by each class at pretest and posttest were used to place the stimuli in rank order, and Spearman's ρ was computed to show the stability with which SOPI portrayed classwide preference rankings. The resulting coefficients ranged from .829 for a 23-day interval to .956 for a 42-day time interval. In a similar procedure Kuhn obtained ρ's of .933 for a 7-day interval and

Table 1
Sound Organization Preference Index

Item	Mnemonic	Generic Style	Composer or Performer/Title	Duration
1.	CWBLUG	Country Western/Bluegrass	Lester Flatt and Earl Scruggs/"Southbound"	:27
2.	CLASIN	Classical Instrumental	Prokofiev/*Classical Symphony*: "Gavotte"	:22
3.	BLACKG	Black Gospel	Harlem Christian Tabernacle Church/"Wings"	:28
4.	CARSND	Ambient Sound	"Triumph Sports Car"	:16
5.	SACHOR	Sacred Choral	Schubert/*Mass in G*: "Kyrie"	:28
6.	ELERAN	Random-Generated Electronic Sounds	Beaver and Krause/"Control Generators/Echo"	:18
7.	DIXIE	Dixieland	Dukes of Dixieland/"Swanee River"	:27
8.	FOLK	Folk	Odetta/"Lowlands"	:30
9.	WIPERS	Ambient Sound	"Windshield Wipers and Rain"	:15
10.	AVANT	Avant-Garde	Penderecki/"Threnody for the Victims of Hiroshima"	:20
11.	MARCH	Band March	Bagley/"National Emblem"	:24
12.	RAGTIM	Ragtime	Joplin/"Maple Leaf Rag"	:22
13.	ELEPOP	Electronic Pop	Beaver and Krause/"Peace Three"	:32
14.	EASLPO	Easy-Listening Pop	The Carpenters/"Sing"	:27
15.	ROCK	Rock	Alice Cooper/"Public Animal #9"	:34
16.	MODSWG	Modern Swing	Miles Davis/Gershwin's Porgy and Bess: "There's a Boat Dat's Leavin' Soon for New York"	:23

.462 for a 168-day interval. The complete reliability analysis of SOPI is presented in Table 2.

Pearson's r was computed between the pretest and posttest total scores of individuals. Those students with higher scores liked more styles or showed a stronger preference for the styles they liked. The total score on SOPI was, therefore, an index of stylistic tolerance or intensity of preference, and its reliability analysis does not furnish information about the reliability with which SOPI measured preference for individual styles.

Pearson's r's were computed between pretest and posttest individual responses to each stimulus as an indication of the stability of individual preference ratings over time. Class means of these coefficients are presented in Table 2. An internal consistency reliability analysis was rejected because of the test's objective of measuring affective response to widely differing music styles. The divergency of styles presented would have contributed to responses of low internal consistency unless the individuals measured had made highly similar responses to each style.

Behavior Observation

Summers (1970) wrote about an individual's underlying attitudes becoming momentarily visible as "outcroppings" in his or her behavior. Cook and Selltiz (1964) listed five sources for making inferences about attitude, beginning with self-report by the subject and observation of the subject's overt behavior. Abeles (Note 4) recommended multiple measures for the study of affective behavior, whereas Campbell and Fiske (1959) view it as a means of convergent validation with one measure's result serving to confirm or deny the result of another. One of the questions posed in this study was whether or not behavioral observation could serve as a rough indicator of student response to different sound stimuli.

Table 2
Test-Retest Reliability Analysis of SOPI

| | Class | | | | | | | |
	1	2	3 [a]	4	5	6	7	8
Spearman's ρ [b]	.956	.953		.918	.906	.881	.935	.829
Pearson's r [c]	.580	.662		.464	.470	.355	.798	.777
Mean of Pearson's r's [d]	.512	.486		.398	.330	.421	.526	.406
Interval between testings in days	42	42		91	84	70	10	23

[a] Posttest data for the third class was discarded because of disorderly classroom conditions at the time of the posttest.
[b] Between pretest and posttest class mean rankings of each stimulus
[c] Between pretest and posttest total score by individuals
[d] Between pretest and posttest individual responses to each stimulus

At the beginning of the study it was impossible to predict the extent to which students' behavior would be easily observable and potentially interpretable in response to the sound stimuli. A tendency toward overt responses was observed during the pilot testing of SOPI, and a standard procedure was developed to encourage these responses so they could be observed and recorded. The researcher made a subjective interpretation of student behavior at the time of testing and checked this later against test results. Observed behavior tended to confirm written indications of preference. Further development of the behavioral observation data is beyond the scope of the present study.

Results

Preference results for 278 fifth-grade students are shown in Table 3. Many students took the test twice as part of the test-retest reliability study, but their initial response to the stimuli is presented here because it represents a more natural sampling of affective behavior than a second encounter with the same test. Mean ratings are shown on a scale of one to seven, with seven indicating highest preference. There were very few instances of omitted responses in the data. When skips did occur, they were encoded

Table 3
Preference Results for 278 Fifth-Grade Students on the First Administration of SOPI

Stimulus[a]	Preference Stability[b]	Rank	Rating	
			Mean	SD
EASLPO	.414	1	6.15	1.59
ROCK	.422	2	5.80	1.88
RAGTIM	.469	3	5.49	1.91
DIXIE	.356	4	5.46	1.85
MARCH	.331	5	5.31	1.87
CWBLUG	.632	6	5.02	2.15
ELERAN	.382	7	4.99	2.16
ELEPOP	.488	8	3.88	2.30
MODSWG	.468	9	3.73	2.13
CARSND	.463	10	3.72	2.29
AVANT	.399	11	3.69	2.26
CLASIN	.518	12	3.00	2.16
BLACKG	.485	13	2.85	2.24
WIPERS	.356	14	2.81	1.92
SACHOR	.437	15	2.70	2.09
FOLK	.421	16	2.23	1.73

Note. Maximum score of 7.00 indicates highest preference.
[a] Stimulus mnemonics are explained in Table 1.
[b] Preference stability is indicated by the mean of Pearson's r's between pretest and posttest individual responses to each stimulus.

as a four or neutral rating. Pearson's r was computed between test and retest individual responses to each stimulus, and the means of these r's are presented in Table 3. The mean r's indicate the stability of preference for each stimulus.

The six stimuli with the highest preference rankings were all clear-cut examples of music as opposed to disorganized sound or ambient noise. All were rated above five on the scale of one to seven, and musically they all shared the characteristic of having an easily perceptible beat. The easy-listening pop music stimulus clearly scored higher than the rock music example, and had the lowest standard deviation of any stimulus on the test. This suggests that students closely agreed that this was the most preferred generic style on the test.

There was a large break in ratings between random-generated electronic sounds and electronic pop music. Both shared quite similar timbres, but the random sounds displayed more energy and the subjective sensation of a faster tempo. The four lowest ranked stimuli all shared a comparatively slow tempo. The sacred choral and folk music examples were preferred less than any of the three ambient sounds.

A Kruskal-Wallis one-way analysis of variance was carried out on the rankings accorded to each stimulus by each class. Stimulus rankings were significantly different at the .001 level (H = 132.38, df = 10), and Dunn's multiple comparison procedure was employed to examine all possible pairwise comparisons using an alpha level of .08. By far the most meaningful result of this analysis was the discovery that none of the seven top ranked styles was significantly more preferred than any of the other members of that group. Each of the first seven styles was preferred significantly more than the five lowest ranking styles. Since the seventh ranking ELERAN stimulus was unique rather than representative of a genre of styles, it was concluded that the six top ranked styles were critical competitors of each other.

Factor Analysis

An exploratory factor analysis of preference response data was conducted to identify some of the stimulus characteristics accounting for the preference response. A factor analysis of principal factors was carried out using the PA2 option in the Statistical Package for the Social Sciences (SPSS) Subprogram FACTOR (Nie, Hull, Jenkins, Steinbrenner, & Bent, 1975). The traditional criterion of eigenvalue $\geq$ one was employed to determine the number of factors extracted in the initial factoring process. Four factors had eigenvalues greater than one, and together they accounted for 50.7% of the total variance. Table 4 presents the results of the initial factoring of SOPI preference responses.

Oblique rather than orthogonal rotation was chosen because there was no logical support for the assumption that the preferred characteristics of preferred stimuli were mutually independent in nature. LeBlanc's model of sources of variation in music taste hypothesizes four stimulus quality variables that are capable of complex interactions with each other, with cultural environment variables, and with personal qualities of the respondent. The model, reproduced here as Figure 1, provides a theoretical basis for expecting oblique rather than orthogonal factors in an analysis of preference responses attributed to stimulus characteristics.

Factors were rotated to an oblique solution using a direct oblimin criterion with the delta parameter set equal to zero as recommended by Harman (1976). Delta influences the obliqueness of the solution, and a delta of zero is said to cause a solution that is fairly to highly oblique (Nie et al., 1975; Harman, 1976). Tables 5 and 6 present the results of oblique rotation and factor pattern correlations, respectively.

Table 4
Initial Factoring of SOPI Responses

Factor	Eigenvalue	Percent of Total Variance	
		Individual	Cumulative
1	3.504	21.9	21.9
2	1.966	12.3	34.2
3	1.396	8.7	42.9
4	1.241	7.8	50.7

Table 5
Direct Oblimin Solution for Oblique Factors of SOPI Responses

Stimulus	Factor F1	Pattern F2	F3	Matrix F4	Factor F1	Structure F2	F3	Matrix F4
CLASIN	.685	.076	.177	−.025	.710	.145	.283	.213
SACHOR	.497	.062	.005	.175	.551	.151	.113	.330
MODSWG	.428	.167	.214	.110	.503	.259	.315	.309
AVANT	.020	.701	.017	−.097	.052	.678	.092	.107
ELERAN	−.045	.657	.051	−.008	.012	.658	.125	.171
WIPERS	.255	.490	−.162	.160	.314	.534	−.039	.341
ELEPOP	.110	.476	.183	−.073	.155	.487	.247	.118
CARSND	−.073	.415	−.213	.152	−.029	.425	−.148	.214
MARCH	.275	−.031	.585	.096	.385	.091	.636	.255
RAGTIM	.118	.018	.584	.096	.231	.126	.618	.225
DIXIE	.081	−.013	.444	.391	.245	.068	.505	.454
EASLPO	−.056	.038	.411	−.032	−.002	.075	.403	.027
FOLK	.108	.099	.019	.533	.265	.258	.130	.594
CWBLUG	−.001	−.004	.127	.511	.158	.153	.206	.529
BLACKG	.161	−.051	−.138	.278	.213	.022	−.078	.286
ROCK	−.240	.155	.120	.276	−.134	.228	.148	.273

The direct oblimin procedure went through 25 iterations with no change in the criterion's first three decimal places on the last four iterations. This was taken as evidence that additional iterations would not meaningfully improve the fit of the solution. Rummel (1970) identified the factor pattern matrix as the best source of information about the clustering of variables,

Table 6
Factor Pattern Correlations

	F1	F2	F3	F4
Factor 1				
Factor 2	.079			
Factor 3	.146	.124		
Factor 4	.275	.279	.157	

Note. Initial value of the direct oblimin criterion, $\delta = 0$, was 8.304. After 25 iterations, it was 4.135. To enhance clarity, stimuli are presented in the order of their highest loadings on succeeding factors.

Figure 1
A Proposed Model of Sources of Variation in Musical Taste

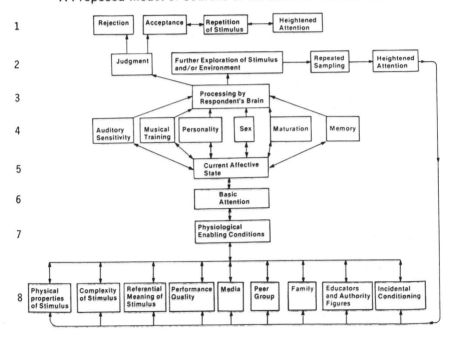

while the factor structure matrix indicated the correlation between each factor and each variable. The factor pattern correlations show the relationships between the factors themselves, and though the highest obtained correlations are moderate, they demonstrate a definite departure from orthogonality.

Although no factor had a loading greater than .71, there was a generally clear separation between higher loading and lower loading stimuli on each factor. Cattell (1966) holds that important factors may never load higher than .30 to .40 in analyses of natural data, and each of the SOPI factors attained a high loading greater than .53, which safely exceeds the range discussed by Cattell.

A preliminary interpretation of the four obtained factors was made by the researcher and a recorded tape was prepared with stimuli grouped according to the factor on which they displayed the highest loading. This tape was played at a symposium of behavioral researchers in music, and the participants were asked to supply as a constructed response their own descriptions of the salient characteristics shared within each stimulus group. The responses of these individuals were used as a cross validation check upon the researcher's factor interpretations.

The classical instrumental stimulus was the one that loaded highest on Factor 1, followed by sacred choral and modern swing. The band march and windshield wipers stimuli had moderate loadings, while the rock stimulus had a moderate negative loading. Focusing upon the three highest loading variables, the factor was characterized by establishment, adult, serious, or "non-fun" music, especially in the mind of the fifth-grade student. Factor 1 was named Establishment Music.

The avant-garde stimulus loaded highest on Factor 2, closely followed by electronic random sounds, and more distantly by windshield wipers, electronic pop music, and the car sound stimulus. Factor 2, characterized by novel timbres and mechanical sounds, was named Novel Timbres.

The band-march and ragtime stimuli displayed virtually identical high loadings on Factor 3, followed by dixieland and easy-listening pop. This factor was characterized by happy, upbeat music with an easily perceptible beat. The high loading stimuli were all examples of popular as opposed to serious styles, and no slow tempos were represented. Factor 3 was named Rhythmic Dynamism.

The folk song and country & western/bluegrass stimuli loaded highest on Factor 4, followed by dixieland, black gospel, and rock. The shared attribute most apparent among these stimuli was their nonestablishment background and portrayal of proletarian life styles. Factor 4 was named People's Music.

Discussion

The first objective of this study was to develop a prototype, group-administered listening test to measure expressed preference for different generic styles of music. This objective was met.

The second objective of the study was test-retest reliability assessment. The Spearman's ρ analysis of classwide stimulus rankings yielded by far the highest reliability coefficients. This analysis would be unaffected by individual preference reversals as long as reversals of comparable number and magnitude were made in the opposite direction. Results indicate excellent stability of classwide preference measurement over time intervals as long as 91 days ($\rho = .918$). This finding closely parallels Kuhn's observation for a similar test.

To compare the test's reliability with that of a widely accepted rank ordering of music listening preferences, the "Hot 100" list published by *Billboard* magazine was examined for stability across time. The "Hot 100" list is a popularity ranking based upon airplay and record sales. Sixteen songs were randomly selected from lists published during the weeks when data was collected for this study, and Spearman's ρ was computed to measure the stability of rankings across time. The ρ's obtained for 7-, 14-, 21-, and 42-day time intervals were .944, .806, .418, and .371, respectively. The ρ's obtained for SOPI range from .956 to .829 over time intervals ranging from 10 to 91 days, which compared quite favorably with the reliability of *Billboard* rankings.

The second reliability analysis undertaken for SOPI reported Pearson's r's between pretest and posttest total scores by individuals. In six out of seven class comparisons, the stability of individual total scores was considerably higher than that of individual responses to each stimulus. This is not surprising because the total score is based upon sixteen measurements compared to the single measurement taken for each stimulus. In this analysis individuals could drastically reverse their ratings of individual stimuli without affecting their total score as long as they made comparable reversals in the opposite direction. These results suggest that as far as individual measurement is concerned, SOPI is more serviceable as an index of stylistic tolerance than an index of style preferences.

The final reliability analysis reported the mean of Pearson's r's between test and retest individual responses to each stimulus. Results of this analysis were disappointing. When the obtained r's were squared to yield coefficients of determination, it was found that the highest amount of variance in an individual's retest response that could be accounted for by that person's first response was about 28%. In 66% of the test-retest comparisons, however, the obtained r showed a relationship greater than chance at the .05 level. SOPI was far more reliable as an indicator of classwide rather than individual preferences. When mean Pearson's r's are presented by stimulus (Table 3) it can be seen that some styles generated a greater stability of preference than others. The most preferred styles did not necessarily enjoy the most stable preferences.

Why was the stability of individual responses so disappointing? A possible answer is offered by the fact that students were visibly impatient with the retest procedure as soon as they discovered that the retest was identical to the test they had already taken. Some students did not respond conscientiously to the retest. The problem of retest restlessness might be avoided in future studies by disguising the retest by presenting stimuli in a different sequence, using a different color of answer sheet, or adding spurious stimuli. The third objective of the study was the exploration of various testing procedures and the use of behavioral observation to gain a rough confirmation or denial of the truthfulness of student responses. With regard to procedure, it was observed that students responded to stimuli before they heard all of the stimulus, and thus did not need the luxury of a 15-second response period. This suggests that more questions could be asked about the same stimulus, or more stimuli could be presented in a given amount of time.

Whether or not students should be allowed to respond before hearing the complete stimulus is another question. Through such action, they may be giving a behavioral clue of the extent to which their own cultural environment stereotypes generic styles of music and the "appropriate" response to these styles. Frequently in this study students showed approval or disapproval behavior within three seconds of the beginning of a popular or classical music stimulus.

The seven-step bipolar response scale used in this study caused no problem. There was no evidence of a directional response set, so alternate forms of the response sheet were not found to be worthwhile in view of the extra effort required when coding responses. There was very little tendency to copy from other students' responses, and this was easily controlled with verbal admonitions. An additional possible control measure would be to print the same answer sheet on paper of different colors.

Similarly, no difficulties were caused by using sound stimuli of varying duration or by using ambient sound to anchor the preference scales. All stimulus durations were found to be long enough to give a true picture of the generic style, and time was saved and music frustration avoided by eschewing the standard 30- or 45-second durations used in some studies.

As previously mentioned, behavioral observation was quite helpful in furnishing data about appropriate response periods and similar administrative matters. Berlyne (1971) presented and discussed observable behavioral correlates of aesthetic perception, and with sufficiently structured behavioral observation, information about the true nature of the listener's affective response could be furnished. Dorow (1977) used videotaping to good advantage in a somewhat similar study. The research task is one of measuring relevant observable behavior in a way that will be unobtrusive, yet accurate.

With regard to stylistic preference, the objective of this study was to identify the most preferred generic style among those presented and to find the critical competitors to that style if any existed. The studies of Greer et al. have consistently found a strong preference for rock music among upper elementary, middle school, and junior high age groups. This finding has generally been supported in other studies, but most of them have not used a comprehensive sampling of other generic styles that benefit from media acceptance, peer group and family endorsement, and that make limited cognitive demands upon the listener. These are the styles most likely to qualify as critical competitors to rock music, and several of these styles were investigated through SOPI.

In this study rock music was not confirmed as the most preferred style. Easy-listening pop music was most preferred, while ragtime, dixieland, band-march, country & western/bluegrass, and randomly generated electronic stimuli earned preference scores statistically comparable to that of rock. In both a practical and a statistical sense these styles qualified as critical competitors. The implication of this finding is that teachers should not consider rock music the only generic style that benefits from an already established degree of student acceptance. This study was limited by the fact that only one example of each generic style was included, and in some cases students may have responded to the idiosyncrasies of a particular music example instead of the actual generic style being measured. This limitation would justify caution in interpreting the present findings.

The exploratory factor analysis conducted in this study disclosed four interpretable factors, which were named Establishment Music, Novel Timbres, Rhythmic Dynamism, and People's Music, respectively. The first two factors seem secure in their characterizations, but questions may be posed about the second two. The high loading stimuli on Factor 3 may represent an optimistic, upbeat ambience as much as they represent rhythmic vitality. Factor 4 has been described as nonestablishment in nature, but it correlates .275 with Factor 1, which represents Establishment Music.

Continued research is probably the best answer to the factor clarification problem, and multiple replications of the same generic style within a test will be most desirable in future studies. This will permit use of the internal consistency model as well as that of test-retest for reliability assessment. Important qualities to vary within a generic style would include tempo, performing medium, and performer's sex when a vocal soloist is prominent. Since the variables thought to underlie taste cannot be fully explored through simple preference statements, a more comprehensive form of response should be investigated. Finally, this line of research should be extended across age levels so that important issues in the chronological development of music taste may be identified for systematic study.

Reference Notes

1. LeBlanc, A. *A preliminary model of sources of variation in musical taste.* Paper presented at the meeting of the Music Educators National Conference, Atlanta, Ga., April 1977.
   LeBlanc, A. *A proposed model of sources of variation in musical taste.* Paper presented to the XIII Congress of the International Society for Music Education, London, Ontario, Canada, August 1978.
2. Forsythe, J. L. Evaluation. In G. R. Corradino, *Muscogee music project* (Title III ESEA Project No. 106-3-70-029). Columbus, Ga.: Muscogee County School District, 1972.

3. Kuhn, T. L. *Reliability of a technique for assessing musical preference in young children.* Paper presented at the meeting of the Music Educators National Conference, Atlantic City, N. J., March 1976.
4. Abeles, H. F. *Value judgments and construction of rating instruments to measure affective behavior.* Paper presented at the meeting of the National Council on Measurement in Education, Chicago, April 1974.

References

Bartlett, D. L. Effect of repeated listenings on structural discrimination and affective response. *Journal of Research in Music Education*, 1973, *21*, 302–317.

Berlyne, D. E. *Aesthetics and psychobiology.* New York: Appleton-Century-Crofts, 1971.

Campbell, D. T., & Fiske, D. W. Convergent and discriminant validation by the multitrait-multimethod matrix. *Psychological Bulletin*, 1959, *56*, 81–105.

Cattell, R. B., & Saunders, D. R. Musical preferences and personality diagnosis: I. A factorization of one hundred and twenty themes. *Journal of Social Psychology*, 1954, *39*, 3–24.

Cattell, R. B. The meaning and strategic use of factor analysis. In R. B. Cattell (Ed.), *Handbook of multivariate experimental psychology.* Chicago: Rand McNally, 1966.

Cook, S. W., & Selltiz, C. A multiple-indicator approach to attitude measurement. *Psychological Bulletin*, 1964, *62*, 36–55.

Dorow, L. G. The effect of teacher approval/disapproval ratios on student music selection and concert attentiveness. *Journal of Research in Music Education*, 1977, *25*, 32–40.

Duerksen, G. L. Some effects of expectation on evaluation of recorded musical performance. *Journal of Research in Music Education*, 1972, *20*, 268–272.

Farnsworth, P. R. *Musical taste: Its measurement and cultural nature.* Stanford, Calif.: Stanford University Press, 1950.

Greer, R. D., Dorow, L. G., Wachhaus, G., & White, E. R. Adult approval and students' music selection behavior. *Journal of Research in Music Education*, 1973, *21*, 345–354.

Greer, R. D., Dorow, L. G., & Randall, A. Music listening preferences of elementary school children. *Journal of Research in Music Education*, 1974, *22*, 284–291.

Harman, H. H. *Modern factor analysis* (3rd ed.). Chicago: University of Chicago Press, 1976.

Hedden, S. K. Listeners' responses to music in relation to autochthonous and experiential factors. *Journal of Research in Music Education*, 1973, *21*, 225–238.

Hevner, K. The affective character of major and minor modes in music. *American Journal of Psychology*, 1935, *47*, 103–118.

Hevner, K. Experimental studies of the elements of expression in music. *American Journal of Psychology*, 1936, *48*, 246–268.

Hevner, K. The affective value of pitch and tempo in music. *American Journal of Psychology*, 1937, *49*, 621–630.

Inglefield, H. G. Conformity behavior reflected in the musical preferences of adolescents. *Contributions to Music Education*, 1972, *1*, 56–65.

Keston, M. J., & Pinto, I. M. Possible factors influencing music preference. *Journal of Genetic Psychology*, 1955, *86*, 101–113.

McMullen, P. T. Influence of number of different pitches and melodic redundancy on preference responses. *Journal of Research in Music Education*, 1974, *22*, 198–204.

McMullen, P. T. Influence of distributional redundancy in rhythmic sequences on judged complexity ratings. *Bulletin of the Council for Research in Music Education*, 1976, *46*, 23–30.

McMullen, P. T., & Arnold, M. J. Preference and interest as functions of distributional redundancy in rhythmic sequences. *Journal of Research in Music Education*, 1976, *24*, 22–31.

Nie, N. E., Hull, C. H., Jenkins, J. G., Steinbrenner, K., & Bent, D. H. *Statistical package for the social sciences* (2nd ed.). New York: McGraw-Hill, 1975.

Radocy, R. D. Effects of authority figure biases on changing judgments of musical events. *Journal of Research in Music Education*, 1976, *24*, 119–128.

Rummel, R. J. *Applied factor analysis.* Evanston, Ill.: Northwestern University Press, 1970.

Summers, G. F. Introduction. In G. F. Summers (Ed.), *Attitude measurement.* Chicago: Rand McNally, 1970.

Wapnick, J. A review of research on attitude and preference. *Bulletin of the Council for Research in Music Education*, 1976, *48*, 1–20.

■ Michigan State University
East Lansing

The purpose of this study was to measure the effects of style, tempo, and performing medium on fifth-rade students' expressed music listening preference. A listening test was administered to 107 students in four classes in central Michigan. Test reliability was evaluated in terms of common factor concentration and stability across time, and behavior observation was used to help interpret results. A preference hierarchy emerged in which the popular styles were most favored and correlation analysis indicated that style was most strongly related to preference. A three-way repeated measures analysis of variance disclosed a significant three-way interaction. An examination of charted cell means indicated a strong effect for style, which was noticeably suppressed by performance in the instrumental medium. Across pooled styles there was a slight preference for faster tempos and the instrumental medium.

Albert LeBlanc *Michigan State University, East Lansing*

JRME 1981, VOLUME 29, NUMBER 2, PAGES 143–156

Effects of Style, Tempo, and Performing Medium on Children's Music Preference

This study is part of a continuing series intended to present, test, and refine a theory of music preference. LeBlanc (1980) has presented a theoretical model that attempts to explain the influences at work on a listener who is making a music preference decision. This model has been revised and incorporated into a formally stated theory.[1] Its most recent revision is presented in Figure 1. The purpose of this study was to test the effects of three physical properties—style, tempo, and performing medium—on children's expressed music preference.

Style is considered a physical property of music because a composer's adherence to a particular one restricts the music devices available at a given point. This restriction is especially evident in the popular styles, with their traditions of tempo and performing medium. Style preference data has often been con-

---

[1]Albert LeBlanc. *An interactive theory of music preference.* Paper presented at the meeting of the College Music Society, San Antonio, Texas, October 1979.

This study was supported by a Michigan State University College of Arts and Letters All-University Research Grant.

Requests for reprints should be sent to Albert LeBlanc, Department of Music, Michigan State University, East Lansing 48824.

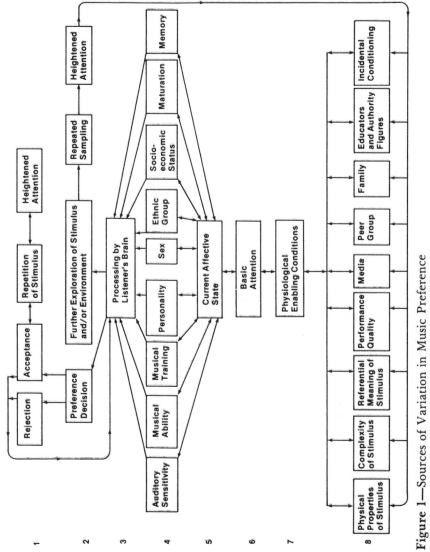

Figure 1—Sources of Variation in Music Preference

sidered a byproduct in studies whose primary focus was on something else. The literature was reviewed by Wapnick (1976).

Many previous studies exploring the effects of tempo and performing medium on listener response have not focused on music preference per se. Schoen and Gatewood (1927), Gundlach (1935), Hevner (1937), Rigg (1940), Middleton, Fay, Kerr, and Amft (1944), and Eagle (1971) have examined the mood effects of music as measured by subjects' responses to descriptive words while listening to music examples. Henkin (1955), Huebner (1976), and LeBlanc (1979) have conducted relevant studies in which the dependent variable was subjects' expressed music preference.

Gundlach (1935), Henkin (1955), and LeBlanc (1979) interpreted factors potentially related to tempo in exploratory factor analyses of listener preference responses as "dynamical," "rhythm," and "rhythmic dynamism," respectively. Henkin's "orchestral color" and LeBlanc's "novel timbres" factors may have some bearing on performing medium.

Hevner (1937) concluded that slow tempos express dignity, calmness, and sadness while fast tempos indicate happiness and restlessness. Rigg (1940) confirmed these findings and speculated that tempo might have more influence over the emotional suggestiveness of music than any other single factor. Examining listener preference responses to art music stimuli, Huebner (1976) found a statistically significant interaction between tempo and different approaches to listening among sixth-grade students.

Wapnick (1980) asked subjects to set piano music excerpts to the most preferred tempo, using a continuously variable control dial linked to a Lexicon Corporation Varispeech II Speed/Time Compressor/Expander. This task could be considered analogous to making a preference response. With college music majors Wapnick found a statistically significant interaction between preferred tempo and excerpt familiarity. When pitch and timbre were held constant through experimental design, Wapnick's subjects showed a bias toward fast tempos. This bias was distinctly greater for music examples familiar to subjects.

In the area of research on performing medium, Schoen and Gatewood (1927) concluded that vocal music had more power than instrumental music to elicit a definite emotional response, attributing this advantage to the presence of words. Middleton, Fay, Kerr, & Amft (1944) found popular vocal music more effective than instrumental waltzes in reducing college students' feelings of tiredness or unpleasantness. In contrast, Eagle (1971) obtained mood responses that were significantly higher for instrumental than for vocal music. He observed that subjects responded differently to vocal and instrumental music even though both performing media may seem to present music that reflects the same mood qualities. Gaston (1951) felt that the most stimulative type of music is that performed in the instrumental medium. He also placed great emphasis on the effect of rhythm in bringing about mood change through the use of music. Gaston's interest in using music factors (physical properties) to encourage mood change in listeners is shared by many music therapists.

The primary objective of this study was to assess the effect of different generic styles, fast and slow tempos, and vocal and instrumental performing media on children's expressed music preference. Secondary objectives were to survey comparative preference for a variety of generic styles and to measure the reliability of the preference test that was developed for this study.

Generic styles were defined here as broad stylistic categories used to specify identifiable types of music within the concert and popular music traditions. It was assumed that a student's confidential self-report was a viable way to measure music preference and that student response to the music examples used was indicative of student response to that style in general. The study was limited to fifth-grade students.

PROCEDURE

A listening tape of music examples was prepared, incorporating fast and slow vocal and instrumental excerpts within the generic styles of rock/pop, country, older jazz, newer jazz, and art music. For exploratory purposes a style category of band music was created. Because of the rarity of solo voice recordings with band, two additional rock/pop examples were paired with these to complete the 24 example tape. The musical phrase determined the length of each excerpt, and excerpts ranged from 26 to 48 seconds in duration, with a mean of 36 seconds.

Examples were chosen according to the way style projected aurally as opposed to relying on the most typical stylistic associations of performers. Assignment to style categories was supported by reference to the generic style popularity charts in *Billboard* magazine and airplay on radio programs devoted to specific styles. Because it was difficult to find pure instrumental examples within the rock/pop and country styles, instrumental sections within vocal compositions were used when necessary.

An effort was made to select examples that would provide a clear contrast of tempo. Slow examples ranged from M.M. beat note = 40 to 80 with a mean of 60, while fast examples ranged from M.M. beat note = 120 to 280 with a mean of 160. There was a danger that very slow examples might be heard subdivided, with each subdivision taken as a beat and very fast examples heard as one beat to the measure. This would cause problems only if it changed the general impression of tempo given by the music example. To check this, three music students independently measured the tempo of each example using an aural/visual electric metronome. In addition to measuring actual tempo, the students were asked to give their subjective categorization of each example as either fast or slow. A few examples were heard subdivided or one beat to the measure, but no reversals were reported between fast and slow tempo. Examples were placed on the tape in random sequence and are shown in Table 1.

The response sheet consisted of 24 seven-step response continua anchored by the words "like" and "dislike." The recorded tape and its response sheet were called the Style, Tempo, and Medium Preference Index (STEMPI).

The preference measure was administered to 107 students from four classes in central Michigan. Three classes were in a predominantly rural area while one was in an urban district. There were few black students, but Hispanic and American Indian minorities were well represented. The overall socioeconomic status of the sample was lower middle class. Behavior observation was carried out during each test administration as a rough check on the truthfulness of student responses, and to gather contextual information useful in interpreting the results of the study.

Table 1—Preference Results on the First Administration of STEMPI

Rank	Rating Mean	SD	Style, Tempo, Medium	Performer/Title	Duration	Record Label, Number
1	6.83	.82	Rock/Pop, Fast, Vocal	Andrew Gold/ "Lonely Boy"[a]	:44	Asylum/1086
2	6.72	.81	Rock/Pop, Fast, Vocal	Heart/ "Barracuda"	:40	Portrait/34799
3	6.61	1.23	Country, Fast, Vocal	Carpenters/ "Sweet, Sweet Smile"	:38	A & M/SP-4703
4	6.46	1.25	Rock/Pop, Slow, Vocal	Carly Simon/ "Nobody Does It Better"[a]	:38	Elektra/E-45413-A
5	6.40	1.46	Rock/Pop, Fast, Instrumental	Queen/"Liar"[b]	:29	Elektra/EKS-75064
6	6.31	1.49	Rock/Pop, Slow, Vocal	Leo Sayer/ "When I Need You"	:48	Warner Bros./BSK 3101
7	5.86	2.02	Rock/Pop, Slow, Instrumental	Peter Gabriel/ "Waiting for the Big One"[b]	:31	Atco/SD36-147
8	5.59	2.15	Country, Slow, Vocal	Cal Smith/ "Come See about Me"	:26	MCA/2266
9	5.48	2.14	Band, Fast, Instrumental	Eastman Wind Ensemble/ "Barnum and Bailey's Favorite"[a]	:33	Mercury/50113
10	5.33	1.97	Country, Slow, Instrumental	Emmylou Harris/ "Making Believe"[b]	:37	Warner Bros./BSK 3115
11	5.29	2.10	Country, Fast, Instrumental	Brown, Sullivan & Co./ "Essence of Sequatchie County"	:30	Sequatchie/NR-1933
12	5.23	1.98	New Jazz, Fast, Instrumental	Shelly Manne and His Men/ "Bernie's Tune"	:27	Contemporary/C 3516
13	4.72	2.38	Old Jazz, Fast, Instrumental	Muggsy Spanier and His Ragtime Band/"At Sundown"	:26	RCA/LPM-1295
14	4.18	2.46	Old Jazz, Fast, Vocal	Lee Wiley/ "Indiana"	:37	Monmouth/MES 7041

Table 1—Continued

Rank	Mean	SD	Style, Tempo, Medium	Performer/Title	Duration	Record Label, Number
15	3.99	2.15	Art Music, Fast, Instrumental	Czech Philharmonic/ "Slavonic Dance No. 5, Op. 46" (Dvořák)	:34	Parliament/PLP-121-2
16	3.83	2.20	New Jazz, Slow, Instrumental	Flip Phillips/ "Around Midnight"	:37	(Taped from broadcast)
17	3.64	2.67	New Jazz, Slow, Vocal	Cleo Laine/ "Send In the Clowns"	:42	RCA/LPL 1-5015
18	3.34	2.32	Old Jazz, Slow, Instrumental	Paul Barbarin/ "Crescent Blues"	:39	Atlantic/1215
19	3.03	2.26	Band, Slow, Instrumental	Eastman Wind Ensemble/ "Song without Words" (Holst)[a]	:36	Mercury/MG50088
20	3.01	2.43	New Jazz, Fast, Vocal	Rita Coolidge/ "Mean to Me"	:34	A & M/SP4531
21	2.98	1.96	Art Music, Slow, Instrumental	Symphony Orchestra of Southwest German Radio/"Allegro Moderato from Seventh Symphony" (Bruckner)	:42	Vox/VBX117
22	2.33	1.96	Old Jazz, Slow, Vocal	Louis Armstrong/"Just a Closer Walk with Thee"	:32	Audio Fidelity/ AFSD5924
23	2.04	1.79	Art Music, Fast, Vocal	Dietrich Fischer-Dieskau/ "Am Feierabend" (Schubert)	:34	Angel/3628 3S
24	1.26	.81	Art Music, Slow, Vocal	Maureen Forrester/"Wenn mein Schatz Hochzeit macht" (Mahler)	:39	RCA/LM-2371

Note. Ratings from one = lowest preference to seven = highest preference
[a] These examples were deleted from the analysis of variance to obtain a balanced design.
[b] Exclusively instrumental segments were excerpted from these vocal compositions.

RESULTS

A test-retest procedure was carried out to measure the test's reliability in terms of the stability of total scores over an eight-day interval. All four classes took the test twice, with 101 students present at both testings. This yielded a Pearson correlation of .87 between test and retest total scores.

Coefficient alpha was computed as an index of common factor concentration, giving the proportion of test variance attributable to common factors among the items. In the case of STEMPI, the presumed common factor would be an individual's preference for listening to various kinds of music. Cronbach (1951) writes that coefficient alpha used with this interpretation serves purposes claimed for indexes of homogeneity. He is critical of test homogeneity as a measurement ideal, and points out that alpha can be high even when items have small intercorrelations. A large alpha indicates that a large proportion of test variance can be attributed to the principal factor running through the test. These considerations would make coefficient alpha a highly appropriate reliability estimate for STEMPI, which attempted to measure comparative listening preference for widely disparate music styles.

An alpha of .88 was obtained for the total test at its first administration, and this rose to .89 at retest. Four of STEMPI's 24 music examples were deleted to balance the analysis of variance design, so alpha was computed for the resulting 20-example test, yielding a coefficient of .86. Very little reliability was lost in deleting the four examples. The style subtests gave alphas of .50 for rock/pop, .73 for country, .79 for older jazz, .68 for newer jazz, and .50 for art music. Each style subtest consisted of four music examples.

Although most students took the test twice, their initial response is presented here in the belief that it is a better sample of affective response (see Table 1). Results confirmed the findings of previous studies (Greer, Dorow, & Randall, 1974; LeBlanc, 1979) that indicated a preference for rock/pop music over art music at this age level. A preference hierarchy emerged (see Table 2).

A correlation analysis was carried out to measure the relationship of the three design variables (style, tempo, and medium) with student preference response. Simple Pearson correlations were computed between the design variables and preference response, resulting in rs of .48 for style ($p < .01$), .17 for tempo, and .01 for medium. Multiple correlations were computed to determine the effect of adding the second and third design variables to a regression

Table 2—Preference Results According to Generic Style

Style	Rank	Rating X	SD
Rock/Pop[a]	1	6.43	0.34
Country	2	5.70	0.62
Band[b]	3	4.25	1.73
New Jazz	4	3.93	0.94
Old Jazz	5	3.64	1.04
Art Music	6	2.57	1.18

[a]Based on six examples
[b]Based on two examples

equation set up to predict preference response from style. When tempo was added to style, R rose from .48 (the value of the simple correlation) to .51. The addition of medium raised R to .53. When these multiple correlations were squared, 23% of preference variation was explained by style, 26% by style and tempo, and 28% by style, tempo, and medium.

The style variable was broken down into its constituent categories and simple correlations computed with preference response. The resulting rs were .42 for rock/pop ($p < .01$); .20 for country ($p < .05$); $-.05$ for band, $-.12$ for newer jazz, and $-.35$ for art music ($p < .01$). A negative correlation indicates a lower preference response in the context of the styles being measured.

Partial correlations were computed to measure the relationship between each design variable and preference response with the effect of other design variables statistically removed. Results in Table 3 show that the highest partial correlations between design variables and preference response are usually obtained by controlling the other design variables.

Significance testing of the effects of the design variables was carried out using a three-way multivariate analysis of variance (Finn, 1974). Two examples of band music had been included in STEMPI for exploratory purposes, and two extra rock/pop examples had been added to maintain a balance between vocal and instrumental examples. These four examples were dropped from the analysis to create a design that was completely balanced on all classification variables. This produced a $5 \times 2 \times 2$ repeated measures design with five levels of generic style, two levels of tempo, and two levels of performing medium. The analysis was based entirely on data from the first test administration.

A multivariate model was chosen over the more traditional mixed model, which uses subjects as a classification, because the multivariate model is not bound by assumptions of equal variances and covariances (compound symmetry) across the repeated measures. In the multivariate model the repeated measures of music preference were not treated as a factor in the sampling design but as multiple intercorrelated responses from the same subjects (Finn & Mattsson, 1978). The effects of each style classification were assessed through an examination of a priori simple contrasts of means using art music as the standard of comparison. Previous research had indicated that art music could be expected to receive the lowest preference score.

Table 3—First and Second Order Partial Correlations between Preference Response and Design Variables

Variables Correlated and Controlled	Partial Correlation
Style Controlling Tempo	.49**
Style Controlling Medium	.50**
Style Controlling Tempo and Medium	.51**
Tempo Controlling Style	.20*
Tempo Controlling Medium	.17
Tempo Controlling Style and Medium	.20*
Medium Controlling Style	.15
Medium Controlling Tempo	.01
Medium Controlling Style and Tempo	.15

*$p < .05$
**$p < .01$

The multivariate null hypothesis posited that the 20 cells of the ANOVA design would have equal means. Rao's approximation of the likelihood ratio criterion yielded $F(19,88) = 128.19$, $p < .01$. The multivariate null hypothesis was rejected because of significant variation attributable to the design variables.

A step-down analysis was conducted to test for the unique effect of each element in the ANOVA design. After the first step-down test, which is the same as a univariate F, the procedure becomes analogous to a set of sequentially ordered analyses of covariance, eliminating the effect of all elements that have already been tested. Because of this, ANOVA elements were organized in a simple-to-complex hierarchy so that complex elements would be tested first for a unique and significant contribution to overall variation. If these complex elements could be eliminated early in the step-down procedure, a more economical explanation of music preference behavior could be advanced. Table 4 presents the results of step-down analysis. The first F to be interpreted indicated a significant three-way interaction of style, tempo, and medium. This meant that none of the ANOVA elements appearing earlier in the order of elimination could validly be tested because their tests were confounded with

Table 4—Multivariate Step-Down Analysis

Source of Variation	df_1, df_2	F^a
Style (S)[b]		
S1	19, 87	311.65**
S2	19, 86	54.53**
S3	19, 85	7.22**
S4	19, 84	43.80**
Tempo (T)	19, 83	8.52**
Medium (M)	19, 82	3.11
Two-Way Interactions		
S1 × T	19, 81	0.12
S2 × T	19, 80	2.08
S3 × T	19, 79	0.45
S4 × T	19, 78	17.81**
S1 × M	19, 77	24.38**
S2 × M	19, 76	12.27**
S3 × M	19, 75	7.72**
S4 × M	19, 74	3.82*
T × M	19, 73	14.06**
Three-Way Interactions		
S1 × T × M	19, 72	1.58
S2 × T × M	19, 71	0.07
S3 × T × M	19, 70	10.37**
S4 × T × M	19, 69	9.43**

Note. Step-down tests should be interpreted from the bottom up.
[a]Differentiation of the step-down Fs
[b]The effect of different styles was assessed by the following symbolic contrasts: S1 = Rock/Pop vs. Art Music, S2 = Country vs. Art Music, S3 = Older Jazz vs. Art Music, and S4 = Newer Jazz vs. Art Music.
*$p < .05$
**$p < .01$

significant variation due to the effect of the last element. Because the significant interaction precluded an interpretation of simple effects, cell means were charted across various combinations of design variables. This facilitated a study of the interaction. The most informative charts are presented in Figures 2 and 3.

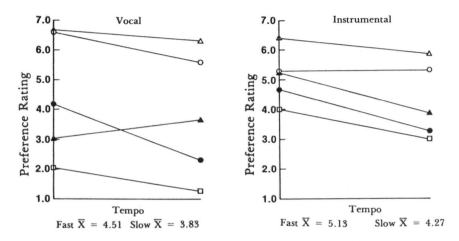

Preference by Style and Tempo within Medium

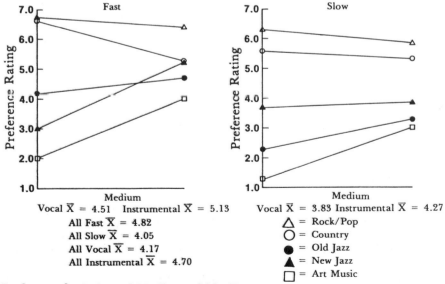

Preference by Style and Medium within Tempo

Figure 2

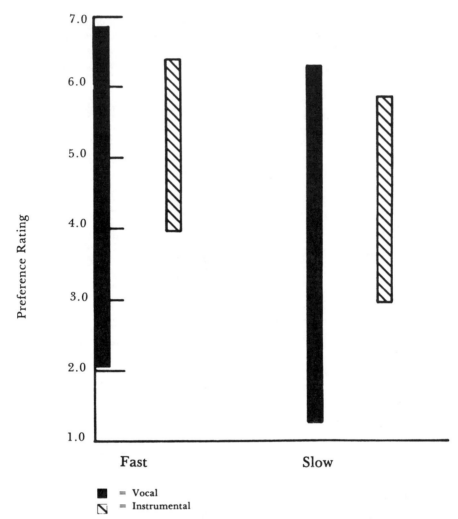

Fast   Slow

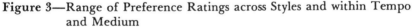 = Vocal

        = Instrumental

Figure 3—Range of Preference Ratings across Styles and within Tempo and Medium

DISCUSSION

Reliability of the test was considered adequate. Music preference results were not surprising in view of previous research findings. Very low standard deviations for "Barracuda," "Lonely Boy," and "Wenn mein Schatz Hochzeit macht" indicate a comparative unanimity of preference for the first two and dislike for the third title. The highest ranking examples are almost exclusively from styles favored by the broadcast media and adolescent peer group. Considered in the light of previous research, this tends to substantiate the influence of the media and peer group variables described in LeBlanc's theoretical model.

That a band music example, "Barnum and Bailey's Favorite," rates fairly high does not argue against this interpretation. That example actually gets a fair amount of airplay in radio and television commercials, and marching bands are supported by the adolescent peer group, as observed at school athletic events. Within the art music category, instrumental examples were preferred over vocal, and fast examples were preferred over slow ones. Vocal art music was ranked at the very bottom.

Behavior observation data may be considered at this point to aid in the interpretation of preference results. Students expressed disappointment when some examples were finished, and 75% of these examples had benefited from recent radio airplay. When students patted their feet to the beat or moved their bodies to the music, 77% of these examples were fast and the remaining ones had a very obvious beat. This observation calls to mind the rhythmic dynamism factor, which emerged in LeBlanc's (1979) factor analysis, and suggests that it is not definable in terms of tempo alone. Students responded to some examples (83% of which were slow) with derision. Vibrato was the most prominent target of mimicry when students made fun of vocal examples (performed by altos or contraltos) they didn't like. The most typical method of mimicking vibrato was rubbing an extended finger up and down the throat while pretending to sing or howl toward the ceiling. The mimicry of instrumental performers occurred whenever there was a prominent instrumental part. This appeared to have no direct connection with the preference results. Interestingly, students never made a mistake in identifying the instrument heard.

Several idiosyncracies of particular examples were spotlighted by behavior observation. Cleo Laine's British accent and the German language in both vocal art music examples received ridicule from student listeners. In every case this ridicule came soon after the vocal entry; students were not critical during the instrumental introduction. Students showed a strong negative reaction to Louis Armstrong's extremely slow performance of "Just a Closer Walk with Thee." Two of the verbal comments made were "Ole Grandpa!" and "That's supposed to be faster, isn't it?" Students were greatly amused by the string bass solo that led into Rita Coolidge's performance of "Mean to Me."

Simple correlation analysis showed that style was by far the strongest design variable in terms of preference response, with tempo showing a moderate relationship to the criterion and medium a negligible one. When multiple correlations were squared, they indicated that tempo and medium contributed 5% to the 28% total of explained criterion variation. Simple correlations of each style with preference response were in agreement with the trend seen in preference ratings. Perhaps the most interesting of the correlation results was the partial correlation analysis, which showed that the relationship of each design variable with the preference rating criterion could be strengthened by controlling the other two design variables. This was especially notable in the case of performing medium, whose correlation with preference rose from .01 to .15 when the effect of style was removed. The presence of the style variable was masking the relationship between performing medium and preference.

The ANOVA finding of significant interactions had been foreshadowed by the partial correlation results. The nature of the interactions and the most important findings of this study may best be approached through a careful study of Figures 2 and 3. In Figure 2, interaction appears as a difference in slope between the charted lines that represent each style. The effect of style is prominent throughout Figure 2, with few reversals of the established preference hierarchy. The styles supported by the broadcast media and adolescent peer group are consistently rated higher. The effect of style is strongest in the vocal medium, and it is noticeably suppressed in the instrumental medium. This suppressing effect operates on both ends of the preference spectrum in fast and slow tempos and is portrayed graphically in Figure 3. Across pooled styles there is a slight preference for faster tempos ($\overline{X}$ = 4.82 for fast, $\overline{X}$ = 4.05 for slow) and for the instrumental medium ($\overline{X}$ = 4.70 for instrumental, $\overline{X}$ = 4.17 for vocal).

Is there a plausible explanation for these unexpected findings? Performing art music in the instrumental medium may remove some of the elements most disliked by young listeners, such as lyrics in a foreign language and the prominent use of vibrato. By the same token, performing rock/pop and country music in the instrumental medium would remove some of the most popular aspects of these styles, such as familiar lyrics in the colloquial native language based on romance, and singers made familiar through media exposure.

CONCLUSIONS

Teachers who want to encourage a positive listener response to jazz and art music should introduce fast instrumental examples first and progress to slow instrumental, fast vocal, and slow vocal examples, in that order. This sequence would take advantage of the entering affect levels found in this study. Use of the instrumental medium seems to negate the strong style-oriented entering preference that works to the disadvantage of art music. There is a slight but general preference for faster tempos and for the instrumental performing medium. Band music seems to be the form of art music most likely to function as a critical competitor to the popular styles. It might be good to introduce it first in a teaching sequence designed to promote listening to art music.

Future research should include a similar study of the effect of tempo and performing medium, using style as a blocking factor with comparatively few levels. As many examples as possible should be used within ANOVA classification cells to reduce the influence of idiosyncratic reaction to specific examples. Extremely fast and slow examples should be avoided because student reaction to extremes of tempo may differ from their reaction to moderate tempo variation. Within the area of vocal music, the effects of a performer's sex, vibrato, vocal range, and language of lyrics are of interest. Preference for marching and concert band music in comparison to other styles should be explored.

REFERENCES

Cronbach, L. J. Coefficient alpha and the internal structure of tests. *Psychometrika*, 1951, *16*, 297-334.

Eagle, C. T., Jr. Effects of existing mood and order of presentation of vocal and instrumental music on rated mood responses to that music. (Doctoral dissertation, University of Kansas, 1971). *Dissertation Abstracts International*, 1971, *32*, 2118A. (University Microfilms No. 71-27,139)

Finn, J. D. *A general model for multivariate analysis*. New York: Holt, Rinehart & Winston, 1974.

Finn, J. D., & Mattsson, I. *Multivariate analysis in educational research*. Chicago: National Educational Resources, 1978.

Gaston, E. T. Dynamic music factors in mood change. *Music Educators Journal*, February 1951, *37*, 42-44.

Greer, R. D., Dorow, L. G., & Randall, A. Music listening preferences of elementary school children. *Journal of Research in Music Education*, 1974, *22*, 284-291.

Gundlach, R. Factors determining the characterization of musical phrases. *American Journal of Psychology*, 1935, *46*, 624-643.

Henkin, R. I. A factorial study of the components of music. *Journal of Psychology*, 1955, *39*, 161-181.

Hevner, K. The affective value of pitch and tempo in music. *American Journal of Psychology*, 1937, *49*, 621-630.

Huebner, M. A. The effect of three listening methods and two tempi on musical attitude of sixth-grade students. (Doctoral dissertation, University of Maryland, 1976). *Dissertation Abstracts International*, 1976, *37*, 3257A. (University Microfilms No. 76-27,394)

LeBlanc, A. Generic style music preferences of fifth-grade students. *Journal of Research in Music Education*, 1979, *27*, 255-270.

LeBlanc, A. Outline of a proposed model of sources of variation in musical taste. *Bulletin of the Council for Research in Music Education*, 1980, *61*, 29-34.

Middleton, W. C., Fay, P. J., Kerr, W. A., & Amft, F. The effect of music on feelings of restfulness-tiredness and pleasantness-unpleasantness. *Journal of Psychology*, 1944, *17*, 299-318.

Rigg, M. G. Speed as a determiner of musical mood. *Journal of Experimental Psychology*, 1940, *27*, 566-571.

Schoen, M., & Gatewood, E. L. The mood effects of music. In M. Schoen (Ed.), *The effects of music*. New York: Harcourt Brace Jovanovich, 1927.

Schoen, M., & Gatewood, E. L. Problems related to the mood effects of music. In M. Schoen (Ed.), *The effects of music*. New York: Harcourt Brace Jovanovich, 1927.

Wapnick, J. A review of research on attitude and preference. *Bulletin of the Council for Research in Music Education*, 1976, *48*, 1-20.

Wapnick, J. Pitch, tempo, and timbral preferences in recorded piano music. *Journal of Research in Music Education*, 1980, *28*, 43-58.

October 28, 1980

This study was designed to investigate empirically the "aesthetic experience" as individually defined by each subject. Subjects (N = 30) were faculty members and advanced graduate students at a large university school of music. Each subject listened to a 20-minute excerpt from Act I of Puccini's La Bohème and simultaneously manipulated the dial of a Continuous Response Digital Interface (CRDI) to indicate perceived aesthetic level. The CRDI dial represented a negative/positive continuum along a 256-degree arc. Data collected were charted graphically to indicate levels of aesthetic response across time. Subjects completed a questionnaire designed to estimate frequency, duration, location, and magnitude of perceived aesthetic experiences and also indicated whether dial manipulation roughly corresponded to these experiences.

Results indicated that there were different responses throughout the excerpt by all subjects. Heightened aesthetic responses were evident during certain parts of the excerpt. "Peak experiences" were relatively short (15 seconds or less in duration), preceded by a period of concentrated focus of attention, and generally followed by an "afterglow" ranging from 15 seconds to several minutes. All subjects reported having at least one aesthetic experience and also reported that movement of the CRDI dial roughly approximated this experience. "Aesthetic responses" for subjects seemed to cluster at many of the same places in the music, with one collective "peak" experience that was represented by the highest and lowest dial movements.

Clifford K. Madsen, Ruth V. Brittin, and Deborah A. Capperella-Sheldon, *Center for Music Research, Florida State University*

JRME 1993, VOLUME 41, NUMBER 1, PAGES 57–69

An Empirical Method for Measuring the Aesthetic Experience to Music

Pleasingness and the representation of beauty in music has current as well as historical significance. For centuries, musicians and philosophers have pondered those attributes of music that give it meaning and lead the listener to a heightened sense of emotion, intellectual engagement, or "aesthetic" responsiveness. Also, certain musical compositions and the need for artistic expression seem to be enduring and timeless in their perennial appeal to listeners.

Langer posited that "*great art is not a direct sensuous pleasure.* If it were, it would appeal—like cake or cocktails—to the untutored as well as to the cultured taste" (1976, p. 205). Langer further states, "Granting ... that the effects do not long outlive their causes, the proposition that music arouses emotions in the listener

For copies of this article, contact Clifford K. Madsen, Center for Music Research, R-71, Florida State University, Tallahassee, Florida 32306-2098.

does not seem, offhand, like a fantastic or mythical assertion" (p. 212–213). Langer maintains that the listener brings a highly individualized and logical imagination to the listening experience. It is the combination of imagination and sound stimulus that generates brief emotional associations and leads to feelingful insight.

Meyer (1956) describes one of the problems in attaining evidence of aesthetic response as the inability of a listener to precisely identify, through time, those musical processes leading to the moment of maximum feelingfulness. Instead, listeners often must rely on inadequate verbal expression in an attempt to convey their experience after it is over. Aesthetic responses in music, which, according to Meyer, are aroused by inhibition of tendencies [creation of tension] and eventual resolution, may be evidenced in two ways: by the observation of overt behavior and by physiological changes.

Reimer (1970) discusses aesthetic experience as being the combination of *both* aesthetic perception (consisting of a number of objective behaviors such as recognizing, discriminating, matching, etc.) and aesthetic reaction. Reimer holds that aesthetic reaction, unlike aesthetic perception, is by nature subjective and thus cannot be taught, controlled, or tested.

Madsen and Madsen (1970) suggest that the "aesthetic experience, which some say represents a somewhat mystical entity, continues to be elusive. Perhaps this 'mystical aesthetic experience' represents the *composite emotional and intellectual responsiveness to music which is modified and reinforced through time and always defined as good*" (p. 44).

The study of aesthetics has a long history that dates from the time of the early Greeks. Scientific or experimental aesthetics, however, represents a relatively new discipline. An important figure in experimental aesthetics was G. T. Fechner, the German psychologist whose *Vorschule der Ästhetik* (1876) established an "experimental" approach to aesthetic study. In this approach, as opposed to metaphysical inquiry, aesthetic pursuits generally take a descriptive form, with researchers attempting to discover, classify, and generalize about works of art and related human activities. Issues of value and meaning are not abandoned, but rather are dealt with indirectly in an attempt to understand the nature of the aesthetic experience and the effects this experience has on human beings. During the mid- to late 19th century, investigators in initial experimental attempts sought to find orders of preference and taste for stimuli such as color, shape, and sound. Berlyne (1974) gave renewed emphasis to this area of empirical investigation when he defined "new" experimental aesthetics. Two key factors involved in the study of aesthetic stimuli and reaction include observation of nonverbal behavior along with verbal descriptions of aesthetic experience, as well as the relationship between psychological and aesthetic response.

Content analysis can be taken to cumbersome extremes, however, as evidenced in the work of Birkoff (1933) who contended that aesthetic measure of a musical stimulus is the "density of the elements of order in the musical structure" (p. 87). Birkoff accounted for every conceivable tangible element in a musical piece, gave it numerical weight according to its consonance or dissonance, and applied those weights to mathematical formulae. The sum was said to represent the aesthetic measure of that music.

Researchers since the early part of the 20th century have compared emotional response to music analysis of structural elements (Birkoff, 1933; Crozier, 1981; Hevner, 1936; Nielzen & Cesarec, 1982). Findings indicate the pairing of mood descriptors with particular musical elements. Adjectives such as "happy, exuberant, joyous, and lively" are most often associated with fast tempi, major modality, loud dynamics, staccato articulations, simple harmonic structures, flowing rhythms, and higher pitches. Descriptors including "sad, reflective, melancholy, longing, and solemn" correspond most often to slower tempi, minor modality, soft dynamics, legato articulations, complex harmonies, firm and slow rhythms, and lower pitches.

Researchers in many studies have attempted to quantify the elements of musical affect. These investigations are largely concerned with considering the effects of isolating and/or manipulating one or more variables and the effects of these variables on listener preference.

Familiarity and complexity in a musical composition have also been examined as variables related to listener preference (Crozier, 1981; Getz, 1966; Hargreaves & Castell, 1987; Heyduk, 1975; Peery & Peery, 1986; Russell, 1986). Conclusions from these studies seem to corroborate Walker's (1981) position that listeners display less liking for simple, consonant tunes and a greater degree of liking as compositions become more structurally complex. As musical pieces become even more complex and dissonant, degree of liking decreases, thus resulting in an inverted U. These findings might explain Berlyne's assertion that there is a point of optimal arousal and that behavior will change to maintain this level.

Other investigations have focused on specific musical elements and their effects on preference (Geringer & Madsen, 1987; LeBlanc, 1981, 1983, 1986, 1988). Results of these studies reveal evidence that music listeners generally select faster tempi when given a choice. Additionally, subjects are more inclined to prefer sharpness or "in-tuneness" to flatness and will preferentially respond to sharp or in-tune intonation over tone quality (Geringer & Madsen, 1981; Madsen & Geringer, 1976).

Some researchers have examined the effects of promotion by disc jockeys, adult approval, peer influence, and group consensus on reported musical preference (Furman & Duke, 1988; Greer, Dorow, Wachaus, & White, 1973; Inglefield, 1982; Russell, 1986). Outcomes of these studies predominantly suggest that each of these variables, to some degree, affect music preference and selection, particularly with young subjects.

Experimental methods of assessment to date have strengthened the available inventory of aesthetic descriptors (i.e., "This music makes me feel happy."). These methods have also provided content analysis to aid the researcher in speculating why the listener responded as he or she did. Self-reports, in the forms of rating scales, checklists, questionnaires, and semantic differentials, have been routinely used in studies concerning liking and preference for music (Goldstein, 1980; Payne, 1983; Russell, 1986; Stratton & Zalanowski, 1984). Yet Crozier stated, "One of the difficulties in evaluating the literature on this topic ... is the interactive nature of aesthetic object and aesthetic response" (p. 433). These self-reports are accurate only to the extent that the listener is able to assess his or her own experience. In most cases, evaluation is made in retrospect, after the stimulus-listener interaction is past.

There are extant and recent methods that offer subjects the opportunity to react to music while responses are being recorded temporally (Clynes & Nettheim, 1982; Hatoh, Kato, Kuwano, & Namba, 1989; Nielsen, 1983, 1987; Namba, Kuwano, Hatch, & Kato, 1989). Nielson (1983) studied what he defined as "tension" by having musically trained subjects press a pair of tongs in accordance with their experienced tension as they listened to Haydn's *Symphony No. 104*, first movement, and Richard Strauss' *Also sprach Zarathustra*, measures 1–75.

Pressure expressed as "tension curves" indicated differentiated tension throughout the examples and an extremely high degree of correspondence between first and second listenings.

Namba and his associates have worked on continuous judgments for years, first applied to loudness levels (Kuwano & Namba, 1985). Recently, they have had subjects press individual adjective keys on a computer that register a corresponding adjective indicative of subjective impression. Using this method of continuous judgment, they suggested that there is some relation between physical properties of musical performance and subject impression; for example, "calm" to tempo and "powerful" to sound intensity levels (Hatoh, Kato, Kuwano, & Namba, 1989).

Clynes (1977) has also used what is described as the "sentograph" to study musical responses as a subject listens to music. Responses are classified into various emotions by subjects' finger-pressure expression.

A most noteworthy study perhaps relating to aspects of the aesthetic experience was reported by Goldstein (1980) who labelled physically felt emotional experiences as "thrills." Goldstein surveyed subjects for information about the "thrills," asking if they had ever experienced them, frequency and duration of the experience, what brought them about, where in the body did these feelings begin, did the feeling spread to other areas of the body, and what did they feel like. Findings indicated that thrills were felt physically and were often begun in the upper spine and back of the neck, subsequently spreading to the rest of the body. Subjects reported that mild thrills lasted only 1 to 5 seconds, while stronger thrills lasted longer. Some subjects noted a relationship between thrills and orgasm. When asked what stimuli result in a thrill, 96% of respondents cited music. Although Goldstein used a questionnaire to obtain thrill information from respondents, he addressed the issue of quantifying duration and intensity of thrills *experienced temporally during music listening* by having subjects raise a particular finger (indicating intensity) and keeping it elevated for the duration of the experience.

It would follow that, since aesthetic experience in music involves a temporal element, some sort of measure through time would be most beneficial in attempting to quantify emotional responsiveness to music. The combination of a microcomputer system and Continuous Response Digital Interface (CRDI) provides this temporal assessment by letting listeners react to musical stimuli in any number of ways while the music is being heard (Brittin, 1991; Gregory, 1989; Madsen, 1990; Madsen & Geringer, 1990; Rentz, 1992; Robinson, 1988). This device has been shown to be a reliable tool in the collection of listener response data. In a study designed to ascertain focus of attention to various musical elements, comparing the responses of musicians and nonmusicians, test-retest reliability for musicians ranged from .82 to .99; nonmusicians from .73 to .91, with an overall mean of .90 (Capperella, 1989). It is conceivable that the CRDI device could have pertinent application in the study of aesthetic experience. Crozier (1981) posited that "an axiom of psychological research in the arts is that response to art is not random" (p. 433). If this is indeed the case, the CRDI may help researchers determine where aesthetic experience (as defined by the listener) occurs within a musical selection as well as allow individual responses to be compared graphically. The CRDI coupled with the listener's assessment of how closely the manipulation of the device reflects aesthetic experience might begin to assuage ambiguity in this area of study.

The purpose of the present study was to investigate empirically what sophisticated musicians considered to be their own aesthetic experience. Purposefully, *no* attempt was made to define the aesthetic experience or to differentiate among the various taxonomic structures or words often used to describe and investigate such concepts as affect, taste, preference, emotion, extramusical variables, musical value, and so on.

There *was* a concerted attempt to select a listening experience deemed free of technical and musical imperfections that was within the common experience of the subjects being tested, and potentially capable of eliciting a differentiated "aesthetic" response.

METHOD

Thirty subjects participated in the study; all were faculty members or advanced graduate students at The Florida State University School of Music. Subjects listened to an excerpt from Puccini's *La Bohème,* recorded by the London Philharmonic with George Solti conducting, Montserrat Caballé, soprano, and Placido Domingo, tenor. The excerpt, familiar to all subjects, consisted of the first act's final 20 minutes and 21 seconds. In part, *La Bohème* was selected because of its familiarity. It was the opera most often presented on Texaco Metropolitan Opera broadcasts since 1940–41 ("'Boheme's' Been Sung," 1989). The excerpt was recorded from a compact disc onto a TDK SA-C60 cassette tape. Listening sessions were conducted using Realistic LV-10 stereo headphones, an Aiwa L50 stereo cassette deck, and a Rotel RX402 receiver. Average intensity level for all subjects was preset at 55 dBA.

Each subject listened to the excerpt and simultaneously manipulated a dial on a Continuous Response Digital Interface (CRDI) device to indicate perceived aesthetic level. The dial was designed to move along a continuum that consisted of a 256-degree arc marked "positive" at the right end and "negative" at the left end (see Figure 1). The dial was affixed to a potentiometer, interfaced with a Sanyo MBC-1250 64k microcomputer using an eight-bit analog-to-digital converter. The interface translated incoming voltage to a digital representation ranging from 0 to 256; that is, placement of the pointer along the dial sent a corresponding voltage that was converted to a numerical rating. These recorded numerical ratings represented the dependent variable across time. With the CRDI's dual-channel capability, subjects were tested in pairs, yet outside each other's viewing of dial manipulation. Data collection was manually initiated with simultaneous keypresses on the cassette player and microcomputer keyboard.

Software, written in C language, was adapted from the extant Continuous Response Observational Data Analysis program developed at the Center for Music Research (Greenfield, 1985). The program provides several samples per second for each channel and, following data collection, charts subjects' responses on temporal graphs. Various sampling rates can be chosen; the sample rate chosen for the present study was five per second.

Subjects were tested in a small laboratory especially arranged for this study. Upon entering the experimental environment, subjects were greeted by one of the experimenters, seated such that the other listener's dial was not visible, and given the following instructions:

"You are going to hear a 20-minute excerpt from Act I of Puccini's *La Bohème.* This study is an attempt to provide ongoing information concerning what you define as the aesthetic experience. As you listen to the music, move the dial corresponding to your aesthetic response. Are there any questions?"

At the listening session's close, participants completed the questionnaire

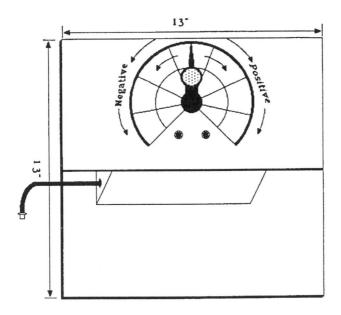

Figure 1. Continuous Response Digital Interface (CRDI) dial.

shown in Figure 2, designed to estimate frequency, duration, location, and magnitude of perceived aesthetic experience. Furthermore, subjects indicated whether manipulation of the dial roughly corresponded to variation of their aesthetic experiences. Four subjects were retested 2 weeks after their initial participation using identical procedures. Reliability for these subjects was assessed by comparing the directionality of responses across each second for both trials (i.e., comparing with 1 second delay the first trial to the second trial across 1221 seconds for direction of response up/down/same). Reliability was calculated by dividing agreements by agreements plus disagreements. Reliability calculated in this manner is not only extremely stringent but retains the contour of the graphic response. Overall, reliability thus calculated was .90.

RESULTS

This study was specifically designed to ascertain empirically the phenomenon of what sophisticated musicians considered to be an aesthetic experience. No attempt was made to define "aesthetic experience." Results of the questionnaire analysis demonstrated that 100% of subjects surveyed ($N = 30$) indicated they had sustained at least one aesthetic experience while listening to the selected excerpt, whereas 70% reported the occurrence of several aesthetic experiences. *All* subjects indicated that movements of the pointer roughly corresponded to variations in their aesthetic experiences. Since this type of empirical demonstration of the aesthetic experience has not been previously established, these findings may represent the major importance of the study in its attempt to quantify this phenomenon.

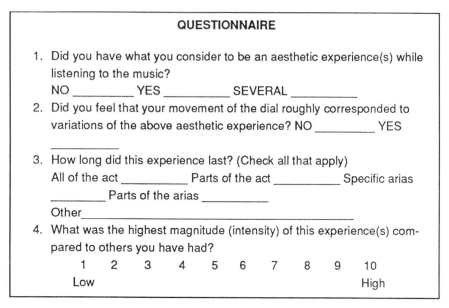

QUESTIONNAIRE

1. Did you have what you consider to be an aesthetic experience(s) while listening to the music?
   NO _____ YES _____ SEVERAL _____
2. Did you feel that your movement of the dial roughly corresponded to variations of the above aesthetic experience? NO _____ YES
   _____
3. How long did this experience last? (Check all that apply)
   All of the act _____ Parts of the act _____ Specific arias
   _____ Parts of the arias _____
   Other_____
4. What was the highest magnitude (intensity) of this experience(s) compared to others you have had?
       1   2   3   4   5   6   7   8   9   10
     Low   High

Figure 2. Questionnaire used in this study.

Additionally, subjects rated the magnitude or intensity of this experience as compared to previous aesthetic experiences on a Likert-type scale ranging from 1 (low) to 10 (high). Results show a mean magnitude rating of 7.32 and a standard deviation of 1.72. Regarding duration and location of peak experiences, subjects indicated heightened experiences in either (a) parts of the act (43%), (b) specific arias (30%) or (c) parts of arias (70%). No participant reported an aesthetic experience lasting the entire excerpt.

Visual analyses of subjects' temporal graphs reveal what seem to be indications of aesthetic experiences, appearing as "peaks," contrasted with areas of lower aesthetic interest, appearing as "valleys." Inspection of individual graphs indicated that various parts of the 20-minute excerpt were perceived somewhat differently by each individual. As an individual subject listened to the excerpt, he/she could move the dial higher, lower, or leave it in the same position. Analyses of individual graphs in temporal relationship to the music indicated that when there was *any* movement of the dial there was, indeed, some "change" in the music that could have stimulated the response. Points of lesser interest generally occurred during musical transitions and points of higher interest occurred during sustained melodic passages. Musical changes could be quite extreme or very subtle: the start of a melody, a slight change in phrase, a change in volume, the slight intensity increase of a singer, or the beginning of a new orchestral texture, to name a few. Obviously, there were many changes occurring during each several seconds. Some dial movement(s) seemed to be more idiosyncratic and experience oriented. For example, one subject who specializes in trumpet turned the dial to its highest position only when the brasses were heard. Similarly, some sopranos moved the dial to its highest position only during the aria "Mi chiamamo Mimi"; tenors during Rudolfo's "Che gelida manina!"

Several of the subjects attempted to "conduct" throughout various parts and commented that it was difficult not to be reminded of past performances. Yet, when indicating high aesthetic responsiveness, most subjects did not hold the dial in its *extreme* position for long duration. Individual subject graphs indicate that most of the extreme high points were of short duration, 15 seconds or less, followed by a gradually descending line.

Figure 3 shows the cumulative graph obtained through the CRDI, although it should be remembered that "group" aesthetic responsiveness is not necessarily the same as individual responsiveness. Also, subjects demonstrated a wide range of responses regarding frequency of change; that is, some listeners continually adjusted the dial, whereas others maintained a stable position for up to several minutes although not at the highest dial setting. When analyzing the composite graph it is evident that the above two "famous arias" represented the highest points for many subjects. However, 100% of responses revealed a critical drop and subsequent peak in aesthetic level between minutes 15 and 18. This is the point in the excerpt just before the final duet, "O soave fanciulla," and the ending of Act I. Because this point represents both the highest and lowest point for *all* subjects in the study, it is analyzed in some detail.

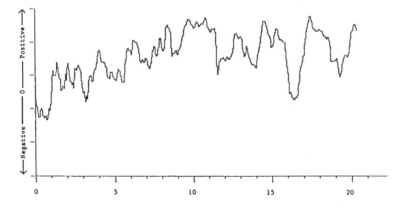

Figure 3. Example of composite graph of data collected with CRDI.

Analysis of responses within this period revealed four points of homogeneity: (a) a substantial drop in aesthetic level (M = 15 minutes, 48 seconds), (b) a low-level plateau (M = 16' 17"), (c) a rise in aesthetic interest (M = 16' 39"), and (d) an aesthetic peak (M = 17' 18"). Means reflect the initiation of each response and correspond with the following musical areas: the close of the soprano's aria, recitative with four men, appearance of the final aria's principal theme, and this theme recurring in the tenor voice being joined by the soprano. Standard deviation of these responses was 22.5 seconds, equivalent to 4.5 measures of the final aria's *Largo sostenuto* tempo as represented in the selected recording. Variables such as individual reaction time, tape speed, manual initiation of data collection, and the microsystem's computational timing are reflected in the standard deviation. That subjects demonstrated complete uniformity in overall response direction, and that mean response times corresponded so closely with specific musical factors seems much more than coincidental and supports the notion that aesthetic experiences may be empirically observed. Furthermore, such experiences may at times be based on some common factor or factors in music and/or its perception. For example, the perceived low point during these measures occurs during a musical transition; the perceived high point begins with a very soft *Largo sostenuto* and return of the main theme, reaching a musical climax with a very loud rendition of the theme sung in unison by tenor and soprano.

Not all subjects, however, indicated the point described in the final aria as the exclusive or highest aesthetic experience. Twenty participants' responses revealed this place represented one of several aesthetic experiences, with others generally occurring during earlier arias. Seven subjects demonstrated a high aesthetic level at this point, although not as high as parts of earlier arias. Three subjects indicated their highest aesthetic peaks at this location only.

Analysis of the questionnaire indicated that the mean number of aesthetic experiences reached during the entire excerpt was 4.5, ranging from one to fourteen with a standard deviation of 3.7. Perceived aesthetic "peaks" and "valleys" as indicated on subjects' graphs appeared somewhat closely grouped perhaps due more to the structure of the aria and recitative, respectively, than to single factors such as dynamic level, tempo, or harmonic complexity, although it is assumed that certain music elements contributed to these more dramatic variations. The excerpt represented a relatively simple diatonic harmonic structure, with little chromatic harmony and few unprepared modulations. Occurrence of the aesthetic experience did not appear, then, to be dependent on compositional complexity; perhaps it related only to melodic and/or dynamic considerations. Melodic attentiveness has been demonstrated as a primary focal point of attention for musicians and attentiveness to dynamics as a focal point for nonmusicians (Madsen & Geringer, 1990).

Regarding the measuring device used, 83% of subjects did not use the entire range of the dial, notably avoiding the lower end of the continuum. It should be remembered that the dial was purposely equally divided between "positive" and "negative" in order not to insure only a positive response. It may be that the designation "negative" deterred the complete use of the dial, assuming subjects did not wish to indicate a negative reaction but merely a "less aesthetic" inclination. It is also possible that the specific configuration of the dial overlay created a measurement artifact. Further research would help isolate this variable.

Test-retest results from several subjects revealed an extremely high correspondence. Reliability was assessed in several different ways. Test-retest trials were examined on the basis of visual overall graphic comparisons of high/low contours. Each graphic comparison overlay was viewed as almost identical although subjects consistently used somewhat more dial on the second hearing. Reliability was also computed for each second comparing test-retest trials. Even after several weeks, reliability across four subjects was .90. This correspondence provides important information in that subjects obviously responded almost identically during the same part(s) of the listening experience.

DISCUSSION

The most important aspect of the pilot investigation described here is that it empirically demonstrates a response to what sophisticated musicians consider to be an aesthetic experience. Every subject had what he or she considered an aesthetic experience and every subject indicated that movement of the CRDI dial roughly corresponded to that aesthetic experience. On purpose, no attempt was made to define the "aesthetic experience" for subjects. Also, the dial that subjects manipulated contained a negative/positive dichotomy in order not to insure only a positive (aesthetic) response. Several subjects stated that they would have preferred a completely positive dial as they had no negative or completely nonaesthetic experiences, and on occasion wanted to move the dial farther toward the positive side. It is important, however, that even subjects who wanted the use of more dial movement made differentiations during the music listening (as did everyone) and did *not* leave the dial in the extreme top position all the time.

Definition of aesthetic responsiveness has had a long and changing history. On the basis of these data, further specificity and some conjecture seem necessary for further research:

1. The "peak aesthetic" experience of which some musicians speak may be temporally very short—15 seconds or less. In order to experience this peak experience, however, it is speculated that one must spend several minutes in highly concentrated focus of attention, especially the 30–45 seconds immediately preceding the peak experience. If concentration is broken (especially by a competing overt experience such as talking), the listening, while pleasant, does not seem to evoke an intense aesthetic response. After the peak aesthetic experience there seems to be an "afterglow" lasting from 15 seconds to several minutes. A peak aesthetic experience is a *thrilling* experience, probably having a substantial physiological component as expressed by subjects as "goose bumps," shivers, full-body excitement, and even infrequent comparisons to orgasm. This thrilling listening response is consistent with some physiological research (Goldstein, 1980).

2. Music capable of eliciting an aesthetic response must be considered by the musically sophisticated subject as extremely substantive and performed very well. The particular selection used in this study was intentionally chosen because it was assumed it would provide an appropriate stimulus to be used with the Continuous Response Digital Interface (CRDI) and might elicit aesthetic responsiveness. Other issues concerning the general quality of music or compositional techniques necessary for an aesthetic experience are left to the interpretation of the reader and subsequent research. A detailed analysis of the music would seem to be especially warranted, particularly that music immediately preceding a "peak" experience.

3. People seem to have the same type of aesthetic response at exactly the same place in the music each time they hear it—if other conditions do not interfere. Test-retest reliability indicated that individual graphs were almost identical to each other with the possible exception that a person's peak experiences were of slightly higher magnitude during the second hearing.

The above speculation is intended to stimulate further research. Obviously, to base any conclusions on a pilot study using one musical selection and thirty subjects is naive at best. These are, however, several issues that seem promising for further inquiry. All subjects indicated that they had at least one aesthetic experience and that movement of the dial roughly approximated this experience. Aesthetic experiences seemed to cluster at several of the same places in the music with one collective peak experience represented by the lowest and highest dial movement across all subject. Also, analyses of subjects' graphs indicate important temporal and musical characteristics fruitful for further investigation.

Issues and questions specific to music education seem manifold. If we can now begin to describe empirically what some aspects of aesthetic sensitivity might be, or at least "the intensity" of a listening response, then we might proceed with additional questions. How should we teach for it? Does this responsiveness happen for all children? If so, when and what are the necessary conditions? Does it happen only with certain music? Is it in part a developmental experience or is it "full blown" and only changes in sophistication level in relationship to more sophisticated music? Will repeated listenings eventually diminish it or increase it? Can it happen while performing? If so, is it the same as when listening? Is "aesthetic sensitivity" a general attribute found throughout certain musical experiences with specific emotional responses nested at certain temporal points? What definition(s) of aesthetic experience is appropriate, or "correct" or meaningful? How do taste, preference, and behavioral or ideational aspects relate to aesthetic responsiveness in music? Although most of these questions remain in the province of the philosopher, others may be clarified by empirical methods. Obviously, more research is needed.

REFERENCES

Berlyne, D. E. (Ed.). (1974). *Studies in the new experimental aesthetics: Steps toward an objective psychology of aesthetic appreciation.* New York: Halstead Press.

Birkoff, G. D. (1933). *Aesthetic measure.* Cambridge, MA: Harvard University.

'Boheme's' been sung 35 times on Texaco shows. (1989, November). *Tallahassee Democrat.*

Brittin, R. V. (1991). The effect of overtly categorizing music on preference for popular music styles. *Journal of Research in Music Education, 39,* 143–151.

Capperella, D. A. (1989). Reliability of the Continuous Response Digital Interface for data collection in the study of auditory perception. *Southeastern Journal of Music Education, 1,* 19–32.

Clynes, M. (1977). *Sentics: The touch of emotions.* New York: Doubleday/Anchor.

Clynes, M., & Nettheim, N. (1982). The living quality of music. In M. Clynes (Ed.), *Music, mind, and brain: The neuropsychology of music.* New York: Plenum Press.

Crozier, J. B. (1981). Information theory and melodic perception: In search of the aesthetic engram. In H. I. Day (Ed.), *Advances in intrinsic motivation and aesthetics* (p. 433–461). New York: Plenum.

Fechner, G. T. (1876). *Vorschule der Ästhetik* (1st ed.). Leipzig: Breitkopk und Häertal.

Furman, C. E., & Duke, R. A. (1988). Effect of majority consensus on preferences for recorded orchestral and popular music. *Journal of Research in Music Education, 36,* 220–231.

Geringer, J. M., & Madsen, C. K. (1981). Verbal and operant discrimination/preference for tone quality and intonation. *Psychology of Music, 9,* 26–30.

Geringer, J. M., & Madsen, C. K. (1987). Pitch and tempo preference in recorded popular music. In C. K. Madsen & C. A. Prickett (Eds.), *Applications of research in music behavior* (pp. 204–212). Tuscaloosa: University of Alabama Press.

Getz, R. P. (1966). The influence of familiarity through repetition in determining music preference. *Journal of Research in Music Education, 14,* 178–192.

Goldstein, A. (1980). Thrills in response to music and other stimuli. *Physiological Psychology, 8,* 126–129.

Greenfield, D. G. (1985). The evaluation of a computer system for behavioral observation training and research. *Journal of Music Therapy*, 22, 95–98.

Greer, R. D., Dorow, L. G., Wachaus, G., & White, E. R. (1973). Adult approval and students' music selection behavior. *Journal of Research in Music Education*, 21, 345–354.

Gregory, D. (1989). Using computers to measure continuous music responses. *Psychomusicology*, 8, 127–134.

Hargreaves, D. J., & Castell, K. C. (1987). Development of liking for familiar and unfamiliar melodies. *Bulletin of the Council for Research in Music Education*, no. 91, 65–69.

Hatoh, T., Kato, M., Kuwano, S., & Namba, S. (1989). Assessment of musical performance using the method of continuous judgement of selected description. *Proceedings of the First International Conference on Music Perception and Cognition* (pp. 33–36), Kyoto, Japan.

Hevner, K. (1936). Experimental studies of the elements of expression in music. *American Journal of Psychology*, 48, 246–268.

Heyduk, R. G. (1975). Rated preference for musical compositions as it relates to complexity and exposure frequency. *Perception and Psychophysics*, 17, 84–91.

Inglefield, H. G. (1982). Conformity behavior reflected in the musical preference of adolescents. In S. H. Barnes (Ed.), *A cross-section of research in music education* (pp. 105–118). New York: University Press of America.

Kuwano, S., & Namba, S. (1985). Continuous judgement of level-fluctuating sounds and the relationship between overall loudness and instantaneous loudness. *Psychological Research*, 47, 27–37.

Langer, S. K. (1976). *Philosophy in a new key* (3rd ed.). Cambridge, MA: Harvard University.

LeBlanc, A. (1981). Effects of style, tempo, and performing medium on children's music preference. *Journal of Research in Music Education*, 29, 143–156.

LeBlanc, A. (1983). Effects of tempo on children's music preference. *Journal of Research in Music Education*, 31, 283–294.

LeBlanc, A. (1986). Effects of vocal vibrato and performer's sex on children's music preference. *Journal of Research in Music Education*, 34, 222–237.

LeBlanc, A. (1988). Tempo preferences of different age music listeners. *Journal of Research in Music Education*, 36, 156–168.

Madsen, C. K. (1990). Measuring musical response. *Music Educators Journal*, 77(3), 26–28.

Madsen, C. K., & Geringer, J. M. (1976). Preference for trumpet tone quality versus intonation. *Bulletin of the Council for Research in Music Education*, no. 46, 13–22.

Madsen, C. K., & Geringer, J. M. (1990). Differential patterns of music listening: Focus of attention of musicians versus nonmusicians. *Bulletin of the Council for Research in Music Education*, no. 105, 45–57.

Madsen, C. K., & Madsen, C. H. (1970). *Experimental research in music.* Englewood Cliffs, NJ: Prentice-Hall.

Meyer, L. B. (1956). *Emotion and meaning in music.* Chicago: University of Chicago Press.

Namba, S., Kuwano, S., Hatoh, T., & Kato, M. (1989). Assessment of musical performance using the method of selected description. *Proceedings of the First International Conference on Music Perception and Cognition* (pp. 29–32), Kyoto, Japan.

Nielsen, F. V. (1983). *Oplevelse af musikalsk spaending* [The experience of musical tension]. Copenhagen: Akademisk Forlag.

Nielsen, F. V. (1987). Musical tension and related concepts. In T. A. Sebeok & J. Umiker-Seboek (Eds.), *The semiotic web '86. An international yearbook* (pp. 491–513). Berlin: Mouton de Gruyter.

Nielzen, S., & Cesarec, Z. (1982). Emotional experience of music as a function of musical structure. *Psychology of Music*, 10(2), 7–17.

Payne, E. (1983). Towards an understanding of music appreciation: Postscript of the report published in Vol. 8, no. 2, 31–41. *Psychology of Music*, 11, 97–100.

Peery, J. C., & Peery, I. W. (1986). Effects of exposure to classical music on the musical preference of preschool children. *Journal of Research in Music Education*, 34(1), 24–33.

Reimer, B. (1970). *A philosophy of music education.* Englewood Cliffs, NJ: Prentice-Hall.

Rentz, E. (1992). Differential aural perception of orchestral instrument families between musicians and nonmusicians using a continuous response digital interface. *Journal of Research in Music Education*, 40, 185–192.

Robinson, C. R. (1988). *Differentiated modes of choral performance evaluation using traditional pro-*

cedures and a Continuous Response Digital Interface device. Unpublished doctoral dissertation, Florida State University, Tallahassee, FL.

Russell, P. A. (1986). Experimental aesthetics of popular music recordings: Pleasingness, familiarity and chart performance. *Psychology of Music, 14*(1), 33–43.

Stratton, V. N., & Zalanowski, A. H. (1984). The relationship between music, degree of liking, and self-reported relaxation. *Journal of Music Therapy, 21*(4), 184–192.

Walker, E. L. (1981). The quest for the inverted-U. In H. I. Day (Ed.), *Advances in intrinsic motivation and aesthetics* (pp. 39–70). New York: Plenum.

April 20, 1992

IX.

REINFORCEMENT

AND

MUSIC

EFFECT OF CONTINGENT MUSIC LISTENING ON INCREASES OF MATHEMATICAL RESPONSES

Clifford K. Madsen
Jere L. Forsythe

JRME 1973, VOLUME 21, NUMBER 2, PAGES 176-181

The use of reinforcement principles to expedite learning has been the focus of increasing educational interest as evidenced by a growing number of behavioral texts, research reports, and institutional programs. Contingent reinforcement has been applied within school settings to shape social behavior, academic behavior, and attitudes toward school and learning in general. The selection of appropriate reinforcers for academic work presents an experimental and educational dilemma, since investigators are disposed to *ex post facto* evaluation concerning effects. Of particular interest in previous investigations was the seemingly infinite variety of reinforcers employed in behavioral shaping. Reinforcing effects have been investigated concerning teacher praise, peer approval, food, material rewards, and free time. Thus, a continuing effort is being made to examine the reinforcing properties of various persons, material things, and activities.

In the present study, the effect of contingent (earned) music listening on academic responses of sixth grade students was investigated. Previous studies concerning reinforcing functions of music listening and music activities have been affirmative.[1] One study revealed that sixth grade black students in a nonintegrated elementary school preferred music listening to candy when given a noncontingent payoff, although candy was slightly preferred when the payoff was contingent on improved scale singing perform-

---

[1] R. D. Greer, A. Randall, and C. Timberlake, "The Discriminate Use of Music Listening as a Contingency for Improvement in Vocal Pitch Acuity and Attending Behavior," *Council for Research in Music Education Bulletin*, No. 26 (Fall 1971), pp. 10-18.

ances.[2] Other studies have reported positive results in the use of contingent music to modify nonmusical behaviors. Claims have long been expressed that music has the power to affect human behavior. The gathering of supportive experimental evidence represents a more recent endeavor. In view of encouraging preliminary evidence, the present investigation of music as a reinforcer for academic responses seemed warranted. The objectives of the study were to determine (1) whether contingent music listening would significantly increase correct responses to mathematical problems compared to other activities and reinforcers, and (2) whether there are significant differences between the reinforcing effects of two types of music listening activities.

Procedures

The study was conducted in a sixth grade pod of an open middle school.[3] A random selection representing half of the school's sixth grade population participated (N = 88). Under the pod arrangement, classroom teachers shared academic instructional duties, combining characteristics of self-contained classrooms with team teaching and teacher area specialization. Mathematics instruction was normally shared by all teachers and supervised by a specialist. Effort was made by the experimenters to avoid a complete diversion from established instructional procedures and materials. An additional concern was to help teachers increase student productivity as well as to satisfy experimental interests.

Mathematical materials selected for the experiment were those with which students had previously been working. This individualized instructional mathematics program provided a test instrument for measuring student performances.[4] Correct responses to mathematical problems served as the basis for determining contingent rewards, as well as for making comparisons among experimental and control groups. Students were randomly assigned to one of the following four groups: dance-listening, earphone-listening, math games control, and contact control. To determine the characteristics of the various contingency groups, experimenters discussed with teachers the nature of contingencies currently operating for mathematical work. Although several teachers employed contingency contracts for other subjects, no teacher had instituted a similar program for mathematical instruction. One teacher had allowed

---

[2] C. K. Madsen and C. H. Madsen, Jr., "Selection of Music Listening or Candy as a Function of Contingent Versus Noncontingent Payoff and Scale Singing," *Journal of Music Therapy*, Vol. 9, No. 4 (1972), pp. 190-198.

[3] Belle Vue Middle School, Tallahassee, Florida. Gratitude is expressed to Freeman Ashmore, Superintendent of Public Instruction, Leon County Schools; Stanley Hilaman, Principal; and the teachers and students in the sixth grade pod.

[4] P. Suppes and M. Jerman, *Individualized Mathematics Drill and Practice Kit* (New York: L. W. Singer Company, Inc., subsidiary of Random House, 1969). An instructional tool designed to account for individual differences and allow each student to progress at a comfortable rate of speed.

students to play mathematical games following completion of mathematics assignments; however, a contingent relationship had not been clearly established. Consequently, experimenters selected mathematical games as an additional control within the present study in order to investigate possible effects of this particular activity.

Comparison of the two types of music listening activities was prompted, in part, by practical considerations regarding the potential application of research findings. That is, if music listening could be used as an effective reinforcer for academic performance, then its practical use in school settings should not depend on availability of unusual or expensive equipment. Most schools have multiple-earphone listening stations, such as those used in the earphone-listening group within the present study. Moreover, tape recorders, record players, and listening rooms are usually common when headsets are not available.

Selection of appropriate reward music was an important aspect of the experiment. Previous studies indicated that sixth-graders in predominantly black elementary schools consistently preferred soul music to traditional music.[5] Reward music in the present study was selected by conducting a survey of a number of sixth grade students who offered specific names of their favorite pop groups, record titles, and tunes. This was the music they liked very much and listened to often. Although the survey was limited, no student who was interviewed expressed a preference for any music other than popular. A tape recording of the music suggested by these students was prepared and used as the contingent-reward music for both the dance- and earphone-listening groups.

The study was conducted daily for one week. Students were seated in groups of six or seven during their regular mathematics class period. A proctor supervised the assigning of materials and the collecting and grading of completed work.[6] Students were instructed to work the mathematical problems on the assigned card from their mathematics kit. On completion of the card, students moved on to the next level card as they were accustomed to doing. Students were told that they could work for only twenty minutes, and that a signal to begin and stop would be given. Following the work period, their cards were graded by the proctors.

Group Contingencies

During the first day's work period, students were not informed of the contingent relationship between their correct responses and the subsequent reward activity. It is assumed that the students discovered this relationship as they were taken to the various reward areas after completing the first day's work. This assumption of initial naiveté is con-

---

[5] C. K. Madsen, D. E. Wolfe, and C. H. Madsen, Jr., "The Effect of Reinforcement and Directional Scalar Methodology in Intonational Improvement," *Council for Research in Music Education Bulletin*, No. 18 (Fall 1969), pp. 22-23.

[6] Students in an undergraduate psychology of music class at Florida State University served as proctors.

sistent with learning theory that suggests that a student must experience a reinforcement before an effect can be established. It is possible that merely telling students of the contingent reward would have affected their performances; however, this aspect was not isolated for study.

The contingency ratio of performance to payoff was designated as two correct responses to one minute of reward time on the first day. The ratio was increased to three correct responses for one minute of listening for the remaining four days. Students spent their total earned time during the time allotted for the experiment. Each day following the twenty-minute work period proctors calculated each student's earned time, wrote it on a small piece of paper, and taped this to the subject's clothing where it could be seen. Students seemed to enjoy comparing their time earnings. This is consistent with past research that suggests that tokens as well as group contingencies probably serve as reinforcers apart from what the tokens can purchase. Reward groups were then taken to the respective areas where subjects spent their earned time. As each student's reward time expired, he was asked to return to the pod where he began working on other subject-matter assignments supervised by the regular teachers.

Students in the contact control group remained in the pod for the duration of the experiment. Following the twenty-minute work period, they were instructed to work on subjects other than mathematics. The math games control group was divided into smaller groups, each headed by a proctor who supervised the playing of a variety of mathematical games. These students were also required to return to work after playing the games. Students in the dance-listening group who earned time were escorted to a nearby room where the prepared tape recording of selected music was played through a stereophonic high-fidelity system. These students were allowed to socialize, dance, or listen to the music. In the earphone-listening group, students listened on individual headsets to the same recorded music as the dance-listening group heard. The wearing of earphones inhibited the earphone-listening group from socializing. However, it was noted that some students looked at each other, smiled, and sometimes sang along with familiar music. At the conclusion of each subject's time, he was tapped on the shoulder and escorted back to the pod.

Results

At the conclusion of the week's experiment, data were collected, tabulated, and analyzed. The four groups were compared on the basis of correct responses assessing effects of the various contingency conditions.[7] A one-way analysis of variance using the F statistic revealed significant

---

[7] The one-way analysis of variance F statistic disclosed no significant differences among the four groups at the beginning of the experiment ($F = .50$).

differences (F = 6.52, p < .01) among the four groups' Monday through Friday gain scores. A summary of this analysis is given in Table 1. The Duncan Multiple Range Test was computed to isolate differences among groups. Results in Table 2 indicate that the data for the earphone-

Table 1
Analysis of Variance Summary Table

Source of Variance	Sum of Squares	df	Mean Square	F
Between Groups	12,119	3	4,040	6.52*
Within Groups	52,083	84	620	
Total	64,202	87		

*p < .01

listening group were significantly different from those of the math games control group and the contact control group (p < .05), but were not significantly different from the other music group. The dance-listening group's data were significantly different from those of both control groups. The two control groups were not significantly different from each other but were each significantly different from both listening groups. Trend analysis of groups over a period of several days indicated that contingency effects were stable by the fifth day for all groups. From these results it appears that (1) contingent music listening activities were effective in significantly increasing correct responses to mathematical problems, and (2) the reinforcing effects of the two types of music listening activities were not significantly different.

Discussion and Conclusions

Investigations of the reinforcing properties of various persons, activities, and material things seem extensive. Previous studies demonstrated

Table 2
Duncan Multiple Range Comparisons

Contact Control (N = 22)	Math Games Control (N = 22)	Dance-Listening (N = 22)	Earphone-Listening (N = 22)
−2.86	.41	16.00	26.05

No significant differences between groups underscored by the same line. All other comparisons between pairs of means significant at the .05 level.

that contingent music activities can effectively reinforce nonmusical behavior. These findings prompted the present investigation concerning effects of contingent music listening on academic responses. Similar results were yielded when the test procedures were replicated, using a complete reversal design extending over a four-week period within a predominately black self-contained sixth grade class (N = 33).[8]

While much more research is needed to investigate the reinforcing effects of music listening activities in expediting learning, some important implications seem apparent from this study. The functional power of music that has traditionally been expressed as a value and supported by personal testimony can be more empirically based in view of research findings and, moreover, might be established contingently and directly. Implications for teachers of subjects other than mathematics may also be gleaned from research results. It should be noted that students worked on mathematical problems for only twenty minutes and that reward time lasted only ten minutes. The regular teachers were impressed with the productivity of their students under these experimental conditions, for in the past they had been spending one hour of each class on mathematics. It would seem that initially shorter periods of on-task work under specific and immediate contingencies is more effective than longer work periods. However, this notion is conjectural since that aspect was not specifically isolated for study. Nonetheless, the practical advantages of establishing contingencies have been implied, while the effect of music listening activities as a possible contingency for other academic behaviors in a school setting has been investigated.

Several problems within this type of study should be noted. Possible "Hawthorne" and "halo" effects are apparent, as well as all noncontrolled variables presumed to be operating within a typical school setting. Also, the addition of any unique element into the normal academic work routine is experimentally suspect, as is any procedure not nested within the teacher's regular classroom procedures.[9] The strength of the present investigation lies in the use of music as a reinforcer when compared to other contrived classroom contingencies. Additionally, the study points to the nonsignificance between the social and the individual music listening treatments. This nonsignificance might indicate that individual music listening, which can be easily dispensed and supervised by a teacher, might be as effective as group social activities, such as dancing and listening, in motivating independent academic work.

■ Florida State University
  Tallahassee, Florida

---

[8] T. Grimes, B. Damron, and T. Kuhn, "A Behavior Modification Study," (unpublished research paper, Florida State University, 1970).

[9] D. T. Campbell and J. C. Stanley, *Experimental and Quasi-Experimental Design for Research* (Chicago: Rand McNally and Company, 1963).

While studies of effective reinforcers for academic subject matter have been extensive, the effect of possible subject matter gain for that subject when used as reinforcement for another subject has only recently been investigated. Initial studies indicated that correct math scores increased as a function of a televised music contingency for subjects who were reinforced for correct academic responses. These studies also demonstrated that subjects showed a significant music subject matter gain. The present study investigated two academic rewards as contingencies for correct math responses: receipt of books and televised music lessons. The study used an extended reversal design and was conducted by a regular classroom teacher. Results indicated that both receipt of books and televised music lessons functioned to increase math performance. More importantly, there was significant pre-, mid-, and posttest gain in music subject matter in direct relationship to subjects' viewing televised lessons.

Clifford K. Madsen *Florida State University, Tallahassee*

JRME 1981, VOLUME 29, NUMBER 2, PAGES 103–110

Music Lessons and Books as Reinforcement Alternatives for an Academic Task

Attempts to delineate motivational factors to stimulate more effective learning have been continuously investigated (Cofer & Appley, 1964; Madsen & Madsen, 1981). Some researchers have been structuring classroom environments in which "token economy systems" help motivate learning. Other investigators have studied possible problems of "intrinsic" motivational factors affected by external influences (Levine & Fasnacht, 1974). Research has adequately demonstrated that one subject can serve as a reward for successful completion of another subject (Premack, 1959). Music listening and performance activities seem especially functional and appropriate as reinforcement for social and academic tasks (Madsen, 1971; Miller, 1974; Madsen & Forsythe, 1973; Madsen & Madsen, 1968, 1972, 1981; Madsen, Wolfe, & Madsen, 1969; Madsen, Madsen, Saudargas, Hammond, Smith, & Edgar, 1970; Madsen, Moore, Wagner, & Yarbrough, 1975; Madsen, Greer & Madsen, 1975). An investigation specifically concerning choice of reinforcement indicated that music lessons presented via television were as effective as free play in increasing academic skills (Madsen & Geringer, 1976).

Requests for reprints should be sent to Clifford K. Madsen, Center for Music Research, Florida State University, Tallahassee 32306.

One study suggested that learning contingencies that offer a learning gain in both the subject matter used as reward and the subject matter that it was intended to reinforce could be designed. The initial study was repeated with an EMR population and relative gains were found to be almost identical (Dorow, 1976), which attested to the generalization of procedures across populations.

Another important aspect of this type of investigation concerns the use of specific individual contingencies nested within larger groups. An entire class is used for research purposes wherein the classroom teacher becomes the "researcher" (Campbell & Stanley, 1963). Music listening and certain other activities seem especially adaptable for this purpose because they can be easily conveyed (individually or collectively) using headphones or television. Therefore, a repetition of the above study was conducted to determine if these procedures could be managed independently by a regular classroom teacher (Madsen, 1979). Results indicated that a classroom teacher could manage all aspects of the study without musical or experimental expertise. This extension also replicated the previous research (Dorow, 1976; Madsen, Dorow, Moore, & Womble, 1976).

Although the progression of this series of investigations is somewhat innovative, trends are being determined and research methodology specified (Greer, 1978). Of primary concern to most investigators of academic behavior, however, is determining and maintaining noncontroversial learning contingencies. Yet, even after these contingencies have been established and maintained, one continues to encounter many questions relating not only to "extrinsic contingencies" but also regarding the nature of "behavioral rewards." It would seem obvious that some motivational factors are in operation when students pursue a difficult academic task. A more important question would seem to relate to maximizing learning gains while providing some personal enjoyment toward long-term educational independence.

The present study compared receipt of books and television viewing as contingencies for academic gain in mathematics in relationship to academic gain in music.

METHOD

A third-grade class randomly chosen from the public school system served as subjects ($n = 26$). Subjects were initially tested on music-listening skills to assess pre-, mid-, and posttest gain over the televised lessons. This test was modeled after student worksheets provided for the televised programs (Leon, 1977) and the original test for televised lessons, which had proven to be an effective instrument with young students (Madsen, Dorow, Moore, & Womble, 1976; Wilson, 1974). Instructions and music examples for the 30-item test were prerecorded on audio tape. The test form consisted of several questions for each lesson that included music listening as well as music concepts and vocabulary questions. For example, to assess a music listening question the student was asked to circle the correct picture indicating "the direction in which the melody is moving." A correct response might be a circle around a picture of arrows pointing up or down. For a concept or vocabulary question, the student was asked true/false, don't know, or multiple choice questions.

To isolate knowledge derived from the specific televised lessons the complete test instrument was given as a pre-, mid-, and posttest. Question items were specific to each lesson and therefore, gain scores across pre/midtest and pre/posttest could be analyzed separately. The music tests were supervised by the classroom teacher. Children were given verbal reinforcement from the teacher for "trying hard" after completion of each page of the test. Also, each student was individually assessed by the teacher on math skills. Students were assigned daily work on the basis of their math performance including addition, subtraction, multiplication, and division. Daily worksheets progressed from easy to difficult with more problems given than could be completed within the 30-minute time limit. The testing procedure was nested within the regular routine of the school program.

DESIGN

The study represented an extended reversal design over a six-week period: baseline, book contingency, music contingency, book contingency, music contingency, and book contingency. Music tests were given before and after the first music contingency and after the last music contingency. Subjects within the book contingency received daily tokens for one week for correct responses on math assignments. These tokens could be exchanged at the end of the week for a small book of the student's choice. During the next week subjects earned tokens that could be exchanged for televised viewing of the music lessons. The lessons were viewed in groups of two or three students with individual headsets from a 12-inch black and white monitor.

In a previous study it was found that sixth-graders who viewed the televised series performed significantly better than nonviewers on a 20-item music achievement test designed to measure the specific subject matter presented throughout these lessons (Shehan, 1979).

Prior to baseline sessions all children had been placed by their classroom teacher in appropriate level academic tasks. Every child was working on individual prescriptions for all academic tasks. Subjects within the music contingency were allowed to "go to the television corner" upon meeting criterion of correct responses as assessed by the teacher. The number and difficulty of assigned tasks per day were individually determined for each student. Data were recorded for both the total number of correct responses and the total number of problems attempted. The attempted problems minus incorrect responses constituted the criterion assessment, which was predetermined by the third-grade teacher.

Each student's progress was charted. Subjects could exchange tokens for books of their choice only at the end of the week. Television viewing could be exchanged daily during each week the television contingency was operating. There was no other television contingency operating within the school setting for any of the subjects prior to or during this study. However, it was hoped that televised music lessons could perhaps share any previously conditioned attraction subjects might have for television viewing in their homes.

All subjects were receiving music instruction from their regular music teacher within the school program. Throughout the study the music specialist knew the children were earning a television viewing contingency but did not know that they were receiving televised music lessons. Traditional classroom music instruction for these children consisted primarily of singing activities that were not directly related to the music instruction concerning music listening discriminations being taught via the televised tapes.

RESULTS

Data were analyzed on the basis of the criterion achievement (percentage of actual minus incorrect responses) and pre-, mid-, posttest gain scores. During the first week (baseline) only three of the 26 students in the class achieved criterion levels every day. During the second week (book contingency) 12 reached the criterion every day. In the third week (first music contingency), 14 students were achieving criterion every day. During the fourth week (book contingency) 15 students continued to achieve criterion throughout the entire week. Nineteen students achieved the daily criterion with the reinstatement of the music contingency and this dropped to 16 students with the final reinstatement of the book contingency. Absences averaged four per day and no subject had more than nine absences throughout the study. However, one subject was dropped from the study because of consistent absences on testing dates, making it impossible to get music test scores.

Mean percentages of correct responses across the entire class are presented in Figure 1. During both contingencies there was a high degree of correct responses. This aspect is interesting when one remembers that not all students were achieving criterion every day. The class mean rose from the baseline rate to a relatively high rate when the first book contingency was instituted. After rising slightly during the first week of the contingency, the mean rose slightly again when the music contingency was initiated. The group average remained relatively high throughout the second book contingency, and rose again with the reinstatement of the music contingency. There was a slight drop with the final reinstatement of the book contingency yet the overall percentage of correct responses was still high.

MUSIC GAIN

The present investigation concerns gain in music-listening skills in a program devised and implemented by the regular classroom teacher. Several previous investigations have determined increases in academic performance, while other studies have determined that contingent music listening increases academic and music skills. The gain in music-listening skills was demonstrated throughout the study in direct relationship to the amount of time students spent viewing the televised music lessons.

The total test had a possible score of 30: 15 test items from the first five lessons (first music contingency) and 15 test items from the last five lessons (second music contingency). A dependent t-test of pretest versus midtest difference scores indicated no significant differences on those 15 items not presented via television. However, pre/midtest difference scores on those 15 items taught via television did demonstrate significant differences ($t = 9.53$, $df = 24$, $p < .01$; Madsen & Moore, 1978). The pre/midtest mean difference score was 2.64 correct responses on the 15 items covered. The total pre/posttest mean difference score was 5.44 ($t = 8.90$, $df = 24$, $p < .01$) indicating that students viewing the music lessons showed significant overall improvement for the 30 test items.

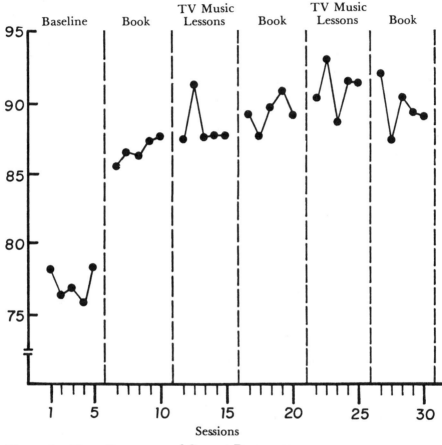

Figure 1—Mean Percentage of Correct Responses

DISCUSSION

The study both repeats and extends previous research (Madsen, Dorow, Moore, & Womble, 1976; Madsen, 1979). Students earning books in the present investigation adds an additional dimension to this line of research. Also, the fact that this research was nested within the regular classroom routine is important. The installation of a small television monitor on top of a cassette video playback unit with several individual headsets provides a pleasant "television corner" within a regular classroom setting. The teacher in the present experiment was already planning to provide some motivational contingency and was delighted to add the televised music/book rotation.

Certain problems arise when attempting research in applied settings, but specific research designs can accommodate most problems. The teacher was highly pleased with the students' performance within this investigation. While marked changes in student performance across contingencies often satisfy researchers, most classroom teachers become apprehensive when students "return to baseline," or indicate a drop in learning performance in other ways. Also, the decision to use the percentage of actual responses completed minus incorrect responses as the basis for students receiving tokens exchanged for books or televised music was determined by the teacher. This method was consistent with past research (Madsen, Dorow, Moore, & Womble, 1976). The classroom teacher advised that the math assignment provide for approximately the same number of completed tasks each day with a slightly changing criterion (number of problems completed) as students progressed through the tasks.

While previous research has used special televised programs not available to teachers, the televised video-cassette tapes used in the present study were provided from WETA-TV, Washington, D.C. Entitled *Music* (a series of 10 30-minute programs), it is available without cost to anyone requesting it. It is accompanied by a curriculum guide that contains objectives, music concepts, a synopsis, preparatory and follow-up activities, recommended classroom listening, and student worksheets (Leon, 1977). Even without the accompanying aspects intended to augment the televised lessons, students in the present study showed learning gains.

Regardless, several research aspects concerning the present study need additional investigation and should be approached with caution. Receipt of selected books and viewing televised music lessons were considered highly desirable and, while it may appear that each might be an attractive choice, isolation of the relative strength concerning each of these, as well as all other contingencies operating in a classroom, needs careful study and more research. Students could receive televised music daily but had to "save" tokens in exchange for weekly books. Therefore, results of the present investigation could possibly be explained solely on the basis of alternative reinforcement schedules. Also, the receipt of tokens (a chart specifying criterion achievement) could be reinforcing regardless of their "backup" exchange.

The music test used in the present study should be considered an initial attempt at developing an effective instrument. The development of valid and reliable instruments to assess all aspects of educational activities needs more careful research, especially in relationship to educational television.

Television viewing does seem widespread within our culture, if not within our school systems.[1] Perhaps, if programming is carefully planned, produced,

---

[1] An NEA survey found that 60% of responding teachers never use television in the classroom. Another 20% use it only once or twice a semester; another 8%, once or twice a month; only 2% use it every day; and 11%, once or twice a week, as reported in *Kapan*, 1980, *62*(1), p. 50.

and tested (as with the above lessons) students will be educationally enriched.[2] More importantly, in attempting to provide the best possible motivation for effective learning, perhaps future research will be able to isolate those reinforcement alternatives that not only stimulate high academic gains and are compatible with teachers' goals but also provide additional worth within themselves. Music instruction as both enrichment and as specific subject matter seems especially appropriate in this regard.

REFERENCES

Campbell, D. T., & Stanley, J. C. *Experimental and quasi-experimental designs for research*. Chicago: Rand McNally, 1963.

Cofer, C. N., & Appley, M. H. *Motivation: Theory and research*. New York: John Wiley & Sons, 1964.

Dorow, L. G. Televised music lessons as educational reinforcement for correct mathematical responses with the educable mentally retarded. *Journal of Music Therapy*, 1976, *13*(2), 77-86.

Greer, R. G. An operant approach to motivation and affect: Ten years of research and theory in music learning. Paper presented at the National Symposium on the Applications of Learning Theory to the Teaching and Learning of Music, Ann Arbor, Michigan, November, 1978.

Leon, R. *Music: Guide to classroom use in intermediate grades*. Arts Programming, WETA-TV, Washington, D. C., 1977.

Levine, F. M., & Fasnacht, G. Token rewards may lead to token learning. *American Psychologist*, 1974, *29*, 816-820.

Madsen, C. H., Jr., & Madsen, C. K. *Teaching/discipline: A positive approach for educational development*, 3rd ed. Boston: Allyn & Bacon, 1981.

Madsen, C. H., Jr., Madsen, C. K., Saudargas, R. A., Hammond, W. R., Smith, J. B., & Edgar, D. E. Classroom RAID (rules, approval, ignore, disapproval): A cooperative approach for professionals and volunteers. *Journal of School Psychology*, 1970, *8*(3), 180-185.

Madsen, C. K. How reinforcement techniques work. *Music Educators Journal*, 1971, *57*(8), 38-41.

Madsen, C. K. The effect of music subject matter as reinforcement for correct mathematics. *Bulletin of the Council for Research in Music Education*, 1979, *59*, 54-58.

Madsen, C. K., Dorow, L. G., Moore, R. S., & Womble, J. U. The effect of music via television as reinforcement for mathematics. *Journal of Research in Music Education*, 1976, *24*, 51-59.

Madsen, C. K., & Forsythe, J. L. Effect of contingent music listening on increases of mathematical responses. *Journal of Research in Music Education*, 1973, *21*, 176-181.

Madsen, C. K., & Geringer, J. M. Choice of televised music lessons versus free play in relationship to academic improvement. *Journal of Music Therapy*, 1976, *13*(4), 154-162.

Madsen, C. K., Greer, R. D., & Madsen, C. H., Jr. (Eds.). *Research in music behavior: Modifying music behavior in the classroom*. New York: Teachers College Press, 1975.

---

[2]The Children's Television Workshop (CTW), producer of educational TV's Sesame Street, is planning a new series aimed at acquainting children with the joys of science. *Science*, 1978, *202* (4369), 730-731.

Madsen, C. K., & Madsen, C. H., Jr. Music as a behavior modification technique with a juvenile delinquent. *Journal of Music Therapy*, 1968, *5*(3), 72-76.

Madsen, C. K., & Madsen, C. H., Jr. Selection of music listening or candy as a function of contingent versus noncontingent reinforcement and scale singing. *Journal of Music Therapy*, 1972, *9*(4), 190-198.

Madsen, C. K., Moore, R. S., Wagner, M. J., & Yarbrough, C. A. Comparison of music as reinforcement for correct mathematical responses versus music as reinforcement for attentiveness. *Journal of Music Therapy*, 1975, *12*(2), 84-95.

Madsen, C. K., & Moore, R. S. *Experimental research in music: Workbook in design and statistical tests.* Raleigh, N.C.: Contemporary Publishing Company, 1978, p. 82.

Madsen, C. K., Wolfe, D. E., & Madsen, C. H., Jr. The effect of reinforcement and directional scalar methodology on intonational improvement. *Bulletin of the Council for Research in Music Education*, 1969, *18*, 22-33.

Miller, D. M. Effects of selected music listening contingencies on arithmetic performance and music preference with educable mentally retarded children. Unpublished doctoral dissertation, Columbia University, 1974.

Premack, D. Toward empirical behavior laws: I. Positive reinforcement. *Psychological Review*, 1959, *66*, 219-233.

Shehan, P. K. The effect of the television series, *Music*, on music listening preferences and achievement of elementary general music students. *Contributions to Music Education*, 1979, *7*, 51-62.

Wilson, J. *Project lispro.* Clinch County Board of Education, Box 177, Homerville, Georgia (Project Summary), 1974.

September 16, 1980

ADULT APPROVAL AND STUDENTS' MUSIC SELECTION BEHAVIOR

R. Douglas Greer
Laura G. Dorow
Gustav Wachhaus
Elmer R. White

JRME 1973, VOLUME 21, NUMBER 4, PAGES 345–354

Many of the variables that influence music selecting behaviors of students are not amenable to influence by teachers.[1] These non-school variables include age, sex, socioeconomic status, and mass media exposure. However, one variable that may be manipulated by the teacher is repeated exposure to music during classroom contact. Much of the available evidence points to the importance of repeated listening or familiarity as an influence on music selection.[2] When this evidence is related to learning theory, whether derived from laboratory research or from research in the nonmusic classroom, it seems that repeated listening increases students' music discriminations.

Acquisition of music discriminations may not result necessarily in increased time spent with those new discriminations but in decreased time spent, since the avoidance of a phenomenon requires discrimination also. Thus, one of the central factors in the familiarity finding is the degree of positive reinforcement associated with the acquisition of music discriminations. Prediction of the amount of time students will spend with new music discriminations is a component of music instruction represented by the construct of

---

[1] Portions of this article were presented at the 1972 National Association of Music Therapy convention in East Lansing, Michigan.

[2] I. K. Bradley, "Repetition as a Factor in the Development of Musical Preferences," *Journal of Research in Music Education*, Vol. 19 (Fall 1971), pp. 295-298; R. P. Getz, "The Influence of Familiarity Through Repetition in Determining Optimum Response of Seventh Grade Children to Certain Types of Serious Music," *Journal of Research in Music Education*, Vol. 14 (Fall 1966), pp. 178-192; H. K. Mull, "The Effect of Repetition Upon the Enjoyment of Modern Music," *The Journal of Psychology*, Vol. 43 (1957), pp. 155-162.

musical attitude (that is, verbal behavior regarding future music selection behaviors). Staats developed a theory partially to explain similar affective learning based on traditional learning theory.[3] The phenomenon of real interest, however, is not the verbal behavior but the future music selection. With the behaviors operationally specified as music selection, it is possible to ask what factors increase, decrease, or do not affect this behavior. Music selection behavior may be studied by looking at the consequences—the music obtained—to determine whether the obtained music acts as a reinforcer. The reinforcing effect of the music can then be represented in terms of time spent listening to the music.

Music teachers' behaviors are associated with students' acquisition of music discriminations, such that teacher-generated approvals are potential reinforcers for students' subsequent music selections. This category of teacher behavior is of considerable importance because music teachers' interactions with their students can terminate in any one of three student music selection behaviors: (1) avoidance of future contact with similar music, (2) increased time spent with the music taught, or (3) no (teacher) influence on music selection behavior. Adult social reinforcement or teacher approval is crucial to classroom management. The results of classroom management research have been implemented in teacher training programs and parent education workshops. More recently, some researchers have begun to investigate the effect of adult social reinforcement on the future reinforcing effects (affective domain) of subject matter.

Related research in teacher approval behavior during music instruction has been conducted by Steele, Kuhn, Forsythe, and Murray.[4] Steele found that adult approval affected children's music selection behavior during the period that social reinforcement was occurring. However, once adult reinforcement was withdrawn, the children reverted to nonreinforced selections. Kuhn found that two approval/disapproval ratios did not differentially affect children's acquisition of music discriminations or attitude toward music class (verbalizations about enjoyment of the classes) but did affect social behavior. His findings concerning social behavior were consistent with previous findings that high approval (80 percent approval to 20 percent disapproval) causes greater adherence to classroom rules than does low approval. Forsythe found that music

---

[3] A. Staats, *Learning, Language, and Cognition* (New York: Holt, Rinehart and Winston, 1968); D. Premack, "Reinforcement Theory," *Nebraska Symposium on Motivation* (Lincoln: University of Nebraska Press, 1965).

[4] J. Forsythe, "The Effect of Teacher Approval, Disapproval and Errors on Student Attentiveness Comparing Music versus Classroom Teachers," in C. K. Madsen, R. D. Greer, and C. H. Madsen, Jr., *Research in Music Behavior* (New York: Teachers College Press, in press); T. L. Kuhn, "The Effect of Teacher Approval and Disapproval on Attentiveness, Musical Achievement, and Attitude of Fifth Grade Students," *Research in Music Behavior;* K. C. Murray, "The Effect of Teacher Approval/ Disapproval on Musical Performance, Attentiveness, and Attitude of High School Choruses," *Research in Music Behavior;* A. L. Steele, "Effects of Social Reinforcement on the Musical Preferences of Mentally Retarded Children," *Journal of Music Therapy,* Vol. 4 (1967), pp. 57-62.

teachers trained in high-approval techniques had more attentive students than teachers of other subjects. However, his data also showed that with approval ratios statistically controlled, students were more attentive in music classes than other classes, a finding consistent with earlier research concerning music as a group reinforcer. Murray found that when high school choral conductors used high approval, their students evidenced a more positive attitude (verbalized preference) toward the pieces rehearsed.

It was determined earlier that attitude was a verbalization regarding future music selection behavior and that the behavior of real interest would seem to be the music selection behaviors. The actual selection behaviors may be studied via a conjugate reinforcement apparatus, a device that contingently presents to the subject alternative channels of music while recording the amount of time the subject selects each channel. The instrument used in this study was designated an operant music listening recorder (OMLR). Similar devices have been suggested by Jeffrey, used by Lovitt for study of episodic reinforcers, and developed and used in music therapy by Cotter.[5] The rationale for this instrumentation and its use as a dependent measure has been discussed previously at length.

Procedures

The present investigation was devised to answer the following questions:

1. Does the rate of adult approval (high approval versus low approval) during music listening lessons affect subjects' posttraining music selection behavior?

2. Does the presentation of music listening lessons by clinician-artists affect posttraining music selection behavior more than repeated listening?

3. What is the rank order of subjects' music selections?

An N of 110 fifth graders of low socioeconomic status served as subjects. The subjects were selected from a school located in the Metropolitan New York area and were classified at low socioeconomic status due to the high percentage of parents (over 35 percent) receiving welfare support. Although all 118 members of the class participated in some portion of the experiment, eight subjects were eliminated from data analyses because of transfers, absenteeism, and (in one case) experimental error. No group biases in mortality were in effect.

---

[5] V. W. Cotter, "Effects of Music on Mentally Retarded Girls' Performance of Manual Tasks," *Dissertation Abstracts*, Vol. B, 1969; Cotter and J. E. Spradlin, "A Non-Verbal Technique for Studying Music Preference," *Journal of Experimental Child Psychology*, Vol. 11 (1971), pp. 357-365; Cotter and S. Toombs, "A Procedure for Determining the Music Preference of Mental Retardates," *Journal of Music Therapy*, Vol. 3 (1966), pp. 57-64; W. E. Jeffrey, "A New Technique for Motivating and Reinforcing Children," *Science*, Vol. 121 (1955), p. 371; T. C. Lovitt, *Narrative Rate Preferences of Normal and Retarded Males as Assessed by Conjugate Reinforcement* (doctoral dissertation, University of Kansas, 1965).

Subjects were pre- and posttested on their music selection behaviors, using the OMLR. The instrument consisted of the following components: three two-track stereophonic tape recorders (two Wollensak 6250, one Revox A77) ; one set of stereophonic earphones (Koss Pro-4AA) ; a press-to-hold microswitch keyboard, adjusted to equal pressure (a small metal box approximately 6" x 10" with five separate telegraph-type keys) ; an electronic switch-relay component that moderated the subjects' control of music contingencies; and a five-pen Esterline Angus chart recorder, which recorded the time spent depressing each key. When the subject depressed a key, a sound contingency was channeled through the earphones. To control for key (microswitch) location, the depression of any key continuously for two minutes triggered a relay switch that relocated all sound sources so that the continuation of a subject's interrupted selection required that he search other keys. Sound contingencies were available to each individual subject for a total of twenty minutes; the time allotment was based on the prior research in the stability of music selection behavior.[6]

The sound contingencies consisted of the following: electronic music, rock music (selected from the top twenty, two years prior to the experiment) , music classics, jazz, and white noise. Each category had eight selections, with each selection running two and one-half minutes. Subjects were randomly assigned to five groups, with four of the groups receiving different instructional treatments and one group acting as a control. Two main effects were studied: (1) high approval (80 percent approval to 20 percent disapproval) versus low approval (20 percent approval to 80 percent disapproval) and (2) clinician-artist presentation versus repeated listening.

All groups except the control group received either six days of music listening or six days of clinician-artist presentation of selected music styles for thirty minutes each day. Listening groups listened to the same style of music that was performed and discussed by the clinician-artist. In addition, the instruction groups (clinician-artist groups) frequently performed in class. Each of the three clinician-artists presented two thirty-minute sessions for two consecutive days in the style of music in which he or she was an authority—electronic music, jazz, or music classics.[7] Clinician-artists were not told which was the high-approval group and which was the low-approval group; group order was rotated daily. Thus, two groups received clinician-artist presentation (one with high-observer approval and one with low-observer approval) , and two groups received listening sessions (one under high-observer approval conditions and one under low-observer approval conditions). None of the compositions taught and presented to subjects were the specific selections tested on the OMLR; compositions taught were similar in style to those tested. Inves-

---

[6] Cotter and Spradlin.

[7] The authors are indebted to Donald Byrd, Mary Jane Bolin, and Susan Yank, who served so well as clinician-artists. In addition, appreciation is expressed to Andrew Randall, Abdul Raquib, and members of the school community at the school in which the research took place.

tigators were interested in generalization of music reinforcers to categories of music.

Approval was dispensed by three observers trained in appropriate observation techniques. Each observer dealt with six to eight subjects at a time. Subject seating was rotated daily. The observer watched for two minutes, then whispered appropriate approval or disapproval to his subjects during a forty-second interaction interval. All observers carried a stopwatch. Approval/disapproval was contingent on whether or not the student followed simple classroom social rules and/or participated in the music behavior requested by clinician-artists. Observers carried cue cards that prescribed a randomly assigned order of approvals and disapprovals. High-approval group cards prescribed eight approvals and two disapprovals per session, while low-approval group cards prescribed two approvals and eight disapprovals. Approvals or disapprovals were dispensed contingently; thus, some children might receive only a few approvals or disapprovals, while other children might receive many. Observers approved only during approval intervals and disapproved only during disapproval intervals.

The control group received no specific music training treatment during the experimental period, but continued with their normal in-school and out-of-school association with music. The high-approval instruction group (HI) was presented with three categories of music for two days each—jazz, electronic music, and music classics—by clinician-artists under high-observer approval conditions. The low-approval instruction group (LI) was presented the same categories for two days each, under low-observer approval conditions. The low-approval listening group (LL) received the same treatment as the LI group, using taped music rather than clinician-artists. Finally the high-approval listening group (HL) received the same treatment as the HI group, using taped music rather than clinician-artists.

The basic design employed was a pre- and posttest (two instructional modes by two approval ratios with one no-treatment control). The design seemed appropriate, since the behaviors of interest were not the behaviors taking place during treatment sessions but the effect of treatment on posttreatment behavior. Classroom rules were posted in the front of the room and orally reviewed each day by one of the experimental personnel. Listening groups were asked to stay in their chairs, keep their feet on the floor, raise their hands to talk, do what the teacher told them, and listen carefully. Children were approved during interaction intervals for following social rules and participating in group music behaviors such as clapping, operating tape recorders, operating Moog V synthesizers, performing on bells, and listening attentively. Approvals consisted of phrases such as, "Good, I like the way you listen." Disapprovals consisted of corrections or mild reprimands such as, "Do it like this." Observers' remarks were whispered in a moderate voice and in a manner that did not allow the subjects' neighbors to overhear the observers' comments. All lessons were videotaped, and data about the clinician's interaction were obtained.

Subjects were tested individually in an appropriate room at the school in which the experiment took place. During the twenty-minute testing period, subjects sat at a desk on which the press-to-hold microswitch box was located. Subjects were screened from other experimental equipment and personnel. The subjects had three alternatives: to press individual or combinations of keys, not to press the keys, or to leave the room (one subject elected this alternative).

Results

Music selection data consisted of the number of seconds that subjects listened to music categories, listened to white noise, or did not listen. Decisions regarding the total groups' rank order of preferences (for example, whether or not differences between ranks were significant at the .01 level) were made using the Wilcoxon matched-pairs signed-ranks test.[8] The rank orders of preferences for all groups combined for the pre- and posttests, as well as combined groups' total time in seconds spent with each sound contingency, are given in Table 1.

Table 1
Rank Order of Preferences for Combined Groups

Sound Contingencies	Total Seconds		Rank	
	Pretest	Posttest	Pretest	Posttest
Rock	59,974	71,235	1	1
Jazz	16,349	12,228	2	3
Electronic	20,606	19,894	2	2
Music Classics	9,317	6,405	3	4
White Noise	4,554	2,692	4	5
Total Time	110,800	112,454		

Analysis of the pretest data using the Kruskall-Wallis test revealed no overall differences between groups. Posttest data were analyzed using the same test, and overall differences between groups were found for electronic music $(p < .01)$, total listening time $(p < .01)$, and white noise $(p < .01)$. Subsequent Mann-Whitney U tests revealed other differences. Results of the Mann-Whitney U tests are found in Table 2.

Posttest selections of categories of music were compared across approval groups to determine approval effects on music selections, particularly those music selection categories that were presented during treatment sessions. The high-approval groups spent more time listening to two of the three music categories taught, indicating that observer-approval ratios affected the music selection behaviors of the subjects, thus reinforcing the effect of the music. Students generalized from specific compositions taught and heard to the general categories tested. High-approval groups also spent more time listening to white noise, less time listening to rock, and

[8] S. Siegel, *Nonparametric Statistics* (New York: McGraw-Hill, 1956).

Table 2
Mann-Whitney *U* Tests Between Groups for the Posttest

Contingencies	HA Groups vs. LA Groups*	L Groups vs. CP Groups**
Electronic Music	p = .0384 (HA > LA)	nonsig.
Music Classics	p = .0084 (HA > LA)	nonsig.
Jazz	nonsig.	nonsig.
White Noise	p = .0023 (HA > LA)	nonsig.
Rock	p = .0351 (HA < LA)	nonsig.
Total Listening Time	p = .0233 (HA < LA)	nonsig.

* HA groups include the high-approval instruction group and the high-approval listening group. LA groups include both the low-approval instruction group and the low-approval listening group.
** L groups include both listening groups, and CP groups include both clinician-performer groups.

less total time listening than low-approval groups. The latter finding indicated that high-approval groups sampled nonrock (treatment music and white noise) categories more than low-approval groups. Conversely, the low-approval groups avoided nonrock categories more than high-approval groups.

Approval treatment effects are further confirmed by the finding that the control group listened more to two of the three music treatment categories than did either the low-approval instruction group or the low-approval listening group. The low-approval groups listened more to rock than the control group—additional evidence that the low-approval treatments caused subjects to avoid treatment categories. Low-approval groups avoided treatment music more than did high-approval groups and the control group. However, high-approval groups did not demonstrate greater selection of taught music than the control group, with the exception of the HL group. Analysis of pre- and posttest change scores normally would help determine whether or not high-approval groups were only maintaining pretest selections, while low-approval groups were decreasing treatment music selection. However, there are difficulties associated with answering these questions by looking at pre- and posttest change scores.

Change scores were analyzed using Wilcoxon matched-pairs signed-ranks tests. One high-approval group increased rock selections (HL, p < .01), while the other high-approval group (HI) maintained rock selection. High-approval groups showing decreases in selection included the HI group and the HL group for white noise (p < .02 and p < .01), HL group for music classics (p < .01), and HL group for electronic music (p < .01). Both high-approval groups maintained their pretest total listening time.

Both low-approval groups increased rock selection (LI, p > .01; LL, p < .01), while they both maintained electronic music selection. The LL group also maintained jazz and white noise selection. Low-approval groups showing decreases included the LI group and the LL group for music classics (p < .01, p < .05, respectively) and the LI group for jazz and white noise (p < .01). Both high-approval groups and low-approval groups showed numerous decreases in all categories except rock (only one high-approval group increased rock selection). Combining change score analyses and posttest score analyses, it is evident that low-approval groups decreased music classics and electronic music more than high-approval groups. However, there are four factors that warrant against saying that the reinforcing effect of the music decreased. First, the lack of validity accorded change scores warrants against acceptance of change score analysis alone. Secondly, an instrument by treatment or instrument novelty effect may have occurred during the experiment. Thirdly, Cotter's finding (with repeated sessions, his subjects increasingly chose more of their first preference) may explain change scores. Finally, the data did not warrant analysis-of-covariance treatment, especially in the light of the possible instrumentation effect.

There are at least three possible interpretations. One interpretation is that the reinforcing effect of the selections decreased with treatments in some instances. Another interpretation is that there was an instrument novelty effect, in which case maintenance of pretest scores indicated an actual increase in the reinforcing effect of the selections. A more cautious interpretation would be to discount change scores and look to posttest scores as the most valid assessment of treatment effects. This later interpretation seems to be the most prudent analysis. Using the most cautious interpretation, it is evident that high-approval groups listened more to two of the three treatment music categories than did the low-approval groups. Low-approval groups listened more to rock and avoided treatment music more than high-approval groups. Nonrock categories were more reinforcing for high-approval groups than for low-approval groups. There was considerable evidence that there were no differences between the instruction groups taught by clinician-artists and repeated listening groups (see Table 2). Although there may have been some interactions between high-approval treatments and instruction treatments, the statistical tests that were used warrant against further comment. Experimental manipulation of discrimination levels and approval ratios simultaneously would seem to be a more valid approach to studying approval and discrimination interaction.

Total group preference order did change somewhat from pretest to posttest, as shown in Table 1. Subjects maintained their pretest electronic music selection, while decreasing their jazz selection. Consequently, electronic music was preferred over jazz on the posttest. It cannot be determined whether jazz became less reinforcing, electronic music more reinforcing, or whether subjects had improved only their ability to find selections. Subjects' rank order of preferences does contribute three interesting findings. The first finding was that subjects in this population did prefer jazz over music classics, countering conjectural arguments that children today find jazz as incomprehensible as music classics. The second finding, duplicating that by Cotter, was that music was preferred over white noise. The third finding was that subjects' unexpected selection of electronic music both on the pretest and posttest raised some interesting questions. What were the discriminations associated with the electronic music selection? Was that selection strictly a novelty effect? If so, why did the control group not decrease electronic selection time between the pre- and posttest?

Discussion and Conclusions

While it is evident from these data that approval was a significant factor in selection behavior, the exact ratios of approval to disapproval were not held completely constant for all groups or for individuals. Although observer approval was held constant for groups (that is, one rate for high-approval groups and one rate for low-approval groups), individual clinician-artist's approval/disapproval rates were not held constant. Observations of videotapes of each clinician-artist's first day of instruction for HI and LI groups were made. These data are presented in Table 3. There was a wide disparity between the jazz approval/disapproval rates; only the jazz category of music selections taught yielded nonsignificant differences. One could infer, therefore, that the low interaction rates, specifically the low approval, from the jazz clinician may have accounted for this inconsistency. Such a conclusion remains a possibility for future research to pursue. Possibly the fact that jazz was taught first, resulted in the nonsignificant difference due to lack of accrued approval associations with jazz. Twenty subjects out of 110 preferred a nonrock selection, and in nineteen of those cases either electronic music or jazz were the preferred selections. Posttest data showed that few subjects changed the first preference and that no group influences were in evidence.

The apparent novelty of the instrument or the instrument x treatment interaction should be controlled in future research. Perhaps the addition

Table 3
Clinician-Artists' Approval/Disapproval
and Inter-Observer Reliability

Day	Music Taught	Group	Approvals	Dis-approvals	Inter-Observer Reliability
1	Jazz	HI*	0	0	1.00
		LI	2	0	1.00
3	Electronic	HI	15	5	.95
		LI	14	5	.95
5	Music Classics	HI	41	17	.96
		LI	43	3	1.00

*HI indicates the high-approval instruction group, while LI indicates the low approval clinician-performer group.

of posttest-only experimental and control groups in conjunction with pre- and posttest experimental and control groups would control for the effect and help pinpoint the nature of the problem. The correlation between subjects' selection behavior (for the rock section) during the first ten minutes and the second ten minutes for the pretest was not exceptionally high (Spearman-Rank, .57) ; thus, preexperimental sampling of the instrument may eliminate some novelty effect. At any rate, such sampling is recommended since these investigators did not obtain the data from one subject. The subject did not depress any of the keys during either the pre- or posttest.

More dramatic approval influences might have been found, had the test assessed the same individual pieces that were presented during treatment. Certainly such a procedure is recommended; yet, the apparent generalizations made by the subjects may be of greater importance. The data, when compared with Murray's findings, point to the importance of music-instructor approval behavior as a potentially valid measure of music teacher competency. Not only has this variable been shown to be important to classroom management, but some evidence of generalization from a social behavior effect to an academic effect in the form of an affective influence has been demonstrated (that is, influence on the children's future association with that subject matter taught). From an analysis of the findings, the following conclusions may be drawn:

1. Subjects receiving music lessons under conditions of adult high approval selected more of that music taught than subjects taught under adult low-approval conditions.

2. No differences between clinician-artist lessons and repeated listening lessons were found.

3. Subjects generalized from specific compositions presented in music lessons to general style categories.

4. The pretest order of group preference, from most preferred to least preferred, was rock music, electronic or jazz, music classics, and white noise; the order of preference on the posttest was rock music, electronic music, jazz, music classics, and white noise.

5. Future research should isolate and control for an instrumentation testing effect.

■ Teachers College, Columbia University
New York, New York

Florida State University
Tallahassee, Florida

University of Maryland
College Park, Maryland

Appalachian State University
Boone, North Carolina

THE EFFECT OF TEACHER APPROVAL/DISAPPROVAL RATIOS ON STUDENT MUSIC SELECTION AND CONCERT ATTENTIVENESS

Laura G. Dorow

JRME 1977, VOLUME 25, NUMBER 1, PAGES 32–40

An application of learning theory to the study of music teacher behavior was made in order to obtain evidence regarding student music selection behavior and concert attentiveness as influenced by ratios of teacher approval to disapproval. Seventy-six fourth- and fifth-grade students were pretested and posttested. The number of seconds subjects selected from three sound contingencies (piano music, rock music, and white noise) on an episodic reinforcement device and student off-task concert behaviors were measured. Subjects were taught piano excerpts under teacher high and low approval/disapproval conditions. Approval ratios were controlled by hand signals (approval/disapproval cues) given to the teacher at predetermined time intervals.

Key Words: aesthetic experience, attitudes, elementary education student, school environment, teaching method, tests.

The study of reinforcement as an independent variable in music education and music therapy has received extensive attention (Greer, Randall, & Timberlake, 1971; Hanley, 1970; Jorgenson, 1970; Madsen, Wolfe, & Madsen, 1969; Madsen & Forsythe, 1973). While the conditioning of reinforcement as a dependent variable has been a subject of considerable research in laboratory experiments (Hendry, 1969; Kelleher, 1966), little attention has been given to the study of conditioned reinforcers as dependent variables within the classroom. There appear to be many educational outcomes related to conditioned reinforcement research, the foremost focusing on the development of interest in the subject matter being taught. Indeed, there are some subjects within the school curriculum for which the study of the conditioning of reinforcers seems to be of paramount concern, specifically the arts.

Related issues, such as attitude as measured by verbal instruments, have been studied in the classroom (Bradley, 1972). However, it appears that little attempt has been made to relate attitude to reinforcement acquisition. Becker (1971) has suggested that a clear operational definition of change in reinforcement is a measure of "time spent" with a given contingency. Instrumentation for the measurement of this "time spent" has been developed by Lovitt (1965) as well as Cotter and Spradlin (1971). These apparati make a limited number of events available to a subject contingent on free operant responding. This instrumentation then can serve as a pretest and posttest measure of the degree of reinforcement of sound contingencies.

Reinforcement has been conditioned in the laboratory by pairing reinforcing stimuli with less reinforcing or non-reinforcing stimuli. Classroom contingencies most frequently associated with subject matter consist of teacher approval or disapproval (Forsythe, 1972; Kuhn, 1972; Murray, 1972; Yarbrough, 1973). The following study was performed to determine whether or not the rate of teacher approval/disapproval used during the instructional treatment influences the posttest selection (time spent listening) of the sound contingencies as well as the concert attending behavior.

Relatively few studies have attempted to change preference with teacher approval (Betancourt & Zeiler, 1971; Steele, 1967). The pioneer study in this area (Greer, Dorow, Wachhaus, & White, 1973) demonstrated an effective use of adult approval in changing music preferences. The results of this study were attributable in part to the sensitive measurement of the episodic reinforcement apparatus and the nature of the research design. Based on the conclusions of the previous research (Greer et al., 1973) the following experiment was designed to assess approval/disapproval effects with some design modifications: (1) a single teacher, rather than teacher aides, gave approvals and disapprovals, (2) a frequency count of the number of approvals and disapprovals received by each subject was obtained, (3) a key manipulation training period was added to the episodic reinforcement apparatus testing sessions, (4) a reduction from five to three sound contingencies was made, with a corresponding reduction in the number of keys, (5) the specific music selections taught were tested on the episodic reinforcement apparatus, and (6) an attempt was made to assess whether or not the approval/disapproval effect carried over from music selection behavior to concert attentiveness.

Method

Seventy-six randomly selected fourth and fifth grade students of low socio-economic backgrounds were randomly assigned to three treatment groups and a posttest-only group. Fifty-seven were pretested and seventy-six posttested individually on the episodic reinforcement apparatus. Three sound contingencies were used: classical piano music, rock music, and white noise. A key manipulation training period at the end of the verbal instruction period familiarized the subjects with the equipment and the sound contingencies. During the training period the experimenter had the subject depress each key for twenty seconds.

Data were also obtained on the subjects' off-task behavior during a pretest and posttest live piano concert. The concert pianist performed the piano pieces that were used on the episodic reinforcement apparatus. The concert audience was videotaped and behavioral observations were taken from the tape. Ten subjects were randomly selected from each of three groups (high approval, high disapproval, concert-only treatment) for a total of thirty ten-minute observations. Forty continuous interval observations were made for each subject. Eight observers were used to help eliminate systematic bias (interobserver reliability averaged .98). The occurrence rather than the frequency of an off-task behavior was recorded for each interval. Off-task behaviors were defined as: talking, turning one's head more than ninety degrees, getting out of one's seat, touching another person, and reading.

The episodic reinforcement apparatus consisted of the following components: (a) two two-track stereophonic tape recorders, (b) one set of earphones, (c) a "press to hold" microswitch keyboard adjusted to equal pressure with three equally spaced telegraph-type keys, (d) an electronic switch relay with timer, and (e) an Esterline Angus Chart Recorder. Music and white noise were channeled through the earphones, contingent on students' depression of keys. The lifting of a key resulted in silence. Continuous depression of any one key for two minutes resulted in a relocation of sound contingencies to keys. In order to continue the same sound contingency the subject had to find the contingency's new key location.

The two-track tape recorders were used to reproduce prerecorded tapes of the three sound contingencies: piano music, rock music as a distractor, and white noise as a sound control. Two and one-half minute segments of eight selections were recorded for each music category. The music performed during the pretest and posttest concert and presented during the treatment period consisted of the same selections as those tested.

Procedure

Subjects were tested individually for twenty minutes in both the pretest and posttest conditions. The duration of the tests was based on the research of Cotter and Spradlin (1971). Subjects were screened from the other components of the apparatus while sitting at a desk on which the "press to hold" keyboard was placed. Verbal instructions similar to those used by Greer, Dorow, Wachhaus, and White (1973) were given.

Two groups ($n_1 = 19$, $n_2 = 19$) received five days of music instruction, one under high teacher approval, and the other under high teacher disapproval. A third group (concert only, $n_3 = 19$) attended the pretest concerts but did not participate in training sessions, and a fourth group (posttest only, $n_4 = 19$) was only posttested. Approval/disapproval ratios were experimentally controlled for both training groups, with the high approval group receiving eighty percent approval and the high disapproval group receiving eighty percent disapproval (Madsen & Madsen, 1974). Approvals and disapprovals were randomly assigned to intervals for each session. The experimenter, located at the back of the classroom, gave approval/disapproval hand signals to the teacher. Signals were given randomly on a rotating fifteen- or thirty-second schedule. All approvals and disapprovals were contingent upon subjects' academic and social behaviors as defined by the posted classroom rules. Approvals were also given using the individual subjects' names. Training sessions were videotaped and a frequency count of approvals and disapprovals received by each subject was determined *ex post facto* for additional control (reliability: .99). During the training sessions, simple aural discriminations were taught, such as singing, playing a melody on the piano, clapping rhythmic patterns, and identifying specific pieces. The music taught consisted of the piano selections used for the pretest and the posttest.

Results

Posttest analysis of the sound contingency selection data using the Mann Whitney U showed the following differences: the approval/disapproval groups and concert-only group had a greater total listening time

Table 1
Summary Mann Whitney U Test Between Groups for the Posttest

Sound Contingencies	Total	X̄	Sig. level (one-tail)	Direction
Piano				
Concert Only	5,726	301.37	.05	Concert Only > Posttest Only
Posttest Only	2,788	146.74	N.S.	
Rock			N.S.	
White Noise				
High Approval	709	37.32	.05	Posttest Only > High Approval
Posttest Only	876	46.11		
Total Listening				
High Approval	21,772	1145.89	.05	High Approval > Posttest Only
Posttest Only	20,938	1102		
High Disapproval	21,242	1118	.05	High Disapproval > Posttest Only
Posttest Only	20,938	1102		
Concert Only	21,675	1140.79	.05	Concert Only > Posttest Only
Posttest Only	20,938	1102		

than a posttest-only group; the high approval group selected less white noise than the posttest-only group; and the concert-only group selected more piano than the posttest-only group. The posttest-only and concert-only data demonstrated an instrumentation effect.

Pretest to posttest change scores were analyzed with the Wilcoxon matched-pairs signed-ranks test. The approval/disapproval treatment groups and the concert-only group maintained their total listening time from pretest to posttest. The high approval group increased their time spent listening to piano music and decreased the amount of time spent listening to white noise. In the high disapproval group, the amount of time spent listening to white noise decreased. Both the disapproval group and the concert-only group maintained their total listening time for the piano and rock music.

Table 2
Pretest-Posttest Change Scores of Treatment Groups by Sound Contingencies

Contingencies	Pretest Total	Posttest Total	Change Total	Mean Change	Sig. Level (one-tail)
Rock					
High Approval	17,102	15,783	−1,319	−69.42	N.S.
High Disapproval	16,605	16,585	−20	−1.05	N.S.
Concert Only	16,714	15,155	−1,559	−82.05	N.S.
Piano					
High Approval	2,941	5,280	+2,339	+123.11	.005
High Disapproval	3,374	4,137	+763	+40.16	N.S.
Concert Only	3,600	5,726	+2,126	+111.89	N.S.
White Noise					
High Approval	1,171	709	−462	−24.32	.01
High Disapproval	1,095	520	−575	−30.26	.01
Concert Only	1,267	794	−473	−24.89	.025

The percentage of approval and disapproval received by each subject was determined. Subsequently, the high approval and the high disapproval groups were divided into two subgroups each, one above and one below the median approval/disapproval percentage for each group (high approval, median—sixty percent approval; high disapproval, median—eighty percent disapproval). Analysis of posttest data for these four new subgroups using the Mann Whitney U revealed the following: (1) Subjects with a higher percentage of approval within the high approval group selected more piano music than subjects with a lower percentage of approval within the same group. (2) Those subjects with a higher percentage of approval within the high approval group also selected more piano music than did those subjects with a higher percentage of disapproval within the high disapproval group. (3) Subjects with a lower percentage of approval in the high approval group selected more rock music than subjects with a higher percentage of approval within the same group.

Table 3
Summary Mann Whitney U Tests Between Approval/Disapproval
Subgroups[1] for the Posttest

Sound Contingencies	Total	X	Sig. level (one-tail)	Direction
Piano				
HA₁	1776	17.76	.05	HA₂ > HA₁
HA₂	3876	38.76		
HA₂	3876	38.76	.05	HA₂ > HD
HD	1809	18.09		
Rock				
HA₁	9649	96.49	.05	HA₁ > HA₂
HA₂	6997	69.97		
White Noise			N.S.	
Total Listening			N.S.	

[1] Subgroups = HA₁ (low percentage high approval)
HA₂ (high percentage high approval)
HD (high percentage high disapproval)

The rank order of preference for each sound contingency in the pretest and posttest was determined using the Wilcoxon matched-pairs signed-ranks test. The group order of preference did not change in the posttest. Rock listening maintained the first position, piano listening the second, and, as would be expected, white noise was last.

The posttest off-task concert behavior observations were analyzed using the Mann Whitney U Test. The most interesting finding was that the

Table 4
Rank Order of Preference for Combined Groups

Sound Contingencies	Total Seconds Pre	Rank	Significance Level	Total Seconds Post	Rank	Significance Level (one-tail)
Rock	50,421	I		47,523	I	
			.00003			.0005
Piano	9,915	II		15,143	II	
			.00003			.0003
White Noise	3,533	III		2,023	III	
Total possible time	68,400			68,400		

high disapproval group had a greater total of off-task behaviors than the high approval group. Differences between groups for each of the sub-categories of off-task behavior are displayed in Table 5.

Table 5
Summary Mann Whitney U Tests Between Groups for the Posttest Concert Observations

Off-Task Behavior	Total	Sig. level (one tail)	Direction
Talking			
High Approval	100	p = .048	High Disapproval > High Approval
High Disapproval	168		
High Approval	100	p = .004	Concert Only > High Approval
Concert Only	249		
High Disapproval	168	p = .041	Concert Only > High Disapproval
Concert Only	249		
Turning Head			
High Disapproval	202	p = .009	High Disapproval > Concert Only
Concert Only	126		
Touching		N.S.	
Out of Seat		N.S.	
Reading			
High Approval	6	p = .041	Concert Only > High Approval
Concert Only	84		
Total Off-Task			
High Approval	298	p = .028	High Disapproval > High Approval
High Disapproval	430		

Conclusions

On the basis of this study the following conclusions were made. Music taught with high approval from the teacher will become more reinforcing (time spent listening will increase). Music taught with high disapproval will become less reinforcing. Treatment effects generalize from music selection behavior to concert attentiveness. The specific approval/disapproval ratio received by individual students is indeed important. These findings replicate and extend those of Greer et al. in 1973.

References

Becker, W. C. *Teaching: A Course in Applied Psychology.* Chicago: Science Research Associates, 1971.

Betancourt, F. W. and M. D. Zeiler. "The Choices and Preferences of

Nursery School Children." *Journal of Applied Behavior Analysis*, Vol. 4, No. 4 (1971), pp. 299-304.

Bradley, I. "Effect on Student Musical Preference of a Listening Program in Contemporary Art Music." *Journal of Research in Music Education*, Vol. 20, No. 3 (Fall 1972), pp. 344-353.

Cotter, V. W. and J. E. Spradlin. "A Non-Verbal Technique for Studying Music Preference." *Journal of Experimental Child Psychology*, Vol. 11, No. 3 (1971), pp. 357-365.

Forsythe, J. "The Effect of Teacher Approval, Disapproval, and Errors on Student Attentiveness Comparing Music versus Classroom Teachers." Unpublished doctoral dissertation (Tallahassee, Florida: Florida State University, 1972).

Greer, R. D., L. G. Dorow, G. Wachhaus, and E. R. White. "Adult Approval and Students' Music Selection Behavior." *Journal of Research in Music Education*, Vol. 21, No. 4 (Winter 1973), pp. 345-354.

Greer, R. D., A. Randall, and C. Timberlake. "The Discriminate Use of Music Listening as a Contingency for Improvement in Vocal Pitch Acuity and Attending Behavior." *Council for Research in Music Education, 1971*, Vol. 26, pp. 10-18.

Hanley, E. M. "Review of Research Involving Applied Behavior Analysis in the Classroom." *Review of Educational Research*, Vol. 40, No. 5 (1970), pp. 597-626.

Hendry, D. P. *Conditioned Reinforcement*. Homewood, Illinois: Dorsey Press, 1969.

Jorgensen, H. "Effect of Contingent Preferred Music in Reducing Two Stereotyped Behaviors of a Profoundly Retarded Child." *Journal of Music Therapy*, Vol. 8 (1971), pp. 139-145.

Kelleher, R. T. "Conditioned Reinforcement in Second-Order Schedules." *Journal of the Experimental Analysis of Behavior*, Vol. 9, No. 5 (1966), pp. 475-485.

Kuhn, T. L. "The Effect of Teacher Approval and Disapproval on Attentiveness, Musical Achievement, and Attitudes of Fifth Grade Students." In C. K. Madsen, R. D. Greer, and C. H. Madsen Jr., *Research in Music Behavior: Modifying Behavior in the Classroom*. New York: Teachers College Press, 1975.

Lovitt, T. C. "Narrative Rate Preferences of Normal and Retarded Males as Assumed by Conjugate Reinforcement." Unpublished doctoral dissertation (Lawrence, Kansas: University of Kansas, 1965).

Madsen, C. K. and J. Forsythe. "The Effect of Contingent Music Listening on Increases of Mathematical Responses." *Journal of Research in Music Education*, Vol. 21, No. 2 (Summer 1973), pp. 176-181.

Madsen, C. H., Jr. and C. K. Madsen. *Teaching-Discipline: A Positive Approach for Educational Development*. Expanded Second Edition for Professionals. Boston: Allyn and Bacon, Inc., 1974.

Madsen, C. K., D. E. Wolfe, and C. H. Madsen. "The Effect of Reinforcement and Directional Scalar Methodology on Intonational Improvement." *Council for Research in Music Education, 1969,* Vol. 18, pp. 22-34.

Murray, K. C. "The Effect of Teacher Approval/Disapproval on Musical Performance, Attentiveness, and Attitude of High School Choruses." Unpublished doctoral dissertation (Tallahassee, Florida: Florida State University, 1972).

Steele, A. L. "Effects of Social Reinforcement on the Musical Preferences of Mentally Retarded Children." *Journal of Music Therapy,* Vol. 4 (1967), pp. 57-62.

Yarborough, C. "The Effect of Magnitude of Conductor Behavior on Musical Performance, Attentiveness, and Attitude of High School Choruses." Unpublished doctoral dissertation (Tallahassee, Florida: Florida State University, 1973).

■ Teachers College, Columbia University
New York City

This meta-analysis evaluated 208 variables derived from 98 studies incorporating music as a contingency for education and therapeutic objectives. Variables were converted to effect sizes (ES) via statistical formulae and compared for determination of characteristics affecting reinforcement value of music. The overall benefits attributable to contingent music were almost three standard deviations greater than control/baseline conditions (ES = 2.90). Results demonstrate that contingent music was more effective than contingent nonmusic stimuli used in these studies and more effective than continuous music. Pairing other stimuli such as food, approval, or visual stimulation with the music decreased its effectiveness as a reinforcer. Uniquely, music functioned as a reinforcer and simultaneously as subject matter, and there was evidence of generalized benefit to other academic and social behaviors that were measured but were not contingently reinforced with music.

Jayne M. Standley, *Florida State University*

JRME 1996, VOLUME 44, NUMBER 2, PAGES 105–133

A Meta-Analysis on the Effects of Music as Reinforcement for Education/Therapy Objectives

As early as 1955, Jeffrey reported success using contingent music to effect behavior change in children. He suggested more research into such use of music since, in his opinion, it had several advantages over other commonly used types of reinforcement. Music was considered preferable to candy, which satiated quickly and was deemed nutritionally unsound; it was also preferable to toys, which he felt were disruptive to the teaching process (Jeffrey, 1955). It was many years before a case study appeared in the literature that demonstrated the successful clinical application of a music contingency (Madsen & Madsen, 1968). In this report, an out-of-control juvenile delinquent male received guitar lessons for reducing hostility toward his mother and for completing his assigned household chores.

Music initiation, participation, or interruption as a contingency for

Jayne M. Standley is a professor of music at the Center for Music Research of the School of Music, Florida State University, Tallahassee, FL 32306-2098. Copyright © 1996 by Music Educators National Conference.

behavior change is now an established education/therapy technique having a vast body of accumulated research. Meta-analysis is a statistical procedure that has become an accepted method for synthesizing such an extant body of literature, describing its characteristics and providing a basis for informed generalization about the results. Specifically, meta-analysis is the application of a variety of formulae to the results of a body of homogeneous research to compute effect sizes—quantitative summaries of the properties and findings of individual studies. Effect sizes can then be compared and contrasted across multiple variables (Glass, McGaw, & Smith, 1984) and these overall results, to some extent, generalized.

Meta-analysis has been criticized by some researchers and statisticians on the basis that it combines data from different studies conducted under varying conditions and that it promulgates an inherent bias through analysis of published articles reflecting screening via the referee process. Experts in the technique have argued that these criticisms are unfounded, since data are not directly pooled but converted via consistent formulae to effect sizes that are comparable (Mann, 1994) and since a meticulous meta-analysis uses all studies located on a specific topic, not just refereed articles (Glass, McGaw, & Smith, 1984). It is the intent and purpose of the meta-analysis to synthesize results of individual studies and all effects, whether significant or not, to identify patterns or trends in a carefully defined area of research. Since an individual study can seldom definitively answer a research question, once a large body of research exists on a specified topic, then some method for synthesizing and interpreting these results seems needed. Despite detractors who prefer statistical analysis of individual studies, meta-analysis is currently being used extensively to effect policy in medicine and the social sciences, where it was endorsed by the National Research Council in 1992 (Mann, 1994).

Meta-analysis has become an accepted research technique in other fields, but there is little evidence that music researchers have used the technique. A recent electronic search of the computerized index PsycINFO (1984 to 1994) revealed 1,805 meta-analyses on a variety of topics in psychology, education, and sociology but included only one music meta-analysis, a 1986 work by Standley. Reasons for the dearth of this type of music research are unknown. Perhaps the field is so young that music researchers do not yet feel confident in the amount of research in specific areas as useful for this type of examination.

Although no meta-analyses on the use of contingent music in educational/therapy settings were located, there are meta-analyses on other contingencies for educational objectives. Wilkinson (1980) analyzed 14 process-product classroom studies and performed a meta-analysis on the relationship between teacher praise and student achievement by converting correlation coefficients. Overall, she found a low correlation between praise and academic achievement ($r = .076$). Correlations were higher for reading achievement ($r = .107$) and for mathematics achievement ($r = .178$) than for other academic areas. Negative correlations were found for academic behavior deemed to be of higher cognitive complexity (spelling, paragraph reading, and mathematics reasoning). Teacher praise was more highly correlated with academic achievement of people from lower socioeconomic backgrounds, whereas negative correlations were revealed for those from higher socioeconomic groups. Praise was also more effective in lower grades than in intermediate grades (Wilkinson, 1980).

Getsie, Langer, and Glass (1985) conducted a meta-analysis on the effects of feedback on discrimination learning in children by computing effect size (ES). Best performance resulted from reward plus punishment (ES = .24), compared to reward alone (ES = – .01) and punishment alone (ES = .20). For bright, upper-class children in the fourth grade or higher, punishment alone was most effective. Overall, computed effects of feedback on learning were modest.

Another analysis synthesized results of 39 studies on all types of classroom reinforcement (Lysakowski & Walberg, 1980). It showed an overall effect size for social and tangible reinforcement to classroom learning equal to 1.17. This indicates that, in general, reinforced students had higher measures of classroom learning than did nonreinforced control students by a little more than one standard deviation. Additionally, there were no significant differences in effect by type of reinforcement categorized as follows: competence, being correct, social praise, contingent activities, tokens, check marks, tangibles, or edibles.

Tenenbaum and Goldring (1989) conducted a meta-analysis on 16 studies of motor skill learning that used what they termed enhanced instruction: cues, participation, reinforcement, and feedback/correctives. An overall mean effect size of .66 was found for studies in which investigators used enhanced instruction versus regular instruction methods. Mean effect sizes were somewhat better for females (.82) than for males (.58), and they were less for elementary students (.46) than for kindergarten (.68), junior high school (.59), and high school students (.81).

A meta-analysis on 36 studies concerning cognitive and behavior treatment of impulsivity in children diagnosed as hyperactive, learning disabled, or having attention deficit disorder, conduct disorder, or behavior disorder revealed that mean effect sizes varied greatly by outcome measure or dependent variable: response latency or measures of slowed behavior (1.73), direct observation or frequency measures (.83), response accuracy (.50), teacher ratings (.35), and parent ratings (–.10) (Baer & Nietzel, 1991). There was no discernible difference between effect sizes for studies in which subjects were trained in cognitive (.52) versus behavioral tasks (.50). Overall, treated groups improved approximately one-third to three-quarters of a standard deviation above control groups.

The only meta-analysis in the related areas of music education/therapy (Standley, 1986) included all uses of music in medical/dental treatment and was recently updated to include more contemporary references (Standley, 1996). The revised data pool from 92 studies and 233 dependent variables showed an overall effect size on primary variables due to music of 1.17. Live music (ES = 1.13) was more effective than recorded music (ES = .86). Studies using the subjects' preferred music showed an overall effect size of 1.40. Effects in medicine were differentiated by age only for infants, with their response (ES = .48) being much lower than that of children and adolescents (ES = .95) or that of adults (ES = .93). Behavioral observation was the most conservative type of dependent measure (ES = .83), with results close to those obtained through physiological measures (ES = .90). Results were greatly differentiated by type of research design, with behavioral designs using subjects as their own control (ES = 1.28) showing a greater effect than studies using an experimental/control group format (ES = .66).

In summary, then, meta-analyses using ES as the statistical comparison conducted on the topic of reinforcement and learning have ranges in overall effect from .24 to 1.17. The only prior meta-analysis on music contained primarily noncontingent techniques and resulted in a similar level of effect (ES = 1.17).

The purpose of this study was to quantify the diverse results of research on the effectiveness of contingent music in educational and therapy settings, to determine the magnitude of music's effect as a reinforcer, and to identify the circumstances that affect its reinforcement value.

METHOD

Procedure

Established practice in meta-analysis involves three primary steps (Getsie, Langer, & Glass, 1985). The first step is a complete literature search to locate all possible sources in the defined population of studies. It is important to include both published and unpublished sources in a meta-analysis to reduce possible biases in the analyzed data that might be created by refereed screening of published results. Next, the relevant characteristics and results of the located articles are identified and categorized. The final step is to use a variety of statistical techniques to convert reported data to comparable effect size measures.

Studies qualified for inclusion in this meta-analysis if they (a) contained empirical data and were reported in English; (b) used music listening initiation, music interruption, or music performance as a contingency for behavior change; (c) used an educational or therapy objective as the dependent variable; and (d) reported results in a format amenable to replicated data analysis. The starting points for a comprehensive literature search were electronic searches of the following data bases: PsycINFO (1967 to 1994), PsycFIRST (1992 to January 1995), ERIC (1967 to 1994), Dissertation Abstracts (1861 to 1994), and MEDLINE (1985 to 1994). Additional articles were identified from the reference lists of articles obtained. The literature search located more than 100 studies on this topic, 98 of which met criteria for inclusion in the meta-analysis. These 98 studies yielded 208 measures of effects on dependent variables.

Estimation of Effect Size

Each dependent variable measure reported in the selected studies was converted to an estimated effect size (ES) according to procedures outlined by Glass, McGaw, and Smith (1984). The ES represents that proportion of a standard deviation that quantifies the experimental effect on the two conditions; i.e., an ES of + 1.00 would indicate that the size of benefit due to the experimental condition was one standard deviation greater than that of the control condition. The effect sizes of experimental results in this analysis were estimated by contrasting the means of experimental/treatment conditions (Exp) and control/baseline conditions (Con) divided by the standard deviation (*SD*) of the control/baseline condition, as in the formula below

$$\frac{\overline{M}_{Exp} - \overline{M}_{Con}}{SD_{Con}} = \text{ES (Estimated Effect Size)}$$

Data not reported in a format that included or allowed computation of means and *SD* were converted via a variety of published statistical formulae (Glass, McGaw, & Smith, 1984).

RESULTS

Ninety-eight studies were included in this meta-analysis and are identified separately in the References section. Table 1 is a comprehensive outline and categorization of study variables grouped by type of education/therapeutic variable. Effect sizes were computed for 208 variables and ranged from ES = 35.44[1] (contingent music effects compared to baseline measures of sitting posture of an adult with a mental disability) to ES = –7.05 (effects of contingent music initiation compared to contingent music interruption on crying of a 10-year-old with a mental disability).

In Table 1, a negative ES value indicates that the second independent variable of the two comparisons was more effective than the first. Of the 208 effect sizes computed, there were 12 that resulted in negative values. Contingent music was less effective than candy (ES = –3.12), lights (ES = –1.60), the voice of infants' mothers (ES = –1.46), or the sound of a heartbeat (ES = –.25). Noncontingent music was less effective than baseline conditions for reducing disruptive school bus behavior (ES = – 1.81) and for reducing crying of infants with colic (ES = –.23). Contingent music was less effective than baseline conditions for increasing treadmill duration of subjects with mental handicaps (ES = –.20) and for reducing self-stimulatory behaviors of subjects with profound mental disabilities (ES = –.04). Contingent music initiation was less effective than contingent music interruption for reducing crying and correcting poor posture with children with mental disabilities (ES = –7.05 and ES = –3.71, respectively). When contingent music was paired with tactile stimulation (ES = –1.22) and with music distortion

Table 1
Variable Categorization and Mean Effect Size

KEY:

Design:
ES = Effect Size
Ss as Con = Subjects as Own Control
Exp = Experimental Group
Con = Control Group

Music:
CM = Contingent Music
M = Music
C = Contingent

Subject Characteristics
MD = Mental Disability
ED = Emotional Disability
LD = Learning Disability
BD = Behavior Disorder
Hyper = Hyperactive
CP = Cerbral Palsey

Other:
R = Reinforcer
Elem. = Elementary

EDUCATIONAL STUDIES

Author (Date)	Design	Subject charac- teristic/age	Dependent variables	Independent variables	ES
ACADEMIC VARIABLES					
Cotter & Spradlin (1971)	Ss as Con	MH/8–16 yrs	Math	CM	1.04
Dorow (1976)	Ss as Con	MH/20 yrs	Math Music listening	CM via TV	.84 7.37
Madsen (1981)	Ss as Con	Normal/3rd gr	Math Music vs. books Music information	CM via TV Books 	1.74 1.62 .55 2.47
Madsen et al. (1976)	Exp/Con	Normal/1st gr	Math Music vs. tutors	CM via TV Tutors 	5.60 9.88 11.98
Madsen & Forsythe (1973)	Exp/Con	Normal/6th gr	Math	CM via ear- phones	 1.16
Madsen et al. (1975)	Exp/Con	Normal/5th gr	Math Attentiveness Generalized math Generalized attention	CM CM 	10.34 3.71 5.17 3.13
McLaughlin & Helm (1993)	Ss as Con	Normal/ middle school	Math	CM	.25
Miller (1977)	Ss as Con	MH/9–14 yrs	Math	CM–Preferred CM–Non- preferred	.51 .74

Table continues on following pages

Author (Date)	Design	Subject charac-teristic/age	Dependent variables	Independent variables	ES
Miller et al. (1974)	Ss as Con	EH/10–13 yrs	Math	CM/Art	1.36
				Nonpreferred activity	.54
Eisenstein (1974)	Ss as Con	Normal/7–8 yrs	Reading in books	CM–Guitar lessons	.76
			Reading from flashcards	CM–Guitar lessons	1.14
Gordon (1977)	Exp/Con	Normal/4th gr	Reading	CM–Lessons	.76
			Watkins Farnum Test		.40
Greer et al. (1975)	Exp/Con	Normal/6th gr	Choice of reinforcer	Music vs. bank	.03
				Music vs. story	.34
				Music vs. candy	–3.12
Madsen & Geringer (1976)	Exp/Con	Normal/5 yrs	Auditory dis-crimination	CM via TV	1.20
				Playtime	1.22
				Choice of R	1.14
				Music vs. playtime	.02
Jacobs (1976)	Ss as Con	Normal/3 yrs	Numbers	CM	6.69
Johnson & Zinner (1974)	Ss as Con	MH/12 yrs	Color discri-mination	CM	.86
				CM	.86
Madsen et al. (1988)	Exp/Con	LD & BD/K & 5th gr	Academic skills	CM for tutors	1.55
Steele (1971)	Ss as Con	Headstart/4–5 yrs	Reading	CM	7.30
			Participation	CM	2.19
Waldron (1977)	Ss as Con	Developmental delay	Telephone numbers	CM/M cue vs. M cue	1.03
Greer et al. (1971)	Exp/Con	Normal/6th gr	Vocal accuracy	Rock vs. silence	.28
				ME series music vs. silence	.05
			Attentiveness	CM	.74
Madsen & Madsen (1972)	Exp/Con	Normal/6th gr	Pitch acuity	CM	.43
			Attending	CM	.60
			Music choice–Soul		.43

SOCIAL VARIABLES

Author (Date)	Design	Subject charac-teristic/age	Dependent variables	Independent variables	ES
Bosco (1974)	Ss as Con	Autistic/8 yrs	Social behavior	CM	.86
Gunter et al. (1993)	Ss as Con	Autistic/14 yrs	Stereotopy	CM	1.00
				Continuous M	.77
				CM vs. continuous M	3.30

Table 1 *(continued)*

Author (Date)	Design	Subject charac-teristic/age	Dependent variables	Independent variables	ES
Hanser (1972)	Ss as Con	EH/Middle school	Social behavior	CM	4.40
Hanser (1974)	Ss as Con	EH/Elem.	Social behavior	CM	11.55
Hill et al. (1989)	Ss as Con	MH/17 yrs	Out-of-seat	CM	2.15
				CM rock	2.49
				CM jazz	2.43
				CM classical	1.06
				CM rap	1.97
Jellison et al. (1984)	Exp/Con	MH & Normal/ 8–15 yrs	Acceptance of MH Ss	CM	.25
			Positive interactions	CM vs. lg group (class)	2.96
			Positive interactions	CM vs. lg group (free time)	.64
Madsen (1982)	Ss as Con	Normal & BD/ 7th & 8th gr	On-task	Approval	1.23
				CM/Approval	1.55
Madsen & Wolfe (1979)	Exp/Con	College Ss	Body move-ment–reading	CM	.82
			Body move-ment–listening	CM	2.42
				Finger snapping	5.63
				Negative practice	7.53
Wilson (1976)	Ss as Con	MH/5–7 yrs	Disruptive be-havior	CM	1.14
Wilson & Hopkins (1973)	Ss as Con	Normal/7th & 8th gr	Home Ec noise	CM	3.36
Wolfe (1982)	Exp/Con	Normal & Hy-per/3rd gr	Body move-ment	CM–Inter-ruption	.17
				CM	.04
			Letters	CM–Inter-ruption	.03
				CM	.10
Yarbrough et al. (1977)	Exp/Con	Normal/5th gr	Attentiveness	CM	.28

MEDICAL STUDIES

PHYSICAL REHABILITATION VARIABLES

Author (Date)	Design	Subject charac-teristic/age	Dependent variables	Independent variables	ES
Ball et al. (1975)	Ss as Con	CP with MH/ 9–17 yrs	Head posture	CM	3.71
Corman (1979)	Ss as Con	CP with MH/ 17–24 yrs	Head extension	CM	1.86

Author (Date)	Design	Subject charac- teristic/age	Dependent variables	Independent variables	ES
Grove et al. (1975)	Ss as Con	CP with MH/ 10–11 yrs	Head extension	CM/Approval	6.84
Kearney & Fussy (1991)	Ss as Con	Neurologic injury/22 yrs	Head posture	CM	4.11
Macurik (1979)	Ss as Con	CP with MH/Elem.	Head posture	CM	2.02
Murphy et al. (1979)	Ss as Con	CP with MH/ 14–19 yrs	Head posture	CM	1.37
Wolfe (1980)	Ss as Con	CP/3–37 yrs	Head posture	CM	.34
				CM/Tone	.52
				CM vs. CM/Tone	.10
Gouvier et al. (1985)	Ss as Con	Physical Impair- ment/21 yrs	Yelling during gait training in PT	CM/ TOK-BAK	4.19
Barrett (1962)	Ss as Con	Neurologic im- pairment/38 yrs	Uncontrol- lable tic	CM/White noise	3.22
Holliday (1987)	Ss as Con	CP/49 yrs	Increased phy- sical skill	CM	6.51
			Decreased inappropriate behavior	CM	.62

OTHER MEDICAL VARIABLES

Author (Date)	Design	Subject charac- teristic/age	Dependent variables	Independent variables	ES
Epstein et al. (1974)	Ss as Con	Headaches/ 39 yrs	EMG tension Amt. of medication	CM	2.48 2.04
Boyle & Greer (1983)	Ss as Con	Coma/31–56 yrs	Overt move- ment	CM	2.50
Butterfield & Siper- stein (1972)	Ss as Con	Neonates/2 days	Sucking patterns	CM	2.00
DeCasper & Carstens (1981)	Ss as Con	Neonates/3 days	Sucking patterns	CM vs. con- tinuous M	1.84
			Activity level	CM vs. con- tinuous M	1.70
Etscheidt (1989)	Ss as Con	Infants with colic/4–7 wks	Crying	CM	1.72
				C attention	2.54
				CM/C attention	3.36
			Alertness	CM	.16
				C attention	1.13
				CM/C attention	1.72
Larson & Ayllon (1990)	Ss as Con	Infants with colic/3–7 wks	Crying	CM	4.95
				Continuous M	–.23
				CM vs. con- tinuous M	4.48

Table 1 *(continued)*

SPORTS STUDIES

Author (Date)	Design	Subject charac-teristic/age	Dependent variables	Independent variables	ES
Caouette & Reid (1985)	Exp/Con	MH/22–30 yrs	Stationary bike duration	CM	.72
				CM/Lights	1.32
				CM vs. Lights	–1.60
Caouette & Reid (1991)	Ss as Con	MH/25 yrs	Stationary bike duration	CM-Preferred	.70
				CM vs. White noise	.13
				CM vs. Pink noise	.91
Ellis et al. (1993)	Ss as Con	MH/18–19 yrs	Treadmill duration	CM	–.20
			Heartrate	CM	.22
Hume & Crossman (1992)	Ss as Con	Swimmers/ 12–16 yrs	Practice behavior	CM	2.26
Silliman & French (1993)	Exp/Con	MH/10–17 yrs	Soccer kick	CM	3.45
				C approval	1.50
				CM vs. C approval	1.52

DEVELOPMENTAL STUDIES
ATTENTION/INTERACTION VARIABLES

Author (Date)	Design	Subject charac-teristic/age	Dependent variables	Independent variables	ES
Allen & Bryant (1985)	Ss as Con	MH/10–11 yrs	Crying	CM	4.81
				CM–Inter-rupted	7.78
				CM vs. CM-Inter-rupted	–7.05
			Sitting up	CM	.48
				CM–Inter-rupted	4.12
				CM vs. CM–Inter-rupted	–3.71
Becker (1983)	Ss as Con	MH/34 yrs	Eye contact	CM	2.60
				CM/Distor-tion	2.50
				CM vs. CM/Distor-tion	.12
Burch et al. (1987)	Ss as Con	MH/31 yrs	Sitting posture	CM	35.44*
Deutsch & Parks (1978)	Ss as Con	MH/14 yrs	Inappropriate behavior	CM	6.61

Author (Date)	Design	Subject characteristic/age	Dependent variables	Independent variables	ES
Dewson & Whiteley (1987)	Ss as Con	MH/11–29 yrs	Head turn	CM/Slides/ Vibration	.60
Dorow (1975)	Ss as Con	MH/9–15 yrs	Follow directions	CM	1.14
				CM/Food	1.52
				CM vs. CM/Food	.42
Dorow (1980)	Ss as Con	MH/15 yrs	Follow directions	CM/Approval	5.16
				CM/Approval/Food	5.18
				C Approval	4.00
				CM/Approval–Maintenance	5.24
				C/Approval/Food–Maintenance	5.29
				C Approval-Maintenance	5.29
Falb (1982)	Ss as Con	MH/6 mo.–3 yrs	Vasoconstriction	CM	3.75
				C heartbeat	4.61
				CM vs. C heartbeat	–.25
Finkelstein & Ramey (1977)	Ss as Con	Infants/8 mo.	Pull toy	CM vs. continuous M	2.69
Holloway (1980)	Ss as Con	MH/30 yrs	Follow directions	CM	1.68
				CM–Playing Instr	1.96
				CM vs. CM–Playing	.28
Konarski (1987)	Ss as Con	MH/21–61 yrs	Pull lever	CM vs. slides	.96
				CM vs. slides w/o response deprivation	1.34
				CM/Response dep. vs. slides	1.58
Metzler (1974)	Exp/Con	MH/16–55 yrs	Imitative behavior	CM	1.27
				Continuous M	.09
				Continuous M	.09
Ramos (1993)	Exp/Con	Abuse hot line callers	Sustain telephone on-hold for counselor	Jazz vs. relaxation M	.99
Remington et al. (1977)	Ss as Con	MH/12.8 yrs	Press bar	Blues M vs. playing drums	.62
Sandford & Tustin (1974)	Ss as Con	Abusive parent of 13-mo.-old	Tolerate infant crying	CM	33.10 *

Table 1 (continued)

Author (Date)	Design	Subject charac-teristic/age	Dependent variables	Independent variables	ES
Saperston et al. (1980)	Exp/Con	MH/28 yrs	Reach for object	CM vs. C juice	.12
Talkington & Hall (1970)	Exp/Con	MH/Elem.	Echoic responses	CM–Preferred CM–Least preferred CM–Most vs. least pre-ferred	1.75 .77 1.26
Underhill & Harris (1974)	Ss as Con	EH/9–13 yrs	Imitation	CM Continuous M CM vs. Con-tinuous M	2.76 .01 2.28
Vollmer & Iwata (1991)	Ss as Con	MH/25–36 yrs	Follow direc-tions	CM vs. food CM vs. social praise	2.28 2.60

SELF-HELP VARIABLES

Luiselli (1991)	Ss as Con	MH/10 yrs	Self-feeding	CM/ Bright light	2.00
Johnson & Babbit (1993)	Ss as Con	MH/4 yrs	Eating solid food	CM	2.80
Garwood (1988)	Ss as Con	MH/21 yrs	Enuresis	CM/Bell pad	.10

TRANSPORTATION VARIABLES

Barmann et al. (1980)	Ss as Con	MH/8 yrs	Disruptive school bus behavior	CM CM vs. con-tinuous M	17.60 12.70
McCarty et al. (1978)	Ss as Con	EH/3–14 yrs	Disruptive school bus behavior	CM Continu-ous M	1.57 –1.81
Reid et al. (1975)	Ss as Con	Autistic/8–10	Disruptive car behavior	CM CM/Ritalin	.94 1.21
Ritschl et al. (1972)	Ss as Con	MH/7–15 yrs	Disruptive school bus behavior	CM	1.54

Author (Date)	Design	Subject charac- teristic/age	Dependent variables	Independent variables	ES
STEREOTOPY VARIABLES					
Borreson & Anderson (1982)	Ss as Con	MH/21 yrs	Rumination	CM	2.16
				CM/Tactile stimulation	−1.22
Carrocio et al. (1976)	Ss as Con	Schizophre- nic/40 yrs	Tics	C Guitar rental	.81
Davis et al. (1983)	Ss as Con	MH/26 yrs	Rumination	CM–10″	1.60
				CM–30″	1.89
				CM/Repri- mand	2.33
				Reprimand	.99
				CM vs. repri- mand	1.57
				CM–30″ vs. CM–20″	.60
			Out-of-seat behavior	CM	1.64
Greenwald (1978)	Ss as Con	MH/7–22 yrs	Self-stimula- tory behavior	CM	−.04
				CM/Distor- tion	−.27
				CM vs. CM/ Distortion	.20
Hauck & Martin (1970)	Ss as Con	Schizophre- nic/5–9	Self-stimula- tory behavior	CM vs. Con- tinuous M	.34
Jorgenson (1971)	Ss as Con	MH/Elem.	Self-stimula- tory behavior	CM	1.95
Jorgenson (1974)	Ss as Con	MH/9 yrs	Stereotopy	CM	2.33
			Follow direc- tions	CM	1.11
McClure et al. (1986)	Ss as Con	MH/9 yrs	Hand-to-mouth stereotopy	CM	7.07
Ritchey (1977)	Exp/Con	MH/17–41 yrs	Self-stimula- tory behaviors	CM	1.04
Ross (1974)	Ss as Con	MH/13–22 yrs	Stereotopy	CM	2.54
				CM–Activity	3.55
				C Play	6.10
Scruggs (1991)	Ss as Con	Geriatric	Wandering	CM	.08
				M Activity	.29
COMPLAINING VARIABLES					
Cook & Freethy (1973)	Ss as Con	Schizophre- nic/43 yrs	Complaining	CM	1.14
				CM/Cue	1.32
				CM vs. CM/Cue	2.90

Table 1 *(concluded)*

Author (Date)	Design	Subject charac-teristic/age	Dependent variables	Independent variables	ES
Williams & Dorow (1983)	Ss as Con	Depression/ 79 yrs	Complaining	CM	2.54
				CM/Repri-mand	2.02
				CM vs. CM/ Reprimand	.56

WORK VARIABLES

Bellamy & Sontag (1973)	Ss as Con	MH/11–12 yrs	Assembly line production	CM–20″	1.98
				CM–30″	.93
				CM–20″ vs. CM–30″	1.64
				CM–20″ vs Continu-ous M	1.57
				CM–30″ vs. Continu-ous M	.43
Clegg (1982)	Ss as Con	MH/22–55 yrs	Work pro-duction	CM	2.40
				Continu-ous M	7.60
				CM vs. Con-tinuous M	2.88
Cotter (1971)	Exp/Con	MH/12–21 yrs	Work pro-duction	CM vs. Con-tinuous M	1.50
Podvin (1967)	Ss as Con	MH/Adults	Work pro-duction	CM vs. Con-tinuous M	1.06

PREFERENCE VARIABLES

Greer et al. (1974)	Ss as Con	Normal/ K–6th gr	Bar press	CM-Rock vs. CM-Nonrock	4.50
Standley & Madsen (1990)	Ss as Con	Infants	Listening preference	CM vs. mother's voice	–1.46
				CM vs. fe-male voice	1.87

Note. All effect size (ES) comparisons with baseline condition unless otherwise stated.

* See Discussion section.

Table 2
Publication Analyses of Included Studies (N = 98)

Publication Year

1960s	1970s	1980s	1990s
2	53	29	14

Publication Source

Music journals	Psychology journals	Mental retardation/ Education journals	Medical journals	Speech therapy journals	Unpublished articles
45	20	16	2	1	14

Reciprocal Citations of Included Studies by Journal Type

Music	Psychology	Mental retardation/Education	Medical	Speech therapy
249	18	52	2	1

(ES = −.27), it was less effective than baseline condition for subjects with mental disabilities.

Table 2 shows the publication source and date of studies included in the meta-analysis. The bulk of the studies were published in the 1970s, with a substantial reduction in number published in the 1980s and 1990s, although the rate across the last 15 years appears to be stable. The source of publication data reveals that music researchers have had a major impact on the development of this topic by having contributed almost half the articles qualified for inclusion. Additionally, this table shows the results of an analysis of the references used by the included studies to determine whether they referenced others' prior work. The music journal authors frequently referenced the prior studies, with 249 citations. Authors of articles published in the mental retardation/education journals also frequently cited these studies ($n = 48$). Authors publishing in psychology journals cited these studies only 18 times, although 20 of the studies in the meta-analysis were published in psychology journals. It seems apparent that educators and those publishing in the field of mental retardation research music as a contingency and quote a large number of prior studies. Psychology journal authors research this topic but do not often quote existing studies. From a historical perspective, it is interesting to note the five articles most referenced by the other meta-analysis studies: Barrett, 1962 ($n = 22$); Madsen and Forsythe, 1973 ($n = 20$); Steele, 1971 ($n = 14$); Cotter, 1971 ($n = 13$); and Greer, Randall, and Timberlake, 1971 ($n = 12$).

Table 3 shows effect sizes for the variety of independent variables as compared to baseline conditions; also shown are effect sizes for contingent music variables as compared to other independent variables.

Table 3
Mean Effect Size for Independent Variable Comparisons (N = 208)

Experimental Conditions versus Baseline

Contingent music	Noncontingent music	Contingent nonmusic stimuli	Contingent music paired with nonmusic stimuli	Generalized dependent variables	Music variations
2.90	2.23	2.37	2.60	4.15	1.99
$n = 105$	$n = 9$	$n = 15$	$n = 22$	$n = 2$	$n = 4$

Contingent Music Conditions versus Other Conditions

Continuous music	Other music	Nonmusic stimuli
2.32	0.24	1.14
$n = 13$	$n = 16$	$n = 22$

The overall effect of contingent music conditions versus baseline conditions was 2.90. This effect is much larger than the 1.17 effect size previously established for social and tangible reinforcement to classroom learning (Lysakowski & Walberg, 1980). In this study, the benefits of noncontingent music over baseline conditions were found to be ES = 2.23. The prior medical meta-analysis on therapeutic uses of music that were primarily noncontingent revealed an overall effect size of 1.17 (Standley, 1996). Contingent music versus continuous music resulted in an ES = 2.32, and contingent music versus nonmusic stimuli as contingencies resulted in an ES = 1.14. In these comparisons, other contingent stimuli included progressive illumination of a string of lights, white noise, heartbeat, bank accounts, stories, candy, projected slides, books, tutor interactions, playtime, juice or food, praise or social approval, and the voices of infants' mothers.

Pairing other stimuli with contingent music (ES = 2.60) slightly reduced its effectiveness. Contingent music paired with nonaversive stimuli such as food, approval, or visual stimulation (ES = 2.63) was more effective than when cessation of contingent music was followed by aversive stimuli such as white noise, music distortion, or loud tones (ES = 1.84).

There were two measures of generalized effect on variables not consequated (contingently reinforced) by the treatment condition (ES = 4.15). In an educational setting, consequating an academic behavior positively affected social behavior and vice versa.

The 105 measures of the effects of contingent music as the sole reinforcement versus baseline conditions were further analyzed. Results are shown in Tables 4–10. Effects by intent of the music contingency are analyzed in Table 4. Procedures intended to increase behavior (ES

Table 4
Mean Effect Size (ES) by Intent of Music Contingency (N = 105)

	Contingency to increase behavior	Contingency to decrease behavior
ES	2.97	2.77
n	69	36

= 2.97) were slightly more effective than those intended to decrease behavior (ES = 2.77).

Table 5 shows differentiated effects by the techniques used to establish the music contingency: initiating music following the desired response (ES = 2.55) versus interrupting ongoing music following an undesirable response (ES = 3.56). It is apparent that music interruption is a more effective contingent music procedure by about one standard deviation.

Table 5
Mean Effect Size by Music Contingency Technique (N = 105)

	Music initiation	Music interruption
ES	2.55	3.56
n	68	37

Timing of the contingency application is analyzed in Table 6. Immediate implementation of the contingency (ES = 3.38) showed greater effect than delayed procedures: (a) those in which tokens, tickets, or points issued for desirable behavior could be exchanged later for music, and (b) those that required sustained correct responding for an extended period before participation in music activities (ES = 1.70). As expected, delay of receipt of contingent music greatly reduced its effects on therapeutic/educational variables.

Table 7 shows analysis by type of educational or therapeutic dependent variable. Effects were greatest for physical rehabilitation (ES = 5.47) and for developmental or daily living variables (3.40). Music contingencies were somewhat less effective for social (ES = 2.04) and academic variables (ES = 2.18) measured in school settings, though these

Table 6
Mean Effect Size by Timing of Music Contingency (N = 105)

	Immediate	Delayed
ES	3.38	1.70
n	75	30

Table 7
Mean Effect Size by Educational/Therapeutic Objective (N = 105)

	EDUCATIONAL Social	Academic	DEVELOPMENTAL Daily living	MEDICAL Health	PHYSICAL Rehabilitation	SPORTS Exercise
ES	2.04	2.18	3.40	2.26	5.47	1.39
n	20	24	38	7	11	5

Table 8
Mean Effect Size by Age (N = 105)

	Infants–4 yrs	5–11 yrs	12–14 yrs	15–18 yrs	Adult	Elderly
ES	3.51	2.53	1.96	1.08	4.51	1.31
n	9	48	16	5	25	2

Table 9
Mean Effect Size by Subject Characteristic (N = 105)

	Normal	Mentally impaired	Emotionally impaired	Medically/ physically impaired
ES	2.99	3.16	2.38	2.25
n	32	48	11	14

effect sizes are much greater than those found in prior meta-analyses of nonmusic reinforcement in the school setting. Music as a contingency was least effective in sports applications (ES = 1.39). In this study, contingent music benefits in medicine (ES = 2.26) were much greater than noncontingent music medical effects (ES = 1.17) noted previously by Standley (1996).

Analyses by age (see Table 8) revealed decreasing effects from infancy (ES = 3.51) through each level of the school years to high school (ES = 1.08). Effect sizes then dramatically increased for uses with adults (ES = 4.51). Least effective were contingent uses of music with the elderly, specifically several studies incorporating Alzheimer's patients (ES = 1.31), although a benefit of greater than one standard deviation for music contingencies on problems of Alzheimer's patients would seem to be a clinically important result.

Table 9 shows effect size for subjects by ability to produce the desired response. The greatest effects were with subjects with mental disabilities (ES = 3.16) and subjects without disabling conditions (ES = 2.99), with little differentiation among other groups, i.e., those with emotional disabilities (ES = 2.38) or those with medical/physical impairments (ES = 2.25). It is interesting that contingent music effects were so large with people with mental disabilities, since the preponderance of these studies used subjects who were categorized as profoundly mentally disabled or multiply disabled.

Table 10 shows that effects varied greatly by type of design, with those studies using subjects as their own control (ES = 3.42) having much greater effect than those involving experimental/control group designs (1.62). A meta-analysis of applied single-subject research involving differential reinforcement (Prochnow-Lagrow, 1984) found a similarly high overall effect size (3.61), although this may be somewhat inflated since the authors modified the analysis procedure by omitting the first three data points for each baseline and treatment condition in order to avoid pollution of treatment results across conditions. In this meta-analysis, all baseline and treatment data points were analyzed. One reason for different effect sizes by design type may be that the studies using subjects as their own control were often single-subject or small-sample studies with contingencies carefully tailored to individual

Table 10
Effect Size by Design Type (N = 105)

	Subjects as own control	Experimental/ Control groups
ES	3.42	1.62
n	75	30

preferences and reinforcement schedules. Such highly individualized techniques are a common aspect of behavioral procedures and are designed to enhance effectiveness.

DISCUSSION

The most conservative, descriptive metric of effect size was used in this study because of the variety of behavioral designs included in which independence between averaged data could not be assumed. Two results are indicated by asterisks in Table 1 and noted as exorbitantly high effect sizes. These reflect the floor-to-ceiling changes from almost no desired behavior under baseline conditions to immediate and high levels of the desired behavior. With only a single subject in each study, a control condition with extremely low variance results, and this produces a very large effect size when divided into the tremendous gain in behavior due to the experimental condition. As a statistical measure of standard deviation, these numbers are impossibly large. As points on the scale of the common metric used for comparison in this study, they accurately reflect the unusual benefits of the music contingency established. The investigator determined that these data should be included, since the numbers carry no inherent value in themselves except within the context of the specific study from which they evolved.

One could argue that no single-subject designs should be included in an analysis of this type on the basis that very small Ns create bias in the results. It seems to the investigator that that argument negates the validity and impact of single-subject research, which is central to behavioral treatment methodology. Although techniques are still evolving, the research literature does demonstrate precedence in including single-subject research in meta-analyses. To rule out the possibility of inflation due to size of N, however, a second analysis of all 208 variables was undertaken by the investigator using Hedges correction factor K (Glass, McGaw, & Smith, 1991, p. 113), a procedure for adjusting ES by the size of the smallest group sample in each study. In the great majority of data points, results were affected by only hundredths of a point, and this adjustment to the 208 variables did not substantially change the overall meta-analysis results.

In summary, these analyses demonstrate that contingent music is more effective than other contingent nonmusic stimuli and is more effective than continuous music, and that pairing other stimuli with contingent music decreases its effectiveness. Music is highly effective as a contingency for either increasing desirable behavior or reducing undesirable behavior, with slightly better results in increasing behavior. Music interruption is more effective than music initiation as the procedure for establishing the contingency, and immediate initiation of the music is more effective than delayed initiation in exchange for tokens or points. In this study, music contingencies were more effective in physical rehabilitation and with developmental behaviors than with medical or educational behaviors. Least effective were sports applications.

Adults and infants, compared with other age-groups, responded best to music contingencies, with effects declining from childhood through the primary- and secondary-school years. Least effects were demonstrated for elderly patients, although effects at the levels demonstrated in these studies would be considered clinically significant. Individuals with mental disabilities and normal subjects demonstrated greater benefits than did those with emotional disabilities or medical/physical impairments. The majority of studies in this analysis used subjects as their own control and demonstrated much greater effect than did studies involving experimental and control groups.

The effects due to contingent music revealed in this study certainly compare favorable to other types of reinforcement assessed through meta-analyses. Perhaps most interesting in this analysis was the widespread and creative use of contingent music across educational and therapeutic objectives. For example, in medicine, contingent music reinforced overt behaviors of comatose patients, decreased crying of infants with colic, improved neck strength and head posture of individuals with neurologic impairments, and reduced headache pain through biofeedback.

The most frequent uses of contingent music have occurred in the field of education. In regular education classrooms, music as subject matter or as pleasurable listening has reinforced other academic achievement, particularly math skills and reading. Contingent music has also reduced noise in Home Economics sewing classes, increased acceptance of children with disabilities in their mainstreamed classes, and improved aural discrimination, vocal pitch acuity, and music information and listening skills. In special education, contingent music has been used to increase self-feeding skill, decrease stereotypical behavior or disruptive behavior, decrease enuresis and rumination (habitual regurgitation), decrease out-of-seat behavior on the school bus, and increase classroom social behaviors such as following directions, imitating, and eye contact.

In physical education and sports, music was played over pool loudspeakers as a group contingency to increase on-task practice time for competitive swimmers, and music reinforcement via tape recorder was used on the soccer field to improve kick accuracy and in the workout room to increase duration of stationary bike riding.

In counseling sessions, one unique study from New Zealand helped an abusive father learn to tolerate the prolonged crying of his infant daughter, a behavior which had previously stimulated physical assault. Contingent music listening following a changing criterion tolerance for the taped crying was paired with videotapes of the child at play and during happy, contented moments (Sandford & Tustin, 1974).

In predicting the effects of music contingencies for future applications, it is interesting to note that several meta-analyses selected for comparison with this study showed decreased reinforcement effects across school grade levels (Getsie, Langer, & Glass, 1985; Wilkinson, 1980), as did this study. Perhaps this is due to preference changes as children develop (LeBlanc, 1981). However, from analysis of these contingent music studies, it seems apparent that such decreases may be more related to the educational values held by the teachers and therapists involved in the studies, namely, that more mature subjects should be expected to delay gratification and benefit from increasingly complex methods of reinforcement. In this study, delay of reinforcement greatly lessened effect, and the studies with older children seemed to incorporate more procedures that provided choices and delayed reinforcement.

A primary criticism of reinforcement for education and therapeutic endeavors has been the contention that reinforcement reduces intrinsic motivation, i.e., the self-engaging participation and pleasure in the activity itself. Cameron and Pierce (1994) conducted a meta-analysis on the relationship between reinforcement, reward, and intrinsic motivation. They concluded that the meta-analysis "results suggest that in the laboratory, overall reward does not negatively impact intrinsic motivation on any of the four measures analyzed" and that "it no longer seems appropriate to argue against the use of incentive systems in applied settings" (p. 394). In the current study, measures of music as subject matter increased simultaneously with music functioning as reinforcement for other academic subjects. Additionally, academic and social behaviors not contingently reinforced showed generalized benefits while other studies demonstrated students' frequent selection of music from a varied menu of possible reinforcers. This meta-analysis demonstrated that music is a powerful contingency, and results showed no evidence of negative effects on either students' academic performance or motivation.

This meta-analysis has shown that demonstrated effects of contingent music are profound, can be creatively designed, and are applicable across a wide variety of educational/therapeutic endeavors. Based on these studies, predicted effects in medicine and counseling seem particularly strong and, if the frequency of research is an indicator, much underutilized in clinical settings. Educational research on contingent music, however, is much more comprehensive in its documentation of uses and procedures. "Music for its own sake" certainly ought to be the core of music education programs; however, more use and creative application of such an effective technique as music reinforcement would seem warranted, especially when it addresses contemporary political desire to improve the basic curriculum (music as reinforcement for other subject matter such as math and reading) while concomitantly improving music knowledge and skills. Clearly, effects are so beneficial across diverse fields of endeavor that knowledge of contingent music techniques would seem to be an important component of the professional skills of all music educators and music therapists.

Those seeking results of research often are frustrated by myriad separate and seemingly incomparable analyses and by the researchers' reluctance to generalize their results. Meta-analysis is a technique for global analysis and synthesis of a carefully defined topic and set of variables specifically for the purpose of generalization of results across multiple studies. Such analyses seem crucial to the professions of music education and therapy as we seek to increase our knowledge of effective techniques from general to specific applications and to affect educational and social policy. Music researchers have not yet incorporated meta-analysis procedures in large numbers, unlike investigators in a number of other fields. It is an additional research method that offers much to enhance our existing methods of inquiry, and pursuit of more research in this area would seem warranted.

Note

1. See Discussion section concerning rationale for inclusion of very large effect sizes.

REFERENCES

References marked with an asterisk indicate studies included in the meta-analysis.

* Allen, L. D., & Bryant, M. C. (1985). A multielement analysis of contingent versus contingent-interrupted music. *Applied Research in Mental Retardation 6* (1), 87–97.
* Ball, T. S., McCrady, R., & Hart, A. (1975). Automated reinforcement of head posture in two cerebral palsied retarded children. *Perceptual and Motor Skills, 40,* 619–622.
Baer, R. A., & Nietzel, M. T. (1991). Cognitive and behavioral treatment of impulsivity in children: A meta-analytic review of the outcome literature. *Journal of Clinical Child Psychology, 20* (4), 400–412.
* Barmann, B. C., Croyle-Barmann, C., & McLain, B. (1980). The use of contingent-interrupted music in the treatment of disruptive bus-riding behavior. *Journal of Applied Behavior Analysis, 13,* 693–698.
* Barrett, B. H. (1962). Reduction in rate of multiple tics by free operant conditioning methods. *The Journal of Nervous and Mental Disease, 135* (3), 187–195.
* Becker, I. (1983). Control of acquisition of eye contact by distorted and undistorted music stimuli. *Journal of Music Therapy, 20* (3), 132–142.
* Bellamy, T., & Sontag, E. (1973). Use of group contingent music to increase assembly line production rates of retarded students in a simulated sheltered workshop. *Journal of Music Therapy, 10,* 125–136.
* Borreson, P. M., & Anderson, J. L. (1982). The elimination of chronic rumination through a combination of procedures. *Mental Retardation, 20* (1), 34–38.
* Bosco, B. K. (1974). *The use of radio control for the contingent application of music with a child exhibiting autistic behaviors: An exploratory study.* Unpublished master's thesis, Florida State University.
* Boyle, M. E., & Greer, R. D. (1983). Operant procedures and the comatose patient. *Journal of Applied Behavior Analysis, 16,* 3–12.
* Burch, M. R., Clegg, J. C., & Bailey, J. S. (1987). Automated contingent reinforcement of correct posture. *Research in Developmental Disabilities, 8* (1), 15–20.
* Butterfield, E. C., & Siperstein, G. N. (1972). Influence of contingent auditory stimulation upon non-nutritional suckle. In J. F. Bosma (Ed.), *Third Symposium on Oral Sensation and Perception: The Mouth of the Infant* (pp. 313–333). Springfield, IL: Charles C Thomas.

Cameron, J., & Pierce, W. D. (1994). Reinforcement, reward, and intrinsic motivation: A meta-analysis. *Review of Educational Research, 64* (3), 363–423.

* Caouette, M., & Reid, G. (1985). Increasing the work output of severely retarded adults on a bicycle ergometer. *Education and Training of the Mentally Retarded, 20* (4), 296–304.

* Caouette, M., & Reid, G. (1991). Influence of auditory stimulation on the physical work output of adults who are severely retarded. *Education and Training in Mental Retardation, 26* (1), 43–52.

* Carroccio, D. F., Latham, S., & Carroccio, B. B. (1976). Rate-contingent guitar rental to decelerate stereotyped head/face-touching of an adult male psychiatric patient. *Behavior Therapy, 7* (1), 104–109.

* Clegg, J. C. (1982). *The effect of non-contingent and contingent music on work production rate of mentally retarded adults in a work activity center.* Unpublished master's thesis, Florida State University.

* Cook, M., & Freethy, M. (1973). The use of music as a positive reinforcer to eliminate complaining behavior. *Journal of Music Therapy, 10,* 213–216.

* Corman, S. E. (1979). *Increasing head extension with the use of automated contingent music.* Unpublished doctoral dissertation, Western Michigan University.

* Cotter, V. W. (1971). Effects of music on performance of manual tasks with retarded adolescent females. *American Journal of Mental Deficiency, 76* (2), 242–248.

* Cotter, V. W., & Spradlin, J. E. (1971). Effects of contingent music on retarded children's performance of addition computations. (Report No. 3). Parsons, KS: Parsons Research Center.

* Davis, W. B., Wieseler, N. A., & Hanzel, T. E. (1983). Reduction of rumination and out-of-seat behavior and generalization of treatment effects using a non-intrusive method. *Journal of Music Therapy, 20* (3), 115–131.

* DeCasper, A. J., & Carstens, A. A. (1981). Contingencies of stimulation: Effects on learning and emotion in neonates. *Infant Behavior and Development, 4,* 19–35.

* Deutsch, M., & Parks, A. L. (1978). The use of contingent music to increase appropriate conversational speech. *Mental Retardation, 16* (1), 33–36.

* Dewson, M. R., & Whiteley, J. H. (1987). Sensory reinforcement of head turning with nonambulatory, profoundly mentally retarded persons. *Research in Developmental Disabilities, 8* (3), 413–426.

* Dorow, L. G. (1975). Conditioning music and approval as new reinforcers for imitative behavior with the severely retarded. *Journal of Music Therapy, 12* (1), 30–39.

* Dorow, L. G. (1976). Televised music lessons as educational reinforcement for correct mathematical responses with the educable mentally retarded. *Journal of Music Therapy, 13* (2), 77–86.

* Dorow, L. G. (1980). Generalization effects of newly conditioned reinforcers. *Journal of Music Therapy, 15* (1), 8–14.

* Eisenstein, S. R. (1974). Effect of contingent guitar lessons on reading behavior. *Journal of Music Therapy, 11,* 138–146.

* Ellis, D. N., Cress, P. J., & Spellman, C. R. (1993). Training students with mental retardation to self-pace while exercising. *Adapted Physical Activity Quarterly, 10* (20), 104–124.

* Epstein, L., Hersen, M., & Hemphill, D. (1974). Music feedback in the treatment of tension headache: An experimental case study. *Journal of Behavior Therapy and Experimental Psychiatry, 5* (1), 59–63.

* Etscheidt, M. A. (1989). *Parent training to reduce the excessive crying associated with infant colic.* Unpublished doctoral dissertation, Georgia State University.

* Falb, M. E. (1982). *The use of operant procedures to condition vasoconstriction in*

profoundly mentally retarded (PMR) infants. Unpublished master's thesis, Florida State University.

* Finkelstein, N. W., & Ramey, C. (1977). Learning to control the environment in infancy. *Child Development, 48,* 806–819.

* Garwood, E. C. (1988). The effect of contingent music in combination with a bell pad on enuresis of a mentally retarded adult. *Journal of Music Therapy, 25* (2), 103–109.

Getsie, R. L., Langer, P., & Glass, G. (1985). Meta-analysis of the effects of type and combination of feedback on children's discrimination learning. *Review of Educational Research, 55* (1), 9–22.

Glass, G., McGaw, B., & Smith, M. (1984). *Meta-analysis in social research.* Beverly Hills, CA: Sage Publications.

* Gordon, M. V. (1977). *The effect of contingent instrumental music instruction on the language reading behavior and musical performance ability of middle school students.* Unpublished doctoral dissertation, Columbia University Teachers College.

* Gouvier, W. D., Richards, J. S., Blanton, P. D., Janert, K., Rosen, L. A., & Drabman, R. S. (1985). Behavior modification in physical therapy. *Archives of Physical Medicine and Rehabilitation, 66* (2), 113–116.

* Greenwald, M. A. (1978). The effectiveness of distorted music versus interrupted music to decrease self-stimulatory behaviors in profoundly retarded adolescents. *Journal of Music Therapy, 15* (2), 58–66.

* Greer, R. D., Dorow, L., & Harrison, L. (1975). Aural discrimination instruction and the preferences of sixth-graders for music listening, story listening, and candy. In C. K. Madsen, R. D. Greer, & C. H. Madsen, Jr. (Eds.), *Research in music behavior* (pp. 97–108). New York: Teachers College, Columbia University Press.

* Greer, R. D., Dorow, L. & Randall, A. (1974). Music listening preferences of elementary school children. *Journal of Research in Music Education, 22,* 284–291.

* Greer, R. D., Randall, A., & Timberlake, C. (1971). The discriminate use of music listening as a contingency for improvement in vocal pitch acuity and attending behavior. *Bulletin of the Council for Research in Music Education,* no. 26, 10–18.

* Grove, D. N., Dalke, B. A., Fredericks, H. D., & Crowley, R. F. (1975). Establishing appropriate head positioning with mentally and physically handicapped children. *Behavioral Engineering, 3* (2), 53–59.

* Gunter, P. L., Fox, J. J., McEvoy, M. A., Shores, R. E., & Denny, R. K. (1993). A case study of the reduction of aberrant, repetitive responses of an adolescent with autism. *Education and Treatment of Children, 16* (2), 187–197.

* Hanser, S. B. (1972). *The effect of contingent music upon the behavior of a group of junior high school students.* Unpublished master's thesis, Florida State University.

* Hanser, S. B. (1974). Group-contingent music listening with emotionally disturbed boys. *Journal of Music Therapy, 11* (4), 220–225.

* Hauck, L. P., & Martin, P. L. (1970). Music as a reinforcer in patient-controlled duration of time-out. *Journal of Music Therapy, 7,* 43–53.

* Hill, J., Brantner, J., & Spreat, S. (1989). The effect of contingent music on the in-seat behavior of a blind young woman with profound mental retardation. *Education and Treatment of Children, 12* (2), 165–173.

* Holliday, A. M. (1987). *Music therapy and physical therapy to habilitate physical disabilities of young children.* Unpublished master's thesis, Florida State University.

* Holloway, M. S. (1980). A comparison of passive and active music reinforcement to increase preacademic and motor skills in severely retarded children

and adolescents. *Journal of Music Therapy, 17* (2), 58–69.

* Hume, K. M., & Crossman, J. (1992). Musical reinforcement of practice behaviors among competitive swimmers. *Journal of Applied Behavior Analysis, 25,* 665–670.

* Jacobs, G. M. (1976). *The effect of music, social-tactile reinforcement, and verbal punishment on the visual discrimination learning of children of low income families.* Unpublished master's thesis, Florida State University

Jeffrey, W. E. (1955). New techniques for motivating and reinforcing children. *Science, 121,* 371.

* Jellison, J. A., Brooks, B., & Huck, A. (1984). Structuring small groups and music reinforcement to facilitate positive interactions and acceptance of severely handicapped students in the regular music classroom. *Journal of Research in Music Education, 32,* 243–264.

* Johnson, C. R., & Babbitt, R. L. (1993). Antecedent manipulation in the treatment of primary solid food refusal. *Behavior Modification, 17* (4), 510–521.

* Johnson, J. M., & Zinner, C. C. (1974). Stimulus fading and schedule learning in generalizing and maintaining behaviors. *Journal of Music Therapy, 11* (2), 84–96.

* Jorgenson, H. (1971). Effects of contingent preferred music in reducing two stereotyped behaviors of a profoundly retarded child. *Journal of Music Therapy, 8* (4), 139–145.

* Jorgenson, H. (1974). The use of a contingent music activity to modify behaviors which interfere with learning. *Journal of Music Therapy, 11,* 41–46.

* Kearney, S., & Fussey, I. (1991). The use of adapted leisure materials to reinforce correct head positioning in a brain-injured adult. *Brain Injury, 5* (3), 295–302.

* Konarski, E., Jr. (1987). Effects of response deprivation on the instrumental performance of mentally retarded persons. *American Journal of Mental Deficiency, 91* (5), 537–542.

* Larson, K., & Ayllon, T. (1990). The effects of contingent music and differential reinforcement on infantile colic. *Behaviour Research and Therapy, 28* (2), 119–125.

LeBlanc, A. (1981). Effects of style, tempo, and performing medium on children's music preference. *Journal of Research in Music Education, 29,* 143–156.

* Luiselli, J. K. (1991). Acquisition of self-feeding in a child with Lowe's syndrome. *Journal of Developmental and Physical Disabilities, 3* (2), 181–189.

Lysakowski, R. S., & Walberg, H. J. (1980). Classroom reinforcement. *Evaluation in Education: An International Review Series, 4,* 115–116.

* Macurik, K. M. (1979). An operant device to reinforce correct head position. *Journal of Behavior Therapy and Experimental Psychiatry, 10,* 237–239.

* Madsen, C. K. (1981). Music lessons and books as reinforcement alternatives for an academic task. *Journal of Research in Music Education, 29,* 103–110.

* Madsen, C. K. (1982). The effect of contingent teacher approval and withholding music performance on improving attentiveness [Special issue]. *Psychology of Music,* 76–81.

* Madsen, C. K., Dorow, L., Moore, R., & Womble, J. (1976). Effect of music via television as reinforcement for correct mathematics. *Journal of Research in Music Education, 24,* 51–59.

* Madsen, C. K., & Forsythe, J. L. (1973). Effect of contingent music listening on increases of mathematical responses. *Journal of Research in Music Education, 21,* 176–181.

* Madsen, C. K., & Geringer, J. (1976). Choice of televised music lessons versus free play in relationship to academic improvement. *Journal of Music Therapy, 13*(4), 154–162.

Madsen, C. K., & Madsen, C. H., Jr. (1968). Music as a behavior modification technique with a juvenile delinquent. *Journal of Music Therapy, 5* (3), 72–76.

* Madsen, C. K., & Madsen, C. H., Jr. (1972). Selection of music listening or candy as a function of contingent versus noncontingent reinforcement and scale singing. *Journal of Music Therapy, 9,* 190–198.

* Madsen, C. K., Moore, R., Wagner, M., & Yarbrough, C. (1975). A comparison of music as reinforcement for correct mathematical responses versus music as reinforcement for attentiveness. *Journal of Music Therapy, 12* (2), 84–95.

* Madsen, C. K., Smith, D. S., & Feeman, C. C., Jr. (1988). The use of music in cross-age tutoring within special education settings. *Journal of Music Therapy, 25* (3), 135–144.

* Madsen, C. K., & Wolfe, D. E. (1979). The effect of interrupted music and incompatible responses on bodily movement and music attentiveness. *Journal of Music Therapy, 16* (1), 17–30.

Mann, C. C. (1994). Can meta-analysis make policy? *Science, 266* (11), 960–962.

* McCarty, B., McElfresh, C., Rice, S., & Wilson, S. (1978). The effect of contingent background music on inappropriate bus behavior. *Journal of Music Therapy, 15* (3), 150–156.

* McClure, J. T., Moss, R. A., McPeters, J. W., & Kirkpatrick, M. A. (1986). Reduction of hand mouthing by a boy with profound mental retardation. *Mental Retardation, 24* (4), 219–222.

* McLaughlin, R. F., & Helm, J. L. (1993). Use of contingent music to increase academic performance of middle-school students. *Psychological Reports, 72,* 658.

* Metzler, R. K. (1974). The use of music as a reinforcer to increase imitative behavior in severely and profoundly retarded female residents. *Journal of Music Therapy, 11* (2), 97–110.

* Miller, D. (1977). Effects of music listening contingencies on arithmetic performance and music preference of EMR children. *American Journal of Mental Deficiency, 81* (4), 371–378.

* Miller, D. M., Dorow, L., & Greer, R. D. (1974). The contingent use of music and art for improving arithmetic scores. *Journal of Music Therapy, 11,* 57–64.

* Murphy, R., Doughty, N., & Nunes, D. (1979). Multielement designs: An alternative to reversal and multiple baseline evaluation strategies. *Mental Retardation, 17* (1), 23–27.

* Podvin, M. G. (1967). The influence of music on the performance of a work task. *Journal of Music Therapy, 4* (2), 52–56.

Prochnow-Lagrow, J. E. (1984). *Meta-analysis of applied single subject research utilizing differential reinforcement of behavior omission.* Unpublished doctoral dissertation, Northern Illinois University.

* Ramos, L. (1993). The effects of on-hold telephone music on the number of premature disconnections to a statewide protective services abuse hot line. *Journal of Music Therapy, 30* (2), 119–129.

* Reid, D. H., Hill, B., Rawers, R., & Montegar, C. (1975). The use of contingent music in teaching social skills to a nonverbal, hyperactive boy. *Journal of Music Therapy, 12* (1), 2–18.

* Remington, R. E., Foxen, T., & Hogg, J. (1977). Auditory reinforcement in profoundly retarded multiply handicapped children. *American Journal of Mental Deficiency, 82* (3), 299–304.

* Ritchey, N. A., Jr. (1977). *A pleasant alternative to a punishment procedure using contingent loud noise to modify self-destructive and self-stimulative behaviors in the non-ambulatory, profoundly and severely retarded.* Unpublished master's thesis, Florida State University.

* Ritschl, C., Mongrella, J., & Presbie, R. J. (1972). Group time-out from rock

and roll music and out-of-seat behavior of handicapped children while riding a school bus. *Psychological Reports, 31,* 967–973.

* Ross, L. E. (1974). *The effects of three treatments involving music on the stereotyped behaviors of profoundly retarded adults.* Unpublished master's thesis, Florida State University.

* Sandford, D. A., & Tustin, R. D. (1974). Behavioural treatment of parental assault on a child. *New Zealand Psychologist, 2,* 76–82.

* Saperston, B. M., Chan, R., Morphew, C. & Carsrud, K. (1980). Music listening versus juice as a reinforcement for learning in profoundly mentally retarded individuals. *Journal of Music Therapy, 17* (4), 174–183.

* Scruggs, S. D. (1991). *The effects of structured music activities versus contingent music listening with verbal prompt on wandering behavior and cognition in geriatric patients with Alzheimer's disease.* Unpublished master's thesis, Florida State University.

* Silliman, L. M., & French, R. (1993). Use of selected reinforcers to improve the ball kicking of youths with profound mental retardation. *Adapted Physical Activity Quarterly, 10* (1), 52–69.

Standley, J. M. (1986). Music research in medical/dental treatment: Meta-analysis and clinical applications. *Journal of Music Therapy, 23* (2), 56–122.

Standley, J. M. (1996). Music research in medical/dental treatment: An update of a prior meta-analysis. In C. E. Furman (Ed.), *Effectiveness of music therapy procedures: Documentation of research and clinical practice* (pp. 1–60). Silver Spring, MD: National Association for Music Therapy.

* Standley, J. M., & Madsen, C. K. (1990). Comparison of infant preferences and responses to auditory stimuli: Music, mother, and other female voice. *Journal of Music Therapy, 27,* 54–97.

* Steele, A. L. (1971). Contingent socio-music listening periods in a preschool setting. *Journal of Music Therapy, 8,* 131–139.

* Talkington, L. W., & Hall, S. M. (1970). A musical application of Premack's hypothesis to low verbal retardates. *Journal of Music Therapy, 7* (3), 95–99.

Tenenbaum, G., & Goldring, E. (1989). A meta-analysis of the effect of enhanced instruction: Cues, participation, reinforcement and feedback and correctives on motor skill learning. *Journal of Research and Development in Education, 22* (3), 53–64.

* Underhill, K. K., & Harris, L. M. (1974). The effect of contingent music on establishing imitation in behaviorally disturbed retarded children. *Journal of Music Therapy, 11,* 156–166.

* Vollmer, T. R., & Iwata, B. (1991). Establishing operations and reinforcement effects. *Journal of Applied Behavior Analysis, 24,* 279–291.

* Waldron, G. M. (1977). *The effect of music as a structural prompt and as a reinforcer on learning a sequential task.* Unpublished master's thesis, University of Minnesota.

Wilkinson, S. S. (1980). *The relationship of teacher praise and student achievement: A meta-analysis of selected research.* Unpublished doctoral dissertation. University of Florida.

* Williams, G., & Dorow, L. G. (1983). Changes in complaints and non-complaints of a chronically depressed psychiatric patient as a function of an interrupted music/verbal feedback package. *Journal of Music Therapy, 20* (3), 143–155.

* Wilson, C. V. (1976). The use of rock music as a reward in behavior therapy with children. *Journal of Music Therapy, 13* (1), 39–48.

* Wilson, C. W., & Hopkins, B. (1973). The effects of contingent music on the intensity of noise in junior high home economics classes. *Journal of Applied Behavior Analysis, 6,* 269–275.

* Wolfe, D. E. (1980). The effect of automated interrupted music on head posturing of cerebral palsied individuals. *Journal of Music Therapy, 17* (4), 184–206.

* Wolfe, D. E. (1982). The effect of interrupted and continuous music on bodily movement and task performance of third grade students. *Journal of Music Therapy, 19* (2), 74–85.

* Yarbrough, C., Charboneau, M., & Wapnick, J. (1977). Music as reinforcement for correct math and attending in ability assigned math classes. *Journal of Music Therapy, 14* (2), 77–88.

Submitted May 15, 1995; accepted August 15, 1995.

X.

Special

Populations

and

Music

Positive interactions of severely handicapped students integrated into four grade levels of elementary music classes were studied under three teaching conditions: (a) large group, (b) small cooperative group, and (c) small cooperative group with a music listening contingency for cooperation. The design consisted of multiple baselines for social interaction with pretest and posttest measures of nonhandicapped students' general acceptance and acceptance of their severely handicapped peers within music. The mean rates of positive interactions were found to increase relative to the degree to which antecedents (small group) and reinforcement (music) were structured for interactions. Mean rates were highest under small group contingency conditions and lowest under large group conditions. Grades with the highest rates of positive interactions indicated significant positive change for music as well as general acceptance. Results indicate that positive social interactions between nonhandicapped and handicapped students in the integrated music classroom with increases in nonhandicapped students' acceptance are not a result of music classroom experiences and music instruction alone but the degree to which teaching conditions specifically structure classroom antecedents and reinforcement for social interaction. Benefits of the integrated music classroom are discussed.

Judith A. Jellison, *University of Texas at Austin*
Barbara H. Brooks, *St. Paul Public Schools*
Ann Marie Huck, *St. Paul, Minnesota*

JRME 1984, VOLUME 32, NUMBER 4, PAGES 243–264

Structuring Small Groups and Music Reinforcement to Facilitate Positive Interactions and Acceptance of Severely Handicapped Students in the Regular Music Classroom

The Education for All Handicapped Children Act (P. L. 94–142), a federal policy that mandates that handicapped children are educated with their nonhandicapped peers to the maximum extent possible, affects both mildly handicapped and severely handicapped students. Numerous researchers and professionals experienced in services for the

---

For reprints of this article, contact Judith A. Jellison, Department of Music, University of Texas at Austin, Austin 78712.

severely handicapped student are particularly supportive of integrated educational experiences. It is generally agreed upon by these professionals that integrated educational experiences are essential if severely handicapped students are to achieve maximum normalization and independence as adults (Brown, Branston, Hamre-Nietupski, Johnson, Wilcox, & Gruenewald, 1979; Brown, Nietupski, & Hamre-Nietupski, 1976; Sontag, Certo, & Button, 1979).

The movement of severely handicapped students into numerous educational environments has generated research on factors that may positively or negatively affect the outcome. Two factors of concern are (a) the attitude of nonhandicapped students toward their handicapped peers and (b) the social interactions between severely handicapped and nonhandicapped students. Research indicates that the attitudes held by nonhandicapped students toward their severely handicapped peers may be changed in a positive direction. Voeltz (1980) studied the attitude of over 2,500 students, grades 2 through 7, toward their severely handicapped peers. Results indicated that, regardless of gender or grade, contact with severely handicapped students was the one variable clearly associated with accepting responses. In a second study, Voeltz (1982) found that an increase in length of contact (i.e., a second school year) resulted in pronounced positive attitudinal changes of students in integrated educational settings. In a study by McHale and Simeonsson (1980), in which contact consisted of play sessions during which 30 nonhandicapped students in small groups of 6 each were instructed to teach their severely handicapped peers how to play, contact was also the variable that appeared to increase nonhandicapped students' understanding of their severely handicapped peers. In these three studies, contact, the variable that positively affected attitudes, was not merely physical proximity of nonhandicapped and handicapped students in the classroom, but physical proximity within environments organized and structured to facilitate social interactions. While the opportunity for contact must first be made available, it does not necessarily result in positive social interactions and attitude change. The critical component to positive interactions between severely handicapped and nonhandicapped students appears to be the way in which instruction is organized (Asher & Taylor, 1981; Hamre-Nietupski & Nietupski, 1981; Stainback, Stainback, & Jaben, 1981). In addition, there have been several reviews of empirical research on instruction variables that affect interactions among handicapped and nonhandicapped students (Stainback & Stainback, 1981; Stainback, Stainback, Raschke, & Anderson, 1981; Strain, 1981). Voeltz (1980) emphasizes the need for empirical research in this area when she points out the following:

Once the opportunity for interaction is available, investigators of the development and quality of longitudinal interactions should commence to collect formative evaluation data through behavioral observation to guide professionals in the optimal design of integrated educational services. (p. 469)

The responsibility for the improvement of educational services for the handicapped extends to music educators and music therapists as well as nonmusic professionals (Alley, 1979; Forsythe & Jellison, 1977; Hazard, 1979; Thompson, 1982). The importance of the integrated music classroom is twofold. Attainment of maximal independence and normalization for the severely handicapped in school and nonschool environments demands classroom integrated music experiences with a focus on teaching functional music and nonmusic skills (Jellison, 1979, 1983). In addition, the music setting is an educational one in which curriculum goals can be modified for the severely handicapped without altering the simultaneous education of the nonhandicapped. Research is necessary to assist music professionals in designing quality music programs. Gilbert and Asmus (1981), in a survey of 789 music educators, concluded that one of the greatest overall needs of teachers related to information about designing and evaluating music programs for handicapped students. In addition, teachers express a need for information about "music as a socializing agent" in the integrated classroom. There are several articles and books that focus on instructional techniques as well as social goals and objectives for the integrated music classroom (Gilbert, 1977; Graham & Beer, 1980; Hardesty, 1979; Lament, 1978; Lathom, 1980; Nocera, 1979; Taylor, 1982). However, to date, there is no published research investigating these techniques or the actual social behavior of handicapped and nonhandicapped students in the integrated music classroom.

The purpose of the present study is to extend previous attitudinal and social interaction research to the integrated music classroom setting. Specifically, the study investigated (a) the frequency and quality of severely handicapped/nonhandicapped social interactions in an integrated music classroom; (b) the degree and type of intervention, if any, that is necessary to facilitate severely handicapped/nonhandicapped interactions in an integrated music classroom; (c) the acceptance by nonhandicapped students of their severely handicapped peers when considering music environments and music activities; and (d) the comparison of the general and music acceptance by nonhandicapped students of their severely handicapped peers before and after integrated music classroom experiences. The social interactions of severely handicapped and nonhandicapped students under three teaching methods (large group, small group, and small group with music contingency) were investigated, as well as attitudinal measures of general acceptance (Voeltz, 1980) and acceptance of nonhandicapped students of their handicapped peers within music.

The three teaching conditions in this study varied in the structuring of antecedents and consequences designed to facilitate social interactions among the severely handicapped students and their nonhandicapped peers. Research literature indicates that structuring antecedents by arranging the classroom into small groups (Nietupski, Hamre-Nietupski, Schuetz, & Ockwood, 1980) as well as small cooperative goal interdependent groups (Johnson & Johnson, 1980) facilitates positive social interactions among handicapped and nonhandicapped students.

Although the small group condition in the present study was based on the cooperative model developed by Johnson and Johnson (1975), there was a major deviation from that model in that no specific group evaluation or other contingency was structured for the completion of the academic task or goal. This decision was based on Cottrell's theory (1968) and supportive evidence by Gottlieb (1982) as well as by Semmel, Gottlieb, and Robinson (1979) that suggest that integrated, academically handicapped children perform more poorly in an evaluative situation. Music listening was structured as the contingency in this study because of its effectiveness as a reinforcer for student academic and social behaviors, as identified in research and reviews by Madsen, Greer, and Madsen (1975) and Greer (1981). A music listening contingency is also very adaptable and can be managed independently by classroom teachers (Dorow, 1976; Madsen, Dorow, Moore, & Womble, 1976; Madsen & Geringer, 1976).

METHOD

Subjects

Subjects were 100 elementary school students, aged 9 to 12, from four classrooms in a regular education public school setting, and 26 severely handicapped (retarded) students, aged 8 to 15, selected from five classrooms in a segregated special education public school setting. Of the severely handicapped students, 21 were ambulatory and 5 were in wheelchairs. Of these students, 14 were able to chain two or more words, 6 used single word responses, 1 was echolalic, 4 were nonverbal, and 1 student used minimal signing to communicate.

No specific selectional factors were used to determine the four classrooms of nonhandicapped students for this study beyond variation of grade level and each classroom teacher's interest. Following the selection of the four nonhandicapped classrooms, five or six handicapped students were selected for integration into each of the four classrooms with an attempt to match as closely as possible the chronological ages of the nonhandicapped students. Handicapped students met the following music and nonmusic criteria: (a) demonstrate attending eye contact, (b) demonstrate awareness of peers, (c) demonstrate appropriate affect, (d) follow one-part directives, (e) remain seated for 25 min and (f) refrain from disruptive or aggressive behaviors. In addition, students selected reacted positively to music and were able to participate or partially participate in the playing of classroom rhythm instruments.

Independent variables

The two independent variables (teaching conditions) studied within the multiple baseline design were: (a) small group and (b) small group with a music contingency. The two conditions varied primarily in the degree of structure of classroom antecedents and consequences to encourage positive social interactions among the severely handicapped and nonhandicapped students. In the large group condition (baseline), students were directed to sit in a single large circle for instruction. No specific antecedents or consequences were structured to facilitate social interactions. Teacher instructions were related to the acquisition of the music objective only. Classroom rules included: (a) participation, (b) following directions, and (c) listening to each other and the teacher. Although no specific reinforcement was structured, the teacher gave students occasional verbal reinforcement for appropriate academic or social behaviors. In the small group condition, major changes were made in the structure of antecedents. Students were assigned to groups of five to six members in which one or two handicapped students were included. Students were instructed to work together within their s®all groups to complete one task (music objective) while ensuring that all members participated in the task. An example of a musical objective would be as follows: Given four rhythm patterns in $\frac{4}{4}$ meter and written on cards, individuals in the group will perform each rhythm pattern; the group will arrange the rhythms into a·rhythm score and perform the rhythm score by clapping or playing percussion instruments. Students were instructed to work cooperatively. The definition of cooperation was read by the teacher each session from a large poster visible to the students. Cooperation was defined as (a) working with everyone, (b) helping everyone, (c) encouraging everyone, and (d) talking about the music activity with everyone. While the groups were working, the teacher monitored the groups and gave assistance when necessary. When appropriate, each group was verbally reinforced once by the teacher for cooperating.

In the small group with music contingency condition, the assignment procedures and teacher instructions to work cooperatively (antecedents) were identical to the small group condition. However, following the definition of cooperation by the teacher, students were told that a rock music listening reward would be given to the small group selected as being the most cooperative.

Dependent variables

Three dependent variables were observed: (a) social interactions, (b) general acceptance, and (c) acceptance within music. The social interaction variable of particular interest that was studied within the multiple baseline design was the frequency of positive heterogeneous (handicapped and nonhandicapped) social interactions. Heterogeneous social interactions were defined as the observation of a sensory exchange (i.e., visual, auditory, or tactile) between handicapped and nonhandicapped students, and were classified into two categories: (a) helping and (b) reciprocal. Helping interactions were those in which the handicapped student received verbal or motor assistance from a nonhandicapped student while the handicapped student was performing, or in order for the student to perform a skill or engage in an activity. Reciprocal interactions were those interactions in which both a handicapped and nonhandicapped student were observed independently engaging in a sensory exchange or were independently alternating verbal or motor actions in an activity with each other. Social interactions were defined as positive when students were socially "on-task" (engaging in social interactions). Interactions were labeled as positive even though the students were academically "off-task" (not following the classroom rules or teacher directives). Social interactions were defined as negative if one or both students were engaging in negative verbal or motor behaviors (i.e., arguing, hitting, name calling).

Negative and positive proximal and isolative behaviors were also observed. These behaviors were defined as noninteraction behaviors in that no heterogeneous sensory or action exchanges were observed. A behavior of a student was defined as proximal when the student was within physical proximity ("an arm's length") of another student and isolative when the student was beyond physical proximity. Proximal and isolative behaviors were defined as positive when the student was (a) academically "on-task" (i.e., following classroom rules and teacher directives) or (b) socially "on-task" (i.e., looking at students or teachers regardless of the academic task). These behaviors were defined as negative when the student was either academically or socially "off-task."

General acceptance was defined as resultant scores on a scale with demonstrated validity and reliability for the measurement of children's attitudes toward handicapped peers (Voeltz, 1980). On this pencil and paper scale, nonhandicapped students responded by marking "yes," "no," or "undecided" to 34 statements concerning handicapped students in regular classrooms and recreational settings and activities. The statements imply varying degrees of nonhandicapped and handicapped peer interactions (i.e., being in the same class, playing together, being friends, etc.).

Acceptance within music was defined as resultant scores of the nonhandicapped students on a scale developed specifically for this study. With permission from the author (Voeltz), music related items were developed to parallel appropriate items on the general acceptance scale (AS). The acceptance within music scale (AMS) consisted of 29 items or statements concerning handicapped students in regular *music* classroom or *music* recreational settings and activities. These items also implied varying degrees of interactions (i.e., being in the same music class, listening to music together, being friends with a handicapped student from music class, etc.). Five of the original 34 items were not appropriate for a music parallel and were included in the AMS without change.

Observation protocol

The focus of the observation was the social interaction behavior of the handicapped students. Data collection sheets were designed to contain general class descriptive information as well as codes for the interaction behavior of each handicapped student being observed and any student or adult with whom the student came into contact. Three main social interaction categories were coded: (a) type of behavior (isolative, proximal, helping, reciprocal), (b) quality (negative or positive), and (c) individual involved in the interaction (none, homogeneous-handicapped, heterogeneous-nonhandicapped, or adult). Four classroom environments were coded: (a) beginning, (b) class, (c) free time, and (d) end.

A 5-sec observe/record interval method was used to collect data. A timed-cue audio tape with a cassette recorder and ear plug was used to structure the observation intervals. The observation order of the handicapped students was determined each session on the basis of the order in which they entered the classroom. After all handicapped and nonhandicapped students were in the classroom and the observation order was determined, the observer marked the code B (beginning of class) and began to hand-record social interaction data. Each student was observed in order for 1 min using the 5-sec observe/record method. For each student, the observer recorded one code from each of the three categories that occurred for most of the 5-sec period. The student observation order was repeated for the duration of the class period until each student being observed left the classroom. Beyond the beginning of the class period, changes in classroom environments (class, free time, and end) were identified and recorded using instructional cues of the music teacher directing the class (i.e., "It's time to begin class.").

Observers

Two trained observers were assigned to two of the four classes and remained as observers for the duration of the study. Two additional trained observers rotated between the two classrooms for reliability. Reliability observations occurred in every condition for every class for a total of 30% of all observation sessions.

Design

A multiple baseline design (Baer, Wolf, & Risley, 1968) was used to test the effects of structuring teaching conditions on the frequency of positive heterogeneous social interactions. All grades received music education classes twice a week for approximately 30 min each session. Each music teacher taught one lower and one upper grade for the duration of the study. A free time period of approximately 5 min in length was scheduled at the end of the second class of each week. Observation data were collected only for the second class of each week. Social interactions and noninteractions were observed in four class environments: (a) before class, (b) class instruction, (c) free time following class instruction, and (d) following class. The number of sessions in each condition for each grade are presented in Figures 1 and 2. Mean times for each observation per class environment per condition are presented in Table 1.

The acceptance of the nonhandicapped students of their handicapped peers in general as well as within music was tested independently in each grade using a pretest-posttest design. Both scales were given during a

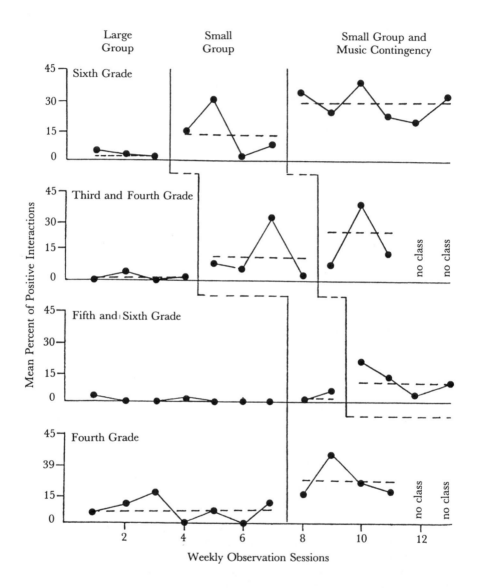

Figure 1. The mean percent of positive interactions (helping and reciprocal) between severely handicapped students and their nonhandicapped peers under three teaching conditions.

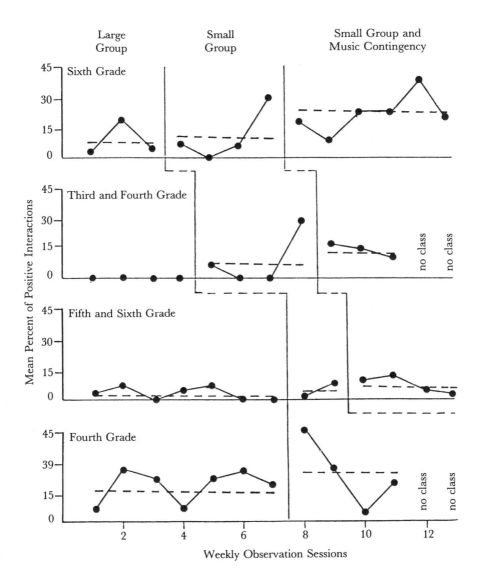

Figure 2. The mean percent of positive interactions (helping and reciprocal) between severely handicapped students and their nonhandicapped peers during free time following three teaching conditions.

Table 1

Mean Frequency and Mean Rate per Session of Positive Noninteraction/Interaction Behaviors of Severely Handicapped Students during Integrated Music Class and Free Time Environments under Three Teaching Conditions

Grade	Environment/ condition	Mean minutes[a]	Non Interaction		Interaction	
			Isolative	Proximal	Helping	Reciprocal
3 & 4	Class					
	Large	6.18	1.80 (.29)	46.00 (7.44)	0 0	1.00 (.16)
	Small	5.30	3.75 (.71)	46.50 (8.77)	1.00 (.19)	6.50 (1.23)
	Contingency	5.11	1.66 (.32)	37.00 (7.24)	1.66 0	11.66 (2.28)
	Free time					
	Large	1.52	4.25 (2.80)	2.75 (1.81)	0 0	0 0
	Small	1.40	8.00 (5.71)	4.50 (3.21)	0 0	1.50 (1.07)
	Contingency	2.30	10.66 (4.63)	12.00 (5.22)	0 0	4.00 (1.72)
4	Class					
	Large	7.27	0 0	60.85 (8.37)	0 0	4.85 (.67)
	Small	6.26	2.75 (.44)	53.00 (8.46)	1.25 (.20)	13.75 (2.20)
	Free time					
	Large	2.35	7.00 (2.98)	9.71 (4.13)	0 0	4.42 (1.88)
	Small	2.38	9.00 (3.78)	8.00 (3.36)	0 0	7.50 (3.15)
5 & 6	Class					
	Large	8.35	3.42 (.41)	6.81 (.82)	0 0	.42 (.05)
	Small	8.32	18.50 (2.22)	60.50 (7.27)	0 0	3.00 (.36)
	Contingency	6.08	6.75 (1.11)	54.75 (9.00)	0 0	6.50 (1.07)
	Free time					
	Large	2.39	5.57 (2.33)	8.14 (3.41)	0 0	.86 (.35)
	Small	2.00	2.50 (1.25)	6.50 (3.25)	0 0	1.00 (.50)
	Contingency	2.60	13.25 (5.10)	8.25 (3.17)	0 0	1.50 (.58)
6	Class					
	Large	5.28	.67 (.13)	35.33 (6.69)	0 0	1.33 (.25)
	Small	4.33	.50 (.12)	40.00 (9.24)	2.00 (.46)	4.50 (1.04)
	Contingency	6.32	3.57 (.56)	45.57 (7.21)	7.28 (1.15)	8.14 (1.29)
	Free time					
	Large	2.38	5.00 (2.10)	7.33 (3.08)	1.66 (.70)	.33 (.14)
	Small	1.28	2.25 (1.75)	8.25 (6.44)	1.50 (1.17)	.25 (.20)
	Contingency	1.76	6.28 (3.57)	6.00 (3.41)	2.85 (1.62)	3.00 (1.70)

[a]Relates to mean minutes of observation per session

Note: Mean rate = mean frequency ÷ mean minutes. Mean rates indicated within parentheses.

single session one week prior to integration and within one week following the last condition. The order for administering the two pretest scales was randomly assigned to two classes. The testing order assigned to each class remained the same for the posttests.

Music curriculum, materials, and listening reward

The music curriculum and materials for each grade level were grade appropriate and based upon the music curriculum developed for the

Table 2
Mean Percent of Positive Homogeneous and Heterogeneous Interactions of Severely Handicapped Students during Integrated Music Class and Free Time Environments under Three Teaching Conditions

Grade	Environment/ condition	Positive interactions[a]		Other[b]
		Homogeneous	Heterogeneous	
3 & 4	Class			
	Large	.28	.87	.99
	Small	0	11.88	2.25
	Contingency	0	20.01	.43
	Free time			
	Large	5.28	0	3.33
	Small	10.23	8.08	1.14
	Contingency	22.22	13.31	22.22
4	Class			
	Large	7.74	5.43	1.09
	Small	0	20.00	.51
	Free time			
	Large	7.00	16.80	6.11
	Small	5.36	26.15	6.86
5 & 6	Class			
	Large	.83	.60	.21
	Small	.46	2.77	.58
	Contingency	.29	10.91	1.48
	Free time			
	Large	9.63	2.53	1.76
	Small	20.84	4.17	14.59
	Contingency	5.42	6.77	4.81
6	Class			
	Large	.93	2.02	.93
	Small	0	13.04	4.45
	Contingency	0	28.13	1.51
	Free time			
	Large	1.52	8.80	10.57
	Small	1.39	10.13	12.59
	Contingency	4.49	21.55	1.50
Total Mean Percent		4.72	10.63	4.54

[a]Helping and reciprocal
[b]Includes classroom teachers and aides

school district. Curriculum objectives were selected from major curriculum domains (i.e., rhythm, melody, dynamics, etc.). Lesson plans were then developed to teach for these objectives using either a large group or small group instructional method.

Reward music consisted of taped "popular-rock" music from two local rock music stations chosen as a result of an informal survey of the students showing their preferences. No formal preference survey was necessary since it has been demonstrated that even nonpreferred music will function as a reinforcer when no choice is involved (Miller, 1977; Miller, Dorow, & Greer, 1974), and when given a choice, rock is preferred over nonrock music (Greer, Dorow, & Harrison, 1975; Greer, Dorow, & Randall, 1974; Madsen & Madsen, 1972).

Setting and equipment

Handicapped students were bused a short distance from their segregated school to the regular school setting. Music classes were held in the regular grade classroom for Grade 3 & 4 and Grade 4. Due to scheduling and accessibility problems, Grade 5 & 6 and Grade 6 met in other rooms in the school for their music classes. Students remained in the classroom setting for the free time period. During the music contingency conditions, students selected for music listening left the regular classroom and listened in a small room adjacent to the class. Cassette tapes of the rock music were played on a Telex Model C130 cassette player equipped with multiple outlets and six headphones.

PROCEDURES

Following the administration of the pretest acceptance scales, all grades were given a brief 40-min orientation session to inform them of the music classes and to answer any general questions regarding "handicapped" or "retarded" students. The integrated music classes began within 1 week of the initial orientation.

Upon entering the music classroom, students were instructed to sit on the floor in a single large circle. No other specific seating instructions were given to the students. For Grade 6, the only grade with students in wheelchairs, nonhandicapped students sat in chairs. Students in wheelchairs were placed throughout the circle of chairs since none were able to move their wheelchairs independently. During baseline, the music teacher proceeded to provide instruction for acquisition of the selected music objective. During the small group and small group music contingency conditions, students initially sat in a single large group for instructions and for a review of cooperative behaviors. Students were then divided into the small heterogeneous groups. During the contingency condition, students were told that the group that was selected as the "most cooperative" would listen to music on headphones during the free time period.

In all conditions, students were told that they could have a free time period after class instruction during which they could engage in free time behaviors such as: (a) moving about the classroom, (b) talking to each other, and (c) playing any instruments that were available from the preceding class activity. During the contingency condition, the group selected as "most cooperative" was announced to the class prior to free time. This group then proceeded to the listening area while the rest of the class engaged in "free time" until the end of the time period.

RESULTS

Social interaction

Observational data for each class session for each grade were first summarized by means of a frequency tally of each of the behavior codes within the three main categories: (a) type of behavior (isolative, proximal, helping, reciprocal), (b) quality (negative or positive), and (c) individual involved in the interaction (none, homogeneous, heterogeneous, or adult). The frequency of the behavior was further summarized within the four environments: (a) beginning, (b) class, (c) free time, and (d) end. Percentages for each behavior code in each environment were derived by dividing the frequency of the behavior by the number of observation intervals. Observation intervals for the beginning and end of class were generally low in frequency (1–5 intervals) for each class. These data were therefore deleted from the study.

Figures 1 and 2 as well as Tables 1 and 2 present data to indicate that structuring antecedents and consequences (small group with music contingency) affects social interactions among severely handicapped students and nonhandicapped peers as to (a) frequency, (b) type of interaction, and (c) the individuals involved in the interactions. Under all conditions, and for all grades, the quality of the interactions as well as noninteractions was positive throughout the study (Table 3). It should also be noted that, for the duration of the study, the highest total mean percent of positive interactions that occurred was heterogeneous (Table 2).

The percentages of positive heterogeneous social interactions were the highest for all grades under the small group music contingency condition and the lowest under the large group condition during class (Figure 1) as well as free time (Figure 2). Figures 1 and 2 also show that the greatest degree of change between conditions occurred for Grade 6 and the least change occurred for Grade 5 & 6. There were also minimal social interactions under the large group condition for all grades with a greater percentage being observed for Grade 6 and Grade 4 during free time (Figure 2).

Interaction data presented in Table 1 indicate that the type of positive heterogeneous interaction that occurred most frequently under the two conditions was reciprocal with the highest mean rate of reciprocals indicated for Grade 3 & 4 and Grade 4 under all conditions. Helping interactions were at a minimum for Grades 3 & 4, 4, and 5 & 6. The highest mean rate of helping interactions occurred for Grade 6 across all conditions with the highest mean rate indicated for the small group music contingency condition. In general, there was an increase in positive heterogeneous reciprocal interactions for all grades during class instruction and free time with the highest mean rate occurring under the small group music contingency condition.

Examination of noninteraction data in Table 1 indicates that the mean rate of proximal behaviors during class is similar for Grade 3 & 4, Grade 4 and Grade 6. The mean rate of proximal behavior was lowest for Grade 5 & 6 under the large group condition with an increase noted for

Table 3

Mean Percent of Positive and Negative Noninteractions and Interactions of Severely Handicapped Students during Integrated Music Class and Free Time Environments

Grade	Environment	Noninteraction[a]		Interaction[b]	
		Positive	Negative	Positive	Negative
3 & 4	Class	69.75	9.67	10.92	.81
	Free time	55.49	8.89	7.13	0
4	Class	64.12	7.53	12.71	.65
	Free time	50.52	1.07	21.47	0
5 & 6	Class	67.69	8.24	4.76	.05
	Free time	48.73	2.06	4.49	1.67
6	Class	65.39	5.63	14.39	0
	Free time	53.71	4.22	13.49	.92

[a]Noninteraction = isolative and heterogenous proximal behaviors
[b]Interaction = heterogeneous helping and heterogeous reciprocal behaviors
Note: Mean percent of three teaching conditions

small group and small group with music contingency. For all grades, with the exception of Grade 3 & 4 free time and Grade 5 & 6 class large group, there is little change noted in proximal behaviors under the three conditions. While there are varying degrees of change in positive isolative behaviors for all grades across conditions during class and free time, no particular trend is observable across grade levels.

The mean reliability for social interaction for all grades was 93% with a range from 78% to 98%. The mean reliability for each class was as follows: Grade 3 & 4 = 91%; Grade 4 = 91%; Grade 5 & 6 = 97%; and Grade 6 = 93%.

Acceptance

Standard scoring and validation procedures (Voeltz, 1982) were used to derive scores for the acceptance scales. Only valid scores from students completing both the pretests and posttests of both scales were included in the analysis. A dependent t test on pretest scores for the two scales indicated no significant differences for testing order. The mean score for the first scale administered was 34.95; for the second, 36.23 ($t(3) = -1.56$, $p > .05$).

Two separate one-way analysis of variance procedures were employed to analyze the pretest data from both scales for the four classes. Significant differences were found among the four classes for the general acceptance (AS) and acceptance within music (AMS) pretest measures (see Table 4). Applications of the Newman-Keuls multiple comparison procedure showed that for general acceptance, Grade 5 & 6 (mean = 30.75) and Grade 6 (mean = 35.93) were not significantly different ($p > .05$). However, students in Grade 5 & 6 had significantly

Table 4

Means, SDs and F Ratios of Measures of Nonhandicapped Students' Acceptance of Severely Handicapped Students in General (AS) and within Music (AMS)

Measure	Third & Fourth		Fourth		Fifth & Sixth		Sixth		
	M	SD	M	SD	M	SD	M	SD	F^a
					Pretest				
General (AS)	37.13	9.20	40.30	7.46	30.75	5.71	35.93	6.83	4.12**
Music (AMS)	38.80	8.70	38.90	5.83	29.92	8.05	33.00	7.98	4.99**
					Posttest				
General (AS)	45.27	5.98	43.55	10.28	28.50	9.99	48.79	5.18	14.59***
Music (AMS)	47.53	6.25	46.55	9.51	27.50	11.75	53.21	5.00	21.98***

[a]Refers to effects between classes: $df = 3/57$
[b]Refers to effects within classes: $c_{df} = 3/53m$ $d_{df} = 3/76$, $e_{df} = 3/44$, $f_{df} = 3/52$
*$p < .05$; **$p < .001$; ***$p < .000$

lower scores than students in Grade 3 & 4 (mean = 37.13) as well as Grade 4 (mean = 40.30). There were no significant differences found for the comparison of means from Grade 6, Grade 3 & 4, and Grade 4.

A Newman-Keuls procedure for the AMS pretest indicated that again there was no significant difference ($p > .05$) between Grade 5 & 6 (mean = 29.92) and Grade 6 (mean = 33.00). There was also no significant difference between Grade 3 & 4 (mean = 38.80) and Grade 4 (mean = 38.90). Both of the lower grades scored significantly higher ($p < .05$) on music acceptance than both of the upper grades.

As a result of significant differences on pretest scores among the four classes, posttest scores for the two acceptance scales were analyzed using two separate one-way analysis of variance procedures and Newman-Keuls multiple comparison procedures. Significant differences were again found among the four classes (see Table 6). However, comparisons of means for general acceptance indicated a different pattern with no significant differences ($p > .05$) for Grade 4 (mean = 43.55), Grade 3 & 4 (mean = 45.27), and Grade 6 (mean = 48.79). The scores from Grades 3 & 4, 4, and 6 were significantly higher ($p < .05$) than those for Grade 5 & 6 (mean = 28.50).

For AMS posttest comparisons, the Newman-Keuls procedure indicated no significant difference ($p > .05$) between Grade 4 (mean = 46.55) and Grade 3 & 4 (mean = 47.53). Grade 6 (mean = 53.21) was not significantly different from Grade 3 & 4 but was significantly higher ($p < .05$) than Grade 4 and Grade 5 & 6 (mean = 27.50). Again the scores from the three grades (3 & 4, 4, and 6) were significantly higher than those from Grade 5 & 6.

Four separate one-way analysis of variance procedures were used to identify differences between the general acceptance and acceptance within music for both pretest and posttest measures within each of the four classes. Significant differences were found for Grade 3 & 4, Grade

4, and Grade 6 although no significant difference was found for Grade 5 & 6 (see Table 4). Application of the Newman-Keuls procedure indicated that for the three grades posttest means for both acceptance scales were significantly higher ($p < .05$) than pretest means for both scales. Also, for all three grades, no significant difference was found between the posttest means for acceptance in general and within music ($p > .05$). There was also no significant difference between the pretest means for general acceptance for each of the classes. For Grade 4, the general acceptance scale posttest (mean = 43.55) was not significantly different from the pretests for both scales for that grade.

An examination of the Grade 6 means for both scales (Table 4) indicates that student responses on the posttests were higher than all other grades although pretest means for Grade 6 were significantly lower than those from Grade 3 & 4 and Grade 4. Since Grade 6 was the only grade with integrated wheelchair students and questions specific to students in wheelchairs appear in both acceptance scales, all posttests were rescored deleting responses to wheelchair items. One way analysis of variance procedures on the rescored tests yielded significant differences for general acceptance, $F (3,57) = 11.63, p < .000$. Newman-Keuls procedures showed no significant differences ($p > .05$) for Grade 4 (mean = 36.70), Grade 3 & 4 (mean = 39.53) and Grade 6 (mean = 40.29). The means for these three grades were significantly higher ($p < .05$) when compared to Grade 5 & 6 (mean = 25.75). Although the means for all grades are lower in this analysis with the wheelchair items deleted, the general comparisons are identical to the comparisons from the initial analysis. Significant differences were found for acceptance within music, $F(3,57) = 16.67, p < .000$. Newman-Keuls procedures again showed no significant differences ($p > .05$) for Grade 4 (mean = 39.40), Grade 3 & 4 (mean = 42.93), and Grade 6 (mean = 43.86). The means for these three grades were significantly higher ($p < .05$) when compared to Grade 5 & 6 (mean = 25.42). These results vary only slightly from the initial analysis.

DISCUSSION

As a result of this study, it can no longer be assumed that the mere integration of severely handicapped students into the music classroom will result in positive, heterogeneous social interactions. The data clearly indicate that the frequency of positive social interactions among severely handicapped and nonhandicapped students in the integrated music classroom is dependent upon the degree to which the teaching method structures antecedents and reinforcement for these interactions. Examination of small group structuring versus small group plus music as a reinforcer revealed that the contingent music held paramount effectiveness as a "socializing agent" for interactions. Although rock music was selected for this study, research suggests that music lessons via television can also serve as a reward for successful completion of academic tasks (Dorow, 1976; Madsen, Dorow, Moore, & Womble, 1976; Madsen & Geringer, 1976). Future research should explore the use of various music contingencies that offer such music and nonmusic learning gains for handicapped/nonhandicapped students in the integrated classroom. Also of great importance from this study is the additional support to research in learning that demonstrates that teaching methods must be structured to ensure that (a) students know specifically what is expected of them, (b) opportunities are provided for students to do what is expected, and (c) contingencies of reinforcement are arranged so that students want to do what is expected. In the present study, all grades were positively affected to some degree by the structuring of antecedents and consequences to encourage heterogeneous interactions. This effect was observed for all grades under class conditions with generalization observable in the free time period.

Particularly encouraging are the data from Grade 6 regarding early intervention and helping behaviors. While this grade did not differ significantly from Grade 5 & 6 on music and general acceptance baseline social interaction data, there were significant differences between these grades at the conclusion of the study. There was minimal positive change observed for Grade 5 & 6 across time, while Grade 6 indicated a high degree of positive change for both acceptance and social interaction measures. Although Grade 6 was the only class with students in wheelchairs, analysis of the acceptance scales with the wheelchair items deleted still resulted in significantly higher scores for Grade 6 than for Grade 5 & 6. Earlier intervention for Grade 6 to the small groups and contingency method may account for the major differences between these grades. Research indicates that the frequency of interaction between severely handicapped and nonhandicapped students is correlated with the level of understanding that the nonhandicapped have of the severely handicapped (McHale & Simeonson, 1980); that greater interpersonal attraction and interaction take place between nonhandicapped and severely handicapped teenagers under cooperative rather than competitive and individualistic conditions (Rynders, Johnson, Johnson, & Schmidt, 1980); and that competitive and individualistic learning activities provide little or no information about handicapped peers and thus allow initial stereotypes to continue and grow (Johnson & Johnson, 1980). Although this study did not particularly structure individualistic or competitive situations, the extended baseline for Grade 5 & 6, during which there was an inordinate deficit of proximal behaviors, did not allow opportunities for nonhandicapped students to interact and gain new information about their handicapped peers.

Although it is unclear from this study if and how helping behaviors may have functioned to increase acceptance and social interactions in Grade 6, the highest mean rate for helping interactions occurred for Grade 6 with minimal helping interactions occurring in the other grades and none occurring for Grade 5 & 6. Future research should examine this type of interaction and possible effects of helping handicapped individuals on attitudinal and behavioral measures. Regardless of the possible effects of helping behaviors, the data from Grade 6 and Grade 5 & 6 would suggest that music teachers should develop strategies that structure antecedents and reinforcers for positive heterogeneous social interaction, and that these strategies should be implemented early in the school year. A delay in implementation may preclude the effectiveness of the strategies.

Although female and male data were not of primary interest to this study, the minimal change for Grade 5 & 6 generated questions regarding acceptance of females and males in all grades. Prior research suggests that females will score higher on acceptance or attitude scales regarding handicapped individuals, and pretest data from the present study supports this finding. (See Table 5.)

However, posttest results indicate that while females may score higher in general than males on initial acceptance of handicapped individuals, this acceptance will not necessarily increase over time and may even decrease without structured interactions to enhance acceptance. The similarity between the posttest data from males in Grade 6 and females from Grades 3 & 4 and 4 suggests that the acceptance of males for their handicapped peers is subject to a high degree of positive change under structured programs designed to bring about that change.

With the exception of data from Grade 5 & 6, which showed no significant difference between pretests and posttests on both acceptance scales, all grades indicated significant positive change and became more accepting of their handicapped peers at the conclusion of the study. All grades indicated no significant difference between general acceptance and acceptance within music for both the pretest and posttest measures. These pretest results suggest that nonhandicapped students with little or no previous experience with severely handicapped peers in the music classroom will generalize their acceptance of these peers to a more specific music acceptance that includes music environments and activities. In addition, the significant positive posttest change as well as the lack of significant differences between scales on the posttest measures indicate additional generalization. It may be concluded that when nonhandicapped students experience positive interactions with their severely handicapped peers in an integrated music classroom, they will be more accepting of these peers in both music and nonmusic environments and activities. The generalization of positive social interactions from the class environment to the free time environment provides some data for the parallel situations of generalization of acceptance across environments. If generalization of acceptance and interactions occurs between environments, then it is critical that music teachers structure antecedents and reinforcement in the integrated music classroom to facilitate positive social interactions between nonhandicapped students and their severely handicapped peers.

CONCLUSIONS

The present study was initiated to provide some preliminary empirical data on the integrated music classroom. Of the utmost importance from this study is the finding that music and music classroom experiences can facilitate positive social interactions between severely handicapped and nonhandicapped students primarily when structured for that purpose.

Table 5
Means of Measures of Female and Male Nonhandicapped Students' Acceptance of Severely Handicapped Students in General (AS) and within Music (AMS)

Grade	Gender		Acceptance Scales						Pre/post mean
			Pretest			Posttest			
			AS	AMS	*M*	AS	AMS	*M*	
3 & 4	Female	(7)	40	43	(41.50)	48	49	(48.50)	45.00
	Male	(8)	34	35	(34.50)	42	46	(44.00)	39.25
4	Female	(10)	42	40	(41.00)	47	51	(49.00)	45.00
	Male	(10)	38	38	(38.00)	40	42	(41.00)	39.50
5 & 6	Female	(5)	33	32	(32.50)	29	29	(29.00)	30.70
	Male	(7)	29	28	(28.50)	28	26	(27.00)	27.75
6	Female	(8)	40	38	(39.00)	51	56	(53.50)	46.25
	Male	(6)	31	27	(29.00)	46	50	(48.00)	38.50

Unfortunately, the mere placement of severely handicapped students in the regular music classroom does not necessarily result in positive heterogeneous interactions. This study demonstrated that heterogeneous helping and reciprocal interactions are facilitated when an early intervention program is implemented that provides (a) opportunities for interactions to occur through small heterogeneous, "cooperative" groups as well as (b) music reinforcement for "cooperative" social interactions. Additionally, results of this study demonstrate that the acceptance of nonhandicapped students of their severely handicapped peers into music and nonmusic environments and activities can be positively affected through positive interactions with their handicapped peers. Since results also indicate that nonhandicapped students generalize their acceptance of severely handicapped students across music and nonmusic environments, the integrated music classroom provides an ideal opportunity for music educators to structure music classroom experiences that will positively influence the values and behaviors of nonhandicapped students. Positive interactions among the severely handicapped and nonhandicapped as students in the music classroom may increase the probability that skills and values will be acquired that are necessary for tolerance and understanding as adults in various integrated community environments.

Based on this initial research, music educators and music therapists can be optimistic regarding the benefits derived for both nonhandicapped and severely handicapped students in the integrated music classroom. It is very likely that positive teacher attitude and behavior will most certainly be identified in future research as variables affecting opportunities for these benefits to be derived. Research on student as well as teacher attitude and behavior in the integrated music classroom must continue in order to ensure the success of the integration movement and ultimately to provide superior music education services to all children.

REFERENCES

Alley, J. M. (1979). Music in the IEP: Therapy/education. *Journal of Music Therapy, 16,* 111–127.

Asher, S. E., & Taylor, A. R. (1981). The social outcomes of mainstreaming: Sociometric assessment and beyond. *Exceptional Education Quarterly, 1*(4), 13–30.

Baer, D. M., Wolf, M. M., & Risley, T. (1968). Some current dimensions of applied behavior analysis. *Journal of Applied Behavior Analysis, 1,* 91–97.

Brown, L., Branston, M. B., Hamre-Nietupski, S., Johnson, F., Wilcox, B., & Gruenewald, L. A. (1979). Rationale for comprehensive longitudinal interactions between severely handicapped students and nonhandicapped students and other citizens. *American Association for the Education of the Severely and Profoundly Handicapped Review, 4*(1), 3–14.

Brown, L., Nietupski, J., & Hamre-Nietupski, S. (1976). Criterion of ultimate functioning. In N. A. Thomas (Ed.), *Hey, don't forget about me!* Reston, VA: Council for Exceptional Children, 8–15.

Cottrell, N. B. (1968). Performance in the presence of other human beings: Mere presence, audience and alienation effects. In E. D. Semmel, R. A. Hoppe, and G. A. Milton (Eds.), *Social facilitation and imitative behavior.* Boston: Allyn & Bacon.

Dorow, L. (1976). Televised music lessons as educational reinforcement for correct mathematical responses with the educable mentally retarded. *Journal of Music Therapy, 13,* 77–86.

Forsythe, J. L., & Jellison, J. A. (1977). It's the law. *Music Educators Journal, 64*(3), 30–35.

Gilbert, J. P. (1977). Mainstreaming in your classroom: What to expect. *Music Educators Journal, 63*(6), 64–68.

Gilbert, J. P., & Asmus, E. P. (1981). Mainstreaming: Music educators' participation and professional needs. *Journal of Research in Music Education, 29,* 31–37.

Gottlieb, B. (1982). Social facilitation influences on the oral reading performance of academically handicapped children. *American Journal of Mental Deficiency, 87,* 153–158.

Graham, R., & Beei, A. (1980). *Teaching music to the exceptional child.* Englewood Cliffs, NJ: Prentice-Hall.

Greer, R. D. (1981). An operant approach to motivation and affect: Ten years of research in music learning. In *Documentary Report of the Ann Arbor Symposium: Applications of Psychology to the Teaching and Learning of Music.* Reston, VA: Music Educators National Conference.

Greer, R. D., Dorow, L. G., & Harrison, L. N. (1975). Aural discrimination instruction and the preferences of sixth graders for music listening, story listening, and candy. In C. K. Madsen, R. D. Greer, and C. H. Madsen, Jr. (Eds.), *Search in music behavior: Modifying music behavior in the classroom.* New York: Teachers College Press.

Greer, R. D., Dorow, L. G., & Randall, A. (1974). Music listening preferences of elementary school children. *Journal of Research in Music Education, 22,* 284–291.

Hamre-Nietupski, S., & Nietupski, J. (1981). Integral involvement of severely handicapped students within regular public schools. *Journal of the Association for the Severely Handicapped, 6*(2), 30–39.

Hardesty, K. W. (1979). *Music for special education.* Morristown, NJ: Silver Burdett.

Hazard, W. R. (1979). A tort is not a piece of cake: Teacher's legal responsibilities. *Music Educators Journal, 65*(8), 26–33.

Jellison, J. (1979). The music therapist in the educational setting: Developing and implementing curriculum for the handicapped. *Journal of Music Therapy, 16,* 128–137.

Jellison, J. (1983). Functional value as criterion for selection and prioritization of nonmusic and music objectives in music therapy. *Music Therapy Perspectives, 1*(2), 17–22.

Johnson, D. W., & Johnson, R. (1975). *Learning together and alone: Cooperation, competition, and individualization.* Englewood Cliffs, NJ: Prentice-Hall.

Johnson, D., & Johnson, R. (1980). Integrating handicapped students into the mainstream. *Exceptional Children, 47,* 90–98.

Lament, M. M. (1978). Reaching the exceptional student through music in the elementary classroom. *Teaching Exceptional Children, 11,* 32–35.

Lathom, W. (1980). *Role of music therapy in the education of handicapped children and youth.* Washington, DC: Hawkins & Associates.

Madsen, C. K., Dorow, L. G., Moore, R. S., & Womble, J. U. (1976). Effect of music lessons via television as reinforcement for correct mathematical responses. *Journal of Research in Music Education, 24,* 50–59.

Madsen, C. K., & Geringer, J. M. (1976). Choice of televised music lessons versus free play in relationship to academic improvement. *Journal of Music Therapy, 13,* 154–162.

Madsen, C. K., Greer, R. D., & Madsen, C. H., Jr. (1975). *Research in music behavior: Modifying music behavior in the classroom.* New York: Teachers College Press.

Madsen, C. K., & Madsen, C. H., Jr. (1972). Selection of music listening or candy as a function of contingent versus noncontingent reinforcement and scale singing. *Journal of Music Therapy, 9,* 190–198.

McHale, S. M., & Simeonsson, R. J. (1980). Effects of interaction on handicapped children's attitudes toward autistic children. *American Journal of Mental Deficiency, 85,* 18–24.

Miller, D. M. (1977). Effects of music listening contingencies on arithmetic performance and music preference of EMR children. *American Journal of Mental Deficiency, 81,* 371–378.

Miller, D. D., Dorow, L. G., & Greer, R. D. (1974). The contingent use of music and art for improving arithmetic scores. *Journal of Music Therapy, 11,* 57–64.

Nietupski, J., Hamre-Nietupski, S., Schuetz, G., & Ockwood, L. (Eds.). (1980). *Severely handicapped students in regular schools.* Milwaukee: Milwaukee Public Schools.

Nocera, S. (1979). *Reaching the special learner through music.* Morristown, NJ: Silver Burdett.

Rynders, J. E., Johnson, R. T., Johnson, D. W., & Schmidt, B. (1980). Producing positive interaction among Down syndrome and nonhandicapped teenagers through cooperative goal structuring. *American Journal of Mental Deficiency, 83,* 268–273.

Semmel, M. J., Gottlieb, J., & Robinson, M. (1979). In D. Berliner (Ed.), *Review of research in education: Vol. 7.* Itasca, IL: Peacock Publisher.

Sontag, E., Certo, N., & Button, J. E. (1979). On a distinction between the education of the severely and profoundly handicapped and a doctrine of limitations. *Exceptional Children, 45,* 604–616.

Stainback, W., & Stainback, S. (1981). A review of research on interactions between severely handicapped and nonhandicapped students. *Journal of the Association for the Severely Handicapped, 6*(2), 23–29.

Stainback, W., Stainback, S., & Jaben, T. (1981). Providing opportunities for interaction between severely handicapped and nonhandicapped students. *Teaching Exceptional Children, 13* 72–75.

Stainback, W., Stainback, S., Raschke, D., & Anderson, R. J. (1981). Three methods for encouraging interactions between severely retarded and nonhandicapped students. *Education and Training of the Mentally Retarded, 16,* 188–192.

Strain, P. (Ed.). (1981). Peer relations of exceptional children and youth [thematic issue]. *Exceptional Education Quarterly, 1*(4), 1–115.

Taylor, R. G. (Ed.). (1982). Music for every child: Teaching special students [thematic issue]. *Music Educators Journal, 68*(8), 25–57.

Thompson, K. (1982). Education of handicapped learners. *Music Educators Journal, 68*(8), 25–28.

Voeltz, L. M. (1980). Children's attitudes toward handicapped peers. *American Journal of Mental Deficiency, 84,* 455–464.

Voeltz, L. M. (1982). Effects of structured interaction with severely handicapped peers on children's attitudes. *American Journal of Mental Deficiency, 86,* 380–390.

January 9, 1984

In this study, 119 sixth- and seventh-grade peer subjects and 90 adult subjects evaluated an 8.5-minute performance by a youth choir made up of children with a variety of mental and physical disabilities. Approximately half the evaluators in each age-group were informed through written instructions of the choir members' disabilities, while this information was omitted from the instructions given to the other half. To control for visual information obtained while viewing the tape, two presentation modes, video plus aural, and aural alone, were used. After watching or listening to the performance, subjects rated the choir using a choral evaluation form. Subjects also responded to two open-ended questions regarding their reactions to the choir. Results indicated a significant three-way interaction among label condition, presentation mode, and age. Within each age-group, the mean rating by the group receiving neither label nor video information was the lowest of the four groups. Otherwise, the two age-groups of subjects seem to have used the information related to disabilities differently.

Jane W. Cassidy, *Louisiana State University*
Wendy L. Sims, *University of Missouri—Columbia*

JRME 1991, VOLUME 39, NUMBER 1, PAGES 23–34

Effects of Special Education Labels on Peers' and Adults' Evaluations of a Handicapped Youth Choir

Mainstreaming of children with handicaps has been an important concern of classroom teachers since the passage of Public Law 94–142 in 1975. Music educators are among those who share the responsibilities of implementing P.L. 94–142 because the general music classroom commonly is considered an appropriate place to begin such an integration process (Meyers, MacMillan, & Yoshida, 1980). A national survey of music educators demonstrated that, by 1981, nearly 63% of the respondents had interacted in the classroom with children with disabilities (Gilbert & Asmus, 1981). More recently, a survey of elementary music teachers from the Southern Division of the Music Educators National Conference reported a weekly average of 717 students serviced by the music specialist, with 5.3% of those being mainstreamed students (Atterbury, 1986).

One of the primary goals of mainstreaming is the development of positive social relationships between handicapped and nonhandicapped children. This seems to be facilitated *not* by the music-class experience itself, but rather by careful structuring of social events by the teacher prior to classroom activity, and sub-

---

For copies of this article, contact Jane W. Cassidy, School of Music, Louisiana State University, Baton Rouge, LA 70803-2504.

sequent reinforcement of desirable social interactions (Jellison, Brooks, & Huck, 1984). In addition to such inducement from the teacher, peer relationships of children are influenced by complex interactions among physical appearance, academic competence, physical prowess, and socially desirable qualities. For children with disabilities, the addition of a label further complicates the social integration process. This has been demonstrated in numerous studies during which subjects were asked to rate characteristics of labeled children on adjective checklists and behavioral intention surveys (Bak & Siperstein, 1986, 1987; Elam & Siegelman, 1983; Gibbons & Kassin, 1982; Voeltz, 1980).

While under some circumstances, labels may help children with handicaps by providing peers with an "explanation" for certain failures, nonhandicapped children seem to maintain low behavioral expectations of retarded children and have attributed retarded peers' success at academic tasks to effort rather than ability (Gibbons & Kassin, 1982; Siperstein, Budoff, & Bak, 1980).

Asmus (1985) reached similar conclusions in music education research related to Attribution Theory with nonhandicapped children. Asmus found that children tended to attribute both success and failure at music tasks to effort, whereas young adults more often attributed them to ability (Asmus, 1986).

Children value academic competence in nonhandicapped and handicapped peers (Johnson, Sigelman, & Falkenberg, 1986; Siperstein & Bak, 1985), and the perception of competent behavior may influence the attitudes of children more than an assigned label (Elam & Sigelman, 1983). Cassity (1981) found that peer acceptance of a group member within a music therapy setting was greatly enhanced when that member performed competently on the piano at the conclusion of regular sessions. Likewise, socially desirable qualities and perceived similarities identified in children with handicaps may affect nonhandicapped children's attitudes in a positive way (Bak & Siperstein, 1987; Freeman & Algozzine, 1980).

Not surprising, adults have similar stereotypical beliefs and expectations of children with stigmatizing labels. As with children, adults attribute success by handicapped children to effort and luck rather than ability, cite lack of ability rather than lack of effort as reason for failures, and predict that such children will be less likely to improve in the future when compared to normal children (Gibbons, Savin, & Gibbons, 1979; Severance & Gasstrom, 1977; Weisz, 1981; Yeates & Weisz, 1985). The biasing effect of labels is clear in the results of several studies in which two groups of adults viewed the same videotape of a normal child performing academic and social tasks (Foster & Keech, 1977; Foster, Yseldyke, & Reese, 1975; Salvia, Clark, & Yseldyke, 1973). Experimental subjects were instructed that the child was mentally retarded, while control subjects were instructed that the child was normal. Comparisons were made between the groups' ratings on personality questionnaires, checklists covering various academic and social skills, and referral forms. When the child was labeled retarded, ratings were consistently lower than when this label was not provided, even though both groups had viewed the *same* normal child. It seems that less is expected from labeled children, and their success is perceived as overachievement (Gibbons, Savin, & Gibbons, 1979).

Since peers' and adults' expectations of children seem to be influenced by knowledge of assigned stigmatizing labels, it is important in the educational setting to determine the relationship between these labels and the evaluation process. Fogel and Nelson (1983) found that labeling did not affect behavioral observations or scoring of academic material (grading a paragraph the target child supposedly copied from the blackboard), but did bias the scoring on a checklist of items containing behaviors characteristic of various exceptionalities.

The effects of disability labels on evaluation in a music setting were observed by Cassidy (1987). Music education, music therapy, and elementary education students rated choral performances by a select children's choir, a handicapped children's choir, and a mainstreamed children's choir. Results indicated that a priori knowledge of "special education" labels had a significant, positive effect on the ratings of music variables.

There is still relatively little known about the function of disability labels on the evaluation of children's music behaviors by teachers or by peers. Since music classes are often selected to provide mainstreaming experiences for children with disabilities, it would seem imperative to the success of this process that music educators understand how children and teachers react to mainstreamed children who are engaged in music-making activities. The study described in this article was designed to replicate and extend Cassidy's (1987) study—to explore further the relationships between disability labels and music evaluations of children with handicaps. Specifically, researchers examined the effects of the presence or absence of labels pertaining to "mental and physical disabilities" on children's and music educators' evaluations of a performance by a handicapped youth choir.

METHOD

Subjects

Peer evaluators serving as subjects were 119 sixth- and seventh-grade students enrolled in a university laboratory school. This age level was selected so that these subjects would represent an age-appropriate peer group to the children they would be evaluating. Another consideration was that all subjects had participated in the school choir for at least one year. Most of these subjects had limited experience with children with disabilities, since no mentally or physically handicapped children attended their school.

Adult evaluators were 90 undergraduate and graduate music majors attending two large state universities, all of whom were either currently majoring in or had a previous degree in music education. Undergraduate ($n = 56$) and graduate ($n = 34$) students were distributed evenly among the four experimental groups.

Independent Variables

Of primary interest was a comparison between responses of evaluators who were informed through written instructions that the choir members were disabled and evaluators who did not receive this information. Peer and adult subjects were assigned to one of these two labeling conditions.

Since a videotaped performance was being evaluated, another variable of interest was whether the visual presentation might function to provide "labeling" information about the singers' handicaps to those evaluators who were not provided with the verbal instructions that included the labels. To control for and examine this possibility, two presentation modes, video including aural, and aural alone, were compared.

The third variable that was considered was age level of the evaluators. Of interest were comparisons between responses of the peer group evaluators and the adult evaluators.

The three factors were examined through use of a label by presentation mode by age design, with two labels of each factor. This design resulted in four groups within each age level: (1) labels/visual (peer n = 28, adult n = 22); (2) labels/no visual (peer n = 30, adult n = 23); (3) no labels/visual (peer n = 32, adult n = 22); and (4) no labels/no visual (peer n = 29, adult n = 23). Intact groups of peers were randomly assigned to treatment conditions, while random assignments of individual adults were made.

Dependent Variables

The dependent variables consisted of subjects' evaluations of the youth choir. The evaluation form was a modified version of the Florida Music Educators Association choral adjudication sheet, consisting of questions relating to the nine categories, or characteristics, of a choral performance. Each of the nine categories listed was followed by a question that clarified the meaning of the characteristic being evaluated. Robinson (1988) found this to be a satisfactory means for middle school students to adjudicate choral performances. Evaluators rated each item on a 5-point scale by circling their choice from among the terms "Poor," "Fair," "Okay," "Good," "Excellent" ("Poor" equaled 1 point; "Fair," 2 points; etc.). The following seven items were included on the forms for all experimental conditions:

1. *Tone*—How would you rate the overall sound of the singing?
2. *Intonation*—How well did the singers sing in tune?
3. *Diction*—How clear and understandable were the words?
4. *Technique*—Did the singers seem to know all the right notes to sing, breathe correctly, and stand with good posture?
5. *Balance*—Could you hear all voices, or did some individual voices or voice parts seem too loud or too soft?
6. *Interpretation*—How would you rate the singers' use of loud and soft singing, proper tempo, and style?
7. *Musical effect*—Did the singers seem to sing well as a group? Were they effective in getting across the feeling and message of the music?

The following two questions were included only on the forms of the subjects in groups who viewed the videotape:

8. *Appearance*—How would you rate the appearance of the group? Did they seem well-disciplined on stage?
9. *Attentiveness*—How well did the students pay attention during the concert?

In addition, all subjects were asked to "list at least three other things you noticed about the group." Peers also responded to the question "Would you like to be a member of this choir?" and adults responded to the question "Given the opportunity, would you choose to work with this group of students?" All the subjects were asked to explain their answer to this question. Demographic information was completed at the end of the evaluation form.

Procedures

The stimulus tape consisted of a videotaped public performance by a choir from a school for children with mental and physical handicaps. Choir members ranged in ages from middle school through high school. Close-ups of children included those in wheelchairs and with Down's syndrome, serving as visual cues as to the handicapping conditions. Students wore matching uniforms, were directed by music educators or music therapists, and stood on or sat in front of risers in a typical choral arrangement.

Three music selections were chosen based on four considerations: (1) the music included solos performed with microphone, in addition to the group singing; (2) the pieces were "popular" in style, thereby increasing potential appeal to peer evaluators; (3) the video had close-up views of most of the choir members; and (4) audience applause was highly enthusiastic after each piece. The duration of the stimulus tape was 8.5 minutes.

Playback of the videotape occurred in classroom or office settings via a VHS videocassette player shown on a color television monitor. Groups of subjects, ranging from 2 to 32 in number, viewed the tape simultaneously, with chairs arranged such that all subjects in the visual groups had an unobstructed view of the screen. To control for sound quality, the video equipment was also used to provide the audio stimulus for the subjects in the "no visual" condition. For these subjects, either the screen was covered, or chairs were arranged such that viewing the screen was impossible.

Written instructions were provided for all subjects, and were also read aloud to the peer subjects to compensate for the possibility of different reading abilities. Instructions for all conditions were similar except that for groups in the condition that received the labels, one extra sentence referring to the singers' disabilities was included. Slight adaptations were also made for visual and no visual conditions. The basic instructions, including the labeling statement (indicated here by all capital letters), and adaptation for visual condition (indicated here in parentheses) read:

> The tape you are about to hear (see) is a prepared public presentation by a group of children. THIS GROUP IS MADE UP OF CHILDREN WITH MENTAL AND PHYSICAL DISABILITIES. After observing the performance, you will be asked to rate the chorus on tone, intonation, diction, technique, balance, interpretation, musical effect, (appearance, and attentiveness). Turn to the Rating Sheet on the next page and read the explanation of each category. In order to make an accurate assessment, you will need to pay attention to both the musical and nonmusical aspects of this performance. Please (watch and) listen to the tape carefully.

Evaluators watched or listened to the entire tape before responding to the performance. During evaluation, the questions were again read aloud to peer evaluators. Once the process was completed, subjects were made aware of the intent of the study, and a discussion of children with disabilities ensued with a second playing of the performance, during which everyone was permitted to view the tape. This concluding discussion served as an opportunity to further the subjects' understanding of children with handicaps and their musical abilities.

RESULTS

A three-way analysis of variance (ANOVA), label condition by presentation mode by age-group, was used to compare ratings from the evaluation forms (see Table 1). For this analysis, the mean for each subject on the seven rating scale items that were common to all groups was considered one data point. Results indicated that there were significant differences due to the main effects of labeling conditions [*M* labels = 2.94, *M* no labels = 2.43, $F(1, 201)$ = 21.93, p = .0001], and presentation mode [*M* visual = 2.83, *M* no visual = 2.53, $F(1, 201)$ = 8.06, p = .005]. The interaction between these two variables was also significant [$F(1, 201)$ = 6.75, p = .01]. While no significant differences were found for the main effects of age level, there was a significant two-way interaction between the age and label variables [$F(1, 201)$ = 9.77, p = .002], as well as a significant three-way interaction, label by presentation mode by age [$F(1, 201)$ = 4.49, p = .035].

Table 1
Summary Table: Three-Way Analysis of Variance Comparing Label Condition, Presentation Mode, and Age.

Source of Variance	Sum of squares	df	Mean squares	F	p*
Label (L)	13.53	1	13.53	21.93	.0001
Presentation mode (P)	4.97	1	4.97	8.06	.005
Age (A)	1.75	1	1.75	2.84	.09
L x P	4.16	1	4.16	6.75	.01
L x A	6.03	1	6.03	9.77	.002
P x A	.16	1	.16	.27	.60
L x P x A	2.77	1	2.77	4.49	.035
Residual	124.62	201	.62		

*p <.05

The significant main effects and lower-order interactions are subsumed within, and best accounted for by, the significant three-way interaction. On inspection of the means for each of the eight groups, the source of this interaction becomes apparent (see Table 2 and Figure 1). All evaluators who received written information describing the choir members' disabilities, with the exception of adult evaluators in the label/visual group, assigned higher ratings than did their counterparts in the no-label conditions. Adult evaluators who received written and visual labeling information rated the choir lower than did the other three label groups, yet their counterparts in the no-labels condition (adults, visual) rated the choir higher than did the other three no-label groups. Within each age level, groups of subjects receiving no labeling statement and no visual information to help identify the singers as handicapped rated the performance lower than all other groups.

Table 2
Means and Standard Deviations for Choral Evaluation Forms (First Seven Items Only)

		Labels		No Labels	
		Video	No Video	Video	No Video
Adults	M	2.55	2.72	2.98	2.05
	SD	.66	.82	.96	.77
	n	22	23	22	23
Peers	M	3.26	3.08	2.54	2.19
	SD	.87	.66	.86	.63
	n	28	30	32	29

The means of the responses to the two items related to appearance and attentiveness (items posed only to the visual presentation groups) were analyzed separately. Results of a two-way ANOVA, label condition by age, indicated no significant differences attributable to main effects or interactions were present.

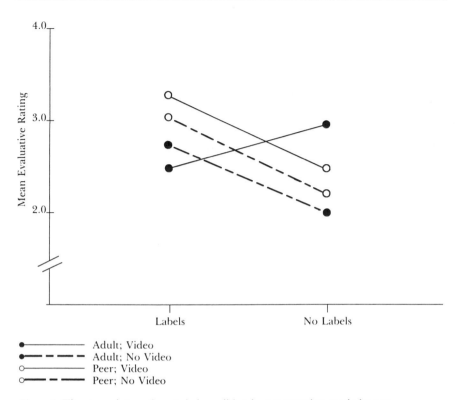

Figure 1. Three-way interaction: Label condition by presentation mode by age.

Responses to the two open-ended questions were analyzed by placing the written statements into three categories. The category "handicap" included any statement pertaining to the singers' handicaps; the category "musical" included any comment related to musical qualities of the performance; and statements related to characteristics of the singer's deportment, such as "enthusiastic" or "on-task" were categorized as "social." In some instances, comments were made about the director or the audience rather than about the performers, and these were placed in a separate "director/audience" category. Interrater reliability, based on a random sample of 30% of the responses that were categorized by two raters, was .90 [agreements ÷ (agreements + disagreements)].

The first open-ended question asked subjects to list at least three things noticed about the group. In each of the four experimental conditions, a substantially higher percentage of peers listed musical aspects of the performance as compared with the adults (see Table 3). High percentages of both adult and peer subjects in the visual conditions listed social characteristics of the group, such as "enthusiastic" or "trying hard." Social characteristics were mentioned less frequently when there was no visual stimulus provided, with different patterns of responses evident between the adults and peers. Comments related to the singers' handicaps were made most frequently by both the adults and peers in the "no labels/visual" condition, with the fewest comments related to handicaps made by members of both age-groups in the "no labels/no visual" condition. A small per-

Table 3
Percentages of Free-Response Comments by Category.

| | Labels | | | | No Labels | | | |
| | Video | | No Video | | Video | | No Video | |
	Adult	Peer	Adult	Peer	Adult	Peer	Adult	Peer
Question 1								
Categories								
Handicap	27	14	4	23	50	56	13	3
Musical	54	68	30	80	27	69	74	90
Social	95	96	78	37	95	81	70	27
Audience/	9	3	17	0	27	9	17	7
Director								
Question 2								
Choice								
Yes	68	21	70	13	73	6	83	3
No	23	79	30	87	27	94	17	97
Undecided	9	0	0	0	0	0	0	0
Categories								
Handicap	32	25	35	33	45	19	13	7
Musical	23	71	43	57	45	62	56	86
Social	64	25	61	13	54	16	78	7
Inadequacy	36	0	35	0	32	0	0	0
Mention								
of handicap	—	—	—	—	73	63	22	7
n	22	28	23	30	22	32	23	29

Note. Results indicate percentages of subjects with responses in the category indicated. Because subjects made multiple responses to most items, all percentages will not add up to 100.

centage of subjects in most groups remarked about the audience response or the directors of the group.

The second open-ended question asked the adult subjects to indicate and explain whether they would like to work with, and the peer subjects whether they would like to participate in, a group such as the one presented. The majority of the adults across the four experimental conditions (68%–83%) indicated that they would like to work with a similar type of group (see Table 3). A large percentage provided explanations that were "social" in nature, such as the desire to work with "such an enthusiastic group," while a number of subjects provided reasons that were musical in nature, such as the desire to "help children learn to sing better." Approximately one-third of these subjects' responses referred to the singers' handicaps as the reason for their decision, while about one-third of the subjects in each group of adults expressed feelings of inadequacy about their ability to work with this type of group (except for the "no labels/no visual" condition, for which subjects did not express feelings about teaching students like those in the choir).

The peers responded somewhat differently to this question, with 79%–97% indicating that they would not like to participate in a choir such as the one presented (see Table 3). The majority of these subjects gave reasons for this response that were related to musical aspects of the performance. These were fairly equally divided between "it was not a good choir" and "I don't like to sing." Overall, less than one-fourth of the peers stated that they would not like to participate in this choir because the singers were handicapped. Five peers stated that they would like to be in the group for reasons related to the handicaps, such as "to get to know and help them," because "it would be fun to sing with disabled children," or "so that the children won't think I don't like them just because they are retarded."

One further characteristic of responses to the open-ended questions was of interest. In an effort to determine whether evaluators in the "no-label" conditions were aware of the singers' handicaps based on the video or audio information only, responses of these subjects were examined for any comments referring to handicaps in their answers. As might be expected, those subjects who viewed the videotape identified the singers as being disabled more frequently than did those subjects who did not view the tape. More than two-thirds of the subjects in the "no labels/visual" condition mentioned the singers' handicaps, while only 15% of the subjects in the "no labels/no visual" groups made comments related to handicaps in their responses.

DISCUSSION

While significant main effects for both label condition and presentation mode were found in the statistical analysis of the ratings, these most appropriately may be accounted for by the presence of a three-way interaction among label conditions, presentation modes, and ages. This interaction seems to be the result of differing patterns of responses between the peer and adult groups. Table 2 and Figure 1 show that subjects in both age-groups who were provided with neither labeling nor visual information related to the performers' handicaps gave the performance the lowest ratings. Otherwise, the two age-groups of subjects seem to have used the information related to the disabilities differently. The students in the peer groups that received instructions including labels gave higher ratings to the singers than did the peers in the groups in which labels were not provided. Even when information about choir members' handicaps was available from the visual stimulus, the young subjects did not respond as positively as when the labels were provided verbally. The adult evaluators in the "no labels/visual" condition, however, rated the choir higher than did the other adult groups—including both groups who received written labeling information.

This may be explained in part by examining the function of the amount of information provided each group. The mean ratings of the adults for the three conditions in which some information pertaining to handicaps was available have a range of only .43. The closeness of these ratings suggests that even in the absence of explicit verbal labels, the visual information may have *functioned* as a label, resulting in little difference among the three "informed" groups. The wider range of means among the peers' ratings for the same three conditions, of .72, seems to indicate that the more explicit the information peers had pertaining to the handicaps, the higher they tended to rate the performance. Given that the mean for the peer group in the "no labels/visual" condition is numerically closest to that of the "no labels/no visual" group, it may be that some of the peer subjects didn't understand or recognize that the singers were handicapped based only on visual information. This conclusion is supported by the results of the analysis of the open-ended questions, which indicated that only two-thirds of this group's subjects mentioned performers' handicaps somewhere in their responses (see Table 3).

The ratings obtained in this study are generally consistent with those obtained by Cassidy (1987). The adult subjects in both studies rated children's musical performances higher when labels were available than when no labels were provided. In the study described in this article, sixth- and seventh-grade students were found to respond in a similar manner. This tendency of subjects to be more generous in ratings of performances when the performers' handicaps were identified may reflect positive attitudes of peers and adults toward the musical efforts of handicapped people. Some ratings, however, may have been higher because the performers exceeded initially low rater expectations; previous research suggests that handicapping labels may bias expectations unfavorably. Further research to explore the effects of prior conceptions on music ratings of musicians with handicaps may provide useful information.

As described above, the pattern of responses to the choral evaluation differed for peer and adult subjects. Differences are also evident between age-groups in response to the open-ended questions. The peer's emphasis on musical characteristics of the performances may reflect children's tendencies to evaluate children with handicaps on the basis of their academic competence rather than on the basis of stigmatizing labels (Elam & Sigelman, 1983; Johnson, Sigelman, & Falkenberg, 1986; Siperstein & Bak, 1985).

It is surprising that the children were more concerned with musical attributes of the performance than were the adults, who were all musicians and current or future educators. This may reflect concerns teachers have about classroom management and their ability to handle exceptional students, or it may indicate that they feel the social aspects of the music program are of more importance or benefit to handicapped children than the musical considerations. Although a high percentage of adults expressed positive feelings about the performance by indicating that they would like to work with such a group, almost a third of the subjects expressed feelings of inadequacy in preparation or the lack of requisite personal characteristics, such as patience. If music educators are to work successfully with children with disabilities in mainstreamed or self-contained settings, they must have clear and realistic ideas both about the goals of mainstreaming and about the musical and social needs and abilities of these students.

The sixth and seventh graders in this study, who were not exposed to children with handicaps in their school, seemed to be sensitive and generous in their evaluations of handicapped peers. While most of the peers responded that they did not want to participate in a choir such as the one presented, their decisions seemed to be based overwhelmingly on considerations about the musical competency of the group, or their own lack of desire to be in a choir, rather than on negative reactions to the handicapped children. Based on these data, it might be recommended that when music teachers or therapists are forming mainstreamed performance groups, or preparing students in regular classrooms to accept mainstreamed peers, they should emphasize the positive musical skills of the mainstreamed students and to maintain a level of competency in the group or class that the nonhandicapped students will find acceptable. Research to explore the attitudes of children who do have regular contact with handicapped peers in their music classes would seem warranted to examine the effects of mainstreaming on peer's musical evaluations of students with handicaps.

For handicapped and nonhandicapped children to be integrated successfully in music classes or activities, the music educator must prepare the students and structure the environment carefully (Jellison, Brooks, & Huck, 1984). Knowledge of nonhandicapped students' attitudes toward handicapped peers, awareness of how disability labels may function, and the realization that the teacher and students may evaluate children with disabilities from different perspectives or based on different criteria may assist the teacher in structuring the most appropriate interactions and expectations with which to accomplish both musical and social goals in the mainstreamed music classroom.

REFERENCES

Asmus, Jr., E. P. (1985). Sixth graders' achievement motivation: Their views of success and failure in music. *Bulletin of the Council for Research in Music Education, 85,* 1–13.

Asmus, Jr., E. P. (1986). Student beliefs about the causes of success and failure in music: A study of achievement motivation. *Journal of Research in Music Education, 34,* 262–278.

Atterbury, B. (1986). A survey of present mainstreaming practices in the southern United States. *Journal of Music Therapy, 23,* 202–207.

Bak, J. J., & Siperstein, G. N. (1986). Protective effects of the label "mentally retarded" on children's attitudes toward mentally retarded peers. *American Journal of Mental Deficiency, 91,* 95–97.

Bak, J. J., & Siperstein, G. N. (1987). Similarity as a factor effecting change in children's attitudes toward mentally retarded peers. *American Journal of Mental Deficiency, 19,* 524–531.

Cassidy, J. W. (1987). The effect of "special education" labels on musicians' and nonmusicians' ratings of selected choirs. *Journal of the International Association of Music for the Handicapped, 3*(2), 25–40.

Cassity, M. T. (1981). The influence of socially valued skills in peer acceptance in a music therapy group. *Journal of Music Therapy, 18,* 148–154.

Elam, J. J., & Sigelman, C. K. (1983). Developmental differences in reactions to children labeled mentally retarded. *Journal of Applied Developmental Psychology, 4,* 303–315.

Fogel, L. S., & Nelson, R. O. (1983). The effects of special education labels on teachers' behavioral observations, checklist scores, and grading of academic work. *Journal of School Psychology, 21,* 241–251.

Foster, G., & Keech, V. (1977). Teacher reactions to the label of educable mentally retarded. *Education and Training of the Mentally Retarded, 12,* 307–311.

Foster, G. G., Yseldyke, J. E., & Reese, J. H. (1975). I wouldn't have seen it if I hadn't believed it. *Exceptional Children, 42,* 469–473.

Freeman, S., & Algozzine, B. (1980). Social acceptability as a function of labels and assigned attributes. *American Journal of Mental Deficiency, 84,* 589–595.

Gibbons, F. X., & Kassin, S. M. (1982). Behavioral expectations of retarded and nonretarded children. *Journal of Applied Developmental Psychology, 3,* 85–104.

Gibbons, F. X., Savin, L. G., & Gibbons, B. N. (1979). Evaluations of mentally retarded persons: "Sympathy" or patronization? *American Journal of Mental Deficiency, 84,* 124–131.

Gilbert, J. P., & Asmus, Jr., E. P. (1981). Mainstreaming: Music educators' participation and professional needs. *Journal of Research in Music Education, 29,* 31–38.

Jellison, J. A., Brooks, B. H., & Huck, A. M. (1984). Structuring small groups and music reinforcement to facilitate positive interactions and acceptance of severely handicapped students in the regular music classroom. *Journal of Research in Music Education, 32,* 243–264.

Johnson, G. G., Sigelman, C. K., & Falkenberg, V. F. (1986). Impacts of labeling and competence on peers' perceptions: Mentally retarded versus nonretarded peers. *American Journal of Mental Deficiency, 90,* 663–668.

Meyers, C. E., MacMillan, D. L. & Yoshida, R. K. (1980). Regular class education of EMR students, from efficacy to mainstreaming: A review of issues and research. In J. Gottlieb (Ed.), *Educating mentally retarded persons in the mainstream* (pp. 176–206). Baltimore, MD: University Park Press.

Robinson, C. R. (1988, March). *The effect of selected variables on choral adjudication ratings assigned by middle school students.* Paper presented at the National Biennial In-Service Conference of the Music Educators National Conference, Indianapolis, IN.

Salvia, J., Clark, G., & Yseldyke, J. (1973). Teacher retention of stereotypes of exceptionality. *Exceptional Children, 39,* 651–652.

Severence, L. J., & Gasstrom, L. L. (1977). Effects of the label "mentally retarded" on causal explanations for success and failure outcomes. *American Journal of Mental Deficiency, 81,* 547–555.

MUSIC EDUCATION RESEARCH

Siperstein, G. N., & Bak, J. J. (1985). Effects of social behavior on children's attitudes toward their mildly and moderately mentally retarded peers. *American Journal of Mental Deficiency, 90*, 319–327.

Siperstein, G. N., Budoff, M., & Bak, J. J. (1980). Effects of the labels "mentally retarded" and "retard" on the social acceptability of mentally retarded children. *American Journal of Mental Deficiency, 84*, 596–601.

Voeltz, L. M. (1980). Children's attitudes toward handicapped peers. *American Journal of Mental Deficiency, 84*, 455–464.

Weisz, J. R. (1981). Effects of the "mentally retarded" label on adult judgments about child failure. *Journal of Abnormal Psychology, 90*, 371–374.

Yeates, K. O., & Weisz, J. R. (1985). On being called "mentally retarded": Do developmental and professional perspectives limit labeling effects? *American Journal of Mental Deficiency, 90*, 349–352.

June 12, 1989

The purpose of this study was to describe, categorize, and compare data concerning music preferences, experiences, and skills obtained from interviews with 228 students labeled "disabled" (n = 73) or "nondisabled" (n = 155). A structured assessment interview was used by university student proctors to collect information from the students in four age-groups. Students identified by their respective schools as eligible for special education services constituted the group labeled "disabled." Questions developed for the interview focused on listening preferences and experiences, musical instrument preferences and performance, and singing and clapping (steady beat) performance. Following procedures consistent with naturalistic inquiry, audiotapes and transcriptions of the interviews were content-analyzed, and categories were developed from the responses. Perhaps the most notable outcome of this study is the similarity of responses between students with disabilities and their nondisabled peers. Results are discussed specific to music curriculum development, the integrated music classroom, and peer/teacher acceptance.

Judith A. Jellison, *The University of Texas at Austin*
Patricia J. Flowers, *The Ohio State University*

JRME 1991, VOLUME 39, NUMBER 4, PAGES 322–333

Talking about Music: Interviews with Disabled and Nondisabled Children

The past two decades have brought about increased public awareness of issues concerning the transition of individuals with disabilities into communities and schools with their nondisabled peers. This awareness, which eventually resulted in the passage of The Education for All Handicapped Children Act of 1975 (Public Law 94–142) (*Federal Register*, 1977b), brought about dramatic changes in educational policy and procedures as well as respective changes in the genre of research questions and methodological practice for professionals concerned with the well-being of individuals with disabilities.

The predominant educational philosophy inherent in the legislative mandates and educational literature throughout the 1970s and 1980s emphasized the process of "normalization"—making available to the disabled patterns and conditions of everyday life that are as close as possible to the norms and patterns of everyday society (Wolfensberger, 1972). Special education curricula and instruction were designed to assist citizens with disabilities to function ultimately as productively

---

For copies of this article, contact Judith A. Jellison, Department of Music, Music Recital Hall, The University of Texas at Austin, Austin, TX 78712-1208.

and independently as possible in integrated environments (Brown, Nietupski, & Hamre-Nietupski, 1976). Music therapists and music educators were encouraged to develop functional music curricula to assist students to be maximally independent in integrated home, school, and community music and nonmusic environments (Jellison, 1979, 1983). The philosophy of "normalization" continues throughout the 1990s, as evidenced by current legislation concerning civil rights for individuals with disabilities.

The regular music classroom is frequently designated on the disabled student's individual educational plan (IEP) as the integrated environment wherein disabled students can engage in "normalizing" activities and interact with nondisabled peers (Alley, 1979). Although there is a substantive research base concerning the therapeutic application of music with disabled children and young people, there is little research that is specifically concerned with the music behaviors of students with disabilities and their nondisabled peers (Jellison, 1988).

The absence of specific behavioral information concerning student performance is particularly consequential if teachers develop expectations for student performance based on the label "disabled" or "handicapped" given to the student receiving special education services. Teachers' overall expectations, for the most part, have been lower for students who are labeled as having a "handicap" or "deficiency" than are the teachers' expectations for the students' nondisabled peers (Foster, Ysseldyke, & Reese, 1975; Reynolds, Wang, & Walberg, 1987; Rolison & Medway, 1985).

In the music setting, music teachers found music objectives to be less important for students labeled "severely handicapped" than for unlabeled students and, similarly, less important for unlabeled students than for students labeled "gifted" (Jellison & Wolfe, 1987). In a study by Cassidy (1987) and an extension by Cassidy and Sims (1989), a priori knowledge of "special education" labels had a significant, positive effect on undergraduate and sixth- and seventh-grade students' ratings of a musical performance by students with disabilities. When the student's actual performance is seen to be unlike that suggested by the label, initial biases have been shown to be overcome (Reschly & Lamprecht, 1979).

A review of findings from several comparative music studies of nondisabled students and students with disabilities indicates that, on several specific music performance and perception tasks (generally related to rhythm activities), the actual performance of students with disabilities is similar, and in some cases, superior to that of their nondisabled peers (Jellison, 1988). Considering the variety of music experiences and types of social interactions that occur in the music classroom, it becomes important not only to obtain and compare data specific to music performance but also to obtain a breadth of information specific to music preferences and experiences that are not easily available using traditional research methodology.

The structured assessment interview, a data source in naturalistic inquiry, provides a useful data collection procedure that can result in obtaining information not easily available using observation or pencil-and-paper methods (Korchin & Schuldberg, 1981; Paget, 1984). The purpose of this study is to describe, categorize, and compare data concerning music preferences, experiences, and skills obtained from interviews with students labeled "disabled" and "nondisabled." Since the intent of this study was to compare behavioral responses within the generic labels "disabled" and "nondisabled," further labeling (i.e. mental retardation, learning disability, etc.) was not determined to be appropriate.

METHOD

Subjects

The subjects were 228 students from four age-groups: 3–5 years (n = 26), 6–8 years n = 83), 9–11 years, (n = 91), and 12–14 years (n = 28). Seventy-three of the students were identified by their respective schools as students eligible for special education services and in the present study made up the group labeled "disabled." The remaining 155 students made up the "nondisabled" group.

Procedure

A structured assessment interview procedure was used to collect data for this paper. In a structured interview procedure, questions are decided upon in advance of the interview and are asked with the same wording and in the same order for all respondents (Maccoby & Maccoby, 1954). The structured interview form has particular advantages in that it allows for comparisons and reliability across interviewers and across time, and it assures that important topics and broad dimensions of behavior are included (Maccoby & Maccoby, 1954). All interviews were audiotaped in order to control for potential sources of error that are critical to reliability and validity (Paget, 1984).

Questions were developed that focused on music preferences, experiences, and skills. Specific questions concerned listening behaviors and interests, music performance experiences, and abilities to sing a favorite song and clap a steady beat (see Figure 1). All interviews were conducted individually and audiotaped. The interviewer was instructed to ask each question in order and to allow the student to respond to the question in his or her own words. The interviewer was not to make suggestions or model singing or clapping unless absolutely necessary.

Interviewers were university students enrolled in music methods courses at The Ohio State University, The University of Texas at Austin, and The University of

---

Questions:
1. Do you like music?
2. What do you like to do while you're listening to music?
3. What is your favorite kind of music? Why do you like this kind of music the best?
4. Is there any other kind of music that you really like?
   (If yes) What is it? Why do you like it?
5. Where do you listen to music most often?
6. Have you ever played a musical instrument?
   (If yes) Which one? Where did you get to play it?
7. Would you like to play a musical instrument?
   (If yes) Which one? Why would you choose this instrument?
8. Do you have music class at your school?
   (If yes) What is your favorite music class activity?
9. What is your favorite song? Would you sing it right now?
10. Can you clap a steady beat? Would you try to clap a steady beat right now?
11. Is there anything else you'd like to tell me about music?

Figure 1.

Texas at San Antonio. The inexperience of the interviewers in assessment techniques of disabled children was not considered to be a factor for concern given (a) the high level of structure for the interview, (b) the audiotaping of the responses, and (c) evidence to suggest that disabled students can perform more strongly with inexperienced examiners who develop rapport than with professionally experienced, unfamiliar examiners (Fuchs, Fuchs, Dailey, & Power, 1985).

Interviewers of disabled students in the present study were instructed to develop rapport through informal interactions (singing, games, talk, and play) with the disabled students prior to the structured interview. Although unfamiliarity of an examiner negatively affects disabled students' performance, it does not seem to be a negative factor for nondisabled students performance (Fuchs, Fuchs, Power, & Dailey, 1985). No specific instructions for the development of rapport were given for students interviewing nondisabled students.

All university interviewers were instructed to obtain information concerning the child's age, grade, and for disabled students, the disabling condition if known, prior to the interview. Audiotaping of the interview process was used to control for (a) errors that may have resulted from individual interviewer effects, (b) the extent to which the standardized procedures were actually followed, (c) clerical errors in the interviewer's written transcription of the verbal responses, (d) misunderstanding of the question by the respondent, and (e) over-prompting of responses. All interviewers provided a written transcription of verbal responses of the audiotaped interview.

RESULTS

Using procedures consistent with naturalistic inquiry, the transcriptions of the interviews were analyzed for content. Following an independent categorization of the data from nondisabled students by one of the investigators, both investigators discussed inconsistencies and refined procedures to arrive at a set of categories for the verbal data.

Categories were also determined for the singing and clapping data. If the subject named and sang his or her favorite song, the singing was analyzed for completeness, tonality (modulation), starting pitch, lowest pitch, and vocal range. More specifically, songs that were sung were assessed to be "complete" or "incomplete." Maintenance of tonality was assessed using procedures established by Flowers and Dunne-Sousa (1990): each singing example was categorized as "modulating," "somewhat modulating," "no modulation," or "indeterminable." Starting pitches were determined using a Korg AT-12 Auto Chromatic Tuner. If the subject clapped when asked to "clap a steady beat," the clapping was categorized as "2 or fewer claps," "steady beat," "steady rhythm," or "unsteady beat." A metronome was used to determine an estimate of the tempo for each response categorized as either "steady beat" or "steady rhythm."

Data from 41 subjects (18%) were used to determine reliability for agreement between written transcriptions and audiotaped versions for subjects' verbal, singing, and clapping responses. An independent reliability observer compared the written transcription of verbal responses recorded by interviewers with the audiotaped responses. Written responses were determined to be accurate (reflecting subject's verbalizations, although every word was not transcribed) or inaccurate. Reliability for accuracy of audiotape to written transcriptions for verbal responses was 100%. For those subjects who sang, tonality was determined using two categories: data from "yes" and "somewhat" were combined to constitute the "modulation" category, and data from "no" made up the "no modulation" category. For those subjects that clapped, categories were also combined: data from "2 or fewer claps" and "unsteady" constituted the "unsteady" category and data from "steady beat" and "steady rhythm" made up the "steady" category. Reliability for both singing modulation and steady/unsteady clapping response categories was 100%.

An additional 41 subjects were selected to determine pitch and tempo reliability. For singing, data from two independent observations were compared for starting pitch, lowest pitch, highest pitch, and range. Pitch data were compared for agreement for exact pitch, pitch within a half step, and pitch within a whole step. Overall exact pitch agreement was low (65%) although there was an overall 95% agreement within a half step and overall 99% agreement within a whole step. A Pearson Product-Moment Correlation calculated on two sets of tempo scores indicated $r = .90$.

When frequency data for respective categories derived from the subjects' responses were examined, a high degree of similarity was noted among age groupings. As a result, the data for several of the response categories that occurred most frequently across age-groups were combined for each of the two groups and are presented in Figures 2 and 3. An examination of the data for Question 4 (see Figure 1) indicated a high level of redundancy when compared with responses from Question 3: data from Question 4 are therefore not included in the final results.

Overall, greater variety was indicated for the response categories for nondisabled students although both groups indicated a similar pattern in responding with greater variety indicated for the 6–8-year-old and 9–11-year-old age groupings and less variety for the 3–5-year-old and 12–14-year-old age groupings.

Of the 228 students, ages 3–14 years, disabled or nondisabled, all but one reported "yes" to liking music. A few responses categorized as "other" for nondisabled students were qualifying responses (e.g. "Depends on the kind of music," or "Some I do and some I don't") and account for the lower percentage for this question (see Figure 2).

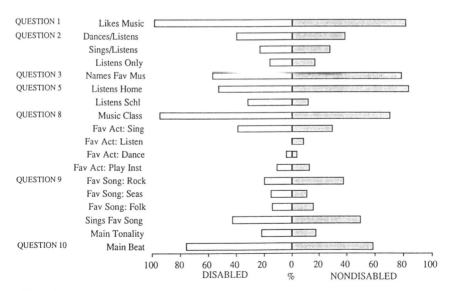

Figure 2.

Responses to Questions 2, 3, 5 and the first part of 9 (see Figure 1) indicated listening preferences and experiences. Responses were most frequently categorized as "dance," "sing," or "listen" for both groups for the question "What do you like to do while you're listening to music?" For Question 2, percentages for students with disabilities for dancing, singing, and listening only "while listening to music" were 40%, 23%, and 16% respectively, and for nondisabled students, 39%, 28%, and 17% respectively (see Figure 2). Figure 2 shows that, for Question 3, 57% of the students with disabilities and 79% of nondisabled students indicated their favorite kind of music by naming style, a particular song, or performer. When responses for Question 5 ("Where do you listen?") were examined, 84% of the responses from nondisabled students were in home-related categories, and 12% were in school-related categories; 53% of the responses from students with disabilities were categorized as home-related and 32% as school-related (see Figure 2). When students named their favorite song (Question 9), most often the category for that song was pop/rock for both groups although seasonal songs and folk songs were also named frequently by students (see Figure 2).

Responses to Questions 6 and 7 indicated preferences and experiences related to music instruments. Figure 3 shows that 89% of the students with disabilities and 67% of the nondisabled students answered that they had played a musical instrument; the category of the instrument played was most frequently percussion for both groups. A large majority of students from both groups also indicated that they wanted to play an instrument with 75% of the students with disabilities and 70% of the nondisabled group indicating interest; instrument categories for responses to the question "Which one?" are presented in Figure 3. When asked "Why you would choose this instrument?" most students in all age groupings indicated that they wanted to play a particular instrument because of its sound; responses that focused on the physical characteristics of the instruments occurred less frequently than did sound-related responses.

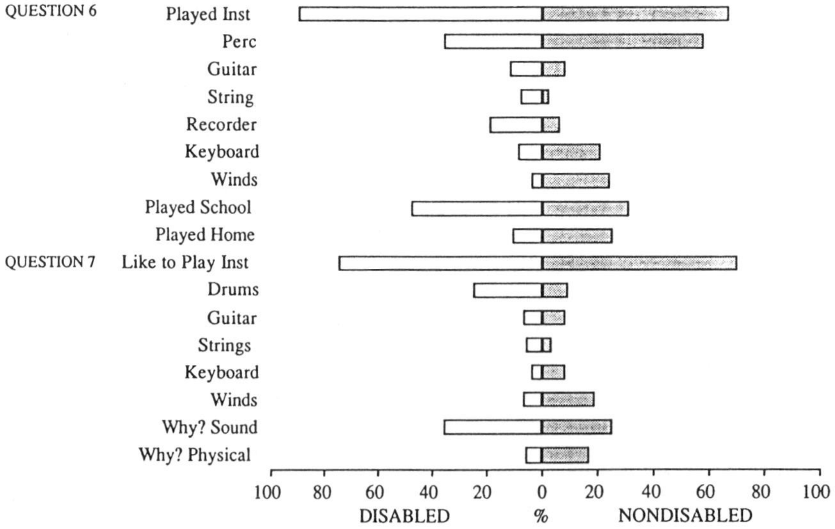

Figure 3.

Table 1
Mean Percentage of Responses of Students with Disabilities and Nondisabled Students for Singing Favorite Song and Clapping Steady Beat

	Age-groups for Disabled (D) and Nondisabled (ND)							
	3–5		6–8		9–11		12–14	
Categories	D	ND	D	ND	D	ND	D	ND
Sings favorite song	75%	73%	30%	57%	66%	36%	0	35%
Mean starting pitch	$C^\#_4$	D_4	A^b_3	$C^\#_4$	$C^\#_4$	C4	-	B_3
Mean lowest pitch	B^b_3	B^b_3	A^b_3	B^b_3	A_3	A_3	-	A_3
Mean highest pitch	F_4	G_4	E_4	G_4	F_4	F_4	-	E_4
Vocal range	A_4	M_6	P_5	M_6	M_6	m_6	-	A_4
Claps steady beat	75%	55%	70%	51%	87%	72%	73%	59%
Steady rhythm[a]	0	0	5%	22%	5%	11%	9%	0
Mean tempo estimate[b]	125	145	102	123	114	97	94	95

Note. Data represents responses to Questions 9 and 10 (see Figure 1).
[a]Students were asked to "Clap a steady beat," although some clapped a steady rhythm.
[b]Tempo estimates were determined using a metronome and are reported in beats per minute.

A majority of the students in both groups answered "yes" that they had music at their school (Question 8): singing was the response mentioned most frequently as a favorite music class activity (see Figure 2). After students named their favorite song (Question 9), 43% of the students with disabilities and 50% of the nondisabled students agreed to sing the song, although most students did not complete the entire song and, for the most part, did not maintain tonality throughout their singing. The tonality data presented in Figure 2 represent only those singing responses that were categorized as "no modulation."

The pitch data presented in Table 1 (starting, lowest pitch, highest pitches) are taken from pitches the students actually sang and does not necessarily represent their possible vocal ranges. Table 1 shows that most students in both groups sang within the range of a sixth (or less) and frequently started their songs around $C^\#_4$, although starting pitches for the 9–11-year-old age grouping for students with disabilities were slightly lower than pitches for nondisabled students.

Figure 2 indicates that, when asked to clap a steady beat (Question 10), 76% of the students with disabilities and 59% of the nondisabled students maintained a steady beat while clapping. Some students clapped a steady rhythm (see Table 1). When steady beat and steady rhythm data are combined, percentages increase to 81% for students with disabilities and 68% for nondisabled students. The tempo of steady beat clapping was determined using a metronome while listening to the audio tape of steady beat responses. In several cases, there were too few claps by single subjects to determine precise data; therefore, tempo data should be considered to be tempo "estimates."

DISCUSSION

Perhaps the most notable outcome of this study is the similarity of responses between students with disabilities and their nondisabled peers. Although the music teacher must take into account individual differences that are important for the development of meaningful music curricula and effective teaching strategies, the label "disabled" or "handicapped" may connote more differences or even a variety of differences that are simply unimportant for day-to-day music classroom instruction and classroom routines. The recognition of similarities and specific areas of difference among the groups in the present study has implications for the development of positive social behavior of students in the integrated music classroom and implications for curriculum and instruction as well.

Issues relating to socialization and classroom social behavior have long been recognized as concerns of educators. The recognition of similarities among people is an important instructional component in preparing teachers and nondisabled students to receive students with disabilities in a positive manner into the regular classroom and subsequently to increase the quality of social interactions in these classrooms (Stainback & Stainback, 1981). Numerous studies and reviews of research show that desegregation alone, without intervention, does not result in peer or teacher acceptance or the development of appropriate academic programs for students with disabilities (Donaldson, 1980). Similarly, in the music setting, Jellison, Brooks, and Huck (1984) found that positive social interactions between nondisabled and disabled students during classroom and free time in the integrated music classroom and nondisabled students' acceptance are not a result of music classroom experiences and music instruction only but are a result of the degree to which the teacher structures small-group experiences and reinforcement for positive interactions.

When social/leisure interactions are promoted between nondisabled students and students with disabilities, similar interests can be identified with resulting increases in positive interactions in the classroom and the development of mutual respect among groups and individuals (Cole, Vandercook, & Rynders, 1989; Voeltz, 1980, 1982). Results of the present study indicate many common music interests and music preferences between students with disabilities and their nondisabled peers. Although these group data are important to help dispel possible attitudes that disabled students are musically very different from their nondisabled peers, direct application of these findings must be treated with caution. Teachers who are aware of similarities between groups of students would be further advised to conduct similar interviews with their own students. Knowledge of a specific individual's preferences and interests is vital to the development of strategies to promote positive interactions in the classroom. Since negative stereotypes persist and may even worsen without early intervention (Jellison, Brooks, & Huck, 1984), music teachers should assess interests and preferences and develop experiences for positive interactions early in the school year.

In addition to implications of this study for attitudes and behaviors in the integrated classroom, several other findings have important implications for the music curriculum and music experiences for students with disabilities. Several researchers have found that it is generally difficult for children to verbally analyze music (Hair, 1981; Flowers, 1983, 1984). In the present study, many similarities were noted between the verbal responses of the two groups; however, a higher frequency of verbal responses and a greater variety of verbal responses were noted among nondisabled students than were noted among students with disabilities. The fact that certain terminology was not used by students with disabilities does not necessarily imply a lack of knowledge. Students with disabilities may simply need more opportunities to "talk" about music with teachers, parents, and friends. Music teachers and music therapists may wish to incorporate functional music conversation into their curricula to assist students in the appropriate use of the vocabulary and terminology that they are learning in the classroom.

Dancing while listening to music was the most preferred activity for both groups. Given that the favorite music for both groups was pop/rock, it is probable that the dancing preferred was informal "social" dancing and not necessarily the type of dance/movement activities traditionally associated with the music classroom. The selection of pop/rock as a listening preference is consistent with numerous studies examining the listening preferences of school-age children (Greer, 1981; LeBlanc, 1979; LeBlanc & McCrary, 1983).

Singing was also a classroom activity highly preferred by both groups, although most students were not generally accurate singers. Findings were consistent with previous literature suggesting that children are more accurate in approximating contours (modulating or somewhat modulating) than pitches (Davidson, McKernon, & Gardner, 1981; Flowers & Dunne-Sousa, 1990). Singing accuracy may have been greater if students were asked to sing a familiar song (one sung often in the classroom) and not necessarily a "favorite" song, particularly given that the favorite was most often a pop/rock favorite. Since the singing of the pop/rock song was often inaccurate, it is possible that students do not necessarily learn the melody of pop/rock tunes but prefer them for dancing. Differences in ratings of singing accuracy between the groups should be interpreted cautiously due to possible variations in difficulty levels of the songs. Overall, older students with disabilities and nondisabled students were less willing to sing than were their younger peers.

Many of the students with disabilities in the present study had opportunities to sing with nondisabled students or to sing the same materials as their nondisabled peers in the public schools. In the review of educational research, Madden and Slavin (1983) found beneficial academic and social gains for students with mild disabilities who were placed in regular classrooms when compared to gains of their disabled peers in segregated special classrooms. Without particular instruction, public school music experiences may have positively influenced the results in the present study in that no striking differences were noted in mean starting pitches between the two groups. Also, it should be noted that students with disabilities in the present study represent a group with a wide range of abilities. When a group of individuals with a single disability classification (retardation) in a segregated setting were studied, their singing ranges and midpoints were generally found to be lower than the ranges and midpoints of their nondisabled peers of the same chronological age (Delio, 1976; Larson, 1977).

In the present study, the mean starting pitches B_3, C_4, and $C\#_4$ across the two groups and age groupings were, for the most part, consistent with results from several studies of students within this age group as reported by Welch (1979). There is no particular explanation for the slightly lower mean starting pitch for students with disabilities in the 6–8-year-old group. Interpretations of vocal range data should be made with caution since students sang a variety of songs and most often sang song fragments.

Similarities were also noted in clapping and clapping tempos. Most students in both groups were able to clap a steady beat, and a few students kept a steady rhythm. Tempos were generally similar between the two groups, with the larger difference for the 9–11-year-old group and the smaller difference for the 12–14-year-old group. Both groups showed an overall "slowing down" of clapping tempo across the age groups.

Few similarities were identified when students responded to questions concerning musical instruments. Percussion instruments were mentioned frequently as having been played by both groups although more nondisabled students had played traditional orchestral or band instruments than had students with disabilities. Guitar and recorder were mentioned more frequently by students with disabilities than by their nondisabled peers. Since data show that few students with disabilities study music outside of the music classroom and that school appears to be the primary environment for music in their lives, it is understandable that classroom instruments would be mentioned more frequently. The inclusion of recorder responses may account for the higher percentage of positive responses among students with disabilities for the question "Have you played a musical instrument?"

Most of the students wanted to play a musical instrument; drums were mentioned more frequently by students with disabilities, and wind instruments more frequently by nondisabled students. For the most part, differences relating to musical instruments appear to be the result of several factors: (a) the definition of "musical instrument"; (b) opportunities for students with disabilities to play traditional keyboard, orchestral, and band instruments; and (c) their knowledge of the names of a variety of traditional orchestral and band instruments.

Writers of several studies (Bruscia & Levinson, 1982; Furman, 1988; Steele, 1984; Staum & Flowers, 1984) and numerous informal articles in music education journals report that students with disabilities are able to read music successfully and learn to play traditional instruments. Although several students in the present study indicated that they had played traditional instruments, the percentage is much lower than is that of their nondisabled peers. Obviously, more opportunities and experiences with traditional instruments need to be made available for students with disabilities. Playing instruments is an experience that readily extends from the school to the home and community and provides, for all students, excellent opportunities for quality social and leisure activities outside the school day.

Music is perceived by society as a highly valued social and leisure activity, and this perception, in part, may account for the selection of music as a curricular subject for students. Although music may be offered in public schools, the music opportunities that are provided for a particular student may differ when that student is known to be "disabled" or "handicapped." Although a student is labeled "disabled" or "handicapped" and is receiving special education services, the present study shows that the student is not "musically disabled" to the extent that preferences, experiences, and skills are dramatically unlike those of nondisabled peers. Knowledge of similarities among students may function to encourage teachers to seek out and use similarities to structure and facilitate positive social and academic growth in their students. The differences that were most notable occurred in the areas of musical instruments and of vocabulary, where knowledge and experiences of students with disabilities have been limited. Findings of the present study suggest future research in strategies for teaching performance skills (playing traditional instruments and singing) and music vocabulary to students with disabilities and subsequent implications for quality musical and social experiences in integrated school and community environments.

REFERENCES

Alley, J. M. (1979). Music in the IEP: Therapy/education. *Journal of Music Therapy, 16,* 111–127.

Brown, L., Nietupski, V., & Hamre-Nietupski, S. (1976). Criterion of ultimate functioning. In M. A. Thomas (Ed.), *Hey, don't forget about me!* (pp. 2–15). Reston, VA: Council for Exceptional Children.

Bruscia, K. E., & Levinson, S. (1982). Predictive factors in Optacon music-reading. *Journal of Visual Impairment & Blindness, 76*, 309–312.

Cassidy, J. W. (1987). The effect of "special education" labels on musicians' and nonmusicians' ratings of selected choirs. *Journal of the International Association of Music for the Handicapped, 3*(2), 25–40.

Cassidy, J. W., & Sims, W. (1989). Effects of special education labels on peers' and music educators' evaluations of a handicapped youth choir. Paper presented at the Eighth National Symposium for Research in Music Behavior, Baton Rouge, LA.

Cole, D. A., Vandercook, T., & Rynders, J. (1989). Comparison of two peer interaction programs: Children with and without severe disabilities. *American Educational Research Journal 25*, 415–439.

Davidson, L., McKernon, P., & Gardner, N.E. (1981). The acquisition of song: A developmental approach. *Documentary report of the Ann Arbor symposium: National symposium on the applications of psychology to the teaching and learning of music* (pp. 301–315). Reston, VA: MENC.

Delio, C. L. (1976). The relationship of diagnostic and social factors to the singing ranges of institutionalized mentally retarded persons. *Journal of Music Therapy, 13*, 17–28.

Donaldson, J. (1980). Changing attitudes toward handicapped persons: A review and analysis of research. *Exceptional Children, 46*, 504–514.

Federal Register (1977a). Education of Handicapped Children. Implementation of Part B of the Education of the Handicapped Act, 42 (163). Part II, Tuesday, August 23, 1977.

Federal Register (1977b). Nondiscrimination of basis of handicap. Part IV, Wednesday, May 4, 1977.

Flowers, P. J. (1983). The effect of instruction in vocabulary and listening on nonmusicians' descriptions of changes in music. *Journal of Research in Music Education, 31*, 179–190.

Flowers, P. J. (1984). Attention to elements of music and effect of instruction in vocabulary of written descriptions of music by children and undergraduates. *Psychology of Music, 12*, 17–24.

Flowers, P. J., & Dunne-Sousa, D. (1990). Pitch pattern accuracy, tonality, and vocal range in the singing of preschool children. *Journal of Research in Music Education, 38*, 102–114.

Foster, G., Ysseldyke, J., Reese, J. (1975). I wouldn't have seen it if I hadn't believed it. *Exceptional Children, 41*, 55–48.

Fuchs, D., Fuchs, L. S., Dailey, A. M., and Power, M. H. (1985). The effects of examiners' personal familiarity and professional experience on handicapped children's test performance. *Journal of Educational Research, 78*, 141–146.

Fuchs, D., Fuchs, L. S., Power, M. H., & Dailey, A. M. (1985). Bias in the assessment of handicapped children. *American Educational Research Journal, 22*, 185–198.

Furman, C. E. (Ed.). (1988). *Effectiveness of music therapy procedures: Documentation of research and clinical practice.* Washington, DC: National Association for Music Therapy.

Greer, R. D. (1981). An operant approach to motivation and affect: Ten years of research in music learning. *Documentary report of the Ann Arbor symposium: National symposium on the applications of psychology to the teaching and learning of music* (pp. 101–121). Reston, VA: MENC.

Hair, H. I. (1981). Verbal identification of music concepts. *Journal of Research in Music Education, 29*, 11–21.

Jellison, J. A. (1979) The music therapist in the education setting: Developing and implementing curriculum for the handicapped. *Journal of Music Therapy, 16*, 128–137.

Jellison, J. A. (1983) Functional value as criterion for selection and prioritization of nonmusic and music educational objectives in music therapy. *Music Therapy Perspectives, 1*(2), 17–22.

Jellison, J. A. (1988). A content analysis of music research with handicapped children and youth (1975–1986): Applications in special education. In C. K. Furman (Ed.), *Effectiveness of music therapy procedures: Documentation of research and clinical practice* (pp. 223–279). Washington, DC: National Association for Music Therapy.

Jellison, J. A., Brooks, B. H., & Huck, A. M. (1984). Structuring small groups and music reinforcement to facilitate positive interactions and acceptance of severely handicapped students in the regular music classroom. *Journal of Research in Music Education, 32*, 243–264.

Jellison, J. A., & Wolfe, D.E. (1987). Educators' ratings of selected objectives for severely handicapped or gifted students in the regular classroom. *Contributions to Music Education, 14*, 36–41.

Korchin, S. J., & Schuldberg, D. (1981). The future of clinical assessment. *American Psychologist, 36,* 1147–1158.

Larson, B. A. (1977). A comparison of singing ranges of mentally retarded and normal children with published songbooks used in singing activities. *Journal of Music Therapy, 14,* 139–143.

LeBlanc, A. (1979). Generic style music preferences of fifth-grade students. *Journal of Research in Music Education, 27,* 255–270.

LeBlanc, A., & McCrary, J. (1983). Effects of tempo and performing medium on children's music preference. *Journal of Research in Music Education, 31,* 283–294.

Maccoby, E. E., & Maccoby, N. (1954). The interview: A tool for social science. In G. Lindzey (Ed.), *Handbook of social psychology* (Vol. 1, pp. 449–487). Cambridge, MA: Addison-Wesley.

Madden, N. A., & Slavin, R. E. (1983). Mainstreaming students with mild handicaps: Academic and social outcomes. *Review of Educational Research, 53,* 519–565.

Paget, K. D. (1984). The structured assessment interview: A psychometric review. *Journal of School Psychology, 22,* 415–427.

Reschley, D. J., & Lamprecht, M. J. (1979). Expectancy effects of labels: Fact or artifact? *Exceptional Children, 46,* 55–58.

Reynolds, M. C., Wang, M. C., & Walberg, H. J. (1987). The necessary restructuring of special and regular education. *Exceptional Children, 53,* 391–398.

Rolison, M. A., & Medway, F. J. (1985). Teachers' expectations and attributions for student achievement: Effects of label, performance pattern, and special education intervention. *American Education Research Journal, 22,* 561–573.

Stainback, S., & Stainback, W. (1981). Educating nonhandicapped students about severely handicapped students: A human differences training model. *Education Unlimited,* March/April, 17–19.

Staum, M. J., & Flowers, P. J. (1984). The use of simulated training and music lessons in teaching appropriate stopping to an autistic child. *Music Therapy Perspectives, 1*(3), 14–17.

Steele, A. L. (1984). Music therapy for the learning disabled: Intervention and instruction. *Music Therapy Perspectives, 1*(3), 2–7.

Voeltz, L. M. (1980). Children's attitudes toward handicapped peers. *American Journal of Mental Deficiency, 84,* 455–464.

Voeltz, L. M. (1982). Effects of structured interaction with severely handicapped peers on children's attitudes. *American Journal of Mental Deficiency, 86,* 380–390.

Welch, G. P. (1979). Vocal range and poor pitch singing. *Psychology of Music, 7,* 13–31.

Wolfensberger, W. (1972). *The principle of normalization in human services.* Toronto: National Institute on Mental Retardation.

August 20, 1990

The primary purpose of this study was to examine the role of music in the deaf culture and to relate the findings to current practices in music education programs for hearing-impaired students. Secondary purposes of the study were to accumulate data that would either substantiate or refute the writings of hearing authors regarding the value of music to the deaf, and to examine factors that determine deaf individuals' involvement with music. Data were collected by (a) a questionnaire sent to a random sample of deaf Americans from across the country, and (b) videotaped personal interviews with a random sample of deaf community members in a large midwestern metropolitan area. Based on their primary language and socialization practices, respondents were identified as members of the deaf culture, members of the hearing culture, or those that interact within both cultures. A summary of the results indicates that (1) cultural identification is a strong influential factor in deaf individuals' involvement with music, (2) deaf individuals that do involve themselves with music do so in ways similar to hearing individuals, (3) musical activities enjoyed most by deaf individuals are singing/signing songs, listening to music, and moving or dancing to music, (4) most respondents believed that music instruction should be optional for deaf students, (5) certain factors related to family involvement with music and musical training seem to be indicators of the role music will play in the lives of deaf individuals, and (6) deaf individuals do not participate to the degree that hearing individuals do in most common ritual uses of music. Quotes from respondents and implications for music educators teaching hearing-impaired students are given.

Alice-Ann Darrow, *University of Kansas*

JRME 1993, VOLUME 41, NUMBER 2, PAGES 93–110

The Role of Music in Deaf Culture: Implications for Music Educators

Culture has been defined as a way of life that identifies a specific group of people. Much has been written about the deaf culture, particularly during the past 10 years. Deaf people in the United States have customs, mores, and institutions that differ from those of the hearing culture. Existing within and in continual relationship with the larger society, the deaf community adopts many of the characteristics of the hearing population; yet, because language is the foundation of culture, the deaf community, whose members communicate in sign language, is also

For copies of this article, contact Alice-Ann Darrow, Department of Art and Music Education and Music Therapy, 311 Bailey Hall, University of Kansas, Lawrence, KS 66045-2344.

unique in many ways. "Taken as a whole, the deaf community emerges as a distinctive societal entity, marked by the satisfaction deaf people usually find in the company of each other" (Schein, 1978, p. 511).

Padden and Humphries (1988) have described a community of Deaf (with a capital "D") people who share a language—American Sign Language—and a culture. They also describe the deaf (with a lowercase "d"): These are individuals who lose their hearing adventitiously through illness, accidents, or old age. This group does not have access to the language, heritage, beliefs, and practices of Deaf people. In addition, a third group of individuals is connected to the deaf community. These people are the hearing children of Deaf parents; the culture bestows on them a similar status, but not necessarily an equal one. A movement has actively begun to recognize the deaf community as a distinct linguistic and cultural minority (Janesick, 1990).

Although the deaf culture is a part of the larger society, it remains enigmatic to most of the hearing population. Knowing little about other cultures often results in ethnocentrism—the tendency to judge other cultures by the standards of one's own. This tendency has often been apparent in regard to the deaf community. Historically, the hearing have taken a paternalistic attitude toward the deaf (Gentry, 1988; Padden & Humphries, 1988) and have made decisions on their behalf for such important issues as speech instruction, the composition and use of various sign systems, and academic instruction and administration. This paternalistic attitude is apparent even in the literature pertaining to the Deaf and music. The earliest account of music education for deaf students was written in the *American Annals of the Deaf and Dumb* (now called *American Annals of the Deaf*) in 1848 (Darrow & Heller, 1985).

Numerous articles pertaining to music and the deaf continue to be published; however, a review of this literature has revealed no entries written by hearing-impaired authors (Darrow, 1989). This situation calls into question the importance of music in the lives of deaf individuals, and underscores the notion that the hearing are speaking for the deaf, perhaps erroneously, regarding this importance and the value of music in educational programs for the deaf.

Gallaudet University, a university in Washington, D.C. for hearing-impaired students, began offering music courses in the fall of 1988. Though the music instructor herself was hearing-impaired, reactions from the deaf community were mixed. While some individuals in the deaf community were in favor of this new opportunity for Gallaudet students, others were disconcerted and believed that it was one more example of "hearing" values being imposed on the deaf (Stewart, 1990). Gallaudet University continues to be an increasingly influential force in the deaf community and in deaf education practices (Kannapell, 1980; Prickett, 1989). In the spring of 1988, after demonstrations, protests, and boycotts, the university inaugurated its first deaf president.

Although no research has been conducted specific to the role of music in the deaf culture, descriptive literature does exist pertaining to the deaf community. The deaf population has grown, doubling its proportion of the total population in the last 40 years. Changes in the nature of the deaf community are occurring along with external events such as the educational practice of mainstreaming, which dramatically reduced enrollment in residential schools.

In the past, state schools for the deaf were the cornerstone of the local deaf community (Schein, 1978). Other educational influences on the deaf community have been the practices of oral-only programs and the implementation (by hearing educators) of English sign systems, which differ greatly from American Sign

Language, the native language of the deaf community (Padden, 1980). Hearing-impaired children educated by these sign systems, and those who have oral skills only, often find it difficult to communicate with other members of the deaf community. Because of these educational practices, hearing-impaired children are often caught between the hearing society and the deaf community, resulting in a lack of personal identity with either cultural group (Sacks, 1989).

Descriptive research related to the deaf community's involvement in the arts has revealed many deaf sculptors, painters, photographers, illustrators, and actors (Gannon, 1981). There are a number of anecdotal accounts of professional musicians with moderate to profound hearing losses (Merchant, 1989). Most, if not all, however have adventitious hearing losses, and consequently would have been able to retain some memory of music from their years prior to acquiring a hearing loss. It is possible, too, that they would not be considered a part of the deaf culture, which is composed primarily of congenitally deaf adults who communicate through sign language rather than speech.

Research studies pertaining to music and the deaf fall into three broad categories: music perception, music performance, and therapeutic uses of music. Much of this research indicates that hearing-impaired individuals are capable of developing various music skills, though perhaps delayed when compared to their hearing counterparts (Darrow, 1989). The question remains as to whether these music skills are reinforcing enough or can be developed sufficiently such that hearing-impaired students will continue to make music a part of their lives.

Music as a means of personal expression often reflects many aspects of the culture. Hamm, Nettl, and Byrnside (1975) stated that "there is no culture known to man, no single civilization of the past, that does not have its own body of music" (p. 71). The deaf culture may be the one exception. The primary purpose of the present study was to examine the role of music in the deaf culture and to relate the findings to current practices in music education programs for hearing-impaired students. Secondary purposes of the study were to accumulate data that would either substantiate or refute the writings of hearing authors regarding the value of music to the deaf, and to examine factors that determine deaf individuals' involvement with music. The research questions were: (1) Do hearing-impaired individuals find music reinforcing enough to make it a functional part of their lives? (2) If so, do they involve themselves with music in ways similar to hearing individuals? (3) What musical experiences, if any, do they find the most rewarding? (4) What is the opinion of the deaf community regarding the role of music in educational programs for hearing-impaired students? (5) Does musical training or involvement with music by other family members have an effect on the function of music in the lives of hearing-impaired individuals? (6) Do deaf individuals participate in common ritual uses of music?

METHOD

Data designed to answer the research questions were collected by (a) a questionnaire sent to a random sample of 300 entries in the *National Telephone Directory for TDD Users,* published by Telecommunications for the Deaf, Inc. (Silver Spring, Maryland), and (b) videotaped personal interviews with a random sample of deaf community members in a large midwestern metropolitan area. Phase 1 of the study consisted of gathering background information necessary for the formulation of questionnaire items that would address the research questions. Leaders in the deaf community were contacted for informal interviews to discuss deaf culture and so that they might offer direction regarding readings that would be helpful in understanding the leisure activities and cultural interests of the deaf community. Attention was also given to Merriam's (1964) 10 major functions of music.

Phase 2 consisted of constructing and piloting the questionnaire and personal interview questions. Construction of the questionnaire and interview questions was a critical part of the study. Hearing-impaired individuals often develop written performance in English that is significantly different from that of their hearing counterparts (Davis & Hardick, 1981; Heward & Orlansky, 1988; Kretschmer & Kretschmer, 1978). Other data indicate that hearing-impaired students often score low on tests such as the Word Meaning and Paragraph Meaning subtests of the Stanford Achievement Test (Moores, 1987). Because of this, advice was sought from members of the deaf community and from professionals knowledgeable in the language development of hearing-impaired individuals. Other traditional resources were used as references for construction of the questionnaire and interview questions (Backstrom & Hursh-César, 1981; Oppenheim, 1966; Payne, 1965). The questionnaire and interview questions were then piloted with a random sample of members from a local deaf community. The questionnaire items and interview questions were revised as indicated by the feedback given during the pilot phase of the study.

Phase 3 consisted of (1) administering the questionnaire, (2) videotaping personal interviews, (3) double-sampling nonrespondents, and (4) compiling and analyzing the data. Due to the language and reading issues discussed in Phase 2, personal interviews were also an extremely important aspect of the study.

The first part of the oral interviews, which were conducted in the native language of the deaf, American Sign Language, was constructed and used for corroboration of the questionnaire data, which were based on written English. Respondents in the pilot study were administered the questionnaire in written form and in sign language. Reliability of responses in written form and sign language was computed at .97. The second part of the oral interviews consisted of open-ended questions used for case study and anecdotal information.

A proportional stratified random sample of 300 individuals was surveyed from all 50 states. Individuals listed in the *National Telephone Directory for TDD Users* (Telecommunications Device for the Deaf) were used as the parent population. This directory was used because listed individuals have hearing losses severe enough such that use of a standard telephone, even with amplification, is infeasible. Using this directory, therefore, increased the likelihood that those sampled would be members of the deaf culture. Following the initial sampling, a second questionnaire was sent to all nonrespondents. The final return rate was 61%. Considering the aforementioned reading issues related to the deaf community, the return rate was considered acceptable.

RESULTS

Responses to Items 1–3 of the questionnaire were used to identify subjects as members of the deaf culture, members of the hearing culture, or those that interact within both cultures. Cultural classification was based on the major identification factors of the deaf community: subjects' use of American Sign Language as the primary language and subjects' level of socialization with the identified cultural groups. Analysis of certain items revealed significant differences between respondents identified as members of these three cultural groups; therefore, responses on these items were examined separately for these three groups. Responses were pooled for items that revealed no significant differences between the cultural groups. Subsequent analyses determined (a) percentage of responses, (b) significant differences between responses, (c) relationships between certain factors and respondents' level of involvement with music, and (d) significant differences between the responses of subjects identified as members of the deaf culture and those identified as either members of the hearing culture or those who interact within both cultures.

Because the second part of the interview questions had an open-ended format rather than a closed-set response format, the data and comments written on the questionnaire were used for case study and anecdotal material. Independent sign-language interpretations of the videotapes, those of the investigator and an RID (Registered Interpreter for the Deaf)-certified interpreter, were compared for reliability of the translations. Reliability was 100% for interpretation of concepts contained in the videotaped interviews.

Cultural Identification

Responses to Items 1–3 of the questionnaire are reported in Table 1. Respondents who associate only or mostly with other deaf individuals and use American Sign Language as their primary language were assigned to the deaf culture group. Respondents who associate equally with deaf and hearing individuals and use spoken English and sign language as their primary languages were assigned to the group that identifies with both the hearing and deaf cultures. Respondents who use only spoken English or signed English and associate mostly or only with hearing individuals were assigned to the hearing culture group. Familial deafness, particularly parental deafness, virtually assures identity with the deaf culture; however, because of the low incidence of hereditary deafness, these data were used only to substantiate already identified members of the deaf culture group based on language use and socialization practices. The breakdown of respondents into groups is reported in Table 2.

Educational Background

The association between educational background and cultural identity can be seen in Table 3. A significant difference was found between the responses of those in the identified culture groups (χ^2= 33.8, df = 4, p < .001). Of those subjects who identify with the deaf culture, the highest percentage attended residential schools for the deaf. Of those subjects who identify with the hearing culture, the highest percentage attended public schools. Of those respondents who identify with both cultures, the highest percentage attended both residential and public schools. Similar associations can be observed between cultural identity groups and respondents who were placed either in mainstreamed classrooms or in self-contained classrooms for the deaf. A significant difference was also found between the responses of those in the identified culture groups (χ^2 = 13.3, df = 6, p < .05). Of those subjects who identify with the deaf culture, the highest percentage of respondents were placed only in self-contained classes for the deaf, and of those subjects who identify with the hearing culture, the highest percentage of respondents were placed in mainstreamed classes. Nearly all subjects were in school prior to Public Law 94–142, the Education for All Handicapped Children Act of 1975.

Table 1
Cultural Identification Responses

Factors	Percentage of respondents

Association

1. Associate only with other deaf individuals	7.4
2. Associate mostly with other deaf individuals	28.4
3. Associate equally with deaf and hearing individuals	54.5
4. Associate mostly with hearing individuals	6.3
5. Associate only with hearing individuals	3.4

Primary language

1. American Sign Language	52.5
2. Signed English	2.8
3. Spoken English	9.0
4. Spoken English and sign language	35.6

Familial deafness

1.Mother and father are (or were) deaf	6.1
2. Mother and father are (or were) hearing	92.2
3. Children are deaf	12.3
4. Children are hearing	48.6
5. Husband or wife is (or was) deaf	53.6
6. Husband or wife is (or was) hearing	11.2

Table 2
Breakdown of Respondents in Culture Identification Groups

Cultural identification groups	Percentage of respondents
Identify with both hearing and deaf cultures	29
Identify with hearing culture	13
Identify with deaf culture	58

Music Education Background

Music education background data are reported in Table 4. A significant difference was found between the responses of those in the identified culture groups (χ^2 = 19.3, df = 4, $p < .001$). Of those subjects who identify with the deaf culture, the highest percentage of respondents never attended music classes, and of those subjects who identify with the hearing culture, the highest percentage of respondents attended music classes regularly. A significant difference was also found between the classifications of music attendance and type of classroom attended

(χ^2 = 15.0, *df* = 4, *p* < .05). The highest percentage of respondents who never attended music classes were placed in self-contained classrooms for the deaf, and the highest percentage of respondents who attended music classes regularly were placed in mainstreamed classrooms. There was no significant difference in the musical activities participated in between those subjects who went to music "regularly" and those that went to music "sometimes." There was also no significant difference in the musical activities participated in based on cultural identification groups. Thus, these data indicate that subjects, regardless of cultural identification or frequency of attendance in music class, participated in similar music classroom activities. Since there were no significant differences in the responses of the culture groups or between those who frequently or sometimes attended music class, the data were combined to give a better or clearer picture of the types of musical activity respondents participated in as students in the music classroom. Of those respondents that attended music classes, the greatest percentage were involved in singing and/or signing songs, listening to music, and moving to music. These activities were also identified as those that were enjoyed the most. Over 50% of the respondents who attended music classes stated that they either loved or liked music class. Only 16% stated that they disliked or hated music class. The remaining respondents were indifferent toward music class. No significant differences were found between the responses of those in the identified culture groups and attitude toward music class.

Table 3
Educational Background

Factors	Percentage of respondents identifying with:		
	Deaf culture	Hearing culture	Both cultures
Type of schooling			
1. Residential school for the deaf	68.6	13.6	39.2
2. Public school	22.5	63.6	25.5
3. Both residential and public school	18.6	22.7	45.1
Public school classroom distribution			
1. Only mainstreamed into regular classes	31.9	66.7	34.2
2. Only in classes for the hearing impaired	38.3	11.1	18.4
3. Mostly in regular classes and sometimes in classes for the hearing impaired	12.8	16.7	26.3
4. Mostly in classes for the hearing impaired and sometimes in regular classes	17.0	5.6	21.1
Pre/Post Public Law 94–142	**Groups combined**		
1. Before 1974	80.9		
2. After 1974	4.6		
3. Both before and after 1974	14.5		

Family and Respondents' Involvement with Music

By means of the questionnaire, I attempted to examine the influence of family interest in music on respondents' interest in music. Participation of family members and respondents in musical activities is reported in Table 5. Also shown in

Table 4
Music Education Background

Factors	Percentage of respondents identifying with:		
	Deaf culture	Hearing culture	Both cultures

Music class attendance

1. Went to music classes regularly	9.6	43.5	23.1
2. Never went to music classes	61.5	21.7	48.1
3. Sometimes went to music classes	28.8	34.8	28.8

Activities in music class   Groups combined

All subjects who went to music regularly/sometimes
1. Sang and/or signed songs	65.9
2. Played instruments	36.4
3. Listened to music	46.6
4. Learned to read music	31.8
5. Moved or danced to music	45.5
6. Learned music facts	20.5
7. Used music only for speech training and/ or auditory training	23.9

Activities enjoyed

1. Singing and/or signing songs	52.8
2. Playing instruments	25.0
3. Listening to music	45.8
4. Learning to read music	20.8
5. Moving or dancing to music	45.8
6. Learning music facts	12.5
7. Using music only for speech training and/ or auditory training	6.9

Enjoyment level

1. Loved music class	26.8
2. Liked music class	25.8
3. Did not care about music class	31.1
4. Did not like music class	8.6
5. Hated music class	7.5

Table 5 are data concerning the family and respondents' home musical environment. Data concerning family and respondents' involvement with musical performances are reported in Table 6. No significant differences were found between the responses of those in the identified culture groups and items concerning family interest in music or respondents' interest in music. No significant associations were found between family interest in music and respondents' interest in music.

Ritual Uses of Music

No significant differences were found between the responses of those in the identified culture groups and items concerned with ritual uses of music. Combined responses (see Table 7) revealed that the highest percentage of respondents: (1) participate in music associated with religious services, (2) listen to (rather than sing or sign) the national anthem, (3) sometimes watch halftime shows at sporting events, and (4) do not participate in holiday music. Approximately one-third of all respondents who were married had music at their weddings.

Musical Preference

No significant differences were found between the responses of those in the identified culture groups and the identification of musical preferences for singers,

Table 5
Home Musical Environment Growing Up and Respondents' Participation Now

Factors	Percentage of responses: Groups combined	
Music activities	**Participation of:**	
	Family members growing up	**Respondents now**
1. Sang and/or signed songs	34.6	21.3
2. Played an instrument	31.4	5.3
3. Read music	17.0	6.0
4. Wrote music	1.3	0.7
5. Listened to music	54.7	26.7
6. Took music lessons	18.9	4.7
7. Were not involved with music	37.7	57.3
Home musical environment		
1. A radio	85.6	75.0
2. A record player or stereo	57.5	66.3
3. Records	46.6	48.1
4. A musical instrument	42.5	28.8
5. A tape player	32.2	59.6
6. Music or music books	32.9	34.6

songs, musical groups, radio stations, and composers (see Table 8). Less than 20% of the respondents identified favorite singers, songs, or musical groups. Ten percent or less of the respondents identified a favorite radio station or composer.

Table 6
Family Involvement with Music Performance Growing Up and Respondents' Involvement Now

Factors	Percentage of responses: Groups combined	
	Involvement of:	
	Family members growing up	**Respondents now**
Attended musical performances		
a. Never	34.2	53.5
b. Rarely	19.1	19.7
c. Sometimes	32.7	21.2
d. Frequently	14.1	5.6
Watched musical performances on TV		
a. Never	23.4	28.9
b. Rarely	19.3	22.9
c. Sometimes	38.0	33.8
d. Frequently	19.3	14.4
Listened to musical performances on the radio or record player		
a. Never	24.1	52.8
b. Rarely	10.3	11.3
c. Sometimes	32.3	17.4
d. Frequently	33.3	18.5
Participated in musical performances		
a. Never	59.3	78.6
b. Rarely	13.8	10.7
c. Sometimes	18.0	7.0
d. Frequently	9.0	3.7
Attended dances		
a. Never	25.1	32.3
b. Rarely	26.7	31.8
c. Sometimes	38.5	27.4
d. Frequently	9.7	8.5

Importance of Music

Responses to the importance of music were weighted according to the degrees of importance, which ranged from "not at all" to "very important." An analysis of variance revealed significant differences ($p = .05$) between the identified culture groups and responses concerning the importance of music (see Table 9). Of those subjects who identify with the deaf culture, the highest percentage of

Table 7
Ritual Uses of Music

Factors	Percentage of responses: Groups combined
Worship services	
1. Music never played	24.3
2. Music rarely played	5.0
3. Music sometimes played	22.5
4. Music always played	38.7
5. Never attend church or synagogue	9.3
National anthem	
1. Sing "The Star-Spangled Banner"	6.0
2. Sign "The Star-Spangled Banner"	15.8
3. Sing and sign "The Star-Spangled Banner"	13.1
4. Listen to "The Star-Spangled Banner"	45.3
5. Never attend sports events	19.6
Sports events	
1. Never watch the halftime show	4.9
2. Seldom watch the halftime show	14.8
3. Sometimes watch the halftime show	40.0
4. Always watch the halftime show	21.7
5. Never attend football games	18.3
Holiday music	
1. Sing Christmas or other holiday music	11.3
2. Sign Christmas or other holiday music	18.2
3. Sing and sign Christmas or other holiday music	23.6
4. Listen to Christmas or other holiday music	18.7
5. Play Christmas or other holiday music	2.4
6. Do not participate in holiday music	25.6
Wedding music	
1. My wedding	32.6

Table 8
Musical Preference

Preference indicated	Percentage of responses: Groups combined
Singer	16.2
Song	17.9
Musical group	15.6
Radio station	10.1
Composer	7.3

Table 9
Analysis of Variance Summary Table for Cultural Groups on Importance of Music

Source	*df*	Sum of squares	Mean squares	*F*	*p*
Between groups	2	18.8	9.4	8.4	.05
Within groups	163	181.0	1.1		
Total	166	199.8			

respondents indicated that music was "not at all important" and of those subjects who identify with the hearing culture, the highest percentage of respondents indicated that music was "very important."

Responses of items related to music background, family involvement with music, individual involvement with music, and ritual uses of music were examined to determine if a relationship existed between these subscales and respondents' response concerning the importance of music in their lives. Within the subscale of music background, significant differences were found between classifications of music attendance and importance of music ($\chi^2 = 30.8$, $df = 6$, $p < .001$), between classifications of music activities enjoyed and importance of music ($\chi^2 = 39.6$, $df = 18$, $p < .05$), and between classifications of attitude toward music class and importance of music ($\chi^2 = 39.6$, $df = 18$, $p < .05$). A significantly greater number of respondents who attended music classes regularly indicated that music was "very important" or "important," a significantly greater number of respondents who had high enjoyment of music scores indicated that music was "very important" or "important," and a significantly greater number of respondents who had positive attitudes toward music class indicated that music was "very important" or "important."

Within the subscale of family involvement with music, significant differences were found between classifications of family participation in musical activities and importance of music ($\chi^2 = 38.7$, $df = 18$, $p < .01$) and between classifications of family involvement with musical performances and importance of music ($\chi^2 = 30.3$, $df = 6$, $p < .001$). A significantly greater number of respondents who had high scores in family participation in music activities indicated that music was "very important" or "important," and a significantly greater number of respondents who had high scores in family involvement with music performance indicated that music was "very important" or "important."

Within the subscale of respondents' involvement with music (see Table 10), significant differences were found between classifications of respondents' participation in musical activities and importance of music (χ^2 = 63.2, df = 18, p < .001) and between classifications of respondents' involvement with musical performance and importance of music (χ^2 = 27.5, df = 6, p < .001). A significantly greater number of respondents who had high "involvement with music" scores indicated that music was "very important" or "important" and a significantly greater number of respondents who had high "involvement with music performance" scores indicated that music was "very important" or "important."

Table 10
Importance of Music

Level of importance	Percentage of respondents identifying with:		
	Deaf culture	Hearing culture	Both cultures
Not at all	46.8	14.3	29.4
Of little importance	19.1	19.0	25.5
Somewhat important	26.6	23.8	27.5
Very important	7.4	42.9	17.6

Within the subscale of respondents' involvement with ritual uses of music, a significant difference was found between classifications of respondents' participation in the national anthem and importance of music (χ^2 = 13.5, df = 3, p < .01). A significantly greater number of respondents who participated in singing the national anthem indicated that music was "very important" or "important."

Finally, respondents were asked their views concerning the music education of hearing-impaired students. No significant differences were found among the identified culture groups. Combined responses indicated that over 75% believed that participation in music education classes should be an option for hearing-impaired students and not a requirement.

DISCUSSION

The primary purpose of this study was to examine the role of music in deaf culture and to relate the findings to current practices in music education programs for hearing-impaired students. Secondary purposes of the study were to accumulate data that would either substantiate or refute the writings of hearing authors regarding the value of music to the deaf, and to examine factors that determine deaf individuals' involvement with music.

A summary of the results indicates that (1) cultural identification is a strong influential factor in deaf individuals' involvement with music; (2) deaf individuals that do involve themselves with music, do so in ways similar to hearing individuals; (3) musical activities enjoyed most by deaf individuals are singing/signing songs, listening to music, and moving or dancing to music; (4) most respondents believed that music instruction should be optional for deaf students; (5) certain factors related to family involvement with music and musical training appear to be indicators of the role music will play in the lives of deaf individuals; and (6) deaf individuals do not participate to the degree that hearing individuals do in most common ritual uses of music.

A review of the literature on music and the deaf (Darrow, 1989; in press) indicates that hearing authors are very positive regarding the value of music to the deaf. The data in this study, however, indicate that some deaf individuals find music to be of little importance or not important at all. A number of respondents also reported that they did not enjoy music class as students. In teaching hearing-impaired students, it may be helpful for music educators to remember that the interests of students from the deaf culture may vary considerably from their hearing peers in regard to music study.

As stated at the beginning of this article, culture has been defined as a way of life that identifies a specific group of people. Factors that contribute to cultural identification are most often language and primary associations. Cultural identification as a result of type of schooling can also be a factor, as seen in Table 3. Most of the subjects from the deaf culture group were educated in residential schools for the deaf or in public school self-contained classes for hearing-impaired students. Likewise, most of the subjects from the hearing culture group were educated in public school mainstreamed classes. The greatest percentage of subjects that identified with the deaf and hearing cultural groups attended both residential schools and public schools.

Table 11
Subscales and Importance of Music

Subscales	Significance *
Music background	
Music class attendance	S
Music class activities involved in	NS
Enjoyment of music class activities	S
Attitude toward music class	S
Family involvement with music	
Music activities involved in	S
Musical items in the home	NS
Watched or participated in musical performances	S
Respondents' involvement with music now	
Music activities involved in	S
Musical items in the home	NS
Watch or participate in musical performances	S
Ritual uses of music	
Involved with music in religious services	NS
Participate in the national anthem	S
Participate in holiday music	NS
Music at wedding	NS

* $p < .05$

Type of school and classroom placement may also play a role in the kind of music education available to hearing-impaired students. The greatest percentage of respondents who identify with the hearing culture were in public schools and mainstreamed into regular classes. This probably accounts for the high percentage of respondents in the hearing culture group that attended music classes regularly. Nearly all subjects attended school prior to P.L. 94-142. This may account for some respondents' lack of participation in music classes either in residential schools or self-contained classrooms in public schools. These data represent a need for music education programs in schools for the deaf and in self-contained classrooms for the deaf. It is possible that such music education programs are rare because music teachers in these schools and classrooms would need to be fluent in sign language.

The music classroom activity in which the greatest number of respondents participated was singing/signing songs. This is still true in music classes for hearing-impaired students today (Darrow & Gfeller, 1991). It is also the activity that the most respondents indicated they enjoyed. The following comments are from respondents:

I enjoying singing and signing any song that I can understand and can relate to ... lyrics mean a lot to me.

I ceased singing in the choir when I could no longer ascertain if I was correctly hitting the right notes. I still sing when alone, but that is all.

I remember many songs and hymns that were sung during my boyhood, and sometimes I find myself humming them—when no one is listening!

I only mouthed the words [in music class], no voice.

I enjoy singing—but it is not very pleasing to the ear, so I only do this in the shower, or when alone, or when with deaf or very close hearing friends.

It is unfortunate that many comments revealed embarrassment at singing in front of others. Perhaps music educators should work on singing skills with hearing-impaired students so that they are comfortable with their voices. Singing songs allows students to become acquainted with musical literature. Singing can also carry over into developing appropriate speech inflection (Darrow & Starmer, 1986).

Other common activities that were enjoyed were moving or dancing to music and listening to music. Many deaf individuals with residual hearing still enjoy listening to music. Some of the comments related to listening and moving to music were:

I was very good at dancing. People thought I felt the vibrations when I danced. They were wrong. When I dance, I feel nothing of the music or the beat at all, but when I sit, I feel the vibrations and beats.

At our club for the deaf, we would use a jukebox or hire live bands. These bands would turn the sound sky-high! How the deaf loved to dance to it!

I still love to listen to music if I can follow the words written down.

Sometimes I listen to orchestra music if all is quiet around me.

Most respondents had positive attitudes toward music class ("I loved music class because I could express myself." "It was fun!"), though some had strong negative feelings ("I hated music class because I felt stupid." "I hated music class because I was punished for not sounding right.") Music educators teaching hearing-impaired students need to plan instructional activities that can assure some success for these students. Though musical training had little to do with respondents' later involvement with music, it had much to do with their attitude toward music and the value they placed on it in their lives. Family involvement with music also did not seem to affect respondents' involvement with music, but did seem to affect respondents' responses regarding the importance of music in their lives ("Music is important to our family and brings us close together. It also helps to keep us in good health." "We do have music in our home, but I think a professional listening to our music would want to leave immediately!") One respondent commented on the lack of encouragement in music by a family member:

> My father was an accomplished musician in his teens. He was a band leader and traveled all over the state. He played piano all his life although in later years he turned away from music to other ventures. My father was probably disappointed that I was born deaf and perhaps there was no encouragement to involve myself in music during my childhood days.

Respondents' family involvement with music was somewhat more active as they were growing up than in their families now. This is understandable since it is usually the parents that initiate musical activity in a family. As the deaf respondents became parents themselves, it would seem less likely, due to their hearing impairment, that they would be as equally involved with music as their hearing parents had been or that they would initiate musical activity as readily. As adults, deaf individuals are more likely to be passive observers or participants in musical activities and not initiators. It is unlikely that their spouses or children would involve them in musical activities to the degree that their parents might have attempted to involve them.

The only ritual use of music with any relation to the importance of music was the singing of the national anthem. It is possible that respondents who value music are not inhibited about singing in general or particularly singing the national anthem.

One respondent stated that many deaf people feel "left out" at Christmas time with the considerable emphasis that is placed on music during this season of the year. Signing songs at Christmas would allow hearing-impaired music education students to become acquainted with and perform traditional holiday music.

A relatively small percentage of respondents identified musical preferences. This could be due to their lack of active involvement with music on a regular basis. Singers and musical groups were identified more often than particular songs, radio stations, or composers. The media's attention on performers rather than their music may account for these results. Preferences for performers and performance groups ranged from the University of Michigan marching band to Madonna. It is the music educator's responsibility to expose all students to a broad range of musical styles so that preferences are informed choices.

Many respondents found music to be an important part of their lives ("Music lifts my spirits when I'm 'down.'"), though fewer respondents did in the deaf culture group. Some respondents were emphatic about its lack of importance. The greatest percentage of respondents believed that music education should be an option for hearing-impaired students and not a requirement ("For the profoundly deaf person, I think music education is absurd! But it's entirely up to the individual.") Perhaps the comments of one respondent point out best why some hearing-impaired individuals should not be required to attend music classes:

> Damn it, I can't hear—why should I talk about music? Even music itself is a complete mystery to me! People seem to be intrigued by all kinds of music, so it must be something. Too bad I'm deaf. You shouldn't be sending out questionnaires like this—it's [a] ridiculous waste of the university's money. Be more sensitive and find time to do better things than this quiz. You know a deaf person can't hear music!

Indeed, for those with no hearing at all, perhaps music education has no place or at least participation in music classes should be up to the individual. For this very small portion of the deaf population, music will probably not find a place in their culture.

The pervasive nature of music in our environment makes it difficult to avoid, even for those who hear very little of it. The results of this study indicate that music has a role in deaf culture, though it is considerably more limited than in the hearing culture. Similarities between the two cultures are more numerous than differences. One similarity is the existence of music within both cultures; one difference is the degree to which music is valued. In a lecture to music educators, Larry Stewart (1990), former professor of psychology at Gallaudet University, stated:

> Everyone has their own values, and many [deaf] people do love music, even if they can't hear much of it. And what they get they appreciate. I personally do feel that way. And so they [hearing people] look at me and wonder how I can enjoy music. I don't know. How do you explain that? ... it is a very individual thing. Others [deaf] say, "Why music?" I don't know how to explain this, but in the deaf world, there is a pecking order ... and music is not always very high in the order.

Music is highly valued in our hearing society, particularly by those, such as music educators, who have made it their life's work. Music educators believe that music is basic and that all students deserve the opportunity to be musically educated—perhaps even those who are Deaf (with a capital "D"). Perhaps we can improve our education of these students by acknowledging and being sensitive to the characteristics of their culture. Until recently, information regarding deaf culture was primarily limited to those who lived within the culture. There are now several excellent resources on the deaf community and the social characteristics of its people (Padden & Humphries, 1988; Sacks, 1989). More important than learning about deaf culture, however, is learning to recognize the similarities and respect the differences between it and our own hearing culture.

REFERENCES

Backstrom, C. H., & Hursh-César, G. (1981). *Survey research.* New York, NY: Macmillan.

Darrow, A. A. (1989). Music and the hearing impaired: A review of the research with implications for music educators. *Update: Applications of Research in Music Education, 7* (2), 10–12.

Darrow, A. A. (in press). Music therapy and the hearing impaired. In T. Wigram, R. West, & B. Saperston (Eds.), *A handbook of music therapy.* Chichester, West Sussex: Carden Publications, Limited.

Darrow, A. A., & Gfeller, K. (1991). A study of public school mainstreaming of hearing impaired students. *Journal of Music Therapy, 28,* 23–39.

Darrow, A. A., & Heller, G. N. (1985). William Wolcott Turner and David Ely Bartlett: Early advocates of music education for the hearing impaired. *Journal of Research in Music Education, 33,* 269–279.

Darrow, A. A., & Starmer, G. J. (1986). The effect of vocal training on the intonation and rate of hearing impaired children's speech: A pilot study. *Journal of Music Therapy, 23,* 194–201.

Davis, J. M., & Hardick, E. J. (1981). *Rehabilitation audiology for children and adults.* New York: John Wiley & Sons.

Gannon, J. R. (1981). *Deaf heritage: A narrative history of deaf America.* Silver Spring, MD: National Association of the Deaf.

Gentry, R. G. (1988). Why we won at Gallaudet. *Gallaudet Today,* May/June, 12–13.

Hamm, C., Nettl, B., & Byrnside, R. (1975). *Contemporary music and music culture.* Englewood Cliffs, NJ: Prentice-Hall, Inc.

Heward, W. L., & Orlansky, M. D. (1988). *Exceptional children.* Columbus, OH: Merrill Publishing.

Janesick, V. J. (1990). Bilingual multicultural education and the deaf: Issues and possibilities. *Journal of Educational Issues of Language Minority Students, 7,* 99–109.

Kannapell, B. (1980). Personal awareness and advocacy in the deaf community. In W. C. Stokoe, *Sign language and the deaf community* (pp. 105–106). Silver Spring, MD: National Association of the Deaf.

Kretschmer, R. R., & Kretschmer, L. W. (1978). *Language development and interaction with the hearing impaired.* Baltimore, MD: University Park Press.

Merchant, D. (1989). Lecture notes for Introduction to Music class at Gallaudet University (Unpublished material).

Merriam, A. P. (1964). *The anthropology of music.* Chicago, IL: Northwestern University Press.

Moores, D. F. (1987). *Educating the deaf* (3rd ed.). Boston: Houghton-Mifflin.

Oppenheim, A. N. (1966). *Questionnaire design and attitude measurement.* New York: Basic Books.

Payne, S. L. (1965). *The art of asking questions.* Princeton, NJ: Princeton University Press.

Padden, C. (1980). The deaf community and the culture of the deaf people. In W. C. Stokoe, *Sign language and the deaf community* (89–104), Silver Spring, MD: National Association of the Deaf.

Padden, C., & Humphries, T. (1988). *Deaf in America: Voices from a culture.* Cambridge, MA: Harvard University Press.

Prickett, H. T. (1989). *Advocacy for deaf children.* Springfield, IL: Charles C Thomas.

Sacks, O. (1989). *Seeing voices.* Berkeley, CA: University of California Press.

Schein, J. D. (1978). The deaf community. In H. Davis & S. R. Silverman (Eds.), *Hearing and deafness* (511–524). New York: Holt, Rinehart, & Winston.

Stewart, L. (1990). Lecture given at the Conference on Music and the Hearing Impaired, Gallaudet University, Washington, DC, July 30.

November 25, 1992

XI.

MULTICULTURAL

ISSUES

AND

MUSIC

Cognitive transfer theory, specifically Thorndike and Woodworth's theory of identical elements, was applied to music preferences. Two separate but related issues were examined in this study: (a) the effect of student familiarity through performance-oriented instruction as a means of increasing preference toward a genre of music and (b) the transfer of preference from taught to untaught pieces of an unfamiliar genre. Traditional African, Asian Indian, Japanese, and Hispanic songs with instrumental accompaniment were taught to 26 sixth-grade students over a 5-week period. A pretest-posttest listening test was administered, incorporating taught and untaught selections from the ethnic genres, as well as current popular and western classical pieces. Results indicated significant preference differences between the taught and untaught selection of the treatment genres. Although instruction increased preference for unfamiliar non-Western songs, there was no transfer of preference to untaught pieces of the same genre.

Patricia K. Shehan, *Washington University, St. Louis*

JRME 1985, VOLUME 33, NUMBER 3, PAGES 149–158

Transfer of Preference from Taught to Untaught Pieces of Non-Western Music Genres

A major goal of the strong multicultural movement in education is to promote respect for a wide range of cultural groups. Multiethnic education in music has sought to explore the ethnic diversity within the American community through representative songs, dances, and selections from the recorded repertoire of musical traditions throughout the world.

While folk, traditional, and non-Western styles of music are not currently supported by the mass media, music educators are largely responsible for the exposure of students to the variety of music styles present throughout the world. It is commonly maintained that instruction in unfamiliar musical styles provides students with a polymusicality

---

For reprints of this article, contact Patricia K. Shehan, Department of Music, Washington University, Campus Box 1032, St. Louis 63130.

and tolerance for approaching other little-known genres. An awareness of the manipulation of musical elements in various world musics may not only increase awareness for one particular style, but should also serve to sensitize perceptions of more familiar music. The development of intelligent value judgments through flexible and broad-minded reception of musical styles are desirable outcomes of school music programs; however, the attitudinal transfer of tolerance and taste for all musics through instruction of selected genres may be presumptuous. Further, little is known about the transfer of preference from familiar to unfamiliar pieces of the same genre.

There are few topics more central to the educative process than the transfer of learning. Defined as the influence of a previously established habit upon the acquisition of a second habit, the transfer principle has been the concern of cognitive theorists since the late 19th century. Several distinctions have appeared in the earlier literature, including lateral vs. vertical transfer (Gagné, 1965), specific and nonspecific transfer (Ellis, 1965; Royer & Cable, 1976), and near and far transfer (Mayer, 1975). Thorndike and Woodworth's theory of identical elements (1901) has heavily influenced many subsequent considerations of transfer theory, suggesting that transfer from one task to another would only occur when both tasks shared similar features. Osgood (1949) indicated that facilitative and inhibitory transfer were functionally related to the similarity and difference relationships between stimuli and responses in an original and transfer task.

In discussing the importance of structure learning, Bruner (1960) postulated two types of transfer of training: specific skills, and principles and attitudes. While educational research frequently documents transfer of knowledge and skills, attitudinal transfer accounts are rare. It is established in the literature that attitudes are learned in a manner similar to the acquisition of cognitive skills, and that once learned, they are stable and not amenable to change.

Attitude research is historically concerned with several constructs, including opinion, taste, and preference. Explained as a predisposition to respond in a favorable or unfavorable manner to objects or situations, attitudes are not directly observable but can be expressed verbally and behaviorally as preferences (Fishbein, 1967). While music instruction has directly affected understanding, attitude, and preference for music, the transfer of preference from taught to untaught pieces within a musical style has not been studied. Familiarity through repeated listening and performance has been a significant determinant of preference (Bradley, 1971; Clary, 1979; Getz, 1966; Hargreaves, 1984). Since pieces within a musical style are identified through the similar treatment of melodic, rhythmic, and textural elements, it would appear that preference for one piece through familiarity with the style would transfer to other pieces of the same style. This paper investigates preference transfer as an extension of cognitive theories of transfer.

When considering related literature in affective responses to music, assessment techniques have included verbalized self-reports, pictographic and written response formats, physiological measures, and behavioral evaluations (Kuhn, 1981). Previous studies have explored factors in the process of music education that may affect the preference of the students (LeBlanc, 1980; Wapnick, 1976). Beyond the "repeated exposure" paradigm that generates preference through familiarity, several other variables have direct implications for the school music curriculum, including peer group approval (Alpert, 1982; Inglefield, 1972; Tanner, 1976), educators and authority approval (Alpert, 1982; Booker, 1969; Dorow, 1977; Greer, Dorow, & Hanser, 1973; Radocy, 1976; Wiebe, 1940), teacher-guided listening (Trammell, 1979), and televised instruction (Brown, 1978; Shehan, 1979).

Children's preferences for current popular music in the elementary grades have been confirmed in the literature (Greer, Dorow, & Hanser, 1973; Greer, Dorow, & Randall, 1974; Greer, Dorow, Wachaus, & White, 1973; LeBlanc, 1979). Competing styles of Western classical, jazz, folk, country and western, and band music have been rated consistently lower by children from preschool through the secondary level. Among nonrock genres, LeBlanc (1981) reported that fast instrumental examples are more likely to elicit positive listener response.

The inclusion of non-Western music as a preference choice has been relatively rare. Flowers (1980) studied the relationship between verbal and operant responses to top-forty and African music selections. Correlations between preference measures were high, and both undergraduates and fourth-graders preferred top-forty over African music. Heingartner and Hull (1974) employed Pakistani music to show that a positive relationship exists between "mere exposure" of music and students' liking for it. In a self-report assessment of fourth- and seventh-grade students' preference for Asian and African styles, Shehan (1982) found that those ethnic styles with greater "rhythmic dynamism" (African and Japanese instrumental) were preferred to the less pulsive and less syncopated selections (Indonesian and Japanese vocal). Indonesian gamelan music was the focus of an investigation of the effects of two instructional methods on verbal and behavioral preference (Shehan, 1984). The performance-oriented heuristic group showed greater gains in overall listening time for gamelan music than did the didactic group. Although current popular music was still the favored style, both groups preferred gamelan music to Western classical music.

The present study attempted to contribute to the considerable body of research in music preference. The investigation sought (a) to determine the effects of student familiarity through performance-oriented instruction in unfamiliar non-Western music as a means of increasing understanding and ultimately affecting preference toward a genre of music and (b) to examine the transfer of preference from taught pieces of an unfamiliar genre to untaught pieces of the same genre. Assuming minimal chance of student exposure to non-Western music beyond the school experience, all subjects had a common experience with the taught and performed music and a lack of experience with the untaught music. The study tested the effects of familiarity through performance of non-Western music on verbally expressed preference. The principle of generalized transfer as applied to preference in music was in question.

METHOD

The subjects for this study were 26 sixth-grade students in a midwestern K–8 parochial school. Students in the suburban community who participated were racially mixed, and the socioeconomic status was judged to be middle class.

A listening tape incorporating 12 music examples was prepared. Two vocal selections with instrumental accompaniment were included for the generic styles of current popular, Asian Indian, African, Hispanic, and Japanese; the Western classical selections were instrumental only. One taught and one untaught piece comprised the selections from the ethnic genres. The non-Western pieces were chosen from the recordings of an elementary textbook series. Authentic regional instruments were employed as accompaniment on the recordings, and children's choirs sang the lyrics in both English and the foreign languages. The inclusion of the more familiar current popular and Western classical styles served as critical competitors, with the intention of showing whether the non-Western styles compete with the peer-approved genre of current popular music or with the less preferred style. Selections were matched on the component of beat/tempo, ranging from M.M. = 170 to 250, with a mean of 210. The 12 music excerpts were arranged in two random orders to control for placement on tape, boredom, and satiation.

Students indicated the degree of preference for a musical selection by checking one response block on a 0–6 continuum. Five bipolar semantic differential scales were utilized for each musical selection: "like–dislike," "good–bad," "interesting–uninteresting," "valuable–worthless," and "buy–would not buy." The last scale provided information on behavioral intention as an extension of verbal preferences. The length of the excerpt was determined by the length of one verse each in English and in the native language, ranging from 43 to 65 sec, with a mean of 54 sec.

The rating scale was thought to provide for the presentation of a greater number of music selections than a behavioral measure. Free operant measures such as the Music Selection Recorder and the Operant Music Listening Recorder require individual testing and can present only a small number of music selections for subject response. While a composite of indexes has been recommended in the assessment of music attitudes and preferences (Kuhn, Sims, & Shehan, 1981), the operant measure was not included because of feasibility problems in fitting the testing of individual subjects into the constrictions of the school schedule.

The investigator taught five weekly 35-min sessions, a time period considered typical for a study unit of non-Western music at the elementary school level. The content of the lessons consisted of listening to the recorded selection of non-Western music, first without and then with the visual aid of notation and lyrics projected on an overhead screen. Students were taught to sing the melody in English by rote, listening and then repeating each individual phrase three times. The complete song was then sung with and without the recording. Simple ostinatos on recorders and percussion instruments were added, and the class was divided into two groups that alternately sang or played the instrumental accompaniment. In this way, all students sang and played the instrumental accompaniment. Due to the time limitation, foreign lyrics were not taught or performed. Closure was provided through a final listening to the recorded song. Folk songs from the four ethnic regions investigated were learned in similar procedure. The fifth class meeting was utilized to review the taught songs by listening to the recording and alternately singing and performing the instrumental ostinato.

RESULTS

Reliability of the listening test examined internal item consistency through the KR–20 formula. A coefficient of .79 was obtained, which was judged suitable and comparable to previous studies.

The mean scores and standard deviations for each of the six styles are presented in Table 1. Pre- and posttreatment preference measures for the 12 music selections indicate current popular as the preferred style, while the Western classical selections drop from a second-place to last-place rating. When the scores for the taught and untaught music of the non-Western styles are combined, preference gains are noted for all, with a substantial increase for Indian, Hispanic, and Japanese music.

Statistical analysis was done using computer program BMDPV2 (Dixon, 1983). The data were analyzed using two-way analyses of variance with repeated measures on both factors. Variables in the study were preference change from pretest to posttest and the effect of instruction of non-Western music on the transfer of preference to untaught pieces of the same styles. Tables 2–5 report analysis of variance (ANOVA) results, while Table 6 displays pretest and posttest cell means and standard deviations for taught and untaught pieces of each treatment style.

Results are similar across styles. While there is no significant testing effect, the taught/untaught variable is significant for all non-Western music styles ($p < .01$). Table 5 reveals the only interaction effect, between tests and taught/untaught pieces of the Hispanic style.

Table 1
Summary of Pretest and Posttest Preference Score Means and Standard Deviations for Combined Taught/Untaught Songs

		African	Indian	Japanese	Hispanic	Western classical	Current popular
Pretest							
	M	60.96	48.64	48.16	59.28	69.88	80.44
	sd	21.94	23.74	19.28	20.68	23.80	22.58
Posttest							
	M	61.68	58.80	58.84	67.96	57.08	75.28
	sd	21.25	25.59	25.54	24.26	23.91	25.59

Table 2

Two-Way Analysis of Variance with Repeated Measures Comparing Tests and Taught/Untaught Pieces on Preference for African Music

Source of variance	SS	df	MS	F	p
Between effects					
Tests	10.24	1	10.24	0.05	.8328
Error	10,914.72	48	227.39		
Within effects					
Taught/untaught	761.76	1	761.76	7.75	.0077
Tests × Taught/untaught	309.76	1	309.76	3.15	.0823
Error	4,720.48	48	98.34		

As F tests alone do not show direction of change, Table 6 indicates that the preference gain for the taught selection is significantly greater than for the untaught selection within each ethnic genre. While Indian and Japanese untaught pieces showed small gains, there is no change in preference for the Hispanic song, and a decrease at the posttest for the African selection.

DISCUSSION

Consistent with previous studies, current popular music is the preferred style among middle school students. Standard rhymed lyrics of a romantic nature and the familiarity of the song and performing group through previous media exposure were likely extramusical factors in the preference choice. Musical influences may have included the clear rhythmic pulse, melodic redundancy, and repeated chordal progressions so typical of current popular genres. The high ranking of Western classical music pieces in the pretest may have reflected familiarity with that genre, which is not surprising when considering current textbook offerings in European and American art music. Indirect teacher approval through previous class lessons that emphasized the standard orchestral repertory may have further prompted the high ratings.

Table 3

Two-Way Analysis of Variance with Repeated Measures Comparing Tests and Taught/Untaught Pieces on Preference for Indian Music

Source of variance	SS	df	MS	F	p
Between effects					
Tests	745.29	1	745.29	2.51	.1199
Error	14,267.96	48	297.25		
Within effects					
Taught/untaught	858.49	1	858.49	11.74	.0013
Tests × Taught/untaught	272.25	1	272.25	3.72	.0595
Error	3,508.76	48	73.09		

Table 4
Two-Way Analysis of Variance with Repeated Measures Comparing Tests and Taught/Untaught Pieces on Preference for Japanese Music

Source of variance	SS	df	MS	F	p
Between effects					
Tests	756.25	1	756.25	3.13	.0831
Error	11,586.56	48	241.39		
Within effects					
Taught/untaught	712.89	1	712.89	8.59	.0052
Tests × Taught/untaught	106.09	1	106.09	1.28	.2637
Error	3,981.52	58	82.95		

Initial preferences reveal a wide disparity between Western and non-Western styles. The lowest ratings for the more "musically exotic" Indian and Japanese selections may indicate response to unusual timbres and textures, as well as to the progressive and nonrepetitive structure of the music. The higher ranking African and Hispanic pieces were organized in repeated verse-refrain form. Although beat/tempo was a controlled variable, the strong rhythmic component and consonant harmonies in thirds inherent in African and Hispanic genres are not matched in the Asian musics. Although new and unusual treatment of musical elements may provide a certain intrigue and attract listener reception to the ethnic genres, the degree of novelty may be significant factor in the direction of the preference response.

According to Thorndike and Woodworth (1901), the conditions for transfer are established when an original learning event and a transfer event share common stimulus properties. If attitudes are learned as skills are acquired, then it follows that music preferences as overt attitudinal expressions might transfer from one musical selection to a second selection of the same style. Songs within one historical period or

Table 5
Two-Way Analysis of Variance with Repeated Measures Comparing Tests and Taught/Untaught Pieces on Preference for Hispanic Music

Source of variance	SS	df	MS	F	p
Between effects					
Tests	515.29	1	515.29	1.97	.1667
Error	12,543.00	48	261.31		
Within effects					
Taught/untaught	2,162.25	1	2,162.25	21.11	.0000
Tests × Taught/untaught	515.29	1	515.29	5.03	.0295
Error	4,915.96	48	102.42		

Table 6
Summary of Pretest and Posttest Cell Means and Standard Deviations for Taught and Untaught Songs of the Non-Western Styles

	African			Indian			Japanese			Hispanic		
	pre	post	both	pre	post	both	pre	post	both	pre	post	both
Taught												
M	31.16	35.32	33.24	25.40	34.16	29.78	25.76	33.32	29.54	32.00	41.08	36.54
sd	13.92	10.78		14.42	15.17		12.38	15.88		14.41	14.45	
Untaught												
M	29.16	26.28	27.72	22.84	25.00	23.92	22.48	25.92	24.20	27.24	27.24	27.24
sd	12.35	13.74		12.17	12.41		9.21	12.57		11.79	13.06	
Both												
M	30.16	30.80	30.48	24.12	29.58	26.85	24.12	29.62	26.87	29.62	34.16	31.89

regional style share a similar treatment of elements and structure and are viewed as communicating in the same musical dialect.

The posttest scores resulted in preference differences between the taught and untaught selection of the treatment genres. The implications are interesting for music education. Cognitive transfer theory has maintained that prior learning and attitudes are retrieved and applied to new settings. The assumption that a transfer of preference follows a similar pattern is discounted in the present study. No generalization of preference response can be inferred, regardless of stylistic similarities between pieces.

The instructional method that emphasized song and instrumental performance resulted in significant preference increases for the treatment selections. Familiarity through repeated listening and participatory experiences were positive influences on the affective response. As in previous research, concrete experiences in active music-making evoked favorable changes in preference.

Further inquiry into the nature of preference transfer might involve a more extended period of exposure to targeted music styles. Acquisition of knowledge about music and any consequent attitudinal change may require study units focused on one specific musical style designed for use in several class sessions. A variety of song, movement, and listening experiences with a number of specific pieces may provide a more thorough exposure to an unfamiliar style. Instruction in non-Western musics may benefit from the combined efforts of music and arts specialists, and classroom and/or social science teachers who can provide a sociocultural context for the music in study.

Although music educators will continue to teach for understanding and the broadening of musical taste, the expectation that study of one representative piece from a style will impact upon interest in other stylistically similar pieces is not supported. Lessons in unfamiliar music, such as the non-Western genres, can hope to provide some flexibility of approach, but care should be taken to differentiate between tolerance and preference.

REFERENCES

Alpert, J. (1982). The effect of disc jockey, peer, and music teacher approval of music on music selection and preference. *Journal of Research in Music Education, 30*, 173–186.

Booker, G. A. (1969). The disc jockey and his impact on teenage musical taste as reflected through a study in three north Florida cities. *Dissertation Abstracts International, 30*, 3038A. (University Microfilms No. 69–30, 424)

Bradley, I. L. (1971). Repetition as a factor in the development of music preferences. *Journal of Research in Music Education, 19*, 295–298.

Brown, A. (1978). Effects of televised instruction on student music selection, music skills, and attitudes. *Journal of Research in Music Education, 26*, 445–455.

Bruner, J. A. (1960). *The process of education.* New York: Vintage Books.

Clary, R. M. (1979). *The effect of rehearsal and performance on high school choir students' preference for choral music.* Unpublished master's thesis, Kent State University, Kent, Ohio.

Dixon, W. J. (Ed.). (1983). *BDMP statistical software.* Berkeley: University of California.

Dorow, L. G. (1977). The effect of teacher approval/disapproval ratios on student music selection behavior and concert attentiveness. *Journal of Research in Music Education, 25*, 32–40.

Ellis, H. C. (1965). *The transfer of learning.* New York: Macmillan.

Fishbein, M. (1967). Attitude and prediction of behavior. In M. Fishbein (ed.), *Readings in attitude theory and measurement.* New York: John Wiley and Sons.

Flowers, P. J. (1980). Relationship between two measures of music preference. *Contributions to Music Education, 8*, 47–54.

Gagné, R. M. (1965). *The conditions of learning.* New York: Holt, Rinehart, and Winston.

Getz, R. P. (1966). The effects of repetition on listening response. *Journal of Research in Music Education, 14*, 178–192.

Greer, R. D., Dorow, L. G., & Hanser, S. (1973). Music discrimination training and the music selection behavior of nursery and primary school children. *Bulletin of the Council for Research in Music Education, 14*, 24–31.

Greer, R. D., Dorow, L. G., & Randall, A. (1974). Music listening preferences of elementary school children. *Journal of Research in Music Education, 22*, 284–291.

Greer, R. D., Dorow, L. G., Wachaus, G., & White, E. R. (1973). Adult approval and students' music selection behavior. *Journal of Research in Music Education, 21*, 345–354.

Hargreaves, D. J. (1984). The effect of repetition on liking for music. *Journal of Research in Music Education, 32*, 35–47.

Heingartner, A., & Hull, J. V. (1974). Affective consequences in adults and children of repeated exposure to auditory stimuli. *Journal of Personality and Social Psychology, 29*, 719–723.

Inglefield, H. G. (1972). Conformity behavior reflected in the musical preferences of adolescents. *Contributions to Music Education, 1*, 56–67.

Kuhn, T. L. (1981). Instrumentation for the measurement of music attitudes. *Contributions to Music Education, 9*, 2–38.

Kuhn, T. L., Sims, W. I., & Shehan, P. K. (1981). Relationship between listening time and like–dislike ratings on three music selections. *Journal of Music Therapy, 18*, 181–192.

LeBlanc, A. (1979). Generic style preferences of fifth-grade students. *Journal of Research in Music Education, 27*, 255–270.

LeBlanc, A. (1980). Outline of a proposed model of sources of variation in musical taste. *Bulletin of the Council for Research in Music Education, 61*, 29–34.

LeBlanc, A. (1981). Effects of style, tempo, and performing medium on children's music preference. *Journal of Research in Music Education, 29*, 143–156.

Mayer, R. E. (1975). Information processing variables in learning to solve problems. *Review of Educational Research, 45*, 525–541.

Osgood, C. E. (1949). The similarity paradox in human learning: A resolution. *Psychological Review, 56*, 132–143.

Radocy, R. E. (1976). Effects of authority figure biases on changing judgments of music events. *Journal of Research in Music Education, 24*, 119–128.

Royer, J. M., & Cable, G. W. (1976). Illustrations, analogies, and facilitative transfer in prose learning. *Journal of Educational Psychology, 68*, 205–209.

Shehan, P. K. (1979). The effect of the television series "Music" on music listening preferences and achievement of elementary general music students. *Contributions to Music Education, 7*, 51–62.

Shehan, P. K. (1982). Student preferences for ethnic music styles. *Contributions to Music Education, 9*, 20–27.

Shehan, P. K. (1984). Effect of instruction method on preference, achievement, and attentiveness for Indonesian gamelan music. *Psychology of Music, 12*, 34–42.

Tanner, F. D. (1976). The effect of disc jockey approval of music and peer approval of music on music selection. *Dissertation Abstracts International, 37*, 3492A. (University Microfilms No. 76–27709)

Thorndike, E. L., & Woodworth, R. S. (1901). The influence of improvement in one mental function upon the efficiency of other functions. *Psychological Review, 8*, 247–261.

Trammel, P. T. (1979). An investigation of the effectiveness of repetition and guided listening in developing enjoyable music listening experiences for second-grade students. *Dissertation Abstracts International, 40*, 2450A. (University Microfilms No. 79–07767)

Wapnick, J. (1976). A review of research on attitude and preference. *Bulletin of the Council for Research in Music Education, 48*, 1–20.

Wiebe, G. (1940). The effect of radio plugging on students' opinions of popular songs. *Journal of Applied Psychology, 24*, 721–727.

October 15, 1984

The purpose of the study was to investigate young children's abilities to discriminate between two chords played as the accompaniment of a melody and played alone with no melody. After receiving brief training in harmonic discrimination, 167 children ages 4 and 5 from four preschools were tested in their ability to discriminate between the chords "I" and "V6/5" in the song "En la Torre de una Iglesia" or between the chords "i" and "VII" in "Drunken Sailor." ANOVAs with repeated measures were performed for age, school, order of stimulus presentation (within variable), and type of stimulus on children's scores for each song. Both analyses indicated that age, type of stimulus, and the interaction of these two variables affected children's performance in the test significantly. In addition, order of presentation was found to be a significant variable of children's scores for the song "Drunken Sailor." Five-year-olds could detect harmonic changes in simple chord progressions, but were unable to do so when a melody was superimposed over the progression. Four-year-olds could not identify the chord changes of either stimuli.

Eugenia Costa-Giomi, *McGill University, Montreal*

JRME 1994, VOLUME 42, NUMBER 1, PAGES 68–85

Recognition of Chord Changes by 4- and 5-Year-Old American and Argentine Children

During the last 30 years, extensive research has focused on young children's music behaviors (McDonald & Simons, 1989; Simons, 1986). Despite the increasing interest in musical growth during the first years of life, the development of young children's harmonic perception has not received as much attention by researchers as has the perceptual development of other musical concepts (Hargreaves, 1986; Radocy & Boyle, 1979; Simons, 1986).

It is known that harmony is one of the most difficult musical concepts for children to grasp. Studies on children's conceptual development have shown that harmonic discrimination occurs later than the discrimination of other concepts such as timbre, loudness, tempo, duration, and pitch (Bentley, 1966; Franklin, 1956; Hufstader, 1977; McDonald & Simons, 1989; Merrion, 1989; Moog, 1976; O'Hearn, 1984; Petzold, 1966; Schultz, 1969; Shuter-Dyson & Gabriel, 1981; Simons, 1986; Taylor, 1969; Vera, 1989; Zimmerman, 1971). There is general agreement that children's ability to discriminate harmony improves noticeably at about age 9 (Imberty, 1969; O'Hearn, 1984; Sloboda, 1985; Taylor, 1969;

This article is based on the author's doctoral dissertation by the same title, accepted in 1981 by The Ohio State University. For copies of this article, contact Eugenia Costa-Giomi, Faculty of Music, Strathcona Music Building, McGill University, 555 Sherbrooke Street West, Montreal QC H3A 1E3.

Valentine, 1913). It is not clear, however, if younger children can actually perceive harmony or if they possess any harmonic discrimination abilities. Although some studies have suggested that young children are not sensitive to harmony (Bentley, 1966; Moog, 1976; Petzold, 1966; Schultz, 1969), there is certain evidence that children are able to perceive harmony at an early age (Buckton, 1982; Hair, 1973; 1987; Hickman, 1969; Pflederer, 1964; Zenatti, 1969).

Conflicting conclusions regarding the harmonic abilities of young children might be the result of differences among the various measures of harmonic perception used in the research literature. The most frequently used measures are based on preference responses, same/different responses, verbal descriptions, and nonverbal responses. These measures have intended to provide young children with simple and accurate means to express what they know and hear. These objectives have not always been accomplished, however.

Measures based on preference responses usually require children to choose the "best" or most appropriate rendition of a musical excerpt played with various harmonic variations. Children's selection of the most consonant version has been generally taken as an indication of their ability to perceive harmony. Studies that used this type of measure found that young children did not necessarily prefer consonant accompaniments to a melody over dissonant accompaniments (Bridges, 1965; Imberty, 1969; Sloboda, 1985; Teplov, 1966; Valentine, 1913; Yoshikawa, 1973; Zenatti, 1974). Moog (1976), who found that children did not show signs of displeasure when listening to a familiar song played with dissonant accompaniments, asserted that preschoolers are incapable of experiencing any sort of harmony at all and that "the child is deaf to harmony at least up till the end of the sixth year, and probably for a long time after that" (p. 136).

Moog's conclusion is questionable since it has been suggested that preference for consonance might be the effect of tonal acculturation rather than an indication of tonal ability (Farnsworth, 1969; Frances 1958/1988; Imberty, 1969; Lundin, 1967; Radocy & Boyle, 1988; Sloboda, 1985; Teplov, 1966; Zenatti, 1974). Sloboda (1985) indicated that the skills measured by tests based on preference for consonance "are the true product of enculturation. They arise from the normal child's intellectual encounters with the music of his culture" (p. 213). There seems to be strong support for this assertion, as all the studies based on preference responses cited earlier—with the exception of Moog (1976)—showed that preference for consonance increased with age. Moog (1976) did not find such an increase among children ranging in age from 6 months to 6 years. There is enough evidence, however, to suggest that measures of harmonic discrimination abilities based on preference responses provide information about the development of children's sense of consonance rather than of their harmonic perception skills.

Measures that require children to indicate whether two or more stimuli are the same or different have been extensively used in music research in early childhood. Although same/different responses are simple to use, they are not free of confusion for the young child. It seems that young children do not always understand the operational meaning of the terms "same" and "different." Children tend to say "same" regardless of the stimulus (Funk, 1977; Hufstader, 1977; Pflederer & Sechrest, 1968, 1970) even when they are able to perceive differences (Hufstader, 1977). It seems that the alteration of the original stimulus has to be very obvious in order for children to say "different" (Funk, 1977). Unfortunately, training in the application of the terms "same" and "different" does not seem to affect children's use or misuse of the terms (DeCarbo, 1981;

Holohan, 1983).

Zenatti (1969), however, who asked children to identify a chord that was different between pairs of short progressions, found that 6-year-olds were able to perform the task above the level of chance. The study also showed that children's ability to identify the chord depended on the number of chords in the progression. This suggests that children might be able to perceive harmonic differences between pairs of stimuli, but have difficulty remembering longer stimuli. In studies in which children's perceptions of concepts other than harmony have been investigated, researchers have also noted that children's correct responses to same/different tasks might be limited by their musical memory (DeNardo, 1988/1989; Gardner, 1973; Klanderman, 1979). Corroborating Zenatti's conclusion that young children can detect harmonic changes, Hair (1973) found that first graders were able to perceive differences between tonic and dominant seventh chords. Also, Pflederer's (1964) findings suggest that young children could perceive harmony: 5- to 8-year-olds identified a melody as different when played with drastic harmonic and rhythmic changes to its accompaniment. On the other hand, Hufstader (1977), who presented children with excerpts altered in rhythm, timbre, melody, and harmony, found that harmonic modifications were the most difficult for children to detect. The study concluded that harmonic listening skills are developed at the seventh-grade level or later.

Studies that use verbalizations to investigate music perception usually present children with one or more variations of a musical stimulus and ask them to verbally describe the differences among them. It is known that it is difficult for young children to describe what they hear because of their limited vocabulary. This seems especially true for harmonic perception. Hair (1981) found that children in Grades 2 to 4 referred to pitch, tempo, and loudness when trying to describe the addition of an accompaniment to a familiar melody. Only 3% of the children used the word "harmony" in their descriptions. Some, however, were able to perceive the difference in the stimulus as suggested by descriptors they used such as "two hands," "together," and "high and low." Pflederer and Sechrest (1968) also noted the originality but inaccuracy of children's descriptions of the difference between a melody played with and without accompaniment. These findings agree with the results of previous studies, which have shown that children are often unable to verbally express their harmonic perception (Teplov, 1966), and that they make references to pitch when describing differences between consonant and dissonant accompaniments (Teplov, 1966) and intervals (Valentine, 1913). It is clear from these studies that children lack the appropriate terms to talk about harmony, and that their descriptions do not necessarily reflect what they can actually hear. The difficulty of measuring children's perception through verbalizations has led researchers to use nonverbal responses when studying children's music perception.

The most common nonverbal measures require children to associate musical elements with kinesthetic or visual representations, or to show their understanding of the concepts through performance. Although these types of responses have been extensively used in research in early childhood, they have rarely been used to investigate children's perception of harmony. It is probably more difficult to find meaningful kinesthetic or visual representations for harmony than for pitch or dynamics. Hair (1987) found that although children in kindergarten through Grade 6 expressed their perception of harmony better through the use of a visual representation than through verbal descriptions, kindergartners and first graders were not able to associate the addition of an accompaniment to a familiar melody with the corresponding visual representation.

It also seems that performance measures appropriate for young children might be difficult to develop because of the complexity involved in performing on most harmonic instruments. In a study that did use performance responses, children were asked to play simple accompaniments to a melody on classroom instruments (Piper & Shoemaker, 1973). The results suggested that children have difficulty in playing harmonic instruments. Children who had not received training on the instruments performed poorly in the task. Other studies that also used performance responses required children to sing familiar songs accompanied by different harmonization. The results of these studies are contradictory. Sterling's (1985) finding that type of accompaniment affected children's singing accuracy suggests that children are indeed sensitive to harmony. Petzold (1966), however, did not find such an effect.

It is obvious that the measurement of young children's harmonic perception is a difficult task. The need to find better ways to study children's musical perception has prompted researchers to find alternate methods to the ones described earlier. A method that has been used in a number of studies requires children to demonstrate their perception of musical concepts in ongoing music that changes noticeably and repeatedly in one concept. In these studies, children were asked to clap (Flowers & Costa-Giomi, 1991), tap a microphone (Montgomery, 1978), press a button (O'Hearn, 1984), move to the music (Sims, 1991), or say a word (Flowers & Costa-Giomi, 1991; Costa-Giomi, 1991) when they heard a change in the music. Results have shown that the method is appropriate to study young children's perception; it seems to have the advantages of nonverbal measures but avoids the problems of questionable visual or kinesthetic representations or performance proficiency. Only one of these studies included harmony among the concepts under investigation (O'Hearn, 1984). Corroborating previous conclusions, O'Hearn (1984) found that harmony is one of the last concepts children grasp, and that a large improvement in the ability to perceive harmonic changes occurs between first and third grade.

Perhaps because research has found that the concept of harmony is difficult for young children to grasp, there is no curricular emphasis on harmony during the first years of elementary school as shown by an analysis of recently published basal series. The Macmillan series (1988) does not include harmony as an independent category in its index until the fourth grade. At that level, activities based on the discrimination between unison and harmony are included among the lessons. No references to harmony are given in the manuals for fifth- and sixth-grade levels. In the Silver Burdett series (1988), the first reference to harmony occurs in first grade in which an activity based on the performance of bells is introduced. No activities on harmony are developed in second grade. Lessons on the difference between unison and harmony are included in third grade. Harmony, described also as texture, is included at the fourth-grade level. The Holt series (1988), on the other hand, introduces the concept of harmony from kindergarten. Two lessons on the simultaneous movement of melody and harmony are included at that level. Three lessons in first grade focus on harmony: simultaneous movement of melody and harmony, performance of tonic and dominant seventh chords on instruments, and aural recognition of instruments playing the accompaniments to melodies. A variety of activities about harmony are included in the lessons at the second-grade level.

The discrepancy among the basal series about the level at which it is best to begin instruction on harmony and the ways in which to provide it to children indi-

Drunken Sailor

Figure 1a. One of the two songs used in the tests.

cates the need for a solid research base in children's development of harmonic perception. The present investigation attempted to contribute to the understanding of one aspect of young children's harmonic perception: their perception of chord changes. The purpose of the study was to investigate the ability of 4- and 5-year-olds to detect harmonic changes in the accompaniment of a song played with and without the melody. Other variables studied were order of stimulus presentation, type of stimulus, preschool attended, and song used.

METHOD

Stimuli

Two songs were selected as stimuli for the test of the study, "En la Torre de una Iglesia" [In the Tower of a Church] and "Drunken Sailor." Only the melodies and the harmony of the songs were used in the study. The words of the songs were not used as part of the stimulus, neither were they taught to the children during the development of the investigation. Both songs were 16 measures long. "En la Torre de una Iglesia" was in $\frac{3}{4}$ meter and in F major, whereas "Drunken Sailor"

En la Torre de una Iglesia

Figure 1b. One of the two songs used in the tests.

was in $^4_4$ and in C Dorian (Figure 1). Each song was played two ways: as an accompanied melody (i.e., melody + harmony), and as accompaniment with no melody (i.e., harmony alone). Therefore, a total of four stimuli were used: (1) accompaniment alone for the song "En la Torre," (2) melody + accompaniment of the song "En la Torre," (3) accompaniment alone for the song "Drunken Sailor," and (4) melody + accompaniment of "Drunken Sailor." To make the test shorter, each child was presented with only two of the four stimuli, the harmony alone and the harmony + melody of one of the two songs. In order to control for order of presentation effects, approximately half the children listened to the harmony alone first and to the harmony + melody later, whereas the other half listened first to the harmony + melody and later to the harmony alone. The stimuli were played at a moderate tempo (MM = 88) on a synthesizer with a piano sound, stored via MIDI on a computer, and recorded on cassette tapes. Four different cassette tapes were prepared, each containing one of the following combinations of stimuli: (1) harmony alone and harmony + melody of "En la Torre" (2) harmony + melody and harmony alone of "En la Torre," (3) harmony alone and harmony + melody of "Drunken Sailor," or (4) harmony + melody and harmony alone of

"Drunken Sailor."

The accompaniment for each melody consisted of block chords played on each beat of the song. The chords used for "En la Torre" were the root position of the tonic and the first inversion of the dominant seventh (i.e., I and V6/5). Those used for "Drunken Sailor" were the root position of the tonic and the root position of the subtonic chord (i.e., i and VII), as shown in Figure 1.

The classroom teacher and 10 children who participated in a pilot study stated that the songs were unknown to the class.

Sample

The subjects who participated in the study were 223 4- and 5-year-old children enrolled in two preschools in Buenos Aires, Argentina, and in two preschools in Columbus, Ohio. The preschools were comparable in their social environment but differed in their music programs. The Argentine preschools had music programs developed by music specialists. Children in those schools received three 30-minute music lessons weekly. In the American preschools, music activities were guided by the classroom teachers throughout the week.

Testing Procedures

During the individual test, children were presented with one of the four tapes described earlier that included the two types of stimuli of either the song "Drunken Sailor" or the song "En la Torre." The proportion of 4- and 5-year-olds who listened to the stimuli of "En la Torre" or "Drunken Sailor" was approximately equal in all four schools. When the first child came into the testing area, she or he was asked to choose one of the four tapes. After the child finished the test, this tape was put aside, and the following child chose one from the three remaining tapes. The third child to be tested chose from the two tapes that had not been previously selected and the fourth child listened to the only tape left. This process was repeated until the test had been administered to all the children. The purpose of this procedure was to obtain proportional sample sizes according to school, age, song, and order of stimulus presentation.

Children were asked to listen carefully to the music and to say the word "change" whenever the music changed. Children were not given any clue about what changed in the music. This method of response was preferred over a nonverbal behavior such as clapping, because there is evidence that children, especially Argentine children, might be less responsive to musical changes through nonverbal behaviors than through simple verbalizations (Costa-Giomi, 1991; Flowers & Costa-Giomi, 1991). I asked those children who remained silent when listening to the music whether the music changed. The question was asked once during the performance of each stimulus, and it was repeated at the end of each performance.

Scoring Procedures

Children's responses were recorded on cassette tape and later analyzed according to the exact beat on which the word "change" was said. If the word "change" was said between beats, it was recorded as falling on the preceding beat.

Children were assigned two scores, one for the harmony-alone stimulus and one for the harmony + melody stimulus. They were given 1 point for each chord change that was correctly identified. Because there were eight chord changes in each stimulus, the maximum possible score per stimulus was 8 points. A chord change was considered to be correctly identified, and given 1 point, if the child said "change" only once after a new chord was played but before the subsequent change. If the child responded more than once after a chord change and prior to the following new chord, the response for that specific harmonic change was considered to be incorrect and given 0 points. When children failed to provide a response after a chord change and prior to the following change, that specific harmonic change was considered to be unidentified and given 0 points.

A reliability judge analyzed the responses of 20% of the children. As established through Pearson Product Moment correlation, interjudge agreement for the harmony-alone scores was .997; for the harmony + melody scores, it was .996.

Comparison of Sample Groups

To investigate whether children attending the four schools differed in their perception of harmonic changes prior to the development of the study, the test was administered to 59 randomly selected children (33 boys, 26 girls). This group included 32 4-year-olds and 27 5-year-olds.

It was found that 86% of the sample obtained scores lower than three (the maximum possible score was 8 points). The poor performance of the children was in general not the result of their responses being incorrect, but of the lack of any kind of verbal response. Most children were silent while listening to the songs and failed to provide verbal cues that denoted their perception of chord changes.

An analysis of variance (ANOVA) with repeated measures was performed for school (between variable) and type of stimulus (within variable) on children's scores to examine whether children's responses differed among preschools. Results of the analysis showed nonsignificant main or interaction effects. Children attending the four preschools did not respond differently to the test. It could be argued that no differences in scores were found among preschools because the test was too difficult for the children. Because a floor effect might have disguised differences among schools, school effects were studied further when testing the entire sample.

Training

During the period of one week, the researcher taught three 15-minute lessons to intact classes of children. There were 15 to 25 children in each class depending on the school. During the training, children engaged in activities that helped them focus their attention on the harmony when listening to music and also helped them respond to harmonic changes verbally. Activities were based on the visual and aural stimuli produced by the researcher playing chords on a keyboard with the left hand only and chords and melodies with both hands. Children were asked to look at the researcher's left hand and to notice how it moved to play different chords and it remained in the same position when repeating a chord. They were asked to say "change" when they saw and heard the hand play a different chord. They were also asked to cover their eyes and to aurally detect chord changes. The music used during the training was improvised according to children's progress. Although Argentine children were taught in Spanish and American children in English, the training followed the same procedures and was consistent among the four preschools.

Table 1
ANOVA Results for the Song "Drunken Sailor"

Source	Sum of squares	df	Mean square	F	p	w^2
School (Sch)	26.16	3	8.72	1.35	.27	.01
Age	211.29	1	211.29	32.79	.00	.28
Order (Ord)	0.30	1	0.30	0.05	.83	.00
Sch x Age	9.62	3	3.21	0.50	.69	.00
Sch x Ord	9.51	3	3.17	0.49	.69	.00
Age x Ord	31.98	1	31.98	4.96	.03	.02
Sch x Age x Ord	4.55	3	1.52	0.30	.87	.00
Error	438.255	68	6.45			
Type of Stimulus (TS)	285.57	1	285.57	60.13	.00	.40
TS x Sch	6.67	3	2.22	0.47	.71	.00
TS x Age	32.39	1	32.36	6.82	0.01	.04
TS x Ord	0.00	1	0.00	0.00	.98	.00
TS x Sch x Age	5.14	3	1.71	0.36	.78	.00
TS x Sch x Ord	20.59	3	6.86	1.45	.24	.01
TS x Age x Ord	10.03	1	10.03	2.11	.15	.00
TS x Sch x Age x Ord	13.37	3	4.46	0.94	.43	.00
Error	322.96	68	4.75			

Test

Following the training, children who participated in all three lessons were administered the test. Thirty-eight children missed at least one training session and consequently were not given the test, and 18 children were absent on the days it was administered. A total of 167 children, 99 girls and 68 boys, took the test. The test was administered within 5 days after the third and last training lesson.

RESULTS

Of the 167 children who took the test, 31 had already taken it prior to the initiation of the training. This preliminary procedure was undertaken to test for possible school differences. It was thought that double testing could have affected children's responses, creating a difference between the performances of children who took the test once and those who took it twice. In order to study this possibility, an ANOVA with repeated measures was conducted for testing condition (single or double testing) and type of stimulus (harmony alone and harmony + melody) on children's scores.

The analysis showed no significant main or interaction effects. Because no differences between the scores of children who took the test once versus twice could be established, the analysis of the data was done with all 167 subjects without excluding those who were tested twice.

To examine how children's responses to each song were affected by age (4 versus 5 years), order of stimulus presentation (harmony alone followed by harmony + melody or vice versa), type of stimuli (within variable: harmony alone and harmony + melody), and school (four preschools), an ANOVA with repeated measures was performed on children's scores for each song. The results of the two analyses were similar. Table 1 shows that the responses of children who listened to "En la Torre" were significantly affected by age, type of stimulus, and by the interaction between age and type of stimulus. Table 2 shows that the responses of children who listened to "Drunken Sailor" were also affected by age, type of stimulus, and the interaction between and age and type of stimulus. In addition, order of presentation was found to affect children's responses to "Drunken Sailor" significantly (Table 2).

Table 2
ANOVA Results for the Song "En la Torre"

Source	Sum of squares	df	Mean square	F	p	w^2
School (Sch)	14.42	3	4.81	0.78	.51	.00
Age	147.91	1	147.91	24.05	.00	.21
Order (Ord)	23.05	1	23.05	3.75	.06	.02
Sch x Age	34.46	3	11.49	1.87	.14	.02
Sch x Ord	10.54	3	3.51	0.57	.64	.00
Age x Ord	3.34	1	3.34	0.54	.46	.00
Sch x Age x Ord	20.32	3	6.77	1.10	.36	.00
Error	412.10	67	6.15			
Type of Stimulus (TS)	212.06	1	212.06	40.80	.00	.32
TS x Sch	2.71	3	0.92	0.17	.91	.00
TS x Age	35.32	1	35.32	6.80	.01	.05
TS x Ord	1.01	1	1.01	0.20	.66	.00
TS x Sch x Age	6.94	3	2.31	0.45	.72	.00
TS x Sch x Ord	19.46	3	6.49	1.25	.30	.01
TS x Age x Ord	1.11	1	1.11	0.21	.65	.00
TS x Sch x Age x Ord	7.63	3	2.55	0.49	.70	.00
Error	348.22	67	5.20			

Children's perception of harmonic change, as expressed through the use of the word "change," was more accurate when listening to the accompaniment of a song without its melody than when listening simultaneously to the song's accompaniment and melody. For both songs, mean scores for the harmony-alone stimuli were significantly higher than for the harmony + melody stimulus (Table 3).

The analysis of children's responses showed that 5-year-olds were able to identify more than half the chord changes of the harmony-alone stimulus, but could identify only two of the eight chord changes of the harmony + melody stimulus. On the other hand, mean scores of 4-year-olds for both the harmony alone and the harmony + melody stimuli were noticeably low. These findings were consistent for both songs (Table 3).

Five-year-olds responded significantly better than did 4-year-olds. The mean composite scores (the average of harmony-alone and harmony + melody scores) obtained by the older children for each song were significantly higher than those obtained by 4-year-olds. It was also observed that 5-year-old children outperformed 4-year-olds regardless of type of stimulus or song; they scored higher than 4-year-olds in both the harmony-alone and the harmony + melody stimuli of each of the songs (Table 3). The presence, however, of a significant age x type of stimu-

Table 3
Mean Scores for 4- and 5-Year-Olds for Each Song

Age	"En la Torre" (n = 83)			"Drunken Sailor" (n = 84)		
	H	H + M	Composite	H	H + M	Composite
4	1.98	0.38	1.18	2.42	0.64	1.53
(n = 82)	(2.76)	(1.04)	(1.51)	(2.94)	(1.28)	(1.75)
5	5.03	1.47	3.25	5.91	2.20	4.05
(n = 85)	(2.84)	(2.84)	(2.06)	(2.11)	(2.11)	(1.66)
Total	3.51	0.93	4.17	1.42		
(n = 187)	(3.24)	(1.87)	(3.22)	(1.90)		

Maximum possible score = 8.00 points
H = Harmony only
H + M = Harmony + Melody
Standard deviations are shown in parentheses.

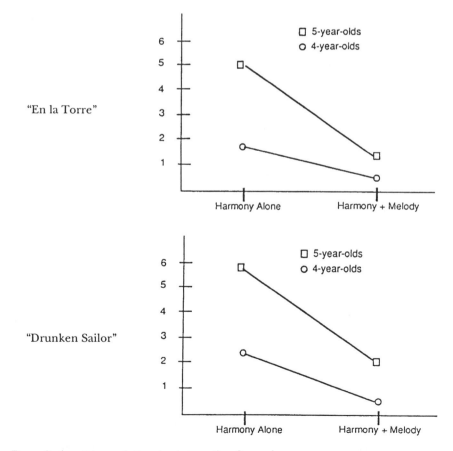

Figure 2. Age X type of stimulus interaction for each song.

lus interaction in each of the ANOVAs indicated that the differences between 4- and 5-year-olds scores were more pronounced for the harmony-alone than for the harmony + melody stimulus (Figure 2).

No significant differences among preschools could be established for children's responses to either song. The lack of difference among preschools existed regardless of age, song, and order of stimulus presentation.

Order of stimulus presentation was found to affect children's scores for the song "Drunken Sailor" significantly. Children's composite scores were higher when presented with the harmony-alone stimulus followed by the harmony + melody stimulus (Mean = 3.01, SD = 2.05) than when presented with the stimuli in the opposite order (Mean = 2.58, SD = 2.34). Although the composite scores for "En la Torre" were also higher when the harmony-alone stimulus was presented first (Mean = 2.64, SD = 2.31) than when presented last (Mean = 1.82, SD = 1.87), the difference was found to be nonsignificant.

To examine whether Argentine and American children responded differently to each of the songs, an ANOVA with repeated measures was conducted for country (between variable) on children's scores (within variable) for each song. No significant differences between the scores of Argentine and American children were found for either song (Table 4).

Table 4
ANOVA Results for Country on Children's Scores for Each Song

	"Drunken Sailor"				
Source	Sum of squares	*df*	Mean square	*F*	*p*
Country	44.02	1	44.02	1.82	.18
Error	2008.98	83	24.21		
Type of stimulus × Country	1.93	1	1.93	0.02	.63
Error	701.07	83	8.45		

	"En la Torre"				
Source	Sum of squares	*df*	Mean square	*F*	*p*
Country	13.09	1	13.09	0.82	.37
Error	1228.02	82	15.95		
Type of stimulus × Country	2.08	1	2.08	0.03	.61
Error	600.87	82	7.80		

The relative magnitude of the variables' effects, that is, the proportion of variability among children's responses that was accounted for by all variables and their interactions, was calculated (see Table 1). According to Cohen (1977), who suggested that in the behavioral sciences, omega-squared values of .15 should be considered large, the effects of age (4- and 5-year-old) and type of stimulus (harmony alone or harmony + melody) are noticeably high. More than 30% of the scores' variance can be explained by type of stimulus effects and more than 20% by age differences.

It was observed that many children remained silent when listening to the stimuli. This was especially true for the younger children; 51% of the 4-year-olds failed to respond to both types of stimuli. The older children were more responsive to the test; only 9% of the 5-year-olds did not respond to either type of stimulus.

Fifty-four children responded to one type of stimulus (harmony alone or harmony + melody), but failed to respond to the other stimulus. Because type of stimulus and age affected children's performance to a greater extent than any other variable, a more detailed analysis of the lack of response of 4- and 5-year olds to each type of stimulus was conducted. It was found that more children failed to respond to the harmony + melody stimulus than to the harmony alone stimulus (Table 5). This was true for both 4- and 5-year-olds. This finding is not surprising, because it corroborates the results of the previous analyses: Children had more difficulty in identifying harmonic changes when listening to the melody + harmony stimulus than to the harmony alone with no melody.

Table 5
Number of Children Who Failed to Respond to Only One Stimulus

Age-group	Harmony alone	Harmony + melody
4 (n = 40)	2 (5%)	22 (55%)
5 (n = 77)	2 (3%)	28 (36%)
Total (n = 117)	4 (3%)	50 (42%)

Although a relatively small number of 5-year olds failed to respond to both types of stimuli, a result that can be attributed to the lack of understanding of test procedures, a large number of them did respond to at least one stimulus, that one most likely being the harmony-alone stimulus. Given that children who responded to one stimulus understood the test procedures, it can be inferred that, for the older children, the harmony + melody stimulus was difficult, not the test procedures. The same cannot be said for younger children: too many 4-year olds failed to respond to either type of stimulus, suggesting that perhaps the test itself was too difficult for them. From Table 5, however, it can be seen that those 4-year olds who were able to provide responses to the stimuli found the harmony + melody stimulus more difficult than the harmony alone.

DISCUSSION

The analysis of mean scores shows that 5-year-old children were able to identify the harmonic changes of the accompaniment alone with no melody. They recognized more than half the chord changes of the harmony-alone stimulus regardless of song. The harmony-alone stimulus was based on the discrimination between two chords, major tonic and dominant seventh (I and V6/5) for the song "En la Torre de una Iglesia" and minor tonic and major subtonic (i and VII) for the song

"Drunken Sailor." Previous research has shown that first graders are able to discriminate between a major tonic and a dominant seventh quite easily (Hair, 1973). The present study showed that kindergartners also can do so. In Hair's study, however, the two chords were paired in such a way as to allow for melodic changes between them; that is, the upper voice of the tonic was always different from that of the dominant seventh chord. It can then be questioned whether children in that study discriminated between chords or just between their melodic pitches. To study this question, one of the stimuli of the present study consisted of positions of the tonic and the dominant seventh chords that allowed the upper voice to remain on the same pitch (see Figure 1b). Kindergartners were able to discriminate between the two chords even when the pitches in their upper voice were the same.

Although 5-year-olds were able to identify most harmonic changes when presented with the accompaniment alone, 4-year-old children could not do so. Four-year-olds' scores for the harmony-alone stimulus were surprisingly low. Neither 5- nor 4-year-olds were able to discriminate between the chords when they were played with a melody. Mean scores for the harmony + melody stimulus were particularly low for both age-groups. It seems that the harmony + melody stimulus was too difficult for the children regardless of age.

Why did children have difficulty in discriminating between chords played simultaneously with a melody? It has been suggested that children focus their attention on the melody rather than on the harmony when presented with both elements simultaneously (Imberty, 1969; Rupp, 1915, reported in Funk, 1977; Zenatti, 1969). However, results of the study provide some evidence that this might not always be true. From those 4- and 5-year-old children who demonstrated an understanding of test procedures by responding to at least one of the stimuli, 42% did not respond to the harmony + melody stimulus, whereas 3% did not respond to the harmony-alone stimulus. That is, even though they were able to respond to the harmony-alone stimulus, many children did not provide any response to the harmony + melody stimulus. Those children did not respond to the harmonic changes of the music, but neither did they respond to other changes in the music such as those of the melody. Future research might help to clarify whether children focus more readily on melody when listening to melody and harmony played simultaneously.

Another possible reason for children's difficulty in identifying harmonic changes when presented with the harmony + melody stimulus is that their attention was diverted to more than one musical element. This could have prevented them from focusing on only the harmony. It has been shown that young children can perceive and demonstrate understanding of musical elements when asked to respond to only one concept at the time, but not when asked to respond to a combination of them (Sims, 1991). In the present study, older children responded quite successfully to the harmony-alone stimulus in which a single musical concept was clearly illustrated, but performed poorly for the harmony + melody stimulus in which more than one concept was represented. It might be possible that the apparent inability of children to perceive harmony is the result of their difficulty to isolate various musical concepts presented simultaneously, rather than their poor harmonic discrimination skills.

Children's difficulty in responding to chord changes when the melody was part of the stimulus was reflected not only in the lower mean scores for the harmony + melody stimulus as compared to those of the harmony alone, but also in the larger number of nonresponses to the more complex stimulus. Interestingly, most children who failed to respond to the harmony-alone stimulus did not respond to the harmony + melody stimulus either. That suggests that if children were unable to identify harmonic changes in the simple stimulus—harmony alone—they were also unable to do so with the more complex one—harmony + melody.

Five-year-old children achieved significantly higher scores than 4-year-old children for both types of stimuli. Even for the harmony + melody stimulus in which children obtained very low scores, 5-year-olds significantly outperformed 4-year-olds. The older children also provided more responses to the stimuli than did the younger ones. These results show that 5-year-old children were not only more accurate in their identification of harmonic changes than were 4-year-olds, but were also more responsive to the tasks of the test.

The most striking difference in performance between 4- and 5-year-olds was found for the harmony-alone stimulus. Five-year-olds were able to identify harmonic changes in the harmony-alone stimulus, but 4-year-olds could not do so. Because the younger children so often failed to respond to the tasks of the test, it could be argued that they did not fully understand the test procedures; this could have produced the differences between age-groups. The study attempted to prevent this problem by providing children with training to familiarize them with the tasks of the test, but it is possible that the training was too brief for the younger children to transfer what they had practiced during the lessons to the test situation. It is also possible, however, that 4-year-olds performed poorly in the harmony-alone task because of their inability to perceive harmonic changes. During the training, younger children were able to easily detect chord changes in simple progression with no melody when watching the instructor play the piano, but could barely do so when asked to close their eyes. Their difficulty in identifying chord changes aurally was true even when presented with chords that differed noticeably in their position and register. Five-year-olds, instead, seemed to be able to perceive the changes aurally quite easily when presented with simple progressions with no melody. These observations suggest that developmental differences in harmonic perception might exist between 4- and 5-year-old children.

The children's responses did not differ among preschools. Children who participated in music classes taught by music specialists did not respond differently than those who engaged in music experiences developed by classroom teachers. Neither did they benefit from the training on harmonic discrimination in a different way than the others. This finding does not support results of previous studies that showed that children who were taught music by classroom teachers performed less well in harmonic discrimination tasks than those who were taught music by music specialists (Bridges, 1965; Piper & Shoemaker, 1973). Interestingly, Argentine and American children did not respond differently to the test. It seems that the ability to identify chord changes is a developmental characteristic. This study suggests that this ability is affected by age but not by culture or instruction.

Children tended to perform better in the test when they were presented with the harmony-alone stimulus first and with the harmony + melody later than with the stimuli in the opposite order. It seems that the presentation of the stimulus that more clearly reflected the harmonic changes at the beginning of the test helped children to identify chord changes more accurately. Only for the song "Drunken Sailor," however, was order of presentation found to significantly affect children's scores. Because the songs differ in so many characteristics, such as mode, melody, frequency of chord changes, and rhythm, it is difficult to speculate about the reasons for this outcome. Future research will examine which characteristics of musical stimuli influence the perception of harmony during the first years of life.

CONCLUSIONS AND IMPLICATIONS

It is unfortunate that most studies in the development of harmonic abilities have found what young children cannot do instead of what they are capable of doing in terms of harmonic perception. Most studies have provided little support for the development of harmonic perception activities in the lower grades of elementary school. The results of the present study, however, suggest that musical experiences that involve the concept of harmony can be introduced at an early age. The following conclusions are expected to provide initial guidelines for the development of harmonic perception activities suitable for young children and for the further study of harmonic abilities in early childhood.

1. Harmonic perception abilities of young children are better than have been previously suggested. Five-year-old children are capable of perceiving harmonic changes in simple stimuli.

2. Development of harmonic perception begins early in life. Differences in harmonic discrimination skills exist between 4- and 5-year-old children.

3. Complexity of the stimulus and age are two important variables in young children's harmonic perception. The addition of a melody to a simple chord progression hinders children's ability to identify chord changes.

4. The apparent inability of children to perceive harmony might be the result of their difficulty to isolate various musical concepts presented simultaneously, rather than their poor harmonic perceptual skills.

5. There is no clear evidence that children focus on the melody rather than on harmony when listening to music. Children are able to discriminate between chords whose upper-voice notes remain the same and allow for no pitch changes. The addition of a melody to a chord progression, however, confuses children of this age and hinders their ability to discriminate harmony.

6. Children tend to perceive harmonic changes better when they are initially presented with simple stimuli that clearly reflect chord changes and later, with complex stimuli in which harmonic changes are combined with other musical concepts.

REFERENCES

Bentley, A. (1966). *Musical ability in children and its measurement.* New York: October House.

Bridges, V. (1965). *An exploratory study of the harmonic discrimination ability of children in kindergarten through grade three in two selected schools.* Unpublished doctoral dissertation, Ohio State University, Columbus.

Buckton, R. (1982). An investigation into the development of musical concepts in young children. *Psychology of Music, 10,*1 17–21.

Cohen, J. (1977). *Statistical power analysis and research results* (Rev. ed.). New York: Academic Press.

Costa-Giomi, E. (1991, February). *Mode discrimination abilities of preschool children.* Paper presented at the meeting of the Ohio Music Educators Association, Cleveland.

De Carbo, J. A. (1981). The effect of same/different discrimination techniques, readiness training, pattern treatment, and sex on aural discrimination ability and singing ability of tonal patterns with kindergarten children. *Dissertation Abstracts International, 42–08A,* 3489. (University Microfilms No. 82–02, 158)

DeNardo, G. F. (1989). An assessment of musical cognitive processes used by children to compare phrases types within a song, 1988. *Dissertation Abstracts International, 50–02A,* 380. (University Microfilms No. 8906517)

Farnsworth, P. R. (1969). *The social psychology of music* (2nd ed.). Ames: Iowa State University Press.

Flowers, P. J., & Costa-Giomi, E. (1991). Verbal and nonverbal identification of pitch changes in a familiar song by English and Spanish speaking preschool children. *Bulletin of the Council for Research in Music Education*, no. 101, 1–12.

Frances, R. (1988). *The perception of music* (W. J. Dowling, trans.). Hillsdale, NJ: Lawrence Erlbaum Associates. (Original work published 1958)

Franklin, E. (1956). *Tonality as a basis for the study of musical talent.* Goteberg: Gumpert.

Funk, J. D. (1977). Some aspects of the development of music perception. *Dissertation Abstracts International*, 38, 1919B (University Microfilms No. 77–20, 301)

Gardner, H. (1973). Children's sensitivity to musical styles. *Merrill-Palmer Quarterly of Behavioral Development*, 19, 67–77.

Hair, H. I. (1973). The effect of training on the harmonic discrimination of first-grade children. *Journal of Research in Music Education*, 73, 85–90.

Hair, H. I. (1981). Verbal identification of music concepts. *Journal of Research in Music Education*, 29, 11–21.

Hair, H. I. (1987). Descriptive vocabulary and visual choices: children's responses to conceptual changes in music. *Bulletin for the Council of Research in Music Education*, no. 91, 59–64.

Hargreaves, D. J. (1986). *The developmental psychology of music.* Cambridge, England: Cambridge University Press

Hickman, A. T. (1969). Some preverbal concepts in music. *Journal of Research in Music Education*, 17, 70–75.

Holohan, J. M. (1983). *The effects of four conditions of same different instruction in the developmental music aptitudes of kindergarten children receiving tonal pattern training.* Unpublished doctoral dissertation, Temple University, Philadelphia, PA.

Hufstader, R. A. (1977). An investigation of a learning sequence of music listening skills. *Journal of Research in Music Education*, 25, 184–196.

Imberty, M. (1969). *L'acquisition des structures tonales chez l'enfant.* [The acquisition of tonal structures in children]. Paris: Klincksieck.

Klanderman, N. Z. (1979). *The development of auditory discrimination and performance of pitch, rhythm, and melody in preschool children.* Unpublished doctoral dissertation. Northwestern University, Evanston, IL.

Lundin, R. W. (1967). *An objective psychology of music.* New York: Ronald Press.

McDonald, D. T., & Simons, G. M. (1989). *Musical growth and development: Birth through six.* New York: Schirmer.

Merrion, M. (1989). *What works: Instructional strategies for music education.* Reston: Music Educators National Conference.

Moog, H. (1976). *The musical experience of the pre-school child.* (C. Clarke, trans.), London: Schott & Co., Ltd. (original work published in 1968)

Montgomery, W. B. (1978). Basic aural discrimination: Third grade children's' perception of changes in music (Doctoral dissertation, Florida State University, Tallahassee). *Dissertation Abstracts International*, 39, 3438A–3439A.

O'Hearn, R. N. (1984). An investigation of the response to change in music events by children in grades one, three, and five. *Dissertation Abstracts International*, 46, 371A.

Petzold, R. G. (1966). *Auditory perception of musical sounds by children in the first six grades* (Cooperative Research Project No.1051). Madison: University of Wisconsin. (ERIC Document Reproduction Service No. ED 010 297).

Pflederer, M. (1964). The responses of children to musical stimulus embodying Piaget's principle of conservation. *Journal of Research in Music Education*, 12, 251–268.

Pflederer, M., & Sechrest, L. (1968). Conservation-type responses of children to musical stimuli. *Bulletin for the Council of Research in Music Education*, no. 13, 19–36.

Pflederer-Zimmerman, M. P., & Sechrest, L. (1970). Brief focused instruction and musical concepts. *Journal of Research in Music Education*, 18, 25–36.

Piper, R. M., & Shoemaker, D. M. (1973). Formative evaluation of a kindergarten music program based on behavioral objectives. *Journal of Research in Music Education*, 21, 145–152.

Radocy, R. E., & Boyle, J. D. (1979). *Psychological foundations of musical behavior.* Springfield, IL: Charles C Thomas.

Radocy, R. E., & Boyle, J. D. (1988). *Psychological foundations of musical behavior* (2nd ed.). Springfield, IL: Charles C Thomas.

Schultz, S. W. (1969). *A study of children's ability to respond to elements of music.* Unpublished doctoral dissertation, Northwestern University, Evanston, IL.

Shuter-Dyson, R., & Gabriel, C. (1981). *The psychology of musical ability.* (2nd ed.). London: Methuen.

Simons, G. (1986). Early childhood musical development: A survey of selected research. *Bulletin of the Council for Research in Music Education,* no. 86, 36–52.

Sims, W. L. (1991). Effects of instruction and task format on preschool children's music concept discrimination. *Journal of Research in Music Education, 39,* 298–310.

Sloboda, J. A. (1985). *The musical mind: The cognitive psychology of music.* Oxford, England: Clarendon Press.

Sterling, P. A. (1985). A developmental study of the effects of accompanying harmonic context on children's vocal pitch accuracy of familiar melodies. *Dissertation Abstracts International, 45,* 2436A.

Taylor, S. (1969). *The musical development of children aged seven to eleven.* Doctoral dissertation. University of Southampton, UK.

Teplov, B. M. (1966). *Psychologie des aptitudes musicales* [The psychology of musical aptitudes]. Paris: Presses Universitaires de France.

Valentine, C. W. (1913). The aesthetic appreciation of musical intervals among school children and adults. *British Journal of Psychology, 6,* 190–216.

Vera, A. (1989). El desarrollo de las destrezas musicales [The development of musical abilities]. *Infancia y Aprendizaje, 45,* 107–121.

Yoshikawa, S. (1973). Yoji no waon-Kan no hattatsu [A developmental study of children's sense of tonality]. *Ongaku-Gaku, 19* (1), 5–72.

Zenatti, A. (1969). Le developpement genetique de la perception musicale [The genetic development of musical perception]. *Monographies Françaises de Psychologie, 17.* Paris: Centre National de la Recherche Scientifique.

Zenatti, A. (1974). Perception et appreciation de la consonance musicale par l'enfant entre 4 et 10 ans [Perception and appreciation of musical consonance by children between the ages of 4 and 10 years]. *Sciences de l'Art, 9* (1 & 2), 1–15.

Zimmerman, M. P. (1971). *Musical characteristics of children.* Washington, DC: Music Educators National Conference.

March 15, 1993

The purpose of this study was to investigate the relationships among musical character-istics and musicians' and nonmusicians' preferences for world musics. World musics were drawn from Africa, Asia, and Latin America. Musical characteristics included tempo, pitch redundancy, tonal centeredness, consonance, brightness in timbre, percus-siveness, loudness, textural complexity, and richness in embellishment. Preference was also examined in relation to familiarity. Subjects were 449 undergraduate students (180 music majors and 269 nonmusic majors). Subjects completed a preference-rating scale that included a total of 36 instrumental excerpts from nine countries. Results showed that all nine musical characteristics were significant sources of variance in world music preferences. The following musical characteristics were preferred by both musicians and nonmusicians: fast tempo, loud, tonal-centered, having many different pitches, conso-nant, moderately embellished, smooth-sounding, and bright timbre. Musicians preferred excerpts with complex texture, whereas nonmusicians preferred moderately complex tex-tures. A positive relationship between familiarity and preference was found across all musical styles. In general, musicians had significantly higher preference means than did nonmusicians.

C. Victor Fung, *University of Minnesota*

JRME 1996, VOLUME 44, NUMBER 1, PAGES 60–83

Musicians' and Nonmusicians' Preferences for World Musics: Relation to Musical Characteristics and Familiarity

The inclusion of world musics in music education programs in the United States has become increasingly important in recent decades. Musics from all cultures began to emerge in music programs, and lis-tening activities have served as a gateway to transmit world musics into

Appreciation is extended to the Archives of Traditional Music at Indiana University, Bloomington, for providing all musical excerpts used in this study. Acknowledgment is also due to Dr. Lizabeth A. Wing for assisting with data collection at the University of Cincinnati—College Conservatory of Music. This article is based on the author's doc-toral dissertation, "Musicians' and Non-musicians' Preferences for World Musics: Relation to Musical Characteristics and Familiarity," accepted in 1994 by Indiana University, Bloomington. C. Victor Fung is an assistant professor of music at the General College, University of Minnesota, 364 Appleby Hall, 128 Pleasant Street Southeast, Minneapolis, MN 55455. Copyright © 1996 by Music Educators National Conference.

American music classrooms. Although a number of researchers have examined various responses to music listening, the use of music other than Western art music and popular genres as stimuli in research is relatively rare. The enormous number of music preference studies can be seen in several reviews of the literature (e.g., Finnäs, 1989; Wapnick, 1976). Music preference is also among the most frequently cited research topics in research articles published in major music education research journals (Schmidt & Zdzinski, 1993).

Both qualitative and quantitative evidence suggests that preference can be an important mediating agent in the process of music education. Although music preference may well be different from aesthetic judgment (Kant 1790/1987), liking for certain musics may be a bridge for development of a musical novice into a musically educated individual who is capable of aesthetic judgment. Asmus (1989) found that, from the standpoint of motivation for music learning, affect for music was one of the five factors that significantly explained motivations in music learning. Therefore, music preference may be a springboard for further music learning.

According to LeBlanc, "music preference decisions are based upon the interaction of input information and the characteristics of the listener, with input information consisting of the musical stimulus and the listener's cultural environment" (LeBlanc, 1987, p. 139). Studies in musical characteristics have explained some variance in preference. Judging from the percentage of variance explained in individual studies, one may postulate that some musical characteristics tend to explain more variance than others. In some studies, tempo, loudness, and complexity have explained more than 50% of the variance (LeBlanc & McCrary, 1983; Martindale & Moore, 1990; Russell, 1982), while timbre and consonance have explained less than 3% of the variance (LeBlanc, 1981; Martindale & Moore, 1990).

As far as can be determined, only one study (Fung, 1992) has involved the use of world music excerpts to investigate the relationship between musical characteristics and preference. In that study, 32 music excerpts were drawn from eight geographic regions: Africa, China, India, Indonesia, Japan, Korea, the Middle East, and Thailand. Results showed that graduate music students indicated higher preferences for the excerpts that were perceived as having fast tempo, regular rhythm, clear melody, tonal centers, consonance, regular phrasing, bright timbre, high complexity, and similarity to Western music. The characteristic of regular rhythm explained 35% of the variance in preference ratings. Other variables explaining variance in preference included complexity (24%), similarity to Western music (23%), melodic clarity (22%), phrasing regularity (19%), tonal centeredness (19%), tempo (17%), consonance (14%), and brightness in timbre (13%). However, pitch register, pitch redundancy, smoothness, and the loudness level of these world music styles were not significantly correlated with preference. The extent to which these relationships generalize to nonmusicians is not known.

Although a number of researchers (e.g., Hargreaves, 1988; Radocy,

1982) have empirically examined the relationship between preference and familiarity, once again, most of these studies have used Western musical stimuli. Two researchers (Geisler, 1990; Hicken, 1992) have examined the familiarity issue with world music excerpts. Geisler (1990) used six Chinese and 13 Western music excerpts while examining the rank-order correlation between preference and familiarity. The rank-order correlation between familiarity and preference for the 19 excerpts was .92 in the United States and .74 in Hong Kong. Hicken (1992) used three world music excerpts (two Japanese and one Indian). Among all predictor variables in the study (familiarity, gender, socioeconomic status, musical experience, music aptitude, and field-dependence/independence), familiarity was the strongest predictor of world music preferences, explaining almost 11% of the variance.

Many music preference studies have examined preferences of nonmusicians. Even though some researchers included both musicians and nonmusicians in the sample (Geringer & Madsen, 1981; Hedden, 1974; Huber & Holbrook, 1980; Radocy, 1982; Sims, 1987), there have been few direct comparisons between the groups' music preferences. In studies that directly compared the preference means between musicians and nonmusicians (Burke & Gridley, 1990; Hargreaves, Messerschmidt, & Rubert, 1980; Smith & Cuddy, 1986), findings consistently indicated that musicians had significantly higher preferences than did nonmusicians regardless of musical style (electronic tones, piano, classical, and popular). However, no such group comparison has been made in preferences for world musics.

Another issue in preference for world musics is sampling of excerpts. The musical styles used in world music preference studies have included African (Flowers, 1980; Fung, 1992, 1994; Nakazawa, 1988; Shehan, 1981, 1985), Chinese (Fung, 1992, 1994; Geisler, 1990), Indian (Fung, 1990, 1992, 1994; Hicken, 1992; May, 1985; Shehan, 1981, 1985), Indonesian (Fung, 1992, 1994; Nakazawa, 1988; Shehan, 1981, 1984), Japanese (Darrow, Haack, & Kuribayashi, 1987; Fung, 1992, 1994; Hicken, 1992; Nakazawa, 1988; Shah, 1990; Shehan, 1981, 1985), Korean (Fung, 1992, 1994), Lao (Shehan, 1987), Malaysian (Shah, 1990), Middle Eastern (Fung, 1992, 1994), Pakistani (Heingartner & Hall, 1974), Persian (Nakazawa, 1988), Puerto Rican (Nakazawa, 1988), and Thai (Fung, 1992, 1994). Most of the cited research used Asian musical styles rather extensively. However, relatively little research attention has been given to Latin American styles and specific music styles found within the continent of Africa.

Given the results of the previous literature, a range of musical characteristics, musical training (i.e., musicians versus nonmusicians), and familiarity emerge as prominent independent variables and predictors of world music preferences. These results are preliminary, however, because of the limited range of world musics found in most of the previous studies. Therefore, the purpose of this study was to investigate the relationships among musical characteristics, familiarity, and musicians' and nonmusicians' preferences for world musics. World musics were drawn from Africa (Congo, Malawi, and Nigeria), Asia (China, Japan, and Korea), and Latin America (Cuba, Mexico, and Peru). Musical characteristics included tempo, pitch redundancy, tonal centeredness, consonance, brightness in timbre, percussiveness, loudness, textural complexity, and richness in embellishment. Musical ·characteristics were limited to those judged by individuals with training in the Western art-music tradition in American music schools. These judgments were not necessarily representative of all musical cultures. Specific research questions included:

1. To what extent did musical characteristics relate to musicians' and nonmusicians' preferences for world musics?

2. To what extent did musical characteristics interact with musicians' and nonmusicians' preference ratings?

3. To what extent did world music preference ratings differ between musicians and nonmusicians?

4. What relationship existed between familiarity and preference ratings across musical styles?

METHOD

This study involved 24 judges and 449 undergraduate students (180 music majors and 269 nonmusic majors). Undergraduate students (N = 449) provided (1) music preference ratings, (2) familiarity ratings, and (3) demographic data. Undergraduate music majors were enrolled in an undergraduate music program at two large midwestern universities. They were recruited from undergraduate music history, music theory, and music education classes. Undergraduate nonmusic majors were enrolled in a nonmusic undergraduate program at a major midwestern university. They were recruited from undergraduate classes in music for elementary education majors, speech and hearing, and physical education.

The age range of the subjects (undergraduate musicians and nonmusicians, N = 449) was 18 to 69 years, with a mean of 20.65 years (*SD* = 3.89). Ninety-four percent of the sample were citizens of the United States. Only 8% of the sample were born outside of the United States, and 5.6% indicated that English was not their native language. The sample could be broken down as follows: 3.6% African/Black, 0.7% American Indian, 4.9% Asian, 87.5% European/White, 1.3% His-panic, and 2% other. The mean number of instruments played by the musician sample was 2.5, and the mean number of years they played such instruments was 18.6. Musicians also had a mean of 16.8 years' ensemble experience. Nonmusicians had played a mean of 1.1 instruments and played for a mean of 4.3 years. They also had a mean of 4.1 years' ensemble experience.

Judges (N = 24) provided ratings of musical characteristics for each excerpt (described below). All judges had earned a master's degree in music and currently were enrolled as majors in one of six doctoral programs in music at a large midwestern university.

Two author-developed instruments were used in this study: the

Musical Characteristics Rating Form (MCRF) and the World Musics Preference Rating Scale (WMPRS). Both instruments contained the same 36 musical excerpts (see Table 1). Each excerpt presented the first 40 seconds of a piece or of a section. Only instrumental excerpts were selected in order to avoid intervening factors such as a language barrier or gender of singer(s). Four instrumental excerpts were sampled from each of the following musical styles: Congo, Malawi, Nigeria, China, Japan, Korea, Cuba, Mexico, and Peru. These nine world-music styles were selected because they provided music samples that reflected some ethnic origins of the major non-European ethnic groups in the United States (i.e., African, Asian, and Latin American). Native American music was not selected due to its heavy emphasis on voice.

To ensure sound quality, all excerpts were drawn from cassette tapes, compact discs, or LP recordings classified as commercial recordings (not field recordings) produced after 1971 and located in the Archives of Traditional Music, Indiana University, Bloomington. To assure a variety of musical characteristics, excerpts were selected randomly from the archives. Seventy items were included in a pilot study. All excerpts were presented in random order. Based on a pilot study of 35 college students' preference ratings using 7-point Likert scales, interitem correlation coefficients were computed among items in each of the nine music styles. Four items in each category with the highest interitem correlation coefficients were selected for the main study.

To examine the reliability of musical characteristic ratings in the pilot study, five music doctoral students rated the excerpts using the following semantic differential pairs, based on Fung (1992) and Lomax (1968), in 7-point scales (1 to 7) for each of the 70 pilot excerpts: (a) slow—fast, (b) irregular rhythm—regular rhythm, (c) short phrasing—long phrasing, (d) irregular phrasing—regular phrasing, (e) low pitch—high pitch, (f) narrow pitch range—wide pitch range, (g) redundant pitches—different pitches, (h) unclear melody—clear melody, (i) nontonal-centered—tonal-centered, (j) dissonant consonant, (k) dull timbre—bright timbre, (l) smooth—percussive, (m) soft—loud, (n) unison/solo—many independent parts, (o) simple texture—complex texture, (p) little or no embellishment—rich embellishment, and (q) similar to Western music—dissimilar to Western music. In Fung's (1992) study, 13 of the 17 scales (all except scales c, f, n, and p) were found to have high reliability coefficients (α range from .82 to .97). Scales c, f, n, and p were adopted from Lomax's (1968) "cantometric coding" and were included in the pilot study. Based on ratings of five judges in the pilot study, scales with low interjudge reliability (irregular phrasing—regular phrasing and short phrasing—long phrasing) were excluded in the main study. Further elimination took place in the main study due to the significant correlations among some scales. The following scales remained for the main analysis: slow—fast, redundant pitches—different pitches, nontonal-centered—tonal centered, dissonant—consonant, dull timbre—bright timbre, smooth—percussive, soft—loud, simple texture—complex texture, and little or no embellishment—rich embellishment.

Judges (N = 24) listened to the musical stimuli recorded on a cassette tape and responded to the MCRF individually. They provided ratings of musical characteristics for each musical excerpt using the semantic differential scales described above. Judges were informed that they could listen to the excerpts as many times as they wished.

The same 36 music excerpts were used in the World Music Preference Rating Scale (WMPRS). The WMPRS had a 10-second interstimulus interval for musicians and nonmusicians to rate their preferences for the excerpts on a 7-point Likert scale (1 = strongly dislike, 7 = strongly like) and to rate their familiarity with the styles on a 3-point scale (1 = unfamiliar, 2 = somewhat familiar, 3 = familiar). Undergraduate musicians (n = 180) and nonmusicians (n = 269) responded to the WMPRS in small groups (n < 35).

RESULTS

On the basis of ratings provided by 24 judges (MCRF), interjudge reliability coefficients for the musical characteristics scales were determined. All coefficients were acceptable and generally high (smooth—percussive: α = .82; slow—fast: α = .83; dull timbre—bright timbre: α = .88; soft—loud: α = .88; simple texture—complex texture: α = .92; little or no embellishment—rich embellishment: α = .92; redundant pitches—different pitches: α = .93; dissonance—consonance: α = .93; nontonal centered—tonal centered: α = .94). Thus, judges' ratings of individual musical characteristics were generally very consistent. In addition, all Pearson correlation coefficients among these nine musical characteristic scales were nonsignificant and were below .45, indicating that, across music excerpts, musical characteristics were generally discrete; that is, the presence or absence of one characteristic did not predict the presence or absence of others. For the composite measure of preference for 36 items (WMPRS), reliability coefficients were consistently high: α = .96; split-halves = .93. Likewise, the composite familiarity measure yielded high reliability coefficients: α = .94; split-halves =.90.

In addition, interitem correlations within each country category were computed for preference and familiarity. All coefficients were significant at .01 level. Median coefficients within each country category ranged from .50 to .68. Furthermore, all four items in each country category correlated highly with preferences for their respective composites at the country level. These coefficients ranged from .72 to .90, with most of the coefficients in the .80 range. Interitem (Spearman) correlations for familiarity ranged from .22 to .65. All coefficients were significant at .01 level. Familiarity was rated on a 3-point scale; correlation coefficients were generally lower than were those for preference. Most of the coefficients were ranged from the .30s to the .50s. As in the preference ratings, all four items in each country category correlated highly with their respective composite familiarity ratings. Intracountry correlation coefficients ranged from .48 to .85, with most of the coefficients ranged from the .60s to the .80s.

Table 1
Titles of Excerpts for the Main Study

Order	Title	Recording & Label
Congo		
7	"Mambala"	*The Music of African Series, Musical Instruments 3. Drums*, Kaleidophone KMA3 (1972)
3	"Congo Bereji"	*The Music of African Series, Musical Instruments 3. Drums*, Kaleidophone KMA3 (1972)
2	"Mishiba"	*The Music of African Series, Musical Instruments 4. Flutes & Horns*, Kaleidophone KMA4 (1972)
21	"Kalubambu tambo abibongo"	*The Music of African Series, Musical Instruments 5. Xylophones*, Kaleidophone KMA5 (1972)
Malawi		
26	"Kukapanda mbale kumaliza"	*Musiker aus Malawi*, Collection Berlin, Museum Collection MC15 (1989)
19	"Makang'ombe"	*Musiker aus Malawi*, Collection Berlin, Museum Collection MC15 (1989)
32	"Maguluve kumala imanga"	Musiker aus Malawi, Collection Berlin, Museum Collection MC15 (1989)
18	"Ulendo wa kumigunda"	*Musiker aus Malawi*, Collection Berlin, Museum Collection MC15 (1989)
Nigeria		
6	Elewe Music: "Ila Rangun"	*Yoruba Bata Drums: Elewe Music and Dance*, Folkways FE4294 (1980)
33	"Asida, Siko"	*Yoruba Bata Drums: Elewe Music and Dance*, Folkways FE4294 (1980)
27	"Ewo"	*Yoruba Bata Drums: Elewe Music and Dance*, Folkways FE4294 (1980)
14	"Wrestling music"	*An Anthology of Africa Music: Nigeria III; Igbo music*, Barenreiter-Musicaphon BM3022311 (1976)
China		
11	"Flying Kites"	*West Meets East*, Folkways FSS37455 (1981)
16	"Thunder in the Drought"	*West Meets East*, Folkways FSS37455 (1981)
1	"La petite pêche rouge"	*Chine Musique du Foukien*, CBS 65574 (1973)
15	"Rythme rapide"	*Chine Musique du Foukien*, CBS 65574 (1973)
20	"Gakkaen"	*Japon: Gagaku*, Ocora C55999018 (1988)
10	"Ajikan"	*Shakuhachi Honkyoku*, Folkways FE4229 (1980)
17	"Shika-no tone"	*Asia, Japan, Musical Atlas*, EMI Italiana C064-17967 (1974)

(Table 1 continues on next page)

Table 1 (continued)
Titles of Excerpts for the Main Study

Order	Title	Recording & Label
Japan		
	"Edo Matsuri Bayashi"	*Asia, Japan, Musical Atlas*, EMI Italiana C064-17967 (1974)
Korea		
9	"Binavi" (2nd section)	*Samul-Nori, Drums and Voices of Korea*, Nonesuch 72093 (1984)
5	"Woodo-kut" (2nd section)	*Samul-Nori, Drums and Voices of Korea*, Nonesuch 72093 (1984)
4	"Kayagum sanjo"	*Sounds of the World, Music of East Asia: Korean*, Music Educators National Conference 3036 (1989)
13	"Tanso I"	*Sounds of the World, Music of East Asia: Korean*, Music Educators National Conference 3036 (1989)
Cuba		
29	"Conga Santiaguera"	*Music of Cuba*, Folkways FE4064 (1985)
31	"Toque a Orunla"	*Antologia de la Musica Afrocubana*, Vol. II, EGREM LD-3995 (1981)
34	"Ayacutá (para Aggayú)"	*Antologia de la Musica Afrocubana*, Vol. II, EGREM LD-3995 (1981)
12	"Toque yubá macota"	*Antologia de la Musica Afrocubana*, Vol. VII, EGREM LD-3606 (1981)
Mexico		
24	"La Zandunga"	*Raíces Musicales*, The National Council for the Traditional Arts (1988)
36	"Luzita"	*Chulas Fronteras*, Arhoolie 3005 (1976)
28	"Muchachos Alegres"	*Chulas Fronteras*, Arhoolie 300 (1976)
30	"Cotula"	*Chulas Fronteras*, Arhoolie 3005 (1976)
Peru		
35	"Corazón I"	*Corazón*, Folkways FSS34035 (1985)
8	"Coca K'intuchay"	*Perou*, Ocora 45586647 (1985)
25	"Wanka"	*Perou*, Ocora 45586647 (1985)
23	"Volcan"	*Perou*, Ocora 45586647 (1985)

Table 2
Groupings of Excerpts by Musical Characteristics (Judge N = 24)

	Slow	Moderate	Fast
Mean rating range	1.5–3.9	4.0–5.1	5.2–6.1
Item numbers	1, 4, 5, 8, 10, 13, 15, 17, 20, 22, 31, 35	2, 7, 9, 11, 16, 18, 21, 23, 24, 25, 34, 36	3, 6, 12, 14, 19, 26, 27, 28, 29, 30, 32, 33

	Redundant pitches	Moderate	Different pitches
Mean rating range	1.5–2.2	2.2–3.8	3.9–5.1
Item numbers	3, 5, 6, 7, 9, 12, 14, 27, 29, 31, 33, 34	2, 4, 8, 10, 17, 18, 19, 20, 21, 22, 26, 32	1, 11, 13, 15, 16, 23, 24 25, 28, 30, 35, 36

	Nontonal	Moderate	Tonal
Mean rating range	1.5–2.9	2.9–4.0	4.9–6.8
Item numbers	3, 5, 6, 7, 9, 12, 27, 29, 31, 32, 33, 34	2, 4, 10, 13, 14, 17, 18, 19, 20, 21, 22, 26	1, 8, 11, 15, 16, 23, 24, 25, 28, 30, 35, 36

	Dissonance	Moderate	Consonance
Mean rating range	3.4–4.2	4.3–5.2	5.7–6.5
Item numbers	2, 4, 12, 19, 20, 21, 27, 29, 31, 32, 33, 34	1, 3, 5, 6, 7, 10, 13, 14, 18, 22, 24, 26	8, 9, 11, 15, 16, 17, 23, 24, 28, 30, 35, 36

	Dull timbre	Moderate	Bright timbre
Mean rating range	2.9–4.0	4.0–5.1	5.2–6.1
Item numbers	2, 3, 4, 5, 7, 9, 10, 12, 19, 26, 27, 33	1, 6, 13, 14, 17, 18, 21, 29, 31, 32, 34, 35	8, 11, 15, 16, 20, 22, 23, 24, 25, 28, 30, 36

	Smooth	Moderate	Percussive
Mean rating range	2.1–4.4	4.4–4.6	6.3–6.8
Item numbers	1, 8, 10, 11, 13, 17, 22, 24, 28, 30, 35, 36	2, 4, 5, 15, 16, 18, 19, 20, 21, 23, 25, 26	3, 6, 7, 9, 12, 14, 27, 29, 31, 32, 33, 34

	Soft	Moderate	Loud
Mean rating range	2.2–4.0	4.1–4.6	4.6–5.6
Item numbers	1, 2, 4, 5, 9, 10, 11, 15, 17, 22, 23, 35	8, 13, 14, 16, 18, 19, 20, 24, 25, 26, 31, 32	3, 6, 7, 12, 21, 27, 28, 29, 30, 33, 34, 36

	Simple texture	Moderate	Complex texture
Mean rating range	1.1–3.1	3.1–3.9	4.1–5.0
Item numbers	4, 5, 10, 11, 13, 15, 17, 20, 22, 23, 30, 35	1, 7, 8, 9, 16, 24, 25, 28, 29, 31, 34, 36	2, 3, 6, 12, 14, 18, 19, 21, 26, 27, 32, 33

	Little/no embellishment	Moderate	Rich embellishment
Mean rating range	2.0–3.0	3.1–3.8	3.8–5.3
Item numbers	4, 5, 6, 7, 9, 19, 21, 29, 30, 31, 32, 34	3, 12, 14, 18, 20, 23, 2 26, 27, 28, 33, 35	1, 8, 10, 11, 13, 15, 16, 17, 22, 24, 25, 36

Table 3
ANOVA Results of Preference with One Between-Subjects Factor and Two Within-Subjects Factors (N = 449)

Source	SS	df	MS	F	p
Between factor					
Musicians/nonmusicians (M)	1839.39926	1	1839.39926	79.98	<.0001
Error	10279.87197	447	22.99748		
Within factors					
Scale (S)	0.92515	8	0.11564	79.93	<.0001
Error	5.17356	3576	0.00145		
Level (L)	287.38382	2	143.69191	405.86	<.0001
Error	316.51264	894	0.35404		
Interactions					
M × S	0.05776	8	0.00722	4.99	<.0001
M × L	13.33969	2	6.66984	18.84	<.0001
S × L	397.59640	16	24.84978	85.01	<.0001
M × S × L	32.23368	16	2.01461	6.89	<.0001

Results by Scale

Scale	SS	df	MS	F	p
Slow/Fast (S/F)	113.01401	2	56.50700	266.32	<.0001
S/F × Musician/nonmusician	2.08443	2	1.04221	4.91	<.05
Redundant/Different					
pitches (R/D)	134.01454	2	67.00727	161.99	<.0001
R/D × Musician/nonmusician	9.96204	2	4.98102	12.04	<.0001
Nontonal/Tonal-centered (N/T)	141.26403	2	70.63202	188.79	<.0001
N/T × Musician/nonmusician	8.88994	2	4.44497	11.88	<.0001
Dissonance/Consonance (D/C)	93.65660	2	46.82830	147.59	<.0001
D/C × Musician/nonmusician	5.55198	2	2.77599	8.75	<.001
Dull/Bright timbre (D/B)	20.02381	2	10.01190	29.95	<.0001
D/B × Musician/nonmusician	5.20938	2	2.60469	7.79	<.001
Smooth/Percussive (S/P)	43.09794	2	21.54897	61.48	<.0001
S/P × Musician/nonmusician	4.92663	2	2.46331	7.03	<.001
Soft/Loud (S/L)	80.90884	2	40.45442	234.19	<.0001
S/L × Musician/nonmusician	5.71876	2	2.85938	16.55	<.001
Simple/Complex texture (S/C)	29.05241	2	14.52621	50.49	<.0001
S/C × Musician/nonmusician	2.96056	2	1.48028	5.14	<.01
Little or no/Rich embellish-					
ment (L/R)	29.94804	2	14.97402	65.07	<.0001
L/R × Musician/nonmusician	0.26964	2	0.13482	0.59	N.S.

Table 4
Preference Means and Standard Deviations Broken Down by Level of Musical Characteristics

Scale	Group	Level of musical characteristics *		
		Low	Moderate	High
Slow/Fast	Both groups (*N* = 449)	3.27 (1.03)	3.88 (1.04)	3.95 (1.13)
	Musicians (*n* = 180)	3.82 (1.06)	4.33 (1.01)	4.38 (1.16)
	Nonmusicians (*n* = 269)	2.91 (0.84)	3.58 (0.95)	3.65 (1.02)
Redundant/Different pitches	Both groups (*N* = 449)	3.75 (1.22)	3.26 (1.10)	4.09 (1.08)
	Musicians (*n* = 180)	4.24 (1.26)	3.86 (1.13)	4.43 (1.03)
	Nonmusicians (*n* = 269)	3.42 (1.07)	2.86 (0.87)	3.86 (1.06)
Nontonal/Tonal centered	Both groups (*N* = 449)	3.67 (1.16)	3.29 (1.10)	4.14 (1.09)
	Musicians (*n* = 180)	4.16 (1.20)	3.87 (1.13)	4.48 (1.03)
	Nonmusicians (*n* = 269)	3.33 (1.01)	2.90 (0.89)	3.91 (1.08)
Dissonance/Consonance	Both groups (*N* = 449)	3.44 (1.16)	3.63 (1.07)	4.11 (1.07)
	Musicians (*n* = 180)	3.98 (1.21)	4.14 (1.09)	4.47 (1.00)
	Nonmusicians (*n* = 269)	3.08 (0.97)	3.29 (0.91)	3.87 (1.05)
Dull/Bright timbre	Both groups (*N* = 449)	3.54 (1.16)	3.70 (1.09)	3.87 (1.08)
	Musicians (*n* = 180)	4.09 (1.20)	4.21 (1.10)	4.24 (1.04)
	Nonmusicians (*n* = 269)	3.17 (0.96)	3.36 (0.94)	3.62 (1.03)
Smooth/Percussive	Both groups (*N* = 449)	3.90 (1.02)	3.44 (1.06)	3.76 (1.25)
	Musicians (*n* = 180)	4.27 (0.97)	3.98 (1.10)	4.28 (1.29)
	Nonmusicians (*n* = 269)	3.65 (0.97)	3.08 (0.87)	3.41 (1.09)
Soft/ Loud	Both groups (*N* = 449)	3.45 (1.02)	3.58 (1.08)	4.07 (1.08)
	Musicians (*n* = 180)	4.01 (1.00)	4.09 (1.11)	4.43 (1.07)
	Nonmusicians (*n* = 269)	3.08 (0.84)	3.25 (0.93)	3.82 (1.01)
Simple/Complex texture	Both groups (*N* = 449)	3.49 (1.02)	3.80 (1.01)	3.81 (1.24)
	Musicians (*n* = 180)	3.98 (1.00)	4.20 (1.02)	4.35 (1.26)
	Nonmusicians (*n* = 269)	3.16 (0.89)	3.53 (0.92)	3.45 (1.08)
No/Rich embellishment	Both groups (*N* = 449)	3.58 (1.08)	3.91 (1.07)	3.61 (1.08)
	Musicians (*n* = 180)	4.03 (1.13)	4.40 (1.08)	4.10 (1.05)
	Nonmusicians (*n* = 269)	3.28 (0.93)	3.59 (0.93)	3.28 (0.97)

Note. Standard deviations indicated in parentheses.
* Low refers to the left side of the musical characteristic scale (e.g., slow), moderate refers to the middle of the scale, and high refers to the right side of the scale (e.g., fast).

On the basis of 24 judges' ratings, a mean was computed for each characteristic for each excerpt. Then excerpts were ranked from the lowest to the highest for each musical characteristic scale. Based on these ranks, the 12 excerpts receiving the lowest 33% of the distribution of means were classified as low in the scale characteristic, the 12 excerpts receiving the middle 33% of the distribution of means were classified as moderate in the scale characteristic, and the 12 excerpts receiving the highest 33% of the distribution of means were classified as high in the scale characteristic. Table 2 presents the distribution of excerpts across the three levels (low, moderate, high) for each musical characteristic. It also presents the ranges of the mean characteristic ratings for each scale level. The 36 excerpts were well distributed across the three levels of each musical characteristic. On the basis of these results, a profile of musical characteristics was derived for each item.

To investigate the relationship between musical characteristics and world music preferences, a mixed-design analysis of variance (ANOVA) was used with one between-subjects factor (musician/nonmusician) and two within-subjects factors: (1) nine musical characteristic scales and (2) three levels within each musical characteristic scale (low/moderate/high). Table 3 shows the results, which revealed significant differences ($p < .0001$) for all main effects and interaction effects. At a general level, results indicated that musicians' and nonmusicians' preferences for world musics were significantly different. As can be seen in Table 4, musicians' means were significantly higher than those for nonmusicians. In addition, different musical characteristic scales were significant in world music preference ratings, and the levels of musical characteristic effects were significant.

Table 3 also shows results for the individual musical characteristic scales. All musical characteristics scales were significant ($p < .0001$). Except for the little or no embellishment—rich embellishment scale, all interaction effects with the between-subjects factor of musician/nonmusician were significant ($p < .05$).

To locate specific mean differences, levels within each musical characteristic scale were compared. All means across the three levels of each scale were significantly different ($p < .05$). Exceptions to this trend were found for mean comparisons between: (1) moderate and high in the levels of simple—complex texture and (2) low and high levels of little or no embellishment—rich embellishment. Means and standard deviations for preference (broken down by musical characteristic) and their levels are presented in Table 4.

Trends of preference means (see Figure 1) indicated that the entire sample ($N = 449$) preferred excerpts that were characterized as relatively fast, having many different pitches, tonal-centered, consonant, bright timbre, smooth, loud, complex or moderately complex in texture, and moderate in the richness of embellishment. The subjects in the sample tended to prefer less those excerpts that were relatively slow, moderately redundant in pitch, moderately tonal-centered, dissonant, of dull timbre, moderately percussive, soft, simple in texture, and with little or no embellishment or rich embellishment. Three

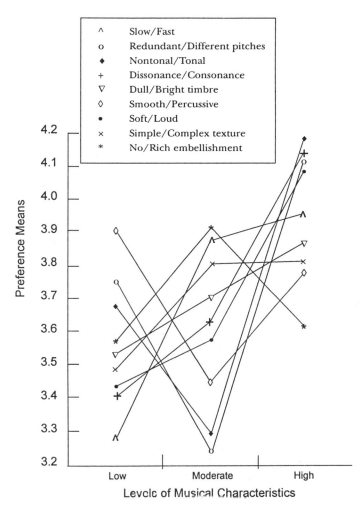

Figure 1. Preference means by levels of musical characteristics.

trends can be observed: (1) mean preferences increased significantly across the low to the high levels in slow/fast, dissonance/consonance, dull/bright timbre, soft/loud, and simple/complex texture scales; (2) a U-shaped relationship with preference (i.e., preference for the extremes) is found for redundant/different pitches, nontonal/tonal-centered, and smooth/percussive scales; and (3) an inverted-U relationship is found between preference and the little or no embellishment/rich embellishment scale (i.e., preference for the moderately embellished excerpts).

While Figure 1 shows the trends of the entire sample ($N = 449$), a different picture emerged when musician/nonmusician characteristics were in interaction with the levels of eight musical characteristics. This was the case for all scales except for the little or no embellishment/rich embellishment scale. Table 4 also presents the preference means broken down according to musical characteristic and the musician/nonmusician subgroups.

Although both musicians and nonmusicians showed a trend of increasing preference means as the level of tempo became faster, the increase (particularly between low and moderate) for nonmusicians was greater than that for musicians. Significant interaction effects were identified in the low and moderate comparison ($p < .01$) and in the low and high comparison ($p < .05$). This indicated that difference in tempo was a more significant factor in nonmusicians' world music preference ratings than for musicians.

Although both musicians and nonmusicians preferred world musical excerpts with greater differences in pitch, this was more the case for nonmusicians than for musicians. Interaction effects were significant in all comparisons for the redundant/different pitches scale. The interaction effect in the low and moderate comparison was significant at .01 level, the interaction effect in the moderate and high comparison was significant at .0001 level, and the interaction effect in the low and high comparison was significant at .05 level. In addition, the highest preference mean for nonmusicians (different pitches) was identical to the lowest preference mean for musicians (moderately redundant pitches).

The results for the nontonal/tonal centered scale presented a very similar case to that presented by the redundant/different pitches scale. Again, a U-shaped relationship was found for both groups; the degree of rise and fall in the curve for nonmusicians was greater than for musicians. The interaction effect in the low and moderate comparison was significant at .01 level, the interaction effect in the moderate and high comparison was significant at .0001 level, and the interaction effect in the low and high comparison was significant at .05 level. In addition, the highest preference mean for nonmusicians (tonal-centered) was very close to the lowest preference mean for musicians (moderately tonal-centered).

Concerning consonance, both musicians and nonmusicians showed higher preference means when the excerpts were more consonant. Significant interaction effects occurred only in the comparisons between the moderate and high levels ($p < .01$) and between the low and high levels ($p < .01$). In both cases, the nonmusician sample showed a larger increase in preference means as the excerpts were more consonant.

Preference means were higher for both musician/nonmusician groups as the timbre of the excerpts was brighter. As with the dissonant/consonant scale, significant interaction effects occurred only in the comparisons between the moderate and high levels ($p < .01$) and between the low and high levels ($p < .01$). In addition, nonmusicians also showed a significantly greater increase in preference means in both cases. As for the slow/fast variable, timbre apparently was a

Table 5
MANOVA Results of Composite Preferences by Musician/Nonmusician

Source	Wilks	df	F	p
Musician/nonmusician	.753	9, 439	16.036	< .001

Univariate *F*-tests with *df* (1, 447)

Source	SS (between)	SS (error)	F	p	r²
Congo	69.342	610.005	50.813	< .001	.10
Malawi	115.408	702.022	73.484	< .001	.14
Nigeria	75.714	734.491	46.078	< .001	.09
China	72.906	631.362	51.617	< .001	.10
Japan	137.818	552.035	111.596	< .001	.20
Korea	79.511	502.166	70.776	< .001	.14
Cuba	68.804	674.563	45.593	< .001	.09
Mexico	1.381	845.457	.730	N.S.	
Peru	64.906	536.665	54.061	< .001	.11

greater factor in preference ratings of nonmusicians than those of musicians.

In the U-shaped trend of the smooth/percussive scale, results showed that nonmusicians preferred smooth excerpts over the percussive ones, while musicians preferred the extremes (smooth and percussive) at about the same level. Significant interaction effects only occurred between the low and moderate comparison ($p < .0001$) and the low and high comparison ($p < .05$). Again, the changes according to level for nonmusicians were greater than those for musicians.

Results also showed that both groups had a higher preference for louder excerpts. As a parallel to the other musical characteristics, the changes according to level in the nonmusician sample were significantly greater than those for the musician sample. Significant interaction effects were found in the comparisons between the moderate and high levels ($p < .0001$) and the low and high levels ($p < .0001$).

The simple/complex texture scale was unique in that a different trend was found for the two samples. Musicians showed a consistently rising trend from the simplest excerpts to the most complex excerpts. For nonmusicians, the increase of preference means from simple to moderate texture was greater than for musicians, and the preference means became slightly declined from the moderate to complex levels, while the musicians continued to increase their preference ratings. Interactions for musician/nonmusician and the low and moderate levels and the moderate and high levels were significant ($p < .01$).

To compare the preference ratings between the two subject groups (musicians and nonmusicians) by country category, a multivariate analysis of variance (MANOVA) was computed. Table 5 shows the MANOVA results of composite preferences for excerpts from the nine countries. The multivariate and univariate results were significant at .001 level except for the composite preference for Mexican excerpts, which was nonsignificant. Musicians had consistently higher preference means than did nonmusicians across all musical styles. Again, all standard deviations were within a reasonably narrow range ($SD = .96$ to 1.39) (see Table 6). Table 6 also shows that both subject groups had the highest mean preference ratings for the Mexican excerpts and the lowest mean preference ratings for the Japanese and Korean excerpts. Where significant differences occurred, the variable of musician/nonmusician explained 9% (Nigerian and Cuban excerpts) to 20% (Japanese excerpts) of variance in preference.

Pearson product-moment correlations between world music preference and familiarity were computed. Based on the ratings of four excerpts within each country category, composite preference and familiarity ratings were used. The last column in Table 6 shows the correlation coefficients between preference and familiarity. All correlations were significant at .01 level. The coefficients were, from the lowest to the highest, .38 (Korea), .41 (Mexico), .44 (Japan), .45 (Congo and Peru), .46 (China), .47 (Cuba), .48 (Malawi), and .49 (Nigeria). With the composite of all categories (36 excerpts), the correlation between preference and familiarity was .47. Thus, there was a significant correlation between preference and familiarity ratings for all world music categories, and approximately 14% to 24% of the variance in preference was explained by familiarity. The familiarity variable for Asian excerpts tended to explain less variance in preference, while familiarity for African excerpts tended to explain relatively more variance in preference.

DISCUSSION

Results showed that musical characteristics, musical training (musicians versus nonmusicians), and familiarity were significant factors in world music preferences. Results also showed that, for each musical characteristic, mean differences among low, moderate, and high levels were significantly different except for that between moderately complex and complex texture and between little or no embellishment and rich embellishment. Therefore, musical characteristics were important in predicting preference across the musical excerpts. The profile of musical characteristics that the entire sample preferred most included fast tempo, loud, tonal-centered, many different pitches, consonant, moderately embellished, smooth sounding, moderate or complex texture, and bright timbre.

As a parallel to the results of literature concerning both Western music preference (e.g., LeBlanc, 1981) and world music preferences (e.g., Fung, 1992), both musicians and nonmusicians preferred faster excerpts in the present study. However, there was a greater increase in preference means between the slow and the moderate excerpts than

Table 6
Descriptive Statistics for Preference by Country and Regional Categories

Combined categories	Number of items	Musicians (n = 180)			Nonmusicians (n = 269)			Combined (N = 449)			
		Mean (SD)	Skew.	Kurt.	Mean (SD)	Skew.	Kurt.	Mean (SD)	Skew.	Kurt.	r*
Congo	4	4.29 (1.25)	-.04	-.40	3.49 (1.11)	.10	-.57	3.81 (1.23)	.14	-.43	.45
Malawi	4	4.10 (1.38)	.04	-.47	3.06 (1.16)	.38	-.18	3.48 (1.35)	.35	-.34	.48
Nigeria	4	4.48 (1.36)	-.21	-.39	3.64 (1.23)	.21	-.53	3.97 (1.35)	.10	-.59	.49
China	4	4.20 (1.25)	.01	.33	3.37 (1.15)	.16	-.55	3.70 (1.25)	.16	-.42	.46
Japan	4	3.65 (1.25)	.39	-.13	2.52 (1.01)	.55	-.44	2.97 (1.24)	.61	.03	.44
Korea	4	3.52 (1.19)	.22	-.13	2.66 (0.96)	.65	.65	3.01 (1.14)	.56	.06	.38
Cuba	4	4.13 (1.34)	-.13	-.52	3.34 (1.15)	.29	-.35	3.66 (1.29)	.20	-.52	.47
Mexico	4	4.68 (1.36)	-.29	-.71	4.57 (1.39)	-.37	-.45	4.61 (1.38)	-.34	-.54	.41
Peru	4	4.56 (1.06)	-.09	-.21	3.78 (1.12)	-.12	-.71	4.09 (1.16)	-.13	-.44	.45
Africa	12	4.29 (1.26)	-.08	-.33	3.40 (1.07)	.17	-.42	3.76 (1.23)	.21	-.35	.50
Asia	12	3.79 (1.09)	.31	.08	2.85 (0.89)	.29	-.17	3.23 (1.08)	.47	.21	.45
Latin America	12	4.46 (0.98)	-.21	.11	3.90 (0.97)	-.22	-.55	4.12 (1.01)	-.17	-.25	.47
World	36	4.18 (1.01)	-.03	.07	3.38 (0.86)	-.08	-.56	3.70 (1.00)	.13	-.09	.47

* Pearson product-moment correlations between preference and familiarity ratings. All coefficients $p < .01$.

between the moderate and fast excerpts. This indicated that there may be an optimal level of tempo increase in relation to preference ratings. Loudness level was another significant musical characteristic. Subjects liked louder excerpts. This seems to contrast with results for pure tone preferences (Hedden, 1974; Martindale & Moore, 1990) in which softer tones were preferred. Listeners may not prefer louder dynamic levels in relatively simpler musical stimuli. In contrast, for music with new, unfamiliar, and perhaps greater amounts of information (world musics), listeners may prefer louder dynamics.

Whether the excerpts were tonal or nontonal also played an important role in subjects' preference ratings. Although the trend was U-shaped in relation to preference ratings, the tonal excerpts received the highest preference mean among all musical characteristics at any level. The moderately tonal excerpts received the lowest preference mean. The preference mean for excerpts categorized as nontonal was in between the two other levels (moderately tonal and tonal). The moderately tonal excerpts seemed to have ambiguous pitch information. In cases where the excerpts were nontonal, non–pitch-related music such as untuned drumming was usually featured. The results suggest that subjects may prefer excerpts with clear tonal patterns. A previous study (Fung, 1992) indicated a significant linear correlation between nontonal/tonal and world music preferences of graduate music students, with 18% of the variance in preference explained by the tonal characteristic. This discrepancy (U-shaped versus linear relationships) may be due to the use of different samples of musics and/or different samples of subjects (graduate students versus undergraduate students).

Similar to the tonal/nontonal characteristics, the relationship between pitch redundancy and preference was U-shaped. Listeners preferred excerpts that had many different pitches, followed by excerpts that were highly redundant in pitch, and the moderate level of pitch redundancy was the least preferred. This result was in contrast to McMullen's (1974) study with objectively defined melodic redundancy. McMullen found that low or intermediate levels of redundancy were preferred over a high redundancy level and that pentatonic and diatonic melodies were preferred over chromatic melodies. The discrepancy in results may be due to one or more of the following reasons: (1) a difference between McMullen's objective definition of redundancy and the present study's use of perceptual judgments of redundancy, (2) the age difference in the samples (4th- to 12th-graders versus college students), and (3) a difference in the sample of musical styles (McMullen's original melodies versus commercial recordings of world musics in this study).

Consonance was another important musical characteristic in that there was a linear relationship between consonance and preference. These results paralleled those of Gibson (1987) and Fung (1992), but were in contrast to those of Martindale and Moore (1990). Although Gibson's (1987) and Martindale and Moore's (1990) studies used electronic tones, subjects in Gibson's study did not provide a rating for consonance, whereas subjects in Martindale and Moore's study provided ratings for both preference and consonance. The present results also parallel those of Fung (1992), in which world music styles were used and a significant linear correlation between preference and consonance was found. It seems that more consonant excerpts may be preferred over the more dissonant ones regardless of electronic tones versus world musics.

Level of embellishment was the only musical characteristic that had an inverted-U relationship with preference in this study. Subjects liked excerpts with moderate levels of embellishment the most. Excerpts with little or no embellishment and excerpts with rich embellishment were least preferred, and the preference means were not significantly different at the two extreme levels of embellishment. The results for degree of embellishment may be related to Walker's (1981) theory of psychological complexity and preference. This may be in line with the results for complexity in Steck and Machotka's (1975) study in which complexity level was defined as the inverse of duration of tones: more complex excerpts had shorter tone durations. When complexity is defined in relation to embellishment, results for excerpts in this study reflect a complete inverted-U relationship with preference.

With a few exceptions, the magnitude of all significant effects of musical characteristics was generally greater for nonmusicians than for musicians. This suggests that musicians may perceive world musics as one large category of music. Individual musical characteristics have somewhat less influence in the preferences of musicians than in the preferences of nonmusicians. Madsen and Geringer (1990) found that, while listening to Western orchestral music, musicians were significantly more attentive to "everything" (combining rhythm, dynamics, timbre, and melody) than were nonmusicians. In addition, musicians significantly focused more on rhythm and melody, while nonmusicians significantly focused more on dynamics and timbre. This difference in the focus of attention between musicians and nonmusicians may have affected the differences in preference responses between the two groups in the present study.

When musicians and nonmusicians were compared, there were significant differences in preference ratings and responses to different levels of musical characteristics. Musicians had significantly higher preference ratings than did nonmusicians. Even for musicians, mean preference ratings indicated only moderate levels of preference.

When the musical styles were examined at the level of country, both musicians and nonmusicians had identical rank orders of preferences for the first seven of nine country styles. The rank order of preference means for the first seven country styles were as follows: Mexico, Peru, Nigeria, Congo, China, Cuba, and Malawi. The order of the last two were reversed among musicians and nonmusicians: Japan followed by Korea for musicians, and Korea followed by Japan for nonmusicians. Results corroborated previous work in world music preferences (Fung, 1992, 1994) in that Korean musical excerpts were preferred least. Korean music might require a longer period of listening or exposure in order to gain higher preference ratings. When examining Korean excerpts in relation to the musical characteristic ratings, these excerpts were generally slow, redundant in pitch, nontonal to moderately tonal, moderately consonant, moderately dull in timbre, moderately percussive, soft, simple in texture, and had little or no embellishment. In contrast, the most preferred excerpts were Mexican excerpts, which tended to be characterized as moderate to fast in tempo, having many different pitches, highly tonal, very consonant, bright in timbre, smooth-sounding, loud, and moderately complex in texture.

When country categories were combined within a region, the rank order of preference means was Latin America, Africa, and Asia. This order of preference was identical for both the musician and nonmusician samples. Due to the cultural and musical influences of the Western world, Latin American musical excerpts received the highest ratings for familiarity and preference. These excerpts tended to emphasize some characteristics that are common to Western music (e.g., tonal, consonant, and having many different pitches). African music, however, possessed some rhythmic characteristics that have influenced Western music. These characteristics include syncopation, complex rhythmic overlay, and percussive sound. Indigenous Asian music has had relatively little influence on Western music, and there are relatively few common characteristics between Asian music and Western music. It is also speculated that this rank order (Latin American, African, and Asian) reflects students' preferences for musical styles from closer geographic regions. Considering the United States as the center, a series of concentric circles may be seen expanding from the center to include further geographic regions. A world music curriculum might begin with the identification of the learner's culture by the student, and then expand to include other cultures and eventually include music from many cultures around the globe. This is rather different from some researchers who have suggested the inclusion of a palette of musical cultures through musical aesthetics, comprehensive musicianship, and creativity approaches (Campbell, 1991; Elliot, 1989, 1990; Standifer, 1990). The question of whether the music itself (e.g., rhythm, tonality) or the cultural origin of the music (e.g., African, Asian) plays a more important role in music preference, perception, and learning is unanswered in this study.

Nevertheless, some practical implications could be drawn for music educators. Music educators could apply results of this study to the presentation of short world music excerpts for listening in music classrooms. When identifying pieces for listening, music teachers would be well-advised to consider musical characteristics present in the pieces they select for college students (both music majors and nonmusic majors). Musical characteristics that were most related to higher preferences included fast, loud, tonal-centered, having many different pitches, consonant, moderately embellished, smooth sounding, moderate or complex in texture, and bright timbre. At least for early listening experiences in world musical styles for college listeners, teachers might select pieces that have these musical characteristics. When college teachers select a musical style among all world music styles for the beginning portion of a curriculum, teachers might select the styles with which their students (mostly European/White) feel closest culturally, such as Latin American styles rather than Asian styles. Teachers may also need to take into account the geographic regions of the music classrooms. It may also be speculated that many Latin American styles reflect some of the most preferred musical characteristics (e.g., tonal, having many different pitches, consonant, and relatively fast).

Familiarity has consistently been a significant factor across studies of music preference representing a range of musical styles. With this in mind, teachers can expand and increase students' preferences by instruction, exposure, or other means that allow students to become more familiar with the musics. The familiarity issue complements the issue of concentric circles. Using the concentric-circle idea described earlier, teachers who are introducing world musics might start with the musical styles with which students are most familiar, and then gradually introduce musical styles from more distant geographic and cultural sources.

Another important practical implication of this study is that teachers need to be aware of the background characteristics of students, particularly their musical training. Teachers who teach world music classes for nonmusicians might choose pieces with careful consideration of musical characteristics, because levels of changes in musical characteristics seem to play a greater role in nonmusicians' preferences. Furthermore, for musicians, world music pieces with higher levels of textural complexity can be presented.

Several directions for further research can be identified. First, future research should expand the sample of world musics. Only instrumental excerpts were used in this study, and these came from only nine countries. Vocal excerpts and excerpts beyond the nine countries should be considered. Other populations such as children and students at different levels should also be included in future research. Second, since this study found that musics from various cultures had different preference ratings, it would be helpful to determine the extent to which cultural sources of musics affect preference. Third, cross-cultural studies are warranted. Campbell (1993) conducted a case study with Indochinese students. However, to date, there has not been a comprehensive study to examine responses of listeners of various cultures. Cultural differences of listeners may interact with the cultural sources of music, and the interaction may vary by cultural group. Fourth, further research is necessary to determine whether results of preference studies are generalizable for longer excerpts, including complete pieces.

The inclusion of world musics in the classroom is imperative. In recent years, some music educators have made a special effort to establish curricular foundations in this area. There is a strong desire to involve a broad range of individuals in the process, including music education researchers and practitioners, ethnomusicologists, and psychologists. Research in world musics and their application to classroom settings will continue to have important implications for music educators. In our increasingly culturally diverse American society, such research results will ultimately enrich education from social, musical, and global perspectives.

REFERENCES

Asmus, E. P. (1989). The effect of music teachers on students' motivation to achieve in music. *Canadian Journal of Research in Music Education, 30,* 14–21.

Burke, M. J., & Gridley, M. C. (1990). Musical preferences as a function of stimulus complexity and listeners' sophistication. *Perceptual and Motor Skills, 71* (2), 687–690.

Campbell, P. S. (1991). *Lessons from the world.* New York, NY: Schirmer Books.

Campbell, P. S. (1993). Cultural issues and school music participation: The new Asians in American schools. *The Quarterly Journal of Music Teaching and Learning, 4* (2), 45–56.

Darrow, A., Haack, P., & Kuribayashi, F. (1987). Descriptors and preferences for Eastern and Western musics by Japanese and American nonmusic majors. *Journal of Research in Music Education, 35,* 237–248.

Elliot, D. J. (1989). Key concepts in multicultural music education. *International Journal of Music Education, 13,* 11–18.

Elliot, D. J. (1990). Music as culture: Toward a multicultural concept of arts education. *Journal of Aesthetic Education, 24* (1), 147–166.

Finnäs, L. (1989). How can musical preferences be modified? *Bulletin of the Council for Research in Music Education,* no. 102, 1–58.

Flowers, P. J. (1980). Relationship between two measures of music preference. *Contributions to Music Education, 8,* 47–54.

Fung, C. V. (1990). *Preferences of selected instrumental students for various tuning systems.* Unpublished master's thesis, Baylor University, Waco, TX.

Fung, C. V. (1992). Musicians' preference and perception for world music. *Southeastern Journal of Music Education, 4,* 178–190.

Fung, C. V. (1994). Undergraduate nonmusic majors' world music preference and multicultural attitudes. *Journal of Research in Music Education, 42* (1), 45–57.

Geisler, H. G. (1990). A cross-cultural exploration of musical preference among Chinese and Western adolescents in Hong Kong (Doctoral dissertation, University of Michigan, 1990). *Dissertation Abstracts International, 51,* 1151A.

Geringer, J. M., & Madsen, C. K. (1981). Verbal and operant discrimination—Preference for tone quality and intonation. *Psychology of Music, 9* (1), 26–30.

Gibson, S. M. (1987). *Judgments of preference on simultaneous sounded bitonal frequencies in the monaural and dichotic conditions.* Paper presented at the annual meeting of the Western Psychological Association in Long Beach, CA.

Hargreaves, D. J. (1988). Verbal and behavioral responses to familiar and unfamiliar music. *Current Psychological Research and Reviews, 6* (4), 323–330.

Hargreaves, D., Messerschmidt, P., & Rubert, C. (1980). Musical preference and evaluation. *Psychology of Music, 8* (1), 13–18.

Hedden, S. K. (1974). Preferences for single tone stimuli. *Journal of Research in Music Education, 22,* 136–142.

Heingartner, A., & Hall, J. V. (1974). Affective consequences in adults and children of repeated exposure to auditory stimuli. *Journal of Personality and Social Psychology, 29* (6), 719–723.

Hicken, L. W. (1992). Relationship among selected listener characteristics and musical preference (Doctoral dissertation, Indiana University, 1991). *Dissertation Abstracts International, 53,* 1089A.

Huber, J., & Holbrook, M. B. (1980). The determinants of esthetic value and growth. *Advances in Consumer Research, 7,* 121–126.

Kant, I. (1987). Critique of judgment (W. S. Pluhar, Trans.). Indianapolis, IN: Hackett Publishing. (Original work published 1790)

LeBlanc, A. (1981). Effects of style, tempo, and performing medium on children's music preference. *Journal of Research in Music Education, 29,* 143–156.

LeBlanc, A. (1987). The development of music preference in children. In J. C. Peery, I. W. Peery, & T. W. Draper (Eds.), *Music and child development* (pp. 137–157). New York: Springer-Verlag.

LeBlanc, A., & McCrary, J. (1983). Effect of tempo on children's music preference. *Journal of Research in Music Education, 31,* 283–294.

Lomax, A. (1968). *Folk song style and culture.* Washington, D.C.: American Association for the Advancement of Science.

Madsen, C. K., & Geringer, J. M. (1990). Differential patterns of music listening: focus of attention of musicians versus nonmusicians. *Bulletin of the Council for Research in Music Education,* no.105, 45–57.

Martindale, C., & Moore, K. (1990). Intensity, dissonance, and preference for pure tones. *Empirical Studies of the Arts, 8* (2), 125–134.

May, W. V. (1985). Musical Style preferences and aural discrimination skills of primary grade school children. *Journal of Research in Music Education, 33,* 7–22.

McMullen, P. T. (1974). Influence of number of different pitches and melodic redundancy on preference responses. *Journal of Research in Music Education, 22,* 198–204.

Nakazawa, N. (1988). School music, environment, and music preferences: a comparison of Japanese students living in Japan and Japanese students living in the United States (Doctoral dissertation, Columbia University Teachers College, 1988). *Dissertation Abstracts International, 49,* 2575A.

Radocy, R. E. (1982). Preference for classical music: a test for the hedgehog. *Psychology of Music,* Special Issue, 91–95.

Russell, P. A. (1982). Relationship between judgments of the complexity, pleasingness and interestingness of music. *Current Psychological Research, 2,* 195–202.

Schmidt, C. P., & Zdzinski, S. F. (1993). Cited quantitative research articles in music education research journals, 1975–1990: A content analysis of selected studies. *Journal of Research in Music Education, 41,* 5–18.

Shah, S. M. (1990). *An investigation of subjects' preferences for music of their own or of other cultural groups.* Unpublished master's thesis, Indiana University, Bloomington, IN.

Shehan, P. K. (1981). Student preferences for ethnic music styles. *Contributions to Music Education, 9,* 21–28.

Shehan, P. K. (1984). The effect of instruction method on preference, achievement and attentiveness for Indonesian gamelan music. *Psychology of Music, 12,* 34–42.

Shehan, P. K. (1985). Transfer of preference from taught to untaught pieces of non-Western music genres. *Journal of Research in Music Education, 33,* 149–158.

Shehan, P. K. (1987). Stretching the potential of music: can it help reduce prejudices? *Update: Applications of Research in Music Education, 5* (2), 17–20.

Sims, W. L. (1987). Effect of tempo on music preference of preschool through fourth-grade children. In C. K. Madsen & C. A. Prickett (Eds.), *Applications of Research in Music Behavior* (pp.15–25). Tuscaloosa: University of Alabama Press.

Smith, K. C., & Cuddy, L. L. (1986). The pleasingness of melodic sequences: contrasting effects of repetition and rule-familiarity. *Psychology of Music, 14*, 17–32.

Standifer, J. A. (1990). Comprehensive musicianship: a multicultural perspective—Looking back to the future. *The Quarterly Journal of Music Teaching and Learning, 1* (3), 10–19.

Steck, L., & Machotka, P. (1975). Preference for musical complexity: effects of context. *Journal of Experimental Psychology: Human Perception and Performance, 104* (2), 170–174.

Walker, E. L. (1981). Hedgehog theory and music education. In Music Educators National Conference, *Documentary report of the Ann Arbor Symposium* (pp. 317–332). Reston, VA: Music Educators National Conference.

Wapnick, J. (1976). A review of research on attitude and preference. *Bulletin of the Council for Research in Music Education,* no. 48, 1–20.

Submitted April 28, 1994; accepted October 20, 1994.

XII.

Other Issues

in

Music Education

The purpose of this study was to examine the amount of time that children of different ages, sexes, and proficiency levels spent on various compositional processes while creating a melody. The author gave 60 children (ages 7, 9, and 11) 10 minutes to compose a song on an electronic keyboard and asked each child to play his or her song and repeat it. Analysis of the 10-minute compositional periods indicated the amount of exploration, development, repetition, and silence subjects used while composing. No significant differences were found in performance between the sexes. Subjects who demonstrated proficiency in replicating their songs differed significantly in the use of repetition and exploration from those subjects who did not. Results suggest that (a) improvisation is a more appropriate creative activity than composition for 7-year-olds; (b) repetition is a necessary process in composing replicable songs; and (c) 9- and 11-year-olds are capable of using exploration, development, and repetition in a manner consistent with reports of adult composers' compositional processes.

John Kratus, *Case Western Reserve University*

JRME 1989, VOLUME 37, NUMBER 1, PAGES 5–20

A Time Analysis of the Compositional Processes Used by Children Ages 7 to 11

Many music educators share the goal of developing creativity in students and advocate the use of creative activities as a means for actively involving students in exploring the dimensions of music (e.g., Biasini, Thomas, & Pogonowski, 1970; Choate, 1968; Choksy, Abramson, Gillespie, & Woods, 1986; Contemporary Music Project, 1966; Lasker, 1971; Marsh, 1970; Music Educators National Conference, 1986; Regelski, 1981). Despite such advocacy, creative activities are rarely used in music classes (Goodlad, 1984; Ling, 1974; Sherman, 1971; Webster, 1987). Schmidt and Sinor (1986) suggested that one reason for the disparity between professed goals and common practice is that little is currently understood about the creative process in music. This is particularly true in the case of music composition. In a discussion of the research related to the process of composition, Sloboda (1985) wrote: ". . . composition is

---

The author is indebted to Julia Budd, Amanda Matthews, and James Tinter for their assistance on this project. For copies of this article, contact John Kratus, Department of Music, Case Western Reserve University, Cleveland 44106.

the least studied and least well understood of all musical processes, and . . . there is no substantial psychological literature to review" (p. 103). A greater understanding of children's approach to composition can guide the development of more appropriate educational goals and activities.

To serve as a basis for creativity research, Webster (1987) developed a comprehensive model of creative thinking in music. According to the model, the nature of the creative process depends on certain enabling skills (e.g., musical aptitudes, conceptual understanding, craftsmanship, and aesthetic sensitivity) and enabling conditions (e.g., motivation, subconscious imagery, supportive environment, and various personality traits). Webster believes that the creative process alternates between two types of thought: divergent thinking, the generation of ideas or possible solutions; and convergent thinking, the selection of a single, "correct" solution based on the evaluation of known possibilities.

Movement between divergent and convergent thought occurs as one progresses through four stages: (a) preparation—understanding the dimensions of the problem and exploration of tentative solutions; (b) incubation—consideration of possible solutions and development of ideas; (c) illumination—arrival at tentative solutions; and (d) verification—evaluation and refinement of the final product.

Essays by adult composers and studies of adults' compositional behaviors tend to support this model. The process of composition, as described in these reports, is one of exploring and developing musical ideas, ultimately resulting in closure on a unique musical product. Sessions (1970) wrote that music composition encompasses a subconscious phase (i.e., preparation) during which musical patterns are improvised and a conscious phase of elaboration and development of musical ideas (i.e., incubation) through application of such musical principles as association, contrast, and balance. As the composer works, the relationships among the parts and the whole of the composition eventually become clear (i.e., illumination), and the composer evaluates the work (i.e., verification). Bennett's (1976) interviews with eight composers resulted in the development of a model of musical composition that follows a similar sequence. According to Bennett, composition begins with the discovery of a germinal idea (preparation), which is then expanded into a first draft (incubation). This is followed by a period of elaboration and refinement (illumination), culminating in a final draft with possible revisions (verification).

The compositional processes used by adult composers in case studies by Reitman (1965) and Sloboda (1985) also coincide with Webster's stages. Although this literature offers some insight into adult compositional processes, there is no published research to suggest that children compose in a similar manner.

Sloboda (1985) suggested four sources of data for studying compositional processes: (a) composers' sketches and notebooks, (b) composers' comments about their compositional processes, (c) interviews with composers at work, and (d) observation of musical improvisation. Each of these approaches poses problems for the study of children's compositional processes. With the exception of some prodigies, most children do not make sketchbooks of musical compositions. Children are unlikely to be able to discuss meaningfully their compositional processes; even adult composers are notoriously unreliable at doing so (Perkins, 1981). Most children are unable to verbalize the reasons for their creative decisions as they compose, because the internalized rules underlying children's acts of production are largely unconscious (Lund & Duchan, 1983) and because comments on one's own cognitive processes are often inaccurate (Nesbit & Wilson, 1977). Although several researchers have examined children's improvisatory behaviors (Flohr, 1979; Freundlich, 1978; Moorhead & Pond, 1941–1951/1978), it would be a mistake to generalize these findings to the study of how children compose. Sloboda (1985) pointed out that "the constraints of improvisation—immediacy and fluency—make it likely that there are processes which improvisation and composition do not share" (p. 103). Unlike improvisation, composition allows time for reflection and revision of the musical product.

A solution to the methodological problem of studying children's compositional processes was suggested by Newell and Simon's investigation (1972) of problem-solving processes. In that study, researchers asked subjects to solve problems of chess, logic, and cryptarithmetic (i.e., arithmetic problems in which letters have been substituted for numbers, as in DONALD + GERALD = ROBERT). Subjects' overt behaviors (i.e., writing and verbalizing) were recorded and used as evidence of internal problem-solving processes. Similarly, the sounds children make on an instrument as they compose can be viewed as an audible analogue of their internal thought processes. In this way, researchers can study three compositional processes: exploration, development, and repetition. As children explore new musical ideas, the music they play sounds unlike music they played previously; as children develop musical ideas, the music they play sounds somewhat like music they played previously; and as children repeat or explore musical ideas, the music they play sounds the same as music they played previously.

Because composition is a dynamic process, researchers analyzing compositional processes should trace changes in the process over time. A time analysis of compositional processes can illustrate how these processes change as an individual child works through a compositional problem. This method of using the sounds made during composition to infer internal creative processes cannot show *why* a subject makes certain compositional decisions, but it does reveal *what* a subject does to explore, develop, and review musical ideas.

One reason for suspecting the existence of developmental differences in children's compositional processes can be found in some recent research that has revealed developmental differences in children's compositional products. Kratus (1985/1986) described developmental differences in the use of rhythm, melody, and motives in songs composed by children ages 5 to 11. Swanwick and Tillman (1986) reported developmental differences between ages 3 and 11 in children's use of structure and expression in their musical compositions. It may be that differences in created products are the result of differences in creative processes.

Distinguishing between process and product can be confusing, because the word *composition* refers to both process (the activity of composing) and product (the resulting music). For the purpose of this study, a composition, when referring to a product, is a unique sequence of pitches and durations that its composer can replicate. A composition reflects closure on a compositional problem. If one cannot replicate an original melody, then it can be inferred that there is no closure, and the music does not exist as a composed product. When referring to a process, composition is the act leading to the production of a unique, replicable sequence of pitches and durations.

The purpose of this study was to examine the use of exploration, development, repetition, and silence by children of different ages, sexes, and proficiency levels who were engaged in composing a melody on an electronic keyboard. The results of the study are reported in two parts. In the first part, I describe age and sex characteristics and differences in subjects' use of composition time. In the second part, I examine the components of the compositional process that are used in children's production of replicable songs. This is done by comparing the amount of time spent on exploration, development, repetition, and silence for those subjects who demonstrated proficiency by successfully composing and repeating a song to the amount of time spent on these compositional processes by subjects who did not demonstrate this proficiency and did not replicate their songs.

METHOD

The subjects were 60 children, ages 7, 9, and 11, including 10 boys and 10 girls from each age-group, chosen randomly from the student population of an elementary school in the suburbs of Cleveland. The 7-year-olds were in the first and second grades, the 9-year-olds were third and fourth graders, and the 11-year-olds were in the fifth and sixth grades. All children in the school participated in two 30-minute general music classes each week taught by a music specialist. The general music curriculum was an eclectic one and did not include compositional activities. To control for prior experience on a keyboard instrument, I excluded from the study any children who had taken piano or organ lessons or who had an electronic keyboard at home.

The sound source used in the composition task was a Casio PT-1, a small (13¼″ × 3¾″ × 1¼″ electronic keyboard with a range of a 17th. The tone setting was set to "piano," and the rhythmic ostinato function was not used.

I tested each subject individually in a small, quiet room in the school. Subjects sat at a table in front of the keyboard. To one side of the subject were a large clock with a second hand and a cassette tape recorder. I sat next to the subject to give instructions but moved to another part of the room once the subject began to compose.

To acquaint subjects with the instrument, I engaged them in several imitative games, requiring subjects to play steps, skips, and repeated notes from one end of the keyboard to the other. Subjects then received the following instructions, which explained the parameters of the task:

Your project this morning is to make up a song on the little piano. Your song will be a brand-new song, one that no one has ever heard before. You may use any white keys you wish, but your song should begin on the key marked with an "X" [middle C]. You will have 10 minutes to make up your song, and I will ask you to play your song two times for the tape recorder. Be sure you can remember your song, so that you can play it the same way two times. Do you have any questions?

Restrictions were placed on the use of available musical materials ("only the white keys") and on the starting pitch (middle C) to provide some degree of guidance and to help subjects begin the task. These restrictions are in accordance with Regelski's (1981) guidelines for using creative activities in general music classes: "If too much free choice is allowed . . . students can quickly become lost, waste time or lose interest for lack of guidance" (p. 294).

After answering questions, I pointed out the 10-minute limit on the clock so that subjects knew exactly when to finish. As necessary, I adjusted the clock to place the minute hand on an even 5-minute interval to make it easier for the subject to keep track of the time. Then I set the cassette tape recorder to "record." Once a subject played the first note of the composition, I started a stopwatch to time the 10-minute period. After 8 minutes, I told subjects, "You have 2 minutes left." At the end of the 10 minutes, I asked subjects to play their songs. After each song was played, I asked the subject to play the same song again.

Analysis of the Compositional Processes and Song Replication

The purpose of the first part of the analysis was to describe the compositional processes used by the subjects during the 10-minute sessions. The 10-minute sessions were divided into 120 intervals of 5 seconds each, and the compositional process used in each interval was categorized as being one of the following:

Exploration: The music sounds unlike music played earlier. No specific references to music played earlier can be heard.

Development: The music sounds similar to, yet different from, music played earlier. Clear references to music played earlier can be heard in the melody, the rhythm, or both.

Repetition: The music sounds the same as music played earlier.

Silence: No music is heard because of subject silence, subject statement or question, or my statement.

The analysis required judges to make an evaluation of the process employed every 5 seconds as they listened to the tapes. Judges recorded their evaluations on printed forms containing 120 numbered blanks by writing "E" (exploration), "D" (development), "R" (repetition), or "S" (silence) in the corresponding blanks. Judges timed the 5-second intervals using a watch with a second hand. If the judges heard more than one process during a single interval, they chose the process that made up most of the interval.

I analyzed all the tapes of the 10-minute composition periods. In addition, two independent judges analyzed 12 of the tapes of the subjects' compositional periods (20% of the total) to check the reliability of my observations. Both independent judges were pursuing graduate degrees in music education and were known to me as excellent musicians. For the reliability check, I selected tapes randomly using a table of random numbers and stratified the selection to include two tapes from members of each sex at each age level. I used a blind procedure of coding the tapes to hide the age and sex of the subjects from the independent judges.

I then totaled the number of observed 5-second intervals of exploration, development, repetition, and silence for each subject. The correlation between the totals that I derived for the 12 tapes and the totals that each of the two judges derived were used as an indicator of the reliability of my evaluations. These coefficients (see Table 1) were quite high, suggesting substantial congruence. Only my evaluations of compositional processes were used as the data for this study.

For the second part of the analysis, the two independent judges evaluated the degree to which each subject's song and its replication sounded alike, using the following 3-point rating scale.

3—Replication is the same as or almost the same as the original.

2—Some sections of the replication are the same as the original.

1—None or almost none of the replication is the same as the original.
The judges evaluated songs and replications from all 60 subjects, and the correlation between the judges' ratings was .71.

RESULTS

Age and Sex Differences

Table 2 shows the mean percentage of time used by subjects for exploration, development, repetition, and silence. (To facilitate the interpretation of the data in Tables 2 and 5 and Figures 1 through 5, I have converted the raw data from "the number of 5-second intervals used" to "the percentage of total time used." For example, sixty 5-second intervals of exploration equal 50% of the total time used.) The 7-year-olds devoted most of their composition time to exploration and spent relatively little time on development, repetition, and silence. For the 9-year-olds, exploration was the process used most often, and approximately one-half of their time was divided between development and repetition. The 11-year-olds divided their time more evenly among exploration, development, and repetition and most often used the development process. Girls and boys were similar in their use of composition time, with the girls using somewhat more repetition and development and less exploration and silence.

To determine whether there were age or sex differences in the use of compositional processes, I performed a series of four two-way analyses of variance on the data, using the number of 5-second intervals for each compositional process (exploration, development, repetition, and silence) as the dependent variables (see Table 3). Results indicated significant age differences in the use of exploration ($p < .001$), develop-

Table 1
Interjudge Reliability of Process Evaluations

Process	Judge 1	Judge 2
Exploration	.95	.92
Development	.76	.86
Repetition	.96	.88
Silence	.98	.98

ment ($p < .001$), and repetition ($p < .01$). No significant age differences ($p > .05$) were found in the use of silence, and there were no significant differences ($p > .05$) between boys and girls in the use of any of the four compositional processes.

Further examination of the differences using the Duncan Multiple Range Test reveals the following significant developmental differences ($p < .05$): 7-year-olds used more exploration than did 9- and 11-year olds, 7-year-olds used less repetition than did 11-year-olds, and 7-year-olds used less development than did 9- and 11-year-olds. No significant differences were found between 7- and 9-year-olds in their use of repetition or between 9- and 11-year-olds in their use of any of the four compositional processes.

A graphic representation of how subjects in the three age-groups used their composition time appears in Figures 1, 2, and 3. These charts illustrate a minute-by-minute composite account of how subjects divided each of the 10 minutes they were given among exploration, development, repetition, and silence.

As shown in Figure 1, exploration was the predominant process that 7-year-olds used throughout the 10-minute period. Although the amount of exploration decreased and the amount of repetition in-

Table 2
Mean Percentages of Time Devoted to Exploration, Development, Repetition, and Silence by Age and Sex

Source	Mean percentage of time use			
	Exploration	Development	Repetition	Silence
Age				
7 years	65.63	15.13	10.83	8.42
9 years	39.67	25.75	24.04	10.54
11 years	29.63	33.13	30.92	6.33
Sex				
Girls	41.42	25.58	26.47	6.53
Boys	48.53	23.75	17.39	10.33

Table 3
Summary of Two-Way Analyses of Variance, Age, and Sex

Source	Sum of squares	df	MS	F	p
		Exploration			
Age	19878.43	2	9939.22	10.63	<.001
Sex	1092.27	1	1092.27	1.17	N.S.
Age x Sex	10.03	2	5.02	0.01	N.S.
Error	50485.20	54	934.91		
Total	71465.93	59			
		Development			
Age	4716.30	2	2358.15	9.66	<.001
Sex	72.60	1	72.60	0.30	N.S.
Age x Sex	569.10	2	284.55	1.17	N.S.
Error	13178.40	54	244.04		
Total	18536.40	59			
		Repetition			
Age	6000.63	2	3000.32	5.17	<.01
Sex	1782.15	1	1782.15	3.07	N.S.
Age x Sex	271.30	2	135.65	0.23	N.S.
Error	31366.90	54	580.87		
Total	39420.98	59			
		Silence			
Age	255.03	2	127.52	0.51	N.S.
Sex	312.82	1	312.82	1.24	N.S.
Age x Sex	99.43	2	49.72	0.20	N.S.
Error	13570.90	54	251.31		
Total	14238.18	59			

Note. N.S. = nonsignificant

creased during the period, these changes were slight, with exploration of new musical material occupying a mean of 58% of the time during the last minute of 7-year-olds' allotted time; there was relatively little development of musical ideas.

For the 9-year-olds (Figure 2) there was a more dramatic and consistent decrease in the amount of exploration used over time from a mean of 63% in the 1st minute to a mean of 26% in the final minute. The type of process that predominated changed over time, as well. In the 6th and 7th minutes, development was used most often, and in the last 3 minutes, repetition was the predominant process used.

Exploration played an even smaller role in the composition periods of the 11-year-olds (see Figure 3). As in the composition periods of the 9-year-olds, the predominant processes used by the 11-year-olds changed

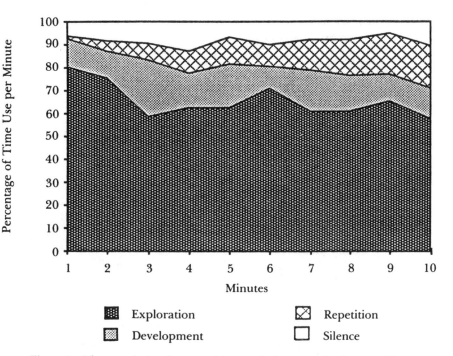

Figure 1. Time analysis of composition period, composite 7-year-olds.

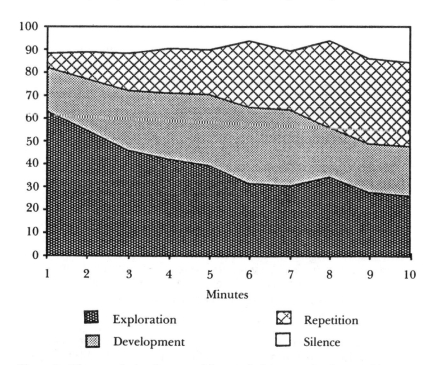

Figure 2. Time analysis of composition period, composite 9-year-olds.

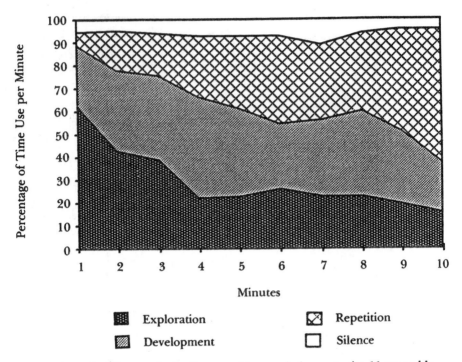

Figure 3. Time analysis of composition period, composite 11-year-olds.

over time from exploration to development to repetition. The 11-year-olds, however, tended to become more quickly engaged in developing and repeating their musical ideas, as shown by the sharp decline in the use of exploration during the first 4 minutes and the corresponding increase in development and repetition.

Replication Group Differences

To compare differences in the compositional processes used by subjects who replicated their songs with those of subjects who did not, I divided the subjects' data into two groups by using the ratings of the two independent judges. Both judges gave 7 subjects replication ratings of 1 (none or almost none of the replication is the same as the original), and both gave 20 subjects ratings of 3 (replication is the same or almost the same as the original). I did not use data from the other 33 subjects in this part of the analysis. The ages and sexes of members of the groups with 1 and 3 ratings are given in Table 4. Although the absolute numbers in Table 4 are too small for meaningful analysis, it is clear that more younger subjects had ratings of 1, whereas more older subjects had ratings of 3.

Table 5 shows the mean percentage of time the groups devoted to exploration, development, repetition, and silence. The subjects with 1 ratings spent more than three-quarters of the 10-minute period on

Table 4
Number of Subjects with Replication Ratings of 1 or 3

	Replication ratings of 1			Replication ratings of 3		
Age	Girls	Boys	Total	Girls	Boys	Total
7 years	2	3	5	1	1	2
9 years	1	1	2	5	2	7
11 years	0	0	0	7	4	11
Total	3	4	7	13	7	20

exploration and relatively little time on development, repetition, and silence. In contrast, the subjects with 3 ratings spent nearly half of their time on repetition. The results of a series of two-tailed t tests on the use of the four compositional processes indicated significant differences between the two groups in the use of exploration ($t = -12.73$, $df = 25$, $p < .001$) and repetition ($t = 6.47$, $df = 25$, $p < .001$). No significant differences ($p > .05$) were found in the use of development ($t = 1.65$, $df = 25$), or silence ($t = 1.72$, $df = 25$).

The composite graphic depictions of time use in Figures 4 and 5 illustrate the marked differences in the compositional processes of subjects in the two replication groups. Subjects who received replication ratings of 1 (see Figure 4) used an extensive amount of exploration throughout the 10-minute period. These subjects rarely, if ever, used repetition. Each successive minute of the composition period was similar to the last for these subjects. Given the lack of repetition, closure on a specific, replicable song could not be reached.

The composite time analysis for the subjects with replication ratings of 3 (Figure 5) illustrates a consistent increase in the use of repetition from 7% in the 1st minute to 67% in the 10th minute. Exploration, which occupied 54% of the 1st minute, quickly decreased to 13% in the 4th

Table 5
Mean Percentages of Time Devoted to Exploration, Development, Repetition, and Silence by Replication Group

Replication group	Mean percentage of time use			
	Exploration	Development	Repetition	Silence
1 Ratings	75.71	16.79	3.21	4.29
3 Ratings	21.85	32.00	49.65	16.50

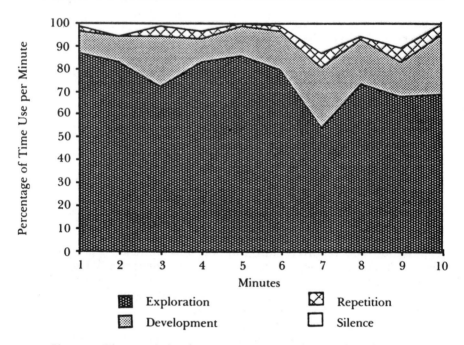

Figure 4. Time analysis of composition period, composite subjects with replication ratings of 1.

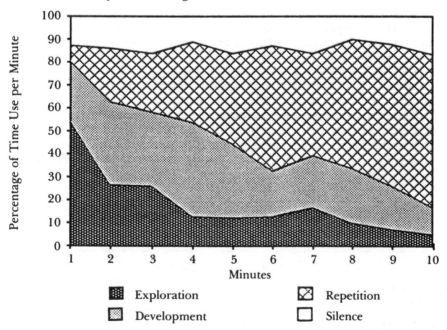

Figure 5. Time analysis of composition period, composite subjects with replication ratings of 3.

minute. Development was the predominant process in the 2nd, 3rd, and 4th minute. The time analysis shows that those subjects with replication ratings of 3 began to develop their musical ideas almost immediately: 26% of the 1st minute and 36% of the 2nd minute was spent on development. During the last few minutes of their compositional time, these subjects were rehearsing and making only minor changes in their songs, as indicated by the small amount of exploration and development. Quick work in exploring and developing during the beginning of the period and sufficient repetition near the end of the period enabled these subjects to produce specific, replicable songs.

DISCUSSION

These findings suggest developmental differences in children's strategies for composing music, and they also suggest that, as children grow from age 7 to 11, development and repetition become more prevalent compositional processes. The 7-year-old subjects "composed" primarily by trying one new musical idea after another (exploration). Reference to previously explored musical ideas was rare, as is shown by the small amount of time that 7-year-olds used to modify ideas (development) or review ideas (repetition). In other words, the creative act of composition for the 7-year-olds was very similar to the act of improvisation, and they used compositional time to explore new ideas rather than modify ideas. The 9- and 11-year-old subjects, on the other hand, used significantly more development and significantly less exploration, and 11-year-olds used significantly more repetition than did 7-year-olds. These results imply that 9- and 11-year-olds use compositional processes that are similar to those used by the adult composers (cited previously; see Bennett, 1976; Reitman, 1965; Sessions, 1970; Sloboda, 1985); both children and adults explore, develop, and repeat musical patterns while composing. The difference between adult composers and children is that adult composers possess a higher degree of enabling skills (Webster, 1987), which allow them to shape their musical materials in a more sophisticated manner.

The 9- and 11-year-old subjects also tended to change from one process to another while composing by emphasizing exploration first, then development, and finally repetition. The data from these subjects support three of the stages in Webster's model of creative thinking (1987). Subjects' emphasis on exploration at the beginning of the composition period is indicative of *preparation*; the emphasis next on development is indicative of *incubation*; and the emphasis on repetition toward the end of the period is indicative of *verification*. The evidence, however, does not imply that these are discrete, clearly defined stages. Subjects did not suddenly shift from using exploration to development to repetition. Rather, they intermingled processes, with one process and then another tending to predominate at various times.

There are at least four possible reasons for the 7-year-old subjects' infrequent use of development and repetition and their inability to change processes while composing: (a) They were unable to hold a melody in their memories while working on it, (b) they did not have strategies for developing musical patterns, (c) they had not formed an understanding of the process for solving problems posed by musical composition, and (d) their interest was directed toward the *process* of making sounds rather than toward the creation of a single *product* of a composed melody. Given the limitations on 7-year-olds' ability to use composition time to refine and repeat their musical ideas, it is reasonable to propose to educators that these students' first creative experiences in music should be improvisatory rather than compositional. This assumption is supported by the results of the second part of the study, which indicate that the composition of a replicable song typically involves substantial repetition. The 7-year-old subjects had no difficulty in generating musical ideas on a keyboard, as shown by their infrequent use of silence. The problem that many 7-year-olds encountered was that they did not or could not develop and review their musical ideas.

It may seem trivial to report that subjects who were able to replicate their songs explored less and repeated more while composing than did subjects who did not replicate their songs. Yet these differences imply great dissimilarities in subjects' approach to solving the given compositional problem. The subjects who replicated their songs understood that solving the problem at hand required repeated reference to the melody they were composing, and they were able to structure their time to leave sufficient time for rehearsal. It could be said that these subjects were *product oriented*; that is, they seemed to be more focused on the task of creating a single product than on exploring new sounds. On the other hand, the subjects who were unable to replicate their songs played one musical idea after another and did not use repetition effectively. Because they lacked reference to earlier material, their ideas did not take shape, and no closure occurred. These subjects could be said to be *process oriented*; that is, the process of exploring new sounds took precedence over the creation of a single composed product. This finding suggests that learning to compose a replicable song requires an understanding of the importance of repetition of musical ideas and a product orientation to the act of composition.

The results of this study suggest two pedagogical questions for further research. First, can children who are unable to compose a replicable song learn to compose? Second, can children who are already able to compose learn to compose in a more sophisticated manner? Results of research described in the educational literature suggest that the answer to both questions is "yes," because creative problem-solving strategies have been taught successfully to children in the context of other subjects (Tuma & Reif, 1980).

Finally, all 60 subjects were able to approach a creative musical task in a meaningful way by working the entire 10 minutes. Even those subjects who were unable to produce a replicable song were enthusiastic about using a keyboard to explore musical sounds. The results of this study imply that students as young as 7 years old can readily engage in creative musical improvisation and that students as young as 9 years old can compose with meaning by shaping their musical ideas. Teachers need not wait until their students' understanding of music is highly developed before introducing creative activities. In fact, creativity may be an important key to helping students gain an understanding of the syntax of music and the process of music making. It is possible that an understanding of the processes children use to compose may lead to a pedagogy based on compositional and improvisational activities to supplement current pedagogies based primarily on performance and listening experiences.

REFERENCES

Bennett, S. (1976). The process of musical creation: Interviews with eight composers. *Journal of Research in Music Education, 24*, 3–13.
Biasini, A., Thomas, R., & Pogonowski, L. (1970). *MMCP interaction.* Bardonia, NY: Media Materials.
Choate, R. A. (Ed.). (1968). *Documentary report of the Tanglewood Symposium.* Washington, DC: Music Educators National Conference.
Choksy, L., Abramson, R. M., Gillespie, A. E., & Woods, D. (1986). *Teaching music in the twentieth century.* Englewood Cliffs, NJ: Prentice-Hall.
Contemporary Music Project. (1966). *Experiments in musical creativity.* Washington, DC: Music Educators National Conference.
Flohr, J. W. (1979). Musical improvisation behavior in young children (Doctoral dissertation, University of Illinois at Urbana-Champaign, 1979). *Dissertation Abstracts International, 40*, 5355A. (University Microfilms No. 8009033)
Freundlich, D. A. (1978). The development of musical thinking: Case studies in improvisation (Doctoral dissertation, Harvard University, 1978). *Dissertation Abstracts International, 39*, 6617A. (University Microfilms No. 7909893)
Goodlad, J. I. (1984). *A place called school.* New York: McGraw-Hill.
Kratus, J. K. (1986). Rhythm, melody, motive, and phrase characteristics of original songs by children aged five to thirteen (Doctoral dissertation, Northwestern University, 1985). *Dissertation Abstracts International, 46*, 3281A. (University Microfilms No. 8600883)
Lasker, H. (1971). *Teaching creative music in secondary schools.* Boston: Allyn and Bacon.
Ling, S. J. (1974). Missing: Some of the most exciting creative moments of life. *Music Educators Journal, 61*(3), 40, 93–95.
Lund, N. J., & Duchan, J. F. (1983). *Assessing children's language in naturalistic contexts.* Englewood Cliffs, NJ: Prentice-Hall.
Marsh, M. V. (1970). *Explore and discover music: Creative approaches to music education in elementary, middle, and junior high schools.* New York: Macmillan.
Moorhead, G. E., & Pond, D. (1978). *Music of young children.* Santa Barbara, CA: Pillsbury Foundation for the Advancement of Music Education. (Original work published 1941–1951)
Music Educators National Conference. (1986). *The school music program: Description and standards* (2nd ed.). Reston, VA: Author.
Nesbit, R. E., & Wilson, J. D. (1977). Telling more than we can know: Verbal reports on mental processes. *Psychological Review, 84*, 231–259.
Newell, A., & Simon, H. A. (1972). *Human problem solving.* Englewood Cliffs, NJ: Prentice-Hall.
Perkins, D. L. (1981). *The mind's best work.* Cambridge, MA: Harvard University Press.
Regelski, T. A. (1981). *Teaching general music.* New York: Schirmer Books.
Reitman, W. R. (1965). *Cognition and thought.* New York: Wiley.

Schmidt, C. P., & Sinor, J. (1986). An investigation of the relationships among music audiation, musical creativity, and cognitive style. *Journal of Research in Music Education, 34,* 160–172.

Sessions, R. (1970). *Questions about music.* Cambridge, MA: Harvard University Press.

Sherman, R. W. (1971). Creativity and the condition of knowing in music. *Music Educators Journal, 58*(2), 18–22.

Sloboda, J. A. (1985). *The musical mind: The cognitive psychology of music.* Oxford, England: Clarendon Press.

Swanwick, K., & Tillman, J. (1986). The sequence of musical development: A study of children's composition. *British Journal of Music Education, 3,* 305–339.

Tuma, D. T., & Reif, F. (Eds.). (1980). *Problem solving and education: Issues in teaching and research.* Hillsdale, NJ: Erlbaum.

Webster, P. R. (1987). Conceptual bases for creative thinking in music. In J. C. Peery, I. W. Peery, & T. W. Draper (Eds.), *Music and child development* (pp. 158–174). New York: Springer-Verlag.

July 27, 1987

The purpose of the study was to ascertain whether significant differences exist in sixth-grade reading, language, and mathematics achievement between students who are excused from regular classroom activities for the study of instrumental music and students not studying instrumental music. Four public school districts from a major metropolitan area were used in the study. The study employed a single-sample multivariate matched-pairs design. Hotelling's T² for correlated samples was applied to the sixth-grade achievement data from the districts individually and computed with the Finn Multivariance program. Results from these analyses indicated that T² was not significant at the .05 level in all four school districts. Therefore, it was concluded that there was no significant difference in sixth-grade reading, language, and mathematics achievement between students who are excused from regular classroom activities for the study of instrumental music and students not studying instrumental music.

Edward J. Kvet, *Loyola University*

JRME 1985, VOLUME 33, NUMBER 1, PAGES 45–54

Excusing Elementary School Students from Regular Classroom Activities for the Study of Instrumental Music: The Effect on Sixth-Grade Reading, Language, and Mathematics Achievement

The scheduling of classes in the elementary school is a professional task that calls for judgments that are as much instructional as administrative. This process, therefore, involves unique challenges for school administrators and teachers. While classroom teachers ultimately are

---

The following article is based on the author's doctoral dissertation at the University of Cincinnati in Ohio, 1982.

For reprints of this article, contact Edward J. Kvet, College of Music, Loyola University, 6363 St. Charles Avenue, New Orleans, LA 70118.

provided with the flexibility to decide the amount, frequency, and timing of instruction for regular academic programs, this same flexibility is not available to either the special teacher or the classroom teacher in the scheduling of special classes.

Related to problems inherent in the scheduling of special classes are the concerns of music educators toward the scheduling of instrumental music in the elementary schools. Various educators have warned of the difficulties in scheduling elementary instrumental music (Edwards, 1969; Ford, 1967; Weerts, 1968). Specifically, Shaw (1968) believes that "this problem [scheduling] is one of the most significant aspects of the elementary instrumental music program in the public schools today" (p. 50).

A widespread scheduling practice in elementary schools is to excuse students from regular classroom activities for instruction in instrumental music. Various authors attest to this scheduling practice in the United States, England, and Israel (Andrews & Cockerville, 1958; Curatilo, 1983; Greckel, 1973; Groff, 1963; Henry, 1978; Kahana, 1980; Kuhn, 1962; Naylor, 1973; Neiding, 1964; Pierce, 1959; Pizar, 1971; Pruitt, 1969; Robitaille & O'Neal, 1981a; Vance, 1965; Weyland, 1960). Andrews and Cockerille (1958) stated that "the major problem in elementary school scheduling is taking pupils out of class for instrumental lessons, choruses, and other groups" (p. 217).

Numerous authors have addressed specific problems inherent in this type of scheduling (Copland, 1960; Curatilo, 1983; Godbey, 1963; Pizar, 1971). One problem is the concern of elementary school educators, administrators, and parents toward the disruption of normal classroom activities caused by the removal of students for instrumental music instruction. Wilson (1941), for example, found that instrumental music schedules that remove students from their regular classroom activities "are not always received with enthusiasm by teachers of academic subjects, who fail to see why their subjects should be interrupted by the music program" (p. 290). Other problems found in this scheduling practice pertain to missed instructional time and how that time is to be rescheduled (Kahana, 1980; Otto, 1971).

The primary attitude on the part of teachers, administrators, and parents about missed instructional time is that a student's academic achievement will be adversely affected by absence from classroom activities. Henry (1978), summarizing these concerns, believes

> if students miss academic classes, even on a rotating basis, the slower students will almost surely have trouble keeping up, and the grades of even the brightest students may fall. Confronted with lower or failing grades, some parents may panic and remove their children from the program. (p. 26)

Many pragmatic solutions have been offered to the problems inherent in this type of scheduling; however, a majority of these are based on anecdotal rather than empirical evidence. The most popular solution is an attempt by teachers and administrators to devise a new or modified instrumental music schedule. The following design options have been offered by various music educators: fixed-period scheduling (Colwell, 1969; Edwards, 1969; Pierce, 1959), rotating schedule (D'Angelo, 1972; Kahana, 1980; Kuhn, 1962; Neiding, 1964; Pizar, 1971), and outside-school scheduling (Biondo, 1958; Roberts, 1961). Another solution is offered by Pizar (1971):

> If the lesson [sic] can be arranged so that they occur during subjects like spelling, general music, art, and physical education, etc., not much harm will be done, except perhaps creating a little animosity between a special teacher and the band director. (p. 49)

Four research studies sought to determine the effect of reducing academic instructional time for instrumental music instruction on an elementary student's academic achievement. Friedman (1959) investigated the effect on reading and arithmetic achievement of children in grades 4 through 6 who were enrolled in experimental instrumental music classes in which the classroom teacher also served as the instrumental music instructor. Results from the study indicated that students in the experimental instrumental music classes did not differ significantly in reading and arithmetic achievement from students enrolled in traditional classrooms who were not studying instrumental music. While the results of this study may have had practical significance for the author's unique situation, the applicability of these findings is limited in situations where students are excused from regular classroom activities for the study of instrumental music.

Groff (1963) studied the effect on total academic achievement of excusing elementary school students from classes to study instrumental music. Instrumental and noninstrumental music students were matched on the variables sex, IQ, and classroom teacher. The author determined that students who are excused from class for instrumental music study did not differ significantly in total academic achievement from students not studying instrumental music.

Robitaille and O'Neal (1981b) attempted to demonstrate that a pupil's academic achievement is enhanced by participation in the instrumental music program. Fifth-grade instrumental music students and noninstrumental students were compared on the basis of reading, mathematics, language, and total battery achievement test scores. The researchers found in all aspects of comparison that the instrumental music students scored higher than the noninstrumental students.

Robitaille and O'Neal (1981a), in a follow-up test, attempted to augment their original findings. Instrumental music students were matched with noninstrumental students on the basis of IQ scores. Results from this comparison revealed no significant differences in achievement scores between the instrumental music students and noninstrumental students.

While the literature abounds with statements regarding the benefits and problems inherent in elementary school instrumental music instruction and scheduling, few of these statements have been substantiated through carefully planned scientific inquiry. Scholarly research related to elementary music scheduling, specifically the problem caused by students being excused for instrumental music instruction during class time, is limited. Finally, music educators, school administrators, and parents need to be assured that the establishment or maintenance of an elementary instrumental music program will not adversely affect the academic progress of the students.

The present study was designed to augment previous research findings by employing stringent matching techniques and multivariate analysis procedures and by increasing external validity. The purpose of the study was to ascertain whether significant differences exist in sixth-grade reading, language, and mathematics achievement between students who are excused from regular classroom activities for the study of instrumental music and students not studying instrumental music. Specific research questions asked were:

1. Is there a significant difference in sixth-grade reading achievement between students who are excused from regular classroom activities for the study of instrumental music and those students not studying instrumental music?

2. Is there a significant difference in sixth-grade language achievement between students who are excused from regular classroom activities for the study of instrumental music and those students not studying instrumental music?

3. Is there a significant difference in sixth-grade mathematics achievement between students who are excused from regular classroom activities for the study of instrumental music and those students not studying instrumental music?

4. Are the results consistent among school districts of differing size, location, socioeconomic status, and racial balance?

METHOD

Subjects

The general setting for the study was a major midwestern metropolitan area with a 1980 population of 1,403,300. Four public school districts that excuse elementary school instrumental music students from regular classroom activities were used in the study. The districts (A, B, C, and D) were selected on the basis of important differences in size, socioeconomic level, setting, and racial composition, as well as similarities in the organization of their elementary instrumental music programs (see Table 1). The initial sample for the study was 2,167 sixth-grade students from 26 elementary schools in Districts A, B, C, and D during the academic year 1980–81.

Procedures

A single-sample multivariate matched-pairs design was employed to determine whether significant differences exist in sixth-grade reading, language, and mathematics achievement between students who are

Table 1
Comparison of School Districts A, B, C, and D

Item	District A	District B	District C	District D
Setting	Suburban city	Suburban township	Rural county	Urban city
Population	8,282	29,078	37,464	385,457
Median income (in dollars)	31,472	22,793	18,628	16,872
Racial composition				
% white	92	98	99	41
% black	7	1	0.5	57
% other	1	1	0.5	2
Minutes of instrumental music instruction per week	70	70	80	70

excused from regular classroom activities for the study of instrumental music and students not studying instrumental music. The subjects were first separated into one of the following groups by school district: (a) *instrumentalists* (I), sixth-grade students who have received instrumental music instruction through the sixth grade; (b) *noninstrumentalists* (NI), sixth-grade students who have not received instrumental music instruction during regular school hours through the sixth grade; and (c) *instrumental students, partial participation* (IPP), sixth-grade students who have received some instrumental music instruction during regular school hours but not continually through the sixth grade.

Students in the IPP category were then discarded from further use in the study. This was done to ensure that the results of the study would not be confounded by this variable. The following information was obtained next for each student in the I and NI groups: (a) sex, (b) race, (c) IQ (before grade 6), (d) cumulative achievement test scores (before grade 6), (e) total reading, mathematics, and language achievement test scores (grade 6), (f) elementary school attended, and (g) sixth-grade classroom teacher. Subjects in the I group were assigned a consecutive even number and the NI subjects a consecutive odd number within the school districts to preserve anonymity.

Students in the I and NI groups from the same school district were matched on the following control variables according to these criteria: (a) sex, (b) race (white, black, or other), (c) IQ (range of ± 1 standard error of measurement), (d) cumulative achievement (range of ± 1 standard error of measurement), (e) elementary school attended (same school during instrumental music study), and (f) sixth-grade classroom teacher (same teacher). If more than one NI student was found to match an I student, one NI student was then randomly assigned to the pair.

After matching on the preceding control variables had been completed, the following information was obtained for each student in the matched pairs: (a) number of days absent during the 1980–81 school year, (b) whether the student was receiving a nonsubsidized, reduced-price, or free lunch (used as a measure of socioeconomic status), (c) whether the student displayed aggressive-disruptive behavior in the sixth-grade classroom, and (d) whether the NI student was studying a musical instrument outside school.

A matched pair was then discarded from the study if any of the following conditions existed: (a) a student was absent for more than 20 days during the 1980–81 school year, (b) a nonmatch between students receiving nonsubsidized, reduced-price, or free lunches, (c) a student displaying aggressive-disruptive behavior determined by the sixth-grade classroom teacher, and (d) a student in the NI group taking instrumental music lessons outside school (including any wind, string, percussion, or keyboard instruments). This matching procedure yielded a final study sample of 17 matched pairs in District A, 42 in District B, 71 in District C, and 45 in District D.

Hotelling's T^2 for correlated samples was applied to the sixth-grade achievement data from Districts A, B, C, and D individually, and computed using the Finn *Multivariance* program (1978). Hotelling's T^2 tested whether the I and NI groups within each district differed on the set of three dependent variables simultaneously. Since the program arrangement for these tests was identical to a single-sample repeated-measures design, the multivariate correlated-samples problem was reduced to a single-sample problem. Within each matched pair, the difference scores between I and NI students on reading, language, and mathematics achievement were used as dependent variables (Tatsuoka, 1971). For testing the significance of T^2, the .05 level was established a priori.

Results

The mean differences and standard deviations for the difference variables from District A, B, C, and D appear in Table 2. Based on the transformation matrix setup (positive mean difference favoring the I group and negative difference favoring the NI group), all mean differences, with the exception of the reading variable in Districts A and B, favor the I group. The values for these two mean differences, however, are quite small.

Table 3 presents the correlation matrices for all four districts. The values obtained show relationships ranging from moderate negative to

Table 2
Mean Differences and Standard Deviations for Difference Variables in Districts A, B, C, and D

Difference variable	District A (n = 17)		District B (n = 17)		District C (n = 71)		District D (n = 45)	
	MD	SD	MD	SD	MD	SD	MD	SD
Reading	– 0.71	8.73	– 0.64	11.84	1.44	10.51	2.13	12.11
Language[a]	1.71	15.36	1.67	9.68	4.25	13.22	–	–
Mathematics	5.76	14.77	3.12	15.04	1.21	10.93	3.18	16.02

Note: n refers to number of matched pairs.
[a]Language achievement data were not available in District D.

Table 3
Correlation Matrices for Difference Variables in Districts A, B, C, and D

Difference variable	District A (n = 17)			District B (n = 42)			District C (n = 71)			District D (n = 45)		
	R	L	M	R	L	M	R	L	M	R	L	M
R	1.00			1.00			1.00			1.00		
L	-0.15	1.00		0.10	1.00		0.36	1.00		—	—	
M	-0.52	0.47	1.00	0.08	-0.28	1.00	0.07	0.07	1.00	-0.27	—	1.00

Note: R = Reading; L = Language; M = Mathematics. n refers to number of matched pairs.

moderate positive, both of which are in District A. However, a majority of the correlations range from weak positive to weak negative. The negative correlations resulted because the correlations were among difference variables and not direct correlations between dependent variables.

Table 4 contains the multivariate analyses and the related effect sizes for the districts. Results from the multivariate analyses revealed that T^2 was not significant at the .05 level in all four school districts. The obtained Mahalanobis D^2 values demonstrated that all of the tests had small effect sizes ($< .20$), not an unusual finding in behavioral research. Therefore, had T^2 been significant, the practical value of such a finding would have been minimal.

The univariate analyses for all the districts are presented in Table 5. Only one of these values, the language variable favoring the I group in District C, reached significance. It was this variable that was responsible for T^2 in District C almost reaching significance. However, based on the findings of Hummel and Sligo (1971), it would be incorrect to interpret the significant univariate F as a real effect without first having had multivariate significance.

DISCUSSION

The data from this study do not warrant the conclusion that the population mean vectors differ. Therefore, the following conclusions are responses to the research questions posed in the initial section.

1. There is no significant difference in sixth-grade reading achievement between students who are excused from regular classroom activi-

Table 4
Multivariate Analyses and Related Effect Sizes for Districts A, B, C, and D

Item	District A (n = 17)	District B (n = 42)	District C (n = 71)	District D (n = 45)
df	3, 14	3, 39	3, 68	2, 43
D^2	0.1838	0.1116	0.1116	0.0555
T^2	3.1253	4.6870	7.9265	2.4993
F	0.9115	1.4861	2.5667	1.2213
p	<.4605	<.2334	<.0617	<.3049

Note: n refers to number of matched pairs.

Table 5
Univariate Analyses for Districts A, B, C, and D

Difference Variable	District A ($n = 17$)	District B ($n = 42$)	District C ($n = 71$)	District D ($n = 45$)
Reading				
df	1, 16	1, 41	1, 70	1, 44
F	*0.1111*	*0.1239*	*1.3257*	*1.3973*
p	$<.7432$	$<.7267$	$<.2535$	$<.2436$
Language				
df	1, 16	1, 41	1, 70	–
F	0.2095	1.2452	7.3527	–
p	$<.6533$	$<.2710$	$<.0085$	–
Mathematics				
df	1, 16	1, 41	1, 70	1, 44
F	2.5907	1.8051	0.8727	1.7697
p	$<.1271$	$<.1865$	$<.3535$	$<.1903$

Note: n refers to number of matched pairs.

ties for the study of instrumental music and students not studying instrumental music.

2. There is no significant difference in sixth-grade language achievement between students who are excused from regular classroom activities for the study of instrumental music and students not studying instrumental music.

3. There is no significant difference in sixth-grade mathematics achievement between students who are excused from regular classroom activities for the study of instrumental music and students not studying instrumental music.

4. The results are consistent among four school districts that differ in size, setting, socioeconomic level, and racial composition.

This study has demonstrated in a variety of educational settings that there is no significant difference in sixth-grade reading, language, and mathematics achievement between students who are excused from regular classroom activities for the study of instrumental music and students not studying instrumental music. Furthermore, the following beliefs of many parents, teachers, and school administrators toward this scheduling practice should be reexamined in light of the results of this study:

1. School administrators' use of scheduling problems as a justification for elimination of instrumental music instruction from the elementary school curriculum.

2. Parents' beliefs that participation by their children in elementary instrumental music will result in lower academic achievement and grades.

3. Removing students from elementary instrumental music instruction as a means for improving academic achievement and grades.

4. Classroom teachers' contention that the disruption caused by removing students from class will adversely affect those students' achievement.

While the results of the study may not be the same in all educational settings, the data obtained should provide educators with additional empirical evidence needed to justify this scheduling practice. However, several issues have emerged that should be considered in subsequent studies.

1. Similar studies should be performed in other educational settings with different instrumental music schedules and achievement measures.

2. Similar studies should be performed in private schools of differing size, socioeconomic level, and racial composition.

3. Further control of socioeconomic status and chronological age variables should be employed in matching.

4. Other methods should be employed for ascertaining whether a student has participated in instrumental music outside school rather than obtaining this information from classroom and instrumental music teachers.

5. Studies should be made at other grade levels if similar scheduling problems exist.

REFERENCES

Andrews, F., & Cockerille, C. (1958). *Your school music program.* Englewood Cliffs, N.J.: Prentice-Hall.

Biondo, C. A. (1958). Starting the instrumental program. *Music Journal, 15*(1), 20, 86.

Colwell, R. (1969). *The teaching of instrumental music.* New York: Appleton-Century-Crofts.

Copland, C. (1960). Instrumental programs in the elementary school. *The Instrumentalist, 14*(7), 32, 36.

Curatilo, J. S. (1983). Scheduling sanity in the elementary schools. *Music Educators Journal, 69*(8), 48–51.

D'Angelo, D. (1972). A type of flexible scheduling for instrumental music. *The Instrumentalist, 27*(1), 59–60.

Edwards, W. (1969). Scheduling instrumental music. *The Instrumentalist, 23*(8), 83–85.

Finn, J. D. (1978). *Multivariance: Univariate and multivariate analysis of variance, covariance, regression, and repeated measures* (Version VI, release 2) [Computer program]. Chicago: National Educational Resources.

Ford, I. (1967). The elementary instrumental music teacher. *The Instrumentalist, 21*(8), 63–64.

Friedman, B. (1959). An evaluation of the achievement in reading and arithmetic of pupils in elementary school instrumental music classes. *Dissertation Abstracts, 20*, 3662–3663. (University Microfilms No. 59–6219)

Godbey, C. C. (1963). Problems involved in scheduling the instrumental music program in the elementary school and proposed solutions. *Dissertation Abstracts, 24*, 5123–5124. (University Microfilms No. 64–5523)

Greckel, W. C. (1973). The music problem and the specialist in elementary education. *The Elementary School Journal, 73*, 251–257.

Groff, F. H. (1963). Effect on academic achievement of excusing elementary school pupils from classes to study instrumental music. *Dissertation Abstracts, 25*, 5014–5015. (University Microfilms No. 64–3536)

Henry, E. (1978). Can you keep them from dropping out? *The Instrumentalist,* *33*(5), 25–27.

Hummel, T. J., & Sligo, J. (1971). Empirical comparison of univariate and multivariate analysis of variance procedures. *Psychological Bulletin, 76*(1), 49–57.

Kahana, S. (1980). Bands in school—A new idea. *Music Educators Journal, 67*(2), 32–33.

Kuhn, W. (1962). *Instrumental music.* Boston: Allyn and Bacon.

Naylor, J. (1973). Instrumental teaching in boarding schools. *Music in Education, 37,* 312–313.

Neiding, K. (1964). *The band director's guide.* Englewood Cliffs, NJ: Prentice-Hall.

Otto, R. A. (1971). *Effective methods for building the high school band.* West Nyack, NY: Parker.

Pierce, A. E. (1959). *Teaching music in the elementary school.* New York: Henry Holt.

Pizar, R. A. (1971). *Administering the elementary band.* West Nyack, NY: Parker.

Pruitt, J. (1969). [Review of *Effect on academic achievement of excusing elementary school pupils from classes to study instrumental music.*] *Bulletin of the Council for Research in Music Education, 15,* 57–59.

Roberts, J. T. (1961). The mechanics necessary to preserve the music program in education. *Music Educators Journal, 48*(1), 66, 71.

Robitaille, J. P., & O'Neal, S. (1981a). Why instrumental music in elementary schools? *Phi Delta Kappan, 63,* 213.

Robitaille, J. P., & O'Neal, S. (1981b). *Why instrumental music in the elementary school!* Unpublished manuscript (available from Albuquerque Public Schools, Albuquerque, New Mexico).

Shaw, G. J. (1968). Problems in scheduling elementary instrumental music. *The School Musician Director and Teacher, 39*(10), 50–51, 65.

Tatsuoka, M. M. (1971). *Multivariate Analysis.* New York: John Wiley and Sons.

Vance, N. N. (1965). Selecting and training instrumentalists in Illinois. *The Instrumentalist, 19* (7), 20–26.

Weerts, R. (1968). The beginning instrumental program in perspective. *The Instrumentalist, 23*(2), 46–47.

Weyland, R. (1960). *A guide to effective music supervision.* Dubuque, IA: William C. Brown.

Wilson, H. R. (1941). *Music in the high school.* New York: Silver Burdett.

June 7, 1984

THE SEX-STEREOTYPING OF MUSICAL INSTRUMENTS

Harold F. Abeles
Susan Yank Porter

JRME 1978, VOLUME 26, NUMBER 2, PAGES 65–75

This series of studies was undertaken to examine musical instrument gender associations. Study 1, which investigated adult musical instrument preferences for children, indicated significant differences (<.05) in instrument selections due to the sex of the child. Study 2 employed a paired-comparison strategy to place eight instruments under investigation on a masculine-feminine continuum. Study 3 investigated children's (K-5) instrumental preferences. Results showed a significant sex by grade interaction. Study 4 examined three procedures for presenting the instruments to preschool children. The results showed a significant sex by method of presentation interaction.

Key Words: attitudes, instrument selection, school environment, sex, teaching method.

The association of gender with musical instruments can, as can stereotyping of any kind, serve to constrict the behavior and thus the opportunities of individuals. Stereotyping is particularly a problem when it is based on characteristics irrelevant to the function of a group of objects, such as the association of maleness with playing the drums and femaleness with playing the violin. The sex-stereotyping of musical instruments, therefore, tends to limit the range of musical experiences available to male and female musicians in several ways, including participation in instrumental ensembles and selection of vocations in instrumental music.

The results of the association of gender with instruments is evidenced in the predominance of males in band programs and the predominance of females in orchestra programs, particularly at the college and secondary school level. Until recently, college marching bands were often the sole domain of males. Lyon (1973) reports that in 1973 less than 10 percent of Purdue University's marching band was female,

Notre Dame marched eight women, and Michigan State University had one woman alto saxophonist.

This pattern of predominantly single sex instrumental ensembles has tended to restrict music vocational opportunities for women. Lyon (1973) reports that women comprise 56 percent of the nation's amateur musicians, 17 percent of all instrumental instructors, and only 5 percent of all public school and college band directors. Lyon concludes, "If women tend to be excluded from the traditionally male bands, then they have to enter the teaching profession with no real experience."

A further illustration of the effect of musical instrument sex-stereotyping can be found by examining the number of women teaching instruments at the university level. A survey of the *College Music Society Directory for 1972–74* shows that although women constitute 25 percent of the string teachers, they account for only 3 percent of the brass and 6 percent of the percussion instructors (Mayer, 1976).

Factors that produce music instrument gender associations and, consequently, the music vocational data previously reported may include parental as well as music educator influences. Associating a gender with musical instruments prior to the time of instrument selection (usually between ages 8 and 12) seems to be a critical factor regarding which instrument a child selects.

Although the outcomes of instrumental sex-stereotyping seem quite evident, little information exists on this behavior in children. The present studies were designed to investigate the parameters of instrumental sex-stereotyping in adults and children, as well as attempt to identify possible causes for musical instrument sex-stereotyping behavior.

Study 1

In the spring of 1975, a survey was conducted in Greensboro, North Carolina, and surrounding communities to determine the extent of musical instrument sex-stereotyping behavior in adults. Respondents were 149 adults (ages 19 to 52), who were chosen from public school and church-related activities.

Each person was given a survey form on which he or she was to indicate age, sex, and any previous instrumental music training. The first paragraph of the form stated that this survey was being undertaken to predict "the likely future demand for musical instruments and for teachers of certain musical instruments in the public schools," and asked the respondents to answer the following hypothetical question. "Your fifth grade daughter has indicated in a school survey that she would like to play a musical instrument . . . ," and then asked the parent to indicate from among the eight instruments taught in the schools—cello, clarinet, drums, flute, saxophone, trombone, trumpet, and violin—the three instruments that they would encourage her to select in first, second, and third choice order. Half of the forms began "Your fifth grade son . . . ;" the other half began "Your fifth grade daughter . . . ." The two forms were distributed alternately, but all other administrative procedures were held constant. No mention was made of the focus of the study during the administration.

The data were analyzed using a Multivariate Analysis of Variance (MANOVA) procedure with the average ranking of each of the eight instruments as the multiple dependent variables. Responses were examined for differences as a function of sex of the respondent, sex of the child, and the presence or absence of past musical experiences in a 2 by 2 by 2 factorial design. The MANOVA tests of significance (Wilks Lambda criterion) for the main effects of sex of respondent, past musical experiences, and all interactions were not significant at the .05 level of confidence. The MANOVA test of significance for the main effect of sex of child was significant beyond the .05 level of confidence (Table 1). The univariate examination shown in Table 1 of the eight instruments' mean rankings indicated that respondents preferred clarinet, flute, and violin for their daughters, and drum, trombone, and trumpet for their sons. The cello and saxophone produced nonsignificant differences at the .05 level due to the sex of the child.

Table 1
MANOVA and ANOVA Analyses of Adults' Instrumental Preferences for Children MANOVA Tests

Source	df	F	p
Sex of Respondent (R)	8,134	1.23	NS
Past Musical Experience (E)	8,134	1.34	NS
Sex of Child (C)	8,134	7.56	<.05
R by E	8,134	1.08	NS
R by C	8,134	.37	NS
E by C	8,134	1.23	NS
R by E by C	8,134	1.96	NS

Univariate F Tests: Sex of Child

Instrument	Male X̄*	Female X̄*	df	F	p
Cello	.272	.458	1,141	1.69	NS
Clarinet	.818	1.527	1,141	5.37	<.05
Drum	.818	.222	1,141	12.76	<.05
Flute	.805	1.807	1,141	29.24	<.05
Saxophone	.610	.388	1,141	2.84	NS
Trombone	.545	.152	1,141	5.76	<.05
Trumpet	1.480	.486	1,141	31.91	<.05
Violin	.779	1.301	1,141	7.48	<.05

*High score equals greater preference.

Study 2

To determine the placement of the eight previously mentioned instruments on a masculine-feminine continuum, 32 music majors and 26 nonmusic majors participated in a paired-comparison ranking of the eight instruments. Students were given a form that listed all possible pairs (28) of the eight instruments under investigation. For each of the pairs the respondents were instructed to circle the instrument that they considered to be the most masculine. Presentation of the pairs was randomly ordered.

The results of the paired-comparison ranking of the instruments yielded a Spearman-Rank Correlation Coefficient of 1.00 between the music majors and nonmusic majors. Subsequently, the data from the groups were pooled and transformed to normalized scale values employing a procedure described by Edwards (1957).

The results of the transformation appear in Table 2. An examination of this table indicates considerable agreement with the results of Study 1. The flute, violin, and clarinet are rated as being the three most feminine instruments and the drums, trombone, and trumpet the most masculine instruments. The cello and saxophone, which were not affected by the sex of the child variable in Study 1, appear in the middle of the scale.

When a person indicated a preference for one of the eight instruments, the choice was assigned the normalized score value for that instrument.

Table 2
Transformations of Instrument-Gender Paired-Comparison Judgments

Instrument	Normalized Gender* Scale Score
Flute	.000
Violin	1.518
Clarinet	1.949
Cello	2.643
Saxophone	3.182
Trumpet	3.261
Trombone	4.143
Drum	4.195

*High score equals more masculine

Study 3

To investigate the musical instrument gender associations of children in the kindergarten through fifth grade, 598 children from three schools, two in Bloomington, Indiana, and one in Wilmington, Delaware, participated in a survey of instrumental preferences.

To ensure that each child participating in the study would be familiar with the eight instruments used, both visual and aural material was prepared. Large cardboard pictures of the instruments were obtained from the Bowmar (1961) *Meet the Instruments* materials. Several of these pictures included small inserts with photographs of a child playing the instrument—typically, a male for those instruments rated near the masculine end of the M-F scale used in Study 2, and a female for those rated near the feminine end. These small photographs were covered with a number used to identify the picture since it was thought likely to affect the child's response.

When preparing the aural material, two factors were thought to be possible confounding variables: the type of melodic material employed, and the range of the instrument. So the same composition, a *Spagnotetta* by Praetorius, was played on each of the eight instruments. Two recordings of the composition were made, one in the instrument's normal playing range, and one in a range centering around middle C. Tempo was held constant for all performances.

The answer sheet used by the students included drawings and the name of each instrument to facilitate the responses of young children. The instruments appeared on the answer sheet in the random order in which they were presented during the study.

At the beginning of the administration, students were told that the researchers were interested in which instruments the students liked. It was made clear to the older students that their selection was not binding with the school instrumental music program. Respondents were instructed not to select an instrument until they had heard all examples. As the recording of each instrument was played, the researcher walked around the room holding the Bowmar picture of the instrument. After all eight instruments were heard, the students were instructed to circle the name of the instrument that they would must like to play if they had the chance. If children knew how to play one of the instruments being examined, their responses were included in the results, whereas the responses of the students who had played an instrument that was not included in the study (e.g. French horn) were not used. Occasionally, kindergarten and first grade students needed some additional instructions in order to understand the task, and these were provided by the researcher.

A pilot study was also conducted to determine the possible effects of the sex of the administrator and range of the instrument's performance on instrument preference with 232 students from kindergarten through fifth grade. Students in each grade were given, in an incomplete factorial design (administrator's sex by range interaction could not be estimated), the instrumental preference survey by a male or female researcher employing the recording of the instruments either in their natural range or around middle C. An analysis of variance applied to the results of this investigation indicated that there was no significant main effect of sex of the administrator ($F = .063$, $df = 1,223$, $p = .99$) or range of the performance ($F = .074$, $df = 1,223$, $p = .99$) on instrumental preference as measured by the normalized gender scale scores. Consequently, other data collections employed recordings of the instruments in their natural ranges and were administered by researchers of either sex.

Additional data on children's instrumental preferences were collected by utilizing the previously mentioned procedures in three schools. As school location was thought to be a possible influence on instrumental preference, a 2 by 2 by 3 (sex by grade by school) randomized blocks design was employed with the school used as a blocking variable. To determine specifically where significant ($<.05$) differences were to be found, *a priori* orthogonal contrasts were employed. The result of this analysis is reported in Table 3.

Table 3
ANOVA of Children's Instrumental
Preferences by Grade and Sex

Source		df	MS	R²	F	p
Sex		1	13.71	.53	24.21	$<.05$
Grade						
$\overline{K, 1, 2}$ vs. $\overline{3, 4, 5}$		1	2.04	.07	9.56	$<.05$
$\overline{K}$ vs. $\overline{1, 2}$		1	.35		1.65	NS
1 vs. 2		1	.01		.05	NS
3 vs. $\overline{4, 5}$		1	.02		.11	NS
4 vs. 5		1	.41		1.92	NS
Sex by Grade						
$\overline{K, 1, 2}$ vs. $\overline{3, 4, 5}$	by Sex	1	1.81	.07	5.78	$<.05$
K vs. $\overline{1, 2}$	by Sex	1	.86		2.75	NS
1 vs. 2	by Sex	1	.13		.41	NS
3 vs. $\overline{4, 5}$	by Sex	1	.00		.00	NS
4 vs. 5	by Sex	1	.03		.10	NS
Sex by School		2	.56			
Grade by School		10	.21			
Sex by Grade by School		10	.31			

Grade		Means	SD
K	M	3.29	.96
	F	3.12	1.23
1	M	3.22	1.00
	F	2.43	1.43
2	M	3.59	.84
	F	2.29	1.59
3	M	3.43	1.00
	F	1.73	1.39
4	M	3.21	1.23
	F	1.49	1.30
5	M	3.30	.82
	F	1.90	1.35

An examination of Table 3 indicates significant (< .05) differences due to the main effects of sex and grade, and sex by grade interaction. Further examination indicates the significant grade effect occurs between the average of the primary grades K, 1, 2, and the average of the intermediate grades 3, 4, 5. Significant sex by grade interaction also occurs between these two groups. A plot of the mean instrumental preference scores by sex and grade appears in Figure 1. To determine the amount of total variance that was

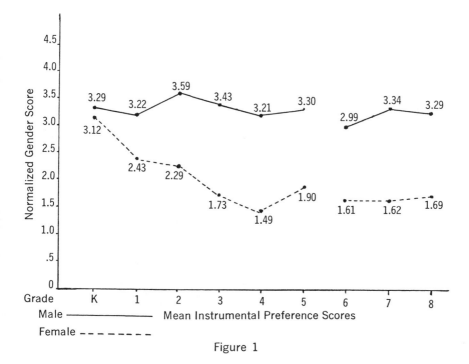

Figure 1

explained by the significant effects, R^2's were calculated. Sixty-seven percent of the total variance was explained by the significant effects, with the effect of sex accounting for a large proportion of the total variance (53 percent).

Additional data were collected on the composition by sex of the instrumental performing groups at the middle schools, to which the elementary school students included in the instrumental preference study would be promoted. The mean normalized instrument gender scores for grades 6-8 also appear in Figure 1, and seem to suggest that a stabilization in instrumental selection occurs.

Study 4

The results in Study 3 (Figure 1) indicate that the sex-stereotyping behavior in musical instrument preference is not very strong in young children (kindergarten) but is more pronounced in children beyond grade 3. This investigation was designed to examine one possible cause for the increase in sex-stereotyping behavior in musical instrument preference—the manner in which children are first introduced to the instruments of the orchestra.

Forty-seven children ages 3 through 5 from a day care center in Bloomington, Indiana, participated in this study. The children were randomly assigned to one of three groups. Group 1 (RCA Group) was presented with the eight instruments (cello, clarinet, flute, saxophone, trombone, trumpet, and violin) from the RCA record *Instruments of the Orchestra* (1962). They were simultaneously shown the pictures of the instruments as described in Study 3. Group 2 (Control Group) was introduced to the eight instruments using both the aural and visual stimuli employed in Study 3, that is, the same melody was played on all of the eight instruments, but the pictures did not show someone playing the instruments. Group 3 (Bowmar Group) heard recorded excerpts from the Bowmar *Meet the Instruments* (1961) materials, and saw the full pictures of the instruments included in the kit, which show children playing several of the instruments.

The administration of all three modes of presentation employed small groups of children (<3), took approximately ten minutes, and generally followed the procedure described in Study 3. The children were asked to point to each instrument on their answer sheet when it was presented as an indication of their ability to associate the aural and visual stimuli with the drawings on their sheets. At the end of the tape the children were asked to draw a circle around the instrument they preferred.

The data collected in the study was analyzed employing a 2 by 2 (sex by group) factorial design with *a priori* orthogonal contrasts used to examine specific hypotheses. The results of this analysis appear in Table 4.

An examination of Table 4 indicates nonsignificant (<.05) results due to the main effects of group and sex, but does indicate a significant difference (<.05) in the interaction hypothesis between the pooled experimental group results (Bowmar and RCA) and the Control Group by sex. A plot of the mean instrumental preference score by sex and group appears in Figure 2. The amount of total variance (R^2) explained by the significant interaction effect was 9 percent.

Discussion

Study 1 was designed to answer the question, "Does the association of gender with musical instruments exist in the general population?" The results of the study suggest that the answer to this question is yes, and that prior musical training or the respondents' sex does not interact with this stereotyping behavior. The design and results of this study also suggest,

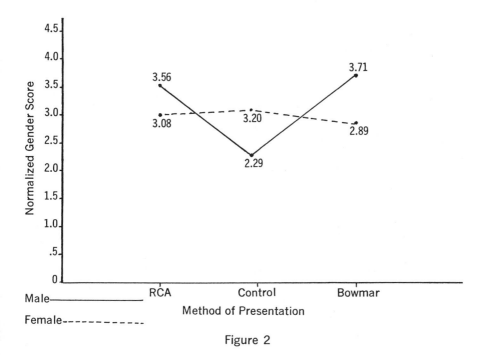

Figure 2

Table 4
Preschool Children's Instrumental Preferences
by Sex and Method of Presentation

Source	df	MS	R²	F	p
Sex	1	.37		.26	NS
Group					
Control vs. Bowmar, RCA	1	4.13		3.00	NS
Bowmar vs. RCA	1	.01		.01	NS
Sex by Group					
Sex by Control vs.					
Bowmar, RCA	1	6.06	.09	4.40	<.05
Sex by Bowmar by RCA	1	2.16		.15	NS
Within Cells	41	1.37			

Group		Means	SD
RCA	M	3.56	.47
	F	3.08	1.63
Control	M	2.29	1.39
	F	3.20	1.10
Bowmar	M	3.71	.51
	F	2.89	1.72

but do not establish, that parents may influence their children to choose certain instruments, depending on the sex of the child. Study 1 indicates, however, that not all instruments are affected by gender associations.

Study 2 was designed to gather further information on the stereotyping of the eight instruments examined. Both musicians and nonmusicians were shown to have similar instrument gender associations. The placement of the instruments on a masculine-feminine scale generally conformed with the results of Study 1 and provided interval scale data for further investigations of instrumental preferences.

The question that Study 3 focused upon was, "At what age does sex-stereotyping of instruments begin?" The study was also designed to suggest possible causes for the behavior, so that additional experimental investigations could be planned. An examination of the results of Study 3 yields several interesting pieces of information. The boys' selections remained relatively stable at the masculine end of the scale from kindergarten through the eventual selection of an instrument. The girls' selections consistently moved toward traditionally feminine instruments, the difference between the sexes maximizing around third and fourth grades. The girls also had consistently larger standard deviations than did the boys, indicating that even when the average instrumental gender score preferences were similar, the girls chose a wider variety of instruments, whereas the boys chose from a relatively restricted group at the masculine end of the scale.

Study 4 was designed to examine one possible cause of the sex-stereotyping of instruments described by the previous studies. This study compared the effects of presenting the instruments using a widely adopted kit for introducing children to orchestral instruments, with an approach that employed only gender associated musical examples, and a third method that was designed to eliminate any gender associations in presenting the instruments. The results indicated that young girls were generally not affected by the mode of presentation, whereas young boys responded differently in the unbiased presentation than in the other two conditions. It should also be noted that both boys and girls tended to choose instruments at the masculine end of the continuum, and that as found in Study 3, girls selected a wider variety of instruments than did boys.

Conclusions

This series of studies suggests that musical instrument gender associations are widespread throughout all age groups, starting with children's initial introduction to the instruments, and may be the dominant factor in instrument selection, possibly having a major effect on the music vocational choices of individuals.

The results of Study 4 suggest that sex-stereotyping of instruments may be diminished if care is taken when initially presenting the instruments, but as these gender associations exist outside the music class as well, consistent reinforcement seems necessary, at least until instrumental selections are made. Special care, therefore, must be taken by the instrumental music teacher when helping children select instruments.

Additional research is needed to examine other variables that may be related to musical instrument gender associations, including the characteristic literature of instruments, the traditional role of instruments in various ensembles (e.g. trumpet in football marching band versus symphony orchestra), and the association of music with traditional feminine characteristics (Keston, 1956).

References

Edwards, Allen L. *Techniques of Attitude Scale Construction*. New York: Appleton-Century-Crofts, Inc., 1957.

Instruments of the Orchestra (RCA Victor, LE6080); New York, 1962.

Keston, M. J. "An Experimental Investigation of the Relationship Between the Factors of the Minnesota Multiphasic Personality Inventory and Musical Sophistication." *American Psychologist*, Vol. II (1956), p. 434.

Lyon, Richard. "Ms. Band Director." *Conn Chord*, Vol. 17, No. 1 (1973), p. 407.

Mayer, Anne. "Women in Applied Music." *The Status of Women in College Music: Preliminary Studies*. Binghamton, New York: College Music Society, 1976, pp. 30–34.

Meet the Instruments (Bowmar, 1715); Glendale, California, 1961.

■ Indiana University
Bloomington, Indiana

Wilmington Public Schools
Wilmington, Delaware

Elementary and secondary music students' achievement motivation was characterized by the reasons they cited for success and failure in music. The students' free responses were classified according to the two-dimensional model of Attribution Theory in which the causes of success and failure are categorized by locus of control, internal or external, and stability through time, stable or unstable. The major findings of the study were that 80% of the reasons cited for success and failure in music were internal in nature, a greater number of stable reasons were cited for success while more external-unstable reasons were cited for failure, females cited more internal-stable reasons than males, the frequency of internal-stable reasons increased with grade level while internal-unstable reasons declined, and the school attended significantly influenced the type of reasons students provided. The importance of these findings to music education practice and their relationship to previous research in achievement motivation was discussed.

Edward P. Asmus, Jr., *University of Utah*

JRME 1986, VOLUME 34, NUMBER 4, PAGES 262–278

Student Beliefs About the Causes of Success and Failure in Music: A Study of Achievement Motivation

Music educators have long realized the importance of motivating students to achieve musically. However, few systematic attempts have been made to study the role of motivation in musical achievement. One means of analyzing motivation is provided by Attribution Theory (Weiner, 1974, 1979). In this theory, the determinants of student action are deduced from reasons students cite about success and failure at a task. The theory holds that what students attribute to be the causes of success and failure at a task will mediate how the task is approached in the future. For instance, a student who attributes success at playing a musical instrument to diligent practice would more likely persist in learning to play a difficult musical work than one who attributes success to a matter of luck. Research has shown that four causal categories can

---

For reprints of this article, contact Edward P. Asmus, Jr., Department of Music, University of Utah, Salt Lake City, Utah 84112.

represent a majority of reasons students cite for success and failure: ability, task difficulty, luck, and effort. The purpose of the present investigation was to utilize Attribution Theory as a basis for understanding the motivational elements inherent in the reasons students cite of why some people are successful in music and others are not.

The present investigation considerably expanded an earlier study (Asmus, 1985) by including a broader spectrum of elementary and secondary school music students from eight grade levels rather than one in the subject population and by employing a greater number of independent variables in the analysis. Five specific null hypotheses guided the course of this investigation: (a) No differences would exist in the observed frequency of attributions between the four major causal categories of Attribution Theory, (b) there would be no differences due to whether the attributions were made about those who are successful in music or those who are not, (c) there would be no differences in attributions due to subject gender, (d) there would be no differences in attributions due to subject grade level, and (e) there would be no differences in attributions due to school attended.

RELATED LITERATURE, MOTIVATION IN MUSIC LEARNING

Influential Factors

The study of motivation in musical achievement assumes that the way students perceive themselves and music influences how much they will strive to learn this art. Raynor (1981a) has indicated that the importance of music activities to an individual is influenced by the same value sources that influence other human activity. The values students place on activities can be identified from the reasons they cite for participating in an activity. A wide variety of reasons are typically cited, which has led to a variety of ways of viewing the determinants of student action (Parsons, 1983; Raynor, 1983).

Self-concept. Raynor (1983) has indicated that individuals who are motivated for music-related activities have self-concepts that are inherently involved with music. The important influence that self-concept can play in determining musical outcomes has been demonstrated by a number of researchers (Covington, 1983; Greenberg, 1970; Michel, 1971; Nolin & Vander Ark, 1977; Vander Ark, Nolin, & Newman, 1980; Wink, 1970; Wolff, 1978). Generally, this research found that positive self-concept was associated with successful task performance and successful task performance, in turn, resulted in positive self-concept.

Reinforcement theory. One perspective of motivation in musical achievement is provided by operant music learning research. This research studies the effects of reinforcement strategies on student behavior. Greer (1981) analyzed operant music learning research for its involvement in motivation and affect through an extensive literature review. In this review, Greer points out that, "Most, if not all operant research has been concerned with motivation" (p. 103). The goal of teaching with operant techniques is to apply reinforcements in order to modify student behavior until success at a learning task is obtained. Raynor (1981b), in response to Greer's presentation, cautions that previous successful experiences have not influenced student motivation in a manner predicted by reinforcement theory. Raynor concluded that the effect of success varies due to individual differences and the particular striving stage of the individual at a task.

Research Findings

Motivation and music teaching. A number of researchers have studied the influence of motivation on the achievement of practicing music educators and those studying to enter this profession. Krueger (1974), in an extensive study of the relationship of personality and motivation to the success of music teachers, concluded that personality and motivation were strongly related to music teaching success. Caimi (1981) and Walker (1979) both used the motivation analysis test (Cattell, Horn, Sweeney, & Radcliffe, 1964) as their measure of motivation. Walker determined that high achieving students in music education courses had positive self-concepts, were strongly attached to loved ones, had low destructive/hostile impulses, and worried little about their safety. Caimi found that the musical performance level of bands was related to the directors' concern for security and attitude toward the parental home while nonperformance musical achievement of band members was related to the directors' concern over the ethical-unselfish self.

Asmus (1986) utilized Attribution Theory to study music education and music therapy students' achievement motivation and self-perceptions of success tendency. These students attributed the success and failure of others to effort while attributing their own success and failure to task difficulty. Self-perceptions of success tendency were found to be strongly related to attributions made of success and failure. In addition, a strong relationship was found between self-attributions in music and self-attributions in academics.

Motivation and student achievement. A few research studies have specifically investigated student motivation in the music learning process. Reimer (1975) employed Attribution Theory to study the affective consequences of teacher-provided casual feedback. College subjects, who believed they were in a piano practicum, received instructions that described causes of piano playing success as due to either ability, effort, task simplicity, or chance. All subjects received feedback that they were successful on their piano performance. Subjects who received internal attribution instructions, ability or effort, had more positive affect toward piano performance and the instructor.

Asmus (1985) classified sixth-grade music students' reasons of why some students succeed in music and why some students do not according to Attribution Theory. The study employed Weiner's (1974) original two-dimensional attribution model of ability, task difficulty, luck, and effort. Results indicated that students attributed success and failure in music as due to the internal reasons of ability and effort. No differences were found between failure or success responses while significant differences among the three participating schools were obtained. Lillemyr (1983), in a study of fourth-grade Norwegian students, found that students with high self-concept tended to have higher perceptions of their cognitive competence, greater interest in school music, more positive self-esteem, higher achievement motivation, and lower levels of failure avoidance than those with low self-concept. Students with a high level of interest in school music tended to have higher perceptions of their musical competence, greater success motivation, more positive perceptions of their ability as students, greater failure avoidance, and lower perceptions of their physical competence than those with low levels of musical interest.

RELATED LITERATURE, ATTRIBUTION THEORY

Description

Attribution Theory assumes that performance on an achievement task is mediated by an individual's beliefs about the causes of success and failure (Bar-Tal, 1978). Weiner (1974) found that students' attributed causes for success and failure at achievement tasks could be organized into four major causal categories: ability, task difficulty, luck, and effort. Ability and task difficulty were found to be perceived as the causes of consistent events while luck and effort were perceived as causes of inconsistent events (Frieze & Weiner, 1971). This allowed the causal categories to be characterized by a stability dimension in which a cause was either stable or unstable. Similarly, ability and effort were perceived as causes originating within the individual while task difficulty and luck were perceived as causes outside the individual. Thus, a second locus of control dimension could characterize the causes as internal or external. This resulted in the original two-dimensional conceptualization of Attribution Theory (Weiner, 1974). Weiner (1979) later expanded the original conceptualization by including a third dimension of controllability, controllable or uncontrollable, and renaming the locus of control dimension to locus of causality. The revised model retained ability, task difficulty, and luck, which were conceived as uncontrollable causes. A new internal-unstable category of mood was added to complete the uncontrollable causes. The four controllable causes consisted of a division of effort into typical effort, internal-stable, and immediate effort, internal-unstable. The controllable causes of teacher bias, external-stable, and unusual help, external-unstable, were added to complete the 2 x 2 x 2 matrix. Most research, however, has employed the two-dimensional model of Attribution Theory.

Summary of Major Research Findings

Numerous investigations employing Attribution Theory have been undertaken in the fields of education and social psychology. This research has been tremendously important in detailing motivation from students' underlying beliefs about the causes of success and failure. A summary of the major findings of this research indicates that: Gender and socioeconomic effects on attribution vary with the task (Bar-Tal, 1978; Bar-Tal, Goldberg, & Knaani, 1984; Raviv, Bar-Tal, Raviv, & Bar-Tal, 1980); expectancy of success at a task generally influences the attributions made (Bardwell, 1984; Chapman & Lawes, 1984; Covington & Onelich, 1979; McMahan, 1973); teachers are affected by the types of attributions students make (Beckman, 1976; Medway & Lowe, 1980; Prawat, Byers, & Anderson, 1983; Ross, Bierbrauer, & Polly, 1974); attributions are correlated with school performance, academic affect, and self-concept (Fitch, 1970; Marsh, Cairns, Relich, Barnes, & Debus, 1984; McFarland & Ross, 1982; Thomas, 1980; Weiner, Russell, & Lerman, 1979); and the two-dimensional conceptualization of student attributions is the most prevalent in the literature.

METHOD

Subjects

The subjects were 589 students enrolled in music courses in grades 4 through 12. The music courses included instrumental, vocal, and general music subject areas. Eight different public schools representing a varied socioeconomic constituency participated in the study.

Procedure

Response Form

The form used in obtaining subject responses was essentially the same as that used by Asmus (1985) with the addition of background items to collect information on subject gender and grade level. The form utilized an open-ended response format in which subjects were to state five reasons why some students do well in music and five reasons why some students do not do well in music.

Open-ended response formats have been utilized successfully in a number of investigations (Asmus, 1985; Elig & Frieze, 1974; Frieze, 1976) and have the advantage of allowing subjects the opportunity to provide a broader variety of attribution responses than is possible with structured approaches (Elig & Freize, 1979). The collection of a broad spectrum of responses through an open-ended approach was perceived as an advantage to the present study because few music education research studies have utilized attributions to investigate motivation and none have focused on the grade levels represented by the subjects of this investigation.

Data Collection

Data were collected from subjects during their regular music classes. The test forms were distributed, instructions for completing the form were given, and sufficient time was provided for subjects to complete their responses. The amount of time varied due to subject grade level; subjects at lower grade levels required more response time than subjects in higher grades. Not all subjects were able to provide five reasons for each of the success and failure response directives. Data from these subjects were retained for analysis if these subjects had seriously applied themselves to the data collection task. A total of 5092 attributions of why some students do well in music and why some do not were provided by the subjects.

Statement Classification

Three judges classified each subject response according to Weiner's original two-dimensional conceptualization of Attribution Theory. The two-dimensional model was utilized rather than the more recent three-dimensional model because it has been the model most frequently used by previous research, it provides a reduced number of dependent measures—four instead of eight—and an initial review of student responses found numerous causes without any control information required to classify statements according to the three-dimensional model. Judges were initially trained to categorize each statement according to the keywords for each cell in the two-dimensional model: ability, task difficulty, luck, and effort. Interjudge reliability of the statements categorized in this manner was found to be extremely poor. After consultation with the judges, it was decided to reclassify all statements according to the dimensional labels of the two-dimensional model: internal-stable, external-stable, external-unstable, and internal unstable. Interjudge reliability for the reclassified responses, as indicated by the intraclass correlation coefficient, was found to be very satisfactory (r = .998).

RESULTS AND DISCUSSION

Distribution of Attributions

A one sample chi-square test (Siegel, 1956) was used to test the hypothesis that attributed causes of success and failure in music were evenly distributed across the four attribution categories. The attribution category scores for all subjects were summed across the success and failure directives to obtain the total number of responses made in each of the four categories. A highly significant difference was obtained between the observed and expected frequencies (Chi-square = 3611.87, $df = 3$, $p < .001$). The relative proportions of responses in each of the attribution categories were as follows: internal-unstable, 38.65%; internal-stable, 42.92%; external-unstable, 9.85%; external-stable, 8.59%. Internal-stable attributions were the most commonly cited ($n = 2314$). Also frequently cited were internal-unstable attributions ($n = 2084$). Much less commonly used were the external attributions, external-stable ($n = 463$) and external-unstable ($n = 521$), which were cited in less than 20% of the cases.

The kinds of attributions made about success and failure in music by these subjects were similar to those observed in a previous study of sixth graders upon which this research was based (Asmus, 1985). The music students attributed the causes of success or failure in music to internal reasons approximately 80% of the time. A slight majority of these reasons were found by the present study to be due to stable causes that have traditionally been described as ability related. This is similar to the results obtained by Frieze and Snyder (1980), who also found that first, third, and fifth graders tend to attribute success and failure in art to internal causes with the majority being ability (internal-stable) rather than effort (internal-unstable) related. The tendency for internal attributions has also been found in college students' views of school situations (Frieze, 1976), teachers referrals of students for special education (Christenson, Ysseldyke, Wang, & Algorzzine, 1983), and attributions made in success settings (Luginbuhl, Crowe, & Kahan, 1975), while the greater use of stable or unstable causes varied among these studies.

A number of implications for music education can be extracted from the results obtained here. Teachers have been shown to attribute student success and failure to effort (Asmus, 1986; Prawat, Byers, & Anderson, 1983). Fortunately, students also attribute a large portion of reasons for success and failure in music to internal-unstable causes. Internal-unstable causes, such as effort, encourage student persistence until a task has been successfully achieved. Unfortunately, students attribute a slightly greater proportion of reasons for success and failure in music to internal-stable causes such as ability. Internal-stable attributions do not promote achievement persistence at the same level as internal-unstable attributions because they rely on the innate capabilities of the student. Recent research by Ames (1984) found that students made more ability attributions in competitive settings than in individually nurturant settings. When music educators make competitive statements such as, "We will audition for who will be section leader," or "Only those who can sing their part will be able to play the drum today," may be forcing students into making internal-stable attributions. Society as a whole promotes the use of internal-stable attributions for musical achievement. Statements frequently made about those who are successful in music include "She has the gift of music" and "He is musically talented," which emphasize internal-stable attributions. If the goal of music education is to promote musical achievement by all students, it would appear that internal-unstable, effort related attributions should be encouraged.

Group and Response Mode Differences

Statistical Analysis

A three-way repeated measures multivariate analysis of variance (MANOVA) was used to test the four hypotheses that dealt with differences in attributions due to response mode, gender, grade level, and school. Gender, grade level, and school were main effects in the analysis, while response mode was the repeated factor. The dependent measures of the analysis were the subjects' four attribution category scores obtained from each of the two response modes. Results of this analysis are presented in Table 1. Because of the large sample size and

Table 1
Repeated Measures Multivariate Analysis of Variance

Source	Wilks lambda	Hypoth. MS	Error MS	F	df	p<
Gender	0.965			4.850	4,541	0.001
Internal-stable		29.007	2.209	13.134	1,544	0.001
Grade	0.715			5.942	32,1997	0.001
Internal-stable		26.663	2.209	12.073	8,544	0.001
Internal-stable		42.767	2.856	14.973	8,544	0.001
External-stable		2.169	0.583	3.723	8,544	0.001
External-unstable		2.441	0.624	3.911	8,544	0.001
School	0.851			3.190	28,1952	0.001
Internal-stable		7.711	2.209	3.492	7,544	0.001
Internal-unstable		13.090	2.856	4.583	7,544	0.001
External-stable		2.064	0.583	3.543	7,544	0.001
External-unstable		2.371	0.624	3.799	7,544	0.001
Gender × grade	0.911			1.602	32,1997	ns
Gender × school	0.952			1.349	20,1795	ns
Grade × school	0.902			1.578	36,2029	ns
Gender × grade × school	0.967			0.758	24,1889	ns
Response mode	0.871			20.080	4,541	0.001
Internal-stable		20.659	0.537	38.507	1,544	0.001
External-stable		2.568	0.204	12.595	1,544	0.001
External-unstable		2.038	0.202	10.088	1,544	0.002
Mode × gender	0.995			0.719	4,541	ns
Mode × grade	0.947			0.931	32,1997	ns
Mode × school	0.897			2.132	28,1952	0.001
External-stable		0.994	0.204	4.874	7,544	0.001
Mode × gender × grade	0.962			0.661	32,1997	ns
Mode × gender × school	0.963			1.030	20,1795	ns
Mode × grade × school	0.910			1.441	36,2029	ns
Mode × gender × grade × school	0.941			1.383	24,1889	ns

the relative ease of obtaining statistical differences with such a large sample size, only alpha levels of .005 or less were considered significant.

Response Mode Differences

A significant difference was obtained between subject attributions assigned for doing well in music and those not doing well in music that indicated that subjects made different attributions in these two response modes. Univariate repeated measures analyses of variance for this significant factor indicated that internal-stable, external-stable, and external-unstable attribution categories contributed significantly to this effect. Subjects made more internal-stable and external-stable attributions to the do well directive while more external-unstable attributions were made to the do not do well directive (Table 2).

The finding of a significant difference due to response mode was opposite that obtained by the earlier study upon which the present research was based (Asmus, 1985). The lack of such a difference in the

Table 2
Means and Standard Deviations for All Significant Main Effects

Variable	Mean	SD	n	Variable	Mean	SD	n
Gender (internal-stable)							
Females	4.205	2.318	332				
Males	3.572	2.280	257				
Grade (internal-stable)				Grade (internal-unstable)			
4	2.211	2.962	38	4	5.579	2.728	38
5	1.921	2.294	38	5	5.868	2.859	38
6	4.346	2.813	26	6	4.077	2.799	26
7	3.783	2.189	120	7	3.983	2.744	120
8	3.854	2.155	171	8	3.491	2.678	171
9	4.190	1.732	58	9	3.086	2.122	58
10	4.612	2.149	49	10	2.184	2.038	49
11	5.070	1.844	43	11	2.256	1.416	43
12	5.304	2.169	46	12	1.848	1.660	46
Grade (external-stable)				Grade (external-unstable)			
4	0.236	0.590	38	4	0.421	0.976	38
5	0.947	1.576	38	5	0.316	0.662	38
6	0.115	0.326	26	6	1.346	1.355	26
7	0.650	1.001	120	7	0.858	1.190	120
8	1.018	1.331	171	8	0.959	1.238	171
9	0.793	0.913	58	9	0.741	0.947	58
10	0.837	1.068	49	10	1.082	1.288	49
11	0.884	1.117	43	11	1.070	0.961	43
12	0.826	0.877	46	12	1.283	1.186	46
School (internal-stable)				School (internal-unstable)			
1	4.688	1.907	80	1	2.088	1.857	80
2	3.831	2.226	65	2	3.877	2.719	65
3	4.226	2.184	62	3	2.468	2.102	62
4	2.052	2.356	77	4	5.766	2.786	77
5	3.484	2.641	62	5	4.210	3.310	62
6	4.480	1.910	100	6	2.870	1.862	100
7	4.851	2.439	67	7	3.373	2.902	67
8	3.697	1.804	76	8	3.868	2.217	76
School (external-stable)				School (external-unstable)			
1	0.688	1.001	80	1	1.150	1.080	80
2	0.508	0.710	65	2	1.015	1.269	65
3	1.484	1.264	62	3	1.290	1.486	62
4	0.584	1.229	77	4	0.364	0.826	77
5	0.436	0.986	62	5	1.177	1.287	62
6	0.900	0.969	100	6	0.970	1.159	100
7	0.791	1.320	67	7	0.508	0.805	67
8	0.895	1.228	76	8	0.803	1.071	76
Response mode (internal-stable)							
Do well	2.097	1.303	589				
Do not	1.832	1.240	589				
Response mode (external-stable)				Response mode (external-unstable)			
Do well	0.440	0.699	589	Do well	0.409	0.639	589
Do not	0.346	0.608	589	Do not	0.492	0.694	589

earlier study may be explained by its limited subject population. That study used only 6th graders as subjects while the current study used 4th through 12th graders. The significant difference due to response mode obtained by the present study implies that music educators will need to consider whether a student has been successful or not when providing feedback after an achievement task to assure that students modify their attributions in a manner conducive to furthering their musical achievement. The significant impact of feedback on students' musical learning has been clearly demonstrated by operant music research (Greer, 1981) and is consistent with the conclusion drawn here.

Gender Differences

A significant gender difference was revealed by the MANOVA which subanalyses of variance indicated to be due to the internal-stable attribution category (Table 1). Females made more internal-stable attributions than males (Table 2). This finding contradicts that of previous research in which females tended toward more external attributions (Bar-Tal, 1978) or no differences due to sex were found (Bar-Tal, Goldberg, & Knaani, 1984; Raviv et al., 1980). One cause of this contradiction could be the generally feminine view society places upon music. Students may learn that it is all right to have musical ability, an internal-stable cause, if you are female, but not if you are male.

Grade Level Differences

A significant grade level main effect was indicated (Table 1). Subanalyses revealed that all attribution variables contributed to this effect. Inspection of the means revealed an interesting trend for the two internal attributions (Table 2), which is displayed graphically in Figure 1. As student grade level gets higher, the number of internal-unstable attributions decreased while the number of internal-stable attributions increased. Students made a shift in their internal attributions from unstable, effort related, to stable, ability related, causes. As pointed out earlier, this may not be desirable and may be a function of learning both in the music class and in life.

Student persistence to attain at achievement tasks is assumed to decrease with such a shift. This finding supports the beginning of formal music instruction and the broad availability of music instruction in the early grades where task persistence may be greater. Current music education practice reduces the availability of music instruction at higher grade levels. An interesting problem for future research would be to determine if the shift to internal-stable attributions is a result of music education practice or if the reduced availability of music instruction at higher grade levels is a result of inherent motivational changes in the students.

The shift from internal-unstable attributions to internal-stable attributions with increasing grade level is consistent with Raynor's (1981a) stages of career striving in which sources of motivational value are time-linked. During early stages of striving, when a student is "becoming,"

Response Mode By School Interaction

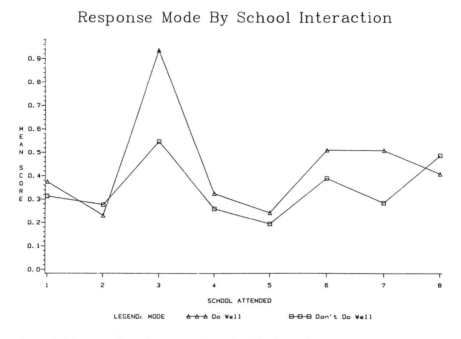

Figure 1. Mean number of responses for each of the internal attribution categories by grade level.

these data suggest a greater use of persistence promoting internal-unstable attributions. As the student matures toward the final stage of "having been," these data indicate a steady shift toward ego protective internal-stable attributions.

The pattern of responses on the external variables is not as clear as that for the internal variables. Generally, the number of external attributions, both stable and unstable, increase with grade level. This would also be consistent with the view that there is an ego protective shift during later stages of striving at a task.

School Differences

Differences in attribution responses were found due to school (Table 1). Like the grade level main effect, these differences were obtained for all four attribution variables. Inspection of the means revealed no clear pattern or trend in the way the attributions were assigned (Table 2). A previous study (Asmus, 1985) also found significant differences between schools, although the differences were not found for external-stable attributions. This difference between studies may again be a result of the restricted sample in the earlier study. Because instrumental, general, and vocal music educators tend to teach all students studying in any of these areas within a particular school, it is proposed that the school effect witnessed in this and the previous research is actually a teacher effect.

Further research, however, will be necessary to provide evidence for this proposition.

Interaction Effects

One significant interaction effect was noted in the MANOVA (Table 1). This interaction was obtained between response mode and school on the external-stable attribution category. The schools indicated by Figure 2 to be responsible for the interaction effect were the two junior high schools participating in the study. Whereas all other schools made higher external-stable attributions to the do well directive, junior high schools made greater external-stable attributions to the do not do well directive (Table 3). This characteristic was unique to the junior high schools and indicates how educational environment can significantly influence students' perceptions of the causes of success and failure in music.

CONCLUSIONS

Summary of Findings

The results of this study indicate that students tend to cite internal reasons for success and failure in music. A majority of the internal

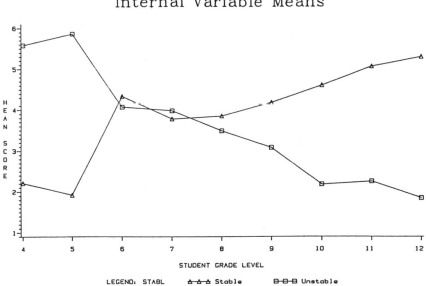

Figure 2. Mean number of external-stable attributions for the significant response mode by school interaction.

Table 3
School by Response Mode Interaction Means and Standard Deviations

		Do well		Don't do well	
School	*n*	*Mean*	*SD*	*Mean*	*SD*
1	80	0.375	0.560	0.313	0.565
2	65	0.231	0.425	0.277	0.484
3	62	0.936	0.903	0.548	0.694
4	77	0.325	0.697	0.260	0.637
5	62	0.242	0.564	0.194	0.507
6	100	0.510	0.611	0.390	0.549
7	67	0.508	0.859	0.284	0.647
8	76	0.408	0.696	0.487	0.702

reasons were found to be stable in nature. Students were found to attribute a greater number of stable attributions when citing reasons why some people do well in music and a greater number of external-unstable reasons when citing reasons why some people do not do well in music. Unlike previous attribution studies, females made more internal-stable attributions than males. Differences in attributed causes were indicated due to grade level. As grade level increased, students increased the number of internal-stable attributions while decreasing the number of internal-unstable attributions. It was also found that with increasing grade level the number of external attributions increased. The school attended significantly influenced how students responded in all four of the attribution categories. It was proposed that this effect actually was indicative of teacher influences. Junior high school students responded with a greater number of external-stable attributions while citing reasons for failure in music while all other schools made greater external-stable attributions when citing reasons for success in music.

Implications for Teaching

A basic tenet of Attribution Theory applied to music education is that beliefs students have about the causes for success and failure at a musical task will influence how the students approach the task in the future. Teachers who encourage students with effort related attributions are more likely to have students who adopt the view that if they try hard and apply themselves, they can achieve in music. Such a view is congruent with the idea that practicing will make a student a better musician and is more likely to result in students who do practice. Those teachers who promote ability related attributions are suggesting to students that it is some innate characteristic that only a few people possess that allows them to be good at music. Students who adopt such a belief pattern are less apt to practice unless they view themselves as an individual with the requisite talent.

This study has shown that students shift their attributions as they get older. When young, students tend to use effort related attributions, while as they get older, their attributions change toward ability related attributions. Young students believe that if they try hard they will succeed at music. Most teachers want their students to apply themselves diligently in their musical pursuits. Unfortunately, the results of this study indicate that the older students get, the less likely it is that their attitudes are conducive for applying themselves at the levels most teachers would want. Therefore, it seems crucial that teachers at all grade levels should encourage students to adopt effort related attributions so that students are motivated to put in the effort required to become proficient at music. It is interesting that the shift between effort related and ability related attributions occurs during the sixth and seventh grades. These are grades when teachers often have trouble keeping students involved with music.

Future Research

A number of future research topics were suggested by the obtained results. During the classification of student responses into the categories suggested by traditional Attribution Theory, it was noted that reasons students cite for success and failure in music did not fall well into the four major Attribution Theory categories as defined by the traditional labels of ability, task difficulty, luck, and effort. A fruitful avenue of research would be to assess the dimensionality of student reasons for success and failure in music through some technique such as factor analysis. An outgrowth of such a study could be a measurement device that would assess student motivation through each of the dimensions identified. Once a reliable and valid measurement device is available, it could be employed with other measures that have been found to be correlated with musical achievement to determine just how large a role motivation plays in musical achievement. Another important avenue of research would be to validate empirically the assumption that teachers have a tremendous influence over the types of attributions their students make. While the present study has provided a number of insights into motivation in musical achievement, a tremendous amount of research effort needs to be expended before a comprehensive understanding of motivation in music is possible.

REFERENCES

Ames, C. (1984). Achievement attributions and self-instructions under competitive and individualistic goal structures. *Journal of Educational Psychology, 76*, 478–487.

Asmus, E. (1985). Sixth graders' achievement motivation: Their views of success and failure in music. *Bulletin of the Council for Research in Music Education, 85*, 1–13.

Asmus, E. (1986). Achievement motivation characteristics of music education and music therapy students as identified by Attribution Theory. *Bulletin of the Council for Research in Music Education, 86*, 71–85.

Bardwell, R. (1984). The development and motivational function of expectations. *American Education Research Journal, 21*, 461–472.

Bar-Tal, D. (1978). Attributional analysis of achievement-related behavior. *Review of Educational Research, 48*, 259–271.

Bar-Tal, D., Goldberg, M., & Knaani, A. (1984). Causes of success and failure and their dimensions as a function of SES and gender: A phenomenological analysis. *British Journal of Educational Psychology, 54*, 51–61.

Beckman, J. L. (1976). Causal attributions of teachers and parents regarding children's performance. *Psychology in the Schools, 13*, 213–218.

Caimi, F. J. (1981). Relationships between motivation variables and selected criterion measures of high school band directing success. *Journal of Research in Music Education, 29*, 183–198.

Cattel, R. B., Horn, J. L., Sweeney, A. B., & Radcliffe, J. A. (1964). *Handbook for the Motivation Analysis Test (MAT)*. Champaign, IL: Institute for Personality Testing.

Chapman, J. W., & Lawes, M. M. (1984). Consistency of causal attributions for expected and actual examination outcome: A study of the expectancy confirmation and egotism models. *British Journal of Educational Psychology, 54*, 177–188.

Christenson, S., Ysseldyke, J. E., Wang, J. J., & Algorzzine, B. (1983). Teachers attributions for problems that result in referral for psychoeducational evaluation. *Journal of Educational Research, 76*, 174–180.

Covington, M. V. (1983). Musical chairs: Who drops out of music instruction and why. In *Motivation and creativity*. Reston, VA: Music Educators National Conference.

Covington, M. V., & Onelich, C. L. (1979). Are causal attributions causal? A path analysis of the cognitive model of achievement motivation. *Journal of Personality and Social Psychology, 37*, 1487–1504.

Elig, T. W., & Frieze, I. H. (1974). A multi-dimensional coding scheme of causal attributions in social and academic situations. *Personality and Social Psychology Bulletin, 1*, 94–96.

Elig, T. W., & Frieze, I. H. (1979). Measuring causal attributions for success and failure. *Journal of Personality and Social Psychology, 37*, 621–634.

Fitch, G. (1970). Effects of self-esteem, perceived performance, and choice on causal attributions. *Journal of Personality and Social Psychology, 16*, 311–315.

Frieze, I. H. (1976). Causal attributions and information seeking to explain success and failure. *Journal of Research in Personality, 10*, 293–305.

Frieze, I. H., & Snyder, H. N. (1980). Children's beliefs about the causes of success and failure in school settings. *Journal of Educational Psychology, 72*, 186–196.

Frieze, I. H., & Weiner, B. (1971). The utilization and attributional judgements for success and failure. *Journal of Personality, 39*, 591–605.

Greenberg, M. (1970). Musical achievement and self-concept. *Journal of Research in Music Education, 18*, 57–64.

Greer, R. D. (1981). An operant approach to motivation and affect: Ten years of research in music learning. In *Documentary report of the Ann Arbor symposium: National symposium on the applications of psychology to the teaching and learning of music*. Reston, VA: Music Educators National Conference.

Krueger, R. J. (1974). *An investigation of personality and music teaching success: Final report*. Washington, DC: Office of Education (DHEW), Regional Research Program. (ERIC Document Reproduction Service No. ED 096 230)

Lillemyr, O. F. (1983, April). *Achievement motivation as a factor in self-perceptions*. Paper presented at the annual meeting of the American Educational Research Association, Montreal, Canada. (ERIC Document Reproduction Service No. ED 237 148)

Luginbuhl, J. E. R., Crowe, D. H., & Kahan, J. P. (1975). Causal attributions for success and failure. *Journal of Personality and Social Psychology, 31*, 86–93.

Marsh, H. W., Cairns, L., Relich, J., Barnes, J., & Debus, R. L. (1984). The relationship between dimensions of self-attributions and dimensions of self-concept. *Journal of Educational Psychology, 76*, 3–32.

McFarland, C., & Ross, M. (1982). The impact of causal attributions on affective reactions to success and failure. *Journal of Personality and Social Psychology, 43*, 937–946.

McMahan, I. D. (1973). Relationships between causal attributions and expectancy of success. *Journal of Personality and Social Psychology, 28*, 108–114.

Medway, F. J., & Lowe, C. A. (1980). Causal attributions for performance by cross-age tutors and tutees. *American Educational Research Journal, 17*, 377–387.

Michel, D. E. (1971). Self-esteem and academic achievement in black junior high school students: Effects of automated guitar instruction. *Bulletin of the Council for Research in Music Education, 24*, 15–23.

Nolin, W. H., & Vander Ark, S. (1977). A pilot study of patterns of attitudes towards school music experiences, self-esteem, and socioeconomic status in elementary and junior high students. *Contributions to Music Education, 5*, 31–46.

Parsons, J. E. (1983). Children's motivation to study music. In *Motivation and Creativity*. Reston, VA: Music Educators National Conference.

Prawat, R. S., Byers, J. L., & Anderson, A. H. (1983). An attributional analysis of teachers' affective reactions to student success and failure. *American Educational Research Journal, 20*, 137–152.

Raviv, A., Bar-Tal, D., Raviv, A., & Bar-Tal, Y. (1980). Causal perceptions of success and failure by advantaged and disadvantaged pupils. *British Journal of Educational Psychology, 30*, 137–146.

Raynor, J. O. (1981a). Motivational determinants of music-related behavior: Psychological careers of student, teacher, performer, and listener. In *Documentary report of the Ann Arbor symposium: National symposium on the applications of psychology to the teaching and learning of music*. Reston, VA: Music Educators National Conference.

Raynor, J. O. (1981b). Response. In *Documentary report of the Ann Arbor symposium: National symposium on the applications of psychology to the teaching and learning of music*. Reston, VA: Music Educators National Conference.

Raynor, J. O. (1983). Step-path theory and the motivation for achievement. In *Motivation and creativity*. Reston, VA: Music Educators National Conference.

Reimer, B. S. (1975). Influence of causal beliefs on affect and expectancy. *Journal of Personality and Social Psychology, 31*, 1163–1167.

Ross, L., Bierbrauer, G., & Polly, S. (1974). Attributions of educational outcomes by professional and nonprofessional instructors. *Journal of Personality and Social Psychology, 29*, 609–618.

Siegel, S. (1956). *Nonparametric statistics for the behavioral sciences*. New York: McGraw-Hill.

Thomas, J. W. (1980). Agency and achievement: Self-management and self-regard. *Review of Educational Research, 50*, 213–240.

Vander Ark, S. D., Nolin, W. H., & Newman, I. (1980). Relationship between musical attitudes, self-esteem, social status, and grade level of elementary children. *Bulletin of the Council for Research in Music Education, 62*, 31–41.

Walker, R. D. (1979). The relationship of selected motivational variables to achievement in the music curriculum. In E. P. Asmus (Ed.), *Proceedings of the research symposium on the psychology and acoustics of music: 1978*. Lawrence, KS: University of Kansas.

Weiner, B. (1974). *Achievement motivation and attribution theory*. Morristown, NJ: General Learning Press.

Weiner, B. (1979). A theory of motivation for classroom experiences. *Journal of Educational Psychology, 71*, 3–25.

Weiner, B., Russell, D., & Lerman, D. (1979). The cognition-emotion process in achievement-related contexts. *Journal of Personality and Social Psychology, 37*, 1211–1220.

Wink, R. L. (1970). The relationship of self-concept and selected personality variables to achievement in music student teaching. *Journal of Research in Music Education, 18*, 234–241.

Wolff, K. L. (1978). The nonmusical outcomes of music education: A review of the literature. *Bulletin of the Council for Research in Music Education, 55*, 1–27.

January 14, 1986

The purpose of this study was to compare the hearing acuity of three groups of music teachers: vocal, elementary instrumental, and high school instrumental. One hundred four music teachers were tested for evidence of hearing loss that could possibly be attributed to Noise-Induced Hearing Loss (NIHL). This type of hearing loss is a permanent loss of hearing acuity resulting from repeated exposure to intense sound levels. Results indicate that some risk of NIHL is involved in high school band directing, but the degree of risk varies widely among individuals.

Robert A. Cutietta, *University of Arizona*
Richard J. Klich, *Kent State University*
David Royse, *Kansas State University*
Harry Rainbolt, *Kansas State University*

JRME 1994, VOLUME 42, NUMBER 4, 318–330

The Incidence of Noise-Induced Hearing Loss among Music Teachers

Noise-induced hearing loss (NIHL) is the permanent loss of some degree of hearing due to exposure to sound at substantially high levels, especially over prolonged periods of time (Willott, 1991). This type of hearing loss results from permanent damage to the hearing nerve (a sensorineural hearing loss) and can affect individuals of any age. It has long been of major concern in industry and in the military, where sound levels must be kept below certain levels and/or protective devices must be worn over the ears. Recently, NIHL has become of interest to professional musicians (see Nodar, 1986).

Several studies have been conducted concerning hearing loss

The authors gratefully recognize the assistance of Judy Cutting in organizing and analyzing the data presented in this article. Robert A. Cutietta is coordinator of music education in the School of Music, The University of Arizona, Tucson AZ 85721. Richard J. Klich is an associate professor in the School of Speech Pathology and Audiology, Kent State University, Kent, OH 44242. David Royse is an assistant professor in the Department of Music, Kansas State University, Manhattan, KS 66502. Harry Rainbolt is an associate professor at the Speech and Hearing Center at Kansas State University, Manhattan, KS 66502. Copyright © 1994 by Music Educators National Conference.

among professional musicians, particularly those involved with symphonic music (Axelsson & Lindgren, 1981; Camp & Horstman, 1987; Jansson & Karlsson, 1983; Johnson, Sherman, Aldridge, & Lorraine 1985, 1986; Karlsson, Lundquist, & Olaussen 1983; Ostri, Eller, Dahlin, & Skylv, 1989; Rabinowitz, Hausler, Bristow, & Rey 1982; Royster, Royster, & Killion, 1991; Schacke, 1987; Westmore & Eversden, 1981; Woolford, Carterette, & Morgan 1988). In all these studies, the majority of subjects demonstrated hearing within normal limits. However, every study found evidence of NIHL in some subjects. For example, violinists usually had a greater loss in the left ear than in the right ear, probably due to the placement of the instrument when playing. The conclusion from these studies seems to be that the risk from orchestral performance is low for most musicians, but some individuals are seemingly more susceptible than others.

Research concerning hearing loss in music educators, or the sound environments in which they work, has been minimal. This lack of research is surprising in light of the importance that hearing acuity has in the professional effectiveness of a music educator and the number of individuals employed in the teaching profession when compared with the numbers employed by symphony orchestras. In particular, the work of Millin (1985, 1987) suggests that the hearing-loss research conducted with symphonic players may not be generalized readily to music educators because of differences in the sound environments in which they work. He found that the typical high school band rehearsal produced sound levels above those legally permitted in industry without requiring ear protection. Furthermore, these levels were 7 to 12 decibels (dB) greater than those produced by symphony orchestras. Perhaps more important, the dynamic range of bands (an average of only 3 dB) was more restricted than in the orchestras (an average of 13 dB), thereby resulting in longer exposure to loud sounds. Thus, with its greater sound levels and reduced dynamic fluctuations, band music seems to present more of a threat to the hearing of a conductor than does symphonic music. In an earlier study (Cutietta, Millin, & Royse, 1989), we tested 32 high school band directors, primarily between the ages of 21 and 49, for evidence of NIHL. The results showed that 41% had signs of NIHL. Encouragingly, most signs were small, and the hearing of most directors was within the range of normal hearing. Still, the 41% incidence of NIHL characteristics was higher than the average 6.6% found in the general population of the United States (Rowland, 1980).

Unfortunately, without a comparison group, the determination of whether NIHL could be unequivocally attributed to band directing was not possible in that study. The purpose of the present study was to compare the incidence of NIHL among three groups of school musicians: choir/general music teachers, teachers of elementary instrumental music, and teachers of high school band. This comparison, together with our earlier findings from the high school band

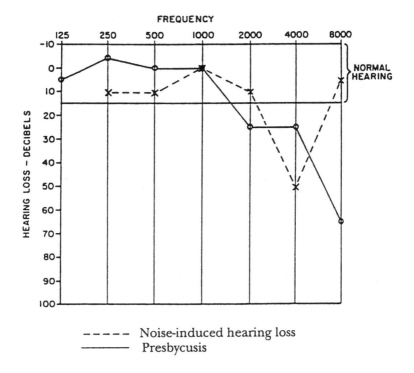

----- Noise-induced hearing loss
———— Presbycusis

Figure 1. Age and noise-related hearing loss patterns.
Note: From Backus, 1969.

directors, should provide a clearer picture of potential risks of NIHL due to high school band directing.

Identification of Hearing Loss

Two types of hearing loss are of primary concern to music educators: presbycusis and NIHL. Characteristic audiometric contours of both types of hearing loss are presented in Figure 1.

Presbycusis is attributable to the natural aging process (see Cutietta, 1981 for a discussion of this condition among music teachers). The characteristic contour on an audiogram that indicates presbycusis is commonly a descending pattern that shows reduced hearing acuity in the higher frequencies.

The audiogram contour for NIHL has a characteristic "notch" that shows reduced hearing acuity in the frequency range around 4000 Hz. Hearing acuity usually is better above and below this range. As in our earlier study (Cutietta, Millan, & Royse, 1989), the hearing level at 4000 Hz in the present study had to be at least 10 dB higher (worse) than at the surrounding frequencies (2000 Hz and 8000 Hz) for the notch to be classified as evidence of possible NIHL.

It should be noted that the signs of presbycusis sometimes resemble or even mask the signs of NIHL, and vice versa. Therefore, any evidence of NIHL found in a study such as this, which includes subjects from a wide age range, may yield only an approximation of the incidence of hearing loss attributable to noise exposure.

METHOD

Subjects

Currently employed music educators who participated in summer music workshops at two Midwestern universities were potential subjects for this study. Of the 114 eligible participants, 104 volunteered and were used as subjects for this study. They were between the ages of 22 and 62 years, with the large majority (76 individuals or 73%) being between 30 and 49 years old. Only 10 (less than 10%) of the subjects were over 50 years old.

Fifty-five subjects (53%) were either choral or general music teachers who taught in various grades from K–12. The commonality among these subjects was that they had no band conducting experience at any time during their teaching careers. Thirty-eight subjects (37%) were high school band directors who had at least 2 years of full-time high school band directing experience. The remaining eleven subjects (11%) were elementary school instrumental music instructors who had no high school band directing experience at any time during their teaching careers. These three groups will be referred to as "vocal," "high school band," and "elementary band," respectively.

Length of teaching service across all subjects ranged from 2 to 34 years. The average was 11.8 years for the vocal group, 12.6 years for the high school band group, and 12.4 years for the elementary band group. The vocal group was slightly older on average than the other two groups. Still, the average ages of the three groups were similar (vocal $M = 39.3$ years, high school band $M = 36.9$ years, elementary band $M = 35.7$ years). The vocal and elementary band groups were predominantly female (85% and 100%, respectively), whereas the high school band group was equally divided between males and females. All three groups had similar percentages reporting regular experience performing with "dance/rock" bands in addition to their school duties (vocal = 11%, high school band = 13%, elementary band = 9%).

Procedures

Hearing tests were administered to all subjects during each workshop. To avoid possible temporary shifts in hearing sensitivity after exposure to loud sounds, care was taken to allow a minimum of 3.5 hours between musical experiences at high sound levels and testing time (Willott, 1991). All testing equipment and facilities met national standards for audiometric testing (ANSI, 1989). The data were collected under the same testing conditions and calibration standards used in the previous study to ensure compatibility between the two sets of data.

Using standardized audiometric procedures, pure tones were produced by a clinical audiometer and played to the subjects over earphones, that is, via air conduction. The subjects were instructed to respond (motion with their hand) when they thought they heard the very soft tones. The levels at which they most consistently responded were recorded as the subjects' thresholds at the test frequencies of 250, 500, 1000, 2000, 4000, and 8000 Hz. An additional test required the subjects to respond to soft tones presented via a bone-conduction oscillator/vibrator placed either behind an ear or on the forehead. This bone-conduction test assessed the integrity of the middle ear mechanism (tympanic membrane and ossicles) that lies between the outer ear canal and inner ear, where the organ of hearing (cochlea) is located. It also helped to indicate whether any damage to the hearing nerve was present. All hearing test results were recorded on standard audiograms (see Figure 1), which show the signal level (in decibels) at which the subject's hearing threshold was found at the different test frequencies.

RESULTS

All audiograms were inspected for evidence of hearing loss at the various test frequencies. In particular, evidence was sought for audiogram contours indicating either presbycusis or NIHL.

Inspection of the data revealed that 15 of the 104 subjects (14%) had audiograms with the contour typical of some degree of hearing loss due to presbycusis. This percentage is high compared to the 4–5% incidence shown in several national surveys with comparable age/gender composition (see Willott, 1991). Eight of these subjects showed a loss in both ears, three in only the left ear, and four in only the right ear. This loss was approximately equally divided between genders.

Elementary and high school instrumental music teachers showed a much higher percentage of age-related loss than did vocal teachers (57%, 23%, and 7%, respectively). Especially noteworthy is that all of the loss in the vocal sample was found in subjects over the age of 40, where one would expect to find this type of loss. Conversely, 45% of this loss was found among instrumental directors under the age of 40. This distribution may suggest an acceleration of the natural age-related loss process due to exposure to excessive sound levels.

Twenty subjects (19%) displayed a notch typical of NIHL. Six of these subjects showed the notch in both ears, nine only in the left ear, and five only in the right ear. Fifteen of the subjects had normal hearing at all the test frequencies, whereas five had hearing outside of normal limits at 4000 Hz. This finding of evidence for NIHL

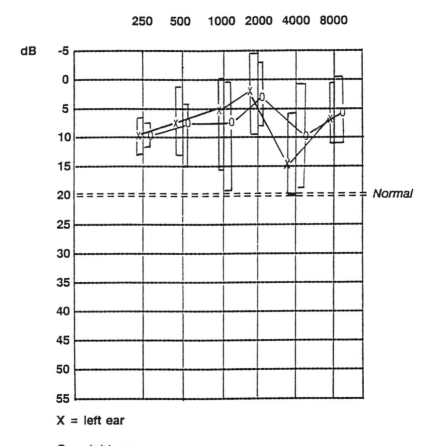

Frequency in Hz

250　500　1000　2000　4000　8000

X = left ear

O = right ear

Figure 2. Composite audiogram for vocal teachers displaying a notch at 4000 Hz.
Note: All composites were obtained by averaging the thresholds across subjects at each test frequency.

among music educators seems to be about the same as it is in the general population, which includes a broad diversity of occupational exposure to noise at various sound levels (Willott, 1991).

Because possible effects of noise were of central importance to this study, we then determined the proportions of subjects with notches in the three groups. Notches were found in 20% of the vocal subjects, 21% of the high school band subjects, and 9% of the elementary band subjects. The similarities between the two larger groups suggested no remarkable difference in the proportion of NIHL between the groups. Cross-breaks by age, group, and type of

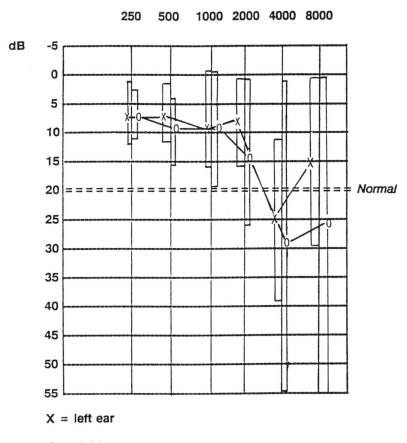

Figure 3. Composite audiogram for high school instrumental teachers displaying a notch at 4000 Hz.

loss produced too many empty cells to be meaningfully analyzed.

Gender seemingly played a role in the incidence of notches found. In both the high school instrumental and vocal groups, 16% of the females in each group had NIHL notches. In the same two groups, 26% of all male high school instrumental directors, and 38% of all males in the vocal group had notches.

The most striking differences among groups were found when comparing the hearing levels (in dB) at which the notches were found. Figure 2 shows the average thresholds and ranges for those vocal subjects who displayed a notch. Although the individual audiograms met our criteria of at least a 10-dB drop at 4000 Hz and a minimum 10-dB recovery at 8000 Hz, the vocal subjects' hearing

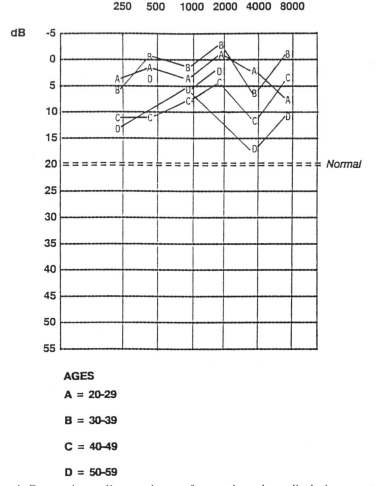

Figure 4. Composite audiogram by age for vocal teachers displaying a notch at 4000 Hz.

remained, in all cases, within the limits of normal hearing. In contrast, notches found in the high school band group, as displayed in Figure 3, show greater average losses and variability among subjects. These subjects' average hearing at 4000 Hz and 8000 Hz fell into the range of mild loss. However, there was wide variability within this group. Some directors showed evidence of severe hearing loss due to NIHL, whereas others had only mild losses and some subjects did not exceed normal limits. The one subject with a notch in the elementary band group had hearing within normal limits.

The degree of NIHL between the two largest groups of subjects (vocal and high school band) was compared by age of subjects. Figures 4 and 5 show the vocal group's hearing had little relation to

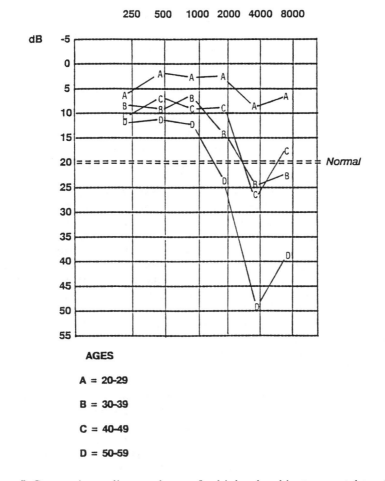

Figure 5. Composite audiogram by age for high school instrumental teachers displaying a notch at 4000 Hz.

age, but the high school band group had a pattern of progressively greater hearing loss as age increased. This supports the notion that their natural age-related change in hearing may be compounded by their ongoing exposure to the sound levels produced by their ensembles (Mills, 1992; Willott, 1991).

DISCUSSION

The purpose of this study was to determine whether high school band directing presents a risk to the hearing of directors. The results indicate that being a high school band director carries a slight degree of risk to the hearing of some individuals. When signs of NIHL were found, the degree of loss was greater among the high school band directors than in the other music-teacher groups. Furthermore, there seemed to be a relationship between the degree of loss and the age of the band directors. Since age and length of service were directly related in all subjects, this, in turn, could be related to length of exposure to high sound levels. This same relationship was not found among teachers of elementary instrumental or vocal music.

Regardless of the type of music taught, these data also suggest that males appear to be more at risk than females. This result agrees with results of other studies, which show a higher incidence of NIHL among males (Boettcher, Gratton, Bancroft, & Spongr, 1992; Borg, Canlon, & Engstrom, 1992; Willott, 1991). This loss is believed to be due to men's traditional employment in more noisy environments, not to any inherent difference in the hearing mechanism (e.g., Rowland, 1980; Willott, 1991). In the present study, approximately 50% of the instrumental subjects at all of the age groupings starting at age 40 were male. Among the vocal subjects, the male percentage for these same age-groups hovered around 20%. Thus, gender cannot be discounted as a confounding variable. Still, the facts that no vocal subjects, male or female, had hearing levels outside normal ranges and that hearing losses were found among both male and female instrumental directors argue in support of their common band-directing experience as the likely cause of the loss. It would be interesting to monitor the hearing of both men and women over the next few decades as the traditional gender roles in music education change.

Although being a high school band director seemingly increases the risk of NIHL, all individuals will not necessarily be equally affected. In this study, fewer than one in five high school band directors showed evidence of NIHL and the degree of loss among them varied widely. This points to the individual variability in susceptibility to NIHL (Borg, Canlon, & Engstrom, 1992).

The NIHL found among band directors may be a function of some other common experience besides their ensemble conducting. For example, it may be that, although the numbers reporting performing in outside dance bands were similar across all groups, the types of bands in which high school directors perform are different from those of the other two groups.

Another possible commonality among high school band directors may be continued practice on louder instruments than those of the other groups. A director who continues daily practice on, for example, the trumpet or percussion is subjected to higher noise levels than an individual who practices on voice or piano.

The variability found among directors may be due to differences in the types of rehearsal/performance rooms among the assorted schools. Although we could not objectively measure the sound levels these directors had been subjected to over the course of their careers, it seems safe to assume that the levels differed because of such factors as room, acoustics, size of bands, and frequency of rehearsals. For example, Bayless (1992) found extreme differences in the acoustical properties of high school band rehearsal rooms. Some newer schools had reverberation times that were more than six times longer than what is recommended in architectural literature. This increased reverberation helps increase the sound level to which the director is exposed. A factor like this may account for some percentage of the individual variations among directors.

This study, in tandem with our earlier study (Cutietta, Millin, & Royse, 1989), suggests that high school band directors need to be cautious about their continued exposure to the sound levels in and out of school. It seems prudent to suggest that directors request periodic hearing tests (e.g., every 12–18 months).

If signs of NIHL are found, there are several potential actions (short of leaving the profession) that could be taken. The first would be for the teacher to request a change to a different line of music teaching, such as elementary band or general music. Unfortunately, for most teachers this would probably not be a desired change.

A second possibility would be for the teacher to wear hearing protection of some sort while directing. This is probably not a realistic avenue to pursue in that existing sound-dampening devices change the quality as well as the quantity of the sound. Furthermore, students might question why the director is wearing ear protection and they are not. Probably the most realistic action for teachers to take is to request that their rehearsal rooms be evaluated for proper acoustical treatment. With professionally installed acoustical treatment, much can be done to reduce the sound levels in a rehearsal room. These suggested safeguards are followed in other environments that pose occupational hazards to hearing, especially industrial and military environments. While the vast majority of directors probably will not be affected by NIHL, all would benefit from regular monitoring of rehearsal and performance sound levels and hearing acuity.

REFERENCES

American National Standards Institute (ANSI). (1989). *American National Standard S3.1-1977, Specifications for audiometers.* New York: Acoustical Society of America.

Axelsson, A., & Lindgren, F. (1981). Hearing in classical musicians. *Acta Oto-laryngologica 3* (Suppl. 1–74).

Backus, J. (1969). *The acoustical foundations of music.* New York: W. W. Norton.

Bayless, R. (1992). *A comparison of reverberation rates of new and older high school instrumental rehearsal rooms.* Unpublished paper, Kent State University, Kent, OH.

Boettcher, F. A., Gratton, M. A., Bancroft, B. R., & Spongr, V. (1992). Interaction of noise and other agents. In A. L. Dancer, D. H. Henderson, R. J. Salvi, & R. P. Hamernik (Eds.), *Noise-induced hearing loss* (pp.

175–187). St. Louis, MO: Mosby Yearbook.

Borg, E., Canlon, B., & Engstrom, B. (1992). Individual variability of noise-induced hearing loss. In A. L. Dancer, D. H. Henderson, R. J. Salvi, & R. P. Hamernik (Eds.), *Noise-induced hearing loss.* (pp. 467–475). St. Louis, MO: Mosby Yearbook.

Camp, J., & Horstman, S. W. (1987). *Report on sound levels for Seattle Symphony Orchestra by the School of Public Health and Environmental Medicine.* Seattle: University of Washington.

Cutietta, R. (1981). Hearing loss due to aging. *The American Music Teacher, 31*(2) (November–December), 30–32.

Cutietta, R. A., Millin, J., & Royse, D. (1989). Noise-induced hearing loss among school band directors. *Bulletin of the Council for Research in Music Education,* no. 101, 41–49.

Jansson, E., & Karlsson, K. (1983). Sound levels recorded within the symphony orchestra and risk criteria for hearing loss. *Scandinavian Audiology, 12,* 215–221.

Johnson, D. W., Sherman, R. E., Aldridge, J., & Lorraine, A. (1985). Effects of instrument type and orchestral position on hearing sensitivity for 0.25 to 20 kHz in the orchestral musician. *Scandinavian Audiology, 14* (4), 215–221.

Johnson, D. W., Sherman, R. E., Aldridge, J., & Lorraine, A. (1986). Extended high frequency hearing sensitivity: A normative threshold study in musicians. *Ann. Otol. Rhinol. Otolaryngol. 95,* 196–202.

Karlsson, K., Lundquist, P. G., & Olaussen, T. (1983). The hearing of symphony orchestra musicians. *Scandinavian Audiology, 12,* 257–264.

Millin, J. (1985). *Sound levels in two high school band rooms in an Ohio school system.* Unpublished report, Kent State University, Kent, OH.

Millin, J. (1987). *Band Room Acoustics in a Northeastern Ohio High School.* Unpublished Report, Kent State University, Kent, OH.

Mills, J. H. (1992). Noise-induced hearing loss: Effects of age and existing hearing loss. In A. L. Dancer, D. H. Henderson, R. J. Salvi, & R. P. Hamernik (Eds.), *Noise-induced hearing loss* (pp. 237–245). St. Louis, MO: Mosby Yearbook.

Nodar, R. H. (1986). The effects of aging and loud music on hearing. *Cleveland Clinic Quarterly* (Spring), 49–92.

Ostri, B., Eller, N., Dahlin, E., & Skylv, G. (1989). Hearing impairment in orchestral musicians, *Scandinavian Audiology, 18,* 243–249.

Rabinowitz, J., Hausler, R., Bristow, & Rey, P. (1982). A study of the effect of loud music on musicians of the Orchestre de la Suisse Romande. *Medicine et Hygiene: Journal Suisse d'Informations Medicales, 19,* 1909–1921.

Rowland, M. (1980). *Basic data on hearing levels of adults, 25–75, U.S., 1971–75.* USDHEW Publication No. (PHS) 80-1663, Series 11, No. 215. Hyattsville, MD: Office of Health Research, Statistics, and Technology.

Royster, J. D., Royster, L. H., & Killion, M. C. (1991). Sound exposures and hearing thresholds of symphony orchestra musicians. *Journal of the Acoustical Society of America 89,* (6), 2793–2803.

Schacke, G. (1987, February). *Sound pressure levels within an opera orchestra and its meaning for hearing.* Paper presented to the 22nd International Congress on Occupational Health, Sydney, Australia.

Westmore, G., & Eversden, I. (1981). Noise-induced hearing loss and orchestral musicians. *Archives of Otolaryngology, 107,* 761–764.

Willott, J. F. (1991). *Aging and the auditory system: Anatomy, physiology, and psychophysics.* San Diego, CA: Singular Publishing.

Woolford, D. H., Carterette, E. C., Edward, C., & Morgan, D. E. (1988).

Hearing impairment among orchestral musicians. *Music Perception,* 5(3), 261–284.

June 28, 1993

XIIII.

The

Past

and the

Future

Cornelia Yarbrough is the recipient of the MENC 1996 Senior Researcher Award. The following speech was presented on April 19, 1996, at a special session of the Society for Research in Music Education at MENC's National Biennial In-Service Conference held in Kansas City, Missouri.

Cornelia Yarbrough
Louisiana State University

JRME 1996, VOLUME 44, NUMBER 3, PAGES 190–203

"The Future of Scholarly Inquiry in Music Education": 1996 Senior Researcher Award Acceptance Address

All of us began as musicians and teachers. We came to research for as many reasons as there are people in this room. Now, as members of the Society for Research in Music Education, most of us are engaged in both teaching and scholarly inquiry.

In the Prologue to *The Canterbury Tales,* we are introduced to an Oxford scholar—too thin, too pale, too nearsighted, and always with his bag of books at hand. Chaucer says of him, simply, "And gladly wolde he lerne and gladly teche."[1] The future of scholarly inquiry in music will require those who share this fundamental ethic of the scholar: to acculturate others through teaching and to lead the culture forward through research. Acculturation requires the skillful organization and communication of extant knowledge, while leading the culture forward requires innovative, creative, and productive research.

The goal of all research in music should be a product that contributes to knowledge about music and musical behavior. Almost every scholar views research as a process during which improvement in research technique occurs. Of course, improvement in scholarly process depends upon repeated research efforts resulting in products that are accepted by a wider scholarly community. Since music research as a

The author wishes to thank the members of the Music Education Research Council and the National Executive Board of MENC for recognizing her contributions through this award. Cornelia Yarbrough is the Derryl and Helen Haymon Professor of Music in the School of Music, Louisiana State University, Baton Rouge, LA 70803. Copyright © 1996 by Music Educators National Conference.

discipline is a relatively recent development, scholarly efforts may be just beginning to have an impact on the training of young musicians and the musical education of our audiences.

Beginning with an update of the content analysis of the *Journal of Research in Music Education* published in 1984, I want to make some recommendations for future research. In this context, I would like to point out (1) the need to broaden ourselves as researchers by developing interdisciplinary knowledge and skills; (2) the importance of nurturing young scholars who understand and can use effectively more than one mode of inquiry; (3) the importance of philosophical inquiry in providing a sense of the big questions and a framework within which smaller hypotheses and topics lie; (4) the importance of building a cogent, focused body of literature in the areas of teaching, preference, performance, perception, and discrimination; (5) the need to define and isolate variables affecting musical performance; and (6) the critical need for timely publication of groundbreaking research.

UPDATE OF 1984 *JRME* CONTENT ANALYSIS

In 1984, my content analysis of the first 31 years of the *Journal of Research in Music Education* was published.[2] In that analysis of 658 studies, I reported frequency counts of articles based on dissertations and theses, and articles using historical, philosophical, experimental, descriptive, and behavioral research methodologies. In addition, I categorized articles within each methodology by general subject matter topic, by sample characteristics of age and training, and by specific research technique where applicable.

I will now present to you an update of this content analysis, a review of the years 1984–1995 of the *JRME*. The procedures and operational definitions of the first content analysis were maintained for the updated analysis. I will follow the order of the first content analysis and make comparisons of the first 31 years with the last 12 years as I proceed.

Results of a frequency count of the number of articles based on theses and dissertations showed that of the total 258 articles examined, 78 (30.23%) were based on dissertations, 5 (1.94%) were based on theses, and 175 (67.83%) were not based on dissertations or theses. As noted in the first content analysis, this percentage appeared to peak during the 10-year period from 1963 to 1972, when approximately 47% of the articles were based on dissertations and theses. A decline to 32% was noted for the last 5 years of the first content analysis, 1979–1983. The current data indicating 32.17% shows that this seems to have stabilized. We must not lose sight of the fact that, in his rationale for establishing the *Journal of Research in Music Education*, Allen Britton stated the need for some way to publish outstanding research in music being conducted by outstanding advanced students at doctoral institutions.[3]

Other observations revealed that 20 senior authors had contributed three or more nonduplicative articles to the *JRME* in the last 12 years (1984–1995). The average number of articles published by these authors was 4.1, with a range of 3 to 9 articles. The 82 articles published

Table 1
Research Methodologies: Frequency and Percentage of Occurrence, Articles and Pages

Research methodology	Articles		Pages	
	Frequency	%	Frequency	%
Historical	31	12.0	449	14.32
Philosophical	1	0.4	12	0.38
Experimental	129	50.0	1,516	48.36
Descriptive	73	28.3	891	28.42
Qualitative	8	3.1	131	4.18
Other	16	6.2	136	4.34
Total	258	100.0	3,135	100.00

by these 20 senior authors represent approximately 30% of the total 258 articles published during this period. These data are similar to those of the first content analysis, with one exception. In the first content analysis, all studies published by the most productive authors were experimental or descriptive in methodology; in this most recent analysis, one historian, Jere Humphreys, appears in the top 20 with three historical studies.

Frequencies and percentages of occurrences of articles and pages for each methodology are presented in Table 1. Data demonstrate that 50% of the studies were classified as experimental in methodology, a gain of about 18% from the last content analysis. Twelve percent of the articles were historical in methodology, a decrease of 5% from the last content analysis; about 28% were descriptive, a decrease of 12%; and there were approximately the same percentage of articles classified as "other." For the first time in the *JRME*, qualitative research is demonstrated in the appearance of eight articles. The most disturbing aspect of these data is the dramatic decrease of philosophical articles: only one philosophical article was found for the last 12 years of the *JRME*.

The frequency and percentage of articles and pages concerning various topics in historical research articles are presented in Table 2. As in the first content analysis, data show a strong interest in the history of music education in the United States and less interest in the history of music education in other countries.

Frequencies and percentages of occurrence of experimental research articles and pages concerning various research topics and number of subjects in each age-group revealed strong interests in the study of teaching (25.58%), perception/discrimination (24.03%), preferences (17.05%), and performance (instrumental, 14.73%; vocal,

Table 2
Frequency and Percentage of Occurrence of Various Topics in Historical Research Articles

Topics	Articles		Pages	
	Frequency	%	Frequency	%
History of Music Education				
United States	22	70.97	323	71.94
Europe	3	9.68	43	9.58
Biography				
United States	4	12.90	58	12.92
Europe	1	3.22	17	3.78
Other	1	3.22	8	1.78
Total	31	99.99*	449	100.00

* Does not total 100% due to rounding procedure.

11.63%). This replicates the 1984 content analysis data, which also demonstrated strong interest in the study of teaching (40% of the articles), perception/discrimination (16.74%), preferences (16.28%), and performance (15.35%). As in the content analysis in 1984, more college-age and elementary students were studied than any other age-groups (see Table 3).

Frequencies and percentages of the occurrence of descriptive research articles and pages with various research topics and number of subjects in each age-group demonstrated that the most space had been devoted to teaching techniques (26.03%), preferences (20.55%), and tests and measurements (17.80%). This is in contrast to the 1984 content analysis, where the most space (39.4% of total descriptive research pages) was devoted to bibliographies, indexes, and lists. The present content analysis showed no occurrence of bibliographies, indexes, and lists. As in the experimental research articles, college-age subjects were more prevalent than other age-groups (see Table 4).

I have indicated the number of subjects studied in both Tables 3 and 4. This is somewhat deceptive, in that it seems that we have more solid results in one area than another. Although there are significant chunks of data focusing on specific aspects of these areas (for example, Al LeBlanc's work in preference in which he builds an empirical data base on a theoretical notion of affective response to music; and the work of several researchers, most notably Clifford Madsen, in the areas of pitch and tempo performance, perception and discrimination), many studies represent one-shot attempts never to be addressed again by other researchers. Only in the area of teaching have many researchers carefully defined effectiveness variables, validated their findings, and con-

Table 3

Frequency and Percentage of Occurrence of Various Topics in Experimental Research with Number of Subjects in Each Age-Group

Topics	Articles		Pages	
	Frequency	%	Frequency	%
1. Teaching techniques, approaches, and teacher training (N = 3,536) a. College (n = 1,719) b. High school (n = 120) c. Junior high (n = 128) d. Elementary (n = 815) e. Preschool (n = 166) f. Music teachers (n = 52) g. Elementary and high school (n = 536)	33	25.58	389	25.66
2. Perception/Discrimination (N = 5,996) a. College (n = 2,275) b. Junior high and high school (n = 116) c. Elementary (n = 1,561) d. Preschool (n = 347) e. College and elementary (n = 365) f. All ages (n = 1,332)	31	24.03	387	25.53
3. Preferences (N = 5792) a. College (n = 1,932) b. College and high school (n = 1,299) c. College and junior high school (n = 221) d. High school and elementary (n = 278) e. Junior high school (n = 179) f. Elementary (n = 965) g. Preschool (n = 45) h. All ages (n = 786) i. Music teachers (n = 87)	22	17.05	259	17.08
4. Performance—Instrumental (N = 1,498) a. College (n = 529) b. College and professionals (n = 75) c. High school and elementary (n = 197) d. Elementary (n = 255) e. All ages (n = 442)	19	14.73	204	13.46

Table 3 continues on next page.

Table 3, concluded
Frequency and Percentage of Occurrence of Various Topics in Experimental Research with Number of Subjects in Each Age-Group

	Articles		Pages	
Topics	Frequency	%	Frequency	%
5. Performance—Vocal (N = 2,343) a. College (n = 91) b. High school (n = 414) c. Junior high school (n = 134) d. Elementary (n = 1,611) e. Preschool (n = 93)	15	11.63	160	10.55
6. Special education (N = 219) a. Adults and junior high school (n = 119) b. Elementary (n = 100)	2	1.55	34	2.24
7. Other (N = 637) a. College (n = 415) b. High School (n = 3) c. Elementary (n = 219)	7	5.43	83	5.47
Total (N = 20,021)	129	100.00	1,516	99.99*

* Does not total 100% due to rounding procedures.

tinued to chip away at solutions to cause-and-effect relationships between teaching and learning.

The appearance of qualitative research methodology is unique to this content analysis. Qualitative research methodology may be defined as that which is based on the notion of context sensitivity. Researchers using this methodology believe that the particular physical, historical, material, and social environments in which people find themselves have great bearing on what they think and how they act. Therefore, techniques for conducting research include, for example, anecdotal accounts, interviews, perusal of materials, transcriptions of musical responses, and demographic information. Since qualitative researchers reject the notion of universal, context-free generalization, the number of subjects observed for a project might be small.[4] The area of musical creativity has been effectively studied by several researchers using this method.

Studies included in the "Other" category of Table 1 are senior researcher addresses, the *Handbook of the Society for Research in Music Education,* discussions of methodology and statistical analysis, and various content analyses.

Table 4

Frequency and Percentage of Occurrence of Various Topics in Descriptive Research with Number of Subjects in Each Age-Group

	Articles		Pages	
Topics	Frequency	%	Frequency	%
1. Teaching techniques and approaches (N = 2,650) a. College (n = 724) b. High school (n = 859) c. Elementary (n = 254) d. Preschool (n = 80) e. All ages (n = 96) f. Music teachers (n = 418) g. Music teachers and high school (n = 60) h. Nonmusic teachers (n = 159) b. Elementary (n = 94)	19	26.03	206	23.12
2. Preferences (N = 5,166) a. College (n = 904) b. High school (n = 234) c. Junior high (n = 990) d. Elementary (n = 542) e. Adult (n = 275) f. Music teachers (n = 284) g. All ages (n = 1,189) h. College and elementary (n = 748)	15	20.55	170	19.08
3. Tests and Measurements (N = 3,893) a. College (n = 733) b. Elementary (n − 443) c. Music teachers (n = 874) d. Music teachers and high school (n = 1,843)	13	17.80	185	20.76
4. Special Education (N = 832) a. Elementary (n = 364) b. Adult (n = 183) c. Music teachers (n = 285)	5	6.85	64	7.18
5. Perception (N = 300) a. College (n = 231) b. College and elementary (n = 69)	4	5.48	41	4.60
6. Student teaching (N = 474)	4	5.48	53	5.95

Table 4 continues on next page.

Table 4, concluded
Frequency and Percentage of Occurrence of Various Topics in Descriptive Research with Number of Subjects in Each Age-Group

	Articles		Pages	
Topics	Frequency	%	Frequency	%
7. Performance—instrumental and vocal (*N* = 1,106) a.High School (*n* = 901) b.Elementary (*n* = 205)	3	4.11	40	4.49
8. Creativity (*N* = 158) a. High school (*n* = 64) b. Elementary (*n* = 94)	3	4.11	44	4.94
9. Home environment (*N* = 229) a. Junior high (*n* = 113) b. Elementary (*n* = 116)	2	2.74	22	2.47
10. Other (*N* = 1,207) a. College (*n* = 484) b. Elementary (*n* = 30) c. Music teachers (*n* = 104) d. Elementary and high school (*n* = 589)	5	6.85	66	7.41
Total (*N* = 16,015)	73	100.00	891	100.00

RECOMMENDATIONS FOR FUTURE RESEARCH

As you know, the presentation of results is normally followed by a discussion section. As I reread the articles published in *JRME* during the past 12 years and typed the abstracts, I began to develop some notions about where we should be going in our research efforts. These notions became compelling recommendations to me, and, as such, seemed a much more interesting route to take in completing this address than merely discussing results. Therefore, I would like to continue by making some recommendations in the areas of interdisciplinary efforts, philosophical inquiry, empirical methodology, research in applied music, and timely publication of research.

Interdisciplinary Knowledge and Research Approaches

It has become more apparent to me from the preceding analysis that, as we approach the 21st century, we, as musicians, teachers, and scholars, need to broaden ourselves by developing *interdisciplinary* knowledge and skills. Music historians need the techniques of anthropology and broad exposure to the humanities and liberal arts; applied music teachers need the skills of psychology and sociology; music educators need the rigor of scientific methodology coupled with strong orientations in the humanities and other liberal arts; and music therapists need the procedures of science, the knowledge of medicine, and the breadth of psychology, sociology, and the humanities. Most important, all of us need research techniques so that we can get outside of our subjectivity and view our musicianship, teaching, and scholarship more objectively.

The ability to change and grow is highly related to success in music performance, teaching, and research. This ability depends on knowledge concerning what has happened in the past, what is happening now, and how we might better ourselves in the future. An interdisciplinary approach allows us to transfer appropriate knowledge and techniques from another area to our own. For example, viewing the Olympics makes clear to us the enormous progress being made in understanding and improving psychomotor skills. Through the use of videotapes of athletes skating, skiing, rowing, and so forth, the subsequent analysis of movement by computer, and, finally, feedback and remediation given directly to the athlete based on the data gathered, dramatic improvement has occurred in highly skilled behaviors. It seems possible that we, as music performers, might learn and apply these techniques, developed by kinesiologists, to the development and refinement of more sophisticated musical, psychomotor skills. Several universities here and abroad are already studying piano performance using computer technology and involving several academic disciplines.

Other academic areas (physics, foreign languages, biology) have been using computers, video laserdiscs, and CD-ROMs to provide interactive learning experiences for students. Given the large research base in music teaching, it seems that it is time for musicians to create interactive learning environments in a variety of areas such as music history, music therapy, music education, music theory, and performance.

Contributions in historiography have been substantive. Attention must be given to nurturing future historians who will provide both researchers and practicing musicians with appropriate perspectives concerning our progress in musical acculturation and innovation. In addition, we must encourage them to apply knowledge and techniques from other fields such as anthropology, sociology, and history to their own research areas.

Importance of Philosophical Inquiry

Much remains to be done regarding the development of young scholars trained in the techniques of philosophical inquiry, including speculation, analysis, and criticism. Although the ability to analyze, criticize, and explore alternative choices logically should be a continuing goal for all researchers, it should be a finely tuned skill for those specializing in philosophical methodology.

The function of philosophical inquiry in the future will be to do what science cannot. Its purpose will be to provide a sense of the big questions, a framework within which smaller hypotheses and topics lie. However, it will be essential for philosophers of music to have an understanding of the progress that has been made through scientific, empirical research. As Patricia Churchland says, knowledge of empirical research is essential "if philosophers are not to remain boxed within the narrow canyons of the commonsense conception of the world or to content themselves with heroically plumping up the pillows of decrepit dogma."[5] For example, prior quantitative research in music has suggested separate functions of cognitive, psychomotor, and affective skills and characteristics. This research indicates that achievement in one of these areas does not necessarily affect achievement in the others. For example, while music appreciation courses may result in students' knowing about the great composers, these same students may not choose to participate in concert attendance where this music is performed. In addition, an advanced level of psychomotor ability in piano performance may not include the ability to play with musical expressiveness.

Philosophical inquiry must examine these connections. Do students need to connect with music through learning to play it, understand it, choose it, or all three of these? If students cannot connect with music, does it then have no value? Does the connection need to be cognitive or emotional or both? Subsequently, future quantitative research must attempt to observe and describe interrelationships between and among the various musical behaviors of performing, composing, listening, teaching, and choosing.

In future perceptual research in music, researchers must understand what is known about the human brain. Immanuel Kant argued that we can know the world only as it appears to us—as it is presented to us—not as it is in itself.[6] However, what we hear as musicians is a function not only of how the world is, but also of how our ears respond to one narrow parameter of the world's properties and of how our brains are formed to manipulate those responses.

For classical empirical philosophers of the 18th and 19th centuries, the only statements given credence were those justified by either direct observation or by inference from other statements already justified. We are now beginning to accept that induction is not the only principle available for empirical justification; we now understand the importance of both inductive and deductive reasoning in the solution of research problems. For example, we now suspect that verbal report may be as valid as empirical observation of behavior.[7]

These are especially important points to consider in empirical research concerning performance, preference, perception, discrimination, and teaching. The characteristics of the musical elements of pitch, dynamics, tempo, style, and timbre may interact in a human brain differently for different musical tasks. Emphasis must be placed on these interactions in musical contexts and new techniques must be welcomed and studied rather than dismissed summarily.

Above all, there is a need for building a focused, cogent body of literature in the areas of teaching, preference, performance, perception, and discrimination. As I mentioned earlier, Al LeBlanc has begun to do this in his work in the area of music preference, and Clifford Madsen, with others, has contributed a large body of empirical knowledge of pitch performance, perception, and discrimination. Empirically, we approach truth as we replicate results.

No other aspect of music behavior has received more focused attention than the study of music teaching. We have analyzed teaching behavior in virtually every K–12 situation available today; we have validated theoretical models of teaching effectiveness; and we have begun to show that certain things are true and generalizable in a music teaching situation. For instance, there is enough data showing the effect of teacher reinforcement on attentiveness and attitude to say without qualification that all teacher education programs should emphasize this in their curricula. We can say also that eye contact is a most significant aspect of effective teaching.

Research in Applied Music

We have not yet solved the problem of what affects a better performance. Several studies serve as models for the study of performance in rehearsal situations. However, much work needs to be done in the applied area of music teaching. For example, a recent article by Anthony Tommasini in the *New York Times* provides a challenge for any researcher looking for a good idea. Tommasini begins the article by saying,

> For an aspiring singer, the mystique of the master class is understandably enticing; within the space of an hour a renowned artist is supposed to size up your problems, impart secret remedies and send you on the sure path to operatic greatness. The truth—and all music students secretly understand this—is that the process of becoming a fine singer and performer is a painstaking effort, and the best support students can have are teachers who stick by them week in and week out for years.[8]

What a wonderful idea for a research project! What is the effect of a master class on solo performance? Is it immediate, lasting, transient, nonexistent? The study of solo performance occurs primarily in a one-to-one teaching situation that is recognized as the most expensive aspect of operating a school of music in a university. Is this the most effective way to teach young artists? Many of my colleagues are now approaching applied study differently by adding voice classes of three to four students and weekly master classes combining two or more studios to the traditional one-to-one method. It seems to me that a good start for an enterprising young researcher would be to capture the great applied teachers, like Dorothy DeLay at The Juilliard School and others, on videotape and to systematically study the techniques used with a variety of students over a long period of time toward the goal of discovering the "it" that makes great and inspired teaching. It may be as simple a solution as, "Give me the five greatest pianists in the world and I'll be the greatest piano teacher."

Researchers must use the technology available to study professional musicians as they practice and during live performances. The careful examination of fine and gross motor behaviors as well as the more subtle nuances of expression should be a priority for those who wish to teach these skills to students.

Timely Publication

Teaching and learning, the essence of our mission as musicians in higher education, require a commitment to the pursuit of greater knowledge about the art and craft of music. With this requirement in mind, our purpose must be not only to broaden knowledge concerning musical scholarship, but also to stimulate active participation in it.

At the completion of the highest university degree, most graduate students are eager to expand their spheres of influence. Some will be superb soloists performing nationally and internationally. Others will expand their spheres of influence through excellent teaching of very fine composers, theorists, performers, and educators. All too few will publish research that will be read by professionals and their students throughout the world for years to come.

Publishing the results of research is the ultimate goal of a serious scholar. More often than not, research manuscripts must be revised to fit the guidelines of a particular journal or publishing house. However, judging the worth of research results may no longer depend on the ability to determine the accuracy of a dependent measure or a statistical analysis. With the rapid development of technological measurement and emerging statistical analyses, keeping apace will only grow more difficult. It may instead be necessary for editorial boards, in the fields of music research that rely on technology, to consider the credentials of the author during the review process. More experienced and productive researchers should be allowed the opportunity to present their research regardless of the inability of the board to instantly comprehend it. There should be an opportunity for controversy, if creative progress is to be made. The question editors should be asking is, "Is this approach workable, possible, foreseeable?"

Elizabeth Minnich makes this point in her award-winning book *Transforming Knowledge:*

> To change the curriculum is by no means to change only what we think about. It is to begin to change who and how we are in the world we share. Teachers joining in this effort become part of an educational project that recalls Plato's dramatic sketch of the cave in *The Republic.* There Socrates makes it clear how well he knows that people do not find it easy to stop watching the same old images reflected on the cave wall, do not like to stand up, turn around, and begin the difficult journey toward a more complete and real knowledge. And he also notes that one who has made the journey and then returned to teach about a fuller reality will be in danger from all those who are used to the one-dimensional images on the cave wall from which all that passes for knowledge—and reality itself—has been derived.
> But if we never startle our students, or any of those with whom we share our

work, our life, and world, if they never feel any anxiety, are never aroused to anger or to sudden, intense, personal engagement by what we say, we ought to be concerned.[9]

The timely publication of research has become an urgent problem. The publication of groundbreaking research must be given priority, even to the extent of pushing other more conservative research aside to make room for it in the earliest possible journal issue. This is already a common practice in the sciences.

In the past, periodicals were considered the best means of staying current in the field. This may no longer be the case. Instead, researchers must rely on professional meetings, symposia, conferences, and the Internet in order to keep abreast of current knowledge. The problem may be due to the fact that music research is similar to that in the scientific fields, where "not only are 80 to 90 percent of all scientists who ever lived alive today, but all of them seem to be publishing."[10]

CONCLUSION

The technology and knowledge available to us today will enable those who choose research as their applied performing area to revolutionize the way we teach and learn music. Information science will speed the process of gathering and sorting bits of knowledge to be used by researchers in expanding and revising the knowledge we now have about music and musical behaviors. Through the combination of technology and information science, we will be able to excite and inspire future generations of music researchers. As Alfred North Whitehead said:

> Art flourishes when there is a sense of adventure, a sense of nothing having been done before, of complete freedom to experiment; but when caution comes in you get repetition, and repetition is the death of art.[11]

Musicians have an opportunity now as never before to put innovation and creativity to work. It is time for young musician-researchers to study how we form our musical ideas, how we communicate them, how we translate them into musical behaviors, and how these musical behaviors affect listeners. In the tradition of Chaucer's scholar who would gladly teach and learn, we must work toward a harmonious blending of teaching and research. A scholarly approach to controlled inquiry in music will be an exciting avenue for gifted musician-scholars of the future.

NOTES

1. Geoffrey Chaucer, *The Canterbury Tales,* edited with an introduction and notes by Jan Halverson (Indianapolis, IN, and New York: Bobs-Merrill Co., 1971), 13.
2. Cornelia Yarbrough, "A Content Analysis of the *Journal of Research in Music*

Education, 1953–1983," *Journal of Research in Music Education, 32* (Winter 1984), 213–222.

3. Allen P. Britton, "Founding *JRME*: A Personal View," *Journal of Research in Music Education, 32* (Fall 1984), 233–242.

4. Mary Lee Smith, "Publishing Qualitative Research," *American Educational Research Journal, 24,* no. 2 (1987), 173–183; John Van Maanen, James M. Dabbs, Jr., and Robert R. Faulkner (Eds.), *Varieties of Qualitative Research* (Beverly Hills, CA: Sage Publications, 1992).

5. Patricia S. Churchland, *Neurophilosophy: Toward a Unified Science of the Mind-Brain* (Cambridge, MA: MIT Press, 1986), 3.

6. Immauel Kant, *Critique of Pure Reason,* rev. 2nd ed., trans F. Max Müller (New York: The MacMillan Co., 1905).

7. Churchland, 242–252.

8. Anthony Tommansini, "Master Classes: The Play vs. 3 Realities," *New York Times,* 28 November 1995, Section C, p. 13.

9. Elizabeth K. Minnich, *Transforming Knowledge* (Philadelphia, PA: Temple University Press, 1990), 80–81.

10. Deanna L. Astle, "Suicide Squeeze: The Escalating Cost of Scholarly Journals," *Academe, 75* (July–August 1989), 14.

11. Alfred North Whitehead, *Dialogues,* as recorded by Lucien Price (Westport, CT: Greenwood Press Publishers, 1954), 173.

JRME Index

Volume 1 (1953)—Volume 45 (1997)

Analysis of State Requirements for College and University Accreditation in Music Education, An. *Raessler.* 18 (3) Fall 1970, 223–233.

Analysis of String Instrumentalists' Performed Intonational Adjustments within an Ascending and Descending Pitch Set, An. *Sogin.* 37 (2) Summer 1989, 104–111.

Analysis of Teacher-Student Interactions in the Piano Lessons of Adults and Children. *Siebenaler.* 45 (1) Spring 1997, 6–20.

Apparent Time Passage and Music Preference by Music and Nonmusic Majors. *Palmquist.* 38 (3) Fall 1990, 206–214.

Applicability of Verbal Processing Strategies to Recall of Familiar Songs. *Booth and Cutietta.* 39 (2) Summer 1991, 121–131.

Application of Information Science Technology to Music Education Materials. *Lane.* 22 (4) Winter 1974, 251–257.

Applied Music Teaching Behavior as a Function of Selected Personality Variables. *Schmidt.* 37 (4) Winter 1989, 258–271.

Approach to the Measurement of Music Appreciation (I), An. *Crickmore.* 16 (3) Fall 1968, 239–253.

Approach to the Measurement of Music Appreciation (II), An. *Crickmore.* 16 (4) Winter 1968, 291–301.

Approach to the Quantitative Study of Dynamics, An. *Gordon.* 8 (1) Spring 1960, 23–30.

Appropriateness of Young Audience Programs for Primary Grade Children, The. *Kyme.* 19 (3) Fall 1971, 366–372.

Are Musical Tastes Indicative of Musical Capacity? *Kyme.* 4 (1) Spring 1956, 44–51.

Art and Music in the Pestalozzian Tradition. *Efland.* 31 (3) Fall 1983, 165–178.

Arts Education as Equal Education Opportunity: The Legal Issues. *Richmond.* 40 (3) Fall 1992, 236–252.

Ascending Music Stimulus Program and Hyperactive Children, An. *Windwer.* 29 (3) Fall 1981, 173–182.

Assessment of Anxiety in Instrumental and Vocal Performances, An. *Hammann.* 30 (2) Summer 1982, 77–90.

Assessment of Motor Music Skill Development in Young Children, An. *Gilbert.* 28 (3) Fall 1980, 167–175.

Assessment of the Classroom Performance of Music Teachers, An. *Taebel.* 38 (1) Spring 1990, 5–23.

Association of Hearing Acuity, Diplacusis, and Discrimination with Music Performance. *Sherbon.* 23 (4) Winter 1975, 249–257.

Attacks and Releases as Factors in Instrumental Identification. *Elliott.* 23 (1) Spring 1975, 35–40.

Attempt to Modify the Musical Preferences of Preschool Children, An. *Schuckert and McDonald.* 16 (1) Spring 1968, 39–44.

Attention and Perseverance Behaviors of Preschool Children Enrolled in Suzuki Violin Lessons and Other Activities. *Scott.* 40 (3) Fall 1992, 225–235.

Bibliography of Sources, 1930–1952, Relating to the Teaching of Choral Music in Secondary Schools. *Modisett.* 3 (1) Spring 1955, 51–60.

Brief Focused Instruction and Musical Concepts. *Zimmerman and Sechrest.* 18 (1) Spring 1970, 25–36.

Career Patterns and Job Mobility of College and University Music Faculty. *Aurand and Blackburn.* 21 (2) Summer 1973, 162–168.

Carl Busch: Danish-American Music Educator. *Love.* 31 (2) Summer 1983, 85–92.

Case Study of a Chromesthetic, A. *Haack and Radocy.* 29 (2) Summer 1981, 85–90.

Causes of Elementary Instrumental Music. *Martignetti.* 13 (3) Fall 1965, 177–183.

Cerebral Dominance for the Perception of Arpeggiated Triads. *Aiello.* 26 (4) Winter 1978, 470–478.

Certain Attitudes toward Occupational Status Held by Music Education Majors. *Bergee.* 40 (2) Summer 1992, 104–113.

Certain Characteristics of Baton Twirlers. *Richardson and Lehman, Jr.* 5 (1) Spring 1957, 31–35.

Chamber Music in Boston: The Harvard Musical Association. *Paige.* 18 (2) Summer 1970, 134–142.

Changes in Musical Attitudes, Opinions, and Knowledge of Music Appreciation Students. *Price and Swanson.* 38 (1) Spring 1990, 39–48.

Changing Aspects of American Culture as Reflected in the MENC. *Molnar.* 7 (2) Fall 1959, 174–184.

Changing In-service Teachers' Self-Perceptions of their Ability to be Effective Teachers of the Arts. *Boyle and Thompson.* 24 (4) 1976, 187–196.

Changing Patterns in the Supervision of Practice Teachers in Music. *McGuire.* 11 (2) Fall 1963, 110–118.

Chapins and Sacred Music in the South and West, The. *Hamm.* 8 (2) Fall 1960, 91–98.

Characteristics of First Year Conservatory Students. *Taylor.* 1 (2) Fall 1953, 105–118.

Characteristics of Motivation for Music and Musical Aptitude of Undergraduate Nonmusic Majors. *Asmus.* 38 (4) Winter 1990, 258–268.

Characteristics of Outstanding High School Musicians. *Garder.* 3 (1), Spring 1955, 11–20.

Children's Ability to Demonstrate Music Concept Discrimination in Listening and Singing. *Sims.* 43 (3) Fall 1995, 204–221.

Children's Age-Related Intellectual Strategies for Dealing with Music and Spatial Analogical Tasks. *Nelson and Barresi.* 37 (2) Summer 1989, 93–103.

Children's Duplication of Rhythmic Patterns. *Gardner.* 19 (3) Fall 1971, 355–360.

Children's Pattern Perception, Accuracy, and Preference in Three Response Modes. *Bennett.* 39 (1) Spring 1991, 74–85.

Children's Singing Accuracy as a Function of Grade Level, Gender, and Individual versus Unison Singing. *Cooper.* 43 (3)Fall, 1995, 222–231.
Children's Strategies for Solving Compositional Problems with Peers. *Wiggins.* 42 (3) Fall 1994, 232–252.
Child-Study Movement and Public School Music Education, The. *Humphreys.* 33 (2) Summer 1995, 79–86.
Christopher Tye and the Musical Dialogue in Samuel Rowley's "When You See Me You Know Me." *Carpenter.* 8 (2) Fall 1960, 85–90.
Cinefluorographic Investigation of Brass Instrument Performance, A. *Merriman and Meidt.* 16 (1) Spring 1968, 31–38.
Cinefluorographic Investigation of Selected Clarinet Playing Techniques, A. *Anfinson.* 17 (2) Summer 1969, 227–239.
Cited Quantitative Research Articles in Music Education Journals, 1975–1990: A Content Analysis of Selected Studies. *Schmidt and Zdzinski.* 41 (1) Spring 1993, 5–18.
Clarinet Choir, The. *Weerts.* 12 (3) Fall 1964, 227–230.
Classification of Recreation Patterns in Listening to Music. *Yingling.* 10 (2) Fall 1962, 105–120.
Classroom Environment as Related to Contest Ratings among High School Performing Ensembles. *Hamann, Mills, Bell, Daugherty,and Koozer.* 38 (3) Fall 1990, 215–224.
Cognitive Flexibility Claim in the Bilingual and Music Education Research Traditions, The. *Bain.* 26 (2) Summer 1978, 76–81.
Collaboration for Music Teacher Education between Higher Education Institutions and K–12 Schools. *Gregory.* 43 (1) Spring 1995, 47–59.
Common Efforts of the Community Orchestra and the School Music Program in Providing Listening Experiences for School Students. *Hoffer.* 6 (1) Spring 1958, 31–42.
Comparative Music Education. *Cykler.* 17 (1) Spring 1969, 149–151.
Comparative Study of Color Association with Music at Various Age Levels, A. *Cutietta and Haggerty.* 35 (2) Summer 1987, 78–91.
Comparative Study of Elementary Music Instruction in Schools of the United States and Great Britain, A. *Anderson.* 13 (2) Summer 1965, 87–92.
Comparative Study of Traditional and Programmed Methods for Developing Music Listening Skills in the Fifth Grade, A. *Rives.* 18 (2) Summer 1970, 126–133.
Comparative Study of Two Methods of Teaching Music Reading to First Grade Children, A. *Klemish.* 18 (4) Winter 1970, 355–364.
Comparative Study of Two Methods of Teaching Sight Singing in the Fourth Grade, A. *Hutton.* 1 (2) Fall 1953, 119–126.
Comparative Study of Two Response Modes in Learning Woodwind Fingerings by Programmed Text, A. *Bigham.* 18 (1) Spring 1970, 70–79.
Comparing Continuous versus Static Measurements in Music Listeners' Preferences. *Brittin and Sheldon.* 43 (1) Spring 1995, 36–46.
Comparison of Faculty, Peer, and Self-Evaluation of Applied Brass Jury Performances, A. *Bergee.* 41(1) Spring 1993, 19–27.

Comparison of First and Third Position Approaches to Violin Instruction, A. *Cowden.* 20 (4) Winter 1972, 505–509.

Comparison of Orff and Traditional Instructional Methods in Music, A. *Siemens.* 17 (3) Fall 1969, 272–285.

Comparison of Preferences for Instructional Objectives between Teachers and Students, A. *Murphy and Brown.* 34 (2) Summer 1986, 134–139.

Comparison of Rhythm Pattern Perception and Performance in Normal and Learning-Disabled Readers, Age Seven and Eight, A. *Atterbury.* 31 (4) Winter 1983, 259–270.

Comparison of Scalar and Root Harmonic Aural Perception Techniques, A. *Alvarez.* 28 (4) Winter 1980, 229–235.

Comparison of Solo and Ensemble Performances with Reference to Pythagorean, Just and Equi-Tempered Intonations. *Mason.* 8 (1) Spring 1960, 31–38.

Comparison of Syllabic Methods for Improving Rhythm Literacy, A. *Colley.* 35 (4) Winter 1987, 221–235.

Comparison of the Motor Music Skills of Non-handicapped and Learning-Disabled Children, A. *Gilbert.* 31 (2) Summer 1983, 147–155.

Comparison of the Singing Formant in the Voices of Professional and Student Singers, A. *Magill and Jacobson.* 26 (4) Winter 1978, 456–469.

Comparison of the Tune Books of Tufts and Walter, A. *Gates.* 36 (3) Fall 1988, 169–193.

Comparison of the Unit Study and Traditional Approaches for Teaching Music through School Band Performance. *Garofalo and Whaley.* 27 (3) Fall 1979, 137–142.

Comparison of Two Approaches to Beginning Band. *Whitener.* 31 (1) Spring 1983, 5–13.

Comparison of Two Approaches to Learning to Detect Harmonic Alterations, A. *de Stwolinski, Faulconer, and Schwarzkopf.* 36 (2) Summer 1988, 83–94.

Comparison of Two Approaches to Teaching Beginning Band. *Whitener.* 30 (4) Winter 1982, 229–235.

Comparison of Two Computer Assisted Instructional Programs in Music Theory, A. *Hullfish.* 20 (3) Fall 1972, 354–361.

Comparison of Verbal Instruction and Nonverbal Teacher-Student Modeling in Instrumental Ensembles, A. *Dickey.* 39 (2) Summer 1991, 132–142.

Comparisons of Beginning Versus Experienced Elementary Music Educators in the Use of Teaching Time. *Wagner and Strul.* 27 (2) Summer 1979, 113–125.

Comparisons of Incipient Music Responses among Very Young Twins and Singletons. *Simons.* 12 (3) Fall 1964, 212–226.

Compositional Technique and Musical Expressivity. *Levy.* 18 (1) Spring 1970, 3–15.

Comprehensive Musicianship in the Contemporary Music Project's

Continuous versus Summative Evaluations of Musical Intensity: A Comparison of Two Methods for Measuring Overall Effect. *Britten and Duke.* 45 (2) Summer 1997, 245–258.

Contributions of Development versus Music Training to Simple Tempo Discrimination, The. *Miller and Eargle.* 38 (4) Winter 1990, 294–301.

Cooperative Promotional Efforts of the Music Supervisors National Conferences and the National Bureau for the Advancement of Music. *Koch.* 38 (4) Winter 1990, 269–281.

Cooperative Research in Programmed Learning: Taped Interval Discrimination Drills. *Spohn and Tarratus.* 15 (3) Fall 1967, 210–214.

Cooperative Research Program. *U.S. Department of Health, Education and Welfare.* 10 (2) Fall 1962, 158.

Course Entry Affect and Its Relationship to Course Grade in Music Education and Music Therapy Classes. *Asmus.* 29 (4) Winter 1981, 257–266.

Criteria of Choral Concert Program Building as Related to an Analysis of the Elements of Music Structure. *Gerow.* 12 (2) Summer 1964, 165–171.

Criteria-Specific Rating Scales in the Evaluation of High School Instrumental Performance. *Saunders and Holahan.* 45 (2) Summer 1997, 259–272.

Critical Days for Music in American Schools. *Pemberton.* 36 (2) Summer 1988, 69–82.

Current Practices in the Evaluation of Student Teachers in Music. *Panhorst.* 19 (2) Summer 1971, 204–208.

Current Trends and New Directions in Educational Research. *Jones.* 5 (1) Spring 1957, 16–22.

Curriculum Planning in Music Education. *Farwell.* 12 (3) Fall 1964, 231–234.

Daniel Batchellor and the American Tonic Sol-fa Movement. *Southcott.* 43 (1) Spring 1995, 60–83.

Definitions of "Knowing": Comparison of Verbal Report versus Performance of Children's Songs. *Killian.* 44 (3) Fall 1996, 215–229.

Demonstration and Recognition of High and Low Contrasts in Teacher Intensity. *Madsen, Standley, and Cassidy.* 37 (2) Summer 1989, 85–92.

Descriptive Study of an Arts-in-Education Project, A. *McGowan.* 36 (1) Spring 1988, 47–57.

Descriptors and Preferences for Eastern and Western Musics by Japanese and American Nonmusic Majors. *Darrow, Haack, and Kuribayashi.* 35 (4) Winter 1987, 237–248.

Design and Trial of a Computer-Assisted Lesson in Rhythm. *Placek.* 22 (1) Spring 1974, 13–23.

Design, Development, and Evaluation of a Systemic Method for English Diction in Choral Performance, The. *Fisher.* 39 (4) Winter 1991, 270–281.

Determination of Musical Experiences Designed to Develop Musical

the First Six Grades, The. *Petzold.* 11 (1) Spring 1963, 21–43.
Development of Aural and Visual Perception through Creative Processes. *Bradley.* 22 (3) Fall 1974, 234–240.
Development of Children Aged Seven to Eleven. *Taylor.* 17 (1) Spring 1969, 100–107.
Development of Music Reading Skills, The. *Bobbitt.* 18 (2) Summer 1970, 143–146.
Development of the Child's Conception of Meter in Music. *Jones.* 24 (3) Fall 1976, 142–154.
Did Puritanism or the Frontier Cause the Decline of Colonial Music? Debated in a Dialogue between Mr. Quaver and Mr. Crotchet. *Covey.* 6 (1) Spring 1958, 68–78.
Different-Age and Mentally Handicapped Listeners' Response to Western Art Music Selections. *Byrnes.* 45 (4) Winter 1997, 568–579.
Dimensionality in High School Student Participants' Perception of the Meaning of Choral Singing Experience. *Hylton.* 29 (4) Winter 1991, 287–304.
Directing Student Attention during Two-Part Dictation. *Beckett.* 45 (4) Winter 1997, 613–625.
Disadvantaged Junior High School Students Compared with Norms of Seashore Measures. *Dawkins and Snyder.* 20 (4) Winter 1972, 438–444.
Discovery Method: Its Relevance for Music Education. *Fowler.* 14 (2) Summer 1966, 126–134.
Discrimination and Interference in the Recall of Melodic Stimuli. *Madsen and Staum.* 31 (1) Spring 1983, 15–31.
Discrimination between Tone Quality and Intonation in Unaccompanied Flute/Oboe Duets. *Madsen and Geringer.* 29 (4) Winter 1981, 305–313.
Discrimination of Modulated Beat Tempo by Professional Musicians. *Kuhn.* 22 (4) Winter 1974, 270–277.
Discrimination of Modulated Music Tempo by Music Majors. *Wang.* 31 (1) Spring 1983, 49–55.
Discrimination of Modulated Music Tempo by String Students. *Wang and Salzberg.* 32 (2) Summer 1984, 123–131.
Discrimination of Pitch Direction by Preschool Children with Verbal and Nonverbal Tasks. *Schlentrich and Webster.* 30 (3) Fall 1982, 151–161.
Discrimination of Tonal Direction on Verbal and Nonverbal Tasks by First Grade Children. *Hair.* 25 (3) Fall 1977, 197–210.
Divergent Production Abilities as Constructs of Musical Creativity. *Gorder.* 28 (1) Spring 1980, 34–42.
Doctoral Dissertations in Music and Music Education. *Gordon.* 13 (1) Spring 1965, 45–59.
Doctoral Dissertations in Music Education. *Gordon.* 14 (1) Spring 1966, 45–57.
Doctoral Dissertations in Music and Music Education. *Gordon.* 15 (1) Spring 1967, 41–59.
Doctoral Dissertations in Music and Music Education. *Gordon.* 17 (3) Fall

1969, 316–346.
Doctoral Dissertations in Music and Music Education. *Gordon.* 18 (3) Fall 1970, 277–297.
Doctoral Dissertations in Music and Music Education. *Gordon.* 22 (2) Summer 1974, 67–111.
Doctoral Dissertations in Music and Music Education, 1957–1963. *Gordon.* 12 (1) Spring 1964, whole issue.
Doctoral Dissertations in Music and Music Education, 1963–1967. *Gordon.* 16 (2) Summer 1968, 88–216.
Doctoral Dissertations in Music and Music Education 1968–1971. *Gordon.* 20 (1) Spring 1972, 9–185.
Doctoral Dissertations in Music and Music Education 1972–1977. *Gordon.* 26 (3) Fall 1978, 127–423.
Duties and Activities of Music Supervisory Personnel in California. *McQuerrey.* 20 (3) Fall 1972, 379–384.
E. Thayer Gaston: Leader in Scientific Thought on Music in Therapy and Education. *Johnson.* 29 (4) Winter 1981, 279–286.
Early Advocates of Music Education for the Hearing Impaired: William Wolcott Turner and David Ely Bartlett. *Darrow and Heller.* 33 (4) Winter 1985, 69–279.
Early Childhood Song Books of Eleanor Smith: Their Affinity with the Philosophy of Friedrich Froebel, The. *Alper.* 28 (2) Summer 1980, 111–118.
Early Clarinet Concertos, The. *Titus.* 13 (3) Fall 1965, 168–169.
Early Public School Music in Columbus, Ohio, 1845–1854. *Kafer.* 15 (30) Fall 1967, 191–200.
Early Twentieth Century Singing Schools in Kentucky Appalachia. *Graham.* 19 (1) Spring 1971, 77–84.
Easy Instructor (1798–1831), The: A History and Bibliography of the First Shape Note Tune Book. *Lowens and Britton.* 1 (1) Spring, 1953, 31–55.
Edgar B. Gordon: A Pioneer of Music Education. *Barresi.* 35 (4) Winter 1987, 259–273.
Educational and Social Factors. *Cleak.* 17 (1) Spring 1969, 152–156.
Edward MacDowell's Critical and Historical Essays (1912). *Lowens.* 19 (1) Spring 1971, 17–34.
Effect of a Music Appreciation Course on Students' Verbally Expressed Preferences for Composers, The. *Price.* 36 (1) Spring 1988, 35–46.
Effect of Appropriate and Inappropriate In-Class Song Performance Models on Performance Preference of Third- and Fourth-Grade Students, The. *Baker.* 28 (1) Spring 1980, 3–17.
Effect of Audience on Music Performance Anxiety. *LeBlanc, Jin, Obert, and Siivola.* 45 (3) Fall 1997, 480–496.
Effect of Authority Figure Biases on Changing Judgments of Musical Events. *Radocy.* 24 (3) Fall 1976, 119–128.
Effect of Color-Coded Notation on Music Achievement of Elementary

Instrumental Students. *Rogers.* 39 (1) Spring 1991, 64–73.

Effect of Concurrent Music Reading and Performance on the Ability to Detect Tempo Change, The. *Ellis.* 37 (4) Winter 1989, 288–297.

Effect of Conductor Academic Task Presentation, Conductor Reinforcement, and Ensemble Practice on Performers' Music Achievement, Attentiveness, and Attitude, The. *Price.* 31 (4) Winter 1983, 245–257.

Effect of Conductor Verbalization, Dynamic Markings, Conductor Gesture, and Choir Dynamic Level on Singers' Dynamic Responses. *Skadsem.* 45 (4) Winter 1997, 509–520.

Effect of Contingent Music Listening on Increases of Mathematical Responses. *Madsen and Forsythe.* 21 (2) Summer 1973, 176–181.

Effect of Delayed Auditory Feedback on Musical Performance. *Havlicek.* 16 (4) Winter 1968, 308–319.

Effect of Differential Teaching Techniques on Achievement, Attitude and Teaching Skills. *Moore.* 24 (3) Fall 1976, 129–141.

Effect of Differentially Focused Observation on Evaluation of Instruction, The. *Duke and Prickett.* 35 (1) Spring 1987, 27–37.

Effect of Disc Jockey, Peer, and Music Teacher Approval of Music on Music Selection and Preference, The. *Alpert.* 30 (3) Fall 1982, 173–186.

Effect of Group Size on Individual Achievement in Beginning Piano Classes, The. *Jackson.* 28 (3) Fall 1980, 162–166.

Effect of Group Vocal Training on the Singing Ability of Nursery School Children, The. *Smith.* 11 (2) Fall 1963, 137–141.

Effect of High Versus Low Teacher Affect and Passive Versus Active Student Activity during Music Listening on Preschool Children's Attention, Piece Preference, Time Spent Listening, and Piece Recognition, The. *Sims.* 34 (3) Fall 1986, 173–191.

Effect of Instruction in Vocabulary and Listening on Nonmusicians' Descriptions of Changes in Music, The. *Flowers.* 31 (3) Fall 1983, 179–189.

Effect of Intensity Training on Pre-service Teachers' Instruction Accuracy and Delivery, The. *Cassidy.* 38 (3) Fall 1990, 164–174.

Effect of Interior Shape and Size of Clarinet Mouthpieces and Intonation and Tone Quality. *Wehner.* 11 (2) Fall 1963, 131–136.

Effect of Interval Direction on Pitch Acuity in Solo Vocal Performance. *Edmonson.* 20 (2) Summer 1972, 246–254.

Effect of Jaw-Thrust Instruction on Trumpet Performance and Overjet of Young Players. *Testa.* 22 (3) Fall 1974, 184–197.

Effect of Keyboard Learning Experiences on Middle School General Music Students' Achievement and Attitudes, The. *Boyle and Wig.* 30 (3) Fall 1982, 163–172.

Effect of Knowledge of Directional Mistunings on the Tuning Accuracy of Beginning and Intermediate Wind Players. *Yarbrough, Karrick, and Morrison.* 43 (3) Fall 1995, 232–241.

The. *Johnson and Darrow,* 45 (2) Summer 1997, 173–184.

Effect of Preparatory Set on Musical Response in College Students, The. *Bartel.* 40 (1) Spring 1992, 47–61.

Effect of Prescribed Rhythmical Movements on the Ability to Read Music at Sight, The. *Boyle.* 18 (4) Winter 1970, 307–318.

Effect of Pretraining Conditions and Age on Pitch Discrimination Ability of Preschool Children, The. *Jordan-DeCarbo.* 37 (2) Summer 1989, 132–145.

Effect of Programmed Materials on the Vocal Development of Selected Children's Choruses, The. *Ten Eyck.* 33 (4) Winter 1985, 231–246.

Effect of Ratio of Positive to Negative Instances on Efficiency to Musical Concept Learning. *Jetter and Wolff.* 33 (1) Spring 1985, 31–43.

Effect of Rehearsal Hierarchy and Reinforcement on Attention, Achievement, and Attitude of Selected Choirs. *Dunn.* 45 (4) Winter 1997, 547–567.

Effect of Repeated Listening on Structural Discrimination and Affective Response. *Bartlett.* 21 (4) Winter 1973, 302–317.

Effect of Repetition on Liking for Music, The. *Hargreaves.* 32 (1) Spring 1984, 35–47.

Effect of Repetition on Tempo Preferences of Elementary Children, The. *Moskovitz.* 40 (3) Fall 1992, 193–203.

Effect of Rhythmic Notation Variables on Sight-Reading Errors, The. *Gregory.* 20 (4) Winter 1972, 462–468.

Effect of Scale Direction on Pitch Acuity in Solo Vocal Performance, The. *Madsen.* 14 (4) Winter 1966, 266–275.

Effect of Subdivision Activity on Rhythmic Performance Skills in High School Mixed Choirs, The. *Major.* 30 (1) Spring 1982, 31–47.

Effect of Task Analysis on Sequential Patterns of Music Instruction, The. *Maclin.* 41 (1) Spring 1993, 48–50.

Effect of Teacher Approval/Disapproval Ratios on Student Music Selection and Concert Attentiveness, The. *Dorow.* 25 (1) Spring 1977, 32–40.

Effect of Teaching Setting and Self-Evaluation on Teacher Intensity Behaviors. *Colwell.* 43 (1) Spring 1995, 6–21.

Effect of Tempo on Children's Music Preference. *LeBlanc and McCrary.* 31 (4) Winter 1983, 283–294.

Effect of Tempo on Music Preferences of Children in Elementary and Middle School. *Montgomery.* 44 (2) Summer 1996, 135–147.

Effect of Tempo on Pitch Perception. *Duke, Geringer, and Madsen.* 36 (2) Summer 1988, 108–125.

Effect of the Timing of Supplementary Materials on Programmed Learning in Music. *Kohn.* 19 (4) Winter 1971, 481–487.

Effect of Three Methods of Supporting the Double Bass on Muscle Tension, The. *Dennis.* 32 (2) Summer 1984, 95–103.

Effect of Timeout from Performance on Attentiveness and Attitude of

Summer 1983, 133–145.

Effects of an Exploratory Program in Instrumental Music on the Aural Perception of Instrumental Timbre. *Kersey.* 14 (4) Winter 1966, 303–308.

Effects of Audio- and Videotape Models on the Performance Achievement of Beginning Clarinetists. *Linklater.* 45 (3) Fall 1997, 402–414.

Effects of Certain Lateral Dominance Traits, Music Aptitude, and Sex Differences with Instrumental Music Achievement. *Schleuter.* 26 (1) Spring 1978, 22–31.

Effects of Competency-Based Methods of Instruction and Self-Observation on Ensemble Directors' Use of Sequential Patterns. *Arnold.* 43 (2) Summer 1995, 127–138.

Effects of Conducting Experience and Programmed Materials on Error Detection Scores of College Conducting Students, The. *DeCarbo.* 30 (3) Fall 1982, 187–200.

Effects of Conducting Instruction on the Musical Performance of Beginning Band Students. *Kelly.* 45 (2) Summer 1997, 295–305.

Effects of Dark-Bright Timbral Variation on the Perception of Flatness and Sharpness. *Wapnick and Freeman.* 28 (3) Fall 1980, 176–184.

Effects of Different Practice Conditions on Advanced Instrumentalists' Performance Accuracy. *Rosenthal.* 36 (4) Winter 1988, 250–257.

Effects of Dynamics, Halves of Exercise, and Trial Sequences on Tempo Accuracy. *Kuhn.* 25 (3) Fall 1977, 222–227.

Effects of Exposure to Classical Music on the Musical Preference of Preschool Children. *Peery and Peery.* 34 (1) Spring 1986, 24–33.

Effects of Finger Markers and Harmonic Context on Performance of Beginning String Students. *Bergonzi.* 45 (2) Summer 1997, 197–211.

Effects of Four Profiles of Oboe Reeds on Intonation, The. *Wehner.* 18 (3) Fall 1970, 242–247.

Effects of Group Breath-Control Training on the Singing Ability of Elementary Students, The. *Phillips.* 33 (3) Fall 1985, 179–191.

Effects of Guided Listening on Musical Enjoyment of Junior High School Students. *Prince.* 22 (1) Spring 1974, 45–51.

Effects of Hand Signs, Syllables, and Letters on First Graders' Acquisition of Tonal Skills. *Martin.* 39 (2) Summer 1991, 161–170.

Effects of Historical and Analytical Teaching Approaches on Music Appreciation. *Halpern.* 40 (1) Spring 1992, 39–46.

Effects of Instruction and Task Format on Preschool Children's Music Concept Discrimination. *Sims.* 39 (4) Winter 1991, 298–310.

Effects of Intensity and Age on Perception of Accent in Isochronous Sequences of a Snare Drum Timbre. *Walls.* 42 (1) Spring 1994, 36–44.

Effects of Learning Procedure, Tempo, and Performance Condition on Transfers of Rhythm Skills in Instrumental Music, The. *Pierce.* 40 (4) Winter 1992, 295–305.

Effects of Listeners' and Performers' Race on Music Preferences. *McCrary.*

Effects of Selected Recruiting Strategies on Beginning Instrumentalists' Participation Decisions. *Nierman and Veak.* 45 (3) Fall 1997, 380–389.

Effects of Self-Assessment and Successive Approximations on "Knowing" and "Valuing" Selected Keyboard Skills. *Kostka.* 45 (2) Summer 1997, 273–282.

Effects of Sequencing, Classifying, and Coding on Identifying Harmonic Functions. *Alvarez.* 29, 1981 (Summer), 135–142.

Effects of Sequential Patterns on Rehearsal Evaluations of High School and Elementary Students, The. *Yarbough and Hendel.* 41 (3) Fall 1993, 246–257.

Effects of Some Aspects of Rhythm on Tempo Perception. *Wang.* 32 (2) Fall 1984, 169–176.

Effects of Special Education Labels on Peers' and Adults' Evaluations of a Handicapped Youth Choir. *Cassidy and Sims.* 39 (1) Spring 1991, 23–34.

Effects of Speed Alterations on Tempo Note Selection, The. *Madsen, Duke, and Geringer.* 34 (2) Summer 1996, 101–110.

Effects of Stimulus Familiarity on Conservation-Type Responses to Tone Sequences: A Cross-Cultural Study, The. *Hargreaves, Castell, and Crowther.* 34 (2) Summer 1986, 88–100.

Effects of Student Teaching on the Classroom Management Beliefs and Skills of Music Student Teachers. *Brand.* 30 (4) Winter 1982, 255–265.

Effects of Style, Tempo, and Performing Medium on Children's Music Preference. *LeBlanc.* 29 (2) Summer 1981, 143–156.

Effects of Tape-Recorded Aural Models on Sight-Reading and Performance Skills. *Anderson.* 29 (1) Spring 1981, 23–30.

Effects of Teaching and Learning Experiences, Tempo, and Mode on Undergraduates' and Children's Symphonic Music Preferences, The. *Flowers.* 36 (1) Spring 1988, 19–34.

Effects of Televised Instruction on Student Music Selection, Music Skills and Attitudes. *Brown.* 26 (4) Winter 1978, 445–455.

Effects of Tempo and Context on Transfer of Performance Skills. *Duke and Pierce.* 39 (2) Summer 1991, 93–100.

Effects of Tempo and Performing Medium on Children's Music Preference. *LeBlanc and Cote.* 31 (1) Spring 1983, 57–66.

Effects of Tempo, Musical Experience, and Listening Modes on Tempo Modulation Perception. *Sheldon.* 42 (3) Fall 1994, 190–202.

Effects of Tempo on Musical Preferences in Children in Elementary and Middle School. *Montgomery.* 44 (2) Summer 1996, 134–147.

Effects of Texture and Number of Parts on the Ability of Music Majors to Detect Performance Errors, The. *Byo.* 45 (1) Spring 1997, 51–66.

Effects of Timbre on College Woodwind Players' Intonational Performance and Perception. *Ely.* 40 (2) Summer 1997, 158–167.

Effects of Traditional and Simplified Methods of Rhythm-Reading Instruction. *Bebeau.* 30 (2) Summer 1982, 107–119.

Effects of Training in Conservation of Tonal and Rhythmic Patterns on

Empirical Method for Measuring the Aesthetic Experience to Music, An. *Madsen, Brittin, and Capperella-Sheldon.* 41(1)Spring 1993, 57–69.

Empirical Testing of an Affective Learning Paradigm. *Asmus.* 28 (3) Fall 1980, 143–154.

Encoding Algorithm and Tables for the Digital Analysis of Harmony (I), An. *Mason.* 17 (3) Fall 1969, 286–300.

Encoding Algorithm and Tables for the Digital Analysis of Harmony (II), An. *Mason.* 17 (4) Winter 1969, 369–387.

Encyclopedia Favoritism toward Native Composers. *Farnsworth.* 17 (4) Winter 1969, 405–407.

Engineering Change in Music Education: A Model of the Political Process underlying the Boston School Music Movement (1829–1838). *Jorgensen.* 31 (1) Spring 1983, 67–75.

Entrance Test Validity. *Frazen.* 17 (1) Spring 1969, 62–68.

Environment—A Factor in Conceptual Listening Skills of Elementary School Children. *McDonald.* 22 (3) Fall 1974, 205–214.

Era of Beginnings in American Music Education (1830–1840), The. *Sunderman.* 4 (1) Spring 1956, 33–39.

Establishment of the Music Supervisors National Conference, 1907–1910, The. *Molnar.* 3 (1) Spring 1955, 40–50.

Ethnographic Research Methodology in Music Education. *Krueger.* 35 (2) Summer 1987, 69–77.

Ethnography of Improvisation Training in a Music Methods Course, An. *Della Pietra and Campbell.* 43 (2) Summer 1995, 112–126.

Evaluation of a Competency-Based Approach to Teaching Aural Interval Identification. *Hofstetter.* 27 (4) Winter 1979, 201–213.

Evaluation of a Sight-Reading Test Administered to Freshman Piano Classes. *Lowder.* 21 (1) Spring 1973, 68–73.

Evaluation of Achievement in Auditory-Visual Discrimination Resulting from Specific Types of Musical Experiences among Junior High School Students, An. *Colwell and Rundell.* 13 (4) Winter 1965, 239–245.

Evaluation of Bentley Measures. *Rowntree.* 17 (1) Spring 1969, 88–89.

Evaluation of Clarinet Tone Quality through the Use of Oscilloscopic Transparencies, The. *Small.* 15 (2) Spring 1967, 11–22.

Evaluation of Three Types of Instructional Strategy for Learner Acquisition of Intervals. *Canelos, Murphy, Blombach, and Heck.* 28 (4) Winter 1980, 243–249.

Evaluation of Various Seating Plans Used in Choral Singing. *Lambson.* 9 (1) Spring 1961, 47–54.

Evolution of Music Education Philosophy from Utilitarian to Aesthetic, The. *Mark.* 30 (1) Spring 1982, 15–21.

Examination of Musical Process as Related to Creative Thinking, An. *Vaughan and Myers.* 19 (3) Fall 1971, 337–341.

Excusing Elementary School Students from Regular Classroom Activities for the Study of Instrumental Music: The Effect of Sixth-Grade

Processes, A. *DeLorenzo.* 37 (3) Fall 1989, 188–200.

First Cry of the Newborn, The: Basis for the Child's Future Musical Development, The. *Fridman.* 21 (3) Fall 1973, 264–269.

First Year Results of a Five-Year Longitudinal Study of the Musical Achievement of Culturally Disadvantaged Students. *Gordon.* 18 (3) Fall 1970, 195–213.

Fixed or Movable Do? *Bentley.* 7 (2) Fall 1959, 163–168.

Flint Central Launches the High School A Cappella Choir Movement. *Kegerreis.* 14 (4) Winter 1966, 254–265.

Focus of Attention and Aesthetic Response. *Madsen.* 45 (1) Spring 1997, 80–90.

Folk Music and Increasing Diversity in American Music Education: 1900–1916. *Volk.* 42 (4) Winter 1994, 285–305.

Foreword to the Papers of the International Seminar on Experimental Research in Music Education. *Bentley.* 17 (1) Spring 1969, 5–6.

Formation of A Cappella Choirs at Northwestern University, St. Olaf College, and Westminster Choir College. *Van Camp.* 13 (4) Winter 1965, 227–238.

Formative Evaluation of a Kindergarten Music Program Based on Behavioral Objectives. *Piper and Shoemaker.* 21 (2) Summer 1973, 145–152.

Formula, Nomogram, and Tables for Determining Musical Interval Relationships. *Mason.* 15 (2) Summer 1967, 110–119.

Founding *JRME:* A Personal View. *Britton.* 32 (4) Winter 1984, 233–242.

Francis Henry Brown, 1818–1891, American Teacher and Composer. *Coolidge.* 9 (1) Spring 1961, 10–36.

Franz Liszt as Pedagogue. *Gervers.* 18 (4) Winter 1970, 385–391.

Fray Pedro de Gante: Pioneer American Music Educator. *Heller.* 27 (1) Spring 1979, 20–28.

Frequently Cited Studies as Indicators of Music Education Research Interests, 1963–1989. *Sample.* 40 (2) Summer 1992, 153–157.

Froebelian Implications in Texts of Early Childhood Songs Published near the Turn of the Century. *Alper.* 30 (1) Spring 1982, 49–60.

Function of Sociability in the Sociology of Music and Music Education. *Riedel.* 12 (2) Summer 1964, 149–158.

Further Investigation of Certain Learning Aspects in the Aural Recognition of Melodic Intervals, A. *Jeffries.* 18 (4) Winter 1970, 399–406.

Future of Scholarly Inquiry in Music Education: 1996 Senior Researcher Award Acceptance Address, The. *Yarbrough.* 44 (3) Fall 1996, 190–204.

Gamut and Solmization in Early British and American Texts, The. *Grashel.* 29 (1) Spring 1981, 63–70.

Gender and Musical Instruments: Winds of Change? *Zervoudakes and Tanur.* 42 (1) Spring 1994, 58–67.

Gender Association of Musical Instruments and Preferences of Fourth-

Spring 1973, 48–54.

History of the Flute and Its Music in the United States, The. *Giroux.* 1 (1) Spring 1953, 68–74.

History of the High School A Cappella Choir. *Kegerreis,* 18 (4) Winter 1970, 319–329.

History of the *Journal of Research in Music Education,* 1953–1965, A. *Warren.* 32 (4) Winter 1984, 223–232.

Illinois School for the Deaf Band, The: A Historical Perspective. *Sheldon.* 45 (4) Winter 1997, 580–600.

Images of Imagination. *Reichling.* 38 (4) Winter 1990, 282–293.

Implications for the Use of the Musical Aptitude Profile with College and University Freshman Music Students. *Gordon.* 15 (1) Spring 1967, 32–40.

Improving Facility in Music Memorization. *Ross.* 12 (4) Winter 1964, 269–278.

Incidence of Noise-Induced Hearing Loss among Music Teachers, The. *Cutietta, Klich, Royse, and Rainbolt.* 42 (4) Winter 1994, 318–330.

Increased Difficulty of Pitch Identification and Electroencephalographic Desynchronization. *Carlson, Chu Wang, and Marple.* 23 (3) Fall 1975, 197–202.

Individualized Instruction, Student Achievement, and Dropout in an Urban Elementary Instrumental Music Program. *McCarthy.* 28 (1) Spring 1980, 59–69.

Individualizing Instruction through New Media Research. *Spohn.* 17 (1) Spring 1969, 94–99.

Influence of Loudness on the Discrimination of Musical Sound Factors. *Haack.* 23 (1) Spring 1975, 67–77.

Influence of Number of Different Pitches and Melodic Redundancy on Preference Responses. *McMullen.* 22 (3) Fall 1974, 198–204.

Influence of Peer Imitation on Expressive Movement to Music, The. *Flohr and Brown.* 27 (3) Fall 1979, 143–148.

Influence of Personality Composition in Applied Piano Groups, The. *Suchor.* 25 (3) Fall 1977, 171–183.

Influence of Selected Factors on Interval Identification. *Buttram.* 17 (3) Fall 1969, 309–315.

Influence of Starting Grade and School Organization on Enrollment and Retention in Beginning Instrumental Music. *Hartley.* 44 (4) Winter 1996, 304.

Influence of Textural and Timbral Factors on the Ability of Music Majors to Detect Performance Errors, The. *Byo.* 41 (2) Summer 1993, 156–167.

Influence of the Meiji Period on Japanese Children's Music. *May.* 13 (2) Summer 1965, 110–120.

Influence of Progressivism on Music Education, 1917–1947. *Miller.* 14 (1) Spring 1966, 3–16.

Information Integration Theory: An Approach to the Study of Cognitive Development in Music. *Demorest.* 40 (2) Summer 1992, 126–138.

In-Service Classroom Teachers' Perceptions of Useful Music Skills and Understandings. *Saunders and Baker.* 39 (3) Fall 1991, 248–261.

Institutional Factors and Job Turnover among Music Administrators at the College Level. *Cornelius.* 37 (4) Winter 1989, 278–287.

Instructional Model for Teaching Identification and Naming of Music Phenomena to Preschool Children, A. *Jetter.* 26 (2) Summer 1978, 97–110.

Instructions Concerning the Teaching of Masterpieces of Art: Introduction and Translation. *Turrentine.* 18 (1) Spring 1970, 37–48.

Instrument Association Skills: Children in First and Second Grades. *Wooderson and Small.* 29 (1) Spring 1981, 39–46.

Instrumental Music Instruction as a Contingency for Increased Reading Behavior. *Gordon.* (2) Summer 1979, 87–102.

Integration of Pitch and Rhythm in Musical Judgment: Testing Age-Related Trends in Novice Listeners. *Demorest and Serlin.* 45 (1) Spring 1997, 67–80.

Intelligence vs. Progress in Music Education. *Holmstrom.* 17 (1) Spring 1969, 76–81.

Intercorrelations among Musical Aptitude Profile and Seashore Measures of Musical Talents Subtests. *Gordon.* 17 (3) Fall 1969, 263–271.

Interference of the Transcription Process and Other Selected Variables on Perception and Memory during Melodic Dictation. *Pembrook.* 34 (4) Winter 1986, 238–261.

Interrelationships among Music Aptitude, IQ, and Auditory Conservation. *Norton.* 28 (4) Winter 1980, 207–217.

Intersensory and Intrasensory Transfer of Melodic Contour Perception by Children. *Olson.* 26 (1) Spring 1978, 41–47.

Interval and Pitch Recognition in and out of Immediate Context. *Shatzkin.* 29 (2) Summer 1981, 111–124.

Interval Recognition in Minimal Context. *Shatzkin.* 32 (1) Spring 1984, 5–14.

Intonational Performance and Perception of Ascending Scales. *Geringer.* 26 (1) Spring 1978, 32–40.

Introduction to Discriminant Analysis, An. *Goodstein.* 35 (1) Spring 1987, 7–11.

Introduction to Seventeenth Century Spanish Music Theory Books. *Forrester.* 21 (1) Spring 1973, 61–67.

Investigation and Analysis of the Public Junior College Music Curriculum with Emphasis on the Problems of the Transfer Music Major, An. *Belford.* 18 (4) Winter 1970, 407–413.

Investigation into Leadership Behaviors and Descriptive Characteristics of High School Band Directors in the United States, An. *Goodstein.* 35 (1) Spring 1987, 13–25.

Investigation of a Learning Sequence of Music Listening Skills, An. *Hufstader.* 25 (3) Fall 1977, 184–196.

Investigation of Growth in Musical Facts and Concepts, Musical Discrimination, and Vocal Performance Proficiency as a Result of Senior High School Music Experiences. *Flom.* 19 (4) Winter 1971, 433–442.

Investigation of Kinesthetics in Violin Playing. *Jacobs.* 17 (1) Spring 1969, 112–114.

Investigation of Musical Achievement among Vocal Students, Vocal-Instrumental Students, and Instrumental Students. *Colwell.* 11 (2) Fall 1963, 123–130.

Investigation of Primary Level Musical Aptitude Profile for Use with Second and Third Grade Students, An. *Harrington.* 17 (4) Winter 1969, 359–368.

Investigation of Reinforcements, Time Use, and Student Attentiveness in Piano Lessons, An. *Kostka.* 32 (2) Summer 1984, 113–122.

Investigation of the Factor Structure of a Scale for the Measurement of Children's Attitudes toward Handicapped Peers within Regular Music Environments, An. *Jellison.* 33 (3) Fall 1985, 167–177.

Investigation of the Relationships among Music Audition, Musical Creativity, and Cognitive Style, An. *Schmidt and Signor.* 34 (3) Fall 1986, 160–172.

Investigation of the Relationships between Music Perception and Music Performance. *Marciniak.* 22 (1) Spring 1974, 35–44.

Investigation of the Relationships between Personality Characteristics and Success in Instrumental Study, An. *Sample and Hotchkiss.* 19 (3) Fall 1971, 307–313.

Investigation of the Use of the Musical Aptitude Profile with College and University Freshman Music Students, An. *Lee.* 15 (4) Winter 1967, 278–288.

Investigation of the Validity of the Musical Aptitude Profile. *Tarrell.* 13 (4) Winter 1965, 195–206.

Is It Research? *Franzen.* 17 (1) Spring 1969, 13–15.

James L. Mursell: An Annotated Bibliography. *Simutis.* 16 (3) Fall 1968, 254–266.

James L. Mursell: An Annotated Bibliography—Addendum (Letters to the Editor). *O'Keeffe.* 17 (2) Summer 1969, 248–251.

Job Satisfaction and Stress among Band Directors. *Heston, Dedrick, Raschke, and Whitehead.* 44 (4) Winter 1996, 319–327.

Johann Conrad Beissel and Music of the Ephrata Cloister. *Blakely.* 15 (2) Summer 1967, 120–138.

Johann Gottfried Schmauk: German-American Music Educator. *Wolf.* 25 (2) Summer 1977, 19–149.

John Tufts' Introduction to the Singing of Psalm-Tunes (1721–1744): The First American Music Textbook. *Lowens.* 2 (2) Fall 1954, 89–102.

Journey to America. *Yarustovsky.* 10 (2) Fall 1962, 121–128.

Judge-Group Differences in the Rating of Secondary School Trumpet

Melodic Memory Tests: A Comparison of Normal Children and Mental Defectives. *Zenatti.* 23 (1) Spring 1975, 41–52.

Members of the Seminar on Experimental Research in Music Education. 17 (1) Spring 1969, 39–40.

MENC Acquires CMP Library and Files. *Willoughby.* 21 (3) Fall 1973, 195–199.

Mendelssohn Quintet Club, The: A Milestone in American Music Education. *Phelps.* 8 (1) Spring 1960, 39–44.

Meta-Analysis on the Effects of Music as Reinforcement for Education/Therapy Objectives, A. *Standley.* 44 (2) Summer 1996, 105–133.

"Missing Males" and Other Gender Issues in Music Education: Evidence from the *Music Supervisors' Journal,* 1914–1924, The. *Koza.* 41 (3) Fall 1993, 212–232.

Model Computer-Assisted Information Retrieval System in Music Education. *Edwards and Douglas.* 20 (4) Winter 1972, 477–483.

Modulated Beat Discrimination among Musicians and Nonmusicians. *Madsen.* 27 (2) Summer 1979, 57–67.

Monotone Problem, The. *Joyner.* 17 (1) Spring 1969, 115–124.

Montessorian Music Method: Unpublished Works. *Rubin.* 31 (3) Fall 1983, 215–226.

Moravian Music Education in America, ca. 1750 to ca. 1830. *Hall.* 29 (3) Fall 1981, 225–234.

Motivation and Perceived Rewards for Research by Music Faculty. *LeBlanc and McCrary.* 38 (1) Spring 1990, 61–68.

Mouth Air Pressure and Intensity Profiles of the Oboe. *Anastasio and Bussard.* 19 (1) Spring 1971, 62–76.

Movement as a Musical Response among Preschool Children. *Metz.* 37 (1) Spring 1989, 48–60.

Multidimensional Scaling Analysis of Musical Style, A. *Eastlund.* 40 (3) Fall 1992, 204–215.

Multivariate Analysis of Degree Persistence of Undergraduate Music Education Majors. *Brown and Alley.* 31 (4) Winter 1983, 271–281.

Multivariate Analysis of Factors in Attitudinal Levels of Wyoming Adults toward Music, A. *Noble.* 25 (1) Spring 1977, 59–67.

Music Abilities and Experiences as Predictors of Error-Detection Skills. *Brand and Burnsed.* 29 (2) Summer 1981, 91–96.

Music Activities of High School Graduates in Two Communities. *Ordway.* 12 (2) Summer 1964, 172–176.

Music and Elementary Education Students' Evaluations of Music-Teaching Scripts. *Wolfe and Jellison.* 38 (4) Winter 1990, 311–321.

Music and Germans in Nineteenth Century Richmond. *Olson.* 14 (1) Spring 1966, 27–32.

Music and Not-Music in Kindergartens. *Kalekin and Fishman.* 34 (1) Spring 1986, 54–68.

Academies. *Fouts.* 20 (4) Winter 1972, 469–476.

Music Instruction in the Nineteenth Century: Views from *Godey's Lady's Book,* 1830–77. *Koza.* 38 (4) Winter 1990, 245–257.

Music Lessons and Books as Reinforcement Alternatives for an Academic Task. *Madsen.* 29 (2) Summer 1981, 103–110.

Music Listening Preferences of Elementary School Children. *Greer, Dorow, and Randall.* 22 (4) Winter 1974, 284–291.

Music Mainstreaming: Practices in Arizona. *Frisque, Niebur, and Humphreys.* 42 (2) Summer 1994, 94–104.

Music Notation Based on E and G. *Fuller.* 14 (3) Fall 1966, 193–196.

Music Reading Ability of Beginning Wind Instrumentalists after Melodic Instruction. *MacKnight.* 23 (1) Spring 1975, 23–34.

Music Reading Films. *Rea.* 2 (2) Fall 1954, 147–155.

Music Reading in the Classroom. *Hewson.* 14 (4) Winter 1966, 289–302.

Music Supervision in the Elementary Schools of New York State. *Banse.* 4 (1) Spring 1956, 26–32.

Music Teachers as Role Models for African-American Students. *Hamann and Walker.* 41 (4) Winter 1993, 303–314.

Music Teaching Competences in California. *Baird.* 6 (1) Spring 1958, 25–31.

Music Teaching in Boston Pubic Schools, 1864–1879. *Howe.* 40 (4) Winter 1992, 316–328.

Music Theory Approach to Beginning Piano Instruction for the College Music Major. *Trantham.* 18 (1) Spring 1970, 49–56.

Musical Abilities and Sex Differences in the Analysis of Aural-Musical Capacities. *Whellams.* 21 (1) Spring 1973, 30–39.

Musical Achievement and the Self-Concept. *Greenberg.* 18 (1) Spring 1970, 57–64.

Musical Activity Preferences of a Selected Group of Fourth-Grade Children. *MacGregor.* 16 (4) Winter 1968, 302–207.

Musical Development in Preschool Disadvantaged Children. *Young.* 22 (3) Fall 1974, 155–169.

Musical Interests of Certain American Literary and Political Figures. *Johnson.* 19 (3) Fall 1971, 272–294.

Musical Intervals and Simple Number Ratios. *Cazden.* 7 (2) Fall 1959, 197–220.

Musical Investigation of the Kamin Effect, A. *Tallaraico.* 21 (2) Summer 1973, 153–161.

Musical Life in Latc Eighteenth Century Richmond. *Stoutamire.* 11 (2) Fall 1963, 99–109.

Musical Style Preferences and Aural Discrimination Skills of Primary Grade School Children. *May.* 33 (1) Spring 1985, 7–22.

Musical Tasks Related to the Development of the Conservation of Metric Time. *Perney.* 24 (4) Winter 1976, 158–168.

Musicians' and Nonmusicians' Aural Perception of Orchestral Instrument Families. *Rentz.* 40 (3) Fall 1992, 185–192.

On the Meaning and Value of Historical Research in Music Education. *Heller.* 33 (1) Spring 1985, 4–6.

Operant Preference for Vocal Balance in Four-Voice Chorales. *Killian.* 33 (1) Spring 1985, 55–67.

Operant Training of Aural Musical Discriminations with Preschool Children. *Fullard.* 15 (3) Fall 1967, 201–209.

Opinions and Practices of Supervisors of Student Teachers in Selected Music Schools. *Clarke.* 6 (1) Spring 1958, 62–67.

Opinions of Classroom Teachers: A Study of Their Role in the Elementary Music Education Program. *Picerno.* 18 (3) Fall 1970, 248–256.

Opinions of Music Teachers Regarding Professional Preparation in Music Education. *Taylor.* 18 (4) Winter 1970, 330–339.

Optimum Length of the Musical Aptitude Profile Subtests, The. *Brown.* 17 (2) Summer 1969, 240–247.

Orchestras in Small Colleges of Northeastern United States. *Banse.* 13 (1) Spring 1965, 39–44.

Organization and Development of the Sectional Conferences, The. *Molnar.* 1 (2) Fall 1953, 127–134.

Origins of the First Music Educators Convention. *John.* 13 (4) Winter 1965, 207–219.

Osbourne McConathy: American Music Educator. *Platt.* 21 (2) Summer 1973, 169–175.

Paradigm for Research on Music Listening, A. *Prince.* 20 (4) Winter 1972, 445–455.

Path Analysis of a Theoretical Model to Describe the Relationship among Five Types of Musical Performance. *McPherson, Bailey, and Sinclair.* 45 (1) Spring 1997, 103–130.

Patrick Conway Military Band School, 1922–1929, The. *Fonder.* 40 (1) Spring 1992, 62–79.

Patterns of Teacher-Student Interaction in Selected Junior High School General Music Classes. *Nolin.* 19 (3) Fall 1971, 314–325.

Peabody Institute: Ideas Implicit in Its Founding, The. *Robinson.* 19 (2) Summer 1971, 216–221.

Pedagogical Philosophy, Methods, and Materials of American Tune Book Introduction: 1801–1860. *Perrin.* 18 (1) Spring 1970, 65–69.

Peer Tutoring Effects on the Music Performance of Tutors and Tutees in Beginning Band Classes. *Alexander and Dorow.* 31 (1) Spring 1983, 33–47.

Perceived Effectiveness of Mainstreaming in Iowa and Kansas Schools. *Gfeller, Darrow, and Hedden.* 38 (2) Summer 1990, 90–101.

Perception and Analysis of the Difference Tone Phenomenon as an Environmental Event. *Asmus, Jr.* 26 (2) Summer 1978, 82–89.

Perception of Tempo Modulation by Listeners of Different Levels of Educational Experience. *Sheldon and Gregory.* 45 (3) Fall 1997, 367–379.

Perception of Tonality in Short Melodies. *Taylor.* 24 (4) Winter 1976,

Bergan. 13 (1) Spring 1965, 15–32.

Pitch, Tempo, and Timbral Preferences in Recorded Piano Music. *Wapnick.* 28 (1) Spring 1980, 43–58.

Place of Music in German Education around 1600, The. *Livingstone.* 19 (2) Summer 1971, 144–167.

Place of Music in German Education from the Beginning through the 16th Century, The. *Livingstone.* 15 (4) Winter 1967, 243–277.

Place of the Performance Area in Training High School Music Teachers. *Peterson.* 4 (1) Spring 1956, 52–56.

Polish Research on the Psychology of Music. *Polakowski.* 20 (2) Summer 1972, 286–288.

Poor Pitch Singing: Response of Monotone Singers to a Program of Remedial Training. *Roberts and Davies.* 23 (4) Winter 1974, 227–239.

Portrait of a Nineteenth-Century School Music Program. *Riley.* 38 (2) Summer 1990, 79–89.

Pragmatic Approach to Certain Aspects of Music Education, A. *McMurray.* 4 (2) Fall 1956, 103–112.

Praise and Corrective Feedback in the Remediation of Incorrect Left-Hand Positions of Elementary String Players. *Salzberg and Salzberg.* 29 (2) Summer 1981, 235–134.

Precursors of Musical Aptitude Testing: From the Greeks through the Works of Francis Galton. *Humphreys.* 41 (4) Winter 1993, 315–327.

Predicting Choral Achievement through Use of Musicality and Intelligence Scores. *Helwig and Thomas.* 21 (3) Fall 1973, 276–280.

Predicting Music Theory Grades: The Relative Efficiency of Academic Ability, Music Experience, and Music Aptitude. *Harrison.* 38 (2) Summer 1990, 124–137.

Predicting Performance Achievement and Retention of Fifth-Grade Instrumental Students. *Klinedinst.* 39 (3) Fall 1991, 225– 238.

Predicting Success in Beginning Instrumental Music through Uses of Selected Tests. *Hufstader.* 22 (1) Spring 1974, 52–57.

Prediction of Academic Success of College Music Majors, The. *Ernest.* 18 (3) Fall 1970, 273–276.

Prediction of Music Achievement in the Elementary School. *Hedden.* 30 (1) Spring 1982, 61–68.

Prediction of Performer Attentiveness Based on Rehearsal Activity and Teacher Behavior. *Yarbrough and Price.* 29 (3) Fall 1981, 209–218.

Preference and Interest as Functions of Distributional Redundancy in Rhythmic Sequences. *McMullen and Arnold.* 24 (1) Spring 1976, 22–31.

Preferences for Single Tone Stimuli. *Hedden.* 22 (2) Summer 1974, 136–142.

Preferences of Elderly Individuals for Selected Music Education Experiences. *Beal-Gilbert.* 30 (4) Winter 1982, 247–253.

Preferences of Undergraduate Music Majors for Sequenced versus Performed Piano Music. *Wapnick and Rosenquist.* 39 (2) Summer 1991,

Recognition of Repeated and Altered Thematic Materials in Music. *Duerksen.* 16 (1) Spring 1968, 3–30.

Rehearsal Organizational Structures Used by Successful High School Choral Directors. *Cox.* 37 (3) Fall 1989, 201–218.

Relation between Six Paintings by Paul Klee and Selected Musical Compositions, The. *Wehner.* 14 (3) Fall 1966, 220–224.

Relationally Analytic and the Impressionistically Concrete Components of Western Music, The. *Northrup.* 19 (4) Winter 1971, 399–407.

Relationship among Aspects of Cognitive Style and Language-Bound/Language-Optional Perception to Musicians' Performance in Aural Discrimination Tasks, The. *Schmidt.* 32 (3) Fall 1984, 159–168.

Relationship among Conductors' Ranking of Three Unfamiliar Wind Band Scores, The. *Fiese.* 39 (3) Fall 1991, 239–247.

Relationship between Academic Preparation and Professional Responsibilities of Secondary School Music Teachers, The. *Franklin.* 19 (4) Winter 1971, 460–466.

Relationship between Creative Behavior in Music and Selected Variables as Measured in High School Students. *Webster.* 27 (4) Winter 1979, 227–242.

Relationship between Curriculum and Learner: Music Composition and Learning Style, The. *Moore.* 38 (1) Spring 1990, 24–38.

Relationship between Grades in Music Theory for Nonmusic Majors and Selected Background Variables. *Harrison.* 44 (4) Winter 1996, 341.

Relationship between Grades in the Components of Freshman Music Theory and Selected Background Variables. *Harrison.* 38 (3) Fall 1990, 175–186.

Relationship between Home Musical Environment and Selected Music Attributes of Second-Grade Children. *Brand.* 34 (2) Summer 1986, 111–120.

Relationship between Humor Perceived in Music and Preferences of Different-Age Listeners. *LeBlanc, Sims, Malin, and Sherrill.* 40 (4) Winter 1992, 269–282.

Relationship between Musical and Social Patterns in American Popular Music, The. *Etzkorn.* 12 (4) Winter 1964, 279–286.

Relationship between Observers' Recorded Teacher Behavior and Evaluation of Music Instruction, The. *Duke and Blackman.* 39 (4) Winter 1991, 290–297.

Relationship between Pitch Recognition and Vocal Pitch Production in Sixth Grade Students, The. *Pedersen and Pedersen* 18 (3) Fall 1970, 265–272.

Relationship between Sightsinging Accuracy and Error Detection in Junior High Singers, The. *Killian.* 39 (3) Fall 1991, 216–224.

Relationship between Teaching Incidents and Taba's Theoretical Construct. *Dorman.* 21 (2) Summer 1973, 182–186.

Relationship of Behavioral Self-assessment to the Achievement of Basic

1981, 183–189.

Relationships between Pitch Memory in Short Melodies and Selected Factors. *Long.* 25 (4) Winter 1977, 272–282.

Relative Effectiveness of Contrasted Music Teaching Styles for the Culturally Deprived. *Reid.* 20 (4) Winter 1972, 484–490.

Relative Effectiveness of Two Approaches to Rhythm Reading for Fourth-Grade Students. *Palmer.* 24 (3) Fall 1976, 110–118.

Relative Effects of Guided Model, Model Only, Guide Only, and Practice Only Treatments on the Accuracy of Advanced Instrumentalists' Musical Performance, The. *Rosenthal.* 32 (4) Winter 1984, 265–273.

Repetition as a Factor in the Development of Musical Preferences. *Bradley.* 19 (3) Fall 1971, 295–298.

Repetition Effects Depend on Duration and Are Enhanced by Continuation of Interrupted Music. *Coppock.* 26 (4) Winter 1978, 436–444.

Replication of a Study on Teaching Singing in the Elementary General Music Classroom. *Froelich.* 27 (1) Spring 1979, 35–45.

Report of an Informal Symposium on the Organization and Administration of Music Education Degree Programs. *Henke.* 17 (3) Fall 1969, 301–308.

Report of the Third International Seminar on Research on Music Education, A. *Petzold.* 21 (2) Summer 1973, 99–105.

Republican Harmony (1795) of Nathaniel Billings, The. *Link.* 18 (4) Winter 1970, 414–419.

Research in Music Education. *Choate.* 13 (2) Summer 1965, 67–86.

Research in the United States. *Britton.* 17 (1) Spring 1969, 108–111.

Research: Philosophy and Esthetics. *Leonard.* 3 (1), Spring 1955, 23–26.

Research Study of a Technique for Adjusting Clarinet Reeds, A. *Intravaia and Resnick.* 16 (1) Spring 1968, 45–58.

Researchers in Music Education/Therapy: Analysis of Publications, Citations and Retrievability of Work. *Brittin and Standley.* 45 (1) Spring 1997, 145–160.

Responses of Children to Musical Tasks Embodying Piaget's Principle of Conservation. *Pflederer.* 12 (4) Winter 1964, 251–268.

Responses of Kindergarten Children to Musical Stimuli and Terminology. *Van Zee.* 24 (1) Spring 1976, 14–21.

Responses to Rhythm Patterns When Presented to Children through Auditory, Visual, and Kinesthetic Modalities. *Persellin.* 40 (4) Winter 1992, 306–315.

Review and Survey of MENC Research Training Institutes. *Nelson and Williams.* 25 (1) Spring 1977, 3–20.

Review of Measures of Musico-Aesthetic Attitude, A. *Bullock.* 21 (4) Winter 1973, 331–344.

Review of the Approaches to the Management of Tension and Stage Fright in Music Performance, A. *Lehrer.* 35 (3) Fall 1987, 143–153.

129–136.

Schools Band Contest of America (1923), The. *Holz.* 10 (1) Spring 1962, 3–12.

Secular Cantata in the United States, The: 1850–1919. *Stopp.* 17 (4) Winter 1969, 388–398.

Selected Bibliography of Works on Music Testing. *Lehman.* 17 (4) Winter 1969, 427–442.

Selected Indexes of the Academic and Professional Preparation of Music Supervisors in Canada. *Jorgensen.* 28 (2) Summer 1980, 92–102.

Selective List of Choral and Vocal Music with Wind and Percussion Accompaniments, A. *Vagner.* 14 (4) Winter 1966, 276–288.

Self-Expressed Adult Music Education Interests and Music Experiences. *Bowles.* 39 (3) Fall 1991, 191–205.

Self-Instructional Drill Materials for Student Conductors. *Sidnell.* 19 (1) Spring 1971, 85–91.

Self-Instructional Program for Musical Concept Development in Preschool Children. *Romanek.* 22 (2) Summer 1974, 129–135.

Self-Reported versus Observed Classroom Activities in Elementary General Music. *Wang and Sogin.* 45 (3) Fall 1997, 444–456.

Senior Researcher Award Acceptance Address. *Madsen.* 36 (3) Fall 1988, 133–139.

Sequential Patterns and the Music Teaching Effectiveness of Elementary Education Majors. *Bowers.* 45 (3) Fall 1997, 428–443.

Sequential Patterns of Instruction in Music. *Yarbrough and Price.* 37 (3) Fall 1989, 179–187.

Sequential Patterns of Music Instruction and Learning to Use Them. *Price.* 40 (1) Spring 1992, 14–29.

Sex Stereotyping of Musical Instruments, The. *Abeles and Porter.* 26 (2) Summer 1978, 65–75.

Sex-Role Associations of Music Instruments and Occupations by Gender and Major. *Griswold and Chroback.* 29 (1) Spring 1981, 57–62.

Short-Term Music Instruction and Young Children's Developmental Music Aptitude. *Flohr.* 29 (3) Fall 1981, 219–224.

Short-Term Retention of Pitch Sequence. *Williams.* 23 (1) Spring 1975, 53–66.

Sight-Reading and Ear-Playing Abilities as Related to Instrumental Music Students. *Luce.* 13 (2) Summer 1965, 101–109.

Sight-Singing Instruction in the Choral Rehearsal: Factors Related to Individual Performance. *Demorest and May.* 43 (2) Summer 1995, 156–167.

Significant Developments in Choral Music Education in Higher Education between 1950–1980. *White.* 30 (2) Summer 1982, 121–128.

Simple Instrument Experiences in School Music Programs from 1900. *Mathis.* 21 (3) Fall 1973, 270–275.

Simulations for Music Education. *Swift.* 19 (4) Winter 1971, 488–491.

Structured and Unstructured Musical Contexts and Children's Ability to Demonstrate Tempo and Dynamic Contrasts. *Flowers, Wapnick, and Ramsey.* 45 (3) Fall 1997, 341–355.

Structuring Small Music Groups and Music Reinforcement to Facilitate Positive Interactions and Acceptance of Severely Handicapped Students in the Regular Music Classroom. *Jellison, Brooks, and Huck.* 32 (4) Winter 1984, 243–264.

Student Beliefs about the Causes of Success and Failure in Music: A Study of Achievement Motivation. *Asmus.* 34 (4) Winter 1986, 262–278.

Student Interpretations of Teacher Verbal Praise in Selected Seventh- and Eighth-Grade Choral Classes. *Taylor.* 45 (4) Winter 1997, 536–546.

Student Participation in Decision-Making Processes Concerning Musical Performance. *Petters.* 24 (4) Winter 1976, 177–186.

Student Perceptions of Characteristics of Effective Applied Music Instructors. *Abeles.* 23 (2) Summer 1975, 147–154.

Student Personality and Instrumental Participation, Continuation, and Choice. *Cutietta and McAllister.* 45 (2) Summer 1997, 282–294.

Student Teachers' Pre-active and Post-active Curricular Thinking. *Schleuter.* 39 (1) Spring 1991, 46–63.

Studies in Music Appreciation: I. A Program of Testing; II. Measuring the Listeners' Recognition of Formal Music; III. Experimental Analysis of the Process. *Mueller.* 4 (1) Spring 1956, 3–25.

Study in Aural Perception, A. *Sherman, A.* 18 (4) Winter 1970, 377–384.

Study in the Correlation of Music Theory Grades with the Seashore Measures of Musical Talents and the Aliferis Music Achievement Test, A. *Roby.* 10 (2) Fall 1962, 137–142.

Study in the Development of Music Listening Skills of Secondary School Students, A. *Haack.* 17 (2) Summer 1969, 193–201.

Study Involving the Visual Arts in the Development of Musical Concepts, A. *Haack.* 18 (4) Winter 1970, 392–398.

Study of a Behaviorally Oriented Training Program for Aural Skills. *Harriss.* 22 (3) Fall 1974, 215–225.

Study of Certain Practices in Music Education in School Systems of Cities over 150,000 Populations. *Ernst.* 5 (1) Spring 1957, 23–30.

Study of Community Attitudes toward Music Education in the Public Schools of Selected Communities in Missouri. *Burmeister.* 3 (2) Fall 1955, 77–91.

Study of Gaston's 'Test of Musicality' as Applied to College Students, A. *Yoder.* 20 (4) Winter 1972, 491–495.

Study of High School Music Participants' Stylistic Preferences and Identification Abilities in Music and the Visual Arts, A. *Haack.* 30 (4) Winter 1982, 213–220.

Study of Internal Validity of the Instrument Timbre Preference Test. *Williams.* 44 (3) Fall 1996, 268–277.

Study of Middle School Band Students' Instrument Choices, A. *Fortney,*

the Rehearsal Setting. *Blocker, Greenwood, and Shellahamer.* 45 (3) Fall 1997, 457–469.

Teaching Clarinet Fingerings with Teaching Machines. *Woelflin.* 12 (4) Winter 1964, 287–294.

Teaching Composition via Schenker's Theory. *Silberman.* 12 (4) Winter 1964, 295–303.

Teaching Effectiveness among Teaching Competency Measures, Pupil Product Measures, and Certain Attribute Variables. *Taebel and Coker.* 28 (4) Winter 1980, 250–264.

Teaching Load and Related Activities of Music Teachers in Indiana Public Schools, 1953–1954, The. *Colbert.* 9 (2), Fall 1961, 125–146.

Teaching Music Fundamentals to the Seventh Grade via Programmed Materials. *Owens.* 21 (1) Spring 1973, 55–60.

Teaching of Music Appreciation, The. *Tischler.* 7 (2) Fall 1959, 169–173.

Techniques for the Evaluation of Musical Status. *Taylor.* 11 (1) Spring 1963, 55–62.

Teen-Age Music Preferences. *Baumann.* 8 (2) Fall 1960, 75–84.

Tempo Perception and Performance of Elementary Students, Grades 3–6. *Ellis.* 40 (4) Winter 1992, 329–341.

Tempo Preferences of Different Age Music Listeners. *LeBlanc, Colman, McCrary, Sherrill, and Malin.* 36 (3) Fall 1988, 156–168.

Temporal Discrimination of Modulated Intensity in Music Excerpts and Tones. *Geringer.* 39 (2) Summer 1991, 113–120.

Tentative Bibliography of Early Wind Instrument Tutors. *Riley.* 6 (1) Spring 1958, 3–24.

Testing Music Hearing in Right and Left Ears of Children Ages Ten, Eleven, and Twelves. *Gollnick.* 26 (1) Spring 1978, 16–21.

Tests and Measures in Higher Education. *Cady.* 15 (2) Summer 1967, 139–150.

Theoretical Relationship between Item Difficulty and the "in Doubt" Response in Music Tests, The. *Levendusky.* 27 (3) Fall 1979, 163–172.

Third Edition of Tufts' Introduction to the Art of Singing Psalm-Tunes, The. *Finney.* 14 (3) Fall 1966, 163–170.

Thomas Harrison's Patented Numeral Notation System. *Elward.* 28 (4) Winter 1980, 218–224.

Time Analysis of the Compositional Processes Used by Children Ages 7 to 11, A. *Kratus.* 37 (1) Spring 1989, 5–20.

Time Use in Instrumental Rehearsals: A Comparison of Experienced, Novice, and Student Teachers. *Goolsby.* 44 (4) Winter 1996, 286–303.

Time-Velocity Ratio Investigation, A. *Bickel.* 32 (2) Summer 1984, 105–111.

Tonality as a Basis for Musical Talent. *Franklin.* 17 (1) Spring 1969, 58–61.

Tone-Word System of Carl Eitz, The. *Jones.* 14 (2) Summer 1966, 84–98.

Total Work Load of High School Music Teachers in Michigan. *Steg.* 3 (2) Fall 1955, 101–118.

Toward an International Solfeggio. *Siler.* 4 (1) Spring 1956, 40–43.

Using a Vertical Keyboard Instrument with the Uncertain Singer. *Jones.* 27 (3) 1979, 173–184.

Using MAP Scores in the Instruction of Beginning Students in Instrumental Music. *Froseth.* 19 (1) Spring 1971, 95–105.

Validation Study of a Measure of Musical Creativity, A. *Baltzer.* 36 (4) Winter 1988, 232–249.

Value of Notated Examples in Learning to Recognize Musical Themes Aurally, The. *Smith.* 1 (2) Fall 1953, 97–104.

Values and Personalities of Selected High School Choral Educators. *Slack.* 25 (4) Winter 1977, 243–255.

Verbal and Operant Responses of Young Children to Vocal versus Instrumental Song Performances. *Sims and Cassidy.* 45 (2) Summer, 234–244.

Verbal Behavior Analysis as a Supervisory Technique with Student Teachers of Music. *Verrastro.* 23 (3) Fall 1975, 171–185.

Verbal Description of Aural Music Stimuli. *Zimmerman.* 19 (4) Winter 1971, 422–432.

Verbal Identification of Music Concepts. *Hair.* 29 (1) Spring 1981, 11–22.

Verbal Instruction in Instrumental Rehearsals: A Comparison of Three Career Levels and Pre-service Teachers. *Goolsby.* 45 (1) Spring 1997, 21–40.

Villa-Lobos as Pedagogue: Music in the Service of the State. *Vassberg.* 23 (30) Fall 1975, 163–170.

Visual Diagnostic Skills Development and College Students' Acquisition of Basic Conducting Skills. *Scott.* 44 (3) Fall 1996, 229–23

Vocal Growth in the Human Adolescent and the Total Growth Process. *Joseph.* 14 (2) Summer 1966, 135–141.

Vocal Growth Measurements in Male Adolescents. *Joseph.* 17 (4) Winter 1969, 423–426.

Vocal Integrity of Elementary Vocal Music Teachers: Personal and Environmental Factors. *Bernstorf and Burk.* 44 (4) Winter 1996, 369–383.

Vocal Music and the Classroom Teacher, 1885 to 1905. *Coffman.* 35 (2) Summer 1987, 92–102.

Vocal Music in the Common Schools of Upper Canada: 1846–1876. *Trowsdale.* 18 (4) Winter 1970, 340–354.

Vocal Self-Identification, Singing Style, and Singing Range in Relationship to a Measure of Cultural Mistrust in African-American Adolescent Females. *Chinn.* 45 (4) Winter 1997, 636–649.

When Tempo Changes Rhythm: The Effect of Tempo on Nonmusicians' Perception of Rhythm. *Duke.* 42 (1) Spring 1994, 28–35.

Willem van de Wall (1887–1953): Organizer and Innovator in Music Education and Music Therapy. *Clair and Heller.* 37 (3) Fall 1989, 165–178.

Wind Instrumentalists' Intonational Performance in Selected Musical